WITHDRAWN

Index of American Periodical Verse: 1994

Rafael Catalá
and
James D. Anderson

assisted by
Martha Park Sollberger

The Scarecrow Press, Inc.
Lanham, Md., & London
1997

SCARECROW PRESS, INC.

Published in the United States of America
by Scarecrow Press, Inc.
4720 Boston Way
Lanham, Maryland 20706

4 Pleydell Gardens, Folkestone
Kent CT20 2DN, England

ISBN 0–8108–3227–5 (cloth : alk. paper)

ISSN 0090-9130

™ The paper used in this publication meets the minimum requirements of American National Standard for Information Sciences—Permanence of Paper for Printed Library Materials, ANSI Z39.48–1984.
Manufactured in the United States of America.

Contents

Preface

This twenty-fourth annual volume of the ***Index*** was produced with the cooperation of 298 participating periodicals from Canada, the United States, and the Caribbean. Nearly 7,000 entries (6,983) for individual poets and translators are included, with 18,793 entries for individual poems. A separate index provides access by title or first line.

The importance of the ***Index*** grows as its necessity becomes more apparent in circles of contemporary poetry research. The increasing demand for inclusion corroborates this fact. The ***Index*** constitutes an objective measure of poetry in North America, recording not only the publication of our own poets in Canada, the U.S., and the Caribbean, but also those from other lands and cultures and from other times. Of course, the ***Index***'s primary purpose is to show what poems have been published by particular poets, what poems have been translated by particular translators, and who wrote poems with particular titles or first lines. But taken together, the ***Index*** reveals trends and influences: the ebb and flow of particular poets, as well as the influence of cultures of other lands and times as represented by their poets published in North American journals.

James D. Anderson has made a major contribution to the ***Index*** by designing and refining computer programs that greatly facilitate the indexing process, proof-reading and error-checking, control of cross-references and consistency in names, sorting, formatting, and typesetting. To him also goes credit for managing relations with participating journals and for seeing that indexing gets done in a timely and accurate manner. Also, I want to express my sincere appreciation to Martha Park Sollberger, librarian *emerita*, for her valuable assistance.

Rafael Catalá
Co-Editor

Introduction

Scope

The ***Index of American Periodical Verse*** indexes poems published in a broad cross-section of poetry, literary, scholarly, popular, general, and "little" magazines, journals, and reviews published in the United States, Canada, and the Caribbean. These periodicals are listed in the "Periodicals Indexed" section, together with names of editors, addresses, issues indexed in this volume, and subscription information. Selection of periodicals to index is the responsibility of the editors, based on recommendations of poets, librarians, literary scholars, and publishers. Publishers participate by supplying copies of all issues to the editors. Criteria for inclusion include the quality of poems, their presentation, and the status or reputation of poets. Within these very broad and subjective guidelines, the editors attempt to include a cross-section of periodicals by type of publisher and publication, place of publication, language, and type of poetry. Periodicals published outside of North America are included only if they have North American editors.

Compilation

Citation data are compiled using the WordStar word-processing program, version 4, on an MS/DOS computer. "Shorthand" macro programs are used to repeat author headings for multiple poems by the same poet, create translator entries from author entries for translated poems, and transform complex author names into cross-reference entries. Sorting is done by "ARISsort," a fast program for sorting very large files written by Fred A. Rowley. Title entries are extracted from the original author entries. Sorted and formatted entries are transferred to a Macintosh computer with laser printer for typesetting and page formatting using Microsoft Word™ and PageMaker™ programs.

Persons interested in the precise details of compilation, including the computer programs used for error-checking, sorting, and formatting, should write to the editors at P.O. Box 38, New Brunswick, NJ 08903-0038. The ***Index*** data for 1982 through 1994 are available from the editors on microcomputer disks.

Names and Cross-References

Because many poets have compound surnames and surnames containing various prefixes, we recognize the need for systematic provision of cross-references from alternative forms of surname to the form chosen for entry in the ***Index***. We have included cross-references whenever the form used for entry does not fall under the last part or element of the name. In addition, many poets publish under different forms of the same name, for example, with or without a middle initial. When poets are known to use different forms of the same name, alternative forms may be indicated using the format authorized by the *Anglo-American Cataloguing Rules*, Second Edition. For example:

WHEATLEY, Pat (Patience)

This heading indicates that this poet has poems published under two forms of name: Pat Wheatley and Patience Wheatley.

When two or more different names refer to the same poet, one name will be chosen, with "see" references to the chosen name from other names. When it is not possible to determine with assurance whether a single poet is using variant forms of name or different poets have similar names, both names will be used. In such cases, "see also" references may be added to headings to remind users to check the variant name forms that might possibly refer to the same poet.

Format and Arrangement of Entries

The basic format and style of the ***Index*** remain unchanged. Poets are arranged alphabetically first by surname, then by forenames. In creating this alphabetical sequence, we have adopted principles of alphanumeric arrangement adopted in 1980 by the American Library Association and the Library of Congress. Names are arranged on the basis of their spelling, rather than their pronunciation, so that, for example, names beginning with "Mac" and "Mc" are placed in separate sections. Similarly, a space has a consistent arrangement value, coming before all numerals or letters. Therefore, similar compound and prefixed surnames are often separated by some distance, as illustrated in the following examples. Note that "De BOLT" precedes "DeBEVOISE" by a considerable number of entries.

De ANGELIS
De BOLT
De GRAVELLES
De LOACH
De PALCHI
De RONSARD
De VAUL
DEAL
DeBEVOISE
DeFOE
DEGUY
Del VECCHIO
DeLISLE
DeMOTT
DENNISON
DER-HOVANESSIAN
DESY
DeYOUNG

Van BRUNT
Van DUYN
Van HALTEREN
Van TOORN
Van TROYER
Van WERT
Van WINCKEL
VANCE
Vander DOES
VANDERBEEK
VanDEVENTER

Abbreviations are also arranged on the basis of spelling, rather than pronunciation or meaning, so that "ST. JOHN" is *not* arranged as "SAINT JOHN," but as "S+T+space+JOHN." Punctuation (including apostrophes and accents), signs, and symbols (other than alphabetic letters and numerals) are not considered, but a hyphen is arranged as if it were a space. Initial articles ("a," "an," "the" and their equivalents in other languages) are ignored in titles of poems and in names of corporate bodies, but they are considered in the arrangement of names of persons and places (e.g., La RUE, El Paso). Numerals, including Roman numerals, are arranged in numerical order preceding alphabetical letters rather than as if they were spelled out.

Under each poet's name, poems are arranged alphanumerically by title or, if there is no title, by first line. Poems with only "Untitled" printed as if it were the title are entered as "Untitled" plus the first line of the poem. Poems whose titles consist only of "Poem" are treated in the same way: the first line is added to this title. In the title index, two entries are provided, one under "Untitled" or "Poem" plus the first line, and one directly under the first line. Numbered poems are handled in the same way. Under poets, initial numbers are treated as the first part of titles, and they are so entered. In the title index, they are entered both under their initial numbers and under the part following the number, if any.

Poem titles and first lines are placed within quotation marks. All significant words of titles are capitalized, but in first lines, only the first word and proper nouns are capitalized. Incomplete excerpts from larger works are followed by the note "Excerpt" or "Excerpts," or, if they are presented as complete sections, by "Selection" or "Selections." The title, first line, or number of excerpts or selections may follow if given in the publication. For example:

WALCOTT, Derek
"Midsummer" (Selections: XXXIV-XXXVI). [Agni] (18) 83, p. 5-7.

WEBB, Phyllis
"The Vision Tree" (Selection: "I Daniel"). [PoetryCR] (5:2) Wint 83-84, p. 11.

WAINWRIGHT, Jeffrey
"Heart's Desire" (Excerpt: "Some Propositions and Part of a Narrative"). [Agni] (18) 83, p. 37.

WATTEN, Barret
"One Half" (Excerpts). [ParisR] (24:86) Wint 82, p. 112-113.

If an excerpt is treated as a complete "sub-work," it receives an independent entry, with reference to the larger work in a note. For example:

ANDERSON, Jack
"Magnets" (from "The Clouds of That Country"). [PoNow] (7:2, #38) 83, p. 23.

Notes about dedications, joint authors, translators, and sources follow the title, enclosed in parentheses. A poem with more than one author is entered under each author. Likewise, a translated poem is entered under each translator, as well as its author(s). Each entry includes the names of all authors and all translators. Multiple authors or translators are indicated by the abbreviation "w.," standing for "with." Translators are indicated by the abbreviation "tr. by," standing for "translated by," and original authors are indicated by the abbreviation "tr. of," standing for "translation of." For example:

AGGESTAM, Rolf
"Old Basho" (tr. by Erland Anderson and Lars Nordström). [NewRena] (16) Spr 83, p. 25.

ANDERSON, Erland
"Old Basho" (tr. of Rolf Aggestam, w. Lars Nordström). [NewRena] (16) Spr 83, p. 25.

NORDSTRÖM, Lars
"Old Basho" (tr. of Rolf Aggestam, w. Erland Anderson). [NewRena] (16) Spr 83, p. 25.

The periodical citation includes an abbreviation standing for the periodical title, followed by volume and issue numbers, date, and page number(s). The periodical abbreviation is enclosed in square brackets. An alphabetical list of these periodical abbreviations is included at the front of the volume, followed by the full periodical titles, names of editors, addresses, the numbers of the issues indexed for this volume of the ***Index***, and subscription information. A separate list of indexed periodicals is arranged by full periodical title, with a reference to the abbreviated title. Volume and issue numbers are included within parentheses. For example, "(16:5)" stands for volume 16, number 5; "(21)" refers to issue or volume 21 for a periodical that uses only one numerical sequence. Dates are given using abbreviations for months and seasons. Year of publication is indicated by the last two digits of the year, for example, 94. Please see the separate list of abbreviations at the front of the volume.

Compiling this year's ***Index*** has been an adventure into the wealth and variety of poetry published in U. S., Caribbean, and Canadian periodicals as well as the intricacies of bringing this richness together and organizing it into a consistent index. The world of poetry publication is a dynamic one, with new periodicals appearing, older periodicals declining, dying, reviving, and thriving. This year saw the loss of nine periodicals and the addition of ten new ones. Two other periodicals that had been dropped were reinstated. Both deleted and newly added periodicals are listed at the front of the volume. Keeping up with these changes is a big job, and we solicit our readers' suggestions as to periodicals that should be included in future volumes of the ***Index***, and also, periodicals that could be dropped. Editors who would like their periodicals considered for inclusion in future volumes should send sample issues to:

Rafael Catalá, Editor
Index of American Periodical Verse
P.O. Box 38
New Brunswick, NJ 08903-0038

Although indexing is indispensable for the organization of any literature, so that particular works can be found when needed and scholarship and research facilitated, it is a tedious business. I know that we have made mistakes. We solicit your corrections and suggestions, which you may send to me at the above address.

James D. Anderson
Co-Editor

Abbreviations

dir., dirs.	director, directors
Dept.	Department
ed., eds.	editor, editors
(for.)	price for foreign countries
(ind.)	price for individuals
(inst.)	price for institutions
(lib.)	price for libraries
NS	new series
p.	page, pages
po. ed.	poetry editor
pub.	publisher
(stud.)	price for students
tr. by	translated by
tr. of	translation of
U.	University
w.	with
yr.	year

Months

Ja	January	Jl	July
F	February	Ag	August
Mr	March	S	September
Ap	April	O	October
My	May	N	November
Je	June	D	December

Seasons

Aut	Autumn	Spr	Spring
Wint	Winter	Sum	Summer

Years

89	1989	92	1992
90	1990	93	1993
91	1991	94	1994

Periodicals Added

Periodical acronyms are followed by titles. Full information may be found in the list of periodicals indexed.

BlackMoon: BLACK MOON

Chain: CHAIN

Image: IMAGE: A Journal of the Arts & Religion

InterQ: INTERNATIONAL QUARTERLY

ModernW: MODERN WORDS: a thoroughly queer international literary journal

Pivot: PIVOT

PlumR: THE PLUM REVIEW

Poz: POZ

SantaBR: SANTA BARBARA REVIEW

War: WAR, LITERATURE, & THE ARTS: An International Journal of the Humanities

Periodicals Deleted

Aerial: AERIAL, Rod Smith, ed., P.O. Box 25642, Washington, DC 20007. No 1992, 1993, or 1994 issues received; letters not answered.

CalQ: CALIFORNIA QUARTERLY, Jack Hicks, ed., Kristin Steege, po. ed., 159 Titus Hall, U. of California, Davis, CA 95616. Publication suspended indefinitely as of September 1, 1993 "due to California state budget cuts."

CityLR: CITY LIGHTS REVIEW, Nancy J. Peters, ed., Lawrence Ferlinghetti, pub., City Lights Books, 261 Columbus Ave., San Francisco, CA 94133. No 1993 or 1994 issues received; letters not answered.

Contact: CONTACT II: A Poetry Review, Maurice Kenny, J. G. Gosciak, eds., P.O. Box 451, Bowling Green, New York, NY 10004. Vol. 11, Nos. 65/66/67 (1993) was the "final issue."

DustyD: DUSTY DOG, John Pierce, ed. & pub., 1904-A Gladden, Gallup, NM 87301. No 1994 issues received. "Poetry magazine and chapbooks suspended."

EmeraldCR: EMERALD COAST REVIEW: West Florida Authors and Artists, Ellen G. Peppler, Charmaine Wellington, eds., West Florida Literary Federation, P.O. Box 1644, Pensacola, FL 32597-1644. No 1992, 1993, or 1994 issues received; letters not answered.

ManhatPR: MANHATTAN POETRY REVIEW, Elaine Reiman-Fenton, ed., P.O. Box 8207, New York, NY 10150-1917. No 1993 or 1994 issues received; letters not answered.

NewMyths: NEW MYTHS, Robert Mooney, ed., State U. of New York, P.O. Box 6000, Binghamton, NY 13902-6000. No 1993 or 1994 issues received; letters not answered.

PacificR: THE PACIFIC REVIEW: A Magazine of Poetry and Prose, Judith Hawkins, ed., James Brown, faculty ed., Derek McKown, po. ed., Dept. of English, California State U., 5500 University Parkway, San Bernardino, CA 92407-2397. No 1993 or 1994 issues received; letters not answered.

Periodicals Indexed

Arranged by acronym, with names of editors, addresses, issues indexed, and subscription information. New titles added to the *Index* in 1994 are marked with an asterisk (*).

13thMoon: 13TH MOON : A Feminist Literary Magazine, Judith Emlyn Johnson, ed., Katie Yates, Emily Novak, Jen Spungin, po. eds., Dept. of English, State U. of NY, Albany, NY 12222. Issues indexed: No 1994 issues received. Subscriptions: $10/1 vol., $18/2 vols., $26/3 vols; Back issues: $6.50-$10/vol.

Abraxas: ABRAXAS, Ingrid Swanberg, ed., 2518 Gregory St., Madison, WI 53711. Issues indexed: No issues published 1992-1994 -- No. 42/43 expected in 1995. Subscriptions: $12/4 issues; Single issue: $3; Double issues: $6.

AfAmRev: AFRICAN AMERICAN REVIEW, Division on Black American Literature and Culture, Modern Language Association, Joe Weixlmann, ed., Dept. of English, Indiana State U., Terre Haute, IN 47809. Issues indexed: (28:1-4). Subscriptions: $24/yr. (ind.), $44/yr. (inst.), $31/yr. (for.), $51/yr. (for. inst.). Single issue: $10, $12 (for.).

Agni: AGNI, Askold Melnyczuk, ed., Creative Writing Program, Boston U., 236 Bay State Rd., Boston, MA 02115. Issues indexed: (39-40). Subscriptions: $12/yr. (2 issues), $23/2 yrs., $34/3 yrs.; $24/yr. (inst.); plus $4/yr. (for.); Single issue: $7.

AlabamaLR: ALABAMA LITERARY REVIEW, Theron Montgomery, ed., Ed Hicks, po. ed., Smith 253, Troy State U., Troy, AL 36082. Issues indexed: (8:1). Subscriptions: $10/yr. (2 issues); Single issue: $5.

Amelia: AMELIA, Frederick A. Raborg, Jr., ed., 329 "E" St., Bakersfield, CA 93304. Issues indexed: (7:3-4, #22-23). Subscriptions: $25/yr. (4 issues), $48/2 yrs., $70/3 yrs.; $27/yr., $52/2 yrs., $76/3 yrs. (Canada, Mexico); $41/yr., $80/2 yrs., $118/3 yrs. (for. air mail); Single issue: $7.95, $8.50 (Canada & Mexico), $12 (for. air mail).

Americas: THE AMERICAS REVIEW, A Review of Hispanic Literature and Art of the USA, Lauro H. Flores, ed., U. of Houston, Houston, TX 77204-2090. Issues indexed: (22:1/2-3/4). Subscriptions: $15/yr. (ind.), $20/yr. (inst.); Single and back issues: $5; Double issues: $10.

AmerLC: AMERICAN LETTERS & COMMENTARY, Jeanne Beaumont, Anna Rabinowitz, eds., 850 Park Ave, Suite 5-B, New York, NY 10021. Issues indexed: (6). Subscriptions: $5/yr. (1 issue).

AmerPoR: THE AMERICAN POETRY REVIEW, Stephen Berg, David Bonanno, Arthur Vogelsang, eds., 1721 Walnut St., Philadelphia, PA 19103. Issues indexed: (23:1-6). Subscriptions: $15/yr., $27/2 yrs., $38/3 yrs.; $18/yr., $33/2 yrs., $47/3 yrs. (for.); classroom rate $7.50/yr. per student; Single issue: $3.25. PA residents add 6% sales tax; Philadelphia residents, 7%.

AmerS: THE AMERICAN SCHOLAR, Joseph Epstein, ed., The Phi Beta Kappa Society, 1811 Q St. NW, Washington, DC 20009. Issues indexed: (63:1-4). Subscriptions: $23/yr., $44/2 yrs., $63/3 yrs. (ind.); $28/yr., $54/2 yrs., $78/3 yrs. (inst.); plus $3/yr. (for.); Single issue: $6.50; $8 (inst.).

AmerV: THE AMERICAN VOICE, Frederick Smock, ed., The Kentucky Foundation for Women, Inc., 332 West Broadway, Suite 1215, Louisville, KY 40202. Issues indexed: (33-35). Subscriptions: $15/yr. (3 issues), $25/2 yrs., $35/3 yrs.; Single and back issues: $5.

AnotherCM: ANOTHER CHICAGO MAGAZINE, Barry Silesky, ed. & pub., 3709 N. Kenmore, Chicago, IL 60613. Issues indexed: (27-28). Subscriptions: $15/yr., $60/5 yrs., $199.95/lifetime; Single issue: $8.

Antaeus: ANTAEUS, Daniel Halpern, ed., The Ecco Press, 100 W. Broad St., Hopewell, NJ 08525. Issues indexed: (73/74, 75/76 "The Final Issue").

AnthNEW: THE ANTHOLOGY OF NEW ENGLAND WRITERS, Frank Anthony, ed., New England Writers/Vermont Poets Association, P.O. Box 483, Windsor, VT 05089. Issues indexed: 6. Single issue: $3.50.

AntigR: THE ANTIGONISH REVIEW, George Sanderson, ed., Box 5000, St. Francis Xavier U., Antigonish, Nova Scotia B2G 2W5 Canada. Issues indexed: (96-99). Subscriptions: $20/4 issues; Single issue: $6.

AntR: THE ANTIOCH REVIEW, Robert S. Fogarty, ed., David St. John, po. ed., P.O. Box 148, Yellow Springs, OH 45387-9910. Issues indexed: (52:1-4). Subscriptions: $30/yr. (4 issues), $53/2 yrs., $75/3 yrs. (ind.); $42/yr., $74/2 yrs., $105/3 yrs. (inst.); plus $9/yr. (for.); Single issue: $6, $7.80 (Canada). Subscription address: P.O. Box 626, Dayton, OH 45459-0626.

ApalQ: APALACHEE QUARTERLY, Barbara Hamby, Bruce Boehrer, Mary Jane Ryals, Monifa Love, Kim MacQueen, Lara Moody, eds., P.O. Box 20106, Tallahassee, FL 32316. Issues indexed: (40/41, 42). Subscriptions: $15/yr. (2 issues, ind.), $30/2 yrs.; $20/yr. (inst.), $30/yr., $50/2 yrs. (for.); Single issue: $6; Double issues: $10.

Arc: ARC: Canada's National Poetry Magazine, John Barton, Nadine McInnis, eds., P.O. Box 7368, Ottawa, Ont. K1L 8E4 Canada. Issues indexed: (32-33). Subscriptions: $20/4 issues (2 years, Canada); $25/yr. (USA); $28/yr. (for.); Single issue: $7.50 (Canada), $8 (USA & for.).

Archae: ARCHAE, Alan Drake, ed., 212 Altamont Pl., Somerville, NJ 08876. Issues indexed: No 1993 or 1994 issues published; #5 published in 1995. Subscriptions: $13/yr. (2 issues); $17/yr. (for.); Single issue: $7, $9 (for.).

Areíto: AREITO, Andrés Gómez, Director, P.O. Box 44-1803, Miami, FL 33144. Issues indexed: Segunda Epoca (5:15-16). Subscriptions: $12/yr. (ind.), $20/yr. (inst.), $18/yr. (for. ind.), $30/yr. (for. inst.).

Arion: ARION: A Journal of Humanities and the Classics, Herbert Golder, ed., 10 Lenox St., Brookline, MA 02146. Issues indexed: (3:1). Subscriptions: $19/yr. (3 issues, ind.), $35/yr. (inst.), $12/yr. (students), plus $3/yr. (for.); Single issue, $7; Back issues, $8. Subscription address: Arion, c/o Office of Scholarly Publications, Boston U., 985 Commonwealth Ave., Boston, MA 02215.

Arshile: ARSHILE: A Magazine of the Arts, Mark Salerno, ed., P.O. Box 3749, Los Angeles, CA 90078. Issues indexed: (3). Subscriptions: $18/2 issues, $36/4 issues (ind.); $24/2 issues, $48/4 issues (inst.); Single issue: $8-$10 plus $2.50 shipping and handling.

Art&Und: ART & UNDERSTANDING: The International Magazine of Literature and Art About AIDS, David Waggoner, ed., 25 Monroe St., Suite 205, Albany, NY 12210. Issues indexed: (3:1-4). Subscriptions: $24.95/yr. (10 issues), $34.95/2 yrs.; Back issues: $5 plus $1 postage and handling; Single issue: $3.95, $4.95 (Canada).

ArtfulD: ARTFUL DODGE, Daniel Bourne, ed., Dept. of English, College of Wooster, Wooster, OH 44691. Issues indexed: (26/27). Subscriptions: $10/4 issues (ind.), $16/4 issues (inst.); Single issue: $5.

Ascent: ASCENT, Audrey Curley, Mark Costello, Paul Friedman, Philip Graham, Carol LeSeure, Jerry Mirskin, Nancy Roberts, George Scouffas, Jean Thompson, Michael Van Walleghen, Kirsten Wasson, eds., P.O. Box 967, Urbana, IL 61801. Issues indexed: (18:2-3, 19:1). Subscriptions: $9/yr. (3 issues), $18/2 yrs.; $5/yr. (for.); Single issue: $3 (bookstore), $3.50 (mail).

Asylum: ASYLUM, Greg Boyd, ed., P.O. Box 6203, Santa Maria, CA 93456. Issues indexed: No 1994 issues received. Subscriptions: $10/yr. (1 annual issue, ind.).

Atlantic: THE ATLANTIC, William Whitworth, ed., Peter Davison, po. ed., 745 Boylston St., Boston, MA 02116-2603. Issues indexed: (273:1-6, 274:1-6). Subscriptions: $17.94/yr., $29.95/2 yrs., $39.95/3 yrs., plus $8/yr. (Canada), $12/yr. (for.); Single issue: $2.95, $3.50 (Canada). Subscription address: Atlantic Subscription Processing Center, Box 52661, Boulder, CO 80322.

Avec: AVEC: A Journal of Writing, Cydney Chadwick, ed., P.O. Box 1059, Penngrove, CA 94951. Issues indexed: (7-8). Subscriptions: $12/2 issues; Single issue: $8.

BambooR: BAMBOO RIDGE: The Hawaii Writers' Quarterly, Eric Chock, Darrell H. Y. Lum, eds., P.O. Box 61781, Honolulu, HI 96839-1781. Issues indexed: (60, 61/62, 63/64). Subscriptions: $16/yr. (2 issues); Single issue, $5; Double issues: $5-8.

BellArk: BELLOWING ARK, Robert R. Ward, ed., P.O. Box 45637, Seattle, WA 98145. Issues indexed: (10:1-6). Subscriptions: $15/yr. (6 issues), $24/2 yrs.; Single and back issues: $3.

BellR: THE BELLINGHAM REVIEW, Knute Skinner, ed., S. Strand Guess, po. ed., The Signpost Press, 1007 Queen St., Bellingham, WA 98226. Issues indexed: (17:1/2, #35/36). Subscriptions: $5/yr. (2 issues), $9.50/2 yrs., $12.50/3 yrs.; plus $1/yr. (for.); through agencies, $6/yr.; Single issue: $2.50; Double issue: $5.

BelPoJ: THE BELOIT POETRY JOURNAL, Marion K. Stocking, ed., RR 2, Box 154, Ellsworth, ME 04605. Issues indexed: (44:3-4, 45:1-2). Subscriptions: $12/yr. (4 issues, ind.), $33/3 yrs.; $18/yr., $49.50/3 yrs. (inst.); plus $3.20/yr. (Canada), $3.70/yr. (for.); Single issue: $4.

BilingR: THE BILINGUAL REVIEW / LA REVISTA BILINGÜE, Gary D. Keller, ed., Hispanic Research Center, Arizona State U., Box 872702, Tempe, AZ 85287-2702. Issues indexed: (18:2/3, 19:1-3). Subscriptions: $18/yr., $34/2 yrs., $48/3 yrs. (ind.); $30/yr. (inst.).

BlackALF: BLACK AMERICAN LITERATURE FORUM *see* AfAmRev: AFRICAN AMERICAN REVIEW (title change).

BlackBR: BLACK BEAR REVIEW, Ave Jeanne, po. ed., 1916 Lincoln St., Croydon, PA 19021. Issues indexed: (18-19). Subscriptions: $10/yr. (2 issues), plus $3 per copy (for.); Single issue: $5.

BlackBread: BLACK BREAD, Jessica Lowenthal, Sianne Ngai, eds., 46 Preston St., #2, Providence, RI 02906. Issues indexed: No 1994 issues received. Subscriptions: $10/2 issues; Single issue: $5.

*BlackMoon: BLACK MOON, Alan Britt, ed. & pub., 233 Northway Rd, Reisterstown, MD 21136. Issues indexed: (1). Single issue: $5.

BlackWR: BLACK WARRIOR REVIEW, Mark S. Drew, ed., Lisa Spadafora, po. ed., U. of Alabama, P.O. Box 2936, Tuscaloosa, AL 35486-2936. Issues indexed: (20:2, 21:1). Subscriptions: $11/yr. (ind.), $17/yr. (inst.); plus $5/yr. (for.); Single issue: $6, plus $3 (for.).

Blueline: BLUELINE, Anthony O. Tyler, ed., Stephanie Coyne DeGhett, po. ed., English Dept., Potsdam College, SUNY, Potsdam, NY 13676. Issues indexed: 15. Single issue: $6.

Bogg: BOGG, John Elsberg, ed., 422 N. Cleveland St., Arlington, VA 22201. Issues indexed: No 1994 issues published; No. 67 published in 1995. Subscriptions: $12/3 issues; Single issue: $4.50.

Bomb: BOMB MAGAZINE, Betsy Sussler, ed. & pub., Roland Legiardi-Laura, po. ed., New Art Publications, P.O. Box 2003, Canal Station, New York, NY 10013. Issues indexed: (46-47, 50); Numbers 48-49 not received. Subscriptions: $18/yr. (4 issues), $32/2 yrs.; $28/yr. (for.); Single issue: $4.

Border: BORDERLANDS: Texas Poetry Review, Dorothy Barnett, Pamela Cook, Liz Garton, Lynn Gilbert, D'Arcy Randall, Polly Robertus, Hazel Ward, dirs, P.O. Box 49818, Austin, TX 78765. Issues indexed: (3-5). Subscriptions: $17/yr. (2 issues, ind.), $33/2 yrs.; $19/yr. (inst.); Single issue: $10.

BostonR: BOSTON REVIEW, Joshua Cohen, ed., Kim Cooper, po. ed., Dept. of Political Science, E53-407, Massachusetts Institute of Technology, Cambridge, MA 02139. Issues indexed: (19:1-2, 3/4, 5-6). Subscriptions: $15/yr., $30/2 yrs. (ind.); $18/yr., $36/2 yrs. (inst.); plus $6/yr. (Canada, Mexico); plus $12/yr. (other for.); Single issue: $4.50.

Boulevard: BOULEVARD, Richard Burgin, ed., Drexel U., P.O. Box 30386, Philadelphia, PA 19103. Issues indexed: (9:1/2, 9:3, #25/26, 27). Subscriptions: $12/3 issues, $20/6 issues, $25/9 issues; Single issue: $6; make checks payable to Opojaz, Inc.

BrooklynR: BROOKLYN REVIEW, Tim Gerken, Michael Gates, Giles Scott, Robert Zverina, po. eds., Lou Asekoff, faculty advisor, English Dept., Brooklyn College, Brooklyn, NY 11210. Issues indexed: (11). Single issue: $5.

Caliban: CALIBAN, Lawrence R. Smith, ed., P.O. Box 561, Laguna Beach, CA 92652. Issues indexed: (14). Subscriptions: $14/yr. (2 issues), $26/2 yrs. (ind.); $24/yr. (inst.); plus $2/yr. (for.); Single issue: $8.

Callaloo: CALLALOO: A Journal of African-American and African Arts and Letters, Charles H. Rowell, ed., Dept. of English, Wilson Hall, U. of Virginia, Charlottesville, VA 22903. Issues indexed: (17:1-4). Subscriptions: $27/yr. (ind.), $54/yr. (inst.); plus $7 (Canada, Mexico); plus $17 (outside North America, air freight); Subscription address: The Johns Hopkins University Press, Journals Publishing Division, 2715 N. Charles St., Baltimore, MD 21218-4319.

Calyx: CALYX: A Journal of Art and Literature by Women, Margarita Donnelly, managing ed., P.O. Box B, Corvallis, OR 97339-0539. Issues indexed: (15:2-3). Subscriptions: $18/yr. (3 issues), $32/2 yrs., $42/3 yrs.; $22.50/yr. (inst.); plus $10/yr. (Canada); plus $18/yr. (for.); $15/yr. (ind. low income); Single issue: $8 plus $1.25 postage.

CanLit: CANADIAN LITERATURE, W. H. New, ed., U. of British Columbia, 2029 West Mall, Vancouver, BC, V6T 1Z2 Canada. Issues indexed: (140-141, 142/143). Subscriptions: $40/yr. (ind.), $55/yr. (inst.) plus $10/yr. outside Canada; Single issue: $15; Double issue: $25.

CapeR: THE CAPE ROCK, Harvey Hecht, ed., Southeast Missouri State U., Cape Girardeau, MO 63701. Issues indexed: (29:1-2). Subscriptions: $7/yr. (2 issues); Single issue: $5.

CapilR: THE CAPILANO REVIEW, Robert Sherrin, ed., 2055 Purcell Way, North Vancouver, BC, V7J 3H5 Canada. Issues indexed: (Series 2:12-14). Subscriptions: $25/yr., $45/2 yrs. (ind.); $30/yr. (inst.); Single issue: $9.

CaribbeanW: THE CARIBBEAN WRITER, Erika J. Waters, ed., Research Publications Center, U. of the Virgin Islands, RR 2, Box 10,000, Kingshill, St. Croix, VI 00850. Issues indexed: (8). Subscriptions: $18/2 yrs. (2 issues); Single issue: $9.

CarolQ: CAROLINA QUARTERLY, Amber Vogel, ed., Julia Stockton, po. ed., Greenlaw Hall CB#3520, U. of North Carolina, Chapel Hill, NC 27599-3520. Issues indexed: (46:2-3, 47:1). Subscriptions: $10/yr. (3 issues, ind.), $12/yr. (inst.); Single issue: $5.

CentR: THE CENTENNIAL REVIEW, R. K. Meiners, ed., College of Arts and Letters, 312 Linton Hall, Michigan State U., East Lansing, MI 48824-1044. Issues indexed: (38:1-3). Subscriptions: $12/yr. (3 issues), $18/2 yrs., plus $4.50/yr. (for.); Single issue: $6.

CentralP: CENTRAL PARK, Stephen-Paul Martin, Eve Ensler, Stacey Schrader, eds., Box 1446, New York, NY 10023. Issues indexed: (23). Subscriptions: $15/yr., 2 issues (ind.), $20/yr. (inst.); Single issue: $7.50 (ind.), $9 (inst).

*Chain: CHAIN, Jena Osman, Juliana Spahr, eds., State U. of New York at Buffalo, 107 14th St., Buffalo, NY 14213. Issues indexed: (1). Subscriptions: $7.95/yr. (1 issue); $14/2 issues. Make checks payable to UB Foundation.

ChamLR: CHAMINADE LITERARY REVIEW, Loretta Petrie, ed., Jim Kraus, po. ed., Chaminade U. of Honolulu, 3140 Waialae Ave., Honolulu, HI 96816. Issues indexed: (14/15); number 12 not received. Subscriptions: $10/yr. (2 issues); $18/2 yrs.; plus $2 (for.).; Single issue: $5; Double issue: $10.

ChangingM: CHANGING MEN: Issues in Gender, Sex and Politics, Michael Biernbaum, Rick Cote, eds., P.O. Box 639, Durham, NH 03825-0639; Bob Vance, po. ed., 1024 Emmet St., Petosky, MI 49770. Issues indexed: (27). Subscriptions: $24/4 issues, $40/4 issues (inst.); $16/4 issues (limited income); $27/4 issues (Canada & Mexico); $40/4 issues (for., air mail); Single issue: $6; Back issues: $5.50.

CharR: THE CHARITON REVIEW, Jim Barnes, ed., Northeast Missouri State U., Kirksville, MO 63501. Issues indexed: (20:1-2). Subscriptions: $9/2 issues; Single issue: $5.

ChatR: THE CHATTAHOOCHEE REVIEW: The DeKalb College Literary Quarterly, Lamar York, ed., Collie Owens, po. ed., 2101 Womack Road, Dunwoody, GA 30338-4497. Issues indexed: (14:2-3). Subscriptions: $15/yr. (4 issues), $25/2 yrs.; Single issue: $4.

Chelsea: CHELSEA, Richard Foerster, ed., P.O. Box 773, Cooper Station, New York, NY 10276-0773. Issues indexed: (56-57). Subscriptions: $12/yr. (2 issues or 1 double issue), $22/2 yrs.; $15/yr., $29/2 yrs. (for.); Single issue: $6.50; Back issues: $3.

ChiR: CHICAGO REVIEW, David Nicholls, ed., Angela Sorby, po. ed., Division of Humanities, U. of Chicago, 5801 S. Kenwood Ave., Chicago, IL 60637. Issues indexed: (40:1, 2/3, 4). Subscriptions: $15/yr. (ind.); $35/yr. (inst.); plus $5/yr. (for.); Single issue: $5; Double issue: $7.

ChironR: CHIRON REVIEW, Michael Hathaway, ed., 522 E. South Ave., St. John, KS 67576-2212. Issues indexed: (13:2-4, #39-41). Subscriptions: $10/yr. (4 issues); $20/yr. (for.); $24/yr. (inst.); Single issue: $3; $6 (for.).

ChrC: THE CHRISTIAN CENTURY: An Ecumenical Weekly, James M. Wall, ed., 407 S. Dearborn St., Chicago, IL 60605-1150. Issues indexed: (111:1-37). Subscriptions: $35/yr.; Single issue: $2.

CimR: CIMARRON REVIEW, Gordon Weaver, ed., Thomas Reiter, Sharon Gerald, Jeff Kersh, Doug Martin, Sally Shigley, Hugh Tribbey, po. eds., 205 Morrill Hall, Oklahoma State U., Stillwater, OK 74078-0135. Issues indexed: (106-109). Subscriptions: $12/yr., $15 (Canada); $30/3 yrs., $40 (Canada); plus $2.50/yr. (for.); Single issue: $3.

CinPR: CINCINNATI POETRY REVIEW, Jeff Hillard, ed., Cincinnati Writers' Project, College of Mt. St. Joseph, 5701 Delhi Rd., Cincinnati, OH 45233. Issues indexed: (24). Subscriptions: $9/4 issues; Single issue: $3; Sample copies: $2.

ClockR: CLOCKWATCH REVIEW: A Journal of the Arts, James Plath, ed., Dept. of English, Illinois Wesleyan Univ., Bloomington, IL 61702-2900. Issues indexed: (9:1/2). Subscriptions: $8/yr. (2 issues); Single issue: $4; Double issues: $8.

CoalC: COAL CITY REVIEW, Brian Daldorph, Sandra Tompson, eds., 1324 Connecticut, Lawrence, KS 66044. Issues indexed: (8). Subscriptions: $6/2 issues; Single issue: $4.

ColEng: COLLEGE ENGLISH, National Council of Teachers of English, Louise Z. Smith, ed., Helene Davis, Thomas Hurley, po. eds., Dept. of English, UMass-Boston, Boston, MA 02125. Issues indexed: (56:1-8). Subscriptions: $40/yr. (ind.), $50/yr. (inst.), plus $6/yr. (for.); Single issue: $6.25; Subscription address: NCTE, 1111 W. Kenyon Rd., Urbana, IL 61801-1096.

ColR: COLORADO REVIEW, David Milofsky, ed., Jorie Graham, po. ed., Dept. of English, Colorado State U., Fort Collins, CO 80523. Issues indexed: (NS 21:1-2). Subscriptions: $15/yr. (2 issues), $28/2 yrs.; $25/yr. (inst.); plus $6/yr. (for.); Single issue: $8. Subscription address: U. Press of Colorado, P.O. Box 849, Niwot, CO 80544.

Colum: COLUMBIA: A Magazine of Poetry & Prose, Airié Dekidjiev, Nick Schaffzin, eds., Scott Hightower, Mark Wunderlich, po. eds., Graduate Writing Division, 404 Dodge Hall, Columbia U., New York, NY 10027. Issues indexed: (21-22) plus "The Lost Issues," a volume "which replace[s] issues 18 & 19." Subscriptions: $7/1 issue, $13/2 issues, $18/3 issues.

Comm: COMMONWEAL, Margaret O'Brien Steinfels, ed., Rosemary Deen, po. ed., 15 Dutch St., New York, NY 10038. Issues indexed: (121:1-22). Subscriptions: $39/yr., $41/yr. (Canada), $44/yr. (for.); $67/2 yrs., $71/2 yrs. (Canada), $77/2 yrs. (for.), plus $35-$44/yr for international airmail; Single issue: $2.

Confr: CONFRONTATION, Martin Tucker, ed., English Dept., C. W. Post Campus of Long Island U., Brookville, NY 11548. Issues indexed: (52/53, 54/55). Subscriptions: $10/yr., $20/2 yrs., $30/3 yrs.; plus $5/yr. (for.).; Single issue: $7; Double issues: $10.

Conjunc: CONJUNCTIONS: Bi-Annual Volumes of New Writing, Bard College, Bradford Morrow, ed., 33 W. 9th St., New York, NY 10011. Issues indexed: (22-23). Subscriptions: Bard College, Annandale-on-Hudson, NY 12504; $18/yr. (2 issues), $32/2 yrs. (ind.); $25/yr., $45/2 yrs. (inst., for.); Back and single issues: $10.

ConnPR: THE CONNECTICUT POETRY REVIEW, Harley More, J. Claire White, eds., P.O. Box 818, Stonington, CT 06378. Issues indexed: (13:1). Single issue: $3 (including postage).

Conscience: CONSCIENCE: A Newsjournal of Prochoice Catholic Opinion, Maggie Hume, ed, Andrew Merton, po. ed., Catholics for a Free Choice, 1436 U St. NW, Washington, DC 20009-3997. Issues indexed: (15:1-4). Subscriptions: $10/yr., free to libraries; Single issue: $3.50; Back issues: $1-3.

ContextS: CONTEXT SOUTH, David Breeden, po. ed., pub., Box 4504, Schreiner College, 2100 Memorial Blvd., Kerrville, TX 78028-5697. Issues indexed: (4:1). Subscriptions: $10/3 issues.

CrabCR: CRAB CREEK REVIEW, Linda Clifton, Carol Orlock, eds., 4462 Whitman Ave. N., Seattle WA 98103. Issues indexed: (8:2/3/9:1/2/3). Subscriptions: $8/3 issues (1 volume), $15/2 volumes, plus $5/volume (for.); Back issues: $3; Anniversary Anthology: $10.

Crazy: CRAZYHORSE, Zabelle Stodola, managing ed., Ralph Burns, po. ed., Dept. of English, U. of Arkansas, 2801 S. University, Little Rock, AR 72204. Issues indexed: (46-47). Subscriptions: $10/yr. (2 issues), $18/2 yrs., $27/3 yrs. Single issue: $5.

CreamCR: CREAM CITY REVIEW, Mark Drechsler, Brian Jung, ed., Cynthia Belmont, Kristin Terwelp, po. eds., English Dept., U. of Wisconsin, P.O. Box 413, Milwaukee, WI 53201. Issues indexed: (18:1-2). Subscriptions: $10/yr. (2 issues), $16/2 yrs.; Single issue: $6; Sample and back issues: $4.50.

CrossCur: CROSSCURRENTS, Linda Brown Michelson, ed., 2200 Glastonbury Road, Westlake Village, CA 91361. Issues indexed: (10:3/4). Subscriptions: $18/yr. (4 issues), $25/2 yrs., $30/3 yrs.; Single issue: $6.

Crucible: CRUCIBLE, Terrence L. Grimes, ed., Barton College, College Station, Wilson, NC 27893. Issues indexed: No 1994 issues received. Subscriptions: $5/yr. (1 issue), $10/2 yrs; Back issues: $5.

CuadP: CUADERNOS DE POÉTICA, Diógenes Céspedes, Director, Apartado Postal 1736, Santo Domingo, Dominican Republic; US Editor: Rafael Catalá, P.O. Box 38, New Brunswick, NJ 08903. Issues indexed: (8:22-23). Subscriptions: America & Europe, $25/yr. (ind.), $30/yr. (inst.); Africa, Asia, & Oceania, $30/yr. (ind.), $40/yr. (inst).

CumbPR: CUMBERLAND POETRY REVIEW, Ingram Bloch, Bob Darrell, Sherry Bevins Darrell, Jeanne Gore, Elizabeth Hahn, Laurence Lerner, Joyce Sommer, Alison Touster-Reed, Eva Touster, Bard Young, eds., Poetics, Inc., P.O. Box 120128, Acklen Station, Nashville, TN 37212. Issues indexed: (13:2, 14:1). Subscriptions: $14/yr, $26/2 yrs. (ind.); $17/yr., $31/2 yrs. (inst.); $23/yr., $37/2 yrs. (for.); Single issue: $7; $10 (for.).

CutB: CUTBANK, Francesca Abbate, C. N. Blakemore, eds., Henrietta Goodman, po. ed., Jocelyn Siler, faculty advisor, Dept. of English, U. of Montana, Missoula, MT 59812. Issues indexed: (41). Subscriptions: $12/yr., $22/2 yrs.; Single issue: $6.95-9.95; Sample copies: $4.

Dandel: DANDELION, Bonnie Benoit, managing ed., Janeen Werner-King, Gordon Pengilly, po. eds., Alexandra Centre, 922 - 9th Ave., S.E., Calgary, Alberta T2G 0S4 Canada. Issues indexed: (20:2, 21:1-2). Subscriptions: $12/yr. (2 issues), $20/2 yrs.; $17/yr. (inst.); Single issue: $7.

DenQ: DENVER QUARTERLY, Donald Revell, ed., U. of Denver, Denver, CO 80208. Issues indexed: (28:3-4, 29:1-2). Subscriptions: $15/yr., $28/2 yrs.; $18/yr. (inst.); plus $1/yr. (for.); Single issue: $5.

Descant: DESCANT, Karen Mulhallen, ed., P.O. Box 314, Station P, Toronto, Ontario M5S 2S8 Canada. Issues indexed: (24:4, 25:1-3/4, #83-86/87). Subscriptions: $20/yr., $35/2 yrs. (ind.); $31.03/yr., $62.06/2 yrs. (inst.); plus $6/yr. (for.); Single issue: $13.91-$15..

DogRR: DOG RIVER REVIEW, Laurence F. Hawkins, ed., Trout Creek Press, 5976 Billings Road, Parkdale, OR 97041-9610. Issues indexed: (13:1-2, #25-26). Subscriptions: $8/yr. (2 issues); Single issue: $4; Sample copy: $3. Plus $2.50 (for.).

Drumvoices: DRUMVOICES: A Confluence of Literary, Cultural & Vision Arts, Eugene B. Redmond, ed., English Dept., Southern Illinois U. at Edwardsville in collaboration with the Eugene B. Redmond Writers Club of East St. Louis, Dept. of English, Box 1431, SIUE, Edwardsville, IL 62026-1431. Issues indexed: No 1994 issues received. Subscriptions: $10/yr. (2 issues); Single issue: $6.

Elf: ELF: Eclectic Literary Forum, C. K. Erbes, ed., P. O. Box 392, Tonawanda, NY 14150. Issues indexed: (4:1-4). Subscriptions: $16/yr. (4 issues), $32/yr. (inst.), plus $8/yr. (for.); Single issue: $5.50.

EngJ: ENGLISH JOURNAL, National Council of Teachers of English, Leila Christenbury, ed., School of Education, Virginia Commonwealth U., P.O. Box 842020, Richmond, VA 23284-2020; David Black, RR 1, Box 396, Louisa, VA 23093. Issues indexed: (83:1-8). Subscriptions: $40/yr. (ind.), $50/yr. (inst.), plus $6/yr. (for.); Single issue: $6.25; Subscription address: 1111 W. Kenyon Rd., Urbana, IL 61801-1096.

Epiphany: EPIPHANY: A Journal of Literature *see* OgalalaR: THE OGALALA REVIEW (title change)

Epoch: EPOCH, Michael Koch, ed., Burlin Barr, po., ed., 251 Goldwin Smith Hall, Cornell U., Ithaca, NY 14853-3201. Issues indexed: (43:1-3). Subscriptions: $11/yr.; $15/yr. (for); Single issue: $5

Event: EVENT: The Douglas College Review: New and Established Writers, Dale Zieroth, ed., Gillian Harding-Russell, po. ed., Douglas College, P.O. Box 2503, New Westminster, BC, V3L 5B2 Canada. Issues indexed: (23:1-3). Subscriptions: $15/yr. + $1.05 GST, $25/2 yrs. + $1.75 GST; Single issue: $6.

EvergreenC: THE EVERGREEN CHRONICLES: A Journal of Gay and Lesbian Literature, Greta Gaard, M. Kiesow Moore, Mark Reschke, eds., P.O. Box 8939, Minneapolis, MN 55408-0936. Issues indexed: (9:1-2). Subscriptions: $15/yr. (2 issues), $28/2 yrs.; $18/yr. (for.); $20/yr. (inst.); Single issue: $7.95.

Eyeball: EYEBALL, Jabari Asim, ed., First Civilizations Inc., P.O. Box 8135, St. Louis, MO 63108. Issues indexed: (3). Subscriptions: $7/yr. (2 issues), $14/2 yrs., $21/3 yrs; $28/yr., $56/2 yrs., $82/3 yrs. (for.); Single issue: $3.50.

Farm: FARMER'S MARKET, Jean C. Lee, John E. Hughes, Lisa Ress, eds., Midwest Farmer's Market, Inc., P.O. Box 1272, Galesburg, IL 61402. Issues indexed: (11:1-2). Subscriptions: $10/yr. (2 issues); Single issue: $6.

Field: FIELD: Contemporary Poetry and Poetics, Stuart Friebert, Alberta Turner, David Walker, David Young, eds., Rice Hall, Oberlin College, Oberlin, OH 44074. Issues indexed: (50-51). Subscriptions: $12/yr., $20/2 yrs.; Single issue: $6; Back issues: $12.

FloridaR: THE FLORIDA REVIEW, Russell Kesler, ed., Dept. of English, U. of Central Florida, Orlando, FL 32816. Issues indexed: (19:2, 20:1). Subscriptions: $7/yr., $11/2 yrs.; Single issue: $4.50.

Footwork: FOOTWORK: The Paterson Literary Review, Maria Mazziotti Gillan, ed., Passaic County Community College, 1 College Blvd., Paterson, NJ 07505-1179. Issues indexed: No 1994 issues received. Subscriptions: $10/issue.

FourQ: FOUR QUARTERS, John J. Keenan, ed., La Salle U., 1900 W. Olney, Philadelphia, PA 19141. Issues indexed: (8:1-2) Second Series. Subscriptions: $8/yr. (2 issues), $13/2 yrs.; Single issue: $4.

FreeL: FREE LUNCH: A Poetry Journal, Free Lunch Arts Alliance, Ron Offen, ed., P.O. Box 7647, Laguna Niguel, CA 92607-7647. Issues indexed: (13). Subscriptions: Free to all serious poets in the U.S.A.; $12/3 issues; $15/3 issues (for.); Single issue: $5, $6 (for.).

Gaia: GAIA: A Journal of Literature & Environmental Arts, Robert S. King, ed., Charles Fishman, po. ed., Whistle Press, Inc., P.O. Box 709, Winterville, GA 30683. Issues indexed: (4). Subscriptions: $9/2 issues, $16/4 issues; plus $4/2 issues (for.); Single issue: $6; Double issue: $8.

GeoR: GEORGIA REVIEW, Stanley W. Lindberg, ed., U. of Georgia, Athens, GA 30602. Issues indexed: (48:1-4). Subscriptions: $18/yr., $30/2 yrs., plus $5/yr. (for.); Single and back issues: $7.

GettyR: GETTYSBURG REVIEW, Peter Stitt, ed., Gettysburg College, Gettysburg, PA 17325-1491. Issues indexed: (7:1-4). Subscriptions: $18/yr., $32/2 yrs., $45/3 yrs.; $26/yr., $48/2 yrs., $69/3 yrs. (for.); Single issue: $7.

GlobalCR: GLOBAL CITY REVIEW, Linsey Abrams, E. M. Broner, eds., Simon H. Rifkind Center for the Humanities, City College of New York, 138th & Convent Ave, New York, NY 10031. Issues indexed: (3-4). Subscriptions: $12/yr. (2 issues); $20/2 yrs.; $15/yr., $25/2 yrs. (inst.); $17/yr., $30/2 yrs. (for.); Single and back issues: $6 plus $1 mailing charge.

GrahamHR: GRAHAM HOUSE REVIEW, Peter Balakian, Bruce Smith, eds., Colgate U. Press, Box 5000, Colgate U., Hamilton, NY 13346; Issues indexed: (18). Subscriptions: $15/2 yrs. (2 issues), $25/4 yrs.; Single issue: $7.50.

Grain: GRAIN, Saskatchewan Writers Guild, Geoffrey Ursell, ed., Elizabeth Philips, interim ed., Judith Krause, po. ed., Box 1154, Regina, Saskatchewan S4P 3B4 Canada. Issues indexed: (21:4, 22:1-2). Subscriptions: $19.95+$1.40 GST/yr., $34.95+$2.45 GST/2 yrs., plus $4/yr. (U.S.), plus $6/yr. (for.); Single issue: $6.95.

GrandS: GRAND STREET, Jean Stein, ed., 131 Varick St. #906, New York, NY 10013. Issues indexed: (12:4, 13:1-2, #48-50). Subscriptions: $30/yr. (4 issues), $50/yr. (for.); Single issue: $10, $12.99 (Canada); Subscription address: Dept. GRS, P.O. Box 3000, Denville, NJ 07834.

GreenMR: GREEN MOUNTAINS REVIEW, Neil Shepard, ed. & po. ed., Johnson State College, Johnson, VT 05656. Issues indexed: (NS 7:1-2). Subscriptions: $12/yr. (2 issues), $18/2 yrs.; Single issue: $7.

GreensboroR: THE GREENSBORO REVIEW, Jim Clark, ed., Julie Funderburk, po. ed., Dept. of English, U. of North Carolina, Greensboro, NC 27412. Issues indexed: (56). Subscriptions: $8/yr. (2 issues), $20/3 yrs.; Single issue: $4.

Gypsy: GYPSY, Belinda Subraman, S. Ramnath, eds., 10708 Gay Brewer Dr., El Paso, TX 79935. Issues indexed: No 1994 issues received. Subscriptions: $14/yr. (2 issues); Single issue: $7.

HampSPR: THE HAMPDEN-SYDNEY POETRY REVIEW, Tom O'Grady, ed., P.O. Box 126, Hampden-Sydney, VA 23943. Issues indexed: Wint 1994. Subscriptions: $5/yr. (1 issue); 1990 Anthology, $12.95.

HangL: HANGING LOOSE, Robert Hershon, Dick Lourie, Mark Pawlak, Ron Schreiber, eds., 231 Wyckoff St., Brooklyn, NY 11217. Issues indexed: (64-65). Subscriptions: $12.50/3 issues, $24/6 issues, $35/9 issues (ind.); $15/3 issues, $30/6 issues, $45/9 issues (inst.); $22/3 issues, $42/6 issues, $62/9 issues (for.); Sample issue: $5 plus $1.50 postage and handling.

Harp: HARPER'S MAGAZINE, Lewis H. Lapham, ed., 666 Broadway, New York, NY 10012. Issues indexed: (288:1724-1729, 289:1730-1735). Subscriptions: $18/yr., plus $2/yr. (USA possessions, Canada), plus $20/yr. (for.); Single issue: $2.95; Subscription address: P.O. Box 7511, Red Oak, IA 51591-0511.

HarvardA: THE HARVARD ADVOCATE, Kyle Waide, Managing ed., Chris Dysard, po. ed., 21 South St., Cambridge, MA 02138. Issues indexed: (128:2-3, 129:1-2). Subscriptions: $15/yr. (ind.), $17/yr. (inst.), $20/yr. (for.); Single issue: $4.

HarvardR: HARVARD REVIEW, Stratis Haviaras, ed., Fred Marchant, po. ed., Poetry Room, Harvard College Library, Cambridge, MA 02138. Issues indexed: (1-2, 6-7). Subscriptions: $12/yr. (2 issues); $16/yr. (for. surface), $24/yr. (for. air mail); Single issue: $8.

HawaiiR: HAWAI'I REVIEW, Robert S. MacBeth, ed., Michelle Viray, Annie Fanning, po. eds., Dept. of English, U. of Hawai'i, 1733 Donaghho Rd., Honolulu, HI 96822. Issues indexed: (18:1, #40). Subscriptions: $15/yr. (3 issues), $25/2 yrs.; Single issue: $5.

HayF: HAYDEN'S FERRY REVIEW, Salima Keegan, managing ed., Erika Lenz, Jonathan Schouten, po. eds., Box 871502, Arizona State U., Tempe, AZ 85287-1502. Issues indexed: (14-15). Subscriptions: $10/yr. (2 issues), $18/2 yrs.; $13/yr., $26/2 yrs. (inst.); Single and back issues: $5 plus $1 postage.

HeavenB: HEAVEN BONE, Steven Hirsch, ed., pub., P.O. Box 486, Chester, NY 10918. Issues indexed: (11). Subscriptions: $16.95/4 issues; Single issue: $6.

Hellas: HELLAS: A Journal of Poetry and the Humanities, Gerald Harnett, ed., The Aldine Press, Ltd., 304 S. Tyson Ave., Glenside, PA 19038. Issues indexed: (5:1-2). Subscriptions: $14/yr. (2 issues), $24/2 yrs.; plus $4/yr. (for.); Single issue: $7.50.

HighP: HIGH PLAINS LITERARY REVIEW, Robert O. Greer, Jr., ed., Joy Harjo, po. ed., 180 Adams St., Suite 250, Denver, CO 80206. Issues indexed: (9:1-3). Subscriptions: $20/yr. (3 issues), $38/2 yrs., plus $5/yr. (for.); Single issue: $7.

HiramPoR: HIRAM POETRY REVIEW, English Dept., Hiram College, Hale Chatfield, ed., P.O. Box 162, Hiram, OH 44234. Issues indexed: (55/56-57). Subscriptions: $8/yr. (2 issues); Single issue: $4.

HolCrit: THE HOLLINS CRITIC, John Rees Moore, ed., Hollins College, VA 24020. Issues indexed: (31:1-5). Subscriptions: $6/yr. (5 issues); $7.50/yr. (for.).

HopewellR: HOPEWELL REVIEW: New Work by Indiana's Best Writers, Joseph F. Trimmer, ed., Erik M. Novak, po. ed., Arts Indiana, Inc., The Majestic Building, 47 S. Pennsylvania St., Suite 701, Indianapolis, IN 46204-3622. Issues indexed: (6). Single issue: $6.95; Back issues: $2.50-$4.95 plus $2.50 shipping.

Hudson: THE HUDSON REVIEW, Paula Deitz, Frederick Morgan, eds., 684 Park Ave., New York, NY 10021. Issues indexed: (46:4, 47:1-3). Subscriptions: $24/yr., $46/2 yrs., $68/3 yrs., plus $4/yr. (for.); Single issue: $7.

IllinoisR: THE ILLINOIS REVIEW, Illinois Writers, Inc., Jim Elledge, ed., Dept. of English, Illinois State U., Campus Box 4240, Normal, IL 61790-4240. Issues indexed: (1:2, 2:1). Subscriptions: $10/yr. (2 issues), $18/yr. (inst.), $15/yr. (prepaid inst.); Single issue: $6.

*Image: IMAGE: A Journal of the Arts & Religion, Gregory Wolfe, ed. and pub., Andrew Hudgins, Denise Levertov, Paul Mariani, po. eds., Richard Wilkinson, managing ed., P.O. Box 674, Kennett Square, PA 19348. Issues indexed: ([2]-8); issue 2, Sum 92, is not numbered. Subscriptions: $30/yr. (4 issues), $60/2 yrs., $40/yr. (for.); Single issue: $10; Subscription address: P.O. Box 3000, Denville, NJ 07834-9351.

IndR: INDIANA REVIEW, Cara Diaconoff, ed., Christopher Green, Jeffrey McKenzie, Adam Sol, po. eds., Indiana U., 316 N. Jordan Ave., Bloomington, IN 47405. Issues indexed: (17:1-2). Subscriptions: $12/2 issues, $15/2 issues (inst.); $22/4 issues (ind.), $25/4 issues (inst.); plus $5/2 issues (for.); Single issue: $7.

Interim: INTERIM, A. Wilber Stevens, ed., Dept. of English, U. of Nevada, 4505 Maryland Parkway, Box 455011, Las Vegas, NV 89154-5011. Issues indexed: (13:1-2). Subscriptions: $8/yr. (2 issues), $13/2 yrs., $16/3 yrs. (ind.); $14/yr. (lib.), $16/yr. (for.); Single issue: $5, $8 (for.).

InterPR: INTERNATIONAL POETRY REVIEW, Mark Smith-Soto, ed., Dept. of Romance Languages, U. of North Carolina, Greensboro, NC 27412-5001. Issues indexed: (20:1-2). Subscriptions: $10/yr. (2 issues, ind.), $15/yr. (inst.); plus $2/yr. (for.); Single issue: $5.

*InterQ: INTERNATIONAL QUARTERLY, Van K. Brock, ed. & pub., P.O. Box 10521, Tallahassee, FL 32302-0521. Issues indexed: (1:1-4). Subscriptions: $22/yr. (4 issues), $38/2 yrs., $50/3 yrs. (ind.); $40/yr., $75/2 yrs., $100/3 yrs. (inst.); plus. $2.50/issue (for.); Single issue: $8.

Inti: INTI: Revista de Literatura Hispánica, Roger B. Carmosino, ed., P.O. Box 20657, Cranston, RI 02920. Issues indexed: (39-40/41). Subscriptions: $30/yr. (2 issues, ind.), $25/yr. (students), $50/yr. (inst.); Single issue: $14.

Iowa: IOWA REVIEW, David Hamilton, ed., 308 EPB, U. of Iowa, Iowa City, IA 52242-1492. Issues indexed: (24:1-3). Subscriptions: $18/yr. (3 issues, ind.), $20/yr. (inst.), plus $3/yr. (for.); Single issue: $6.95.

Jacaranda: JACARANDA, Cornel Bonca, ed., English Dept., California State U., Fullerton, CA 92634. Issues indexed: (4:2, 5:1, 10); Vol. 4, no. 2 (Spr 90) and vol. 5, no. 1 (Wint-Spr 91) had not been received previously for indexing. "There is no vol. 5, no. 2." "Jacaranda went temporarily dark after vol. 6:1/2 [indexed in 1992 vol.], and reappeared in 1994 with a new issue, numbered simply "10." Subsequent issues will be numbered 11, 12, 13, and so on" -- Cornel Bonca, ed. Subscriptions: $10/yr. (2 issues, ind.), $14/yr. (inst.); Sample issues: $6.

JamesWR: THE JAMES WHITE REVIEW, A Gay Men's Literary Journal, Phil Willkie, pub., Clif Mayhood, po. ed., P.O. Box 3356, Butler Quarter Station, Minneapolis, MN 55403. Issues indexed: (11:2-5). Subscriptions: $12/yr., $20/2 yrs.; $16/yr., $30/2 yrs. (Canada); $20/yr. (other for.); Single issue: $3, $4 (Canada); Back issues: $1 (for minimum order of $10).

JINJPo: THE JOURNAL OF NEW JERSEY POETS, Sander Zulauf, ed., Center for Teaching Excellence, County College of Morris, 214 Center Grove Rd., Randolph, NJ 07869-2086. Issues indexed: (16:1-2). Subscriptions: $7/yr. (2 issues), $12/2 yrs.; Single issue: $4.

Journal: THE JOURNAL, Kathy Fagan, Michelle Herman, eds., The Ohio State U., Dept. of English, 164 W. 17th Ave., Columbus, OH 43210. Issues indexed: (18:1-2). Subscriptions: $8/yr. (2 issues), $16/2 yrs., $24/3 yrs.; Single issue: $5.

Kaleid: KALEIDOSCOPE, International Magazine of Literature, Fine Arts, and Disability, Darshan Perusek, ed., Chris Hewitt, po. ed. (51 W. 86th ST., #404, New York, NY 10024), United Disability Services, 326 Locust St., Akron, OH 44302-1876. Issues indexed: (28-29, plus "Special Issue 1994"). Subscriptions: $9/yr. (2 issues, ind.), $14/yr. (inst.), plus $5/yr. (Canada); plus $8/yr. (other for.); Single issue: $5, $7 (for.); Sample issue: $4. Also available on audio cassette.

Kalliope: KALLIOPE: A Journal of Women's Art, Mary Sue Koeppel, ed., Florida Community College at Jacksonville, 3939 Roosevelt Blvd., Jacksonville, FL 32205. Issues indexed: (16:1-3). Subscriptions: $12.50/1 yr. (3 issues), $22/2 yrs. (ind.); $20/yr. (inst.); plus $6/yr. (for.); free to women in prison; Single issue: $7, plus $2 (for.), $3 (for., double issue); Back issues: $4-8.

KenR: KENYON REVIEW, Marilyn Hacker, ed., Kenyon College, Gambier, OH 43022. Issues indexed: (NS 16:1-4). Subscriptions: Kenyon Review, P.O. Box 8062, Syracuse, NY 13217; $22/yr., $40/2 yrs., $60/3 yrs. (ind.); $24/yr. (inst.); plus $8 (for.); Single issue: $8, including postage; Back issues: $10.

Lactuca: LACTUCA, Mike Selender, ed., P.O. Box 621, Suffern, NY 10901. Issues indexed: No 1994 issues received. Subscriptions: $10/3 issues, $13/3 issues (for.), $17/6 issues, $23/6 issues (for.); Single issue: $4, plus $2 (for.).

LaurelR: LAUREL REVIEW, William Trowbridge, David Slater, Beth Richards, eds., GreenTower Press, Dept. of English, Northwest Missouri State U., Maryville, MO 64468. Issues indexed: (28:1-2). Subscriptions: $8/yr. (2 issues), $14/2 yrs.; $11/yr., $20/2 yrs. (for.); Single issue: $5; Back issues: $4.50.

Light: LIGHT: A Quarterly of Humorous, Occasional, Ephemeral & Light Verse, John Mella, ed., Box 7500, Chicago, IL 60680. Issues indexed: (9-12). Subscriptions: $16/yr. (4 issues), $28/2 yrs.; $24/yr. (for.); Single issue: $6; Back issues: $4.

LindLM: LINDEN LANE MAGAZINE, Belkis Cuza Malé, ed., 6724 Crooked Palm Terr., Miami Lakes, FL 33014. Issues indexed: (13:1). Subscriptions: $12/yr. (ind.), $22/yr. (inst.), $22/yr. (Latin America, Europe); Single issue: $2.

LitR: THE LITERARY REVIEW: An International Journal of Contemporary Writing, Walter Cummins, ed., Fairleigh Dickinson U., 285 Madison Ave., Madison, NJ 07940. Issues indexed: (37:2-4, 38:1). Subscriptions: $18/yr., $21/yr. (for.); $30/2 yrs., $36/2 yrs. (for.); Single issue: $5, $6 (for.).

LouisL : LOUISIANA LITERATURE: A Review of Literature and Humanities, David C. Hanson, ed., Dept. of English, SLU-792, Southeastern Louisiana U., Box 792, Hammond, LA 70402. Issues indexed: (11:1-2). Subscriptions: $10/yr. (2 issues, ind.); $12.50/yr. (inst.); plus $5/yr. (Canada), plus $10/yr. (other for.).

LullwaterR: LULLWATER REVIEW, Daniel A. Atkins, ed., Box 22036, Emory U., Atlanta, GA 30322. Issues indexed: No 1994 issues received. Subscriptions: $12/yr. (2 issues), plus $3 (for.); Single issue: $5.

Luz: LUZ: En Arte y Literatura, Verónica Miranda, Directora/Editora, Luz Bilingual Publishing, P.O. Box 571062, Tarzana, CA 91357-1062. Issues indexed: (6-7). Subscriptions: $25/yr. (3 issues), $45/2 yrs., $65/3 yrs.; $35/yr. (for.); Single issue: $8, plus $3 (for.).

MalR: THE MALAHAT REVIEW, U. of Victoria, Derk Wynand, ed., P.O. Box 1700, Victoria, BC, Canada V8W 2Y2. Issues indexed: (106-109). Subscriptions: $18 plus $1.26 GST/yr. (4 issues), $32 plus $2.24 GST/2 yrs.; $20/yr. US Funds (U.S.); Single issue: $7.

ManhatR: THE MANHATTAN REVIEW, Philip Fried, ed., 440 Riverside Dr., #45, New York, NY 10027. Issues indexed: No 1994 issues received. Subscriptions: $10/2 issues (ind.), $14/2 issues (inst.), plus $3/issue (outside USA & Canada); Back issues: $5 (ind.), $7 (inst); include 6" x 9" envelope and $1.45 for postage.

Manoa: MANOA: A Pacific Journal of International Writing, Robert Shapard, Frank Stewart, eds., Frank Stewart, po. ed., English Dept., U. of Hawaii, Honolulu, HI 96822. Issues indexed: (6:1-2). Subscriptions: $18/yr. (2 issues), $32/2 yrs. (ind.); $22/yr., $40/2 yrs. (inst.); $21/yr., $38/2 yrs. (for. ind.); $26/yr., $47/2 yrs. (for. inst.); plus $12/yr. (for. air mail); Single issue: $15. Subscription address: U. of Hawaii Press, 2840 Kolowalu St., Honolulu, HI 96822.

MassR: THE MASSACHUSETTS REVIEW, Jules Chametzky, Mary Heath, Paul Jenkins, eds., Martín Espada, Anne Halley, Paul Jenkins, po. eds., Memorial Hall, U. of Massachusetts, Amherst, MA 01003. Issues indexed: (35:1-3/4). Subscriptions: $15/yr. (4 issues, ind.), $20/yr. (lib.), $25/yr. (for.); Single issue: $5.

Mester: MESTER, José Ramón Núñez-Astray, ed., Dept. of Spanish and Portuguese, U. of California, Los Angeles, CA 90024-1532. Issues indexed: (22:2/23:1). Subscriptions: $18/yr. (2 issues, ind.), $30/yr. (inst.), $12/yr. (stud.), $24/yr. (Latin America), plus $5/yr. outside U.S., Canada, Mexico.

MichQR: MICHIGAN QUARTERLY REVIEW, Laurence Goldstein, ed., 3032 Rackham Bldg., U. of Michigan, Ann Arbor, MI 48109. Issues indexed: (33:1-4). Subscriptions: $18/yr., $36/2 yrs. (ind.), $20/yr. (inst.); Single issue: $5; Back issues: $2.50.

MidAR: MID-AMERICAN REVIEW, Robert Early, George Looney, eds., Doug Martin, po. ed., 106 Hanna Hall, Dept. of English, Bowling Green State U., Bowling Green, OH 43403. Issues indexed: (14:2). Subscriptions: $12/yr. (2 issues), $20/2 yrs., $28/3 yrs; Single issue: $7; Sample issue: $5.

MidwQ: THE MIDWEST QUARTERLY: A Journal of Contemporary Thought, James B. M. Schick, ed., Stephen E. Meats, po. ed., Pittsburg State U., Pittsburg, KS 66762-5889. Issues indexed: (35:2-4, 36:1). Subscriptions: $12/yr. plus $4 (for.); Single issue: $4.

MinnR: THE MINNESOTA REVIEW: a journal of committed writing, Jeffrey Williams, ed., Rebecca Wee, Michael Huff, po. eds., Dept. of English, East Carolina U., Greenville, NC 27858-4353. Issues indexed: (NS 40). Subscriptions: $12/yr. (2 issues); $24/yr. (inst., for.), plus $5/yr. (for. air mail); Single and back issues: $7.50; Double issue: $12.50.

MissouriR: THE MISSOURI REVIEW, Speer Morgan, ed., College of Arts & Science, 1507 Hillcrest Hall, U. of Missouri, Columbia, MO 65211. Issues indexed: (17:1-3). Subscriptions: $15/yr. (3 issues), $27/2 yrs., $36/3 yrs.; Single issue: $6.

MissR: MISSISSIPPI REVIEW, Frederick Barthelme, ed., The Center for Writers, U. of Southern Mississippi, Box 5144, Hattiesburg, MS 39406-5144. Issues indexed: (22:3, 23:1/2). Subscriptions: $15/yr. (2 issues), $28/2 yrs., $40/3 yrs., plus $2/yr. (for.); Single issue: usually $12.

*ModernW: MODERN WORDS: a thoroughly queer international literary journal, Garland Richard Kyle, ed. & pub., 350 Bay St., No. 100, Box 325, San Francisco, CA 94133. Issues indexed: (1-2). Subscriptions: $25/3 issues, $100/lifetime; Single issue: $10.

MoodySI: MOODY STREET IRREGULARS: A Jack Kerouac Newsletter, Joy Walsh, Mike Basinski, eds., P.O. Box 157, Clarence Center, NY 14032. Issues indexed: 28 (labeled 29 on p. 2): "The Last Word: Final Issue."

Nat: THE NATION, Katrina vanden Heuvel (acting), Victor Navasky (on leave), eds., Grace Schulman, po. ed., 72 Fifth Ave., New York, NY 10011. Issues indexed: (258:1-25, 259:1-22); 258:1-16 not received. Subscriptions: $48/yr., $80/2 yrs., plus $18/yr. (for.); Single issue: $2.25, $2.75 (Canada); Back issues: $4, $5 (for.). Send subscription correspondence to: P.O. Box 10763, Des Moines, IA 50340-0763.

NegC: NEGATIVE CAPABILITY, Sue Walker, ed., 62 Ridgelawn Dr. East, Mobile, AL 36608. Issues indexed: (13:1-2/3, 14:1/2). Subscriptions: $15/yr. (3 issues, ind.), $20/yr. (inst., for.); Single issue: $5.

NewAW: NEW AMERICAN WRITING, Maxine Chernoff, Paul Hoover, eds., OINK! Press, 2920 West Pratt, Chicago, IL 60645. Issues indexed: (12). Subscriptions: $18/3 issues; $24/3 issues (inst.); plus $7/3 issues (for.); Single issue: $7.

NewDeltaR: NEW DELTA REVIEW, Nicola Mason, Catherine Williamson, eds., Brook Haley, po. ed., James Gordon Bennett, faculty advisor, Creative Writing Program, English Dept., Louisiana State U., Baton Rouge, LA 70803-5001. Issues indexed: (10:1-2, 11:1-2). Subscriptions: $7/yr. (2 issues); Single issue: $4.

NewEngR: NEW ENGLAND REVIEW, Middlebury Series, David Huddle, acting ed., Middlebury College, Middlebury, VT 05753. Issues indexed: (16:1-4). Subscriptions: $23/yr. (4 issues), $43/2 yrs., $62/3 yrs. (ind.); $40/yr., $75/2 yrs., $108/3 yrs. (lib., inst.); plus $10/yr. (for. surface) or $20/yr. (for. air mail); Single issue: $7, $9 (for. surface), $10 (for. air mail); subscription address: U. Press of New England, 23 S. Main St., Hanover, NH 03755-2048.

NewL: NEW LETTERS, James McKinley, ed., U. of Missouri-Kansas City, 5100 Rockhill Rd., Kansas City, MO 64110. Issues indexed: (60:2-4, 61:1). Subscriptions: $17/yr. (4 issues), $28/2 yrs., $55/5 yrs. (ind.); $20/yr., $34/2 yrs., $65/5 yrs. (lib.); Single issue: $5, $6 (Canada).

NewOR: NEW ORLEANS REVIEW, Ralph Adamo, ed., Box 195, Loyola U., New Orleans, LA 70118. Issues indexed: (20:1/2-3/4). Subscriptions: $18/yr. (ind.), $21/yr. (inst.), $24/yr. (for.); Single issue: $9.

NewRena: THE NEW RENAISSANCE, Louise T. Reynolds, ed., James E. A. Woodbury, po. ed., 9 Heath Road, Arlington, MA 02174-3614. Issues indexed: (9:1, #27). Subscriptions: $19.50/3 issues, $37.50/6 issues; $21/3 issues, $39/3 issues (Canada); $23/3 issues, $41/6 issues (other for.); Single issue: $9, $9.50 (for.).

NewRep: THE NEW REPUBLIC, Andrew Sullivan, ed., Mary Jo Salter, po. ed., 1220 19th St. NW, Washington, DC 20036. Issues indexed: (210:1-26, 211:1-26). Subscriptions: $69.97/yr., $84.97/yr. (Canada), $99.97/yr. (elsewhere). Back issues: $3.50. Single issue: $2.95. Subscription Service Dept., The New Republic, P.O. Box 602, Mount Morris, IL 61054.

NewYorker: THE NEW YORKER, Pamela Maffei McCarthy, managing ed., 20 W. 43rd St., New York, NY 10036. Issues indexed: (69:45-50, 70:1-43). Subscriptions: $32/yr., $52/2 yrs.; $65.27/yr. (Canada); $76/yr. (other for.); Single issue: $1.95; Subscription correspondence to: Box 56447, Boulder, CO 80322.

NewYorkQ: THE NEW YORK QUARTERLY, William Packard, ed., P.O. Box 693, Old Chelsea Station, New York, NY 10113. Issues indexed: (53). Subscriptions: $15/yr., $30/2 yrs., $45/3 yrs.; $25/yr. (lib.); plus $5/yr. (for.); Single issue: $6.

NewYRB: THE NEW YORK REVIEW OF BOOKS, Robert B. Silvers, Barbara Epstein, eds., 250 W. 57th St., New York, NY 10107. Issues indexed: (41:1/2-21). Subscriptions: $49.50/yr.; Single issue: $3.25, $4.60 (Canada); NY Review of Books, P.O. Box 420384, Palm Coast, FL 32142-0384.

Nimrod: NIMROD, Francine Ringold, ed., Manly Johnson, po. ed., Arts and Humanities Council of Tulsa, 2210 S. Main St., Tulsa, OK 74114. Issues indexed: (37:2, 38:1). Subscriptions: $11.50/yr. (2 issues), $21/2 yrs., $30.50/3 yrs.; plus $3/yr. (for.); Single issue: $6.95.

NoAmR: THE NORTH AMERICAN REVIEW, Robley Wilson, ed., Peter Cooley, po. ed., U. of Northern Iowa, Cedar Falls, IA 50614-0516. Issues indexed: (279:1-6). Subscriptions: $18/yr., $25/yr. (Canada), $28/yr. (elsewhere); Single issue: $4, $5.25 (Canada).

NoCarLR: NORTH CAROLINA LITERARY REVIEW, Alex Albright, ed., English Dept., East Carolina U., Greenville, NC 27858-4353. Issues indexed: (2:1). Subscriptions: $17/yr. (2 issues), $31/2 yrs.; plus $5/yr. (for.); Single issues: 10.50.

Noctiluca: NOCTILUCA: An International Magazine of Poetry, Judy Katz-Levine, ed., 10 Hillshire Ln., Norwood, MA 02062-3009. Issues indexed: (3). Subscriptions: $10/3 issues.

NoDaQ: NORTH DAKOTA QUARTERLY, Robert W. Lewis, ed., Jay Meek, po. ed., U. of North Dakota, Grand Forks, ND 58202-7209. Issues indexed: (62:1-4). Subscriptions: $20/yr., $24/yr. (inst.); $23/yr. (for. ind.), $28/yr. (for. inst.); Single issue: $5 (ind.), $7 (for.); Special issues: $10, $12 (for.).

Northeast: NORTHEAST, John Judson, ed., Juniper Press, 1310 Shorewood Dr., La Crosse, WI 54601. Issues indexed: (Ser. 5:10-11). Subscriptions: $33 (2 issues, including books and gifts of the press, ind.), $38 (inst.); Single issue: $4.

NorthStoneR: THE NORTH STONE REVIEW, James Naiden, ed., D Station, Box 14098, Minneapolis, MN 55414. Issues indexed: No 1994 issues published; No. 12 published in 1995. Subscriptions: $15/yr. (2 issues); Single issue: $8.

NowestR: NORTHWEST REVIEW, John Witte, ed. & po. ed., 369 PLC, U. of Oregon, Eugene, OR 97403. Issues indexed: (32:1-3). Subscriptions: $14/yr. (3 issues), $26/2 yrs., $35/3 yrs.; $12/yr., $22/2 yrs. (stud.); plus $2/yr. (for.); Single issue: $5.

Nuez: LA NUEZ: Revista Internacional de Arte y Literatura, Rafael Bordao, ed., P.O. Box 023617, Brooklyn, NY 11202. Issues indexed: (5:13-15): last issue.

Obs: OBSIDIAN II: Black Literature in Review, Gerald Barrax, ed. & po. ed., Dept. of English, Box 8105, North Carolina State U., Raleigh, NC 27695-8105. Issues indexed: (9:1-2). Subscriptions: $12/yr. (2 issues), $20/2 yrs.; $13/yr. (Canada), $15/yr. (other for.); Single issue: $5; Double issues: $10.

OgalalaR: THE OGALALA REVIEW, Gordon Grice, Tracy Hiatt Grice, eds., P.O. Box 2699, U. of Arkansas, Fayetteville, AR 72701. Issues indexed: (5:1); 4:1 not received. Subscriptions: $10/yr. (2 issues), $18/2 yrs; Single issue: $5.

OhioR: THE OHIO REVIEW, Wayne Dodd, ed., Ellis Hall, Ohio U., Athens, OH 45701-2979. Issues indexed: (51-52). Subscriptions: $16/yr. (3 issues), $40/3 yrs.; Single issue: $6.

Ometeca: OMETECA: Ciencia y Literatura, Science & Literature, Ciência e literatura, Rafael Catalá, ed., P.O. Box 38, New Brunswick, NJ 08903-0038. Issues indexed: No 1994 issues published. Subscriptions: $20/yr. (2 issues, ind.), $35/yr. (inst., USA, Canada, Mexico); $33/yr. (elsewhere).

OnTheBus: ONTHEBUS: A New Literary Magazine, Jack Grapes, ed., Bombshelter Press, 6421-1/2 Orange St., Los Angeles, CA 90048. Issues indexed: No 1994 issues received. Subscriptions: $28/3 issues (ind.), $33/3 issues (inst.); Single issue: $11, plus $1 postage; Double issue: $13.50 plus $1.50 postage.

OntR: ONTARIO REVIEW, Raymond J. Smith, ed., 9 Honey Brook Dr., Princeton, NJ 08540. Issues indexed: (40-41). Subscriptions: $12/yr. (2 issues), $22/2 yrs., $30/3 yrs., plus $2/yr. (for.); Single issue: $6.

Os: OSIRIS, Andrea Moorhead, ed., P.O. Box 297, Deerfield, MA 01342. Issues indexed: (38-39). Subscriptions: $12/2 issues; Single issue: $6.

Outbr: OUTERBRIDGE, Charlotte Alexander, ed., English Dept., College of Staten Island (CUNY), 2800 Victory Blvd., Staten Island, NY 10314. Issues indexed: (25). Subscriptions: $5/yr. (1 issue).

OxfordM: OXFORD MAGAZINE, Constance Pierce, editorial advisor, Dept. of English, Bachelor Hall, Miami U., Oxford, OH 45056. Issues indexed: No 1994 issues received. Single issue: $5.

Paint: PAINTBRUSH: A Journal of Contemporary Multicultural Literature, Ben Bennani, ed., Northeast Missouri State U., Kirksville, MO 63501. Issues indexed: (21). Subscriptions: $15/yr. (1 issue, ind.), $20/yr. (inst.); Single and back issues: $7.

PaintedB: PAINTED BRIDE QUARTERLY, Kathy Volk Miller, Brian Brown, Marion Wrenn, eds., Painted Bride Arts Center, 230 Vine St., Philadelphia, PA 19106. Issues indexed: (53/54). Subscriptions: $16/yr. (4 issues), $28/2 yrs., $20/yr. (lib., inst.); Single issue: $5. Distributed free to inmates.

PaintedHR: PAINTED HILLS REVIEW, Michael Ishii, Kara D. Kosmatka, eds., 2950 Portage Bay West #411, Davis, CA 95616. Issues indexed: (11). Subscriptions: $10/3 issues, $18/6 issues (USA & Canada); $14/3 issues, $24/6 issues (other for.); Single issue: $3.50.

ParisR: THE PARIS REVIEW, George A. Plimpton, Peter Matthiessen, Donald Hall, Robert Silvers, Blair Fuller, Maxine Groffsky, Jeanne McCulloch, James Linville, eds., Richard Howard, po. ed., Box S, 541 East 72nd St., New York, NY 10021. Issues indexed: (36:130-133). Subscriptions: $34/4 issues, plus $7/4 issues (for.); Single issue: $10, $13 (Canada); Subscription address: 45-39 171st Place, Flushing, NY 11358.

Parting: PARTING GIFTS, Robert Bixby, ed. and pub., March Street Press, 3413 Wilshire Dr., Greensboro, NC 27408-2923. Issues indexed: (7:1-2). Subscriptions: $5/yr. (2 issues), $9/2 yrs., $13/3 yrs.; Single issue: $3.

PartR: PARTISAN REVIEW, William Phillips, ed., Boston U., 236 Bay State Rd., Boston, MA 02215. Issues indexed: (61:1-4). Subscriptions: $22/yr. (4 issues), $40/2 yrs., $56/3 yrs.; $28/yr., $56/2 yrs. (for.); $32/yr. (inst.); Single issue: $6, plus $1.50 per issue postage and handling.

PassN: PASSAGES NORTH, Anne Ohman Youngs, ed., Conrad Hilberry, po. ed., English Dept., Northern Michigan U., Marquette, MI 49855-5363. Issues indexed: (15:1-2); spine of 15:2, Wint 94 has "16:2". Subscriptions: $10/yr., $18/2 yrs; plus $9/yr. (for.); Single issue: $6.

Pearl: PEARL, Joan Jobe Smith, Marilyn Johnson, Barbara Hauk, eds., 3030 E. 2nd St., Long Beach, CA 90803. Issues indexed: (20). Subscriptions: $15/yr. (3 issues, ind.); $20/yr. (lib.); $30/yr. (patrons); Single issue: $6.

Pembroke: PEMBROKE MAGAZINE, Shelby Stephenson, ed., Box 60, Pembroke State U., Pembroke, NC 28372. Issues indexed: (26). Subscriptions: $5/issue (USA, Canada, Mexico), $5.50/issue (other for.).

PennR: THE PENNSYLVANIA REVIEW, Ed Ochester, executive ed., Julie Parson-Nesbitt, po. ed., 526 Cathedral of Learning, U. of Pittsburgh, Pittsburgh, PA 15260. Issues indexed: (5:2). Subscriptions: $10/yr. (2 issues), $18/2 yrs.; Single issue: $6.

Pequod: PEQUOD, Mark Rudman, ed., Dept. of English, Room 200, New York U., 19 University Pl., New York, NY 10003. Issues indexed: (37-38). Subscriptions: $12/yr. (2 issues), $20/2 yrs. (ind.); $18/yr., $34/2 yrs. (inst).; plus $3/yr. (for.); Single issue: $7.50-$10.

PikeF: THE PIKESTAFF FORUM, Robert D. Sutherland, James R. Scrimgeour, eds./pubs., P.O. Box 127, Normal, IL 61761. Issues indexed: No 1994 issues received. Subscriptions: $12/6 issues; Single issue: $3.

*Pivot: PIVOT, Martin Mitchell, ed., Sibyl Barsky Grucci, pub., 221 S. Barnard St., State College, PA 16801. Issues indexed: 41-42. Subscriptions: $14/3 yrs. (3 issues), $15/3 yrs. (for.); Single issue: $5, $6 (for.).

Plain: PLAINSONGS, Dwight Marsh, ed., Dept. of English, Hastings College, Hastings, NE 68902. Issues indexed: (14:2-3, 15:1). Subscriptions: $9/yr. (3 issues).

Ploughs: PLOUGHSHARES, DeWitt Henry, executive dir., David Daniel, po. ed., Emerson College, 100 Beacon St., Boston, MA 02116-1596. Issues indexed: (20:1, 2/3, 4). Subscriptions: $19/yr., $36/2 yrs. (ind.); $24/yr. (for. ind.); $22/yr. (inst.), $27/yr. (for. inst.). Single issue: $8.95.

*PlumR: THE PLUM REVIEW, Mike Hammer, Christina Daub, eds., P.O. Box 3557, Washington, DC 20007. Issues indexed: (7). Subscriptions: $14/yr. (2 issues), $28/2 yrs., $40/3 yrs. Subscription address: P.O. Box 1347, Philadelphia, PA 19105-1347.

Poem: POEM, Huntsville Literary Association, Nancy Frey Dillard, ed., c/o English Dept., U. of Alabama, Huntsville, AL 35899. Issues indexed: (71-72). Subscriptions: $10/yr.; Back issues: $5; Subscription address: Huntsville Literary Association, P.O. Box 919, Huntsville, AL 35804.

PoetC: POET AND CRITIC, Neal Bowers, ed., Dept. of English, 203 Ross Hall, Iowa State U., Ames, IA 50011-1201. Issues indexed: (25:2-3, 26:1). Subscriptions: Iowa State U. Press, South State St., Ames, IA 50010; $18/yr. (3 issues), $21/yr. (for.); $46/3 yrs., $55/3 yrs. (for.); Single issue: $8.

PoetL: POET LORE, Philip K. Jason, Geraldine Connolly, executive eds., The Writer's Center, 4508 Walsh St., Bethesda, MD 20815. Issues indexed: (89:1-4). Subscriptions: $10/yr. (Writer's Center members); $15/yr. (ind.); $24/yr. (inst.), plus $5/yr. (for.); Single issue: $4.50, plus $1 postage and handling; Samples: $4.

Poetry: POETRY, Joseph Parisi, ed., 60 W. Walton St., Chicago, IL 60610. Issues indexed: (163:4-6, 164:1-6, 165:1-3). Subscriptions: $25/yr. (ind.); $31/yr. (for.); $27/yr. (inst.); $33/yr. (for. inst.); Single issue: $2.50 plus $1 postage; Back issues: $3 plus $1 postage.

PoetryC: POETRY CANADA, Barry Dempster, po. ed., P.O. Box 1061, Kingston, Ont. K7L 4Y5 Canada. Issues indexed: (14:2-4, 15:1). Subscriptions: $19.26/4 issues (ind.); $38.52/4 issues (inst.); Back issues: $5; Single issue: $4.95; Double issue: $7.95.

PoetryE: POETRY EAST, Richard Jones, ed., Dept. of English, 802 W. Belden Ave., DePaul U., Chicago, IL 60614. Issues indexed: (37/38). Subscriptions: $12/yr.; Single issue: $7, Double issue: $8.

PoetryNW: POETRY NORTHWEST, David Wagoner, ed., U. of Washington, 4045 Brooklyn Ave. NE, Seattle, WA 98105. Issues indexed: (35:1-4). Subscriptions: $10/yr., $12/yr. (for.); Single issue: $3, $3.50 (for.).

PoetryUSA: POETRY USA, Jack Foley, ed., 2569 Maxwell Ave., Oakland, CA 94601. Issues indexed: No 1994 issues received. Subscriptions: $10/4 issues; Single issue: $1; Double issue: $2.

PottPort: THE POTTERSFIELD PORTFOLIO, Ian Colford, ed., The Gatsby Press, 5280 Green St., P.O. Box 22094, Halifax, Nova Scotia, Canada B3H 4M8. Issues indexed: No 1994 issues published; recommencing Fall 1995. Subscriptions: $18/yr. (3 issues, Canada), $24/yr. (USA); Single issue: $7.

*Poz: POZ, Sean O'Brien Strub, exec. ed., Richard Pérez-Feria, ed., P.O. Box 1279 Old Chelsea Station, New York, NY 10113-1279. Issues indexed: (1:1-4). Subscriptions: $19.95/yr. (6 issues); $79.95/yr. (inst.); available without cost to low-income HIV positive persons; Single copy: $3.95, $4.95 (Canada).

PraF: PRAIRIE FIRE: A Canadian Magazine of New Writing, Andris Taskans, ed., Méira Cook, Catherine Hunter, po. eds., 423-100 Arthur St., Winnipeg, Manitoba R3B 1H3 Canada. Issues indexed: (15:1-4, #66-69). Subscriptions: $24/yr., $44/2 yrs. (ind.); $32/yr. (inst.), plus $4 (USA), plus $6 (for.); Single issue: $11.95.

PraS: PRAIRIE SCHOONER, Hilda Raz, ed., 201 Andrews Hall, U. of Nebraska, Lincoln, NE 68588-0334. Issues indexed: (68:1-4). Subscriptions: $20/yr., $35/2 yrs., $46/3 yrs. (ind.); $22/yr. (lib.); Single issue: $6.45

Prima: PRIMAVERA, Arlene Zide, Ruth Young, Lisa Grayson, William Falloon, Martha Ann Selby, Kathleen Kuiper, eds., Box 37-7547, Chicago, IL 60637. Issues indexed: No 1994 issues received. Single issue: $9; Back issues: $5.

ProseP: THE PROSE POEM: An International Journal, Peter Johnson, ed., English Dept., Providence College, Providence, RI 02918. Issues indexed: (3). Subscriptions: $8/annual issue.

Quarry: QUARRY, Steven Heighton, ed., P.O. Box 1061, Kingston, Ontario K7L 4Y5 Canada. Issues indexed: (42:4, 43:1-3). Subscriptions: $22.47/yr. (4 issues), $39.85/2 yrs. (8 issues); Single issue: $6.95.

QRL: QUARTERLY REVIEW OF LITERATURE, T. & R. Weiss, eds., 26 Haslet Ave., Princeton, NJ 08540. Issues indexed: No 1994 issues received. Subscriptions: $20/2 volumes (paper), $20/volume (cloth, inst.).

QW: QUARTERLY WEST, M. L. Williams, ed., Sally Thomas, Margot Schilpp, po. eds., 317 Olpin Union Hall, U. of Utah, Salt Lake City, UT 84112. Issues indexed: (38-39). Subscriptions: $11/yr. (2 issues), $20/2 yrs.; $14/yr., $26/2 yrs. (for.); Single issue: $6.50; Back issues: $5.

RagMag: RAG MAG, Beverly Voldseth, ed. & pub., Black Hat Press, Box 12, 508 2nd Ave., Goodhue, MN 55027. Issues indexed: (12:1). Subscriptions: $10/yr. (2 issues), $15/2 yrs.; plus $5/yr. (for.); Single issue: $6; Back issues: $4.

Raritan: RARITAN: A Quarterly Review, Richard Poirier, ed., Rutgers U., 31 Mine St., New Brunswick, NJ 08903. Issues indexed: (13:3-4, 14:1-2). Subscriptions: $16/yr., $26/2 yrs. (ind.); $20/yr., $30/2 yrs. (inst.); plus $5.50/yr (for.); Single issue: $5; Back issues: $6.

RedBass: RED BASS, Jay Murphy, ed., 105 W. 28th St., 3rd floor, New York, NY 10001. Issues indexed: No 1994 issues received. Subscriptions: $20/2 issues (ind.), $35 (inst., for.); Single issue: $8.50; Back issues: $5.

RiverC: RIVER CITY, Paul Naylor, ed., Dept. of English, U. of Memphis, Memphis, TN 38152. Issues indexed: (14:2). Subscriptions: $9/yr. (ind., 2 issues), $10/yr. (inst).; Single issue: $5.

RiverS: RIVER STYX, Lee Fournier, ed., 3207 Washington Ave., St. Louis, MO 63103. Issues indexed: (40). Subscriptions: $20/3 issues, $38/6 issues; Single issue: $7.

Rosebud: ROSEBUD: For People Who Enjoy Writing, Roderick Clark, ed., P.O. Box 459, Cambridge, WI 53523. Issues indexed: (1:2-3). Subscriptions: $14/4 issues, plus $7 (for.); Single copy: $5.50, $6.50 (Canada); Subscription address: Beth Swan, 4218 Barnett St., Madison, WI 53704.

Salm: SALMAGUNDI: A Quarterly of the Humanities and Social Sciences, Robert Boyers, ed., Skidmore College, Saratoga Springs, NY 12866. Issues indexed: (101/102, 103, 104/105). Subscriptions: $15/yr., $25/2 yrs. (ind.); $22/yr., $37/2 yrs. (inst.); plus $10/yr. (for.); Sample issues: $6; Single issue: $8.

*SantaBR: SANTA BARBARA REVIEW, Patricia Stockton Leddy, ed., 1309-A State St., Santa Barbara, CA 93101. Issues indexed: (1:1-2, 2:1-2). Subscriptions: $10/yr. (2 issues), plus $7/yr. (for.) or $23/yr. (for. air mail); Single issue: $6, plus $2.40 postage and handling.

SenR: SENECA REVIEW, Deborah Tall, ed., Hobart and William Smith Colleges, Geneva, NY 14456. Issues indexed: (24:1-2). Subscriptions: $8/yr. (2 issues), $15/2 yrs.; Single issue: $5.

Sequoia: SEQUOIA: Stanford Literary Magazine, Carlos Rodriguez, managing ed., Ruth Porritt, Carlos Rodriguez, po. eds., Storke Publications Building, Stanford U., Stanford, CA 94305. Issues indexed: No 1994 issues received. Subscriptions: $10/yr. (1 issue), $12/yr. (for.).

SewanR: THE SEWANEE REVIEW, George Core, ed., U. of the South, Sewanee, TN 37383-1000. Issues indexed: (102:1-4). Subscriptions: $16/yr., $28/2 yrs., $40/3 yrs. (ind.); $20/yr., $38/2 yrs., $55/3 yrs. (inst.); plus $5/yr. (for.); Single issue: $5.75; Back issues: $8.

ShadowP: SHADOW PLAY, Jan Bender, ed., 99 Reynolds Rd., Grand Isle, VT 05458. Issues indexed: (4). Single issue: $4.

Shen: SHENANDOAH: The Washington and Lee University Review, Dabney Stuart, ed., Box 722, Lexington, VA 24450. Issues indexed: (44:1-4). Subscriptions: $11/yr., $18/2 yrs., $25/3 yrs.; $14/yr., $24/2 yrs., $33/3 yrs. (for.); Single issue: $3.50; Back issues: $6.

Shiny: SHINY: The Magazine of the Future, Michael Friedman, ed. and pub., 3188 - 10th St., Boulder, CO 80304. Issues indexed: No issues published 1993 or 1994; next issue expected Summer 1995. Subscriptions: $28/4 issues; Single issue: $5; Double issue: $10.

SilverFR: SILVERFISH REVIEW, Rodger Moody, ed., P.O. Box 3541, Eugene, OR 97403. Issues indexed: No 1994 issues received. Subscriptions: $12/3 issues (ind.), $15/3 issues (inst.); Single issue: $4-5.

SingHM: SING HEAVENLY MUSE!: Women's Poetry and Prose, Ruth Berman, Joline Gitis, Carol Masters, Donna Carlson, Karen Karsten, D. Perry Kidder, Carrie Wicks, Sue Ann Martinson, Corinna Nelson, Shirley Whiting, Mazi Johnson, Linda Webster, eds., P.O. Box 13320, Minneapolis, MN 55414. Issues indexed: (21). Subscriptions: $15/2 issues, $20/3 issues, $38/6 issues (ind.); $22/3 issues, $41/6 issues (inst.); $16/3 issues (low income); Single issue: $8 plus $2 postage and handling.

SinW: SINISTER WISDOM: A Journal for the Lesbian Imagination in the Arts and Politics, Elana Dykewomon, managing ed., P.O. Box 3252, Berkeley, CA 94703. Issues indexed: (52-54). Subscriptions: $17/yr. (4 issues), $30/2 yrs. (ind.); $30/yr. (inst.); $22/yr. (for.); $8-15/yr. (hardship); Free on request to women in prisons and mental institutions; Single issue: $5.

SlipS: SLIPSTREAM, Robert Borgatti, Livio Farallo, Dan Sicoli, eds., P.O. Box 2071, Niagara Falls, NY 14301. Issues indexed: (14). Subscriptions: $15/2 issues plus 2-3 chapbooks; Single issue: $5.

SmPd: THE SMALL POND MAGAZINE OF LITERATURE, Napoleon St. Cyr, ed., pub., P.O. Box 664, Stratford, CT 06497. Issues indexed: (31:1-3, #90-92). Subscriptions: $8/yr. (3 issues), $15/2 yrs., $22/3 yrs., plus $1.50/yr. (for.); Single issue: $3; Random back issues: $2.50.

SnailPR: THE SNAIL'S PACE REVIEW: A Biannual Little Magazine of Contemporary Poetry, Ken Denberg, Darby Penney, eds., RR 2 Box 363 Brownell Rd., Cambridge, NY 12816. Issues indexed: No 1994 issues received. Subscriptions: $7/yr. (ind.), $12/yr. (inst.); Single issue: $4.

Sonora: SONORA REVIEW, Bill Brymer, ed., Cori Brackett, Daniel LaBeau, po. eds., Dept. of English, U. of Arizona, Tucson, AZ 85721. Issues indexed: (27-28). Subscriptions: $12/yr. (2 issues), $24/2 yrs.; Single issue: $6.

SoCaR: SOUTH CAROLINA REVIEW, Frank Day, Carol Johnston, eds., Dept. of English, Clemson U., Strode Tower, Box 341503, Clemson, SC 29634-1503. Issues indexed: (26:2, 27:1/2). Subscriptions: $10/yr., $18/2 yrs., $26/3 yrs. (USA, Canada); plus $3/yr. (other for.); Sample issue: $10.

SoCoast: SOUTH COAST POETRY JOURNAL, John J. Brugaletta, ed., English Dept., California State U., Fullerton, CA 92634. Issues indexed: (16-17). Subscriptions: $10/yr. (2 issues), $18/2 yrs. (ind.); $12/yr. (inst.); Single issue: $6.

SoDakR: SOUTH DAKOTA REVIEW, John R. Milton, ed., Dept. of English, U. of South Dakota, Box 111, U. Exchange, Vermillion, SD 57069. Issues indexed: (32:1-4). Subscriptions: $15/yr., $25/2 yrs. (USA, Canada); plus $1/yr. elsewhere; Single issue: $5.

SouthernHR: SOUTHERN HUMANITIES REVIEW, Dan R. Latimer, R. T. Smith, eds., 9088 Haley Center, Auburn U., AL 36849. Issues indexed: (28:1-4). Subscriptions: $15/yr.; Single issue: $5.

SouthernPR: SOUTHERN POETRY REVIEW, Ken McLaurin, ed., English Dept., U. of North Carolina, Charlotte, NC 28223. Issues indexed: (34:1-2). Subscriptions: $8/yr.

SouthernR: SOUTHERN REVIEW, James Olney, Dave Smith, eds., Louisiana State U., 43 Allen Hall, Baton Rouge, LA 70803-5005. Issues indexed: (30:1-4). Subscriptions: $18/yr., $32/2 yrs., $45/3 yrs.; $35/yr., $55/2 yrs., $80/3 yrs. (inst.); Single issue: $5, $10 (inst.).

SouthwR: SOUTHWEST REVIEW, Willard Spiegelman, ed., Southern Methodist U., Dallas, TX 75275. Issues indexed: (79:1, 2/3, 4). Subscriptions: $20/yr., $35/2 yrs., $50/3 yrs. (ind.); $25/yr. (inst.); Single issue: $5.

Sparrow: SPARROW, Felix Stefanile, Selma Stefanile, eds., pubs., 103 Waldron St., West Lafayette, IN 47906. Issues indexed: No 1994 issues received. Single issue: $5, $7.50 (libs., inst.), $10 (for.).

Spirit: THE SPIRIT THAT MOVES US, Morty Sklar, ed., pub., P.O. Box 820, Jackson Heights, NY 11372. Issues indexed: No 1992, 1993 or 1994 issues published; #12 expected in 1994 but not received.

SpiritSH: SPIRIT: A Magazine of Poetry, David Rogers, ed., Dept. of English, Seton Hall U., South Orange, NJ 07079. Issues indexed: (59). Subscriptions: $4/yr. (2 issues); Single issue: $2; Back issues: $3.

Spitball: SPITBALL: The Literary Baseball Magazine, Mike Shannon, ed., William J. McGill, po. ed., 5560 Fox Rd., Cincinnati, OH 45239. Issues indexed: (46-47). Subscriptions: $16/yr. (4 issues); $22/yr. (Canada, U.S. funds); Single issue: $5.

SpoonR: THE SPOON RIVER POETRY REVIEW (formerly Spoon River Quarterly), Lucia Cordell Getsi, ed., English Dept., Campus Box 4240, Illinois State U., Normal, IL 61790-4240. Issues indexed: (19:1). Subscriptions: $12/yr. (2 issues); $15/yr. (inst.); Single issue: $8.

Stand: STAND MAGAZINE, Daniel Schenker, Amanda Kay, U.S. eds., 122 Morris Rd., Lacey's Spring, AL 35754. Issues indexed: (35:2-4, 36:1). Subscriptions: $25/yr., $46/2 yrs.; $22/yr. (students, unwaged); Single issue: $7; U.S.A. distributor: Anton J. Mikovsky, 50 E. 42nd St. Ste. 1809, New York, NY 10017.

Sulfur: SULFUR: A Literary Bi-Annual of the Whole Art, Clayton Eshleman, ed., English Dept., Eastern Michigan U., Ypsilanti, MI 48197. Issues indexed: (14:1-2, #34-35). Subscriptions: $14/2 issues (ind.), $20/2 issues (inst.), plus $4 (for.) or $10 (for. air mail postage); Single issue: $9.

Sun: SUN: A Magazine of Ideas, Sy Safransky, ed., 107 N. Roberson St., Chapel Hill, NC 27516. Issues indexed: (217-228). Subscriptions: $32/yr., $60/2 yrs., $150/5 yrs., $300/10 yrs., $1,000 lifetime, plus $10/yr. (for.); Single issue: $3.50. The Sun, Subscription Service, P.O. Box 6706, Syracuse, NY 13217.

SycamoreR: SYCAMORE REVIEW, Michael Manley, ed., Michelle Byrne, po. ed., Dept. of English, Heavilon Hall, Purdue U., West Lafayette, IN 47906. Issues indexed: (6:1-2). Subscriptions: $9/yr., $11/yr. (for.); Single issue: $5.

Talisman: TALISMAN: A Journal of Contemporary Poetry and Poetics, Edward Foster, ed., Box 1117, Hoboken, NJ 07030. Issues indexed: (12-13). Subscriptions: $11/yr. (2 issues); $15/yr. (inst.); plus $2/yr. (for.); Single issue: $6.

TampaR: TAMPA REVIEW: Literary Journal of the University of Tampa, Richard Mathews, ed., Donald Morrill, Kathryn Van Spanckeren, po. eds., Box 19F, U. of Tampa, 401 W. Kennedy Blvd., Tampa, FL 33606-1490. Issues indexed: (8-9). Subscriptions: $10/yr. (2 issues); plus $4/yr. (for.); Single issue: $5.95.

TarRP: TAR RIVER POETRY, Peter Makuck, ed., Dept. of English, General Classroom Bldg., East Carolina U., Greenville, NC 27858-4353. Issues indexed: (33:2, 34:1). Subscriptions: $10/yr (2 issues), $18/2 yrs.; Single issue: $5.50.

TexasR: TEXAS REVIEW, Paul Ruffin, ed., Division of English and Foreign Languages, Sam Houston State U., Huntsville, TX 77341. Issues indexed: (15:1/2). Subscriptions: $10/yr., $18/2 yrs., $26/3 yrs.; $10.50/yr. (Canada), $11/yr. (for.); Single issue: $5.

Thirteenth Moon: *See* 13thMoon *at beginning of file.*

Thrpny: THE THREEPENNY REVIEW, Wendy Lesser, ed., pub., P.O. Box 9131, Berkeley, CA 94709. Issues indexed: (56-59). Subscriptions: $16/yr., $28/2 yrs., $30/yr. (for.); Single issue: $4.

TickleAce: TICKLEACE: A Journal of Literary and Visual Art, Susan Ingersoll, Lawrence Mathews, Bruce Porter, Michael Winter, eds., P.O. Box 5353, St. John's, NF, A1C 5W2 Canada. Issues indexed: (28); No. 27 not received. Subscriptions: $14/yr. (2 issues), $17/yr. (inst.), plus $5/yr. (U.S.), plus $7/yr. (other for.); Single issue: $8.

Trans: TRANSLATION, The Journal of Literary Translation, Lori M. Carlson, Frank MacShane, eds., The Translation Center, 412 Dodge Hall, Columbia U., New York, NY 10027. Issues indexed: (29). The Translation Center's "activities were suspended during the summer, following the unanticipated retirement of the Director of the Center for health reasons" -- Peter Smith, Dean, School of the Arts, Columbia U., 12-22-94.

Trasimagen: TRASIMAGEN: Revista Latinoamericana de Literatura y Arte, Lillian Haddock, directora; Lillian Haddock, Jose Luis Colon-Santiago, eds., P.O. Box 2581, Stuyvesant Station, New York, NY 10009. Issues indexed: No 1994 issues received. Subscriptions: $20/yr. (2 issues); $24/yr. (inst.); $30/yr. (for.); Single issue: $10.

Tricycle: TRICYCLE: The Buddhist Review, Helen Tworkov, ed., The Buddhist Ray, Inc., 163 W. 22nd St., New York, NY 10011. Issues indexed: No 1994 issues received. Subscriptions: $20/yr. (4 issues), $38/2 yrs., $57/3 yrs., plus $5/yr. (for. surface mail), $15/yr. (for. air mail); Single copy: 6. Subscription address: Dept. TRI, P.O. Box 3000, Denville, NJ 07834-9897.

TriQ: TRIQUARTERLY, Reginald Gibbons, Susan Hahn, eds., Northwestern U., 2020 Ridge Ave., Evanston, IL 60208. Issues indexed: (90-92). Subscriptions: $20/yr. (3 issues), $36/2 yrs., $500/life (ind.); $30/yr., $48/2 yrs., $500/life (inst.), plus $5/yr. (for.); Single issue: cost varies; Sample copies: $4.

Turnstile: TURNSTILE, Daniel Bial, Lindsey Crittenden, Meghan Daum, Ann Biester Deane, Vira DeFilippo, Twisne Fan, Ann McKay Farrell, Kit Haines, Marian Lizzi, Mitchell Nauffts, George Witte, eds., 175 Fifth Ave., Suite 2348, New York, NY 10010. Issues indexed: No 1994 issues received; Vol. 5, no. 1 published in 1995. Subscriptions: $12/2 issues, $22/4 issues; Single issue: $6.50.

US1: US 1 WORKSHEETS, Irene Willis, coordinating ed., Rebekah Nicholson, Mark Scott, po. eds., US 1 Poets' Cooperative, P.O. Box 1, Ringoes, NJ 08551-0001. Issues indexed: No issues published in 1994; No. 30/31 published in 1995. Subscriptions: $10/2 double issues; Single (double) issue: $6.

Verse: VERSE, Henry Hart, U. S. ed., Dept. of English, College of William and Mary, Williamsburg, VA 23185. Issues indexed: (11:1-2). Subscriptions: $15/yr. (3 issues), $21/yr. (lib.); Single issue: $5.

VirQR: THE VIRGINIA QUARTERLY REVIEW: A National Journal of Literature and Discussion, Staige D. Blackford, ed., Gregory Orr, po. consultant, One West Range, Charlottesville, VA 22903. Issues indexed: (70:1-4). Subscriptions: $15/yr., $22/2 yrs., $30/3 yrs. (ind.); $22/yr., $30/2 yrs., $50/3 yrs. (inst.); plus $3/yr. (for.); Single issue: $5.

Vis: VISIONS INTERNATIONAL, Bradley R. Strahan, po. ed., pub., Black Buzzard Press, 1110 Seaton Lane, Falls Church, VA 22046. Issues indexed: (44-46). Subscriptions: $14/yr. (3 issues), $27/2 yrs. (ind.); $42/3 yrs. (lib.); Single issue: $4.50-$5.

*War: WAR, LITERATURE, & THE ARTS: An International Journal of the Humanities, Donald Anderson, ed., Dept. of English, 2354 Fairchild Dr., Ste 6D35, U.S. Air Force Academy, CO 80840-6242. Will Hochman, po. ed., Dept. of English, U. of Southern Colorado, Pueblo, CO 81001. Issues indexed: (6:1-2). Subscriptions: $10/yr. (2 issues), $18/2 yrs., $24/3 yrs. (ind.); $20/yr., $36/2 yrs., $48/3 yrs. (inst.); plus $5/yr. (for.). Make checks payable to: Academic Support Fund (WLA).

WashR: WASHINGTON REVIEW, Clarissa K. Wittenberg, ed., P.O. Box 50132, Washington, DC 20091-0132. Issues indexed: (19:5-6; 20:1-4). Subscriptions: $12/yr. (6 issues), $20/2 yrs.; Single issue: $3.

WeberS: WEBER STUDIES: An Interdisciplinary Humanities Journal, Neila C. Seshachari, ed., Weber State U., Ogden, UT 84408-1214. Issues indexed: (11:1-3). Subscriptions: $10/yr. (3 issues), $20/yr. (inst.); plus actual extra postage costs per year (for.); Back and single issues: $7.

WebR: WEBSTER REVIEW, Nancy Schapiro, Robert Boyd, Greg Marshall, eds., English Dept., SLCC-Meramec, 11333 Big Bend Rd., St. Louis, MO 63122. Issues indexed: (18). Subscriptions: $5/yr. (1 issue).

WestB: WEST BRANCH: a twice-yearly magazine of poetry and fiction, Karl Patten, Robert Love Taylor, eds., Bucknell Hall, Bucknell U., Lewisburg, PA 17837. Issues indexed: (34-35). Subscriptions: $7/yr. (2 issues), $11/2 yrs.; Single issue: $4; Double issue: $7.

WestCL: WEST COAST LINE: A Journal of Contemporary Writing and Criticism, Roy Miki, ed., 2027 East Academic Annex, Simon Fraser U., Burnaby, BC V5A 1S6 Canada. Issues indexed: (28:1/2-3, #13/14-15). Subscriptions: $20/yr. (ind., 3 issues), $30/yr. (inst.); Single issue: $10.

WestHR: WESTERN HUMANITIES REVIEW, Barry Weller, ed., Richard Howard, po. ed., U. of Utah, Salt Lake City, UT 84112. Issues indexed: (48:1-4). Subscriptions: $20/yr. (4 issues, ind.), $26/yr. (inst.); Single issue: $6.

WilliamMR: THE WILLIAM AND MARY REVIEW, Andrew J. Zawacki, ed., Brian T. Henry, Stephanie Jones, po. eds., College of William and Mary, P.O. Box 8795, Williamsburg, VA 23187. Issues indexed: (32). Subscriptions: $5.00/single issue, plus $1.50 (for.); Single issue: $5.50.

WillowR: WILLOW REVIEW, Paulette Roeske, ed., College of Lake County, 19351 W. Washington St., Grayslake, IL 60030. Issues indexed: (21). Subscriptions: $13/3 issues, $20/5 issues; Single issue: $5.

WillowS: WILLOW SPRINGS, Nance Van Winckel, ed., Laurel Darrow, po. ed., Eastern Washington U., MS-1, Cheney, WA 99004. Issues indexed: (34). Subscriptions: $8/yr. (2 issues), $15/2 yrs., $22/3 yrs.; Single issue: $4.50.

Wind: WIND, Steven R. Cope, Charlie G. Hughes, eds., P.O. Box 24548, Lexington, KY 40524. Issues indexed: (73-74). Subscriptions: $10/yr. (2 issues, ind.), $12/yr. (inst.), $14/yr. (for.); Single issue: $6.

WindO: THE WINDLESS ORCHARD, Robert Novak, ed., English Dept., Indiana-Purdue U., Fort Wayne, IN 46805. Issues indexed: (58). Subscriptions: $10/3 issues; Single issue: $4.

Witness: WITNESS, Peter Stine, ed., Oakland Community College, Orchard Ridge Campus, 27055 Orchard Lake Road, Farmington Hills, MI 48334-4579. Issues indexed: (8:1-2). Subscriptions: $12/yr. (2 issues), $22/2 yrs.; $18/yr., $34/2 yrs. (inst.); plus $4/yr. (for.); Single copies: $7.

WorldL: WORLD LETTER, Jon Cone, ed., 2726 E. Court St., Iowa City, IA 52245. Issues indexed: (5). Subscriptions: $9/2 issues (U.S.), $12/2 issues (Canada); Single issue: $5 (U.S.), $7 (Canada).

WorldO: WORLD ORDER, Firuz Kazemzadeh, Betty J. Fisher, Howard Garey, Robert H. Stockman, James D. Stokes, eds., Herbert Woodward Martin, po. consultant, National Spiritual Assembly of the Bahá'ís of the United States, 415 Linden Ave., Wilmette, IL 60091. Issues indexed: (25:3-4, 26:1-2). Subscriptions: $15/yr. (4 issues), $28/2 yrs.; $15/yr., $28/2 yrs. (for.); $20/yr., $38/2 yrs. (for. airmail); Single issue: $3.

WormR: THE WORMWOOD REVIEW, Marvin Malone, ed., P.O. Box 4698, Stockton, CA 95204-0698. Issues indexed: (34:1-4; #133-136). Subscriptions: $12/4 issues; $24/4 issues (patrons); Single and back issues: $4.

Writ: WRIT, Roger Greenwald, ed., Innis College, U. of Toronto, 2 Sussex Ave., Toronto, Canada M5S 1J5. Issues indexed: (26). Subscriptions: $18/2 issues (ind.), $20/2 issues (inst.); same amount in U.S. funds outside Canada; Back issues: $10-20.

Writer: THE WRITER, Sylvia K. Burack, ed., pub., 120 Boylston St., Boston, MA 02116-4615. Issues indexed: (107:1-12). Subscriptions: $27/yr., $50/2 yrs., $74/3 yrs.; plus $8/yr. (for.); $10/5 issues for new subscribers; Single issue: $2.25.

WritersF: WRITERS' FORUM, Alexander Blackburn, ed., Victoria McCabe, po. ed., P.O. Box 7150, U. of Colorado, Colorado Springs, CO 80933-7150. Issues indexed: (20). Subscriptions: $8.95/yr. (1 issue) plus $1.05 postage and handling; Back issue sample: $5.95 plus $1.05 postage and handling.

XavierR: XAVIER REVIEW, Thomas Bonner, Jr., ed., Box 110C, Xavier U., New Orleans, LA 70125. Issues indexed: (14:1-2). Subscriptions: $10/yr. (2 issues, ind.), $15/yr. (inst.).

YaleR: THE YALE REVIEW, J. D. McClatchy, ed., Yale U., P.O. Box 208243, New Haven, CT 06520-8243. Issues indexed: (82:1-4). Subscriptions: $22/yr., $39.50/2 yrs., $59.50/3 yrs. (ind.); $33/yr., $59.50/2 yrs., $89.50/3 yrs. (for. ind.); $46/yr. (inst.), $51/yr. (for. inst.); Single issues: $7.50 (ind.), $15 (inst.), $11 (for. ind.), $16 (for. inst.); Subscription address: Subscriber Services Coordinator, Blackwell Publishers, 238 Main St., Cambridge, MA 02142; make checks payable to Blackwell Publishers.

YellowS: YELLOW SILK, Journal of Erotic Arts, Lily Pond, ed., pub., P.O. Box 6374, Albany, CA 94706. Issues indexed: (11:4, 12:1-3, #44-47). Subscriptions: $30/yr. (4 issues, ind.), $38/yr. (lib., inst.), plus $8/yr. (for. surface) or $22/yr. (for. air). Single issue: $7.50.

Zyzzyva: ZYZZYVA: The Last Word, West Coast Writers & Artists, Howard Junker, ed., 41 Sutter St., Suite 1400, San Francisco, CA 94104-4903. Issues indexed: (10:1-4, #37-40). Subscriptions: $28/yr. (4 issues), $48/2 yrs. (ind.); $36/yr. (inst.); $48/yr. (for.); Single issue: $10.

Alphabetical List of Journals Indexed, with Acronyms

13th Moon: A Feminist Literary Magazine : 13th Moon

Abraxas : Abraxas
African American Review : AfAmRev
Agni : Agni
Alabama Literary Review : AlabamaLR
Amelia : Amelia
American Letters & Commentary : AmerLC
The American Poetry Review : AmerPoR
The American Scholar : AmerS
The American Voice : AmerV
The Americas Review: A Review of Hispanic Literature and Art of the USA : Americas
Another Chicago Magazine : AnotherCM
Antaeus : Antaeus
The Anthology of New England Writers : AnthNEW
The Antigonish Review : AntigR
The Antioch Review : AntR
Apalachee Quarterly : ApalQ
Arc : Arc
Archae : Archae
Areíto : Areíto
Arion: A Journal of Humanities and the Classics : Arion
Arshile: A Magazine of the Arts : Arshile
Art & Understanding: The International Magazine of Literature and Art About AIDS : Art&Und
Artful Dodge : ArtfulD
Arts Indiana Literary Supplement: *See* Hopewell Review *(title change)*
Ascent : Ascent
Asylum : Asylum
The Atlantic : Atlantic
Avec: A Journal of Writing : Avec

Bamboo Ridge: The Hawaii Writers' Quarterly : BambooR
The Bellingham Review : BellR
Bellowing Ark : BellArk
The Beloit Poetry Journal : BelPoJ
The Bilingual Review / La Revista Bilingüe : BilingR
Black American Literature Forum: *See* African American Review *(title change)*
Black Bear Review : BlackBR
Black Bread : BlackBread
Black Moon : BlackMoon
Black Warrior Review : BlackWR
Blueline : Blueline
Bogg : Bogg
Bomb Magazine : Bomb
Borderlands: Texas Poetry Review : Border
Boston Review : BostonR
Boulevard : Boulevard
Brooklyn Review : BrooklynR

Caliban : Caliban
Callaloo: A Journal of African-American and African Arts and Letters : Callaloo
Calyx: A Journal of Art and Literature by Women : Calyx
Canadian Literature : CanLit
The Cape Rock : CapeR
The Capilano Review : CapilR
The Caribbean Writer : CaribbeanW
Carolina Quarterly : CarolQ
The Centennial Review : CentR
Central Park : CentralP
Chain : Chain
Chaminade Literary Review : ChamLR
Changing Men: Issues in Gender, Sex and Politics : ChangingM
The Chariton Review : CharR
The Chattahoochee Review: The DeKalb College Literary Quarterly : ChatR
Chelsea : Chelsea
Chicago Review : ChiR
Chiron Review : ChironR
The Christian Century: An Ecumenical Weekly : ChrC
Cimarron Review : CimR
Cincinnati Poetry Review : CinPR
Clockwatch Review: A Journal of the Arts : ClockR
Coal City Review : CoalC
College English : ColEng
Colorado Review : ColR
Columbia: A Magazine of Poetry & Prose : Colum
Commonweal : Comm
Confrontation : Confr
Conjunctions: Bi-Annual Volumes of New Writing : Conjunc
The Connecticut Poetry Review : ConnPR
Conscience: A Newsjournal of Prochoice Catholic Opinion : Conscience
Context South : ContextS
Crab Creek Review : CrabCR
Crazyhorse : Crazy
Cream City Review : CreamCR
Crosscurrents : CrossCur
Crucible : Crucible
Cuadernos de Poética : CuadP
Cumberland Poetry Review : CumbPR
Cutbank : CutB

Dandelion : Dandel
Denver Quarterly : DenQ
Descant : Descant
Dog River Review : DogRR
Drumvoices: A Confluence of Literary, Cultural & Vision Arts : Drumvoices

Elf: Eclectic Literary Forum : Elf
English Journal : EngJ
Epiphany: A Journal of Literature : *See* The Ogalala Review *(title change)*
Epoch : Epoch
Event: The Douglas College Review : Event
The Evergreen Chronicles: A Journal of Gay & Lesbian Literature : EvergreenC
Eyeball

Farmer's Market : Farm
Field: Contemporary Poetry and Poetics : Field
The Florida Review : FloridaR
Footwork: The Paterson Literary Review : Footwork
Four Quarters : FourQ
Free Lunch: A Poetry Journal : FreeL

Gaia: A Journal of Literature & Environmental Arts : Gaia
Georgia Review : GeoR
Gettysburg Review : GettyR

Global City Review : GlobalCR
Graham House Review : GrahamHR
Grain : Grain
Grand Street : GrandS
Green Mountains Review : GreenMR
The Greensboro Review : GreensboroR
Gypsy : Gypsy

The Hampden-Sydney Poetry Review : HampSPR
Hanging Loose : HangL
Harper's Magazine : Harp
The Harvard Advocate : HarvardA
Harvard Review : HarvardR
Hawai'i Review : HawaiiR
Hayden's Ferry Review : HayF
Heaven Bone : HeavenB
Hellas: A Journal of Poetry and the Humanities : Hellas
High Plains Literary Review : HighP
Hiram Poetry Review : HiramPoR
The Hollins Critic : HolCrit
Hopewell Review: New Work by Indiana's Best Writers : HopewellR
The Hudson Review : Hudson

The Illinois Review : IllinoisR
Image: A Journal of the Arts & Religion : Image
Indiana Review : IndR
Interim : Interim
International Poetry Review : InterPR
International Quarterly : InterQ
Inti: Revista de Literatura Hispánica : Inti
Iowa Review : Iowa

Jacaranda : Jacaranda
The James White Review: A Gay Men's Literary Journal : JamesWR
The Journal : Journal
The Journal of New Jersey Poets : JlNJPo

Kaleidoscope: International Magazine of Literature, Fine Arts, and Disability : Kaleid
Kalliope: A Journal of Women's Art : Kalliope
Kenyon Review : KenR

Lactuca : Lactuca
Laurel Review : LaurelR
Light: A Quarterly of Humorous, Occasional, Ephemeral & Light Verse : Light
Linden Lane Magazine : LindLM
The Literary Review: An International Journal of Contemporary Writing : LitR
Louisiana Literature: A Review of Literature and Humanities : LouisL
Lullwater Review : LullwaterR
Luz: En Arte y Literatura : Luz

The Malahat Review : MalR
The Manhattan Review : ManhatR
Manoa: A Pacific Journal of International Writing : Manoa
The Massachusetts Review : MassR
Memphis State Review: *See* River City *(title change)*
Mester : Mester
Michigan Quarterly Review : MichQR
Mid-American Review : MidAR
The Midwest Quarterly: A Journal of Contemporary Thought : MidwQ
The Minnesota Review: a journal of committed writing : MinnR
Mississippi Review : MissR
The Missouri Review : MissouriR
Modern Words: a thoroughly queer international literary journal : ModernW
Moody Street Irregulars: A Jack Kerouac Newsletter : MoodySI

The Nation : Nat
Negative Capability : NegC
New American Writing : NewAW
New Delta Review : NewDeltaR
New England Review : NewEngR
New Letters : NewL
New Orleans Review : NewOR
The New Renaissance : NewRena
The New Republic : NewRep
The New York Quarterly : NewYorkQ
The New York Review of Books : NewYRB
The New Yorker : NewYorker
Nimrod : Nimrod
Noctiluca: An International Magazine of Poetry : Noctiluca
The North American Review : NoAmR
North Carolina Literary Review : NoCarLR
North Dakota Quarterly : NoDaQ
The North Stone Review : NorthStoneR
Northeast : Northeast
Northwest Review : NowestR
La Nuez: Revista Internacional de Arte y Literatura : Nuez

Obsidian II: Black Literature in Review : Obs
The Ogalala Review : OgalalaR
The Ohio Review : OhioR
Ometeca: Ciencia y Literatura, Science & Literature : Ometeca
Ontario Review : OntR
OnTheBus: A New Literary Magazine : OnTheBus
Osiris : Os
Outerbridge : Outbr
Oxford Magazine : OxfordM

Paintbrush: A Journal of Contemporary Multicultural Literature : Paint
Painted Bride Quarterly : PaintedB
Painted Hills Review : PaintedHR
The Paris Review : ParisR
Parting Gifts : Parting
Partisan Review : PartR
Passages North : PassN
Pearl : Pearl
Pembroke Magazine : Pembroke
The Pennsylvania Review : PennR
Pequod : Pequod
The Pikestaff Forum : PikeF
Pivot : Pivot
Plainsongs : Plain
Ploughshares : Ploughs
The Plum Review : PlumR
Poem : Poem
Poet And Critic : PoetC
Poet Lore : PoetL
Poetry : Poetry
Poetry Canada : PoetryC
Poetry East : PoetryE
Poetry Northwest : PoetryNW
Poetry USA : PoetryUSA
The Pottersfield Portfolio : PottPort
Poz : Poz
Prairie Fire: A Canadian Magazine of New Writing : PraF
Prairie Schooner : PraS
Primavera : Prima
The Prose Poem: An International Journal : ProseP

Quarry : Quarry
Quarterly Review of Literature : QRL
Quarterly West : QW

Rag Mag : RagMag
Raritan: A Quarterly Review : Raritan
Red Bass : RedBass
River City : RiverC
River Styx : RiverS
Rosebud: For People Who Enjoy Writing : Rosebud

Salmagundi: A Quarterly of the Humanities and Social Sciences : Salm
Santa Barbara Review : SantaBR
Seneca Review : SenR
Sequoia: Stanford Literary Magazine : Sequoia
The Sewanee Review : SewanR
Shadow Play : ShadowP
Shenandoah: The Washington and Lee University Review : Shen
Shiny: The Magazine of the Future : Shiny
Silverfish Review : SilverFR
Sing Heavenly Muse!: Women's Poetry and Prose : SingHM
Sinister Wisdom: A Journal for the Lesbian Imagination in the Arts and Politics : SinW
Slipstream : SlipS
The Small Pond Magazine of Literature : SmPd
The Snail's Pace Review: A Biannual Little Magazine of Contemporary Poetry : SnailPR
Sonora Review : Sonora
South Carolina Review : SoCaR
South Coast Poetry Journal : SoCoast
South Dakota Review : SoDakR
Southern Humanities Review : SouthernHR
Southern Poetry Review : SouthernPR
Southern Review : SouthernR
Southwest Review : SouthwR
Sparrow : Sparrow
Spirit: A Magazine of Poetry : SpiritSH
The Spirit That Moves Us : Spirit
Spitball: The Literary Baseball Magazine : Spitball
The Spoon River Poetry Review (*formerly* The Spoon River Quarterly) : SpoonR
Stand Magazine : Stand
Sulfur: A Literary Bi-Annual of the Whole Art : Sulfur
Sun: A Magazine of Ideas : Sun
Sycamore Review : SycamoreR

Talisman: A Journal of Contemporary Poetry & Poetics : Talisman
Tampa Review: Literary Journal of the University of Tampa : TampaR
Tar River Poetry : TarRP
Texas Review : TexasR
Thirteenth Moon: *See* 13th Moon *(at beginning of list)*
The Threepenny Review : Thrpny
TickleAce: A Journal of Literary and Visual Art : TickleAce
Translation: The Journal of Literary Translation : Translation
Trasimagen: Revista Latinoamericana de Literatura y Arte : Trasimagen
Tricycle: The Buddhist Review : Tricycle
Triquarterly : TriQ
Turnstile : Turnstile

US 1 Worksheets : US1

Verse : Verse
The Virginia Quarterly Review: A National Journal of Literature and Discussion : VirQR
Visions International : Vis

War, Literature, & the Arts: An International Journal of the Humanities : War
Washington Review : Wash
Weber Studies: An Interdisciplinary Humanities Journal : WeberS
Webster Review : WebR

West Branch: A twice-yearly magazine of poetry and fiction : WestB
West Coast Line: A Journal of Contemporary Writing and Criticism (*formerly* West Coast Review) : WestCL
Western Humanities Review : WestHR
The William and Mary Review : WilliamMR
Willow Review : WillowR
Willow Springs : WillowS
Wind : Wind
The Windless Orchard : WindO
Witness : Witness
World Letter : WorldL
World Order : WorldO
The Wormwood Review : WormR
Writ : Writ
The Writer : Writer
Writers' Forum : WritersF

Xavier Review : XavierR

The Yale Review : YaleR
Yellow Silk: Journal of Erotic Arts : YellowS

Zyzzyva: The Last Word, West Coast Writers and Artists : Zyzzyva

The Author Index

AAL, Katharyn Machan
See MACHAN, Katharyn Howd
1. AARNES, William
"Dawn." [Pivot] (42) 94, p. 4.
"Homework, 1964." [Pembroke] (26) 94, p. 106.
"Plight." [PoetC] (25:2) Wint 94, p. 21.
"Promise." [Pivot] (42) 94, p. 4.
2. AARON, Jonathan
"Street Scene." [PartR] (61:4) Fall 94, p. 706.
ABDULLAH, Ahmad Khamal B.
See KEMALA
3. ABERNETHY, Hugh, Jr.
"Lost Coney Island Romance." [Confr] (54/55) Fall 94-Wint 95, p. 315-316.
4. ABICH, Tina Maria
"Leaving *Sesame Street*." [Kalliope] (16:3) 94, p. 7.
5. ABOUD, James C.
"Inamorata." [Agni] (40) 94, p. 171.
"The Regulations." [Agni] (40) 94, p. 172.
"The Weight of Things." [Agni] (40) 94, p. 173.
6. ABRAHAMSON, Karen
"Love Under Water." [Arc] (33) Fall 94, p. 50.
7. ABRAM, Patricia
"Anonymous." [AntigR] (96) Wint 94, p. 41-42.
"Murney Tower, Kingston." [AntigR] (96) Wint 94, p. 40.
8. ABRAMS, Bill
"Directions for Breaking In." [Interim] (13:2) Fall-Wint 94-95, p. 3.
9. ABSE, Dannie
"Beautiful Dead Poets." [Pivot] (41) 93, p. 29.
"Chocolate Box." [Poetry] (165:2) N 94, p. 88.
"In the Villa Borghese." [Poetry] (165:2) N 94, p. 89.
"Just One of Those Days, William." [Pivot] (41) 93, p. 28-29.
"Talking to Blake." [Poetry] (165:2) N 94, p. 87.
"Two Photographs." [Poetry] (165:2) N 94, p. 90.
10. ABSHER, Thomas D.
"Acts of Prayer." [ChrC] (111:32) 9 N 94, p. 1048.
11. ACKER, Ally
"White Noise at Midnight." [Ploughs] (20:4) Wint 94-95, p. 7.
12. ACKERMAN, Diane
"City of Dreams." [Poetry] (164:6) S 94, p. 336.
"Natural Wonders." [Poetry] (164:6) S 94, p. 334-335.
13. ACOSTA, Feliciano
"The Land Is Screaming" (tr. by Leyzman Salim and Lauren Schick). [InterQ] (1:4) 94, p. 22.
"Pomberi" (in Guaraní and English, tr. by Leyzman Salim and Lauren Schick). [InterQ] (1:4) 94, p. 23.
"Yvy Sapukài." [InterQ] (1:4) 94, p. 22.
14. ACOSTA, Luzmarina
"Being With You" (tr. by Preston Browning and Lang Gomez). [LitR] (37:4) Sum 94, p. 580.
15. ACOSTA POSADA, Juan Armando David
"Weather" (from *Migrations to Solitude*). [JamesWR] (11:4) Sum 94, p. 1.
16. ACREE, Carolyn
"Field." [Sun] (225) S 94, p. 19.
"In Montana." [Sun] (228) D 94, p. 19.
17. ACUFF, Gale
"Chin Music." [Spitball] (47) Sum 94, p. 8-9.

18. ADAMS, Anna
"McFadden." [NewYorkQ] (53) 94, p. 60.
19. ADAMS, B. B.
"Out of the Frying Pan, into the Fire." [Light] (12) Wint 94-95, p. 12.
20. ADAMS, Barbara
"True Name" (tr. of Yves Bonnefoy). [PoetryE] (37/38) Spr 94, p. 215.
21. ADAMS, Cindy L.
"The City of New Orleans." [NegC] (13:2/3) 93, p. 177.
22. ADAMS, Cyd
"Omens." [Border] (3) Fall 93, p. 1.
"Revival." [Border] (5) Fall-Wint 94, p. 1.
23. ADAMS, Hannah B.
"Earth with Her Consort, Sun, Meet in a Treetop." [BellArk] (10:3) My-Je 94, p. 26.
"Fire Grazing." [BellArk] (10:3) My-Je 94, p. 26.
"Heart Song in September." [BellArk] (10:3) My-Je 94, p. 26.
"How Families Continue to Gather." [BellArk] (10:3) My-Je 94, p. 26.
"Midnight with Susan." [BellArk] (10:3) My-Je 94, p. 26.
"Name Change." [BellArk] (10:3) My-Je 94, p. 26.
"A Question and an Answer." [BellArk] (10:3) My-Je 94, p. 26.
"Unbraiding." [BellArk] (10:3) My-Je 94, p. 26.
24. ADAMS, Hazard
"Meditations in the Sixties." [Interim] (13:2) Fall-Wint 94-95, p. 28-32.
25. ADAMS, Jefferson
"Fear As a River, My Body the Chosen Landscape." [HiramPoR] (55/56) Fall 93-Sum 94, p. 5.
26. ADAMS, Terry
"After the Laying-on of Hands for Jonathan, Dying of Cancer." [Sun] (223) Jl 94, p. 34.
"Breath." [Sun] (222) Je 94, p. 33-34.
27. ADAMSON, Robert
"The Australian Crawl." [MalR] (107) Sum 94, p. 146-147.
"Folk Song." [MalR] (107) Sum 94, p. 148-149.
28. ADANG, Mark
"Frostbite." [WindO] (58) Sum 94, p. 12-13.
"Holding Sheet Music." [WindO] (58) Sum 94, p. 10-11.
29. ADANG, Rick
"Fat Man." [ChiR] (40:4) 94, p. 56.
"Kitty, Before the Breakdown" ("Letter From Kitty Dukakis: Between the Election and the Breakdown," from the Spring issue of *The Paris Review*). [Harp] (289:1732) S 94, p. 34.
"Letter from Kitty Dukakis: Between the Election and the Breakdown." [ParisR] (36:130) Spr 94, p. 250-251.
30. ADCOCK, Betty
"In Another Life." [SouthernR] (30:1) Ja, Wint 94, p. 76-78.
"Lines to a Past Love." [SouthernR] (30:4) Aut 94, p. 699-700.
"Living for Awhile in the Country." [Pembroke] (26) 94, p. 51.
"Names." [Shen] (44:4) Wint 94, p. 88-89.
"The Swan Story" (to Don). [Pembroke] (26) 94, p. 52-56.
"Time After Time." [GeoR] (48:2) Sum 94, p. 240.
"Time at the Movies." [TarRP] (33:2) Spr 94, p. 30-31.
"The Widow Speaking." [SouthernR] (30:4) Aut 94, p. 700-701.
31. ADDINGTON, Christie
"I Don't Know Your Alphabet." [Pearl] (20) Spr 94, p. 45.
32. ADDINGTON, Rosa Lea
"Leonardo's Notebooks." [Border] (3) Fall 93, p. 2.
33. ADDONIZIO, Kim
"Metaphors for the Body in Extremis" (First Sue Saniel Elkind National Poetry Award, Finalist). [Kalliope] (16:2) 94, p. 12.
34. ADISA, Opal Palmer
"Cotton Cane Tobacco." [CaribbeanW] (8) 94, p. 27-28.
"Pan-Africanism." [CaribbeanW] (8) 94, p. 31.
"She Traveling." [CaribbeanW] (8) 94, p. 29-30.
"Sisters in Misery and Womanism." [CaribbeanW] (8) 94, p. 32-35.
35. ADLER, Cori
"Tomato Salad" (Memory piece for Fannie, Karen, and Efi). [SingHM] (21) 94, p. 49-51.

36. ADLER, Lucile
"The Red Pear Tree." [SouthwR] (79:4) Aut 94, p. 661.
37. ADNAN, Etel
"Untitled: There are no frogs in this wide sky." [Bomb] (50) Wint 94-95, p. 80-81.
38. ADOLPH, Andrea
"26 and Single." [Pearl] (20) Spr 94, p. 46.
"Autism." [CimR] (106) Ja 94, p. 69.
"Improvisation." [SantaBR] (1:2) Fall-Wint 93, p. 98.
"Little Wants" (for Dorianne Laux). [CimR] (106) Ja 94, p. 70.
39. ADONIS
"Celebrating Her" (tr. by Khaled Mattawa). [InterQ] (1:3) 94, p. 126-127.
"The Desert: Diary of Beirut under Siege, 1982" (tr. by Samuel Hazo). [LitR] (37:3) Spr 94, p. 453-459.
"Mount Suneen" (tr. by Samuel Hazo). [LitR] (37:3) Spr 94, p. 452.
"The Passage" (tr. by Samuel Hazo). [LitR] (37:3) Spr 94, p. 451-452.
"Tree of Fire" (tr. by Samuel Hazo). [LitR] (37:3) Spr 94, p. 452.
40. AESCHYLUS
"Agamemnon: A Modern Adaptation" (Two Excerpts, tr. by Robert Auletta). [HarvardR] (7) Fall 94, p. 86-94.
41. AFIF, Kaissar
"Homeleaving Dreams of the Walls of Homeland" (tr. by Mansour Ajami). [LitR] (37:3) Spr 94, p. 460-462.
"The Minaret" (tr. by Mansour Ajami). [LitR] (37:3) Spr 94, p. 462.
"Nakedness" (tr. by Mansour Ajami). [LitR] (37:3) Spr 94, p. 462.
"The Poem: This woman stands between spring and the field" (tr. by Mansour Ajami). [LitR] (37:3) Spr 94, p. 463.
42. AGARD, John
"Prospero Caliban Cricket" (for CLR James). [MassR] (35:3/4) Aut-Wint 94, p. 546-548.
43. AGGEN, Gail
"Flamenca Blood." [CoalC] (8) Ap 94, p. 15-16.
44. AGOSIN, Marjorie
"Gabriela's Elqui." [Agni] (39) 94, p. 107.
"In Oaxaca" (tr. by Richard Schaaf). [HarvardR] (6) Spr 94, p. 168.
AGOSTINO, James d'
See D'AGOSTINO, James
45. AGOSTINO, Paul
"Dental Analogies." [Pearl] (20) Spr 94, p. 58.
46. AGRICOLA, Sandra
"The Jewelry Store." [OhioR] (52) 94, p. 77.
47. AGUERO, Kathleen
"A Visit to the Psychic at 41." [HarvardR] (2) Fall 92, p. 127.
48. AGÜEROS, Jack
"Sonnet for Alejandro Roman, Remarkable Rider." [HangL] (64) 94, p. 6.
"Sonnet for the Bicycle Rider's Leg." [HangL] (64) 94, p. 5.
"Sonnet: The History of Puerto Rico." [HangL] (64) 94, p. 5.
"To Julia de Burgos" (tr. of Julia de Burgos). [Callaloo] (17:3) Sum 94, p. 672-673.
AGUIAR, Fred d'
See D'AGUIAR, Fred
AGUILAR, Joaquín Vásquez
See VASQUEZ AGUILAR, Joaquín
AHEBEE, Octavia McBride
See McBRIDE-AHEBEE, Octavia
49. AHSEN, Akhter
"Manhunt in the Desert" (Excerpt). [HeavenB] (11) 94, p. 31-33.
50. AICHEL, Shirley
"Simplicities." [HiramPoR] (57) Fall 94-Wint 95, p. 5.
"Wyeth's Helga." [HiramPoR] (57) Fall 94-Wint 95, p. 6.
51. AIDOO, Ama Ata
"Spices" (for Pandi (Mutuma)). [Field] (50) Spr 94, p. 94-98.
52. AIELLO, Joan
"Aubade." [SoCoast] (17) Je 94, p. 9.
53. AIKEN, William
"Early Loss." [Wind] (74) 94, p. 3-4.
"Fractals." [Poetry] (165:1) O 94, p. 19-20.
"Hardee's." [PoetL] (89:2) Sum 94, p. 47.

"Hotel Clifton." [CreamCR] (18:2) Fall 94, p. 136-137.
"Landfill." [Plain] (14:3) Spr 94, p. 29.
"Last Word." [NoDaQ] (62:1) Wint 94-95, p. 109-110.
"Oil." [PoetL] (89:2) Sum 94, p. 45-46.
"The Party Hat at New Years." [WillowR] (21) Spr 94, p. 20.
"Poem Against the Phoenix." [WillowR] (21) Spr 94, p. 21.

54. AISENBERG, Nadya
"Army of the Ordinary." [BellR] (17:1/2) Spr-Fall 94, p. 93.
"Conversation." [AnthNEW] (6) 94, p. 6.
"The River." [BellR] (17:1/2) Spr-Fall 94, p. 92.

55. AIZENBERG, Susan
"Flying West." [LaurelR] (28:2) Sum 94, p. 80-81.
"Nights Mutable as Water Revise Themselves Into the Shape of Our Extravagant Past." [Agni] (39) 94, p. 189.
"Winter Photograph of Brighton Beach, Brooklyn." [Kalliope] (16:1) 94, p. 16.

56. AJAMI, Mansour
"The Box" (tr. of Shawqi Abi Shaqra). [LitR] (37:3) Spr 94, p. 449.
"Don't Let Them Take Me Away" (tr. of Mansour Rahbani). [LitR] (37:3) Spr 94, p. 512-513.
"Every Land, a Voice" (tr. by the author). [LitR] (37:3) Spr 94, p. 466-467.
"Fire" (tr. of Sa'id 'Aql). [LitR] (37:3) Spr 94, p. . [LitR] (37:3) Spr 94, p. 470-471.
"A Hand Not Ready for Birds" (tr. of Muhammad 'Ali Shams al-Din). [LitR] (37:3) Spr 94, p. 523-524.
"Homeleaving Dreams of the Walls of Homeland" (tr. of Kaissar Afif). [LitR] (37:3) Spr 94, p. 460-462.
"I Shall Put You in My Eyes" (tr. of Sa'id 'Aql). [LitR] (37:3) Spr 94, p. . [LitR] (37:3) Spr 94, p. 471-473.
"Is It for Your Eyes?" (tr. of Sa'id 'Aql). [LitR] (37:3) Spr 94, p. . [LitR] (37:3) Spr 94, p. 468-469.
"A Kiss" (tr. of Michel Trad). [LitR] (37:3) Spr 94, p. 526.
"The Minaret" (tr. of Kaissar Afif). [LitR] (37:3) Spr 94, p. 462.
"Nakedness" (tr. of Kaissar Afif). [LitR] (37:3) Spr 94, p. 462.
"The Neighbors Think I Am a Star" (tr. of Shawqi Abi Shaqra). [LitR] (37:3) Spr 94, p. 447-448.
"Neither One Is Staying With the Other" (tr. of Mansour Rahbani). [LitR] (37:3) Spr 94, p. 513-514.
"Only My Homeland Remains" (tr. of Sa'id 'Aql). [LitR] (37:3) Spr 94, p. . [LitR] (37:3) Spr 94, p. 473-474.
"Pictures" (tr. of Shawqi Bzai'). [LitR] (37:3) Spr 94, p. 477-479.
"The Poem: This woman stands between spring and the field" (tr. of Kaissar Afif). [LitR] (37:3) Spr 94, p. 463.
"Quintrain" (tr. of Sa'id 'Aql). [LitR] (37:3) Spr 94, p. . [LitR] (37:3) Spr 94, p. 473.
"The Road" (tr. of Shawqi Abi Shaqra). [LitR] (37:3) Spr 94, p. 450.
"A Sigh for Beirut" (tr. by the author). [LitR] (37:3) Spr 94, p. 464-465.
"Souvenir" (tr. of Michel Trad). [LitR] (37:3) Spr 94, p. 526.
"We Have a Cottage" (tr. of Michel Trad). [LitR] (37:3) Spr 94, p. 525.

57. AJAY, Stephen
"From the Ghats." [Confr] (54/55) Fall 94-Wint 95, p. 322.
"The Stroke." [Zyzzyva] (10:4) Wint 94, p. 71-73.

AKEMI, Tomioka
See TOMIOKA, Akemi

58. AKHMATOVA, Anna
"And to die in haughty consciousness" (tr. by Judith Hemschemeyer). [InterQ] (1:1) [93?], p. 17.
"Clenched hands under the dark shawl" (tr. by David Helwig). [Quarry] (43:1) Je 94, p. 31.
"Dante" (tr. by Virginia Starrett). [SoCoast] (17) Je 94, p. 62.
"I am not among those who flung" (tr. by David Helwig). [Quarry] (43:1) Je 94, p. 32.
"I am still at home today" (tr. by Judith Hemschemeyer). [InterQ] (1:1) [93?], p. 18.
"In the face of your agonizing death" (tr. by Judith Hemschemeyer). [InterQ] (1:1) [93?], p. 17.
"Leave me alone with music" (tr. by Judith Hemschemeyer). [InterQ] (1:1) [93?], p. 17.
"The memory of sun in the heart grows weak" (tr. by David Helwig). [Quarry] (43:1) Je 94, p. 31-32.

"Necessity herself has finally submitted" (tr. by Judith Hemschemeyer). [InterQ] (1:1) [93?], p. 19.
"Off in the distance hung some sort of bridge" (tr. by Judith Hemschemeyer). [InterQ] (1:1) [93?], p. 19.
"On the right, the Dnieper, on the left, maple trees" (tr. by Judith Hemschemeyer). [InterQ] (1:1) [93?], p. 16.
"Our boys, they defended us" (tr. by Judith Hemschemeyer). [InterQ] (1:1) [93?], p. 17.
"Sonnet: I would have crowned you myself, Fate!" (tr. by Judith Hemschemeyer). [InterQ] (1:1) [93?], p. 18.

AKIKO, Yosano (ca. 1900)
See YOSANO, Akiko (ca. 1900)

59. AKIN, Gülten
"Woman's Song" (tr. by Ruth Christie). [Stand] (35:2) Spr 94, p. 70.

60. AKUTAGAWA
Haiku [AmerPoR] (23:4) Jl-Ag 94, p. 20.

61. AKUTAGAWA, Fusei (1912-1971)
"Autumn Grasses Renga" (w. Araki Yasusada and Ozaki Kusatao, tr. by Tosa Motokiyu, Ojiu Norinaga and Okura Kyojin). [Conjunc] (23) 94, p. 72-73.
"Sentences for Jack Spicer Renga" (w. Araki Yasusada, tr. by Tosa Motokiyu, Ojiu Norinaga and Okura Kyojin). [Conjunc] (23) 94, p. 75-76.
"Suitor Renga" (w. Araki Yasusada and Ozaki Kusatao, tr. by Tosa Motokiyu, Ojiu Norinaga and Okura Kyojin). [Conjunc] (23) 94, p. 74.

62. Al-DIN, Muhammad 'Ali Shams
"A Hand Not Ready for Birds" (tr. by Mansour Ajami). [LitR] (37:3) Spr 94, p. 523-524.

63. Al-DINE, Jawdat Fakhr
"Beware of Our Death in the South" (tr. by Sabah al-Ghandour). [LitR] (37:3) Spr 94, p. 480.
"A Handful of the Southern Wind" (tr. by Sabah al-Ghandour). [LitR] (37:3) Spr 94, p. 481.

64. Al-FAQIH, Zuheir
"Ghurba — In an Alien Land" (tr. of May Rihani). [LitR] (37:3) Spr 94, p. 519-520.
"Voyage 2" (tr. of May Rihani). [LitR] (37:3) Spr 94, p. 520.

65. Al-GHANDOUR, Sabah
"Beware of Our Death in the South" (tr. of Jawdat Fakhr al-Dine). [LitR] (37:3) Spr 94, p. 480.
"A Handful of the Southern Wind" (tr. of Jawdat Fakhr al-Dine). [LitR] (37:3) Spr 94, p. 481.

66. Al-HAJ, Ounsi
"I Was Born Under the sign of Leo" (tr. by Najwa Nasr). [LitR] (37:3) Spr 94, p. 488.
"A Scattered Hymn" (tr. by Najwa Nasr). [LitR] (37:3) Spr 94, p. 486.
"The Silence Which Passes by Like Scandal" (Excerpt, tr. by Najwa Nasr). [LitR] (37:3) Spr 94, p. 487-488.
"Under Logs of Anger" (tr. by Najwa Nasr). [LitR] (37:3) Spr 94, p. 489-490.

67. Al-KHAL, Yusuf
"Quartet for the Last Days" (tr. by Adnan Haydar and Michael Beard). [LitR] (37:3) Spr 94, p. 506-507.

68. Al-MAGHUT, Mohammad
"The Human Excess" (tr. by Allen Hibbard and Osama Isber). [CimR] (108) Jl 94, p. 15.
"Terror and Sex" (tr. by Allen Hibbard and Osama Isber). [CimR] (108) Jl 94, p. 16-17.

69. Al-NAAMANI, Houda
"A.U.B. Melancholy." [LitR] (37:3) Spr 94, p. 510.
"Fear, You Are Drunk" (tr. by Adnan Haydar and Michael Beard). [LitR] (37:3) Spr 94, p. 509-510.
"Healing." [LitR] (37:3) Spr 94, p. 511.
"I Am the Truth" (tr. by Adnan Haydar and Michael Beard). [LitR] (37:3) Spr 94, p. 508-509.
"To R.K." [LitR] (37:3) Spr 94, p. 511.

70. Al-SAYED, Mahmud
"Becoming a Hyena" (tr. by Allen Hibbard and Osama Isber). [CimR] (108) Jl 94, p. 18.
"Marlboro" (tr. by Allen Hibbard and Osama Isber). [CimR] (108) Jl 94, p. 18.
"Surrealism" (tr. by Allen Hibbard and Osama Isber). [CimR] (108) Jl 94, p. 19.

"The Trojan Horse" (tr. by Allen Hibbard and Osama Isber). [CimR] (108) Jl 94, p. 18.
"Why, Oh Arab?" (tr. by Allen Hibbard and Osama Isber). [CimR] (108) Jl 94, p. 19.

71. ALBAN, Laureano
"Flour" (from *Enciclopedia de maravillas*, tr. by Fred Fornoff). [ArtfulD] (26/27) 94, p. 132-133.
"The Giraffe" (from *Enciclopedia de maravillas*, tr. by Fred Fornoff). [ArtfulD] (26/27) 94, p. 134-135.
"The Iceberg" (from *Enciclopedia de maravillas*, tr. by Fred Fornoff). [ArtfulD] (26/27) 94, p. 136-137.
"The Magnet" (from *Enciclopedia de maravillas*, tr. by Fred Fornoff). [ArtfulD] (26/27) 94, p. 138-139.
"The Printing Press" (from *Enciclopedia de maravillas*, tr. by Fred Fornoff). [ArtfulD] (26/27) 94, p. 140-141.
"The Sheet" (from *Enciclopedia de maravillas*, tr. by Fred Fornoff). [ArtfulD] (26/27) 94, p. 142-143.
"The Skirt" (from *Enciclopedia de maravillas*, tr. by Fred Fornoff). [ArtfulD] (26/27) 94, p. 144-145.

72. ALBERGOTTI, Dan
"Methuselah at the Gates." [SoCaR] (27:1/2) Fall 94-Spr 95, p. 10.

73. ALBERTINA, Diane
"Hair on his chest." [Amelia] (7:4, #23) 94, p. 42.

74. ALBERTS, John R.
"Your mother's at her ironing board." [Amelia] (7:3, #22) 94, p. 40.

75. ALBIACH, Anne-Marie
"Gradiva" (from "Anawratha," tr. by Norma Cole). [Avec] (7:1) 94, p. 13.
"Travail Vertical et Blanc." [Conjunc] (23) 94, p. 207-209.

76. ALBON, George
"Childplay in the Dessert." [Talisman] (12) Spr 94, p. 251-252.

77. ALBRECHT, Malaika King
"Tenses." [QW] (39) Sum-Fall 94, p. 196-197.

78. ALCALA, Rigoberto
"The Flight South of the Monarch Butterfly." [Americas] (22:3/4) Fall-Wint 94, p. 63-64.
"Ghost Story." [Americas] (22:3/4) Fall-Wint 94, p. 65-66.
"The Güare from Michoacán." [Americas] (22:3/4) Fall-Wint 94, p. 67.
"Show and Tell" (For my grandmother María, the illiterate woman who taught me to read Spanish). [Americas] (22:3/4) Fall-Wint 94, p. 68-70.

79. ALCALAY, Ammiel
"7 Lines on the Miraculous Yarkon" (tr. of Ronny Someck). [LitR] (37:2) Wint 94, p. 341.
"Acrid Memory" (tr. of Sami Shalom Chetrit). [LitR] (37:2) Wint 94, p. 359.
"Bad Dream" (tr. of Sami Shalom Chetrit). [LitR] (37:2) Wint 94, p. 362-364.
"A Bird Between Continents" (Selections: 10 poems, tr. of Erez Bitton). [LitR] (37:2) Wint 94, p. 277-283.
"The Crusader Man" (tr. of Shelley Elkayam). [LitR] (37:2) Wint 94, p. 328.
"Curfew" (prose poem, tr. of Semezdin Mehmedinovic). [Conjunc] (23) 94, p. 269-270.
"Day Blood — Night Blood" (tr. of Yehezkel Kedmi). [LitR] (37:2) Wint 94, p. 321-322.
"Dimona Blues" (tr. of Ronny Someck). [LitR] (37:2) Wint 94, p. 342.
"Embroidered Rag. Poem on Umm Kulthum" (tr. of Ronny Someck). [LitR] (37:2) Wint 94, p. 343.
"The Extent of the Tragedy" (tr. of Tikva Levi). [LitR] (37:2) Wint 94, p. 346.
"Fleeting Thrill" (tr. of Shlomo Avayou). [LitR] (37:2) Wint 94, p. 284.
"Gideon Was Thinking About Bread" (tr. of Shelley Elkayam). [LitR] (37:2) Wint 94, p. 329.
"The Girl and the Butcher's Window" (tr. of Ronny Someck). [LitR] (37:2) Wint 94, p. 341-342.
"Glass" (prose poem, tr. of Semezdin Mehmedinovic). [Conjunc] (23) 94, p. 268.
"HaMasger Street. Wedding Singer" (tr. of Ronny Someck). [LitR] (37:2) Wint 94, p. 343.
"Handcuffs. Street Poem" (tr. of Ronny Someck). [LitR] (37:2) Wint 94, p. 342.
"Jasmine. Poem on Sandpaper" (tr. of Ronny Someck). [LitR] (37:2) Wint 94, p. 344.
"Lamenting of the Birds" (tr. of Moshe Sartel). [LitR] (37:2) Wint 94, p. 291-303.
"Letter to Ibn Gabirol" (tr. of Lev Hakak). [LitR] (37:2) Wint 94, p. 313.
"Lion's" (prose poem, tr. of Semezdin Mehmedinovic). [Conjunc] (23) 94, p. 270.

"A Martyr's Resting Place" (prose poem, tr. of Semezdin Mehmedinovic). [Conjunc] (23) 94, p. 269.
"My People, Knowledge, and I" (tr. of Yehezkel Kedmi). [LitR] (37:2) Wint 94, p. 324-326.
"Nelson. Trafalgar Square" (tr. of Ronny Someck). [LitR] (37:2) Wint 94, p. 344.
"A Night of Scuds" (tr. of Sami Shalom Chetrit). [LitR] (37:2) Wint 94, p. 359-360.
"Niva" (tr. of Ronny Someck). [LitR] (37:2) Wint 94, p. 341.
"Not Equal to Them the Easterner" (tr. of Yehezkel Kedmi). [LitR] (37:2) Wint 94, p. 319-321.
"Odalisque of the Levant / an Ode" (tr. of Shlomo Avayou). [LitR] (37:2) Wint 94, p. 285-286.
"Poems in Another Land" (Selections: 1-29, tr. of Sami Shalom Chetrit). [LitR] (37:2) Wint 94, p. 356-359.
"Poor Bertolt Brecht Came from the Black Forest" (tr. of Tikva Levi). [LitR] (37:2) Wint 94, p. 346.
"Poverty Line" (tr. of Ronny Someck). [LitR] (37:2) Wint 94, p. 340.
"Purim Sequence" (tr. of Tikva Levi). [LitR] (37:2) Wint 94, p. 347-355.
"Raging Soul" (tr. of Yehezkel Kedmi). [LitR] (37:2) Wint 94, p. 322-324.
"Seven Stanzas to an Indian Chief" (tr. of Shelley Elkayam). [LitR] (37:2) Wint 94, p. 327-328.
"Song of the Architect" (2 selections, tr. of Shelley Elkayam). [LitR] (37:2) Wint 94, p. 330-331.
"A Stone I Lay from Marble of Marmara" (tr. of Moshe Sartel). [LitR] (37:2) Wint 94, p. 288-290.
"Sunscape" (tr. of Ronny Someck). [LitR] (37:2) Wint 94, p. 342.
"The Time of the Singing Birds" (tr. of Amira Hess). [LitR] (37:2) Wint 94, p. 307-310.
"To the Life of Plants on the Road" (tr. of Tikva Levi). [LitR] (37:2) Wint 94, p. 345.
"White Death" (prose poem, tr. of Semezdin Mehmedinovic). [Conjunc] (23) 94, p. 268-269.
"Who Is a Jew and What Kind of Jew?" (tr. of Sami Shalom Chetrit). [LitR] (37:2) Wint 94, p. 360-362.
"Wildweed" (tr. of Shlomo Avayou). [LitR] (37:2) Wint 94, p. 285.
"With Help" (tr. of Shelley Elkayam). [LitR] (37:2) Wint 94, p. 329.
"Yes Indeed I'll Answer God" (tr. of Shelley Elkayam). [LitR] (37:2) Wint 94, p. 332-334.
"You Have to Abandon Jerusalem" (tr. of Shlomo Avayou). [LitR] (37:2) Wint 94, p. 286-287.

80. ALDAN, Daisy
"Again This Stone." [Chelsea] (57) 94, p. 66-67.
"I Awake in These Hills." [Chelsea] (57) 94, p. 65.
"Out of Her Exile." [Chelsea] (57) 94, p. 65-66.
"The Polish Rider" (painting by Rembrandt van Rijn). [Chelsea] (57) 94, p. 69-70.
"The Sheep Shearing" (Limerick, Ireland). [Chelsea] (57) 94, p. 68.
"Whispers" (for Mamma, Anais, and Zina). [Chelsea] (57) 94, p. 67.

81. ALDRIDGE, Richard
"Gently Down the Tubes." [Light] (12) Wint 94-95, p. 13.
"This Time." [Light] (11) Aut 94, p. 12.

82. ALEKSA, Vainis
"Husband." [AnotherCM] (27) 94, p. 5-6.

83. ALESHIRE, Joan
"Door to Door." [Jacaranda] (10) 94, p. 78-79.

84. ALESSIO, Carolyn
"Listening to Mussorgsky in Mary's Garage." [ChiR] (40:2/3) 94, p. 73-74.
"Peatmoss." [SycamoreR] (6:2) Sum 94, p. 44-45.
"Skywriting." [Rosebud] (1:2) Sum 94, p. 83.

85. ALEXANDER, Charles
"Exposures" (1-12). [Talisman] (12) Spr 94, p. 113-116.
"The Short Spreadsheet of Transition." [Talisman] (12) Spr 94, p. 110-112.

86. ALEXANDER, Elizabeth
"At the Beach" (for M.). [Callaloo] (17:2) Sum 94, p. 418.
"At the Beach" (For M.). [Poetry] (163:5) F 94, p. 277.
"The Child Collects." [ChiR] (40:2/3) 94, p. 109.
"Cure." [Callaloo] (17:2) Sum 94, p. 419.
"Dream." [Callaloo] (17:2) Sum 94, p. 417-418.
"Dream." [KenR] (NS 16:1) Wint 94, p. 13-14.

"Frank Willis." [ChiR] (40:2/3) 94, p. 110.
"Haircut." [KenR] (NS 16:1) Wint 94, p. 14-15.
"In the Small Rooms." [KenR] (NS 16:1) Wint 94, p. 12-13.
"L.A. by Night." [Poetry] (163:5) F 94, p. 276.
"Memphis." [Eyeball] (3) 93, p. 4.
"Sonnet." [Eyeball] (3) 93, p. 4.

87. ALEXANDER, Pamela
"Look Here." [Atlantic] (273:6) Je 94, p. 72.
"Manners." [Agni] (39) 94, p. 105.

88. ALEXANDER, Will
"The Serpentine Fusion of Occult Solar Riddles" (w. Andrew Joron). [Caliban] (14) 94, p. 20-29.

89. ALEXIE, Sherman
"The Alcoholic Love Poems." [Callaloo] (17:1) Wint 94, p. 18-20.
"All I Wanted to Do Was Dance" (for Diane). [Callaloo] (17:1) Wint 94, p. 15-16.
"Cline." [Callaloo] (17:1) Wint 94, p. 17.
"Drum as Love, Fear, and Prayer" (for Diane). [Ploughs] (20:1) Spr 94, p. 44-50.
"Fire as Verb and Noun." [Caliban] (14) 94, p. 48-51.
"Mother" (for Lillian). [Caliban] (14) 94, p. 46-47.
"Political Science." [Caliban] (14) 94, p. 52.
"Running from the Mafia" (for Diane). [Callaloo] (17:1) Wint 94, p. 22-23.
"Sittin' on the Dock of the Bay." [Callaloo] (17:1) Wint 94, p. 21.
"Things (for an Indian) to Do in New York (City)." [BelPoJ] (45:2) Wint 94-95, p. 14-19.

90. ALEXIS, Austin
"To the Woman in Venice." [SantaBR] (2:1) Spr-Sum 94, p. 93.

91. ALFRED, William
"For Jess B. Bessinger on His Retirement." [HarvardR] (Premier Issue) Spr 92, p. 67.

ALI, Aga Shahid
See ALI, Agha Shahid

92. ALI, Agha Shahid
"The Bird, Peripatetically." [WilliamMR] (32) 94, p. 59.
"The Blesséd Word: A Prologue on Kashmir" (for Irfan). [TriQ] (91) Fall 94, p. 189-191.
"The City of Daughters: A Poem About Kashmir." [TriQ] (91) Fall 94, p. 192-195.
"The Correspondent." [DenQ] (28:4) Spr 94, p. 5-6.
"Eleven Stars Over Andalusia" (tr. of Mahmoud Darwish, w. Mona Anis, Nigel Ryan and Ahmad Dallal). [GrandS] (12:4, #48) Wint 94, p. 100-111.
"A History of Paisley" (for Anuradha Dingwaney). [ParisR] (36:131) Sum 94, p. 208-210.
"I See Kashmir from New Delhi at Midnight." [DenQ] (28:4) Spr 94, p. 7-9.
"Kashmir without a Post Office" (for James Merrill). [GrahamHR] (18) Wint 94-95, p. 94-97.
"Some Vision of the World Cashmere." [HarvardR] (7) Fall 94, p. 28-29.

93. ALI, Ahmed
"Dialogue with Lee San." [InterQ] (1:3) 94, p. 172-173.

94. ALIESAN, Jody
"Fate." [CrabCR] (8:2/3/9:1/2/3) 94, p. 45-46.

95. ALKAIOS
Translations by Nicholas Rockel [Descant] (25:1, #84) Spr 94, p. 25-26, 35.

96. ALKALAY-GUT, Karen
"Ashkelon Beach" (tr. of Yehuda Amichai). [InterQ] (1:3) 94, p. 102.
"Calm Reconciliation or Latest Impressions" (tr. of Gad Yaacobi). [AmerLC] (6) 94, p. 125-126.
"Housewife." [InterQ] (1:3) 94, p. 100.
"Poetry in the Middle East." [InterQ] (1:3) 94, p. 101.

ALKLAI-GUT, Keren
See ALKALAY-GUT, Karen

97. ALKMAN
Translations by Nicholas Rockel [Descant] (25:1, #84) Spr 94, p. 33.

98. ALLARDT, Linda
"Wood." [BelPoJ] (44:4) Sum 94, p. 5.

99. ALLBERY, Debra
"After the Auction of My Grandmother's Farm." [TriQ] (91) Fall 94, p. 200.
"After Vermeer." [TriQ] (91) Fall 94, p. 196-199.
"Instinct." [Writer] (107:8) Ag 94, p. 22.

"Next-Door Neighbors." [Writer] (107:8) Ag 94, p. 22.
100. ALLEGRE, Marla Rowe
"City of Diamonds." [Amelia] (7:3, #22) 94, p. 91.
101. ALLEN, Dick
"Animus." [Pivot] (42) 94, p. 31.
"Innocence." [Pivot] (42) 94, p. 30-31.
"Phase Transitions." [ChiR] (40:2/3) 94, p. 115-116.
102. ALLEN, Fergus
"Genealogy." [NewYorker] (69:49) 7 F 94, p. 58-59.
103. ALLEN, Gilbert
"Cars and the Man" (Robert Penn Warren Poetry Prize Winner: Third Prize). [CumbPR] (14:1) Fall 94, p. 10-11.
"The Great Smoky Mountain Railway." [Shen] (44:4) Wint 94, p. 47.
"Live Oaks in the Piedmont" (for Linda and Aubrey, who lived there). [SouthernHR] (28:4) Fall 94, p. 348-349.
104. ALLEN, Jed
"The Kiss." [ChironR] (13:2) Sum 94, p. 10.
105. ALLEN, Judith
"The Lover." [SouthernPR] (34:2) Wint 94, p. 28-29.
106. ALLEN, Samuel
"Law and Order: The Immigrant." [AmerPoR] (23:5) S-O 94, p. 19-20.
107. ALLEN, Susan Munden
"Blackberries." [SouthernHR] (28:3) Sum 94, p. 268.
108. ALLEN, Valerie Martínez
"Absence, Luminescent." [PraS] (68:4) Wint 94, p. 142-145.
"It Is Not." [PraS] (68:4) Wint 94, p. 141.
"Nocturne." [PraS] (68:4) Wint 94, p. 146.
"Tesoro" (For Timothy Trujillo, 1951-1991). [PraS] (68:4) Wint 94, p. 147-148.
109. ALLEN, William
"Buchenwald Landscape." [GlobalCR] (4) Fall 94, p. 91.
"Connecticut Shoreline." [ConnPR] (13:1) 94, p. 4.
110. ALLEY, Rick
"Cleaning." [WillowS] (34) Sum 94, p. 54.
"Folklore." [Caliban] (14) 94, p. 107.
"In Spring Air." [Caliban] (14) 94, p. 105.
"On the Way." [Caliban] (14) 94, p. 106.
"With Gratitude, In-Depth & Sweet." [WillowS] (34) Sum 94, p. 55.
111. ALLMAN, John
"'35 Dodge." [NoDaQ] (62:3) Sum 94-95, p. 55.
112. ALLNUTT, Gillian
"Lighthouse, Ardnamurchan, Argyll." [Jacaranda] (5:1) Wint-Spr 91, p. 36.
113. ALLRED, Joanne
"Between Worlds." [ColR] (21:2) Fall 94, p. 84-85.
"Cocoon." [CreamCR] (18:2) Fall 94, p. 100-101.
114. ALMBERG, Evangeline
"Discourse from an Immortal" (tr. of Lawrence Wong, w. Andrew Parkin). [PoetryC] (14:3) My 94, p. 22.
"The Shattered Cliff" (tr. of Lawrence Wong, w. Andrew Parkin). [PoetryC] (14:3) My 94, p. 22.
115. ALMON, Bert
"Nell Campion Rausch" (Uttoxeter, 1907 / Stettler, Alberta, 1988). [PraF] (15:1, #66) Spr 94, p. 140-141.
"Ode to the Hot Water Bottle" (Grain Contest Winners, Prose Poem: Honourable Mention). [Grain] (21:4) Spr 94, p. 21.
"The Sun Tan Parlor in Lahaina." [ChamLR] (14/15) Spr-Fall 94, p. 118.
116. ALMON, Margaret
"The Suit of Women" (for Erin). [HayF] (14) Spr-Sum 94, p. 48-49.
117. ALPAUGH, David
"After the Perfect Dive." [Zyzzyva] (10:3) Fall 94, p. 73-74.
118. ALTER, Michael
"To Be a Hand." [HiramPoR] (57) Fall 94-Wint 95, p. 7-8.
119. ALTHAUS, Keith
"Poem of the Dump Sticker Salesman." [Jacaranda] (10) 94, p. 117-118.
120. ALVAREZ, María Auxiliadora
"It's Not Fair" (tr. by Tess O'Dwyer). [Trans] (29) Spr 94, p. 90-91.
"The Red Bird of My Air" (tr. by Tess O'Dwyer). [Trans] (29) Spr 94, p. 92.

ALVAREZ, Pansy Maurer
See MAURER-ALVAREZ, Pansy
121. ALVELO, Wilfredo
"Desde Aquí." [Nuez] (5:13/14/15) 94, p. 18.
122. AMABILE, George
"Canon." [Nimrod] (37:2) Spr-Sum 94, p. 1.
AMARAL, José Vázquez
See VAZQUEZ-AMARAL, José
AMARI, Hayashi
See HAYASHI, Amari
123. AMATO, Christianne
"Lettuce Leaves." [AntigR] (96) Wint 94, p. 75.
124. AMATO, Mike
"The Malignancy: Like the Stones in Van Gogh's Garden." [FreeL] (13) Spr 94, p. 31-33.
125. AMATUZIO, Anna
"Jane Avril." [SoCoast] (16) Ja 94, p. 32.
126. AMES, Allen
"John Muir in the Western Mountains" (for Han Shan, ca. 700-780). [ChatR] (14:2) Wint 94, p. 42-43.
127. AMICHAI, Yehuda
"Ashkelon Beach" (tr. by Karen Alkalay-Gut). [InterQ] (1:3) 94, p. 102.
128. AMIDON, Richard
"The Churches Are Doing Well." [SlipS] (14) 94, p. 70.
129. AMIRTHANAYAGAM, Indran
"Drop Out." [KenR] (NS 16:3) Sum 94, p. 119-120.
"Kiss." [Jacaranda] (10) 94, p. 118-119.
"Monsoon in the West." [KenR] (NS 16:3) Sum 94, p. 118-119.
130. AMMONS, A. R.
"Following Tragedy." [HarvardR] (2) Fall 92, p. 18.
"Keeping Track." [NoCarLR] (2:1) Spr 94, p. 21.
"Reading Ta'o Chien." [SouthernR] (30:4) Aut 94, p. 791.
"Sentiment." [NewYorker] (70:1) 21 F 94, p. 76.
131. AMSEL, Philip
"Quebec." [InterPR] (20:2) Fall 94, p. 109.
132. AMYUNI, Mona Takyeddine
"Beirut" (tr. of Clarie Gebeyli). [LitR] (37:3) Spr 94, p. 485.
"Beirut! O Queen of the World" (tr. of Nizar Kabbani). [LitR] (37:3) Spr 94, p. 498-502.
"A Man Is Dead" (tr. of Clarie Gebeyli). [LitR] (37:3) Spr 94, p. 483-484.
"On Every Roof a Bond" (tr. of Clarie Gebeyli). [LitR] (37:3) Spr 94, p. 483.
"A Porch" (tr. of Clarie Gebeyli). [LitR] (37:3) Spr 94, p. 482.
133. ANAKREON (563-478 B.C.)
"You, boy, with the girlish eyes" (tr. by Robin Skelton). [Arc] (32) Spr 94, p. 38.
134. ANDERSEN, Astrid Hjertenaes
"The House in the Dream" (tr. by Aina Gerner-Mathisen and Suzanne Bachner). [SpoonR] (19:1) Wint-Spr 94, p. 94-95.
"The House on the Meadow" (tr. by Aina Gerner-Mathisen and Suzanne Bachner). [SpoonR] (19:1) Wint-Spr 94, p. 96.
"Red Branches" (tr. by Aina Gerner-Mathisen and Suzanne Bachner). [SpoonR] (19:1) Wint-Spr 94, p. 93.
135. ANDERSON, Alice
"Communion." [NewYorkQ] (53) 94, p. 100.
"The Split." [PlumR] (7) [94?], p. 41-43.
"To the Wolves." [PlumR] (7) [94?], p. 44-45.
136. ANDERSON, Barbara
"Chrystal: 2:14 AM." [PassN] (15:1) Sum 94, p. 26-28.
"Night." [PassN] (15:1) Sum 94, p. 25.
137. ANDERSON, Ben
"Education." [NewYorkQ] (53) 94, p. 101.
"Passing Mention." [MinnR] (41/42) Fall 93-Spr 94 (published Mr 95), p. 31.
138. ANDERSON, Catherine
"Wonderland." [HarvardR] (6) Spr 94, p. 90.
139. ANDERSON, Curt
"Domestic." [Talisman] (12) Spr 94, p. 242.
"Hairstyles of the Gods." [PoetryE] (37/38) Spr 94, p. 21.

140. ANDERSON, Doug
"Blues." [MassR] (35:1) Spr 94, p. 149-151.
141. ANDERSON, Erland
"Another David." [ContextS] (4:1) 94, p. 11.
"False Discoveries" (for Jean Charlot). [AmerS] (63:2) Spr 94, p. 258.
142. ANDERSON, Gary
"The Martins." [Amelia] (7:4, #23) 94, p. 107.
"What Stays." [Amelia] (7:4, #23) 94, p. 107.
143. ANDERSON, Jack
"Beggars." [HangL] (64) 94, p. 6.
"Light Sources." [Caliban] (14) 94, p. 117.
"Transcendence." [Chelsea] (56) 94, p. 94-95.
"A Window in the Poem." [ProseP] (3) 94, p. 6-7.
144. ANDERSON, Jon
"The Effluvium." [PassN] (15:1) Sum 94, p. 5.
"Ken" (aids, august 1993). [PassN] (15:1) Sum 94, p. 4.
"Machines of Loving Grace." [PassN] (15:1) Sum 94, p. 7.
"Quentin Boyar's Grand Canyon Decision." [PassN] (15:1) Sum 94, p. 3.
"Timor Mortis Conterbat Me." [PassN] (15:1) Sum 94, p. 6-7.
145. ANDERSON, Kathleen
"Wanting." [CrabCR] (8:2/3/9:1/2/3) 94, p. 85.
146. ANDERSON, Kemmer
"Hebron 1994." [ChrC] (111:11) 6 Ap 94, p. 356.
147. ANDERSON, Mia
"The Shambles." [PoetryC] (15:1) N 94, p. 4-5.
148. ANDERSON, Robert K.
"A Circle Closes" (Excerpt). [EvergreenC] (9:1) Wint-Spr 94, p. 86.
149. ANDERSON-REECE, Erik
"At the end of linear time." [AnotherCM] (27) 94, p. 7-8.
"Raison d' *Elvis*." [ChiR] (40:2/3) 94, p. 123-131.
150. ANDRADE, Carlos Drummond de
"Friendly Song" (printed on the Brazilian 50 Cruzeiros note, tr. by Lloyd Schwartz). [HarvardR] (Premier Issue) Spr 92, p. 109.
151. ANDRADE, Eugenio de
"17. I find my friends with ease" (From *Solar Matter*, 1955, tr. by Alexis Levitin). [NewRena] (9:1, #27) 94, p. 113.
"17. São fáceis de encontrar, os meus amigos." [NewRena] (9:1, #27) 94, p. 112.
"34. Aqui oiço o trabalho do outono." [NewRena] (9:1, #27) 94, p. 114.
"34. Here I listen to the work of autumn" (From *Solar Matter*, 1995, tr. by Alexis Levitin). [NewRena] (9:1, #27) 94, p. 115.
"35. It doesn't startle me if an arm of the river" (From *Solar Matter*, 1995, tr.tr. by Alexis Levitin). [NewRena] (9:1, #27) 94, p. 117.
"35. Não me espanta se vir aproximar-se." [NewRena] (9:1, #27) 94, p. 116.
"Adagio" (in Portuguese). [Os] (39) Fall-Wint 94, p. 22.
"Adagio" (tr. by Alexis Levitin). [Os] (39) Fall-Wint 94, p. 23.
"Adagio Quasi Andante" (tr. by Alexis Levitin). [JamesWR] (11:4) Sum 94, p. 4.
"Almost Nothing" (tr. by Alexis Levitin). [Os] (39) Fall-Wint 94, p. 19.
"Between March and April" (tr. by Alexis Levitin). [ApalQ] (40/41) 94, p. 76-77.
"By Chance" (tr. by Alexis Levitin). [Os] (38) Spr 94, p. 19.
"Casualmente." [Os] (38) Spr 94, p. 18.
"Com Os Juncos." [NewRena] (9:1, #27) 94, p. 118.
"Dunes" (tr. by Alexis Levitin). [HarvardR] (6) Spr 94, p. 172.
"From Summer's Side" (tr. by Alexis Levitin). [CrabCR] (8:2/3/9:1/2/3) 94, p. 73.
"In Memoriam" (F.G.L., in Portuguese). [Os] (39) Fall-Wint 94, p. 20.
"In Memoriam" (tr. by Alexis Levitin). [Os] (39) Fall-Wint 94, p. 21.
"Last Poem" (tr. by Alexis Levitin). [WebR] (18) Fall 94, p. 26.
"Lines of Winter" (tr. by Alexis Levitin). [WebR] (18) Fall 94, p. 25.
"No chão agora claro dança o Ar—." [NewRena] (9:1, #27) 94, p. 120.
"Nocturne" (tr. by Alexis Levitin). [Os] (39) Fall-Wint 94, p. 23.
"Nocturno." [Os] (39) Fall-Wint 94, p. 22.
"On Ground Now Bright Dances Air" (From *Shadow's Weight*, tr. by Alexis Levitin). [NewRena] (9:1, #27) 94, p. 121.
"A Paixão." [Os] (38) Spr 94, p. 20.
"Passeio Allegre" (tr. by Alexis Levitin). [WebR] (18) Fall 94, p. 25.
"Passion" (tr. by Alexis Levitin). [Os] (38) Spr 94, p. 21.
"Provisional Title" (tr. by Alexis Levitin). [PoetL] (89:3) Fall 94, p. 17-18.

"Quase Nada." [Os] (39) Fall-Wint 94, p. 19.
"Solar Matter 38" (tr. by Alexis Levitin). [MidAR] (14:2) 94, p. 65.
"Those Bodies" (tr. by Alexis Levitin). [Sun] (223) Jl 94, p. 27.
"The Visit" (tr. by Alexis Levitin). [Os] (38) Spr 94, p. 19.
"A Visita." [Os] (38) Spr 94, p. 18.
"With the Rushes" (From *Another Name for Earth*, tr. by Alexis Levitin). [NewRena] (9:1, #27) 94, p. 119.

152. ANDRE, Jean
"Unside Down, and, Possibly, Backward." [Elf] (4:4) Wint 94, p. 40.

153. ANDREWS, Bruce
"Lip Service" (2 selections). [WashR] (19:5) F-Mr 94, p. 11.
"Lip Service" (Selection: "Primum Mobile 4"). [Talisman] (12) Spr 94, p. 9-12.
"Lip Service" (Selections: "Earth 4," "Earth 5"). [Caliban] (14) 94, p. 38-40.
"Mars" (8 & 10, from *Lip Service*). [NewAW] (12) Spr-Sum 94, p. 73-80.

154. ANDREWS, Claudia Emerson
"Bone." [Crazy] (47) Wint 94, p. 47.
"The Boundaries of Her Voice." [Crazy] (47) Wint 94, p. 46.
"Pinion." [NewEngR] (16:1) Wint 94, p. 24-25.
"The Pit." [Crazy] (47) Wint 94, p. 45.
"The Proof-Meter." [Crazy] (47) Wint 94, p. 48.
"The Rapture." [NewEngR] (16:1) Wint 94, p. 22-23.
"What Waits for You." [NewEngR] (16:1) Wint 94, p. 23-24.

155. ANDREWS, Linda
"All the Calliopes in Montana." [Gaia] (4) Je 94, p. 36-37.
"The Bathers." [Gaia] (4) Je 94, p. 38.
"Io, One Summer." [Gaia] (4) Je 94, p. 36.
"Late Sky" (at Bend, Oregon). [Gaia] (4) Je 94, p. 36.
"Plains at Belle Fourche" (South Dakota). [Gaia] (4) Je 94, p. 37.
"When a Daughter Is Missing." [Calyx] (15:3) Wint 94-95, p. 42-43.

156. ANDREWS, Nin
"Advice to Don Juan: Orgasms to Avoid." [SpoonR] (19:1) Wint-Spr 94, p. 8.
"The Book of Lies." [ParisR] (36:133) Wint 94, p. 121.
"The Disappearance." [SpoonR] (19:1) Wint-Spr 94, p. 9.
"Like an Angel." [SpoonR] (19:1) Wint-Spr 94, p. 7.
"The Orgasm Beyond." [AnotherCM] (27) 94, p. 10.
"The Right Time." [AnotherCM] (27) 94, p. 9.
"The Secret." [AnotherCM] (27) 94, p. 11.

157. ANDREWS, Shari
"Instruction to the Intending Emigrant" (after reading N.B. as a Home for Emigrants . . .). [CanLit] (141) Sum 94, p. 50-51.
"What Little Light There Is" (Grain Contest Winners, Prose Poem: Honourable Mention). [Grain] (21:4) Spr 94, p. 22.

158. ANDREWS, Tom
"Cinema Vérité: Scenes from a Marriage." [Journal] (18:1) Spr-Sum 94, p. 66-67.
"Logician's Sonnet." [PoetryE] (37/38) Spr 94, p. 22.
"My World Record" (From "Codeine Diary" in *The Hemophiliac's Motorcycle*, University of Iowa Press, winner of the Iowa Poetry Prize). [Harp] (289:1730) Jl 94, p. 32-34.
"Unwritten Sonnet." [PoetryE] (37/38) Spr 94, p. 23.

159. ANDROLA, Ron
"First Diane Smiled." [ChironR] (13:3) Aut 94, p. 2.
"I Am Beginning to Question My Fate." [ChironR] (13:3) Aut 94, p. 3.
"I Talked about Steve Richmond to My Daughter." [ChironR] (13:3) Aut 94, p. 2.
"The Poet Better." [ChironR] (13:3) Aut 94, p. 3.
"Reading Fred Voss." [ChironR] (13:3) Aut 94, p. 5.
"Singing Against the Hyenas of Hope" (for kurt cobain, r.i.p.). [ChironR] (13:3) Aut 94, p. 3.
"A Syrian Poem." [Pearl] (20) Spr 94, p. 52.
"Usual Day at the Factory." [ChironR] (13:3) Aut 94, p. 28.
"What They Want." [ChironR] (13:3) Aut 94, p. 3.

160. ANGEL, George
"Novena." [Sulfur] (34) Spr 94, p. 65.
"Octave." [Sulfur] (34) Spr 94, p. 64-65.
"Septic." [Sulfur] (34) Spr 94, p. 64.
"The stone is dead." [Sulfur] (34) Spr 94, p. 63.
"Untitled: Hill whether there was howling." [Caliban] (14) 94, p. 123.

"The word blood is dead." [Sulfur] (34) Spr 94, p. 63-64.
ANGELO, Mary d'
See D'ANGELO, Mary
161. ANIS, Mona
"Eleven Stars Over Andalusia" (tr. of Mahmoud Darwish, w. Nigel Ryan, Aga Shahid Ali and Ahmad Dallal). [GrandS] (12:4, #48) Wint 94, p. 100-111.
ANNA, Lynnette (Dueck) d'
See D'ANNA, Lynnette (Dueck)
162. ANONYMOUS
"We Hear Music." [Eyeball] (3) 93, p. 3.
163. ANONYMOUS (11th c., Early Celtic)
"Autumn" (from "The Guesting of Athirne," tr. by Jennifer E. Boyle). [SoCoast] (17) Je 94, p. 59.
"Autumn" (from "The Guesting of Athirne"). [SoCoast] (17) Je 94, p. 59.
164. ANONYMOUS (Egyptian, circa 1550-1080 B.C.)
"Egyptian Love Lyrics" (tr. by Barbara Hughes Fowler). [GrandS] (13:2, #50) Fall 94, p. 110-112.
165. ANONYMOUS (from *Bodleian Latin Miscellany,* ca. 1500)
"Mittitur." [SoCoast] (16) Ja 94, p. 60.
"The Tokens (Mittitur)" (tr. by Mary Black Vigil and John J. Brugaletta). [SoCoast] (16) Ja 94, p. 61.
166. ANONYMOUS (Mother Goose)
"Georgie Porgie, puddin' and pie" (Traditional Mother Goose Version). [Harp] (288:1726) Mr 94, p. 30.
"Peter, Peter, pumpkin eater" (Traditional Mother Goose Version). [Harp] (288:1726) Mr 94, p. 30.
167. ANONYMOUS (Six Survivors of Childhood Sexual Abuse, September 17, 1990)
"I Remember." [SingHM] (21) 94, p. 81.
168. ANONYMOUS (The Sumerian Beer Tablet)
"The Hymn to Ninkasi" (tr. by Miguel Civl). [SantaBR] (2:2) Fall-Wint 94, p. 42-43.
169. ANONYMOUS (traditional Hebrew prayer)
"Rebond Shel Olam" (tr. by Dan Jaffe). [DenQ] (29:1) Sum 94, p. 46.
170. ANSAY, A. Manette
"American Family Values." [PoetryNW] (35:4) Wint 94-95, p. 29-30.
"A Cartography" (for JWS). [PoetryNW] (35:4) Wint 94-95, p. 30-31.
"First Steps." [PoetryNW] (35:4) Wint 94-95, p. 28.
"Ponies" (for Laurie Nelson). [WillowS] (34) Sum 94, p. 32.
"Reasons to Behave." [NewL] (60:3) 94, p. 102-103.
171. ANSEL, Talvikki
"From Stone." [HayF] (14) Spr-Sum 94, p. 46.
172. ANSTETT, Aaron
"Big World Full of Uneasy Sleepers." [CreamCR] (18:1) Spr 94, p. 18.
"Five Definitions." [PaintedB] (53/54) 94, p. 49.
"The Ticket Taker Speaks." [BlackWR] (20:2) Spr-Sum 94, p. 120.
173. ANTHONY, Luke
"Trains" (For the Serbs fighting fascism). [NewYorkQ] (53) 94, p. 79.
174. ANTLER
"Hearing the Echo." [HeavenB] (11) 94, p. 56.
"Hearing the Echo." [NewYorkQ] (53) 94, p. 56.
"Kicking the Habit." [Sun] (223) Jl 94, p. 24.
"Solution." [JamesWR] (11:2) Wint 94, p. 7.
"Stars in My Brain." [HeavenB] (11) 94, p. 57.
"Workers Should Be Happy." [Sun] (224) Ag 94, p. 24.
175. ANZALDUA, Gloria
"The Basque *Brujas* — c. 1492" (for Angie Arrien). [SinW] (54) Wint 94-95, p. 115-121.
176. AOYAMA, Miyuki
"Ah, my pocketbook" (Tanka, tr. of Motoko Michiura, w. Akemi Tomioka and Leza Lowitz). [Zyzzyva] (10:2) Sum 94, p. 61.
"Haiku: Someone else's wife" (tr. of Nobuko Katsura, w. Leza Lowitz). [YellowS] (11:4, #44) Wint 93-94, p. 44.
"My nipples still erect" (Tanka, tr. of Motoko Michiura, w. Akemi Tomioka and Leza Lowitz). [Zyzzyva] (10:2) Sum 94, p. 61.
"The Second to Last Kiss (Tanka)" (tr. of Amari Hayashi, w. Leza Lowitz). [YellowS] (11:4, #44) Wint 93-94, p. 45.

"Someday I'll turn to water" (Tanka, tr. of Motoko Michiura, w. Akemi Tomioka and Leza Lowitz). [Zyzzyva] (10:2) Sum 94, p. 61.
"Whenever I see poppies" (Tanka, tr. of Motoko Michiura, w. Akemi Tomioka and Leza Lowitz). [Zyzzyva] (10:2) Sum 94, p. 61.

177. APOLLINAIRE, Guillaume
"Annie" (tr. by Donald Revell). [AmerPoR] (23:6) N-D 94, p. 5.
"Autumn" (tr. by Donald Revell). [AmerPoR] (23:6) N-D 94, p. 5.
"The Brazier" (tr. by Donald Revell). [Colum] (22) Wint 94, p. 112-114.
"The Door" (tr. by Donald Revell). [AmerPoR] (23:6) N-D 94, p. 5.
"An Evening" (tr. by Donald Revell). [PartR] (61:4) Fall 94, p. 629-630.
"The Farewell" (tr. by Donald Revell). [Pequod] (38) 94, p. 100.
"The Harvest Month" (tr. by Donald Revell). [Pequod] (38) 94, p. 90-95.
"Hunting Horns" (tr. by Donald Revell). [AmerPoR] (23:6) N-D 94, p. 5.
"Marie" (tr. by Donald Revell). [WillowS] (34) Sum 94, p. 67.
"Palace" (to Max Jacob, tr. by Donald Revell). [Pequod] (38) 94, p. 98-99.
"Poem Read at the Marriage of André Salmon" (July 13, 1909, tr. by Donald Revell). [SenR] (24:1) Spr 94, p. 53-54.
"Rosemonde" (to André Derain, tr. by Donald Revell). [SenR] (24:1) Spr 94, p. 55.
"Saltimbanques" (tr. by Donald Revell). [AmerPoR] (23:6) N-D 94, p. 5.
"Sickly Autumn" (tr. by Donald Revell). [PartR] (61:4) Fall 94, p. 630.
"Singer" (tr. by Donald Revell). [AmerPoR] (23:6) N-D 94, p. 5.
"The Traveller" (to Fernand Fleuret, tr. by Donald Revell). [Pequod] (38) 94, p. 96-97.
"The Wind by Night" (tr. by Donald Revell). [WillowS] (34) Sum 94, p. 66.
"Zone" (tr. by Donald Revell). [AmerPoR] (23:6) N-D 94, p. 3-5.

178. APPEL, Dori
"Legacy." [PraS] (68:3) Fall 94, p. 60-61.
"My Grandmother's Education." [PraS] (68:3) Fall 94, p. 58-60.

179. APPELBAUM, David
"The Earthworm Jar." [Comm] (121:8) 22 Ap 94, p. 14.

180. APPELL, David
"Reaching." [HawaiiR] (18:1, #40) Spr 94, p. 65.

181. APPLEGATE, Tim
"Roberts Bay." [DogRR] (26) Wint 94-95, p. 42.
"Utah." [DogRR] (26) Wint 94-95, p. 42.

182. APPLEMAN, Marjorie
"Getting Somewhere." [Confr] (54/55) Fall 94-Wint 95, p. 283-284.

183. APPLEMAN, Philip
"Parable of the Talents." [Confr] (54/55) Fall 94-Wint 95, p. 275-276.

184. APPLEWHITE, James
"Remembering Home Movies on Water." [Writer] (107:10) O 94, p. 26-27.
"A Run with the Double River." [Writer] (107:10) O 94, p. 27.

APPOLLINAIRE, Guillaume
See APOLLINAIRE, Guillaume

185. 'AQL, Sa'id
"Fire" (tr. by Mansour Ajami). [LitR] (37:3) Spr 94, p. . [LitR] (37:3) Spr 94, p. 470-471.
"I Shall Put You in My Eyes" (tr. by Mansour Ajami). [LitR] (37:3) Spr 94, p. . [LitR] (37:3) Spr 94, p. 471-473.
"Is It for Your Eyes?" (tr. by Mansour Ajami). [LitR] (37:3) Spr 94, p. . [LitR] (37:3) Spr 94, p. 468-469.
"Only My Homeland Remains" (tr. by Mansour Ajami). [LitR] (37:3) Spr 94, p. . [LitR] (37:3) Spr 94, p. 473-474.
"Quintrain" (tr. by Mansour Ajami). [LitR] (37:3) Spr 94, p. . [LitR] (37:3) Spr 94, p. 473.

AQUIAR, Fred d'
See D'AGUIAR, Fred

186. ARAGON, Francisco
"The Calendar." [Zyzzyva] (10:4) Wint 94, p. 91-92.

187. ARAKI, Yasusada
"Autumn Grasses Renga" (w. Ozaki Kusatao and Akutagawa Fusei, tr. by Tosa Motokiyu, Ojiu Norinaga and Okura Kyojin). [Conjunc] (23) 94, p. 72-73.
"Dream and Charcoal" (tr. by Tosa Motokiyu, Ojiu Norinaga and Okura Kyojin). [Conjunc] (23) 94, p. 69-70.
"Geisha and Iris" (tr. by Tosa Motokiyu, Ojiu Norinaga and Okura Kyojin). [Conjunc] (23) 94, p. 70-71.

"Horsehide and Sunspot" (July 17, 1962, Hiroshima Municipal Stadium, tr. by Tosa Motokiyu, Ojiu Norinaga and Okura Kyojin). [Conjunc] (23) 94, p. 72.
"Sentences for Jack Spicer Renga" (w. Akutagawa Fusei, tr. by Tosa Motokiyu, Ojiu Norinaga and Okura Kyojin). [Conjunc] (23) 94, p. 75-76.
"Suitor Renga" (w. Ozaki Kusatao and Akutagawa Fusei, tr. by Tosa Motokiyu, Ojiu Norinaga and Okura Kyojin). [Conjunc] (23) 94, p. 74.
"Telescope with Urn" (tr. by Tosa Motokiyu, Ojiu Norinaga and Okura Kyojin). [Conjunc] (23) 94, p. 69.
"Untitled Haiku" (tr. by Tosa Motokiyu, Ojiu Norinaga and Okura Kyojin). [Conjunc] (23) 94, p. 71.
"Utterances and Hepatica" (tr. by Tosa Motokiyu, Ojiu Norinaga and Okura Kyojin). [Conjunc] (23) 94, p. 76-77.

188. ARANCIO, Lawrence
"Answer Man." [Iowa] (24:3) Fall 94, p. 144.
"The Fear of Death." [Iowa] (24:3) Fall 94, p. 146.
"Role Reversal." [Iowa] (24:3) Fall 94, p. 145.
"Veronicas." [Iowa] (24:3) Fall 94, p. 144.

189. ARASANAYAGAM, Jean
"Fire in the Village" (Kangra Painting from Tira-Sujanpur, Plate 28 — Kangra Valley Painting). [KenR] (NS 16:4) Fall 94, p. 87-90.

190. ARBUTHNOT, Nancy
"White Shark." [CrabCR] (8:2/3/9:1/2/3) 94, p. 77.

191. ARCA SARAVIA, Marco Tulio del
"Fatherland, I Do Not Forget You" (tr. by Carroll E. Mace). [XavierR] (14:2) Fall 94, p. 65.
"Patira, Yo No Te Olvido." [XavierR] (14:2) Fall 94, p. 65.

192. ARCANGELINI, M. J.
"Triptych — Three Studies for a Portrait of Francis Bacon." [JamesWR] (11:5) Fall 94, p. 15.

193. ARCENEAUX, Therese
"Cottonwood Wash, Navajo Reservation." [BellArk] (10:5) S-O 94, p. 25.
"Glory, Glory." [BellArk] (10:3) My-Je 94, p. 25.
"Here in This Morning." [BellArk] (10:1) Ja-F 94, p. 14.
"Lapidarian Landscapes." [SouthernPR] (34:2) Wint 94, p. 50.
"October Wind." [BellArk] (10:5) S-O 94, p. 25.
"The Singing Tree." [BellArk] (10:3) My-Je 94, p. 25.
"Tenant's Song." [BellArk] (10:1) Ja-F 94, p. 14.
"These Atoms That I Call Myself." [BellArk] (10:1) Ja-F 94, p. 14.
"Time Dancer, Earth Dancer." [BellArk] (10:1) Ja-F 94, p. 14.

194. ARCHILOCHOS
Translations by Nicholas Rockel [Descant] (25:1, #84) Spr 94, p. 28.

195. ARCOS, Jorge Luis
"Epistle to Jose Luis Ferrer (From Havana to Miami)" (tr. by David Frye). [MichQR] (33:3) Sum 94, p. 469-471.

196. ARENAS, Marion
"Visiting My Brother in California After Many Years." [SingHM] (21) 94, p. 52.

197. ARGÜELLES, Ivan
"Love & Nihilism." [YellowS] (11:4, #44) Wint 93-94, p. 45.
"Ulysses: A Companion Guide" (Selection: XXV-XXVIII). [Caliban] (14) 94, p. 93-99.

198. ARGUETA, Manlio
"The Chinchintora" (from his collection *La Guerra Florida*, tr. by Chuck Wachtel). [HangL] (64) 94, p. 12-14.
"The Chronicler of the Indies, 1548" (from his collection *La Guerra Florida*, tr. by Chuck Wachtel). [HangL] (64) 94, p. 8-9.
"Gentle Homeland" (from his collection *La Guerra Florida*, tr. by Chuck Wachtel). [HangL] (64) 94, p. 10.
"Head-Hunters" (from his collection *La Guerra Florida*, tr. by Chuck Wachtel). [HangL] (64) 94, p. 11.
"A Horizon of Dogs" (tr. by Chuck Wachtel). [Pequod] (37) 94, p. 125-126.
"My Country" (tr. by Chuck Wachtel). [Pequod] (37) 94, p. 127.

199. ARIDJIS, Chloe
"Dawn" (tr. of Homero Aridjis). [HarvardR] (6) Spr 94, p. 7.
"Trees" (tr. of Homero Aridjis). [HarvardR] (6) Spr 94, p. 8-13.

200. ARIDJIS, Homero
"Dawn" (tr. by Chloe Aridjis). [HarvardR] (6) Spr 94, p. 7.

"Trees" (tr. by Chloe Aridjis). [HarvardR] (6) Spr 94, p. 8-13.
201. ARIF, Hafiz
"Ainal Adnin: A Love Song" (tr. of Kemala). [InterQ] (1:3) 94, p. 180-184.
202. ARIN, Jennifer
"Persephone." [Chain] (1) Spr-Sum 94, p. 256-257.
203. ARIZA, René
"Apuradores." [LindLM] (13:1) Mr 94, p. 7.
"Los Barcos Encallados de la Noche." [LindLM] (13:1) Mr 94, p. 7.
"Carteles." [LindLM] (13:1) Mr 94, p. 7.
"Vals Ciudadano." [LindLM] (13:1) Mr 94, p. 7.
204. ARJONA, Ramon, IV
"Barking Sands." [ChamLR] (14/15) Spr-Fall 94, p. 135.
"Song for Chinese Lanterns" (For Eve). [ChamLR] (14/15) Spr-Fall 94, p. 136-137.
ARKEL, Jo van
See Van ARKEL, Jo
205. ARMER, Sondra Audin
"Burnt Offerings." [Amelia] (7:4, #23) 94, p. 37.
206. ARMITAGE, Simon
"Baby." [SouthernR] (30:2) Ap, Spr 94, p. 264-265.
"Bastards." [SouthernR] (30:2) Ap, Spr 94, p. 262-263.
"Convictions." [SouthernR] (30:2) Ap, Spr 94, p. 264.
"Lines Thought to Have Been Written on the Eve of the Execution of a Warrant for His Arrest." [Jacaranda] (10) 94, p. 132-133.
"Poem: And if it snowed and snow covered the drive." [Jacaranda] (5:1) Wint-Spr 91, p. 37.
"Swine." [SouthernR] (30:2) Ap, Spr 94, p. 263-264.
"White Christmas." [Verse] (11:2) Sum 94, p. 9.
"Work." [SouthernR] (30:2) Ap, Spr 94, p. 262.
207. ARMSTRONG, Gene
"Arroyo." [BellArk] (10:1) Ja-F 94, p. 25.
208. ARMSTRONG, Mary
"Hindsight." [CreamCR] (18:1) Spr 94, p. 52-53.
"The Police Ask Questions." [SpoonR] (19:1) Wint-Spr 94, p. 16-17.
"Transparencies." [SpoonR] (19:1) Wint-Spr 94, p. 18-19.
"A Turbulence of Wings" (Los Angeles, May, 1992). [SpoonR] (19:1) Wint-Spr 94, p. 14-15.
209. ARMSTRONG, Patricia Mees
"Low-Cost Senior Housing." [Writer] (107:5) My 94, p. 21.
210. ARNETT, Harold
"Plowing in the Dark." [CapeR] (29:1) Spr 94, p. 3.
211. ARNOLD, Bob
"Peaceable Kingdom." [ShadowP] (4) 94, p. 20-26.
"Woods Work." [DogRR] (26) Wint 94-95, p. 52.
ARPINO, Tony d'
See D'ARPINO, Tony
212. ARRAIZ LUCCA, Rafael
"IX. Once I heard you say" (tr. by Pamela Carmell). [Trans] (29) Spr 94, p. 133.
"Leningrad" (tr. by Pamela Carmell). [Trans] (29) Spr 94, p. 132.
"A Poet (Disconcerted) Asks Himself" (tr. by Pamela Carmell). [Trans] (29) Spr 94, p. 134-135.
"Things" (tr. by Pamela Carmell). [Trans] (29) Spr 94, p. 131.
213. ARRIETA, Marcia
"Feeding on Air." [MidwQ] (35:2) Wint 94, p. 162-163.
"Fragile." [Elf] (4:1) Spr 94, p. 41.
214. ARROWOOD, Gayle F.
"My Oil." [Wind] (73) 94, p. 1.
215. ARROYO, Rane (Rane Ramón)
"Broom Salsa." [Eyeball] (3) 93, p. 33.
"The Field." [ApalQ] (42) Fall 94, p. 35-38.
"Mateo Is Turning into a Piñata Tonight." [AnotherCM] (27) 94, p. 12.
"The Singing Shark Dream, or Toto, I Don't Think We're in Tegucigalpa." [PennR] (6:1) 94, p. 8-13.
216. ARROYO SHAGHAGHI, María Luisa
"Un Compromiso." [Americas] (22:3/4) Fall-Wint 94, p. 61.
"Un Hombre Cambiado." [Americas] (22:3/4) Fall-Wint 94, p. 62.
"Sundays, los Domingos." [Americas] (22:3/4) Fall-Wint 94, p. 59-60.

217. ARTAUD, Antonin
"Here Lies" (tr. by Clayton Eshleman. w. Bernard Bador). [GrandS] (12:4, #48) Wint 94, p. 187-208.
"Interjections" (Excerpts, tr. by Clayton Eshleman, w. Bernard Bador). [Sulfur] (35) Fall 94, p. 50-61.
218. ARTHUR, Chris
"Book Burning." [Descant] (25:1, #84) Spr 94, p. 94.
"Departures." [Descant] (25:1, #84) Spr 94, p. 93.
"Forecasts." [Descant] (25:1, #84) Spr 94, p. 90-91.
"Not Quite a Lament for Susan." [Event] (23:3) Wint 94-95, p. 46.
"Satori Splinters." [Descant] (25:1, #84) Spr 94, p. 92.
219. ARTMAN, Deborah
"Cruel." [Vis] (46) 94, p. 16.
220. ARTOPOEUS, Otto
"Sparrows." [ChrC] (111:15) 4 My 94, p. 460.
221. ARVIO, Sarah
"Hello Goodbye." [ParisR] (36:130) Spr 94, p. 239-240.
222. ASCHER/STRAUS
"As It Returns." [NewAW] (12) Spr-Sum 94, p. 87-105.
223. ASEKOFF, L. S.
"Crossing into Brooklyn." [BrooklynR] (11) 94, p. 118.
"Death's Candy." [BrooklynR] (11) 94, p. 117.
"Feeding the Deer." [Jacaranda] (5:1) Wint-Spr 91, p. 3.
"The Third Circle." [Jacaranda] (5:1) Wint-Spr 91, p. 1-2.
"Yesenin" (Hotel d'Angleterre Moscow, 1923). [Salm] (101/102) Wint-Spr 94, p. 158-159.
"Yesenin" (Hotel d'Angleterre, St. Petersburg, 1925). [Salm] (103) Sum 94, p. 109-110.
ASERET SIN
See WASHINGTON, Teresa (Aseret Sin)
224. ASH, John
"The Other Great Composers." [Jacaranda] (5:1) Wint-Spr 91, p. 66.
225. ASHANTI, Baron James
"Little Dipper" (for Louis Armstrong). [Eyeball] (3) 93, p. 5.
226. ASHBERY, John
"Another Example." [HarvardR] (Premier Issue) Spr 92, p. 7.
"Bromeliads." [PartR] (61:1) Wint 94, p. 150.
"Dangerous Moonlight." [Antaeus] (75/76) Aut 94, p. 234-235.
"Free Nail Polish." [NewYorker] (69:50) 14 F 94, p. 88.
"Locations" (tr. of Pascalle Monnier). [Conjunc] (23) 94, p. 274-278.
"My Philosophy of Life." [AmerPoR] (23:6) N-D 94, p. 64.
"Para Siempre Teresita? Para Siempre Rodrigo" (tr. of Pascalle Monnier). [Conjunc] (23) 94, p. 272-274.
"Pretty Questions." [ColR] (21:1) Spr 94, p. 62-63.
"Spring Cries." [PartR] (61:1) Wint 94, p. 151.
"Tuesday Evening." [GrandS] (13:1, #49) Sum 94, p. 123-139.
"World's End." [NewYorker] (70:2) 28 F 94, p. 88.
227. ASHEAR, Linda
"There once was a lady named Kitten" (Honorable Mention, The A & C Limericks Awards). [Amelia] (7:4, #23) 94, p. 18.
"Vigil." [LaurelR] (28:1) Wint 94, p. 125.
228. ASHLEY, Renée
"Embers, the light." [PoetL] (89:1) Spr 94, p. 28.
"Nemesis." [AmerV] (34) 94, p. 156.
"Obsolete Angel." [SycamoreR] (6:1) Wint 94, p. 10.
"On the Death of Proteus." [AntR] (52:3) Sum 94, p. 492.
"Sort of a Love Poem." [Poetry] (163:5) F 94, p. 283-284.
"What She Wanted." [SycamoreR] (6:1) Wint 94, p. 11-12.
"What We Don't Understand." [SycamoreR] (6:1) Wint 94, p. 13-14.
229. ASHTON, Jennifer
"Apocalypse Is an Elegy." [ParisR] (36:132) Fall 94, p. 20-21.
"Privileges of Travel." [ParisR] (36:132) Fall 94, p. 19-20.
230. ASPEN
"Fat Woman Strides." [SinW] (52) Spr-Sum 94, p. 89.
231. ASTOR, M. C.
"Blue Crocodile." [ChironR] (13:4) Wint 94, p. 13.

"Colors of the Night" (second prize in the 1994 *Chiron Review* Poetry Contest). [ChironR] (13:4) Wint 94, p. 13.

232. ASTRACHAN, Samuel
"Festschrift." [PraS] (68:1) Spr 94, p. 39.
"Lamb Chops." [PraS] (68:1) Spr 94, p. 40-41.
"Weiss and Giovanucci." [PraS] (68:1) Spr 94, p. 40.

233. ATHEY, David
"Above Duluth." [BellArk] (10:3) My-Je 94, p. 11.
"After Easter." [BellArk] (10:3 [i.e. 10:4]) Jl-Ag 94, p. 7.
"Alden Nowlan." [AntigR] (97) Spr 94, p. 44.
"At the Cabin." [BellArk] (10:5) S-O 94, p. 23.
"Coffee." [BellArk] (10:2) Mr-Ap 94, p. 14.
"The Death of Old Age." [SoDakR] (32:3) Fall 94, p. 109.
"Fishing (Part Two)." [SoDakR] (32:3) Fall 94, p. 106.
"Forty Days and Forty Years." [Northeast] (5:11) Wint 94-95, p. 4.
"Genesis." [BellArk] (10:5) S-O 94, p. 23.
"Great Whisper." [SoDakR] (32:3) Fall 94, p. 107.
"My Father's Directions for Exploring Minnesota." [BellArk] (10:3) My-Je 94, p. 11.
"Proposition." [BellArk] (10:3) My-Je 94, p. 11.
"This Morning." [Northeast] (5:11) Wint 94-95, p. 3.
"Vincent." [SoDakR] (32:3) Fall 94, p. 108.
"Vision." [BellArk] (10:3 [i.e. 10:4]) Jl-Ag 94, p. 7.

234. ATIL, Yesho
"By the Red Tulips." [Kalliope] (16:1) 94, p. 20.
"Duck Hunting." [NewDeltaR] (11:2) Spr-Sum 94, p. 38-39.
"Grandmother Taking a Bath." [InterQ] (1:3) 94, p. 170.

235. ATKINS, Cynthia
"Morning Song." [Pivot] (42) 94, p. 34.
"Storybook." [Pivot] (41) 93, p. 38.
"This House Divided." [TarRP] (34:1) Fall 94, p. 13.

236. ATKINS, Priscilla
"Hawk Cemetery." [HopewellR] (6) 94, p. 85.
"Letter from the Prairie." [HopewellR] (6) 94, p. 86.
"On Receiving Your Gift of Narcissus." [BambooR] (60) Wint 94, p. 89-90.

237. ATKINSON, Alan
"Bouquet." [Plain] (14:2) Wint 94, p. 15.
"Invention at Crescent City." [RagMag] (12:1) Sum 94, p. 49.

238. ATKINSON, Jennifer
"Extradition." [Poetry] (164:1) Ap 94, p. 24-25.

239. ATKINSON, Michael
"American Mile Zero." [Chelsea] (56) 94, p. 30-31.
"Cassandra near Sleep." [Chelsea] (56) 94, p. 32-33.
"Children Playing War in the Shadows of the North American Forest." [PraS] (68:1) Spr 94, p. 52.
"Cicadas." [ConnPR] (13:1) 94, p. 17.
"The Holy Bloom." [PoetryE] (37/38) Spr 94, p. 14-15.
"Lost." [PraS] (68:1) Spr 94, p. 53-54.
"Murnau on the Road" (The great German director died in a car crash on March 11, 1931, at the age of 42). [PraS] (68:1) Spr 94, p. 55-56.
"Waiting for Cocteau's Chimney to Fall." [GrahamHR] (18) Wint 94-95, p. 15-16.

240. ATWOOD, Margaret
"Bored." [Atlantic] (274:6) D 94, p. 102.
"Daphne and Laura and So Forth." [Field] (51) Fall 94, p. 48.
"King Lear in Respite Care." [Field] (51) Fall 94, p. 52-53.
"Man in a Glacier." [Field] (51) Fall 94, p. 54-55.
"Questioning the Dead." [Field] (51) Fall 94, p. 49.
"Red Fox." [Field] (51) Fall 94, p. 50-51.
"Sekhmet, the Lion-Headed Goddess of War, Violent Storms, Pestilence, and Recovery From Illness, Contemplates the Desert in the Metropolitan Museum of Art." [NewL] (60:4) 94, p. 28-29.
"Statuary." [NewL] (60:4) 94, p. 30-31.
"Up." [NewL] (60:4) 94, p. 31-32.

241. AUDEN, W. H.
"Early Morning Bathing." [NewYorker] (70:24) 8 Ag 94, p. 61.
"Friendship." [NewYorker] (70:24) 8 Ag 94, p. 60.
"A Visit." [NewYorker] (70:24) 8 Ag 94, p. 61.

242. Auf der HEIDE, Lisl
"Heron." [SantaBR] (1:1) Spr-Sum 93, p. 57.
243. AUGUSTINE, Laura
"Going Back." [HiramPoR] (55/56) Fall 93-Sum 94, p. 6.
"How It Is." [PoetryE] (37/38) Spr 94, p. 33.
244. AULETTA, Robert
"Agamemnon: A Modern Adaptation" (Two Excerpts, tr. of Aeschylus). [HarvardR] (7) Fall 94, p. 86-94.
245. AUSTIN, Annemarie
"Aunt Alexandra." [Verse] (11:1) Spr 94, p. 37.
246. AUTREY, Ken
"Circulation." [PoetryNW] (35:1) Spr 94, p. 45-46.
"Sahel." [PoetryNW] (35:1) Spr 94, p. 46-47.
247. AUTRY, Rick
"Visions." [Kaleid] (28) Wint-Spr 94, p. 41.
248. AUVINEN, Karen
"Hands: a Distillation." [Plain] (15:1) Fall 94, p. 28-29.
249. AUXEMERY, Jean-Paul
"Xenias" (tr. by Charlotte Mandell). [Sulfur] (35) Fall 94, p. 131-138.
250. AVAKIAN, Sona
"A Loon Has No Regrets." [Zyzzyva] (10:3) Fall 94, p. 29-31.
251. AVAYOU, Shlomo
"Fleeting Thrill" (tr. by Ammiel Alcalay). [LitR] (37:2) Wint 94, p. 284.
"Odalisque of the Levant / an Ode" (tr. by Ammiel Alcalay). [LitR] (37:2) Wint 94, p. 285-286.
"Wildweed" (tr. by Ammiel Alcalay). [LitR] (37:2) Wint 94, p. 285.
"You Have to Abandon Jerusalem" (tr. by Ammiel Alcalay). [LitR] (37:2) Wint 94, p. 286-287.
252. AVELINO, Andrés
"Irrupcion." [CuadP] (8:22) Enero-Abril 94, p. 81.
253. AVENA, Thomas
"Two and a Half Dreams for Max Jacob." [Art&Und] (3:3) Ag 94, p. 10.
254. AVERY, Brian C.
"The Emperor's Dreams." [HayF] (14) Spr-Sum 94, p. 18.
AVILA, Inés Hernández
See HERNANDEZ-AVILA, Inés
255. AVILA, Marita
"Connection Between Womyn." [SinW] (54) Wint 94-95, p. 94-96.
256. AVOTCJA
"Halleluyah Y'all." [SinW] (54) Wint 94-95, p. 51.
257. AWAD, Joseph
"Feeling Struggling for Form." [Hellas] (5:2) Fall-Wint 94, p. 35.
"Magnolia." [Hellas] (5:2) Fall-Wint 94, p. 36.
258. AWIAKTA, Marilou
"The Real Thing" (For Bernice). [Callaloo] (17:1) Wint 94, p. 31-32.
"Star Vision." [Callaloo] (17:1) Wint 94, p. 30.
"Where Mountain and Atom Meet." [Callaloo] (17:1) Wint 94, p. 29.
259. AXELROD, David
"After a Fast, Walking in a Field of Germinated Wheat." [ProseP] (3) 94, p. 8.
"At the Smokejumper's Trailer." [CrabCR] (8:2/3/9:1/2/3) 94, p. 138-139.
"The Day the Neighbors Divorced." [ChironR] (13:3) Aut 94, p. 7.
"How It Is with Us Human Beings" (four variations from Japanese). [WebR] (18) Fall 94, p. 40-41.
"Materialism." [WebR] (18) Fall 94, p. 42-43.
"Things Blow Up and That's OK." [WebR] (18) Fall 94, p. 43-45.
260. AXINN, Donald Everett
"The Exit." [WritersF] (20) 94, p. 69.
261. AXTELL, Kathie
"White Underwear Makes Me Love Bad Boys." [Dandel] (21:2) 94, p. 62-63.
262. AYALA, Naomi
"Abuelo's Garden." [Callaloo] (17:3) Sum 94, p. 937.
"Airborne." [Callaloo] (17:3) Sum 94, p. 849-850.
"Fifteen-Ten." [Callaloo] (17:3) Sum 94, p. 935.
"For Late Nite Poems." [Callaloo] (17:3) Sum 94, p. 936.
"For 'S'." [Callaloo] (17:3) Sum 94, p. 848.
"Haiti." [Callaloo] (17:3) Sum 94, p. 847.

"If We Passed You." [Callaloo] (17:3) Sum 94, p. 745-746.
"Imigrant's Voice." [Callaloo] (17:3) Sum 94, p. 743-744.
"Words." [Callaloo] (17:3) Sum 94, p. 747.

263. AYCOCK, Allan
"The Barkeaters." [ProseP] (3) 94, p. 9.

264. AYERS, Robert A.
"My Grandfather Knew Every County in Texas." [Border] (5) Fall-Wint 94, p. 2.

265. AZEVEDO, Kathleen de
"Girl from Ipanema." [HangL] (65) 94, p. 7.
"Nuns." [HangL] (65) 94, p. 5-6.

266. AZRAEL, Mary
"Afterward the Tree." [PraS] (68:2) Sum 94, p. 149.
"A Singsong about What Happens." [PraS] (68:2) Sum 94, p. 150.

BAASTAD, Erling Friis
See FRIIS-BAASTAD, Erling

267. BABSTOCK, Ken
"Waiting on a Transplant." [Quarry] (43:2) S 94, p. 106.
"West Ray Dreamscape." [Quarry] (43:2) S 94, p. 107.
"White Dog." [Quarry] (43:2) S 94, p. 108.

268. BACA, Jimmy Santiago
"Healing Earthquakes." [Callaloo] (17:1) Wint 94, p. 52-61.

269. BACCHAN
"The Honey-Hall" (Selections: 3, 6, 21, 99, 119, 128, tr. by R. Lightbulb Winders). [GrahamHR] (18) Wint 94-95, p. 60-61.

270. BACH, Glenn
"Bushido." [ChironR] (13:2) Sum 94, p. 30.
"Kill Poets." [Pearl] (20) Spr 94, p. 6.
"She Hobbles Around on One Leg and Waits to Die, Like a Bird" (Selection: 64). [CoalC] (8) Ap 94, p. 9-10.

271. BACHARACH, Deborah
"Knife in a Vegetarian Kitchen." [SlipS] (14) 94, p. 47.
"Vegetable Spreads for Spring." [SlipS] (14) 94, p. 48.

272. BACHE-SNYDER, Kaye
"Camping Beside Lost Creek" (Eyster Prize, Winner in Poetry). [NewDeltaR] (10:1) Fall 92-Wint 93, p. 1.
"If What's Remembered Never Was." [Plain] (14:2) Wint 94, p. 12-13.

273. BACHMANN, Ingeborg
"After This Flood" (tr. by Peter Filkins). [AmerPoR] (23:2) Mr-Ap 94, p. 35.
"Early Noon" (tr. by Peter Filkins). [AmerPoR] (23:2) Mr-Ap 94, p. 36.
"Every Day" (tr. by Steven Vincent Frattali). [GrahamHR] (18) Wint 94-95, p. 42.
"In Apulia" (tr. by Peter Filkins). [ParisR] (36:131) Sum 94, p. 141.
"In the Storm of Roses" (tr. by Peter Filkins). [AmerPoR] (23:2) Mr-Ap 94, p. 35.
"In Twilight" (tr. by Peter Filkins). [Sulfur] (35) Fall 94, p. 156.
"Letter in Two Drafts" (tr. by Peter Filkins). [ParisR] (36:131) Sum 94, p. 142-143.
"March Stars" (tr. by Peter Filkins). [AmerPoR] (23:2) Mr-Ap 94, p. 36.
"The Native Land" (tr. by Peter Filkins). [AmerPoR] (23:2) Mr-Ap 94, p. 35.
"Psalm" (tr. by Peter Filkins). [Sulfur] (35) Fall 94, p. 157-158.
"Shadows Roses Shadow" (tr. by Peter Filkins). [AmerPoR] (23:2) Mr-Ap 94, p. 35.

274. BACHNER, Suzanne
"The House in the Dream" (tr. of Astrid Hjertenaes Andersen, w. Aina Gerner-Mathisen). [SpoonR] (19:1) Wint-Spr 94, p. 94-95.
"The House on the Meadow" (tr. of Astrid Hjertenaes Andersen, w. Aina Gerner-Mathisen). [SpoonR] (19:1) Wint-Spr 94, p. 96.
"Red Branches" (tr. of Astrid Hjertenaes Andersen, w. Aina Gerner-Mathisen). [SpoonR] (19:1) Wint-Spr 94, p. 93.

275. BADESCU, Horia
"Caudine Forks" (tr. by Eveline L. Kanes and Mihai Zaharia). [InterPR] (20:1) Spr 94, p. 77.
"Furcile Caudine." [InterPR] (20:1) Spr 94, p. 76.
"The Lamentations of Solomon" (X, XXVI, tr. by Eveline L. Kanes and Mihai Zaharia). [InterPR] (20:1) Spr 94, p. 83, 85.
"Lied" (1-2). [InterPR] (20:1) Spr 94, p. 78, 80.
"Maieutica." [InterPR] (20:1) Spr 94, p. 86.

"Maieutics" (tr. by Eveline L. Kanes and Mihai Zaharia). [InterPR] (20:1) Spr 94, p. 87.
"Plingerie Lui Solomon" (X, XXVI). [InterPR] (20:1) Spr 94, p. 82, 84.
"Song" (1-2, tr. by Eveline L. Kanes and Mihai Zaharia). [InterPR] (20:1) Spr 94, p. 79, 81.

276. BADOR, Bernard
"Here Lies" (tr. of Antonin Artaud, w. Clayton Eshleman). [GrandS] (12:4, #48) Wint 94, p. 187-208.
"Interjections" (Excerpts, tr. of Antonin Artaud, w. Clayton Eshleman). [Sulfur] (35) Fall 94, p. 50-61.

277. BAECHLER, Wolfgang
"Rachel" (tr. by Reinhold Grimm). [Pembroke] (26) 94, p. 133.
"Two Marital Idyls" (tr. by Reinhold Grimm). [Pembroke] (26) 94, p. 131-132.

278. BAER, Tom
"The High Life." [Grain] (21:4) Spr 94, p. 135.

279. BAERT, Nicolas
"Gene or Eugene Grey or Gray." [NewYorkQ] (53) 94, p. 114.

280. BAGGETT, Rebecca
"Georgia O'Keeffe's *Blue and Green Music*." [MidAR] (14:2) 94, p. 61-62.
"Mid-Thirties." [Gaia] (4) Je 94, p. 14.

281. BAGLEY, Jeanette C.
"Autumn Ritual." [WeberS] (11:2) Spr-Sum 94, p. 42.
"Departure." [WeberS] (11:2) Spr-Sum 94, p. 41-42.

282. BAHLER, Beth
"Engagement." [Parting] (7:1) Sum 94, p. 23-24.

283. BÄHLER, Malena
"La Mirada del Alba." [Luz] (6) My 94, p. 41-42.
"Tiempo." [Luz] (6) My 94, p. 42.

284. BAHLINGER, Lisa
"Traps." [GreenMR] (NS 17:2) Fall-Wint 94-95, p. 123-124.

285. BAILEY, Clay
"Process Serving." [Pearl] (20) Spr 94, p. 73.

286. BAILEY, Rebecca
"Ripe Sun Flower." [Wind] (74) 94, p. 4.

287. BAIN, Frederika
"The Dragon Killer." [HawaiiR] (18:1, #40) Spr 94, p. 97.
"Eucharist." [HawaiiR] (18:1, #40) Spr 94, p. 96.

288. BAINES, Mercedes
"Age of Innocence." [WestCL] (28:1/2, #13/14) Spr-Fall 94, p. 196-197.
"Brown Child" (dedicated to my mother Dorise). [WestCL] (28:1/2, #13/14) Spr-Fall 94, p. 194-195.
"Sadie Mae's Mane." [WestCL] (28:1/2, #13/14) Spr-Fall 94, p. 198.

289. BAIRD, Ansie
"Half My Life." [DenQ] (28:4) Spr 94, p. 10.

290. BAKER, Brian
"The Bully." [Dandel] (20:2) 93, p. 15-16.

291. BAKER, David
"Abandoned Barn." [Poetry] (164:1) Ap 94, p. 4-5.
"Childless." [SouthernHR] (28:4) Fall 94, p. 376.
"Dust to Dust." [Poetry] (163:4) Ja 94, p. 205-207.
"Home." [ParisR] (36:130) Spr 94, p. 107.
"Memento" (for Andrew Hudgins). [SouthernHR] (28:4) Fall 94, p. 377.
"Missionary Position." [NewEngR] (16:2) Spr 94, p. 72-73.
"Old Barn in Darkness." [ColEng] (56:3) Mr 94, p. 318.
"Predatory." [PraS] (68:2) Sum 94, p. 37-39.
"Rain Barrel." [PraS] (68:2) Sum 94, p. 36-37.
"Thanksgiving in Time of AIDS." [PraS] (68:2) Sum 94, p. 40.
"The Third Person." [ParisR] (36:130) Spr 94, p. 106-107.
"The Women." [Poetry] (164:1) Ap 94, p. 6.
"Yellow Lilies and Cypress Swamp." [Antaeus] (73/74) Spr 94, p. 151-152.

292. BAKER, June Frankland
"For One Now Living Somewhere Else." [HiramPoR] (57) Fall 94-Wint 95, p. 10.
"In Lock-flight." [HiramPoR] (57) Fall 94-Wint 95, p. 9.
"Watching the Doves, Day Before the New Year." [HiramPoR] (57) Fall 94-Wint 95, p. 11.

293. BAKER, Marie Annharte
"Porkskin Panorama." [Callaloo] (17:1) Wint 94, p. 214-218.
294. BAKER, Melinda
"Entitled to One Moon Poem." [MidwQ] (36:1) Aut 94, p. 53.
"For the Absent." [MidwQ] (36:1) Aut 94, p. 52.
295. BAKER, Nicholson
"From the Index of First Lines." [NewYorker] (70:43) 26 D 94-2 Ja 95, p. 83.
296. BAKOWSKI, Peter
"The Committee's Decision." [WormR] (34:4, #136) 94, p. 160.
"Country Road." [WormR] (34:4, #136) 94, p. 160.
"Croak." [WormR] (34:4, #136) 94, p. 160.
"Definition of an Apple." [WormR] (34:4, #136) 94, p. 159.
"The History of Ripples." [WormR] (34:4, #136) 94, p. 160.
"Invention of the Umbrella." [WormR] (34:4, #136) 94, p. 160.
"Navigating Insomnia." [WormR] (34:4, #136) 94, p. 160.
"The New Melancholia." [WormR] (34:4, #136) 94, p. 160.
"Nostalgia." [WormR] (34:4, #136) 94, p. 160.
"Observation Number Five." [WormR] (34:4, #136) 94, p. 160.
"The Old Women of Bulgaria." [Event] (23:1) Spr 94, p. 38-39.
"Post Card from a Richmond Summer." [Vis] (44) 94, p. 13.
"The Procrastinator." [WormR] (34:4, #136) 94, p. 160.
"Rooming House, Grey Street, St. Kilda, 1991." [Event] (23:1) Spr 94, p. 40-41.
"Seeing a Beautiful Girl in the Streets." [WormR] (34:4, #136) 94, p. 160.
"Snail." [WormR] (34:4, #136) 94, p. 160.
"Somewhere, a Choir." [Vis] (46) 94, p. 21.
"The Trapeze Artist." [WormR] (34:4, #136) 94, p. 160.
"Walking the Streets of Venice and Santa Monica, Los Angeles, 1984." [Pearl] (20) Spr 94, p. 11.
"Writer's Block." [WormR] (34:4, #136) 94, p. 160.
297. BALABAN, John
"Letters from Across the Sea." [Poetry] (164:1) Ap 94, p. 26-28.
"Some Notes on Miami." [Witness] (8:2) 94, p. 30-34.
298. BALAKIAN, Peter
"18th Hole." [IllinoisR] (1:2) Spr 94, p. 11.
"Sneakers" (tr. of Artem Haroutiunian, w. the author). [GrahamHR] (18) Wint 94-95, p. 33-37.
299. BALAZ, Joe
"Da Skatebordahs of Ke Alanui Lane." [HawaiiR] (18:1, #40) Spr 94, p. 81-86.
300. BALAZS, Mary
"Diaper Change: Sidewalk Cafe." [Kalliope] (16:3) 94, p. 6.
301. BALCARCEL, Rebecca
"Ferry Crossing." [ClockR] (9:1/2) 94-95, p. 140.
302. BALDERSTON, Jean
"Nuclear Screening Services" (found in the 1988-1989 *IPAT Catalog of Psychological Assessment Instruments, Computer Interpretive Services and Books*). [NewYorkQ] (53) 94, p. 116.
303. BALDWIN, Joseph
"Radiology Dept." [PoetryE] (37/38) Spr 94, p. 36.
304. BALDWIN, Tama
"Angel." [IllinoisR] (1:2) Spr 94, p. 31.
"A Full Day Moon, August." [OhioR] (52) 94, p. 120.
"Vox Dei." [IllinoisR] (1:2) Spr 94, p. 24-25.
305. BALK, Christianne
"Armistice." [Ploughs] (20:4) Wint 94-95, p. 10-11.
"Dear Hippopotamus." [NewRep] (211:19) 7 N 94, p. 48.
"Departure." [Ploughs] (20:4) Wint 94-95, p. 8-9.
"Dress-Me-Up David." [MichQR] (33:1) Wint 94, p. 68-69.
"Where the Long, Lazy Mothers Stroll." [Ploughs] (20:4) Wint 94-95, p. 12-13.
306. BALL, Angela
"Burning" (tr. of Xi Murong, w. Zheng Jianqing). [LitR] (37:4) Sum 94, p. 684.
"Dominica" (from "Jean Rhys"). [Field] (50) Spr 94, p. 70-71.
"Jean Rhys: England, 16." [SouthernR] (30:2) Ap, Spr 94, p. 267.
"Jean Rhys: Lancelot." [SouthernR] (30:2) Ap, Spr 94, p. 267-269.
"Jean Rhys: World's End." [SouthernR] (30:2) Ap, Spr 94, p. 266.
307. BALL, Joseph H.
"The Duncan Yo-Yo Guy." [Wind] (73) 94, p. 2-3.

"Epidaurus." [Wind] (73) 94, p. 1-2.

308. BALL, Roger
"Cottonwood." [CoalC] (8) Ap 94, p. 39.
"Slice of Granite." [CoalC] (8) Ap 94, p. 31.

309. BALL, Sally
"Nocturnal." [SouthwR] (79:1) Wint 94, p. 82-83.
"Peeper Says Put Up Your Dukes." [NewEngR] (16:4) Fall 94, p. 157-158.

310. BALLESTEROS, Katherine A.
"One Last and Lonely Cry of Owls." [Amelia] (7:3, #22) 94, p. 40.

311. BALLON, Richard
"Death Appeared." [Parting] (7:2) Wint 94-95, p. 38.
"Grasping God." [Parting] (7:2) Wint 94-95, p. 40.
"Summer Camp." [ChangingM] (27) Wint 94, p. 47.
"The Woodcuts." [Vis] (44) 94, p. 38.

312. BALLOU, Emily
"Lorraine Who Was Lost Does Yoga." [CreamCR] (18:1) Spr 94, p. 8-11.

313. BALOIAN, James
"A Beginning." [SmPd] (31:2, #91) Spr 94, p. 20.

BALTATZI, Adamandia (Adamantia García)
See GARCIA-BALTATZI, Adamantia

314. BALTIMORE, Susan
"Choosing Dominion." [Parting] (7:2) Wint 94-95, p. 37.
"Flowers." [Parting] (7:2) Wint 94-95, p. 61.
"Stairs." [Parting] (7:2) Wint 94-95, p. 36.
"Woman." [Parting] (7:2) Wint 94-95, p. 2.

315. BANAS, Kathy
"Spring Planting." [BellArk] (10:3 [i.e. 10:4]) Jl-Ag 94, p. 10.

316. BANDLER, Rhoda
"Public Notice." [Light] (10) Sum 94, p. 17.

317. BANERJEE, Paramita
"Crow" (tr. of Anuradha Mahapatra, w. Carolyne Wright). [PartR] (61:1) Wint 94, p. 155.
"The Earth Chooses Her Own Husband" (tr. of Mallika Sengupta, w. Carolyne Wright). [Calyx] (15:2) Sum 94, p. 59.
"He Gets Well" (tr. of Debarati Mitra, w. Carolyne Wright). [InterQ] (1:2) 93, p. 156.
"I Go" (tr. of Rama Ghosh, w. Carolyne Wright). [BostonR] (19:2) Ap-My 94, p. 9.
"In White Moonlight" (tr. of Debarati Mitra, w. Carolyne Wright). [InterQ] (1:2) 93, p. 155.
"Ravaged Blossom" (tr. of Chitra Lahiri, w. Arlene Zide). [InterQ] (1:2) 93, p. 189.
"Street Drama" (tr. of Chaitali Chattopadhyay, w. Arlene Zide). [InterQ] (1:2) 93, p. 187.
"Tambura" (tr. of Anuradha Mahapatra, w. Carolyne Wright). [Calyx] (15:2) Sum 94, p. 61.
"That's Not for Puti" (tr. of Vijaya Mukhopadhyay, w. Carolyne Wright). [KenR] (NS 16:4) Fall 94, p. 93.
"Thirty-Five Parganas" (tr. of Gita Chattopadhyay, w. Carolyne Wright). [Calyx] (15:2) Sum 94, p. 60.
"Thou Art Durga" (tr. of Gita Chattopadhyay, w. Carolyne Wright). [InterQ] (1:2) 93, p. 157.
"Where There Is No Rest" (tr. of Chitra Lahiri, w. Arlene Zide). [InterQ] (1:2) 93, p. 188.

318. BANG, Mary Jo
"The Oracle." [DenQ] (29:2) Fall 94, p. 5.

319. BANGS, Carol Jane
"Falsehood" (To the woman who spent the weekend at the ocean with my husband the weekend he was supposed to be on a personal retreat, the weekend our son came down with the chicken pox). [Zyzzyva] (10:4) Wint 94, p. 75.

320. BANKHEAD, Patricia Kennedy
"Under the Mountain." [SouthernPR] (34:2) Wint 94, p. 17.

321. BANKIER, Joanna
"La Lugubre Gondola No. 2" (tr. of Tomas Tranströmer). [ParisR] (36:130) Spr 94, p. 236-238.

322. BANKS, K. Morrison
"Devouring Beauty." [SantaBR] (1:1) Spr-Sum 93, p. 58.

323. BANKS, Kenneth
"Homecoming: Four Variations on a Theme." [AntigR] (99) Aut 94, p. 22-25.

324. BANKS-RICHARDSON, S. (Stan)
"Before I Became Like Everyone Else — and Then Decided to Stop." [BelPoJ] (45:1) Fall 94, p. 29.
"Deaths Elsewhere, Death's Elsewhere" (conceived while reading the obituaries of Tuesday, March 29, 1994). [WindO] (58) Sum 94, p. 32-33.
325. BAÑUELOS, Juan
"Nobody Lives in My Country Anymore" (tr. by Reginald Gibbons). [TriQ] (91) Fall 94, p. 95-96.
326. BANUS, Maria
"The Arena" (tr. by Brenda Walker). [PoetryC] (14:4) S 94, p. 24.
"At the Table" (To Sorin, tr. by Brenda Walker). [PoetryC] (14:4) S 94, p. 24.
BAOLIN, Cheng
See CHENG, Baolin
327. BAPTISTA, Annabelle
"Sun Dazed." [Obs] (9:2) Fall-Wint 94, p. 71.
328. BARAKA, Amiri
"The City of New Ark: A Poem of Destiny" (Selection from Book One). [Sulfur] (34) Spr 94, p. 158-171.
"Tom Ass Clarence." [Agni] (39) 94, p. 17-18.
329. BARANCZAK, Stanislaw
"Allegro Ma Non Troppo" (tr. of Wislawa Szymborska, w. Clare Cavanagh). [Salm] (103) Sum 94, p. 266-267.
"A Byzantine Mosaic" (tr. of Wislawa Szymborska, w. Clare Cavanagh). [HarvardR] (2) Fall 92, p. 150-151.
"Coloratura" (tr. of Wislawa Szymborska, w. Clare Cavanagh). [Salm] (103) Sum 94, p. 268-269.
"Epitaph" (tr. of Wislawa Szymborska, w. Clare Cavanagh). [PartR] (61:4) Fall 94, p. 633.
"Lament 19 or: A Dream" (From *Laments*, tr. of Jan Kochanowski, w. Seamus Heaney). [HarvardR] (7) Fall 94, p. 7-10.
"May 16, 1973" (tr. of Wislawa Szymborska, w. Clare Cavanagh). [HarvardR] (7) Fall 94, p. 36-37.
"On the Banks of the Styx" (tr. of Wislawa Szymborska, w. Clare Cavanagh). [Salm] (103) Sum 94, p. 269-270.
"Poetry Reading" (tr. of Wislawa Szymborska, w. Clare Cavanagh). [PartR] (61:4) Fall 94, p. 634.
"Sky" (tr. of Wislawa Szymborska, w. Clare Cavanagh). [Agni] (39) 94, p. 20-21.
"We're Extremely Fortunate" (tr. of Wislawa Szymborska, w. Clare Cavanagh). [Salm] (103) Sum 94, p. 270-271.
330. BARANOW, Joan
"To My Lover About My Father." [CreamCR] (18:2) Fall 94, p. 124-125.
331. BARATIER, David
"Found with a Tatooed UPC Code." [BlackBR] (18) Wint-Spr 94, p. 34.
"A New Cardboard Box." [BlackBR] (18) Wint-Spr 94, p. 29.
332. BARATTA, Edward
"Bringing the Dog Back." [Confr] (54/55) Fall 94-Wint 95, p. 309-310.
"A December Poem." [JlNJPo] (16:2) Aut 94, p. 1.
333. BARAW, Charles
"Trouble." [NewEngR] (16:3) Sum 94, p. 131.
334. BARBEE, Sam
"Visitation." [Pembroke] (26) 94, p. 146-147.
335. BARBER, David
"Lines on a Yankee Aphorism" (The tongue is ever turning to the aching tooth). [TriQ] (92) Wint 94-95, p. 84-85.
"Little Overture." [Poetry] (164:3) Je 94, p. 145.
"Mysteries of the Deep." [Boulevard] (9:3, #27) Fall 94, p. 143-144.
"The Spirit Level." [PartR] (61:1) Wint 94, p. 155-156.
"To the Trespasser." [Poetry] (164:3) Je 94, p. 146.
"Zooms and Pans." [TriQ] (92) Wint 94-95, p. 86-87.
336. BARBER, Jennifer
"After a Night of Not Speaking to Each Other." [Journal] (18:1) Spr-Sum 94, p. 50.
"Copper Beech." [Journal] (18:1) Spr-Sum 94, p. 51.
337. BARBOUR, Douglas
"For L.N." [Nimrod] (37:2) Spr-Sum 94, p. 2.
"The Gift of Your Poems" (for Tom Pow). [Nimrod] (37:2) Spr-Sum 94, p. 3.
"Prairie Magpie." [Nimrod] (37:2) Spr-Sum 94, p. 2.

338. BARCLAY, Heather Haas
"Bicycles at the Language Institute." [Dandel] (21:2) 94, p. 68.
339. BARD, Karen S.
"The Poet and the Poet's Wife" (for Robert Bly. First Sue Saniel Elkind National Poetry Award, Finalist). [Kalliope] (16:2) 94, p. 13-14.
340. BARDEN, Louise
"Through the Ice." [SmPd] (31:1, #90) Wint 94, p. 18.
341. BARDOLPH, Richard
"Apprehensions for the Future of Hereditary Monarchy." [Light] (9) Spr 94, p. 14.
342. BARDWELL, Leland
"Letter to My Teacher." [QW] (38) Winter-Spr 93-94, p. 196-197.
343. BARFIELD, Steve
"The Banjo's Carnival." [DarkMoon] (1) 94, p. 82.
"The Prodigal Poet." [DarkMoon] (1) 94, p. 81.
344. BARGEN, Walter
"5. Just the Motion." [CharR] (20:2) Fall 94, p. 92.
"Even an Entire Evening sitting in Lawn Chairs." [CharR] (20:2) Fall 94, p. 96-97.
"The Falling Osage." [SpoonR] (19:1) Wint-Spr 94, p. 29-30.
"The Final Act." [Wind] (74) 94, p. 5-6.
"Living Happily Ever After." [Wind] (74) 94, p. 6-7.
"Map to the Party." [CapeR] (29:1) Spr 94, p. 25.
"No Matter How Hard We Try." [CharR] (20:2) Fall 94, p. 94-95.
"Shadows of Swimmers." [CharR] (20:2) Fall 94, p. 91.
"Snake Act: The Movie." [NewL] (60:3) 94, p. 65-69.
"Stopping at the Edge of Paradise." [SycamoreR] (6:1) Wint 94, p. 41-42.
"Transatlantic Gesture." [SpoonR] (19:1) Wint-Spr 94, p. 27-28.
"A Turning of Degrees." [CharR] (20:2) Fall 94, p. 93.
345. BARGOWSKI, John D., Sr.
"'61 Yankees." [JlNJPo] (16:2) Aut 94, p. 5-6.
"After Reading About the Bleeding." [JlNJPo] (16:2) Aut 94, p. 3.
"Alphabetical Order." [JlNJPo] (16:2) Aut 94, p. 2.
"Decoration Day." [JlNJPo] (16:2) Aut 94, p. 4.
"First Memory of the Gang Wars in Hoboken 1957." [SlipS] (14) 94, p. 56.
"Tying Knots." [SlipS] (14) 94, p. 55-56.
346. BARKAN, Stanley
"The Worm in the Book" (for Alfred Van Loen). [Confr] (54/55) Fall 94-Wint 95, p. 330.
347. BARKER, Helene
"Divorce, Walking Alone." [PoetL] (89:1) Spr 94, p. 17.
"Evidence of Habit." [HiramPoR] (55/56) Fall 93-Sum 94, p. 7-11.
"White Flowers." [Border] (4) Spr-Sum 94, p. 1.
348. BARKER, Penny
"The Fruit Sellers of St. Vincent's." [SoDakR] (32:4) Wint 94, p. 65.
349. BARKER, Wendy
"Inheritance." [Border] (4) Spr-Sum 94, p. 2.
"Stylist." [NoAmR] (279:3) My-Je 94, p. 40.
350. BARKS, Coleman
"Currycombing." [GeoR] (48:3) Fall 94, p. 554-555.
351. BARNES, Dick
"Winter to Spring in the Middle West." [AntR] (52:2) Spr 94, p. 322-323.
352. BARNES, Jim
"Late Fall" (tr. of Dagmar Nick). [DenQ] (29:1) Sum 94, p. 92.
"Monet's Lilies" (Musée de l'Orangerie, Bastille Day 1991). [GeoR] (48:2) Sum 94, p. 352.
"Picasso's Chair." [Confr] (54/55) Fall 94-Wint 95, p. 297.
"Poem on His Birthday." [Callaloo] (17:1) Wint 94, p. 247-248.
"Proust's Way: July 1991." [SouthernHR] (28:3) Sum 94, p. 276-277.
"Rodin's Garden." [GeoR] (48:2) Sum 94, p. 350-351.
"Rousseau Primitive." [Confr] (54/55) Fall 94-Wint 95, p. 298.
"Vision and Prayer" (Notre Dame, 12.vii.91). [GettyR] (7:2) Spr 94, p. 246-247.
"Word." [GettyR] (7:2) Spr 94, p. 248.
353. BARNES, Kate
"Hayricks." [Light] (10) Sum 94, p. 8.
"The Rhetoric of Fiction." [NewEngR] (16:4) Fall 94, p. 166-175.

354. BARNES, Kay
"Grandmother in the Living Room" (tr. of Jean Ethier-Blais). [InterPR] (20:2) Fall 94, p. 81.
355. BARNES, Kim
"Calling the Coyotes In." [Shen] (44:2) Sum 94, p. 90-91.
"Family Travel." [Shen] (44:2) Sum 94, p. 88-89.
"Last Ride." [Manoa] (6:2) Wint 94, p. 215.
"Near the Eye: Oklahoma, 1988" (For my great uncle, Rudolf Valentino York). [IllinoisR] (1:2) Spr 94, p. 16.
"Sunday Outing." [Manoa] (6:2) Wint 94, p. 216.
356. BARNES, Randy
"Hand-Jive." [Vis] (45) 94, p. 35-36.
357. BARNES, Richard
"Adrogué" (tr. of Jorge Luis Borges, w. Robert Mezey). [Descant] (25:1, #84) Spr 94, p. 65-66.
" *Ein Traum*" (tr. of Jorge Luis Borges). [AmerPoR] (23:1) Ja-F 94, p. 27.
"Endymion on Latmos" (tr. of Jorge Luis Borges, w. Robert Mezey). [Descant] (25:1, #84) Spr 94, p. 67-68.
"The Enigmas" (tr. of Jorge Luis Borges, w. Robert Mezey). [Agni] (40) 94, p. 119.
"Flowing or Being" (tr. of Jorge Luis Borges, w. Robert Mezey). [Agni] (40) 94, p. 121.
"Góngora" (tr. of Jorge Luis Borges). [WestHR] (48:3) Fall 94, p. 235.
" *Inferno*, V, 129" (tr. of Jorge Luis Borges, w. Robert Mezey). [AmerPoR] (23:1) Ja-F 94, p. 27.
"Invocation to Joyce" (tr. of Jorge Luis Borges). [AmerPoR] (23:1) Ja-F 94, p. 28.
"Luke XXIII" (tr. of Jorge Luis Borges, w. Robert Mezey). [Agni] (40) 94, p. 120.
"Matthew XXV, 30" (tr. of Jorge Luis Borges, w. Robert Mezey). [AmerPoR] (23:1) Ja-F 94, p. 27.
"Matthew XXV, 30" (tr. of Jorge Luis Borges, w. Robert Mezey). [Descant] (25:1, #84) Spr 94, p. 74.
"The Odyssey, Book XXIII" (tr. of Jorge Luis Borges, w. Robert Mezey). [AmerPoR] (23:1) Ja-F 94, p. 27.
"Rain" (tr. of Jorge Luis Borges). [AmerPoR] (23:1) Ja-F 94, p. 25.
"La Recoleta" (tr. of Jorge Luis Borges, w. Robert Mezey). [AmerPoR] (23:1) Ja-F 94, p. 28.
"The Suicide" (tr. of Jorge Luis Borges). [OhioR] (52) 94, p. 76.
"Swords" (tr. of Jorge Luis Borges, w. Robert Mezey). [Descant] (25:1, #84) Spr 94, p. 69.
"Tankas" (tr. of Jorge Luis Borges). [Descant] (25:1, #84) Spr 94, p. 70-71.
"To Manuel Mujica Lainez" (tr. of Jorge Luis Borges, w. Robert Mezey). [AmerPoR] (23:1) Ja-F 94, p. 26.
358. BARNET, Miguel
"Pilgrims of the Dawn" (To the crew of the "Sirene," 1836, tr. by David Frye). [MichQR] (33:4) Fall 94, p. 805-806.
359. BARNETT, Ruth Anderson
"Dixie Remembers the Runway." [NewL] (60:2) 94, p. 122-123.
"Phaedra in Hades." [GreenMR] (NS 17:2) Fall-Wint 94-95, p. 90.
"To the Teenaged Girl Across the Street, Crouched Behind Her Mother's Car" (for Marcia). [SouthernPR] (34:2) Wint 94, p. 18-21.
360. BARNEY, Anne
"Learning" (For My Mother). [SingHM] (21) 94, p. 31.
361. BARNSTEAD, John
"The End of Volume Two" (tr. of Mikhail Kuzmin, with Scholia). [AntigR] (99) Aut 94, p. 58-61.
362. BARNSTONE, Aliki
"The Bell." [PraS] (68:3) Fall 94, p. 85-87.
"Greek Easter." [PraS] (68:3) Fall 94, p. 84-85.
"Spirals." [ChiR] (40:2/3) 94, p. 119-120.
363. BARNSTONE, Tony
"Memory" (tr. of Bei Ling, w. Xi Chuan). [Talisman] (12) Spr 94, p. 175.
"Void" (tr. of Bei Ling, w. Xi Chuan). [Talisman] (12) Spr 94, p. 175.
"You Asked About My Life. I Send You, Pei Di, These Lines" (tr. of Wang Wei, w. Willis Barnstone and Xu Haixin). [NewEngR] (16:3) Sum 94, p. 31.
364. BARNSTONE, Willis
"Federico in August." [PartR] (61:2) Spr 94, p. 311-312.

"You Asked About My Life. I Send You, Pei Di, These Lines" (tr. of Wang Wei, w. Tony Barnstone and Xu Haixin). [NewEngR] (16:3) Sum 94, p. 31.

365. BARON, Enid L.
"The Courting of the Blue-Footed Booby." [Rosebud] (1:2) Sum 94, p. 74.
"Encampment." [Rosebud] (1:2) Sum 94, p. 63.

366. BARON, Todd
"Day : Book." [Talisman] (13) Fall 94-Wint 95, p. 200-204.

367. BARONE, Dennis
"September." [Talisman] (12) Spr 94, p. 20.

368. BARQUET, Jesús J.
"Entre Bambalinas." [Nuez] (5:13/14/15) 94, p. 42.
"Vérrazano-Narrows Bridge" (tr. by Jeff Longwell and the author). [MichQR] (33:3) Sum 94, p. 636-637.

369. BARR, Tina
"Armless." [HarvardR] (2) Fall 92, p. 59-60.
"Lethe." [DenQ] (28:4) Spr 94, p. 11-12.

370. BARRACK, Jack
"The Hiroshima Horse." [Poetry] (164:4) Jl 94, p. 194.

371. BARRATT, Amy
"Life on the Winter Island." [AntigR] (99) Aut 94, p. 134-135.
"The Mountain" (for S.A.). [AntigR] (99) Aut 94, p. 136-137.
"Picking Raspberries, Late Summer." [AntigR] (99) Aut 94, p. 138.

372. BARRAX, Gerald
"And Tell the Girls to Pray for Me." [SouthernR] (30:4) Aut 94, p. 719-722.
"Reunion Birthday Poem." [Shen] (44:2) Sum 94, p. 107.
"Sainthood." [Shen] (44:2) Sum 94, p. 106.
"Sunday, 24 May 1992, 10:30 A.M." [AmerPoR] (23:4) Jl-Ag 94, p. 12.

373. BARRESI, Dorothy
"Crow Sermon." [GrahamHR] (18) Wint 94-95, p. 88-90.
"On First Looking into Wells Fargo and Seeing a Rock Star." [PassN] (15:1) Sum 94, p. 33-35.
"On the Poisoning of a Neighborhood Cat." [PassN] (15:1) Sum 94, p. 36-37.

374. BARRETT, Michael
"Variations on a Theme by Einstein." [QW] (39) Sum-Fall 94, p. 190-193.

375. BARRETT, Nick
"Free Wood: South Lot, Swope Park Municipal." [IndR] (17:2) Fall 94, p. 58-59.
"Plotting Land" (for Teresa, and Benito Martinez). [Farm] (11:1) Spr-Sum 94, p. 62-64.
"Train." [IndR] (17:2) Fall 94, p. 60-61.

376. BARRIE, Jill
"The Pragmatist." [CimR] (107) Ap 94, p. 89.

377. BARRIENTOS, Raúl
"Cellophane" (tr. by Ben A. Heller). [GrahamHR] (18) Wint 94-95, p. 38-39.

378. BARRINGER, Margaret
"The Dreamer." [HarvardR] (7) Fall 94, p. 48.

379. BARROWS, Anita
"Quelque Lecons des Tenebres." [PraS] (68:1) Spr 94, p. 32-38.

380. BART, Anna
"Downtown Buffalo." [Border] (3) Fall 93, p. 3.

381. BART, Jill
"Faded Silk, Dark Voices." [ChamLR] (14/15) Spr-Fall 94, p. 218-220.
"Gauguin's 'Aita Parari'." [ChamLR] (14/15) Spr-Fall 94, p. 223.
"The Naked and the Nude." [ChamLR] (14/15) Spr-Fall 94, p. 221-222.

382. BARTH, Laurie
"Almost Really Real." [DenQ] (28:3) Wint 94, p. 5-6.

383. BARTHELME, Steven
"Morning." [NegC] (14:1/2) 94, p. 93.

384. BARTLETT, Brian
"A Basement Tale" (for Andrew). [Quarry] (43:2) S 94, p. 135-136.
"A Bear-Hunt Tale." [Arc] (33) Fall 94, p. 63-64.
"Massacre Jigsaw Puzzle." [Quarry] (43:2) S 94, p. 137-139.
"Thanksgiving in an Old House" (for Karen). [MalR] (109) Wint 94, p. 91-92.

385. BARTOLOMÉ, Efraín
"Flood" (tr. by Reginald Gibbons). [TriQ] (91) Fall 94, p. 117.

386. BARTON, Bruce
"Cancellations." [WestB] (35) 94, p. 30-31.

387. BARTON, John
"Academy Performance." [MalR] (109) Wint 94, p. 88-90.
"Beyond Recognition." [PoetryC] (14:4) S 94, p. 18.
"Chicken Boy." [MalR] (106) Spr 94, p. 60-62.
"Continuity." [Quarry] (42:4) Mr 94, p. 90-91.
"Dementia." [CapilR] (2:13) Spr 94, p. 76-77.
"Ecology." [Quarry] (42:4) Mr 94, p. 88-89.
"Eros." [JamesWR] (11:4) Sum 94, p. 8.
"From a Journey Around the World." [PoetryC] (14:4) S 94, p. 18-19.
"Loose-strife." [JamesWR] (11:4) Sum 94, p. 9.
"Mississippi." [CapilR] (2:13) Spr 94, p. 78-80.
"A Near Antipodes." [EvergreenC] (9:2) Sum-Fall 94, p. 85-86.
"Number Theory." [CapilR] (2:13) Spr 94, p. 73-75.
"Patriarchy." [PraF] (15:3, #68) Aut 94, p. 52-54.
"Saranac Lake Vacation." [CapilR] (2:13) Spr 94, p. 84-88.
"Le Tombeau de Sylvia Plath." [PoetryC] (14:4) S 94, p. 19.
"Undercurrent." [CapilR] (2:13) Spr 94, p. 81-83.
388. BARTOW, Stuart
"Bored by Reading Lacan All Morning, I Go Outside to Waste Time in the Garden." [WindO] (58) Sum 94, p. 29.
389. BASHEVA, Miriana
"Morning" (tr. by Lisa Sapinkopf, w. Georgi Belev). [CrabCR] (8:2/3/9:1/2/3) 94, p. 109.
390. BASHO (1644-1694)
Haiku [AmerPoR] (23:4) Jl-Ag 94, p. 17.
391. BASILIADIS, Nic
"Vasiliki." [CoalC] (8) Ap 94, p. 22.
392. BASINSKI, Michael
"Questions." [WashR] (20:4) D 94-Ja 95, p. 29.
"Saw the Word Which." [WashR] (20:4) D 94-Ja 95, p. 29.
393. BASKETT, Franz (Franz K.)
"The Calico Bull." [NewOR] (20:3/4) Fall-Wint 94, p. 133.
"Marley." [Pearl] (20) Spr 94, p. 85.
394. BASNEY, Lionel
"You Know What It Was." [SewanR] (102:3) Sum 94, p. 376.
395. BASSETT, Fred
"Regrets to a Red-Winged Black Bird." [NegC] (14:1/2) 94, p. 16.
396. BATCHELOR, Rhonda
"Jealousy and Desire" (Grain Contest Winners, Prose Poem: Honourable Mention). [Grain] (21:4) Spr 94, p. 23.
397. BATEMAN, Claire
"Bed." [CreamCR] (18:2) Fall 94, p. 140-141.
"Friction." [NewEngR] (16:1) Wint 94, p. 65-66.
"Hair." [ParisR] (36:132) Fall 94, p. 123.
"Sky." [NewEngR] (16:1) Wint 94, p. 66-67.
"Stitching the Bride." [ParisR] (36:132) Fall 94, p. 122-123.
"Yes." [CreamCR] (18:2) Fall 94, p. 142.
398. BATES, Andrea
"Commitment." [HighP] (9:1) Spr 94, p. 81.
399. BATES, Jefferson D.
"King Oliver Tries Out a New Piano Player" (after T.S. Eliot). [Light] (9) Spr 94, p. 16.
"Slumming at the Showboat" (With a tip of the old fedora to Thomas Hardy). [Light] (10) Sum 94, p. 20.
400. BATES, Jennifer
"What I Have to Offer." [Parting] (7:2) Wint 94-95, p. 34.
401. BATES, Marilyn
"Ex." [PennR] (6:1) 94, p. 26.
402. BATES, Robert L.
"Abbreviated." [Light] (10) Sum 94, p. 12.
"Baffled." [Light] (9) Spr 94, p. 8.
"Exalted." [Light] (9) Spr 94, p. 13.
"They'll Do It Every Time, Specially on the Interstate." [Light] (11) Aut 94, p. 8.
403. BATESON, Catherine
"What I Dreamed About." [ProseP] (3) 94, p. 10.

404. BATHANTI, Joseph
"The Cartographer." [WeberS] (11:2) Spr-Sum 94, p. 94.
"A Dream of the Dead on Good Friday." [NoCarLR] (2:1) Spr 94, p. 154.
"John." [CumbPR] (13:2) Spr 94, p. 6-7.
"Living Together." [WeberS] (11:2) Spr-Sum 94, p. 95.
"The Scar." [NoCarLR] (2:1) Spr 94, p. 156-157.
"Turns." [Pembroke] (26) 94, p. 107-108.
405. BATTIN, Wendy
"Like the Second Hand on a Very Slow Watch." [Thrpny] (58) Sum 94, p. 23.
"Practice at Dawn." [Poetry] (163:5) F 94, p. 274.
406. BAUDELAIRE, Charles
"The Cat" (tr. by Leslie H. Whitten). [Outbr] (25) 94, p. 88-89.
"Le Chat." [Light] (11) Aut 94, p. 20.
407. BAUER, Grace
"Café au Lait." [NegC] (13:2/3) 93, p. 1-3.
"Life and Death on the Freret Bus." [NegC] (13:2/3) 93, p. 4.
408. BAUGH, Edward
"Detail from 'Ritual of the River'." [MalR] (107) Sum 94, p. 142.
"Hedge Trimming." [MalR] (107) Sum 94, p. 143.
409. BAUMANN, Iren
"Tuesday" (tr. by Gary Sea). [Vis] (45) 94, p. 23.
410. BAUMEL, Judith
"New, New York." [Pivot] (41) 93, p. 2-3.
"Philips Street, Andover." [Agni] (39) 94, p. 182-183.
411. BAUMGAERTNER, Anna
"The Accompanist." [Vis] (46) 94, p. 19.
412. BAVETTA, Ruth
"Red." [Writer] (107:5) My 94, p. 21.
413. BAXTER, E. R., III
"After a Long Illness." [SlipS] (14) 94, p. 82.
"Death in America." [SlipS] (14) 94, p. 81-82.
414. BAYDOUN, 'Abbas
"The Poem of Tyre" (Excerpts, tr. by Sharif S. Elmusa). [LitR] (37:3) Spr 94, p. 475-476.
415. BAYER, Deanne
"Changes in the Colors of Love." [CapeR] (29:2) Fall 94, p. 17.
"Disappearance of a Virtuoso." [SoDakR] (32:2) Sum 94, p. 30.
"The Persistence of Forgetting." [SoDakR] (32:2) Sum 94, p. 29.
"A Rothko Nocturne." [Plain] (14:2) Wint 94, p. 19.
"There Is No 221B Baker Street." [Elf] (4:3) Fall 94, p. 25.
416. BAYER, Deborah
"SWF." [Parting] (7:1) Sum 94, p. 75.
"Thieves' Market." [Parting] (7:2) Wint 94-95, p. 28-29.
417. BAYLEY, Edgar
"I Can't Say It Any Other Way" (tr. by Geoffrey Brock). [InterQ] (1:4) 94, p. 30.
"No Puedo Decirlo de Otro Modo." [InterQ] (1:4) 94, p. 30.
418. BEACH, Judi K.
"Dinosaur National Monument." [TarRP] (33:2) Spr 94, p. 7.
419. BEAKE, Fred
"Psychic." [Stand] (35:3) Sum 94, p. 68.
BEAR, Ray Young (Ray A. Young)
See YOUNG BEAR, Ray (Ray A.)
BEAR, Shining
See SHINING BEAR
420. BEARD, Michael
"After the Ice" (tr. of Khalil Hawi, w. Adnan Haydar). [LitR] (37:3) Spr 94, p. 494-497.
"Digoenes / Pillar of Salt" (tr. of Henri Zoghaib, w. Adnan Haydar). [LitR] (37:3) Spr 94, p. 533-535.
"Fear, You Are Drunk" (tr. of Houda al-Naamani, w. Adnan Haydar). [LitR] (37:3) Spr 94, p. 509-510.
"I Am the Truth" (tr. of Houda al-Naamani, w. Adnan Haydar). [LitR] (37:3) Spr 94, p. 508-509.
"I Long for a Moment" (tr. of Henri Zoghaib, w. Adnan Haydar). [LitR] (37:3) Spr 94, p. 532.

"The Mariner and the Dervish" (tr. of Khalil Hawi, w. Adnan Haydar). [LitR] (37:3) Spr 94, p. 491-494.
"Memoirs in Exile" (Selections: 9, 28, 31, 42-44, 46, 47, 60-61, 65, tr. of Joseph Abi Daher, w. Adnan Haydar). [LitR] (37:3) Spr 94, p. 444-446.
"Quartet for the Last Days" (tr. of Yusuf al-Khal, w. Adnan Haydar). [LitR] (37:3) Spr 94, p. 506-507.

421. BEARDSLEY, Douglas
"Wrestling with the Angel" (for John Atkinson, 1941-1983). [Pivot] (42) 94, p. 37.

422. BEASLEY, Bruce
"Ultrasound." [Antaeus] (73/74) Spr 94, p. 82-84.

423. BEATTY, Christy
"Farther Down." [CutB] (41) Wint 94, p. 74-75.

424. BEAUCHAMP, Steven (J. Steven)
"Notes on a Scale." [EngJ] (83:5) S 94, p. 54.
"Rain Dance." [Blueline] (15) 94, p. 41.

425. BEAUMONT, Jeanne
"The Last Blue Place." [SenR] (24:1) Spr 94, p. 39.
"Marilyns" (after Warhol). [Jacaranda] (5:1) Wint-Spr 91, p. 8.
"Road Trip." [Pivot] (41) 93, p. 51-52.
"The Town by Heart." [Pivot] (41) 93, p. 51.
"A Vase." [PoetryE] (37/38) Spr 94, p. 108-109.
"Wig." [PoetryE] (37/38) Spr 94, p. 107.

426. BEAUSOLEIL, Claude
"Grand Hôtel des Étrangers" (Excerpt). [InterPR] (20:2) Fall 94, p. 40, 42.
"The Grand Hotel of Foreigners" (Excerpt, tr. by Jed English). [InterPR] (20:2) Fall 94, p. 41, 43.

427. BEAVER, Bruce
"Slate Workers." [MalR] (107) Sum 94, p. 65.

428. BECK, Art
"Depression Album." [ArtfulD] (26/27) 94, p. 81.

429. BECK, Dian
"Frank Finds an Orbit." [Sonora] (28) Fall 94, p. 23-24.

430. BECKER, Richard
"Driving to Santa Fe." [Colum] (21) Fall 93, p. 42.
"Lagoon on the James." [Colum] (21) Fall 93, p. 41.

431. BECKER, Robin
"The Roast Chicken." [AmerPoR] (23:1) Ja-F 94, p. 31.
"Shopping." [AmerPoR] (23:1) Ja-F 94, p. 31.

432. BECKETT, Larry
"Sonnet: At noon, it hits us, it's everywhere: anger." [Zyzzyva] (10:2) Sum 94, p. 42.

433. BECKOVIC, Matija
"If I Knew I'd Bear Myself Proudly" (tr. by Charles Simic). [HarvardR] (Premier Issue) Spr 92, p. 75.

434. BEDICHEK, Don
"West Texas After Much Thinking." [SmPd] (31:3, #92) Fall 94, p. 35.

435. BEDIENT, Calvin (Cal)
"Blue Fire." [NewAW] (12) Spr-Sum 94, p. 122.
"Spring Rights." [DenQ] (29:1) Sum 94, p. 6-7.
"White Snow Falling Without Wind" (Thanksgiving Day, Foss River Grove). [Poetry] (165:2) N 94, p. 79-80.

BEEK, Edith van
See Van BEEK, Edith

436. BEEMAN, Katherine
"The Measure of Time" (tr. of Janou Saint-Denis). [InterPR] (20:2) Fall 94, p. 77.

437. BEGLEY, T.
"Vowel Imprint" (w. Olga Broumas). [AmerV] (33) 94, p. 95-99.

438. BEHAN, Marie
"Roman Fall." [SouthernPR] (34:1) Sum 94, p. 65-67.

439. BEHAR, Ruth
"After Papa" (tr. of Carilda Oliver Labra). [MichQR] (33:3) Sum 94, p. 599-600.
"A Chronicle That Swoons Before the Immigrant Tree" (tr. of Nancy Morejón). [MichQR] (33:3) Sum 94, p. 623.
"Dangers of Speaking and Staying Quiet. Language of Silence" (based on a poem of Francisco de Quevedo, tr. of Marilyn Bobes). [MichQR] (33:3) Sum 94, p. 541.
"The Islands" (tr. of Reina María Rodríguez). [MichQR] (33:4) Fall 94, p. 783-784.

"Knots in the Handkerchief" (tr. of Ernesto Santana). [MichQR] (33:4) Fall 94, p. 677.
"The Last Days." [Witness] (8:1) 94, p. 138-139.
"Letter to a Woman Friend" (tr. of Reina María Rodríguez). [MichQR] (33:4) Fall 94, p. 784.
"My Name (A Family Anti-Elegy)" (Excerpts, tr. of Excilia Saldaña, w. David Frye). [MichQR] (33:3) Sum 94, p. 543-547.
"Nothing Lost Will Come Back with the Rain" (tr. of Victor Fowler Calzada). [MichQR] (33:3) Sum 94, p. 592-593.
"Poem for the Woman Who Talks to Herself in the Park" (tr. of Linea de Feria). [MichQR] (33:4) Fall 94, p. 781-782.
"Prayer to Lourdes" (For Lourdes Casal, poet, scholar, bridge). [MichQR] (33:3) Sum 94, p. 417-418.
"Soil" (tr. of Carilda Oliver Labra). [MichQR] (33:3) Sum 94, p. 598.
"The Thing." [MichQR] (33:1) Wint 94, p. 217-218.
"Two Figures on a Bridge" (tr. of Zaida Del Río). [MichQR] (33:3) Sum 94, p. 638.
"The Wall" (tr. of María Elena Cruz Varela). [MichQR] (33:4) Fall 94, p. 803.

440. BEHLEN, Charles
"Cow in the Suburbs." [Border] (5) Fall-Wint 94, p. 3-4.
"Miss Edna's Boardinghouse." [Border] (4) Spr-Sum 94, p. 3.
"Shell." [Border] (4) Spr-Sum 94, p. 4-5.

441. BEHM, Richard
"Dreaming of Fish." [HampSPR] Wint 94, p. 26.
"On the North Country Trail." [HampSPR] Wint 94, p. 26.

442. BEHN, Robin
"Five O'Clock" (for S.). [Iowa] (24:1) Wint 94, p. 76.
"Windy Popples, Late October." [Iowa] (24:1) Wint 94, p. 75.

443. BEHRENDT, Stephen C.
"Mt. Moriah Dawn." [WeberS] (11:2) Spr-Sum 94, p. 86.
"Noon Roses." [WeberS] (11:2) Spr-Sum 94, p. 83-84.
"Reading the News I Had Expected" (for John). [WeberS] (11:2) Spr-Sum 94, p. 84-85.
"To the Young Man from the East Coast Who Has Inquired about Graduate Study in English." [WeberS] (11:2) Spr-Sum 94, p. 85-86.

BEI, Dao
See BEI DAO

444. BEI, Ling
"The Face, Also, Has Bruised Dignity" (tr. by Jin Zhong and William Slaughter). [Manoa] (6:1) Sum 94, p. 82-83.
"Memory" (tr. by Tony Barnstone and Xi Chuan). [Talisman] (12) Spr 94, p. 175.
"Morning, Looking into the Distance" (tr. by G. Wiersma). [Manoa] (6:1) Sum 94, p. 82.
"Void" (tr. by Tony Barnstone and Xi Chuan). [Talisman] (12) Spr 94, p. 175.
"Words of Autumn" (tr. by Jin Zhong and Wang Weiqing). [Manoa] (6:1) Sum 94, p. 81.

445. BEI DAO
"Apple and Brute Stone" (tr. by David Hinton). [Sulfur] (34) Spr 94, p. 15-16.
"Background" (tr. by David Hinton). [Conjunc] (23) 94, p. 134.
"Flash" (tr. by David Hinton). [InterQ] (1:2) 93, p. 40.
"Folding Procedure" (tr. by David Hinton). [Sulfur] (34) Spr 94, p. 17-18.
"For T. Tranströmer" (tr. by David Hinton). [Talisman] (12) Spr 94, p. 181.
"Lament" (tr. by David Hinton). [Sulfur] (34) Spr 94, p. 15.
"Morning" (tr. by David Hinton). [Conjunc] (23) 94, p. 133.
"Musical Variations" (tr. by David Hinton). [Sulfur] (34) Spr 94, p. 18.
"New Century" (tr. by Donald Finkel and Chen Xueliang). [Manoa] (6:1) Sum 94, p. 110-111.
"Other Than Tomorrow" (tr. by David Hinton). [InterQ] (1:2) 93, p. 43.
"Pastoral" (tr. by David Hinton). [InterQ] (1:2) 93, p. 41.
"Playwright" (tr. by David Hinton). [Talisman] (12) Spr 94, p. 181.
"Playwright" (tr. by Donald Finkel and Chen Xueliang). [Manoa] (6:1) Sum 94, p. 110.
"Questioning the Sky" (tr. by Donald Finkel and Chen Xueliang). [Manoa] (6:1) Sum 94, p. 111.
"Realm" (tr. by David Hinton). [Conjunc] (23) 94, p. 135.
"Records" (tr. by David Hinton). [InterQ] (1:2) 93, p. 42.
"Seeing Double" (tr. by David Hinton). [Conjunc] (23) 94, p. 133-134.

"This Day" (tr. by David Hinton). [Conjunc] (23) 94, p. 134-135.
"Toxin" (tr. by David Hinton). [Sulfur] (34) Spr 94, p. 16.
"Untitled: At the mother tongue's line of defense" (tr. by David Hinton). [Sulfur] (34) Spr 94, p. 17.

446. BEJEL, Emilio
"El Libro Regalado" (Selections: I-II, tr. by Stephen Clark). [MichQR] (33:3) Sum 94, p. 472-476.

447. BELEV, Georgi
"And When the Winter Wind Rushed Straight into My Heart" (tr. of Georgi Borisov, w. Lisa Sapinkopf). [InterQ] (1:1) [93?], p. 86.
"Arrival" (tr. of Fedya Filkova, w. Lisa Sapinkopf). [InterQ] (1:1) [93?], p. 85.
"Attraction" (tr. of Georgi Rupchev, w. Lisa Sapinkopf). [CrabCR] (8:2/3/9:1/2/3) 94, p. 111.
"Ballad for the Future" (tr. of Ivan Radoev, w. Lisa Sapinkopf). [InterQ] (1:1) [93?], p. 77.
"Four Seekers of the Great Metaphor" (tr. of Vladimir Levchev, w. Lisa Sapinkopf). [PartR] (61:2) Spr 94, p. 319-320.
"Grass" (tr. of Blaga Dimitrova, w. Lisa Sapinkopf). [InterQ] (1:1) [93?], p. 79.
"Hotel Room (Vienna, 1966)" (tr. of Blaga Dimitrova, w. Lisa Sapinkopf). [InterQ] (1:1) [93?], p. 78-79.
"Morning" (tr. of Miriana Basheva, w. Lisa Sapinkopf). [CrabCR] (8:2/3/9:1/2/3) 94, p. 109.
"Ortamezar — The Jewish Quarter" (tr. of Ivan Teofilov, w. Lisa Sapinkopf). [InterQ] (1:1) [93?], p. 82-83.
"Repentance" (tr. of Blaga Dimitrova, w. Lisa Sapinkopf). [InterQ] (1:1) [93?], p. 80.
"Silence" (tr. of Marin Georgiev, w. Lisa Sapinkopf). [InterQ] (1:1) [93?], p. 81.
"Song" (tr. by Lisa Sapinkopf and the author). [InterQ] (1:1) [93?], p. 87.
"A Tale That's Not a Tale" (tr. of Binyo Ivanov, w. Lisa Sapinkopf). [CrabCR] (8:2/3/9:1/2/3) 94, p. 109-110.
"Teenagers" (tr. of Ivan Teofilov, w. Lisa Sapinkopf). [InterQ] (1:1) [93?], p. 84.
"Vulnerability" (tr. of Fedya Filkova, w. Lisa Sapinkopf). [InterQ] (1:1) [93?], p. 85.
"The Wind Is Coming and I Love You" (tr. of Binyo Ivanov, w. Lisa Sapinkopf). [PartR] (61:2) Spr 94, p. 320-321.

448. BELGUM, Erik
"Untitled: They wore their brains around their heads like turbans." [Caliban] (14) 94, p. 144.

449. BELHERT, Dean
"White Supremacy on the Shirt Circuit." [Light] (11) Aut 94, p. 13.

450. BELIEU, Erin
"All Distance." [Journal] (18:2) Fall-Wint 94, p. 6-7.
"Bee Sting." [Journal] (18:2) Fall-Wint 94, p. 9.
"The Dream, After Surgery" (for Carl Phillips). [Journal] (18:2) Fall-Wint 94, p. 11.
"The Exploding Madonna" (III. The Hour of Lead). [HarvardR] (7) Fall 94, p. 42-43.
"Outside the Hotel Ritz." [Journal] (18:2) Fall-Wint 94, p. 8.
"The Rescue Ship" (In memoriam for J.G.). [Journal] (18:2) Fall-Wint 94, p. 12-13.
"Tick." [Journal] (18:2) Fall-Wint 94, p. 10.

451. BELITT, Ben
"Four Epigrams" (tr. of Gonzalo Rojas). [Colum] (22) Wint 94, p. 154.
"Numen" (tr. of Gonzalo Rojas). [Colum] (22) Wint 94, p. 152-153.

452. BELL, Marvin
"The Book of the Dead Man" (Selections: #12, #24, #32). [DenQ] (28:3) Wint 94, p. 7-13.

453. BELL, Sally C. (Sally Cheney)
"Blue Solitude" (tr. of Fanny Carrión de Fierro). [PoetL] (89:1) Spr 94, p. 26.
"Green Solitude" (tr. of Fanny Carrión de Fierro). [PoetL] (89:1) Spr 94, p. 25.
"Only You" (tr. of Fanny Carrión de Fierro). [WebR] (18) Fall 94, p. 13.
"Red Solitude" (tr. of Fanny Carrión de Fierro). [PoetL] (89:1) Spr 94, p. 27.

454. BELL, Wade
"Blue Morning." [MoodySI] (28, also labeled 29) Fall 94, p. 28.

455. BELLI, Carlos Germán
"Al Pintor Giovanni Donato da Montorfano (1440-1510)." [Inti] (39) Primavera 94, p. 247-248.
"El Corazon Hambriento." [Inti] (39) Primavera 94, p. 249-250.
"El Hablante Contento." [Inti] (39) Primavera 94, p. 250-251.
"Variations for My Brother Alfonso" (tr. by Rose Passalacqua). [Conjunc] (23) 94, p. 111-114.

456. BELLIN, Steven
"A Dunking." [CreamCR] (18:2) Fall 94, p. 103.
457. BELLM, Dan
"Before Words." [Poetry] (164:2) My 94, p. 67.
458. BELLMAN, Carl Michael
"On an Unexpected Farewell, Announced at Ulla Winblad's Breakfast One Summer Morning in the Country" (Pastoral Dedicated to Ryl. Secretary Leopold, tr. by Michael Thompson). [Quarry] (43:1) Je 94, p. 46-48.
"To Shit-Disturber Lövberg at the Dantobom Death-House, Written at Graveside" (Dedicated to Doctor Blad, tr. by Michael Thompson). [Quarry] (43:1) Je 94, p. 44-45.
"To Ulla in the Window at Fiskartorp, about Noon, One Summer's Day" (Pastoral Dedic. to Herr Assessor Lunström, tr. by Michael Thompson). [Quarry] (43:1) Je 94, p. 42-43.
459. BELLOWS, Timothy
"Hemingway. A Restaurant. High Speeds." [SoCoast] (17) Je 94, p. 34-35.
460. BELOIT/FUDAN TRANSLATION WORKSHOP
"The City" (4 selections, tr. of Gu Cheng, w. Chen Yanbing and John Rosenwald). [Manoa] (6:1) Sum 94, p. 118-120.
461. BEN-LEV, Dina
"The Agency Called Us Temporary Saviors." [PoetryNW] (35:1) Spr 94, p. 42.
"Broken Helix." [Field] (50) Spr 94, p. 13-14.
"Psalm for a Second Marriage." [PoetryE] (37/38) Spr 94, p. 50.
"The Return." [PoetryE] (37/38) Spr 94, p. 46-47.
"The Screamers." [PoetryE] (37/38) Spr 94, p. 44.
"A Sensualist Speaks on Faith." [PoetryE] (37/38) Spr 94, p. 48-49.
"Turning Off the News at Night." [PoetryE] (37/38) Spr 94, p. 45.
"Unfinished City in Burnt Sienna." [PoetryNW] (35:1) Spr 94, p. 43.
462. BEN-TOV, S.
"Armored Pines on Mount Pollino." [SouthernPR] (34:2) Wint 94, p. 52.
"The Arrival Gate." [MissouriR] (17:3) 94, p. 177.
"The Gate of Babylon." [MissouriR] (17:3) 94, p. 180-181.
"The Lighthouse." [MissouriR] (17:3) 94, p. 176.
"Meteor Elegy" (For Itzhak Bentov ne Imrich Tobias, 1923-79). [MissouriR] (17:3) 94, p. 178-179.
"Mono Lake, Moonrise." [ConnPR] (13:1) 94, p. 6-7.
"Nocturne for the Treaty Signing" (Jerusalem, September 1993, for Raphi Amram). [Ploughs] (20:1) Spr 94, p. 134.
"Shah Jahan in Prison." [MissouriR] (17:3) 94, p. 175.
"Turtle Beach." [MissouriR] (17:3) 94, p. 182.
463. BENARI, Joseph
"Letter to My Daughter." [SingHM] (21) 94, p. 36-37.
464. BENBOW, Margaret
"May and the Misdiagnosis: Fighting Back." [GeoR] (48:2) Sum 94, p. 290.
"The Mother's Night Thoughts." [GeoR] (48:2) Sum 94, p. 289.
465. BENDALL, Molly
"4. Pastoral" (from "Five Masques for the Body"). [Jacaranda] (10) 94, p. 127.
"All the Nights" (tr. of Joyce Mansour). [DenQ] (29:1) Sum 94, p. 89.
"Conversation with Eva Hesse." [Jacaranda] (5:1) Wint-Spr 91, p. 10-11.
"Conversations on the Plurality of Worlds" (After Bernard le Bovier de Fontenelle). [Poetry] (163:6) Mr 94, p. 311-315.
"Fête on the Lake." [Poetry] (164:5) Ag 94, p. 264-265.
"Going and Coming of Sequins" (tr. of Joyce Mansour). [AmerPoR] (23:4) Jl-Ag 94, p. 16.
"In the Gloom on the Left" (tr. of Joyce Mansour). [AmerPoR] (23:4) Jl-Ag 94, p. 15.
"Mirror" (tr. of Joyce Mansour). [DenQ] (29:1) Sum 94, p. 90.
"Modesty" (tr. of Joyce Mansour). [AmerPoR] (23:4) Jl-Ag 94, p. 15.
"The Sun in Capricorn" (tr. of Joyce Mansour). [AmerPoR] (23:4) Jl-Ag 94, p. 15.
466. BENEDETTI, Mario
"The Art of Poetry" (tr. by Richard Zenith). [AmerPoR] (23:3) My-Je 94, p. 49.
"Everything Is Distant" (tr. by Richard Zenith). [AmerPoR] (23:3) My-Je 94, p. 50.
"I Am My Guest" (tr. by Richard Zenith). [AmerPoR] (23:3) My-Je 94, p. 49.
"Life This Parenthesis" (tr. by Richard Zenith). [AmerPoR] (23:3) My-Je 94, p. 49.
"Transgressions" (tr. by Richard Zenith). [AmerPoR] (23:3) My-Je 94, p. 49.
"Traveling" (tr. by Richard Zenith). [AmerPoR] (23:3) My-Je 94, p. 49.

467. BENEDICT, Elinor
"Chinavision." [Parting] (7:2) Wint 94-95, p. 3.
"Cross Country." [HayF] (15) Fall-Wint 94, p. 98.
"Paper Flowers" (Hall of Revolutionary Martyrs, Tianjin, China, January 14, 1980. ELF 1994 Poetry Competition: Honorable Mention). [Elf] (4:2) Sum 94, p. 22.
"Sea Change." [Parting] (7:2) Wint 94-95, p. 63.
468. BENEDIKT, Michael
"Cafe Life (I)." [ProseP] (3) 94, p. 13-14.
"The Committals." [ProseP] (3) 94, p. 11-12.
"Elegy for Eddie (My Stepfather, Briefly)" (For my Mother, Helen Davis Benedikt Sachs, b. 1911-d. 1988, who re-married in 1978, & in Memory of Edward Sachs, b. 1909-d. 1979). [NewYorkQ] (53) 94, p. 52-55.
"Of Granny Smith's Apples, or, of the Revolutionizing of Life in Small but Efficacious Ways" (Dedicated to Granny Smith, inventor of the Granny Smith-type apple). [ParisR] (36:130) Spr 94, p. 246-249.
469. BENET, Maria M.
"Desolation Sound: A Weekend Tryst on the B.C. Coast." [PraF] (15:3, #68) Aut 94, p. 22-23.
"Quae Amissa, Salve" (— What has been lost is safe). [PraF] (15:3, #68) Aut 94, p. 20-21.
470. BENITEZ, Luis
"Caricatures." [ConnPR] (13:1) 94, p. 9.
"Poemas de la Tierra y la Memoria" (3 poems). [Luz] (6) My 94, p. 51-53.
471. BENNET, Elvira
"Apple Tree." [CumbPR] (13:2) Spr 94, p. 18-19.
"Mrs. Podolski Explains How She Wants Me to Look at the World." [PlumR] (7) [94?], p. 58.
"Mrs. Podolski Offers Me Ten Pieces of Advice." [CarolQ] (46:3) Sum 94, p. 26-27.
"Mrs. Podolski Tells Me a Little About Her Marriage." [CarolQ] (46:3) Sum 94, p. 28.
"Poet, Dance, Tree." [SoDakR] (32:2) Sum 94, p. 62.
"Prenatal Parental Paternal." [WestHR] (48:1) Spr 94, p. 89-91.
"Toccata." [DogRR] (26) Wint 94-95, p. 21.
472. BENNETT, Bruce
"An Assistant Professor Foresees His Dismissal" (after Yeats). [TarRP] (34:1) Fall 94, p. 12.
"Battleground." [TarRP] (33:2) Spr 94, p. 28.
"The Committee." [TarRP] (33:2) Spr 94, p. 29.
"Discourse." [TarRP] (33:2) Spr 94, p. 29.
"Framed, Smiling." [LaurelR] (28:2) Sum 94, p. 101.
"Frippery." [Light] (9) Spr 94, p. 19.
"Gertrude's Ear." [Ploughs] (20:4) Wint 94-95, p. 14.
"The Guild." [TarRP] (33:2) Spr 94, p. 28.
"Learning from Experience." [HarvardR] (Premier Issue) Spr 92, p. 120.
"Sic Transit." [TarRP] (33:2) Spr 94, p. 29.
"Speeder's Epitaph." [Light] (12) Wint 94-95, p. 13.
"Spring Term: Week Six." [SoCoast] (17) Je 94, p. 51.
"To a Not-So-Sweet Singer." [Light] (11) Aut 94, p. 10.
"Vintage Reagan?" [Light] (9) Spr 94, p. 8.
473. BENNETT, Lynda
"Dear Phil." [ColEng] (56:3) Mr 94, p. 320.
"Unlatched." [ColEng] (56:3) Mr 94, p. 319.
474. BENNETT, Mary
"Introvert." [Zyzzyva] (10:3) Fall 94, p. 53.
475. BENSE, Robert
"Afterlife in a Chinese Garden." [Poem] (71) My 94, p. 18.
"Confiteor." [SoDakR] (32:4) Wint 94, p. 63.
"Madrigal for Five Voices" (Homage to Carlo Gesualdo: musician and murderer). [Poem] (71) My 94, p. 16-17.
"Prospect of Infinity." [SoDakR] (32:4) Wint 94, p. 64.
"Staying in Touch." [Poem] (71) My 94, p. 15.
"Twice in October." [HiramPoR] (55/56) Fall 93-Sum 94, p. 12.
476. BENSEN, Robert
"Isis at Caroni" (Caroni Bird Sanctuary, Trinidad, for Derek Walcott). [Verse] (11:2) Sum 94, p. 126-127.
"The Long Season." [Pivot] (42) 94, p. 1.

477. BENSKO, John
"Crab Pickers." [PoetL] (89:2) Sum 94, p. 12.
"Do You Know What High School You Went To?" [PoetL] (89:2) Sum 94, p. 13.
"A Passing Blow." [GettyR] (7:1) Wint 94, p. 142-143.
"The Pet Store." [SouthernR] (30:2) Ap, Spr 94, p. 270-271.
478. BENSON, Andrew
"All She Can Eat." [War] (6:2) Fall-Wint 94, p. 61-62.
479. BENSON, Diane E.
"Potlatch Ducks." [Callaloo] (17:1) Wint 94, p. 135.
"Recovery." [Callaloo] (17:1) Wint 94, p. 136.
480. BENSON, Gerard
"Bomb Poem: An Urban Sestina." [Pivot] (42) 94, p. 20.
"Dance of the Scarecrows." [Pivot] (42) 94, p. 21.
"The Hat." [Pivot] (42) 94, p. 21.
481. BENTLEY, Nelson
"The Moosead" (An epic fragment in five books: Book Five). [BellArk] (10:1) Ja-F 94, p. 17-21.
482. BENTLEY, Roy
"The Beasts of the Fields." [ArtfulD] (26/27) 94, p. 148.
"News of God." [SouthernR] (30:3) Sum 94, p. 522-523.
"The Politics of Spit." [SouthernR] (30:3) Sum 94, p. 524-525.
"Row Houses." [ArtfulD] (26/27) 94, p. 149.
"Speaking with a Single Tongue" (for David Baker). [ArtfulD] (26/27) 94, p. 150-152.
"The Whore Is Born in Texas." [SouthernR] (30:3) Sum 94, p. 523-524.
483. BENTTINEN, Ted
"Louhi." [NegC] (14:1/2) 94, p. 47-48.
"Lullaby Across the Gap." [Confr] (52/53) Wint-Spr 94, p. 305.
484. BERARD, Anne Tysen
"Love's needle." [Amelia] (7:3, #22) 94, p. 48.
485. BERDESHEVSKY, Margo
"Air." [BambooR] (63/64) Sum-Fall 94, p. 7-9.
"Short and the Long of It." [BambooR] (63/64) Sum-Fall 94, p. 10-11.
486. BERG, Nancy
"I Could Have Danced All Night If I Hadn't Spontaneously Combusted" (Previously published in *Negative Capability Magazine*). [ChamLR] (14/15) Spr-Fall 94, p. 231-235.
"Portrait de Mademoiselle Riviere." [ChamLR] (14/15) Spr-Fall 94, p. 229-230.
487. BERG, Stephen
"The Gaze." [DenQ] (29:1) Sum 94, p. 8-9.
488. BERGAMINI, Giacomo
"A Lucia." [Os] (39) Fall-Wint 94, p. 37-38.
489. BERGAMINO, Gina
"Bergen-Belsen, 1945." [NewYorkQ] (53) 94, p. 63-66.
"Blue Boy." [ChironR] (13:4) Wint 94, p. 18.
"The Candle." [ChironR] (13:4) Wint 94, p. 18.
"Language." [ChironR] (13:4) Wint 94, p. 18.
"Lower East Side." [ChironR] (13:4) Wint 94, p. 18.
"Secret Garden." [ChironR] (13:4) Wint 94, p. 18.
"Twisted Kind of Love." [ChironR] (13:4) Wint 94, p. 18.
"Wall." [ChironR] (13:4) Wint 94, p. 18.
490. BERGAN, Brooke
"Pastorals" (Excerpt, tr. of Guillevic). [PoetryE] (37/38) Spr 94, p. 231-232.
"The Thirty-Three Names of God: Essay from a Journal with No Dates or Personal Pronouns" (tr. of Marguerite Yourcenar). [PoetryE] (37/38) Spr 94, p. 203-207.
491. BERGER, Margi
"Skeleton." [Poetry] (165:2) N 94, p. 84.
492. BERGMAN, Denise
"Berries, Bread and Blue Sweater." [SingHM] (21) 94, p. 7-9.
493. BERKE, Judith
"The Bridge at Asnieres." [NewL] (60:4) 94, p. 90.
"Salome." [DenQ] (28:3) Wint 94, p. 14.
"The Van Gogh Poems" (Selections: 4 poems. Errata note in #51, p. 106: title should be "Four Poems After Van Gogh" "woman" should be "women" in next-to-last line of first poem, "Boots"). [Field] (50) Spr 94, p. 27-30.

494. BERLAND, Bruce
"Horace Has a Bad Day" (tr. of György Petri, w. Mária Körösy). [Poetry] (164:2) My 94, p. 85.
495. BERLAND, Dinah
"Hotel at the End of the World." [AntR] (52:2) Spr 94, p. 297.
496. BERLATSKY, Noah
"Budgy the Magus and His Demon, Gruff, at the Bus Stop." [Parting] (7:1) Sum 94, p. 32-33.
497. BERLIND, Bruce
"Accident on a Stretch of Interstate 94 Between Chicago and Milwaukee" (tr. of Ottó Orbán, w. Mária Körösy). [Boulevard] (9:1/2, #25/26) Spr 94, p. 226.
"According to My Friend H." (tr. of Imre Oravecz). [DenQ] (29:1) Sum 94, p. 93.
"American Station" (In the Grand Canyon, tr. of Agnes Nemes Nagy, w. Mária Körösy). [AnotherCM] (27) 94, p. 147.
"And Afterwards You Came" (tr. of Imre Oravecz). [DenQ] (29:1) Sum 94, p. 94.
"Daydream" (tr. of György Petri, w. Mária Körösy). [AmerPoR] (23:1) Ja-F 94, p. 34.
"The Drawbacks of Redemption" (tr. of György Petri, w. Mária Körösy). [SenR] (24:2) Fall 94, p. 57.
"Elegy" (tr. of György Petri, w. Mária Körösy). [AmerPoR] (23:1) Ja-F 94, p. 32.
"Execrable Cold" (tr. of Gyula Illyés, w. Mária Korösy)." [WebR] (18) Fall 94, p. 6.
"From the Insomnia Songs" (In memory of Arnold Schönberg, tr. of György Petri, w. Mária Körösy). [AmerPoR] (23:1) Ja-F 94, p. 33.
"I Came Again" (tr. of Imre Oravecz). [Nimrod] (38:1) Fall-Wint 94, p. 133.
"I Like" (tr. of György Petri, w. Mária Körösy). [Chelsea] (56) 94, p. 113.
"In the Garden" (to Lajos Aprily and Zoltán Jékely, tr. of Agnes Nemes Nagy). [AmerPoR] (23:1) Ja-F 94, p. 34.
"A Miscarried Meeting with János Pilinszky" (tr. of Sándor Kányádi, w. Mária Körösy). [SenR] (24:2) Fall 94, p. 59.
"Night Song of the Personal Spook" (tr. of György Petri, w. Mária Körösy). [AmerPoR] (23:1) Ja-F 94, p. 33.
"The Onion Speaks" (tr. of György Petri, w. Mária Körösy). [Chelsea] (56) 94, p. 111.
"Our Relationship begins to be Intimate" (tr. of György Petri, w. Mária Körösy). [AmerPoR] (23:1) Ja-F 94, p. 32.
"Remembering My First Master" (tr. of Szabolcs Várady, w. Mária Körösy). [SenR] (24:2) Fall 94, p. 60-61.
"Self-Portrait 1990" (tr. of György Petri, w. Mária Körösy). [Chelsea] (56) 94, p. 112.
"Shipwreck" (tr. of Agnes Gergely). [InterQ] (1:1) [93?], p. 34-39.
"Snow" (tr. of Agnes Nemes Nagy, w. Mária Körösy). [AnotherCM] (27) 94, p. 148.
"The Sun's Gone Down" (tr. of Agnes Nemes Nagy, w. Mária Körösy). [AnotherCM] (27) 94, p. 149.
"There Will Be No War" (tr. of Gyula Illyes, w. Mária Körösy). [ConnPR] (13:1) 94, p. 23.
"To A." (tr. of György Petri, w. Mária Körösy). [AmerPoR] (23:1) Ja-F 94, p. 33.
"Today I Had to Wait Outside a Door" (tr. of Imre Oravecz). [DenQ] (29:1) Sum 94, p. 95.
"White" (tr. of Gyula Illyés, w. Mária Korösy)." [WebR] (18) Fall 94, p. 5-6.
"With a Consignment of Poems" (tr. of György Petri, w. Mária Körösy). [Chelsea] (56) 94, p. 112.
"Woodcut" (tr. of Sándor Kányádi, w. Mária Körösy). [SenR] (24:2) Fall 94, p. 58.
498. BERNARD, Artis
"Securing Yellow." [ParisR] (36:133) Wint 94, p. 227-228.
"Stockyard Cafe." [Border] (5) Fall-Wint 94, p. 5.
499. BERNARD, Kenneth
"The Poet Speakee." [Confr] (52/53) Wint-Spr 94, p. 330-331.
500. BERNARD, Pam (Pamela)
"Ghosts of Las Colinas." [TriQ] (90) Spr-Sum 94, p. 170.
"Group Portrait with Incest." [Nimrod] (38:1) Fall-Wint 94, p. 24.
"Is, Big and Fatal." [TriQ] (90) Spr-Sum 94, p. 171-172.
"The Past As Gentile de Fabriano's Flight Into Egypt." [Nimrod] (38:1) Fall-Wint 94, p. 26.
"Raking the Prairie." [SingHM] (21) 94, p. 23.
"Return from School After the Storm" (3rd Prize, 8th Annual Contest). [SoCoast] (16) Ja 94, p. 10.
"September 13" (The Pablo Neruda Prize for Poetry: Second Prize). [Nimrod] (38:1) Fall-Wint 94, p. 23.

"Ward B: Daytrip to an Exhibition of Photographs by Edward Steichen." [SingHM] (21) 94, p. 80.
"The Whole History." [Nimrod] (38:1) Fall-Wint 94, p. 25.

501. BERNATH, James Greenfield
"Weathering." [SmPd] (31:3, #92) Fall 94, p. 27.

502. BERNHARD, Jim
"Break In" (January 1953). [BellArk] (10:3) My-Je 94, p. 16.
"The Loss of the Lmno P" (The first grade, fall of 1950). [BellArk] (10:5) S-O 94, p. 31.
"Pat Chaffin." [BellArk] (10:3 [i.e. 10:4]) Jl-Ag 94, p. 3.
"Political Speech." [BellArk] (10:3 [i.e. 10:4]) Jl-Ag 94, p. 3.
"Sasha, Seven Years, Old at Breakfast." [BellArk] (10:3) My-Je 94, p. 16.

503. BERNHARD, Thomas
"An Evening" (tr. by James Reidel). [ArtfulD] (26/27) 94, p. 61.
"Living and Dead" (tr. by James Reidel). [ArtfulD] (26/27) 94, p. 62.
"My Parents' House" (tr. by James Reidel). [ArtfulD] (26/27) 94, p. 60.

504. BERNSTEIN, Carole
"Torcello." [HangL] (65) 94, p. 8-9.

505. BERNSTEIN, Charles
"Circumstraint." [RiverC] (14:2) Spr 94, p. 86-89.
"Echo Off (Use Other Entrace)." [Sulfur] (34) Spr 94, p. 126-131.
"Memories." [AmerPoR] (23:6) N-D 94, p. 54.
"Work Vertical and Blank" (working around and through "Travail Vertical et Blanc" by Anne-Marie Albiach). [Conjunc] (23) 94, p. 210-214.

506. BERNSTEIN, J. B.
"Live Long, Die Short." [NegC] (14:1/2) 94, p. 21.
"Stripped." [NegC] (14:1/2) 94, p. 20.

507. BERNSTEIN, Lisa
"Insulin Shock." [KenR] (NS 16:3) Sum 94, p. 91.
"The Old Contract." [KenR] (NS 16:3) Sum 94, p. 91-92.
"Watching the Sea." [KenR] (NS 16:3) Sum 94, p. 90.

508. BERRETT, Jean
"Crossing Tripp Lake." [Northeast] (5:11) Wint 94-95, p. 36.
"The River That Rises in My Bones." [Northeast] (5:11) Wint 94-95, p. 35-36.

509. BERRIGAN, Anselm
"Listening to a Funeral." [Talisman] (13) Fall 94-Wint 95, p. 230.
"Sterile Poem." [Talisman] (13) Fall 94-Wint 95, p. 229.

510. BERRIGAN, Daniel
"Death No Dominion" (John St. George, +11/26/'93). [Elf] (4:4) Wint 94, p. 21-24.

511. BERRIGAN, Edmund
"United States." [Talisman] (13) Fall 94-Wint 95, p. 152.
"What Can I Do with My Ribcage" (— Boris Pasternak). [Talisman] (13) Fall 94-Wint 95, p. 151.

512. BERRY, D. C.
"Anniversary Rose." [LaurelR] (28:2) Sum 94, p. 59.
"Cigarette." [Poetry] (163:5) F 94, p. 261.
"Daddy" (1911-1984). [NewEngR] (16:4) Fall 94, p. 136.
"Earrings." [PoetC] (26:1) Fall 94, p. 14.
"Golfball." [SouthernHR] (28:4) Fall 94, p. 380.
"Kid." [GettyR] (7:1) Wint 94, p. 113.
"Mardi Gras at Middle Age." [NegC] (13:2/3) 93, p. 5.
"Marina Lounge." [Shen] (44:4) Wint 94, p. 107.
"Piano Recital." [GettyR] (7:1) Wint 94, p. 114.
"Saddam." [NegC] (13:2/3) 93, p. 6.
"Tadpoles." [PoetC] (26:1) Fall 94, p. 13.

513. BERRY, J. D.
"Feasting Green." [BlackBR] (18) Wint-Spr 94, p. 32-33.

514. BERRY, Jake
"Antiquities." [HeavenB] (11) 94, p. 16.
"Poem: Turbulence in Matrius." [HeavenB] (11) 94, p. 16.
"Umgathama." [HeavenB] (11) 94, p. 76.

515. BERRY, Wendell
"Sabbaths 1992." [SouthernR] (30:4) Aut 94, p. 861-868.

516. BERRYMAN, John
"The Ball Poem." [NewEngR] (16:3) Sum 94, p. 45-46.
"Fare Well." [NewEngR] (16:3) Sum 94, p. 44.

"The Lake Isle of Innisfree." [NewEngR] (16:3) Sum 94, p. 40.
"A Professor's Song." [NewEngR] (16:3) Sum 94, p. 43.
"The Song of the Tortured Girl." [NewEngR] (16:3) Sum 94, p. 42.

517. BERSSENBRUGGE, Mei-mei
"Daughter." [Avec] (7:1) 94, p. 100-102.
"Fragrance." [Chelsea] (57) 94, p. 46-49.

518. BERTIN, Kate
"Just a Friendly Game." [Amelia] (7:4, #23) 94, p. 83.

519. BERTOLA, Carla
"Era, Maw." [RagMag] (12:1) Sum 94, p. 38-39.

520. BERTOLINO, James
"As Above, So Below." [BellR] (17:1/2) Spr-Fall 94, p. 34.
"As Above, So Below." [CrabCR] (8:2/3/9:1/2/3) 94, p. 55.
"The Wave." [CrabCR] (8:2/3/9:1/2/3) 94, p. 55.

521. BERTRAM, Lena Krogh
"Untitled: Embrace me" (tr. by Per Brask and Patrick Friesen). [PoetryC] (14:2) Mr 94, p. 20.

522. BERTSCHMAN, Don
"Untitled: I think of the sea at night." [Elf] (4:4) Wint 94, p. 33.

523. BESSMAN, Joan C.
"An Elegy for e.e.c." [NegC] (14:1/2) 94, p. 31.

524. BETCHER, Jeffrey
"Elegy." [KenR] (NS 16:3) Sum 94, p. 41.

525. BETHEL, Marion
"Of Pirates and Junkanoo." [CaribbeanW] (8) 94, p. 38.
"Taino Rebirth." [MassR] (35:3/4) Aut-Wint 94, p. 562.

526. BEUKEL, Karlien van den
"In the Laboratory." [Stand] (35:2) Spr 94, p. 66-67.

527. BEYER, Lynne
"Career." [Talisman] (12) Spr 94, p. 233.
"What's Allowed." [Talisman] (12) Spr 94, p. 233.

528. BEZNER, Kevin
"After My Father's Death." [Elf] (4:3) Fall 94, p. 26.
"Starlings Gather, Morning." [Elf] (4:3) Fall 94, p. 27.

529. BHATT, Sujata
"Fate" (i.m. A.K. Ramanujan, 1929-1993). [MalR] (107) Sum 94, p. 106-107.
"An India of the Soul." [MalR] (107) Sum 94, p. 105.
"Lizard, Iguana, Chameleon, Salamander" (for Jakobine von Dömming. A response to a series of Dömming's paintings). [MalR] (107) Sum 94, p. 103-104.
"Ninniku." [MalR] (107) Sum 94, p. 108-110.

530. BIALA, Arlene
"An Evening with Michel." [SoCoast] (17) Je 94, p. 11.

531. BIBLE. O.T. Lamentations
"The Book of Lamentations" (Selections: 1-5, tr. by Susan Stewart). [DenQ] (29:1) Sum 94, p. 47-52.

532. BIBLE. O.T. Psalms
"The Psalms: A New Translation" (14, 51, 58, 88, 90, 131, 139, tr. by Eugene H. Peterson). [Image] (5) Spr 94, p. 21-28.

533. BICKEL, Claudia
"The Slickour of His Hair" (— Sharon Olds). [AntigR] (97) Spr 94, p. 38.

534. BICKERSTAFF, Patsy Ann
"Wildlife Hospital." [EngJ] (83:6) O 94, p. 76.

535. BIDAR, Trinidad
"Babysitting." [NowestR] (32:2) 94, p. 15.
"Drivin' with Ma." [Zyzzyva] (10:2) Sum 94, p. 64-66.
"Father of Snow." [Zyzzyva] (10:2) Sum 94, p. 62-63.

536. BIDART, Frank
"Catullus: Excrucior." [HarvardR] (Premier Issue) Spr 92, p. 47.
"A Coin for Joe, with the Image of a Horse, c.350-325 BC." [Antaeus] (75/76) Aut 94, p. 236.

537. BIDGOOD, Ruth
"Surrogates." [MalR] (107) Sum 94, p. 196.
"Sweetness (Trefeca Fawr)." [MalR] (107) Sum 94, p. 197.

538. BIEHL, Michael
"The Anniversary." [Image] (6) Sum 94, p. 75-76.
"Back in a California Supermarket." [Image] (6) Sum 94, p. 76-78.

"February." [Image] (6) Sum 94, p. 74-75.

539. BIELAWA, Michael J.
"The Day Gehrig Died, Again." [Spitball] (47) Sum 94, p. 88.

540. BIELE, Joelle
"Chinese Boxes." [PoetryNW] (35:1) Spr 94, p. 27-28.

541. BIEN, Jeff
"Poem on St. Laurent." [Descant] (25:3/4, #86/87) Fall-Wint 94, p. 58-60.

542. BIENEK, Horst
"Flight, in Vain" (Selections: 33, 35-36, tr. by Patricia Pollock Brodsky). [DenQ] (29:1) Sum 94, p. 53-54.

543. BIERDS, Linda
"The Air: Pasteur at Villeneuve l'Etang." [Journal] (18:1) Spr-Sum 94, p. 106-107.
"The Bats: Beethoven, 1810." [Journal] (18:1) Spr-Sum 94, p. 100-101.
"Held." [KenR] (NS 16:4) Fall 94, p. 28-29.
"Hunter." [MassR] (35:1) Spr 94, p. 43-44.
"The Iceland Spar." [Journal] (18:1) Spr-Sum 94, p. 102.
"It." [Field] (50) Spr 94, p. 47.
"Lautrec." [Journal] (18:1) Spr-Sum 94, p. 98-99.
"Memento of the Hours." [NewYorker] (70:15) 30 My 94, p. 67.
"Ne Plus Ultra — Thomas Wedgwood, 1771-1805." [Journal] (18:1) Spr-Sum 94, p. 103-105.
"Phantom Pain" (Josiah Wedgwood, 1795). [Field] (50) Spr 94, p. 49-50.
"The Reversals." [NewYorker] (70:31) 3 O 94, p. 108.
"Seizure." [Field] (50) Spr 94, p. 48.
"The Skater, 1775" (Susannah Wedgwood at Ten). [NewYorker] (70:38) 21 N 94, p. 89.
"Westray." [KenR] (NS 16:4) Fall 94, p. 27-28.
"Windows." [Atlantic] (274:5) N 94, p. 104.
"The Winter, 1748" (Erasmus Darwin, 1731-1802). [NewYorker] (70:38) 21 N 94, p. 88.

544. BIESPIEL, David
"Hideaway." [Zyzzyva] (10:2) Sum 94, p. 113.
"Ruth in the Fields" (two poems for my mother). [Zyzzyva] (10:2) Sum 94, p. 111.

545. BIG EAGLE, Duane
"New York Times in the Supermarket." [Callaloo] (17:1) Wint 94, p. 268-269.
"What I Carry Away." [ColR] (21:2) Fall 94, p. 152-153.

546. BILBROUGH, Paola
"On Angels." [MalR] (107) Sum 94, p. 175.

547. BILGERE, George
"Big Bang." [NewEngR] (16:2) Spr 94, p. 35-36.
"Laundromat." [NewEngR] (16:2) Spr 94, p. 36-37.
"Mastodon" (at the British Museum). [NewEngR] (16:2) Spr 94, p. 34-35.
"Splendor." [Field] (51) Fall 94, p. 100-103.

548. BILL, Jim
"Elegy for April." [Border] (5) Fall-Wint 94, p. 6.
"My Desert or Yours." [FreeL] (13) Spr 94, p. 13.

549. BILOTSERKIVETS, Natalka
"100 Years of Youth" (tr. by Michael M. Naydan). [Agni] (39) 94, p. 42.

550. BILYEU, Jody
"The Art of Bad Field Softball." [LaurelR] (28:1) Wint 94, p. 123-124.
"At the High School Choral Festival, May 1981" (for my mother). [QW] (39) Sum-Fall 94, p. 195.

551. BIRNEY, Dion
"First Death" (For Mildred Tibbetts Marsh). [BrooklynR] (11) 94, p. 14-15.

552. BISHOP, David A.
"Holiday at Normandy." [SmPd] (31:2, #91) Spr 94, p. 24.

553. BISHOP, Judith
"Beachcombing." [InterQ] (1:2) 93, p. 133.
"A Suite for Charles Blackman." [InterQ] (1:2) 93, p. 130-132.

554. BISHOP, Wendy
"Bwana Tembu" (after Isak Dinesen). [Border] (3) Fall 93, p. 4.
"Los Caballos." [EngJ] (83:7) N 94, p. 79.
"Shower." [EngJ] (83:3) Mr 94, p. 103.
"Thunderstorm" (Tsaile, Arizona). [CapeR] (29:1) Spr 94, p. 31.
"To Start My Father's Heart." [ColEng] (56:3) Mr 94, p. 317.

555. BISWAL, Manorama Mahapatra
"My Whole Life for Him" (tr. by Arlene Zide and J. P. Das). [InterQ] (1:2) 93, p. 177.
556. BITAR, Walid
"Andes From Strangers." [CutB] (41) Wint 94, p. 78-79.
"Our Lady of the Iguanas." [CutB] (41) Wint 94, p. 76-77.
557. BITNEY, Katharine
"Everything I Knew." [PraF] (15:2, #67) Sum 94, p. 93-94.
"A Prayer for Vernal Equinox." [PraF] (15:2, #67) Sum 94, p. 95.
558. BITTON, Erez
"A Bird Between Continents" (Selections: 10 poems, tr. by Ammiel Alcalay). [LitR] (37:2) Wint 94, p. 277-283.
559. BLACK, David
"Fish or Cut Bait." [DogRR] (13:1, #25) Spr-Sum 94, p. 9.
"Time Pieces." [BellArk] (10:5) S-O 94, p. 16.
560. BLACK, Ralph W.
"The Assassin." [GeoR] (48:1) Spr 94, p. 45-46.
561. BLACK, Sophie Cabot
"Against the Steep Side of Wind." [AmerV] (34) 94, p. 30.
"Angel." [Bomb] (47) Spr 94, p. 76.
"August." [Colum] (22) Wint 94, p. 15.
"Invisible Bride." [AmerV] (33) 94, p. 31.
"November." [Colum] (22) Wint 94, p. 160.
"Report from Nirvana." [Bomb] (47) Spr 94, p. 76.
"The Rest Area." [Bomb] (47) Spr 94, p. 76.
562. BLACKSHEAR, Helen
"The Hardware Store." [NegC] (14:1/2) 94, p. 153.
563. BLADES, Joe
"At Malagash." [Nimrod] (37:2) Spr-Sum 94, p. 4.
564. BLAGG, Krista
"212 Sewell Street." [ProseP] (3) 94, p. 15.
565. BLAIKLOCK, Noreen
"Grey Feather." [AnthNEW] (6) 94, p. 37.
566. BLAIR, Elizabeth
"Divided Light" (Selections: a 5-poem sequence from a collection about the Lewis and Clark expedition of 1804-1806). [Gaia] (4) Je 94, p. 15-17.
567. BLAIR, Guy
"Generations." [CreamCR] (18:1) Spr 94, p. 37-40.
568. BLAIR, John
"Mercy." [HampSPR] Wint 94, p. 21-22.
569. BLAIR, Peter
"Blossick After Work, January 17, 1991." [PoetryE] (37/38) Spr 94, p. 116.
"Monster Truck Show." [PoetryE] (37/38) Spr 94, p. 114-115.
"State of the Union, January 1991." [PoetryE] (37/38) Spr 94, p. 117.
BLAIS, Jean Ethier
See ETHIER-BLAIS, Jean
570. BLAKE, Rosemary
"Catechism." [AntigR] (97) Spr 94, p. 46.
571. BLAKE, Sarah
"Entrance" (for Nona). [HarvardR] (6) Spr 94, p. 81.
572. BLAKELY, Paul
"The Farthest Place." [PoetC] (26:1) Fall 94, p. 33.
573. BLAKER, Margaret
"Burial at Natchez, 1725." [AnthNEW] (6) 94, p. 7.
BLANC, Jean le
See LeBLANC, Jean
574. BLANCHARD, Eliza
"If I Wanted." [AntigR] (96) Wint 94, p. 91.
575. BLANCHARD, Len
"Cause for Dancing." [Outbr] (25) 94, p. 7-8.
"The Chum and I." [Outbr] (25) 94, p. 5-6.
"Life Cycle." [BellArk] (10:3 [i.e. 10:4]) Jl-Ag 94, p. 26.
"Life Provoking." [BellArk] (10:3) My-Je 94, p. 8.
"Love Like Water." [JamesWR] (11:5) Fall 94, p. 9.
"Meditation on a Suicide." [SmPd] (31:2, #91) Spr 94, p. 28.
"Sloughed Skin and Other Harvests." [Outbr] (25) 94, p. 3-4.

576. BLANDIANA, Ana
"Bisericile N-au Acoperisuri." [InterPR] (20:1) Spr 94, p. 24.
"The Churches Have No Roofs" (tr. by Eveline L. Kanes and Mihai Zaharia). [InterPR] (20:1) Spr 94, p. 25.
"The Father" (tr. by Eveline L. Kanes and Mihai Zaharia). [InterPR] (20:1) Spr 94, p. 33.
"Hell" (tr. by Eveline L. Kanes and Mihai Zaharia). [InterPR] (20:1) Spr 94, p. 31.
"Un Infern." [InterPR] (20:1) Spr 94, p. 30.
"Molecule de Calciu." [InterPR] (20:1) Spr 94, p. 26.
"Molecules of Calcium" (tr. by Eveline L. Kanes and Mihai Zaharia). [InterPR] (20:1) Spr 94, p. 27.
"Poem: Cine si ce sa viseze." [InterPR] (20:1) Spr 94, p. 34.
"Poem: Who can still dream, and of what" (tr. by Eveline L. Kanes and Mihai Zaharia). [InterPR] (20:1) Spr 94, p. 35.
"Psalm: Tu care ai invatat ursii sa doarma." [InterPR] (20:1) Spr 94, p. 28.
"Psalm: You who have taught bears" (tr. by Eveline L. Kanes and Mihai Zaharia). [InterPR] (20:1) Spr 94, p. 29.
"Tatal." [InterPR] (20:1) Spr 94, p. 32.

577. BLANKENSHIP, Bethany L.
"Autumn Apples." [SpiritSH] (59) 94, p. 28.
"The First Egg." [SpiritSH] (59) 94, p. 29.

578. BLASING, Randy
"At Length." [Poetry] (164:2) My 94, p. 78.
"The Birth" (tr. of Nazim Hikmet, w. Mutlu Konuk). [AmerPoR] (23:2) Mr-Ap 94, p. 37.
"Country Song." [SewanR] (102:3) Sum 94, p. 378.
"Last Letter to My Son" (tr. of Nazim Hikmet, w. Mutlu Konuk). [AmerPoR] (23:2) Mr-Ap 94, p. 38-39.
"The Mailman" (from Hungarian travel notes, tr. of Nazim Hikmet, w. Mutlu Konuk). [AmerPoR] (23:2) Mr-Ap 94, p. 38.
"One A.M." (tr. of Nazim Hikmet, w. Mutlu Konuk). [AmerPoR] (23:2) Mr-Ap 94, p. 37.
"Some Memories" (tr. of Nazim Hikmet, w. Mutlu Konuk). [AmerPoR] (23:2) Mr-Ap 94, p. 40-41.
"Thirty Years Ago" (tr. of Nazim Hikmet, w. Mutlu Konuk). [AmerPoR] (23:2) Mr-Ap 94, p. 41.
"To Samet Vurgun" (tr. of Nazim Hikmet, w. Mutlu Konuk). [AmerPoR] (23:2) Mr-Ap 94, p. 39.
"Visionary Company." [SewanR] (102:3) Sum 94, p. 377.
"Windows" (tr. of Nazim Hikmet, w. Mutlu Konuk). [AmerPoR] (23:2) Mr-Ap 94, p. 39-40.

579. BLATNER, Barbara
"The Pope in Space." [ApalQ] (40/41) 94, p. 54-57.

580. BLAUNER, Laurie
"Elegy for Burlesque." [QW] (38) Winter-Spr 93-94, p. 131.
"The Furniture of Thought." [AmerPoR] (23:3) My-Je 94, p. 46.
"Killing Time." [Poetry] (165:3) D 94, p. 146.
"The Person You've Never Kissed." [AmerPoR] (23:3) My-Je 94, p. 46.

581. BLAZEVIC, Neda Miranda
"Metaphor — Simulation" (tr. by Dasha Culic Nisula). [InterQ] (1:1) [93?], p. 120-121.

582. BLEHERT, Dean
"James Boswell." [Light] (11) Aut 94, p. 18.
"Samuel Johnson." [Light] (11) Aut 94, p. 18.
"The Worm Doesn't Know Which Way to Turn." [Light] (9) Spr 94, p. 18.

583. BLEOCA, Liviu
"Around the Fire" (tr. of Aurel Rau, w. Adam J. Sorkin). [HiramPoR] (55/56) Fall 93-Sum 94, p. 100.
"The Gift" (tr. of Aurel Rau, w. Adam J. Sorkin). [HiramPoR] (55/56) Fall 93-Sum 94, p. 99.
"Writing with a Ballpoint" (tr. of Aurel Rau, w. Adam J. Sorkin). [HiramPoR] (55/56) Fall 93-Sum 94, p. 101.

584. BLEVINS, Tippi N.
"Branded." [Amelia] (7:4, #23) 94, p. 114.

585. BLEVINS-CHURCH, Adrian
"The Man Who Went Out for Cigarettes." [Vis] (45) 94, p. 29.

"On the Island, Thinking of Home." [PaintedB] (53/54) 94, p. 91.
"Storm." [Plain] (15:1) Fall 94, p. 10-11.
"Swallows." [SouthernPR] (34:2) Wint 94, p. 69-70.

586. BLICKLEY, Mark
"Tangier." [Parting] (7:2) Wint 94-95, p. 25-27.

587. BLITCH, Lynn
"Condolences to God." [NegC] (14:1/2) 94, p. 139.
"The Harrowed Don't Talk." [NegC] (14:1/2) 94, p. 140.

588. BLOCH, Chana
"Alone on the Mountain" (on my birthday). [SantaBR] (1:1) Spr-Sum 93, p. 65.
"Crossing the Table." [SantaBR] (1:1) Spr-Sum 93, p. 64.
"Crying at the Movies." [Field] (50) Spr 94, p. 34.
"Day-Blind." [SantaBR] (1:1) Spr-Sum 93, p. 66.
"The Family." [SantaBR] (1:1) Spr-Sum 93, p. 62.
"How Pain Gets Passed Around." [Field] (50) Spr 94, p. 36.
"Practicing" (for Benjamin, prestissimo). [SantaBR] (1:1) Spr-Sum 93, p. 63.
"Self-Portrait at Eleven-Thirty P.M." [Field] (50) Spr 94, p. 35.

589. BLOCH, Talia
"Zwischen (Between)." [SycamoreR] (6:2) Sum 94, p. 50.

590. BLOCK, Laurie
"Downhill From Here" (3rd Place, 1994 Poetry Contest). [Dandel] (21:1) 94, p. 7-8.

591. BLOCK, Ron
"Cartoon Noire from The Twilight Drive-In." [AnotherCM] (28) 94, p. 24.
"Shame." [NoDaQ] (62:1) Wint 94-95, p. 15-16.

592. BLOMAIN, Karen
"Husband." [AnthNEW] (6) 94, p. 13.

593. BLOOM, Ronna
"The Chairs." [AntigR] (99) Aut 94, p. 102.
"Landlady." [AntigR] (99) Aut 94, p. 103.

594. BLOOMENSTEIN, Ellen P.
"In the Made for TV Movie." [Sonora] (28) Fall 94, p. 26.

595. BLOOMFIELD, Lisa
"Untitled Biographer." [SantaBR] (1:1) Spr-Sum 93, p. 60-61.

596. BLOOMFIELD, Maureen
"La Grande Châsse." [ParisR] (36:131) Sum 94, p. 94.
"Postulant." [ParisR] (36:131) Sum 94, p. 95-96.

597. BLOSSOM, Laurel
"Baboon Liver Transplant Poem." [ParisR] (36:130) Spr 94, p. 252-253.

598. BLOUNT, Roy, Jr.
"There Once Was a Lady Who Did, and Other 'Do-Me Feminist' (I Believe the Expression Is) Limericks." [Antaeus] (75/76) Aut 94, p. 333-341.

599. BLUESTONE, Stephen
"Anniversary Song." [BostonR] (19:6) D-Ja 94-95, p. 28.
"Beethoven Does Not Lie Here" (Franz Schubert's last words). [BostonR] (19:6) D-Ja 94-95, p. 28.
"A Circumstance of the Porch." [BostonR] (19:6) D-Ja 94-95, p. 28.
"First Voices." [BostonR] (19:6) D-Ja 94-95, p. 28.
"Thomson's Gazelle." [BostonR] (19:6) D-Ja 94-95, p. 28.

600. BLUGER, Marianne
"After Stein." [PoetryC] (14:3) My 94, p. 5.
"Blessé." [PoetryC] (14:3) My 94, p. 5.

601. BLUM, Anne Marie
"On a Line from Carolyn Forche." [Vis] (44) 94, p. 5.

602. BLUM, Ray
"Pollock." [SmPd] (31:2, #91) Spr 94, p. 8.

603. BLUMENREICH, Julia
"When He Died" (to H.T.). [Chain] (1) Spr-Sum 94, p. 145-147.

604. BLUMENTHAL, Jay
"The Homecoming." [Jacaranda] (4:2) Spr 90, p. 76-77.
"'The Red Roofs' of Pissarro." [Jacaranda] (4:2) Spr 90, p. 77.

605. BLUMENTHAL, Michael
"The Accountant" (For Don Jamieson & Leslie Epstein). [Poetry] (164:3) Je 94, p. 152.
"The Forces." [Poetry] (164:3) Je 94, p. 150.
"Never to Have Loved a Child." [Poetry] (164:3) Je 94, p. 151.

"A Poem for Catherine Ann Heaney" (To accompany a fossil fish ... from the Harvard Museum of Comparative Zoology). [HarvardR] (Premier Issue) Spr 92, p. 70.

606. BLY, Robert
"After My Father's Funeral." [Field] (50) Spr 94, p. 15.
"The Boy Who Had One Thought." [ProseP] (3) 94, p. 17.
"The Buried Train." [Nat] (259:12) O 17 94, p. 431.
"The Cuckoo" (tr. of Tomas Tranströmer). [Field] (50) Spr 94, p. 101.
"The Dispersed Woman" (tr. of Pedro Salinas). [HarvardR] (6) Spr 94, p. 165.
"Early Morning." [Boulevard] (9:3, #27) Fall 94, p. 66.
"Early Morning." [Image] (8) Wint 94-95, p. 84.
"His Hair" (tr. of Mirabai). [HarvardR] (6) Spr 94, p. 113.
"The Kingdom of Uncertainty" (tr. of Tomas Tranströmer). [Field] (50) Spr 94, p. 100.
"Letter to James Wright." [GettyR] (7:4) Aut 94, p. 559.
"The Life of Samson." [GettyR] (7:4) Aut 94, p. 562.
"Marie." [Image] (8) Wint 94-95, p. 84.
"Melancholy inside Families" (tr. of Pablo Neruda, w. James Wright). [Field] (51) Fall 94, p. 8-9.
"The New Animal." [Sun] (223) Jl 94, p. 19.
"Nudging a Poem." [PlumR] (7) [94?], p. 40.
"The Pine Cone." [ProseP] (3) 94, p. 16.
"Robert Frost and His Enemies." [HarvardR] (6) Spr 94, p. 33.
"St. George, the Dragon, and the Virgin" (A sculpture made by Bernt Notke in 1489 for the Stockholm Cathedral). [GettyR] (7:4) Aut 94, p. 560-561.
"Standing by the Road." [Sun] (223) Jl 94, p. 19.
"That Story." [Boulevard] (9:3, #27) Fall 94, p. 65.
"Things My Brother and I could Do" (For W.S.). [DarkMoon] (1) 94, p. 3.
"Thoughts in the Cabin." [KenR] (NS 16:1) Wint 94, p. 97.
"Where We meet." [DarkMoon] (1) 94, p. 4.

607. BLYTH, Steven J.
"Highlands." [Verse] (11:1) Spr 94, p. 118.

608. BOBES, Marilyn
"Dangers of Speaking and Staying Quiet. Language of Silence" (based on a poem of Francisco de Quevedo, tr. by Ruth Behar). [MichQR] (33:3) Sum 94, p. 541.

609. BOBROWSKI, Johannes
"Holderlin in Tubingen" (tr. by Mark Rudman). [Pequod] (37) 94, p. 128.
"In the Torrent" (tr. by Mark Rudman). [Pequod] (37) 94, p. 129.

610. BOCCIA, Michael
"One More Round." [LitR] (37:4) Sum 94, p. 572.

BOCK, Kristan
See BOCK, Kristin L.

611. BOCK, Kristin L.
"The Local Brothel." [NewYorkQ] (53) 94, p. 78.
"They Still Stink of Bleach." [Dandel] (21:1) 94, p. 40-41.

612. BOCK, Lee Walker
"August Morning." [RagMag] (12:1) Sum 94, p. 48.

613. BODEEN, Jim
"At the Council of Churches Meeting on Just War My Townspeople Speak Up." [CrabCR] (8:2/3/9:1/2/3) 94, p. 47.

614. BODO, Murray
"The Earth Moves at Midnight" (for my mother). [WestHR] (48:1) Spr 94, p. 92.

615. BOE, Marilyn J.
"Cod Liver Oil." [PoetryE] (37/38) Spr 94, p. 11.

616. BOEHM, S.
"The Bear." [HiramPoR] (55/56) Fall 93-Sum 94, p. 13.

617. BOGEN, Don
"Among Appliances." [ParisR] (36:133) Wint 94, p. 114-115.

618. BOGEN, Laurel Ann
"Cold, Cold, Cold." [ChironR] (13:3) Aut 94, p. 8.
"For B.B. King, My 44th Birthday and You, Too." [ChironR] (13:3) Aut 94, p. 8.
"Wings / That Which Takes Fight" (for Raymond Levin and Tom Mauldin). [ChironR] (13:3) Aut 94, p. 8.

619. BOGGAN, Larry
"McKinley County Jail, 1989." [ClockR] (9:1/2) 94-95, p. 105.

620. BOGIN, Magda
"On the Edge of Pleasure" (tr. of Rosario Castellanos). [Calyx] (15:2) Sum 94, p. 34-35.
621. BOGIN, Nina
"Going Up the Hudson After Twenty Years." [Poetry] (164:6) S 94, p. 316.
"Halabja." [Hudson] (47:2) Sum 94, p. 257.
"Inside the Chimney." [Hudson] (47:2) Sum 94, p. 255-256.
"March 1992." [Hudson] (47:2) Sum 94, p. 258.
"Yugoslavia in Ruins." [Hudson] (47:2) Sum 94, p. 256-257.
622. BOHANAN, Audrey
"Speaking from the Wings." [Boulevard] (9:3, #27) Fall 94, p. 141-142.
623. BOHANNON, J. P.
"A Thing on Paper." [SantaBR] (2:1) Spr-Sum 94, p. 73.
BOIS, Melanie du
See Du BOIS, Melanie
624. BOISSEAU, Michelle
"Auld Lang Syne." [Journal] (18:1) Spr-Sum 94, p. 57-58.
"Blood Sonata." [Journal] (18:1) Spr-Sum 94, p. 59-61.
"Cardinality." [GettyR] (7:1) Wint 94, p. 140-141.
"Likeness." [CreamCR] (18:2) Fall 94, p. 104-113.
625. BOKOVEC, Vera
"The Skeleton of A Whale" (tr. of Jaroslav Seifert). [Vis] (45) 94, p. 32-33.
626. BOLAND, Eavan
"Anna Liffey." [AmerPoR] (23:2) Mr-Ap 94, p. 25-27.
"The Black Lace Fan My Mother Gave Me." [AmerPoR] (23:2) Mr-Ap 94, p. 31.
"The Black Lace Fan My Mother Gave Me." [QW] (38) Winter-Spr 93-94, p. 185-186.
"In a Bad Light." [PartR] (61:1) Wint 94, p. 154-155.
"Love." [NewYorker] (69:45) 10 Ja 94, p. 56.
"Story." [QW] (38) Winter-Spr 93-94, p. 138-139.
"The Water Clock." [NewYorker] (70:9) 18 Ap 94, p. 63.
"We Are the Only Animals That Do This." [SenR] (24:1) Spr 94, p. 14-16.
"What Language Did." [KenR] (NS 16:1) Wint 94, p. 1-2.
"What We Lost." [Jacaranda] (5:1) Wint-Spr 91, p. 38-39.
"A Woman Painted on a Leaf." [YaleR] (82:1) Ja 94, p. 82-83.
627. BOLI, Todd
"The March of Extinctions." [PartR] (61:1) Wint 94, p. 157.
"The Veneration of Relics." [PartR] (61:1) Wint 94, p. 157.
628. BOLING, Lucy
"In Bird Light." [AntR] (52:4) Fall 94, p. 608-609.
629. BOLLS, Imogene
"Blue-Pox." [ClockR] (9:1/2) 94-95, p. 81.
"Incense of Apple." [SoDakR] (32:2) Sum 94, p. 75.
"Just a Thought." [SoDakR] (32:2) Sum 94, p. 76.
"Stone People." [ClockR] (9:1/2) 94-95, p. 79.
"Such Pure Light." [ClockR] (9:1/2) 94-95, p. 82.
"This Poem Is My House." [ClockR] (9:1/2) 94-95, p. 80.
630. BOLSTER, Stephanie
"25 April 1856." [CapilR] (2:12) Wint 94, p. 6-7.
"Alice's Adventures under Ground." [CanLit] (141) Sum 94, p. 52-53.
"Alice's Socks." [CanLit] (141) Sum 94, p. 54.
"Derivations." [CapilR] (2:12) Wint 94, p. 10-11.
"Half-Sick of Shadows." [CapilR] (2:12) Wint 94, p. 14.
"In Which Alice Visits Pacific Rim National Park." [CanLit] (141) Sum 94, p. 53-54.
"The Real Alice." [CapilR] (2:12) Wint 94, p. 15-16.
"The Scream" (After the painting by Edvard Munch, 1893). [Grain] (22:1) Sum 94, p. 63.
"To Susanna: with Belated Consolations." [CapilR] (2:12) Wint 94, p. 12-13.
"Vortex." [CapilR] (2:12) Wint 94, p. 5.
"Whichever Rabbit." [CapilR] (2:12) Wint 94, p. 8-9.
631. BOLT, Thomas
"Wedgwood." [SouthwR] (79:4) Aut 94, p. 683-690.
632. BOLTON, Joe
"Resurrections" (tr. of Julio Florez). [NewRena] (9:1, #27) 94, p. 37.
"The Sleeping Garden" (To Jose Vasconcelos, tr. of Enrique González Martínez). [NewRena] (9:1, #27) 94, p. 35.

"Study" (Fragment, tr. of Joaquín González Camargo). [NewRena] (9:1, #27) 94, p. 39.

633. BOMBA, Bernard
"Miserere in the Shrouds." [SouthernPR] (34:2) Wint 94, p. 41.
"Wish" (for a young friend's marriage). [Outbr] (25) 94, p. 9.

634. BONCHO (?-1714)
Haiku [AmerPoR] (23:4) Jl-Ag 94, p. 18.

635. BOND, Bruce
"Confederate Dead." [SewanR] (102:3) Sum 94, p. 379-380.

636. BOND, Joan
"Crows." [Dandel] (21:1) 94, p. 39.
"He Keeps Her." [AntigR] (99) Aut 94, p. 47.
"Mr. Stewart, the Banker." [Dandel] (21:1) 94, p. 38.

637. BONDS, Diane S.
"Eclipse." [ClockR] (9:1/2) 94-95, p. 139.

638. BONNEFOY, Yves
"De Natura Rerum" (tr. by Lisa Sapinkopf). [HarvardR] (2) Fall 92, p. 155.
"Psyché and the Palace of Love" (tr. by Lisa Sapinkopf). [BostonR] (19:1) Fe-Mr 94, p. 17.
"True Name" (tr. by Barbara Adams). [PoetryE] (37/38) Spr 94, p. 215.
"Wind and Smoke" (tr. by John Naughton). [GrahamHR] (18) Wint 94-95, p. 7-11.

639. BONTOGON, Eric
"Black Night" (Surfacing 2). [WestCL] (28:1/2, #13/14) Spr-Fall 94, p. 199.

640. BOOKER, Stephen Todd
"Faith." [BlackWR] (20:2) Spr-Sum 94, p. 23.
"The Pied-Piper of Murderloin Downs." [KenR] (NS 16:1) Wint 94, p. 101.
"Sandii." [KenR] (NS 16:1) Wint 94, p. 102-104.
"To the Owner of a Pet." [Confr] (54/55) Fall 94-Wint 95, p. 311.

641. BOOKEY, Ted
"Bad Luck Bird" (tr. of Erich Kastner). [Vis] (44) 94, p. 8.
"May" (tr. of Erich Kastner). [Vis] (44) 94, p. 8-9.

642. BOOTH, Philip
"Again." [DenQ] (28:4) Spr 94, p. 13.
"Backcountry." [AmerPoR] (23:5) S-O 94, p. 15.
"First Night." [BelPoJ] (44:4) Sum 94, p. 18.
"First Song." [BelPoJ] (44:4) Sum 94, p. 18.
"Fog-Talk." [AmerPoR] (23:5) S-O 94, p. 14.
"Half-Life." [AmerPoR] (23:5) S-O 94, p. 15.
"Lightly." [DenQ] (28:4) Spr 94, p. 14.
"Sentences." [AmerPoR] (23:5) S-O 94, p. 15.
"Seventy." [BelPoJ] (44:4) Sum 94, p. 18.
"Sixty-Six." [AmerPoR] (23:5) S-O 94, p. 14.
"Talk About Walking." [AmerPoR] (23:5) S-O 94, p. 15.
"Three Awakenings in New England." [NewEngR] (16:3) Sum 94, p. 100-101.

643. BORAN, Pat
"Passport." [NoDaQ] (62:4) Fall 94-95, p. 140.

644. BORDAO, Rafael
"Corona del Desterrado." [Nuez] (5:13/14/15) 94, p. 55.
"De la Caida." [Luz] (6) My 94, p. 32.
"Del Devenir." [Luz] (6) My 94, p. 33.
"Himno al Follaje." [Nuez] (5:13/14/15) 94, p. 41.
"Pájaros Insomnes." [Nuez] (5:13/14/15) 94, p. 54.
"Postrimeria de la Eternidad." [Luz] (6) My 94, p. 31.
"El Robo de la Libertad." [Nuez] (5:13/14/15) 94, p. 54.

645. BORDISNE, Eva
"Ecclesiastes Ch. 1, V. 9" (tr. of Sandor Knayadi, w. Len Roberts). [Boulevard] (9:3, #27) Fall 94, p. 138-139.

646. BORDWELL, Harold
"Chacun à Son Goût." [Light] (11) Aut 94, p. 18.
"A Thoroughly Disgusting Dream." [Light] (11) Aut 94, p. 21.

647. BORG, Shannon
"After the Earthquake, You Left California." [PoetryNW] (35:3) Aut 94, p. 25.
"One Version of a Summer Night." [WillowS] (34) Sum 94, p. 57.
"When We Lived Above Star Plumbing Supply and Wanted to See the Ocean." [PoetryNW] (35:3) Aut 94, p. 24.

648. BORGES, Jorge Luis
"1972" (tr. by Robert Mezey). [AmerPoR] (23:1) Ja-F 94, p. 26.
"A Francia." [SoCoast] (17) Je 94, p. 22.
"Adrogué" (tr. by Robert Mezey and Richard Barnes). [Descant] (25:1, #84) Spr 94, p. 65-66.
"Alexander Selkirk" (tr. by Robert Mezey). [Descant] (25:1, #84) Spr 94, p. 61.
"Alexander Selkirk" (tr. by Robert Mezey). [WestHR] (48:3) Fall 94, p. 234.
"Blake" (tr. by Robert Mezey). [AmerPoR] (23:1) Ja-F 94, p. 25.
"Einar Tambarskelver (Heimskringla, I, 117)" (tr. by Robert Mezey). [AmerPoR] (23:1) Ja-F 94, p. 29.
"Elegy for a Park" (tr. by Robert Mezey). [NewYRB] (41:21) 22 D 94, p. 22.
"Elvira de Alvear" (tr. by Robert Mezey). [AmerPoR] (23:1) Ja-F 94, p. 25.
"Endymion on Latmos" (tr. by Robert Mezey and Richard Barnes). [Descant] (25:1, #84) Spr 94, p. 67-68.
"The Engraving" (tr. by Robert Mezey). [PartR] (61:4) Fall 94, p. 631.
"The Enigmas" (tr. by Robert Mezey and Richard Barnes). [Agni] (40) 94, p. 119.
"Flowing or Being" (tr. by Robert Mezey and Richard Barnes). [Agni] (40) 94, p. 121.
"Fragments of an Apocryphal Evangelist" (12 selections, tr. by Robert Mezey). [Poetry] (164:2) My 94, p. 72.
"G. A. Bürger" (in Spanish). [SoCoast] (17) Je 94, p. 24.
"G. A. Bürger" (tr. by Robert Mezey). [SoCoast] (17) Je 94, p. 25.
"Góngora" (tr. by Richard Barnes). [WestHR] (48:3) Fall 94, p. 235.
"Hengist Wants Men (449 A.D.)" (tr. by Robert Mezey). [AmerPoR] (23:1) Ja-F 94, p. 29.
"*Inferno*, V, 129" (tr. by Robert Mezey and Richard Barnes). [AmerPoR] (23:1) Ja-F 94, p. 27.
"Invocation to Joyce" (tr. by Richard Barnes). [AmerPoR] (23:1) Ja-F 94, p. 28.
"Luke XXIII" (tr. by Robert Mezey and Richard Barnes). [Agni] (40) 94, p. 120.
"Matthew XXV, 30" (tr. by Robert Mezey and Richard Barnes). [AmerPoR] (23:1) Ja-F 94, p. 27.
"Matthew XXV, 30" (tr. by Robert Mezey and Richard Barnes). [Descant] (25:1, #84) Spr 94, p. 74.
"Metaphors of the Thousand and One Nights" (tr. by Robert Mezey). [Descant] (25:1, #84) Spr 94, p. 72-73.
"Metaphors of the Thousand and One Nights" (tr. by Robert Mezey). [WestHR] (48:3) Fall 94, p. 236-237.
"Mexico" (tr. by Robert Mezey). [Thrpny] (56) Wint 94, p. 30.
"The Mirror" (tr. by Robert Mezey). [AmerPoR] (23:1) Ja-F 94, p. 25.
"Museum" (tr. by Robert Mezey). [PartR] (61:4) Fall 94, p. 631-632.
"Nineteen Twenty-something" (tr. by Robert Mezey). [AmerPoR] (23:1) Ja-F 94, p. 25.
"The Odyssey, Book XXIII" (tr. by Robert Mezey and Richard Barnes). [AmerPoR] (23:1) Ja-F 94, p. 27.
"On His Blindness" (tr. by Robert Mezey). [Poetry] (164:2) My 94, p. 71.
"The Other" (tr. by Robert Mezey). [WestHR] (48:3) Fall 94, p. 233.
"Rain" (tr. by Richard Barnes). [AmerPoR] (23:1) Ja-F 94, p. 25.
"La Recoleta" (tr. by Robert Mezey and Richard Barnes). [AmerPoR] (23:1) Ja-F 94, p. 28.
"Ricardo Güiraldes" (tr. by Robert Mezey). [Descant] (25:1, #84) Spr 94, p. 64.
"Saturdays" (To C.G., tr. by Robert Mezey). [AmerPoR] (23:1) Ja-F 94, p. 26.
"The Suicide" (tr. by Richard Barnes). [OhioR] (52) 94, p. 76.
"The Suicide" (tr. by Sandra Maley). [PlumR] (7) [94?], p. 67.
"Swords" (tr. by Robert Mezey and Richard Barnes). [Descant] (25:1, #84) Spr 94, p. 69.
"Tamerlane (1336-1405)" (tr. by Robert Mezey). [Descant] (25:1, #84) Spr 94, p. 62-63.
"Tankas" (tr. by Richard Barnes). [Descant] (25:1, #84) Spr 94, p. 70-71.
"To France" (tr. by Robert Mezey). [SoCoast] (17) Je 94, p. 23.
"To Francisco López Merino" (tr. by Robert Mezey). [AmerPoR] (23:1) Ja-F 94, p. 26.
"To Manuel Mujica Lainez" (tr. by Robert Mezey and Richard Barnes). [AmerPoR] (23:1) Ja-F 94, p. 26.
"To the One Reading Me" (tr. by Robert Mezey). [Descant] (25:1, #84) Spr 94, p. 60.
"Ein Traum" (tr. by Richard Barnes). [AmerPoR] (23:1) Ja-F 94, p. 27.

"The Unending Rose" (to Susana Bombal, tr. by Sandra Maley). [PlumR] (7) [94?], p. 66.

649. BORINSKY, Alicia
"Canción de los Amantes Suicidas." [InterQ] (1:4) 94, p. 28.
"Estaciones." [InterQ] (1:4) 94, p. 29.
"Seasons" (tr. by Cola Franzen). [InterQ] (1:4) 94, p. 29.
"Song of the Suicidal Lovers" (tr. by Cola Franzen). [InterQ] (1:4) 94, p. 28.

650. BORISOV, Georgi
"And When the Winter Wind Rushed Straight into My Heart" (tr. by Lisa Sapinkopf and Georgi Belev). [InterQ] (1:1) [93?], p. 86.

651. BORKHUIS, Charles
"Corpse and Counting." [CentralP] (23) Spr 94, p. 133-135.
"Inside Language." [Talisman] (13) Fall 94-Wint 95, p. 4-6.

652. BORKOVEC, Vera
"Poetry" (tr. of Libuse Cacalová). [HampSPR] Wint 94, p. 38.
"Summer Afternoon" (tr. of Libuse Cacalová). [HampSPR] Wint 94, p. 39.

653. BORN, Anne
"A Recollection from 1967" (tr. of Henrik Nordbrandt). [ProseP] (3) 94, p. 70.
"The Train" (tr. of Henrik Nordbrandt). [ProseP] (3) 94, p. 69.

654. BOROWSKI, Tadeusz
"The Sun of Auschwitz" (tr. by Rafferty, Meryl, Natchez, Pioro). [NewEngR] (16:2) Spr 94, p. 151-152.

655. BORRERO, Antonia
"Rice Is My Name." [CaribbeanW] (8) 94, p. 56-57.

656. BORSON, Roo
"Among the Vines." [PoetryC] (14:2) Mr 94, p. 6.
"Everyone Dies." [PoetryC] (14:2) Mr 94, p. 6.
"Happiness in the Great Lakes." [PoetryC] (14:2) Mr 94, p. 7.
"A Kind of Song." [Nimrod] (37:2) Spr-Sum 94, p. 5.
"Milk." [PoetryC] (14:2) Mr 94, p. 7.
"Sleep in the Afternoon." [Nimrod] (37:2) Spr-Sum 94, p. 6.
"Vocation." [Nimrod] (37:2) Spr-Sum 94, p. 7.
"Whuff." [Nimrod] (37:2) Spr-Sum 94, p. 7.
"With March." [PoetryC] (14:2) Mr 94, p. 7.

657. BORUCH, Marianne
"At the Watercolor Gallery." [NewEngR] (16:4) Fall 94, p. 16.
"By the Sea." [NewEngR] (16:4) Fall 94, p. 18.
"Cello." [AmerV] (35) 94, p. 94.
"Crushed Birds." [NewEngR] (16:4) Fall 94, p. 15.
"Flowers." [AmerV] (35) 94, p. 95.
"Hospital Greenhouse." [Field] (51) Fall 94, p. 79.
"I Notice on My Walk." [Field] (51) Fall 94, p. 80.
"In the Street, Men Working." [NewEngR] (16:4) Fall 94, p. 17.
"Lament." [Field] (51) Fall 94, p. 77-78.
"Late Winter Fog." [Boulevard] (9:3, #27) Fall 94, p. 140.
"Nesting Boxes." [AmerV] (35) 94, p. 91.
"Sewing." [NewEngR] (16:4) Fall 94, p. 19.
"Snow Falling." [AmerV] (35) 94, p. 93.
"Stained Glass Windows." [AmerV] (35) 94, p. 92.
"The Vietnam Birthday Lottery, 1970." [GeoR] (48:4) Wint 94, p. 656-657.

658. BORUN-JAGODZINSKA, Katarzyna
"My Name Is Jocasta" (tr. by Kathleen Snodgrass, w. Justyna Kostkowska). [ArtfulD] (26/27) 94, p. 22.
"A Patriotic Song" (tr. by Kathleen Snodgrass, w. Justyna Kostkowska). [ArtfulD] (26/27) 94, p. 21.

659. BORVICK, Yonina
"Aliza Says" (tr. of Bracha Serri). [LitR] (37:2) Wint 94, p. 337-338.
"And As Far As What I Wanted" (tr. of Amira Hess). [LitR] (37:2) Wint 94, p. 306.
"And to Return, Who Is a Jew?" (tr. of Bracha Serri). [LitR] (37:2) Wint 94, p. 338-339.
"The History of Literature: Poets" (tr. of Lev Hakak). [LitR] (37:2) Wint 94, p. 311.
"I Am the Daughter of Lot" (tr. of Bracha Serri). [LitR] (37:2) Wint 94, p. 335.
"Poem Contemplating Poets" (tr. of Lev Hakak). [LitR] (37:2) Wint 94, p. 312.
"Wife of Lot" (tr. of Bracha Serri). [LitR] (37:2) Wint 94, p. 336-337.

660. BOS, Gerard A.
"Old Grayton Beach." [NegC] (14:1/2) 94, p. 39.

"Seaside, Florida." [NegC] (14:1/2) 94, p. 40.

661. BOSCH, Daniel

"Dear Mom." [Agni] (40) 94, p. 159-160.
"Erato in Hollywood." [Agni] (40) 94, p. 161.
"For Paul." [PraS] (68:1) Spr 94, p. 81-82.
"The Prodigal: At the Buffet." [HarvardR] (2) Fall 92, p. 159.
"Sleeping Standing Up." [PraS] (68:1) Spr 94, p. 80-81.

662. BOSCO, Monique

"Folles Amoureuses." [Os] (38) Spr 94, p. 9.
"Langue Première." [Os] (38) Spr 94, p. 9.
"Minotaure." [Os] (38) Spr 94, p. 8.
"Sans Honte Ni Pudeur." [Os] (38) Spr 94, p. 8.
"Tapis Verts." [Os] (38) Spr 94, p. 10.

663. BOSS, Todd Ryan

"After Her Bath." [RagMag] (12:1) Sum 94, p. 91.
"Echo." [RagMag] (12:1) Sum 94, p. 88-89.
"I Could Have Written It." [RagMag] (12:1) Sum 94, p. 87.
"In His Best Suit." [RagMag] (12:1) Sum 94, p. 92.
"Ironing Board." [MidwQ] (35:4) Sum 94, p. 405.
"The Night We Stayed Up." [RagMag] (12:1) Sum 94, p. 90.

664. BOSSELAAR, Laure-Anne

"Genesis" (tr. of Herman de Coninck, w. Kurt Brown). [MassR] (35:1) Spr 94, p. 104.
"Leek Street" (For Jay Schneiders, killed in the Six-Day War and identified by the numbers on his arm). [InterQ] (1:1) [93?], p. 26-27.
"Paris, May 1st" (in the Jewish war memorial, tr. of Herman de Coninck, w. Kurt Brown). [MassR] (35:1) Spr 94, p. 103.
"The Plural of Happiness" (Excerpt, tr. of Herman de Coninck, w. Kurt Brown). [MassR] (35:1) Spr 94, p. 104.

BOSSENCE, S. Chapman

See CHAPMAN-BOSSENCE, S.

665. BOSVELD, Jennifer

"Her English Mays and Junes in Cornwall." [NegC] (14:1/2) 94, p. 162.
"Loving War." [NegC] (14:1/2) 94, p. 159-161.

666. BOTKIN, Nancy

"Mother." [SlipS] (14) 94, p. 44.

667. BOTTOMS, David

"Free Grace at Rose Hill" (for Martin Bresnick). [SouthernR] (30:4) Aut 94, p. 768-769.
"Heron Blues" (a Monty Dolack poster). [SouthernR] (30:4) Aut 94, p. 769-770.
"Home Maintenance." [Poetry] (165:2) N 94, p. 68.
"Homebuyer." [Poetry] (165:2) N 94, p. 69.
"Night Company." [InterQ] (1:4) 94, p. 106.
"Sleepless Nights." [SouthernR] (30:4) Aut 94, p. 770-771.
"Warbler at Howell's Drive-In." [Poetry] (165:2) N 94, p. 70.

668. BOUCHERON, Robert

"Corydon." [Hellas] (5:1) Spr-Sum 94, p. 49-51.

669. BOUCK, Laurie

"Brown Bat Huddled on My Shoulder Confesses." [Caliban] (14) 94, p. 138-139.

670. BOURASSA, Sylvie

"A Day at the All Saints' Café" (For Rippon, Gerry, Jahmel, Mehdi, Bob and Benoit who all earned their wings). [Grain] (22:1) Sum 94, p. 93-94.

671. BOURKE, Lawrence

"Driving to Kosciusko, Away from Academics." [MalR] (107) Sum 94, p. 84.
"The Manawatu." [MalR] (107) Sum 94, p. 82-83.

672. BOURNE, Daniel

"As If Franz Kafka Were a Great Southern Writer." [ClockR] (9:1/2) 94-95, p. 133.
"My Stomach" (tr. of Ryszard Holzer). [NewRena] (9:1, #27) 94, p. 149.
"The Possession." [NoDaQ] (62:1) Wint 94-95, p. 95.
"The Surpise" (tr. of Ryszard Holzer). [NewRena] (9:1, #27) 94, p. 147.
"The Weak." [SoCaR] (27:1/2) Fall 94-Spr 95, p. 3.

673. BOUVARD, Marguerite

"Waking." [SouthernHR] (28:4) Fall 94, p. 379.

674. BOWDAN, Janet

"Snell's Limbs and Braces." [NewDeltaR] (10:2) Spr-Sum 93, p. 27-28.
"Telling Them Louisiana Is Water." [NewDeltaR] (10:2) Spr-Sum 93, p. 28-29.

675. BOWEN, Kevin
"A Conical Hat" (for Le Cao Dai and Vu Giang Hung). [HayF] (14) Spr-Sum 94, p. 33-34.
"The Quiet Americans" (for To Nhuan Vy). [Ploughs] (20:1) Spr 94, p. 143.
676. BOWEN, Nancy K.
"Ice Skating." [SouthernPR] (34:1) Sum 94, p. 20-21.
"Tangles." [TarRP] (33:2) Spr 94, p. 25.
677. BOWERING, George
"Summer 1964. Mexico." [CanLit] (142/143) Fall-Wint 94, p. 182.
678. BOWERING, Marilyn
"How Were the People Made?" (in which the author replies to the Bible, Darwin and Mr. Emery, her grade six school teacher). [MalR] (108) Fall 94, p. 5-16.
"Now the Horses Come Out." [PoetryC] (14:4) S 94, p. 4.
"When I Speak to You." [PoetryC] (14:4) S 94, p. 4.
"You Paint the Dark Walls." [PoetryC] (14:4) S 94, p. 4.
679. BOWERS, Cathy Smith
"For the Body." [NewEngR] (16:4) Fall 94, p. 106-107.
"Snow." [GeoR] (48:4) Wint 94, p. 722.
"Women Dancing with Babies on Their Hips." [SouthernPR] (34:2) Wint 94, p. 24.
680. BOWERS, Cherie
"Spam." [EvergreenC] (9:1) Wint-Spr 94, p. 33-34.
681. BOWERS, Neal
"The Ladder in the Graveyard." [SouthernHR] (28:1) Wint 94, p. 44.
"Making It Up." [Poetry] (165:3) D 94, p. 151.
"Memories of Love." [SewanR] (102:4) Fall 94, p. 537-538.
"The Music Never Gets Any Older." [Poetry] (165:3) D 94, p. 150.
"Party Postmortem." [Poetry] (165:3) D 94, p. 150-151.
"RSVP" (Excerpt). [AmerS] (63:4) Aut 94, p. 547.
"Seized by the Days." [Poetry] (165:3) D 94, p. 149.
"Shared Stars" (for Nancy). [SouthernHR] (28:2) Spr 94, p. 168.
"Tenth-Year Elegy" (Excerpt). [AmerS] (63:4) Aut 94, p. 546.
682. BOWLES, Brad
"Beware the Random Scratchings." [CumbPR] (13:2) Spr 94, p. 16.
"Fifty Eyes." [CumbPR] (13:2) Spr 94, p. 17.
683. BOWLING, Tim
"Sturgeon." [Arc] (33) Fall 94, p. 8-11.
BOX, Annette le
See LeBOX, Annette
684. BOYCE, Charles
"Gloucester Near Winter." [SmPd] (31:1, #90) Wint 94, p. 32.
685. BOYCE, Pleuke
"Angels" (tr. of Adriaan Morrien). [Quarry] (43:1) Je 94, p. 24-25.
"In the Other" (tr. of Ed Leeflang). [Quarry] (43:1) Je 94, p. 28.
"Letters to Leporello" (tr. of Ed Leeflang). [Quarry] (43:1) Je 94, p. 29-30.
"Longing to Fly" (tr. of Adriaan Morrien). [Quarry] (43:1) Je 94, p. 23.
"Love and Friendship" (tr. of Adriaan Morrien). [Quarry] (43:1) Je 94, p. 27.
"Old Age" (tr. of Adriaan Morrien). [Quarry] (43:1) Je 94, p. 26.
"Ten Lines" (tr. of Adriaan Morrien). [Quarry] (43:1) Je 94, p. 22.
BOYD, Liz Walsh
See WALSH-BOYD, Liz
BOYD-WALSH, Liz
See WALSH-BOYD, Liz
686. BOYER, Dale W.
"Columbus in the Plague Years." [JamesWR] (11:4) Sum 94, p. 9.
687. BOYLE, Jennifer E.
"Autumn" (from "The Guesting of Athirne," tr. of Early Celtic anonymous poem, 11th c.). [SoCoast] (17) Je 94, p. 59.
"Glose." [Vis] (44) 94, p. 4.
"The Prostitute Speaks about Her Former Life." [NegC] (14:1/2) 94, p. 90-92.
688. BOYLE, Kevin
"Before Bed." [NoAmR] (279:4) Jl-Ag 94, p. 34.
"The Church Universal." [SouthernPR] (34:1) Sum 94, p. 34-35.
"Recall." [PoetL] (89:4) Wint 94-95, p. 19.
"Town and Through It." [VirQR] (70:2) Spr 94, p. 304-305.
689. BOZANIC, Nick
"Please." [YellowS] (12:3, #47) Fall-Wint 94-95, p. 21.

690. BRACHO, Coral
"Of Their Ornate Eyes of Crystalline Sand" (tr. by Forrest Gander). [Conjunc] (23) 94, p. 79-80.
"Untitled: Your voice (in your body rivers stir" (tr. by Forrest Gander). [Conjunc] (23) 94, p. 81-82.
"Your Life Refracts Me Like an Enigma" (tr. by Forrest Gander). [Conjunc] (23) 94, p. 80-81.
691. BRACKENBURY, Alison
"And the Legend." [Jacaranda] (5:1) Wint-Spr 91, p. 86-87.
"It Is." [Stand] (36:1) Wint 94-95, p. 78.
692. BRACKER, Jonathan
"Book." [SouthernPR] (34:2) Wint 94, p. 57-58.
"How to Understand Poetry." [Elf] (4:4) Wint 94, p. 31.
693. B'RACZ, Emoke
"It is painful to feel desire" (tr. of Katalin Ladik). [Vis] (46) 94, p. 18.
694. BRADEN, Allen
"Bear Poison" (for Mark Strand). [SouthernPR] (34:2) Wint 94, p. 13-15.
695. BRADLEY, Bill
"As a Feminist Drag Queen." [Zyzzyva] (10:2) Sum 94, p. 32-33.
696. BRADLEY, Burt
"Postcards to Caravaggio (and the Boys)" (5 selections). [QW] (39) Sum-Fall 94, p. 185-189.
697. BRADLEY, George
"Blue That Believes in Nothing." [Poetry] (164:2) My 94, p. 92.
"Museum-Quality Amour." [ParisR] (36:130) Spr 94, p. 162.
"Progress of Myth at East Haddam." [ParisR] (36:130) Spr 94, p. 163.
698. BRADLEY, John
"Angelus: From *The Book of Arson*." [PoetryE] (37/38) Spr 94, p. 132-133.
"For Want of a Candle." [PoetryE] (37/38) Spr 94, p. 134-135.
"Heat." [SlipS] (14) 94, p. 28.
"Speaking-Spoken-Spun" (for Frida Kahlo). [PoetryE] (37/38) Spr 94, p. 136.
699. BRADLEY, Lawrence
"Garcia Lorca Writes for America." [MidwQ] (35:3) Spr 94, p. 305-306.
700. BRADLEY, Robert
"A Dry Wake for Ex." [Ploughs] (20:4) Wint 94-95, p. 15-16.
701. BRADY, Philip
"The Dream My Father Radios." [CentR] (38:3) Fall 94, p. 504-505.
"Lullaby for Me." [ChatR] (14:2) Wint 94, p. 32.
"Mazembé." [CentR] (38:1) Wint 94, p. 111-119.
"The Naked Grandmother" (for Robert Lunday). [SpoonR] (19:1) Wint-Spr 94, p. 99-101.
"Poem Beginning with a Found Line." [CentR] (38:3) Fall 94, p. 503.
702. BRAGGS, Earl S.
"The Baseball Boys of 1964." [AfAmRev] (28:4) Wint 94, p. 585-587.
"Our Town Was Any Town, but Motown Was Heaven." [AfAmRev] (28:4) Wint 94, p. 587-588.
"Simon and Naomi." [AfAmRev] (28:4) Wint 94, p. 589-590.
703. BRAHIC, Beverley
"Cassis." [InterQ] (1:4) 94, p. 145.
"Dear Anne." [AntigR] (97) Spr 94, p. 143.
"History." [AntigR] (97) Spr 94, p. 144.
"Low Rent." [AntigR] (97) Spr 94, p. 145.
"Spider." [InterQ] (1:4) 94, p. 146.
704. BRAHMAN, Calico
"The Nature of Attainable Alchemy." [HeavenB] (11) 94, p. 50-55.
705. BRAID, Kate
"Blue Tattoo." [MalR] (108) Fall 94, p. 114-117.
706. BRAININ-PASSEK, Valeri
"Dialogue" (tr. by Don Share and Deborah Cohen). [PartR] (61:2) Spr 94, p. 315-316.
BRAKEMAN, Diane Seuss
See SEUSS-BRAKEMAN, Diane
707. BRAME, Gloria Glickstein
"Even After." [Elf] (4:4) Wint 94, p. 28.
708. BRAND, Alice G.
"Calendars That Cross Time and Place But Cannot Erase what Is Not There." [Blueline] (15) 94, p. 57-58.

"Meadow Stars." [MidwQ] (36:1) Aut 94, p. 54-55.
"Moon and Breeze Festival" (First Sue Saniel Elkind National Poetry Award, Finalist). [Kalliope] (16:2) 94, p. 15-16.
"To the Body at Calm." [SlipS] (14) 94, p. 57-58.

709. BRAND, Ken
"Swagger." [PraF] (15:2, #67) Sum 94, p. 27.

710. BRANDÃO, Fiama Hasse Pais
"#47" (from *White Space*, tr. by Alexis Levitin). [MassR] (35:1) Spr 94, p. 105.
"#49" (from *White Space*, tr. by Alexis Levitin). [MassR] (35:1) Spr 94, p. 106.
"Graphic 2" (tr. by Alexis Levitin). [Vis] (46) 94, p. 20.

711. BRANDI, John
"I Forgot Myself Last Night." [Caliban] (14) 94, p. 120-122.
"To Move On — In the Way One Breathes." [Caliban] (14) 94, p. 122.

712. BRANDL, Mark Staff
"Dusk, North Side of Tortola" (for Cornelia). [CaribbeanW] (8) 94, p. 17-18.

713. BRANDLER, Marcielle
"The Ceremony." [BlackBR] (19) Fall-Wint 94, p. 33.
"Ituri Forest." [BlackBR] (19) Fall-Wint 94, p. 34.

714. BRANDON, Sherry
"The Archeology of Argument." [CrabCR] (8:2/3/9:1/2/3) 94, p. 75-76.
"Libyan Laundry 1956." [Parting] (7:2) Wint 94-95, p. 2.
"Prospecting." [Parting] (7:2) Wint 94-95, p. 15.
"Smoking Anna Akhmatova's Words." [Parting] (7:2) Wint 94-95, p. 51.
"Some Thoughts Are All Thunder." [CrabCR] (8:2/3/9:1/2/3) 94, p. 75.

715. BRANDT, Di
"A busload of silly Christians, with silly hats, touring." [Quarry] (42:4) Mr 94, p. 34.
"How badly she wants peace, this wise woman" (for Carol Rose). [PraF] (15:1, #66) Spr 94, p. 58.
"I didn't want it to be like this, a nightmare in living colour." [Quarry] (42:4) Mr 94, p. 36.
"Inside the bound woman is another, who loves to dance" (for Diana). [PraF] (15:1, #66) Spr 94, p. 59.
"Jerusalem, the golden, city of my dreams, dreaming." [Quarry] (42:4) Mr 94, p. 30.
"The knives in the kitchen, leaping up at me" (for Clarise). [PraF] (15:1, #66) Spr 94, p. 55.
"Little poet, is this what you meant by *important*." [PraF] (15:1, #66) Spr 94, p. 60.
"Occupied Territories: An Argument in Poetry" (w. Carol Rose). [Quarry] (42:4) Mr 94, p. 29-37.
"The trees of Jerusalem, so much sadder than Winnipeg trees." [PraF] (15:1, #66) Spr 94, p. 56.
"Waking up in Jerusalem, the voice on the minaret." [PraF] (15:1, #66) Spr 94, p. 57.
"We are the lucky ones, they whisper, hugging to themselves." [PraF] (15:1, #66) Spr 94, p. 61.
"When you told me about the Wall, where the women go." [Quarry] (42:4) Mr 94, p. 32.

716. BRANNEN, Jonathan
"Thing Is the Anagram of Night" (Selections). [Talisman] (12) Spr 94, p. 238.

717. BRANNON, Melissa
"Lena, Waiting for the Mail." [QW] (39) Sum-Fall 94, p. 243-244.

718. BRANNON, R. Frost, Jr.
"Late Lunch" (from "A Kenning of Roses"). [AmerPoR] (23:1) Ja-F 94, p. 30.

719. BRANTINGHAM, James M.
"Book I, v: Quis Multis Gracilis" (tr. of Horace). [CrabCR] (8:2/3/9:1/2/3) 94, p. 105.
"Epode III" (tr. of Horace). [CrabCR] (8:2/3/9:1/2/3) 94, p. 103.
"Sermones II, iv" (Excerpt, tr. of Horace). [CrabCR] (8:2/3/9:1/2/3) 94, p. 104.

720. BRASCHI, Giannina
"Empire of Dreams" (tr. by José Vazquez-Amaral and Tess O'Dwyer). [ApalQ] (40/41) 94, p. 49-53.
"From two slow roads, two fast stops, I take the wind" (tr. by Tess O'Dwyer). [ProseP] (3) 94, p. 20.
"I always knew that a bit farther or closer but never in the exact spot" (tr. by Tess O'Dwyer). [ProseP] (3) 94, p. 19.
"I Don't Have It, and I Wanted It" (from *Empire of Dreams*, tr. by Tess O'Dwyer). [Callaloo] (17:3) Sum 94, p. 938.
"Sure, it's true" (tr. by Tess O'Dwyer). [ProseP] (3) 94, p. 18.

721. BRASFIELD, James
"Surge" (tr. of Blas de Otero). [Talisman] (12) Spr 94, p. 200-201.
722. BRASK, Per
"Civilization's Children" (tr. of Nina Malinovski, w. Patrick Friesen). [PoetryC] (14:2) Mr 94, p. 22.
"Hotel" (tr. of Ulrikka S. Gernes, w. Patrick Friesen). [PoetryC] (14:2) Mr 94, p. 21.
"The House Is Open" (tr. of Ulrikka S. Gernes, w. Patrick Friesen). [PoetryC] (14:2) Mr 94, p. 21.
"Show Me Your Breasts" (tr. of Niels Hav, w. Patrick Friesen). [PoetryC] (14:2) Mr 94, p. 22.
"Untitled: Embrace me" (tr. of Lena Krogh Bertram, w. Patrick Friesen). [PoetryC] (14:2) Mr 94, p. 20.
"Untitled: In dreams" (tr. of Nina Malinovski, w. Patrick Friesen). [PoetryC] (14:2) Mr 94, p. 22.
"Untitled: You cannot steal lines from a dancer my love" (tr. of Camilla Christensen, w. Patrick Friesen). [PoetryC] (14:2) Mr 94, p. 20.
"Visit from My Father" (tr. of Niels Hav, w. Patrick Friesen). [PoetryC] (14:2) Mr 94, p. 21.
723. BRASS, Deborah
"Traveling Alone." [Colum] (22) Wint 94, p. 73.
"The U.S." [Colum] (22) Wint 94, p. 72.
724. BRASS, Perry
"Keith." [Art&Und] (3:4) O-N 94, p. 29.
725. BRAUCHER, Karen
"Open Mind, Open Heart" (from "Song of Hard Journey." The Nimrod / Hardman Wards: Finalist). [Nimrod] (38:1) Fall-Wint 94, p. 73-74.
726. BRAUD, Janice L.
"Indian Time." [BellArk] (10:6) N-D 94, p. 26.
"A Moment of Rest for a Dragline Operator." [BellArk] (10:3 [i.e. 10:4]) Jl-Ag 94, p. 11.
"Ripples." [BellArk] (10:6) N-D 94, p. 8.
"Trailer Trash." [BellArk] (10:3 [i.e. 10:4]) Jl-Ag 94, p. 11.
"Winter Revisited." [BellArk] (10:3 [i.e. 10:4]) Jl-Ag 94, p. 31.
727. BRAUN, Graal
"Beethoven Concert." [Hellas] (5:2) Fall-Wint 94, p. 99.
"Freedom." [Hellas] (5:2) Fall-Wint 94, p. 98.
728. BRAUN, Volker
"Desert Storm" (tr. by Reinhold Grimm). [Pembroke] (26) 94, p. 138.
729. BRAWLEY, Eleanor
"No Mc Neill Man Past Fifty Has Ever Been Worth Shooting." [Pembroke] (26) 94, p. 124.
730. BRAWLEY, Lisa
"Emma Jean's Violets." [CumbPR] (13:2) Spr 94, p. 35-36.
731. BRAXTON, Joanne M.
"Zoning" (for MMB). [AfAmRev] (28:4) Wint 94, p. 597.
732. BRAY, Tara
"The Chapelle Vase." [Poem] (72) N 94, p. 48.
733. BRAYMEN-CLEARY, Lee
"Pamela's First Steelie." [NegC] (14:1/2) 94, p. 49-50.
734. BRAZIL, Janice H.
"I Sit Here Writing." [Outbr] (25) 94, p. 10.
"Questioning." [Outbr] (25) 94, p. 11.
735. BREBNER, Diana
"Aegis." [PoetryC] (14:2) Mr 94, p. 18.
"Explosions." [PoetryC] (14:2) Mr 94, p. 18.
"Facing Buddha." [PoetryC] (14:2) Mr 94, p. 18.
"The Green Canoe." [PoetryC] (14:2) Mr 94, p. 19.
"Letters from Moscow." [PoetryC] (14:2) Mr 94, p. 19.
"The Path of Mercury." [PoetryC] (14:2) Mr 94, p. 18.
"The Swimmer." [PoetryC] (14:2) Mr 94, p. 19.
"Water Serpents." [PoetryC] (14:2) Mr 94, p. 19.
736. BRECHNER, Kenny
"Departure." [Northeast] (5:11) Wint 94-95, p. 32.
"In the Same Dance" (tr. of Konstantin Kavafis). [Northeast] (5:11) Wint 94-95, p. 32.
"The Lighthouse." [Northeast] (5:11) Wint 94-95, p. 33.

737. BREEN, Shannon
"The Utility Player." [Spitball] (46) Spr 94, p. 9.
BRENDAN-BROWN, Sean
See BROWN, Sean (Sean Brendan)
738. BRENNAN, Scott
"The Virtual Little." [ChiR] (40:1) 94, p. 50.
739. BRENNAN, Sherry
"Domestic Bliss / Dominus Patrus" (to Julia Blumenrich). [Chain] (1) Spr-Sum 94, p. 138-144.
740. BRESLIN, Julia Galligan
"American Beech." [Boulevard] (9:1/2, #25/26) Spr 94, p. 225.
"Webs." [Boulevard] (9:1/2, #25/26) Spr 94, p. 225.
"Weeds." [Boulevard] (9:1/2, #25/26) Spr 94, p. 224.
741. BRETON, André
"Femme et Oiseau." [NewRena] (9:1, #27) 94, p. 76.
"Woman and Bird" (tr. by Jeanie Puleston Fleming and Christopher Merrill). [NewRena] (9:1, #27) 94, p. 77.
742. BRETT, Mark
"Wrestling Dada." [MinnR] (41/42) Fall 93-Spr 94 (published Mr 95), p. 48.
743. BREWER, Gay
"After Trying to Teach Thoreau to the Sophomores." [Border] (4) Spr-Sum 94, p. 6.
"American Parable." [NoDaQ] (62:1) Wint 94-95, p. 127.
"Another Saturday." [Border] (5) Fall-Wint 94, p. 7.
"Apologies Accepted." [ContextS] (4:1) 94, p. 32.
"Considering the Ph.D." [PaintedHR] (11) Spr-Sum 94, p. 8.
"Espionage in Mind." [PaintedHR] (11) Spr-Sum 94, p. 9.
"Glen Campbell Signs His New Autobiography *Rhinestone Cowboy*." [Border] (5) Fall-Wint 94, p. 8.
"Legend of the Porch." [ChironR] (13:4) Wint 94, p. 7.
"Sitting with Dog, I Assume His Mood." [ChironR] (13:4) Wint 94, p. 7.
"Students and Master." [ChironR] (13:4) Wint 94, p. 7.
744. BREWER, Kenneth W.
"D Tuning." [Plain] (14:2) Wint 94, p. 25.
745. BRICKHOUSE, Robert
"At Food King." [HampSPR] Wint 94, p. 7.
"March Surprise." [Light] (9) Spr 94, p. 7.
"Passing Through Nelson County Again at Christmas." [ChatR] (14:3) Spr 94, p. 28.
"Persephone." [Light] (11) Aut 94, p. 12.
746. BRICUTH, John
"Talking Big." [MidwQ] (35:2) Wint 94, p. 130.
747. BRIDGFORD, Kim
"Before Anything Happened." [SpoonR] (19:1) Wint-Spr 94, p. 61-62.
"Blue." [WritersF] (20) 94, p. 193.
"Crying." [Wind] (74) 94, p. 8-9.
"The Eating Ritual." [NegC] (14:1/2) 94, p. 53.
"Half a Heart." [Witness] (8:1) 94, p. 18.
"Life Coils." [SpoonR] (19:1) Wint-Spr 94, p. 60.
"Scissor-Lightning." [XavierR] (14:2) Fall 94, p. 52.
"Stones." [NegC] (14:1/2) 94, p. 52.
"A Sympathetic Woman." [Witness] (8:1) 94, p. 19.
"What You Might Say If a Friendship Ends Unhappily." [NegC] (14:1/2) 94, p. 51.
748. BRIGGS, John
"Miracle in Patagonia." [AntigR] (96) Wint 94, p. 56.
"Morning." [AntigR] (96) Wint 94, p. 57.
749. BRILLEMBOURG, Carlos
"I believe in architecture." [Bomb] (46) Wint 94, p. 22.
750. BRILLIANT, Alan D.
"Shopping for Love." [Sun] (217) Ja 94, p. 33.
751. BRINGHURST, Robert
"Dogen." [CanLit] (140) Spr 94, p. 82-85.
"Dongshan Liangjie." [CanLit] (140) Spr 94, p. 79.
"Xuedou Zhongxian." [CanLit] (140) Spr 94, p. 80.
"Yongjia Xuanjue." [CanLit] (140) Spr 94, p. 81.
752. BRISTER, J. G.
"Dear John." [NewYorkQ] (53) 94, p. 105.

753. BRITO, Silvester
"Back Road Lift." [Callaloo] (17:1) Wint 94, p. 318-319.
754. BRITT, Alan
"Awake." [DarkMoon] (1) 94, p. 85.
"Bodies of Lightning." [CharR] (20:2) Fall 94, p. 106.
"The Dream Tyger." [MidwQ] (36:1) Aut 94, p. 56-57.
"Dreaming." [DarkMoon] (1) 94, p. 88-89.
"Haitian Sugar." [DarkMoon] (1) 94, p. 86-87.
"A Little Poem About Darkness & a Driver." [DarkMoon] (1) 94, p. 84.
"Our Lost Poet" (for Steve Barfield). [DarkMoon] (1) 94, p. 83.
"The Quicksilver Poet" (For Silva Scheibli-Clare). [CharR] (20:2) Fall 94, p. 105.
755. BROBST, Richard
"Sunlight at Dusk." [SouthernPR] (34:1) Sum 94, p. 41.
756. BROCK, Geoffrey
"I Can't Say It Any Other Way" (tr. of Edgar Bayley). [InterQ] (1:4) 94, p. 30.
757. BROCK, James
"To the Coronor Who Did Not Have to Draw My Blood." [NowestR] (32:2) 94, p. 16-17.
758. BROCK, Van K.
"Night on a Notebook" (tr. of Dong Jiping, w. the author). [InterQ] (1:2) 93, p. 47-49.
"Sunday Morning with Prokofiev." [AmerV] (33) 94, p. 105-106.
759. BROCK-BROIDO, Lucie
"Carrowmore." [NewYorker] (70:17) 13 Je 94, p. 88.
"Dominus." [ColR] (21:1) Spr 94, p. 152-153.
"Evangelical." [Antaeus] (75/76) Aut 94, p. 237.
"Everybody Has a Heart, Except Some People." [Agni] (39) 94, p. 43.
"His Apprentice." [Agni] (39) 94, p. 44.
"In the Attitude Desired for Exhibition." [HarvardR] (6) Spr 94, p. 34-35.
"Radiating Naïveté." [HarvardR] (Premier Issue) Spr 92, p. 61.
"Treason." [ColR] (21:1) Spr 94, p. 150-151.
"You Can't Always Get What You Want." [Agni] (39) 94, p. 45.
760. BROCKI, Anselm
"Cross-purposes." [ChamLR] (14/15) Spr-Fall 94, p. 181-182.
761. BROCKWELL, Stephen
"Birch Messages." [Arc] (33) Fall 94, p. 61.
762. BRODERICK, Richard
"December." [PraS] (68:3) Fall 94, p. 134.
"The Hobo Camp." [PraS] (68:3) Fall 94, p. 135.
763. BRODINE, Karen
"Driving Home." [CrabCR] (8:2/3/9:1/2/3) 94, p. 16.
764. BRODSKY, Joseph
"Angel." [NewYorker] (69:45) 10 Ja 94, p. 50.
"Anti-Shenandoah: Two Skits and a Chorus of Going East." [Antaeus] (75/76) Aut 94, p. 238-240.
"Infinitive" (To Ulf Linde). [NewYRB] (41:13) 14 Jl 94, p. 13.
"Porta San Pancrazio" (tr. by the author). [NewYorker] (70:4) 14 Mr 94, p. 52.
"Törnfallet." [NewYorker] (70:24) 8 Ag 94, p. 46.
765. BRODSKY, Louis Daniel
"Benjy's Fences." [CimR] (107) Ap 94, p. 92-93.
"Circusgoer." [Confr] (54/55) Fall 94-Wint 95, p. 312-313.
"Helen Among the 12 Disciples" (For Margaret and Dick Haxel). [Amelia] (7:4, #23) 94, p. 93-94.
"Intimations in Spring." [Confr] (52/53) Wint-Spr 94, p. 318-319.
"The Isle of Lesbos." [Amelia] (7:4, #23) 94, p. 95-96.
"Lovesong." [Amelia] (7:3, #22) 94, p. 61.
"Oxford Nocturne." [NegC] (14:1/2) 94, p. 82-83.
"Spinning Tops." [NegC] (14:1/2) 94, p. 81.
"Tipton's Hidden Treasures." [Amelia] (7:4, #23) 94, p. 94-95.
766. BRODSKY, Patricia Pollock
"Flight, in Vain" (Selections: 33, 35-36, tr. of Horst Bienek). [DenQ] (29:1) Sum 94, p. 53-54.
767. BRODY, Harry
"The Return: Easter '89." [NegC] (14:1/2) 94, p. 89.
768. BROGAN, Matthew
"The Metamorphosis" (for Michael Stortz). [Zyzzyva] (10:1) Spr 94, p. 133.

BROIDO, Lucie Brock
See BROCK-BROIDO, Lucie
769. BROMIGE, David
"Slow Lake (Skylark)." [RiverC] (14:2) Spr 94, p. 18-22.
770. BRONER, Sari
"Recording." [GlobalCR] (4) Fall 94, p. 12.
771. BRONK, William
"The Abnegation." [NoDaQ] (62:2) Spr 94-95, p. 214.
"At Hand." [NoDaQ] (62:2) Spr 94-95, p. 214-215.
"The Shaker Chair." [NoDaQ] (62:2) Spr 94-95, p. 215.
772. BROOK, Donna
"Message to Mary Ferrari in Jo'burg." [HangL] (65) 94, p. 11-12.
773. BROOKS, Brenda
"I Came to See You." [Grain] (22:1) Sum 94, p. 104.
"Local Honey." [Arc] (32) Spr 94, p. 64-65.
"There Is No One in My Heart." [Arc] (32) Spr 94, p. 63.
774. BROOKS, Cleanth
"Abner Gardner, Tired Business Man." [SoCaR] (27:1/2) Fall 94-Spr 95, p. 17.
"Birth of Aphrodite." [SoCaR] (27:1/2) Fall 94-Spr 95, p. 17-18.
"Geometry of Sunset." [SoCaR] (27:1/2) Fall 94-Spr 95, p. 18.
"The Maelstrom." [SoCaR] (27:1/2) Fall 94-Spr 95, p. 19-20.
"Portrait of an Intellectual." [SoCaR] (27:1/2) Fall 94-Spr 95, p. 18-19.
775. BROSMAN, Catharine Savage
"Artichokes." [NewOR] (20:1/2) Spr-Sum 94, p. 147.
"Asparagus." [SouthwR] (79:4) Aut 94, p. 659.
"Fragments from the Customs House." [SewanR] (102:4) Fall 94, p. 539-540.
"Into the Wind." [SewanR] (102:2) Spr 94, p. 244-245.
"Madame d'Epinay Writes to Her Lover" (At Château La Chevrette, the tenth of May). [NewOR] (20:1/2) Spr-Sum 94, p. 150-151.
"Mushrooms." [NewOR] (20:1/2) Spr-Sum 94, p. 148.
"Old Priests." [SouthernR] (30:1) Ja, Wint 94, p. 79.
"On Mobile Bay." [SouthernR] (30:4) Aut 94, p. 761.
"Passages." [SouthernR] (30:1) Ja, Wint 94, p. 80-81.
"Saguache." [NewOR] (20:1/2) Spr-Sum 94, p. 146.
"Tulips." [SouthernR] (30:4) Aut 94, p. 761-762.
"Verbena, Yucca, Sage." [NewOR] (20:1/2) Spr-Sum 94, p. 149.
776. BROSSARD, Chandler
"Traditionally a Place of Banishment" (dedicated to Maria Ewing Huffman — Excerpts). [WorldL] (5) 94, p. 4-7.
777. BROSSARD, Nicole
"Flesh, Song(e) et Promenade" (in French and English, tr. by Lola Lemire Tostevin). [WestCL] (28:3, #15) Wint 94-95, p. 6-25.
778. BROTT, Andrea Adam
"Fat Girl at Twelve." [Calyx] (15:3) Wint 94-95, p. 52-53.
"Saturday Night on the Lower East Side." [CimR] (108) Jl 94, p. 83-84.
"When They Come for Me." [CapeR] (29:2) Fall 94, p. 34-35.
779. BROUGHTON, Irv
"Back." [CimR] (106) Ja 94, p. 82-84.
780. BROUGHTON, T. Alan
"Dolorosa." [FourQ] (8:1) Spr 94, p. 12.
"Parable." [FourQ] (8:1) Spr 94, p. 11.
"Praise for the Core and Crust of Earth." [VirQR] (70:1) Wint 94, p. 100-103.
781. BROUMAS, Olga
"Vowel Imprint" (w. T. Begley). [AmerV] (33) 94, p. 95-99.
782. BROWDER, Clifford
"Affinity." [ChatR] (14:3) Spr 94, p. 31-32.
783. BROWN, Allan
"Aquinas." [AntigR] (97) Spr 94, p. 47.
"Ghazal" (for Kim). [MalR] (109) Wint 94, p. 19.
"Two Biblical Sonatas" (in mem. W. J. Barnes). [MalR] (109) Wint 94, p. 20-21.
784. BROWN, Bill
"Columbine." [SouthernPR] (34:1) Sum 94, p. 13-14.
"Early Mornings at the Silver Castle." [CumbPR] (14:1) Fall 94, p. 41.
"From the Night Porch." [LitR] (37:4) Sum 94, p. 576-577.
"Soul Train Carpe Diem." [Pearl] (20) Spr 94, p. 44.

785. BROWN, Bobbie
"Leo Sprinkle's Body." [AntR] (52:2) Spr 94, p. 306-309.
786. BROWN, Clarence
"The Stalin Epigram" (tr. of Osip Mandelstam, w. W. S. Merwin). [Agni] (39) 94, p. 94-95.
787. BROWN, Cory
"All All." [WestB] (34) 94, p. 30.
"Symbolism." [Farm] (11:1) Spr-Sum 94, p. 146.
788. BROWN, Glen
"After His Witnessing an Argument with My Father." [PoetC] (25:3) Spr 94, p. 28.
"Hell." [SpoonR] (19:1) Wint-Spr 94, p. 97.
"No." [NegC] (14:1/2) 94, p. 27.
"Rip from Space." [Elf] (4:2) Sum 94, p. 37.
789. BROWN, Gregg (Gregg G.)
"Architecture." [Plain] (14:2) Wint 94, p. 29.
"Illness Is a Calumny." [Blueline] (15) 94, p. 59-60.
790. BROWN, Harry
"Backyard Yorick." [Wind] (73) 94, p. 3.
"One upon a Pillow, Or, Now Never Two." [Wind] (73) 94, p. 3.
791. BROWN, Jamie
"Words for the Village Revolutionary." [NegC] (14:1/2) 94, p. 75.
792. BROWN, Kurt
"Genesis" (tr. of Herman de Coninck, w. Laure-Anne Bosselaar). [MassR] (35:1) Spr 94, p. 104.
"Paris, May 1st" (in the Jewish war memorial, tr. of Herman de Coninck, w. Laure-Anne Bosselaar). [MassR] (35:1) Spr 94, p. 103.
"The Plural of Happiness" (Excerpt, tr. of Herman de Coninck, w. Laure-Anne Bosselaar). [MassR] (35:1) Spr 94, p. 104.
793. BROWN, Lee Ann
"August Valentine for Anne Leslie Waldman." [Talisman] (13) Fall 94-Wint 95, p. 116.
"Deep Gossip Not" (to Katie Yates). [Chain] (1) Spr-Sum 94, p. 158.
"Renga" (February 9, 1994, Chinese New Year's Eve, w. Judith Goldman, Lisa Jarnot, and Sianne Ngai). [Chain] (1) Spr-Sum 94, p. 197-199.
794. BROWN, Robert
"Afternoon in Algoma." [Elf] (4:1) Spr 94, p. 30-31.
"At My Father-in-Law's Art Show." [Elf] (4:1) Spr 94, p. 32-33.
"The Mind's Eye." [NewDeltaR] (11:2) Spr-Sum 94, p. 17.
"Sleepers Awake!" [Elf] (4:1) Spr 94, p. 31.
795. BROWN, Sean (Sean Brendan)
"The Dark Side of Dazzle." [WeberS] (11:1) Wint 94, p. 115.
"Don't Know Him Too Far." [CapeR] (29:1) Spr 94, p. 50.
"An Irish Nun at Ypres, 1917" (for Les Dames Irlandaises of the Royal Benedictine Abbey). [CoalC] (8) Ap 94, p. 20.
"Last Station." [SmPd] (31:1, #90) Wint 94, p. 15.
"Pit of the Stomach." [CoalC] (8) Ap 94, p. 19.
"Recovering" (First Place Winner, Social Concern Poetry Competition, 1993). [BlackBR] (18) Wint-Spr 94, p. 39-40.
"Returning from Ulster." [WeberS] (11:1) Wint 94, p. 113-114.
"Spaniard." [BlackBR] (18) Wint-Spr 94, p. 18.
"Strangers." [WeberS] (11:1) Wint 94, p. 114.
"White Chrysanthemums." [Plain] (15:1) Fall 94, p. 6-7.
796. BROWN, Stephanie
"Boys." [YellowS] (12:1, #45) Spr-Sum 94, p. 9.
"Commencement Address." [YellowS] (12:1, #45) Spr-Sum 94, p. 8.
"Fitness: A Triptych." [AmerPoR] (23:4) Jl-Ag 94, p. 8.
"Marginalia." [AmerPoR] (23:4) Jl-Ag 94, p. 9.
"No, No Nostalgia!" [AmerPoR] (23:4) Jl-Ag 94, p. 8.
"Schadenfreude." [AmerPoR] (23:4) Jl-Ag 94, p. 9.
"Unfasten, Lift Up." [YellowS] (12:1, #45) Spr-Sum 94, p. 8.
797. BROWN, Steve
"Night." [Pearl] (20) Spr 94, p. 71.
798. BROWN, Steven Ford
"First Evocation" (tr. of Angel Gonzalez). [InterQ] (1:1) [93?], p. 154-155.
"My Profound Vocation" (tr. of Angel Gonzalez, w. Moira Perez). [InterQ] (1:1) [93?], p. 153.

"This Moment" (tr. of Angel González). [MidAR] (14:2) 94, p. 136-137.
799. BROWN, Susan E.
"The Den" (for my mother). [WritersF] (20) 94, p. 202.
800. BROWN-DAVIDSON, Terri
"Puppets." [Ledge] (17) Wint 94, p. 14-17.
"Three Marys." [TriQ] (90) Spr-Sum 94, p. 75-77.
801. BROWNE, Laynie
"A Body of Such Stories" (for Brad Davidson). [Talisman] (13) Fall 94-Wint 95, p. 197-198.
802. BROWNING, Janisse
"Yes, and More." [WestCL] (28:1/2, #13/14) Spr-Fall 94, p. 85-86.
803. BROWNING, Preston
"Being With You" (tr. of Luzmarina Acosta, w. Lang Gomez). [LitR] (37:4) Sum 94, p. 580.
804. BRUCE, Debra
"Follow-Up Exam." [Poetry] (164:4) Jl 94, p. 213.
805. BRUCE, George
"Epistle 1, Confessional Response." [Interim] (13:1) Spr-Sum 94, p. 6-7.
806. BRUCE, Rae Marie
"Looking Out Toward Nahant Island from the Oral Surgeon's Chair While Wearing Braces at 54, I Realized That." [SpoonR] (19:1) Wint-Spr 94, p. 64.
"Trans-Atlantic Connection." [SpoonR] (19:1) Wint-Spr 94, p. 65.
807. BRUCHAC, Joseph
"A Bear Song" (for N. Scott Momaday). [Paint] (21) Aut 94, p. 119.
"Corners." [Callaloo] (17:1) Wint 94, p. 104.
"Dog Song" (Baffin Island, June 1992). [Callaloo] (17:1) Wint 94, p. 99-101.
"For Littlecoon in Oklahoma Two Years After His Death." [Callaloo] (17:1) Wint 94, p. 102.
"Oligawi." [Callaloo] (17:1) Wint 94, p. 103.
808. BRUGALETTA, John J.
"Answers to Five Important Questions Posed by the Smithsonian Institution." [Zyzzyva] (10:1) Spr 94, p. 38-39.
"Bill Ferrell." [NegC] (14:1/2) 94, p. 184.
"Epitaph of a Boxer" (tr. of Lukilius, mid-1st c. A.D.). [SoCoast] (16) Ja 94, p. 57.
"The Exile" (tr. of Theògnis of Mègara, late-6th - early-5th c. B.C.). [SoCoast] (16) Ja 94, p. 57.
"First among the lovely things I leave" (tr. of Praxìlla of Sìcyon, mid-5th c. B.C.). [SoCoast] (16) Ja 94, p. 57.
"In Memoriam: For William Stafford." [NegC] (14:1/2) 94, p. 299.
"Nola and Lola." [NegC] (13:2/3) 93, p. 210.
"On Being Asked How One Should Clean Mushrooms." [NegC] (14:1/2) 94, p. 183.
"Three Similes from Dante's *Commedia*" (tr. of Dante). [SoCoast] (17) Je 94, p. 63-65.
"The Tokens (Mittitur)" (tr. of anonymous poem from *Bodleian Latin Miscellany,* ca. 1500, w. Mary Black Vigil). [SoCoast] (16) Ja 94, p. 61.
"Tourist, take this message to your hawkish nation" (tr. of Simònides of Ceos, 556-468 B.C.). [SoCoast] (16) Ja 94, p. 57.
809. BRUHWILER, Ryland
"Today I Wasted My Life" (for Thich Nhat Hanh). [BelPoJ] (45:1) Fall 94, p. 37.
810. BRUNET, David
"Deconstructing Aristotle." [MinnR] (41/42) Fall 93-Spr 94 (published Mr 95), p. 49.
BRUNO, Carmen Michael la
See LaBRUNO, Michael (Carmen Michael)
BRUNO, Michael la (Michael C. la)
See LaBRUNO, Michael (Carmen Michael)
BRUNT, Lloyd van
See Van BRUNT, Lloyd
811. BRUTUS, Dennis
"February, 1990." [InterQ] (1:3) 94, p. 17.
"For WCJB: My Brother, Who Died in Exile." [InterQ] (1:3) 94, p. 16.
812. BRYAN, L. E.
"God's Mole." [HayF] (15) Fall-Wint 94, p. 95.
813. BRYAN, Sharon
"Weird Niece." [QW] (38) Winter-Spr 93-94, p. 113.
814. BRYANT, Philip S.
"Father's Bouquet." [Obs] (9:2) Fall-Wint 94, p. 74-75.

"Passover Hamburgers." [Obs] (9:2) Fall-Wint 94, p. 74.
"Picking Wild Flowers." [Obs] (9:2) Fall-Wint 94, p. 72-73.
"Sermon on a Perfect Spring Day." [Obs] (9:2) Fall-Wint 94, p. 72.
"TittyBoat." [Obs] (9:1) Spr-Sum 94, p. 90.

815. BRYNER, Jeanne
"Butterfly." [PoetryE] (37/38) Spr 94, p. 102-103.
"The Emperor's Blind Daughter." [PraS] (68:2) Sum 94, p. 27-28.
"Freedom Counter." [PraS] (68:2) Sum 94, p. 29-30.
"I'm Trying to Be Accurate." [PraS] (68:2) Sum 94, p. 28-29.
"Letter from Ward Three." [PraS] (68:2) Sum 94, p. 30-31.
"The Mill's Annual Picnic, 1960, Conneaut Lake Park, Pa." [CreamCR] (18:1) Spr 94, p. 44.
"The Rabbit." [PoetryE] (37/38) Spr 94, p. 100-101.
"Strawberries." [WestB] (34) 94, p. 32-33.
"Why It Happens." [PoetryE] (37/38) Spr 94, p. 99.

816. BUCHANAN, C. J.
"Bog People: A Planxty to Peat." [WestHR] (48:2) Sum 94, p. 124.
"Bog People — The Windeby Girl" (for my sister). [SoDakR] (32:4) Wint 94, p. 9-10.
"Leda." [SoDakR] (32:4) Wint 94, p. 12-13.
"White As the Holes in Heaven" (Ariadne-Arachne). [SoDakR] (32:4) Wint 94, p. 11.

817. BUCHANAN, Paul
"Tying Flies in My Windowless Office." [SoCoast] (16) Ja 94, p. 24.

818. BUCHMAN, Ruth
"Beads." [HarvardR] (6) Spr 94, p. 123.

819. BUCKHOLTS, Claudia
"Bride of Vichy." [ConnPR] (13:1) 94, p. 21.
"Thirteenth Dayl." [ConnPR] (13:1) 94, p. 3.

820. BUCKLEY, B. J.
"Pantheón, Creole-Cajun Cemetery at the Old Spanish Fort, Pascagoula, Mississippi Feast of All Souls, 1992" (Robert Penn Warren Poetry Prize Winner: First Prize). [CumbPR] (14:1) Fall 94, p. 2-3.
"The Woman and Water." [CumbPR] (14:1) Fall 94, p. 4-6.

821. BUCKLEY, Christopher
"Alisos Canyon Contract." [Crazy] (46) Spr 94, p. 117-120.
"Corot at Chartres" (La Cathedrale de Chartres, 1830). [QW] (38) Winter-Spr 93-94, p. 103-104.
"Equinox." [Poetry] (164:6) S 94, p. 332-333.
"Jonah." [DenQ] (29:2) Fall 94, p. 6-8.
"Late Schoolyard." [BlackWR] (20:2) Spr-Sum 94, p. 99-101.
"Rain/Light." [QW] (38) Winter-Spr 93-94, p. 101-102.
"Singing." [YellowS] (11:4, #44) Wint 93-94, p. 43.
"There & Then." [SantaBR] (2:1) Spr-Sum 94, p. 80.
"Washing the Body." [PoetL] (89:1) Spr 94, p. 21-22.

822. BUCKNAVAGE, John
"Jim Carpenter, Former Slave." [HawaiiR] (18:1, #40) Spr 94, p. 109-110.

823. BUCKNER, Sally
"Maintenance." [CrabCR] (8:2/3/9:1/2/3) 94, p. 29-32.

824. BUCPAPA, Uk
"Debts" (tr. of Xhevahir Spahiu, w. Henry Israeli). [DenQ] (29:1) Sum 94, p. 103.
"The Forest at Night" (tr. of Frederik Rreshpja, w. Henry Israeli). [DenQ] (29:1) Sum 94, p. 101.
"The Sea" (tr. of Frederik Rreshpja, w. Henry Israeli). [DenQ] (29:1) Sum 94, p. 102.

BUDBILL, David
See MOUNTAIN, Judevine

825. BUDENZ, Julia
"Exile" (corrections for the printing in #45, Wint 93). [Crazy] (46) Spr 94, p. 6.
"Sonetti Petrarcheschi" (Selections: 9-10, 12, 14-16, 18-23, 26-32, from *The Gardens of Flora Baum*). [Crazy] (46) Spr 94, p. 171-180.
"Umbra" (Three Passages, from *The Gardens of Flora Baum*). [Crazy] (46) Spr 94, p. 121-170.

826. BUDY, Andrea Hollander
"Beginning and Ending with Lines from Shakespeare." [Pivot] (42) 94, p. 6.
"Blue." [Pivot] (42) 94, p. 6-7.
"Ellis Island, September 1907." [Poetry] (165:2) N 94, p. 94.
"History." [Poetry] (165:2) N 94, p. 93.

"The Line." [LaurelR] (28:1) Wint 94, p. 98.
827. BUELL, Janet
"Canyons." [Writer] (107:1) Ja 94, p. 24.
828. BUFFONI, Franco
"The Carmelite Nun" (tr. by the author and Dave Smith). [SouthernR] (30:2) Ap, Spr 94, p. 272-274.
829. BUGEJA, Michael J.
"Boy Talk." [Hellas] (5:2) Fall-Wint 94, p. 72.
"Calamity's Eye" (to Cheryl, my niece sent to school in a hurricane). [Pembroke] (26) 94, p. 157-158.
"Creation, Apocalypse: All the Acts Between." [Elf] (4:3) Fall 94, p. 23.
"Girl Talk." [Hellas] (5:2) Fall-Wint 94, p. 71.
"Man Talk." [Hellas] (5:2) Fall-Wint 94, p. 73.
"Poet of Greenpeace and Sierra." [Elf] (4:3) Fall 94, p. 24.
"Porpoise in the Passaic" (for Diane Ackerman). [Elf] (4:3) Fall 94, p. 22.
"Storybook" (The Douglas Manning Smith Epic/Heroic Poetry Award). [Amelia] (7:4, #23) 94, p. 56-59.
"Trinity." [Poetry] (163:6) Mr 94, p. 316-317.
"Voice of America." [JlNJPo] (16:2) Aut 94, p. 7.
"Woman Talk." [Hellas] (5:2) Fall-Wint 94, p. 74.
830. BUHROW, B. J.
"Closet Child." [CreamCR] (18:1) Spr 94, p. 76-78.
"In Reverse, the Accident." [CreamCR] (18:1) Spr 94, p. 75.
"Mona Lisa in the Mall." [CreamCR] (18:1) Spr 94, p. 79.
831. BUKOWSKI, Charles
"The Announcer (1982)." [WormR] (34:3, #135) 94, p. 129-130.
"Between the Earthquake, the Volcano and the Leopard." [Antaeus] (75/76) Aut 94, p. 241-246.
"Cold Summer." [Poetry] (164:4) Jl 94, p. 214-215.
"Dead." [ChironR] (13:4) Wint 94, p. 5.
"Feeling Fairly Good Tonight (1985)." [WormR] (34:1, #133) 94, p. 47.
"First Poem Back from Hell." [PaintedB] (53/54) 94, p. 101.
"The Fool." [NewYorkQ] (53) 94, p. 37-39.
"For Those Who Can't Wait." [SlipS] (14) 94, p. 127.
"From the Inward Eye." [PaintedB] (53/54) 94, p. 100.
"He Left (1983)." [WormR] (34:3, #135) 94, p. 130-131.
"Here." [PaintedB] (53/54) 94, p. 99.
"Hey, Buddy, Let's Deal." [Jacaranda] (10) 94, p. 4-5.
"The Highschool Girls (1984)." [WormR] (34:1, #133) 94, p. 45-46.
"The Laughing Heart." [PraS] (68:2) Sum 94, front cover.
"Musings." [Antaeus] (73/74) Spr 94, p. 77-79.
"O Tempora! O Mores! (1984)." [WormR] (34:3, #135) 94, p. 131.
"One More Day." [Jacaranda] (10) 94, p. 8-9.
"Progress? (1983)." [WormR] (34:4, #136) 94, p. 179-180.
"The Rivers." [NewYorkQ] (53) 94, p. 40.
"The Skaters (1984)." [WormR] (34:4, #136) 94, p. 181.
"Snake Eyes." [Jacaranda] (10) 94, p. 10-11.
"The Strange Workings of the Dark Life." [Jacaranda] (10) 94, p. 6-7.
"They Rolled the Whole Bed Out of There." [NewYorkQ] (53) 94, p. 41-42.
"This Is an Advertisement." [Jacaranda] (10) 94, p. 3.
"Trouble with Spain." [ChironR] (13:2) Sum 94, p. 9.
"The Uninitiated (1984)." [WormR] (34:4, #136) 94, p. 180-181.
"Who's Who in America: 1984-1985, Forty-Third Edition (1985)." [WormR] (34:1, #133) 94, p. 46-47.
"Wise." [Boulevard] (9:3, #27) Fall 94, p. 33.
"The Word." [ChironR] (13:4) Wint 94, p. 5.
"You're Out." [NewYorkQ] (53) 94, p. 43.
832. BULLARD, Christopher
"The Ballad of the Rat King." [Hellas] (5:2) Fall-Wint 94, p. 108-109.
"Inherent Vice." [Hellas] (5:1) Spr-Sum 94, p. 87-88.
"Movie-Going." [Hellas] (5:1) Spr-Sum 94, p. 86.
"'The Swing' by Fragonard." [Hellas] (5:2) Fall-Wint 94, p. 105-106.
"Time-Keeping." [Hellas] (5:2) Fall-Wint 94, p. 107.
"A Wall." [Hellas] (5:1) Spr-Sum 94, p. 89-90.
833. BULLOCK, Lawrence
"Profane." [Sun] (221) My 94, p. 30.

834. BUMPS, Susan
"Annie's Magic." [SantaBR] (2:2) Fall-Wint 94, p. 92.
"Giving Homage to the Summer Fruit God." [SantaBR] (2:2) Fall-Wint 94, p. 93.
835. BUNTIN, Stimmons B.
"Indigo Bunting." [SouthernHR] (28:3) Sum 94, p. 246.
836. BURD, Jennifer J.
"Neck X-Ray." [SouthernPR] (34:2) Wint 94, p. 22.
837. BURGESS, Lynne
"Ancestors." [Northeast] (5:11) Wint 94-95, p. 16.
838. BURGOS, Julia de
"Call Out My Number" (tr. by Julio Marzán). [Callaloo] (17:3) Sum 94, p. 671.
"Pentachromatic" (tr. by Julio Marzán). [Callaloo] (17:3) Sum 94, p. 705-706.
"Pentacromia." [Callaloo] (17:3) Sum 94, p. 706.
"Poem of the Intimate Agony" (tr. by Julio Marzán). [Callaloo] (17:3) Sum 94, p. 670.
"Poem with the Final Tune" (tr. by Julio Marzán). [Callaloo] (17:3) Sum 94, p. 669.
"Río Grande de Loíza" (tr. by Grace Schulman). [Callaloo] (17:3) Sum 94, p. 667.
"To Julia de Burgos" (tr. by Jack Agüeros). [Callaloo] (17:3) Sum 94, p. 672-673.
839. BURK, Ronnie
"Cuahtemoc." [Caliban] (14) 94, p. 71.
"Excavations." [Caliban] (14) 94, p. 72.
840. BURKARD, Michael
"His." [CentralP] (23) Spr 94, p. 85-86.
841. BURKE, Marianne
"Astoria." [SouthwR] (79:1) Wint 94, p. 108-110.
842. BURKE, Michael
"Meditations on a Drawing." [JlNJPo] (16:2) Aut 94, p. 8-9.
843. BURLESON, Derick
"Democracy" (Buatre, Rwanda, November 3, 1992). [Poetry] (164:4) Jl 94, p. 197.
"In This Country." [Poetry] (164:4) Jl 94, p. 198-199.
844. BURNHAM, D. S. (P. S.?)
"Natural Language." [ApalQ] (40/41) 94, p. 73-74.
845. BURNHAM, Deborah
"Saving Remnants." [WestB] (35) 94, p. 51.
846. BURNS, Cullen Bailey
"In This World." [PassN] (15:2) Wint 94, p. 8.
"Milk Money." [PassN] (15:2) Wint 94, p. 9.
"To War and Arms." [PassN] (15:2) Wint 94, p. 10.
847. BURNS, Gerald
"August 31, 1991." [Boulevard] (9:1/2, #25/26) Spr 94, p. 60-62.
"For Messrs. Sampsell and Tibbetts." [Talisman] (13) Fall 94-Wint 95, p. 268-269.
"The Other Language." [NewAW] (12) Spr-Sum 94, p. 106-108.
"Procès-Verbaux." [NewAW] (12) Spr-Sum 94, p. 109-111.
848. BURNS, Heather
"Lesson on a Hot Night." [EngJ] (83:5) S 94, p. 54.
849. BURNS, Joanne
"Better Than One: for the Occasional Traveller." [InterQ] (1:2) 93, p. 125-129.
850. BURNS, Ralph
"Aunt." [Field] (51) Fall 94, p. 93-94.
"A Boat Is a Lever" (after Simone Weil). [Field] (51) Fall 94, p. 92.
"Force." [IndR] (17:1) Spr 94, p. 26.
"Stella." [Field] (51) Fall 94, p. 87-91.
851. BURNSIDE, John
"1964." [Pivot] (42) 94, p. 17.
"(Detail)." [Verse] (11:2) Sum 94, p. 18.
"First School." [Verse] (11:2) Sum 94, p. 20.
"Learning Gaelic." [Pivot] (41) 93, p. 45.
"Listen with Mother." [Verse] (11:2) Sum 94, p. 18.
"Naiad." [Pivot] (42) 94, p. 17.
"On Fulford Burn." [NewYorker] (70:33) 17 O 94, p. 54.
"Pisces." [Pivot] (41) 93, p. 45.
"Segovia." [Verse] (11:2) Sum 94, p. 19.
852. BURNSTEEL, Gerald
"Atlantic City Memoir." [HarvardR] (2) Fall 92, p. 118-119.
853. BURR, Gray
"Run, Don't Walk." [Hellas] (5:2) Fall-Wint 94, p. 44-45.

854. BURRIS, Sidney
"The Celebration." [Shen] (44:1) Spr 94, p. 25.
"The Compensation." [IllinoisR] (2:1) Fall 94, p. 7-8.
"For an Audience." [Shen] (44:1) Spr 94, p. 22-24.
"How to Read American Poetry." [Shen] (44:1) Spr 94, p. 21.
855. BURROWS, E. G.
"The Appearance of Being in Charge." [SantaBR] (2:2) Fall-Wint 94, p. 65.
"Bachelor." [SantaBR] (2:2) Fall-Wint 94, p. 66-67.
"Boundaries." [Ascent] (18:3) Spr 94, p. 11.
"Detroit." [ContextS] (4:1) 94, p. 30.
"Experimental Species." [SantaBR] (2:2) Fall-Wint 94, p. 66.
"Now." [SantaBR] (2:2) Fall-Wint 94, p. 67.
"Opera." [GettyR] (7:2) Spr 94, p. 338.
"Sleeping It Off." [Ascent] (18:3) Spr 94, p. 12.
"Toward Pasco." [SantaBR] (2:2) Fall-Wint 94, p. 68.
"The Troubled Shore." [Ascent] (18:3) Spr 94, p. 10.
"The Unholy Ones." [Crazy] (47) Wint 94, p. 18-19.
856. BURSK, Christopher (Chris)
"Cell Count." [NewEngR] (16:4) Fall 94, p. 52-53.
"Compromising Pictures." [Sun] (219) Mr 94, p. 36-37.
"Don't Worry." [Poetry] (165:1) O 94, p. 7-8.
"First Offense." [Crazy] (47) Wint 94, p. 76.
"The Group." [NewEngR] (16:4) Fall 94, p. 54-59.
"The Ice Man." [NewEngR] (16:4) Fall 94, p. 51-52.
"A Sudden Draft." [NewEngR] (16:4) Fall 94, p. 49.
"Tiny." [NewEngR] (16:4) Fall 94, p. 50.
857. BURSKY, Rick
"The Art of Indifference." [BrooklynR] (11) 94, p. 73.
"Brain Tumor." [NewOR] (20:3/4) Fall-Wint 94, p. 134.
"Catacomb." [HayF] (15) Fall-Wint 94, p. 61.
"Instincts." [BrooklynR] (11) 94, p. 72.
"The Last Man on Earth." [PoetL] (89:2) Sum 94, p. 34.
"The Narrow Language." [NewOR] (20:3/4) Fall-Wint 94, p. 135.
"Obligation." [InterPR] (20:1) Spr 94, p. 100.
"Origins." [Verse] (11:1) Spr 94, p. 85.
"Surviving the Titanic." [PaintedB] (53/54) 94, p. 86.
"Testament." [SouthernPR] (34:1) Sum 94, p. 23-24.
"The Tragedy of Tourism" (for Janis). [InterPR] (20:1) Spr 94, p. 101.
858. BURT, John
"Anna Peterson: Ashfield, Massachusetts, February, 1849" (for Rhys and Eleanor Williams). [SouthwR] (79:4) Aut 94, p. 608-622.
"Formalities" (a Sapphic). [ParisR] (36:130) Spr 94, p. 161.
"Love" (a Sapphic). [ParisR] (36:130) Spr 94, p. 161.
"A Spring Night" (a Sapphic). [ParisR] (36:130) Spr 94, p. 161.
"Water" (a Sapphic). [ParisR] (36:130) Spr 94, p. 161.
859. BURT, Paul J.
"Under the Porch" (from "A Time for Reflection"). [AmerPoR] (23:3) My-Je 94, p. 24.
860. BURT, Stephen
"Mods." [HarvardA] (128:2) Wint 94, p. 9.
"Unpleasant Facts." [HarvardA] (128:2) Wint 94, p. 26.
861. BURTCH, Mary
"Every Morning." [ChrC] (111:20) 29 Je-6 Jl 94, p. 628.
862. BUSCH, Trent
"Even Should I Knock." [Outbr] (25) 94, p. 13.
"Gaunt Ships." [Outbr] (25) 94, p. 12.
"I. T. Davis." [AmerS] (63:4) Aut 94, p. 542-543.
"The Uncle." [Thrpny] (59) Fall 94, p. 28.
863. BUSH, Duncan
"The Sunday the Power Went Off." [MalR] (107) Sum 94, p. 186-187.
864. BUSH, Peter
"The Marx Family Saga" (Excerpt, tr. of Juan Goytisolo). [Conjunc] (23) 94, p. 150-165.
865. BUSH, Rebecca
"Afternoon States March." [HeavenB] (11) 94, p. 63.

866. BUSON (1715-1783)
Haiku [AmerPoR] (23:4) Jl-Ag 94, p. 17.Chiyo-Jo, Lady (1701-1775) Haiku [AmerPoR] (23:4) Jl-Ag 94, p. 18.
867. BUSTAMANTE, Ann
"Waiting Our Turn." [HopewellR] (6) 94, p. 87.
868. BUSTAMANTE, Cecilia
"Visiting the Relatives." [Border] (3) Fall 93, p. 5.
869. BUTCHER, Grace
"Fashion Statement." [WestB] (35) 94, p. 75.
"Hunting the Deer." [WestB] (35) 94, p. 76-77.
"Last Concert." [TarRP] (33:2) Spr 94, p. 35.
BUTE, Jing
See JING, Bute
870. BUTLER, Lollie
"The Riddle King" (for my father). [Vis] (46) 94, p. 14.
871. BUTLER, Lorinda T.
"Antigua Me Come From." [CaribbeanW] (8) 94, p. 70-75.
872. BUTLER, Lynne Burris
"Fruit in Autumn." [Ascent] (19:1) Fall 94, p. 50.
"Instructions to the Departing Husband" (Honorable Mention, 8th Annual Contest). [SoCoast] (16) Ja 94, p. 30.
"Playing Dead." [PraS] (68:1) Spr 94, p. 86-87.
873. BUTSON, Barry
"Anna Mae's." [AntigR] (99) Aut 94, p. 35-36.
874. BUTSON, Joe
"Phenomenal Batting Average." [Spitball] (47) Sum 94, p. 29.
875. BUTTERCUP, Timothy
"Queer Queer? Queer!" [ChangingM] (27) Wint 94, p. 17.
876. BUTTERS, Christopher
"Garden." [ChangingM] (27) Wint 94, p. 42.
877. BUTTON, Margo
"Schizophrenic." [Event] (23:1) Spr 94, p. 34-35.
878. BUTTS, W. E.
"Father's Shirt." [PoetL] (89:2) Sum 94, p. 44.
879. BUZBEE, Lewis
"Sunday, Tarzan in His Hammock." [Zyzzyva] (10:1) Spr 94, p. 99-100.
"Sunday, Tarzan in His Hammock" (From the Spring *ZYZZYVA*, a special "all colleague" issue of written work by people in the West Coast publishing industry ...). [Harp] (288:1729) Je 94, p. 33.
880. BYRD, Gregory
"Deer Hunting in the Everglades." [InterQ] (1:4) 94, p. 98.
"Late Epithalamion." [TampaR] (9) Fall 94, p. 52.
881. BYRD, Sigman
"The Child Astronomer." [Border] (4) Spr-Sum 94, p. 7.
882. BYRD, Vicki
"Fishing." [SpiritSH] (59) 94, p. 34-35.
"Round Robbins' Barn." [SpiritSH] (59) 94, p. 33.
883. BYRKIT, Becky
"Couplet" (1994 Sonora Review Poetry Award Winner). [Sonora] (28) Fall 94, p. 67-68.
"I Drink Alone." [Sonora] (28) Fall 94, p. 69-71.
884. BYRNE, Edward
"Solitude: A Meditation in Four Fragments (After Keats)." [SouthernPR] (34:2) Wint 94, p. 44.
885. BYRNE, Elena Karina
"Breaking Unbalance" (Elegy for Lynne). [AmerPoR] (23:6) N-D 94, p. 42.
"Thirst for Them." [Jacaranda] (10) 94, p. 57.
886. BZAI', Shawqi
"Pictures" (tr. by Mansour Ajami). [LitR] (37:3) Spr 94, p. 477-479.

887. CABACUNGAN, Darryl Keola
"Fall into Winter." [ChamLR] (14/15) Spr-Fall 94, p. 150.
"Ha'ina — The Echo." [ChamLR] (14/15) Spr-Fall 94, p. 151.
"Kona Storm Wait." [ChamLR] (14/15) Spr-Fall 94, p. 145.
"Mah Jong Moon Songs." [ChamLR] (14/15) Spr-Fall 94, p. 148.

"Maple Splendor." [ChamLR] (14/15) Spr-Fall 94, p. 143.
"Mid-Autumn Full Moon." [ChamLR] (14/15) Spr-Fall 94, p. 144.
"November Storm." [ChamLR] (14/15) Spr-Fall 94, p. 142.
"October Storm." [ChamLR] (14/15) Spr-Fall 94, p. 141.
"Prelude." [ChamLR] (14/15) Spr-Fall 94, p. 149.
"September Moon." [ChamLR] (14/15) Spr-Fall 94, p. 147.
"September Waning." [ChamLR] (14/15) Spr-Fall 94, p. 140.
"Summer into Fall." [ChamLR] (14/15) Spr-Fall 94, p. 146.

888. CABALLERO-ROBB, Maria Elena
"Harm's Way." [IndR] (17:1) Spr 94, p. 130.

889. CABALQUINTO, Luis
"Spring Concert." [PraS] (68:4) Wint 94, p. 188.

890. CABLE, Gerald
"Falling in a Field." [CrabCR] (8:2/3/9:1/2/3) 94, p. 86.
"Frost." [CrabCR] (8:2/3/9:1/2/3) 94, p. 87.

891. CABRERA, Ramón
"Tu Voz." [Areíto] (4:15) Marzo 94, p. 44.

892. CACALOVA, Libuse
"Poetry" (tr. of Vera Borkovec). [HampSPR] Wint 94, p. 38.
"Summer Afternoon" (tr. by Vera Borkovec). [HampSPR] Wint 94, p. 39.

893. CACOS, James
"Flat tire." [HiramPoR] (57) Fall 94-Wint 95, p. 13.
"The Red Bird." [HiramPoR] (57) Fall 94-Wint 95, p. 12.

894. CADDY, David
"Lines for Sarah at Easter." [Stand] (35:2) Spr 94, p. 27.

895. CADENAS, Rafael
"Amante" (poem excerpts: I, III, tr. by Margaret Sayers Peden). [Trans] (29) Spr 94, p. 48-49.
"The Great Forgotten" (tr. by Margaret Sayers Peden). [Trans] (29) Spr 94, p. 46.
"In the Midst of Uncertainty" (tr. by Margaret Sayers Peden). [Trans] (29) Spr 94, p. 50-51.
"Late, I Take Up the Thread" (tr. by Margaret Sayers Peden). [Trans] (29) Spr 94, p. 45.
"Wish" (tr. by Andrea Galeano and Gail Ghai). [Vis] (45) 94, p. 8.
"You Tear Me" (tr. by Margaret Sayers Peden). [Trans] (29) Spr 94, p. 47.

896. CADER, Teresa
"Invisible Order." [TriQ] (90) Spr-Sum 94, p. 152.
"Six Entries on the Invention of Paper." [TriQ] (90) Spr-Sum 94, p. 150-151.

897. CADERS, Teresa
"Spirit Papers." [Agni] (39) 94, p. 122.

898. CADET, Maurice
"Bitter Strata" (tr. by Jean-Claude Michel). [InterPR] (20:2) Fall 94, p. 25.
"Strates Amères." [InterPR] (20:2) Fall 94, p. 24.

899. CADNUM, Michael
"Anatomy of an Eye." [WillowS] (34) Sum 94, p. 58-59.
"Beach." [PoetryNW] (35:2) Sum 94, p. 22.
"Dry Heat." [NewDeltaR] (10:1) Fall 92-Wint 93, p. 31.
"I Left Out Nearly Everything." [PoetryNW] (35:2) Sum 94, p. 23.
"Mojave River." [SoDakR] (32:1) Spr 94, p. 105.
"Pigeon." [WritersF] (20) 94, p. 110.
"Skeleton of a Whale." [QW] (38) Winter-Spr 93-94, p. 106.

900. CAFAGÑA, Marcus
"Black Girl on the Overpass." [SenR] (24:1) Spr 94, p. 76.
"Eastern High, 1967." [Border] (4) Spr-Sum 94, p. 8-9.
"Gas." [Border] (4) Spr-Sum 94, p. 10-11.
"Justice." [HarvardR] (6) Spr 94, p. 151.
"Remission." [Iowa] (24:3) Fall 94, p. 33.

901. CAGAN, Penny
"Winning the Prize." [Calyx] (15:3) Wint 94-95, p. 56-57.

902. CAIMBEUL, Maoileas
"Cánan." [Verse] (11:2) Sum 94, p. 37.
"Impire Na Mara." [Verse] (11:2) Sum 94, p. 37.
"Language." [Verse] (11:2) Sum 94, p. 37.
"Sea Emperor." [Verse] (11:2) Sum 94, p. 37.

903. CAINE, Shulamith Wechter
"In Japan." [SouthernPR] (34:1) Sum 94, p. 35-36.

904. CAIRNS, Scott
"Farming the Salt Flats." [WeberS] (11:2) Spr-Sum 94, p. 39.
"From 'The Recovered Midrashim of Rabbi Sab'." [Image] (5) Spr 94, p. 50-52.
"Necropolitan." [ParisR] (36:132) Fall 94, p. 26.
"Susceptibilities." [WeberS] (11:2) Spr-Sum 94, p. 39-40.
"Three Sisters." [WeberS] (11:2) Spr-Sum 94, p. 40.
905. CAIRNS, Tom
"A History of Rhubarb." [WestHR] (48:2) Sum 94, p. 166-167.
906. CALABRESE
"Butter." [Dandel] (21:2) 94, p. 60.
"Ida-Mae." [Dandel] (21:2) 94, p. 59.
"Pet Names." [Dandel] (21:2) 94, p. 61.
907. CALBERT, Cathleen
"The Apple Way." [AmerV] (33) 94, p. 120-124.
"In Praise of My Young Husband." [ParisR] (36:131) Sum 94, p. 147-148.
"Trinity." [TriQ] (92) Wint 94-95, p. 81-83.
"The Woman Who Loved Things." [HarvardR] (6) Spr 94, p. 67.
908. CALDER, Alison
"Imagine a Picture" (1st Place, 1994 Poetry Contest). [Dandel] (21:1) 94, p. 5.
"Sometimes She." [Dandel] (21:2) 94, p. 5.
909. CALDWELL, Beverly
"Confessions of a Lapsed Baptist." [Border] (4) Spr-Sum 94, p. 12.
"Life Sentences." [Border] (4) Spr-Sum 94, p. 14.
910. CALENDRILLO, Linda
"The Tree Is Flammable." [NegC] (14:1/2) 94, p. 94.
911. CALEY, Matthew
"Piss-Flowers." [Verse] (11:2) Sum 94, p. 89.
"Thirst." [Verse] (11:2) Sum 94, p. 89.
912. CALHOUN, Laurie
"A Million Little Frogs." [Outbr] (25) 94, p. 14.
913. CALL, Jennifer
"As." [HayF] (14) Spr-Sum 94, p. 47.
914. CALLAHAN, Madelyn Ravotto
"Winter's Children." [PoetL] (89:2) Sum 94, p. 53-54.
915. CALLAN, Anne
"Histories." [MalR] (106) Spr 94, p. 33-34.
"Lament for Odysseus." [MalR] (106) Spr 94, p. 32.
916. CALLIN, Richard
"Naming." [BlackWR] (21:1) Fall-Wint 94, p. 146-148.
"A New Life." [HiramPoR] (55/56) Fall 93-Sum 94, p. 18-19.
"Rope." [HiramPoR] (55/56) Fall 93-Sum 94, p. 14-15.
"Woman on a Train." [HiramPoR] (55/56) Fall 93-Sum 94, p. 16-17.
CALLIS, Amparo Sanz
See SANZ CALLIS, Amparo
917. CALLOWAY, Martha Cowell
"The Oleander Grove." [Blueline] (15) 94, p. 16.
CALVET, Rey Diaz
See DIAZ CALVET, Rey
918. CALVO, Luis Raúl
"Calles Asiáticas." [Nuez] (5:13/14/15) 94, p. 18.
"Los Comedores de Patatas." [Nuez] (5:13/14/15) 94, p. 18.
919. CALZADA, Victor Fowler
"Nothing Lost Will Come Back with the Rain" (tr. by Ruth Behar). [MichQR] (33:3) Sum 94, p. 592-593.
CAMARGO, Joaquín González
See GONZALEZ CAMARGO, Joaquín
920. CAMERON, Juan
"Cámera Oscura" (Selections: Cantos 11, 18, tr. by Cola Franzen). [WorldL] (5) 94, p. 13-14.
"Happening" (tr. by Cola Franzen). [InterQ] (1:1) [93?], p. 140.
"She Who Is Hiding" (tr. by Cola Franzen). [InterQ] (1:1) [93?], p. 141.
921. CAMERON, Mary
"Dreaming Cormorant." [Arc] (33) Fall 94, p. 45.
"The Fall." [MalR] (106) Spr 94, p. 93.
"Ironic Photograph of Lost Love." [MalR] (106) Spr 94, p. 92.
"Things That Are Taught." [MalR] (106) Spr 94, p. 91.

CAMILLO, Kevin Thomas Patrick di
See Di CAMILLO, Kevin Thomas Patrick
922. CAMPBELL, Barbara
"Anita." [ClockR] (9:1/2) 94-95, p. 136-137.
"Australia." [IndR] (17:2) Fall 94, p. 74-75.
"Letter to Roger Mitchell." [ClockR] (9:1/2) 94-95, p. 138.
"Notes on Form." [NewAW] (12) Spr-Sum 94, p. 123-124.
923. CAMPBELL, Carolyn E.
"In Search of Mom's Cafe." [Rosebud] (1:2) Sum 94, p. 12-13.
924. CAMPBELL, Elizabeth
"Passing." [BellR] (17:1/2) Spr-Fall 94, p. 32.
925. CAMPBELL, Joan
"Tonight, a Tree" (Sestina for Drum). [AmerV] (33) 94, p. 5-6.
926. CAMPBELL, Karen Gegax
"Portrait of My Father." [Zyzzyva] (10:4) Wint 94, p. 50.
927. CAMPBELL, Marty
"Dubby Shoonk, Frederiksted." [CaribbeanW] (8) 94, p. 64-65.
928. CAMPBELL, P. Michael
"Our Lady of the Canned Foods." [SantaBR] (2:2) Fall-Wint 94, p. 150.
929. CAMPBELL, Rick
"Even the Ohio Can Change." [MissouriR] (17:2) 94, p. 90.
"Morrison's, 1968." [MissouriR] (17:2) 94, p. 93.
"On Missing the First Step on the Moon." [MissouriR] (17:2) 94, p. 91.
"The Poem in the River." [InterQ] (1:4) 94, p. 87-90.
"Setting Pins, 1966." [MissouriR] (17:2) 94, p. 89.
"The Spring in Tevebaugh Hollow." [MissouriR] (17:2) 94, p. 92.
"To Jennifer, Thinking of Li Po." [MissouriR] (17:2) 94, p. 88.
930. CAMPBELL, Robert
"The Screened Porch." [Atlantic] (273:2) F 94, p. 81.
931. CAMPBELL, Susan Maxwell
"Exile in North Texas." [Border] (4) Spr-Sum 94, p. 15.
932. CAMPBELL, Victor
"The faces of old indians stare at me out of dreams." [HiramPoR] (57) Fall 94-Wint 95, p. 16.
"It is opposite the blues." [HiramPoR] (57) Fall 94-Wint 95, p. 15.
"Rumi is like the message in a bottle." [HiramPoR] (57) Fall 94-Wint 95, p. 14.
933. CAMPERT, Remco
"Message About the Times" (tr. by Manfred Wolf). [GrahamHR] (18) Wint 94-95, p. 18.
"Poetry" (tr. by Manfred Wolf). [GrahamHR] (18) Wint 94-95, p. 19.
"Sunday" (tr. by Manfred Wolf). [GrahamHR] (18) Wint 94-95, p. 20.
934. CAMPIGLIO, Stephen
"News of the Road We're Riding." [LitR] (37:4) Sum 94, p. 605.
935. CAMPION, Dan
"Anachronism." [Light] (12) Wint 94-95, p. 20.
"The Censor." [Light] (9) Spr 94, p. 20.
"A Collation for John Frederick Nims." [Light] (9) Spr 94, p. 23-25.
"Suspense." [Border] (4) Spr-Sum 94, p. 16.
936. CAMPO, Rafael
"The 10,000th AIDS Death in San Francisco" (January 1993). [PraS] (68:4) Wint 94, p. 48-49.
"Aida." [AmerV] (34) 94, p. 41-42.
"Aunt Toni's Heart." [BostonR] (19:1) Fe-Mr 94, p. 34.
"The Battle Hymn of the Republic." [Ploughs] (20:1) Spr 94, p. 144-145.
"The Cuban Sky." [PraS] (68:4) Wint 94, p. 47-48.
"Five Patients." [Thrpny] (57) Spr 94, p. 17.
"In English That Is Spanish." [PraS] (68:4) Wint 94, p. 49-50.
"Madrid." [PraS] (68:4) Wint 94, p. 47.
"My Voice." [Nat] (259:12) O 17 94, p. 432.
"Song Before Death." [KenR] (NS 16:4) Fall 94, p. 131-138.
937. CAMPOS, Javier
"Carpe Diem." [Inti] (39) Primavera 94, p. 254.
"El Poeta Joven" (Para Carolyn Kost y Nick Hill). [Inti] (39) Primavera 94, p. 253-254.
938. CANNER, Niko
"Acts of Indemnity and Oblivion." [HarvardA] (129:1) Sum 94, p. 31.

"The Book of Modest Invention." [HarvardA] (129:1) Sum 94, p. 27.

939. CANNON, Harold C.
"The River Zambesi." [Light] (11) Aut 94, p. 24.

940. CANNON, Melissa
"The King of Handcuffs" (2nd Prize, 8th Annual Contest). [SoCoast] (16) Ja 94, p. 28.

941. CANNON, William
"A Benediction:" (for Eugene A. Nolan, S.J.). [CumbPR] (14:1) Fall 94, p. 33.
"How I Would Say It." [Wind] (74) 94, p. 10.

942. CANTOR, Ellen
"A Family History" (for Jane). [NewEngR] (16:1) Wint 94, p. 78-79.
"Making Meat." [NewEngR] (16:1) Wint 94, p. 81-82.
"This Eye." [NewEngR] (16:1) Wint 94, p. 79-80.

943. CANTRELL, Charles
"The Dog Inside." [SoCoast] (17) Je 94, p. 29.

944. CANTU, Norma
"Action. Thought. Spirit." [PraS] (68:4) Wint 94, p. 163-164.

945. CANTWELL, B. A.
"Conspiracy, the Crest." [XavierR] (14:1) Spr 94, p. 47.
"Dormant." [XavierR] (14:1) Spr 94, p. 46.
"Jasper." [Amelia] (7:3, #22) 94, p. 90.

946. CANTWELL, Billie Lou
"Balance." [Border] (4) Spr-Sum 94, p. 17.
"Homecoming." [Border] (4) Spr-Sum 94, p. 19-20.

947. CAPEK, Karel
"We Are Two" (tr. by Bernard S. Mikofsky). [WorldL] (5) 94, p. 40.

948. CAPPELLO, Rosemary
"The Great Depression." [Pearl] (20) Spr 94, p. 80.

CARBEAU, Mitchell Les
See LesCARBEAU, Mitchell

949. CARBO, Nick
"English as a Second Language." [WestHR] (48:1) Spr 94, p. 14-15.
"Scarborough Beach" (for Denise). [WestHR] (48:1) Spr 94, p. 13.

950. CARDENAS, Rene F.
"Hebbronville, Texas: Summer, 1955." [Callaloo] (17:2) Sum 94, p. 597.
"Modern Mexican Instructions." [MidwQ] (35:4) Sum 94, p. 406.
"Persons Who Hesitate in Doorways." [SmPd] (31:3, #92) Fall 94, p. 25.
"Rage, Torment and Peace." [XavierR] (14:1) Spr 94, p. 48.
"Reunion and Eclipse in San Antonio, June 1992." [Callaloo] (17:2) Sum 94, p. 590-596.

951. CARDONA-HINE, Alvaro
"Farina." [DarkMoon] (1) 94, p. 25.
"In the Month of May." [DarkMoon] (1) 94, p. 23.
"Milkmusic." [DarkMoon] (1) 94, p. 24.
"New Mexico Night." [DarkMoon] (1) 94, p. 27.
"Short Bio." [DarkMoon] (1) 94, p. 26.

952. CARDUCCI, Lisa
"A Certain Sea" (tr. by Genni Gunn). [InterPR] (20:2) Fall 94, p. 37.
"Une Certaine Mer." [InterPR] (20:2) Fall 94, p. 36.

953. CAREY, Barbara
"Being of This World." [Quarry] (42:4) Mr 94, p. 58.

954. CAREY, Michael
"Clearing the Yard of Fallen Branches" (for Andrew McCullagh Carey, age 5). [ChrC] (111:7) 2 Mr 94, p. 212.
"Standing by a Field of Virgin Prairie." [ChrC] (111:18) 1-8 Je 94, p. 563.

955. CARIAGA, Catalina
"No Moon." [Zyzzyva] (10:1) Spr 94, p. 131.

956. CARILLO, Isolina
"Dos Gardenias." [Areíto] (4:15) Marzo 94, p. 42.

957. CARLBOM, Arthur
"Class Act." [AnthNEW] (6) 94, p. 31.

958. CARLIN, Kim
"Washington Street." [SouthernPR] (34:1) Sum 94, p. 70-72.

959. CARLIN, Vuyelwa
"The Madwoman Buries Her Imaginary Child." [Stand] (35:3) Sum 94, p. 69.

960. CARLSON, Barbara Siegel
"Geode." [SpoonR] (19:1) Wint-Spr 94, p. 105-106.
"Symphonic." [SpoonR] (19:1) Wint-Spr 94, p. 103-104.
961. CARLSON, C. A.
"Crush." [ChiR] (40:2/3) 94, p. 132-133.
962. CARLSON, Nancy Naomi
"Carriage Hill Adagio" (For Great-aunt Shirley). [Wind] (73) 94, p. 4-5.
963. CARMELL, Pamela
"IX. Once I heard you say" (tr. of Rafael Arráiz Lucca). [Trans] (29) Spr 94, p. 133.
"Ignorance" (tr. of Hanni Ossott). [Trans] (29) Spr 94, p. 89.
"The Illness" (tr. of Hanni Ossott). [Trans] (29) Spr 94, p. 86-88.
"Leningrad" (tr. of Rafael Arráiz Lucca). [Trans] (29) Spr 94, p. 132.
"Ownership" (tr. of Hanni Ossott). [Trans] (29) Spr 94, p. 89.
"A Poet (Disconcerted) Asks Himself" (tr. of Rafael Arráiz Lucca). [Trans] (29) Spr 94, p. 134-135.
"Things" (tr. of Rafael Arráiz Lucca). [Trans] (29) Spr 94, p. 131.
964. CARMEN, George
"Parchment." [Ledge] (17) Wint 94, p. 12-13.
965. CARMEN, Marilyn Elain
"Found Poetry." [Grain] (21:4) Spr 94, p. 130.
966. CARMONA, Lucia
"Y Dios Entre los Paramos" (Selections: 2 poems). [Luz] (6) My 94, p. 27-29.
967. CARNECI, Magda
"Ars Exilum Mundi" (tr. by Adam J. Sorkin, w. the author). [Vis] (46) 94, p. 29.
968. CARNEY, Rob
"Cain and Job Shoot Pool." [CreamCR] (18:1) Spr 94, p. 5.
"Don't Be Afraid, the Clown's Afraid Too." [Callaloo] (17:4) Fall 94, p. 1125-1126.
"A Love Supreme." [BellArk] (10:2) Mr-Ap 94, p. 30.
"Once Upon a Time, There Was a Holding Corporation Called Old America." [Callaloo] (17:4) Fall 94, p. 1123-1124.
"Salt in Lot's Wounds." [CreamCR] (18:1) Spr 94, p. 7.
"Song of the Underground Railroad." [Zyzzyva] (10:4) Wint 94, p. 135-138.
"Still-Life with Magdelene and Wind." [CreamCR] (18:1) Spr 94, p. 6.
969. CARPENTER, Carol
"Collage." [BellR] (17:1/2) Spr-Fall 94, p. 54-55.
"Epistemology." [FourQ] (8:1) Spr 94, p. 50.
970. CARPENTER, Jillyn
"I Have Pictures." [Amelia] (7:4, #23) 94, p. 177-178.
"January in Logan, Utah." [Amelia] (7:4, #23) 94, p. 176.
"Message." [Amelia] (7:4, #23) 94, p. 176-177.
971. CARPENTER, Lucas
"Amerika, Du Hast Es Besser" (— Goethe). [Poem] (71) My 94, p. 30.
"Commencement 1992." [WebR] (18) Fall 94, p. 65-66.
"Commencement 1993." [Poem] (71) My 94, p. 25.
"Fourth of July" (Scottsbluff, Nebraska). [Poem] (71) My 94, p. 28-29.
"Perils of the Affect." [Journal] (18:2) Fall-Wint 94, p. 45.
"Sitting on the Front Porch of Andalusia." [Poem] (71) My 94, p. 26-27.
972. CARPER, Thomas
"Harry's Anemometers." [Pivot] (42) 94, p. 18.
"Her Handbag." [Pivot] (42) 94, p. 18.
"Roses in the Garden." [Pivot] (41) 93, p. 52.
"Rozemaryn's Phone Call." [Journal] (18:2) Fall-Wint 94, p. 88.
"The Salvation of Faust." [Poetry] (163:5) F 94, p. 267.
"Sisyphus's Pet Rock." [Poetry] (163:5) F 94, p. 268.
"Step by Step." [Pivot] (41) 93, p. 53.
973. CARRIER, Warren
"On the River." [OhioR] (52) 94, p. 121.
974. CARRION de FIERRO, Fanny
"Blue Solitude" (tr. by Sally Cheney Bell). [PoetL] (89:1) Spr 94, p. 26.
"Green Solitude" (tr. by Sally Cheney Bell). [PoetL] (89:1) Spr 94, p. 25.
"Only You" (tr. by Sally C. Bell). [WebR] (18) Fall 94, p. 13.
"Red Solitude" (tr. by Sally Cheney Bell). [PoetL] (89:1) Spr 94, p. 27.
975. CARROLL, Miriam
"Imani." [SinW] (53) Sum-Fall 94, p. 54.
976. CARRUTH, Hayden
"August 1945." [NewRep] (210:15) 11 Ap 94, p. 38.

"The Brook." [TriQ] (91) Fall 94, p. 161.
"What To Do." [TriQ] (91) Fall 94, p. 162.

977. CARRYL, Guy Wetmore
"The Sycophantic Fox and the Gullible Raven." [Light] (12) Wint 94-95, p. 24.

978. CARSON, Anne
"The Fall of Rome: A Traveller's Guide." [Pequod] (38) 94, p. 15-44.
"The Glass Essay." [Raritan] (13:3) Wint 94, p. 25-63.

979. CARSON, Jeffrey
"The Elegies of Jutting Rock" (Selections: 6 poems, tr. of Odysseus Elytis, w. Nikos Sarris). [AmerPoR] (23:6) N-D 94, p. 27-30.
"Elegy of Grüningen" (In memory of Friedrich von Hardenberg. Tr. of Odysseus Elytis, w. Nikos Sarris).). [NoDaQ] (62:4) Fall 94-95, p. 9-10.
"The Garden Was Entering the Sea" (tr. of Odysseus Elytis, w. Nikos Sarris). [NoDaQ] (62:4) Fall 94-95, p. 7-8.
"The Icon" (tr. of Odysseus Elytis, w. Nikos Sarris). [AmerPoR] (23:4) Jl-Ag 94, p. 48.

980. CARTARESCU, Mircea
"Memory of an October Evening in 1984" (tr. by Adam J. Sorkin and Ileana Ciocarlie). [AnotherCM] (27) 94, p. 13-14.
"Not a Thing About Survival Technique" (tr. by Adam J. Sorkin and Ileana Ciocârlie). [NewDeltaR] (10:2) Spr-Sum 93, p. 68.
"Our Love Has Gone" (tr. by Adam J. Sorkin and Ileana Ciocarlie). [AnotherCM] (27) 94, p. 15-16.

981. CARTER, Albert Howard, III
"Golden Man." [HiramPoR] (55/56) Fall 93-Sum 94, p. 20.

982. CARTER, Anne Babson
"Three Blocks from San Marco." [ParisR] (36:131) Sum 94, p. 211-212.

983. CARTER, Ellin
"Cosmology." [HayF] (15) Fall-Wint 94, p. 99.

984. CARTER, Jared
"The Burial." [WebR] (18) Fall 94, p. 71-73.
"Linen." [Poetry] (165:3) D 94, p. 155.
"Wind Egg." [LaurelR] (28:1) Wint 94, p. 24-25.

985. CARTER, Jimmy
"The Ballad of Tom Gordy." [NewOR] (20:1/2) Spr-Sum 94, p. 19-20.
"A Battle Prayer." [NewOR] (20:1/2) Spr-Sum 94, p. 25.
"Considering the Void." [NewOR] (20:1/2) Spr-Sum 94, p. 26.
"Contemplation of What Has Been created, and Why." [NegC] (14:1/2) 94, p. 4.
"The County Boss Explains How It Is." [NewOR] (20:1/2) Spr-Sum 94, p. 16-17.
"The Day No One Came to the Peanut Picker." [NewOR] (20:1/2) Spr-Sum 94, p. 18.
"The History of a Point." [NewOR] (20:1/2) Spr-Sum 94, p. 21.
"Hollow Eyes, Bellies, Hearts." [NegC] (14:1/2) 94, p. 2-3.
"It Can Fool the Sun." [NewOR] (20:1/2) Spr-Sum 94, p. 22.
"Itinerant Songsters Visit Our Village." [NewOR] (20:1/2) Spr-Sum 94, p. 27.
"Miss Lillian." [NewOR] (20:1/2) Spr-Sum 94, p. 24.
"Of Possum and Fatback." [NewOR] (20:1/2) Spr-Sum 94, p. 13-14.
"Plains." [NewOR] (20:1/2) Spr-Sum 94, p. 15.
"A President Expresses Concern on a Visit to Westminster Abbey." [NewOR] (20:1/2) Spr-Sum 94, p. 23.
"Prosperity Doesn't Suit Everyone." [NewEngR] (16:3) Sum 94, p. 93.
"A Reflection of Beauty in Washington." [NegC] (14:1/2) 94, p. 1.
"A Winter Morning." [NegC] (14:1/2) 94, p. 5.

986. CARTER, Michaela
"Coming of Age." [AntR] (52:4) Fall 94, p. 613.

987. CARTER, Stephen W.
"Reflex." [HiramPoR] (55/56) Fall 93-Sum 94, p. 21.

988. CARTER, Steve
"Humor As an Occult Art." [Plain] (15:1) Fall 94, p. 16.
"In the Fullness of Time." [ChamLR] (14/15) Spr-Fall 94, p. 184-185.
"New World." [LitR] (37:4) Sum 94, p. 603.

989. CARTER, Terry Anne
"Grammar Lesson." [Dandel] (21:1) 94, p. 35.

990. CARTER-JONES, Sheila
"How Far Down." [PennR] (6:1) 94, p. 19.
"Sweet Mulberries." [PennR] (6:1) 94, p. 18.

CARTERET, Mark de
See DeCARTERET, Mark
991. CARTLEDGE-HAYES, Mary
"Lost Souls." [ChrC] (111:9) 16 Mr 94, p. 270.
992. CARTWRIGHT, Keith
"The Bridge." [Shen] (44:2) Sum 94, p. 66-67.
993. CARTWRIGHT, William (17th c.)
"No Platonique Love." [SoCoast] (16) Ja 94, p. 62.
994. CASAL, Lourdes
"For Ana Veldford" (tr. by David Frye). [MichQR] (33:3) Sum 94, p. 415-416.
995. CASE, David Allen
"Alexandrian Vespers." [CarolQ] (46:2) Wint 94, p. 78.
"Back Home." [Jacaranda] (10) 94, p. 93.
"The Skin of Grief." [Jacaranda] (10) 94, p. 92.
996. CASELLA, Paul
"Wednesdays Seem to Be My Day." [Plain] (14:3) Spr 94, p. 28.
997. CASEY, Brenda
"I Know" (tr. of Pierre Morency, w. Elizabeth Hahn). [InterPR] (20:2) Fall 94, p. 75.
"I Must Say" (tr. of Pierre Morency, w. Elizabeth Hahn). [InterPR] (20:2) Fall 94, p. 73.
998. CASEY, Deb
"The Man with No Sons." [PraS] (68:3) Fall 94, p. 110-111.
"Mortality and a Spoon." [PraS] (68:3) Fall 94, p. 113-114.
"Preparation." [PraS] (68:3) Fall 94, p. 117.
"Returning the Chain Saw." [PraS] (68:3) Fall 94, p. 115-116.
"The Tall Man Smiles" (The Ruins of *Palenque*). [PraS] (68:3) Fall 94, p. 111-113.
999. CASEY, Richard C.
"Noli Me Tangere." [SmPd] (31:3, #92) Fall 94, p. 29.
1000. CASSADORE, D. R.
"Home of Cowboy Poetry: Elko, NV." [Interim] (13:2) Fall-Wint 94-95, p. 6.
"Watermelon Seeds." [Interim] (13:2) Fall-Wint 94-95, p. 7.
1001. CASSELMAN, Barry
"Channel Selections." [SantaBR] (2:2) Fall-Wint 94, p. 144-145.
1002. CASSIN, Maxine
"2901 II." [NewOR] (20:1/2) Spr-Sum 94, p. 109.
"Autumnal." [NewOR] (20:1/2) Spr-Sum 94, p. 101.
"A Bouquet from St. Martinville." [NewOR] (20:1/2) Spr-Sum 94, p. 105.
"Canaries" (for Vassar). [NewOR] (20:1/2) Spr-Sum 94, p. 104.
"Czeslaw Milosz." [NewOR] (20:1/2) Spr-Sum 94, p. 103.
"Dandelion." [NewOR] (20:1/2) Spr-Sum 94, p. 102.
"Dear Emily." [NewOR] (20:1/2) Spr-Sum 94, p. 106.
"Encounter with Nancy." [NewOR] (20:1/2) Spr-Sum 94, p. 108.
"Study in White: New Orleans by Moonlight." [NegC] (13:2/3) 93, p. 7.
"Willingness to Stumble in Learning." [NewOR] (20:1/2) Spr-Sum 94, p. 107.
1003. CASSITY, Turner
"Crime and Punishment." [ChiR] (40:2/3) 94, p. 9-10.
1004. CASTEDO, Elena
"She's Got Wrinkles." [PraS] (68:4) Wint 94, p. 149-150.
1005. CASTELLANOS, Rosario
"On the Edge of Pleasure" (tr. by Magda Bogin). [Calyx] (15:2) Sum 94, p. 34-35.
1006. CASTILLO, Efraim
"1- El Rostro del Estafador." [CuadP] (8:22) Enero-Abril 94, p. 19-22.
"2- Esta Ventana Que Abro." [CuadP] (8:22) Enero-Abril 94, p. 22-24.
1007. CASTILLO, Joyce Mc. Gregor del
"El Cumpleaños" (tr. of Joan Peternel). [Luz] (6) My 94, p. 35.
"La Familia" (tr. of Joan Peternel). [Luz] (6) My 94, p. 37.
"¿Propulsion o Traccion?" (tr. of Joan Peternel). [Luz] (6) My 94, p. 39.
1008. CASTILLO, Lenora
"History." [PraS] (68:4) Wint 94, p. 87-88.
"The Summer of Good-bys." [PraS] (68:4) Wint 94, p. 89.
1009. CASTLEBERRY, R. T.
"What Lovers Say." [Vis] (46) 94, p. 15.
1010. CATLIN, Alan
"The Bartender at Pauly's." [WormR] (34:3, #135) 94, p. 99.
"She Was Running." [WormR] (34:3, #135) 94, p. 99.

1011. CATULLUS
"Catullus 65" (tr. by Roger Greenwald). [Pequod] (37) 94, p. 65.
Translations by Nicholas Rockel [Descant] (25:1, #84) Spr 94, p. 27, 30-32, 34.
1012. CAUFIELD, Tom
"Appreciating the Classics." [WormR] (34:1, #133) 94, p. 6.
"Eddie." [WormR] (34:1, #133) 94, p. 8-9.
"Full Color." [WormR] (34:1, #133) 94, p. 6-7.
"Memphis, Art Show." [WormR] (34:1, #133) 94, p. 9-10.
"Naked by the Train Tunnel." [WormR] (34:1, #133) 94, p. 7-8.
"No, I Don't Remember That." [WormR] (34:1, #133) 94, p. 7.
"Walmart Has Everything That a Man Could Want." [WormR] (34:1, #133) 94, p. 5.
1013. CAULFIELD, Carlota
"Landscapes of the Mind." [MichQR] (33:4) Fall 94, p. 701.
"El Tiempo Es una Mujer Que Espera" (Selections: 3 poems). [Luz] (6) My 94, p. 17-19.
1014. CAVAFY, Constantine (C. P., Constantine P.)
"Intervention of the Gods" (tr. by John Rodenbeck). [Iowa] (24:1) Wint 94, p. 162.
"On the Actual Site" (tr. by John Rodenbeck). [Iowa] (24:1) Wint 94, p. 162.
"The Ships" (tr. by Edmund Keeley and Dimitri Gondicas). [Antaeus] (75/76) Aut 94, p. 247-249.
1015. CAVALIERI, Grace
"The Protest." [IndR] (17:1) Spr 94, p. 15.
1016. CAVALLO, Diana
"Requiem for Louise Varèse." [Confr] (54/55) Fall 94-Wint 95, p. 279-281.
1017. CAVANAGH, Clare
"Allegro Ma Non Troppo" (tr. of Wislawa Szymborska, w. Stanislaw Baranczak). [Salm] (103) Sum 94, p. 266-267.
"A Byzantine Mosaic" (tr. of Wislawa Szymborska, w. Stanislaw Baranczak). [HarvardR] (2) Fall 92, p. 150-151.
"Coloratura" (tr. of Wislawa Szymborska, w. Stanislaw Baranczak). [Salm] (103) Sum 94, p. 268-269.
"Epitaph" (tr. of Wislawa Szymborska, w. Stanislaw Baranczak). [PartR] (61:4) Fall 94, p. 633.
"May 16, 1973" (tr. of Wislawa Szymborska, w. Stanislaw Baranczak). [HarvardR] (7) Fall 94, p. 36-37.
"On the Banks of the Styx" (tr. of Wislawa Szymborska, w. Stanislaw Baranczak). [Salm] (103) Sum 94, p. 269-270.
"Poetry Reading" (tr. of Wislawa Szymborska, w. Stanislaw Baranczak). [PartR] (61:4) Fall 94, p. 634.
"Sky" (tr. of Wislawa Szymborska, w. Stanislaw Baranczak). [Agni] (39) 94, p. 20-21.
"We're Extremely Fortunate" (tr. of Wislawa Szymborska, w. Stanislaw Baranczak). [Salm] (103) Sum 94, p. 270-271.
1018. CAVANAUGH, Elaine
"In Painter's Words." [AnthNEW] (6) 94, p. 11.
1019. CAVANAUGH, William C.
"After the Seventh Season, Tiresias." [HopewellR] (6) 94, p. 88.
1020. CAYLE
"Acts/Ax of Love." [AfAmRev] (28:4) Wint 94, p. 591.
"Death Says." [AfAmRev] (28:4) Wint 94, p. 591-592.
"The Driven Who Ride Anyway." [AfAmRev] (28:4) Wint 94, p. 595-596.
"For Etheridge Knight (1933—March 10, 1991)." [AfAmRev] (28:4) Wint 94, p. 592-594.
"The Hand That Forgets." [AfAmRev] (28:4) Wint 94, p. 594-595.
1021. CECIL, Richard
"Elegy for Minnie." [HopewellR] (6) 94, p. 92-93.
"Lucullus Dines Alone." [HopewellR] (6) 94, p. 89-91.
"Rip Van Winkle." [Crazy] (47) Wint 94, p. 69-70.
"Room with View / Radio." [Crazy] (47) Wint 94, p. 71-72.
"Swing Low, Sweet Chariot." [Crazy] (47) Wint 94, p. 73-75.
"Unwritten Elegy" (For Cleo, 1971-1992). [Crazy] (47) Wint 94, p. 66.
"Words for Robert Lowell." [Crazy] (47) Wint 94, p. 67-68.
1022. CEFOLA, Ann
"How My Father Looked Like Superman." [Confr] (54/55) Fall 94-Wint 95, p. 319.

1023. CELAN, Paul
"A Boomerang on Breath" (tr. by Niko and Heather McHugh). [SenR] (24:1) Spr 94, p. 48.
"Chance Having Been Rigged" (tr. by Niko and Heather McHugh). [SenR] (24:1) Spr 94, p. 46.
"The Island of the Visible" (tr. by Niko and Heather McHugh). [SenR] (24:1) Spr 94, p. 47.
"Out of Angel Substance" (tr. by Niko and Heather McHugh). [SenR] (24:1) Spr 94, p. 52.
"Pain, the Syllable" (tr. by Niko and Heather McHugh). [SenR] (24:1) Spr 94, p. 50-51.
"Trajectile" (tr. by Cid Corman). [WorldL] (5) 94, p. 12.
"What Is Required of Stars" (tr. by Cid Corman). [WorldL] (5) 94, p. 12.
"You with the Dark Slingshot" (tr. by Niko and Heather McHugh). [SenR] (24:1) Spr 94, p. 49.
"You with the Darkscantling" (tr. by Cid Corman). [WorldL] (5) 94, p. 12.
1024. CELAYA, Gabriel
"Marea del Silencio — 41" (tr. by Martin Paul and José A. Elgorriaga). [GrandS] (13:1, #49) Sum 94, p. 222-223.
1025. CERAVOLO, Joseph
"Autumn-Time, Wind and the Planet Pluto." [AmerPoR] (23:4) Jl-Ag 94, p. 4.
"Caught in the Swamp." [AmerPoR] (23:4) Jl-Ag 94, p. 3.
"Dangers of the Journey to the Happy Land." [AmerPoR] (23:4) Jl-Ag 94, p. 6.
"Data." [AmerPoR] (23:4) Jl-Ag 94, p. 3.
"Grow." [AmerPoR] (23:4) Jl-Ag 94, p. 3.
"Ho Ho Ho Caribou" (for Rosemary). [AmerPoR] (23:4) Jl-Ag 94, p. 4.
"Lighthouse." [AmerPoR] (23:4) Jl-Ag 94, p. 3.
"Pain Songs." [AmerPoR] (23:4) Jl-Ag 94, p. 5.
"Soul in Migration." [AmerPoR] (23:4) Jl-Ag 94, p. 6.
"Warmth." [AmerPoR] (23:4) Jl-Ag 94, p. 3.
"White Fish in Reeds." [AmerPoR] (23:4) Jl-Ag 94, p. 3.
"Wild Provoke of the Endurance Sky." [AmerPoR] (23:4) Jl-Ag 94, p. 3.
1026. CERNUDA, Luis
"Impressions of Exile" (1-2, tr. by Eddie Flintoff). [Stand] (35:2) Spr 94, p. 34-35.
1027. CESARIC, Dobrisa
"Fruit Tree, After a Rain" (tr. by P. H. Liotta). [InterQ] (1:3) 94, p. 187.
1028. CHACE, Joel
"Mushrooms." [Pembroke] (26) 94, p. 113.
1029. CHACON, Alfredo
"I Want to Talk to You, Word" (tr. by Tess O'Dwyer). [Trans] (29) Spr 94, p. 146.
"Once the Voice Is Herself" (tr. by Tess O'Dwyer). [Trans] (29) Spr 94, p. 145.
"Utter" (tr. by Tess O'Dwyer). [Trans] (29) Spr 94, p. 144.
1030. CHADWICK, William
"Dwarf Tossing Contest." [Descant] (24:4, #83) Wint 93-94, p. 70-71.
"The Education of Dwarf." [Descant] (24:4, #83) Wint 93-94, p. 65-66.
"Loose-hilted Dwarf." [Descant] (24:4, #83) Wint 93-94, p. 68-69.
"Nice Dwarf." [Descant] (24:4, #83) Wint 93-94, p. 64.
"Periodontal Dwarf." [Descant] (24:4, #83) Wint 93-94, p. 72-73.
"Tournaments." [Descant] (24:4, #83) Wint 93-94, p. 67.
1031. CHALIFOUX, Kristine
"The Trial of Harry Crosby." [ClockR] (9:1/2) 94-95, p. 36-37.
1032. CHALLENDER, Craig
"Shadow Dancing." [MidwQ] (35:2) Wint 94, p. 164.
1033. CHAMBERLAIN, Cara
"Siberia." [Parting] (7:1) Sum 94, p. 26-27.
"The Taming." [PoetL] (89:1) Spr 94, p. 36.
"Van Eyck." [Parting] (7:1) Sum 94, p. 61.
1034. CHAMBERS, John
"Hearing Callas in the Spring." [NegC] (14:1/2) 94, p. 169-170.
"Turning Over" (A Memory of Gracie and George Miller). [NegC] (14:1/2) 94, p. 171-173.
1035. CHAMLEE, Kenneth
"Change of Season." [CumbPR] (14:1) Fall 94, p. 17.
"The English Professor's Flag Football Game" (Robert Penn Warren Poetry Prize Winner: Honorable Mention). [CumbPR] (14:1) Fall 94, p. 15-16.
"The Pull." [CumbPR] (14:1) Fall 94, p. 18-19.

1036. CHANDLER, Tom
"1943 Steel Penny." [BrooklynR] (11) 94, p. 102.
"Alcyone." [BrooklynR] (11) 94, p. 104.
"The Lumper." [PoetL] (89:4) Wint 94-95, p. 34.
"The University of When." [BrooklynR] (11) 94, p. 103.
1037. CHANDONNET, Ann Fox
"On Being Asked by a Gay Friend to Lend Him a Bra for Halloween." [Border] (3) Fall 93, p. 6.
1038. CHANDRA, G. S. Sharat
"Shadows and Dreams." [InterQ] (1:2) 93, p. 176.
1039. CHANG, Diana
"Second Nature." [InterQ] (1:2) 93, p. 36-37.
1040. CHANG, Edmond
"Tumor" (tr. of Hsiang Ming). [Talisman] (12) Spr 94, p. 159.
1041. CHANG, Mo
"Temple of Thirty-Three Rooms" (tr. by Wai-lim Yip). [Talisman] (12) Spr 94, p. 154-155.
CHANG, Soo Ko
See KO, Chang-soo
1042. CHANG, Victoria M.
"The Laws of the Garden." [HawaiiR] (18:1, #40) Spr 94, p. 107.
"My Parents' Restaurant, Dragon Inn." [HawaiiR] (18:1, #40) Spr 94, p. 105.
CHANG, Yanbing
See CHEN, Yanbing
1043. CHANG, Young-hee
"The Female Buddha" (at The Delivery Room in Severance General Hospital, tr. of Kim Seung-Hee). [BambooR] (63/64) Sum-Fall 94, p. 21-22.
1044. CHANGA, Ras
"Born Again." [MassR] (35:3/4) Aut-Wint 94, p. 544-545.
1045. CHAPMAN, I. M.
"The Ascetic Chauvinist, or, What Is the Chief End of Man?" [Wind] (73) 94, p. 5-6.
1046. CHAPMAN, Jane Autenrieth
"Mother, You Called Me." [CreamCR] (18:1) Spr 94, p. 72.
1047. CHAPMAN, Mark
"To One Who Was a Muse." [JINJPo] (16:1) Spr 94, p. 1.
1048. CHAPMAN, Robin S.
"1/17, Banff." [Northeast] (5:11) Wint 94-95, p. 5.
"Dreaming the Rainforest." [Nimrod] (38:1) Fall-Wint 94, p. 90.
"Eopsaltria Australis: Dawn Singer." [Nimrod] (38:1) Fall-Wint 94, p. 89.
1049. CHAPMAN-BOSSENCE, S.
"The Cat and the Lady" (Honorable Mention, The Amelia Awards). [Amelia] (7:4, #23) 94, p. 45-47.
1050. CHAPPELL, Fred
"XXIII Literary Critic." [NewEngR] (16:2) Spr 94, p. 157.
"XXV Another." [NewEngR] (16:2) Spr 94, p. 156.
"XXVII ANOTHER." [NewEngR] (16:2) Spr 94, p. 157.
"XXXIII Grace Before Meat." [NewEngR] (16:2) Spr 94, p. 155.
"XXXIV Another." [NewEngR] (16:2) Spr 94, p. 155-156.
"LXXXIX in the Garden." [NewEngR] (16:2) Spr 94, p. 157.
"The Rose and Afterward." [SouthernHR] (28:1) Wint 94, p. 66.
1051. CHAR, René
"Man Flees" (tr. by Susanne Dubroff). [HampSPR] Wint 94, p. 9.
"The Owl" (tr. by Richard Jones). [PoetryE] (37/38) Spr 94, p. 237.
1052. CHARACH, Ron
"At Catwalk Level." [MalR] (109) Wint 94, p. 75.
CHARME, Mark du
See DuCHARME, Mark
CHARRO, Francisco Dominguez
See DOMINGUEZ CHARRO, Francisco
1053. CHARTRAND, Lina
"Doctor Xiabo." [Grain] (21:4) Spr 94, p. 63-64.
1054. CHASE, Aleka
"Beginnings" (2 poems). [PoetryE] (37/38) Spr 94, p. 83-84.
"First Moscow Poem." [PoetryE] (37/38) Spr 94, p. 81-82.
"Home." [Vis] (44) 94, p. 15.

1055. CHASE, Karen
"Kazimierz Square." [AnotherCM] (27) 94, p. 17-25.
1056. CHASE, Linda
"Sun Hats." [Verse] (11:1) Spr 94, p. 95.
1057. CHASE, Naomi Feigelson
"I Can Tell You Now." [HarvardR] (2) Fall 92, p. 92.
1058. CHATILLON, Pierre
"Les Mots." [InterPR] (20:2) Fall 94, p. 16-20.
"Words" (tr. by Judith Cowan). [InterPR] (20:2) Fall 94, p. 17-21.
1059. CHATTOPADHYAY, Chaitali
"Street Drama" (tr. by Arlene Zide and Paramita Banerjee). [InterQ] (1:2) 93, p. 187.
1060. CHATTOPADHYAY, Gita
"Thirty-Five Parganas" (tr. by Carolyne Wright, w. Paramita Banerjee). [Calyx] (15:2) Sum 94, p. 60.
"Thou Art Durga" (tr. by Carolyne Wright and Paramita Banerjee). [InterQ] (1:2) 93, p. 157.
1061. CHAVEZ, Denise
"Watching Mrs. Sedillo." [PraS] (68:4) Wint 94, p. 33-36.
1062. CHAVEZ, José Luis
"A Mi Madre." [BilingR] (19:2) My-Ag 94, p. 167.
"Ponte los Huaraches, Chicano." [BilingR] (19:2) My-Ag 94, p. 165-166.
1063. CHAVEZ, Lisa D.
"After the Prom." [Jacaranda] (5:1) Wint-Spr 91, p. 6-7.
CHE-HUNG, Yuen
See YUEN, Che-hung
1064. CHEE, Alex
"Blazing." [JamesWR] (11:3) Spr 94, p. 5.
"Thieves." [JamesWR] (11:3) Spr 94, p. 4.
"Threes Are Sixes Now" (A pantoum, with Christopher Marlowe). [JamesWR] (11:3) Spr 94, p. 5.
"Two." [JamesWR] (11:3) Spr 94, p. 4.
1065. CHEE, Norla
"On the Down Beat." [Kalliope] (16:3) 94, p. 8-9.
1066. CHEN, Dongdong
"Garden" (tr. by Yanbing Chen and John Rosenwald). [AnotherCM] (27) 94, p. 75.
"In Sickness" (tr. by Yanbing Chen and John Rosenwald). [AnotherCM] (27) 94, p. 74.
"The North" (tr. by Yanbing Chen and John Rosenwald). [AnotherCM] (27) 94, p. 72.
"Poetry" (tr. by Yanbing Chen and John Rosenwald). [AnotherCM] (27) 94, p. 73.
CHEN, Juliette
See LINH, Tran Ngoc
CHEN, Rajandaye Ramkissoon
See RAMKISSOON-CHEN, Rajandaye
1067. CHEN, Shi-Zheng
"Game of Lies" (tr. of Yang Lian, w. Heather S. J. Steliga). [Manoa] (6:1) Sum 94, p. 157-158.
"Winter Garden" (tr. of Yang Lian, w. Heather S. J. Steliga). [Manoa] (6:1) Sum 94, p. 158-159.
1068. CHEN, Xueliang
"New Century" (tr. of Bei Dao, w. Donald Finkel). [Manoa] (6:1) Sum 94, p. 110-111.
"Playwright" (tr. of Bei Dao, w. Donald Finkel). [Manoa] (6:1) Sum 94, p. 110.
"Questioning the Sky" (tr. of Bei Dao, w. Donald Finkel). [Manoa] (6:1) Sum 94, p. 111.
1069. CHEN, Yanbing
"Blank" (tr. of Song Lin). [AnotherCM] (27) 94, p. 70-71.
"The Cat at a Friend's House" (tr. of Zhang Zhen, w. John Rosenwald). [AnotherCM] (27) 94, p. 76-77.
"The Cemetery of Language" (tr. of Meng Lang). [AnotherCM] (27) 94, p. 65.
"The City" (4 selections, tr. of Gu Cheng, w. John Rosenwald and the Beloit/Fudan Translation Workshop). [Manoa] (6:1) Sum 94, p. 118-120.
"Garden" (tr. of Chen Dongdong, w. John Rosenwald). [AnotherCM] (27) 94, p. 75.
"In Sickness" (tr. of Chen Dongdong, w. John Rosenwald). [AnotherCM] (27) 94, p. 74.

"The North" (tr. of Chen Dongdong, w. John Rosenwald). [AnotherCM] (27) 94, p. 72.
"Not Letting Grief Go" (tr. of Meng Lang). [AnotherCM] (27) 94, p. 67.
"Poetry" (tr. of Chen Dongdong, w. John Rosenwald). [AnotherCM] (27) 94, p. 73.
"The Prop Gun" (tr. of Meng Lang). [AnotherCM] (27) 94, p. 66.
"Sickroom" (tr. of Song Lin). [AnotherCM] (27) 94, p. 69.
"Winter" (tr. of Meng Lang). [AnotherCM] (27) 94, p. 68.

1070. CHEN, Yue Ming
"The Pride of Illiteracy." [CanLit] (140) Spr 94, p. 49.

1071. CHENEY-COKER, Syl
"Hallucination of a Refugee." [MalR] (107) Sum 94, p. 144.
"War Bulletins." [MalR] (107) Sum 94, p. 145.

1072. CHENG, Baolin
"Aiming" (tr. of Jing Bute, w. Richard Terrill). [AnotherCM] (27) 94, p. 87.
"An Anonymous Woman Visited My Home" (tr. by the author and Richard Terrill). [AnotherCM] (27) 94, p. 97.
"Awakening at Dawn" (tr. of Lu Yimin, w. Richard Terrill). [AnotherCM] (27) 94, p. 90.
"Blowing Wind" (tr. of Xi Chuan, w. Richard Terrill). [AnotherCM] (27) 94, p. 85.
"Correspondent" (tr. of Yu Jian, w. Richard Terrill). [NoDaQ] (62:1) Wint 94-95, p. 93-94.
"Experience" (tr. of Xi Chuan, w. Richard Terrill). [AnotherCM] (27) 94, p. 86.
"Fish" (tr. by the author and Richard Terrill). [AnotherCM] (27) 94, p. 93.
"Glass" (tr. by the author and Richard Terrill). [AnotherCM] (27) 94, p. 91.
"Growing Grapes" (tr. by the author and Richard Terrill). [AnotherCM] (27) 94, p. 95.
"Homeland" (tr. of Shang Zhongmin, w. Richard Terrill). [TampaR] (9) Fall 94, p. 9.
"Mother" (tr. of Shang Zhongmin, w. Richard Terrill). [TampaR] (9) Fall 94, p. 8.
"Occurrence" (tr. by the author and Richard Terrill). [AnotherCM] (27) 94, p. 98.
"Running Across My Wife at a Subway Station" (tr. by the author and Richard Terrill). [AnotherCM] (27) 94, p. 92.
"Sand Castle" (tr. of Lu Yimin, w. Richard Terrill). [AnotherCM] (27) 94, p. 88.
"Spring" (tr. by the author and Richard Terrill). [AnotherCM] (27) 94, p. 94.
"The Sunset Above the Square" (tr. of Xi Chuan, w. Richard Terrill). [AnotherCM] (27) 94, p. 84.
"Tympanist" (tr. by the author and Richard Terrill). [AnotherCM] (27) 94, p. 96.
"Walt Whitman" (tr. of Wang Yin, w. Richard Terrill). [NowestR] (32:1) 94, p. 110.
"Wind and Rain Were Approaching" (tr. of Lu Yimin, w. Richard Terrill). [AnotherCM] (27) 94, p. 89.

CHENG, Gu
See GU, Cheng

1073. CHERRY, Kelly
"On Looking at a Painting by Van Gogh." [Image] (4) Fall 93, p. 66.
"Renaissance Da Vinci Wheel." [Image] (4) Fall 93, p. 66.
"The Return to a New Place." [Image] (4) Fall 93, p. 65.
"The Rose." [MidwQ] (35:2) Wint 94, p. 127-128.
"Your Voice." [IllinoisR] (2:1) Fall 94, p. 9.

1074. CHERRY, Nancy
"Flying to Montana." [Parting] (7:2) Wint 94-95, p. 27.
"Playing House." [Parting] (7:2) Wint 94-95, p. 39-40.

1075. CHESNE, Sabrina
"Canon." [AntR] (52:2) Spr 94, p. 298.
"Excerpts of a Letter from Southern California to Okinawa (June 21, 1945)." [SoCoast] (17) Je 94, p. 37.
"Violet Vinegar." [AntR] (52:2) Spr 94, p. 299.
"Woman Working Alone in Her Restaurant (New Year's Eve, 1988)." [AntR] (52:2) Spr 94, p. 300-301.

1076. CHESS, Richard
"David's Body." [Confr] (54/55) Fall 94-Wint 95, p. 282.
"Tzimtzum: Contraction." [Ploughs] (20:1) Spr 94, p. 95-96.
"Witnesses." [TampaR] (9) Fall 94, p. 11.

1077. CHETRIT, Sami Shalom
"Acrid Memory" (tr. by Ammiel Alcalay). [LitR] (37:2) Wint 94, p. 359.
"Bad Dream" (tr. by Ammiel Alcalay). [LitR] (37:2) Wint 94, p. 362-364.
"A Night of Scuds" (tr. by Ammiel Alcalay). [LitR] (37:2) Wint 94, p. 359-360.

"Poems in Another Land" (Selections: 1-29, tr. by Ammiel Alcalay). [LitR] (37:2) Wint 94, p. 356-359.
"Who Is a Jew and What Kind of Jew?" (tr. by Ammiel Alcalay). [LitR] (37:2) Wint 94, p. 360-362.

1078. CHICHETTO, James Wm.
"Father Corby's Account of the Battle of Gettysburg." [Poem] (72) N 94, p. 1.
"God Told Massasoit Dream." [Poem] (72) N 94, p. 2.
"Good Friday, 1994." [Poem] (72) N 94, p. 4.
"Osceola Dream." [Poem] (72) N 94, p. 3.

1079. CHILCOTE, S. M.
"Jottings in Snow." [TickleAce] (28) Fall-Wint 94, p. 104.

1080. CHILD, Abigail
"Necrorealism." [Chain] (1) Spr-Sum 94, p. 183-187.
"Two Countries" (to Gail Scott). [Chain] (1) Spr-Sum 94, p. 164-171.

1081. CHILD, Don
"Landscape in Five Dimensions." [WorldO] (25:4) Sum 94, p. 33-39.

1082. CHILDERS, Joanne
"Polestar: The Seventh Star of the Little Dipper." [Kalliope] (16:3) 94, p. 15.

1083. CHIN, Justin
"Looking for Kansas." [EvergreenC] (9:1) Wint-Spr 94, p. 62-65.

1084. CHIN, Sung
"River Tale" (tr. by Leonard Schwartz and Mingxia Li). [Talisman] (12) Spr 94, p. 177-178.

CH'ING-CHAO, Li
See LI, Ch'ing-Chao

1085. CHINN, Daryl Ngee
"Practice." [ArtfulD] (26/27) 94, p. 41-43.

1086. CHIPMAN, Peter
"History of History: Paleolithic Times." [CumbPR] (13:2) Spr 94, p. 30.

1087. CHISHOLM, Stephen
"Nothing Works Around Here Anyway." [Pearl] (20) Spr 94, p. 63.

1088. CHITWOOD, Michael
"Church Piano." [Poetry] (164:2) My 94, p. 76-77.
"Fish." [QW] (39) Sum-Fall 94, p. 199-200.
"On the Roof of the Angle Plant, Rocky Mount, Virginia." [Thrpny] (56) Wint 94, p. 29.
"Photograph of Five Men Crossing a Creek." [SouthernR] (30:1) Ja, Wint 94, p. 82.
"What Day Is This?" [Poetry] (164:2) My 94, p. 77.
"Who Knows?" [Poetry] (163:5) F 94, p. 260.
"Why the Nazis Feared Jazz." [QW] (39) Sum-Fall 94, p. 201.

1089. CHO, Jung-kwon
"Fruit" (tr. by Chang Soo Ko). [Vis] (45) 94, p. 17.

1090. CHO, Wen-chün
"Alas and alas" (tr. by Arthur Waley). [NewYorkQ] (53) 94, p. 7.

1091. CHOCRON, Sonia
"This Is My City" (tr. by David Unger). [Trans] (29) Spr 94, p. 179.
"Through the Streets" (tr. by David Unger). [Trans] (29) Spr 94, p. 179.

1092. CHONG, Hyon-Jong
"Body Movements" (tr. by Peter Fusco). [CrabCR] (8:2/3/9:1/2/3) 94, p. 70.
"The Death God of Civilization" (in Korean and English, tr. by Peter Fusco). [PennR] (6:1) 94, p. 22-23.

1093. CHORLTON, David
"The Ensign Bearer." [DogRR] (26) Wint 94-95, p. 30.
"Jajce." [Pembroke] (26) 94, p. 143.
"The Locksmith." [Poem] (72) N 94, p. 10.
"Metamorphoses." [HeavenB] (11) 94, p. 23.
"El Mozote." [DogRR] (26) Wint 94-95, p. 29.
"The Octogenarians." [Poem] (72) N 94, p. 8.
"Old Couple in a Storm." [CumbPR] (13:2) Spr 94, p. 71.
"Owl." [HeavenB] (11) 94, p. 23.
"The Sacristan." [Poem] (72) N 94, p. 9.
"Sand Dream." [DogRR] (13:1, #25) Spr-Sum 94, p. 25.
"Sarajevo Wedding." [WebR] (18) Fall 94, p. 68-69.
"Shepherds." [Poem] (72) N 94, p. 7.
"Spring." [CumbPR] (13:2) Spr 94, p. 70.
"A Sudden Sleep." [CumbPR] (13:2) Spr 94, p. 72.

1094. CHOU, Ching Chuan
"A Sixteen Character Lyric" (in Chinese and English, tr. by Wang Hui-Ming). [PaintedB] (53/54) 94, p. 92-93.
1095. CHOULIARAS, Yiorgos
"Freud's Dream" (tr. by the author). [HarvardR] (7) Fall 94, p. 37.
"September 1971" (to D.K. who wrote, tr. by David Mason and the author). [Pequod] (37) 94, p. 119.
1096. CHOW, Edmond
"Grandpa." [AntigR] (98) Sum 94, p. 29.
"The Past." [AntigR] (98) Sum 94, p. 30.
1097. CHRISTENSEN, Camilla
"Untitled: You cannot steal lines from a dancer my love" (tr. by Per Brask and Patrick Friesen). [PoetryC] (14:2) Mr 94, p. 20.
1098. CHRISTENSEN, Marc D.
"A Barely Audible Echo Speaks Five." [MinnR] (41/42) Fall 93-Spr 94 (published Mr 95), p. 27-28.
1099. CHRISTENSEN, Paul
"Fall, and Sunset." [Border] (5) Fall-Wint 94, p. 9-10.
"The Image Peddler." [Border] (3) Fall 93, p. 7-10.
"The Sleeper." [Border] (3) Fall 93, p. 11-12.
1100. CHRISTIE, Ruth
"Fathers Far Off" (tr. of Tugrul Tanyol). [Stand] (35:2) Spr 94, p. 69.
"Woman's Song" (tr. of Gülten Akin). [Stand] (35:2) Spr 94, p. 70.
1101. CHRISTOPHER, Irvin Walter
"From the Sea by All Beloved." [NewOR] (20:1/2) Spr-Sum 94, p. 145.
1102. CHRISTOPHER, Nicholas
"5°" (Selections: 8, 14, 16, 24). [GrandS] (13:2, #50) Fall 94, p. 90-96.
"After a Long Illness." [Poetry] (163:4) Ja 94, p. 222-223.
"The Fire at the Foundling Hospital." [Poetry] (164:6) S 94, p. 331.
"May Day, 1992." [Colum] ("The Lost Issues", [i.e. 18-19]) 93, p. 147-149.
"The Recording Angel." [Colum] ("The Lost Issues", [i.e. 18-19]) 93, p. 145-146.
1103. CHRISTOV, Boris
"Body" (tr. by Robert Pinsky). [PartR] (61:1) Wint 94, p. 159.
"Spirit" (tr. by Robert Pinsky). [PartR] (61:1) Wint 94, p. 158.
1104. CHRISTY, Ana
"Party Night in New Hope." [MoodySI] (28, also labeled 29) Fall 94, p. 26.
1105. CHU, Bao-Long
"This Is the House I Pass Through Daily." [WestHR] (48:2) Sum 94, p. 136.
CHU, Jim Wong
See WONG-CHU, Jim
CHUAN, Chou Ching
See CHOU, Ching Chuan
CHUAN, Xi
See XI, Chuan
1106. CHUN, Lisa
"On Being Ordinary." [PlumR] (7) [94?], p. 52-53.
CHURCH, Adrian Blevins
See BLEVINS-CHURCH, Adrian
1107. CHUTE, Robert
"Driving to the Beach on Carl Orff's Birthday." [Vis] (44) 94, p. 16.
1108. CIESLINSKI, L. John
"Grounds for Dismissal." [Amelia] (7:3, #22) 94, p. 129.
1109. CINELLI, Joan Eheart
"Epiphany." [ChrC] (111:1) 5-12 Ja 94, p. 18.
1110. CIOCARLIE, Ileana
"Memory of an October Evening in 1984" (tr. of Mircea Cartarescu, w. Adam J. Sorkin). [AnotherCM] (27) 94, p. 13-14.
"Not a Thing About Survival Technique" (tr. of Mircea Cartarescu, w. Adam J. Sorkin). [NewDeltaR] (10:2) Spr-Sum 93, p. 68.
"Our Love Has Gone" (tr. of Mircea Cartarescu, w. Adam J. Sorkin). [AnotherCM] (27) 94, p. 15-16.
1111. CIOFFARI, Philip
"Small Blessings." [MidwQ] (35:4) Sum 94, p. 407.
1112. CIRINO, Leonard
"A Slip of the Tongue." [ContextS] (4:1) 94, p. 35.

1113. CISCEL, Dennis
"An Old Man's Song." [Border] (4) Spr-Sum 94, p. 89.
1114. CISNEROS, Sandra
"Still-Life with Potatoes, Pearls, Raw Meat, Rhinestones, Lard, and Horse Hooves." [NewYorker] (70:14) 23 My 94, p. 68-69.
1115. CITINO, David
"Bread for the Dead." [SouthernHR] (28:2) Spr 94, p. 166-167.
"Broken Symmetry." [OgalalaR] (5:1) Wint 94, p. 64-65.
"Children Find Body at Beach" (Cleveland Plain Dealer). [OgalalaR] (5:1) Wint 94, p. 66-67.
"The Coat." [TarRP] (33:2) Spr 94, p. 19.
"The Dancing of the Bees, The Progress of Multiple Sclerosis." [DenQ] (29:1) Sum 94, p. 10.
"Egyptian Tomb Painting, Aztec Sacrifice, Central Ohio Autopsy." [LitR] (37:4) Sum 94, p. 599-600.
"The House of Death." [OgalalaR] (5:1) Wint 94, p. 61.
"The House of Pain." [NewEngR] (16:4) Fall 94, p. 134-135.
"Large Bear Deceives Me" (Chippewa Death-song). [OgalalaR] (5:1) Wint 94, p. 62-63.
"A Matter of Perspective." [CentR] (38:2) Spr 94, p. 318.
"The Meaning of April." [LaurelR] (28:1) Wint 94, p. 96.
" *Name That Tune* in the Foro Romano." [LaurelR] (28:1) Wint 94, p. 94-95.
"The Other White Meat." [Salm] (104/105) Fall 94-Wint 95, p. 180-181.
"Phil Ochs Is Dead." [CentR] (38:2) Spr 94, p. 315-317.
"Potato." [LaurelR] (28:2) Sum 94, p. 31.
"A Promise of Tuna." [OgalalaR] (5:1) Wint 94, p. 58-60.
"Real Man Delivers an Anti-Pastorale to the Columbus Chamber of Commerce." [FloridaR] (20:1) Fall 94, p. 81.
"Smelling the Snow." [Poetry] (165:3) D 94, p. 128.
1116. CIVITAREALE, Pietro
"Sombras Dibujadas" (tr. by Carlos Vitale). [Luz] (7) N 94, p. 47-48.
1117. CIVL, Miguel
"The Hymn to Ninkasi" (tr. from The Sumerian Beer Tablet). [SantaBR] (2:2) Fall-Wint 94, p. 42-43.
1118. CLAMPITT, Amy
"Birdham." [NewRep] (210:1) 3 Ja 94, p. 40.
"The Equinoctial Disturbances." [NewYorker] (70:4) 14 Mr 94, p. 66.
"Pot Nomads" (for Robert Hosmer). [WilliamMR] (32) 94, p. 46-47.
1119. CLANCY, Joseph P.
"Racing Pigeons" (tr. of Bobi Jones). [Verse] (11:1) Spr 94, p. 114-115.
1120. CLARK, Elizabeth B.
"Ballad of Things Lost" (For Giovanni Quessep, tr. of Mario Rivero). [ApalQ] (42) Fall 94, p. 44-48.
"Suddenly Someone Is Knocking" (tr. of Mario Rivero). [ApalQ] (42) Fall 94, p. 43.
1121. CLARK, Gary P., Jr.
"A Lakeside Toast." [NewEngR] (16:1) Wint 94, p. 160-161.
"Mouthwash." [NewEngR] (16:1) Wint 94, p. 159-160.
1122. CLARK, Jeanne E.
"Neicie Louise Who Still Lives at Home, Gets a Call from Rosamond Harland, Her Friend and an Auto Show Girl." [Parting] (7:2) Wint 94-95, p. 62.
"Plains" (after the photograph by Wright Morris). [Parting] (7:2) Wint 94-95, p. 63.
1123. CLARK, Jeff
"Things Are Not As We Would Have Them Be." [AmerPoR] (23:1) Ja-F 94, p. 40.
1124. CLARK, Jenny
"Tearing the Veil." [HiramPoR] (55/56) Fall 93-Sum 94, p. 23.
"What I Remembered When I Saw My Friend's Granddaughter's Picture." [HiramPoR] (55/56) Fall 93-Sum 94, p. 22.
1125. CLARK, Jim
"Others Dream of Flying." [CumbPR] (14:1) Fall 94, p. 42-43.
1126. CLARK, Jo Ann
"Dinarzad." [WestHR] (48:1) Spr 94, p. 24-25.
"Halley's comet." [WestHR] (48:1) Spr 94, p. 26.
1127. CLARK, John Livingstone
"Core/Respondence: Love" (two excerpts: 11, 18). [Grain] (22:2) Fall 94, p. 26.
"Four Studies: Configuring Love." [Grain] (22:2) Fall 94, p. 24-25.

1128. CLARK, Kevin
"The Price" (for Norman Dubie). [DenQ] (28:4) Spr 94, p. 15-17.
1129. CLARK, M. Riesa
"Mashriqu'l-Adhkár" ("Mother Temple" of the West). [WorldO] (25:3) Spr 94, p. 47.
1130. CLARK, Mary
"One Way Love." [NewEngR] (16:4) Fall 94, p. 45.
"She No Longer Looks at Herself." [NewEngR] (16:4) Fall 94, p. 47-48.
"Your Place." [NewEngR] (16:4) Fall 94, p. 46-47.
1131. CLARK, Matt
"Menard, Texas." [Border] (5) Fall-Wint 94, p. 11-12.
1132. CLARK, Nancy Bigelow
"Of Heroes and Heron." [BellArk] (10:3) My-Je 94, p. 28.
"Sky, Fuchsia, Chartreuse" (for Todd). [BellArk] (10:3) My-Je 94, p. 13.
1133. CLARK, Stephen
"El Libro Regalado" (Selections: I-II, tr. of Emilio Bejel). [MichQR] (33:3) Sum 94, p. 472-476.
1134. CLARK, Susan
"I want someone to say what you say" (w. Catriona Strang and Lisa Robertson). [Chain] (1) Spr-Sum 94, p. 29.
"Theatre of the New World of the Time." [Avec] (7:1) 94, p. 94-99.
"To Wound, To Wind." [Chain] (1) Spr-Sum 94, p. 275-277.
1135. CLARK, Tom
"Maid in Waiting at the Court of Venus." [Talisman] (13) Fall 94-Wint 95, p. 207.
"Pastimes of the Early Tudor Court." [Talisman] (13) Fall 94-Wint 95, p. 208.
"Saeta." [Talisman] (13) Fall 94-Wint 95, p. 207.
1136. CLARK, William
"The Aphasiac." [Boulevard] (9:3, #27) Fall 94, p. 126.
1137. CLARKE, George Elliott
"April." [Nimrod] (37:2) Spr-Sum 94, p. 22.
"Violets for Your Furs" (For C.). [Nimrod] (37:2) Spr-Sum 94, p. 21.
1138. CLARKE, Ian
"Pale Spring" (16 March, Gettysburg). [LaurelR] (28:1) Wint 94, p. 97.
"Perch." [GreensboroR] (56) Sum 94, p. 96.
1139. CLARKE, Kalo
"Life Hinted at But Invisible." [BellR] (17:1/2) Spr-Fall 94, p. 24.
1140. CLARKE, Raymond
"Bus Ride." [Obs] (9:2) Fall-Wint 94, p. 77.
"Father." [Obs] (9:2) Fall-Wint 94, p. 76.
1141. CLAY, Willy
"In Our Museum." [Poetry] (163:5) F 94, p. 251.
"On Me, the Imported Skies." [Poetry] (165:2) N 94, p. 95-96.
1142. CLAYTON, Christine
"In Utero" (tr. of Durs Grünbein, w. Douglas Clayton). [AnotherCM] (28) 94, p. 57.
"Insomnia" (tr. of Durs Grünbein, w. Douglas Clayton). [AnotherCM] (28) 94, p. 58.
"Variations on No Theme" (Excerpt, tr. of Durs Grünbein, w. Douglas Clayton). [AnotherCM] (28) 94, p. 59.
1143. CLAYTON, Douglas
"In Utero" (tr. of Durs Grünbein, w. Christine Clayton). [AnotherCM] (28) 94, p. 57.
"Insomnia" (tr. of Durs Grünbein, w. Christine Clayton). [AnotherCM] (28) 94, p. 58.
"Variations on No Theme" (Excerpt, tr. of Durs Grünbein, w. Christine Clayton). [AnotherCM] (28) 94, p. 59.
CLEARY, Lee Braymen
See BRAYMEN-CLEARY, Lee
1144. CLEARY, Suzanne
"All at Once." [PoetryNW] (35:4) Wint 94-95, p. 34-35.
"Almost Away" (After "Old Gold Over White" by Mark Rothko). [PoetryNW] (35:4) Wint 94-95, p. 36-37.
"Floodplain, 1987." [AmerPoR] (23:3) My-Je 94, p. 45.
CLEMENS, Samuel Langhorne
See TWAIN, Mark
1145. CLEMENT, Jennifer
"Only This Instant." [AmerV] (33) 94, p. 4.

1146. CLEMENTS, Brian
"Fall." [SycamoreR] (6:1) Wint 94, p. 24.
"Winning, Losing." [SycamoreR] (6:1) Wint 94, p. 25-26.
1147. CLEMENTS, Marcyn Del
"The Back Nine." [Wind] (74) 94, p. 10-11.
"In the Forest of Cardóns." [Wind] (74) 94, p. 11-12.
"Ramifications." [HolCrit] (31:2) Ap 94, p. 16.
1148. CLEVE, Emerald
"Grandfather Clock." [SpiritSH] (59) 94, p. 20.
"Two Cats." [SpiritSH] (59) 94, p. 19.
1149. CLEWELL, David
"In Case of Rapture" (From the Spring 1993 issue of *The Missouri Review*). [Harp] (288:1724) Ja 94, p. 30-31.
"The Magician's Assistant Dreams of One Day Coming Clean." [LaurelR] (28:1) Wint 94, p. 19-22.
"She Dreamed She Was Writing a Love Poem." [Shen] (44:2) Sum 94, p. 68-69.
1150. CLIFF, Michelle
"From the Artichoke Capital of the World, Namesake of Fidel, As Is the Queer Part of San Francisco." [KenR] (NS 16:1) Wint 94, p. 160-162.
1151. CLIFT, G. W.
"Speed Merchant." [Border] (4) Spr-Sum 94, p. 21.
1152. CLIFTON, Linda J.
"Moon." [CrabCR] (8:2/3/9:1/2/3) 94, p. 54.
1153. CLINTON, James H.
"Black Wool, Red Satin Lining." [XavierR] (14:1) Spr 94, p. 78.
1154. CLIPMAN, William
"Skinning Coyote." [SouthernPR] (34:1) Sum 94, p. 15-16.
1155. CLOUGH, Sheryl
"Seattle Sestina" (for Nelson Bentley). [BellArk] (10:5) S-O 94, p. 11.
1156. CLOVER, Joshua
"1/23/91." [BostonR] (19:1) Fe-Mr 94, p. 28.
"1/23/91." [ColR] (21:1) Spr 94, p. 70-71.
"Family Romance" (4 MH). [BostonR] (19:1) Fe-Mr 94, p. 28.
"Field Effect." [DenQ] (29:1) Sum 94, p. 11.
"Hunger in St. Petersburg." [Iowa] (24:1) Wint 94, p. 191-192.
"Map of the City" (16 November, Mecca Normal). [BostonR] (19:1) Fe-Mr 94, p. 28.
"The Nevada Glassworks." [BostonR] (19:1) Fe-Mr 94, p. 28.
"The Orchid Project." [BostonR] (19:1) Fe-Mr 94, p. 28.
"The Plaza: Trotsky in Exile." [Iowa] (24:1) Wint 94, p. 193-194.
"Radiant City." [ColR] (21:1) Spr 94, p. 72-75.
"Rilke's Apollo's Torso." [Iowa] (24:1) Wint 94, p. 192.
"Romeoville & Joliet." [ColR] (21:1) Spr 94, p. 76-77.
CLUE, Charlotte de
See DeCLUE, Charlotte
1157. CLUTE, Mitchell
"Journey." [DenQ] (28:4) Spr 94, p. 18.
1158. CLUTINGER, Thomas H.
"Light's Economy." [Amelia] (7:3, #22) 94, p. 148.
1159. COATES, Carrol F.
"The Song of Nedjma" (For Kateb, tr. of Manden Wara). [Callaloo] (17:2) Sum 94, p. 605-607.
1160. COCCIMIGLIO, Vic
"Night Prayer." [Poetry] (163:6) Mr 94, p. 335.
"The Party." [Pearl] (20) Spr 94, p. 22.
"Robinson's First Wife on the Fifteenth Anniversary of His Departure" (after Weldon Kees). [Thrpny] (59) Fall 94, p. 25.
"Travel." [Callaloo] (17:4) Fall 94, p. 1127-1128.
1161. COCORAN, Kathleen
"Marie Therese." [BlackBR] (18) Wint-Spr 94, p. 12-13.
1162. CODRESCU, Andrei
"Sunday Sermon." [NewAW] (12) Spr-Sum 94, p. 52.
1163. CODY, Suzanne
"Black Widow." [SlipS] (14) 94, p. 78.

1164. COE, Dina
"Doves on a Tar Roof." [Pivot] (41) 93, p. 13.
1165. COELHO, Art
"Soul Seal." [Amelia] (7:3, #22) 94, p. 15.
"Two Prices: No Yields." [Americas] (22:3/4) Fall-Wint 94, p. 56-58.
1166. COFER, Judith Ortiz
"Black Silk Shirt." [ColR] (21:2) Fall 94, p. 130.
"First Job: The Southern Sweets Sandwich Shop and Bakery." [SouthernR] (30:4) Aut 94, p. 710-713.
"Photographs of My Father." [PraS] (68:4) Wint 94, p. 61-62.
"Saint, Hair, Water." [ColR] (21:2) Fall 94, p. 131.
1167. COGGINS, Melissa
"My Last Morning at the Gadsden County Farm." [ApalQ] (40/41) 94, p. 111-112.
1168. COHEE, Marcia
"Before Thanksgiving." [Pearl] (20) Spr 94, p. 9.
"First Trimester." [Parting] (7:2) Wint 94-95, p. 10.
"Saturday Night at the Laundromat." [Border] (3) Fall 93, p. 13-14.
"Slow Time." [Parting] (7:2) Wint 94-95, p. 22.
"The Twilight." [Parting] (7:2) Wint 94-95, p. 23.
1169. COHEN, Bruce
"The Fourth Wall." [PaintedHR] (11) Spr-Sum 94, p. 45.
"The Invention of Baseball." [PaintedHR] (11) Spr-Sum 94, p. 47.
"Spring Baseball." [PaintedHR] (11) Spr-Sum 94, p. 46.
"The Whispering Campaign." [Ploughs] (20:4) Wint 94-95, p. 27-28.
1170. COHEN, Carole
"The Potato Poems." [CapeR] (29:1) Spr 94, p. 12.
1171. COHEN, Deborah
"Dialogue" (tr. of Valeri Brainin-Passek, w. Don Share). [PartR] (61:2) Spr 94, p. 315-316.
1172. COHEN, Diana
"Poem for Survivors Trying to Love" (performance piece for poet and film strip). [SpoonR] (19:1) Wint-Spr 94, p. 88-90.
1173. COHEN, Elizabeth
"Courtyard at Hotel D'Arlatan." [NegC] (14:1/2) 94, p. 30.
"Drive By Shooting." [RiverS] (40) 94, p. 34.
"The Spin Cycle." [RiverS] (40) 94, p. 35.
1174. COHEN, Ira
"Gold & Ivory." [Caliban] (14) 94, p. 131.
"Rocket Dream" (for Gaëlle). [Caliban] (14) 94, p. 130.
1175. COHEN, Miriam A.
"November the Time." [DogRR] (26) Wint 94-95, p. 7.
1176. COHEN, Nancy
"Distinguished Poet of a Small Country" (The Nimrod / Hardman Wards: Finalist). [Nimrod] (38:1) Fall-Wint 94, p. 75-76.
COKER, Syl Cheney
See CHENEY-COKER, Syl
1177. COKINOS, Christopher
"Ancient Shark Jaw." [WeberS] (11:3) Fall 94, p. 108-109.
"Bobcat Tracks along the Kaw River Edge." [LouisL] (11:2) Fall 94, p. 79-80.
"The Skin Sings the Season Home, You." [PoetC] (26:1) Fall 94, p. 32.
1178. COLBURN, Jean
"Material Unpossessions" (with thanks to Mark Johannes). [CapeR] (29:1) Spr 94, p. 30.
"The Statue." [ConnPR] (13:1) 94, p. 12.
1179. COLBY, Joan
"Gifts." [IllinoisR] (1:2) Spr 94, p. 26-27.
"Song: An Appendix." [IllinoisR] (1:2) Spr 94, p. 18.
1180. COLE, Henri
"Carnations." [NewYorker] (70:35) 31 O 94, p. 71.
"Eating Figs Under the White Rocks." [HarvardR] (6) Spr 94, p. 57.
"Three Aurelian Moons." [Colum] ("The Lost Issues", [i.e. 18-19]) 93, p. 117-118.
1181. COLE, James
"April." [Light] (9) Spr 94, p. 7.
"Elegance in Winter." [Light] (12) Wint 94-95, p. 7.
1182. COLE, Lyllian D.
"Butterfly." [Amelia] (7:3, #22) 94, p. 87.

"Curled brown oak." [Amelia] (7:3, #22) 94, p. 87.
"Monarch butterflies." [Amelia] (7:3, #22) 94, p. 87.

1183. COLE, Michael
"An Extended Pause" (After Paul Klee's Gewölk über BOR, 1928). [ArtfulD] (26/27) 94, p. 47.

1184. COLE, Norma
"Contrafact: Amas." [Chelsea] (57) 94, p. 61.
"Contrafact: Conditions Maritimes." [Chelsea] (57) 94, p. 59-60.
"Contrafact: *for Chain*" (to Laura Moriarty). [Chain] (1) Spr-Sum 94, p. 176-178.
"Contrafact: M for Moira." [Avec] (7:1) 94, p. 140.
"The Exhibition" (tr. of Anne Portugal). [Chelsea] (57) 94, p. 62-64.
"Gradiva" (from "Anawratha," tr. of Anne-Marie Albiach). [Avec] (7:1) 94, p. 13.

1185. COLE, Peter
"Island to Island" (Excerpt, tr. of Harold Schimmel). [Conjunc] (23) 94, p. 105-110.
"Speech's Hedge Where the Honey" (Selections: 1-4, 8, 11-12, 20). [Conjunc] (23) 94, p. 222-234.

1186. COLE, William Rossa
"I thought I'd found my El Dorado." [Light] (10) Sum 94, p. 24.
"On Lac Leman, in a grand hotel." [Light] (11) Aut 94, p. 24.
"On the River Meramek." [Light] (9) Spr 94, p. 22.
"Seen on Any Subway." [Light] (9) Spr 94, p. 13.

1187. COLEMAN, Anita (Anita Louise)
"Bernard Loves Edward." [HopewellR] (6) 94, p. 95-96.
"Cabbage Soup" (For my mother, Thelma Louise Coleman, 1913-1993). [HopewellR] (6) 94, p. 94.

1188. COLEMAN, Earl
"Good Dog Blount." [Light] (11) Aut 94, p. 8.
"Hard Dick." [SmPd] (31:3, #92) Fall 94, p. 30.

1189. COLEMAN, Wanda
"American Sonnet (4)." [Jacaranda] (10) 94, p. 51.
"American Sonnet (29)" (after Wolfgang Hildesheimer). [Caliban] (14) 94, p. 101.
"American Sonnet (30)" (after Chris Gilbert). [Caliban] (14) 94, p. 102.
"American Sonnet (32)" (for Bliss Carnochan). [Caliban] (14) 94, p. 103.
"Ar'ioch." [Jacaranda] (10) 94, p. 51.
"Meanwhile in Manhattan." [Jacaranda] (10) 94, p. 47-49.
"Sudden Vacancy." [Jacaranda] (10) 94, p. 50.

1190. COLES, Katharine
"Death Valley" (After a painting by Maureen O'Hara Ure). [QW] (39) Sum-Fall 94, p. 179-184.
"The History of the Bicycle, Munich, 1993." [WestHR] (48:4) Wint 94, p. 341-347.
"Natural Disasters" (for T.P., 1936-1993). [ParisR] (36:132) Fall 94, p. 114-118.

1191. COLGIN, Paul David
"Fresh Produce." [Border] (4) Spr-Sum 94, p. 22.

1192. COLLIER, James
"Clutching a Small Piece of the World." [PoetryNW] (35:3) Aut 94, p. 14-15.

1193. COLLIER, Michael
"Archimedes." [PassN] (15:1) Sum 94, p. 40-41.
"The French Horn." [NewEngR] (16:2) Spr 94, p. 9-10.
"The House of Being." [DenQ] (28:3) Wint 94, p. 15-17.
"The Raccoon." [NewEngR] (16:2) Spr 94, p. 7.
"The Secretary." [NewEngR] (16:2) Spr 94, p. 8-9.
"Vietnam." [PassN] (15:1) Sum 94, p. 38-39.
"The Water Dream." [NewEngR] (16:2) Spr 94, p. 11-13.

1194. COLLIER, Phyllis K.
"The Beginning of Fear." [CapeR] (29:2) Fall 94, p. 30-31.
"Listening to the Word." [SoDakR] (32:2) Sum 94, p. 63.

1195. COLLINGS, Michael R.
"Aftershock rumbles." [Amelia] (7:4, #23) 94, p. 119.

1196. COLLINS, Andrea V.
"Hiroshima Day at the Riviera Coffeeshop." [SingHM] (21) 94, p. 24-25.

1197. COLLINS, Billy
"The Blues." [Journal] (18:1) Spr-Sum 94, p. 35.
"Center." [TriQ] (92) Wint 94-95, p. 88-89.
"The City of Tomorrow." [Boulevard] (9:3, #27) Fall 94, p. 191-192.
"Days." [Poetry] (164:6) S 94, p. 348.
"Dear Reader." [Poetry] (163:4) Ja 94, p. 219.

"Deathbeds." [Poetry] (165:1) O 94, p. 29-30.
"Design." [TriQ] (92) Wint 94-95, p. 90.
"Directions." [TriQ] (92) Wint 94-95, p. 91-92.
"Exploring the Coast of Birdland." [Journal] (18:1) Spr-Sum 94, p. 36-37.
"Forgetfulness" (read by the author at the 40th annual Poetry Day in Chicago). [Harp] (289:1733) O 94, p. 38.
"Medium." [Poetry] (163:4) Ja 94, p. 217-218.
"Memento Mori." [Jacaranda] (5:1) Wint-Spr 91, p. 18.
"Modern Peasant." [Jacaranda] (5:1) Wint-Spr 91, p. 19.
"Romanticism." [Poetry] (163:5) F 94, p. 252.
"Still Life." [QW] (38) Winter-Spr 93-94, p. 111.

1198. COLLINS, Loretta
"Fetish." [TriQ] (92) Wint 94-95, p. 67-70.
"The Twelve Foot Neon Woman on Top of Marla's Exotik Pleasure Palace Speaks." [QW] (38) Winter-Spr 93-94, p. 94-95.

1199. COLLINS, Martha
"Likes." [AmerV] (33) 94, p. 3.
"Re: House(s)." [ColR] (21:2) Fall 94, p. 122-125.

1200. COLLINS, Richard
"A Confession" (tr. of Nichita Stanescu). [Vis] (46) 94, p. 8.

1201. COLUMBUS, Claudette Kemper
"Demonstration and Death." [BilingR] (19:1) Ja-Ap 94, p. 61.

1202. COMANESCU, Danisa
"The Family's Wednesday" (tr. by Brenda Walker). [PoetryC] (14:4) S 94, p. 23.

1203. COMNIOS, Susan
"Upstate, April." [Blueline] (15) 94, p. 38.

1204. COMPANIOTTE, John
"Pitching to James Joyce." [Border] (3) Fall 93, p. 15.
"The Rabbits." [Border] (3) Fall 93, p. 16.

1205. CONANT, Jeff
"Concrete Remains." [WashR] (19:6) Ap-My 94, p. 16.
"However aware, however alert." [Talisman] (12) Spr 94, p. 150.
"What Tidings?" (for Diana). [WashR] (19:6) Ap-My 94, p. 16.

1206. CONAWAY, Frank
"Over Your Shoulder." [PoetC] (25:3) Spr 94, p. 8.
"The Water Bearer." [BelPoJ] (45:1) Fall 94, p. 16.

1207. CONCEL, Mary A.
"Bless This Night." [MassR] (35:1) Spr 94, p. 85.
"Love Poem." [MassR] (35:1) Spr 94, p. 86.

1208. CONDEE, Nancy
"15 Wise Exhortations" (tr. of Dmitrii Aleksandrovich Prigov, w. Vladimir Padunov). [MinnR] (41/42) Fall 93-Spr 94 (published Mr 95), p. 11-12.
"Telegrams" (tr. of Dmitrii Aleksandrovich Prigov, w. Vladimir Padunov). [MinnR] (41/42) Fall 93-Spr 94 (published Mr 95), p. 12-14.
"The Weather on the Planet" (tr. of Dmitrii Aleksandrovich Prigov, w. Vladimir Padunov). [MinnR] (41/42) Fall 93-Spr 94 (published Mr 95), p. 14-15.

1209. CONE, Jon
"Taking Leave." [WorldL] (5) 94, p. 41.

1210. CONGDON, T. R.
"Dr. D." [AnthNEW] (6) 94, p. 34.

1211. CONINCK, Herman de
"Genesis" (tr. by Laure-Anne Bosselaar and Kurt Brown). [MassR] (35:1) Spr 94, p. 104.
"Paris, May 1st" (in the Jewish war memorial, tr. by Laure-Anne Bosselaar and Kurt Brown). [MassR] (35:1) Spr 94, p. 103.
"The Plural of Happiness" (Excerpt, tr. by Laure-Anne Bosselaar and Kurt Brown). [MassR] (35:1) Spr 94, p. 104.

1212. CONKLING, Helen
"In 1933." [PraS] (68:3) Fall 94, p. 52.
"In 1945." [PraS] (68:3) Fall 94, p. 54.
"In Janet's Room." [PraS] (68:3) Fall 94, p. 57.
"Perfume." [PraS] (68:3) Fall 94, p. 55-56.
"War." [PraS] (68:3) Fall 94, p. 53.

1213. CONLEY, Susan
"Kinetics." [TarRP] (33:2) Spr 94, p. 9.
"Winter in San Diego." [TarRP] (33:2) Spr 94, p. 8.

1214. CONLON, Christopher
"Soweto" (1989). [Wind] (74) 94, p. 12-13.
1215. CONN, Jan
"Fin-de-Siècle Blues, Corpus Christi." [AntigR] (96) Wint 94, p. 26.
"The Great Awakening." [AntigR] (96) Wint 94, p. 27.
"Train. Camels. Sponges." [MalR] (109) Wint 94, p. 41-42.
"Villa Tunari." [AntigR] (96) Wint 94, p. 24-25.
1216. CONN, Stewart
"Air and Water: John Muir" (for James Rankin). [SouthernR] (30:2) Ap, Spr 94, p. 275-276.
"The American Girl." [SouthernR] (30:2) Ap, Spr 94, p. 277.
"The Blue House." [SouthernR] (30:2) Ap, Spr 94, p. 276-277.
"White Tulips." [Verse] (11:1) Spr 94, p. 52.
1217. CONNELLAN, Leo
"Blueberry Boy." [NegC] (14:1/2) 94, p. 198.
"Boxing." [NegC] (14:1/2) 94, p. 204.
"Crossing America" (Selections: I-II)." [NegC] (14:1/2) 94, p. 212.
"Dark Horses Rushing." [NegC] (14:1/2) 94, p. 210-211.
"Garbage Truck." [NegC] (14:1/2) 94, p. 200.
"A Hen Crossing the Road." [NegC] (14:1/2) 94, p. 201.
"Mudelein on the Michigan." [NegC] (14:1/2) 94, p. 207.
"Old Gravestones." [NegC] (14:1/2) 94, p. 197.
"On the Eve of My Becoming a Father." [NegC] (14:1/2) 94, p. 196.
"Out Jim Moore's Window." [NegC] (14:1/2) 94, p. 199.
"Scott Huff." [NegC] (14:1/2) 94, p. 202.
"Shadows." [NegC] (14:1/2) 94, p. 203.
"Shooter." [NegC] (14:1/2) 94, p. 213.
"Tomorrow." [NegC] (14:1/2) 94, p. 214-215.
"The Treachery of Flame." [NegC] (14:1/2) 94, p. 205.
"Watching Jim Shoulders." [NegC] (14:1/2) 94, p. 209.
"Wawenock." [NegC] (14:1/2) 94, p. 206.
"A Witness." [NegC] (14:1/2) 94, p. 208.
1218. CONNELLY, Karen
"I Kneel to Kiss the Ice." [Descant] (25:1, #84) Spr 94, p. 10-12.
"Rat Laughter." [Descant] (25:1, #84) Spr 94, p. 13-15.
"Stray Cat." [Arc] (33) Fall 94, p. 51-54.
1219. CONNOLLY, Geraldine
"My Daughter's Hair." [HampSPR] Wint 94, p. 43.
"The New World." [Poetry] (163:4) Ja 94, p. 189-190.
1220. CONNOLLY, Tristianne J.
"The Short-Haired Girls." [AntigR] (97) Spr 94, p. 61.
1221. CONNOR, Joan
"Driving in Provence" (Near Arles). [SmPd] (31:1, #90) Wint 94, p. 22-23.
1222. CONNOR, Tony
"The Man at the End of the Street." [Pivot] (41) 93, p. 34.
"A Provocation." [Pivot] (41) 93, p. 35.
1223. CONOLEY, Gillian
"3/1/91   4/29/92." [AmerPoR] (23:1) Ja-F 94, p. 6.
"Lamentation for Martha Graham." [AmerPoR] (23:1) Ja-F 94, p. 6.
"Red Couch." [NewAW] (12) Spr-Sum 94, p. 115.
"The Truth." [NegC] (13:2/3) 93, p. 8-9.
1224. CONRAD, C. A.
"Familiar Spring." [ChironR] (13:4) Wint 94, p. 12.
"For Love." [ChironR] (13:4) Wint 94, p. 12.
"R.S.V.P." (first prize in the 1994 *Chiron Review* Poetry Contest). [ChironR] (13:4) Wint 94, p. 12.
1225. CONRAD, Fran
"Soweto Hands" (honorable mention, Social Concern Poetry Competition, 1993). [BlackBR] (18) Wint-Spr 94, p. 43.
1226. CONRAN, Tony
"Gametes." [Jacaranda] (5:1) Wint-Spr 91, p. 80.
1227. CONTI, Edmund
"MCMXCIC" (or is it Memorex?). [Light] (12) Wint 94-95, p. 20.
"At Bay." [JINJPo] (16:1) Spr 94, p. 2.
"Ogden Nash Considers His Options." [Light] (9) Spr 94, p. 17.
"Sailing all around the Delta." [Light] (10) Sum 94, p. 24.

"Sailing on the River Thames." [Light] (11) Aut 94, p. 24.
"Sailing on the Sea of Azov." [Light] (12) Wint 94-95, p. 24.
"Sailing on the Zuider Zee" (Third Prize, Second Annual River Rhyme Competition). [Light] (9) Spr 94, p. 22.
"Sunday." [Light] (11) Aut 94, p. 13.
"What's an Eskimo Son to Do?" [Light] (10) Sum 94, p. 19.
"Zen and Zensibility." [Light] (11) Aut 94, p. 10.

1228. CONTOSKI, Victor
"Envoy." [HangL] (65) 94, p. 14.
"Oranges." [HangL] (65) 94, p. 13-14.

1229. CONYNE, Barbara
"Sweet Thing" (First Sue Saniel Elkind National Poetry Award, Finalist). [Kalliope] (16:2) 94, p. 17-18.

1230. COOK, Méira
"Days of Water" (Honourable Mention, Long Poem Category). [PraF] (15:4, #69) Wint 94-95, p. 78-84.
"The Fallen Here." [WestCL] (28:1/2, #13/14) Spr-Fall 94, p. 120-121.

1231. COOK, Nancy
"A Concise History of Aviation." [ChamLR] (14/15) Spr-Fall 94, p. 46-47.

1232. COOK, Rebecca
"Cousin" (A Plainsongs Award Poem). [Plain] (15:1) Fall 94, p. 5.

1233. COOK, Steve
"Not Even a Comma on Anyone's Page." [SantaBR] (1:2) Fall-Wint 93, p. 61.
"Playing at the Father's Art." [SantaBR] (1:2) Fall-Wint 93, p. 60.
"Pulling Back the Water Ahead." [SantaBR] (2:1) Spr-Sum 94, p. 78.

1234. COOKE, Robert P.
"Something Important." [Plain] (14:2) Wint 94, p. 32.

1235. COOLEY, Nicole
"Alice in Paradise." [WillowS] (34) Sum 94, p. 42-43.
"The Family History." [Nat] (259:21) D 19 94, p. 774.
"Good Friday." [WillowS] (34) Sum 94, p. 44-45.
"Maison Blanche." [Nat] (259:14) O 31 94, p. 498.
"Romance." [Nat] (258:19) My 16 94, p. 673.

1236. COOLEY, Peter
"The Boy Child." [NegC] (13:2/3) 93, p. 222.
"Father and Children." [NegC] (13:2/3) 93, p. 224.
"Poem for the Moment of My Death." [NegC] (13:2/3) 93, p. 10.
"Poem on the First Day of School." [Poetry] (164:6) S 94, p. 347.
"The Soul." [NegC] (13:2/3) 93, p. 227-228.
"To Emily Dickinson in New Orleans." [NegC] (13:2/3) 93, p. 229-230.

1237. COOLIDGE, Clark
"Missing Times." [NewAW] (12) Spr-Sum 94, p. 1-7.
"On the Pumice of Morons (The Unaugural Poem)" (w. Larry Fagin). [Sulfur] (34) Spr 94, p. 4-7.

1238. COOPER, Bernard
"Tone Poem." [ParisR] (36:130) Spr 94, p. 102-104.

1239. COOPER, Courtney Anne
"The Odysseus Lover." [NegC] (13:2/3) 93, p. 11.

1240. COOPER, Jane
"Being Southern." [GlobalCR] (3) Spr 94, p. 1-2.
"Clementene." [KenR] (NS 16:2) Spr 94, p. 10-11.
"From the Journal Concerning My Father." [KenR] (NS 16:2) Spr 94, p. 11-14.
"How Can I Speak for Her?" [KenR] (NS 16:2) Spr 94, p. 15-16.
"The Infusion Room." [AmerPoR] (23:1) Ja-F 94, p. 46.
"The Past." [AmerPoR] (23:1) Ja-F 94, p. 47.
"Seventeen Questions about *King Kong*." [ParisR] (36:131) Sum 94, p. 307-308.
"Wanda's Blues." [AmerPoR] (23:1) Ja-F 94, p. 46.

1241. COOPER, John Charles
"I will Flee to the Dharma, I Will Flee to the Sangha, I Will Flee to the Buddha" (For Thomas Merton). [Wind] (73) 94, p. 6-7.

1242. COOPER, Lisa
"Singing." [Border] (3) Fall 93, p. 18.

1243. COOPER, Richard
"Symphony in Black" (an extract). [Stand] (35:3) Sum 94, p. 75.

1244. COOPER-STONE, Robin
"Lazarus Unveiled." [AnotherCM] (28) 94, p. 28-29.

1245. COOPERMAN, Matthew
"Tending towards Water." [CumbPR] (13:2) Spr 94, p. 22-23.
1246. COOPERMAN, Robert
"Arsinoe II, Wife and Sister of Ptolemy, Just Before Her Death in a Suspicious Fire, 190 B.C." [Parting] (7:1) Sum 94, p. 28.
"As Kindly As You Can." [SoDakR] (32:2) Sum 94, p. 61.
"The Bull's Eye." [HampSPR] Wint 94, p. 37.
"Corinna, Cook for Ovid's Wife, Drusilla." [PraF] (15:1, #66) Spr 94, p. 135.
"Dinner at the Aegean Isles." [Outbr] (25) 94, p. 15.
"Louis VII Tightens the Siege at Qundar, the Second Crusade." [Plain] (15:1) Fall 94, p. 14.
"Motor Mania" (for H.A.). [Plain] (14:2) Wint 94, p. 14.
"Mrs. Lottie Crawford, After Her Husband Was Butted to Death by Their Pet Goat: Coleman, Georgia." [SoCoast] (17) Je 94, p. 14.
"New York to Cleveland by Train, 1945." [Outbr] (25) 94, p. 17.
"The Newly-Crowned Emperor Tiberius Receives a Petition of Amnesty on Behalf of the Exiled Poet Ovid." [Poem] (71) My 94, p. 9.
"Perilla, Step-Daughter of the Exiled Poet Ovid, After Her Audience with the Emperor Tiberius." [Poem] (71) My 94, p. 10-11.
"Pirate Treasure." [Outbr] (25) 94, p. 16.
"Roland of Nantes Speaks through an Interpreter to Yusef-al-Durr, Leader of the Turkish Stronghold of Qundar, 1147." [DogRR] (13:1, #25) Spr-Sum 94, p. 38-39.
"A Touch." [Parting] (7:1) Sum 94, p. 45.
"Walking the Civil War Battlefield of Gaines Court House: Richmond Virginia." [Plain] (14:3) Spr 94, p. 6.
"Young as an Angel." [Border] (3) Fall 93, p. 19-20.
"Yusuf-al-Durr Replies to the Demands of Robert of Nantes, 1147." [DogRR] (13:1, #25) Spr-Sum 94, p. 39-40.
1247. COPE, David
"The Abandoned City" (from "Coming Home"). [AmerPoR] (23:6) N-D 94, p. 38.
"After the Long Hard Day" (Excerpt. From "Fragments from the Stars"). [AmerPoR] (23:6) N-D 94, p. 38.
"The Great Tree Down" (From "On the Bridge"). [AmerPoR] (23:6) N-D 94, p. 38.
"Strafing in El Salvador" (Excerpt. From "Quiet Lives"). [AmerPoR] (23:6) N-D 94, p. 38.
1248. COPE, Steven
"Woman in the Stacks." [CoalC] (8) Ap 94, p. 41.
1249. COPE, Wendy
"Ever So Cute" (after A.A. Milne). [Light] (10) Sum 94, p. 11.
1250. COPELAND, Todd
"Beachcombing on Matagorda Island, Texas." [Journal] (18:2) Fall-Wint 94, p. 65-66.
"In Medias Res — Port O'Connor, Texas." [Journal] (18:2) Fall-Wint 94, p. 67-68.
"Intercoastal, Mid-May." [Journal] (18:2) Fall-Wint 94, p. 63-64.
"Priorities." [Journal] (18:2) Fall-Wint 94, p. 61-62.
"Susan Taking Samples." [SouthernPR] (34:1) Sum 94, p. 14-15.
"Two." [Border] (4) Spr-Sum 94, p. 23.
1251. COPELLO, Fernando M.
"Calle de Galileo, Madrid." [Nuez] (5:13/14/15) 94, p. 16.
"La Costa Opuesta." [Nuez] (5:13/14/15) 94, p. 16.
"Ultimas Instrucciones." [Nuez] (5:13/14/15) 94, p. 16.
1252. CORBETT, William
"O, July 1992." [HarvardR] (2) Fall 92, p. 135.
1253. CORBIN, Joan
"A Surprise." [SinW] (53) Sum-Fall 94, p. 23.
1254. CORDA, Carol
"Arizona Memorial." [NegC] (14:1/2) 94, p. 127.
"Like a Courtesan." [NegC] (14:1/2) 94, p. 126.
1255. CORDARY, J.
"The Catfish Song." [BelPoJ] (45:1) Fall 94, p. 34.
"Daffodil." [BelPoJ] (45:1) Fall 94, p. 35.
"I Want." [BelPoJ] (45:1) Fall 94, p. 34.
1256. CORDING, Robert
"AA Meeting." [SouthernR] (30:1) Ja, Wint 94, p. 83-85.
"Astapovo." [Poetry] (164:2) My 94, p. 82-83.

"Crossed Song." [AmerS] (63:2) Spr 94, p. 214.
"For Sarah Wincester." [CreamCR] (18:1) Spr 94, p. 54-55.
"Letting in the Day." [SewanR] (102:3) Sum 94, p. 383-385.
"Pop-up Book." [GettyR] (7:4) Aut 94, p. 605-607.
"Prayer." [TarRP] (33:2) Spr 94, p. 23-24.
"Soccoro." [GettyR] (7:4) Aut 94, p. 608-609.
"Unfinished Sampler." [Poetry] (163:5) F 94, p. 278-279.
"Washing the Body." [NewEngR] (16:2) Spr 94, p. 33.

1257. COREY, Kathy
"The Woman That Picked Beets in the Field." [Plain] (14:2) Wint 94, p. 35.

1258. COREY, Stephen
"Dirt." [Pembroke] (26) 94, p. 145.
"Editing Poems During a Hospital Deathwatch." [Poetry] (163:4) Ja 94, p. 224.
"Living Hands." [YellowS] (12:3, #47) Fall-Wint 94-95, p. 18-19.

1259. CORISH, Denis
"The Place Not Lived In." [CumbPR] (13:2) Spr 94, p. 86.

1260. CORKERY, Caleb
"South Haven" (for Joe). [BrooklynR] (11) 94, p. 60-61.

1261. CORKERY, Christopher Jane
"The Chosen." [PartR] (61:2) Spr 94, p. 314-315.
"Jigsaw Puzzle in Pregnancy." [Atlantic] (273:6) Je 94, p. 110.

1262. CORLEY, Elisabeth Lewis
"Going on." [SouthernPR] (34:1) Sum 94, p. 43.

1263. CORMAN, Cid
"Anon." [CreamCR] (18:2) Fall 94, p. 270-271.
"Trajectile" (tr. of Paul Celan). [WorldL] (5) 94, p. 12.
"What Is Required of Stars" (tr. of Paul Celan). [WorldL] (5) 94, p. 12.
"You with the Darkscantling" (tr. of Paul Celan). [WorldL] (5) 94, p. 12.

1264. CORMIER, Richard A.
"The Calling." [Amelia] (7:3, #22) 94, p. 157.

CORMIER-SHEKERJIAN, Regina de
See DeCORMIER, Regina

1265. CORN, Alfred
"After Neruda." [Verse] (11:2) Sum 94, p. 129.
"The Alfama." [Salm] (104/105) Fall 94-Wint 95, p. 182-184.
"Caesarea." [Nat] (259:18) N 28 94, p. 666.
"Canto XXX." [Colum] (21) Fall 93, p. 141-145.
"The Cloak of Invisibility." [NewRep] (211:5) 1 Ag 94, p. 42.
"Insertion Arias." [ParisR] (36:131) Sum 94, p. 203-204.
"Lago di Como: the Cypresses." [NewRep] (210:26) 27 Je 94, p. 38.
"Mikhail Baryshnikov Dances *Three Preludes* for Mark Morris." [Salm] (104/105) Fall 94-Wint 95, p. 184-185.
"Olfactory." [ApalQ] (42) Fall 94, p. 24-25.
"Sugar Cane." [KenR] (NS 16:2) Spr 94, p. 63-65.
"To Hermes." [KenR] (NS 16:2) Spr 94, p. 65.

1266. CORNEJO, Ursula
"Exilio de Cuerpo" (Fragmentos: III, V-VII, X, XII, XVII, XXII). [Inti] (39) Primavera 94, p. 255-257.

1267. CORNFORD, Adam
"Animus" (from The Cyborg's Path). [Talisman] (12) Spr 94, p. 18.
"Suit" (Lucky Market, East 18th and Lakeshore). [Caliban] (14) 94, p. 124.

1268. CORNISH, James
"In a Tub." [Amelia] (7:4, #23) 94, p. 79.

1269. CORNWELL, Ted
"Dear John." [ModernW] (1) Summer 94, p. 11.

1270. CORONA, Manuel
"Mercedes." [Areíto] (4:15) Marzo 94, p. 43.

1271. CORRALES, José
"El Viejo Bugarrón." [Nuez] (5:13/14/15) 94, p. 28.

1272. CORRIGAN, Michael T.
"All These Years." [Poem] (72) N 94, p. 53.
"Rehearsal." [Poem] (72) N 94, p. 52.
"Summer." [Spitball] (47) Sum 94, p. 28.
"That Which Sustains Us." [BellArk] (10:3 [i.e. 10:4]) Jl-Ag 94, p. 12.
"Those Who Left." [Poem] (72) N 94, p. 54.
"To My Niece and Friend, Sixteen." [BellArk] (10:3 [i.e. 10:4]) Jl-Ag 94, p. 9.

1273. CORTEZ, Jayne
"Cultural Operations 1992." [Sulfur] (35) Fall 94, p. 152-153.
"I Wake Up Early." [Sulfur] (35) Fall 94, p. 150-151.
"States of Motion." [Sulfur] (35) Fall 94, p. 154-155.
1274. CORY, Jim
"By the Balls." [ChironR] (13:3) Aut 94, p. 7.
1275. COSTA, Horacio
"The Book of Fracta" (Selections, tr. by Charles A. Perrone). [Sulfur] (34) Spr 94, p. 150-157.
1276. COSTA, Maren
"The Promise." [RagMag] (12:1) Sum 94, p. 97.
1277. COSTOPOULOS, Olga
"Aloe (Quaecumquae) Vera." [Nimrod] (37:2) Spr-Sum 94, p. 24.
"Club Sandwiches." [Nimrod] (37:2) Spr-Sum 94, p. 23.
"A Short Course in Modern Poetry." [Light] (10) Sum 94, p. 12.
1278. COTRAU, Liviu
"Kind of Bright" (tr. of Ion Mircea, w. Adam J. Sorkin). [HayF] (14) Spr-Sum 94, p. 15.
"River in the Dark" (tr. of Ion Mircea, w. Adam J. Sorkin). [HayF] (14) Spr-Sum 94, p. 16.
1279. COTTER, Dennis
"The Source of the Name" (7 poems, excerpted from the longer version which includes a verse for all 28 major league teams). [Spitball] (47) Sum 94, p. 35-41.
1280. COULEHAN, Jack
"First Blood" (for Anne). [NegC] (14:1/2) 94, p. 99-100.
1281. COUNSIL, Wendy
"Before Making Love." [FreeL] (13) Spr 94, p. 12.
"A Curiosity." [ChironR] (13:2) Sum 94, p. 15.
"Titania Wakes." [CreamCR] (18:1) Spr 94, p. 86.
COURCY, Peter de
See DeCOURCY, Peter
1282. COURSEN, H. R.
"Recalling August." [TarRP] (34:1) Fall 94, p. 27.
"Rhyme Royal for Autumn Storm" (elegy for the 14th-century Geoffrey Chaucer). [HolCrit] (31:1) F 94, p. 11-12.
1283. COUTO, Nancy Vieira
"Angie Appropriates a Bar or Two." [GettyR] (7:4) Aut 94, p. 635-636.
"They Double Up Around the Absence of Campfires." [GettyR] (7:4) Aut 94, p. 633.
"They Will See Rita Hayworth." [GettyR] (7:4) Aut 94, p. 634.
1284. COUTO, Peter
"The City of the Forbidden" (tr. of Suzanne Pellerin, w. the author). [InterPR] (20:2) Fall 94, p. 45, 47.
1285. COUTURIER, John
"Christmas List." [Pearl] (20) Spr 94, p. 21.
1286. COVEY, Patricia
"*Pietas*, For Jessie Helms." [NewYorkQ] (53) 94, p. 67.
1287. COWAN, Judith
"Childhood" (tr. of Alphonse Piché). [InterPR] (20:2) Fall 94, p. 67.
"A Love Poem to Humanity" (Excerpt, to Kypris, tr. of Guy Marchamps). [InterPR] (20:2) Fall 94, p. 87-91.
"Newly Married at Niagara" (to the bride, tr. of Marcel Nadeau). [InterPR] (20:2) Fall 94, p. 35.
"A Prayer to India" (tr. of Yolande Villemaire). [InterPR] (20:2) Fall 94, p. 93, 95.
"The Recluses" (tr. of Marcel Nadeau). [InterPR] (20:2) Fall 94, p. 33.
"Sailor Song" (tr. of Alphonse Piché). [InterPR] (20:2) Fall 94, p. 69.
"Snow Solo" (tr. of Clément Marchand). [InterPR] (20:2) Fall 94, p. 63, 65.
"Words" (tr. of Pierre Chatillon). [InterPR] (20:2) Fall 94, p. 17-21.
1288. COWEE, Bill
"The Mathematics of Generations." [SmPd] (31:3, #92) Fall 94, p. 26.
"Meditations of Joseph." [Conscience] (15:3) Aut 94, p. 23.
1289. COWING, Sue
"Fever." [NegC] (14:1/2) 94, p. 128.
"You Deserved That." [NegC] (14:1/2) 94, p. 129-130.

1290. COWLES, Christopher
"Farewell beyond Mortality." [Comm] (121:8) 22 Ap 94, p. 20.
"To a Nun Seen on Her Way to Prayers." [Comm] (121:8) 22 Ap 94, p. 20.
1291. COX, Brian
"Left-Eye Cataract." [Hudson] (47:1) Spr 94, p. 25-26.
"Lindow Man at Manchester Museum." [Hudson] (47:1) Spr 94, p. 24-25.
1292. COX, Carol
"Cerulean Blue." [Pivot] (41) 93, p. 38-39.
"Excuses." [HangL] (64) 94, p. 26.
"Hope." [HangL] (64) 94, p. 27.
"In the Upper Delta, The Pecan Trees Flash Their New Green Leaves." [HangL] (64) 94, p. 28.
"Note." [HangL] (64) 94, p. 25.
1293. COX, Joe (Joseph)
"Looking for Odd Jobs, Walt Whitman Repairs Emily Dickinson's Back Porch Door — May 14th, 1850." [Nimrod] (38:1) Fall-Wint 94, p. 91.
"Nesting." [AntR] (52:2) Spr 94, p. 305.
1294. COX, Mark
"The Cord." [ChiR] (40:2/3) 94, p. 37-38.
"Sonata." [Poetry] (164:2) My 94, p. 70.
1295. COX, Wayne
"Desert of the Days" (tr. of Miquel Martí i Pol, w. Lourdes Manyé i Martí). [SouthernHR] (28:2) Spr 94, p. 157.
"The Other Struggle" (tr. of Miquel Martí i Pol, w. Lourdes Manyé i Martí). [SouthernHR] (28:2) Spr 94, p. 159.
CRABBE, Chris Wallace
See WALLACE-CRABBE, Chris
1296. CRAIG, M. Earl
"Autumn Pastoral." [CutB] (41) Wint 94, p. 9-10.
1297. CRAIG, Mary Christie
"¡No Arriba Amœbæ!" (With apologies to Arthur Guiterman). [Light] (10) Sum 94, p. 9.
1298. CRAMER, Steven
"The Cloud Chamber." [NewEngR] (16:4) Fall 94, p. 75-76.
"The Glen." [BostonR] (19:3/4) Je-S 94, p. 35.
"My Dream as Jacob." [HarvardR] (7) Fall 94, p. 46.
"The Night We Knew for Sure." [Atlantic] (274:1) Jl 94, p. 88.
"On Fire." [IndR] (17:1) Spr 94, p. 23.
"When the Snow Thundered." [GreensboroR] (56) Sum 94, p. 18-19.
"The Work." [Poetry] (164:2) My 94, p. 96.
1299. CRANDALL, Jeff
"Carp, Pike Place Market." [CreamCR] (18:1) Spr 94, p. 57.
1300. CRANE, Hart
"Ten Poems." [Antaeus] (75/76) Aut 94, p. 350-353.
1301. CRANSTON, Edwin A.
"Dora's Island" (tr. of Mizuno Ruriko). [TriQ] (91) Fall 94, p. 58-59.
"Hänsel and Gretel's Island" (tr. of Mizuno Ruriko). [TriQ] (91) Fall 94, p. 56-57.
"On the Island of Elephant Trees" (tr. of Mizuno Ruriko). [TriQ] (91) Fall 94, p. 62-63.
"The Sky Where the Moas Were" (tr. of Mizuno Ruriko). [TriQ] (91) Fall 94, p. 60-61.
"The Tree House" (tr. of Mizuno Ruriko). [TriQ] (91) Fall 94, p. 64-65.
1302. CRASNARU, Daniela
"After the Fall" (tr. by Brenda Walker). [PoetryC] (14:4) S 94, p. 22.
"Cheshire Cat" (tr. by Adam J. Sorkin and Mia Nazarie). [PraS] (68:1) Spr 94, p. 67-68.
"Curtsy" (tr. by Adam J. Sorkin and Maria-Ana Tupan). [PraS] (68:1) Spr 94, p. 68.
"In Praise of the Month of April" (tr. by Brenda Walker). [PoetryC] (14:4) S 94, p. 22.
"Scripta" (tr. by Adam J. Sorkin and Ioana Ieronim). [Vis] (46) 94, p. 39.
"Slope" (tr. by Adam J. Sorkin). [Vis] (44) 94, p. 16.
1303. CRATE, Joan
"The Year of the Coyote." [Dandel] (20:2) 93, p. 10-12.
1304. CRAWFORD, Neta C.
"Diva Girl." [SinW] (52) Spr-Sum 94, p. 78.

1305. CRAWFORD, Robert
"Photonics." [Jacaranda] (5:1) Wint-Spr 91, p. 60.
"Thomas Hardy Works at Texaco." [Light] (10) Sum 94, p. 13.
"To My Son" (for Adam). [NegC] (14:1/2) 94, p. 114.
1306. CREEDON, Carolyn
"Bonepsalm." [AmerPoR] (23:3) My-Je 94, p. 44.
1307. CREELEY, Robert
"Sky." [HarvardR] (Premier Issue) Spr 92, p. 27.
"The Window." [WestHR] (48:2) Sum 94, p. 151.
1308. CRISICK, Maureen Micus
"Suppose." [Poetry] (164:4) Jl 94, p. 191.
1309. CRISP, Shelley
"Naming the Animals." [CreamCR] (18:1) Spr 94, p. 21-22.
1310. CRIST, Larry
"Appetizer." [SlipS] (14) 94, p. 59-60.
1311. CRIST-EVANS, Craig
"Heaven." [PassN] (15:2) Wint 94, p. 14.
1312. CRONWALL, Brian
"Wars and Rumors of Wars." [ChamLR] (14/15) Spr-Fall 94, p. 48.
1313. CROOKER, Barbara
"Concerning Things That Can Be Doubled." [WestB] (35) 94, p. 31.
"Grating Parmesan." [Kaleid] (Special Issue) 94, p. 15.
1314. CROSS, Mary
"The Concept of Force." [SouthernPR] (34:1) Sum 94, p. 42.
1315. CROSS, William
"High Time" (tr. of Richard Exner). [LitR] (37:4) Sum 94, p. 609.
1316. CROTEAU, Paul G.
"One of these mornings" (tr. of Daniel Dargis, w. Ronald Léger). [InterPR] (20:2) Fall 94, p. 23.
1317. CROW, Pamela
"Here." [Calyx] (15:3) Wint 94-95, p. 50.
"True North." [Calyx] (15:3) Wint 94-95, p. 51.
1318. CROWE, Anna
"Pittenweem Beach" (for Jessica Crowe and Janet Cornfoot). [Stand] (35:3) Sum 94, p. 11.
1319. CROWN, Kathleen
"The Holy Ghost Flies into Second Baptist on Airline Highway in Baton Rouge." [Calyx] (15:3) Wint 94-95, p. 5.
"The Holy Ghost Gets Seasonal Work at Far West Fisheries, Alaska." [Calyx] (15:3) Wint 94-95, p. 6-7.
"The Holy Ghost Swoops Down on the Observation Deck of the Creole Nature Trail" (Sabine Wildlife Refuge, Louisiana, Christmas 1991). [Calyx] (15:3) Wint 94-95, p. 8-10.
"Hurricane Season on Chimes Street in Baton Rouge." [Calyx] (15:2) Sum 94, p. 36-37.
1320. CROZIER, Lorna
"Beauty in All Things." [SouthernR] (30:2) Ap, Spr 94, p. 280-281.
"Behind the Camera." [PoetryC] (14:4) S 94, p. 6.
"Dressage." [Nimrod] (38:1) Fall-Wint 94, p. 95.
"The End of Love." [Nimrod] (38:1) Fall-Wint 94, p. 92.
"Finding the Name." [NoDaQ] (62:2) Spr 94-95, p. 8.
"For the Child Who Is Scared of the Dark." [Nimrod] (38:1) Fall-Wint 94, p. 96.
"A Good Day to Start a Journal." [Nimrod] (38:1) Fall-Wint 94, p. 99-100.
"Height of Summer." [PoetryC] (14:4) S 94, p. 6.
"He's Only a Cat." [PoetryC] (14:4) S 94, p. 7.
"How Things Get Started." [Nimrod] (38:1) Fall-Wint 94, p. 97-98.
"Last Rites." [Nimrod] (37:2) Spr-Sum 94, p. 26-27.
"The Magpie Dance." [NoDaQ] (62:2) Spr 94-95, p. 9-10.
"My sister's Eyes." [Nimrod] (37:2) Spr-Sum 94, p. 25.
"Night." [Grain] (21:4) Spr 94, p. 102.
"The Old Order." [Grain] (21:4) Spr 94, p. 99-101.
"Photograph, Not of Me or Little Billie, Circa 1953." [SouthernR] (30:2) Ap, Spr 94, p. 278-280.
"A Sabbath Hymn." [PoetryC] (14:4) S 94, p. 7.
"Seeing My Father in the Neighbours' Cockatoo." [Nimrod] (38:1) Fall-Wint 94, p. 93-94.

"What Diminishes across the Water." [NoDaQ] (62:2) Spr 94-95, p. 7.
"The White Planet." [Grain] (21:4) Spr 94, p. 103-104.

1321. CRUMBLE, Rachel Landrum
"Forgetting French." [SouthernPR] (34:1) Sum 94, p. 16-17.

1322. CRUMMEY, Michael
"Almost Everything." [Arc] (33) Fall 94, p. 13.
"Cigarettes." [CapilR] (2:12) Wint 94, p. 34-35.
"Cod (1)." [CapilR] (2:12) Wint 94, p. 29-30.
"Cod (2)." [CapilR] (2:12) Wint 94, p. 31.
"David Donnell's Schlong." [MalR] (106) Spr 94, p. 46-47.
"Lilacs." [CapilR] (2:12) Wint 94, p. 32-33.
"Morning Labrador Coast." [CapilR] (2:12) Wint 94, p. 27-28.
"Near Jack's Pond Park." [MalR] (106) Spr 94, p. 45.
"News from Home: Metamorphosis." [Event] (23:1) Spr 94, p. 28-29.
"Precedents: A Meditation on the Bobbitts." [PoetryC] (14:4) S 94, p. 28.
"River / Roads." [Quarry] (42:4) Mr 94, p. 85.
"South of Badger." [CapilR] (2:12) Wint 94, p. 25-26.

1323. CRUNK, T.
"Sunday Afternoon, Waiting for the Funeral to Start." [QW] (39) Sum-Fall 94, p. 177.

1324. CRUZ VARELA, María Elena
"The Wall" (tr. by Ruth Behar). [MichQR] (33:4) Fall 94, p. 803.

1325. CSAMER, Mary Ellen
"The Death Sonnets." [Event] (23:2) Sum 94, p. 7-12.

1326. CSOORI, Sándor
"The Day after Easter" (tr. by Len Roberts). [SouthernR] (30:2) Ap, Spr 94, p. 282-283.
"Diary, Early Fall of 1982" (tr. by Len Roberts). [NowestR] (32:2) 94, p. 24.
"Fleeing Soldier, 1944" (tr. by Len Roberts). [NowestR] (32:2) 94, p. 25.
"Holy and Wicked Time" (tr. by Len Roberts and Miklos Horvath). [NowestR] (32:2) 94, p. 26.
"I Look Back and Don't See Myself" (tr. by Len Roberts). [AnotherCM] (28) 94, p. 30-31.
"I Shall Go, I'm Going" (tr. by Len Roberts). [NowestR] (32:2) 94, p. 29.
"I Surrender Myself" (tr. by Len Roberts and László Vertes). [NowestR] (32:2) 94, p. 28.
"If I Had Believed" (tr. by Len Roberts and Laszlo Vertes). [AnotherCM] (28) 94, p. 32.
"Injured Poem" (For Ferenc Kiss, who's learning to speak after his stroke. Tr. by Len Roberts). [DenQ] (29:1) Sum 94, p. 55.
"People, Branches" (tr. by Nicholas Kolumban). [InterQ] (1:1) [93?], p. 92.
"The Smile of My Exile" (tr. by Len Roberts and Miklos Horvath). [NowestR] (32:2) 94, p. 23.
"There Are Only Days" (tr. by Len Roberts). [NowestR] (32:2) 94, p. 27.

1327. CUDDEBACK, Nicole
"A Fifth Grader Writes a Letter to Herself." [CimR] (109) O 94, p. 62.
"Last Trip to Florida." [SoCoast] (17) Je 94, p. 16.

1328. CUDDIHY, Michael
"Listening to Beethoven's Piano and Cello Sonata in A Major." [Comm] (121:12) 17 Je 94, p. 21.

1329. CULHANE, Brian
"Naxos (I)." [SenR] (24:2) Fall 94, p. 34-35.
"Naxos (II)." [SenR] (24:2) Fall 94, p. 36.
"On Seeing *Shoah*." [Boulevard] (9:1/2, #25/26) Spr 94, p. 197-198.

1330. CULLAR, Carol
"The Alaska Question." [ChironR] (13:4) Wint 94, p. 25.
"He's Crossed the River." [Border] (4) Spr-Sum 94, p. 25.
"Last Night Over." [CoalC] (8) Ap 94, p. 4.
"Sum of All the Years." [Border] (4) Spr-Sum 94, p. 26-27.

1331. CULLY, Barbara
"Biographical." [AmerPoR] (23:2) Mr-Ap 94, p. 7.
"Far From the World." [AmerPoR] (23:2) Mr-Ap 94, p. 7.
"In an Open View." [AmerPoR] (23:2) Mr-Ap 94, p. 6.
"Nureyev." [DenQ] (29:1) Sum 94, p. 12.
"Solo." [AmerPoR] (23:2) Mr-Ap 94, p. 6.
"The Wounding We Call the Windy Forest." [AmerPoR] (23:2) Mr-Ap 94, p. 6.

1332. CULVER, Irene
"After Hermes." [BellArk] (10:2) Mr-Ap 94, p. 3.
"The Dear Dwaddler." [BellArk] (10:3 [i.e. 10:4]) Jl-Ag 94, p. 24.
"Falling in Love with Old Women." [BellArk] (10:3) My-Je 94, p. 25.
"Family Conference after a Fight." [BellArk] (10:2) Mr-Ap 94, p. 3.
"Going to a Coffee House on a Sunday Afternoon Just to Read the Paper." [BellArk] (10:6) N-D 94, p. 4.
"In the House of One Loft." [BellArk] (10:2) Mr-Ap 94, p. 3.
"Keyshates." [BellArk] (10:3 [i.e. 10:4]) Jl-Ag 94, p. 24.
"Mundane's New Gate." [BellArk] (10:3 [i.e. 10:4]) Jl-Ag 94, p. 24.
"The Neva Cycle" (Selections: 5 poems). [BellArk] (10:1) Ja-F 94, p. 6-7.
"The Neva Poems" (Selections: 3 poems). [BellArk] (10:5) S-O 94, p. 28-29.
"Still Life." [BellArk] (10:2) Mr-Ap 94, p. 3.
"Sunrise Avenue." [BellArk] (10:3) My-Je 94, p. 25.
"Twynklen Daunen." [BellArk] (10:6) N-D 94, p. 11.
1333. CUMBERLAND, Sharon (Sharon L.)
"Habit." [Ploughs] (20:1) Spr 94, p. 68.
"On Going In." [Ploughs] (20:1) Spr 94, p. 69-71.
"The Rape of the Sabine Women" (First Sue Saniel Elkind National Poetry Award, Finalist). [Kalliope] (16:2) 94, p. 19-20.
"What You Have." [Ploughs] (20:1) Spr 94, p. 67.
1334. CUMMING, Patricia
"Atoning." [AnotherCM] (28) 94, p. 33.
1335. CUMMING, R. B.
"Morning Walk." [Wind] (73) 94, p. 7-8.
"Seasons." [Wind] (73) 94, p. 7.
1336. CUMMINGS, Darcy
"Dating Hephaestus" (First Sue Saniel Elkind National Poetry Award, Finalist). [Kalliope] (16:2) 94, p. 21.
"Early to Rise." [Kalliope] (16:3) 94, p. 12.
1337. CUMMINS, Deborah
"In the State of Absence." [NewEngR] (16:1) Wint 94, p. 154-155.
1338. CUMMINS, James
"An *Ars Poetica* for You." [ParisR] (36:132) Fall 94, p. 232.
"Outside the Paul Laurence Dunbar House, the Grifter Sees Us Coming." [WestHR] (48:2) Sum 94, p. 135.
"Sestina." [ParisR] (36:132) Fall 94, p. 230-231.
"Turista." [WestHR] (48:2) Sum 94, p. 134.
1339. CUMPIANO, Ina
"After Each Storm." [Americas] (22:3/4) Fall-Wint 94, p. 51.
"Anaphora for a First Grandchild." [DenQ] (29:2) Fall 94, p. 9.
"Metonymies." [Americas] (22:3/4) Fall-Wint 94, p. 52-53.
"The Spit" (for Wayne). [Americas] (22:3/4) Fall-Wint 94, p. 54-55.
"Yo, la Malinche" (From a long biographical poem in progress). [Americas] (22:3/4) Fall-Wint 94, p. 46-50.
1340. CUNNINGHAM, Brent
"The Pyromaniac and the Gas Station Girl." [CreamCR] (18:1) Spr 94, p. 30-31.
1341. CURBELO, Silvia
"The Blackbirds Take Over the Sky." [YellowS] (12:1, #45) Spr-Sum 94, p. 38.
"Dreaming Horse" (after the painting by Franz Marc). [PraS] (68:4) Wint 94, p. 31-32.
"Drinking Song" (after Schumann). [PraS] (68:4) Wint 94, p. 32-33.
"Photograph of My Parents." [PraS] (68:4) Wint 94, p. 30-31.
"Tonight I Can Almost Hear the Singing." [KenR] (NS 16:2) Spr 94, p. 71.
"Tourist Weather." [Caliban] (14) 94, p. 42.
"Wish." [Caliban] (14) 94, p. 41.
1342. CURRIER, Jameson
"Tokyo." [JamesWR] (11:4) Sum 94, p. 14.
1343. CURRY, Germaine
"Baptismal White Tanks Baptist Church, Buckeye, Arizona." [SouthernPR] (34:2) Wint 94, p. 21-22.
1344. CURTIS, David
"The Common." [Writer] (107:5) My 94, p. 20.
"Had 'Starry' Vere a Star?" [FourQ] (8:1) Spr 94, p. 37.
"Marianne Moore Because." [FourQ] (8:1) Spr 94, p. 38.

1345. CURTIS, Richard
"At the Byzantine Monastery" (Eastern Turkey, 1976). [Journal] (18:1) Spr-Sum 94, p. 80-81.
"The Fruits of Winter." [Journal] (18:1) Spr-Sum 94, p. 82-83.
1346. CURTIS, Tony
"Wearing the Trousers." [MalR] (107) Sum 94, p. 46.
1347. CURZON, David
"Identities." [Pivot] (41) 93, p. 12.
"Instructions From the Mustard Seed Manual on Chinese Landscape Painting." [Antaeus] (73/74) Spr 94, p. 150.
"An Old Master." [Pivot] (41) 93, p. 11.
"This Dream-World" (Job 39:26 and 42:3). [Confr] (52/53) Wint-Spr 94, p. 309.
1348. CUSAC, Anne-Marie
"Marsh Hawk." [AmerS] (63:1) Wint 94, p. 129.
1349. CUSHING, James
"End of May." [ArtfulD] (26/27) 94, p. 146.
"Personal Problems." [SycamoreR] (6:2) Sum 94, p. 38-39.
"Some of These Days." [NegC] (14:1/2) 94, p. 41.
1350. CUSHMAN, Stephen
"Adoration." [PoetL] (89:4) Wint 94-95, p. 43.
"Boy on Horseback." [SouthwR] (79:1) Wint 94, p. 80.
"Except I Shall See." [SouthernR] (30:3) Sum 94, p. 526-527.
"Invidia." [PoetL] (89:4) Wint 94-95, p. 41-42.
1351. CUTLER, Bruce
"The Father." [SpoonR] (19:1) Wint-Spr 94, p. 31.
1352. CZEKANOWICZ, Anna
"Mother and Daughter" (tr. by Katarzyna Kietlinska and David Malcolm). [InterQ] (1:1) [93?], p. 106.
"Report from a Distant City" (tr. by Katarzyna Kietlinska and David Malcolm). [InterQ] (1:1) [93?], p. 107.
"To Get Through the Night" (tr. by Katarzyna Kietlinska and David Malcolm). [InterQ] (1:1) [93?], p. 108-109.
1353. CZURY, Craig
"Obit Hotel" (Selections: 4 poems, for John Waugh). [WashR] (20:2) Ag-S 94, p. 17.

1354. DAALEN, Maria van
"Boeing." [SouthernR] (30:2) Ap, Spr 94, p. 326-327.
1355. DABNEY, Janice
"Above the Path of Those Who Soar" (for Jim). [BellArk] (10:6) N-D 94, p. 4.
1356. DABYDEEN, David
"Trotter." [MalR] (107) Sum 94, p. 33-35.
1357. DACEY, Philip
"The 15th Zagreb Literary Talks (May 12, 1988)" (from *Cycle for Yugoslavia*). [CreamCR] (18:1) Spr 94, p. 41.
"Death Cocoa." [MidwQ] (35:2) Wint 94, p. 167-168.
"Elegy in the Present Tense." [Journal] (18:2) Fall-Wint 94, p. 54.
"Eskimo Joe." [MidwQ] (35:2) Wint 94, p. 165-166.
"Insomnia." [PoetryNW] (35:1) Spr 94, p. 35.
"The Mark." [Journal] (18:2) Fall-Wint 94, p. 55.
"The New American Stations of the Cross." [Farm] (11:1) Spr-Sum 94, p. 20-22.
"The Orphan." [Shen] (44:4) Wint 94, p. 61-62.
"Stigmata." [SoCoast] (16) Ja 94, p. 36-37.
1358. DACUS, Rachael (Rachel)
"Earth Whale." [BellArk] (10:3) My-Je 94, p. 12.
"Oldest Night, New Moon." [BellArk] (10:6) N-D 94, p. 9.
"On What Isle." [BellArk] (10:6) N-D 94, p. 4.
"Things Women Do Alone." [BellArk] (10:2) Mr-Ap 94, p. 9.
1359. DAGGETT, Lyle
"The Dawn Rocked Its Shoulders." [RagMag] (12:1) Sum 94, p. 8-9.
1360. D'AGOSTINO, James
"Half Notes." [AnotherCM] (27) 94, p. 28-29.
"Untying." [AnotherCM] (27) 94, p. 26-27.
1361. D'AGUIAR, Fred
"At Sea." [MassR] (35:3/4) Aut-Wint 94, p. 380.

"Black Ink." [Jacaranda] (5:1) Wint-Spr 91, p. 40.
"Dead Again." [Pivot] (41) 93, p. 33.
"Fog Area." [SouthernR] (30:2) Ap, Spr 94, p. 284-285.
"Transport." [Shen] (44:3) Fall 94, p. 60-62.

1362. DAHER, Joseph Abi
"Memoirs in Exile" (Selections: 9, 28, 31, 42-44, 46, 47, 60-61, 65, tr. by Adnan Haydar and Michael Beard). [LitR] (37:3) Spr 94, p. 444-446.

1363. DAHLEN, Beverly
"A Reading" (Excerpts, June 20-July 1, 1993, For V.H.). [RiverC] (14:2) Spr 94, p. 28-34.

1364. DAIGON, Ruth
"Aunt Katya." [Kalliope] (16:3) 94, p. 27.
"For the First Time." [MidwQ] (36:1) Aut 94, p. 58-59.
"Perspectives." [XavierR] (14:1) Spr 94, p. 62.
"Running for His Life" (for my son Glenn). [PoetL] (89:1) Spr 94, p. 23-24.
"Things." [CapeR] (29:1) Spr 94, p. 46.

1365. DALACHINSKY, Steve
"Jack's House (Rap for Kerouac)." [MoodySI] (28, also labeled 29) Fall 94, p. 28-29.

1366. DALEY, Michael
"Kali Bushtit." [CumbPR] (13:2) Spr 94, p. 8.
"Original Sin." [Ploughs] (20:4) Wint 94-95, p. 29-30.

1367. DALIN, Joan
"Hegel's Dialectic As Rabbit" (for Gerald Burns). [Confr] (54/55) Fall 94-Wint 95, p. 285.

1368. DALKEY, Victoria
"Crows" (for Tom Phillipe). [CimR] (109) O 94, p. 73-74.

1369. DALLAL, Ahmad
"Eleven Stars Over Andalusia" (tr. of Mahmoud Darwish, w. Mona Anis, Aga Shahid Ali and Nigel Ryan). [GrandS] (12:4, #48) Wint 94, p. 100-111.

1370. DALLAS, Jon
"Alcheringa." [Plain] (14:3) Spr 94, p. 30.
"The Length of Breath." [WindO] (58) Sum 94, p. 51.
"On Your Toes" (Ray Bolger 1904-1987). [Plain] (14:2) Wint 94, p. 33.
"She Starts from Sleep in Winter." [WindO] (58) Sum 94, p. 50.

1371. DALLAT, C. L.
"On the Island." [Verse] (11:1) Spr 94, p. 51.

1372. DALSHEIMER, Alex
"Nature / Nurture." [SinW] (54) Wint 94-95, p. 123.

1373. DALY, Brian
"Watching Roses Die." [SmPd] (31:2, #91) Spr 94, p. 27.

1374. DALY, Catherine
"Before Sun Shines." [Pivot] (41) 93, p. 13.

1375. DALY, Chris
"The Bruno Effect." [WormR] (34:4, #136) 94, p. 144.
"Dwarf's Life." [WormR] (34:4, #136) 94, p. 142-143.
"Executioner's Tune." [SlipS] (14) 94, p. 80.
"Lover." [WormR] (34:4, #136) 94, p. 141-142.
"Richard." [WormR] (34:4, #136) 94, p. 142.
"Tanning Psalm." [WormR] (34:4, #136) 94, p. 143.

1376. DALY, Robert
"The Passion of the Aardwolf and the Spoon: A Libretto." [ChiR] (40:2/3) 94, p. 136-156.

1377. DAMBOWIC, Bernice
"A Lesbian Voice." [SinW] (53) Sum-Fall 94, p. 31.

1378. DAME, Enid
"Blue." [Pivot] (41) 93, p. 20.
"Breaking." [Pivot] (41) 93, p. 19.

1379. DAMIANOV, Damian
"The Time of the Blue Haze" (tr. by Karl Elder and Zhana Mihailova). [AnotherCM] (28) 94, p. 34.

1380. DANA, Robert
"Almost All" (Helsinki, Finland). [Manoa] (6:2) Wint 94, p. 29.
"How Desire Keeps Us Young." [GeoR] (48:4) Wint 94, p. 757.
"Morning, Noon, and Night." [Manoa] (6:2) Wint 94, p. 30.

"On the Murder of Two Orphan Children by Sniper Fire, Sarajevo, 1992." [Manoa] (6:2) Wint 94, p. 30-31.
"Rapture." [Manoa] (6:2) Wint 94, p. 31.

1381. DANERI, Juan José
"Marina II" (de *Retaguardia de la Vanguardia*, Viña del Mar, 1992). [Os] (38) Spr 94, p. 26.

1382. DANFORD, Douglas
"A merchant who lives on the Tyne" (First Prize, Second Annual River Rhyme Competition). [Light] (9) Spr 94, p. 22.

1383. D'ANGELO, Mary
"Black Out." [CapeR] (29:1) Spr 94, p. 28.
"City Safari." [CapeR] (29:1) Spr 94, p. 29.
"Nemesis, Nemesis." [CapeR] (29:1) Spr 94, p. 27.

1384. DANIEL, Barbara
"The Sierra Nevada." [Blueline] (15) 94, p. 15-16.

1385. DANIEL, David
"Blue Ridge Blue." [Agni] (39) 94, p. 208.
"My Mother's Mornings." [Agni] (39) 94, p. 209.

1386. DANIEL, Matthew
"It Has Already Happened" (written after a visit to Dachau, Nazi concentration camp). [BlackBR] (19) Fall-Wint 94, p. 44-46.

1387. DANIEL, Shoshana T.
"After the Storm" (2nd Prize, The Amelia Awards). [Amelia] (7:4, #23) 94, p. 28.

1388. DANIELL, Rosemary
"Chocolate Eclairs." [AmerV] (33) 94, p. 127.

1389. DANIELS, Barbara
"The Fortune Teller." [FourQ] (8:1) Spr 94, p. 58.
"I Stole Your Book." [Outbr] (25) 94, p. 18-19.

1390. DANIELS, Carl M.
"Details Details." [SlipS] (14) 94, p. 71-72.
"Life Is Like a Multiple-Choice Test." [ChironR] (13:2) Sum 94, p. 28-29.
"WASP Guilt." [ChironR] (13:4) Wint 94, p. 25.

1391. DANIELS, Jim
"Blizzard." [WestB] (34) 94, p. 67.
"Blood." [NewEngR] (16:3) Sum 94, p. 102-104.
"The Holy Waters of the New World." [ConnPR] (13:1) 94, p. 13-14.
"Looking It Up." [Witness] (8:2) 94, p. 92-94.
"Outside the Arcade." [Witness] (8:2) 94, p. 94-95.
"What I Did." [WestB] (34) 94, p. 68-69.

1392. DANIELS, Peter
"The Mormons in Sicily." [Verse] (11:2) Sum 94, p. 84.
"River." [Colum] (22) Wint 94, p. 71.

1393. DANKLEFF, Richard
"With the Sun Rising." [AmerS] (63:2) Spr 94, p. 192.

1394. D'ANNA, Lynnette (Dueck)
"Untitled: When push comes to shove you shove, I push." [PoetryC] (14:3) My 94, p. 24.

1395. DANSDILL, Phil
"12 Across, 19 Down." [EngJ] (83:8) D 94, p. 32.

1396. DANTE ALGIERHI
"Canto XXI — The Inferno of Dante Algierhi" (tr. by Robert Pinsky). [Colum] (21) Fall 93, p. 7-13.
"Dante, Inferno XXVI: Ulysses" (tr. by Robert Pinsky). [HarvardR] (6) Spr 94, p. 137-140.
"Dante's *Inferno*, Canto XVIII: Among the Pimps and Seducers" (tr. by Robert Pinsky). [Verse] (11:1) Spr 94, p. 59-62.
"Dante's *Inferno*, Canto XXV: Among the Thieves" (tr. by Robert Pinsky). [Raritan] (14:1) Sum 94, p. 18-25.
"Dante's *Inferno*, Canto XXXI: The Giants" (tr. by Robert Pinsky). [QW] (39) Sum-Fall 94, p. 150-157.
"Dante's *Inferno*, Canto XXXIV (The Final Canto)" (tr. by Robert Pinsky). [Agni] (39) 94, p. 242-246.
"Inferno, Canto II: The Beginning of the Journey" (tr. by Robert Pinsky). [AmerPoR] (23:4) Jl-Ag 94, p. 36-37.
"Three Similes from Dante's *Commedia*" (in Italian and English, tr. by John J. Brugaletta). [SoCoast] (17) Je 94, p. 63-65.

DAO, Bei
See BEI DAO
D'AQUIAR, Fred
See D'AGUIAR, Fred
1397. DARGIS, Daniel
"Un matin." [InterPR] (20:2) Fall 94, p. 22.
"One of these mornings" (tr. by Paul G. Croteau and Ronald Léger). [InterPR] (20:2) Fall 94, p. 23.
1398. DARLING, Frances Marr
"Spring Equinox Meditation." [AnthNEW] (6) 94, p. 22.
1399. DARLING, Robert
"Mural." [Pivot] (42) 94, p. 41.
"The Woman on the Train." [Pivot] (42) 94, p. 40-41.
1400. DARLINGTON, Tenaya
"Sea Braids." [BelPoJ] (45:1) Fall 94, p. 20-21.
1401. D'ARPINO, Tony
"Bikini." [InterQ] (1:2) 93, p. 13.
"The Path of Water." [XavierR] (14:1) Spr 94, p. 61.
"The Voyage." [InterQ] (1:2) 93, p. 12.
1402. DARRAGH, Simon
"Clerihew: Thomas Alva Edison." [Light] (11) Aut 94, p. 22.
"The Fence" (tr. of Christian Morgenstern). [Light] (11) Aut 94, p. 9.
1403. DARRAGH, Tina
"May to meet the road you rise" (to Beth Joselow). [Chain] (1) Spr-Sum 94, p. 190-191.
"Stones / us piece the middle" (to Diane Ward). [Chain] (1) Spr-Sum 94, p. 242-243.
1404. DARWEESH, Mohammed
"The Ants" (tr. of Sami Mahdi). [Vis] (45) 94, p. 37.
1405. DARWISH, Mahmoud (Mahmud)
"Eleven Stars Over Andalusia" (tr. by Mona Anis and Nigel Ryan, with Aga Shahid Ali and Ahmad Dallal. Stanza VI also in Arabic). [GrandS] (12:4, #48) Wint 94, p. 100-111.
"Eyeless in Gaza" (w. Gary Geddes, accompanying a photo essay by Larry Towell). [Quarry] (42:4) Mr 94, p. 39-54.
1406. DAS, J. P.
"The Fish — 2" (tr. of Gagan Gill, w. Arlene Zide and Madhu Joshi). [InterQ] (1:2) 93, p. 184.
"My Whole Life for Him" (tr. of Manorama Mahapatra Biswal, w. Arlene Zide). [InterQ] (1:2) 93, p. 177.
"Poem in Motion" (tr. of Sunanda Tripathy, w. Arlene Zide). [InterQ] (1:2) 93, p. 186.
1407. DASWANI, Tilottama
"8" (tr. of D. M. Lone, w. Arlene Zide). [InterQ] (1:2) 93, p. 161.
1408. DAUER, Lesley
"Elegies for Living People." [NewEngR] (16:4) Fall 94, p. 115-116.
"The Fat Lady." [NewEngR] (16:4) Fall 94, p. 115.
1409. DAUMAL, René
"Heaven Is Convex" (Section III of *The Anti-Heaven*, tr. by Jordan Jones). [HeavenB] (11) 94, p. 64-68.
1410. DAVID, Nat
"This Ain't No Video Game — This Is War." [ChamLR] (14/15) Spr-Fall 94, p. 72.
1411. DAVIDSON, Daniel
"Desire" (Excerpt). [Talisman] (13) Fall 94-Wint 95, p. 37-40.
1412. DAVIDSON, Lisa
"Madam, Your Daughter Is Molting" (Selections: 9 poems). [BellArk] (10:2) Mr-Ap 94, p. 4-5.
"Post Card." [BellArk] (10:3 [i.e. 10:4]) Jl-Ag 94, p. 7.
1413. DAVIDSON, Michael
"The Arcades Project" (5 selections). [RiverC] (14:2) Spr 94, p. 1-5.
1414. DAVIDSON, Phebe
"And How She Turned." [JINJPo] (16:1) Spr 94, p. 3.
"Breathing in the light." [Amelia] (7:3, #22) 94, p. 26.
"Canticles / Snow" (3rd Prize, The Amelia Awards). [Amelia] (7:4, #23) 94, p. 33.
"Flying into Newark." [Amelia] (7:3, #22) 94, p. 25.
"The Hill Girl Wakes." [LitR] (37:4) Sum 94, p. 657.

"Incarnation." [Amelia] (7:3, #22) 94, p. 24.
"The Mower Spits Leaves." [JlNJPo] (16:1) Spr 94, p. 4.
"Object-d'Art." [SouthernPR] (34:1) Sum 94, p. 11.
"Old Man Czmielski" (Montegue Wade Poetry Award). [Amelia] (7:4, #23) 94, p. 31-33.
"One for Beth" (without metronome). [Amelia] (7:3, #22) 94, p. 24-25.
"Putting in the Jacks" (from "The Silence and Other Poems"). [AmerPoR] (23:6) N-D 94, p. 22.
"Tell, Persephone." [ColEng] (56:6) O 94, p. 683.
"What Matters." [ColEng] (56:3) Mr 94, p. 318.

DAVIDSON, Terri Brown
See BROWN-DAVIDSON, Terri

1415. DAVIES, John
"Bluegrass Awdl." [MalR] (107) Sum 94, p. 166.
"Climbing with the Wrong Person." [MalR] (107) Sum 94, p. 167.
"Say Hello to Phoenix" (for Song Ho). [CrabCR] (8:2/3/9:1/2/3) 94, p. 142-143.
"Wings." [Jacaranda] (5:1) Wint-Spr 91, p. 67.

1416. DAVIES, Robert A.
"Paiute House." [DogRR] (26) Wint 94-95, p. 52.

1417. DAVIGNON, Richard
"Alice Triptych." [CrabCR] (8:2/3/9:1/2/3) 94, p. 99-100.

1418. DAVIS, Angela J.
"Blue to Rose." [YellowS] (12:1, #45) Spr-Sum 94, p. 10.
"Blue to White." [YellowS] (12:1, #45) Spr-Sum 94, p. 10.
"Time over Time." [YellowS] (12:1, #45) Spr-Sum 94, p. 10.

1419. DAVIS, Barbara
"Happen to Be." [Vis] (46) 94, p. 13.

1420. DAVIS, Barbara Kerr
"People Tell Me." [Sun] (224) Ag 94, p. 19.

1421. DAVIS, Christopher
"Introducing Thy Salt Bride." [CutB] (41) Wint 94, p. 42-43.
"Mission District Sunrise." [CutB] (41) Wint 94, p. 44-45.

1422. DAVIS, Cortney (Courtney)
"The Barking Dog." [Hudson] (47:1) Spr 94, p. 52.
"The Body Flute." [Hudson] (47:1) Spr 94, p. 49-51.
"To the Mother of the Burned Children." [Kaleid] (Special Issue) 94, p. 33.

1423. DAVIS, Ellen
"In Autumn" (after Rilke). [Agni] (40) 94, p. 153.
"Solace." [Agni] (40) 94, p. 152.
"Tufa." [Border] (3) Fall 93, p. 21.
"Woman with Numberless Dreams." [HarvardR] (7) Fall 94, p. 48.

1424. DAVIS, Frederick
"The Cure" (from "Suite Polonaise"). [AmerPoR] (23:3) My-Je 94, p. 24.

1425. DAVIS, Glover
"Ashes." [QW] (38) Winter-Spr 93-94, p. 132.

1426. DAVIS, Heather
"Garden Party." [CreamCR] (18:1) Spr 94, p. 23.

1427. DAVIS, John
"Harold's First Day of Vacation." [NewDeltaR] (10:2) Spr-Sum 93, p. 54.
"Reference Desk Woman." [BelPoJ] (45:2) Wint 94-95, p. 5.
"Seventy-ninth Birthday." [LaurelR] (28:2) Sum 94, p. 105.

1428. DAVIS, Jon
"American Night." [AmerLC] (6) 94, p. 8-11.
"The Campaign Manager Talks Shop." [OntR] (41) Fall-Wint 94, p. 85-87.
"Contingency: Crazy Horse, Custer, Richard Rorty." [AmerLC] (6) 94, p. 12-14.
"The Ochre World" (Selections: 22, 24-25, 36-37). [ProseP] (3) 94, p. 21-27.
"A Party of Sorts." [Sonora] (28) Fall 94, p. 45.
"To Mr. Jefferson on the Occasion of My 'Madness'." [OntR] (41) Fall-Wint 94, p. 83-84.

1429. DAVIS, Jordan
"O it really is terrifying." [HangL] (65) 94, p. 31.

1430. DAVIS, Melody
"Akins 12th Avenue Discount Fruit and Vegetable." [WestB] (34) 94, p. 34.

1431. DAVIS, Olena Kalytiak
"Thirty Years Rising." [MichQR] (33:2) Spr 94, p. 295-296.

1432. DAVIS, Peggy
"Formica." [PoetryNW] (35:2) Sum 94, p. 19.
"Obliteration." [PoetryNW] (35:2) Sum 94, p. 20-21.
"When my mother fixed liver." [PoetryNW] (35:2) Sum 94, p. 18.
1433. DAVIS, R. M.
"To a Hungarian Poet from the Provinces" (from the outskirts of Lubbock, Texas). [Border] (4) Spr-Sum 94, p. 28.
1434. DAVIS, Sarah
"Camera." [CutB] (41) Wint 94, p. 73.
1435. DAVIS, William Virgil
"Again." [ArtfulD] (26/27) 94, p. 92.
"At the Cemetery." [ArtfulD] (26/27) 94, p. 95.
"Castles in the Air." [FourQ] (8:2) Fall 94, p. 17.
"The Closet." [ArtfulD] (26/27) 94, p. 96.
"Dog Days." [Amelia] (7:3, #22) 94, p. 108.
"Family Portraits." [Northeast] (5:11) Wint 94-95, p. 17.
"The Holes." [ArtfulD] (26/27) 94, p. 94.
"In Far Fields." [ArtfulD] (26/27) 94, p. 91.
"The Morning After." [MidAR] (14:2) 94, p. 138-139.
"The Service." [XavierR] (14:1) Spr 94, p. 82.
"Their Dance." [ArtfulD] (26/27) 94, p. 90.
"Their Death and Life." [ArtfulD] (26/27) 94, p. 93.
"To a Fly, Who Died of Poetry." [Amelia] (7:4, #23) 94, p. 40.
1436. DAVIS-SHEA, Rachael
"Crouch." [BambooR] (60) Wint 94, p. 93.
"Ether." [BambooR] (63/64) Sum-Fall 94, p. 12.
"Finishing School." [BambooR] (60) Wint 94, p. 91-92.
"Protuberances of My Father." [BambooR] (60) Wint 94, p. 94-95.
"Sixteenth Birthday." [BambooR] (63/64) Sum-Fall 94, p. 13.
1437. DAVISON, Peter
"The Narcissists." [NewRep] (210:10) 7 Mr 94, p. 42.
"The Unfrocked Governess" (for Elizabeth Bishop). [Atlantic] (274:2) Ag 94, p. 52.
1438. DAVISON, Scott
"San Martino Summer (Indian Summer)" (tr. of Cesare Pavese). [PraS] (68:1) Spr 94, p. 114.
"Two Poems of 1946" (tr. of Cesare Pavese). [PraS] (68:1) Spr 94, p. 113.
1439. DAY, Jean
"Adventure" (Selections: 8 poems). [Avec] (7:1) 94, p. 63-68.
"Coming upon ourselves impatient in the wilderness" (to Jennifer Moxley). [Chain] (1) Spr-Sum 94, p. 206.
1440. DAY, Lucille
"Homage to Henrietta Swan Leavitt and Annie Jump Cannon." [Wind] (74) 94, p. 14-15.
"The Owl." [PoetL] (89:3) Fall 94, p. 24.
DE . . .
See also names beginning with "De" without the following space, filed below in their alphabetic positions, e.g., DeFOE.
DE ANDRADE, Carlos Drummond
See ANDRADE, Carlos Drummond de
DE ANDRADE, Eugenio
See ANDRADE, Eugenio de
DE AZEVEDO, Kathleen
See AZEVEDO, Kathleen de
DE BURGOS, Julia
See BURGOS, Julia de
De CONINCK, Herman
See CONINCK, Herman de
De FERIA, Linea
See FERIA, Linea de
De FIERRO, Fanny Carrión
See CARRION de FIERRO, Fanny
DE IZAGUIRRE, Ester
See IZAGUIRRE, Ester de

1441. De KAY, Ormonde
"Who Do We Appreciate?" [Light] (10) Sum 94, p. 22.
1442. De la HOUSSAYE, Harry
"Elegy for the Swamp." [NewOR] (20:3/4) Fall-Wint 94, p. 138.
"The Prison Cemetery." [NewOR] (20:3/4) Fall-Wint 94, p. 139.
1443. De la MARE, Walter
"Drugged." [SoCoast] (16) Ja 94, p. 63.
DE LOS SANTOS, Marisa
See SANTOS, Marisa de los
DE OTERO, Blas
See OTERO, Blas de
1444. De ROECK, Galina
"Duchenku" (tr. of Anna Khodzher). [Manoa] (6:2) Wint 94, p. 176-177.
"Kumbiak Kayuka" (tr. of Anna Khodzher). [Manoa] (6:2) Wint 94, p. 177-178.
"Old Tale" (tr. of Zoya Nenlyumkina). [Manoa] (6:2) Wint 94, p. 179-180.
"Patterns Sing" (tr. of Anna Khodzher). [Manoa] (6:2) Wint 94, p. 176.
"The Third Degree of Freedom" (2 selections, tr. of Alexander Petrovich Romanenko). [Manoa] (6:2) Wint 94, p. 80-81.
"Under the Wing of My Yaranga" (tr. of Antonina Kymytval'). [Manoa] (6:2) Wint 94, p. 181.
1445. De VITO, E. B.
"Even Angels." [Comm] (121:18) 21 O 94, p. 12.
"Imitation of Art." [Comm] (121:2) 28 Ja 94, p. 21.
1446. DEAGON, Andrea Webb
"At the Fence." [SouthernPR] (34:1) Sum 94, p. 43-44.
"Into My Hands." [TarRP] (33:2) Spr 94, p. 6-7.
1447. DEAL, Kathleen Gunton
"Kindling." [FreeL] (13) Spr 94, p. 23.
"Something Untamed." [SingHM] (21) 94, p. 83.
1448. DEAN, Debra Kang
"Emblems of Faith." [CimR] (107) Ap 94, p. 94-95.
1449. DEBELJAK, Ales
"A Face in the Delta" (New Orleans, December 1988, tr. by the author and Christopher Merrill). [NegC] (13:2/3) 93, p. 12.
"North African Afternoon." [Border] (3) Fall 93, p. 22-23.
DeBURGOS, Julia
See BURGOS, Julia de
1450. DeCARTERET, Mark
"Four Hi-Techu." [ChiR] (40:2/3) 94, p. 76.
"Saint Francis." [SoCoast] (16) Ja 94, p. 41.
1451. DECKER, Diana
"Evohé" (tr. of Cristina Peri Rossi). [AmerV] (33) 94, p. 19-25.
1452. DECKER, Donna
"Dialects." [AmerV] (33) 94, p. 147-148.
1453. DECKER, Mike
"The River." [ParisR] (36:131) Sum 94, p. 213.
1454. DeCLUE, Charlotte
"Four Hands." [NewL] (60:4) 94, p. 36-37.
1455. deCORMIER, Regina
"Colometa" (for Mercè Rodoreda, who wrote *The Time of the Doves*. First Sue Saniel Elkind National Poetry Award, Finalist). [Kalliope] (16:2) 94, p. 22-23.
1456. DeCOURCY, Peter
"Algoma Steel Exports." [Dandel] (20:2) 93, p. 45.
1457. DEDORA, Brian
"Stump Smoke" (Excerpt). [Arc] (32) Spr 94, p. 12-13.
1458. DeFOE, Mark
"Blood Bond." [IllinoisR] (1:2) Spr 94, p. 47.
"Bystanders." [IllinoisR] (1:2) Spr 94, p. 50.
"Legend." [LitR] (37:4) Sum 94, p. 660.
1459. DeFREES, Madeline
"Everything Starts with the Fall" (From *When Sky Lets Go*, 1982). [NewL] (60:4) 94, p. 105-106.
"The Walnut Tree on the One-Yard Line." [TarRP] (33:2) Spr 94, p. 13.

1460. DeFREESE, Allison
"And Her Feet She Hid" (Associated Writing Programs Intro Award poem). [IndR] (17:2) Fall 94, p. 112-113.
"Foreign Student." [Border] (3) Fall 93, p. 24-25.
1461. DeGHETT, Stephanie Coyne
"Fringillirosadae." [NewEngR] (16:3) Sum 94, p. 117-118.
DEIGHAN, Shannon Nelson
See NELSON-DEIGHAN, Shannon
1462. DEISLER, Julia
"4 Seasons / 4 Poems." [Elf] (4:3) Fall 94, p. 32-33.
DeKAY, Ormonde
See De KAY, Ormonde
Del ARCA SARAVIA, Marco Tulio
See ARCA SARAVIA, Marco Tulio del
Del CLEMENTS, Marcyn
See CLEMENTS, Marcyn Del
1463. Del RIO, Zaida
"Two Figures on a Bridge" (tr. by Ruth Behar). [MichQR] (33:3) Sum 94, p. 638.
1464. DELANO, Page Dougherty
"The Agit-Prop Train *V.I. Lenin No. 1*." [OntR] (40) Spr-Sum 94, p. 62-63.
"Going to China Girls." [OntR] (40) Spr-Sum 94, p. 61-62.
"Not Everybody Loves a Uniform." [OntR] (40) Spr-Sum 94, p. 63-64.
1465. DELANTY, Greg
"The Crossing." [Pivot] (41) 93, p. 37.
"On a Marriage." [NewRep] (210:13) 28 Mr 94, p. 42.
"On the Renovation of Ellis Island." [ColEng] (56:4) Ap 94, p. 454.
"While Reading *Poets in Their Youth*." [Pivot] (41) 93, p. 37.
1466. DeLAURENTIS, Louise Budde
"After Hanging a Dead Possum Outside My Window" (Halloween 1992). [Outbr] (25) 94, p. 20.
1467. DELEA, Christine
"The Boston Strangler: A Victim's Mother Speaks." [SlipS] (14) 94, p. 120.
1468. DELFINER, Ellen
"The Funeral." [SmPd] (31:2, #91) Spr 94, p. 30.
1469. DELIGIORGIS, Stavros
"Piece (Sic) 1972" (Excerpt: "Map"). [WorldL] (5) 94, p. 30.
1470. DellaROCCA, L. (Lenny)
"For Janet." [BellArk] (10:3 [i.e. 10:4]) Jl-Ag 94, p. 9.
"The Man Who Slept on Roofs." [ApalQ] (40/41) 94, p. 102-104.
"To Irina Ratushkinskaya." [BellArk] (10:6) N-D 94, p. 7.
1471. DELMONICO, Neal
"3.36 Young Maiden" (from the 16th c. Sanskrit treatise *Blazing Sapphire*, tr. of Rupa Gosvamin, w. Elizabeth Otten). [WebR] (18) Fall 94, p. 37.
"4.35 Bashful Radha" (from the 16th c. Sanskrit treatise *Blazing Sapphire*, tr. of Rupa Gosvamin, w. Elizabeth Otten). [WebR] (18) Fall 94, p. 37.
1472. DELSON-KARAN, Myrna
"1. New England View" (tr. of René Lapierre). [AntigR] (98) Sum 94, p. 67.
"2. Wreath" (tr. of René Lapierre). [AntigR] (98) Sum 94, p. 69.
"3. Night Tunnel" (tr. of René Lapierre). [AntigR] (98) Sum 94, p. 71.
"4. Salamander's Nest" (tr. of René Lapierre). [AntigR] (98) Sum 94, p. 73.
"Grasses of Eternity" (tr. of René Lapierre). [InterPR] (20:2) Fall 94, p. 57.
"New York 1957" (tr. of René Lapierre). [InterPR] (20:2) Fall 94, p. 53.
"Promise" (tr. of René Lapierre). [InterPR] (20:2) Fall 94, p. 55.
1473. DeLUNA, Blas Manuel
"Bitter Earth, Part III." [QW] (39) Sum-Fall 94, p. 245-246.
1474. DEMCAK, Andrew
"Crossing." [ChironR] (13:3) Aut 94, p. 13.
"Popsicle." [CoalC] (8) Ap 94, p. 25.
"Waiting." [SlipS] (14) 94, p. 93-94.
"Wife." [ChironR] (13:3) Aut 94, p. 13.
"Xmas Cards." [Pearl] (20) Spr 94, p. 74.
1475. DEMING, Len
"Insomnia." [Plain] (15:1) Fall 94, p. 32-33.
1476. DeMONT, Steve
"Chrysanthemum." [DarkMoon] (1) 94, p. 76.
"Ensemble Fourteen." [DarkMoon] (1) 94, p. 78.

"Urban Dwellings." [DarkMoon] (1) 94, p. 77.
1477. DeMOTT, Robert
"Deer in the Yard." [TarRP] (34:1) Fall 94, p. 8.
"The Name He Gave It." [TarRP] (34:1) Fall 94, p. 9.
"Nantucket" (for Andrea). [SmPd] (31:3, #92) Fall 94, p. 29.
1478. DEMPSTER, Barry
"A Bird in the House." [Arc] (33) Fall 94, p. 33.
"Birds." [Event] (23:2) Sum 94, p. 13.
"Bleeding Hearts." [MalR] (109) Wint 94, p. 82.
"Next Life." [Event] (23:2) Sum 94, p. 14.
"Octaves." [MalR] (109) Wint 94, p. 80-81.
"Unconditional Love." [Arc] (33) Fall 94, p. 31-32.
1479. DENBERG, Ken
"Common Birds." [DenQ] (28:4) Spr 94, p. 19.
1480. DENGLER, Mary
"Jane Austen's Falling Women." [Interim] (13:2) Fall-Wint 94-95, p. 8.
1481. DENIGNI, Michael
"Verso Piano." [Amelia] (7:4, #23) 94, p. 64.
1482. DeNIORD, Chard
"Borderline." [Pequod] (38) 94, p. 107.
"Dream of a New World Order." [HarvardR] (7) Fall 94, p. 26-27.
"Lilith." [Pequod] (38) 94, p. 108.
"Sleeping Lessons." [SenR] (24:1) Spr 94, p. 77-88.
"A Woman's Force." [Pequod] (38) 94, p. 110.
"The Women." [Pequod] (38) 94, p. 109.
1483. DeNIRO, Alan
"Grace." [GrahamHR] (18) Wint 94-95, p. 62-69.
1484. DENISOFF, Dennis
"Phantom Limb." [Arc] (32) Spr 94, p. 54.
1485. DENNIS, Carl
"As If." [Poetry] (164:6) S 94, p. 341-342.
"Fall." [Nat] (259:12) O 17 94, p. 431.
"The Great Soul." [Pivot] (42) 94, p. 11.
"Loss." [Poetry] (164:2) My 94, p. 86-87.
"More Art." [AmerV] (34) 94, p. 113-114.
"Starry Night." [VirQR] (70:2) Spr 94, p. 305-306.
"Still Life." [Poetry] (164:2) My 94, p. 87.
"To Reason." [Poetry] (163:5) F 94, p. 258-259.
"Your City." [VirQR] (70:2) Spr 94, p. 306-307.
1486. DENNIS, Rodney G. (Rodney Gove)
"Carolyn." [BelPoJ] (44:4) Sum 94, p. 8-14.
"Gypsies." [HarvardR] (2) Fall 92, p. 97-98.
"Psalmody." [HarvardR] (6) Spr 94, p. 19.
1487. DENNY, Alma
"Champagne's to Blame." [Light] (12) Wint 94-95, p. 8.
"Jots and Tittles of Vittles." [Light] (11) Aut 94, p. 11.
"Who Let Them Down?" [Light] (10) Sum 94, p. 11.
1488. DENNY, David
"Smokers." [ContextS] (4:1) 94, p. 4.
1489. DENT, Tory
"Make Costly Your Tears." [Agni] (40) 94, p. 126-127.
1490. DEPPE, Theodore (Ted)
"The Book of God" (Children's Unit, St. Dymphna's Hospital, 1994). [CreamCR] (18:2) Fall 94, p. 166-167.
"The Funeral March of Adolf Wolfli" (From an oral history of Lisa Becker taken in Berne, Switzerland, 1970). [GreenMR] (NS 17:2) Fall-Wint 94-95, p. 18-20.
"Set Design for the City" (for David Dawson). [BelPoJ] (45:1) Fall 94, p. 18-19.
Der HEIDE, Lisl Auf
See Auf der HEIDE, Lisl
1491. DER-HOVANESSIAN, Diana
"Antiquers." [Light] (10) Sum 94, p. 11.
"From a Letter I Did Not Recieve." [Agni] (39) 94, p. 19.
"The Polished One." [Light] (10) Sum 94, p. 15.
"Sexist Poem." [AmerS] (63:1) Wint 94, p. 110.
"Valentine for Endless Love." [GrahamHR] (18) Wint 94-95, p. 85.

1492. DERRICOTTE, Toi
"1993 Inventory." [PraS] (68:3) Fall 94, p. 82.
"After a Reading at a Black School." [Callaloo] (17:2) Sum 94, p. 467.
"At a Cocktail Party Honoring a Noted Old Southern Writer" (for Mary Helen Washington). [PraS] (68:3) Fall 94, p. 78.
"Black Boys Play the Classics." [PraS] (68:3) Fall 94, p. 83.
"Bookstore." [PraS] (68:3) Fall 94, p. 79.
"Brother." [Callaloo] (17:2) Sum 94, p. 466.
"Clitoris." [KenR] (NS 16:2) Spr 94, p. 87.
"Family Secrets." [PraS] (68:3) Fall 94, p. 82.
"For Black Women Who Are Afraid." [Callaloo] (17:2) Sum 94, p. 468.
"For My First Grade Teacher and Her Special Messenger." [PraS] (68:3) Fall 94, p. 80.
"From a Letter: About Snow." [PraS] (68:3) Fall 94, p. 81.
"In the Mountains." [AmerPoR] (23:3) My-Je 94, p. 16.
"Passing." [KenR] (NS 16:2) Spr 94, p. 88.
"Quandary." [KenR] (NS 16:2) Spr 94, p. 87.
"Tender." [KenR] (NS 16:2) Spr 94, p. 87-88.
"Three Poems Written on the Back Flap of a Book by Moshe Dor." [KenR] (NS 16:2) Spr 94, p. 86-87.
"Workshop on Racism." [PraS] (68:3) Fall 94, p. 77.
1493. DERRY, Alice
"Camping at Klahane." [PraS] (68:2) Sum 94, p. 31-33.
1494. DESAI, Sanskritirani
"An Uproar." [MalR] (107) Sum 94, p. 115.
1495. DESNOS, Robert
"As Beautiful As You Are" (tr. by Carolyn Forché). [Jacaranda] (4:2) Spr 90, p. 6-9.
"Let's Be Serious" (tr. by Carolyn Forché). [Jacaranda] (4:2) Spr 90, p. 10-11.
"Nights" (tr. by Carolyn Forché). [Jacaranda] (4:2) Spr 90, p. 3.
"A Tale" (tr. by Carolyn Forché). [Jacaranda] (4:2) Spr 90, p. 4.
"Tale of a Bear" (tr. by Carolyn Forché). [Jacaranda] (4:2) Spr 90, p. 12-13.
"Tale of a Camel" (tr. by Carolyn Forché). [Jacaranda] (4:2) Spr 90, p. 5.
"Verses on the Butcher" (tr. by Carolyn Forché). [Jacaranda] (4:2) Spr 90, p. 15.
"Window" (tr. by Carolyn Forché). [Jacaranda] (4:2) Spr 90, p. 14.
1496. DesPREZ, Eleanor
"Prayer." [CumbPR] (13:2) Spr 94, p. 73.
1497. DesRUISSEAUX, Pierre
"Les Mots Arrêtés" (extraits, à Susan Glickman). [Os] (39) Fall-Wint 94, p. 14-15.
1498. DESY, Peter
"Almost a Perfect Day for Fishing." [Jacaranda] (4:2) Spr 90, p. 80.
"Anxiety." [FourQ] (8:1) Spr 94, p. 35.
"Aunt Belinda." [BrooklynR] (11) 94, p. 101.
"Departures." [HawaiiR] (18:1, #40) Spr 94, p. 104.
"Driving from Columbus, Ohio to Detroit, March 1989." [Jacaranda] (4:2) Spr 90, p. 81.
"Even Then." [FourQ] (8:1) Spr 94, p. 36.
"Last Fight." [HawaiiR] (18:1, #40) Spr 94, p. 103.
"The Participant." [ProseP] (3) 94, p. 28.
"Why I'll Never Write That Novel." [QW] (39) Sum-Fall 94, p. 176.
1499. DEUTCH, Richard
"Floating the Woman" (for Theodore Weiss). [WestHR] (48:3) Fall 94, p. 232.
1500. DEVI, Rajlakshimi
"Household Shrine" (tr. by Carolyne Wright and Mithi Mukherjee). [InterQ] (1:2) 93, p. 158.
DEVITO, E. B.
See De VITO, E. B.
DEVORA, Barbara Griest
See GRIEST-DEVORA, Barbara
1501. DEWALT, Bryan
"Prowlers." [Arc] (33) Fall 94, p. 55.
1502. DeWINTER, Corrine
"Before the Kiss." [Parting] (7:2) Wint 94-95, p. 53.
"Mata Hari." [Plain] (14:2) Wint 94, p. 37.
"Mythology." [Parting] (7:2) Wint 94-95, p. 52.
"Womb" (A Plainsongs Award Poem). [Plain] (14:2) Wint 94, p. 21.

DEWITT, Susan Kelly
See KELLY-DeWITT, Susan
1503. DHARMARAJ, Ramola
"If I Could Speak to You." [IndR] (17:1) Spr 94, p. 76-78.
"In the Name of Treatment — Electric Current, Side-Effects Permanent" (for Wonnie). [IndR] (17:1) Spr 94, p. 71-73.
"In the Valley of the Shadow." [IndR] (17:1) Spr 94, p. 79.
"Return to India: Questions." [IndR] (17:1) Spr 94, p. 74-75.
DI, Xue
See XUE, Di
Di . . .
See also names beginning with "Di" without the following space, filed below in their alphabetic positions, e.g., DiPALMA
1504. Di CAMILLO, Kevin Thomas Patrick
"The Man with the Olive-Loaf Tie." [SlipS] (14) 94, p. 77-78.
1505. Di PIERO, W. S.
"22nd Street" (After Giacomo Leopardi's "A Silvia"). [Pequod] (37) 94, p. 66.
"The Depot." [Thrpny] (56) Wint 94, p. 13.
"Shrine with Flowers." [TriQ] (91) Fall 94, p. 163-169.
"Windy Hill." [YaleR] (82:3) Jl 94, p. 31-32.
1506. Di PRIMA, Diane
"Airplane Note (Another Travel Poem)." [HeavenB] (11) 94, p. 87.
"How to Deal with the Mysteries of the World." [HeavenB] (11) 94, p. 6-7.
"Ishtar — 1" (from *Loba*). [NewAW] (12) Spr-Sum 94, p. 47.
"Psyche and the Maidens" (from *Loba*). [NewAW] (12) Spr-Sum 94, p. 48.
1507. Di PRISCO, Joseph
"Sir Walter Scott." [Thrpny] (59) Fall 94, p. 39.
1508. DIAL, Bob
"Above Sacandaga." [Blueline] (15) 94, p. 21.
"Winter Night in Schenectady." [Ledge] (17) Wint 94, p. 90-91.
DIAZ, René Vazquez
See VAZQUEZ DIAZ, René
1509. DIAZ CALVET, Rey
"Me Gustas" (Bolero). [Areíto] (4:15) Marzo 94, inside front cover.
DiCAMILLO, Kevin Thomas Patrick
See Di CAMILLO, Kevin Thomas Patrick
1510. DICK, Alexander
"Peggy's Cove." [AntigR] (99) Aut 94, p. 26-27.
1511. DICKERSON, Grace Stuart
"Fresh ground coffee perks." [Amelia] (7:4, #23) 94, p. 17.
1512. DICKEY, James
"Last Hours" (for Tom). [SouthernR] (30:4) Aut 94, p. 693-698.
1513. DICKEY, William
"Dancer IV." [Art&Und] (3:2) Je-Jl 94, p. 11.
"The Weather of This World." [Art&Und] (3:2) Je-Jl 94, p. 10.
1514. DICKINSON, Laura
"Clearing Deadwood." [SoDakR] (32:2) Sum 94, p. 111-112.
1515. DICKINSON, Stephanie
"Rock Saloon." [Border] (4) Spr-Sum 94, p. 30-31.
1516. DICKMAN, Susan
"Speaking to the Dead." [CimR] (107) Ap 94, p. 96.
"Touch Wood." [BlackWR] (20:2) Spr-Sum 94, p. 7.
"Visible Woman" (First Sue Saniel Elkind National Poetry Award, Finalist). [Kalliope] (16:2) 94, p. 24.
"Ways of Sleep." [CumbPR] (14:1) Fall 94, p. 62.
1517. DICKSON, John
"The Arena." [Elf] (4:2) Sum 94, p. 34-35.
"Desire Under the Oaks." [Elf] (4:2) Sum 94, p. 32-33.
"Echoes of a Native Land." [Poetry] (164:3) Je 94, p. 137.
"In Fitful Sleep." [IllinoisR] (2:1) Fall 94, p. 10-11.
"Pavane for Victrola and Kazoo." [WillowR] (21) Spr 94, p. 3.
"Still Life with Birds." [Elf] (4:4) Wint 94, p. 26-27.
1518. DICKSON, Les
"Deluge." [Dandel] (21:2) 94, p. 72.
1519. DICKSON, Ray Clark
"Breakfast with Buford." [WormR] (34:3, #135) 94, p. 104-105.

"Buford & the Wall Street Trader." [WormR] (34:3, #135) 94, p. 105.
"Buford at Cooking School." [WormR] (34:3, #135) 94, p. 103.
"Buford at the County Hospital." [WormR] (34:3, #135) 94, p. 105.
"Buford on the Shady Side." [WormR] (34:3, #135) 94, p. 104.
"Buford's Buckshot Saturday Night." [WormR] (34:3, #135) 94, p. 103.
"Uncle Buford and the Electric Slide." [WormR] (34:3, #135) 94, p. 104.

1520. DIDSBURY, Peter
"Next." [Verse] (11:1) Spr 94, p. 3.
"The Old Masters." [Verse] (11:1) Spr 94, p. 4-5.
"One Mile Wide." [Verse] (11:1) Spr 94, p. 5.
"The Shore." [Verse] (11:1) Spr 94, p. 4.
"That Old-Time Religion." [Jacaranda] (5:1) Wint-Spr 91, p. 62-63.

1521. DIEGO, Eliseo
"Comienza un Lunes." [Areíto] (4:16) Junio 94, p. 37.
"Cuadernillo de Bella Sola." [Areíto] (4:16) Junio 94, inside back cover.
"El Día de Los Otros." [Areíto] (4:16) Junio 94, inside front cover.
"Testamento." [Areíto] (4:16) Junio 94, p. 39.

1522. DIESEL, Eric
"Each Morning a New Courtship Dawns." [EvergreenC] (9:1) Wint-Spr 94, p. 8.

1523. DIETZ, Sheila
"For Lota de Macedo Soares." [AmerPoR] (23:4) Jl-Ag 94, p. 35.
"The Murmuring of Fish." [MidAR] (14:2) 94, p. 42-44.
"Spirits Rising." [AntR] (52:3) Sum 94, p. 486-489.
"Train A Comin'." [Crazy] (47) Wint 94, p. 44.

1524. DIETZE, Susanne
"Rapunzel." [SoCoast] (16) Ja 94, p. 13.

1525. DIGGES, Deborah
"Rune for the Parable of Despair." [Antaeus] (75/76) Aut 94, p. 250-251.
"Tombs of the Muses" (for S.P.D.). [Antaeus] (73/74) Spr 94, p. 63-64.

1526. DILL, Emil P.
"Catskill Mts, NY." [IndR] (17:1) Spr 94, p. 149-150.
"The Peace Machine." [IndR] (17:1) Spr 94, p. 147-148.
"Sonny." [Wind] (73) 94, p. 8.

1527. DILLARD, Annie
"Consider, Please, Arches." [Image] (8) Wint 94-95, p. 76.
"Deathbeds." [NewL] (60:4) 94, p. 34-35.
"Everyone Knows." [Image] (8) Wint 94-95, p. 76.
"Mayakovsky in New York: A Found Poem" (Lifted, with permission, from Vladimir Mayakovsky's "My Discovery of America," 1926). [Atlantic] (274:3) S 94, p. 64.
"Pastoral." [Antaeus] (75/76) Aut 94, p. 252.

1528. DILLARD, Gavin Geoffrey
"Haiku" (2 poems). [Amelia] (7:4, #23) 94, p. 145.
"Humbly, we took pride in this" (from *Yellow Snow*). [Amelia] (7:3, #22) 94, p. 37.
"Three." [ModernW] (1) Summer 94, p. 9.

1529. DILLON, Andrew
"Above the Frozen Grass." [ApalQ] (40/41) 94, p. 67.
"At Eighty-Eight." [CapeR] (29:1) Spr 94, p. 35.
"Later." [ApalQ] (40/41) 94, p. 66.
"A Main Street." [CapeR] (29:2) Fall 94, p. 47.
"Reading the Fragments of Sappho." [ApalQ] (40/41) 94, p. 68.

1530. DILLON, Mike
"Maybe the First Modern Laugh." [ChironR] (13:4) Wint 94, p. 30.

1531. DILSAVER, Paul
"Alternative Medicine." [DogRR] (26) Wint 94-95, p. 22-23.
"Hospital Poem: Fading." [SlipS] (14) 94, p. 83-84.
"The Judge Ambulates." [SlipS] (14) 94, p. 84.
"Scales." [DogRR] (13:1, #25) Spr-Sum 94, p. 34-35.

1532. DIMITROVA, Blaga
"Grass" (tr. by Lisa Sapinkopf and Georgi Belev). [InterQ] (1:1) [93?], p. 79.
"Hotel Room (Vienna, 1966)" (tr. by Lisa Sapinkopf and Georgi Belev). [InterQ] (1:1) [93?], p. 78-79.
"Repentance" (tr. by Lisa Sapinkopf and Georgi Belev). [InterQ] (1:1) [93?], p. 80.

1533. DINE, Carol
"Acorns." [ColEng] (56:7) N 94, p. 825.
"For My Son in Autumn." [SouthernPR] (34:2) Wint 94, p. 12-13.

"My Son's Film in Black and White." [Kalliope] (16:3) 94, p. 14.

1534. DINESCU, Mircea

"Autumn Exhibition" (tr. by Eveline L. Kanes and Mihai Zaharia). [InterPR] (20:1) Spr 94, p. 19.

"Death has climbed on our house" (tr. by Eveline L. Kanes and Mihai Zaharia). [InterPR] (20:1) Spr 94, p. 13.

"The Hypocritical Corpse" (tr. by Eveline L. Kanes and Mihai Zaharia). [InterPR] (20:1) Spr 94, p. 23.

"Jericho Waltz" (tr. by Eveline L. Kanes and Mihai Zaharia). [InterPR] (20:1) Spr 94, p. 15.

"Medical Advice" (tr. by Eveline L. Kanes and Mihai Zaharia). [InterPR] (20:1) Spr 94, p. 21.

"Moartea s-a suit pe casa noastra." [InterPR] (20:1) Spr 94, p. 12.

"Mortul Fatarnic." [InterPR] (20:1) Spr 94, p. 22.

"Salonul de Toamna." [InterPR] (20:1) Spr 94, p. 18.

"Sfatul Medicului." [InterPR] (20:1) Spr 94, p. 20.

"Trace of a Voyage" (tr. by Eveline L. Kanes and Mihai Zaharia). [InterPR] (20:1) Spr 94, p. 17.

"Urma Calatoriei." [InterPR] (20:1) Spr 94, p. 16.

"Valsul Ierihonului." [InterPR] (20:1) Spr 94, p. 14.

1535. DINGS, Fred

"Dissertation on Dogs." [HighP] (9:2) Ag 94, p. 102-103.

"Ode to My Tongue." [QW] (39) Sum-Fall 94, p. 194.

"Planes." [HighP] (9:2) Ag 94, p. 100-101.

1536. DIORIO, Margaret

"Blizzard." [Amelia] (7:4, #23) 94, p. 172.

1537. DiPALMA, Ray

"Afterburner." [NewAW] (12) Spr-Sum 94, p. 64.

"Along the Tongue." [NewAW] (12) Spr-Sum 94, p. 62.

"The Man on the Wheel / Steam Navigation and the Application of Chemistry." [NewAW] (12) Spr-Sum 94, p. 65.

"Transcription" (Excerpts). [Talisman] (13) Fall 94-Wint 95, p. 291-293.

"Warehouse." [NewAW] (12) Spr-Sum 94, p. 63.

DiPIERO, W. S.

See Di PIERO, W. S.

DiPRIMA, Diane

See Di PRIMA, Diane

DiPRISCO, Joseph

See Di PRISCO, Joseph

1538. DISCH, Tom (Thomas M.)

"Bird Feeder." [Light] (12) Wint 94-95, p. 10.

"Buying a Used Car." [Boulevard] (9:3, #27) Fall 94, p. 108.

"The Dark Old House." [KenR] (NS 16:4) Fall 94, p. 67-68.

"Frames of the Annenberg Collection." [Hudson] (46:4) Wint 94, p. 640.

"A Girl and Her Horse." [Light] (9) Spr 94, p. 15.

"Making It Yours." [SouthwR] (79:1) Wint 94, p. 110-111.

"Signs of Spring in a Depressed Economy." [Poetry] (164:1) Ap 94, p. 8.

"Smile!" [Hudson] (46:4) Wint 94, p. 639.

"Sunday Morning, in the Laundry Room." [Hudson] (46:4) Wint 94, p. 638.

"Tracy Dreams of the Ball." [KenR] (NS 16:4) Fall 94, p. 66-67.

"Trees in the Park." [KenR] (NS 16:4) Fall 94, p. 66.

1539. DISCHELL, Stuart

"The Talking Cure." [Ploughs] (20:4) Wint 94-95, p. 31-32.

1540. DISKIN, Trayce

"The House on Tamarack." [BrooklynR] (11) 94, p. 30.

1541. DITTA, Joseph M.

"Anniversary." [PoetC] (25:3) Spr 94, p. 21.

"The Boys, the Ball, and the Flicker." [WeberS] (11:2) Spr-Sum 94, p. 38.

"Our House." [GreenMR] (NS 17:2) Fall-Wint 94-95, p. 111.

"Seeing the Morning." [SouthernPR] (34:2) Wint 94, p. 74.

"To My Mother." [WeberS] (11:2) Spr-Sum 94, p. 38.

1542. DIXON, John

"The Girl in the Street." [Verse] (11:1) Spr 94, p. 70.

1543. DIXON, K. Reynolds

"The White Peacocks." [PraS] (68:2) Sum 94, p. 64-65.

1544. DIXON, Melvin
"And These Are Just a Few." [Callaloo] (17:2) Sum 94, p. 420-421.
1545. DJANIKIAN, Gregory
"Absences." [Poetry] (164:6) S 94, p. 311-312.
"At Stanley Bay" (Alexandria, 1954). [AntR] (52:2) Spr 94, p. 324-325.
"Shooting Star." [PoetL] (89:2) Sum 94, p. 31-32.
"Walking My Children Home from School." [TarRP] (33:2) Spr 94, p. 10-11.
1546. DJEBAR, Assia
"Blue Sky" (tr. by Joanna Goodman). [DenQ] (29:1) Sum 94, p. 56.
1547. DOBLER, Patricia
"Choir." [PoetL] (89:4) Wint 94-95, p. 18.
"For George." [PoetL] (89:4) Wint 94-95, p. 17.
1548. DOBYNS, Stephen
"Artistic Matters." [GreensboroR] (56) Sum 94, p. 76-77.
"Dead Poet Ha Ha." [GreensboroR] (56) Sum 94, p. 78.
"Painful Fingers" (for Joel Brouwer). [Antaeus] (75/76) Aut 94, p. 253.
"The Privileges of Philosophy." [GeoR] (48:3) Fall 94, p. 534-535.
"Quiet Time." [GeoR] (48:4) Wint 94, p. 761-762.
"Santiago: Five Men in the Street." [HarvardR] (Premier Issue) Spr 92, p. 106.
"Santiago: La Avenida Pedro de Valdivia." [Border] (3) Fall 93, p. 28.
"Santiago: Market Day in Winter." [Border] (3) Fall 93, p. 26.
1549. DODD, Elizabeth
"At Scott's Bluff, Nebraska." [VirQR] (70:3) Sum 94, p. 449-450.
"The Bog at Quoddy Head" (in Maine, at the United States' easternmost edge). [LaurelR] (28:2) Sum 94, p. 54.
"The Cave." [PoetC] (25:2) Wint 94, p. 25.
"The Hudson River School." [PoetC] (25:2) Wint 94, p. 24.
"March, 1993." [SycamoreR] (6:1) Wint 94, p. 19.
"The Piebald Robin." [WestB] (34) 94, p. 41.
"Reading American." [VirQR] (70:3) Sum 94, p. 448-449.
1550. DODGE, Robert
"The New Nursing Home." [Interim] (13:2) Fall-Wint 94-95, p. 9-10.
1551. DODSON, Keith A.
"Fourth Anniversary." [ChironR] (13:3) Aut 94, p. 16.
"Middle Age." [ChironR] (13:3) Aut 94, p. 16.
"My Daughters." [ChironR] (13:3) Aut 94, p. 16.
"Never Thought." [ChironR] (13:3) Aut 94, p. 16.
1552. DOERR, Ken H.
"Prayer" (for Brian Doerr). [CumbPR] (13:2) Spr 94, p. 74.
1553. DOFFLEMYER, John C.
"Wild Senses." [BlackBR] (19) Fall-Wint 94, p. 22-23.
1554. DOGEN, Eihei
"Poem on the Treasury of the Clear-seeing Eye" (tr. by Jane Hirshfield). [NewEngR] (16:3) Sum 94, p. 32.
1555. DOHERTY, Dennis
"The snake's shed skin." [Amelia] (7:4, #23) 94, p. 27.
1556. DOINAS, Stefan A.
"Cronica Sobolanilor." [InterPR] (20:1) Spr 94, p. 70.
"Declaratia Lui Lorenzo." [InterPR] (20:1) Spr 94, p. 64.
"Excursie in Lumina." [InterPR] (20:1) Spr 94, p. 66.
"Guilty Star" (tr. by Eveline L. Kanes and Mihai Zaharia). [InterPR] (20:1) Spr 94, p. 69.
"Journey into the Light" (tr. by Eveline L. Kanes and Mihai Zaharia). [InterPR] (20:1) Spr 94, p. 67.
"Lorenzo's Decree" (tr. by Eveline L. Kanes and Mihai Zaharia). [InterPR] (20:1) Spr 94, p. 65.
"Marele Mutilat." [InterPR] (20:1) Spr 94, p. 72.
"Stea Vinovata." [InterPR] (20:1) Spr 94, p. 68.
"The Story of the Rats" (tr. by Eveline L. Kanes and Mihai Zaharia). [InterPR] (20:1) Spr 94, p. 71.
"Ulise." [InterPR] (20:1) Spr 94, p. 74.
"Ulysses" (tr. by Eveline L. Kanes and Mihai Zaharia). [InterPR] (20:1) Spr 94, p. 75.
"The Wounded Veteran" (tr. by Eveline L. Kanes and Mihai Zaharia). [InterPR] (20:1) Spr 94, p. 73.

1557. DOLIN, Sharon
"The Bear." [Boulevard] (9:1/2, #25/26) Spr 94, p. 97.
"Heart Work." [Confr] (54/55) Fall 94-Wint 95, p. 296.
1558. DOMIN, Hilde
"Catalogue" (tr. by Sarah Kafatou). [HarvardR] (7) Fall 94, p. 144.
"Not to Tire" (tr. by Sarah Kafatou). [HarvardR] (7) Fall 94, p. 144.
"Summons" (tr. by Sarah Kafatou). [HarvardR] (7) Fall 94, p. 144.
1559. DOMINA, Lynn
"Black Holes." [PraS] (68:2) Sum 94, p. 35-36.
"If I Am Not Real, Then This Is Not Happening." [PraS] (68:2) Sum 94, p. 35.
"Silk." [PraS] (68:2) Sum 94, p. 34.
1560. DOMINGUEZ, Frank
"Imagenes." [Areíto] (4:15) Marzo 94, p. 43.
"Tu Me Acostumbraste." [Areíto] (4:15) Marzo 94, p. 41.
1561. DOMINGUEZ CHARRO, Francisco
"A Grace M. de los Santos: Poetisa del Aliento." [CuadP] (8:22) Enero-Abril 94, p. 114.
1562. DOMINIC, Magie L.
"Notes from the Cover." [Arc] (32) Spr 94, p. 27-29.
1563. DONAGHY, Daniel
"Anchor." [WestB] (35) 94, p. 84.
1564. DONAGHY, Michael
"Arcadia." [Pivot] (41) 93, p. 55.
"The Brother." [Jacaranda] (5:1) Wint-Spr 91, p. 41.
"Cage." [Jacaranda] (5:1) Wint-Spr 91, p. 41.
"Caliban's Books." [NewYorker] (70:11) 2 My 94, p. 69.
"A Sicilian Defense." [Pivot] (41) 93, p. 55.
1565. DONAHUE, Joseph
"Christ Enters Manhattan (IV)." [CentralP] (23) Spr 94, p. 76-80.
"Christ Enters Manhattan (VI)." [Talisman] (12) Spr 94, p. 142-144.
"Lulu at the Beach" (for Stephen-Paul Martin). [CentralP] (23) Spr 94, p. 81-84.
1566. DONALD, Merlin
"Global Villagers." [AntigR] (98) Sum 94, p. 125.
"In the Stomach of Leviathan." [AntigR] (98) Sum 94, p. 126-127.
"Scholars." [AntigR] (98) Sum 94, p. 127.
"Shadow to Sun." [AntigR] (98) Sum 94, p. 129.
"Tom Thompson." [AntigR] (98) Sum 94, p. 128.
"Vigil." [AntigR] (98) Sum 94, p. 130.
1567. DONG, Jiping
"Night on a Notebook" (tr. by the author and edited with Van K. Brock). [InterQ] (1:2) 93, p. 47-49.
"Taboo Words" (tr. by the author). [ProseP] (3) 94, p. 29.
DONGDONG, Chen
See CHEN, Dongdong
1568. DONHAUSER, Michael
"The Poplar" (tr. by Helga Karin Kidder). [SpoonR] (19:1) Wint-Spr 94, p. 113.
"San Giustina. Night" (tr. by Helga Karin Kidder). [SpoonR] (19:1) Wint-Spr 94, p. 114.
"Your Back" (tr. by Helga Karin Kidder). [SpoonR] (19:1) Wint-Spr 94, p. 115.
1569. DONIO, Greg
"Sweet Bouquet of Haiku." [Writer] (107:5) My 94, p. 20.
1570. DONLAN, John
"Blotter Eyes." [PoetryC] (14:3) My 94, p. 23.
"Geranium Lake." [MalR] (109) Wint 94, p. 54.
"Ghosts." [Event] (23:2) Sum 94, p. 17.
"Goodbye." [Event] (23:2) Sum 94, p. 16.
"Leicester" (for Philip Larkin). [MalR] (109) Wint 94, p. 55.
"Milkweed" (for Rhea Tregabov). [PoetryC] (14:3) My 94, p. 23.
"Our Mothers" (On my birthday). [Event] (23:2) Sum 94, p. 15.
"Out of It." [PoetryC] (14:3) My 94, p. 23.
"A Sod." [PoetryC] (14:3) My 94, p. 23.
"Wear" (for Miriam Clavir). [PoetryC] (14:3) My 94, p. 23.
1571. DONLON, Tom
"Saipan." [PoetL] (89:2) Sum 94, p. 19.
1572. DONNELLY, Laura
"Untitled: Land of my birth." [ChironR] (13:3) Aut 94, p. 31.

1573. DONNELLY, P. N. W.
"Oheawai." [Vis] (44) 94, p. 28.
1574. DONOHUE, Angelin Moran
"A Couple Views Magritte at the Metropolitan." [Elf] (4:2) Sum 94, p. 44.
1575. DONOHUE, Sheila P.
"Angels." [NewEngR] (16:4) Fall 94, p. 42-43.
"Palinode: To a Husband." [NewEngR] (16:4) Fall 94, p. 43.
1576. DONOVAN, Gerard
"Synge of Aran." [Stand] (35:2) Spr 94, p. 63.
1577. DOOLEY, David
"Beauty." [Hudson] (46:4) Wint 94, p. 668.
"The Waiter." [Hudson] (46:4) Wint 94, p. 667.
"Zoramel." [Hudson] (46:4) Wint 94, p. 665-666.
1578. DOONAN, Elizabeth
"Epilogue" (In memoriam Nelson Arrunátegui, tr. of Luis Rebaza-Soraluz). [PlumR] (7) [94?], p. 2-3.
"The Lake" (for Stephanie — 2 March 1983, tr. of Luis Rebaza-Soraluz). [PlumR] (7) [94?], p. 1.
1579. DOORTY, John
"The Dan Daley Dialogues" (Selections: 7 poems). [BellR] (17:1/2) Spr-Fall 94, p. 9-15.
1580. DOR, Moshe
"After the Storm" (tr. by William Matthews and the author). [TarRP] (34:1) Fall 94, p. 29.
"Angels and Cave" (tr. by William Matthews and the author). [TarRP] (34:1) Fall 94, p. 28.
"Anti-Abstract Poem" (tr. by Barbara Goldberg). [PraS] (68:1) Spr 94, p. 31.
"Balance of Power" (tr. by Barbara Goldberg). [WebR] (18) Fall 94, p. 8.
"Bruise" (tr. by Barbara Goldberg). [PraS] (68:1) Spr 94, p. 31-32.
"Circe" (tr. by Henry Taylor). [WebR] (18) Fall 94, p. 9.
"The Herons Have Returned" (tr. by Bernhard Frank). [WebR] (18) Fall 94, p. 12.
"I'm Inside" (tr. of Yisrael Eliraz, w. Reed Whittemore). [HarvardR] (7) Fall 94, p. 32-34.
"Magnets" (tr. by Catherine Harnett Shaw). [WebR] (18) Fall 94, p. 11.
"Open City" (tr. by William Matthews and the author). [TarRP] (34:1) Fall 94, p. 29.
"Refuge" (tr. by William Matthews and the author). [TarRP] (34:1) Fall 94, p. 28.
"Shelter" (tr. by Barbara Goldberg). [WebR] (18) Fall 94, p. 7.
"The Silence of the Builder" (tr. by Barbara Goldberg, w. the author). [HarvardR] (7) Fall 94, p. 35.
"Stubbornness" (tr. by William Matthews and the author). [TarRP] (34:1) Fall 94, p. 29.
"Time Zones" (tr. by Elaine Magarrell). [WebR] (18) Fall 94, p. 10.
"Town" (tr. by Laura Fargas). [WebR] (18) Fall 94, p. 7.
1581. DORCELY, Gina
"La Source" (to Grandmother, Port-au-Prince, Haiti, August 1991). [Ploughs] (20:1) Spr 94, p. 113-114.
1582. DORESKI, William
"Beginning Russian." [HiramPoR] (55/56) Fall 93-Sum 94, p. 24-25.
"Factory Work." [HarvardR] (2) Fall 92, p. 131.
"Home Places." [Poem] (71) My 94, p. 38.
"Huron." [Poem] (71) My 94, p. 39.
"Medieval History." [LitR] (37:4) Sum 94, p. 678.
"Porcupine Treed." [ChatR] (14:2) Wint 94, p. 34.
"Rheingold." [HarvardR] (7) Fall 94, p. 11.
"The Story of Our Lives." [CentR] (38:1) Wint 94, p. 122-123.
1583. DORF, Marilyn
"Harp in the Willows." [Plain] (15:1) Fall 94, p. 30.
"This Sidewalk." [Plain] (14:2) Wint 94, p. 34.
1584. DORFNER, John
"Lowell Celebrates Kerouac 1992." [MoodySI] (28, also labeled 29) Fall 94, p. 17.
1585. DORIS, Stacy
"Born Bad." [Avec] (7:1) 94, p. 75.
"Charities." [Avec] (7:1) 94, p. 74.
"Heists" (to Kim Rosenfield). [Chain] (1) Spr-Sum 94, p. 194.
"Know Ledge." [Avec] (7:1) 94, p. 74.
"Lip — Steal." [Avec] (7:1) 94, p. 76.

"Several Bawdy Acts." [Conjunc] (22) 94, p. 158-167.
"Valapuke." [Avec] (7:1) 94, p. 76.
"Vavoid." [Avec] (7:1) 94, p. 78.
"Version — Worm — Wall." [Avec] (7:1) 94, p. 77.
"Walk." [Avec] (7:1) 94, p. 77.
"Whelm." [Avec] (7:1) 94, p. 75.
"Win — Venerate." [Avec] (7:1) 94, p. 73.

1586. DORN, Alfred
"The Island." [Hellas] (5:2) Fall-Wint 94, p. 96.
"Reminder." [Hellas] (5:2) Fall-Wint 94, p. 97.

1587. DORPH, Doug
"I'm Good When It Comes to Little Things." [BrooklynR] (11) 94, p. 69.
"Offspring." [HangL] (65) 94, p. 15.
"Pumice." [ChironR] (13:4) Wint 94, p. 24.

1588. DORSETT, Robert
"Leaving My Father." [NegC] (14:1/2) 94, p. 55.

1589. DORSEY, Candas Jane
"Cynthia." [PraF] (15:1, #66) Spr 94, p. 109.
"More Schrödinger's Cat." [PraF] (15:1, #66) Spr 94, p. 108.
"A poem is as long as the space that contains it." [PraF] (15:1, #66) Spr 94, p. 107.
"Schrödinger's Cat and Doppler's Dog." [PraF] (15:1, #66) Spr 94, p. 110.
"Stone Blind Love." [PraF] (15:1, #66) Spr 94, p. 111.
"Unfinished Business." [CanLit] (141) Sum 94, p. 34.

1590. DOTY, Mark
"Crepe de Chine." [GlobalCR] (3) Spr 94, p. 30-33.
"Grosse Fuge." [Boulevard] (9:3, #27) Fall 94, p. 34-40.
"Homo Will Not Inherit." [Witness] (8:2) 94, p. 130-133.
"Long Point Light." [Atlantic] (274:6) D 94, p. 70.
"March." [CarolQ] (47:1) Fall 94, p. 37-38.
"Migratory." [CarolQ] (47:1) Fall 94, p. 35-36.

1591. DOUBIAGO, Sharon
"Love on the Streets of Manhattan Beach." [AmerV] (33) 94, p. 72.

1592. DOUGALL, Lucy
"Maiti Devi." [BellArk] (10:6) N-D 94, p. 9.

1593. DOUGHERTY, Sean
"Friday in the Fin de siecle." [CoalC] (8) Ap 94, p. 16.

1594. DOUGLAS, Kristen
"Black." [Wind] (74) 94, p. 17.
"Planetarium." [Wind] (74) 94, p. 15-16.

1595. DOVE, Richard
"Footnote" (tr. of Michael Kruger). [NewYorker] (69:48) 31 Ja 94, p. 44.

1596. DOVE, Rita
"The Darker Face of the Earth" (Selection: Eleventh scene. Drama in verse). [Callaloo] (17:2) Sum 94, p. 374-380.
"Rive d'Urale." [Callaloo] (17:2) Sum 94, p. 366-370.
"Statistic: The Witness." [GeoR] (48:3) Fall 94, p. 474.
"Vacation." [NewYorker] (70:43) 26 D 94-2 Ja 95, p. 102.

1597. DOWD, Juditha
"Stokes State Berceuse." [JlNJPo] (16:1) Spr 94, p. 5.

1598. DOWES, George
"A Bent-Standing Small Workman." [Writer] (107:1) Ja 94, p. 26-27.

1599. DOWNES, Gwladys
"Kissing Cousins." [CanLit] (140) Spr 94, p. 71.
"Lucy's Children." [CanLit] (140) Spr 94, p. 72.

1600. DOWNIE, Glen
"I Dream of My Grandfather, Who Died in '32." [Nimrod] (37:2) Spr-Sum 94, p. 28.

1601. DOWNING, Ben
"Hiroshima without Adjectives" (after John Henry). [ParisR] (36:131) Sum 94, p. 145.
"Inside the Horse." [CarolQ] (47:1) Fall 94, p. 34.
"Marathon" (for B.M.M.). [CarolQ] (47:1) Fall 94, p. 33.
"Naming the Ford" (Marianne Moore, 1955). [Poetry] (165:2) N 94, p. 73.
"The Object." [ParisR] (36:131) Sum 94, p. 144.
"The Valley of Its Saying." [Nat] (259:12) O 17 94, p. 431.
"The Weather." [ParisR] (36:131) Sum 94, p. 145.

1602. DOWNS, Stuart
"From the Inside." [Confr] (52/53) Wint-Spr 94, p. 325.
"Zinnias and a Wrench." [SouthernPR] (34:2) Wint 94, p. 9-10.
1603. DOXEY, William
"The Good Ol' Boy." [ChatR] (14:2) Wint 94, p. 30.
1604. DOYLE, Lynn
"Arrows Shoot Through Us." [VirQR] (70:2) Spr 94, p. 300-301.
"Disaster, Us." [WestHR] (48:2) Sum 94, p. 171-172.
"The Muse, I Am." [WestHR] (48:2) Sum 94, p. 172.
"There Being, Something Wrong" (for B.C.). [WestHR] (48:2) Sum 94, p. 170.
1605. DOYLE, Owen
"The Heron." [SoCoast] (17) Je 94, p. 20-21.
1606. DOYON, Paule
"Automne." [InterPR] (20:2) Fall 94, p. 60.
"Autumn" (tr. by Roger Noël). [InterPR] (20:2) Fall 94, p. 61.
"Printemps." [InterPR] (20:2) Fall 94, p. 58.
"Spring" (tr. by Roger Noël). [InterPR] (20:2) Fall 94, p. 59.
1607. DRABIK, Grazyna
"Writing a Curriculum Vitae" (tr. of Wislawa Szymborska, w. Austin Flint). [Crazy] (47) Wint 94, p. 100-101.
1608. DRAEGER, Amy B.
"For Pat Aletky, Mark Plotkin, Carolyn King, and Gracie, the Blind Dog Who Love Washington D.C." [AmerLC] (6) 94, p. 52-53.
"View of River at the Hilton, 1993." [AmerLC] (6) 94, p. 53.
1609. DRAGONWAGON, Crescent
"Bat in the Dining Room" (A Children's Story. Illustrated by Sunny Kwak). [NoAmR] (279:5) S-O 94, p. 23-34.
1610. DRAKE, Alan
"Rongorongo as Transcultural Imaginative Idiom." [HeavenB] (11) 94, p. 39.
1611. DRAKE, David
"Alger Hiss" (a double clarihew). [Light] (12) Wint 94-95, p. 29.
1612. DRAKE, Jennifer
"Andrew Wyeth's Place." [NewYorkQ] (53) 94, p. 110.
1613. DRAYCOTT, Catherine
"IV. In truth there were many falls." [Chain] (1) Spr-Sum 94, p. 235.
1614. DRENNAN, Ellen
"Recipe for Time." [Dandel] (21:1) 94, p. 75-76.
"Skating Lessons." [Grain] (22:1) Sum 94, p. 87.
"Strong Roots." [Dandel] (21:1) 94, p. 77.
1615. DRESBACH, D. P.
"The Recommendation, Ferrara" (for Linda). [Blueline] (15) 94, p. 77-78.
DRESSAY, Anne Le
See Le DRESSAY, Anne
1616. DREXEL, John
"Commutations (I)." [Verse] (11:2) Sum 94, p. 87.
"A Slavic Elegy." [SenR] (24:1) Spr 94, p. 72.
DREYFUS, William Louis
See LOUIS-DREYFUS, William
1617. DRINKARD, Tom
"Old Soldiers." [NegC] (14:1/2) 94, p. 32-34.
"Waiting for the Parade." [NegC] (14:1/2) 94, p. 35-37.
1618. DRISCOLL, Mary
"The Attic Window." [Plain] (14:3) Spr 94, p. 27.
1619. DRIZHAL, Peter
"Mirror Spilled a Wide." [BlackBR] (19) Fall-Wint 94, p. 10.
1620. DRUCKER, Trudy
"The Fifth Voyage" (From the diary of Mrs. Gulliver). [Light] (12) Wint 94-95, p. 17.
"Interpreting Hamlet." [Light] (11) Aut 94, p. 16.
1621. DRUMMOND, Robbie Newton
"Limber Pine." [Dandel] (21:2) 94, p. 8.
"Private Room in the Nursing Home." [Dandel] (20:2) 93, p. 43-44.
DRUMMOND DE ANDRADE, Carlos
See ANDRADE, Carlos Drummond de
1622. DRURY, John
"The Center of the Block." [ParisR] (36:131) Sum 94, p. 149.

"Summer Jobs." [ParisR] (36:131) Sum 94, p. 150-151.

1623. DRYANSKY, Amy
"Black Crumbs." [GreenMR] (NS 17:2) Fall-Wint 94-95, p. 23-24.
"Out of Here." [GreenMR] (NS 17:2) Fall-Wint 94-95, p. 21-22.

1624. DU, Fu
"In Praise of Rain" (tr. by Sam Hamill). [CrabCR] (8:2/3/9:1/2/3) 94, p. 50.

Du . . .
See also names beginning with "Du" without the following space, filed below in their alphabetic positions, e.g., DuPLESSIS.

1625. Du BOIS, Melanie
"Rug on the Floor of My Mind." [Poetry] (165:3) D 94, p. 156.

1626. DUARTE, Ernesto
"Bajate de Esa Nube" (Bolero). [Areíto] (4:15) Marzo 94, inside back cover.

1627. DUBIE, Norman
"At the Death of Peasants." [ColR] (21:1) Spr 94, p. 91-92.
"For a Fifteenth Century Zen Master" (for Stephen Scafidi). [CutB] (41) Wint 94, p. 7-8.

1628. DUBIN, Miriam
"Street Light." [Farm] (11:2) Fall-Wint 94-95, p. 128.
"Woman Inside a Poem." [Farm] (11:2) Fall-Wint 94-95, p. 127.

1629. DUBNOV, Eugene
"A Polonaise of Oginski" (tr. by Chris Newman, w. the author). [Grain] (21:4) Spr 94, p. 98.
"White Night" (tr. by Christopher Newman and Carol Rumens). [SouthernPR] (34:2) Wint 94, p. 42-43.

DuBOIS, Melanie
See Du BOIS, Melanie

1630. DUBRAVA, Patricia
"Joven Mexicano, Puerto Escondido." [InterQ] (1:4) 94, p. 86.
"Upon Reading a Man's Poem About Fishing with Father." [PaintedHR] (11) Spr-Sum 94, p. 50.

1631. DUBROFF, Susanne
"Man Flees" (tr. of René Char). [HampSPR] Wint 94, p. 9.

1632. DuCHARME, Mark
"Purgative Verticals" (Selections: 9/8, 12/2). [Talisman] (12) Spr 94, p. 97.
"Speech at the Window." [WashR] (20:3) O-N 94, p. 14.
"Studies: In the Dark." [WashR] (20:3) O-N 94, p. 14.

1633. DUDER, Celeste
"Proposal in the Village." [Border] (5) Fall-Wint 94, p. 13.

1634. DUDLEY, Ellen
"Avgas in Aden." [Agni] (40) 94, p. 149.
"Body Betrayal." [GreenMR] (NS 17:2) Fall-Wint 94-95, p. 84.
"Catalpa Tree and River." [GreenMR] (NS 17:2) Fall-Wint 94-95, p. 83.
"Dangerous Men." [GreenMR] (NS 17:2) Fall-Wint 94-95, p. 82.

1635. DUEHR, Gary
"Cuts." [CrabCR] (8:2/3/9:1/2/3) 94, p. 113.

1636. DUEMER, Joseph
"General Semantics." [YellowS] (12:1, #45) Spr-Sum 94, p. 38.
"The Human Voice." [Ploughs] (20:1) Spr 94, p. 102.
"Theory of Tragedy." [AmerPoR] (23:1) Ja-F 94, p. 5.

1637. DUFAULT, Peter Kane
"February Variations." [NewRep] (210:12) 21 Mr 94, p. 36.
"Nephelogic." [NewRep] (211:7) 15 Ag 94, p. 42.
"Unified Field." [NewRep] (211:15) 10 O 94, p. 46.

1638. DUFFIN, Brent
"Dogs Have Rights, Too (Except This One)." [SoCoast] (17) Je 94, p. 30-31.

1639. DUFFIN, K. E.
"Generations." [HarvardR] (6) Spr 94, p. 35.
"Houses." [HarvardR] (2) Fall 92, p. 34.

1640. DUFFY, Carol Ann
"Warming Her Pearls." [AmerPoR] (23:2) Mr-Ap 94, p. 30.
"Warming Her Pearls." [Jacaranda] (5:1) Wint-Spr 91, p. 61.

1641. DUFFY, James
"Fat Tuesday." [Ploughs] (20:4) Wint 94-95, p. 49-50.

1642. DUFFY, Patty
"Brainwashing" (1st Prize, The A & C Limericks Awards). [Amelia] (7:4, #23) 94, p. 11.
1643. DUGAN, Alan
"Prothalamion of Quantum Mechanics and Astrophysics." [HarvardR] (Premier Issue) Spr 92, p. 1-3.
1644. DUGAN, Lawrence
"Locked in: A Lenten Talk." [TarRP] (34:1) Fall 94, p. 34-35.
"Near the Cathedral." [TarRP] (34:1) Fall 94, p. 35.
"St. Michael-in-Peril-of-the-Sea." [TarRP] (34:1) Fall 94, p. 35.
DUGGAN, Devon Miller
See MILLER-DUGGAN, Devon
1645. DUHAMEL, Denise
"Always Leave One Hand on the Body." [PraF] (15:4, #69) Wint 94-95, p. 85.
"Apocalyptic Barbie." [BambooR] (60) Wint 94, p. 97.
"The Asparagus." [WormR] (34:4, #136) 94, p. 148.
"Barbie's Molester." [ChiR] (40:2/3) 94, p. 12.
"Bisexual Barbie." [ChiR] (40:2/3) 94, p. 13.
"Class." [WestB] (34) 94, p. 42.
"The Crazy Man" (after stories of Kinnaq as told by Asatchaq). [AmerPoR] (23:4) Jl-Ag 94, p. 35.
"A Different Kind of Birth" (from the Inuit tale *The Man Who Was a Mother*). [Ploughs] (20:4) Wint 94-95, p. 51.
"Differently-Abled Barbies." [ChiR] (40:2/3) 94, p. 14.
"Elegy." [SlipS] (14) 94, p. 5.
"Georgie Porgie, Pudding and Pie, Kissed the Girls and Made Them Cry." [ArtfulD] (26/27) 94, p. 105.
"How the Sky Fell." [ArtfulD] (26/27) 94, p. 104.
"The Invisible Men" (from the Inuit tale). [PoetL] (89:2) Sum 94, p. 17-18.
"It Ends When Mr. Clean's Wife Finds Out about Us." [NoDaQ] (62:2) Spr 94-95, p. 181-182.
"The Names Have Been Changed." [ChatR] (14:3) Spr 94, p. 33-34.
"Pea Pods and Bladders" (from Inuit tales). [GreenMR] (NS 17:2) Fall-Wint 94-95, p. 110.
"The Putting Away of Dolls" (from tales of the Inuit). [PoetL] (89:2) Sum 94, p. 14.
"Raw Material." [BellR] (17:1/2) Spr-Fall 94, p. 25.
"The Rumpless Ones" (from the Netsilik and Iglulik tales). [AmerPoR] (23:4) Jl-Ag 94, p. 34.
"Secretary." [WormR] (34:4, #136) 94, p. 148-149.
"Sleeping Beauty's Dreams." [ArtfulD] (26/27) 94, p. 103.
"The Starving Baby" (from the Inuit legend Okailuk's Story of Kotzebue). [PoetL] (89:2) Sum 94, p. 15-16.
"Things I Could Never Tell My Mother" (for Edward Field). [HarvardR] (2) Fall 92, p. 30.
"Three Blind Mice." [ChatR] (14:3) Spr 94, p. 35-36.
"Upside Down" (from the Eskimo tale *Kakuarshuk*). [HangL] (64) 94, p. 29-30.
"Whole." [BrooklynR] (11) 94, p. 10-11.
"The Woman Who Was Kind to Insects" (from the West Greenland Inuit tale). [FreeL] (13) Spr 94, p. 7.
"The Woman with Two Vaginas" (From the Baffin Island Inuit tale, *Arnatsiq*). [FreeL] (13) Spr 94, p. 8-9.
"A Woman's Story Comes to Life" (after the Tikigaq legend). [AmerPoR] (23:4) Jl-Ag 94, p. 34.
1646. DUKE, Lee
"Bad News." [FreeL] (13) Spr 94, p. 10.
1647. DULLAGHAN, F. J.
"Homecoming." [Verse] (11:1) Spr 94, p. 47.
1648. DUMAS, Gerald
"In 1903." [Atlantic] (273:5) My 94, p. 121.
1649. DUMITRU, Cyra Sweet
"Enough Water." [Nimrod] (38:1) Fall-Wint 94, p. 101.
1650. DUMONT, Marilyn
"The Pay Wickets." [Grain] (21:4) Spr 94, p. 120.
"What More Than Dance." [Dandel] (20:2) 93, p. 41-42.
1651. DUNCAN, David
"Pantoum." [Amelia] (7:3, #22) 94, p. 78-79.

1652. DUNCAN, Graham
"Chip-on-the-Shoulder Poet." [Plain] (14:2) Wint 94, p. 33.
"Emblems." [Pivot] (41) 93, p. 10.
"Mourning Doves." [Pivot] (42) 94, p. 8.
"Short Convalescence After the Winter Solstice." [Pivot] (42) 94, p. 9.
1653. DUNETZ, Lora
"Does It Matter?" [Hellas] (5:1) Spr-Sum 94, p. 78.
"Resignation" (The Amelia Encore Award). [Amelia] (7:4, #23) 94, p. 147.
1654. DUNGLINSON, Margaret
"Dead." [Stand] (35:3) Sum 94, p. 51.
"Easter." [Stand] (35:3) Sum 94, p. 52-53.
"Letter." [Stand] (35:3) Sum 94, p. 50.
1655. DUNHAM, Vera S.
"Untitled: A poet's talent only clutters" (tr. of Galina Gamper). [Elf] (4:3) Fall 94, p. 37.
"Untitled: My childhood is a glass menagerie" (tr. of Galina Gamper). [Elf] (4:3) Fall 94, p. 36.
1656. DUNHILL, Christina
"The Darts." [Verse] (11:1) Spr 94, p. 95.
1657. DUNN, Stephen
"Afterlife." [GeoR] (48:1) Spr 94, p. 152-153.
"At the School for the Deaf." [NewEngR] (16:2) Spr 94, p. 138.
"Bank Street." [Poetry] (164:3) Je 94, p. 136.
"Criminal" (After Tonya & Nancy). [QW] (39) Sum-Fall 94, p. 202.
"Decorum." [KenR] (NS 16:2) Spr 94, p. 82-83.
"The Gasoline Sportcoat." [CarolQ] (46:3) Sum 94, p. 15-16.
"Grace" (After the 1993 World Series). [Iowa] (24:3) Fall 94, p. 70-71.
"Imagining Myself My Father." [SouthernR] (30:2) Ap, Spr 94, p. 289-290.
"The Living." [Antaeus] (75/76) Aut 94, p. 254-255.
"Power." [Iowa] (24:3) Fall 94, p. 71.
"Road Stop." [SouthernR] (30:2) Ap, Spr 94, p. 287-288.
"Something Like Happiness." [Antaeus] (73/74) Spr 94, p. 65-66.
"Tiger Face." [Nat] (259:1) Jl 4 94, p. 30.
"The Voice." [SouthernR] (30:2) Ap, Spr 94, p. 286-287.
1658. DUNWOODY, Michael
"Invocation." [PoetryC] (14:4) S 94, p. 17.
"Notre Dame." [PoetryC] (14:4) S 94, p. 17.
"Still Life with Flowers and Nude and a Touch of Frost." [PoetryC] (14:4) S 94, p. 17.
"Strollin' Thru the Plaka with My Honey." [PoetryC] (14:4) S 94, p. 17.
"Tantalus in the Dark." [EvergreenC] (9:2) Sum-Fall 94, p. 81.
1659. DUO, Duo
"The Boy Who Catches Wasps" (tr. by Gregory Lee). [Manoa] (6:1) Sum 94, p. 155.
"When I Knew the Bell Sound Was Green" (tr. by Gregory Lee). [Manoa] (6:1) Sum 94, p. 156.
"When the People Arose from Cheese" (tr. by Donald Finkel and Li Guohua). [AnotherCM] (27) 94, p. 216-217.
"When the People Rise from Cheese" (Statement #1, tr. by John Rosenwald). [AnotherCM] (27) 94, p. 216.
1660. DuPLESSIS, Rachel Blau
"Draft 21: Cardinals." [Chelsea] (57) 94, p. 82-88.
1661. DUPLIJ, Steven
"Being Delirious." [CrabCR] (8:2/3/9:1/2/3) 94, p. 108.
"Window." [Vis] (46) 94, p. 18.
1662. DUPRÉ, Louise
"Au Centre du Visage." [Os] (38) Spr 94, p. 34-38.
1663. DUPREE, Edison
"A Tree." [PoetryNW] (35:4) Wint 94-95, p. 42.
"Wet Night at My Grandmother's." [PoetryNW] (35:4) Wint 94-95, p. 43.
1664. DUPUIS, Howard
"A Simple, Honest Poem." [CumbPR] (13:2) Spr 94, p. 34.
"Thinking About the Universe Over Lunch and Dinner." [MidwQ] (36:1) Aut 94, p. 60.
1665. DURAKOVIC, Ferida
"Beauty and the Beast" (tr. by Amela Simic). [AntR] (52:2) Spr 94, p. 213.

"November, Raging Through the Rooms" (tr. by Amela Simic). [AntR] (52:2) Spr 94, p. 215.
"Paper Tea" (tr. by Mario Susko). [AntR] (52:2) Spr 94, p. 217.

1666. DURAND, Marcella
"Letter from the Cathedral II." [BrooklynR] (11) 94, p. 34-35.
"Sestina for a Fish." [Talisman] (12) Spr 94, p. 220-221.

1667. DURDAG, Kerem
"The Fall." [CrabCR] (8:2/3/9:1/2/3) 94, p. 71.

1668. DUREPOS, Fernand
"Lonely" (to Marjorie Caron). [InterPR] (20:2) Fall 94, p. 98.
"Solitaire" (à Marjorie Caron, tr. by the author). [InterPR] (20:2) Fall 94, p. 99.

1669. DUTTON, G. F.
"November in Angus." [MalR] (107) Sum 94, p. 190.
"Vatersay." [MalR] (107) Sum 94, p. 191.

1670. DWORKIN, Joy
"Special Troikas: A Corps" (tr. of Nina Iskrenko, w. Forrest Gander). [Conjunc] (23) 94, p. 145-149.

1671. DWYER, Deirdre
"Highland Games, Portree, the Isle of Skye." [Dandel] (20:2) 93, p. 40.
"Thieves of a Nowhere Time" (Grain Contest Winners, Prose Poem: Honourable Mention). [Grain] (21:4) Spr 94, p. 20.
"The Thin Walls of Japan." [CanLit] (140) Spr 94, p. 30.

1672. DYBEK, Stuart
"Alphabet Soup." [ProseP] (3) 94, p. 30-31.
"Today, Tonight." [Poetry] (163:6) Mr 94, p. 328-329.

1673. DYE, Jeffrey L.
"Au Cameroun." [Vis] (46) 94, p. 31-32.
"Elemental Lessons." [LitR] (37:4) Sum 94, p. 686.
"Samantha." [HiramPoR] (57) Fall 94-Wint 95, p. 17.

1674. DYER, Eric
"Transmission." [NegC] (14:1/2) 94, p. 109.

1675. DYER, Kevin
"Love as Lost Form." [DenQ] (29:1) Sum 94, p. 13-14.

1676. DYKEWOMON, Elana
"When to Answer." [Zyzzyva] (10:2) Sum 94, p. 132-133.

1677. DYKSTRA, Kristin
"View from Chellis Road." [Parting] (7:2) Wint 94-95, p. 23.

1678. EACKER, Sandra
"Knotweed." [CrabCR] (8:2/3/9:1/2/3) 94, p. 76.

1679. EADIE, Tom
"Dead Reconing." [AntigR] (96) Wint 94, p. 28.
"Death." [AntigR] (96) Wint 94, p. 30.
"Endings." [AntigR] (96) Wint 94, p. 29.
"The Lessons of Heraclitis." [AntigR] (97) Spr 94, p. 130.

1680. EADY, Cornelius
"Chuck Berry." [PennR] (6:1) 94, p. 16-17.
"Going Down Slow." [GlobalCR] (4) Fall 94, p. 16.
"I Ain't Got No Home." [ColR] (21:2) Fall 94, p. 117-118.
"Johnny on the Mainline." [ColR] (21:2) Fall 94, p. 119.
"Money (That's What I Want)." [GlobalCR] (4) Fall 94, p. 17.
"Paradiso." [Agni] (39) 94, p. 1.

1681. EAGLE, Amy
"Commerce." [Farm] (11:2) Fall-Wint 94-95, p. 16.

EAGLE, Duane Big
See BIGEAGLE, Duane

1682. EARLE, Jean
"Storm Lobsters." [MalR] (107) Sum 94, p. 127.
"Water and Wire." [MalR] (107) Sum 94, p. 128.

1683. EASLEY, Jason
"Bronzed blond swinging Big." [Amelia] (7:3, #22) 94, p. 119.

1684. EASTER, Mary Moore
"The World Falls on the Poet's Head." [RagMag] (12:1) Sum 94, p. 32-33.

1685. EASTMAN, Bruce
"Cockamania." [CharR] (20:2) Fall 94, p. 90.

"Losing a Finger." [CharR] (20:2) Fall 94, p. 90.

1686. EASTMAN, Deborah

"Spying on Alcatraz." [AnthNEW] (6) 94, p. 19.

1687. EATON, Charles Edward

"The Bugler." [ConnPR] (13:1) 94, p. 10-11.
"Catwalk." [LaurelR] (28:2) Sum 94, p. 60.
"The Downside." [CharR] (20:1) Spr 94, p. 80.
"The Fling." [Amelia] (7:3, #22) 94, p. 12-13.
"The Fox and I." [ChatR] (14:3) Spr 94, p. 37.
"The Gold Tooth." [CentR] (38:3) Fall 94, p. 509.
"Petrified Forest." [CentR] (38:3) Fall 94, p. 508.
"The Pond." [Comm] (121:2) 28 Ja 94, p. 16.
"Red Carpet Treatment." [ColEng] (56:3) Mr 94, p. 321.
"Summer Night." [CarolQ] (46:2) Wint 94, p. 23.
"The Vise." [CharR] (20:1) Spr 94, p. 81.
"Water Wings." [Salm] (101/102) Wint-Spr 94, p. 163-164.
"White Flag." [CharR] (20:1) Spr 94, p. 79.
"Zombie." [CharR] (20:1) Spr 94, p. 82.

1688. EAVES, Will

"Small Hours." [Verse] (11:2) Sum 94, p. 82.

1689. EBERLY, Kathryn

"My Dog and I." [EvergreenC] (9:2) Sum-Fall 94, p. 29.

1690. EBERSOLE, Glenda

"Immersion." [SpoonR] (19:1) Wint-Spr 94, p. 119.

1691. ECHEVERRIA, Sophie Dominik

"Remembering Jesus and the Last Supper of My Father." [Sun] (221) My 94, p. 23.

1692. ECONOMOU, George

"The Cats of St. Nicholas" (tr. of George Seferis). [HarvardR] (2) Fall 92, p. 123-124.
"Century Dead Center." [Sulfur] (34) Spr 94, p. 55-58.

1693. EDDY, Elizabeth

"Alone." [PennR] (6:1) 94, p. 7.
"Black Raspberries." [Light] (10) Sum 94, p. 21.

1694. EDELMANN, Carolyn Foote

"Captain." [JlNJPo] (16:2) Aut 94, p. 10.
"Chefs of August." [JlNJPo] (16:2) Aut 94, p. 11-12.
"Mas la Cascade." [JlNJPo] (16:2) Aut 94, p. 13-14.

1695. EDELSTEIN, Carol

"Charm to Be Read in the Year 3494." [GeoR] (48:4) Wint 94, p. 723-724.

1696. EDKINS, Anthony

"The Bulls of Guisando." [SpiritSH] (59) 94, p. 10.
"City" (tr. of Alvaro Mutis). [WebR] (18) Fall 94, p. 22.
"The Death of Captain Cook" (tr. of Alvaro Mutis). [WebR] (18) Fall 94, p. 24.
"Heartsight." [SpiritSH] (59) 94, p. 9.
"Landscape with Hawk." [SpiritSH] (59) 94, p. 11.
"Sonata" (tr. of Alvaro Mutis). [WebR] (18) Fall 94, p. 23.
"Spanish Character." [SpiritSH] (59) 94, p. 8.
"When This Saxon Dies." [SpiritSH] (59) 94, p. 12.

1697. EDMOND, Lauris

"The Guest Speaker Speaks." [MalR] (107) Sum 94, p. 68.
"Summer, Golden Bay." [MalR] (107) Sum 94, p. 69.

1698. EDMONDSON, Dorothea

"Footbottoms Up." [TriQ] (90) Spr-Sum 94, p. 178.
"Mulgrave" (for my grandparents). [TriQ] (90) Spr-Sum 94, p. 176-177.

1699. EDMUNDS, Martin

"The Fire." [Agni] (39) 94, p. 134-136.
"November." [PartR] (61:2) Spr 94, p. 316-317.
"Stone." [Boulevard] (9:1/2, #25/26) Spr 94, p. 256.

1700. EDNEY, Julian

"Foldings." [SantaBR] (2:2) Fall-Wint 94, p. 151.
"Mesopotamia to Teach Drawing." [SmPd] (31:3, #92) Fall 94, p. 21.
"Miles." [SoCoast] (17) Je 94, p. 38.
"Providence." [SoCoast] (17) Je 94, p. 17.

1701. EDSON, Russell

"The Birth of a Small Pink Elephant." [ProseP] (3) 94, p. 32.
"Cheese." [ProseP] (3) 94, p. 35.

"The Old Man Who Flew." [ProseP] (3) 94, p. 34.
"This Encounter." [ProseP] (3) 94, p. 33.

1702. EDWARDS, Anne
"Fly Fishing in White River Junction." [AntigR] (98) Sum 94, p. 105.
"Insufficient Heart." [NewEngR] (16:2) Spr 94, p. 139-140.

1703. EDWARDS, Elizabeth
"Lindo Man." [FloridaR] (20:1) Fall 94, p. 80.
"Lunar Eclipse." [CreamCR] (18:2) Fall 94, p. 96.
"Walking Home Hungry after Church." [CarolQ] (46:3) Sum 94, p. 11.

1704. EDWARDS, Geoffrey
"Behind the little woolly clouds the sky is writing its anguish" (tr. of Clarisse Tremblay). [InterPR] (20:2) Fall 94, p. 39.
"I am a blood thought pierced with rebellious dawns" (tr. of Clarisse Tremblay). [InterPR] (20:2) Fall 94, p. 39.

1705. EDWARDS, Mike J.
"Traveler." [HiramPoR] (55/56) Fall 93-Sum 94, p. 26.

1706. EDWARDS, Robert
"Endurance." [CapeR] (29:2) Fall 94, p. 19.
"GI Joe Talks to the Army Psychiatrist." [ChamLR] (14/15) Spr-Fall 94, p. 58-59.
"Grandma." [Vis] (44) 94, p. 23.
"Mars Hill." [DogRR] (13:1, #25) Spr-Sum 94, p. 49-50.
"Permanent Lodger" (for Scott). [DogRR] (13:1, #25) Spr-Sum 94, p. 29-31.
"Tired Arms." [DogRR] (13:1, #25) Spr-Sum 94, p. 51.
"Tired Arms." [Elf] (4:3) Fall 94, p. 27.

1707. EDZHUBOVA, Nina
"I want to close my eyes and sink into oblivion." [Amelia] (7:3, #22) 94, p. 81.
"It's Autumn." [Amelia] (7:3, #22) 94, p. 81.

1708. EGAN, Michael
"Letter to Rosanne." [Colum] ("The Lost Issues", [i.e. 18-19]) 93, p. 120-121.

1709. EGAN, Moira
"Love & Death." [Boulevard] (9:3, #27) Fall 94, p. 178-179.

1710. EGEJURU, Phanuel
"Cock and Moon Story." [NewOR] (20:1/2) Spr-Sum 94, p. 112.
"Ihe Kwuru, Ihe Akwudebe Ya." [NewOR] (20:1/2) Spr-Sum 94, p. 111.
"See It All When You Die." [NewOR] (20:1/2) Spr-Sum 94, p. 110.

1711. EGEMO, Constance
"Photograph, Fall of '41." [AmerS] (63:1) Wint 94, p. 117-118.

1712. EHRHART, W. D.
"The Lotus Cutters of Ho Tay." [DogRR] (26) Wint 94-95, p. 62-63.
"Making Love in the Garden." [AmerPoR] (23:6) N-D 94, p. 63.
"Mostly Nothing Happens." [War] (6:2) Fall-Wint 94, p. 55-59.
"Sleeping with General Chi." [AmerPoR] (23:6) N-D 94, p. 63.
"What I Know About Myself." [AmerPoR] (23:6) N-D 94, p. 63.

1713. EHRLICH, Linda
"Cades Cove." [SouthernPR] (34:1) Sum 94, p. 13.

1714. EICHER, Diana J.
"Sisu" (strength in Finnish). [BambooR] (60) Wint 94, p. 98.

1715. EIMERS, Nancy
"Absent Bird Moon." [PoetryNW] (35:3) Aut 94, p. 12-13.
"Everlastings" (for my mother). [PoetryNW] (35:3) Aut 94, p. 11-12.
"A History of Navigation." [PoetryNW] (35:4) Wint 94-95, p. 3-7.
"Inventions." [IndR] (17:2) Fall 94, p. 32-33.
"Old Things." [TriQ] (91) Fall 94, p. 179-182.
"Space Life" (for Lynda Schraufnagel, in memory). [TriQ] (91) Fall 94, p. 176-178.
"World of Tomorrow." [IndR] (17:2) Fall 94, p. 30-31.

1716. EINZIG, Barbara
"The Grandmother Who Was a Baby." [Chelsea] (57) 94, p. 75-78.

1717. EISEN, Christine
"Prison of Air." [BellArk] (10:1) Ja-F 94, p. 15.
"Raisa." [BellArk] (10:6) N-D 94, p. 13.
"Spring" (for Kaki). [BellArk] (10:3 [i.e. 10:4]) Jl-Ag 94, p. 15.
"Spring" (for Kaki). [BellArk] (10:3) My-Je 94, p. 11.
"White Cat." [BellArk] (10:6) N-D 94, p. 13.

1718. EISENBERG, Susan
"Separated." [Kalliope] (16:3) 94, p. 30.

1719. EISENLOHR, Kurt
"Here Is." [BlackBR] (19) Fall-Wint 94, p. 37-41.

1720. EISENSTEIN, Linda
"Coming Out at Parties" (Halloween, 1992). [Kalliope] (16:1) 94, p. 54-55.
"Four Cats Are Too Much with Us." [CumbPR] (13:2) Spr 94, p. 13.

1721. EISNER, Amy
"Of Vague and Incorrect Definitions" (After Madison, *Federalist* 37). [HarvardA] (129:1) Sum 94, p. 14.
"Truth Against the World" (Mrs. Frank Lloyd Wright). [HarvardA] (129:1) Sum 94, p. 12.
"Uncle Mel at the Breakfast Table." [HarvardA] (129:1) Sum 94, p. 19.

1722. EISNER, Keith
"Sister Sadie." [Sun] (221) My 94, p. 13-15.

1723. EKLUND, George
"Her." [Plain] (14:2) Wint 94, p. 31.
"The Sorrow of the King." [PoetC] (25:2) Wint 94, p. 14.
"Strange." [HiramPoR] (57) Fall 94-Wint 95, p. 18.
"The Wasp." [PoetC] (25:2) Wint 94, p. 15.
"The Winter Chair." [Plain] (15:1) Fall 94, p. 38.

1724. ELDER, Karl
"The Time of the Blue Haze" (tr. of Damian Damianov, w. Zhana Mihailova). [AnotherCM] (28) 94, p. 34.

1725. ELDER, Mary
"Stonechat." [SouthernPR] (34:1) Sum 94, p. 58.

1726. ELEISH, Parinaz
"On the Way to Caucasus (Crossing the Delijan Pass)." [InterQ] (1:3) 94, p. 158.

1727. ELGORRIAGA, José A.
"Marea del Silencio — 41" (tr. of Gabriel Celaya, w. Martin Paul). [GrandS] (13:1, #49) Sum 94, p. 222-223.

1728. ELIRAZ, Yisrael
"I'm Inside" (tr. by Reed Whittemore, w. Moshe Dor). [HarvardR] (7) Fall 94, p. 32-34.

1729. ELIZABETH, Martha
"Ambiguous Love Poem." [GeoR] (48:4) Wint 94, p. 721.
"Darlene Catches Up with Wilson." [Jacaranda] (4:2) Spr 90, p. 113.
"Seeing the Elephant." [Sun] (222) Je 94, p. 38.
"Wilson's Reunion with Darlene." [Jacaranda] (4:2) Spr 90, p. 112.

1730. ELKAYAM, Shelley
"The Crusader Man" (tr. by Ammiel Alcalay). [LitR] (37:2) Wint 94, p. 328.
"Gideon Was Thinking About Bread" (tr. by Ammiel Alcalay). [LitR] (37:2) Wint 94, p. 329.
"Seven Stanzas to an Indian Chief" (tr. by Ammiel Alcalay). [LitR] (37:2) Wint 94, p. 327-328.
"Song of the Architect" (2 selections, tr. by Ammiel Alcalay). [LitR] (37:2) Wint 94, p. 330-331.
"With Help" (tr. by Ammiel Alcalay). [LitR] (37:2) Wint 94, p. 329.
"Yes Indeed I'll Answer God" (tr. by Ammiel Alcalay). [LitR] (37:2) Wint 94, p. 332-334.

1731. ELKIND, Sue Saniel
"Perspectives." [Kalliope] (16:2) 94, p. 53.

1732. ELLEDGE, Jim
"The Fable of ∞ That I Tell the Man I Love." [Os] (39) Fall-Wint 94, p. 25.
"The Man I Love and I Shop at Jewel." [BlackWR] (21:1) Fall-Wint 94, p. 92-93.
"The Man I Love Befriends the Serpents." [ChiR] (40:2/3) 94, p. 113-114.
"The Man I Love Has a Bad Hair Day." [BlackWR] (21:1) Fall-Wint 94, p. 90-91.

1733. ELLEFSON, J. C.
"Back on the Ghost Road." [HampSPR] Wint 94, p. 5.
"An Incident at Wrong Town." [HampSPR] Wint 94, p. 4.
"Muscle and Bone." [HampSPR] Wint 94, p. 5-6.
"The Return of the Inscrutable Miss Mei Li." [ChamLR] (14/15) Spr-Fall 94, p. 208-209.

1734. ELLEN
"Angels Falsifying the Moves." [Plain] (15:1) Fall 94, p. 8-9.

1735. ELLERY, Chris
"We Are Sorry to Say." [Border] (3) Fall 93, p. 29.

1736. ELLINGSON, Alice
"The Waters of the City." [Vis] (45) 94, p. 17.
ELLINGSON, Alice Olds
See OLDS-ELLINGSON, Alice
1737. ELLIOT, Joe
"The Flower." [GlobalCR] (4) Fall 94, p. 10.
"Happy." [GlobalCR] (4) Fall 94, p. 9.
"If Words Were Ever Definite Enough." [GlobalCR] (4) Fall 94, p. 11.
1738. ELLIOTT
"Ravaged." [BlackBR] (18) Wint-Spr 94, p. 35-36.
"Soul." [BlackBR] (18) Wint-Spr 94, p. 19.
1739. ELLIOTT, Harley
"Living to Tell About It." [HangL] (64) 94, p. 31.
"New Birds." [HangL] (64) 94, p. 32.
"Some Tramps." [HangL] (64) 94, p. 32.
1740. ELLIS, R. Virgil (Ron)
"Feeding Birds" (for my father). [CimR] (109) O 94, p. 67.
"The Old Surprise." [CimR] (109) O 94, p. 67-69.
1741. ELLIS, S. A.
"Things You Can't Say." [Dandel] (21:1) 94, p. 36-37.
1742. ELLIS, Scott
"Night Basketball." [AntigR] (96) Wint 94, p. 92-93.
1743. ELLIS, Stephen
"Forgottens Recalled." [Talisman] (13) Fall 94-Wint 95, p. 206.
"In the Meter." [Talisman] (13) Fall 94-Wint 95, p. 205.
"A Morning Round." [Talisman] (13) Fall 94-Wint 95, p. 206.
"Within an Arc of Surging Stems." [Talisman] (13) Fall 94-Wint 95, p. 205.
1744. ELLIS, Thomas Sayers
"Cowbell." [KenR] (NS 16:1) Wint 94, p. 132.
"The Moonlite Inn." [KenR] (NS 16:1) Wint 94, p. 131-132.
"Sticks." [Agni] (39) 94, p. 85-86.
"Tapes." [KenR] (NS 16:1) Wint 94, p. 132-133.
1745. ELLIS, Timothy
"Tension." [AntigR] (99) Aut 94, p. 66.
1746. ELLYN, Wendy
"Daddy." [Sun] (217) Ja 94, p. 13.
1747. ELMESSIRI, Abdelwahab
"The Dream Tree" (tr. of Badr Tawfiq). [Vis] (45) 94, p. 20-21.
1748. ELMUSA, Sharif S.
"An Epitaph for a Mass Grave in Sabra and Shatilla." [NewL] (60:3) 94, p. 107.
"The Poem of Tyre" (Excerpts, tr. of 'Abbas Baydoun). [LitR] (37:3) Spr 94, p. 475-476.
1749. ELOVIC, Barbara
"Angels." [Pivot] (41) 93, p. 14.
"Cozumel Cemetery." [Pivot] (41) 93, p. 15.
"Parade" (for Cathleen). [Pivot] (42) 94, p. 14.
"The Sad Magicians." [Pivot] (42) 94, p. 15-16.
1750. ELSBERG, John
"English Tea." [Amelia] (7:4, #23) 94, p. 51.
1751. ELSE, Vicotria
"The Daughter's Ballad." [WestHR] (48:1) Spr 94, p. 9.
"Lines Written Some Years after Visiting Tintern Abbey." [WestHR] (48:1) Spr 94, p. 10-11.
"The Sinkhole." [WestHR] (48:1) Spr 94, p. 8.
1752. ELSON, Rebecca A. W.
"These Two Candles, Saint Pantelehm." [Poetry] (164:6) S 94, p. 322-323.
1753. ELUARD, Paul
"Boat Scene" (tr. by Barbara Goldman and Richard Jones). [PoetryE] (37/38) Spr 94, p. 217.
"Fish" (tr. by Barbara Goldman and Richard Jones). [PoetryE] (37/38) Spr 94, p. 220.
"The Law" (tr. by Barbara Goldman and Richard Jones). [PoetryE] (37/38) Spr 94, p. 218.
"Of One and of Two, of All" (tr. by Barbara Goldman and Richard Jones). [PoetryE] (37/38) Spr 94, p. 219.

"So Many Dreams in the Air" (tr. by Barbara Goldman and Richard Jones). [PoetryE] (37/38) Spr 94, p. 221.
"The Two of Us" (tr. by Barbara Goldman and Richard Jones). [PoetryE] (37/38) Spr 94, p. 216.

1754. ELYTIS, Odysseus
"The Elegies of Jutting Rock" (Selections: 6 poems, tr. by Nikos Sarris and Jeffrey Carson). [AmerPoR] (23:6) N-D 94, p. 27-30.
"Elegy of Grüningen" (In memory of Friedrich von Hardenberg. Tr. by Jeffrey Carson and Nikos Sarris).). [NoDaQ] (62:4) Fall 94-95, p. 9-10.
"The Garden Was Entering the Sea" (tr. by Jeffrey Carson and Nikos Sarris). [NoDaQ] (62:4) Fall 94-95, p. 7-8.
"The Icon" (tr. by Jeffrey Carson and Nikos Sarris). [AmerPoR] (23:4) Jl-Ag 94, p. 48.

1755. EMANUEL, Lynn
"Art Class." [AntR] (52:3) Sum 94, p. 494.
"Bad Painting." [AntR] (52:3) Sum 94, p. 493.
"Blue Movie." [AmerPoR] (23:3) My-Je 94, p. 14.
"Film Noir: At the Ritz." [AntR] (52:3) Sum 94, p. 496-497.
"Film Noir: Train Trip Out of Metropolis." [AntR] (52:3) Sum 94, p. 495.

1756. EMMETT, Elaine
"Arcadia." [TexasR] (15:1/2) Spr-Sum 94, p. 82.
"The Old Sanitarium." [TexasR] (15:1/2) Spr-Sum 94, p. 83.

1757. EMMONS, Jeanne
"Jacks" (for Eleanor). [LaurelR] (28:1) Wint 94, p. 38-39.

1758. ENCKE, Jeffrey
"New God, In Training." [CreamCR] (18:1) Spr 94, p. 59-61.

1759. ENDO, Russell Susumu
"Zodiac." [NewL] (60:3) 94, p. 104-105.

1760. ENGEL, David
"Hunter in the Bower of the Quadruped God." [Amelia] (7:3, #22) 94, p. 39.

1761. ENGELS, John
"Death Trip." [NewEngR] (16:1) Wint 94, p. 125-127.
"For Carolyn Kelver, after Forty Years." [NewEngR] (16:4) Fall 94, p. 132-133.
"Hummingbird on a Telephone Wire." [NewEngR] (16:1) Wint 94, p. 127-128.
"Rat." [SouthernR] (30:3) Sum 94, p. 528.
"Stink." [TriQ] (90) Spr-Sum 94, p. 78-82.

1762. ENGLER, Robert Klein
"The Lamp of Many Filigree" (To the memory of Eugene Feldman). [OgalalaR] (5:1) Wint 94, p. 68.
"Temple of the Crows." [EvergreenC] (9:2) Sum-Fall 94, p. 90.

1763. ENGLISH, Jed
"The Grand Hotel of Foreigners" (Excerpt, tr. of Claude Beausoleil). [InterPR] (20:2) Fall 94, p. 41, 43.

1764. ENGMAN, John
"What I Did and What They Did about It When They Caught Me." [PraS] (68:2) Sum 94, p. 59-60.
"Work." [PraS] (68:2) Sum 94, p. 58.

1765. ENRIGHT, Sean
"Blind Woman Knitting." [Thrpny] (57) Spr 94, p. 22.
"Heart and Soul." [AmerS] (63:2) Spr 94, p. 212-213.
"May Queen." [SewanR] (102:4) Fall 94, p. 542-543.
"The Other Life" (after Baudelaire). [SewanR] (102:4) Fall 94, p. 541-542.
"Perfect Pitch." [CumbPR] (14:1) Fall 94, p. 44-45.

1766. ENRIQUEZ, Mario
"Speeding Ticket, Broke." [Amelia] (7:3, #22) 94, p. 79-80.

1767. ENSLIN, Theodore
"Autumnal Rime." [Talisman] (12) Spr 94, p. 37-69.
"Stone's Fall, Wind's Rising." [WorldL] (5) 94, p. 31-35.

1768. ENTREKIN, Gail Rudd
"In Hospital." [CimR] (108) Jl 94, p. 91-92.
"This Time" (For Benjamin). [CimR] (108) Jl 94, p. 92-93.

1769. ENZENSBERGER, Hans Magnus
"Atmosphere of Departure" (Berlin, 1990, tr. by Reinhold Grimm). [NewL] (60:3) 94, p. 41.
"Consistency" (tr. by Reinhold Grimm). [NewL] (60:3) 94, p. 39.
"The Hardware Store" (tr. by Reinhold Grimm). [NewL] (60:3) 94, p. 40.

"Old Couples" (tr. by Reinhold Grimm). [NewL] (60:3) 94, p. 42.
"Strange Attractor" (tr. by Reinhold Grimm). [Pembroke] (26) 94, p. 136.

1770. EPLING, Kathy
"Letters from Nineveh." [PraS] (68:3) Fall 94, p. 26-28.
"What We Know." [PraS] (68:3) Fall 94, p. 25.

1771. EPPSTEIN, Maureen
"In My Sister's Garden." [BellArk] (10:5) S-O 94, p. 25.
"The Running of the Deer." [BellArk] (10:5) S-O 94, p. 25.

1772. EPSTEIN, Daniel Mark
"After Reading 'Le Démon de l'Analogy'." [MichQR] (33:2) Spr 94, p. 297-299.

1773. EQUI, Elaine
"Detail." [NewAW] (12) Spr-Sum 94, p. 26-27.
"Hot Pink." [Caliban] (14) 94, p. 53.
"Later." [AmerPoR] (23:2) Mr-Ap 94, p. 18.
"Little Landscape." [NewAW] (12) Spr-Sum 94, p. 25.
"The Lost Language." [Caliban] (14) 94, p. 54.
"So What." [Caliban] (14) 94, p. 55.
"Sometimes I Get Distracted" (for Philip Whalen). [NewAW] (12) Spr-Sum 94, p. 24.

1774. ERB, Elke
"The Kitchen" (tr. by Rosmarie Waldrop). [WorldL] (5) 94, p. 11.
"Ruppiner Street" (tr. by Rosmaire Waldrop). [WorldL] (5) 94, p. 11.
"Visit" (tr. by Rosmarie Waldrop). [WorldL] (5) 94, p. 10.
"Vivat, Crescat, Floreat!" (tr. by Rosmarie Waldrop). [WorldL] (5) 94, p. 10.

1775. ERBA, Luciano
"American Suite" (tr. by Ann Snodgrass). [QW] (39) Sum-Fall 94, p. 149.

1776. ERMINI, Flavio
"Pena e Peccato" (Selections: III, VII). [Os] (39) Fall-Wint 94, p. 16-17.

1777. ERNEST, R. M.
"The Clutch" (to Carter McKenzie). [Chain] (1) Spr-Sum 94, p. 254.

1778. ERNST, Myron
"Florida-Mid-Winter." [CumbPR] (14:1) Fall 94, p. 38.
"In the Canyon de Chelly" (Eastern Arizona). [HiramPoR] (55/56) Fall 93-Sum 94, p. 27.
"The Sing." [HiramPoR] (55/56) Fall 93-Sum 94, p. 29.
"St. Johns" (Northeastern Arizona). [HiramPoR] (55/56) Fall 93-Sum 94, p. 28.

1779. ERWIN, Christine
"A Few General Hints." [Event] (23:1) Spr 94, p. 48-49.
"It's So Alive." [Quarry] (43:3) n 94, p. 130.
"Nets at Your Feet." [Quarry] (42:4) Mr 94, p. 16.

1780. ERWIN, Séan
"Recovery." [Poetry] (164:4) Jl 94, p. 216.

1781. ESAREY, Debra
"Ballistics." [IndR] (17:1) Spr 94, p. 36.
"Clarity." [IndR] (17:1) Spr 94, p. 35.
"Incarnate." [IndR] (17:1) Spr 94, p. 33-34.

1782. ESCANDELL, Noemi
"Ah, Autumn Garden" (tr. of Fina García Marruz, w. Daniella Gioseffi). [CaribbeanW] (8) 94, p. 91-92.
"Farewell" (tr. of Fina García Marruz, w. Daniella Gioseffi). [CaribbeanW] (8) 94, p. 93.
"I Want to See" (tr. of Fina García Marruz, w. Daniella Gioseffi). [CaribbeanW] (8) 94, p. 91.
"Is It I Who Sheds — ?" (tr. of Fina García Marruz, w. Daniella Gioseffi). [CaribbeanW] (8) 94, p. 94.
"Longing to Go Out" (tr. of Fina García Marruz, w. Daniella Gioseffi). [CaribbeanW] (8) 94, p. 93-94.
"On the Small Table" (tr. of Fina García Marruz, w. Daniella Gioseffi). [CaribbeanW] (8) 94, p. 90.
"A Sweet Snow Falls" (From *Lost Glances*, tr. of Fina García Marruz, w. Daniella Gioseffi). [CaribbeanW] (8) 94, p. 92.

1783. ESHLEMAN, Clayton
"Circa 1926" (tr. of Cesar Vallejo, w. Jorge Guzmán). [PartR] (61:4) Fall 94, p. 635-636.
"A Cross Section of the Incarnation." [GrandS] (12:4, #48) Wint 94, p. 120-121.
"Debris." [Agni] (39) 94, p. 200-203.

"Guyton Place" (based on Tyree Guyton's "Heidelberg Project" in Detroit in the late 1980s). [Agni] (39) 94, p. 204-207.
"Here Lies" (tr. of Antonin Artaud, w. Bernard Bador). [GrandS] (12:4, #48) Wint 94, p. 187-208.
"Homuncula." [ParisR] (36:131) Sum 94, p. 304-306.
"I Awake at 5 AM Seeing a Serbian Bayonet." [Talisman] (12) Spr 94, p. 205.
"Interjections" (Excerpts, tr. of Antonin Artaud, w. Bernard Bador). [Sulfur] (35) Fall 94, p. 50-61.
"The Not-So-Mysterious Koan." [GrandS] (12:4, #48) Wint 94, p. 116.
"Outtakes." [KenR] (NS 16:3) Sum 94, p. 76-77.
"Quotidian Spectres." [KenR] (NS 16:3) Sum 94, p. 77-79.
"Some Fugal Lubrication." [GrandS] (12:4, #48) Wint 94, p. 117-119.
"White Nights." [Talisman] (12) Spr 94, p. 204.

1784. ESKINDE, Veleka
"Sleeper's Lullaby." [XavierR] (14:1) Spr 94, p. 80.

1785. ESPADA, Martín
"The Good Liar Meets His Executioners" (for Nelson Azócar, Valparaíso, Chile). [NoDaQ] (62:3) Sum 94-95, p. 5-7.
"Imagine the Angels of Bread, 1994" (for National Public Radio, January 2, 1994). [MassR] (35:1) Spr 94, p. 24-25.
"Thomas Jefferson and the Declaration of Food Stamps" (Madison, Wisconsin, 1982). [NoDaQ] (62:3) Sum 94-95, p. 8-9.

1786. ESPAILLAT, Rhina P.
"Gardening." [Poetry] (164:3) Je 94, p. 141.
"In the Garden." [Pivot] (41) 93, p. 54.
"The Jury" (1st Prize, The Amelia Awards). [Amelia] (7:4, #23) 94, p. 29-30.

1787. ESPMARK, Kjell
"Route Tournante" (tr. by Joan Tate). [ParisR] (36:130) Spr 94, p. 100-101.

ESQUIBEL, David Young
See YOUNG-ESQUIBEL, David

1788. ESTABROOK, Michael
"1931." [CoalC] (8) Ap 94, p. 35.
"Blue Collar Place." [NegC] (14:1/2) 94, p. 43.
"Cold Kiss." [CoalC] (8) Ap 94, p. 35.
"Dirt." [DogRR] (13:1, #25) Spr-Sum 94, p. 22-23.
"It Was a Close Game." [SlipS] (14) 94, p. 16-18.
"Lemming" (in memory of Ann Sexton). [Wind] (74) 94, p. 18.
"The Meaning of Life." [DogRR] (26) Wint 94-95, p. 61.
"Railroad Spike." [NewYorkQ] (53) 94, p. 106-107.
"Waiting." [Wind] (74) 94, p. 18.

1789. ESTEBAN, Cooper
"Selma, '63." [Border] (4) Spr-Sum 94, p. 32.

1790. ESTELLÉS, Vicent Andrés
"I Can't Say Your Name" (tr. by Nathaniel Smith). [SenR] (24:2) Fall 94, p. 62.
"Tarragona" (tr. by Nathaniel Smith and Lynette McGrath). [SenR] (24:2) Fall 94, p. 63.

1791. ESTES, Angie
"Conversation on the Line" (First Sue Saniel Elkind National Poetry Award, Finalist). [Kalliope] (16:2) 94, p. 25.

1792. ESTESS, Sybil Pittman
"Esther Decides." [ParisR] (36:130) Spr 94, p. 105.

ESTRADA, Alfredo Silva
See SILVA ESTRADA, Alfredo

1793. ESTREICH, George
"Astronomy: Three Families." [PassN] (15:2) Wint 94, p. 40.
"Looking." [MidwQ] (35:2) Wint 94, p. 169.
"The Magician's Rehearsal." [Pivot] (41) 93, p. 56.
"Reverse." [PassN] (15:2) Wint 94, p. 41.

1794. ESTRIN, Jerry
"Nudes" (From "Rome, a Mobile Home"). [Avec] (7:1) 94, p. 1-5.
"Our Commonality." [Avec] (7:1) 94, p. 6.

1795. ETCHEVERRY, Jorge
"Strategy" (tr. by the author and Sharon Khan). [CanLit] (142/143) Fall-Wint 94, p. 62.

1796. ETHIER-BLAIS, Jean
"Grand-Mère au Salon." [InterPR] (20:2) Fall 94, p. 80.

"Grandmother in the Living Room" (tr. by Kay Barnes). [InterPR] (20:2) Fall 94, p. 81.
"Hermine and Her Mother" (tr. by Roch Smith). [InterPR] (20:2) Fall 94, p. 83.
"Hermine et Sa Mere." [InterPR] (20:2) Fall 94, p. 82.

ETSUKO, Saito
See SAITO, Etsuko

1797. ETTER, Carrie
"After the Attack." [BelPoJ] (45:1) Fall 94, p. 43.
"History of Western Civilization, Part I: Final Exam" (for Elliott Kai-Kee). [PoetC] (26:1) Fall 94, p. 18.
"Sunday in the Park." [PoetC] (26:1) Fall 94, p. 17.
"When I Am Especially Prolific." [WestB] (35) 94, p. 81.

1798. ETTER, Dave
"Nancy Eastwick" (Jericho Township). [WestB] (35) 94, p. 101.

1799. ETTY, Robert
"Some Points the Critics Make About Cézanne." [Stand] (35:2) Spr 94, p. 64.

1800. EUBANKS, Georgann
"Dr. Strickland Gives Up Hypnotism" (Atlanta, 1932). [NewDeltaR] (10:2) Spr-Sum 93, p. 47-49.

1801. EURIPIDES
"The Daughters of Troy" (Excerpts, tr. by Mark Rudman and Katharine Washburn). [DenQ] (29:1) Sum 94, p. 57-78.

1802. EVANS, Christine
"Conflict in Your Car." [HangL] (65) 94, p. 94.

EVANS, Craig Crist
See CRIST-EVANS, Craig

1803. EVANS, David Allen
"Bullfrogs" (for Ernie, Larry, and Bob). [EngJ] (83:1) Ja 94, p. 87.

1804. EVANS, David, Jr.
"Poem for Ray Smith Who Showed Me Why I Should Hate." [FreeL] (13) Spr 94, p. 6.

1805. EVANS, George
"A Walk in the Garden of Heaven" (A Letter to Vietnam for Hu'u Thinh, Le Minh Khue, and Nguyen Quang Thieu). [NewL] (61:1) 94, p. 99-107.

1806. EVANS, Jack
"The Ancient Gods Went Broke." [FreeL] (13) Spr 94, p. 29-30.
"Good News." [DogRR] (26) Wint 94-95, p. 55.

1807. EVANS, Jamie Lee
"Lesbians and the Even Steven Syndrome, or For White Class Privileged Dykes Who Should Know Better" (a sarcastic pissed off poem). [SinW] (52) Spr-Sum 94, p. 75-77.

1808. EVANS, John
"Charlie's Dream of Mine" (Selections: 7-8). [Zyzzyva] (10:1) Spr 94, p. 41.

1809. EVANS, Judson
"Elegy." [CumbPR] (13:2) Spr 94, p. 24-25.

1810. EVANS, Kathy
"Cunt." [YellowS] (12:3, #47) Fall-Wint 94-95, p. 25.
"The Dream Before St. Valentine's Day." [YellowS] (12:3, #47) Fall-Wint 94-95, p. 24.
"Thirst." [YellowS] (12:3, #47) Fall-Wint 94-95, p. 24.

1811. EVANS, Leigh
"Lightning." [WebR] (18) Fall 94, p. 109.

1812. EVANS, Michael
"Between Likeness & Unlikeness." [Sonora] (28) Fall 94, p. 46-47.
"The Blacksmith Considers Form." [IndR] (17:1) Spr 94, p. 31-32.
"Buffalo Bill Was Not My Hero." [ChiR] (40:2/3) 94, p. 77-80.
"Instructions for the Funeral." [TarRP] (34:1) Fall 94, p. 15.
"Walking the Winter Orchard." [CreamCR] (18:2) Fall 94, p. 169.

1813. EVARTS, Prescott
"Commas." [CimR] (109) O 94, p. 70.
"The Question." [CimR] (109) O 94, p. 70-71.

1814. EVASCO, Marjorie M.
"Dancing a Spell." [TampaR] (9) Fall 94, p. 17.

1815. EWART, Gavin
"The Drugs of the Fifties." [Light] (9) Spr 94, p. 12.

"In the Tone of an Echo from the Bosom of a Ruined Sepulchre." [Light] (11) Aut 94, p. 16.
"Pickled." [Light] (10) Sum 94, p. 28.
"South London Criminals." [Light] (12) Wint 94-95, p. 11.

1816. EWY, Lael
"Crows." [SantaBR] (2:1) Spr-Sum 94, p. 76.
"Old Swing Set." [SantaBR] (2:1) Spr-Sum 94, p. 77.

1817. EXNER, Richard
"High Time" (tr. by William Cross). [LitR] (37:4) Sum 94, p. 609.

1818. FABILLI, Mary
"Advent 1960." [Talisman] (13) Fall 94-Wint 95, p. 185.
"Apes for Sale." [Talisman] (13) Fall 94-Wint 95, p. 186.
"Cut the Sark." [Talisman] (13) Fall 94-Wint 95, p. 190-191.
"Denizens of Deep Waters." [Talisman] (13) Fall 94-Wint 95, p. 189.
"Go Now." [Talisman] (13) Fall 94-Wint 95, p. 188.
"In Lake Maracaibo." [Talisman] (13) Fall 94-Wint 95, p. 181-182.
"In Memoriam." [Talisman] (13) Fall 94-Wint 95, p. 187.
"In That Curtailment of Desire." [Talisman] (13) Fall 94-Wint 95, p. 189.
"In the Silurian Depths." [Talisman] (13) Fall 94-Wint 95, p. 184-185.
"An Inclined Plane." [Talisman] (13) Fall 94-Wint 95, p. 186.
"Letter to Robert." [Talisman] (13) Fall 94-Wint 95, p. 181.
"My Body." [Talisman] (13) Fall 94-Wint 95, p. 191-192.
"Out of the Ground." [Talisman] (13) Fall 94-Wint 95, p. 179.
"Outside the Room." [Talisman] (13) Fall 94-Wint 95, p. 187.
"Pink Tripe." [Talisman] (13) Fall 94-Wint 95, p. 180.
"Poem: We who in dream discount the horses whose broken hooves." [Talisman] (13) Fall 94-Wint 95, p. 183-184.
"Sauerkraut." [Talisman] (13) Fall 94-Wint 95, p. 188.
"This Is the Day of Freedom." [Talisman] (13) Fall 94-Wint 95, p. 182-183.
"The Undertaker Relied on Roses." [Talisman] (13) Fall 94-Wint 95, p. 190.
"You Go to Bed at Night." [Talisman] (13) Fall 94-Wint 95, p. 179.

1819. FABRY, Sarah L. G.
"I Know the Blue." [JINJPo] (16:1) Spr 94, p. 6.
"Offering Chrism." [OgalalaR] (5:1) Wint 94, p. 28-29.

1820. FACKLER, Elizabeth
"Wes Hardin's Grave." [Writer] (107:5) My 94, p. 19.

1821. FACKNITZ, Susan V.
"What Happens." [PoetryE] (37/38) Spr 94, p. 24-25.

1822. FAGAN, Kathy
"Apostasy" (In Two Parts). [LaurelR] (28:1) Wint 94, p. 59-60.
"Moving & St rage" (billboard on Ohio State Route 36). [Agni] (40) 94, p. 128-129.
"Revisionary Instruments" (for Jackie). [MissouriR] (17:1) 94, p. 158-163.
"Triptych." [MissouriR] (17:1) 94, p. 164-166.

1823. FAGIN, Larry
"On the Pumice of Morons (The Unaugural Poem)" (w. Clark Coolidge). [Sulfur] (34) Spr 94, p. 4-7.

1824. FAHEY, Diane
"Thirteen." [Verse] (11:2) Sum 94, p. 16.

1825. FAHEY, W. A.
"Air." [Confr] (54/55) Fall 94-Wint 95, p. 323.

1826. FAHRBACH, Helen
"House of the Blue Horse." [RagMag] (12:1) Sum 94, p. 68.
"If You Live Near Water." [RagMag] (12:1) Sum 94, p. 69.

1827. FAIN, Sharon
"Losing the Drought." [HangL] (65) 94, p. 54.

1828. FAINLIGHT, Ruth
"Agua de Colonia." [NewYorker] (69:49) 7 F 94, p. 74.
"Buds." [SouthernR] (30:2) Ap, Spr 94, p. 291.
"Inward" (from *Twelve Sibyls*). [Atlantic] (274:4) O 94, p. 90.

1829. FAIRCHILD, B. H.
"Body and Soul" (Winner, 1994 Guy Owen Contest, Stephen Dobyns, judge). [SouthernPR] (34:2) Wint 94, p. 5-7.
"Scenes from the Academy." [SewanR] (102:4) Fall 94, p. 511-514.

1830. FAIRCHILD, John
"Generations of Promises, Long Ago." [DarkMoon] (1) 94, p. 79.
"The Grasshopper Lies Lightly." [DarkMoon] (1) 94, p. 80.
1831. FAIVRE, Rob
"Of the Good Places for Revelation, Insight, etc." (to Steve). [Blueline] (15) 94, p. 76.
1832. FAIZ, Faiz Ahmed
"Five Beirut Poems" (tr. by Andrew McCord). [Conjunc] (23) 94, p. 84-88.
1833. FALK, John
"Bright Vapor." [Os] (38) Spr 94, p. 17.
"Moon Gone Calcified." [Os] (38) Spr 94, p. 16.
"On the Line." [Os] (39) Fall-Wint 94, p. 13.
1834. FALSBERG, Elizabeth
"Lines." [BellArk] (10:6) N-D 94, p. 10.
"Sighting." [BellArk] (10:6) N-D 94, p. 10.
1835. FALZONE, Kelly Cass
"I Cry for a Man I Despise." [CumbPR] (14:1) Fall 94, p. 76-77.
"Pig Opening." [CumbPR] (14:1) Fall 94, p. 74-75.
1836. FANDEL, John
"At the Hearing." [FourQ] (8:2) Fall 94, p. 18.
"Sermon." [Comm] (121:1) 14 Ja 94, p. 19.
1837. FANNING, Roger
"Plumbing's Underworld." [Jacaranda] (10) 94, p. 126.
1838. FARACO, Carlos
"Like a White Wolf the Moon Took Flight" (tr. by Forrest Gander). [Caliban] (14) 94, p. 143.
1839. FARAWELL, Martin Jude
"Platitudes." [HiramPoR] (57) Fall 94-Wint 95, p. 20.
"Two a.m." [HiramPoR] (57) Fall 94-Wint 95, p. 19.
"While Shaving." [Amelia] (7:3, #22) 94, p. 137.
1840. FARGAS, Laura
"Timshel" (Hebrew for 'thou mayest'). [PlumR] (7) [94?], p. 74-75.
"Town" (tr. of Moshe Dor). [WebR] (18) Fall 94, p. 7.
1841. FARGNOLI, Patricia
"The Memory of Roses." [NegC] (14:1/2) 94, p. 44-45.
1842. FARMER, Candace O'Bannon
"Chesterfield Pkwy." [Callaloo] (17:1) Wint 94, p. 267.
1843. FARMER, Harold
"The Hunter and the Moon" (Poem after the /xam). [SenR] (24:1) Spr 94, p. 45.
"The Hunters" (Poem after the /xam). [SenR] (24:1) Spr 94, p. 41.
"The Singing" (Poem after the /xam). [SenR] (24:1) Spr 94, p. 40.
"Young Man Carried off by Lion" (Poem after the /xam). [SenR] (24:1) Spr 94, p. 42-44.
1844. FARMER, Rod
"The Clause." [BellArk] (10:1) Ja-F 94, p. 23.
"Indian Bazaar." [BellArk] (10:1) Ja-F 94, p. 24.
"Swan Dive." [HampSPR] Wint 94, p. 40.
"When." [Elf] (4:3) Fall 94, p. 33.
1845. FARMER, Wayne
"Memoir." [GrandS] (13:2, #50) Fall 94, p. 214-221.
1846. FARNSWORTH, Robert
"Eminent Domain." [Hudson] (47:3) Aut 94, p. 427.
"Eudaemonics." [DenQ] (28:3) Wint 94, p. 18-19.
"Sins Since." [NoDaQ] (62:2) Spr 94-95, p. 85-86.
"Work." [NoDaQ] (62:2) Spr 94-95, p. 83-84.
1847. FARRELL, Hansen
"Which Way." [Callaloo] (17:1) Wint 94, p. 177.
1848. FARRELL, Kate
"Flowers of St. Francis." [AntigR] (98) Sum 94, p. 44.
"Greetings from Modesto California" (For Wendy). [AntigR] (98) Sum 94, p. 40.
"Real Estate." [AntigR] (98) Sum 94, p. 41.
"Slug." [AntigR] (98) Sum 94, p. 43.
"What Makes You Happy." [AntigR] (98) Sum 94, p. 42.
1849. FARRÉS, Osvaldo
"Acercate Mas." [Areíto] (4:15) Marzo 94, p. 42.

1850. FASEL, Ida
"Celestial Advice." [ChrC] (111:12) 13 Ap 94, p. 386.
"Fossil." [ChrC] (111:30) 26 O 94, p. 974.
"Geologist" (Deuteronomy 32:4). [ChrC] (111:24) 24-31 Ag 94, p. 772.
"The Meeting." [ChrC] (111:29) 19 O 94, p. 943.
FATE, Tom Montgomery
See MONTGOMERY-FATE, Tom
1851. FAUDREE, Paja
"A Jar of Pig Lips" (Elmo's Filling Station, Highway 61, Mississippi." [CarolQ] (46:3) Sum 94, p. 77.
"The Shattered Park." [Sonora] (27) Spr 94, p. 142-145.
1852. FAY, Steve
"Crossings." [Ascent] (19:1) Fall 94, p. 28-29.
"Girl with Catfish." [IllinoisR] (1:2) Spr 94, p. 22-23.
1853. FAZZINI, Marco
"Other Still Lives" (Excerpts, tr. of Valerio Magrelli, w. Douglas Reid Skinner). [Verse] (11:1) Spr 94, p. 44-45.
1854. FEARING, Kenneth
"Dirge." [FreeL] (13) Spr 94, p. 26-27.
"Scheherazade." [FreeL] (13) Spr 94, p. 25.
"SOS." [FreeL] (13) Spr 94, p. 27-28.
1855. FEATHERSTON, Dan
"Ofrenda." [Talisman] (13) Fall 94-Wint 95, p. 255-257.
1856. FEDO, David
"Echolalia." [TexasR] (15:1/2) Spr-Sum 94, p. 84-85.
1857. FEDORIW, Diana
"Why L.A.?" [Zyzzyva] (10:2) Sum 94, p. 29.
1858. FEELA, David
"Deduction." [SouthernPR] (34:1) Sum 94, p. 45.
1859. FEHLER, Gene
"Incident at Maggie's Cafe." [Pearl] (20) Spr 94, p. 72.
"Scholar's Ecstasy." [Light] (12) Wint 94-95, p. 16.
1860. FEIERSTEIN, Ricardo
"Diptych: I. Cycle, II. Transmission" (tr. by J. Kates and Stephen Sadow). [PlumR] (7) [94?], p. 55-57.
1861. FEIGENBAUM, Erika
"Andante for Four Chairs and Two Lovers." [HiramPoR] (57) Fall 94-Wint 95, p. 21.
1862. FEIN, Richard
"Cetacean Creed." [SmPd] (31:2, #91) Spr 94, p. 7.
"The Clouds." [PartR] (61:4) Fall 94, p. 637.
1863. FEINFELD, D. A.
"To Construct a Maze." [HiramPoR] (55/56) Fall 93-Sum 94, p. 30.
1864. FEINSTEIN, Robert N.
"Bones." [Amelia] (7:3, #22) 94, p. 118-119.
"Diet." [Amelia] (7:3, #22) 94, p. 133.
"Graffiti." [Light] (11) Aut 94, p. 19.
"Little Mary." [Light] (9) Spr 94, p. 19.
1865. FEINSTEIN, Sandy
"Vallø." [Border] (3) Fall 93, p. 30.
1866. FEINSTEIN, Sascha
"Amulets." [HayF] (15) Fall-Wint 94, p. 66-67.
"Isis" (for a woman in Don Maung airport). [GreenMR] (NS 17:2) Fall-Wint 94-95, p. 89.
"Orchid: Three Portraits, One Night." [Confr] (54/55) Fall 94-Wint 95, p. 290-291.
"Singapore, July 4th." [Confr] (54/55) Fall 94-Wint 95, p. 292.
"Sonnets for Stan Gage (1945-1992)." [HayF] (15) Fall-Wint 94, p. 64-65.
1867. FELDMAN, Irving
"The Celebrities." [Atlantic] (273:2) F 94, p. 100.
"The Girlfriend." [Confr] (54/55) Fall 94-Wint 95, p. 269-270.
"Kiss and Tell." [Raritan] (14:1) Sum 94, p. 26-30.
"The Little Children of Hamelin." [ParisR] (36:131) Sum 94, p. 89-93.
"She Knows." [Nat] (259:10) O 3 94, p. 358.
"Terminal Laughs." [YaleR] (82:1) Ja 94, p. 24-25.

1868. FELDMAN, Ruth
"For Adolf Eichmann" (tr. of Primo Levy, w. Brian Swann). [NewEngR] (16:2) Spr 94, p. 149.
1869. FELICIANO, Margarita
"Agujero del Diablo" (Cataratas del Niágara). [CanLit] (142/143) Fall-Wint 94, p. 11.
"Carretera." [CanLit] (142/143) Fall-Wint 94, p. 9.
"Devil's Hole" (Niagara Falls). [CanLit] (142/143) Fall-Wint 94, p. 10.
"Highway." [CanLit] (142/143) Fall-Wint 94, p. 8.
FEMINA, Gerry La
See LaFEMINA, Gerry
1870. FENG, Anita N.
"Graffitti at the Peak of Folded Brocade Hill." [IllinoisR] (2:1) Fall 94, p. 13.
"The Last Piece." [IllinoisR] (2:1) Fall 94, p. 12-13.
1871. FENTON, James
"Hinterhof." [NewYRB] (41:9) 12 My 94, p. 14.
1872. FERGUS, Howard
"At Fifty-Five (July 1993)." [CaribbeanW] (8) 94, p. 52-53.
1873. FERGUSON, Judith
"Faith." [Border] (4) Spr-Sum 94, p. 33-34.
1874. FERGUSON, Scott
"There and There Again." [AmerLC] (6) 94, p. 107-108.
1875. FERIA, Linea de
"Poem for the Woman Who Talks to Herself in the Park" (tr. by Ruth Behar). [MichQR] (33:4) Fall 94, p. 781-782.
1876. FERINE, Timothy
"The Human Beings." [ChironR] (13:3) Aut 94, p. 21.
"Sorrow." [ChironR] (13:3) Aut 94, p. 21.
1877. FERLINGHETTI, Lawrence
"In the Diner." [Vis] (45) 94, p. 41-42.
1878. FERNANDEZ, Amando
"Corporeidad." [Nuez] (5:13/14/15) 94, p. 9.
"Espejo de Bronce." [Nuez] (5:13/14/15) 94, p. 9.
"La Figura de Héctor." [Nuez] (5:13/14/15) 94, p. 9.
"El Fuego." [MichQR] (33:4) Fall 94, p. 785-786.
1879. FERNANDEZ, Pablo Armando
"Cities" (tr. by Daniela Gioseffi and Enildo Garcia). [Vis] (46) 94, p. 23.
1880. FERRA, Lorraine
"After Passing a Revival Tent." [BellArk] (10:3) My-Je 94, p. 12.
"Winter Solstice." [PoetC] (25:3) Spr 94, p. 9.
1881. FERRY, David
"Ode I.23. To Chloë" (tr. of Horace). [PartR] (61:4) Fall 94, p. 628-629.
"Ode: II.14, to Postumus" (tr. of Horace). [Thrpny] (59) Fall 94, p. 13.
"Ode III.13. To a Fountain" (tr. of Horace). [PartR] (61:4) Fall 94, p. 628.
1882. FESSLER, Michael
"The Year of the Lotus." [Wind] (74) 94, p. 19-20.
1883. FETTERS, Clifford Paul
"On Looking Up After Love." [Elf] (4:3) Fall 94, p. 29.
"Power and Weakness." [FourQ] (8:1) Spr 94, p. 57.
"Strange Display." [Plain] (14:3) Spr 94, p. 26.
FICK, Marlon Ohnesorge
See OHNESORGE-FICK, Marlon
1884. FICKERT, Kurt
"Arrivals and Departures." [Wind] (73) 94, p. 9.
"Five Sisters." [Wind] (73) 94, p. 9-10.
1885. FIELD, Edward
"Old Acquaintance." [MichQR] (33:1) Wint 94, p. 219-220.
"Vocalise." [Pearl] (20) Spr 94, p. 57.
1886. FIELD, Valerie
"Madame Chairman." [SingHM] (21) 94, p. 39.
FIERRO, Fanny Carrión de
See CARRION de FIERRO, Fanny
1887. FIGLER, Dayvid J.
"Everytime." [ChironR] (13:4) Wint 94, p. 30.
"Look It Up." [ChironR] (13:4) Wint 94, p. 11.

1888. FIGUEREDO, A. E.
"The Littlest Iliad" (St. Thomas, During the Annual Eel Run, 1973, for Bruce and Cutty). [CaribbeanW] (8) 94, p. 55.
1889. FIGUEROA, Luis Andrés
"Pieza Blanca" (Para Andrés, de *Velas en al Agua*, Valparaíso, Chile, 1992). [Os] (38) Spr 94, p. 27.
1890. FILER, Damien
"You Just Have to Hope." [DogRR] (26) Wint 94-95, p. 7.
1891. FILES, Meg
"The Love Hunter" (For Larry Stallings, murdered 10/3/92). [ColEng] (56:3) Mr 94, p. 322.
1892. FILKINS, Peter
"After This Flood" (tr. of Ingeborg Bachmann). [AmerPoR] (23:2) Mr-Ap 94, p. 35.
"Early Noon" (tr. of Ingeborg Bachmann). [AmerPoR] (23:2) Mr-Ap 94, p. 36.
"Hidden Meadow." [AmerS] (63:2) Spr 94, p. 257.
"In Apulia" (tr. of Ingeborg Bachmann). [ParisR] (36:131) Sum 94, p. 141.
"In the Storm of Roses" (tr. of Ingeborg Bachmann). [AmerPoR] (23:2) Mr-Ap 94, p. 35.
"In Twilight" (tr. of Ingeborg Bachmann). [Sulfur] (35) Fall 94, p. 156.
"Letter in Two Drafts" (tr. of Ingeborg Bachmann). [ParisR] (36:131) Sum 94, p. 142-143.
"March Stars" (tr. of Ingeborg Bachmann). [AmerPoR] (23:2) Mr-Ap 94, p. 36.
"The Native Land" (tr. of Ingeborg Bachmann). [AmerPoR] (23:2) Mr-Ap 94, p. 35.
"Psalm" (tr. of Ingeborg Bachmann). [Sulfur] (35) Fall 94, p. 157-158.
"Shadows Roses Shadow" (tr. of Ingeborg Bachmann). [AmerPoR] (23:2) Mr-Ap 94, p. 35.
1893. FILKOVA, Fedya
"Arrival" (tr. by Lisa Sapinkopf and Georgi Belev). [InterQ] (1:1) [93?], p. 85.
"Vulnerability" (tr. by Lisa Sapinkopf and Georgi Belev). [InterQ] (1:1) [93?], p. 85.
1894. FINALE, Frank
"Anecdote of the Rifle" (With apologies to Wallace Stevens). [NegC] (14:1/2) 94, p. 22.
1895. FINCH, Peter
"The Poem" (teaching at Merthyr Tydfil). [MalR] (107) Sum 94, p. 118-119.
1896. FINCH, Roger
"International Conference on Speech and Speechlessness." [CapeR] (29:1) Spr 94, p. 4.
1897. FINCKE, Gary
"Coughing Through the Brambles." [MissouriR] (17:3) 94, p. 40-41.
"The Doctrine of Signatures." [PoetryNW] (35:1) Spr 94, p. 15.
"The Dream of Alchemy." [NewDeltaR] (11:1) Fall 93-Wint 94, p. 99-101.
"The Etymology of Angels." [MissouriR] (17:3) 94, p. 46-47.
"Filling the Hands." [TarRP] (34:1) Fall 94, p. 33.
"The Great Chain" (From "The Great Chain of Being," a ten-part poem, in the Fall 1993 *Missouri Review*). [Harp] (288:1726) Mr 94, p. 34.
"The High Rise Evergreen." [PoetL] (89:1) Spr 94, p. 47.
"Memorizing the Dead." [Pivot] (41) 93, p. 25.
"The Method-Acting for Affliction." [PraS] (68:1) Spr 94, p. 66-67.
"The Near-Death Fervor." [MissouriR] (17:3) 94, p. 42.
"The One Birds." [MissouriR] (17:3) 94, p. 43.
"The Outlaw under the Floor." [PraS] (68:1) Spr 94, p. 65-66.
"The Pardoner." [GreenMR] (NS 17:2) Fall-Wint 94-95, p. 48-50.
"The Pointillism of Abuse." [PoetL] (89:1) Spr 94, p. 46.
"The Punishment Seminar." [ProseP] (3) 94, p. 36.
"The Quest for the Clean Hang." [LaurelR] (28:1) Wint 94, p. 79-80.
"The Resting Heartbeat." [Pivot] (42) 94, p. 9-10.
"Sealing the Porn Shop." [PraS] (68:1) Spr 94, p. 64-65.
"The Simple Language Which Damns Us." [WestB] (34) 94, p. 28-29.
"Sparklers." [LaurelR] (28:2) Sum 94, p. 106-107.
"The Wonderful Resolve to Breathe." [MissouriR] (17:3) 94, p. 44-45.
1898. FINE, Saralee Gelman
"Aging." [NegC] (14:1/2) 94, p. 185.
1899. FINK, Janie
"The Hostess Describes Her Party." [Pembroke] (26) 94, p. 77.
1900. FINK, Robert A.
"Laying on of Hands." [GrahamHR] (18) Wint 94-95, p. 43.

"March in West Texas." [Border] (5) Fall-Wint 94, p. 14.
"Rowena's This Lady Stylist Down at Wilmer's Barber Shop." [Border] (3) Fall 93, p. 31-32.

1901. FINKE, Gary
"The Immunity Shark." [PoetL] (89:4) Wint 94-95, p. 20.

1902. FINKEL, Donald
"In the Clearing." [YaleR] (82:3) Jl 94, p. 66-75.
"New Century" (tr. of Bei Dao, w. Chen Xueliang). [Manoa] (6:1) Sum 94, p. 110-111.
"Playwright" (tr. of Bei Dao, w. Chen Xueliang). [Manoa] (6:1) Sum 94, p. 110.
"A Question of Seeing." [DenQ] (28:3) Wint 94, p. 20.
"Questioning the Sky" (tr. of Bei Dao, w. Chen Xueliang). [Manoa] (6:1) Sum 94, p. 111.
"When the People Arose from Cheese" (tr. of Duo Duo, w. Li Guohua). [AnotherCM] (27) 94, p. 216-217.

1903. FINKELSTEIN, Caroline
"1950." [WillowS] (34) Sum 94, p. 30.
"Against Closing." [GeoR] (48:3) Fall 94, p. 558.
"Brief." [Poetry] (164:5) Ag 94, p. 253.
"Fabric." [GeoR] (48:3) Fall 94, p. 556-557.
"An Opinion." [Poetry] (164:5) Ag 94, p. 254.
"The Rescue." [WillowS] (34) Sum 94, p. 31.
"A Round with Envy." [SenR] (24:2) Fall 94, p. 52.
"Vacation." [Poetry] (164:5) Ag 94, p. 252.

1904. FINKELSTEIN, Norman
"Prayer for Steven." [DenQ] (28:3) Wint 94, p. 109.
"Track" (Excerpts). [Talisman] (13) Fall 94-Wint 95, p. 251-253.
"Yes Then No" (for M. P.). [DenQ] (28:4) Spr 94, p. 20-21.

1905. FINLEY, Anne
"A Day in the Life of Two-Deer." [Callaloo] (17:1) Wint 94, p. 178.

1906. FINLEY, Mike
"The Audience." [ChironR] (13:4) Wint 94, p. 19.
"Four Lousy Miracles." [ChironR] (13:4) Wint 94, p. 19.
"This Gun Shoots Black Holes." [ChironR] (13:4) Wint 94, p. 19.

1907. FINLEY, Ross Thompson
"Red Hands." [AntigR] (99) Aut 94, p. 37-38.

1908. FINNEGAN, James
"After the Experiments." [Confr] (54/55) Fall 94-Wint 95, p. 308.
"Of Evil or Lust." [CentR] (38:2) Spr 94, p. 339.

1909. FINNELL, Dennis
"The Generic Manifesto." [IllinoisR] (2:1) Fall 94, p. 14-15.
"Martyrdom." [PassN] (15:2) Wint 94, p. 28.
"Real Poetik." [DenQ] (28:4) Spr 94, p. 22-24.

1910. FINNERTY, Tracey Erin
"A Little Necrophilia Can Go a Long Way." [AnotherCM] (27) 94, p. 50.

1911. FIORENTINI, Monica Teresa
"Hey, Baby, What's Your Sign?" [ModernW] (2) Wint 94, p. 15.

1912. FIRAN, Carmen
"The Face of Smoke" (tr. by Brenda Walker). [PoetryC] (14:4) S 94, p. 23.
"Separation" (tr. by Brenda Walker). [PoetryC] (14:4) S 94, p. 23.

1913. FISCHER, Allen (Allen C.)
"Ballet of a Dead Tree." [Pivot] (42) 94, p. 54-55.
"Barbecuing." [IndR] (17:2) Fall 94, p. 51-52.
"Chaos." [Pivot] (42) 94, p. 55.
"Fireflies." [Pivot] (41) 93, p. 11.
"The Happy Hour." [RiverS] (40) 94, p. 32-33.
"Temper." [SouthernPR] (34:2) Wint 94, p. 54.
"Vaudevillian." [Vis] (44) 94, p. 6.

1914. FISCHER, Henry G.
"Clothes." [Light] (10) Sum 94, p. 12.
"Winter's End." [Hellas] (5:1) Spr-Sum 94, p. 74.

1915. FISHER, Barbara
"Minnesota Woods." [SantaBR] (1:2) Fall-Wint 93, p. 49.
"Speed Graphic." [SantaBR] (1:2) Fall-Wint 93, p. 48.

1916. FISHER, Steve
"Boosted Dream Poem Written on a Stolen Typewriter." [Pearl] (20) Spr 94, p. 8.

"Controlled Populations #2." [ChironR] (13:4) Wint 94, p. 8.
"Responding to Minions." [ChironR] (13:4) Wint 94, p. 8.
"Skull Monkeys." [ChironR] (13:4) Wint 94, p. 9.

1917. FISHER-SMITH, Jordan
"Bird Life Heart." [Sun] (222) Je 94, p. 17.

1918. FISHMAN, Charles
"All Beginnings Are Difficult." [Elf] (4:3) Fall 94, p. 28.
"Grateful for the Earth." [Elf] (4:3) Fall 94, p. 29.
"Jerusalem Snow." [InterQ] (1:3) 94, p. 161-162.
"Natural Selection." [ColEng] (56:1) Ja 94, p. 66.

1919. FISHMAN, Lisa
"Abundance." [CutB] (41) Wint 94, p. 13-14.
"The Fire of Love." [AntR] (52:1) Wint 94, p. 86-87.
"For All We Know." [IndR] (17:1) Spr 94, p. 80-81.
"The Hills Have Gone into the Country." [HayF] (15) Fall-Wint 94, p. 96.
"Leelanau." [AntR] (52:1) Wint 94, p. 84-85.
"Story for Lacan." [IndR] (17:1) Spr 94, p. 82.
"Stratton, 1983." [AntR] (52:1) Wint 94, p. 83.

1920. FISK, Brent
"Frostbite." [Pearl] (20) Spr 94, p. 45.

1921. FISK, Molly
"A Long Year of Hands and Mouths" (for W.). [ChironR] (13:4) Wint 94, p. 30.
"Surface Tension." [Zyzzyva] (10:2) Sum 94, p. 107.
"Surrender." [Sun] (220) Ap 94, p. 28.
"Veterans." [Calyx] (15:2) Sum 94, p. 56-57.

1922. FITTERMAN, Rob
"Ameresque: The Snap Wyatt Poems" (3 selections). [WashR] (19:5) F-Mr 94, p. 23.

1923. FITTERMAN, Robert
"Propose." [ShadowP] (4) 94, p. 41.

1924. FITTS, Gus
"There once was a hippie on Haight" (2nd Prize, The A & C Limericks Awards). [Amelia] (7:4, #23) 94, p. 12.
"A Thorny Horny." [Amelia] (7:3, #22) 94, p. 139.
"Turning Dearth" (2nd Prize, The Amelia Short Humor Awards). [Amelia] (7:4, #23) 94, p. 91.

1925. FITZ-RANDOLPH, Meg Hill
"The Love of Horses" (For J.B.). [YellowS] (12:2, #46) Sum-Fall 94, p. 28.

1926. FITZPATRICK, Mark
"That Last Little Bit." [Parting] (7:2) Wint 94-95, p. 42.

1927. FITZSIMMONS, Thomas
"Time Twist." [Vis] (44) 94, p. 37.

1928. FIX, Charlene
"Dream of a Pig." [HiramPoR] (55/56) Fall 93-Sum 94, p. 31.
"Mannequin Hand." [ChiR] (40:2/3) 94, p. 71-72.
"The Wise Girls Walk." [HiramPoR] (55/56) Fall 93-Sum 94, p. 32.

1929. FIXEL, Lawrence
"A Little Kitchen Music." [ProseP] (3) 94, p. 37-38.

FLACCUS, Statyllius (1st Century B.C./A.D.)
See STATYLLIUS FLACCUS (1st Century B.C./A.D.)

1930. FLANAGAN, Brenda
"The Girl From Bahia." [Caliban] (14) 94, p. 18-19.

1931. FLANDERS, Jane
"Stone Wings." [Confr] (52/53) Wint-Spr 94, p. 313.

1932. FLAVIN, Jack
"Old Flame." [ApalQ] (42) Fall 94, p. 49.
"Two Fragments" (tr. of Sappho). [ApalQ] (40/41) 94, p. 69-70.

1933. FLEET, Chris
"Skin Man." [BlackBR] (18) Wint-Spr 94, p. 30-31.

1934. FLEMING, Anne
"Questions for Isabelle Gunn" (who joined the Hudson's Bay Company as John Fubister, 1806). [PraF] (15:1, #66) Spr 94, p. 136-139.
"Swim Before Dinner." [Arc] (33) Fall 94, p. 58.

1935. FLEMING, Jeanie Puleston
"Woman and Bird" (tr. of André Breton, w. Christopher Merrill). [NewRena] (9:1, #27) 94, p. 77.

1936. FLENNIKEN, Kathleen
"Fear of Blindness." [BellArk] (10:5) S-O 94, p. 25.
"Ivory Rose." [Interim] (13:2) Fall-Wint 94-95, p. 11.
"The Laying On of Hands." [Interim] (13:2) Fall-Wint 94-95, p. 13.
"My Archeologist." [Interim] (13:2) Fall-Wint 94-95, p. 12.
"This One I Hold." [BellArk] (10:5) S-O 94, p. 25.

1937. FLETCHER, Dorothy K.
"Fifteen." [Outbr] (25) 94, p. 29.

1938. FLETCHER, John Gould
"The Last Frontier." [SoCaR] (27:1/2) Fall 94-Spr 95, p. 265.
"London Excursion: Station." [SoCaR] (27:1/2) Fall 94-Spr 95, p. 264.

1939. FLINT, Austin
"Writing a Curriculum Vitae" (tr. of Wislawa Szymborska, w. Grazyna Drabik). [Crazy] (47) Wint 94, p. 100-101.

1940. FLINT, Roland
"The Fidelity Pasta." [ColR] (21:2) Fall 94, p. 132.
"Grief November." [ColR] (21:2) Fall 94, p. 135-136.
"Park River Memento." [ColR] (21:2) Fall 94, p. 133-134.

1941. FLINTOFF, Eddie
"Impressions of Exile" (1-2, tr. of Luis Cernuda). [Stand] (35:2) Spr 94, p. 34-35.

1942. FLOCK, Miriam
"Fight or Flight." [Salm] (104/105) Fall 94-Wint 95, p. 172-173.

1943. FLOREA, Ted
"Bringing in the Sheaves." [Northeast] (5:11) Wint 94-95, p. 10-11.

1944. FLORES, Fernando Esteban
"Altared States." [Americas] (22:1/2) Spr-Sum 94, p. 81-82.
"Amá." [Americas] (22:1/2) Spr-Sum 94, p. 83-86.

1945. FLORES, Toni
"For John and Anthony, in Case of Accident." [SenR] (24:2) Fall 94, p. 45.
"This Mare Wants to Roll." [SenR] (24:2) Fall 94, p. 46.

1946. FLOREZ, Julio
"Resurrecciones." [NewRena] (9:1, #27) 94, p. 36.
"Resurrections" (tr. by Joe Bolton). [NewRena] (9:1, #27) 94, p. 37.

1947. FLOURNOY, Bret
"Diving." [JamesWR] (11:3) Spr 94, p. 6.
"For Michael, like the Junipers." [JamesWR] (11:3) Spr 94, p. 7.
"To No One in Particular, Myself." [JamesWR] (11:3) Spr 94, p. 7.
"Waiting Outside Penny's." [JamesWR] (11:3) Spr 94, p. 7.

1948. FLYNN, John
"Spring: March 22, 1958." [CimR] (107) Ap 94, p. 98.
"Waiting for the Samaritan." [CimR] (107) Ap 94, p. 97.

1949. FLYNN, Kelly
"Locust Trees." [GrahamHR] (18) Wint 94-95, p. 91-92.
"Nervous." [GrahamHR] (18) Wint 94-95, p. 93.

1950. FOAKES, R. A.
"Proud Flesh" (In Memoriam B.M.F., selections from a nine sonnet sequence: 2, 5, 9). [Jacaranda] (5:1) Wint-Spr 91, p. 110-111.

FOE, Mark de
See DeFOE, Mark

1951. FOERSTER, Richard
"The Clearing." [Poetry] (164:6) S 94, p. 324.
"The Failure of Similes." [Poetry] (164:6) S 94, p. 325.
"Holyrood Abbey." [Poetry] (164:6) S 94, p. 326.

1952. FOGARTY, Mark
"What I Lived For." [Elf] (4:4) Wint 94, p. 27.

1953. FOGEL, Alice B.
"Beholden." [Ploughs] (20:4) Wint 94-95, p. 54.
"Grassfire." [BelPoJ] (45:1) Fall 94, p. 17.
"Grief." [Ploughs] (20:4) Wint 94-95, p. 52-53.

1954. FOGLE, Andy
"Mercy." [Parting] (7:2) Wint 94-95, p. 1.
"Wreck." [Parting] (7:2) Wint 94-95, p. 16.

1955. FOLKART, Barbara
"A Quiconque A Perdu Ce Qui Ne Se Retrouve Jamais, Jamais" (Charles Baudelaire, "Le Cygne"). [MalR] (106) Spr 94, p. 57.
"D'Avoir Cédé sur Son Désir." [MalR] (106) Spr 94, p. 59.

"Easter Eggs." [Event] (23:1) Spr 94, p. 42.
"Old Woman Beside a Geranium Bush." [AntigR] (96) Wint 94, p. 82.
"Quelquefois dans un Beau Jardin." [MalR] (106) Spr 94, p. 58.

1956. FOLLETT, C. B.
"Bossy Nova." [SoCoast] (17) Je 94, p. 46-47.
"Christmas Eve." [Parting] (7:1) Sum 94, p. 44.
"The Fall of a Tree" (honorable mention, Social Concern Poetry Competition, 1993). [BlackBR] (18) Wint-Spr 94, p. 44-45.
"If She Could Keep the Sky" (Second Place Winner, Social Concern Poetry Competition, 1993). [BlackBR] (18) Wint-Spr 94, p. 41-42.

FOND, Carolyn Street la
See LaFOND, Carolyn Street

1957. FONG, Herman
"The 11:48 North" (Associated Writing Programs Intro Award poem). [IndR] (17:2) Fall 94, p. 98-99.
"Sacramento River, Early April" (Associated Writing Programs Intro Award poem). [IndR] (17:2) Fall 94, p. 100-101.

FONTAINE, Jean de la
See La FONTAINE, Jean de

1958. FONTANA, Jennie
"Milk." [Stand] (36:1) Wint 94-95, p. 4-8.

1959. FONTANA, Michael
"All that's left home is me" (in "Into the Crocodile's Jaws"). [IndR] (17:1) Spr 94, p. 177.
"The happiness is a lie" (in "Into the Crocodile's Jaws"). [IndR] (17:1) Spr 94, p. 175.
"I am an orphan" (in "Into the Crocodile's Jaws"). [IndR] (17:1) Spr 94, p. 174.
"The past is a curse" (in "Into the Crocodile's Jaws"). [IndR] (17:1) Spr 94, p. 178-179.

1960. FONTENOT, Ken
"A Fan Reminds Me of a Morning Long Ago." [SouthernR] (30:3) Sum 94, p. 529.

1961. FOOTMAN, Jennifer
"Sewer Rat." [Arc] (33) Fall 94, p. 42-43.
"The Wandering Womb, or Why the Fuck Don't You Stay Still." [Quarry] (43:2) S 94, p. 93-94.

1962. FORCHÉ, Carolyn
"As Beautiful As You Are" (tr. of Robert Desnos). [Jacaranda] (4:2) Spr 90, p. 6-9.
"Let's Be Serious" (tr. of Robert Desnos). [Jacaranda] (4:2) Spr 90, p. 10-11.
"Nights" (tr. of Robert Desnos). [Jacaranda] (4:2) Spr 90, p. 3.
"A Tale" (tr. of Robert Desnos). [Jacaranda] (4:2) Spr 90, p. 4.
"Tale of a Bear" (tr. of Robert Desnos). [Jacaranda] (4:2) Spr 90, p. 12-13.
"Tale of a Camel" (tr. of Robert Desnos). [Jacaranda] (4:2) Spr 90, p. 5.
"Verses on the Butcher" (tr. of Robert Desnos). [Jacaranda] (4:2) Spr 90, p. 15.
"Window" (tr. of Robert Desnos). [Jacaranda] (4:2) Spr 90, p. 14.

1963. FORD, Cathy
"The Pariah Dress" (for Linda Rogers). [Quarry] (43:1) Je 94, p. 99-101.

1964. FORD, Linda
"Beach Glass." [BellR] (17:1/2) Spr-Fall 94, p. 33.

1965. FORD, Maria
"Cream Separators." [Event] (23:2) Sum 94, p. 18-19.

1966. FORD, Michael C.
"Sometimes We Provide for Ourselves Our Own Horror" (to Veda Ann Borg, her movies). [Pearl] (20) Spr 94, p. 12.

1967. FORD, William
"Love in Middle Age." [Poetry] (164:5) Ag 94, p. 256.

1968. FORMAN, Ruth
"For Your Information." [Callaloo] (17:4) Fall 94, p. 1274.

1969. FORNOFF, Fred
"Flour" (from *Enciclopedia de maravillas*, tr. of Laureano Albán). [ArtfulD] (26/27) 94, p. 132-133.
"The Giraffe" (from *Enciclopedia de maravillas*, tr. of Laureano Albán). [ArtfulD] (26/27) 94, p. 134-135.
"The Iceberg" (from *Enciclopedia de maravillas*, tr. of Laureano Albán). [ArtfulD] (26/27) 94, p. 136-137.
"The Magnet" (from *Enciclopedia de maravillas*, tr. of Laureano Albán). [ArtfulD] (26/27) 94, p. 138-139.

"The Printing Press" (from *Enciclopedia de maravillas*, tr. of Laureano Albán). [ArtfulD] (26/27) 94, p. 140-141.
"The Sheet" (from *Enciclopedia de maravillas*, tr. of Laureano Albán). [ArtfulD] (26/27) 94, p. 142-143.
"The Skirt" (from *Enciclopedia de maravillas*, tr. of Laureano Albán). [ArtfulD] (26/27) 94, p. 144-145.

1970. FORREST, Matthew
"Frosted Glass" (tr. of Etsuko Saito, w. Henry Hughes). [SycamoreR] (6:2) Sum 94, p. 95.
"I Learned on the Right Side of the Sea" (tr. of Etsuko Saito, w. Henry Hughes). [SycamoreR] (6:2) Sum 94, p. 97-98.

1971. FORT, Charles
"T. S. Eliot Was a Negro." [ProseP] (3) 94, p. 39.

1972. FORTH, Steven
"Distractions." [WestCL] (28:3, #15) Wint 94-95, p. 77-80.

1973. FOSCO, Cory Alan
"Baggage" (for Steve Trahan). [ChironR] (13:3) Aut 94, p. 7.

1974. FOSTER, Barbara
"Dorothy Parker on Avenue C." [Light] (12) Wint 94-95, p. 20.

1975. FOSTER, Ed
"Dear Image Maker." [RiverC] (14:2) Spr 94, p. 75-76.
"The Ruins of Midas." [RiverC] (14:2) Spr 94, p. 74.

1976. FOSTER, Leslie D.
"Socrates on Trial." [ChrC] (111:14) 27 Ap 94, p. 448.

1977. FOSTER, Linda Nemec
"Bad Art at the Clarkston Motor Inn." [Rosebud] (1:2) Sum 94, p. 82.
"Tabloid Headlines." [Parting] (7:1) Sum 94, p. 42-43.
"Village of the Mermaids: After Delvaux" (for Judith Barrington). [QW] (39) Sum-Fall 94, p. 198.
"Woman Suffering from Seizures of Ecstasy." [Parting] (7:1) Sum 94, p. 30.

1978. FOSTER, Michael
"Seven Love Poems." [OgalalaR] (5:1) Wint 94, p. 43-44.

1979. FOSTER, Robert
"Carburry Dunes" (for Allisan). [Arc] (33) Fall 94, p. 14-15.
"Clare" (Born April 26, 1988). [AntigR] (97) Spr 94, p. 62-64.
"For Many Voices" (Act III, Der Rosenkavalier). [AntigR] (97) Spr 94, p. 65.

1980. FOSTER, Sesshu
"Postcard to Akemi Miyazawa, 115 Eastern Avenue, East Los, CA 90032." [PennR] (6:1) 94, p. 24.
"Untitled: It was hot in El Paso, the streets of Juarez busy and dusty." [HangL] (65) 94, p. 17.

1981. FOSTER, Shirley
"Isadora Duncan's Children" (A Paper Collage). [HiramPoR] (55/56) Fall 93-Sum 94, p. 33.

1982. FOUSHEE, Sandra Claire
"A Place to Live in." [SouthernPR] (34:2) Wint 94, p. 33-34.

FOUST, Michelle Mitchell
See MITCHELL-FOUST, Michelle

FOUST, Mimi Plevin
See PLEVIN-FOUST, Mimi

1983. FOWLER, Anne Carol
"Tea Roses." [CumbPR] (13:2) Spr 94, p. 20-21.

1984. FOWLER, Barbara Hughes
"Egyptian Love Lyrics" (tr. of Egyptian hieroglyphics, circa 1550-1080 B.C.). [GrandS] (13:2, #50) Fall 94, p. 110-112.

1985. FOWLER, Dale
"The Exile Makes a Comeback." [WorldO] (25:4) Sum 94, p. 51.
"I Eat My Words." [WorldO] (25:4) Sum 94, p. 19.

1986. FOWLER, Dorothy
"6:15 Sestina." [SinW] (53) Sum-Fall 94, p. 18-19.

1987. FOWLER, Ezra
"Your Eyes." [HeavenB] (11) 94, p. 93.

1988. FOWLER, James
"The Rime of Cockaigne." [SoCoast] (17) Je 94, p. 40-41.

1989. FOWLER, Russell
"Requiem." [ColEng] (56:2) F 94, p. 190.

1990. FOX, Charles
"Monsieur Ilagro, the Prince of Deception, Solves the Problem of Conjuring." [CreamCR] (18:1) Spr 94, p. 87.

1991. FOX, Faulkner
"Fatherland." [AnotherCM] (27) 94, p. 51-52.

1992. FOX, Linda L.
"The Snow Peas and the Crones." [CreamCR] (18:1) Spr 94, p. 56.

1993. FOXCROFT, Bill
"The Zeppelin Anchored / to the Hill of Dreams?" (— Frank O'Hara, 'Ashes on Saturday Afternoon'). [Event] (23:3) Wint 94-95, p. 47-48.

1994. FOY, John
"Rue des Martyrs" (Selections: 3, 15, 21). [Poetry] (165:3) D 94, p. 147-148.

1995. FRAIND, Lori C.
"The Day That *Guernica* Moved to Bosnia." [ContextS] (4:1) 94, p. 10.

1996. FRAKES, Clint
"The Enduring Drought." [Caliban] (14) 94, p. 100.

1997. FRALEY, Michael
"Zoo Keeper." [Amelia] (7:4, #23) 94, p. 30.

1998. FRANCIS, Lee
"Star Dancer." [Callaloo] (17:1) Wint 94, p. 77-78.

1999. FRANCIS, Scott
"The Cab Delivers Fox and Clown to Corporate Headquarters." [PaintedB] (53/54) 94, p. 28.
"In the Elevator, Clown and Fox Rise." [PaintedB] (53/54) 94, p. 29.
"In the Top Office, Fox Intuits Clown's Disaster." [PaintedB] (53/54) 94, p. 30.

2000. FRANCO, Michael
"Beautiful beyond all" (for Michael and Norma SF '93). [Agni] (40) 94, p. 174.
"A Book of Measure: Second Circumference" (Excerpt). [Talisman] (12) Spr 94, p. 243.

2001. FRANGIEH, Bassam
"I Wear You" (tr. of Nizar Kabbani). [LitR] (37:3) Spr 94, p. 505.
"The Orange" (tr. of Nizar Kabbani). [LitR] (37:3) Spr 94, p. 503.
"When You Find a Man" (tr. of Nizar Kabbani). [LitR] (37:3) Spr 94, p. 502.
"With a Newspaper" (tr. of Nizar Kabbani). [LitR] (37:3) Spr 94, p. 504.
"You Are So Beautiful" (tr. of Nizar Kabbani). [LitR] (37:3) Spr 94, p. 504.

2002. FRANK, Bernhard
"Buddha" (tr. of Rainer Maria Rilke). [HeavenB] (11) 94, p. 38.
"The Glory of Buddha" (tr. of Rainer Maria Rilke). [HeavenB] (11) 94, p. 38.
"The Herons Have Returned" (tr. of Moshe Dor). [WebR] (18) Fall 94, p. 12.
"A Year Later" (tr. of M. Winkler). [WebR] (18) Fall 94, p. 12.

2003. FRANK, David
"Truck Talk." [AntigR] (98) Sum 94, p. 33-34.

2004. FRANK, Della
"Shimasani / My Grandmother" (For Rose Mitchell). [Callaloo] (17:1) Wint 94, p. 306-308.

2005. FRANK, Diane
"Lunar Eclipse." [CimR] (106) Ja 94, p. 67-68.

2006. FRANK, R.
"Bound for Oblivion." [Light] (11) Aut 94, p. 8.
"Diatribe." [Light] (12) Wint 94-95, p. 8.

2007. FRANKLIN, Michael
"Dr. Seuss Enters into Heaven on the Best Day of Summer." [JamesWR] (11:4) Sum 94, p. 1.

2008. FRANZEN, Cola
"Cámera Oscura" (Selections: Cantos 11, 18, tr. of Juan Cameron). [WorldL] (5) 94, p. 13-14.
"Happening" (tr. of Juan Cameron). [InterQ] (1:1) [93?], p. 140.
"Power of Pérez" (tr. of Jorge Guillén). [GrahamHR] (18) Wint 94-95, p. 48-59.
"Seasons" (tr. of Alicia Borinsky). [InterQ] (1:4) 94, p. 29.
"She Who Is Hiding" (tr. of Juan Cameron). [InterQ] (1:1) [93?], p. 141.
"Song of the Suicidal Lovers" (tr. of Alicia Borinsky). [InterQ] (1:4) 94, p. 28.

2009. FRASER, Caroline
"Ratty Go Batty." [NewYorker] (70:40) 5 D 94, p. 102.

2010. FRASER, Gregory
"Ars Poetica." [WestHR] (48:4) Wint 94, p. 386-390.

2011. FRASER, Kathleen
"The Disappeared." [Chelsea] (57) 94, p. 53-55.
"Lampi e Acqua" (Excerpt, tr. of Maria Obino). [Avec] (7:1) 94, p. 83-88.
"Photogene." [NewAW] (12) Spr-Sum 94, p. 8-11.
"Trailwin.g." [Chelsea] (57) 94, p. 56.
2012. FRASIER, Carrie
"Irises." [MidwQ] (35:3) Spr 94, p. 307.
2013. FRATER, Anne
"Aghaidh Choimheach." [Verse] (11:2) Sum 94, p. 38.
"Caisteal." [Verse] (11:2) Sum 94, p. 39.
"Castle." [Verse] (11:2) Sum 94, p. 39.
"Mabel" (in Gaelic and English). [Verse] (11:2) Sum 94, p. 40-41.
"Mask." [Verse] (11:2) Sum 94, p. 38.
2014. FRATTALI, Steven Vincent
"Every Day" (tr. of Ingeborg Bachmann). [GrahamHR] (18) Wint 94-95, p. 42.
2015. FRAZEUR, Joyce
"Where the Storks Nest." [ContextS] (4:1) 94, p. 6.
2016. FRAZIER, Hood
"Snow Angels." [EngJ] (83:5) S 94, p. 31.
2017. FRAZIER, Jan
"Black Bananas." [HighP] (9:2) Ag 94, p. 74-75.
"Cotton" (for Annie Chamblee, 1890-1941). [HighP] (9:2) Ag 94, p. 76-77.
2018. FREDE, Richard
"At the Auto Sales & Service." [Poetry] (165:2) N 94, p. 76.
"Vitae." [Poetry] (165:2) N 94, p. 77-78.
2019. FREDERICKSON, Yahya
"Cattle from Ethiopia." [CreamCR] (18:2) Fall 94, p. 130.
"Leaving Islands." [CreamCR] (18:2) Fall 94, p. 129.
"Malarial." [RiverS] (40) 94, p. 52.
"Requiem for Al-Mocha" (for J. L.). [RiverS] (40) 94, p. 53.
2020. FREEK, George
"Postscript from Magritte." [CapeR] (29:2) Fall 94, p. 12.
2021. FREELAND, Charles
"Concerning Immunization." [LaurelR] (28:1) Wint 94, p. 126.
"The Flood." [CarolQ] (47:1) Fall 94, p. 18.
"The Method." [HayF] (15) Fall-Wint 94, p. 22-23.
2022. FREEMAN, Eliezer
"My She-Whale" (tr. of Ya'aqov Halevi Haramgaal). [ProseP] (3) 94, p. 46.
2023. FREEMAN, Glenn
"No Strings Attached." [Plain] (14:2) Wint 94, p. 8-9.
"Snake Dance." [Outbr] (25) 94, p. 30-32.
2024. FREEMAN, Grace B.
"In the Dark." [Pembroke] (26) 94, p. 90.
2025. FREEMAN, Jan
"Caught." [AmerV] (33) 94, p. 82.
2026. FREEMAN, Jody
"Gloria" (in English). [InterPR] (20:2) Fall 94, p. 100, 102.
"Gloria" (in French, tr. by Jean-Pierre Pelletier). [InterPR] (20:2) Fall 94, p. 101, 103.
2027. FREEMAN, Suzanne
"Orionids." [Border] (4) Spr-Sum 94, p. 35.
2028. FREERICKS, Charles Avakian
"Car Show, 1976." [JlNJPo] (16:2) Aut 94, p. 15-16.
FREES, Madeline de
See DeFREES, Madeline
FREESE, Allison de
See DeFREESE, Allison
2029. FREIMAN, Marcelle
"Memories." [Stand] (35:4) Aut 94, p. 78-79.
2030. FRENCH, Catherine
"One Day in the Whale." [QW] (38) Winter-Spr 93-94, p. 105.
2031. FRENCH, Paula
"Credo in Pink." [AmerV] (33) 94, p. 109.
2032. FRIDSMA, Bernard, Sr.
"As a Rule" (tr. of Margryt Poortstra). [Vis] (46) 94, p. 10.

2033. FRIEBERT, Stuart
"Abasicky." [Shen] (44:4) Wint 94, p. 111.
"Annie-Over" (For LoLo). [WeberS] (11:2) Spr-Sum 94, p. 135.
"Beaver Poison." [ArtfulD] (26/27) 94, p. 88.
"Big Eye." [WeberS] (11:2) Spr-Sum 94, p. 133.
"Brauche." [CentR] (38:2) Spr 94, p. 319.
"Call-Up-A-Storm." [CentR] (38:2) Spr 94, p. 320.
"Don Eagle." [WebR] (18) Fall 94, p. 107.
"The Farkleberry Tree." [ArtfulD] (26/27) 94, p. 87.
"First-and-Last Snake" (for Anne Finch, Countess of Chilsea). [WeberS] (11:2) Spr-Sum 94, p. 136.
"Gaumy." [Shen] (44:4) Wint 94, p. 112.
"The Hairy Woodpecker." [ArtfulD] (26/27) 94, p. 86.
"I'll Bring Him Back in an Iron Cage." [ChironR] (13:3) Aut 94, p. 9.
"In the End They'll Say We Were Wrong To." [ChironR] (13:3) Aut 94, p. 9.
"Iron Dragon" (for Diane). [WeberS] (11:2) Spr-Sum 94, p. 135-136.
"It's Raining." [WeberS] (11:2) Spr-Sum 94, p. 134.
"Jasmine Bush" (tr. of Judita Vaiciunaite, w. Viktoria Skrupskelis). [Field] (51) Fall 94, p. 64.
"Kingfisher." [Crazy] (47) Wint 94, p. 23.
"Mayfly." [Crazy] (47) Wint 94, p. 25.
"Mother, Fishing." [WestB] (35) 94, p. 82-83.
"Old Chainsides." [Crazy] (47) Wint 94, p. 24.
"Purse Seine." [Shen] (44:4) Wint 94, p. 110.
"Records." [CentR] (38:2) Spr 94, p. 321.
"Shoebill." [ChironR] (13:3) Aut 94, p. 9.
"Still Life with Window Frosted Over" (tr. of Judita Vaiciunaite, w. Viktoria Skrupskelis). [Field] (51) Fall 94, p. 65.
"Voltaire" (For David). [WillowR] (21) Spr 94, p. 22.
"Wild Plum Bushes, Black Against the Drifts." [WebR] (18) Fall 94, p. 108.

2034. FRIED, Erich
"Answer" (tr. by Lane Jennings). [Vis] (45) 94, p. 43.
"Going Under" (tr. by Lane Jennings). [Vis] (44) 94, p. 7.

2035. FRIED, Mark
"Story of the Parrot's Resurrection" (tr. of Eduardo Galeano, w. illustrations by José Francisco Borges). [Conjunc] (23) 94, p. 191-192.

2036. FRIEDLANDER, Benjamin
"Anthemic." [Sulfur] (35) Fall 94, p. 7.
"Cast out his son." [Sulfur] (35) Fall 94, p. 6.
"Holding a Pencil." [Sulfur] (35) Fall 94, p. 6.
"Poem: Contradiction." [Sulfur] (35) Fall 94, p. 8.
"This is the fairy handle." [Sulfur] (35) Fall 94, p. 5.
"Why I Am Not." [Sulfur] (35) Fall 94, p. 7-8.

2037. FRIEDMAN, Alan H.
"The Garden of Earthly Dilemmas." [Raritan] (14:2) Fall 94, p. 11-12.

2038. FRIEDMAN, Debbie
"Swift." [Calyx] (15:2) Sum 94, p. 46-47.

2039. FRIEDMAN, Dorothy
"Blackberry Pies." [Writer] (107:1) Ja 94, p. 25.

2040. FRIEDMAN, Ed
"Heading for Manhattan by Train." [HangL] (64) 94, p. 35.
"On Contradiction." [HangL] (64) 94, p. 33.
"Rocket To Stardom." [HangL] (64) 94, p. 34.

2041. FRIEDMAN, Jeff
"The Names of Things." [NewEngR] (16:2) Spr 94, p. 41-42.

2042. FRIEDMAN, Lisa
"Seeing God." [Calyx] (15:3) Wint 94-95, p. 12-13.

2043. FRIEDMAN, Michael
"Head." [HangL] (65) 94, p. 16.
"Lecture." [HangL] (65) 94, p. 16.
"Wave." [HangL] (65) 94, p. 16.

2044. FRIEDMAN, Robert
"Clarity." [HeavenB] (11) 94, p. 87.

2045. FRIEL, Raymond
"De Profundis." [Verse] (11:1) Spr 94, p. 116.
"Husband." [Verse] (11:1) Spr 94, p. 115.

"May, 1967." [Verse] (11:2) Sum 94, p. 85.
"Posterity." [Verse] (11:1) Spr 94, p. 117.
"Small Hours." [Verse] (11:1) Spr 94, p. 117.
"Spring." [Verse] (11:1) Spr 94, p. 116.

2046. FRIES, Kenny
"The Canoe Ride." [KenR] (NS 16:1) Wint 94, p. 9-10.
"Islands." [KenR] (NS 16:1) Wint 94, p. 10-11.
"Love Poem." [EvergreenC] (9:2) Sum-Fall 94, p. 77.

2047. FRIESEN, Patrick
"Civilization's Children" (tr. of Nina Malinovski, w. Per Brask). [PoetryC] (14:2) Mr 94, p. 22.
"Finding God." [PoetryC] (14:3) My 94, p. 18.
"Hotel" (tr. of Ulrikka S. Gernes, w. Per Brask). [PoetryC] (14:2) Mr 94, p. 21.
"The House Is Open" (tr. of Ulrikka S. Gernes, w. Per Brask). [PoetryC] (14:2) Mr 94, p. 21.
"Looking for a Tattoo." [PoetryC] (14:3) My 94, p. 19.
"My Movie." [PoetryC] (14:3) My 94, p. 19.
"Resurrection." [PoetryC] (14:3) My 94, p. 18.
"Show Me Your Breasts" (tr. of Niels Hav, w. Per Brask). [PoetryC] (14:2) Mr 94, p. 22.
"Untitled: Embrace me" (tr. of Lena Krogh Bertram, w. Per Brask). [PoetryC] (14:2) Mr 94, p. 20.
"Untitled: In dreams" (tr. of Nina Malinovski, w. Per Brask). [PoetryC] (14:2) Mr 94, p. 22.
"Untitled: You cannot steal lines from a dancer my love" (tr. of Camilla Christensen, w. Per Brask). [PoetryC] (14:2) Mr 94, p. 20.
"Visit from My Father" (tr. of Niels Hav, w. Per Brask). [PoetryC] (14:2) Mr 94, p. 21.

2048. FRIIS-BAASTAD, Erling
"The Poet Attempts a Novel." [DogRR] (13:1, #25) Spr-Sum 94, p. 15.

2049. FRIMAN, Alice
"At St. John's Monastery." [WritersF] (20) 94, p. 220-222.
"Forgive and Forget." [IndR] (17:1) Spr 94, p. 146.
"The Good News" (for the mosquitoes of Minnesota). [CreamCR] (18:1) Spr 94, p. 24-25.
"Letter to My Husband." [LaurelR] (28:2) Sum 94, p. 55.
"Pigeon Drop" (from a first line by Carolyn Kizer). [HopewellR] (6) 94, p. 97.
"Speaking of Cats" (— The Samburu, Kenya). [NoDaQ] (62:1) Wint 94-95, p. 128.
"A Walk at the End of the Century." [BelPoJ] (45:1) Fall 94, p. 28.

2050. FRITZ, Walter Helmut
"A Man before His Bookcase" (tr. by Reinhold Grimm). [Pembroke] (26) 94, p. 137.

2051. FROME, Carol
"Afterlife." [HiramPoR] (55/56) Fall 93-Sum 94, p. 34.
"Examination." [NowestR] (32:3) 94, p. 28.
"Mother's Day." [NowestR] (32:3) 94, p. 29.
"Snow Angels." [HiramPoR] (55/56) Fall 93-Sum 94, p. 35.

2052. FROST, Carol
"Apology." [TriQ] (90) Spr-Sum 94, p. 136.
"Art." [AmerPoR] (23:3) My-Je 94, p. 15.
"Balance." [VirQR] (70:1) Wint 94, p. 99.
"Crying Wolf." [TriQ] (90) Spr-Sum 94, p. 137.
"Denial." [GreenMR] (NS 17:2) Fall-Wint 94-95, p. 16.
"Desire." [NewEngR] (16:2) Spr 94, p. 74.
"Envy." [NoDaQ] (62:2) Spr 94-95, p. 112.
"Expectation." [GreenMR] (NS 17:2) Fall-Wint 94-95, p. 17.
"Failure." [AmerV] (35) 94, p. 107.
"Fate." [VirQR] (70:1) Wint 94, p. 98.
"Fury." [TriQ] (90) Spr-Sum 94, p. 133.
"Help." [NoDaQ] (62:2) Spr 94-95, p. 113.
"Horror." [AmerPoR] (23:3) My-Je 94, p. 15.
"Judgment." [TriQ] (90) Spr-Sum 94, p. 135.
"Laws." [PartR] (61:2) Spr 94, p. 313.
"Nothing." [NewEngR] (16:2) Spr 94, p. 75.
"Obedience" (the nuns). [AmerPoR] (23:3) My-Je 94, p. 15.
"The Past." [AmerV] (35) 94, p. 109.
"Pride." [AmerV] (35) 94, p. 108.

"Recompense." [AmerPoR] (23:3) My-Je 94, p. 15.
"Secrecy." [ColR] (21:2) Fall 94, p. 148.
"Sexual Jealousy." [VirQR] (70:1) Wint 94, p. 99.
"Shame." [NewEngR] (16:2) Spr 94, p. 74-75.
"Small." [AmerPoR] (23:3) My-Je 94, p. 15.
"Thrill." [Atlantic] (274:1) Jl 94, p. 70.
"Truth." [TriQ] (90) Spr-Sum 94, p. 134.

2053. FROST, Celestine
"Pretense, rage and shame." [Talisman] (13) Fall 94-Wint 95, p. 259-260.

2054. FROST, Elisabeth
"My Mother Made Us Smoke." [Colum] ("The Lost Issues", [i.e. 18-19]) 93, p. 139-140.
"These Roses." [Jacaranda] (10) 94, p. 29.

2055. FROST, Helen
"Charlie." [AntR] (52:3) Sum 94, p. 490-491.

2056. FROST, Richard
"For a Brother." [NoAmR] (279:4) Jl-Ag 94, p. 39.
"The Mummified Cat." [Pivot] (42) 94, p. 56.
"The Old Hedonist's Dwindling Sestina." [GeoR] (48:2) Sum 94, p. 278-279.
"Old Photo." [SenR] (24:1) Spr 94, p. 23.

2057. FRYE, David
"Ana Mendieta" (tr. of Nancy Morejón). [MichQR] (33:3) Sum 94, p. 618-620.
"Before a Mirror" (To Sonia Rivera Valdés, tr. of Nancy Morejón). [MichQR] (33:3) Sum 94, p. 621-622.
"Epistle t Jose Luis Ferrer (From Havana to Miami)" (tr. of Jorge Luis Arcos). [MichQR] (33:3) Sum 94, p. 469-471.
"For Ana Veldford" (tr. of Lourdes Casal). [MichQR] (33:3) Sum 94, p. 415-416.
"Lunch" (tr. of José Kozer). [MichQR] (33:3) Sum 94, p. 577.
"Moving" (November 1983, tr. of Mirtha N. Quintanales). [MichQR] (33:3) Sum 94, p. 590-591.
"My Key" (tr. of Yanai Manzor). [MichQR] (33:4) Fall 94, p. 731.
"My Name (A Family Anti-Elegy)" (Excerpts, tr. of Excilia Saldaña, w. Ruth Behar). [MichQR] (33:3) Sum 94, p. 543-547.
"Pilgrims of the Dawn" (To the crew of the "Sirene," 1836, tr. of Miguel Barnet). [MichQR] (33:4) Fall 94, p. 805-806.

FU, Du
See DU, Fu

2058. FU, Lo
"Walking Toward Wang Wei (1989)" (tr. by Yip Wai-lim). [InterQ] (1:2) 93, p. 56-57.

FU, Tu
See DU, Fu

2059. FUGALLI, Tom
"In Search of Sharks." [WestHR] (48:3) Fall 94, p. 255.
"Revelation" (Branch Davidian). [WestHR] (48:3) Fall 94, p. 256.

2060. FUKUNAGA, Todd
"Angels" (For Marisa). [HawaiiR] (18:1, #40) Spr 94, p. 89.
"Leviathan." [HawaiiR] (18:1, #40) Spr 94, p. 88.

2061. FULLER, Kate
"Zuni Goodbye." [BellArk] (10:6) N-D 94, p. 4.

2062. FULLER, William
"On Baudelaire's 'Une Charogne'." [ApalQ] (40/41) 94, p. 90.

2063. FULLINGIM, Dwight
"View of Myself (Alone) on the Coast." [Border] (5) Fall-Wint 94, p. 17.

2064. FULTON, Alice
"By Her Own Hand." [ChiR] (40:1) 94, p. 1-2.
"Fuzzy Feelings." [ChiR] (40:1) 94, p. 3-6.
"Garish" (M. C. T., my aunt). [ChiR] (40:1) 94, p. 7-9.
"Give: A Sequence Reimagining Daphne and Apollo" (3 selections). [Pequod] (38) 94, p. 58-70.
"Give: A Sequence, Reimagining Daphne and Apollo" (3 selections). [TriQ] (92) Wint 94-95, p. 56-66.
"Give: A Sequence, Reimagining Daphne and Apollo" (Excerpt). [AmerV] (35) 94, p. 161-171.
"Trespass." [Epoch] (43:1) 94, p. 76-77.
"Unwanting." [Epoch] (43:1) 94, p. 78-79.

2065. FULTON, Robin
"Vaughan Williams — One of His Tunes." [MalR] (107) Sum 94, p. 67.
"The Village." [MalR] (107) Sum 94, p. 66.
2066. FUNDORA, Yolanda V.
"In the Way of Fortune" (tr. of Georgina Herrera). [MichQR] (33:4) Fall 94, p. 773.
"Letter to César Vallejo" (tr. of Georgina Herrera). [MichQR] (33:4) Fall 94, p. 771.
2067. FUNGE, Robert
"Apples." [HiramPoR] (55/56) Fall 93-Sum 94, p. 37.
"The Field." [CumbPR] (14:1) Fall 94, p. 35.
"From the Ave Maria Chapel." [CumbPR] (14:1) Fall 94, p. 34.
"The Gambler's Special." [Border] (5) Fall-Wint 94, p. 18-19.
"On Reading David Wagoner's 'My Father's Ghost'." [CrabCR] (8:2/3/9:1/2/3) 94, p. 119.
"Storm." [HiramPoR] (55/56) Fall 93-Sum 94, p. 36.
"Upon Dozing Off at a Poetry Reading, I Dreamed." [HolCrit] (31:3) Je 94, p. 18.
2068. FUNK, Allison
"Insomnia." [PoetryNW] (35:3) Aut 94, p. 19.
"Snake Road." [PoetryNW] (35:3) Aut 94, p. 17-18.
"Stalactites." [CimR] (107) Ap 94, p. 83-84.
2069. FUNKHOUSER, Erica
"Secular Gardening." [AmerV] (35) 94, p. 116.
"Striper." [AmerV] (35) 94, p. 114-115.
"Weave." [AmerV] (35) 94, p. 113.
2070. FUQUA, C. S.
"Ashes." [ChironR] (13:3) Aut 94, p. 24.
"Connecting Lots." [ChironR] (13:2) Sum 94, p. 16.
"Emeute" (for Andrew). [ChironR] (13:2) Sum 94, p. 16.
"On Reading 'Emeute' to the College Girl." [ChironR] (13:2) Sum 94, p. 16.
"Parent Child." [ChironR] (13:2) Sum 94, p. 16.
"The Second Stroke." [CoalC] (8) Ap 94, p. 21.
2071. FUQUEN, Ruth V. Tams
"Baptismal Song for Twins, Daughter and Son" (for Andria, Lilia and Ingrid). [PoetryNW] (35:4) Wint 94-95, p. 10-11.
"The Gardener." [PoetryNW] (35:4) Wint 94-95, p. 9-10.
"Introduction: Statement of Course." [PoetryNW] (35:4) Wint 94-95, p. 8-9.
2072. FURBISH, Dean
"Morning (Awakening of the Elements)" (tr. of Daniil Kharms). [ChironR] (13:2) Sum 94, p. 7.
"Untitled: Everyone in the end advances" (tr. of Daniil Kharms). [ChironR] (13:2) Sum 94, p. 7.
"Untitled: Spring arrived" (tr. of Daniil Kharms). [ChironR] (13:2) Sum 94, p. 7.
"Wicked Gathering of the Faithless" (tr. of Daniil Kharms). [ChironR] (13:2) Sum 94, p. 7.
2073. FUSCO, Peter
"Body Movements" (tr. of Hyon-Jong Chong). [CrabCR] (8:2/3/9:1/2/3) 94, p. 70.
"The Death God of Civilization" (tr. of Chong Hyon-Jong). [PennR] (6:1) 94, p. 22-23.
FUSEI, Akutagawa
See AKUTAGAWA, Fusei
2074. FUSEK, Serena
"High Noon." [SlipS] (14) 94, p. 37.
"Wings (Tattoo)." [SlipS] (14) 94, p. 36.
2075. FYMAN, Cliff
"Atlantic Hotel in Long Beach." [Sun] (225) S 94, p. 26.

2076. GABBARD, G. N.
"An Epitaph for the Artist As a Young Man." [Light] (11) Aut 94, p. 19.
"Kwacho" (a bird and flower print). [Light] (10) Sum 94, p. 21.
"Number Ten Little Engine." [Light] (12) Wint 94-95, p. 13.
"Oracle." [Light] (9) Spr 94, p. 16.
2077. GABIS, Rita
"Letter." [YellowS] (11:4, #44) Wint 93-94, p. 29.
"Sleeping Together." [YellowS] (11:4, #44) Wint 93-94, p. 28.
"Solitude." [YellowS] (11:4, #44) Wint 93-94, p. 29.
"These Eggs." [YellowS] (11:4, #44) Wint 93-94, p. 28.

"Washing Beans" (corrected reprint from issue #20). [Colum] (21) Fall 93, p. 157.
2078. GABRIEL, Margaret
"Christmas Song." [MalR] (108) Fall 94, p. 113.
"Dream Shore." [PoetryC] (14:2) Mr 94, p. 16.
"The Genius of Flora." [PraF] (15:4, #69) Wint 94-95, p. 100.
"If for No Reason." [PoetryC] (14:2) Mr 94, p. 16.
"Picasso Negro." [PoetryC] (14:2) Mr 94, p. 16.
"Turn Away." [PraF] (15:4, #69) Wint 94-95, p. 98-99.
2079. GADE, Lisa
"It's Top Forty in My Head." [Agni] (39) 94, p. 186-187.
2080. GAGNON, Madeleine
"Lentement, le soleil fait son oeuvre." [Os] (38) Spr 94, p. 15.
"Voici un jour de rêve, le temps s'est arrêté." [Os] (38) Spr 94, p. 14.
2081. GAHETE JURADO, Manuel
"A Imagen." [Nuez] (5:13/14/15) 94, p. 22.
"Dilogía." [Nuez] (5:13/14/15) 94, p. 22.
2082. GAINER, Joseph
"The Deaf-Blind Egg Lady." [HawaiiR] (18:1, #40) Spr 94, p. 90.
2083. GAJCY, Tadeusz
"Beggar of Sorrow" (tr. by David Sparenberg and Aleksandra Szostalo). [WebR] (18) Fall 94, p. 14.
2084. GALEANO, Andrea
"Wish" (tr. of Rafael Cadenas, w. Gail Ghai). [Vis] (45) 94, p. 8.
2085. GALEANO, Eduardo
"Story of the Parrot's Resurrection" (tr. by Mark Fried, w. illustrations by José Francisco Borges). [Conjunc] (23) 94, p. 191-192.
2086. GALEF, David
"Dis-Orienting." [Light] (9) Spr 94, p. 8.
"Questions." [Light] (12) Wint 94-95, p. 22.
"Sonnet 129, Postprandial Version." [Light] (12) Wint 94-95, p. 17.
2087. GALLADER, Jordan
"End." [NewDeltaR] (11:1) Fall 93-Wint 94, p. 90-91.
2088. GALLAGHER, Jean
"Arches of Bridge Break Ranks* (Or, My New Marriage)" (*A 1937 charcoal-on-cloth by Paul Klee). [Comm] (121:11) 3 Je 94, p. 14.
2089. GALLAGHER, Lois
"Axiom." [GlobalCR] (4) Fall 94, p. 65.
2090. GALLAGHER, Tess
"The Kiss Eats a Loaf of Bread." [AmerV] (35) 94, p. 20-21.
"The Kiss in Her Bath." [AmerV] (35) 94, p. 13-14.
"Lynx Light." [AmerV] (35) 94, p. 15.
"Moment with Thunder" (for Tess, tr. of Liliana Ursu, w. the poet). [Kalliope] (16:2) 94, p. 68.
"Motoring Toward Seattle, The Kiss Considers Capital Punishment." [BlackWR] (21:1) Fall-Wint 94, p. 86-87.
"Two Bracelets." [AmerV] (35) 94, p. 18-19.
"Urgent Story." [AmerV] (35) 94, p. 16-17.
"With Her Words Beside Me." [SantaBR] (1:2) Fall-Wint 93, p. 47.
"Your Hair Is Red in Sunlight" (for Mihnea). [SantaBR] (1:2) Fall-Wint 93, p. 46.
2091. GALLAHER, Cynthia
"The Egg Man." [SlipS] (14) 94, p. 46-47.
2092. GALLAHER, Edwin
"Scaring Charles Wright on the Highway." [Border] (4) Spr-Sum 94, p. 36.
2093. GALLAHER, John
"Medallions." [Border] (4) Spr-Sum 94, p. 37-38.
2094. GALLER, David
"Bach." [PraS] (68:3) Fall 94, p. 138-139.
"Clearing Away Maples." [PraS] (68:3) Fall 94, p. 136.
"A Story." [PraS] (68:3) Fall 94, p. 137-138.
2095. GALLIK, Daniel
"Their Marriage Is Prose or Worse" (from the journals of Thoreau, August 11, 1853). [Elf] (4:3) Fall 94, p. 30.
"You Cannot Escape a Large Distance from a Black Hole" (for Grace Butcher). [HiramPoR] (55/56) Fall 93-Sum 94, p. 38.
2096. GALVIN, Brendan
"Grove." [GeoR] (48:2) Sum 94, p. 323.

"Is." [SenR] (24:1) Spr 94, p. 27.
"Potato Variations" (Skibbereen, W. Cork, Ireland — Deer Island, Boston Harbor, USA). [BlackWR] (20:2) Spr-Sum 94, p. 104-106.
"Sentence." [Agni] (39) 94, p. 188.
"Talking to Anne from Her Dream." [BlackWR] (20:2) Spr-Sum 94, p. 102-103.

2097. GALVIN, James
"Agriculture" (for Richard Borgmann). [Iowa] (24:1) Wint 94, p. 128.
"More Like It." [Iowa] (24:1) Wint 94, p. 130-131.
"On Exploration." [Iowa] (24:1) Wint 94, p. 132.
"Resurrection Update." [Iowa] (24:1) Wint 94, p. 128-129.
"Two Horses and a Dog." [Iowa] (24:1) Wint 94, p. 129-130.
"Untitled, 1968" (for Mark Rothko). [Iowa] (24:1) Wint 94, p. 133-134.

2098. GALVIN, Martin
"Arms." [PoetL] (89:4) Wint 94-95, p. 23.
"Freshman Year." [FourQ] (8:1) Spr 94, p. 22.
"Lessons of the Hand." [PoetL] (89:4) Wint 94-95, p. 21-22.
"Mating Owls." [FourQ] (8:1) Spr 94, p. 21.
"P." [FourQ] (8:2) Fall 94, p. 10.
"Prevision." [FourQ] (8:1) Spr 94, p. 20.
"Universal Donor." [Poetry] (164:4) Jl 94, p. 219.

2099. GAMALINDA, Eric
"Five Tango Sensations." [InterQ] (1:4) 94, p. 41.
"The Sensual Imagination, after Fernando Botero." [InterQ] (1:4) 94, p. 38-40.

2100. GAMBILL, Gina
"All Sex'd Up." [YellowS] (11:4, #44) Wint 93-94, p. 36.

2101. GAMPER, Galina
"Untitled: A poet's talent only clutters" (tr. by Vera S. Dunham). [Elf] (4:3) Fall 94, p. 37.
"Untitled: My childhood is a glass menagerie" (tr. by Vera S. Dunham). [Elf] (4:3) Fall 94, p. 36.

2102. GANASSI, Ian
"The More I Know." [Amelia] (7:4, #23) 94, p. 178.
"The Reason." [AnotherCM] (27) 94, p. 55-56.
"The Roommate Trap." [YaleR] (82:2) Ap 94, p. 74-75.
"Sports of All Sorts." [AnotherCM] (27) 94, p. 53-54.
"The Swim Team." [Ploughs] (20:4) Wint 94-95, p. 55-56.
"The Usual Sirens." [AmerLC] (6) 94, p. 99-100.

2103. GANDER, Forrest
"Decree for Rain." [HarvardR] (7) Fall 94, p. 45.
"Like a White Wolf the Moon Took Flight" (tr. of Carlos Faraco). [Caliban] (14) 94, p. 143.
"Of Their Ornate Eyes of Crystalline Sand" (tr. of Coral Bracho). [Conjunc] (23) 94, p. 79-80.
"Special Troikas: A Corps" (tr. of Nina Iskrenko, w. Joy Dworkin). [Conjunc] (23) 94, p. 145-149.
"Untitled: Your voice (in your body rivers stir" (tr. of Coral Bracho). [Conjunc] (23) 94, p. 81-82.
"Your Life Refracts Me Like an Enigma" (tr. of Coral Bracho). [Conjunc] (23) 94, p. 80-81.

2104. GANDLEVSKY, Sergey
"Untitled: It's time to change the record" (tr. by Philip Metres, w. Dmitry Psurtsev). [ArtfulD] (26/27) 94, p. 15.
"Untitled: Oh, how the lilacs are this May!" (tr. by Philip Metres, w. Dmitry Psurtsev). [ArtfulD] (26/27) 94, p. 14.
"Untitled: To land a job at the garage" (tr. by Philip Metres, w. Dmitry Psurtsev). [ArtfulD] (26/27) 94, p. 13.

2105. GANICK, Peter
"No Soap Radio" (Excerpts). [Talisman] (12) Spr 94, p. 13-15.
"Untitled (an Ocean)" (Excerpt). [WashR] (20:3) O-N 94, p. 25.

2106. GANSWORTH, Eric L.
"Walking a Mile in His Wingtips." [SlipS] (14) 94, p. 74-75.

2107. GARCIA, Albert
"I Watch You Paint." [PraS] (68:4) Wint 94, p. 93-95.

2108. GARCIA, Carlos Ernesto
"Guaro Even 100 Proof Fails" (tr. by Elizabeth Gamble Miller). [InterQ] (1:4) 94, p. 32.

"No Hay Guaro Que Valga." [InterQ] (1:4) 94, p. 32.
2109. GARCIA, Enildo
"Cities" (tr. of Pablo Armando Fernandez, w. Daniela Gioseffi). [Vis] (46) 94, p. 23.
2110. GARCIA, José
"3 x 111 Tristychs" (Selections, tr. of Yannis Ritsos, w. Adamantia García-Baltatzi). [PaintedHR] (11) Spr-Sum 94, p. 28.
2111. GARCIA, Ramón
"Miss Primavera Contest." [Americas] (22:3/4) Fall-Wint 94, p. 71-72.
"Salmo: Para El" (for Marisela Norte). [Americas] (22:3/4) Fall-Wint 94, p. 73-75.
2112. GARCIA, Richard
"A Death in Larkspur Canyon." [PraS] (68:4) Wint 94, p. 90-91.
"Drifting with the Crowd." [PraS] (68:4) Wint 94, p. 91-92.
"El Zapato." [PraS] (68:4) Wint 94, p. 92-93.
2113. GARCIA-BALTATZI, Adamantia
"3 x 111 Tristychs" (Selections, tr. of Yannis Ritsos, w. José García). [PaintedHR] (11) Spr-Sum 94, p. 28.
2114. GARCIA MARRUZ, Fina
"Ah, Autumn Garden" (tr. by Daniella Gioseffi, w. Noemi Escandell). [CaribbeanW] (8) 94, p. 91-92.
"Farewell" (tr. by Daniella Gioseffi, w. Noemi Escandell). [CaribbeanW] (8) 94, p. 93.
"I Want to See" (tr. by Daniella Gioseffi, w. Noemi Escandell). [CaribbeanW] (8) 94, p. 91.
"Is It I Who Sheds — ?" (tr. by Daniella Gioseffi, w. Noemi Escandell). [CaribbeanW] (8) 94, p. 94.
"Longing to Go Out" (tr. by Daniella Gioseffi, w. Noemi Escandell). [CaribbeanW] (8) 94, p. 93-94.
"On the Small Table" (tr. by Daniella Gioseffi, w. Noemi Escandell). [CaribbeanW] (8) 94, p. 90.
"A Sweet Snow Falls" (From *Lost Glances*, tr. by Daniella Gioseffi, w. Noemi Escandell). [CaribbeanW] (8) 94, p. 92.
2115. GARDAM, Heather
"The Others." [Dandel] (21:1) 94, p. 12.
2116. GARDIEN, Kent
"The Belgian Poem." [ParisR] (36:132) Fall 94, p. 119-120.
"Calle San Jerónimo." [WeberS] (11:1) Wint 94, p. 76.
"The Fluffy Doldrums." [ParisR] (36:132) Fall 94, p. 120-121.
"The Telephone Book." [ParisR] (36:132) Fall 94, p. 121.
2117. GARDIPE, Amber
"The Bush Cracks." [Callaloo] (17:1) Wint 94, p. 179-180.
"Oh Great Eagle." [Callaloo] (17:1) Wint 94, p. 181.
2118. GARDNER, Charity
"Unhooking Catfish." [Boulevard] (9:1/2, #25/26) Spr 94, p. 239.
2119. GARDNER, Drew
"August." [Talisman] (13) Fall 94-Wint 95, p. 220.
"The book in the human mind." [Talisman] (12) Spr 94, p. 147.
"Near Hermes." [Zyzzyva] (10:4) Wint 94, p. 94-95.
2120. GARDNER, Geoffrey
"Behind This Faded Sky" (tr. of Jules Supervielle). [CrabCR] (8:2/3/9:1/2/3) 94, p. 136.
"This Innocent Child" (tr. of Jules Supervielle). [CrabCR] (8:2/3/9:1/2/3) 94, p. 137.
2121. GARDNER, Hillary J.
"Eau Folle (1)" (tr. of Olga Xirinacs). [DenQ] (29:1) Sum 94, p. 113.
2122. GARDNER, Jennie
"Intimations of Mortality from Failure to Recollect Early Childhood." [Light] (10) Sum 94, p. 14.
2123. GARDNER, John
"Art, Life and Tom Kinsella." [QW] (38) Winter-Spr 93-94, p. 74-85.
2124. GARDNER, Mary
"Old Bones." [Wind] (73) 94, p. 10-11.
2125. GARDNER, Stephen
"Eva McCann's Diary: 4/14/80: Fort Smith, Arkansas" (Eyster Prize, Winner in Poetry). [NewDeltaR] (11:2) Spr-Sum 94, p. 1-2.
2126. GARDUÑO, Raúl
"Found in the Armory of a Cyclone" (tr. by Reginald Gibbons and Ambar Past). [TriQ] (91) Fall 94, p. 146-147.

2127. GARLAND, Max
"Lessons from a Fifties Childhood." [CarolQ] (47:1) Fall 94, p. 62.
"Memories of Pentecost." [CarolQ] (47:1) Fall 94, p. 61.
"Mirror." [Poetry] (163:4) Ja 94, p. 199.
2128. GARLINGTON, Jack
"Travel Note." [Light] (9) Spr 94, p. 9.
2129. GARNETT, Ruth
"Barrage." [RiverS] (40) 94, p. 61-62.
"Concerning Violence" (for Fanon). [RiverS] (40) 94, p. 60.
2130. GARNIER, Pierre
"Fortified Churches of the Thierarche." [RagMag] (12:1) Sum 94, p. 76-77.
"Ode to Those Who Were Shot in the Citadel." [RagMag] (12:1) Sum 94, p. 80-82.
"Recollections from My Adolescence." [RagMag] (12:1) Sum 94, p. 78-79.
2131. GARRETT, Dana
"Blown Branch." [Amelia] (7:4, #23) 94, p. 111.
2132. GARRETT, George
"Jacob." [CarolQ] (46:3) Sum 94, p. 13-14.
2133. GARRISON, David
"Loss." [Poem] (71) My 94, p. 53.
"The Poet Kneading Bread at 40." [ChironR] (13:3) Aut 94, p. 16.
"Portrait of Nina." [BellArk] (10:3 [i.e. 10:4]) Jl-Ag 94, p. 7.
"Time Zone in the Act of Recovery." [Poem] (71) My 94, p. 52.
2134. GARRISON, Deborah
"Husband, Not at Home." [NewYorker] (70:21) 18 Jl 94, p. 54.
2135. GARTEN, Bill
"Frame 145." [Blueline] (15) 94, p. 6.
"Frame 210: Father." [RagMag] (12:1) Sum 94, p. 28.
"Frame 211: If Matter." [RagMag] (12:1) Sum 94, p. 29.
"Frame 214." [RagMag] (12:1) Sum 94, p. 30.
2136. GARTHE, Karen
"Carpenter." [GlobalCR] (4) Fall 94, p. 21.
"Curly Travel." [GlobalCR] (4) Fall 94, p. 20.
2137. GARZA, Elisa A.
"Wearing Elena's Earrings." [PoetL] (89:2) Sum 94, p. 48.
"Why I Make the Best Barrels." [Verse] (11:1) Spr 94, p. 50.
2138. GARZA, José
"Stars, Tadpoles and Water." [Callaloo] (17:1) Wint 94, p. 126-127.
2139. GASPAR, Frank
"Coal." [GeoR] (48:4) Wint 94, p. 642.
"Crows." [Nimrod] (38:1) Fall-Wint 94, p. 105.
"His Book of Days." [TampaR] (9) Fall 94, p. 39-41.
"Log." [Nimrod] (38:1) Fall-Wint 94, p. 104.
"Psalm." [Nimrod] (38:1) Fall-Wint 94, p. 102-103.
2140. GASPAR, Gail
"Safe Passage." [Pivot] (41) 93, p. 15-16.
2141. GASPARINI, Leonard
"New Orleans Nocturne." [NegC] (13:2/3) 93, p. 13.
"The Night After Christmas." [Quarry] (42:4) Mr 94, p. 38.
2142. GATES, Beatrix
"Negotiations" (for my parents). [NoDaQ] (62:1) Wint 94-95, p. 22-25.
2143. GATES, Edward
"For Gabriel Dumont." [PraF] (15:4, #69) Wint 94-95, p. 95.
2144. GAVIN, Gaynell
"Stations." [SmPd] (31:3, #92) Fall 94, p. 36-37.
2145. GAVIN, Tim
"First Communion." [SoDakR] (32:2) Sum 94, p. 46.
"Learning the ABC's." [SoDakR] (32:2) Sum 94, p. 47.
2146. GAVRON, Jackie
"The Truant." [NewYorkQ] (53) 94, p. 108.
2147. GAY, Zan
"On a Steamroller." [SouthernPR] (34:2) Wint 94, p. 29-30.
2148. GEBEYLI, Clarie
"Beirut" (tr. by Mona Takyeddine Amyuni). [LitR] (37:3) Spr 94, p. 485.
"A Man Is Dead" (tr. by Mona Takyeddine Amyuni). [LitR] (37:3) Spr 94, p. 483-484.

"On Every Roof a Bond" (tr. by Mona Takyeddine Amyuni). [LitR] (37:3) Spr 94, p. 483.
"A Porch" (tr. by Mona Takyeddine Amyuni). [LitR] (37:3) Spr 94, p. 482.

2149. GECEWICZ, Donald
"Spaces" (tr. of Gabriella Sobrino). [Vis] (46) 94, p. 37.

2150. GEDDES, Gary
"Canada Park." [Nimrod] (37:2) Spr-Sum 94, p. 34-35.
"Christene's Poem." [Nimrod] (37:2) Spr-Sum 94, p. 36.
"Eyeless in Gaza" (w. Mahmud Darwish, accompanying a photo essay by Larry Towell). [Quarry] (42:4) Mr 94, p. 39-54.
"Green Line." [Nimrod] (37:2) Spr-Sum 94, p. 37.
"The Prize." [SouthernPR] (34:2) Wint 94, p. 67-68.

2151. GEIGER, Timothy
"Another Atmosphere" (2 selections). [NewDeltaR] (11:2) Spr-Sum 94, p. 52-53.

2152. GELMAN, Juan
"Otras Partes." [InterQ] (1:4) 94, p. 51-52.
"Somewhere Else" (tr. by Joan Lindgren). [InterQ] (1:4) 94, p. 50-51.

2153. GEMIN, Pamela
"Almost Winter." [Farm] (11:1) Spr-Sum 94, p. 132.
"In Gratitude." [BellArk] (10:3) My-Je 94, p. 28.
"The Knots." [BellArk] (10:3) My-Je 94, p. 28.
"Rosie's Poem." [BellArk] (10:3) My-Je 94, p. 28.

2154. GENOWAYS, Ted
"The Dead Have a Way of Returning." [SouthernPR] (34:2) Wint 94, p. 73.
"For My Father, Who Does Not Dance." [NoDaQ] (62:1) Wint 94-95, p. 37.
"Guaraches' Smile." [HighP] (9:2) Ag 94, p. 78-79.
"My Grandfather Speaks to Me Still." [CapeR] (29:1) Spr 94, p. 13.
"The Weight of Memory." [Ploughs] (20:1) Spr 94, p. 99-101.

2155. GENTILCORE, Roxanne M.
"Figure, circa 3,000 B.C." [AntigR] (98) Sum 94, p. 56.

2156. GENTRY, Jane
"My Mother's Clothes." [AmerV] (34) 94, p. 65.

GEOK, Leong Liew
See LEONG, Liew Geok

2157. GEORGE, Alice Rose
"A Humdrum Life." [Atlantic] (273:3) Mr 94, p. 75.

2158. GEORGE, Anita
"From Sappho" (Fragments: 105(a), 105(c))." [Poetry] (164:3) Je 94, p. 140.
"Three Fragments from Sappho." [AntigR] (97) Spr 94, p. 66.

2159. GEORGE, Anne
"The Old Woman As Rose, Mountain, Wind." [NegC] (14:1/2) 94, p. 151-152.

2160. GEORGE, Emery
"Ravensbrück Passion" (from "Metropolitan Icons," tr. of János Pilinszky). [AmerPoR] (23:6) N-D 94, p. 22.
"Under a Winter Sky" (For Tamás Cholnoky, tr. of János Pilinszky). [DenQ] (29:1) Sum 94, p. 96.

2161. GEORGE, Gerald
"Visit to a Nursing Home." [ColEng] (56:8) D 94, p. 936-937.

2162. GEORGE, Tom
"News." [FloridaR] (19:2) 94, p. 25.

2163. GEORGIEV, Marin
"Silence" (tr. by Lisa Sapinkopf and Georgi Belev). [InterQ] (1:1) [93?], p. 81.

2164. GERARD-MOORE, Cynthia
"The Antithesis." [HiramPoR] (57) Fall 94-Wint 95, p. 23.
"Grandma's Still Life." [HiramPoR] (57) Fall 94-Wint 95, p. 22.

2165. GEREIGHTY, Andrea
"Summer: New Orleans." [NegC] (13:2/3) 93, p. 14-15.

2166. GERGELY, Agnes
"Shipwreck" (tr. by Bruce Berlind). [InterQ] (1:1) [93?], p. 34-39.

2167. GERNER-MATHISEN, Aina
"The House in the Dream" (tr. of Astrid Hjertenaes Andersen, w. Suzanne Bachner). [SpoonR] (19:1) Wint-Spr 94, p. 94-95.
"The House on the Meadow" (tr. of Astrid Hjertenaes Andersen, w. Suzanne Bachner). [SpoonR] (19:1) Wint-Spr 94, p. 96.
"Red Branches" (tr. of Astrid Hjertenaes Andersen, w. Suzanne Bachner). [SpoonR] (19:1) Wint-Spr 94, p. 93.

2168. GERNES, Sonia
"A Chair, a Table, a Yellow Balloon." [PoetryNW] (35:2) Sum 94, p. 24.
"Rings." [HopewellR] (6) 94, p. 98.
"Sight Is a Species of Touch." [HopewellR] (6) 94, p. 99.
2169. GERNES, Ulrikka S.
"Hotel" (tr. by Per Brask and Patrick Friesen). [PoetryC] (14:2) Mr 94, p. 21.
"The House Is Open" (tr. by Per Brask and Patrick Friesen). [PoetryC] (14:2) Mr 94, p. 21.
2170. GERSTLER, Amy
"Ash Wednesday." [AmerV] (35) 94, p. 73-74.
"Commentary." [NewAW] (12) Spr-Sum 94, p. 32-33.
"Four Meditations on an Ice Puddle." [AntR] (52:3) Sum 94, p. 478-479.
"Introducing: The Clouds." [AmerV] (35) 94, p. 71-72.
"Mixed Messages." [Colum] (22) Wint 94, p. 44-45.
"My Hero." [AmerV] (35) 94, p. 67-68.
"Nowadays." [AmerV] (35) 94, p. 69-70.
"Sworn Statement." [AntR] (52:3) Sum 94, p. 480-481.
"The Wanderer." [NewAW] (12) Spr-Sum 94, p. 34.
2171. GERVAIS, Marty
"The Affairs of Death." [Descant] (25:1, #84) Spr 94, p. 108.
"The Dark Sounds of Night." [Descant] (25:1, #84) Spr 94, p. 113.
"In That Voice." [Descant] (25:1, #84) Spr 94, p. 112.
"The Last Pie." [Descant] (25:1, #84) Spr 94, p. 109-111.
GERVEN, Claudia van
See Van GERVEN, Claudia
2172. GERY, John
"Decisions." [SpiritSH] (59) 94, p. 31.
"For the Duration." [SpiritSH] (59) 94, p. 32.
"Lie #1: That Penelope Resisted Scores of Suitors." [ParisR] (36:133) Wint 94, p. 178-179.
"Lie #2: That Parkman Almost Died on the Oregon Trial" (The Ogillallah Village, 1846). [ParisR] (36:133) Wint 94, p. 179-180.
"Lie #4: That Frances Osgood Slept with E. A. Poe." [KenR] (NS 16:4) Fall 94, p. 30-31.
"Lie #6: That Hart Crane Crawled in Bed between the Cowleys." [KenR] (NS 16:4) Fall 94, p. 31-32.
"Promiscuous Spirit." [SpiritSH] (59) 94, p. 30.
"Promises." [Pivot] (42) 94, p. 45-46.
2173. GETTLER, Andrew
"Heat." [Confr] (52/53) Wint-Spr 94, p. 317.
2174. GEVIRTZ, Susan
"Echo Orbit." [Avec] (7:1) 94, p. 31-38.
"Prosthesis." [Avec] (8:1) 94, p. 25-36.
2175. GEWANTER, David
"Boy's Poem." [BostonR] (19:5) O-N 94, p. 21.
"Shield" (*Aeneid*, VIII.729-731). [HarvardR] (6) Spr 94, p. 143.
"The Work-Towers." [Thrpny] (56) Wint 94, p. 26.
2176. GHAI, Gail
"Wish" (tr. of Rafael Cadenas, w. Andrea Galeano). [Vis] (45) 94, p. 8.
GHETT, Stephanie Coyne
See DeGHETT, Stephanie Coyne
2177. GHIGNA, Charles
"Cabbage Patched." [Light] (12) Wint 94-95, p. 22.
"The Existential Brunch." [Light] (11) Aut 94, p. 11.
"Musery Loves Company." [Light] (10) Sum 94, p. 12.
2178. GHOLSON, Christien
"All the Beautiful Dead Along the Side of the Road." [Gaia] (4) Je 94, p. 19.
"Cars! Cars! Cars!" [ContextS] (4:1) 94, p. 5.
"Cirque Baalazar, Flanders: An Aquatint Etching." [Parting] (7:1) Sum 94, p. 41.
"The Hours of St. Christophe: Fragment of a Manuscript Illumination." [BellArk] (10:6) N-D 94, p. 24.
"I Am Goofing on the Conspiracy of Life" (for don, veronica and wendell ray). [BellArk] (10:1) Ja-F 94, p. 21.
"I Am Goofing on the Conspiracy of Life" (for don, veronica and wendell ray). [BellArk] (10:2) Mr-Ap 94, p. 13.
"I Am One of the Escaped Dogs on This Street." [BellArk] (10:3) My-Je 94, p. 11.

"In the Middle of the Continent, in the Middle of Winter." [BellArk] (10:6) N-D 94, p. 24.
"In the Night Sea." [Gaia] (4) Je 94, p. 18-19.
"In the Realm of the Foghorn King: Fragment of a Manuscript Illumination." [Parting] (7:1) Sum 94, p. 40.
"Lovers: A Winter Landscape." [BellArk] (10:6) N-D 94, p. 24.
"Night, Hunting Its Own Tail." [BellArk] (10:3) My-Je 94, p. 11.
"Resurrection: Black Ink on White Rice Paper." [BellArk] (10:1) Ja-F 94, p. 23.
"The Sea of Forgetting, the Hourglass of Feathers." [Parting] (7:2) Wint 94-95, p. 65.
"Solstice: Nightscape Made from Reflected Light." [BellArk] (10:6) N-D 94, p. 24.
"Sunday Afternoon Matinee: Collage Made from Refuse Found on a Movie Theater Floor." [BellArk] (10:1) Ja-F 94, p. 23.
"Woman Facing Storm Waves: A Watercolor." [Parting] (7:2) Wint 94-95, p. 66.
"You Can Tell a Lot About People by the Way They Hand Out Leaflets During Rush Hour." [BellArk] (10:5) S-O 94, p. 12.

2179. GHOSE, Zulfikar
"The Church and the Tree." [InterQ] (1:3) 94, p. 174-175.

2180. GHOSH, Rama
"I Go" (tr. by Carolyne Wright, w. Paramita Banerjee). [BostonR] (19:2) Ap-My 94, p. 9.

2181. GIANNINI, David
"Ellipses" (for Mark Farrington). [Talisman] (13) Fall 94-Wint 95, p. 159-162.
"Wellfleet — Audubon Sanctuary" (for Ted Enslin). [Talisman] (12) Spr 94, p. 82.

2182. GIBB, Robert
"At the Steelworkers' Monument During the 100th Anniversary of the Homestead Strike of 1892." [MissouriR] (17:2) 94, p. 180-181.
"The Employments of Time in Homestead." [MissouriR] (17:2) 94, p. 182-185.
"First Day." [MissouriR] (17:2) 94, p. 178-179.
"In the House of Memory." [IllinoisR] (2:1) Fall 94, p. 18-19.
"A Late Winter Blues." [IllinoisR] (2:1) Fall 94, p. 16-17.
"N. Easton-Belmont Pike." [PoetryNW] (35:2) Sum 94, p. 45-47.
"Night Moves." [MissouriR] (17:2) 94, p. 177.
"Saying Farewell to the Displays in the Carnegie Museum." [Poetry] (164:6) S 94, p. 317-318.
"Swimming Lessons." [IllinoisR] (2:1) Fall 94, p. 17-18.

2183. GIBBONS, Reginald
"All the Buried Voices" (tr. of Jaime Sabines). [TriQ] (91) Fall 94, p. 147.
"Family Portrait" (in memory of Old Emeterio, my father. Tr. of Joaquín Vásquez Aguilar, w. Ambar Past). [TriQ] (91) Fall 94, p. 154-155.
"Flood" (tr. of Efraín Bartolomé). [TriQ] (91) Fall 94, p. 117.
"Found in the Armory of a Cyclone" (tr. of Raúl Garduño, w. Ambar Past). [TriQ] (91) Fall 94, p. 146-147.
"Landscape with Dead Anthems" (tr. of Ambar Past). [TriQ] (91) Fall 94, p. 115-116.
"Like the Night" (tr. of Jaime Sabines). [TriQ] (91) Fall 94, p. 107.
"Nobody Lives in My Country Anymore" (tr. of Juan Bañuelos). [TriQ] (91) Fall 94, p. 95-96.

2184. GIBBONS, Robert
"Voyeur." [CapeR] (29:2) Fall 94, p. 33.

2185. GIBBONS, Robert Jerome
"The Nineteen-Seventy-Three Annual Coon Valley Wisconsin American Legion Fourth of July Lawn Tractor Pull Competition and Picnic." [Northeast] (5:11) Wint 94-95, p. 25-27.

2186. GIBBS, Robert
"Dreams in All Colours." [TickleAce] (28) Fall-Wint 94, p. 38.
"The Irishness of Summer." [TickleAce] (28) Fall-Wint 94, p. 37.
"Three Poems from '1492/1992'." [TickleAce] (28) Fall-Wint 94, p. 39.

2187. GIBSON, Margaret
"Elegy to a Sculptor." [SouthernR] (30:4) Aut 94, p. 826-830.
"Grief" (For Connie). [SpoonR] (19:1) Wint-Spr 94, p. 23.
"Home Ground." [Shen] (44:4) Wint 94, p. 108-109.
"Stubborn." [SpoonR] (19:1) Wint-Spr 94, p. 24.

2188. GIBSON, Stephen
"Blue Underwear." [NewEngR] (16:4) Fall 94, p. 100-101.
"The Bra." [ParisR] (36:131) Sum 94, p. 102.

"Christmas in Radio City." [NowestR] (32:3) 94, p. 25.
"Ciano's Overcoat: The Execution of Galeazzo Ciano, Mussolini's Son-In-Law, Ordered by the Duce, Verona, January 11, 1944" (from a photograph). [Epoch] (43:2) 94, p. 184.
"The Duel After the Masquerade" (by Gerome). [Boulevard] (9:1/2, #25/26) Spr 94, p. 199-200.
"The Novelist: Notes for a Story on a Train Ride to Naples, 1943" (adapted from a short story by Luigi Pirandello). [Epoch] (43:2) 94, p. 185.
"Rembrandt's Flayed Ox." [HayF] (15) Fall-Wint 94, p. 52.

2189. GIBSON, Stephen Robert
"Buildings I Have Seen Between the End of the Day and My Life." [PoetryNW] (35:2) Sum 94, p. 11.

2190. GIDLOW, Elsa
"California Valley with Girls." [Arc] (32) Spr 94, p. 41.
"Never Any Fear." [Arc] (32) Spr 94, p. 42.

2191. GIGLIO, Katheryn
"The Shaving Poem." [Kalliope] (16:1) 94, p. 14.

2192. GILBERT, Alan
"Witnesses." [Pequod] (37) 94, p. 103-104.

2193. GILBERT, Christopher
"Ad Hoc." [IllinoisR] (2:1) Fall 94, p. 22.
"Metaphor for Something That Plays Us / Remembering Eric Dolphy." [IllinoisR] (2:1) Fall 94, p. 20-22.

2194. GILBERT, Jack
"Adulterated." [AmerPoR] (23:1) Ja-F 94, p. 16.
"Almost Happy." [Iowa] (24:1) Wint 94, p. 83.
"Gift Horses." [Iowa] (24:1) Wint 94, p. 82.
"The History of Men." [VirQR] (70:2) Spr 94, p. 299.
"Man at a Window." [AmerPoR] (23:1) Ja-F 94, p. 16.
"Michiko Dead." [VirQR] (70:2) Spr 94, p. 300.
"Music Is the Memory of What Never Happened" (for Gerald Stern). [VirQR] (70:2) Spr 94, p. 298.
"Older Women." [VirQR] (70:2) Spr 94, p. 299.
"Prospero without His Magic." [NewYRB] (41:5) 3 Mr 94, p. 19.
"Recovering Amid the Farms." [AmerPoR] (23:1) Ja-F 94, p. 17.
"Searching for Pittsburgh." [PoetryE] (37/38) Spr 94, p. 38.
"Steel Guitars." [PoetryE] (37/38) Spr 94, p. 39.
"Tasters for the Lord." [PoetryE] (37/38) Spr 94, p. 37.
"Tear It Down." [AmerPoR] (23:1) Ja-F 94, p. 16.
"To See If Something Comes Next." [AmerPoR] (23:1) Ja-F 94, p. 16.
"The White Heart of God." [AmerPoR] (23:1) Ja-F 94, p. 17.

2195. GILBERT, Margaret
"A Letter." [NewYorkQ] (53) 94, p. 111.
"Swallow Barn." [Crazy] (46) Spr 94, p. 31-37.

2196. GILBERT, Sandra M.
"Water Music." [Poetry] (164:1) Ap 94, p. 29-38.

2197. GILBERT, Virginia
"Driving." [PraS] (68:3) Fall 94, p. 106-109.

2198. GILBERT-LECOMTE, Roger
"Testament" (tr. by Michel Palma and Lee Whittier). [PoetryE] (37/38) Spr 94, p. 236.
"The Wind After, The Wind Before" (tr. by Michel Palma and Lee Whittier). [PoetryE] (37/38) Spr 94, p. 234-235.

2199. GILDNER, Gary
"The Bunker in the Parsley Fields." [Field] (51) Fall 94, p. 69-70.
"The Cougar." [PoetryNW] (35:3) Aut 94, p. 36.
"Dogtoothed Violets." [PoetryNW] (35:3) Aut 94, p. 33.
"Flicker." [PoetryNW] (35:3) Aut 94, p. 34-35.
"My Polish Grandfather." [ColR] (21:2) Fall 94, p. 158-161.
"Picked Out a Toka, a Stanley." [Field] (51) Fall 94, p. 71-72.
"Song: One Summer Afternoon in the Country." [GeoR] (48:2) Sum 94, p. 250-251.

2200. GILES, Ron
"The Painting at the Dentist's Office." [SouthernHR] (28:4) Fall 94, p. 350.

2201. GILGUN, John
"How Jeff Gets the Necessary Grieving Done." [Arc] (33) Fall 94, p. 60.
"Myself, 1952." [JamesWR] (11:4) Sum 94, p. 14.

2202. GILL, Gagan
"The Fish — 2" (tr. by Arlene Zide, J. P. Das and Madhu Joshi). [InterQ] (1:2) 93, p. 184.
2203. GILL, James Vladimir
"Literature and Poetry" (from *Le cornet à dés*, tr. of Max Jacob). [ProseP] (3) 94, p. 53.
"Rilkeing." [ProseP] (3) 94, p. 40-41.
"The Soldier of Marathon" (from *Le cornet à dés*, tr. of Max Jacob). [ProseP] (3) 94, p. 51.
"True Anecdote" (from *Le cornet à dés*, tr. of Max Jacob). [ProseP] (3) 94, p. 52.
2204. GILL, Michael J.
"Fifteen Lines." [Parting] (7:1) Sum 94, p. 61.
"Twenty-Four Lines." [HiramPoR] (55/56) Fall 93-Sum 94, p. 39.
2205. GILL-LONERGAN, Janet
"Winter Solstice." [BellArk] (10:6) N-D 94, p. 9.
2206. GILLAM, Ken
"George Washington Goes Down at the Help-ee Self-ee Laundromat." [NewEngR] (16:2) Spr 94, p. 126-129.
2207. GILLAN, Maria Mazziotti
"How Transparent We Are." [NegC] (14:1/2) 94, p. 17.
2208. GILLETT, Mary Jo Firth
"Your Mouth." [Calyx] (15:2) Sum 94, p. 48-49.
2209. GILLEY, Amy Bragdon
"The Dark Husband." [SantaBR] (2:1) Spr-Sum 94, p. 98-99.
"Fred's Idea." [SantaBR] (2:1) Spr-Sum 94, p. 100.
2210. GILLIAN, Maria Mazziotti
"The Curved Bridge." [Border] (5) Fall-Wint 94, p. 20-21.
2211. GILLIE, Paul
"The World and Mima Road." [BellR] (17:1/2) Spr-Fall 94, p. 8.
2212. GILLIS, Susan
"The Vacant Lot a Landing Pad." [PraF] (15:2, #67) Sum 94, p. 19.
2213. GILLMAN, Richard
"Notes for My Mother's Biographer." [NewEngR] (16:2) Spr 94, p. 38-40.
2214. GILSDORF, Ethan
"Ask Your Angel / Calling All Angels." [NewDeltaR] (11:1) Fall 93-Wint 94, p. 57-58.
"The Blue-Gray Church." [NewDeltaR] (11:1) Fall 93-Wint 94, p. 56-57.
"Equation." [Pivot] (42) 94, p. 26.
"Incentive." [Pivot] (42) 94, p. 26.
"Moonscape." [NewYorkQ] (53) 94, p. 66.
"Passing Through Unkempt Vermont." [GreenMR] (NS 17:2) Fall-Wint 94-95, p. 114.
"To My Old Photograph." [GreenMR] (NS 17:2) Fall-Wint 94-95, p. 115.
2215. GILSON, Michael
"Credo" (tr. of Marcel Olscamp). [InterPR] (20:2) Fall 94, p. 49, 51.
GINEBRA, Arminda Valdés
See VALDÉS GINEBRA, Arminda
2216. GINSBERG, Allen
"Apocolypse of Les Halles." [Antaeus] (75/76) Aut 94, p. 256-257.
"The Charnel Ground." [AmerPoR] (23:3) My-Je 94, p. 5.
"Fun House Antique Store." [AmerPoR] (23:3) My-Je 94, p. 3.
"Imitation of K.S." [AmerPoR] (23:3) My-Je 94, p. 3.
"Not Dead Yet." [AmerPoR] (23:3) My-Je 94, p. 4.
"Salutations to Fernando Pessoa." [Thrpny] (57) Spr 94, p. 5.
"A Thief Stole This Poem." [AmerPoR] (23:3) My-Je 94, p. 4.
"When the Light Appears" (Lento). [AmerPoR] (23:3) My-Je 94, p. 3.
"Who Eats Who?" [AmerPoR] (23:3) My-Je 94, p. 4.
"Yiddishe Kopf." [AmerPoR] (23:3) My-Je 94, p. 4.
2217. GIOIA, Dana
"Descent to the Underworld" (translation taken from Act III of Seneca's *Hercules Furens*). [Image] (3) Spr 93, p. 13-15.
"Hercules Conquers the Underworld" (Choral Ode from the tragedy *Hercules Furens*, tr. of Seneca). [CarolQ] (46:2) Wint 94, p. 76-77.
2218. GIOSEFFI, Daniela
"Ah, Autumn Garden" (tr. of Fina García Marruz, w. Noemi Escandell). [CaribbeanW] (8) 94, p. 91-92.

"Cities" (tr. of Pablo Armando Fernandez, w. Enildo Garcia). [Vis] (46) 94, p. 23.
"Farewell" (tr. of Fina García Marruz, w. Noemi Escandell). [CaribbeanW] (8) 94, p. 93.
"I Want to See" (tr. of Fina García Marruz, w. Noemi Escandell). [CaribbeanW] (8) 94, p. 91.
"Is It I Who Sheds — ?" (tr. of Fina García Marruz, w. Noemi Escandell). [CaribbeanW] (8) 94, p. 94.
"Longing to Go Out" (tr. of Fina García Marruz, w. Noemi Escandell). [CaribbeanW] (8) 94, p. 93-94.
"On the Small Table" (tr. of Fina García Marruz, w. Noemi Escandell). [CaribbeanW] (8) 94, p. 90.
"A Sweet Snow Falls" (From *Lost Glances*, tr. of Fina García Marruz, w. Noemi Escandell). [CaribbeanW] (8) 94, p. 92.

2219. GIOVANNI, Nikki
"November." [Elf] (4:3) Fall 94, p. 19.
"A Poem (For Langston Hughes)." [Elf] (4:3) Fall 94, p. 20.

2220. GIPPS, Marina Pilar
"Price." [MoodySI] (28, also labeled 29) Fall 94, p. 26.

2221. GITZEN, Julian
"Created for the Night." [CapeR] (29:2) Fall 94, p. 26.
"A Man of Several Homes." [NegC] (14:1/2) 94, p. 68.
"Why Frugal Farm Women Need Patience." [NegC] (14:1/2) 94, p. 69.

2222. GIZZI, Michael
"Too Big Canader: A Travelogue" (for Christopher Dewdney). [Agni] (40) 94, p. 138-141.

2223. GIZZI, Peter
"Imitation of Life." [RiverC] (14:2) Spr 94, p. 43-45.
"On the Condition of the Father in Ayres: A Masque" (Selections: 13 poems). [Avec] (8:1) 94, p. 68-76.

2224. GLADDING, Jody
"Asparagus." [YaleR] (82:2) Ap 94, p. 72.
"Winter Walk." [WestB] (34) 94, p. 91.

2225. GLADE, Jon Forrest
"The Bull Riders' Lover." [Pearl] (20) Spr 94, p. 62.

2226. GLADHART, Amalia
"Remains." [SouthernPR] (34:2) Wint 94, p. 63-64.

2227. GLADUN, Chris
"Kitsch." [Writ] (26) 94, p. 15.
"Lullaby." [Writ] (26) 94, p. 18-19.
"Run Silent Run Deep." [Writ] (26) 94, p. 16-17.
"Sad." [Writ] (26) 94, p. 12-14.

2228. GLANCY, Diane
"*Concerto for Piano and Orchestra*, Aram Khachaturian, Tucson Symphony Orchestra." [Journal] (18:1) Spr-Sum 94, p. 68.
"I Hear a Medicine Man." [Callaloo] (17:1) Wint 94, p. 250.
"*I raro te Oviri* (Under the Pandanus)" (— Paul Gauguin). [IndR] (17:1) Spr 94, p. 14.
"If I Were to Tell a Story." [Callaloo] (17:1) Wint 94, p. 249.
"Minimal Indian." [Ploughs] (20:1) Spr 94, p. 56-66.
"Pele." [IndR] (17:1) Spr 94, p. 13.
"Pow Wow Pipes." [IndR] (17:1) Spr 94, p. 12.
"Rejoining the Tongue." [IndR] (17:1) Spr 94, p. 10-11.
"There's a Story." [NewL] (60:4) 94, p. 199.

2229. GLANCY, Gabrielle
"At the Equator." [ColR] (21:2) Fall 94, p. 163-164.
"Martha." [ColR] (21:2) Fall 94, p. 162.

2230. GLASER, Elton
"After Bonnard." [PoetryNW] (35:4) Wint 94-95, p. 23.
"Bifocal." [Border] (4) Spr-Sum 94, p. 39.
"Box Elder." [SouthernHR] (28:3) Sum 94, p. 275.
"Ibrahim and Ahmed." [LaurelR] (28:2) Sum 94, p. 87-88.
"Eine Kleine Nachtmusik." [GeoR] (48:3) Fall 94, p. 472-473.
"Posies for a Late Valentine." [LaurelR] (28:2) Sum 94, p. 89.
"Purge." [LaurelR] (28:2) Sum 94, p. 86-87.
"Regenerate Shores." [GettyR] (7:3) Sum 94, p. 477-479.
"Slum Hisself, Mouth Open." [CreamCR] (18:1) Spr 94, p. 88-89.

"Undead White European Male" (for Charles Simic). [GettyR] (7:3) Sum 94, p. 480-482.
"Without Permission." [Pivot] (41) 93, p. 42.

2231. GLASS, Jesse, Jr.
"Gnostic Doll." [Confr] (52/53) Wint-Spr 94, p. 310.

2232. GLASS, Malcolm
"Mornings" (for Julie Chandler). [PoetC] (26:1) Fall 94, p. 27.
"Wings of the Owl." [PoetC] (26:1) Fall 94, p. 28.

2233. GLASSER, Jane Ellen
"At the End of Down." [Kalliope] (16:3) 94, p. 16.

2234. GLASSER, Marvin
"On the Elements." [Parting] (7:2) Wint 94-95, p. 14.
"Something Else." [Parting] (7:2) Wint 94-95, p. 13.

2235. GLAZE, Andrew
"Light Boat." [Pivot] (42) 94, p. 16.
"Old Clerks." [Pivot] (41) 93, p. 5.
"What Are We, Stars?" [Pivot] (42) 94, p. 16.

2236. GLAZER, Michele
"Boar Baroque." [Field] (51) Fall 94, p. 73-74.
"Corkscrew: A Short History of a Short Relationship." [ColR] (21:1) Spr 94, p. 97-99.
"The Purpose of Design Is to Make the Whole Greater Than the Sum of Its Parts." [ColR] (21:1) Spr 94, p. 95-96.
"Real Life #2: Scraps." [Ploughs] (20:4) Wint 94-95, p. 72.
"Star-Spangled." [ColR] (21:1) Spr 94, p. 100-102.
"Variations on a Fixed Target." [AmerLC] (6) 94, p. 94-96.

2237. GLAZIER, Loss Pequeño
"Octave(Accord)" (Excerpt). [Os] (39) Fall-Wint 94, p. 3.

2238. GLAZIER, Lyle
"Searching for Amy" (Selections: III-IV). [ShadowP] (4) 94, p. 42-61.

2239. GLAZNER, Greg
"December of Minutes." [QW] (39) Sum-Fall 94, p. 203.
"Untitled: How do you approach the two bowls of milk." [QW] (39) Sum-Fall 94, p. 204.

2240. GLOEGGLER, Tony
"Rain Poem." [NewYorkQ] (53) 94, p. 94.

2241. GLOVER, Beaird
"Loving You." [NewYorkQ] (53) 94, p. 82.

2242. GLÜCK, Louise
"Mock Orange." [AmerPoR] (23:2) Mr-Ap 94, p. 31.
"Symposium." [Antaeus] (75/76) Aut 94, p. 258.

2243. GODDARD, Linda M.
"Penny's Sink." [Kalliope] (16:1) 94, p. 57.

2244. GODDEN, Richard
"The Condition of England, 1979-1991." [NewOR] (20:3/4) Fall-Wint 94, p. 145-146.
"Losing It." [NewOR] (20:3/4) Fall-Wint 94, p. 147.
"Shoah" (to those killed in the Warsaw Ghetto Uprising, April-May, 1943). [NewOR] (20:3/4) Fall-Wint 94, p. 148-149.

2245. GODOY, Iliana
"Lente Púrpura." [Nuez] (5:13/14/15) 94, p. 43.
"Morada." [Nuez] (5:13/14/15) 94, p. 43.
"Umbrales." [Nuez] (5:13/14/15) 94, p. 43.

2246. GODWIN-JACKSON, Betty J.
"Why Johnny Can't." [Obs] (9:2) Fall-Wint 94, p. 78-80.

2247. GOEDICKE, Patricia
"Cousins." [Ploughs] (20:1) Spr 94, p. 172-174.
"In the Long Run Like Governments." [TriQ] (91) Fall 94, p. 230-232.
"Private / Property." [WestB] (35) 94, p. 54-55.
"Stop the World." [KenR] (NS 16:4) Fall 94, p. 6-8.
"Stream." [Hudson] (47:1) Spr 94, p. 85-86.
"What Love Does ('With Tear-Floods and Sigh-Tempests')." [TriQ] (91) Fall 94, p. 233-237.

2248. GOEL, Edith
"Poema I." [Nuez] (5:13/14/15) 94, p. 39.
"Poema II." [Nuez] (5:13/14/15) 94, p. 39.

2249. GOERNER, Leslie
"Before the Cart." [BellArk] (10:6) N-D 94, p. 12.
"Campfire Song." [BellArk] (10:6) N-D 94, p. 12.
"The Life of Light" (Selections: 4 poems). [BellArk] (10:5) S-O 94, p. 22.
"Lost and Found." [BellArk] (10:6) N-D 94, p. 30.
"Prospect." [BellArk] (10:6) N-D 94, p. 12.
"Sifting Through." [BellArk] (10:6) N-D 94, p. 12.
"Somewhere Love Discovers." [BellArk] (10:6) N-D 94, p. 12.
"Tide Journal." [BellArk] (10:1) Ja-F 94, p. 26-27.
"Vigil." [BellArk] (10:6) N-D 94, p. 12.
2250. GOETSCH, Douglas
"Colorblind." [HangL] (64) 94, p. 44.
"Father's Day, 1993." [HangL] (64) 94, p. 47.
"Folds." [HangL] (64) 94, p. 45.
"Foul Shots." [Ledge] (17) Wint 94, p. 86.
"Haikus" (2 poems). [Ledge] (17) Wint 94, p. 87.
"Mrs. Britt's." [HangL] (64) 94, p. 46.
"Three Blind Dates." [Ledge] (17) Wint 94, p. 88-89.
2251. GOETT, Lise
"1933." [ParisR] (36:133) Wint 94, p. 123-124.
"After Twenty Years of Marriage." [ParisR] (36:133) Wint 94, p. 125.
"Conversion." [ParisR] (36:133) Wint 94, p. 126-127.
"Donna de Casa." [Colum] (21) Fall 93, p. 51-52.
2252. GOFF, Madeline
"The Boy Next Door." [RagMag] (12:1) Sum 94, p. 94.
"Cinquains." [RagMag] (12:1) Sum 94, p. 95.
"Ellipses." [RagMag] (12:1) Sum 94, p. 96.
2253. GOFF, Paula
"Groundhog, Shadow Speaking." [SoCaR] (26:2) Spr 94, p. 8.
"Our Lady of Office Supply." [SoCaR] (26:2) Spr 94, p. 8.
GOH, Poh Seng
See SENG, Goh Poh
2254. GOHURRY, John
"Prelude." [Verse] (11:1) Spr 94, p. 52.
2255. GOLAY, Michael K.
"On Deck." [Amelia] (7:4, #23) 94, p. 63.
2256. GOLDBARTH, Albert
"Art History." [PoetryNW] (35:4) Wint 94-95, p. 38-39.
"Away." [Poetry] (164:6) S 94, p. 343-344.
"A Blank Wide Face." [WestHR] (48:2) Sum 94, p. 125-127.
"The Book of Human Anomalies" (based on Mark Sloan's *Hoaxes, Humbugs and Spectacles*). [LaurelR] (28:2) Sum 94, p. 66-67.
"Cheese." [ColR] (21:1) Spr 94, p. 175-179.
"Cityscape." [Witness] (8:2) 94, p. 115.
"Contest! Name the Crayon Colors!" [CreamCR] (18:1) Spr 94, p. 84-85.
"Even, Equal." [CreamCR] (18:1) Spr 94, p. 83.
"Fantasy Toy." [ChiR] (40:2/3) 94, p. 15-24.
"Forever Half-Done." [Colum] ("The Lost Issues", [i.e. 18-19]) 93, p. 155-156.
"'Here' and 'There'." [AmerLC] (6) 94, p. 101-106.
"In Praise of Bathos." [OntR] (40) Spr-Sum 94, p. 59-60.
"On the Level." [IllinoisR] (2:1) Fall 94, p. 23.
"Proportion." [CreamCR] (18:1) Spr 94, p. 82.
"Raisings." [PoetryNW] (35:4) Wint 94-95, p. 38.
"Saying." [IllinoisR] (2:1) Fall 94, p. 24.
"Song: Doubt and Limitation." [PoetryNW] (35:1) Spr 94, p. 30-31.
"Spring Nights." [LaurelR] (28:2) Sum 94, p. 64-65.
"A Still Life, Symbolic of Lines." [SouthwR] (79:4) Aut 94, p. 680-682.
"The Two Domains: In Several Voices" (Chapbook 21). [BelPoJ] (44:3) Spr 94, p. 1-46.
"The Undergrain / My Father." [PoetryNW] (35:1) Spr 94, p. 29-30.
"What the Poem Is Actually About." [BlackWR] (21:1) Fall-Wint 94, p. 123-129.
"Y'Call Someplace Paradise, Kiss It Goodbye" (— The Eagles, "The Last Resort"). [Poetry] (164:6) S 94, p. 345-346.
2257. GOLDBERG, Barbara
"Anti-Abstract Poem" (tr. of Moshe Dor). [PraS] (68:1) Spr 94, p. 31.
"Balance of Power" (tr. of Moshe Dor). [WebR] (18) Fall 94, p. 8.

"Bruise" (tr. of Moshe Dor). [PraS] (68:1) Spr 94, p. 31-32.
"In Your Absence." [HarvardR] (6) Spr 94, p. 114.
"Shelter" (tr. of Moshe Dor). [WebR] (18) Fall 94, p. 7.
"The Silence of the Builder" (tr. of Moshe Dor, w. the author). [HarvardR] (7) Fall 94, p. 35.

2258. GOLDBERG, Beckian Fritz
"Being Pharaoh." [Field] (50) Spr 94, p. 16-19.
"How Many Live Here." [Pivot] (41) 93, p. 10.
"In the Gardenia." [GreenMR] (NS 17:2) Fall-Wint 94-95, p. 11.
"The Lying Childhood." [GreenMR] (NS 17:2) Fall-Wint 94-95, p. 9-10.
"Multiple Adam." [PoetryNW] (35:3) Aut 94, p. 10.
"My Mouth." [Pivot] (41) 93, p. 9.
"The Painted Adam." [Iowa] (24:1) Wint 94, p. 108.
"Sometimes White." [Sonora] (28) Fall 94, p. 3-4.
"The Weight." [PassN] (15:1) Sum 94, p. 8-10.
"Whitman's Confession: In the Cleft of Eternity." [WestHR] (48:1) Spr 94, p. 62-63.

2259. GOLDBERG, Susan J.
"Summer 1985." [EngJ] (83:7) N 94, p. 30.

2260. GOLDENSOHN, Barry
"Arch of Titus." [Poetry] (165:2) N 94, p. 92.
"Before Beethoven's Creation of Music As Personal Expression" (A vigil for Lorrie). [Poetry] (165:1) O 94, p. 25.
"Law and Sensibility." [Poetry] (165:2) N 94, p. 91.

2261. GOLDENSOHN, Lorrie
"I Did Speak of Some Distressful Stroke." [Salm] (104/105) Fall 94-Wint 95, p. 177-179.

2262. GOLDFARB, David
"June 8 Vision." [SenR] (24:1) Spr 94, p. 69.

2263. GOLDMAN, Barbara
"Boat Scene" (tr. of Paul Eluard, w. Richard Jones). [PoetryE] (37/38) Spr 94, p. 217.
"Fish" (tr. of Paul Eluard, w. Richard Jones). [PoetryE] (37/38) Spr 94, p. 220.
"The Law" (tr. of Paul Eluard, w. Richard Jones). [PoetryE] (37/38) Spr 94, p. 218.
"Of One and of Two, of All" (tr. of Paul Eluard, w. Richard Jones). [PoetryE] (37/38) Spr 94, p. 219.
"So Many Dreams in the Air" (tr. of Paul Eluard, w. Richard Jones). [PoetryE] (37/38) Spr 94, p. 221.
"The Two of Us" (tr. of Paul Eluard, w. Richard Jones). [PoetryE] (37/38) Spr 94, p. 216.

2264. GOLDMAN, Judith
"Renga" (February 9, 1994, Chinese New Year's Eve, w. Lee Ann Brown, Lisa Jarnot, and Sianne Ngai). [Chain] (1) Spr-Sum 94, p. 197-199.

2265. GOLDMAN, Judy
"Pantoum for the Children, So They Will Know Yiddish." [KenR] (NS 16:2) Spr 94, p. 21-22.
"Sestina Edged in Odds." [OhioR] (52) 94, p. 35-36.

2266. GOLDMAN, Paula
"Almost a Love Poem." [PoetL] (89:4) Wint 94-95, p. 25-26.
"Michelangelo's Last Pietà (1475-1564)." [CreamCR] (18:1) Spr 94, p. 35.
"O'Keeffe's Black Door." [CreamCR] (18:1) Spr 94, p. 36.

2267. GOLDSMITH, Ellen
"Chelsea Foods." [SingHM] (21) 94, p. 38.

2268. GOLDSTEIN, Laurence
"Permissive Entry: A Sermon on Fame." [TampaR] (8) Spr 94, p. 22-23.
"The Sports Complex." [MichQR] (33:1) Wint 94, p. 146-147.

2269. GOLDTHWAITE, Melissa A.
"The Wedding Ring." [ChrC] (111:3) 26 Ja 94, p. 68.

2270. GOLIARD, Peter
"Eat, Drink." [Light] (11) Aut 94, p. 11.
"A Frivolous Ditty of Dewlaps and Furbelows." [Light] (9) Spr 94, p. 15.

2271. GOLL, Yvan
"The Gardener" (tr. by J. Kates). [PoetryE] (37/38) Spr 94, p. 214.
"Intimate Hurts" (tr. by J. Kates). [PoetryE] (37/38) Spr 94, p. 211.
"Song of the Civilized" (tr. by J. Kates). [PoetryE] (37/38) Spr 94, p. 213.
"Washing the Dead" (tr. by J. Kates). [PoetryE] (37/38) Spr 94, p. 212.

2272. GOMEZ, Lang
"Being With You" (tr. of Luzmarina Acosta, w. Preston Browning). [LitR] (37:4) Sum 94, p. 580.
2273. GOMPERT, Chris
"Sailing to My Lai." [TarRP] (34:1) Fall 94, p. 3.
2274. GONCALVES, Egito
"Dedikation" (Selections from the poem-cycle: #4, #8, tr. by Alexis Levitin). [ArtfulD] (26/27) 94, p. 50-51.
"Dedikation" (Selection: #9, tr. by Alexis Levitin). [ConnPR] (13:1) 94, p. 26.
2275. GONDICAS, Dimitri
"The Ships" (tr. of C. P. Cavafy, w. Edmund Keeley). [Antaeus] (75/76) Aut 94, p. 247-249.
2276. GONET, Jill
"Immune Deficiency." [RiverS] (40) 94, p. 24.
"Simulacra." [RiverS] (40) 94, p. 23.
2277. GONZALEZ, Angel
"First Evocation" (tr. by Steven Ford Brown). [InterQ] (1:1) [93?], p. 154-155.
"My Profound Vocation" (tr. by Steven Ford Brown and Moira Perez). [InterQ] (1:1) [93?], p. 153.
"This Moment" (tr. by Steven Ford Brown). [MidAR] (14:2) 94, p. 136-137.
2278. GONZALEZ, Jane
"At the Dressing Table." [SmPd] (31:3, #92) Fall 94, p. 14.
2279. GONZALEZ, Rafael Jesus
"The Consecration of Coffee" (For Archbishop Oscar A. Romero). [Vis] (44) 94, p. 29.
"Rune." [Vis] (44) 94, p. 28.
2280. GONZALEZ, Ray
"Fifty Years." [PraS] (68:4) Wint 94, p. 26.
"Four Poems to Survive the Next Century." [PraS] (68:4) Wint 94, p. 27-29.
"The Grandfather." [PraS] (68:4) Wint 94, p. 22.
"Three Snakes, Strawberry Canyon, Berkeley" (for Phil Woods). [PraS] (68:4) Wint 94, p. 22-23.
"Twelve Thousand Clay Bowls, Twelve Million Fossils." [PraS] (68:4) Wint 94, p. 25.
"Without Sorrow." [PraS] (68:4) Wint 94, p. 24.
2281. GONZALEZ CAMARGO, Joaquín
"Estudiando" (Fragmento). [NewRena] (9:1, #27) 94, p. 38.
"Study" (Fragment, tr. by Joe Bolton). [NewRena] (9:1, #27) 94, p. 39.
2282. GONZALEZ MARTINEZ, Enrique
"El Jardin Que Sueña" (A José Vasconcelos). [NewRena] (9:1, #27) 94, p. 34.
"The Sleeping Garden" (To Jose Vasconcelos, tr. by Joe Bolton). [NewRena] (9:1, #27) 94, p. 35.
2283. GONZALEZ-T., César A.
"Más — Allá." [PraS] (68:4) Wint 94, p. 173-176.
2284. GOOBIE, Beth
"Permission" (Grain Contest Winners, Prose Poem: First). [Grain] (21:4) Spr 94, p. 14-15.
"What They Could Tell Me." [MalR] (106) Spr 94, p. 77-79.
2285. GOODAN, Kevin
"Something Like Blood." [CutB] (41) Wint 94, p. 32.
GOODEN, Denise Gray
See GRAY-GOODEN, Denise
2286. GOODIN, Thom
"What the Fisherman Told Me." [CapeR] (29:1) Spr 94, p. 11.
2287. GOODMAN, Brent
"Garlic." [TampaR] (9) Fall 94, p. 66.
2288. GOODMAN, Joanna
"Blue Sky" (tr. of Assia Djebar). [DenQ] (29:1) Sum 94, p. 56.
"The Dry Spell." [MassR] (35:1) Spr 94, p. 26.
"What Brought Them There." [IndR] (17:2) Fall 94, p. 21.
2289. GOODMAN, Miriam
"Dreaming of Sex in Atlanta." [HarvardR] (Premier Issue) Spr 92, p. 84.
2290. GOODMAN, Ryah Tumarkin
"Against Each Other." [Amelia] (7:4, #23) 94, p. 71.
2291. GOODWIN, Leigh Clifton
"Boulangerie." [CrabCR] (8:2/3/9:1/2/3) 94, p. 22.

2292. GOODWIN, Norman
"The Politics of Innocence." [Jacaranda] (10) 94, p. 43.
"The Rendering Van." [Jacaranda] (10) 94, p. 44-45.

GOOSE, Mother
See ANONYMOUS (Mother Goose)

2293. GORDON, Carol
"Bundy." [CrabCR] (8:2/3/9:1/2/3) 94, p. 44.
"Message Home" (Centrum Writers' Conference, 1984). [CrabCR] (8:2/3/9:1/2/3) 94, p. 23.

2294. GORDON, David
"Autumn Lift" (tr. of Lu Yu). [WorldL] (5) 94, p. 17.
"In Twin Clear Hall, a Night Piece" (tr. of Lu Yu). [WorldL] (5) 94, p. 19.
"Neighbor Without Food Being Taken to the Outskirts: Pitying Him I Wrote This" (tr. of Lu Yu). [WorldL] (5) 94, p. 18.

2295. GORDON, Kirpal
"When All Else Fails." [HeavenB] (11) 94, p. 78-79.

2296. GORDON, Mary
"A Reading Problem." [GlobalCR] (4) Fall 94, p. 69-70.

2297. GORDON, Maureen
"Mussels." [MalR] (109) Wint 94, p. 76.

2298. GORDON, Myles
"The Meeting." [ChangingM] (27) Wint 94, p. 45.
"Mother and Daughter." [ChironR] (13:2) Sum 94, p. 19.

2299. GORDON, Ricia
"Dragonflies." [NewEngR] (16:2) Spr 94, p. 71.

2300. GORDON, Robert
"Between Dog and Wolf." [WritersF] (20) 94, p. 29.
"Black Drake, Jangling and Waiting for the Messiah." [WritersF] (20) 94, p. 28.
"Clouded Crystal Ball." [SoCoast] (16) Ja 94, p. 29.

2301. GORDON, Sarah
"Deposits." [ApalQ] (40/41) 94, p. 82-83.

2302. GORMAN, John
"A Good Boy from the 1950s." [LaurelR] (28:1) Wint 94, p. 23.

2303. GORST, Norma W.
"A Gift of Horses" (for H.M.G.). [BambooR] (63/64) Sum-Fall 94, p. 14-15.

2304. GORST, Norma Wunderlich
"Castle Mnemonic." [ChamLR] (14/15) Spr-Fall 94, p. 8-9.
"Plover in August." [ChamLR] (14/15) Spr-Fall 94, p. 10-11.

GORY, Michael la
See LaGORY, Michael

2305. GOSNELL, W. C.
"Answer" (for Janet). [NegC] (14:1/2) 94, p. 42.

2306. GOSVAMIN, Rupa
"3.36 Young Maiden" (from the 16th c. Sanskrit treatise *Blazing Sapphire*, tr. by Neal Delmonico and Elizabeth Otten). [WebR] (18) Fall 94, p. 37.
"4.35 Bashful Radha" (from the 16th c. Sanskrit treatise *Blazing Sapphire*, tr. by Neal Delmonico and Elizabeth Otten). [WebR] (18) Fall 94, p. 37.

2307. GOTO, Hiromi
"The Body Politic." [WestCL] (28:1/2, #13/14) Spr-Fall 94, p. 218-221.

2308. GOTTESMAN, Carl A.
"The Bishop's Dream. The Lady in Flames." [SoCaR] (27:1/2) Fall 94-Spr 95, p. 1-2.

2309. GOTTLIEB, Arthur G.
"Hearts." [Ledge] (17) Wint 94, p. 8-9.
"Social Intercourse." [Ledge] (17) Wint 94, p. 7.
"Work Force." [Ledge] (17) Wint 94, p. 10-11.

2310. GOUDE, Gary
"1969." [WormR] (34:4, #136) 94, p. 149.
"Factory Life." [WormR] (34:4, #136) 94, p. 149.
"Making Things." [WormR] (34:4, #136) 94, p. 149-150.
"My Bitch." [WormR] (34:4, #136) 94, p. 150.
"Working Class." [WormR] (34:4, #136) 94, p. 150.

2311. GOULD, C. E., Jr.
"Post Script." [Light] (10) Sum 94, p. 22.
"Sheep Up or Cheep Out." [Light] (10) Sum 94, p. 22.

2312. GOULD, Charles E., Jr.
"Recipe." [Light] (12) Wint 94-95, p. 9.
2313. GOULD, Janice
"I Learn a Simple Lesson About Our Society." [Callaloo] (17:1) Wint 94, p. 105-107.
2314. GOUMAS, Yannis
"Ascent" (tr. of Alexándra Plastíra). [Os] (38) Spr 94, p. 12.
"Endowment" (tr. of Alexándra Plastíra). [Os] (38) Spr 94, p. 13.
"The Lord's Day" (tr. of Alexándra Plastíra). [Os] (38) Spr 94, p. 11.
2315. GOYETTE, Susan
"For Robyn." [PoetryC] (15:1) N 94, p. 16.
"For the Unrejoiced." [PoetryC] (15:1) N 94, p. 16.
"October." [PoetryC] (15:1) N 94, p. 16.
"Ryan." [PoetryC] (15:1) N 94, p. 16.
"The True Names of Birds." [PoetryC] (15:1) N 94, p. 16.
2316. GOYTISOLO, Juan
"The Marx Family Saga" (Excerpt, tr. by Peter Bush). [Conjunc] (23) 94, p. 150-165.
2317. GRABILL, James
"Suddenly Tonight I Am Listening." [WillowS] (34) Sum 94, p. 29.
2318. GRAF, Nico
"Spain" (tr. by W. Martin). [ArtfulD] (26/27) 94, p. 16-20.
2319. GRAF, Ted
"What He Said to Me Without Speaking." [NewEngR] (16:4) Fall 94, p. 109.
2320. GRAFFEO, Ignatius
"Hard Copy." [CoalC] (8) Ap 94, p. 31.
2321. GRAHAM, Adelle
"The Entry Into." [ChironR] (13:3) Aut 94, p. 24.
2322. GRAHAM, David
"Accidental Blessings." [SycamoreR] (6:2) Sum 94, p. 32.
"Flyway." [PraS] (68:2) Sum 94, p. 62-64.
"July Wind." [PraS] (68:2) Sum 94, p. 61.
"Posters the Sun Is Erasing." [SycamoreR] (6:2) Sum 94, p. 33.
"This Old Man." [SycamoreR] (6:2) Sum 94, p. 30-31.
"Tricky Fingers." [Pivot] (42) 94, p. 42.
2323. GRAHAM, Desmond
"The Accompanist." [AntigR] (98) Sum 94, p. 53.
"Budapest (April 1992)" (for Kunos Laszlo). [AntigR] (98) Sum 94, p. 51-52.
"For Milena" (aged two). [AntigR] (98) Sum 94, p. 54.
"The Liebestod Poems." [AntigR] (98) Sum 94, p. 55.
"Lupins." [Quarry] (42:4) Mr 94, p. 118.
"The Ninth Month" (December 1990). [Quarry] (42:4) Mr 94, p. 116-117.
2324. GRAHAM, Jorie
"Against Eloquence." [SenR] (24:2) Fall 94, p. 20-21.
"Flood." [Antaeus] (75/76) Aut 94, p. 259-264.
"In Hidden Place So Let My Days Forth Pass." [SenR] (24:2) Fall 94, p. 26-27.
"Indeterminacy: A Quartet." [HarvardR] (2) Fall 92, p. 6-13.
"The Turning." [SenR] (24:2) Fall 94, p. 22-25.
2325. GRAHAM, Neile
"The Game of Cards." [PoetL] (89:1) Spr 94, p. 16.
"Loving the Green Man" (for Bette). [PoetL] (89:1) Spr 94, p. 15.
2326. GRAHAM, Taylor
"Afraid of Flying." [PaintedHR] (11) Spr-Sum 94, p. 44.
"Improvisation." [CoalC] (8) Ap 94, p. 5.
"In Her Sleep." [Amelia] (7:3, #22) 94, p. 158.
"The Pin Widow." [Ascent] (18:3) Spr 94, p. 45.
"Since the Fire." [CoalC] (8) Ap 94, p. 5.
2327. GRANDE, Félix
"La Persistencia del Imperio." [Nuez] (5:13/14/15) 94, p. 69-70.
2328. GRANT, Monica
"Think of It This Way, My Dears." [Event] (23:2) Sum 94, p. 20.
2329. GRANT, Paul
"Crossroads" (Blues for the Seven Simeons). [SoCaR] (26:2) Spr 94, p. 180-181.
"Shaggy Dog Sonnet." [Hellas] (5:1) Spr-Sum 94, p. 71.
"The Star Chamber." [HiramPoR] (57) Fall 94-Wint 95, p. 24.
"The Territories." [SoDakR] (32:1) Spr 94, p. 102.

2330. GRAPES, Jack
"Break Down." [ChatR] (14:2) Wint 94, p. 28.
"The Lost Things." [CreamCR] (18:2) Fall 94, p. 116-117.
2331. GRAVES, Michael
"A Graceful Celebrant." [HolCrit] (31:4) O 94, p. 20.
"Persecution." [WritersF] (20) 94, p. 220.
2332. GRAVES, Steven
"Rains." [HarvardR] (2) Fall 92, p. 168-169.
2333. GRAVIS, Cheryl Lynne
"The Daughters of Lot" (Selection: "Older Daughter"). [Nimrod] (38:1) Fall-Wint 94, p. 115.
"Lefse" (for Tina). [Nimrod] (38:1) Fall-Wint 94, p. 117-118.
"Manumission." [Nimrod] (38:1) Fall-Wint 94, p. 116.
2334. GRAY, Douglas
"Falling Off from the Upper Ranges" (for Bob Canzoneri). [ChironR] (13:3) Aut 94, p. 31.
"Incidents after the Heartbreak." [ChironR] (13:3) Aut 94, p. 31.
"Peashooter." [NewDeltaR] (10:2) Spr-Sum 93, p. 52-53.
2335. GRAY, Janet
"Gayle's Valentine." [CentralP] (23) Spr 94, p. 114-115.
2336. GRAY, Mary
"Chameleon." [LitR] (37:4) Sum 94, p. 604.
"Offering." [WeberS] (11:3) Fall 94, p. 117.
"Simple." [WeberS] (11:3) Fall 94, p. 118.
2337. GRAY, Rich
"The last dance held in Troy." [Amelia] (7:4, #23) 94, p. 80.
2338. GRAY-GOODEN, Denise
"Dear Laureate." [CaribbeanW] (8) 94, p. 44.
2339. GRAYHURST, Allison
"It Is Not Like Hell." [CapeR] (29:2) Fall 94, p. 41.
2340. GREEN, Andrew
"To Denise Pelan." [EngJ] (83:6) O 94, p. 78.
GREEN, Carmen Rogers
See ROGERS-GREEN, Carmen
2341. GREEN, Daniel
"Lives of Poets" (After reading Larkin's Biography). [Outbr] (25) 94, p. 35.
"Pumper 1912." [Outbr] (25) 94, p. 33.
"Souvenirs." [Outbr] (25) 94, p. 34.
2342. GREEN, David H.
"Stretch Limerick." [Light] (10) Sum 94, p. 15.
2343. GREEN, Martin
"At Fort Benjamin Harrison, Indiana." [Amelia] (7:3, #22) 94, p. 73.
2344. GREEN, Paul Eliot
"Going Over on the *Talthybius*." [NoCarLR] (2:1) Spr 94, p. 39-40.
"Guard Duty at Camp Sevier (Waiting to Go Over)." [NoCarLR] (2:1) Spr 94, p. 37-38.
"In Picardy." [NoCarLR] (2:1) Spr 94, p. 37.
"In the Dark Night." [NoCarLR] (2:1) Spr 94, p. 41.
"The Making of a Bolshevist." [NoCarLR] (2:1) Spr 94, p. 42-43.
"Song of the Dead 'America First!'." [NoCarLR] (2:1) Spr 94, p. 45.
2345. GREEN, Pete
"Nightmare Session." [Border] (5) Fall-Wint 94, p. 22.
2346. GREEN, Peter
"Tristia III.3" (tr. of Ovid). [SouthernHR] (28:1) Wint 94, p. 42-44.
2347. GREEN, Samuel
"At the Pond's Edge." [Poetry] (164:5) Ag 94, p. 257.
"Fiddle Trees." [YellowS] (12:2, #46) Sum-Fall 94, p. 21.
"In a Borrowed House on the Mainland After the Blizzard." [YellowS] (12:2, #46) Sum-Fall 94, p. 21.
"You Ask Me About Birds and I Tell You." [YellowS] (12:2, #46) Sum-Fall 94, p. 21.
2348. GREENBAUM, Jessica
"Outside La Roque-Gageac." [SenR] (24:2) Fall 94, p. 40-41.
2349. GREENBERG, Alvin
"Against Dreaming" (Winner of the Chelsea Award for Poetry). [Chelsea] (56) 94, p. 14.

"The Cars of Young Men." [GreenMR] (NS 17:2) Fall-Wint 94-95, p. 26.
"The Corridors of Power." [MinnR] (41/42) Fall 93-Spr 94 (published Mr 95), p. 35.
"Crematorium." [TarRP] (33:2) Spr 94, p. 18.
"A Critique of the Theory of the Death of the Author." [GreenMR] (NS 17:2) Fall-Wint 94-95, p. 27.
"Equinox: 9/23, 7:10 a.m." [GreenMR] (NS 17:2) Fall-Wint 94-95, p. 25.
"Happiness" (2 october 1992. Winner of the Chelsea Award for Poetry). [Chelsea] (56) 94, p. 13.
"I Wish I Knew America Better" (Winner of the Chelsea Award for Poetry). [Chelsea] (56) 94, p. 8-9.
"A Loss for Words." [MinnR] (41/42) Fall 93-Spr 94 (published Mr 95), p. 34.
"Pleurisy." [WillowS] (34) Sum 94, p. 56.
"Quotidian" (Winner of the Chelsea Award for Poetry). [Chelsea] (56) 94, p. 12.
"The Search for a Unified Theory" (Winner of the Chelsea Award for Poetry). [Chelsea] (56) 94, p. 10-11.
"Some Days." [SantaBR] (1:2) Fall-Wint 93, p. 21.
"Something Amazing." [GettyR] (7:1) Wint 94, p. 130-131.
"Wintering Over at the End of the Century" (Winner of the Chelsea Award for Poetry). [Chelsea] (56) 94, p. 15-16.

2350. GREENBERG, Diana Lita
"You Wonder My Rage." [HangL] (65) 94, p. 93-94.

2351. GREENBERG, Pam
"Parable of the Fish" (A Plainsongs Award Poem). [Plain] (15:1) Fall 94, p. 20-21.

2352. GREENE, Jeffrey
"The Balance." [Boulevard] (9:1/2, #25/26) Spr 94, p. 201-202.
"Physics" (after Stephen Hawking). [Ploughs] (20:1) Spr 94, p. 97-98.

2353. GREENE, Renee
"Portrait of Jerry: A Love Poem." [PraS] (68:2) Sum 94, p. 101.
"Waterseal." [PraS] (68:2) Sum 94, p. 102.

2354. GREENE, Richard
"The Swimmers." [TickleAce] (28) Fall-Wint 94, p. 36.

2355. GREENE, Robin
"Liberty Clinic." [Farm] (11:1) Spr-Sum 94, p. 147.

2356. GREENHALGH, Chris
"Love Songs" (Selections: III, VII-VIII, XI, XIV, XVI-XVIII, XX). [Verse] (11:1) Spr 94, p. 34-36.
"Sin." [Verse] (11:1) Spr 94, p. 33.

2357. GREENHART, Susan
"Fighting." [AnthNEW] (6) 94, p. 17.

2358. GREENING, John
"Birch." [Stand] (36:1) Wint 94-95, p. 61.
"Rufus." [Verse] (11:1) Spr 94, p. 64.

2359. GREENLAW, Lavinia
"The Innocence of Radium." [Jacaranda] (10) 94, p. 134-135.

2360. GREENSLADE, David
"Pocket Guides." [ProseP] (3) 94, p. 43.
"Speak Up." [ProseP] (3) 94, p. 42.

2361. GREENWALD, Robert
"The Silent Ringmaster." [Kaleid] (Special Issue) 94, p. 34-35.

2362. GREENWALD, Roger
"A" (tr. of Pia Tafdrup). [Pequod] (38) 94, p. 50.
"Catullus 65" (tr. of Catullus). [Pequod] (37) 94, p. 65.
"De Profundis" (tr. of Pia Tafdrup). [Pequod] (38) 94, p. 54.
"Destination" (tr. of Pia Tafdrup). [Pequod] (38) 94, p. 57.
"Farther and Farther Away" (to a Writer, tr. of Tarjei Vesaas). [Pequod] (37) 94, p. 118.
"Frost Chord" (tr. of Pia Tafdrup). [Pequod] (38) 94, p. 51.
"Leaf-fall among Red Oaks in Maine" (tr. of Pia Tafdrup). [Pequod] (38) 94, p. 55.
"Lumière Cendrée" (tr. of Pia Tafdrup). [Pequod] (38) 94, p. 56.
"Shadow-figure" (tr. of Pia Tafdrup). [Pequod] (38) 94, p. 52.
"Tabernacles" (tr. of Pia Tafdrup). [Pequod] (38) 94, p. 53.

2363. GREENWAY, William
"Bayou." [SouthernPR] (34:2) Wint 94, p. 45-46.
"Beneath the Plaza of Illustrious Hombres." [Poetry] (164:6) S 94, p. 337-339.
"Depth of Field." [Parting] (7:2) Wint 94-95, p. 20.
"Dreams of the Blind Girl." [Poetry] (164:6) S 94, p. 340.

"Free Radicals." [CapeR] (29:2) Fall 94, p. 27.
"General Boot." [HiramPoR] (57) Fall 94-Wint 95, p. 25.
"Hands" (for Phil Brady). [PoetC] (25:2) Wint 94, p. 29.
"Mama." [SpoonR] (19:1) Wint-Spr 94, p. 98.
"Matthew, 1947-1992." [PoetC] (25:2) Wint 94, p. 27-28.
"Nineveh." [FloridaR] (19:2) 94, p. 24.
"One Owner." [Poetry] (165:2) N 94, p. 71.
"Progress." [Poetry] (163:4) Ja 94, p. 203-204.
"The Song of Calling Rain to Rain." [Parting] (7:2) Wint 94-95, p. 45.
"Tenderhooks." [PoetryNW] (35:1) Spr 94, p. 44-45.
"Them." [Poetry] (163:4) Ja 94, p. 202.
"Toothache." [Poetry] (165:1) O 94, p. 13.

2364. GREGA, Gina
"Intoxication." [BellArk] (10:3 [i.e. 10:4]) Jl-Ag 94, p. 10.

2365. GREGER, Debora
"The Body Translated into Heaven." [SouthwR] (79:1) Wint 94, p. 79-80.
"The Cloud of Unknowing" (Hanford, Nagasaki). [Poetry] (165:3) D 94, p. 141-142.
"The Dead of Summer." [NewRep] (211:14) 3 O 94, p. 34.
"The Desert Father: The Flagpole-Sitter." [Nat] (259:12) O 17 94, p. 431.
"The Dictionary of Silence." [Colum] ("The Lost Issues", [i.e. 18-19]) 93, p. 125-126.
"I Dinosauri di Venezia." [NewYorker] (70:3) 7 Mr 94, p. 46.
"Il Diluvio Universale (Particolare)." [SewanR] (102:4) Fall 94, p. 544-546.
"In the Eternal City." [Nat] (259:4) Jl 25-Ag 1 94, p. 138.
"Lives of the North American Martyrs." [Poetry] (165:3) D 94, p. 139-140.
"The Love of Ruins." [Nat] (259:14) O 31 94, p. 502.
"Psyche and Eros in Florida." [Poetry] (163:5) F 94, p. 262.
"Sacre Conversazioni." [Poetry] (165:3) D 94, p. 138-139.
"Ship Burial: Hanford, Washington." [Nat] (259:1) Jl 4 94, p. 30.
"The Twilight of England." [Poetry] (164:4) Jl 94, p. 200-201.
"The White Hands of Isolde." [Colum] ("The Lost Issues", [i.e. 18-19]) 93, p. 122-124.

2366. GREGERMAN, Debra
"The A Train." [AnotherCM] (27) 94, p. 57-58.
"Beyond Doubt." [LitR] (37:4) Sum 94, p. 601.
"Sonnet of One Head Clapping." [IndR] (17:1) Spr 94, p. 94.
"Triage." [IndR] (17:1) Spr 94, p. 95.
"Valentine." [IndR] (17:1) Spr 94, p. 96.

2367. GREGERSON, Linda
"Creation Myth" (Wheel-thrown stoneware, Richard DeVore). [ColR] (21:1) Spr 94, p. 180-185.
"Good News." [BostonR] (19:2) Ap-My 94, p. 14.
"Saints' Logic." [BostonR] (19:2) Ap-My 94, p. 14.
"Sold." [BostonR] (19:2) Ap-My 94, p. 14.

2368. GREGG, Linda
"Asking for Directions." [GettyR] (7:1) Wint 94, p. 48.
"Maybe Leave-Taking." [GettyR] (7:1) Wint 94, p. 47.

2369. GREGOR, Arthur
"Cycling in Autumn (Breteau-en Puisaye)." [CumbPR] (14:1) Fall 94, p. 24-25.
"Father and Son at Saint Benoit." [KenR] (NS 16:3) Sum 94, p. 126-127.
"Geraniums." [KenR] (NS 16:3) Sum 94, p. 125-126.
"Gesualdo." [CumbPR] (14:1) Fall 94, p. 22-23.
"In Conclusion." [KenR] (NS 16:3) Sum 94, p. 124.
"In This Tranquility" (For My Friends at Les Rabutteloires). [CumbPR] (14:1) Fall 94, p. 20-21.
"Memory Fragments." [Hudson] (47:2) Sum 94, p. 221-226.
"Memory Fragments" (2 selections: "Lazne Luhacovic," "Trivandrum"). [Pivot] (42) 94, p. 2-3.
"Memory Fragments" (Excerpts). [Interim] (13:1) Spr-Sum 94, p. 15.
"Mozart in Chatillon." [Hudson] (47:2) Sum 94, p. 220-221.
"Rachmaninoff's 'Symphonic Dances'." [Nat] (258:17) My 2 94, p. 607.
"Vespers." [Nat] (258:17) My 2 94, p. 607.

2370. GREGORIO, Renée
"The Other Voices." [HeavenB] (11) 94, p. 96.

2371. GREGORY, Michael
"The Larger Circles" (on the first anniversary of the Tiananmen Square massacre). [SouthernPR] (34:2) Wint 94, p. 30-31.

2372. GREGORY, Robert
"Charm Against Captain Poison & Captain Seafish." [Caliban] (14) 94, p. 134-135.

2373. GREGSON, Ian
"The Hawk at the Shrink." [Jacaranda] (5:1) Wint-Spr 91, p. 78-79.
"The Housekeeper Reflects on Her Employer." [Jacaranda] (4:2) Spr 90, p. 60-61.

2374. GRENNAN, Eamon
"30/4/93." [CarolQ] (46:3) Sum 94, p. 46-47.
"After a Death, a Walk in the Country." [Field] (50) Spr 94, p. 72-73.
"Ants." [Field] (50) Spr 94, p. 74.
"At the Falls." [AmerPoR] (23:6) N-D 94, p. 17.
"Bits of My Father." [Thrpny] (59) Fall 94, p. 26.
"Blaze." [Verse] (11:1) Spr 94, p. 75.
"Border Incident." [NewRep] (210:21) 23 My 94, p. 48.
"Cave and Awakening." [Vis] (45) 94, p. 7.
"Clearance." [SouthernHR] (28:1) Wint 94, p. 15.
"Correspondence." [Verse] (11:1) Spr 94, p. 76-77.
"Design." [Pivot] (42) 94, p. 32.
"Figures." [CarolQ] (46:3) Sum 94, p. 50.
"First of May." [Pivot] (42) 94, p. 31-32.
"From the Plane Window." [AmerPoR] (23:6) N-D 94, p. 16.
"Glasshouse and Prayer." [Shen] (44:1) Spr 94, p. 33.
"Raking." [Field] (50) Spr 94, p. 79.
"Robin." [Field] (50) Spr 94, p. 75-76.
"Roses." [CarolQ] (46:3) Sum 94, p. 48-49.
"Rough Art." [Shen] (44:1) Spr 94, p. 34-35.
"Sea Creatures." [SouthernHR] (28:3) Sum 94, p. 229.
"Somewhere in Ireland" (Early Spring 1991). [Vis] (45) 94, p. 6.
"Spring Fever." [NewYorker] (70:14) 23 My 94, p. 80.
"Swan in Winter." [Verse] (11:1) Spr 94, p. 72-75.
"These Northern Fields At Dusk" (Near Newbliss, Co. Monaghan). [AmerPoR] (23:6) N-D 94, p. 16.
"Towards Dusk the Porcupine." [Shen] (44:1) Spr 94, p. 36-37.
"Waiting Room." [Field] (50) Spr 94, p. 77-78.
"Women Going." [NewYorker] (70:36) 7 N 94, p. 198.

2375. GREY, John
"After So Many Years." [DogRR] (26) Wint 94-95, p. 16-17.
"Backyard Pool." [ProseP] (3) 94, p. 44.
"Bubbling Under" (Eyster Prize, Winner in Poetry). [NewDeltaR] (11:1) Fall 93-Wint 94, p. 1-2.
"Coffee House." [ChironR] (13:4) Wint 94, p. 11.
"Computers That Talk Back." [CapeR] (29:2) Fall 94, p. 49.
"Counting." [Outbr] (25) 94, p. 36.
"I Remember Jack." [HiramPoR] (55/56) Fall 93-Sum 94, p. 40.
"The Rain Opens Up Possibilities." [Parting] (7:2) Wint 94-95, p. 1.
"Snapshots." [Border] (5) Fall-Wint 94, p. 23.
"Soft Shell of Parting." [Outbr] (25) 94, p. 37.
"This Day Is Part of the Journey." [Amelia] (7:3, #22) 94, p. 60.
"Wave." [Parting] (7:2) Wint 94-95, p. 64.

2376. GREY, Lucinda
"In Either Tongue" (for Bernard). [PoetC] (26:1) Fall 94, p. 5-8.
"Reclaiming a Language." [TarRP] (33:2) Spr 94, p. 27.
"Trotsky, Coyoacán, 1937." [Wind] (74) 94, p. 20-21.

2377. GREYHAWK, Gregory
"Hill 239." [NewL] (61:1) 94, p. 98.

2378. GRICE, Gordon
"Echo." [Plain] (14:2) Wint 94, p. 30.
"Garden." [Plain] (14:3) Spr 94, p. 38.
"Hog Farmer." [Farm] (11:1) Spr-Sum 94, p. 148.
"Peter Kurten and the Swan." [Plain] (14:3) Spr 94, p. 33.
"Windfall." [Amelia] (7:4, #23) 94, p. 98.

2379. GRIEST-DEVORA, Barbara
"Positioning Kilims." [Border] (4) Spr-Sum 94, p. 40.

2380. GRIFFIN, Andrew Grimes
"Theme Song" (for Neil and Tony). [Arc] (32) Spr 94, p. 51.
2381. GRIFFIN, Gillie
"My Father Becomes a Chicken." [Quarry] (43:1) Je 94, p. 67-68.
2382. GRIFFIN, Shaun T.
"Magpie Funeral." [WritersF] (20) 94, p. 42.
"Wildflower." [WeberS] (11:3) Fall 94, p. 84.
2383. GRIFFIN, Susan
"Thicket" (a one act play). [KenR] (NS 16:2) Spr 94, p. 130-157.
2384. GRIFFIN, Walter
"The Descent." [DogRR] (26) Wint 94-95, p. 19.
"Dirt." [IndR] (17:2) Fall 94, p. 72.
2385. GRIFFITH, Gail
"One Day in Modesto." [Vis] (44) 94, p. 18.
2386. GRIFFITH, Jeri
"Window." [Border] (4) Spr-Sum 94, p. 41.
2387. GRIFFITH, Kevin
"Avoidance Behavior." [Pivot] (41) 93, p. 46.
"In the Forest of the Dead." [Pivot] (41) 93, p. 46.
"The MLA Waste Land." [MinnR] (41/42) Fall 93-Spr 94 (published Mr 95), p. 50-52.
"Reading in Bed." [PoetL] (89:4) Wint 94-95, p. 49.
2388. GRIGGS, Darrin
"A Man Plows His Field." [GreensboroR] (56) Sum 94, p. 3.
2389. GRILLO, Paul
"A Day Like Today." [Parting] (7:2) Wint 94-95, p. 49.
"The Hinterland of Lost Familiars" (for Garth Hudson). [Caliban] (14) 94, p. 128-129.
"Prime Time." [Parting] (7:2) Wint 94-95, p. 46.
2390. GRIM, Jessica
"Untitled (for Chain series)" (to Jean Day). [Chain] (1) Spr-Sum 94, p. 202-205.
2391. GRIMM, Reinhold
"Atmosphere of Departure" (Berlin, 1990, tr. of Hans Magnus Enzensberger). [NewL] (60:3) 94, p. 41.
"Consistency" (tr. of Hans Magnus Enzensberger). [NewL] (60:3) 94, p. 39.
"Desert Storm" (tr. of Volker Braun). [Pembroke] (26) 94, p. 138.
"Early November" (tr. of Ursula Krechel). [Pembroke] (26) 94, p. 134.
"From My Life History" (tr. of Guenter Kunert). [Pembroke] (26) 94, p. 139.
"The Hardware Store" (tr. of Hans Magnus Enzensberger). [NewL] (60:3) 94, p. 40.
"A Man before His Bookcase" (tr. of Walter Helmut Fritz). [Pembroke] (26) 94, p. 137.
"Manhattan Transfer" (tr. of Holger Teschke). [Pembroke] (26) 94, p. 135.
"Old Couples" (tr. of Hans Magnus Enzensberger). [NewL] (60:3) 94, p. 42.
"Rachel" (tr. of Wolfgang Baechler). [Pembroke] (26) 94, p. 133.
"Strange Attractor" (tr. of Hans Magnus Enzensberger). [Pembroke] (26) 94, p. 136.
"Two Marital Idyls" (tr. of Wolfgang Baechler). [Pembroke] (26) 94, p. 131-132.
2392. GRISHAM, Sam L.
"Blue." [ChatR] (14:2) Wint 94, p. 46.
2393. GRISWOLD, Jay
"Amphora." [SpoonR] (19:1) Wint-Spr 94, p. 36.
"Herons" (for Adrian Louis). [HayF] (14) Spr-Sum 94, p. 31-32.
"The Insomnia of Loneliness." [Elf] (4:1) Spr 94, p. 25.
"The Jogger" (for Randall Jarrell). [SouthernPR] (34:2) Wint 94, p. 68-69.
"Sleep." [SpoonR] (19:1) Wint-Spr 94, p. 37.
"Sunday." [ChamLR] (14/15) Spr-Fall 94, p. 161-162.
2394. GROGG, Charles
"Two Days Before Spring, Normal, Illinois." [WebR] (18) Fall 94, p. 102.
2395. GROLMES, Sam
"In the Place of Experience." [Talisman] (12) Spr 94, p. 96.
2396. GROSHOLZ, Emily
"Balloon." [Pivot] (41) 93, p. 48.
"The Great Blizzard" (January 1992). [Poetry] (165:3) D 94, p. 133-134.
"Variations on Rain, Moonlight, Nightingales, and the Incalculable." [TarRP] (34:1) Fall 94, p. 36-39.
"Watering." [NewL] (60:4) 94, p. 81.

2397. GROSS, Pamela
"Crow's Visit." [Journal] (18:1) Spr-Sum 94, p. 12.
"EKG: Heart, Resting." [Journal] (18:1) Spr-Sum 94, p. 13-14.
"Eyes of the Luna Moth." [Journal] (18:1) Spr-Sum 94, p. 11.
"Golden Oriole / *Yarrell's History of British Birds*." [Journal] (18:1) Spr-Sum 94, p. 15.
"Louisiana Accession, 1988" (collection obtained by the Burke Museum, University of Washington). [Journal] (18:1) Spr-Sum 94, p. 8-9.
"M44, From Messier's Album." [Journal] (18:1) Spr-Sum 94, p. 10.
2398. GROSS, Philip
"Figure in Landscape: China Clay." [Pivot] (42) 94, p. 54.
"Fillings." [Pivot] (42) 94, p. 53.
"A Guest of the Atlantic." [Stand] (35:2) Spr 94, p. 32-33.
2399. GROSSBERG, Benjamin Scott
"First Contact." [GreenMR] (NS 17:2) Fall-Wint 94-95, p. 91-92.
2400. GROSSMAN, Andrew
"A child's boot tracks." [DogRR] (13:1, #25) Spr-Sum 94, p. 35.
"Coming back." [DogRR] (13:1, #25) Spr-Sum 94, p. 33.
"Fastest way home." [DogRR] (13:1, #25) Spr-Sum 94, p. 33.
"Her hand in the lake." [DogRR] (13:1, #25) Spr-Sum 94, p. 33.
"Sound of a chainsaw." [DogRR] (13:1, #25) Spr-Sum 94, p. 35.
"Through stop signs." [DogRR] (13:1, #25) Spr-Sum 94, p. 33.
"With their graves here." [DogRR] (13:1, #25) Spr-Sum 94, p. 35.
2401. GROSSMAN, Rebekah
"Bathsheba." [Confr] (54/55) Fall 94-Wint 95, p. 289.
2402. GROVE, C. L.
"Arachnamor." [Light] (10) Sum 94, p. 16.
"The Legend of Arthur." [Light] (12) Wint 94-95, p. 21.
"Says Pat, on the shore of the Irish Sea" (Honorable Mention, Second Annual River Rhyme Competition). [Light] (9) Spr 94, p. 22.
"The Shark." [Light] (9) Spr 94, p. 19.
"When Cleopatra sailed the Nile." [Light] (10) Sum 94, p. 24.
2403. GROVER, Teji
"Song of Separation" (tr. by Arlene Zide and Aruna Sitesh, with the author). [InterQ] (1:2) 93, p. 190-191.
2404. GRUE, Lee Meitzen
"Naming the Hurricane." [NegC] (13:2/3) 93, p. 16-17.
2405. GRUENDING, Dennis
"Cauca Valley." [CanLit] (142/143) Fall-Wint 94, p. 97.
2406. GRUMMER, Greg
"Satan, Enlisting the Aid of a Pack of Dogs." [PlumR] (7) [94?], p. 38-39.
2407. GRÜNBEIN, Durs
"In Utero" (tr. by Christine Clayton and Douglas Clayton). [AnotherCM] (28) 94, p. 57.
"Insomnia" (tr. by Christine Clayton and Douglas Clayton). [AnotherCM] (28) 94, p. 58.
"Variations on No Theme" (Excerpt, tr. by Christine Clayton and Douglas Clayton). [AnotherCM] (28) 94, p. 59.
2408. GRYNIEWICZ, Eugene R.
"A Poem." [Elf] (4:1) Spr 94, p. 29.
"Survival." [WindO] (58) Sum 94, p. 34.
2409. GU, Cheng
"The City" (4 selections, tr. by Chen Yanbing, John Rosenwald and the Beloit/Fudan Translation Workshop). [Manoa] (6:1) Sum 94, p. 118-120.
2410. GUENTHER, Charles
"A Clan" (for John Osborne). [Light] (12) Wint 94-95, p. 19.
2411. GUENTHER, Gabriele
"The Bathroom Series" (based on a sequence of sketches by On Kawara at the Museum für Moderne Kunst in Frankfurt am Main). [MalR] (109) Wint 94, p. 56-57.
"Elsewhere." [MalR] (109) Wint 94, p. 58.
"In Brief." [AntR] (52:4) Fall 94, p. 610-611.
"Small Talk Cafe, Holland." [AntR] (52:4) Fall 94, p. 612.
2412. GUERIN, Bonnie
"Bath." [ChamLR] (14/15) Spr-Fall 94, p. 100-101.

2413. GUERNSEY, Bruce
"Epitaph." [AmerS] (63:4) Aut 94, p. 582.
2414. GUESS, Carol
"The Driven." [PoetryNW] (35:3) Aut 94, p. 29-30.
"Five." [PoetryNW] (35:3) Aut 94, p. 30.
2415. GUESS, S. Strand
"A Genius of Sorts." [BellR] (17:1/2) Spr-Fall 94, p. 48.
"Mozart's Swimming Lessons." [BellR] (17:1/2) Spr-Fall 94, p. 49-50.
2416. GUEST, Barbara
"Motion Pictures" (1-8). [AmerPoR] (23:1) Ja-F 94, p. 3-4.
"Ojjiba." [Conjunc] (22) 94, p. 76-80.
"Parachutes, My Love, Could Carry Us Higher." [AmerPoR] (23:2) Mr-Ap 94, p. 54.
2417. GUEVARA, Maurice Kilwein
"Eco." [PennR] (6:1) 94, p. 34.
"The Yellow Borges: An Answer to a Question." [PennR] (6:1) 94, p. 35.
2418. GUILFORD, Chuck
"In the Burnt Hills." [CrabCR] (8:2/3/9:1/2/3) 94, p. 144.
2419. GUILLÉN, Jorge
"Power of Pérez" (tr. by Cola Franzen). [GrahamHR] (18) Wint 94-95, p. 48-59.
2420. GUILLEVIC
"Pastorals" (Excerpt, tr. by Brooke Bergan). [PoetryE] (37/38) Spr 94, p. 231-232.
GUIN, Ursula K. le
See Le GUIN, Ursula K.
2421. GUINEE, Trudy
"Hyacinths." [SpoonR] (19:1) Wint-Spr 94, p. 43-44.
"My Mother's Wedding Dresss." [SpoonR] (19:1) Wint-Spr 94, p. 41-42.
"Trailmaker" (for my father). [AlabamaLR] (8:1) 94, p. 24-25.
2422. GUMERAID, Mairi Nic
"A' Bhean Impidh." [Verse] (11:2) Sum 94, p. 64.
"The Fairy Tale." [Verse] (11:2) Sum 94, p. 63.
"Mo Chota Sabainn." [Verse] (11:2) Sum 94, p. 65.
"My Sunday Coat." [Verse] (11:2) Sum 94, p. 66.
"Sgeul Nan Sithichean." [Verse] (11:2) Sum 94, p. 62.
"Woman of Persuasion." [Verse] (11:2) Sum 94, p. 64-65.
2423. GUMINA, Shirley
"Fly in Amber." [Light] (10) Sum 94, p. 10.
2424. GUNDY, Jeff
"How the Boy Jesus Resisted Taking Out the Trash." [LaurelR] (28:2) Sum 94, p. 49.
2425. GUNN, Genni
"A Certain Sea" (tr. of Lisa Carducci). [InterPR] (20:2) Fall 94, p. 37.
2426. GUNN, L. S.
"Keeping Score." [Vis] (44) 94, p. 11.
2427. GUNN, Mark
"The Altar in Saint Peter's Basilica" (Good Friday, 1993). [Comm] (121:6) 25 Mr 94, p. 14.
2428. GUNN, Thom
"Arachne." [NewYorker] (70:39) 28 N 94, p. 104.
"Weegee V: Coffee Shop." [Thrpny] (56) Wint 94, p. 19.
2429. GUNNARS, Kristjana
"Exiles Among You" (16-21). [Event] (23:2) Sum 94, p. 21-26.
"Exiles Among You" (Selections: 27, 29-32). [PoetryC] (15:1) N 94, p. 6-7.
"Exiles Among You" (Selections: 46-47, 50). [AntigR] (99) Aut 94, p. 39-40.
"Scent of Cedar" (Selections). [PraF] (15:1, #66) Spr 94, p. 27-41.
2430. GUNSTROM, Nickie J.
"City of One." [Kalliope] (16:1) 94, p. 31.
GUOHUA, Li
See LI, Guohua
2431. GUPPY, Stephen
"Three Frames After Photographs by Diane Arbus" (from *Blind Date with the Angel: the Diane Arbus Poems*). [PoetryC] (14:2) Mr 94, p. 28.
2432. GUPTA, Nila
"Your Love Has Undone Me" (for Sharmini). [Arc] (32) Spr 94, p. 30-31.
2433. GURKIN, Kathryn B.
"Talking Heads." [Parting] (7:1) Sum 94, p. 73.

2434. GURLEY, James
"Biophilia" (at the nature reserve outside London, Ontario). [Arc] (33) Fall 94, p. 16-17.
"On the Harmonic Sounds of Flame" (John Tyndall, 1857). [AntigR] (98) Sum 94, p. 95-96.
"The Universe As a Work of Art" (Magic Lantern Show, 1860). [AntigR] (98) Sum 94, p. 97-98.
2435. GURNIS, Peter
"Boat-Builder." [Agni] (39) 94, p. 184.
"The Lover." [Agni] (39) 94, p. 185.
2436. GUSTAFSON, Jim
"First Sonnet." [Arshile] (3) 94, p. 13.
2437. GUSTIN, Annie
"For the Two Little Girls." [InterQ] (1:4) 94, p. 31.
GUT, Karen Alkalay
See ALKALAY-GUT, Karen
GUT, Keren Alklai
See ALKALAY-GUT, Karen
GUTIÉRREZ, Amparo Pérez
See PÉREZ GUTIÉRREZ, Amparo
2438. GUTIÉRREZ, Julio
"Un Poquito de Tu Amor." [Areíto] (4:15) Marzo 94, p. 43.
2439. GUY, Shirley
"Skin Dress." [Zyzzyva] (10:1) Spr 94, p. 35-36.
GUZMAN, Esteban Torres
See TORRES-GUZMAN, Esteban
2440. GUZMAN, Jorge
"Circa 1926" (tr. of Cesar Vallejo, w. Clayton Eshleman). [PartR] (61:4) Fall 94, p. 635-636.
2441. GWYNN, R. S.
"Chang Eng" (Mount Airy, N.C., January, 1874). [Elf] (4:4) Wint 94, p. 25.

2442. H. T.
"Carousel" (to Susan Smith Nash). [Chain] (1) Spr-Sum 94, p. 148-152.
"Vanishing Act." [AmerLC] (6) 94, p. 122-123.
"Voiceunder / Recognition." [WashR] (19:6) Ap-My 94, p. 16.
HA, Jin
See JIN, Ha
2443. HAAREN, Michael
"Baby Boomer Fantasy #1992." [Amelia] (7:3, #22) 94, p. 93.
"There is no frigate like a wig." [Amelia] (7:3, #22) 94, p. 55.
2444. HABER, Leo
"The Grinder Baruch Espinosa." [ProseP] (3) 94, p. 45.
2445. HABOVA, Dana
"The Good Kings Wenceslases" (tr. of Miroslav Holub, w. David Young). [HarvardR] (Premier Issue) Spr 92, p. 52.
"Intensive Care Unit" (tr. of Miroslav Holub, w. David Young). [InterQ] (1:1) [93?], p. 93.
"Pompeii" (tr. of Miroslav Holub, w. David Young). [HarvardR] (Premier Issue) Spr 92, p. 117.
"Pompeii" (tr. of Miroslav Holub, w. David Young). [InterQ] (1:1) [93?], p. 94-95.
2446. HACKER, Marilyn
"August Journal." [PraS] (68:1) Spr 94, p. 24-28.
"Cancer Winter" (for Rafael Campo and Hayden Carruth). [ParisR] (36:131) Sum 94, p. 296-303.
"Days of 1992." [ColR] (21:2) Fall 94, p. 104-106.
"Exploded Landscape" (tr. of Claire Malroux). [ColR] (21:2) Fall 94, p. 108.
"The Lamp Set Down" (tr. of Claire Malroux). [ColR] (21:2) Fall 94, p. 109-111.
"Precepts" (tr. of Claire Malroux). [Agni] (39) 94, p. 210.
"The rain shakes a disheveled head" (tr. of Claire Malroux). [PraS] (68:1) Spr 94, p. 29.
"She speaks to us of a country not our own" (tr. of Claire Malroux). [PraS] (68:1) Spr 94, p. 30.
"Time Has Doors Has Windows" (tr. of Claire Malroux). [ColR] (21:2) Fall 94, p. 107.

2447. HACKER, Neva Vinetta
"Light for Deborah." [SoCoast] (16) Ja 94, p. 14-15.
2448. HACKETT, Robert
"Eel Season" (tr. of Jean-Claude Pinson). [ConnPR] (13:1) 94, p. 18-19.
2449. HADARI, Atar
"Jewelry Salesman." [PoetL] (89:4) Wint 94-95, p. 47.
"Matches." [PoetL] (89:4) Wint 94-95, p. 46.
2450. HADAS, Rachel
"Along Edges." [DenQ] (28:3) Wint 94, p. 21-22.
"Correspondences." [Thrpny] (56) Wint 94, p. 7.
"Four Lives, Stirring." [NewYorker] (70:7) 4 Ap 94, p. 68.
"Helen" (tr. of Paul Valéry). [HarvardR] (6) Spr 94, p. 143.
"How Young" (tr. of Konstantine Karyotakis). [HarvardR] (Premier Issue) Spr 92, p. 40.
"July Midnight." [Pivot] (41) 93, p. 58.
"The Last Movie." [NewRep] (210:18) 2 My 94, p. 40.
"Ophelia" (tr. of Arthur Rimbaud). [HarvardR] (Premier Issue) Spr 92, p. 21-22.
"Preveza" (tr. of Konstantine Karyotakis). [HarvardR] (Premier Issue) Spr 92, p. 56.
"Problems of Summer." [Colum] (22) Wint 94, p. 13-14.
"Recoveries." [KenR] (NS 16:3) Sum 94, p. 28-31.
"Revision." [Pivot] (42) 94, p. 38-39.
"The Sacrifice." [Pivot] (41) 93, p. 58.
"Skirts." [HarvardR] (6) Spr 94, p. 113.
"Summer Night." [HarvardR] (7) Fall 94, p. 16.
"Windows" (tr. of Stéphane Mallarmé). [HarvardR] (6) Spr 94, p. 158-159.
"The Wolf in the Bed." [Colum] (22) Wint 94, p. 12.
2451. HADAYIA, Jennifer M.
"Inheritance." [Calyx] (15:3) Wint 94-95, p. 44-45.
2452. HADDAWAY, J. L.
"The Language of Parents" (for W.M.H.). [Wind] (73) 94, p. 11-12.
"The Persistence of Memory." [SmPd] (31:3, #92) Fall 94, p. 15.
2453. HADDUCK, Kevin
"Breathe into This Body." [ChrC] (111:21) 13-20 Jl 94, p. 686.
"Hand Writing." [ChrC] (111:24) 24-31 Ag 94, p. 782.
2454. HADEN, Amy Clark
"Foulbrood." [NegC] (14:1/2) 94, p. 9.
2455. HADFIELD, Charles
"Heat Haze." [Os] (39) Fall-Wint 94, p. 24.
2456. HAFFNER, John
"The Question Concerning Martin Heidegger and Lou Reed." [AntigR] (96) Wint 94, p. 58.
2457. HAGER, Stephanie
"Almost 24." [PoetryE] (37/38) Spr 94, p. 111.
"A Bad Thing." [WormR] (34:3, #135) 94, p. 100.
"Instead of Running." [PoetryE] (37/38) Spr 94, p. 110.
"Kansas." [WormR] (34:3, #135) 94, p. 100-101.
"The Things We Do." [SycamoreR] (6:1) Wint 94, p. 45.
2458. HAGUE, Richard
"Time-Lapse Photography: A Mouse Corpse Devoured by Maggots." [Poetry] (163:6) Mr 94, p. 331-332.
2459. HAHN, Elizabeth
"I Know" (tr. of Pierre Morency, w. Brenda Casey). [InterPR] (20:2) Fall 94, p. 75.
"I Must Say" (tr. of Pierre Morency, w. Brenda Casey). [InterPR] (20:2) Fall 94, p. 73.
"Maxine Kumin Writes of Pairing Geese." [MinnR] (41/42) Fall 93-Spr 94 (published Mr 95), p. 40.
"With a Fine-Toothed Comb." [AntigR] (98) Sum 94, p. 65.
2460. HAHN, Kimiko
"The Crab." [HangL] (65) 94, p. 20.
"For My Once Mother-in-Law, for Asaye." [Manoa] (6:2) Wint 94, p. 24-25.
"Four Weeks After Mother's funeral." [Manoa] (6:2) Wint 94, p. 26.
"The Old Woman's Breast." [HangL] (65) 94, p. 19.
"The Snake." [HangL] (65) 94, p. 21.
"The Swimmer's Blood" (for v). [Manoa] (6:2) Wint 94, p. 25-26.
"Wisteria." [PennR] (6:1) 94, p. 27-33.

2461. HAHN, Robert
"Copying." [WestHR] (48:4) Wint 94, p. 308-315.
2462. HAHN, Susan
"The Fifth Amendment." [AmerV] (35) 94, p. 99-100.
"Mens Rea." [AmerV] (35) 94, p. 101-103.
"The New Age." [Boulevard] (9:3, #27) Fall 94, p. 105-106.
"Passover, Easter, Hitler's Birthday." [Shen] (44:4) Wint 94, p. 90-91.
"Poem in Late May." [Boulevard] (9:3, #27) Fall 94, p. 107.
"Song of Estrogen." [AmerV] (35) 94, p. 104.
"Yeast." [Shen] (44:4) Wint 94, p. 92.
2463. HAIGHT, Robert
"Nymphs." [Northeast] (5:11) Wint 94-95, p. 7.
"This River." [Northeast] (5:11) Wint 94-95, p. 6.
2464. HAINES, John
"The House of the Injured." [Elf] (4:3) Fall 94, p. 47.
"Shepherd's Purse." [Atlantic] (274:3) S 94, p. 78.
2465. HAIR, Jennie
"Mountains Rising and Falling." [CrabCR] (8:2/3/9:1/2/3) 94, p. 53.
HAIXIN, Xu
See XU, Haixin
HAJIME, Kijima
See KIJIMA, Hajime
2466. HAKAK, Lev
"The History of Literature: Poets" (tr. by Yonina Borvick). [LitR] (37:2) Wint 94, p. 311.
"Letter to Ibn Gabirol" (tr. by Ammiel Alcalay). [LitR] (37:2) Wint 94, p. 313.
"Poem Contemplating Poets" (tr. by Yonina Borvick). [LitR] (37:2) Wint 94, p. 312.
2467. HALBERSTADT, Alex
"New Year's with My Father, Moscow" (Jacob deceives Isaac, Genesis 27). [Zyzzyva] (10:3) Fall 94, p. 33-35.
HALE, Ellen Turlington Johnston
See JOHNSTON-HALE, Ellen Turlington
2468. HALE, Robert V.
"Revisited." [DenQ] (28:4) Spr 94, p. 25.
2469. HALES, Corrinne
"Alive." [QW] (39) Sum-Fall 94, p. 213-214.
"Life After Death." [NoAmR] (279:6) N-D 94, p. 25.
"What Actually Happens." [QW] (39) Sum-Fall 94, p. 211-212.
2470. HALEVI, Samuel Michael
"Eros" (tr. of Rainer Maria Rilke, w. Jane Hirshfield). [DenQ] (29:1) Sum 94, p. 97.
"Untitled: From almost all things, It flashes toward feeling" (tr. of Rainer Maria Rilke, w. Jane Hirshfield). [DenQ] (29:1) Sum 94, p. 98.
2471. HALL, Barry
"A Proposal." [Vis] (44) 94, p. 14.
2472. HALL, C. B.
"Quite Another Eternity" (Selections: 1-6, 68-70, tr. of Leevi Lehto). [Talisman] (12) Spr 94, p. 198-199.
2473. HALL, Christine
"Long Legs." [NewYorkQ] (53) 94, p. 103.
2474. HALL, Donald
"The Corner." [HarvardR] (6) Spr 94, p. 159.
"Family Values." [Nat] (259:18) N 28 94, p. 656.
"Flying." [SewanR] (102:2) Spr 94, p. 210.
"Friends Now." [Boulevard] (9:3, #27) Fall 94, p. 103.
"Going Out." [OntR] (41) Fall-Wint 94, p. 120.
"His Face." [Boulevard] (9:3, #27) Fall 94, p. 104.
"The Hurricane." [Thrpny] (56) Wint 94, p. 11.
"The Night of the Day." [GettyR] (7:2) Spr 94, p. 211-218.
"Nunc Est Bibendum." [HarvardR] (2) Fall 92, p. 109.
"Savin Rock." [SewanR] (102:2) Spr 94, p. 209.
"Stephen's Wrist." [PartR] (61:2) Spr 94, p. 309-310.
"Sundays." [SewanR] (102:2) Spr 94, p. 208.
"The Turning Point." [PartR] (61:2) Spr 94, p. 310.
2475. HALL, Elizabeth
"A Visit with Auntie." [Amelia] (7:4, #23) 94, p. 72.

2476. HALL, H. Palmer
"The Marine Sulfur Queen" (lost at sea, February, 1963). [Border] (4) Spr-Sum 94, p. 42-43.
"While Visiting a Friend Just before His Divorce." [Border] (4) Spr-Sum 94, p. 44-45.

2477. HALL, Judith
"St. Peregrinus' Cancer." [WestHR] (48:2) Sum 94, p. 122-123.
"Sundays in the Ladies' Room, a Ritual." [Journal] (18:1) Spr-Sum 94, p. 64-65.
"Touched Relics." [Journal] (18:1) Spr-Sum 94, p. 62-63.

2478. HALL, Kathryn
"Before Bed." [FourQ] (8:1) Spr 94, p. 47.
"Medici's Order." [SoDakR] (32:2) Sum 94, p. 31.
"What the Nation Needed." [SycamoreR] (6:2) Sum 94, p. 25-26.

2479. HALL, Keith
"Gennesaret." [SouthernPR] (34:1) Sum 94, p. 38-39.

2480. HALLERMAN, Victoria
"Apology." [Pivot] (42) 94, p. 57.
"The Bends." [GlobalCR] (3) Spr 94, p. 104.
"The Body Opened." [SouthernPR] (34:2) Wint 94, p. 59-62.
"Egret." [Poetry] (165:3) D 94, p. 130.
"Hudson River Frozen Across at Rhinecliff." [Pivot] (42) 94, p. 56-57.
"The Woman in the Magic Show." [GlobalCR] (3) Spr 94, p. 105.

2481. HALLIDAY, Mark
"1946." [Poetry] (163:5) F 94, p. 255.
"About Time." [VirQR] (70:3) Sum 94, p. 456-457.
"Castle Strange." [IndR] (17:2) Fall 94, p. 35-36.
"Crosstown Tirade." [ChiR] (40:2/3) 94, p. 103-105.
"Hectic." [Agni] (39) 94, p. 60-61.
"Horrible." [ChiR] (40:2/3) 94, p. 102.
"No Promise." [IndR] (17:2) Fall 94, p. 34.
"Threads." [VirQR] (70:3) Sum 94, p. 457-458.

2482. HALLMAN, Mark
"Mathematician as a Child." [EvergreenC] (9:2) Sum-Fall 94, p. 28.

2483. HALLMUNDSSON, Hallberg
"Myth" (a meditation of Iceland's thousand years, tr. of Matthias Johannessen). [Vis] (44) 94, p. 35-37.

2484. HALM, Cindra
"Drought." [Kalliope] (16:3) 94, p. 10-11.
"An Inheritance of Windows." [Kalliope] (16:3) 94, p. 11.

2485. HALME, Kathleen
"Carnivores." [AmerV] (35) 94, p. 44.
"A Celibate Imagination." [AmerV] (35) 94, p. 48.
"Delilah in Dixie." [AmerV] (35) 94, p. 41-42.
"Desire Lines." [AmerV] (35) 94, p. 43.
"The Everlasting Universe of Things" (— Shelley). [AmerV] (35) 94, p. 45-47.
"A World without Words." [LaurelR] (28:1) Wint 94, p. 77.

2486. HALPERIN, Mark
"Nameless Indiscretions." [CrabCR] (8:2/3/9:1/2/3) 94, p. 18.
"Trembling." [CrabCR] (8:2/3/9:1/2/3) 94, p. 123.

2487. HALPERN, Reuben
"Woman in the Wings." [ChangingM] (27) Wint 94, p. 18.

2488. HAMANN, Shannon
"Fragment." [QW] (39) Sum-Fall 94, p. 158-160.

2489. HAMBRICK, Jack
"Keeping the Skull." [Shen] (44:4) Wint 94, p. 87.

2490. HAMBURGER, Michael
"The Withering Away of the State." [Stand] (35:2) Spr 94, p. 14-15.

2491. HAMBY, Barbara
"James Atkins, Irlandese." [Iowa] (24:1) Wint 94, p. 100-101.
"The Ovary Tattoo." [Iowa] (24:1) Wint 94, p. 98-99.
"St. Anthony of the Floating Larynx." [Iowa] (24:1) Wint 94, p. 102-103.
"Toska." [Iowa] (24:1) Wint 94, p. 104-105.

2492. HAMELIN, Claude
"The Actor" (tr. by the author). [InterPR] (20:2) Fall 94, p. 29.
"Black Screen" (tr. by the author). [InterPR] (20:2) Fall 94, p. 27.
"Le Comédien." [InterPR] (20:2) Fall 94, p. 28.

"Écran Noir." [InterPR] (20:2) Fall 94, p. 26.
"Rue Ste-Famille." [InterPR] (20:2) Fall 94, p. 30.
"Ste-Famille Street" (tr. by the author). [InterPR] (20:2) Fall 94, p. 31.

2493. HAMER, Forrest
"Pica." [CreamCR] (18:2) Fall 94, p. 122.

2494. HAMILL, Sam
"Abstract." [AmerPoR] (23:4) Jl-Ag 94, p. 12.
"Another Duffer." [AmerPoR] (23:4) Jl-Ag 94, p. 12.
"Everything Melts" (tr. of Jaan Kaplinski, w. the author). [CrabCR] (8:2/3/9:1/2/3) 94, p. 49.
"I Make My Home in the Mountains" (tr. of Li Po). [NewEngR] (16:3) Sum 94, p. 31.
"In Praise of Rain" (tr. of Tu Fu). [CrabCR] (8:2/3/9:1/2/3) 94, p. 50.
"Our Shadows" (tr. of Jaan Kaplinski, w. the author). [CrabCR] (8:2/3/9:1/2/3) 94, p. 48.
"To the Tune 'The Washing Stream'" (tr. of Li Ch'ing-Chao). [CrabCR] (8:2/3/9:1/2/3) 94, p. 50.

2495. HAMILTON, Alfred Starr
"Artisan Work." [WormR] (34:3, #135) 94, p. 91.
"Law." [JlNJPo] (16:2) Aut 94, p. 17.
"Sanctified." [WormR] (34:3, #135) 94, p. 91.
"Stairway." [WormR] (34:3, #135) 94, p. 90.
"Tiger." [WormR] (34:3, #135) 94, p. 91.

2496. HAMILTON, Brian Christopher
"Hungry." [CharR] (20:2) Fall 94, p. 88-89.

2497. HAMILTON, Carol
"First Memories." [Amelia] (7:3, #22) 94, p. 92.
"Parsimony." [MidwQ] (35:2) Wint 94, p. 170.

2498. HAMILTON, Colin
"In Passing." [MichQR] (33:2) Spr 94, p. 349.
"The Nightwatchman." [MichQR] (33:2) Spr 94, p. 348.

2499. HAMILTON, Fritz
"4:30 a.m. I could." [MidwQ] (36:1) Aut 94, p. 61.
"Trying to" (for Phil). [SmPd] (31:3, #92) Fall 94, p. 11.

2500. HAMILTON, J. A.
"Eat It" (for Elise). [Arc] (32) Spr 94, p. 66.
"The Sick Boy." [PoetryC] (15:1) N 94, p. 25.
"Special Needs" (Honourable Mention, Long Poem Category). [PraF] (15:4, #69) Wint 94-95, p. 62-77.

2501. HAMILTON, Kitty
"The Ragpicker." [PraS] (68:2) Sum 94, p. 103.
"While Reading about Emily Dickinson." [PraS] (68:2) Sum 94, p. 104-105.

2502. HAMILTON, Mark
"Uncle Lowell." [HopewellR] (6) 94, p. 100-101.

2503. HAMILTON, Robb
"Poetry Fun Fact: Ukiah Is Haiku Spelled Backward." [SantaBR] (2:1) Spr-Sum 94, p. 74.

2504. HAMILTON, Saskia
"Dream at Eighty-four." [Thrpny] (57) Spr 94, p. 13.

2505. HAMMOND, Blaine
"Performing for the Crowds." [FreeL] (13) Spr 94, p. 24.

2506. HAMMOND, Catherine
"Alna the Night Nurse" (János Kórbáz Klinika, Budapest, Hungary). [LaurelR] (28:2) Sum 94, p. 32-34.

2507. HAN, Shan
"After Dinner, I Close My Door" (tr. by Peter Stambler). [SouthernHR] (28:4) Fall 94, p. 347.
"Carelessly, I Drop My Inkstone in the Pool" (tr. by Peter Stambler). [GrahamHR] (18) Wint 94-95, p. 74.
"Every Morning, He Takes Breakfast with Me" (tr. by Peter Stambler). [GrahamHR] (18) Wint 94-95, p. 75.
"Leaping Upwards, I Clap My Heels and Bruise Them" (tr. by Peter Stambler). [SouthernHR] (28:4) Fall 94, p. 347.
"Useless, These Absent Thoughts" (tr. by Peter Stambler). [Stand] (35:3) Sum 94, p. 54.
"The Uses of Poetry" (tr. by Peter Stambler). [GrahamHR] (18) Wint 94-95, p. 77.

"We Come Ashore Far from Home" (tr. by Peter Stambler). [GrahamHR] (18) Wint 94-95, p. 76.

2508. HANAZONO, Emperor (1297-1348)
"Civil War" (tr. by Graeme Wilson). [Jacaranda] (5:1) Wint-Spr 91, p. 116.

2509. HANDLER, Joan Cusack
"Another Life" (After a Hysterectomy). [Kalliope] (16:1) 94, p. 21.
"Family." [Confr] (52/53) Wint-Spr 94, p. 301-302.
"Glory." [Agni] (39) 94, p. 169.

2510. HANLEN, Jim
"By Angela's Hometown." [EngJ] (83:2) F 94, p. 90.

2511. HANLEY, Aedan
"Woman Crying During a Flood." [Callaloo] (17:4) Fall 94, p. 967-968.

2512. HANNIGAN, Paul
"Credo." [HarvardR] (Premier Issue) Spr 92, p. 87.
"The Greatest Gift." [HarvardR] (Premier Issue) Spr 92, p. 88.
"The Imps in Hell." [HarvardR] (Premier Issue) Spr 92, p. 87.
"Noblesse Oblige." [HarvardR] (Premier Issue) Spr 92, p. 88-89.
"Il Principle Nuovo." [HarvardR] (Premier Issue) Spr 92, p. 87.
"Santa Miseria." [HarvardR] (Premier Issue) Spr 92, p. 89-90.
"Ten Thousand Cries of Pain" (2 poems). [HarvardR] (Premier Issue) Spr 92, p. 89.

2513. HANSEN, Tom
"Dim Light before Sunrise." [ColEng] (56:7) N 94, p. 826.
"X at Sea." [FloridaR] (20:1) Fall 94, p. 35.

2514. HANSEN, Twyla
"Behind My Back." [Kalliope] (16:1) 94, p. 42.

2515. HANSON, Kenneth O.
"At My Grandfather's Funeral." [Interim] (13:1) Spr-Sum 94, p. 4-5.
"The Road Home." [Interim] (13:1) Spr-Sum 94, p. 3.

2516. HANTOVER, Jeffrey
"Protestations." [BambooR] (63/64) Sum-Fall 94, p. 17-18.
"The Speed of Light at Thien Mu Pagoda." [BambooR] (63/64) Sum-Fall 94, p. 16.

2517. HANZLICEK, C. G.
"Osprey" (for Dianne). [QW] (39) Sum-Fall 94, p. 215-216.

2518. HARALDSSON, Arni
"The Phoenix" (with photograph). [WestCL] (28:3, #15) Wint 94-95, p. 86-87.
"The West Royal" (with photograph). [WestCL] (28:3, #15) Wint 94-95, p. 84-85.

2519. HARAMGAAL, Ya'aqov Halevi
"My She-Whale" (tr. by Eliezer Freeman). [ProseP] (3) 94, p. 46.

2520. HARBAUGH, C. A.
"Nude Beach." [Amelia] (7:3, #22) 94, p. 69.

2521. HARDENBROOK, Yvonne
"After you leave." [Amelia] (7:3, #22) 94, p. 31.
"The Last Dance." [Amelia] (7:3, #22) 94, p. 148.

2522. HARDGROVE, Theodore
"The Laughing Lady, His Candle and a Soothing Cup of Tea." [JamesWR] (11:2) Wint 94, p. 9.
"On Lee's Pond." [JamesWR] (11:2) Wint 94, p. 9.

2523. HARDIN, Jeff
"As a Man Must Do." [FloridaR] (20:1) Fall 94, p. 84-85.
"The Held Book." [HayF] (15) Fall-Wint 94, p. 59.
"Weekend Trip." [PoetC] (26:1) Fall 94, p. 16.

2524. HARDY, Myronn
"Blue Song." [Eyeball] (3) 93, p. 36.
"Building a Country." [Eyeball] (3) 93, p. 36.

2525. HARDY, Naomi
"God of Goldfish." [BellArk] (10:3) My-Je 94, p. 13.
"The Lecture." [BellArk] (10:3) My-Je 94, p. 13.
"Yellow." [BellArk] (10:3 [i.e. 10:4]) Jl-Ag 94, p. 10.

2526. HARER, Katherine
"Hubba-Hubba." [HangL] (65) 94, p. 23.
"In June." [HangL] (65) 94, p. 22.

2527. HARJO, Joy
"The Creation Story." [InterQ] (1:4) 94, p. 101.
"Insomnia and the Seven Steps to Grace." [InterQ] (1:4) 94, p. 99-100.
"The Other Side of Yellow to Blue." [AmerPoR] (23:6) N-D 94, p. 20.
"A Postcolonial Tale." [AmerPoR] (23:6) N-D 94, p. 20.

"The Song of the House in the House." [AmerPoR] (23:6) N-D 94, p. 18.
"The Woman Who Fell from the Sky." [AmerPoR] (23:6) N-D 94, p. 18-19.

2528. HARMON, Joshua
"Ex-Husband." [WestHR] (48:3) Fall 94, p. 271.
"Her Sister's Theory of Love." [WestHR] (48:3) Fall 94, p. 274.
"The Other Man." [WestHR] (48:3) Fall 94, p. 273.
"Summer Storm." [WestHR] (48:3) Fall 94, p. 272.

2529. HARMON, William
"Anaphora." [Agni] (39) 94, p. 116-118.
"Becoming's Signature." [CarolQ] (46:3) Sum 94, p. 31.
"Dan Pope's Daughters' Names." [CarolQ] (46:3) Sum 94, p. 32-33.

2530. HARMS, James
"Los Angeles." [IllinoisR] (1:2) Spr 94, p. 29-30.
"As Always." [Journal] (18:1) Spr-Sum 94, p. 52-53.
"First Elegy, Pasadena." [Crazy] (46) Spr 94, p. 113-116.
"From Ocean Park to Healdsburg" (Richard Diebenkorn, 1922-1993). [Poetry] (164:2) My 94, p. 93-94.
"Mariner Without a Moon." [NewEngR] (16:2) Spr 94, p. 31-32.
"Mrs. Worthington." [Poetry] (164:1) Ap 94, p. 23.
"Reel around the Shadow." [ChiR] (40:2/3) 94, p. 134-135.
"Theoretical Life." [HayF] (14) Spr-Sum 94, p. 55.
"Tribe and Country." [IndR] (17:1) Spr 94, p. 160.
"Whenever You Hang Your Head." [NewEngR] (16:2) Spr 94, p. 30.

2531. HARNACK, Curtis
"Early Camera-Work." [SewanR] (102:3) Sum 94, p. 381-382.

2532. HAROUTIUNIAN, Artem
"Sneakers" (tr. by the author and Peter Balakian). [GrahamHR] (18) Wint 94-95, p. 33-37.

2533. HARPER, Cynthia
"French Quarter August." [NegC] (13:2/3) 93, p. 18-19.

2534. HARPER, L. L. (Linda Lee)
"Almost Born Agin." [SoCoast] (17) Je 94, p. 6-7.
"Crossing the Border." [LaurelR] (28:1) Wint 94, p. 99-100.
"Liberties." [WindO] (58) Sum 94, p. 17-18.
"My Favorite Dream." [WindO] (58) Sum 94, p. 19.
"Separation." [WindO] (58) Sum 94, p. 25.
"Violets." [WindO] (58) Sum 94, p. 20.

2535. HARPER, Lea
"The Basket." [Descant] (25:3/4, #86/87) Fall-Wint 94, p. 116-118.
"I Have the Power." [Descant] (25:3/4, #86/87) Fall-Wint 94, p. 120.
"The Prisoner God." [Descant] (25:3/4, #86/87) Fall-Wint 94, p. 113-115.
"Singer." [Descant] (25:3/4, #86/87) Fall-Wint 94, p. 119.

2536. HARPER, Michael S.
"Impertinent Correspondences." [Callaloo] (17:4) Fall 94, p. 1017-1018.

2537. HARPER, William
"Poetry Slam?" [TriQ] (91) Fall 94, p. 243-244.

2538. HARRIS, Arnold
"Wise Man." [WorldO] (25:3) Spr 94, p. 57.

2539. HARRIS, Bill
"Yardbird Suite" (Side One: 1920-1940, a biopoem fictionalized accounts of events real and imagined from the life of Charles Yardbird Parker, jazz musician 29 August 1920-12 March 1955). [Eyeball] (3) 93, p. 9-10.

2540. HARRIS, James
"Aphasia." [Manoa] (6:1) Sum 94, p. 94-95.
"Balance." [YellowS] (12:3, #47) Fall-Wint 94-95, p. 12.
"Byzantine." [Manoa] (6:1) Sum 94, p. 95-96.
"Courtship." [PoetryE] (37/38) Spr 94, p. 28.
"Extravagances." [YellowS] (12:3, #47) Fall-Wint 94-95, p. 12.
"Heat." [YellowS] (12:3, #47) Fall-Wint 94-95, p. 13.
"Living a Life." [Manoa] (6:1) Sum 94, p. 94.
"Witness." [YellowS] (12:3, #47) Fall-Wint 94-95, p. 13.

2541. HARRIS, Jana
"Bad Daughter Poem." [Jacaranda] (10) 94, p. 120-123.
"Committing the Landscape to Memory" (Cristal McLeod (Mourning Dove), Okanogan writer, age 12, 1900). [Calyx] (15:2) Sum 94, p. 38-42.
"Fever" (Nameless of Spring Coulee, 1889). [Calyx] (15:2) Sum 94, p. 43-45.

2542. HARRIS, Joseph
"On the Prospects of Fame." [Light] (11) Aut 94, p. 17.
2543. HARRIS, Judith
"Blessing." [MidwQ] (35:3) Spr 94, p. 308.
"Indian Summer at the Estate Sale." [Boulevard] (9:1/2, #25/26) Spr 94, p. 222-223.
"Jewish Holidays." [PoetL] (89:3) Fall 94, p. 31-32.
"The Model." [AntR] (52:2) Spr 94, p. 303.
2544. HARRIS, Maureen
"Everything Is Changed" (For Shirley, January 28, 1934—December 4, 1992). [Event] (23:3) Wint 94-95, p. 49-53.
"Flowers for My Mother." [PoetryC] (14:3) My 94, p. 25.
2545. HARRIS, Nancy C.
"Learning to Fish with Crickets" (for Peggy Ranson). [NewOR] (20:1/2) Spr-Sum 94, p. 136-137.
"Memento Mori: The Black Box" (For Everette Hawthorne Maddox). [NegC] (13:2/3) 93, p. 70-73.
"New Orleans: All Saints Day" (For Julie Kane). [NegC] (13:2/3) 93, p. 20-21.
2546. HARRISON, Dennis
"Good Girl." [BellArk] (10:6) N-D 94, p. 23.
"The Quiet." [BellArk] (10:6) N-D 94, p. 23.
2547. HARRISON, Jeffrey
"The Birds That Woke Us: An Urban Pastoral." [Nat] (259:12) O 17 94, p. 432.
"Hitting Golfballs off the Bluff." [YaleR] (82:2) Ap 94, p. 73.
"A Private Part of the Dance." [HarvardR] (7) Fall 94, p. 51.
2548. HARRISON, Jim
"Sonoran Radio" (Freely translated). [Antaeus] (75/76) Aut 94, p. 265-273.
2549. HARRISON, Nicki
"Sound." [DogRR] (13:1, #25) Spr-Sum 94, p. 51.
2550. HARROD, Lois Marie
"The Heretic Sonnet." [Verse] (11:2) Sum 94, p. 81.
"Horseshoe Crabs" (Brigantine Wildlife Refuge, 1992). [LitR] (37:4) Sum 94, p. 597-598.
"M. C. Escher's *Day and Night*." [PraS] (68:1) Spr 94, p. 83-84.
"Milk and Cookies at Midnight." [PraS] (68:1) Spr 94, p. 85-86.
"New Grange, County Meath, Ireland." [SoCoast] (17) Je 94, p. 8.
"Rabid Animals." [AmerPoR] (23:2) Mr-Ap 94, p. 18.
"Somniloquy." [XavierR] (14:2) Fall 94, p. 53-54.
"The Sonnet of Blue Windows." [Verse] (11:2) Sum 94, p. 81.
"Thousands of Miles from Familiar Surroundings." [Conscience] (15:3) Aut 94, p. 13.
"Tongues." [PraS] (68:1) Spr 94, p. 84-85.
"The Way Dust Makes Light Visible." [HiramPoR] (55/56) Fall 93-Sum 94, p. 41.
2551. HARRYMAN, Carla
"Fish Speech." [Avec] (7:1) 94, p. 107.
"Monongahela" (After Amy Trachtenberg). [Avec] (7:1) 94, p. 104-105.
"Self Portrait" (for Amy Trachtenberg). [Avec] (7:1) 94, p. 105-106.
2552. HARRYMAN, William
"Chasing Shadows." [DogRR] (26) Wint 94-95, p. 17.
2553. HARSHMAN, Marc
"Perhaps a Religious Poem." [Pembroke] (26) 94, p. 144.
2554. HART, Frank
"Oh God." [SlipS] (14) 94, p. 119.
2555. HART, Henry
"The Black Mit." [ConnPR] (13:1) 94, p. 15.
"The Last Visit." [WilliamMR] (32) 94, p. 56-57.
"The Tree Ladder." [Hudson] (47:1) Spr 94, p. 87-88.
2556. HART, James
"The Slaughterhouse." [PoetryNW] (35:1) Spr 94, p. 41.
"Walking the Dark." [PoetryNW] (35:1) Spr 94, p. 40.
2557. HART, Jonathan
"Lotus." [HarvardR] (6) Spr 94, p. 148.
2558. HART, Kevin
"How Hast Thou Counselled Him." [InterQ] (1:2) 93, p. 112.
"Rain." [InterQ] (1:2) 93, p. 111.
"September Rain." [InterQ] (1:2) 93, p. 113.

2559. HART, Mark
"Getting the Writing Down." [Amelia] (7:4, #23) 94, p. 137.
2560. HART, Susan
"Till the Music Stops" (ELF 1994 Poetry Competition: Honorable Mention). [Elf] (4:2) Sum 94, p. 23.
2561. HART, William
"Parking lot." [Amelia] (7:3, #22) 94, p. 23.
2562. HARTEL, Heather
"Gramma's Dishes." [Elf] (4:1) Spr 94, p. 28.
2563. HARTMAN, Charles O.
"Limpet." [SouthwR] (79:1) Wint 94, p. 81-82.
"Tuxedo" (nocturne). [TriQ] (91) Fall 94, p. 213-215.
2564. HARTMAN, Geoffrey H.
"Curfew" (for Aharon Appelfeld). [ParisR] (36:131) Sum 94, p. 153-154.
"Homecoming" (to Germany, in the 1950s). [ParisR] (36:131) Sum 94, p. 155-157.
"Night Thoughts East" (Jerusalem, 1988). [ParisR] (36:131) Sum 94, p. 152-153.
"Words." [ParisR] (36:131) Sum 94, p. 154-155.
2565. HARTMAN, Steven
"Welcome to the Terrordome." [DogRR] (13:1, #25) Spr-Sum 94, p. 36-37.
2566. HARTNETT, Annie
"Leaving Big Bend State Park." [Border] (5) Fall-Wint 94, p. 24.
2567. HARTZEL, Catherine
"Theory Breaking into Three Unresolved Parts." [Outbr] (25) 94, p. 43-44.
"This Blue Dream." [Outbr] (25) 94, p. 42.
2568. HARVEY, Gayle Elen
"After Everyone Has Gone Home." [TickleAce] (28) Fall-Wint 94, p. 11.
"Even the Rain Smells of Apples." [TickleAce] (28) Fall-Wint 94, p. 9.
"In the Presence of the Bear" (for Bjornson). [TickleAce] (28) Fall-Wint 94, p. 10.
"The News Is of Congress." [ColEng] (56:2) F 94, p. 189.
"Poplars on the Banks of the Epte" (after Monet). [TickleAce] (28) Fall-Wint 94, p. 12.
"The Practice of Dissonance" (after Shostakovitch — the "8th Quartet" — for Katie). [InterQ] (1:4) 94, p. 107.
2569. HARVEY, Jack D.
"Apples." [Vis] (46) 94, p. 25-26.
2570. HARVEY, John
"The Adventure of the Speckled Band." [PoetL] (89:3) Fall 94, p. 7-9.
"Behind the Door the Television Is On Again." [PoetL] (89:3) Fall 94, p. 10.
2571. HARVOR, Elisabeth
"A Breast, Our Hearts." [PoetryC] (14:2) Mr 94, p. 12.
"Childhood: Summer Night." [MalR] (109) Wint 94, p. 14-15.
"Like Any Lost Thing." [MalR] (109) Wint 94, p. 18.
"Notes on a Lost Poem, 1993." [MalR] (109) Wint 94, p. 16-17.
"Toxic Inventory" (For my mother in 1993, memories of glazing days, July, 1949). [PoetryC] (14:2) Mr 94, p. 13.
2572. HASAN, Rabiul
"Where One Shall Find a Refuge." [WritersF] (20) 94, p. 99.
2573. HASHIMOTO, Sharon
"Because You Showed Me a Piece of Barbed Wire." [Shen] (44:2) Sum 94, p. 50.
"A Picture of My Sister and Me on the Porch, Summer 1957." [Shen] (44:2) Sum 94, p. 51.
"Watchmaker." [CrabCR] (8:2/3/9:1/2/3) 94, p. 13.
2574. HASHMI, Alamgir
"According to the Scriptures." [LitR] (37:4) Sum 94, p. 711.
"Diary." [LitR] (37:4) Sum 94, p. 712.
"Taxila / Margalla." [LitR] (37:4) Sum 94, p. 713.
"The Trojans." [LitR] (37:4) Sum 94, p. 706.
2575. HASKINS, Lola
"The Making of *T. Clarkson Preaches at the Antislavery Convention:* Sundry Discourses by the Painter, B. Haydon." [BelPoJ] (44:4) Sum 94, p. 24-29.
"Mama." [NewYorkQ] (53) 94, p. 57.
"Matanzas." [PassN] (15:2) Wint 94, p. 17.
"Times." [GeoR] (48:2) Sum 94, p. 252.
"Tuning." [PassN] (15:2) Wint 94, p. 16.
"Typing in the Rainy Season." [InterQ] (1:4) 94, p. 129.
"Los Viejitos" (Patzcuaro, Mexico). [InterQ] (1:4) 94, p. 128.

2576. HASS, Robert
"At a Certain Age" (tr. of Czeslaw Milosz, w. the author). [NewYorker] (69:46) 17 Ja 94, p. 68.
"The Bridge" (tr. of Oscar V. de L. Milosz, w. Czeslaw Milosz). [Thrpny] (58) Sum 94, p. 11.
"Dragonflies Mating." [Antaeus] (75/76) Aut 94, p. 274-277.
"Layover" (followed by Notes). [Agni] (40) 94, p. 122-125.
"Realism" (tr. of Czeslaw Milosz, w. the author). [NewYorker] (70:8) 11 Ap 94, p. 70.
"This World" (tr. of Czeslaw Milosz, w. the author). [Antaeus] (75/76) Aut 94, p. 304.
2577. HASS, Robert B.
"Boston Market." [PoetryNW] (35:1) Spr 94, p. 17.
"Humpback." [Poetry] (163:6) Mr 94, p. 333-334.
"Lullaby for the Mathematician." [Poetry] (163:6) Mr 94, p. 334.
"Why I Am Afraid to Have a Son." [CumbPR] (13:2) Spr 94, p. 26.
"Why I Am Afraid to Have a Son." [SouthernPR] (34:2) Wint 94, p. 16.
2578. HASTINGS, John R.
"The Last Will and Testament of Sir Patrick Spens." [DogRR] (13:1, #25) Spr-Sum 94, p. 32-33.
2579. HASTINGS, Nancy Peters
"Agnes." [Plain] (15:1) Fall 94, p. 26.
2580. HATHAWAY, Michael
"Dogcatcher's Lament." [JamesWR] (11:2) Wint 94, p. 18.
"If the Shoe Fits." [JamesWR] (11:2) Wint 94, p. 18.
"Stumbling into Light." [JamesWR] (11:2) Wint 94, p. 18.
2581. HATHAWAY, Rosemary
"Anniversary." [SinW] (53) Sum-Fall 94, p. 96.
"Ode to an Old Woman From an Old Woman." [SinW] (53) Sum-Fall 94, p. 50.
2582. HATHAWAY, William
"Homecooking." [NoAmR] (279:5) S-O 94, p. 12.
"The Last Cowboy." [CharR] (20:1) Spr 94, p. 63.
"Triggering Corinth, NY." [SouthernR] (30:3) Sum 94, p. 530-532.
2583. HATHAWAY, William T.
"City Spring." [SoDakR] (32:4) Wint 94, p. 59.
"Our Groundling Gap: The Sonnet Mock'd." [SoDakR] (32:4) Wint 94, p. 60.
2584. HATMAKER, Elizabeth
"Throwback." [Epoch] (43:2) 94, p. 190-191.
2585. HATTERSLEY, Michael E.
"Taking the Century by the Throat." [Poetry] (163:4) Ja 94, p. 200-201.
HAU-RAN, Meng
See MENG, Hau-ran
2586. HAV, Niels
"Show Me Your Breasts" (tr. by Per Brask and Patrick Friesen). [PoetryC] (14:2) Mr 94, p. 22.
"Visit from My Father" (tr. by Per Brask and Patrick Friesen). [PoetryC] (14:2) Mr 94, p. 21.
2587. HAVEN, Stephen
"Homage to Agee." [Salm] (101/102) Wint-Spr 94, p. 168-169.
"W.D. Snodgrass and the Owl." [Salm] (101/102) Wint-Spr 94, p. 170-171.
2588. HAWI, Khalil
"After the Ice" (tr. by Adnan Haydar and Michael Beard). [LitR] (37:3) Spr 94, p. 494-497.
"The Mariner and the Dervish" (tr. by Adnan Haydar and Michael Beard). [LitR] (37:3) Spr 94, p. 491-494.
2589. HAWKHEAD, John
"Ante Natal." [SoCoast] (16) Ja 94, p. 47.
"The Return." [SoCoast] (16) Ja 94, p. 33.
2590. HAWKINS, Bruce
"Ripeness." [Vis] (44) 94, p. 17.
2591. HAWKINS, James
"Evensong." [MidwQ] (35:3) Spr 94, p. 310.
"Odium." [MidwQ] (35:3) Spr 94, p. 309.
2592. HAWKS, Thomas
"I Return to the Green Bridge." [WestHR] (48:3) Fall 94, p. 214.
"The Invisible Man" (for Claude Rains). [WestHR] (48:3) Fall 94, p. 215.

"The Myth of the Metals" (for Susanna). [WestHR] (48:3) Fall 94, p. 213.
"The New Regionalism." [WestHR] (48:3) Fall 94, p. 216-217.

2593. HAXTON, Brooks
"The Aubade of the Blown Rose" (after the anonymous French). [Jacaranda] (10) 94, p. 87.
"The Body of My Brother Osiris Is in the Mustard Seed." [Atlantic] (273:5) My 94, p. 88.
"Dilemma." [Jacaranda] (10) 94, p. 89.
"From the Outside." [Hudson] (46:4) Wint 94, p. 696.
"Limpopo, Orinoco, or Yazoo." [Hudson] (46:4) Wint 94, p. 694.
"Memoires Nostalgiques de Cockaigne." [Hudson] (46:4) Wint 94, p. 695.
"On the Essential Goodness of True Art." [Jacaranda] (10) 94, p. 88.
"One Drop Spilled from Psyche's Lamp." [BelPoJ] (45:1) Fall 94, p. 5.
"Saturday." [OntR] (40) Spr-Sum 94, p. 30.
"A Shell." [SouthwR] (79:1) Wint 94, p. 113-114.

2594. HAYASHI, Amari
"The Second to Last Kiss (Tanka)" (tr. by Miyuki Aoyama and Leza Lowitz). [YellowS] (11:4, #44) Wint 93-94, p. 45.

2595. HAYDAR, Adnan
"After the Ice" (tr. of Khalil Hawi, w. Michael Beard). [LitR] (37:3) Spr 94, p. 494-497.
"Digoenes / Pillar of Salt" (tr. of Henri Zoghaib, w. Michael Beard). [LitR] (37:3) Spr 94, p. 533-535.
"Fear, You Are Drunk" (tr. of Houda al-Naamani, w. Michael Beard). [LitR] (37:3) Spr 94, p. 509-510.
"I Am the Truth" (tr. of Houda al-Naamani, w. Michael Beard). [LitR] (37:3) Spr 94, p. 508-509.
"I Long for a Moment" (tr. of Henri Zoghaib, w. Michael Beard). [LitR] (37:3) Spr 94, p. 532.
"The Mariner and the Dervish" (tr. of Khalil Hawi, w. Michael Beard). [LitR] (37:3) Spr 94, p. 491-494.
"Memoirs in Exile" (Selections: 9, 28, 31, 42-44, 46, 47, 60-61, 65, tr. of Joseph Abi Daher, w. Michael Beard). [LitR] (37:3) Spr 94, p. 444-446.
"Quartet for the Last Days" (tr. of Yusuf al-Khal, w. Michael Beard). [LitR] (37:3) Spr 94, p. 506-507.

2596. HAYDEN, Dolores
"Private Geography, 1990." [Hellas] (5:1) Spr-Sum 94, p. 44.

2597. HAYDON, Rich
"Camas and Corn." [DogRR] (13:1, #25) Spr-Sum 94, p. 5.
"Mapping the River" (for Lisa). [BellArk] (10:2) Mr-Ap 94, p. 14.
"Out in the River." [BellArk] (10:2) Mr-Ap 94, p. 11.

2598. HAYES, Ann
"Natural Disaster on TV: Raccoon, Illinois, Kansas, Missouri, Mississippi Rivers in Flood." [Confr] (54/55) Fall 94-Wint 95, p. 273.
"Villanelle for Some Baseball Cards." [Confr] (54/55) Fall 94-Wint 95, p. 274.

2599. HAYES, Carol Porter
"From a Stranger." [Poem] (72) N 94, p. 49.
"What to Do for You." [Poem] (72) N 94, p. 50-51.

2600. HAYES, Daniel
"In Bed with Lola." [TriQ] (90) Spr-Sum 94, p. 21-52.

HAYES, Mary Cartledge
See CARTLEDGE-HAYES, Mary

2601. HAYES, Noreen
"Naked Going." [SpiritSH] (59) 94, p. 2.

2602. HAYMAN, Dick
"At Least!" [Light] (12) Wint 94-95, p. 22.
"Cat-Ching." [Light] (11) Aut 94, p. 9.
"Chicken?" [Light] (9) Spr 94, p. 19.
"Monumental Savings." [Light] (10) Sum 94, p. 17.

2603. HAYNA, Lois Beebe
"Elegy in the Desert." [Vis] (46) 94, p. 27.

2604. HAYNES, Linda Collins
"Remnants of a Country Church." [HopewellR] (6) 94, p. 102-103.

2605. HAYS, Angelyn
"The Ugly Show" (New York Times, 1906). [FloridaR] (19:2) 94, p. 26-27.

2606. HAYWARD, David
"Sister." [Thrpny] (57) Spr 94, p. 35.
2607. HAZELDINE, Nigel
"Great Words." [SantaBR] (2:1) Spr-Sum 94, p. 72.
"To Caroline on Our Eleventh Anniversary." [Amelia] (7:4, #23) 94, p. 167.
2608. HAZELTON, Hugh
"America" (tr. of Alfredo Lavergne). [InterPR] (20:2) Fall 94, p. 108.
"Communiqué" (in English). [InterPR] (20:2) Fall 94, p. 104.
"Communiqué" (in French, tr. by the author). [InterPR] (20:2) Fall 94, p. 105.
2609. HAZEN, James
"Getting Used to It." [ChatR] (14:3) Spr 94, p. 38.
"The Pipe Burns Low." [CumbPR] (13:2) Spr 94, p. 69.
"Portrait." [WebR] (18) Fall 94, p. 47.
2610. HAZNERS, Dainis
"Where the Water Goes." [CrabCR] (8:2/3/9:1/2/3) 94, p. 14-15.
2611. HAZO, Samuel
"Aristotle and the Snow." [Image] (6) Sum 94, p. 40-41.
"Balamand" (tr. of Nadia Tuéni). [LitR] (37:3) Spr 94, p. 529.
"Beirut" (tr. of Nadia Tuéni). [LitR] (37:3) Spr 94, p. 527-528.
"Beit-Eddine" (tr. of Nadia Tuéni). [LitR] (37:3) Spr 94, p. 528-529.
"The Desert: Diary of Beirut under Siege, 1982" (tr. of Adonis). [LitR] (37:3) Spr 94, p. 453-459.
"For Bill." [Hudson] (47:1) Spr 94, p. 81-82.
"In the Lebanese Mountains" (tr. of Nadia Tuéni). [LitR] (37:3) Spr 94, p. 528.
"Mount Suneen" (tr. of Adonis). [LitR] (37:3) Spr 94, p. 452.
"Older Ways to See, Younger Ways to Say." [Image] (6) Sum 94, p. 39-40.
"Panache." [TarRP] (33:2) Spr 94, p. 14-15.
"The Passage" (tr. of Adonis). [LitR] (37:3) Spr 94, p. 451-452.
"Tree of Fire" (tr. of Adonis). [LitR] (37:3) Spr 94, p. 452.
HE, Li
See LI, He
2612. HEADDON, Bill
"Rats." [CoalC] (8) Ap 94, p. 24.
2613. HEADLEY, Robert
"Milagro." [ChironR] (13:2) Sum 94, p. 17.
2614. HEANEY, Seamus
"viii. The annals say: when the monks of Clonmacnoise." [GrahamHR] (18) Wint 94-95, p. 108.
"At the Wellhead." [NewYorker] (70:6) 28 Mr 94, p. 74.
"Damson." [Antaeus] (75/76) Aut 94, p. 278-279.
"Far Away." [NewYorker] (70:43) 26 D 94-2 Ja 95, p. 88.
"An Invocation." [HarvardR] (2) Fall 92, p. 25-26.
"Lament 19 or: A Dream" (From *Laments*, tr. of Jan Kochanowski, w. Stanislaw Baranczak). [HarvardR] (7) Fall 94, p. 7-10.
"Tollund." [NewYorker] (70:31) 3 O 94, p. 92.
2615. HEATH-STUBBS, John
"The Centaur Cheiron." [Interim] (13:1) Spr-Sum 94, p. 8.
"Lycian Chimera: Bellerophon on Pegasus." [Interim] (13:1) Spr-Sum 94, p. 9.
"Not on the Palatine." [Confr] (54/55) Fall 94-Wint 95, p. 43.
"Stheno and Euryale." [Interim] (13:1) Spr-Sum 94, p. 9.
2616. HÉBERT, Anne
"Day Has No Equal But Night" (tr. by A. Poulin, Jr.). [AmerPoR] (23:4) Jl-Ag 94, p. 10.
"The Executed" (tr. by A. Poulin, Jr.). [AmerPoR] (23:4) Jl-Ag 94, p. 10.
"The Old" (tr. by A. Poulin, Jr.). [AmerPoR] (23:4) Jl-Ag 94, p. 10.
"The Piano" (tr. by A. Poulin, Jr.). [AmerPoR] (23:4) Jl-Ag 94, p. 10.
2617. HECHT, Anthony
"Death the Patient." [SewanR] (102:3) Sum 94, p. 386.
"Death the Whore." [YaleR] (82:4) O 94, p. 13-16.
"Prospects." [NewYorker] (70:30) 26 S 94, p. 90.
"Terms" (For Derek Walcott). [Verse] (11:2) Sum 94, p. 91-92.
2618. HEDEEN, Paul M.
"Locke Was Right?" [NoAmR] (279:3) My-Je 94, p. 39.
2619. HEDIN, Laura
"Panes." [CoalC] (8) Ap 94, p. 39.

2620. HEDLUND, Dorothy Swaner
"Smoky Mountains smoking." [Amelia] (7:3, #22) 94, p. 89.
2621. HEEKIN, Billy
"Paul." [Poz] (1:3) Ag-S 94, p. 30.
2622. HEFFERNAN, Michael
"The Boulevardier." [TarRP] (33:2) Spr 94, p. 12.
"Lake Isle." [TarRP] (33:2) Spr 94, p. 12.
2623. HEFLIN, Jack
"First Grade Physics." [HiramPoR] (57) Fall 94-Wint 95, p. 28.
"I-90 East, Exit 120." [HiramPoR] (57) Fall 94-Wint 95, p. 26.
"Wind River Canyon." [HiramPoR] (57) Fall 94-Wint 95, p. 27.
HEIDE, Lisl Auf der
See Auf der HEIDE, Lisl
2624. HEIGHTON, Steven (Steve)
"Elegy, Apollo 1." [CanLit] (141) Sum 94, p. 49.
"Elegy As a Message Left on an Answering Machine" (for Tom Marshall). [CanLit] (140) Spr 94, p. 161-162.
"Happens a Man" (tr. of Rainer Maria Rilke). [Quarry] (43:3) n 94, p. 42.
"Stone Mountain Elegy" (For Chris). [Descant] (25:3/4, #86/87) Fall-Wint 94, p. 76.
"Stone Mountain Postscript." [Descant] (25:3/4, #86/87) Fall-Wint 94, p. 77-78.
"Were You to Die." [Descant] (25:3/4, #86/87) Fall-Wint 94, p. 79-80.
2625. HEIM, Scott
"Winterkill." [Pearl] (20) Spr 94, p. 79.
2626. HEINE, Heinrich
"Götterdämmerung" (tr. by W. D. Jackson). [Stand] (35:3) Sum 94, p. 4-5.
2627. HEINE-KOEHN, Lala
" ΛΑΓΙΑΡΝΕ, The Favourite One." [Arc] (33) Fall 94, p. 34-35.
2628. HEISE, Thomas
"16 June, 1944: Dachau." [NewYorkQ] (53) 94, p. 112.
"Dancing." [ChatR] (14:2) Wint 94, p. 33.
"Ghazal: Houdini." [WormR] (34:1, #133) 94, p. 18.
"Minneapolis Hotel." [WormR] (34:1, #133) 94, p. 19.
2629. HEISLER, Eva
"Hermione at the End of Part One." [Journal] (18:1) Spr-Sum 94, p. 69-71.
"Pilgrim." [ProseP] (3) 94, p. 47.
2630. HEITHAUS, Joe
"Paul's Poem" (for my brother 1952-1991). [SouthernPR] (34:2) Wint 94, p. 62-63.
2631. HEITZMAN, Judy Page
"Choosing Colors." [Pearl] (20) Spr 94, p. 83.
2632. HEJINIAN, Lyn
"My Life in the Nineties" (Selection: "We Are Citizens of Process"). [Chelsea] (57) 94, p. 41-43.
2633. HELD, Dennis
"First Blues." [Plain] (15:1) Fall 94, p. 27.
"Two Ships in Broad Daylight." [IllinoisR] (2:1) Fall 94, p. 25.
2634. HELD, George
"Ava Doll." [PoetC] (26:1) Fall 94, p. 19.
"On a Lock of Hair" (Walt Whitman Centennial Exhibition). [Confr] (52/53) Wint-Spr 94, p. 337.
2635. HELLER, Ben A.
"Cellophane" (tr. of Raúl Barrientos). [GrahamHR] (18) Wint 94-95, p. 38-39.
2636. HELLER, Dorothy
"No nudist need fear an arrest." [Amelia] (7:4, #23) 94, p. 188.
2637. HELLER, Michael
"Without Ozymandias." [Arshile] (3) 94, p. 14-16.
2638. HELLMAN, Sheila
"Sensitive Skin." [JlNJPo] (16:1) Spr 94, p. 7.
"Turkish Coffee in the Arab Market." [JlNJPo] (16:1) Spr 94, p. 8.
2639. HELMUTH, Willard
"Dinner at the Red Lobster." [Kaleid] (Special Issue) 94, p. 20.
2640. HELSTERN, Linda Lizut
"Matrilineal." [Border] (5) Fall-Wint 94, p. 25-26.
2641. HELWIG, David
"Clenched hands under the dark shawl" (tr. of Anna Akhmatova). [Quarry] (43:1) Je 94, p. 31.
"Departures." [Event] (23:1) Spr 94, p. 20-21.

"Dogdays." [Grain] (22:1) Sum 94, p. 43.
"For Tom" (for Tom Marshall). [CanLit] (140) Spr 94, p. 158-160.
"I am not among those who flung" (tr. of Anna Akhmatova). [Quarry] (43:1) Je 94, p. 32.
"The memory of sun in the heart grows weak" (tr. of Anna Akhmatova). [Quarry] (43:1) Je 94, p. 31-32.
"Three Parts." [Grain] (22:1) Sum 94, p. 40-41.
"Untitled: The body in the dream mirror." [Grain] (22:1) Sum 94, p. 42.
"Widows: Vancouver Island." [Event] (23:1) Spr 94, p. 22-23.

2642. HELWIG, Maggie
"As Leaves" (after Meister Eckhart). [Quarry] (43:1) Je 94, p. 130-131.
"Talk Like a Wire." [MalR] (106) Spr 94, p. 103-106.
"Trouble in the Graveyard (Another Poem for War-Time)." [MalR] (106) Spr 94, p. 101-102.
"You in the Morning." [Quarry] (43:1) Je 94, p. 132.

2643. HELWIG, Susan L.
"Sister." [Dandel] (21:1) 94, p. 72.
"Tourist." [AntigR] (96) Wint 94, p. 64.
"Zumburger." [AntigR] (96) Wint 94, p. 63.

2644. HEMAN, Bob
"The Next Day." [Caliban] (14) 94, p. 89.
"Representations." [Caliban] (14) 94, p. 90.
"Scope." [Caliban] (14) 94, p. 89.
"Standing Forces." [Caliban] (14) 94, p. 90.
"Synapse." [Caliban] (14) 94, p. 90.
"System." [Caliban] (14) 94, p. 89.

2645. HEMP, Christine
"Loosening the Ties." [EngJ] (83:4) Ap 94, p. 109.

2646. HEMPEL, Elise
"October from a Passing Car." [Parting] (7:1) Sum 94, p. 62.

2647. HEMPEL, Wes
"Eager for Light." [LitR] (37:4) Sum 94, p. 661.

2648. HEMSCHEMEYER, Judith
"And to die in haughty consciousness" (tr. of Anna Akhmatova). [InterQ] (1:1) [93?], p. 17.
"I am still at home today" (tr. of Anna Akhmatova). [InterQ] (1:1) [93?], p. 18.
"In the face of your agonizing death" (tr. of Anna Akhmatova). [InterQ] (1:1) [93?], p. 17.
"Leave me alone with music" (tr. of Anna Akhmatova). [InterQ] (1:1) [93?], p. 17.
"Necessity herself has finally submitted" (tr. of Anna Akhmatova). [InterQ] (1:1) [93?], p. 19.
"Off in the distance hung some sort of bridge" (tr. of Anna Akhmatova). [InterQ] (1:1) [93?], p. 19.
"On the right, the Dnieper, on the left, maple trees" (tr. of Anna Akhmatova). [InterQ] (1:1) [93?], p. 16.
"Our boys, they defended us" (tr. of Anna Akhmatova). [InterQ] (1:1) [93?], p. 17.
"Sonnet: I would have crowned you myself, Fate!" (tr. of Anna Akhmatova). [InterQ] (1:1) [93?], p. 18.

2649. HENDERSHOT, Cynthia
"Buried." [HeavenB] (11) 94, p. 40.

2650. HENDERSON, Archibald
"Seeing Blind." [NegC] (14:1/2) 94, p. 54.

2651. HENDERSON, Brian
"The Heart Is a Knife." [Descant] (25:3/4, #86/87) Fall-Wint 94, p. 82.
"In an Airplane." [Descant] (25:3/4, #86/87) Fall-Wint 94, p. 84.
"Standing in Starlight." [Descant] (25:3/4, #86/87) Fall-Wint 94, p. 81.
"Tourist in Mexico." [CanLit] (142/143) Fall-Wint 94, p. 188-190.
"Valediction." [Descant] (25:3/4, #86/87) Fall-Wint 94, p. 85.
"You Say." [Descant] (25:3/4, #86/87) Fall-Wint 94, p. 83.

2652. HENDERSON, Donna
"The Apple." [Calyx] (15:3) Wint 94-95, p. 14-16.
"The Moth." [Calyx] (15:2) Sum 94, p. 54-55.

2653. HENDERSON, Stewart
"High Wire Act." [SoCoast] (16) Ja 94, p. 49.
"The Unicorn in the Slaughterhouse." [SoCoast] (16) Ja 94, p. 50-51.
"Went to." [SoCoast] (16) Ja 94, p. 52.

HENDY, Gerry von
See Von HENDY, Gerry

2654. HENKIN, David
"Woman at 12 Elm." [PoetL] (89:1) Spr 94, p. 45.

2655. HENNEDY, Hugh
"Crossing the Bridge." [TarRP] (33:2) Spr 94, p. 32-33.
"Il Sera la Lumiere du Monde." [SmPd] (31:2, #91) Spr 94, p. 27.
"Jeremiah Before Dawn and After." [Parting] (7:1) Sum 94, p. 16.

2656. HENNESSEY, Bill
"Fable for My Father." [CapeR] (29:2) Fall 94, p. 22.
"Mi Nonno" (for my wife). [SlipS] (14) 94, p. 86.
"Something I Ate." [SlipS] (14) 94, p. 85-86.

2657. HENNESSY, Eileen
"Buffalo." [ParisR] (36:132) Fall 94, p. 23.
"Crossing." [ParisR] (36:132) Fall 94, p. 22.
"Electra Hissed at by a Swan." [ParisR] (36:132) Fall 94, p. 25.
"It Is the Usual Spring." [ParisR] (36:132) Fall 94, p. 24.

2658. HENNING, Dianna
"Avon Calling." [Vis] (44) 94, p. 33.
"Crows." [Vis] (46) 94, p. 7-8.
"For the Love of Hands." [CapeR] (29:1) Spr 94, p. 20-21.
"Getting Cream Off Bordens Milk Before My Sister Beats Me To It." [SingHM] (21) 94, p. 34.
"Love as a Form of Gravity." [InterQ] (1:4) 94, p. 63.
"The Mourners." [CapeR] (29:1) Spr 94, p. 22.
"Natural." [HayF] (15) Fall-Wint 94, p. 34.

2659. HENRIQUEZ, Francisco
"Un Decimista en Paris" (A Severo Sarduy — recuerdo). [Nuez] (5:13/14/15) 94, p. 61.

2660. HENRY, B. T.
"Border Crossing" (Cameron Lake, Alberta, Canada). [HiramPoR] (57) Fall 94-Wint 95, p. 29.

2661. HENRY, Carla L.
"Navajo Changing Woman." [Blueline] (15) 94, p. 43.

2662. HENRY, Paul
"Recital." [MalR] (107) Sum 94, p. 177.
"Smoke." [MalR] (107) Sum 94, p. 176.

2663. HENRY VIII, King
"Love Ever Green" (attributed to King Henry VIII, about 1515). [SoCoast] (17) Je 94, p. 60.

2664. HENSLEY, Becca
"Interrogative Bread Poem." [ContextS] (4:1) 94, p. 7.
"There's Strength in Numbers." [NewYorkQ] (53) 94, p. 88.

HENSON, Sandra Meek
See MEEK-HENSON, Sandra

2665. HENSON, Stuart
"Introductory Offer." [CumbPR] (14:1) Fall 94, p. 61.
"Long Island Trains" (for Susan & Bill Guditus). [CumbPR] (14:1) Fall 94, p. 59-60.

2666. HENTZ, Robert R.
"The Arbiters of Art." [DogRR] (13:1, #25) Spr-Sum 94, p. 11.
"Choose Something Like a Balloon." [Hellas] (5:2) Fall-Wint 94, p. 38.

2667. HERBERT, Kristin
"Tintinnabulation." [AntR] (52:2) Spr 94, p. 310.

2668. HERBERT, Mary K. (Mary Kennan)
"Days of Horses, Dreams of Horses." [HiramPoR] (57) Fall 94-Wint 95, p. 30.
"The Deer at Midleap." [HampSPR] Wint 94, p. 11.
"The Whines of Summer." [ColEng] (56:5) S 94, p. 573.

2669. HERBERT, W. N.
"BC." [Verse] (11:2) Sum 94, p. 7.
"Corbandie." [Verse] (11:2) Sum 94, p. 6.
"Ode to Scotty." [Verse] (11:2) Sum 94, p. 4.
"Okehampton Doldrum." [Verse] (11:2) Sum 94, p. 8.
"Remote Control." [Verse] (11:2) Sum 94, p. 5.

2670. HERBERT, Zbigniew
"I Would Like to Describe." [Manoa] (6:1) Sum 94, p. 98-100.

"I Would Like to Describe" (tr. by Czeslaw Milosz and Peter Dale Scott). [NewEngR] (16:1) Wint 94, p. 105-106.
"Shame" (tr. by Charles Kraszewski). [NewYorker] (69:48) 31 Ja 94, p. 52.

2671. HERBST, Nikki
"Esther." [CentR] (38:2) Spr 94, p. 326-328.
"Five People (Homeless)." [CentR] (38:2) Spr 94, p. 323-325.
"My Father at Ninety." [DenQ] (29:1) Sum 94, p. 15.
"Rain." [CreamCR] (18:2) Fall 94, p. 95.

2672. HERD, Tracey
"The Nightmare of the Gallops-Watcher." [Verse] (11:2) Sum 94, p. 22.
"Summer '76." [Verse] (11:2) Sum 94, p. 20-21.
"The Survivors." [Verse] (11:2) Sum 94, p. 21.

2673. HERLANDS, E. Ward
"Jogging Past Her Mailbox." [ProseP] (3) 94, p. 48.

2674. HERNANDEZ, Elizabeth
"Travelling Baggage" (tr. of Magaly Quiñones). [Callaloo] (17:3) Sum 94, p. 808.

2675. HERNANDEZ, Miguel
"The World Is As It Appears" (tr. by Don Share). [HarvardR] (2) Fall 92, p. 140.

2676. HERNANDEZ-AVILA, Inés
"For Nelson — Leader, Tribal Person, Elder" (Summer 1988, on the occasion of Mandela's 70th birthday, when the South African government offered him a six hour visit with his family). [Callaloo] (17:1) Wint 94, p. 94-96.
"Oaxaca — summer 1989." [Callaloo] (17:1) Wint 94, p. 89-93.
"Shapechanger" (Appeared in a different version in *Hurricane Alice*, Winter 93). [Callaloo] (17:1) Wint 94, p. 97-98.

2677. HERNANDEZ-RAMDWAR, Camille
"Baited Illusion." [WestCL] (28:1/2, #13/14) Spr-Fall 94, p. 56.
"Colour Bar." [WestCL] (28:1/2, #13/14) Spr-Fall 94, p. 57.

2678. HERNCANE, Michael Bruce
"Once." [WestB] (35) 94, p. 77-78.

2679. HEROLD, Andre-ferdinand
"Falling on Earth" (tr. by Carol Poster). [PoetryE] (37/38) Spr 94, p. 233.

2680. HERRERA, Georgina
"In the Way of Fortune" (tr. by Yolanda V. Fundora). [MichQR] (33:4) Fall 94, p. 773.
"Letter to César Vallejo" (tr. by Yolanda V. Fundora). [MichQR] (33:4) Fall 94, p. 771.

2681. HERRINGTON, Neva
"Overnight." [Wind] (74) 94, p. 21.

2682. HERSCHBACH, Robert
"An Epic." [QW] (39) Sum-Fall 94, p. 209-210.

2683. HERSHEY, Laura
"A Mother Tells." [Kaleid] (Special Issue) 94, p. 25.

2684. HERSHON, Robert
"Clint Eastwood and the Perfect Smile." [WilliamMR] (32) 94, p. 32.
"The German Lunatic" (for Paul Violi). [Sulfur] (35) Fall 94, p. 62-64.

2685. HERZ, Steve
"Cross Country Ski." [SmPd] (31:2, #91) Spr 94, p. 26.

2686. HERZBERG, Judith
"Song" (tr. by Shirley Kaufman, w. the author). [Field] (50) Spr 94, p. 45.
"Target" (tr. by Shirley Kaufman, w. the author). [Field] (50) Spr 94, p. 46.

2687. HESKETH, Phoebe
"The Rivals." [Stand] (35:2) Spr 94, p. 30.

2688. HESS, Amira
"And As Far As What I Wanted" (tr. by Yonina Borvick). [LitR] (37:2) Wint 94, p. 306.
"Then Slake Him From" (tr. by Marsha Weinstein). [LitR] (37:2) Wint 94, p. 307.
"The Time of the Singing Birds" (tr. by Ammiel Alcalay). [LitR] (37:2) Wint 94, p. 307-310.

2689. HESS, Scott
"Important Things" (for my mother). [HiramPoR] (55/56) Fall 93-Sum 94, p. 44.
"My Father at the Piano." [HiramPoR] (55/56) Fall 93-Sum 94, p. 42-43.

2690. HESS, Sonya
"The Colorist." [Caliban] (14) 94, p. 73.
"Names." [WestB] (34) 94, p. 17.
"Quaint Songs." [HiramPoR] (55/56) Fall 93-Sum 94, p. 45.

2691. HETTICH, Michael
"A Dance Called Leaping." [LitR] (37:4) Sum 94, p. 569.
"For One Entire Day." [Sun] (221) My 94, p. 9.
"From Day to Day." [LitR] (37:4) Sum 94, p. 568.
"A Marriage." [LitR] (37:4) Sum 94, p. 570.
2692. HEWITT, Christopher
"Privilege of Dreams" (after paintings by Beatrice Ost). [LaurelR] (28:1) Wint 94, p. 63.
"Valentine's Day" (after paintings by Beatrice Ost). [LaurelR] (28:1) Wint 94, p. 64.
2693. HEWITT, Geroge
"The Metaphysician at Maplewood Park." [SoCoast] (16) Ja 94, p. 38-39.
2694. HEYEN, William
"Aloha." [ChamLR] (14/15) Spr-Fall 94, p. 25-26.
"The American Civil War." [SouthernR] (30:3) Sum 94, p. 533-535.
"Anticipatory Breach." [Crazy] (47) Wint 94, p. 43.
"The Beautiful Daughter." [SouthernR] (30:3) Sum 94, p. 535-536.
"Bison." [WormR] (34:4, #136) 94, p. 151-152.
"Blackbird Spring." [OntR] (41) Fall-Wint 94, p. 104.
"Christmas Celebration of SS Guards in Neuengamme." [CreamCR] (18:2) Fall 94, p. 172.
"The Grid." [WormR] (34:4, #136) 94, p. 150-151.
"The Institute of Brain, 1991." [CreamCR] (18:2) Fall 94, p. 173.
"Leper Memory." [ChamLR] (14/15) Spr-Fall 94, p. 27.
2695. HIBBARD, Allen
"Becoming a Hyena" (tr. of Mahmud Al-Sayed, w. Osama Isber). [CimR] (108) Jl 94, p. 18.
"The Human Excess" (tr. of Mohammad Al-Maghut, w. Osama Isber). [CimR] (108) Jl 94, p. 15.
"I Am Trying to Save the Last Female Before the Arrival of the Tartars" (tr. of Nizar Kabbani, w. Osama Isber). [CimR] (108) Jl 94, p. 12-14.
"Marlboro" (tr. of Mahmud Al-Sayed, w. Osama Isber). [CimR] (108) Jl 94, p. 18.
"Surrealism" (tr. of Mahmud Al-Sayed, w. Osama Isber). [CimR] (108) Jl 94, p. 19.
"Terror and Sex" (tr. of Mohammad Al-Maghut, w. Osama Isber). [CimR] (108) Jl 94, p. 16-17.
"The Trojan Horse" (tr. of Mahmud Al-Sayed, w. Osama Isber). [CimR] (108) Jl 94, p. 18.
"Why, Oh Arab?" (tr. of Mahmud Al-Sayed, w. Osama Isber). [CimR] (108) Jl 94, p. 19.
2696. HIBBARD, Tom
"Clandestine Passage" (tr. of Pierre Reverdy). [WillowS] (34) Sum 94, p. 65.
"Wedding Day" (tr. of Francis Jammes). [WillowS] (34) Sum 94, p. 64.
2697. HICKMAN, Lou Ella
"Easter Vigil." [SpiritSH] (59) 94, p. 27.
"Emmaus." [SpiritSH] (59) 94, p. 25.
"Eve's Lament." [SpiritSH] (59) 94, p. 24.
"Finding the Child Jesus in the Temple." [SpiritSH] (59) 94, p. 24.
"Prairie Evening." [Blueline] (15) 94, p. 34.
"Purgatory — Song of the Beloved." [SpiritSH] (59) 94, p. 26.
"The Visitor." [Blueline] (15) 94, p. 34.
2698. HICKMAN, Trenton L.
"Homecoming." [TarRP] (33:2) Spr 94, p. 4.
2699. HICOK, Bob
"In Her Hands." [PoetryNW] (35:4) Wint 94-95, p. 32-33.
"Memory." [RiverS] (40) 94, p. 50-51.
"My Job as It Relates to Bruegel's" (Netherlandish Proverbs). [Iowa] (24:3) Fall 94, p. 150-151.
"Nigger." [Iowa] (24:3) Fall 94, p. 151-152.
"Prodigal." [RiverS] (40) 94, p. 49.
"Surgery." [PoetryNW] (35:4) Wint 94-95, p. 31.
"Visiting the Wall." [TarRP] (33:2) Spr 94, p. 20-22.
2700. HIDGE, Jan D.
"Spelt in the Hoboes' Signs" (1st Prize, 8th Annual Contest). [SoCoast] (16) Ja 94, p. 34-35.
2701. HIESTAND, Emily
"This Other God." [Image] (8) Wint 94-95, p. 95-96.

"What They Were Sacrificing" (Columbus Day, 1992, after the Maya and Aztec). [Image] (8) Wint 94-95, p. 96-99.

2702. HIGGINS, Dick
"A Three-Part Cat Names 'Rillo'." [Talisman] (13) Fall 94-Wint 95, p. 286-288.

2703. HIGH, John
"In the Back Yard." [Talisman] (12) Spr 94, p. 239.

2704. HIGHFIELD, Arnold
"Tether." [AnthNEW] (6) 94, p. 32.

2705. HIGHTOWER, Scott
"The Application of Force" (*Die Geisselung Christi*, Adriaen van der Werff, 1710). [Salm] (101/102) Wint-Spr 94, p. 160-162.
"Tartessos" (Rhys Carpenter's 1925 *Greeks in Spain*). [Hellas] (5:2) Fall-Wint 94, p. 66-67.

2706. HIKMET, Nazim
"The Birth" (tr. by Randy Blasing and Mutlu Konuk). [AmerPoR] (23:2) Mr-Ap 94, p. 37.
"Last Letter to My Son" (tr. by Randy Blasing and Mutlu Konuk). [AmerPoR] (23:2) Mr-Ap 94, p. 38-39.
"The Mailman" (from Hungarian travel notes, tr. by Randy Blasing and Mutlu Konuk). [AmerPoR] (23:2) Mr-Ap 94, p. 38.
"One A.M." (tr. by Randy Blasing and Mutlu Konuk). [AmerPoR] (23:2) Mr-Ap 94, p. 37.
"Some Memories" (tr. by Randy Blasing and Mutlu Konuk). [AmerPoR] (23:2) Mr-Ap 94, p. 40-41.
"Thirty Years Ago" (tr. by Randy Blasing and Mutlu Konuk). [AmerPoR] (23:2) Mr-Ap 94, p. 41.
"To Samet Vurgun" (tr. by Randy Blasing and Mutlu Konuk). [AmerPoR] (23:2) Mr-Ap 94, p. 39.
"Windows" (tr. by Randy Blasing and Mutlu Konuk). [AmerPoR] (23:2) Mr-Ap 94, p. 39-40.

2707. HILBERRY, Conrad
"The Calvinist." [GettyR] (7:4) Aut 94, p. 693.
"Domestic Animals." [Shen] (44:1) Spr 94, p. 81.
"The Eye." [Shen] (44:4) Wint 94, p. 28-30.
"Falling in Love." [GettyR] (7:4) Aut 94, p. 694-695.
"Martha Dancing." [Shen] (44:1) Spr 94, p. 82-83.
"Omens." [VirQR] (70:2) Spr 94, p. 301-302.
"Player Piano." [Shen] (44:1) Spr 94, p. 84-85.

2708. HILBERRY, Jane
"Craft." [VirQR] (70:4) Aut 94, p. 675-676.
"Free Coffee." [VirQR] (70:4) Aut 94, p. 677-678.
"My Mother's Beauty." [Northeast] (5:11) Wint 94-95, p. 22-23.
"Nude" (after a painting by William McGregor Paxton). [Northeast] (5:11) Wint 94-95, p. 20-21.
"Train." [VirQR] (70:4) Aut 94, p. 674-675.

2709. HILBERT, Donna
"Code Green" (16 poems). [Pearl] (20) Spr 94, p. 23-41.

2710. HILBERT, Ernie, Jr.
"White House." [BlackBR] (18) Wint-Spr 94, p. 10-11.

2711. HILDEBRAND, William C.
"Remember When the Legend Was a Yodel." [Amelia] (7:3, #22) 94, p. 77.

2712. HILL, Craig
"Ulysses' Shipmates" (tr. of Jean de La Fontaine). [Raritan] (13:4) Spr 94, p. 19-21.

2713. HILL, Eric
"Saint John's Crows." [TickleAce] (28) Fall-Wint 94, p. 112-113.

2714. HILL, Gerald
"The Talking Cure." [Event] (23:2) Sum 94, p. 27-28.

2715. HILL, Henry F.
"All in the Family." [Light] (10) Sum 94, p. 18.
"Queer Ducks." [Light] (12) Wint 94-95, p. 10.
"Turnabout." [Light] (11) Aut 94, p. 15.

2716. HILL, Lindsay
"Birth." [Sulfur] (35) Fall 94, p. 119.
"He-dog and Spine." [RiverC] (14:2) Spr 94, p. 49.
"Inferno." [Sulfur] (35) Fall 94, p. 121-122.
"Jackal Say." [RiverC] (14:2) Spr 94, p. 48.

"Mendelevium." [Sulfur] (35) Fall 94, p. 120.
"Receiver." [RiverC] (14:2) Spr 94, p. 46-47.
"Terror Pantoum." [Sulfur] (35) Fall 94, p. 120-121.

2717. HILL, Pamela Steed
"A Close Finish." [Vis] (44) 94, p. 19.
"Learning to Walk." [Epoch] (43:1) 94, p. 86-87.
"The Proofer." [FourQ] (8:2) Fall 94, p. 52-53.
"Saddling the Gods (or How to Live Through a Tornado)." [Epoch] (43:1) 94, p. 88-89.
"Wanting to Swim." [FourQ] (8:2) Fall 94, p. 54.

2718. HILL, Rick
"The Forerunner." [HayF] (15) Fall-Wint 94, p. 97.

2719. HILL, Selima
"The Birds." [GrahamHR] (18) Wint 94-95, p. 12.
"Eating Chocolates in the Dark." [Jacaranda] (5:1) Wint-Spr 91, p. 56-57.
"The Island." [GrahamHR] (18) Wint 94-95, p. 13.
"Silence" (for Padraig Daly). [GrahamHR] (18) Wint 94-95, p. 14.

2720. HILLAR, Malgorzata
"Request of Thyme" (tr. by David Sparenberg and Aleksandra Szostalo). [WebR] (18) Fall 94, p. 15.

2721. HILLILA, Bernhard
"Pulling the Plug." [Light] (11) Aut 94, p. 8.

2722. HILLMAN, Brenda
"The Unbeginning." [Antaeus] (75/76) Aut 94, p. 280.

2723. HILLMAN, Grady
"Dancers of the Hyperinflation Waltz." [Border] (3) Fall 93, p. 33.

2724. HILTON, David
"For Samantha at 14." [PoetryNW] (35:3) Aut 94, p. 16-17.
"For William Stafford." [PoetL] (89:2) Sum 94, p. 59.
"Love-Life." [PoetL] (89:2) Sum 94, p. 57-58.
"The Old Hog Farm." [PoetL] (89:2) Sum 94, p. 56.
"A Root Canal Afternoon." [Parting] (7:2) Wint 94-95, p. 43.

HINE, Alvaro Cardona
See CARDONA-HINE, Alvaro

2725. HINE, Richard
"Angels." [Parting] (7:2) Wint 94-95, p. 67-68.

2726. HINNANT, Coleman
"About the Detached Hand in the Photograph." [Outbr] (25) 94, p. 45-46.
"Blue." [PlumR] (7) [94?], p. 46-47.
"Like Stones and Sunsets." [PlumR] (7) [94?], p. 48-49.

2727. HINTON, David
"Apple and Brute Stone" (tr. of Bei Dao). [Sulfur] (34) Spr 94, p. 15-16.
"Background" (tr. of Bei Dao). [Conjunc] (23) 94, p. 134.
"Flash" (tr. of Bei Dao). [InterQ] (1:2) 93, p. 40.
"Folding Procedure" (tr. of Bei Dao). [Sulfur] (34) Spr 94, p. 17-18.
"For T. Tranströmer" (tr. of Bei Dao). [Talisman] (12) Spr 94, p. 181.
"Lament" (tr. of Bei Dao). [Sulfur] (34) Spr 94, p. 15.
"Morning" (tr. of Bei Dao). [Conjunc] (23) 94, p. 133.
"Musical Variations" (tr. of Bei Dao). [Sulfur] (34) Spr 94, p. 18.
"Other Than Tomorrow" (tr. of Bei Dao). [InterQ] (1:2) 93, p. 43.
"Pastoral" (tr. of Bei Dao). [InterQ] (1:2) 93, p. 41.
"Playwright" (tr. of Bei Dao). [Talisman] (12) Spr 94, p. 181.
"Realm" (tr. of Bei Dao). [Conjunc] (23) 94, p. 135.
"Records" (tr. of Bei Dao). [InterQ] (1:2) 93, p. 42.
"Seeing Double" (tr. of Bei Dao). [Conjunc] (23) 94, p. 133-134.
"This Day" (tr. of Bei Dao). [Conjunc] (23) 94, p. 134-135.
"Toxin" (tr. of Bei Dao). [Sulfur] (34) Spr 94, p. 16.
"Untitled: At the mother tongue's line of defense" (tr. of Bei Dao). [Sulfur] (34) Spr 94, p. 17.
"Way" (for Tu Fu). [Talisman] (12) Spr 94, p. 92-93.

2728. HINTON, Grady
"Brown's Blues." [Eyeball] (3) 93, p. 27.

2729. HIPOLITO, Terry
"Exit Portatus Crudusque Rex." [SoCoast] (17) Je 94, p. 57.

2730. HIPPERT, Rebecca
"The Names I Can't Remember" (for Bob). [HiramPoR] (57) Fall 94-Wint 95, p. 31-33.
2731. HIPPOLYTE, Kendel
"Bed-Time Story, W. I." [MassR] (35:3/4) Aut-Wint 94, p. 385-386.
"Castries" (for John Robert Lee). [MassR] (35:3/4) Aut-Wint 94, p. 465-470.
"Three Sonnets for Mister Kent." [MassR] (35:3/4) Aut-Wint 94, p. 463-464.
HIROAKI, Sato
See SATO, Hiroaki
2732. HIRSCH, Edward
"Blue Hydrangea." [NewYorker] (70:13) 16 My 94, p. 84.
"The Burning of the Midnight Lamp." [ParisR] (36:133) Wint 94, p. 216-218.
"Days of 1968." [Antaeus] (75/76) Aut 94, p. 281.
"Hotel Window." [NewRep] (210:22) 30 My 94, p. 40.
"Idea of the Holy" (New York City, 1975). [ParisR] (36:133) Wint 94, p. 215-216.
"The Ordeal of Civility." [GlobalCR] (4) Fall 94, p. 92-93.
"Traveller" (St. Lucia, 1985). [NewYorker] (69:50) 14 F 94, p. 68.
2733. HIRSCH, Gene
"Prayer." [HiramPoR] (55/56) Fall 93-Sum 94, p. 46-47.
2734. HIRSCH, Neisha
"The Day of the Rose." [HeavenB] (11) 94, p. 85.
2735. HIRSCH, Steven
"Health Foods." [HeavenB] (11) 94, p. 77.
2736. HIRSCHMAN, Jack
"The Season of Reckonings" (In Memory of My Brother, the Writer Guy F. Laraque, Assassinated Under the Cedras Regime, tr. of Paul Laraque). [CentralP] (23) Spr 94, p. 70-72.
2737. HIRSHFIELD, Jane
"A Breakable Spell." [Manoa] (6:1) Sum 94, p. 19-20.
"Cycladic Figure: The Harp Player (ca. 3000 B.C.E.)." [Antaeus] (73/74) Spr 94, p. 154-155.
"An Earthly Beauty." [AmerPoR] (23:4) Jl-Ag 94, p. 11.
"Eros" (tr. of Rainer Maria Rilke, w. Samuel Michael Halevi). [DenQ] (29:1) Sum 94, p. 97.
"The Gods Are Not Large." [AmerPoR] (23:4) Jl-Ag 94, p. 11.
"Happiness." [Manoa] (6:1) Sum 94, p. 18-19.
"The Love of Aged Horses." [Atlantic] (273:2) F 94, p. 81.
"Lying." [Atlantic] (274:5) N 94, p. 72.
"Poem on the Treasury of the Clear-seeing Eye" (tr. of Eihei Dogen). [NewEngR] (16:3) Sum 94, p. 32.
"A Recurring Possibility." [Manoa] (6:1) Sum 94, p. 18.
"Untitled: From almost all things, It flashes toward feeling" (tr. of Rainer Maria Rilke, w. Samuel Michael Halevi). [DenQ] (29:1) Sum 94, p. 98.
2738. HIX, H. L.
"I Was Never in Control." [LaurelR] (28:2) Sum 94, p. 82-83.
"The Spindle Turns on the Knees of Necessity" (— Plato, *Republic*). [Ploughs] (20:4) Wint 94-95, p. 73.
"This Morally Neutralized Domain of Intercourse" (— Habermas, *Communication and the Evolution of Society*). [Ploughs] (20:4) Wint 94-95, p. 75.
"What One Would See If One Did Not" (— Wittgenstein, *Remarks on Colour*). [Ploughs] (20:4) Wint 94-95, p. 74.
2739. HIXON, India
"Mulberry comes through in you." [Talisman] (12) Spr 94, p. 109.
2740. HLAVSA, Virginia (Virginia V.)
"Connecting the Dots." [Comm] (121:10) 20 My 94, p. 22.
"Declensions." [SmPd] (31:3, #92) Fall 94, p. 31.
"Obligations." [Comm] (121:7) 8 Ap 94, p. 10.
"Power Lines." [CumbPR] (13:2) Spr 94, p. 39.
2741. HO, Louise
"Jet-Lagged in Boston." [PoetryC] (14:3) My 94, p. 20.
2742. HOAGLAND, Everett
"Cookin'." [AmerPoR] (23:3) My-Je 94, p. 36.
"Good Bloods and Bad Water." [AmerPoR] (23:3) My-Je 94, p. 35.
"Keeping the Faith" (for my great-grandfather, William David Holmes, Union Army Soldier). [AmerPoR] (23:3) My-Je 94, p. 36.

"Kinda Blue: Miles Davis Died Today" (for Michael S. Harper). [AmerPoR] (23:3) My-Je 94, p. 35.
2743. HOAGLAND, Tony
"Jet." [Ploughs] (20:4) Wint 94-95, p. 76.
"Lucky." [PassN] (15:2) Wint 94, p. 35-36.
"Mission." [HarvardR] (6) Spr 94, p. 68.
"Self-Improvement." [Ploughs] (20:4) Wint 94-95, p. 77-78.
"Totally." [PassN] (15:2) Wint 94, p. 33-34.
2744. HOARE, Deirdre
"The Dead Turn at the Gate to Hands, Leaves, and Days." [Pivot] (42) 94, p. 36.
HOBBES, James
See HOBBS, James
2745. HOBBS, Blair
"Beatings." [PraS] (68:2) Sum 94, p. 131-132.
"Sister Psychic." [PraS] (68:2) Sum 94, p. 132-133.
2746. HOBBS, James
"The Antiquarians." [BellArk] (10:2) Mr-Ap 94, p. 9.
"Book Learning." [BellArk] (10:3 [i.e. 10:4]) Jl-Ag 94, p. 25.
"Brief Candle." [BellArk] (10:1) Ja-F 94, p. 23.
"Co-sine." [BellArk] (10:1) Ja-F 94, p. 25.
"Reluctance." [BellArk] (10:3) My-Je 94, p. 7.
"Rhythm" (Road XY, Morgan County). [BellArk] (10:3) My-Je 94, p. 9.
2747. HODGE, Margaret
"After a Purse Snatching Led Me to Jenny." [BellArk] (10:6) N-D 94, p. 5.
"For a Fifth Anniversary." [BellArk] (10:3) My-Je 94, p. 7.
"A Hike at the End of Cape Flattery." [BellArk] (10:5) S-O 94, p. 12.
"Late Spring on Campus." [BellArk] (10:5) S-O 94, p. 12.
"Letter to Alice from Her Restored House While House Sitting" (for Ken Strunk, 13). [BellArk] (10:3 [i.e. 10:4]) Jl-Ag 94, p. 9.
"The Prince of 317 Avenue B, Snohomish." [BellArk] (10:1) Ja-F 94, p. 16.
"A Small Tweed Suitcase." [BellArk] (10:6) N-D 94, p. 5.
"A Stuffed Seal." [BellArk] (10:6) N-D 94, p. 5.
"Sunny Labor Day at Shilshole Bay." [BellArk] (10:6) N-D 94, p. 5.
2748. HODGES, Gregg
"After the Fire." [TarRP] (33:2) Spr 94, p. 35.
2749. HODGINS, Philip
"At the Sheep-Parasite Field Day." [NewYorker] (69:46) 17 Ja 94, p. 62.
"Carracci's Self-Portrait." [MalR] (107) Sum 94, p. 76.
"The Prey." [MalR] (107) Sum 94, p. 77.
2750. HODNETT, Edda
"Brotherhood" (tr. of Doris Runge). [SouthernHR] (28:3) Sum 94, p. 256.
"Dressed Up" (tr. of Doris Runge). [SouthernHR] (28:3) Sum 94, p. 257.
"Flying" (tr. of Doris Runge). [SouthernHR] (28:3) Sum 94, p. 251.
"Hunting Song" (tr. of Doris Runge). [SouthernHR] (28:3) Sum 94, p. 259.
"The Last Line" (tr. of Doris Runge). [SouthernHR] (28:3) Sum 94, p. 254.
"Market Woman in Siena" (tr. of Doris Runge). [SouthernHR] (28:3) Sum 94, p. 253.
"Night Asylum" (tr. of Doris Runge). [SouthernHR] (28:3) Sum 94, p. 255.
"Ophelia's Flowers" (tr. of Doris Runge). [SouthernHR] (28:3) Sum 94, p. 252.
2751. HODOR, Timothy
"The Down's Syndrome Woman." [NegC] (14:1/2) 94, p. 29.
"The Self-Portrait, 1652." [NegC] (14:1/2) 94, p. 28.
2752. HOEKSEMA, Kurt
"The Abridged Brother Tiger" (4 poems taken from a longer sequence, "The Very Rich Hours of Brother Tiger"). [Image] (3) Spr 93, p. 82-84.
2753. HOEPPNER, Edward Haworth
"Eyelid." [Journal] (18:2) Fall-Wint 94, p. 78.
"On White." [Journal] (18:2) Fall-Wint 94, p. 79-82.
"Rain." [Journal] (18:1) Spr-Sum 94, p. 43-44.
"Something Rather Than Nothing." [Journal] (18:1) Spr-Sum 94, p. 45-46.
"Surrender." [Journal] (18:1) Spr-Sum 94, p. 41-42.
2754. HOEY, Allen
"Another Sunday Morning." [CimR] (107) Ap 94, p. 85-86.
"Suppose." [Hudson] (47:1) Spr 94, p. 84.
"Up Before Dawn." [Hudson] (47:1) Spr 94, p. 83.

2755. HOFER, Marianna
"In My Own Secret Heart." [Parting] (7:1) Sum 94, p. 58-59.
2756. HOFF, Jennifer
"Part 2 (The Reluctant Subject)." [Chain] (1) Spr-Sum 94, p. 216-217.
2757. HOFFMAN, Barbara
"Good Girl." [SlipS] (14) 94, p. 64.
"Hot Bread." [SlipS] (14) 94, p. 65.
2758. HOFFMAN, Daniel
"Blizzard." [Hudson] (47:3) Aut 94, p. 418-419.
"Bob." [Hudson] (47:3) Aut 94, p. 417-418.
"Scott Nearing's Ninety-Eighth Year." [GeoR] (48:3) Fall 94, p. 515-516.
2759. HOFFMANN, Roald
"Havana, 1990-1517." [ColR] (21:2) Fall 94, p. 102.
"How Exactly Was This Done?" [PraS] (68:3) Fall 94, p. 6.
"Juan de Prado in Amsterdam, 1656." [ColR] (21:2) Fall 94, p. 100-101.
"Olive Tree Master." [ColR] (21:2) Fall 94, p. 103.
"The Scientific Method." [NewL] (60:3) 94, p. 106.
2760. HOFMANN, Michael
"Intimations of Immortality" (for F. C. Delius). [Antaeus] (75/76) Aut 94, p. 282-283.
2761. HOGAN, Linda
"Great Measures." [Callaloo] (17:1) Wint 94, p. 25-26.
"Nothing." [Callaloo] (17:1) Wint 94, p. 24.
"Other, Sister, Twin." [Callaloo] (17:1) Wint 94, p. 27-28.
"The Truth Is." [EngJ] (83:3) Mr 94, p. 100.
2762. HOGAN, Michael
"A Room on the North Side." [Pembroke] (26) 94, p. 111.
2763. HOGAN, Wayne
"Consciousness and Book Reviews." [Light] (11) Aut 94, p. 17.
"My Elvis Sighting." [Light] (12) Wint 94-95, p. 19.
"The People, Well, Maybe." [SlipS] (14) 94, p. 92.
"Performance Poet." [HiramPoR] (57) Fall 94-Wint 95, p. 34.
"The Philosophers, the Sociologists." [DogRR] (13:1, #25) Spr-Sum 94, p. 24.
"When Guitarists Were Gods." [DogRR] (26) Wint 94-95, p. 6.
2764. HOGGARD, Lynn
"Laughing Ladies." [XavierR] (14:2) Fall 94, p. 67.
"Poteaux d'Angle (Angle Markers)" (tr. of Henri Michaux). [GrahamHR] (18) Wint 94-95, p. 81-82.
2765. HOGNESS, Deborah
"To Fiskadoro from Bangor." [CrabCR] (8:2/3/9:1/2/3) 94, p. 112.
2766. HOGUE, Cynthia
"Crossing Brooklyn Bridge" (for an unknown man, and for Ed). [SouthernR] (30:1) Ja, Wint 94, p. 86-87.
"Love Story." [NoAmR] (279:2) Mr-Ap 94, p. 42.
"Moving South During Summer." [NegC] (13:2/3) 93, p. 22.
"We All Shine On" (for J. W., April 1992). [CentralP] (23) Spr 94, p. 5-6.
2767. HOLAHAN, Susan
"Dear Editor Kirby, Even in This Facility." [Agni] (39) 94, p. 106.
"In the Easy Dream." [PlumR] (7) [94?], p. 10.
"Talk *This* Way." [SenR] (24:1) Spr 94, p. 11-12.
"Wind My Chair Makes." [SenR] (24:1) Spr 94, p. 13.
2768. HOLAS, Nicole
"Colour." [WestCL] (28:1/2, #13/14) Spr-Fall 94, p. 170-171.
2769. HOLDEN, Elizabeth W.
"Eel Grass." [ChatR] (14:3) Spr 94, p. 39-40.
"Stillness." [Kalliope] (16:1) 94, p. 56.
2770. HOLDEN, Jonathan
"Gould." [NewEngR] (16:4) Fall 94, p. 151-153.
"La Nauseé." [NewEngR] (16:4) Fall 94, p. 153-154.
"The Wicked Witch Is Dead" (Margaret Hamilton, 82, Dies — Played Wicked Witch in 'Oz'). [NewEngR] (16:4) Fall 94, p. 155-156.
2771. HOLDER, Barbara
"One Sunday." [Wind] (74) 94, p. 22.
2772. HÖLDERLIN, Friedrich
"The Ages of Life" (tr. by Mark Irwin). [DenQ] (29:1) Sum 94, p. 79.
"The Middle of Life" (tr. by Mark Irwin). [DenQ] (29:1) Sum 94, p. 80.

"To Nature" (tr. by Karl Kirchwey). [Antaeus] (73/74) Spr 94, p. 160-162.

2773. HOLENDER, Barbara D.
"But Is It Art?" [Light] (11) Aut 94, p. 19.

2774. HOLINGER, Richard
"Coma Ward." [Boulevard] (9:1/2, #25/26) Spr 94, p. 57.
"Treasure." [Boulevard] (9:1/2, #25/26) Spr 94, p. 58-59.

2775. HOLLADAY, Hilary
"Flurried." [WestB] (35) 94, p. 53.
"Mothers of Antiquity." [WestB] (35) 94, p. 52.

2776. HOLLAHAN, Eugene
"Metairie." [NegC] (13:2/3) 93, p. 23.
"The Tadpole in the Tide Pool." [CumbPR] (13:2) Spr 94, p. 1-3.
"Wind for the Misbegotten." [CumbPR] (13:2) Spr 94, p. 4-5.

2777. HOLLAND, Andrea Claire
"Delivering." [PaintedHR] (11) Spr-Sum 94, p. 5.

2778. HOLLAND, Nelson
"Mind's Eye." [WillowS] (34) Sum 94, p. 38.
"Night and Day." [WillowS] (34) Sum 94, p. 39.
"Slight of Hands." [WillowS] (34) Sum 94, p. 40-41.

2779. HOLLAND, Walter
"Examining Rooms" (for Yves Lubin). [JamesWR] (11:5) Fall 94, p. 16.

2780. HOLLANDER, John
"Figurehead." [NewRep] (211:3/4) 18-25 Jl 94, p. 46.
"Forget How to Remember, How to Forget." [Poetry] (165:3) D 94, p. 153-154.
"So Red." [NewYorker] (70:33) 17 O 94, p. 95.

2781. HOLLEY, Margaret
"Bread of Angels." [SouthernHR] (28:1) Wint 94, p. 60-61.
"Fire-Watch." [SouthernHR] (28:1) Wint 94, p. 58-59.
"Honeymoon." [SouthernHR] (28:1) Wint 94, p. 62.
"Neanderthal." [GeoR] (48:4) Wint 94, p. 815-816.

2782. HOLLO, Anselm
"At That Point" (tr. of Jouni Inkala). [GrandS] (12:4, #48) Wint 94, p. 63-64.
"Publication Date First of October." [Talisman] (12) Spr 94, p. 208.
"Small Door at Far End." [NewAW] (12) Spr-Sum 94, p. 49-51.

2783. HOLLOWAY, Eachan
"Hostage." [DenQ] (29:1) Sum 94, p. 16.
"The Morning Patriot." [QW] (39) Sum-Fall 94, p. 168.

2784. HOLLOWAY, Glenna
"Rosalind and Orlando" (Act VI at Rowland House). [Amelia] (7:3, #22) 94, p. 120.
"To John Singer Sargent's Madam X on Tour." [SoCoast] (17) Je 94, p. 52-53.

2785. HOLLY, Margaret
"Dreaming Demeter." [GettyR] (7:2) Spr 94, p. 322-323.

2786. HOLM, Bill
"Girl Eating Rice." [WeberS] (11:1) Wint 94, p. 40.
"In Arches Park: Moab, Utah." [WeberS] (11:1) Wint 94, p. 38.
"The New Music, the Old Song." [WeberS] (11:1) Wint 94, p. 40.
"Racial Confusion in China." [WeberS] (11:1) Wint 94, p. 39.
"To Priests and Therapists of Whatever Denomination. Driving up Price Canyon to Spanish Fork along the Old Union Pacific Tracks." [WeberS] (11:1) Wint 94, p. 39.
"What Brigham Young Said." [WeberS] (11:1) Wint 94, p. 38.

2787. HOLMAN, Bob
"Let's Get Butt Naked and Write Poetry." [Talisman] (13) Fall 94-Wint 95, p. 140-142.

2788. HOLMES, Darryl
"Michael Jackson Meets Bob Marley." [Eyeball] (3) 93, p. 14.
"Spotlight." [BrooklynR] (11) 94, p. 115.

2789. HOLMES, J. J. Jackie
"Walking Home Against the Crowd." [Amelia] (7:3, #22) 94, p. 80.

2790. HOLMES, Janet
"Against the Literal." [GeoR] (48:2) Sum 94, p. 314.
"Post-Solstice." [PassN] (15:2) Wint 94, p. 32.

2791. HOLMES, John Clellon
"Fear in the Afternoon." [AmerPoR] (23:6) N-D 94, p. 55.

2792. HOLMES, Nancy
"The Adulteress and Her Specialty." [Event] (23:3) Wint 94-95, p. 55-56.

"The Adulteress and the Poem." [Event] (23:3) Wint 94-95, p. 54.
"The Adulteress in a Ditch." [Event] (23:3) Wint 94-95, p. 57.

2793. HOLTMAN, Janet
"Family Tobacco" (for my brother). [GreensboroR] (56) Sum 94, p. 32-33.

2794. HOLTMAN, Jason
"Squirrel Hunting." [SycamoreR] (6:1) Wint 94, p. 34-35.

2795. HOLTON, Brian
"Before Daybreak" (tr. of Yang Lian). [Conjunc] (23) 94, p. 43.
"The Foundations of Terror" (tr. of Yang Lian). [Conjunc] (23) 94, p. 46.
"The Garden on a Winter's Day, 1" (tr. of Yang Lian). [Conjunc] (23) 94, p. 44.
"The Garden on a Winter's Day, 3" (tr. of Yang Lian). [Conjunc] (23) 94, p. 45.
"Mountain Valley" (tr. of Yang Lian). [Conjunc] (23) 94, p. 43-44.

2796. HOLUB, Miroslav
"The Good Kings Wenceslases" (tr. by Dana Hábová and David Young). [HarvardR] (Premier Issue) Spr 92, p. 52.
"Intensive Care Unit" (tr. by Dana Hábová and David Young). [InterQ] (1:1) [93?], p. 93.
"Pompeii" (tr. by Dana Hábová and David Young). [HarvardR] (Premier Issue) Spr 92, p. 117.
"Pompeii" (tr. by Dana Hábová and David Young). [InterQ] (1:1) [93?], p. 94-95.

2797. HOLZER, Ryszard
"Mój Brzuchu." [NewRena] (9:1, #27) 94, p. 148.
"My Stomach" (tr. by Daniel Bourne). [NewRena] (9:1, #27) 94, p. 149.
"Niespodzianka." [NewRena] (9:1, #27) 94, p. 146.
"The Surpise" (tr. by Daniel Bourne). [NewRena] (9:1, #27) 94, p. 147.

2798. HOMER, Art
"Autumn Walk, the Old Neighborhood." [WritersF] (20) 94, p. 191.
"A Heart Attack in the Men's Shower." [SouthernR] (30:3) Sum 94, p. 537-538.
"I'm Not He Is." [PraS] (68:2) Sum 94, p. 122.
"Three Day California Honky Tonking Weekend." [GreenMR] (NS 17:2) Fall-Wint 94-95, p. 119-120.
"Winter Sonnet for an Absent Friend." [PraS] (68:2) Sum 94, p. 122-123.

2799. HONES, Karen Lee
"The Cowboy Sestinas." [YellowS] (11:4, #44) Wint 93-94, p. 4-7.

2800. HONGO, Garrett
"Ministry: Homage to Kilauea." [WillowR] (21) Spr 94, p. 65-66.

2801. HONIG, Edwin
"Arising at Mount San Angelo." [HarvardR] (6) Spr 94, p. 49.

2802. HONYCHURCH, Lennox
"The Arawak Curse." [CaribbeanW] (8) 94, p. 84-86.
"Twaleyba (Remember)" (for Althea). [CaribbeanW] (8) 94, p. 87-88.

2803. HOOD, James W.
"A Peculiar Mercy." [ChrC] (111:34) 23-30 N 94, p. 1103.

2804. HOOD, Mary A.
"Obscene Letter" (First Sue Saniel Elkind National Poetry Award, Finalist). [Kalliope] (16:2) 94, p. 26.

2805. HOOD, Mary Winifred
"His Vision of the Angel of Death." [Poetry] (165:3) D 94, p. 135.
"St. Caspar del Bufalo." [Poetry] (165:3) D 94, p. 136.
"St. Catherine Dei Ricci." [Poetry] (165:3) D 94, p. 136-137.

2806. HOOD, Thomas
"Hood on Hood." [Light] (11) Aut 94, p. 16.

2807. HOOGLAND, Cornelia
"Now. Here." [PraF] (15:1, #66) Spr 94, p. 132-133.

2808. HOOPER, Patricia
"Afterward." [HiramPoR] (55/56) Fall 93-Sum 94, p. 49.
"In the Park." [HiramPoR] (55/56) Fall 93-Sum 94, p. 48.
"The Power Failure." [ConnPR] (13:1) 94, p. 24.
"Remainders." [Pivot] (41) 93, p. 53.
"Sickness in July." [LitR] (37:4) Sum 94, p. 680.

2809. HOOPER, Virginia
"Permission to Visit." [AmerPoR] (23:6) N-D 94, p. 53.
"Vessels." [AmerPoR] (23:6) N-D 94, p. 53-54.

2810. HOOVER, Paul
"Beauty." [NewAW] (12) Spr-Sum 94, p. 21.
"Distance." [RiverC] (14:2) Spr 94, p. 39-42.

"Fog and Smoke on Snow." [RiverC] (14:2) Spr 94, p. 37-38.
"Reason's Eye." [NewAW] (12) Spr-Sum 94, p. 22-23.
"The Water Engine." [RiverC] (14:2) Spr 94, p. 35-36.

2811. HOPE, Akua Lezli
"Shredded Swells of Memory." [Eyeball] (3) 93, p. 44.
"Song Through the Wall." [Eyeball] (3) 93, p. 44.

2812. HOPE, Warren
"Change of Tenants." [Hellas] (5:1) Spr-Sum 94, p. 42.
"Day's End." [Hellas] (5:1) Spr-Sum 94, p. 42.

2813. HOPES, David
"On the Day You Were Born" (for David Joshua Adam, August 17, 1993). [Vis] (45) 94, p. 5.
"The Wild Woman's Song." [Vis] (44) 94, p. 12.

2814. HOPPE, W. Joe
"On Flag Day." [Border] (5) Fall-Wint 94, p. 27.

2815. HOPPER, Christopher James
"Filling Hollow Places." [BlackBR] (19) Fall-Wint 94, p. 4.

2816. HORACE
"Book I, v: Quis Multis Gracilis" (tr. by James M. Brantingham). [CrabCR] (8:2/3/9:1/2/3) 94, p. 105.
"Epode III" (tr. by James M. Brantingham). [CrabCR] (8:2/3/9:1/2/3) 94, p. 103.
"Ode I.23. To Chloë" (tr. by David Ferry). [PartR] (61:4) Fall 94, p. 628-629.
"Ode: II.14, to Postumus" (tr. by David Ferry). [Thrpny] (59) Fall 94, p. 13.
"Ode III.13. To a Fountain" (tr. by David Ferry). [PartR] (61:4) Fall 94, p. 628.
"Odes" (Selections: 4.7, 2.14, tr. by L.L. Lee). [CharR] (20:1) Spr 94, p. 77-78.
"Sermones II, iv" (Excerpt, tr. by James M. Brantingham). [CrabCR] (8:2/3/9:1/2/3) 94, p. 104.
"A welcome spring breeze dulls the whetted edge of the winter" (I.4, tr. by Joseph S. Salemi). [CarolQ] (46:3) Sum 94, p. 51.

2817. HORNE, Lewis
"Shortcuts." [CumbPR] (13:2) Spr 94, p. 52-53.
"Winter Mating." [Nimrod] (37:2) Spr-Sum 94, p. 48-49.

2818. HORNER, Carl S.
"Rising Somewhere Far Away." [ApalQ] (42) Fall 94, p. 53.

2819. HORNER, Carolyn
"Blue Moon." [RagMag] (12:1) Sum 94, p. 11.

2820. HORNER, Jan
"Banker Poet." [PraF] (15:1, #66) Spr 94, p. 19-20.
"Cat Woman." [PraF] (15:1, #66) Spr 94, p. 21.
"Lost Bride." [PraF] (15:1, #66) Spr 94, p. 15-16.
"A Poem About Buses." [PraF] (15:1, #66) Spr 94, p. 14.
"Red Roses, Blue Kitchen." [PraF] (15:1, #66) Spr 94, p. 12.
"She Opened the Car Door." [PraF] (15:1, #66) Spr 94, p. 13.
"While the Abortion Debate Drones on in Parliament." [PraF] (15:1, #66) Spr 94, p. 17-18.

2821. HORNIK, Jessica
"At Steepletop." [NewRep] (210:7) 14 F 94, p. 44.
"The Closed Forest" (In memory of J.L.W.). [Atlantic] (273:1) Ja 94, p. 82.
"The Less I See." [SouthwR] (79:1) Wint 94, p. 107-108.

2822. HOROWITZ, Mikhail
"Lascaux." [HeavenB] (11) 94, p. 44.
"Rene Magritte: Rap Sheet." [HeavenB] (11) 94, p. 45.

2823. HORTON, Barbara Savadge
"Like a Bird." [PoetryNW] (35:3) Aut 94, p. 20-21.
"Mother Sips Sherry Evenings." [PoetryE] (37/38) Spr 94, p. 26-27.
"One Hundred Eight." [AnotherCM] (27) 94, p. 59-60.
"Tulips." [PoetryNW] (35:3) Aut 94, p. 22-23.

2824. HORTSCH, Dan
"Gift from a Word Man." [SoCoast] (17) Je 94, p. 4.

2825. HORVATH, Brooke
"Children in the Bedroom." [TexasR] (15:1/2) Spr-Sum 94, p. 86-87.
"Evangelist with Child." [TexasR] (15:1/2) Spr-Sum 94, p. 88-89.
"The Green Flash." [NegC] (14:1/2) 94, p. 124-125.
"Hello." [TarRP] (34:1) Fall 94, p. 16-17.
"Lake Glass" (For Barbara Felt). [Boulevard] (9:3, #27) Fall 94, p. 182-184.
"The Mary Haggadot" (Selections: 2, 7). [DenQ] (28:4) Spr 94, p. 26-29.

2826. HORVATH, Elemér
"Sarcophagus" (tr. by Nicholas Kolumban). [ArtfulD] (26/27) 94, p. 12.
2827. HORVATH, Miklos
"Holy and Wicked Time" (tr. of Sándor Csoóri, w. Len Roberts). [NowestR] (32:2) 94, p. 26.
"The Smile of My Exile" (tr. of Sándor Csoóri, w. Len Roberts). [NowestR] (32:2) 94, p. 23.
2828. HORVITZ, Lori
"Warning." [BrooklynR] (11) 94, p. 33.
2829. HOSPITAL, Carolina
"A Daughter for Raisa" (A Eulogy). [PraS] (68:4) Wint 94, p. 123-124.
"How the Cubans Stole Miami." [PraS] (68:4) Wint 94, p. 121-122.
"The Lost Hammock" (after Diego Vicente Tejera). [PraS] (68:4) Wint 94, p. 125-126.
2830. HOST, R. M.
"The Jester" (I, III). [DogRR] (13:1, #25) Spr-Sum 94, p. 46-48.
"Meaning." [DogRR] (26) Wint 94-95, p. 20.
2831. HOSTOVSKY, Paul
"Late Bloom." [JlNJPo] (16:2) Aut 94, p. 18.
"Miss Williams." [JlNJPo] (16:2) Aut 94, p. 19.
2832. HOTHAM, Gary
"Haiku" (2 poems). [Northeast] (5:11) Wint 94-95, p. 24.
"Haiku" (5 poems). [Northeast] (5:10) Sum 94, p. 35.
"Half heard rain." [BelPoJ] (44:4) Sum 94, p. 39.
"She comes back." [BelPoJ] (44:4) Sum 94, p. 39.
"Time to go." [BelPoJ] (44:4) Sum 94, p. 39.
2833. HOUCHIN, Ron
"Barns and Churches." [ClockR] (9:1/2) 94-95, p. 18.
"Living on the Land" (after Gauguin's *La Perte de pucelage*). [HawaiiR] (18:1, #40) Spr 94, p. 108.
2834. HOUGHTALING, C. J.
"Barbie's Midlife Crisis." [SoCoast] (16) Ja 94, p. 12.
2835. HOUSLEY, Kathleen L.
"Apostate." [ChrC] (111:28) 12 O 94, p. 918.
"Grieving Knows No Drouth in Its Verdant Season." [ChrC] (111:34) 23-30 N 94, p. 1110.
HOUSSAYE, Harry de la
See De la HOUSSAYE, Harry
2836. HOUSTON, Beth
"Crows." [FloridaR] (19:2) 94, p. 64-65.
"Fan." [Confr] (52/53) Wint-Spr 94, p. 338-339.
"Moment of Truth." [ColEng] (56:1) Ja 94, p. 69-70.
"Watermelon." [YaleR] (82:3) Jl 94, p. 36-37.
2837. HOUSTON, Douglas
"Judgement." [Jacaranda] (5:1) Wint-Spr 91, p. 70-71.
2838. HOUSTON, Lisa
"The House Codex" (from *fragments for navigation*). [Chain] (1) Spr-Sum 94, p. 155-156.
HOVANESSIAN, Diana Der
See DER-HOVANESSIAN, Diana
2839. HOWARD, Ben
"Spitting Forgiven" (Dublin, 1947). [SenR] (24:2) Fall 94, p. 69-80.
"Westward." [Poetry] (163:4) Ja 94, p. 220.
"The Word from Dublin, 1944." [SewanR] (102:2) Spr 94, p. 246-254.
2840. HOWARD, Dale
"View From a Hot Air Balloon." [Elf] (4:1) Spr 94, p. 36.
2841. HOWARD, H. Wendell
"A Hot Day's End." [Hellas] (5:1) Spr-Sum 94, p. 72.
2842. HOWARD, Julie Kate
"Oz." [ChatR] (14:2) Wint 94, p. 31.
2843. HOWARD, Matthew
"Half-Life." [ChiR] (40:1) 94, p. 61.
2844. HOWARD, Maureen
"Counters" (for Richard Santino). [Raritan] (14:1) Sum 94, p. 31-33.
2845. HOWARD, Richard
"Homage to Antonio Canaletto." [Antaeus] (75/76) Aut 94, p. 284-287.

"The Manatee" (New Smyrna Beach, Florida). [Boulevard] (9:3, #27) Fall 94, p. 67-68.
2846. HOWARD, Ted
"A Few Points Malthus Overlooked." [QW] (38) Winter-Spr 93-94, p. 128.
2847. HOWE, Alvah K.
"Three Metamorphoses." [BelPoJ] (44:4) Sum 94, p. 15-17.
2848. HOWE, Fanny
"The Apophatic Path." [GrandS] (12:4, #48) Wint 94, p. 183-185.
"Basic Science." [GrandS] (12:4, #48) Wint 94, p. 181-182.
"Feel the Manifest As a Magnet." [Chelsea] (57) 94, p. 31.
"Next Time I'll Travel by Dream." [Chelsea] (57) 94, p. 30.
2849. HOWE, Ken
"Bee Speaks." [PraF] (15:1, #66) Spr 94, p. 142-143.
2850. HOWE, Marie
"What the Living Do." [Atlantic] (273:4) Ap 94, p. 68.
2851. HOWELL, Cameron
"Fragments Before Waking." [Shen] (44:3) Fall 94, p. 87.
"Night Sets In." [Shen] (44:3) Fall 94, p. 88-90.
2852. HOWELL, Christopher
"Indeed." [PoetryNW] (35:1) Spr 94, p. 28.
"Kipling Visits Portland and the West." [NoDaQ] (62:2) Spr 94-95, p. 193-194.
2853. HOWER, Mary
"The First Time." [VirQR] (70:2) Spr 94, p. 302-303.
"Mother's Jackal." [VirQR] (70:2) Spr 94, p. 303-304.
2854. HOWES, Victor
"The Judgment of Paris." [Hellas] (5:1) Spr-Sum 94, p. 77.
"Narcissus for the Defense." [Hellas] (5:1) Spr-Sum 94, p. 76.
2855. HOWLAND, Ronald N. (Ron)
"Death Outside." [NegC] (14:1/2) 94, p. 24.
"Mending Nets." [PoetL] (89:4) Wint 94-95, p. 31-33.
2856. HOWSER, Jack A.
"Seasons." [SmPd] (31:1, #90) Wint 94, p. 23.
2857. HOYLMAN, Loana
"Hotel Molokai." [ChamLR] (14/15) Spr-Fall 94, p. 115-117.
2858. HRYNIEWICZ-YARBROUGH, Ewa
"School of Survival" (tr. of Krzysztof Lisowski). [QW] (39) Sum-Fall 94, p. 148.
2859. HSIANG, Ming
"Tumor" (tr. by Edmond Chang). [Talisman] (12) Spr 94, p. 159.
2860. HSU, Hsuan
"Lost and Losing." [SoCoast] (16) Ja 94, p. 42.
HSUAN, Hsu
See HSU, Hsuan
HUANG KUO-PIN
See WONG, Lawrence
2861. HUBBELL, Brian
"Mail Order Stomp." [BelPoJ] (45:1) Fall 94, p. 6-9.
"Measuring E. B. White's Boathouse." [BelPoJ] (45:1) Fall 94, p. 10-11.
2862. HUDA, Mohammad Nurul (Mohammed Nurul)
"The Game in Reverse" (tr. of Taslima Nasreen, w. Carolyne Wright and the author). [IndR] (17:1) Spr 94, p. 97.
"Happy Marriage" (tr. of Taslima Nasrin, w. Carolyne Wright and the author). [NewYorker] (70:28) 12 S 94, p. 55.
"I'll Go Away and I Won't Say a Thing" (tr. of Nasima Sultana, w. Carolyne Wright). [InterQ] (1:2) 93, p. 160.
"Let There Be Some Rage" (tr. of Nasima Sultana, w. Carolyne Wright and the author). [IndR] (17:1) Spr 94, p. 98.
2863. HUDDLE, David
"So Long." [SouthernR] (30:4) Aut 94, p. 705-707.
2864. HUDECHEK, Robin D.
"Bathtub." [CreamCR] (18:2) Fall 94, p. 115.
2865. HUDGINS, Andrew
"Blue Danube." [SouthernR] (30:1) Ja, Wint 94, p. 88.
"Grandmomma's Toenails." [SouthernR] (30:4) Aut 94, p. 764-765.
"My Wife: An Ode." [SouthernR] (30:4) Aut 94, p. 763-764.
"O Say Can You See?" [ColR] (21:2) Fall 94, p. 120.
"Seventeen." [SouthernR] (30:1) Ja, Wint 94, p. 89-90.

"Slap." [ColR] (21.2) Fall 94, p. 121.
"The Social Order." [NewEngR] (16:1) Wint 94, p. 157-158.
"Tools: An Ode." [Poetry] (164:3) Je 94, p. 155.

2866. HUDSON, Ann
"Grief." [PoetryE] (37/38) Spr 94, p. 34.

2867. HUDSON, Carolyn
"There Is No Map." [BellArk] (10:3 [i.e. 10:4]) Jl-Ag 94, p. 7.

2868. HUDSON, Gwendolyn
"Immanuel on Clinic Day." [Conscience] (15:2) Sum 94, p. 30.

2869. HUDSON, June
"I Once Could Fly." [Calyx] (15:2) Sum 94, p. 16.
"Rainy Day Schedule." [SoCoast] (16) Ja 94, p. 17.

2870. HUEBNER, Lisa
"Traitor." [SinW] (52) Spr-Sum 94, p. 58-59.

2871. HUERTA, Efraín
"Here They Are" (tr. by Jim Normington). [Talisman] (12) Spr 94, p. 202-203.

2872. HUFF, Michael
"A Radio Summer Evening in Nevada." [SouthernPR] (34:1) Sum 94, p. 29-30.

2873. HUFFSTICKLER, Albert
"I Never Slept in a Laundromat." [CoalC] (8) Ap 94, p. 42.

2874. HUGGINS, Peter
"Angels Bearing Swords of Fire." [NegC] (13:2/3) 93, p. 24-25.
"Solo." [Parting] (7:1) Sum 94, p. 25.

2875. HUGHES, Benedict
"Jean." [BrooklynR] (11) 94, p. 106.

2876. HUGHES, Glenn
"Door." [PraS] (68:2) Sum 94, p. 23.
"First Things." [PraS] (68:2) Sum 94, p. 22.
"On the Birth of a Friend's Son." [PraS] (68:2) Sum 94, p. 22.

2877. HUGHES, Henry
"Frosted Glass" (tr. of Etsuko Saito, w. Matthew Forrest). [SycamoreR] (6:2) Sum 94, p. 95.
"I Learned on the Right Side of the Sea" (tr. of Etsuko Saito, w. Matthew Forrest). [SycamoreR] (6:2) Sum 94, p. 97-98.

2878. HUGHES, Langston
"Syllabic Poem." [AmerPoR] (23:2) Mr-Ap 94, p. 53.

2879. HUGHES, P.
"On a Roll-on Deodorant Ball Pierced and Used as an Earring." [Pearl] (20) Spr 94, p. 56.

2880. HUGHES, Pamela
"Bangladesh, May 1991" (for the dead and the living). [FourQ] (8:2) Fall 94, p. 40.

2881. HUGHES, Ted
"The Locket." [Antaeus] (75/76) Aut 94, p. 288-289.

HUI-MING, Wang
See WANG, Hui-Ming

2882. HULL, Coral
"Afternoon Tea with Mum." [Iowa] (24:1) Wint 94, p. 195-196.
"An Hour After Suicide." [Iowa] (24:1) Wint 94, p. 197-198.
"Night Light." [TampaR] (9) Fall 94, p. 42-43.
"Pilbarra Roadside." [AnotherCM] (27) 94, p. 61.
"Sparrow." [NoAmR] (279:4) Jl-Ag 94, p. 38.
"Umbrella Tree." [TampaR] (8) Spr 94, p. 20.

2883. HULL, David M.
"Thanksgiving Variations" (Selections: #6, #13, #19). [Ascent] (19:1) Fall 94, p. 48-49.

2884. HULSE, John
"Eng-ka." [ChamLR] (14/15) Spr-Fall 94, p. 204.

2885. HULSE, Michael
"Send Her a Fax" (with apologies to Waller). [AntigR] (99) Aut 94, p. 104.

2886. HUME, Christine
"Dirty Money." [IndR] (17:2) Fall 94, p. 50.
"Flush." [Ploughs] (20:4) Wint 94-95, p. 79-80.
"Obedience of Two." [HayF] (14) Spr-Sum 94, p. 56.

2887. HUMES, Harry
"Aunt Tink." [PoetryNW] (35:4) Wint 94-95, p. 41.
"Dead Hawk." [PoetryNW] (35:1) Spr 94, p. 36-37.

"The Mink." [PoetryNW] (35:1) Spr 94, p. 37-38.
"My Father Made Bamboo Fly Rods." [WestB] (35) 94, p. 29.
"Nature." [QW] (39) Sum-Fall 94, p. 166-167.
"The Shovel." [WestB] (35) 94, p. 28.
"Snake Man." [PoetryNW] (35:1) Spr 94, p. 36.
"This Morning." [WestB] (35) 94, p. 27.
"Vultures." [PoetryNW] (35:1) Spr 94, p. 38.

2888. HUMMER, T. R.
"Mechanics." [QW] (38) Winter-Spr 93-94, p. 88-89.
"Ohio Abstract: Hart Crane." [QW] (38) Winter-Spr 93-94, p. 86-87.
"Under the Sign of the Color of Smoke or Stars." [QW] (38) Winter-Spr 93-94, p. 90-91.

2889. HUMPHREY, Paul
"Ghosts." [Writer] (107:5) My 94, p. 21.
"Love Knot." [Light] (11) Aut 94, p. 9.
"Party Line." [Light] (11) Aut 94, p. 21.
"Speedies." [Light] (9) Spr 94, p. 13.

2890. HUMPHREYS, Helen
"Elbows / Wrists." [Nimrod] (37:2) Spr-Sum 94, p. 51.
"Pigs Can See the Wind." [Nimrod] (37:2) Spr-Sum 94, p. 50.
"Winter Aconite." [Nimrod] (37:2) Spr-Sum 94, p. 52.

2891. HUNDLEY, Lynne
"Candy Smokes." [ChironR] (13:2) Sum 94, p. 25.
"Nothing." [Pearl] (20) Spr 94, p. 81.
"Packing." [ChironR] (13:2) Sum 94, p. 19.
"Waiting." [Pearl] (20) Spr 94, p. 81.

2892. HUNOLD, Rose Marie
"Bayjan White." [Obs] (9:2) Fall-Wint 94, p. 82-83.
"The Mammy Quartet." [Kalliope] (16:3) 94, p. 18.
"Plume of the Confederacy." [Obs] (9:2) Fall-Wint 94, p. 81-82.

2893. HUNT, Laird
"Book of the Dead 1: Preparation." [Talisman] (12) Spr 94, p. 250.
"Book of the Dead 2: Retrieval." [Talisman] (12) Spr 94, p. 250.

2894. HUNT, Nan
"Good Women." [Border] (4) Spr-Sum 94, p. 46-47.

2895. HUNTER, Allison
"The Doppler Effect." [CapeR] (29:1) Spr 94, p. 17.
"Gathering by the Blanco." [Pivot] (41) 93, p. 1.

2896. HUNTER, Bruce
"December Arson in Cabbagetown" (for Andrew Wreggett). [PoetryC] (15:1) N 94, p. 23.
"Slow Train Home." [PoetryC] (15:1) N 94, p. 23.

2897. HUNTER, Catherine
"Gender Relations." [PraF] (15:2, #67) Sum 94, p. 105.
"Moon Poem for Z." [PraF] (15:2, #67) Sum 94, p. 50.

2898. HUNTER, Walt
"The Coco Mar Motel" (Puerto Rico, 1969). [CreamCR] (18:2) Fall 94, p. 128.

2899. HURDELSH, Mark D.
"I Can't Resist Making It an Ocean." [SmPd] (31:1, #90) Wint 94, p. 20.
"Leaving Pennsylvania." [Wind] (73) 94, p. 12.

2900. HURDLE, Crystal
"Aqua Velva." [Event] (23:3) Wint 94-95, p. 58-60.

2901. HURFORD, Chris
"The Garden God." [Verse] (11:2) Sum 94, p. 28.

2902. HURLEY, Maureen
"Dream Vessels #2: Earth Palette" (from a collage by Marsha Connell. First Sue Saniel Elkind National Poetry Award, Finalist). [Kalliope] (16:2) 94, p. 27-28.

2903. HURLOW, Marcia (Marcia L.)
"Aliens Are Intercepting My Brain Waves." [ChiR] (40:2/3) 94, p. 117-118.
"Consellations from Andromeda" (for Marjorie Hurlow Stump). [PoetC] (25:3) Spr 94, p. 26.
"Madame Rhonda's Next Predictions." [PoetC] (25:3) Spr 94, p. 27.
"Milin an Elorn." [Poetry] (165:2) N 94, p. 86.
"Other Evidence." [Poetry] (165:2) N 94, p. 85-86.
"The Pantheist Who Loved His Wife." [PraS] (68:2) Sum 94, p. 167.

"Suspended." [PraS] (68:2) Sum 94, p. 166.
2904. HURSEY, Brett
"A Jesus Like Everybody Else's." [ChironR] (13:2) Sum 94, p. 24.
"The Treatment." [HayF] (15) Fall-Wint 94, p. 108.
2905. HUSSEY, Charlotte
"Mohawk Villanelle." [Arc] (33) Fall 94, p. 49.
2906. HUSSEY, Susan
"The Color of Death Is Not Red." [Kalliope] (16:1) 94, p. 59.
"The Empty Pool." [Kalliope] (16:1) 94, p. 59.
2907. HUSSMANN, Mary
"Rodeo Lips." [KenR] (NS 16:2) Spr 94, p. 84-85.
2908. HUTCHINGS, Pat
"The Day We Found the Dead Cows." [ClockR] (9:1/2) 94-95, p. 57.
"Jessica Has Her Baby." [ClockR] (9:1/2) 94-95, p. 56.
2909. HUTCHISON, Joseph
"The Dreamers." [WritersF] (20) 94, p. 100.
"Foregone Conclusions." [DenQ] (29:2) Fall 94, p. 10.
"Instructions Received in a Dream." [WritersF] (20) 94, p. 99.
"A Midsummer Night's Tennis Match." [Northeast] (5:10) Sum 94, p. 7.
"The Net." [WritersF] (20) 94, p. 100.
2910. HUTCHISON, Scott Travis
"Apples and Seeds." [Poem] (72) N 94, p. 12.
"Collection." [Poem] (72) N 94, p. 11.
2911. HUYLER, Frank
"My Mother's Hair." [GeoR] (48:1) Spr 94, p. 65.
2912. HYETT, Barbara Helfgott
"American Burying Beetle" (First Sue Saniel Elkind National Poetry Award, Finalist). [Kalliope] (16:2) 94, p. 29.
"Atlantic Ridley Sea Turtle." [NewRep] (211:10) 5 S 94, p. 48.
"The River." [ColEng] (56:5) S 94, p. 571.
"Schaus Swallowtail Butterfly." [ColEng] (56:5) S 94, p. 572.
2913. HYMANS, Don
"Delicate Seeming." [BlackWR] (21:1) Fall-Wint 94, p. 122.
2914. HYMAS, June Hopper
"As Cranes Pick Corn from Snow." [HiramPoR] (55/56) Fall 93-Sum 94, p. 53-55.
"Dimensional Images." [HiramPoR] (55/56) Fall 93-Sum 94, p. 50-52.
2915. HYNES, Maureen
"Aubade." [PoetryC] (14:3) My 94, p. 12.
"Brain Sketch." [MalR] (106) Spr 94, p. 30-31.
"The Bus, the Rain, the Destination and the Towns Between." [PoetryC] (14:3) My 94, p. 12.
"Remedy." [PoetryC] (14:3) My 94, p. 12.
"Roof Tiles." [Quarry] (43:3) N 94, p. 126-127.
"The River Industry of Ants." [MalR] (106) Spr 94, p. 29.
"Withrow Avenue." [TickleAce] (28) Fall-Wint 94, p. 117-118.
HYON-JONG, Chong
See CHONG, Hyon-Jong

2916. IBACETA, Herminia D.
"Todo el Mundo Calla." [Nuez] (5:13/14/15) 94, p. 14.
2917. IBARRA, Raúl
"En la Ciudad." [LindLM] (13:1) Mr 94, p. 22.
"La Lancha Nocturna en la Bahía." [LindLM] (13:1) Mr 94, p. 22.
"Pequeña Historia." [LindLM] (13:1) Mr 94, p. 22.
"Vivo sin Vivir en Mí." [LindLM] (13:1) Mr 94, p. 22.
2918. IBSEN, Arni
"You Who Are High and Dry" (tr. by Peter Ridgewell and the author). [Vis] (45) 94, p. 18-19.
2919. IBYKOS
Translations by Nicholas Rockel [Descant] (25:1, #84) Spr 94, p. 29.
2920. IDDINGS, Kathleen
"My Class — Fifth Grade." [EngJ] (83:2) F 94, p. 91.
2921. IERONIM, Ioana
"At the Bus Stop, in Winter" (tr. by Adam Sorkin). [ChatR] (14:3) Spr 94, p. 41.
"Partisans" (tr. by Adam J. Sorkin and the author). [Vis] (46) 94, p. 28.

"Scripta" (tr. of Daniela Crasnaru, w. Adam J. Sorkin). [Vis] (46) 94, p. 39.

2922. IFEDERMAN, Raymond
"The Interrogators." [Caliban] (14) 94, p. 142.

2923. IGNATOW, David
"Conditions." [Caliban] (14) 94, p. 34.
"Dawn." [Caliban] (14) 94, p. 34.
"Forever." [Caliban] (14) 94, p. 34.
"Forever." [ProseP] (3) 94, p. 49.
"One Can." [ProseP] (3) 94, p. 50.
"Thank You." [Caliban] (14) 94, p. 33.

2924. IINO, Tomoyuki
"Fuji" (tr. of Mitsuharu Kaneko, w. Jon Silkin). [Stand] (35:3) Sum 94, p. 18.

2925. ILINSKA, Zofia
"I Lament." [CumbPR] (13:2) Spr 94, p. 82.
"Madame Gautreau to Her Biographer" (Famous American beauty married to a French banker, painted by John Singer Sargent 1856-1925). [CumbPR] (13:2) Spr 94, p. 80.
"Sailing Out of Tilbury." [CumbPR] (13:2) Spr 94, p. 81.

2926. ILLICK, Peter
"You Can Check Out, but You Can Never Leave, 'Hotel California' The Eagles." [WeberS] (11:1) Wint 94, p. 97-98.

2927. ILLYÉS, Gyula
"Execrable Cold" (tr. by Bruce Berlind, w. Mária Korösy)." [WebR] (18) Fall 94, p. 6.
"There Will Be No War" (tr. by Bruce Berlind, w. Mária Körösy). [ConnPR] (13:1) 94, p. 23.
"White" (tr. by Bruce Berlind, w. Mária Korösy)." [WebR] (18) Fall 94, p. 5-6.

2928. IMAM, Hina Faisal
"Dream Cycle." [Amelia] (7:3, #22) 94, p. 106.

2929. IMAMATSURIBE no Yosafu
"Conscript" (written in 755, tr. by Graeme Wilson). [Jacaranda] (5:1) Wint-Spr 91, p. 116.

2930. INADA, Lawson Fusao
"Kicking the Habit." 46-47 [EngJ] (83:5) S 94, p. 46-47.
"Sushi or Not Sushi." [FreeL] (13) Spr 94, p. 35-36.

2931. INCE, Özdemir
"Caka Bey" (tr. by Saliha Paker, for Anthony Bryer). [Talisman] (13) Fall 94-Wint 95, p. 250.

2932. INEZ, Colette
"Admonitions." [IndR] (17:1) Spr 94, p. 120.
"The Attorney General's Garden." [Light] (12) Wint 94-95, p. 13.
"August Atoms." [ColR] (21:2) Fall 94, p. 172-173.
"Basho Takes an Upland Journey to Visit Poets in the North." [Hudson] (47:3) Aut 94, p. 420-421.
"Clerihew: Percy Bysshe Shelley." [Light] (11) Aut 94, p. 17.
"The Composer." [Pivot] (42) 94, p. 28.
"Dream Shore." [ColR] (21:2) Fall 94, p. 171.
"Encounter in the Square." [NewYorkQ] (53) 94, p. 51.
"Hard Muse." [Hudson] (47:3) Aut 94, p. 421-422.
"I Clasp Another Woman's Hand in Mine as if She Were My Child." [NewEngR] (16:4) Fall 94, p. 77-78.
"In a Garden." [SycamoreR] (6:1) Wint 94, p. 36.
"Moth Dream of My Late Therapist." [IndR] (17:1) Spr 94, p. 119.
"The Music Box." [NewEngR] (16:4) Fall 94, p. 78-79.
"Ruminations." [WestB] (35) 94, p. 5.
"Son and Ma." [WestB] (35) 94, p. 6-7.
"A Statue Travels from a Desert Quarry to Stare Behind Glass." [Pivot] (41) 93, p. 4.
"A Story." [SycamoreR] (6:1) Wint 94, p. 37-38.
"Teaching Junior High at Castle Hill." [WestB] (35) 94, p. 5-6.
"Thinking of Charlotte Corday and My Childhood in America." [Shen] (44:1) Spr 94, p. 49.
"The Visit." [IndR] (17:1) Spr 94, p. 118.
"The Wedding's Off, Sing the Mourning Doves, Hoo-Hooing." [Pivot] (42) 94, p. 28-29.

2933. INGERSOLL, Glenn
"The Crane in Flight." [BelPoJ] (44:4) Sum 94, p. 32.
"King of the Mountain." [BelPoJ] (44:4) Sum 94, p. 33.
2934. INGERSON, Martin I.
"The Lutenist" (in praise of music and other muses). [BellArk] (10:1) Ja-F 94, p. 15.
"This Winter Light" (at the Bon Marché, South Center). [BellArk] (10:1) Ja-F 94, p. 15.
2935. INGRAM, Katie
"The Day of the Dead." [SantaBR] (1:1) Spr-Sum 93, p. 50.
"Saying Good-bye." [SantaBR] (1:1) Spr-Sum 93, p. 50.
2936. INGRAM, Paul
"Clerihew: John James Audubon." [Light] (11) Aut 94, p. 22.
2937. INKALA, Jouni
"At That Point" (tr. by Anselm Hollo). [GrandS] (12:4, #48) Wint 94, p. 63-64.
2938. INMAN, Will
"Territorial Ears." [ChamLR] (14/15) Spr-Fall 94, p. 199-200.
2939. IOANNOU, Susan
"Appointment Above Florence: Visiting Sir Harold Action" (for Merla McMurray, March 1990). [Dandel] (21:1) 94, p. 26-28.
2940. IONESCU, Eugene
"Ballade" (tr. by Aurelia Roman, w. Bradley R. Strahan). [Vis] (46) 94, p. 5.
"Croquis Humoristique" (tr. by Aurelia Roman, w. Bradley R. Strahan). [Vis] (46) 94, p. 4.
"The Exhausted One" (tr. by Aurelia Roman, w. Bradley R. Strahan). [Vis] (46) 94, p. 5.
2941. IONNA-VERONIKA
"Circe." [Jacaranda] (5:1) Wint-Spr 91, p. 108.
"Scheherezade." [Jacaranda] (5:1) Wint-Spr 91, p. 109.
"What to Say to a Bear." [Jacaranda] (5:1) Wint-Spr 91, p. 106-107.
2942. IRIMIA, Mihaela A.
"The Herald's Ballad" (Excerpt, tr. of Dan Verona, w. Adam J. Sorkin). [Vis] (46) 94, p. 30.
2943. IRONS, J. (Jamie)
"At the Teaching Hospital." [Zyzzyva] (10:4) Wint 94, p. 133.
"Sahel." [Vis] (45) 94, p. 33.
2944. IRWIN, Mark
"The Ages of Life" (tr. of Friedrich Hölderlin). [DenQ] (29:1) Sum 94, p. 79.
"Airport." [Boulevard] (9:1/2, #25/26) Spr 94, p. 111.
"The Middle of Life" (tr. of Friedrich Hölderlin). [DenQ] (29:1) Sum 94, p. 80.
"Rodeo." [Journal] (18:2) Fall-Wint 94, p. 89-96.
"Tock." [Agni] (39) 94, p. 172.
"We." [MidAR] (14:2) 94, p. 159.
"Wing." [Journal] (18:1) Spr-Sum 94, p. 72.
2945. ISAACSON, Lisa
"1979." [Sulfur] (34) Spr 94, p. 36-38.
"Heroes and Saints." [Sulfur] (34) Spr 94, p. 33-35.
"Zaire." [Sulfur] (34) Spr 94, p. 35-36.
2946. ISBER, Osama
"Becoming a Hyena" (tr. of Mahmud Al-Sayed, w. Allen Hibbard). [CimR] (108) Jl 94, p. 18.
"The Human Excess" (tr. of Mohammad Al-Maghut, w. Allen Hibbard). [CimR] (108) Jl 94, p. 15.
"I Am Trying to Save the Last Female Before the Arrival of the Tartars" (tr. of Nizar Kabbani, w. Allen Hibbard). [CimR] (108) Jl 94, p. 12-14.
"Marlboro" (tr. of Mahmud Al-Sayed, w. Allen Hibbard). [CimR] (108) Jl 94, p. 18.
"Surrealism" (tr. of Mahmud Al-Sayed, w. Allen Hibbard). [CimR] (108) Jl 94, p. 19.
"Terror and Sex" (tr. of Mohammad Al-Maghut, w. Allen Hibbard). [CimR] (108) Jl 94, p. 16-17.
"The Trojan Horse" (tr. of Mahmud Al-Sayed, w. Allen Hibbard). [CimR] (108) Jl 94, p. 18.
"Why, Oh Arab?" (tr. of Mahmud Al-Sayed, w. Allen Hibbard). [CimR] (108) Jl 94, p. 19.
2947. ISHIGAKI, Rin
"At the Bathhouse" (tr. by Leith Morton). [Stand] (35:3) Sum 94, p. 17.
"Cliff" (tr. by Leith Morton). [Stand] (35:3) Sum 94, p. 16.

"Living" (tr. by Leith Morton). [Stand] (35:3) Sum 94, p. 16.

2948. ISHIHARA, Yoshiro
"Figure" (tr. by Hiroaki Sato). [Conjunc] (23) 94, p. 220.
"Horse and Riot" (tr. by Hiroaki Sato). [Conjunc] (23) 94, p. 215-216.
"Mist & Town" (tr. by Hiroaki Sato). [Conjunc] (23) 94, p. 219-220.
"Myth" (tr. by Hiroaki Sato). [Conjunc] (23) 94, p. 217.
"Night Robbers" (tr. by Hiroaki Sato). [Conjunc] (23) 94, p. 216-217.
"Song of the Ringing in the Ear" (tr. by Hiroaki Sato). [Conjunc] (23) 94, p. 218.
"Structure" (tr. by Hiroaki Sato). [Conjunc] (23) 94, p. 215.

2949. ISHIKAWA, Takuboku
"Poems to Eat" (12 poems tr. by Carl Sesar). [InterQ] (1:2) 93, p. 60-61.

2950. ISISCHILD, Ixtlan Wales
"The Meeting." [NewDeltaR] (10:1) Fall 92-Wint 93, p. 16-17.

2951. ISKRENKO, Nina
"Special Troikas: A Corps" (tr. by Forrest Gander, w. Joy Dworkin). [Conjunc] (23) 94, p. 145-149.

2952. ISRAEL, Charles, Jr.
"Shuddering Goddesses." [SouthernPR] (34:1) Sum 94, p. 22-23.

2953. ISRAELI, Henry
"Debts" (tr. of Xhevahir Spahiu, w. Uk Bucpapa). [DenQ] (29:1) Sum 94, p. 103.
"The Forest at Night" (tr. of Frederik Rreshpja, w. Uk Bucpapa). [DenQ] (29:1) Sum 94, p. 101.
"Headrush." [Nimrod] (37:2) Spr-Sum 94, p. 53.
"Retreat." [Nimrod] (37:2) Spr-Sum 94, p. 53.
"The Sea" (tr. of Frederik Rreshpja, w. Uk Bucpapa). [DenQ] (29:1) Sum 94, p. 102.

2954. ISSA (1763-1827)
Haiku [AmerPoR] (23:4) Jl-Ag 94, p. 17.

2955. ISSAIA, Nan
"Old." [NewRena] (9:1, #27) 94, p. 176.

2956. ITO, Susan K.
"Amanita Phalloides." [SantaBR] (1:2) Fall-Wint 93, p. 6-7.
"Mileva." [SantaBR] (2:1) Spr-Sum 94, p. 101-102.
"Sébaco." [SantaBR] (2:1) Spr-Sum 94, p. 103-104.

2957. IVANOFF, Stephanie (Stephanie E.)
"#3 North Normal Street." [AmerV] (35) 94, p. 129-130.
"Father Accountant and Deus Ex Machina." [AmerV] (35) 94, p. 131.
"Honey." [PaintedB] (53/54) 94, p. 81.
"The Nettles" (for my Mother). [AmerV] (35) 94, p. 127-128.

2958. IVANOV, Binyo
"A Tale That's Not a Tale" (tr. by Lisa Sapinkopf, w. Georgi Belev). [CrabCR] (8:2/3/9:1/2/3) 94, p. 109-110.
"The Wind Is Coming and I Love You" (tr. by Lisa Sapinkopf and Georgi Belev). [PartR] (61:2) Spr 94, p. 320-321.

2959. IVES, Rich
"True Stories." [NowestR] (32:1) 94, p. 116.

2960. IVEY, John Mark
"The Great Man Theory." [Obs] (9:2) Fall-Wint 94, p. 84.

2961. IWANAGA, Ryan
"Washing Rice." [SouthernPR] (34:2) Wint 94, p. 10-11.

2962. IWIN, Mark
"Grand Canyon." [Shen] (44:1) Spr 94, p. 64-65.

2963. IZAGUIRRE, Ester de
"A una Joven Pareja Que Se Abraza en la Calle." [Luz] (6) My 94, p. 14.
"The One Who Never Was" (tr. by Angela McEwan). [Luz] (6) My 94, p. 11.
"El Que No Fue." [Luz] (6) My 94, p. 10.
"Teatro." [Luz] (6) My 94, p. 12.
"Theatre" (tr. by Angela McEwan). [Luz] (6) My 94, p. 13.
"To a Young Couple Embracing in the Street" (tr. by Angela McEwan). [Luz] (6) My 94, p. 15.

2964. JABES, Edmond
"Dante's Hell" (tr. by Rosmarie Waldrop). [Avec] (7:1) 94, p. 141-147.

JACKSON, Betty J. Godwin
See GODWIN-JACKSON, Betty J.

2965. JACKSON, Fleda Brown
"Barbara." [Shen] (44:4) Wint 94, p. 31.
"Bat." [WestB] (35) 94, p. 49-50.
"Chat." [TarRP] (34:1) Fall 94, p. 19-20.
"The Doe Across from Aberdeen." [Shen] (44:3) Fall 94, p. 24.
"Dog in the Manger." [PoetL] (89:4) Wint 94-95, p. 45.
"The Fox and the Grapes." [PoetL] (89:4) Wint 94-95, p. 44.
"Hagar." [Shen] (44:3) Fall 94, p. 22-23.
"I Escape with My Mother in the Desoto." [WestB] (35) 94, p. 50-51.
"Kitten." [IndR] (17:1) Spr 94, p. 128-129.
"Sunday Morning." [Shen] (44:3) Fall 94, p. 20-21.
"Wilmington Women Rout Holy Family" (sports page, Wilmington, Delaware *News-Journal*). [Shen] (44:3) Fall 94, p. 25.
"Woman in Gauze." [WestB] (34) 94, p. 79.

2966. JACKSON, John
"Farmer's Market." [LaurelR] (28:2) Sum 94, p. 57.
"The Middle of Vacation" (Clark's Point, Maine). [LaurelR] (28:2) Sum 94, p. 56-57.

2967. JACKSON, Katherine
"Learning to Sketch Carmella's Garden." [PartR] (61:4) Fall 94, p. 640.
"Visitations" (a musical fiction, c1875). [CumbPR] (13:2) Spr 94, p. 83-84.

2968. JACKSON, Noel
"The Gourd." [HampSPR] Wint 94, p. 19.
"St. Luke Painting the Virgin." [HampSPR] Wint 94, p. 19.
"This Hand's Praise." [HampSPR] Wint 94, p. 20.

2969. JACKSON, W. D.
"Götterdämmerung" (tr. of Heinrich Heine). [Stand] (35:3) Sum 94, p. 4-5.

2970. JACOB, John
"Kaposi's Sarcoma." [AnotherCM] (28) 94, p. 81.

2971. JACOB, Max
"1889-1916" (tr. by William Kulik). [AmerPoR] (23:2) Mr-Ap 94, p. 3.
"1914" (tr. by William Kulik). [AmerPoR] (23:2) Mr-Ap 94, p. 3.
"Achilles' Wheel" (tr. by William Kulik). [AmerPoR] (23:2) Mr-Ap 94, p. 4.
"Ballad of the Night Visitor" (tr. by William Kulik). [AmerPoR] (23:2) Mr-Ap 94, p. 4.
"A Bit of Art Criticism" (tr. by William Kulik). [AmerPoR] (23:2) Mr-Ap 94, p. 3.
"Burial in Quimper" (tr. by William Kulik). [AmerPoR] (23:2) Mr-Ap 94, p. 5.
"Christian Families" (tr. by William Kulik). [AmerPoR] (23:2) Mr-Ap 94, p. 5.
"The Dice Cup" (4 selections, tr. by William Kulik). [DenQ] (29:1) Sum 94, p. 81-82.
"Fear" (tr. by William Kulik). [AmerPoR] (23:2) Mr-Ap 94, p. 3.
"The Feminist Question" (tr. by William Kulik). [AmerPoR] (23:2) Mr-Ap 94, p. 3.
"Hell Has Gradations" (tr. by William Kulik). [AmerPoR] (23:2) Mr-Ap 94, p. 4.
"If Guillaume's Death Had Been Christian" (tr. by William Kulik). [AmerPoR] (23:2) Mr-Ap 94, p. 5.
"Infernal Visions" (tr. by William Kulik). [AmerPoR] (23:2) Mr-Ap 94, p. 5.
"Jean Jacques" (tr. by William Kulik). [AmerPoR] (23:2) Mr-Ap 94, p. 4.
"The Key" (tr. by William Kulik). [AmerPoR] (23:2) Mr-Ap 94, p. 3.
"Literature and Poetry" (from *Le cornet à dés*, tr. by James Vladimir Gill). [ProseP] (3) 94, p. 53.
"Poem: To erase the heads of the generals of the Empire!" (tr. by William Kulik). [AmerPoR] (23:2) Mr-Ap 94, p. 3.
"Reconstruction" (tr. by William Kulik). [AmerPoR] (23:2) Mr-Ap 94, p. 5.
"The Soldier of Marathon" (from *Le cornet à dés*, tr. by James Vladimir Gill). [ProseP] (3) 94, p. 51.
"True Anecdote" (from *Le cornet à dés*, tr. by James Vladimir Gill). [ProseP] (3) 94, p. 52.

2972. JACOBIK, Gray
"The Turning." [Pivot] (41) 93, p. 26.

2973. JACOBIK, Jane
"Sandwoman." [SouthernPR] (34:2) Wint 94, p. 26-27.

2974. JACOBOWITZ, Judah
"Last Days of Ravel." [CapeR] (29:1) Spr 94, p. 15.

2975. JACOBS, Bruce A.
"Black on Black." [Obs] (9:2) Fall-Wint 94, p. 85-86.
"Manners." [Obs] (9:2) Fall-Wint 94, p. 86-87.

"Mentoring." [Obs] (9:2) Fall-Wint 94, p. 87-88.
2976. JACOBS, J. L.
"A Cord of Stone." [Talisman] (12) Spr 94, p. 222-225.
2977. JACOBS, Kathryn
"The Weed." [Elf] (4:4) Wint 94, p. 37.
2978. JACOBS, Sage Meridyth
"Letters to Kerouac" (a blues in 3 parts). [MoodySI] (28, also labeled 29) Fall 94, p. 20.
2979. JACOBSEN, Josephine
"First Woman." [NewYorker] (70:16) 6 Je 94, p. 58.
"Invisibilities: Even If You Listen." [AmerV] (35) 94, p. 157.
"Invisibilities: The Fish Tank Room." [AmerV] (35) 94, p. 156.
"Invisibilities: The Trip." [AmerV] (35) 94, p. 158.
"Invisibilities: Traveler." [AmerV] (35) 94, p. 155.
"Midnight Moose." [NewL] (61:1) 94, p. 154.
"Noon." [NewYorker] (70:21) 18 Jl 94, p. 59.
"The Ugly Old Lady." [Poetry] (164:3) Je 94, p. 139.
2980. JACOME-ROCA, Daniel
"Juventud." [LindLM] (13:1) Mr 94, p. 30.
2981. JAEGER, Lowell
"The Dinosaur." [ClockR] (9:1/2) 94-95, p. 106-107.
2982. JAFFE, Dan
"Eden After" (tr. of Lev Mak). [DenQ] (29:1) Sum 94, p. 86.
"In a Holocaust Memorial Garden" (Temple Beth Shalom, Sarasota, Florida). [NewL] (60:4) 94, p. 188-189.
"Rebond Shel Olam" (tr. of traditional Hebrew prayer). [DenQ] (29:1) Sum 94, p. 46.
2983. JAFFE, Maggie
"Gustav Mahler" (for the '67 Green Line). [ChironR] (13:4) Wint 94, p. 28.
"Luz Parra." [ChironR] (13:4) Wint 94, p. 28.
"Police/State." [SingHM] (21) 94, p. 5-6.
"Van Gogh's Whore." [ChironR] (13:4) Wint 94, p. 28.
JAGODZINSKA, Katarzyna Borun
See BORUN-JAGODZINSKA, Katarzyna
2984. JAHANNES, Ja
"I Hear You Margaret." [Obs] (9:2) Fall-Wint 94, p. 89-91.
2985. JAKIELA, Lori
"A Personal History of Hands." [ChiR] (40:2/3) 94, p. 69-70.
"A Personal History of Hands." [WestB] (34) 94, p. 20.
2986. JALOWICA, Daniel
"New Rule." [CanLit] (142/143) Fall-Wint 94, p. 212.
2987. JAMES, Cynthia
"Port-of-Spain by Night." [MassR] (35:3/4) Aut-Wint 94, p. 395-396.
2988. JAMES, David
"The Curse." [Parting] (7:2) Wint 94-95, p. 54.
"Getting Out of the Fast Lane." [LitR] (37:4) Sum 94, p. 681.
"The Meaning of Life." [SoCoast] (16) Ja 94, p. 4-5.
"Refusing to Acknowledge the Past." [Parting] (7:2) Wint 94-95, p. 55.
"The Vision of an Idiot." [SycamoreR] (6:2) Sum 94, p. 29.
2989. JAMES, Joyce
"Lies." [SouthernR] (30:4) Aut 94, p. 766-767.
2990. JAMES, Lysa
"A Wish." [Conscience] (15:2) Sum 94, p. 26.
2991. JAMES, Sibyl
"The Geomancy of Restaurants." [ProseP] (3) 94, p. 54.
"Learning to Live in Police States." [ProseP] (3) 94, p. 55.
"The Sisters of Saida Manoubia." [Calyx] (15:2) Sum 94, p. 14-15.
"Whether to *Cumbia.*" [Vis] (44) 94, p. 10.
2992. JAMES, Stewart
"Vanessa." [ParisR] (36:132) Fall 94, p. 253-269.
2993. JAMIE, Kathleen
"Ships / Rooms." [Jacaranda] (5:1) Wint-Spr 91, p. 65.
"Wee Wifey." [Jacaranda] (5:1) Wint-Spr 91, p. 64.
2994. JAMMES, Francis
"Wedding Day" (tr. by Tom Hibbard). [WillowS] (34) Sum 94, p. 64.

2995. JANABI, Hatif
"Questions and Their Retinue" (tr. by Khaled Mattawa). [InterQ] (1:3) 94, p. 128-130.
2996. JANECZKO, Paul B.
"How to Hug Your Three-Year-Old Daughter." [EngJ] (83:4) Ap 94, p. 109.
2997. JANES, Percy
"St. Thomas: Summer." [TickleAce] (28) Fall-Wint 94, p. 106.
"St. Thomas: Winter." [TickleAce] (28) Fall-Wint 94, p. 105.
2998. JANKOWSKI-SMITH, Shelli
"Renunciation." [Agni] (40) 94, p. 130.
2999. JANOWITZ, Phyllis
"Children and Animals." [Jacaranda] (4:2) Spr 90, p. 57-58.
"Nowhere." [Colum] (22) Wint 94, p. 57-58.
"Points of View." [Jacaranda] (4:2) Spr 90, p. 56-57.
"Reproduction." [Elf] (4:2) Sum 94, p. 28-29.
3000. JANZEN, Jean
"Cover Me." [Image] (8) Wint 94-95, p. 28.
"The Jewish Bride." [WestB] (35) 94, p. 55-56.
"Looking for the Soul." [Image] (8) Wint 94-95, p. 29-30.
"Order." [SoCoast] (17) Je 94, p. 5.
"Photographs of the Wild." [Image] (8) Wint 94-95, p. 26-27.
"Women of the Cloth." [WestB] (35) 94, p. 56-57.
3001. JANZEN, Rhoda
"An Incident of Cost." [InterPR] (20:1) Spr 94, p. 94-97.
"The Presence in the Room Beneath." [CumbPR] (14:1) Fall 94, p. 27.
"Two Sisters Return for a Fresno Christmas." [CumbPR] (14:1) Fall 94, p. 26.
3002. JARDINE, Gerri
"Reno to Wendover." [CutB] (41) Wint 94, p. 59.
3003. JARMAN, Mark
"Four Unholy Sonnets." [AmerPoR] (23:5) S-O 94, p. 33.
"How My Sister, My Mother, and I Still Travel Down Balwearie Road." [IllinoisR] (2:1) Fall 94, p. 26.
"In Front of the Children." [NewYorker] (70:38) 21 N 94, p. 96.
"In Via Est Cisterna." [Hudson] (46:4) Wint 94, p. 682.
"Nine Unholy Sonnets." [Hudson] (47:3) Aut 94, p. 413-416.
"Second Day." [SouthernHR] (28:3) Sum 94, p. 232.
"Three Unholy Sonnets." [AmerPoR] (23:3) My-Je 94, p. 56.
"Unholy Sonnet" (2 poems). [BlackWR] (20:2) Spr-Sum 94, p. 73-74.
3004. JARNAGIN, Willa
"Little Death." [Agni] (39) 94, p. 173.
3005. JARNOT, Lisa
"Renga" (February 9, 1994, Chinese New Year's Eve, w. Judith Goldman, Lee Ann Brown, and Sianne Ngai). [Chain] (1) Spr-Sum 94, p. 197-199.
3006. JARRARD, Kyle
"The Arnold & Ann Show." [WormR] (34:1, #133) 94, p. 13-15.
"The Decline of America." [WormR] (34:1, #133) 94, p. 16-18.
"Melodrama, Live." [WormR] (34:1, #133) 94, p. 16.
"Modern Man." [WormR] (34:1, #133) 94, p. 15.
"Old Cowboy." [WormR] (34:1, #133) 94, p. 15.
"Saved: 2." [WormR] (34:1, #133) 94, p. 15.
"Trash: 2." [WormR] (34:1, #133) 94, p. 18.
3007. JARVIS, C. D. Runyon
"Hevra Kadisha." [SouthernPR] (34:2) Wint 94, p. 70-73.
3008. JASPER, Pat
"Part III, Chapter XIV, Wherin Fresh from Defeat in a Recent Skirmish the Ingenious Gentleman Sallies Forth to Skydome in Quest of a Victory." [CanLit] (142/143) Fall-Wint 94, p. 75-76.
3009. JASTERMSKY, Karen
"On Mayakovsky's Shoulders." [AnthNEW] (6) 94, p. 8.
"The Pitch." [EvergreenC] (9:1) Wint-Spr 94, p. 14-15.
3010. JAUSS, David
"After the End of the World" (Sun Ra and His Intergalactic Research Arkestra, Berlin, 1976). [MissouriR] (17:2) 94, p. 42-43.
"Allegedly." [IndR] (17:1) Spr 94, p. 115-116.
"Estate Sales." [SouthernHR] (28:2) Spr 94, p. 142.

"The Hatchet" (Thelonious Monk, "Round Midnight," New York, April 5, 1957). [Shen] (44:4) Wint 94, p. 59-60.
"Homage to John Cage." [Poetry] (165:1) O 94, p. 16-17.
"Improvising Rivers." [MissouriR] (17:2) 94, p. 39-41.
"The Master Musicians of Joujouka" (Ornette, Coleman, Joujouka, Morocco, January 17, 1973). [MissouriR] (17:2) 94, p. 44.
"Nohant, 1876" (from *Saint Flaubert*). [PoetryE] (37/38) Spr 94, p. 35.
"Star Ledger" (in memory of L.H.). [Crazy] (47) Wint 94, p. 7.
"Style" (James P. Johnson, The Jungles Casino, New York, February, 1909). [Shen] (44:4) Wint 94, p. 57-58.

3011. JAVA
"Patent Leather Blue." [AnotherCM] (27) 94, p. 107-108.

3012. JEBB, Keith
"Beachcombing." [Verse] (11:1) Spr 94, p. 48.

3013. JEFFERS, Jamaal
"Beautiful Things." [CaribbeanW] (8) 94, p. 37.

3014. JEFFERS, Meg
"Ordnance." [MidAR] (14:2) 94, p. 135.

3015. JELUSIC, Bozica
"Famous Surrealist's Slippers" (tr. by Dasha Culic Nisula and the author). [InterQ] (1:1) [93?], p. 124-125.
"The Ground in Labrador (After Lawrence)" (tr. by Dasha Culic Nisula and the author). [InterQ] (1:1) [93?], p. 122-123.
"Key of the Vanishing Kingdom" (Homage to Sylvia Plath, tr. by Dasha Culic Nisula). [PennR] (6:1) 94, p. 21.
"Kljuc Nestajucega Kraljevstva" (Homage a Sylvia Plath). [PennR] (6:1) 94, p. 20.

3016. JENCKES, Norma
"The Last time I Saw Paris." [WestHR] (48:2) Sum 94, p. 128.
"Messy Things." [WestHR] (48:2) Sum 94, p. 129.

3017. JENKINS, Alan
"The London Dissector" (Excerpt). [Jacaranda] (5:1) Wint-Spr 91, p. 68-69.

3018. JENKINS, Louis
"Corkscrew." [ProseP] (3) 94, p. 57.
"New Mexico." [Sun] (224) Ag 94, p. 18.
"Sainthood." [CimR] (109) O 94, p. 66.
"Spontaneous Combustion." [ProseP] (3) 94, p. 56.
"Your Baby." [ProseP] (3) 94, p. 58.

3019. JENKINS, Mike
"The Building." [Jacaranda] (5:1) Wint-Spr 91, p. 72-73.
"Implanting of Stone." [CharR] (20:2) Fall 94, p. 86-87.

3020. JENKINS, Paul
"How Animals Think" (I, II. Associated Writing Programs Intro Award poem). [IndR] (17:2) Fall 94, p. 145-146.

3021. JENKINSON, J. S.
"Missing Person." [WindO] (58) Sum 94, p. 45.

3022. JENKS, Shane
"The Pit." [Callaloo] (17:1) Wint 94, p. 182.

3023. JENNINGS, Carol
"Shanghai." [Amelia] (7:3, #22) 94, p. 117.

3024. JENNINGS, Elizabeth
"Angels." [Image] ([2]) Sum 92, p. 25-26.

3025. JENNINGS, Lane
"Answer" (tr. of Erich Fried). [Vis] (45) 94, p. 43.
"Going Under" (tr. of Erich Fried). [Vis] (44) 94, p. 7.

3026. JENSEN, Laura
"Minus Tide." [Crazy] (46) Spr 94, p. 106-112.
"The Sparkler." [Crazy] (47) Wint 94, p. 60-62.

3027. JESELNICK, Mary
"Night Sky." [Parting] (7:1) Sum 94, p. 68.
"Protective Coloration." [Parting] (7:1) Sum 94, p. 6.

3028. JESSEPH, Jennifer J.
"Birthing the Boats." [Calyx] (15:3) Wint 94-95, p. 46-47.

3029. JEWELL, Andrew
"Requiem for a Circus Clown." [Plain] (15:1) Fall 94, p. 7.

3030. JEWELL, Michael
"Woodcutter's Song." [AnthNEW] (6) 94, p. 35.

JIA-XIN, Wang
See WANG, Jiaxin
JIAN, Yu
See YU, Jian
JIANQING, Zheng
See ZHENG, Jianqing
JIMENEZ, Domingo Moreno
See MORENO JIMENEZ, Domingo
3031. JIMÉNEZ, Ydilia
"A Dulce Maria Loynaz." [Nuez] (5:13/14/15) 94, p. 5.
3032. JIN, Ha
"Ways of Talking." [Poetry] (164:4) Jl 94, p. 196.
3033. JIN, Zhong
"The Face, Also, Has Bruised Dignity" (tr. of Bei Ling, w. William Slaughter). [Manoa] (6:1) Sum 94, p. 82-83.
"Words of Autumn" (tr. of Bei Ling, w. Wang Weiqing). [Manoa] (6:1) Sum 94, p. 81.
3034. JING, Bute
"Aiming" (tr. by Cheng Baolin and Richard Terrill). [AnotherCM] (27) 94, p. 87.
JIPING, Dong
See DONG, Jiping
3035. JOHANNESSEN, Matthias
"Myth" (a meditation of Iceland's thousand years, tr. by Hallberg Hallmundsson). [Vis] (44) 94, p. 35-37.
JOHANNESSEN, Mattias
See JOHANNESSEN, Matthias
3036. JOHANSSEN, Kerry
"When Her Hands Pulled the Baby Out." [DenQ] (29:1) Sum 94, p. 17.
3037. JOHNSON, Allen, Jr.
"Come South with Me." [Light] (11) Aut 94, p. 13.
"Heed the Call of Home." [Light] (12) Wint 94-95, p. 7.
3038. JOHNSON, Corrine
"Brothers." [PoetryE] (37/38) Spr 94, p. 79.
"Introductions." [PoetryE] (37/38) Spr 94, p. 80.
"Roof." [PoetryE] (37/38) Spr 94, p. 78.
3039. JOHNSON, Edward
"Hate Speech." [ChironR] (13:2) Sum 94, p. 18.
"Remains." [ChironR] (13:2) Sum 94, p. 18.
3040. JOHNSON, Gerald J.
"An Antique Rime" (An epithalamion for Terri and Stephen). [FourQ] (8:2) Fall 94, p. 55.
3041. JOHNSON, Jacqueline Joan
"Clara." [Eyeball] (3) 93, p. 39.
"Moseka's Way" (for Aminata Moseka / Abbey Lincoln). [Eyeball] (3) 93, p. 38.
3042. JOHNSON, Jonathan
"For My Communist Grandfather Downcast by Current Affairs." [HawaiiR] (18:1, #40) Spr 94, p. 111.
"Skinhead Execution of One of Their Own." [Sonora] (27) Spr 94, p. 30-31.
"Three Locations" (for Peter). [HayF] (15) Fall-Wint 94, p. 50-51.
"Unmarked Stop in Front of Westmond General Store, Westmond, Idaho." [CimR] (109) O 94, p. 63-64.
"Working Without Brothers." [HawaiiR] (18:1, #40) Spr 94, p. 112.
3043. JOHNSON, Kimberly
"In the City of Eventual Peace." [NewYorker] (70:29) 19 S 94, p. 80.
3044. JOHNSON, Marael
"A Ritual Lie." [SlipS] (14) 94, p. 53-54.
3045. JOHNSON, Margot
"12 Months a Year." [Pearl] (20) Spr 94, p. 48-49.
3046. JOHNSON, Mark Allan
"The Burning Barrel." [BellArk] (10:3) My-Je 94, p. 7.
"The Circle Unbroken." [BellArk] (10:2) Mr-Ap 94, p. 15.
3047. JOHNSON, Martin
"Do Not Confuse Yourself." [ChatR] (14:3) Spr 94, p. 42.
3048. JOHNSON, Michael L.
"All Is Vanity." [SoCoast] (17) Je 94, p. 10.

"Georgia O'Keeffe's Music — Pink and Blue I" (for Andrew Svedlow). [Amelia] (7:3, #22) 94, p. 94.
"Live Nude Girls." [WeberS] (11:1) Wint 94, p. 122.
"My Last Visit with Ed Ruhe." [Amelia] (7:3, #22) 94, p. 94.
"Oldest Known Hummingbird in North America Is Captured." [Amelia] (7:3, #22) 94, p. 95.

3049. JOHNSON, Nancy
"Shopping: The Lipstick Channel." [MassR] (35:1) Spr 94, p. 83-84.

3050. JOHNSON, Nick
"Back Home." [Confr] (54/55) Fall 94-Wint 95, p. 305.

3051. JOHNSON, P. K.
"Smallest Miracles." [BellArk] (10:6) N-D 94, p. 4.

3052. JOHNSON, Peter
"Artiste Manquée." [NoDaQ] (62:4) Fall 94-95, p. 32.
"Pirates." [NoDaQ] (62:4) Fall 94-95, p. 33.
"Universal Medicine." [DenQ] (29:2) Fall 94, p. 11.

3053. JOHNSON, Sam
"My Two Cents" (culled entirely from Larry King's column in *USA Today* by Sam Johnson and Chris Marcil). [NewRep] (211:1) 4 Jl 94, p. 9.

3054. JOHNSON, Sheila Golburgh
"A Quest for Cranes." [ApalQ] (42) Fall 94, p. 59.

3055. JOHNSON, Stacey Land
"Flood Season." [HangL] (65) 94, p. 24.
"A Romance." [NoAmR] (279:3) My-Je 94, p. 30-31.

3056. JOHNSON, Susan
"The Steady Business of Shadows." [Interim] (13:1) Spr-Sum 94, p. 10.
"Symphony." [QW] (39) Sum-Fall 94, p. 241-242.
"Woman Walking Shore." [Interim] (13:1) Spr-Sum 94, p. 11-12.

3057. JOHNSON, Thomas L.
"Found Poem" (from *The Atlanta Constitution*). [SoCaR] (26:2) Spr 94, p. 204-207.

3058. JOHNSON, William
"At Sheep Lake." [WeberS] (11:3) Fall 94, p. 131.
"Burning the Raspberry Canes." [PoetryNW] (35:1) Spr 94, p. 34.
"Chinese Ruins on the Salmon." [WeberS] (11:3) Fall 94, p. 132.
"Dipper." [WeberS] (11:3) Fall 94, p. 132-133.
"Hawks." [WeberS] (11:3) Fall 94, p. 133.
"Icefishing on Lost Valley Reservoir." [PoetryNW] (35:1) Spr 94, p. 33.
"Root Cellar." [PoetryNW] (35:1) Spr 94, p. 32.

3059. JOHNSTON, Allan
"A Clear Glass." [WeberS] (11:2) Spr-Sum 94, p. 64-65.
"A Painter Thinks of Icarus" (from "Tasks of Survival"). [AmerPoR] (23:2) Mr-Ap 94, p. 33.
"Pavane." [WeberS] (11:2) Spr-Sum 94, p. 66.
"To See Water." [WeberS] (11:2) Spr-Sum 94, p. 66.
"Waking." [WeberS] (11:2) Spr-Sum 94, p. 65.

3060. JOHNSTON, Fred
"Balance." [AntigR] (96) Wint 94, p. 39.
"Boat Dreaming." [AntigR] (96) Wint 94, p. 38.
"Letter to Joaquín." [SouthernHR] (28:2) Spr 94, p. 160.
"Light Out of Smoak" (for Sean O Murchú). [SenR] (24:2) Fall 94, p. 42-43.
"Repudiation." [NewL] (60:3) 94, p. 38.

3061. JOHNSTON, Gary
"Blue Sweet: The Dying Testament of Huddie Ledbetter 1888-1949." [Eyeball] (3) 93, p. 37-38.

3062. JOHNSTON, Marilyn
"Falling from the Mirror." [SmPd] (31:3, #92) Fall 94, p. 19.
"I Knew a Man." [SmPd] (31:1, #90) Wint 94, p. 29.
"Icarus's Sister." [SmPd] (31:1, #90) Wint 94, p. 28.
"Lake Congamond, Before Shut Eye." [SmPd] (31:1, #90) Wint 94, p. 30-32.
"Transformations." [SmPd] (31:3, #92) Fall 94, p. 19.

3063. JOHNSTON, Mark
"Knife's Song." [SoCoast] (16) Ja 94, p. 25.
"The Parachutists." [SoCoast] (16) Ja 94, p. 26-27.
"Permutations: Starting Again at Zero." [ChironR] (13:3) Aut 94, p. 30.
"Reverse Aubade for Layne." [WebR] (18) Fall 94, p. 67.

3064. JOHNSTON, Stella
"The Clown Doll." [WestHR] (48:1) Spr 94, p. 60-61.
"Julian." [ParisR] (36:131) Sum 94, p. 214-216.
3065. JOHNSTON, Sue Ann
"For Pioneering Women Whose Babies Died." [CanLit] (141) Sum 94, p. 13.
"True Story." [Event] (23:1) Spr 94, p. 44-47.
3066. JOHNSTON-HALE, Ellen Turlington
"Summer Night." [NoCarLR] (2:1) Spr 94, p. 60.
3067. JOLLIFF, William
"The Blood Groove." [SouthernPR] (34:2) Wint 94, p. 15-16.
"Hot Apples." [QW] (38) Winter-Spr 93-94, p. 92.
"Monroe at Rail Fence Park." [CumbPR] (14:1) Fall 94, p. 78.
"Praying the Name." [WritersF] (20) 94, p. 40.
"Rafting on Fulton Creek." [Pivot] (41) 93, p. 18-19.
"Sister Runkle's Flannelgraph: Noah's Children." [Border] (4) Spr-Sum 94, p. 48.
"Telling Fortunes." [CapeR] (29:2) Fall 94, p. 16.
"Tonight My Son Would Be a Priest." [FloridaR] (19:2) 94, p. 84.
3068. JOLLIMORE, Troy
"Three Poems." [AntigR] (99) Aut 94, p. 28.
3069. JONES, Alice
"Christmas Morning." [LaurelR] (28:2) Sum 94, p. 79.
"The Dream." [Poetry] (163:5) F 94, p. 273.
"Failure to Thrive." [ColR] (21:2) Fall 94, p. 149.
"Swimming." [ColR] (21:2) Fall 94, p. 150-151.
"Thirst." [Poetry] (163:5) F 94, p. 272.
"Thirteen." [Poetry] (163:5) F 94, p. 271.
3070. JONES, Bobi
"Racing Pigeons" (tr. by Joseph P. Clancy). [Verse] (11:1) Spr 94, p. 114-115.
3071. JONES, Cy Keith
"Wondering." [JlNJPo] (16:2) Aut 94, p. 20.
3072. JONES, D. G.
"Confronting the sea, the shift of skies, beauty" (tr. of Louise Warren). [PoetryC] (14:4) S 94, p. 28.
"In my house there are no mirrors" (tr. of Louise Warren). [PoetryC] (14:4) S 94, p. 28.
"Stream of lightning, I love sweat" (tr. of Louise Warren). [PoetryC] (14:4) S 94, p. 28.
"Your belly betrays light tremors" (tr. of Louise Warren). [PoetryC] (14:4) S 94, p. 28.
JONES, Deryn Rees
See REES-JONES, Deryn
3073. JONES, F.
"Money." [Verse] (11:2) Sum 94, p. 86.
3074. JONES, Glory Lee
"Belt" (After talking on *Hot Daddy* phone sex line). [JamesWR] (11:3) Spr 94, p. 9.
"Cleopatra." [JamesWR] (11:3) Spr 94, p. 8.
"The Evenings and the Nights of Cole Porter Years After the Accident." [JamesWR] (11:3) Spr 94, p. 9.
"School Prayers for Alec Scudder" (for E.M. Forster). [JamesWR] (11:3) Spr 94, p. 9.
3075. JONES, Janis Montgomery
"Poor Women." [NegC] (14:1/2) 94, p. 38.
3076. JONES, Jill
"Dancing in the Diamond Light" (for Loretta). [Vis] (44) 94, p. 18.
3077. JONES, Jordan
"Heaven Is Convex" (Section III of *The Anti-Heaven*, tr. of René Daumal). [HeavenB] (11) 94, p. 64-68.
3078. JONES, Joy
"Dizzy" (for the late jazz trumpeter Dizzy Gillespie). [AfAmRev] (28:4) Wint 94, p. 600.
3079. JONES, Paul
"At the Hunter's Stew." [SouthernR] (30:3) Sum 94, p. 539-540.
"Pastoral." [SouthernR] (30:3) Sum 94, p. 540-541.
"Wild Ginger." [SouthernHR] (28:4) Fall 94, p. 334.

3080. JONES, Richard
"Boat Scene" (tr. of Paul Eluard, w. Barbara Goldman). [PoetryE] (37/38) Spr 94, p. 217.
"Fish" (tr. of Paul Eluard, w. Barbara Goldman). [PoetryE] (37/38) Spr 94, p. 220.
"The Law" (tr. of Paul Eluard, w. Barbara Goldman). [PoetryE] (37/38) Spr 94, p. 218.
"The Novel." [TriQ] (91) Fall 94, p. 202-210.
"Of One and of Two, of All" (tr. of Paul Eluard, w. Barbara Goldman). [PoetryE] (37/38) Spr 94, p. 219.
"The Owl" (tr. of René Char). [PoetryE] (37/38) Spr 94, p. 237.
"Sacrifices." [Os] (38) Spr 94, p. 6-7.
"So Many Dreams in the Air" (tr. of Paul Eluard, w. Barbara Goldman). [PoetryE] (37/38) Spr 94, p. 221.
"The Two of Us" (tr. of Paul Eluard, w. Barbara Goldman). [PoetryE] (37/38) Spr 94, p. 216.

3081. JONES, Robert
"Failed Poet Grading Vocabulary Quizzes" (for my students). [PoetryNW] (35:2) Sum 94, p. 28-29.

3082. JONES, Rodney
"In the Spirit of Limuel Hardin." [SouthernR] (30:4) Aut 94, p. 846-848.
"Indian Turnip." [SouthernR] (30:4) Aut 94, p. 848-849.
"Perfection." [SouthernR] (30:4) Aut 94, p. 851-854.
"The Troubles That Women Start Are Men." [SouthernR] (30:4) Aut 94, p. 850-851.

3083. JONES, Roger
"Owl." [ColEng] (56:4) Ap 94, p. 452.
"Sulphur River." [Border] (5) Fall-Wint 94, p. 28.

JONES, Sheila Carter
See CARTER-JONES, Sheila

3084. JONKER, Jason
"Father's Song." [ChangingM] (27) Wint 94, p. 45.
"Joel Was Eight Years Older and Seemed a God to Me." [ChangingM] (27) Wint 94, p. 23.

3085. JONSON, Ben
"Mab." [Light] (10) Sum 94, p. 24.

3086. JOPP, Jessica
"Imbrium Basin in the Sea of Rains." [PlumR] (7) [94?], p. 37.

3087. JORDAN, Barbara
"II. Impending thoughtfulness" (to Monica Raymond). [Chain] (1) Spr-Sum 94, p. 233.
"Anchorites." [Image] (7) Fall 94, p. 45-46.
"Common Ephemeral." [Image] (7) Fall 94, p. 46-47.
"Crucible." [Image] (7) Fall 94, p. 47-48.

3088. JORDAN, Faris
"Undoing the Knot." [SlipS] (14) 94, p. 31.

3089. JORDAN, MaryKate
"The Impact of Silence." [BellArk] (10:6) N-D 94, p. 15.
"Masquerade." [BellArk] (10:1) Ja-F 94, p. 11.
"Priestly Office." [BellArk] (10:6) N-D 94, p. 15.

3090. JORDAN, Richard
"Canned Dreams." [Obs] (9:2) Fall-Wint 94, p. 92.
"In Voluntary Servitude." [Obs] (9:2) Fall-Wint 94, p. 92-93.

3091. JORON, Andrew
"A Beautiful Disease." [HeavenB] (11) 94, p. 42.
"Peculiar Roots Have Reason's Eyes." [Sulfur] (35) Fall 94, p. 123.
"The Serpentine Fusion of Occult Solar Riddles" (w. Will Alexander). [Caliban] (14) 94, p. 20-29.

3092. JOSELOW, Beth
"Cross the Palms." [NewAW] (12) Spr-Sum 94, p. 129.
"Tina, I Said." [Chain] (1) Spr-Sum 94, p. 192.

3093. JOSEPH, Allison
"At the Clinic." [Callaloo] (17:2) Sum 94, p. 460-461.
"Backing Vocals." [Eyeball] (3) 93, p. 13.
"For Mother, After the Reading." [CapeR] (29:2) Fall 94, p. 14-15.
"For Shame." [AmerV] (33) 94, p. 80-81.
"Good Advice." [Callaloo] (17:2) Sum 94, p. 462-463.
"Hometown." [Plain] (14:2) Wint 94, p. 26.

"Hospice." [Plain] (15:1) Fall 94, p. 22-23.
"In the Bookstore." [Callaloo] (17:2) Sum 94, p. 464-465.
"Instructions." [PoetC] (25:2) Wint 94, p. 3.
"Livelihood." [PoetC] (25:2) Wint 94, p. 4-5.
"Pledge." [SouthernR] (30:4) Aut 94, p. 708-709.
"Soul Train." [Eyeball] (3) 93, p. 13.

3094. JOSEPH, Jenny
"Patriotic Poem Against Nationalism" (for a newborn child). [PartR] (61:3) Sum 94, p. 511-513.

3095. JOSEPH, Stephen
"Epigram." [Confr] (54/55) Fall 94-Wint 95, p. 324.

3096. JOSHI, Madhu
"The Fish — 2" (tr. of Gagan Gill, w. Arlene Zide and J. P. Das). [InterQ] (1:2) 93, p. 184.

3097. JOYCE, James
"XXXVI. I hear an army charging upon the land." [SoCoast] (16) Ja 94, p. 65.

JUDEVINE MOUNTAIN
See MOUNTAIN, Judevine

3098. JUDGE, Michael
"The Drowned." [PoetL] (89:3) Fall 94, p. 23.
"Poem: My sister follows me behind the barn." [DogRR] (13:1, #25) Spr-Sum 94, p. 23.

3099. JUDSON, John
"Autumn Soliloquy in Morning Mist." [OhioR] (52) 94, p. 122.

3100. JULES, Jacqueline
"The Starfish." [SantaBR] (2:1) Spr-Sum 94, p. 75.
"Terror's Dominion." [SmPd] (31:3, #92) Fall 94, p. 20.

3101. JULIANO, Gary
"Dance Lessons" (for Kate). [CapeR] (29:2) Fall 94, p. 36-37.
"Towels." [PaintedB] (53/54) 94, p. 31.

JUNG-KWON, Cho
See CHO, Jung-kwon

3102. JUNIPER, Dean
"My Father's Watch." [Verse] (11:1) Spr 94, p. 67.

3103. JUNKINS, Donald
"Walking to Indian Camp." [NoDaQ] (62:2) Spr 94-95, p. 140.
"Xi'an: The Underground Terra Cotta Warriors of Emperor Qin Shi Huang (221 B.C.)." [Salm] (103) Sum 94, p. 105-106.

JURADO, Manuel Gahete
See GAHETE JURADO, Manuel

3104. JUREK, Richard
"A Letter in German Typed on an Old Schreibmaschine." [AntigR] (96) Wint 94, p. 59-60.
"Palermo." [AntigR] (96) Wint 94, p. 61-62.

3105. JUSTER, A. M.
"Rejection Letter." [Hellas] (5:1) Spr-Sum 94, p. 75.

3106. JUSTICE, Donald
"Pantoum of the Depression Years." [NewYorker] (70:15) 30 My 94, p. 86.
"Sadness, an Improvisation." [SouthernR] (30:4) Aut 94, p. 723-724.
"Sonnet: The wall surrounding them they never saw." [PlumR] (7) [94?], p. 80.

K., W. T.
See W. T. K.

3107. KABBANI, Nizar
"Beirut! O Queen of the World" (tr. by Mona Takyeddine Amyuni). [LitR] (37:3) Spr 94, p. 498-502.
"I Am Trying to Save the Last Female Before the Arrival of the Tartars" (tr. by Allen Hibbard and Osama Isber). [CimR] (108) Jl 94, p. 12-14.
"I Wear You" (tr. by Bassam Frangieh). [LitR] (37:3) Spr 94, p. 505.
"The Orange" (tr. by Bassam Frangieh). [LitR] (37:3) Spr 94, p. 503.
"When You Find a Man" (tr. by Bassam Frangieh). [LitR] (37:3) Spr 94, p. 502.
"With a Newspaper" (tr. by Bassam Frangieh). [LitR] (37:3) Spr 94, p. 504.
"You Are So Beautiful" (tr. by Bassam Frangieh). [LitR] (37:3) Spr 94, p. 504.

3108. KACZMAREK, Scott
"The Cure." [Amelia] (7:3, #22) 94, p. 51.

3109. KAFATOU, Sarah
"Catalogue" (tr. of Hilde Domin). [HarvardR] (7) Fall 94, p. 144.
"Convergings, Vanishings." [CumbPR] (13:2) Spr 94, p. 85.
"Not to Tire" (tr. of Hilde Domin). [HarvardR] (7) Fall 94, p. 144.
"Summons" (tr. of Hilde Domin). [HarvardR] (7) Fall 94, p. 144.
3110. KAHN, Lisa
"Today I Commanded the Wind / Heute Befahl Ich dem Wind" (Selections from a bilingual English/German lyrical volume). [AmerPoR] (23:2) Mr-Ap 94, p. 33.
3111. KAISER, Timothy
"Highway Number 1." [AntigR] (99) Aut 94, p. 98-99.
"Home." [AntigR] (99) Aut 94, p. 100-101.
3112. KALAMARAS, George
"Cuff-links." [SycamoreR] (6:2) Sum 94, p. 54-56.
"Entering the Corridors of Breath." [Elf] (4:1) Spr 94, p. 26-27.
"Hiroshima as Inscribed in the Book of Questions." [RiverS] (40) 94, p. 1-3.
"The Mountain." [YellowS] (12:2, #46) Sum-Fall 94, p. 13.
"Of One Breath Passing into Another" (for Jim Grabill). [Elf] (4:2) Sum 94, p. 43.
"The Phenomenology of Space" (upon meeting Rosa). [YellowS] (12:3, #47) Fall-Wint 94-95, p. 10.
"The Stretch for Sound." [YellowS] (12:2, #46) Sum-Fall 94, p. 12.
"Sunday Morning Sleep." [HayF] (15) Fall-Wint 94, p. 32-33.
"Thursday's Meditation." [WorldL] (5) 94, p. 24-25.
"Woman Handing Man an Envelope, Chinese Servant with Moth Wings, Standing on a Floor of Water" (for Max Ernst). [HopewellR] (6) 94, p. 104-105.
"A Word." [Nimrod] (38:1) Fall-Wint 94, p. 113.
3113. KALDAS, Pauline
"A Calm Moment" (tr. of May Mudhaffar). [InterQ] (1:3) 94, p. 156.
"Egypt, the war of 1967." [InterQ] (1:3) 94, p. 153.
"Home." [InterQ] (1:3) 94, p. 154-155.
"A Man and a Woman" (tr. of May Mudhaffar). [InterQ] (1:3) 94, p. 157.
3114. KALENDEK, Julie
"Broken." [Chain] (1) Spr-Sum 94, p. 282.
3115. KALINSKI, Todd
"3 Generations." [ChironR] (13:2) Sum 94, p. 11.
"The Minister of the Hot Coals." [ChironR] (13:2) Sum 94, p. 11.
"Mr. Neptune." [ChironR] (13:2) Sum 94, p. 11.
"The New, the Bigs, the Blues." [SlipS] (14) 94, p. 107-108.
"Thru the Present Weavingly." [CoalC] (8) Ap 94, p. 30.
3116. KALLENBERG, Garrett
"Natural Philosophy 3 Divination." [Talisman] (12) Spr 94, p. 218.
3117. KALLET, Marilyn
"At the Edge of You." [ShadowP] (4) 94, p. 18-19.
"Forbidden Verses." [ShadowP] (4) 94, p. 16-17.
"Ghost Sonnet #2." [ShadowP] (4) 94, p. 15.
"Letter from Sweet Briar." [ShadowP] (4) 94, p. 16.
"Sick of Words." [ShadowP] (4) 94, p. 10-11.
"Turning Back the Body." [ShadowP] (4) 94, p. 11-12.
"Warning." [ShadowP] (4) 94, p. 12-13.
"Why I Wear My Hair Long." [ShadowP] (4) 94, p. 9.
"You Occupy Everything." [ShadowP] (4) 94, p. 14-15.
3118. KALOGERIS, George
"Solomos at Zakynthos." [PartR] (61:2) Spr 94, p. 312.
3119. KALOIDIS, Elliot
"The Afternoon Our Guide Explained Where the Mountains Will Grow." [PaintedB] (53/54) 94, p. 90.
3120. KALZ, Jill
"Sex Behind the Mill Road Cafe" (for Michelle). [CreamCR] (18:1) Spr 94, p. 80-81.
3121. KAMADA, Roy Osamu
"Prelude: October, 1969." [BambooR] (63/64) Sum-Fall 94, p. 19-20.
3122. KAMAL, Daud
"The Blue Wind." [Vis] (45) 94, p. 23.
"Poem: There is a silence that delves for pain" (tr. of Mansour Y. Sheikh). [Vis] (45) 94, p. 21.
"Still Life" (tr. of Mansoor Y. Sheikh). [Vis] (46) 94, p. 10.

3123. KAMENETZ, Rodger
"Pilpul." [Sun] (225) S 94, p. 37.
3124. KANE, April
"Yellow Rubber Gloves." [EvergreenC] (9:1) Wint-Spr 94, p. 20.
3125. KANE, Julie
"Everything But Blue" (Everette Hawthorne Maddox, 1944-1989). [NegC] (13:2/3) 93, p. 69.
"Ode to the Big Muddy." [NegC] (13:2/3) 93, p. 26-27.
3126. KANE, Peter
"Inescapable, the Rain" (Associated Writing Programs Intro Award poem). [IndR] (17:2) Fall 94, p. 122.
3127. KANEKO, Mitsuharu
"Fuji" (tr. by Tomoyuki Iino and Jon Silkin). [Stand] (35:3) Sum 94, p. 18.
3128. KANELOS, Peter
"In the Cave of Skulls" (Patmos, 1990). [Poetry] (164:6) S 94, p. 320-321.
3129. KANES, Eveline L.
"Another Hour" (tr. of Ileana Malancioiu, w. Mihai Zaharia). [InterPR] (20:1) Spr 94, p. 37.
"The Art of Poetry" (tr. of Nichita Stanescu, w. Mihai Zaharia). [InterPR] (20:1) Spr 94, p. 61, 63.
"Autumn Exhibition" (tr. of Mircea Dinescu, w. Mihai Zaharia). [InterPR] (20:1) Spr 94, p. 19.
"Cain and Abel" (tr. of Nichita Stanescu, w. Mihai Zaharia). [InterPR] (20:1) Spr 94, p. 51.
"Caudine Forks" (tr. of Horia Badescu, w. Mihai Zaharia). [InterPR] (20:1) Spr 94, p. 77.
"The Churches Have No Roofs" (tr. of Ana Blandiana, w. Mihai Zaharia). [InterPR] (20:1) Spr 94, p. 25.
"Death has climbed on our house" (tr. of Mircea Dinescu, w. Mihai Zaharia). [InterPR] (20:1) Spr 94, p. 13.
"The Father" (tr. of Ana Blandiana, w. Mihai Zaharia). [InterPR] (20:1) Spr 94, p. 33.
"Guilty Star" (tr. of Stefan A. Doinas, w. Mihai Zaharia). [InterPR] (20:1) Spr 94, p. 69.
"Hell" (tr. of Ana Blandiana, w. Mihai Zaharia). [InterPR] (20:1) Spr 94, p. 31.
"The Hypocritical Corpse" (tr. of Mircea Dinescu, w. Mihai Zaharia). [InterPR] (20:1) Spr 94, p. 23.
"Jericho Waltz" (tr. of Mircea Dinescu, w. Mihai Zaharia). [InterPR] (20:1) Spr 94, p. 15.
"The Jester" (tr. of Ileana Malancioiu, w. Mihai Zaharia). [InterPR] (20:1) Spr 94, p. 43.
"Journey into the Light" (tr. of Stefan A. Doinas, w. Mihai Zaharia). [InterPR] (20:1) Spr 94, p. 67.
"The Lamentations of Solomon" (X, XXVI, tr. of Horia Badescu, w. Mihai Zaharia). [InterPR] (20:1) Spr 94, p. 83, 85.
"The Last Memory" (tr. of Ileana Malancioiu, w. Mihai Zaharia). [InterPR] (20:1) Spr 94, p. 45.
"Like a Rabbit" (tr. of Ileana Malancioiu, w. Mihai Zaharia). [InterPR] (20:1) Spr 94, p. 39.
"Lorenzo's Decree" (tr. of Stefan A. Doinas, w. Mihai Zaharia). [InterPR] (20:1) Spr 94, p. 65.
"Maieutics" (tr. of Horia Badescu, w. Mihai Zaharia). [InterPR] (20:1) Spr 94, p. 87.
"Medical Advice" (tr. of Mircea Dinescu, w. Mihai Zaharia). [InterPR] (20:1) Spr 94, p. 21.
"Molecules of Calcium" (tr. of Ana Blandiana, w. Mihai Zaharia). [InterPR] (20:1) Spr 94, p. 27.
"On the Field of Stone" (tr. of Nichita Stanescu, w. Mihai Zaharia). [InterPR] (20:1) Spr 94, p. 53.
"Poem: Who can still dream, and of what" (tr. of Ana Blandiana, w. Mihai Zaharia). [InterPR] (20:1) Spr 94, p. 35.
"Poem: You float like a nocturnal dream" (tr. of Nichita Stanescu, w. Mihai Zaharia). [InterPR] (20:1) Spr 94, p. 49.
"Psalm: You who have taught bears" (tr. of Ana Blandiana, w. Mihai Zaharia). [InterPR] (20:1) Spr 94, p. 29.
"Song" (1-2, tr. of Horia Badescu, w. Mihai Zaharia). [InterPR] (20:1) Spr 94, p. 79, 81.

"The Story of the Rats" (tr. of Stefan A. Doinas, w. Mihai Zaharia). [InterPR] (20:1) Spr 94, p. 71.
"Testament" (tr. of Nichita Stanescu, w. Mihai Zaharia). [InterPR] (20:1) Spr 94, p. 55, 57.
"Trace of a Voyage" (tr. of Mircea Dinescu, w. Mihai Zaharia). [InterPR] (20:1) Spr 94, p. 17.
"Ulysses" (tr. of Stefan A. Doinas, w. Mihai Zaharia). [InterPR] (20:1) Spr 94, p. 75.
"Victim of My Dream" (tr. of Ileana Malancioiu, w. Mihai Zaharia). [InterPR] (20:1) Spr 94, p. 41.
"Vigil Near Metals" (tr. of Nichita Stanescu, w. Mihai Zaharia). [InterPR] (20:1) Spr 94, p. 59.
"When I Sailed" (tr. of Ileana Malancioiu, w. Mihai Zaharia). [InterPR] (20:1) Spr 94, p. 47.
"The Wounded Veteran" (tr. of Stefan A. Doinas, w. Mihai Zaharia). [InterPR] (20:1) Spr 94, p. 73.

3130. KANTOR, Marisa G.
"Chocolate Rabbits." [LouisL] (11:2) Fall 94, p. 77-78.

3131. KANYADI, Sándor
"Ecclesiastes Ch. 1, V. 9" (tr. by Len Roberts and Eva Bordisne). [Boulevard] (9:3, #27) Fall 94, p. 138-139.
"A Miscarried Meeting with János Pilinszky" (tr. by Bruce Berlind and Mária Körösy). [SenR] (24:2) Fall 94, p. 59.
"Woodcut" (tr. by Bruce Berlind and Mária Körösy). [SenR] (24:2) Fall 94, p. 58.

3132. KAPLAN, Jonathan
"Halcyon Days (New Jersey)." [TexasR] (15:1/2) Spr-Sum 94, p. 90.

3133. KAPLAN, Robert
"Driving." [ModernW] (1) Summer 94, p. 55-61.
"Rooster Poem." [ModernW] (2) Wint 94, p. 95-100.

3134. KAPLINSKI, Jaan
"Everything Melts" (tr. by the author and Sam Hamill). [CrabCR] (8:2/3/9:1/2/3) 94, p. 49.
"Our Shadows" (tr. by the author and Sam Hamill). [CrabCR] (8:2/3/9:1/2/3) 94, p. 48.

KARAN, Myrna Delson
See DELSON-KARAN, Myrna

3135. KARLIN, Wayne
"Meeting — Boston 1993" (for Le Minh Khue). [PoetL] (89:1) Spr 94, p. 31-32.

3136. KAROL, Pamala
"Crib Death." [AnotherCM] (27) 94, p. 109-112.

3137. KARP, Vickie
"Harm." [NewYorker] (70:32) 10 O 94, p. 67.

3138. KARR, J. Rodney
"Algolagnia" (London, 1892). [Iowa] (24:3) Fall 94, p. 147-148.
"How to Write a Love Poem" (for S.M.). [Iowa] (24:3) Fall 94, p. 149.

3139. KARR, Mary
"Bayou" (for Pete Karr). [HarvardR] (Premier Issue) Spr 92, p. 94.

3140. KARR, Muriel
"Botanical Drawing Class." [ChironR] (13:2) Sum 94, p. 25.
"Imported Braid." [BellArk] (10:6) N-D 94, p. 31.
"Inside the Box." [BellArk] (10:6) N-D 94, p. 31.
"Life the Mystery." [BellArk] (10:3) My-Je 94, p. 15.
"Mirror" (in the old MGM Hotel — Reno, Nevada). [BellArk] (10:3) My-Je 94, p. 15.
"Muriel Mating Call." [ChironR] (13:2) Sum 94, p. 25.
"My Mother Dies of Cancer." [BellArk] (10:3) My-Je 94, p. 15.
"Sequins in an Empty Room" (toward a definition of happiness). [BellArk] (10:5) S-O 94, p. 27.
"We Avoid the Words 'Heaven' and 'Light'." [BellArk] (10:6) N-D 94, p. 31.
"Wing Detachment, Wing Repair." [BellArk] (10:3) My-Je 94, p. 15.
"You Joke, We Laugh, Every Bit of It Works." [BellArk] (10:6) N-D 94, p. 31.
"You Start Flapped." [BellArk] (10:5) S-O 94, p. 11.

3141. KARRER, Pearl
"Some People Can Tell Time by Looking at the Sun But I Have Never Been Able to Make Out the Numbers." [Gaia] (4) Je 94, p. 50.
"Stained Glass." [Vis] (44) 94, p. 30-32.

3142. KARYOTAKIS, Konstantine
"How Young" (tr. by Rachel Hadas). [HarvardR] (Premier Issue) Spr 92, p. 40.
"Preveza" (tr. by Rachel Hadas). [HarvardR] (Premier Issue) Spr 92, p. 56.
3143. KASDORF, Julia
"Flu" (1919, 1992). [ColEng] (56:8) D 94, p. 935.
"Sixth Anniversary." [SouthernHR] (28:1) Wint 94, p. 27.
"The Streak." [ArtfulD] (26/27) 94, p. 83.
3144. KASHNER, Sam
"Don Quixote in America." [WilliamMR] (32) 94, p. 22.
3145. KASISCHKE, Laura
"45. The sky is cream-colored in summer." [WillowS] (34) Sum 94, p. 46-47.
"Arms." [CrabCR] (8:2/3/9:1/2/3) 94, p. 114-115.
"Bells of Ice." [CrabCR] (8:2/3/9:1/2/3) 94, p. 116-118.
"Black Bear Paw $20." [WillowS] (34) Sum 94, p. 48-49.
"Exploding Homes." [IndR] (17:1) Spr 94, p. 165-166.
"Fatima." [KenR] (NS 16:2) Spr 94, p. 80-81.
"Housekeeping in a Dream." [NewEngR] (16:1) Wint 94, p. 122-123.
"Pall." [NewEngR] (16:1) Wint 94, p. 123-124.
"Parrot, Fever." [Chelsea] (56) 94, p. 71-73.
"The Poem of O." [IndR] (17:1) Spr 94, p. 162-164.
3146. KASPER, Michael
"The January Star" (tr. of Piotr Sommer, w. the author). [Thrpny] (56) Wint 94, p. 30.
3147. KASSELL, Nancy
"Exile." [SouthernPR] (34:1) Sum 94, p. 46-47.
KASTEN, Alfonso Larrahona
See LARRAHONA KASTEN, Alfonso
3148. KASTNER, Erich
"Bad Luck Bird" (tr. by Ted Bookey). [Vis] (44) 94, p. 8.
"May" (tr. by Ted Bookey). [Vis] (44) 94, p. 8-9.
3149. KATES, J.
"Among Black Trees" (tr. of Olga Popova). [CrabCR] (8:2/3/9:1/2/3) 94, p. 46.
"Diptych: I. Cycle, II. Transmission" (tr. of Ricardo Feierstein, w. Stephen Sadow). [PlumR] (7) [94?], p. 55-57.
"France" (tr. of Jean-Pierre Rosnay). [PoetryE] (37/38) Spr 94, p. 210.
"The Gardener" (tr. of Yvan Goll). [PoetryE] (37/38) Spr 94, p. 214.
"I Write Books" (tr. of Jean-Pierre Rosnay). [PoetryE] (37/38) Spr 94, p. 208.
"Intimate Hurts" (tr. of Yvan Goll). [PoetryE] (37/38) Spr 94, p. 211.
"Paradise County Seat" (tr. of Sergey Maged). [Writ] (26) 94, p. 20-27.
"Poete Maudit" (tr. of Mikhail Okun). [PlumR] (7) [94?], p. 8.
"The Professor's Posy." [Light] (11) Aut 94, p. 14.
"Song of the Civilized" (tr. of Yvan Goll). [PoetryE] (37/38) Spr 94, p. 213.
"There Is No Heaven" (tr. of Jean-Pierre Rosnay). [PoetryE] (37/38) Spr 94, p. 209.
"Washing the Dead" (tr. of Yvan Goll). [PoetryE] (37/38) Spr 94, p. 212.
3150. KATROVAS, Richard
"Laffite." [NegC] (13:2/3) 93, p. 28-30.
3151. KATSIMPALIS, Melissa
"The Crocodile and the Model" (Australia, 3/25/87). [SpoonR] (19:1) Wint-Spr 94, p. 81.
"The Indians Tell My Son." [SpoonR] (19:1) Wint-Spr 94, p. 85.
"Memorial Day." [SpoonR] (19:1) Wint-Spr 94, p. 87.
"Rabbit Killed." [SpoonR] (19:1) Wint-Spr 94, p. 78-79.
"Sheep." [SpoonR] (19:1) Wint-Spr 94, p. 77.
"Snapping Beans." [SpoonR] (19:1) Wint-Spr 94, p. 84.
"Their Field Lifts in Great Wings of Melting Snow." [SpoonR] (19:1) Wint-Spr 94, p. 76.
"Time Change." [SpoonR] (19:1) Wint-Spr 94, p. 83.
"To the Field This Was Simply a Boy." [SpoonR] (19:1) Wint-Spr 94, p. 80.
"Widower." [SpoonR] (19:1) Wint-Spr 94, p. 82.
"The Women Are the Field." [SpoonR] (19:1) Wint-Spr 94, p. 86.
3152. KATSURA, Nobuko
"Haiku: Someone else's wife" (tr. by Miyuki Aoyama and Leza Lowitz). [YellowS] (11:4, #44) Wint 93-94, p. 44.
3153. KATZ, Jeffrey
"Enough." [CumbPR] (14:1) Fall 94, p. 48.
"Romantic Comedy." [CumbPR] (14:1) Fall 94, p. 47.

3154. KATZ, Susan A.
"No Easy Choices." [NegC] (14:1/2) 94, p. 148.
3155. KATZ-LEVINE, Judy
"Birth" (for Cid Corman). [ShadowP] (4) 94, p. 1-2.
"Calligraphy Creek." [ShadowP] (4) 94, p. 7.
"Connecting with an Old Poet." [ShadowP] (4) 94, p. 3.
"Ghazal After a Decision." [ShadowP] (4) 94, p. 5.
"Renga" (2 poems, w. Miriam Sagan). [Noctiluca] (3) 94, p. 39-44.
"Ruthlessness in saying what you do (what you are " (— Cid Corman). [ShadowP] (4) 94, p. 2.
"Seed Glowing in a Mirror" (34 poems). [Noctiluca] (3) 94, p. 1-37.
"There." [ShadowP] (4) 94, p. 8.
"Trying to Pierce Ruthlessness." [ShadowP] (4) 94, p. 3.
"Underbrush." [ShadowP] (4) 94, p. 5.
"Underneath All." [ShadowP] (4) 94, p. 7.
"Walking Home" (for Cid). [ShadowP] (4) 94, p. 4.
3156. KATZEMAN, J.
"Finders Keepers." [JamesWR] (11:5) Fall 94, p. 6.
3157. KAUFFMAN, Elizabeth Doonan
"Of the Sonorous Labyrinth" (for Pilar and José Luis Malpartida, tr. of Luis Rebaza-Soraluz). [Boulevard] (9:1/2, #25/26) Spr 94, p. 257-258.
3158. KAUFMAN, Margaret
"Lot's Wife" (after Akhmatova). [Ploughs] (20:1) Spr 94, p. 75.
3159. KAUFMAN, Shirley
"Song" (tr. of Judith Herzberg, w. the author). [Field] (50) Spr 94, p. 45.
"Target" (tr. of Judith Herzberg, w. the author). [Field] (50) Spr 94, p. 46.
"Vows." [Field] (51) Fall 94, p. 95-96.
3160. KAUNE, Gayle Rogers
"Degrees of Light in an Affluent City." [CrabCR] (8:2/3/9:1/2/3) 94, p. 106-107.
3161. KAUR, Kanwaljit
"Other Voices." [WestCL] (28:1/2, #13/14) Spr-Fall 94, p. 163.
3162. KAVAFIS, Konstantin
"In the Same Dance" (tr. by Kenny Brechner). [Northeast] (5:11) Wint 94-95, p. 32.
KAVAFIS, Konstantin
See also CAVAFY, Constantine (C. P., Constantine P.)
3163. KAVANAGH, Ed
"For Keith Douglas" (1920-1940). [TickleAce] (28) Fall-Wint 94, p. 71-73.
"Villanelle" (from the Life of a Liquid Acrobat). [TickleAce] (28) Fall-Wint 94, p. 70.
3164. KAVEN, Bob
"I Fabricate Memories of High School in the Fifties." [Agni] (40) 94, p. 157-158.
3165. KAY, Margaret
"Granddaughter and Ancestors." [AmerS] (63:1) Wint 94, p. 58-59.
KAY, Ormonde de
See De KAY, Ormonde
3166. KAZANTZIS, Judith
"From Bratislava to the High Tatry: Tales of Old Slovakia." [Verse] (11:1) Spr 94, p. 66-67.
"The Named Land." [Stand] (35:4) Aut 94, p. 5-11.
3167. KAZENBROOT, Nelly
"Horses." [PoetryC] (14:3) My 94, p. 17.
"House." [PoetryC] (14:3) My 94, p. 17.
"Qualicum Beach." [AntigR] (96) Wint 94, p. 94-95.
"Road Kill." [PoetryC] (14:3) My 94, p. 17.
"Sick." [AntigR] (96) Wint 94, p. 96.
"Weeds." [Dandel] (20:2) 93, p. 46.
3168. KEANE, Katherine
"City of Peace, Nature, Science — City of Oneness" (w. Jonathan Sinagub). [Caliban] (14) 94, p. 74-88.
3169. KEARNEY, Kevin
"Horizons." [NewRena] (9:1, #27) 94, p. 75.
3170. KEARNS, Josie
"New Numbers." [PoetryNW] (35:3) Aut 94, p. 3-9.
3171. KEARNS, Rick
"Have It Your Way." [ChiR] (40:2/3) 94, p. 28.

3172. KEATS, John
"On Death." [SoCoast] (16) Ja 94, p. 64.
3173. KECKLER, W. B.
"H.I.V. Test." [Ledge] (17) Wint 94, p. 18-19.
"Mountain Under Sea." [Os] (39) Fall-Wint 94, p. 2.
3174. KEDMI, Yehezkel
"Day Blood — Night Blood" (tr. by Ammiel Alcalay). [LitR] (37:2) Wint 94, p. 321-322.
"My People, Knowledge, and I" (tr. by Ammiel Alcalay). [LitR] (37:2) Wint 94, p. 324-326.
"Not Equal to Them the Easterner" (tr. by Ammiel Alcalay). [LitR] (37:2) Wint 94, p. 319-321.
"Raging Soul" (tr. by Ammiel Alcalay). [LitR] (37:2) Wint 94, p. 322-324.
3175. KEEFER, Janice Kulyk
"Travelling Alone." [AmerV] (33) 94, p. 107-108.
3176. KEEGAN, James
"Mule" (for my father). [SouthernPR] (34:1) Sum 94, p. 31-32.
3177. KEEGAN, Linda
"Back Forty." [CapeR] (29:2) Fall 94, p. 21.
"The Laboratory." [PoetL] (89:4) Wint 94-95, p. 14.
3178. KEELAN, Claudia
"The Body You Love May Be Your Own." [Colum] (22) Wint 94, p. 142.
"Rushing the Gates of Empirical Gardens." [Agni] (39) 94, p. 156-157.
"Same Question." [NewAW] (12) Spr-Sum 94, p. 127.
"The Secularist." [AmerLC] (6) 94, p. 5-7.
"To My Teacher." [Pequod] (37) 94, p. 46-48.
3179. KEELEY, Edmund
"The Ships" (tr. of C. P. Cavafy, w. Dimitri Gondicas). [Antaeus] (75/76) Aut 94, p. 247-249.
3180. KEEN, Paul
"Covenant" (for J.L.K., in memoriam). [Quarry] (42:4) Mr 94, p. 96.
"Frontiers" (for J.L.K. in memory). [Quarry] (42:4) Mr 94, p. 92-93.
"Paperweight from Oban (1990)." [Quarry] (42:4) Mr 94, p. 94.
"Paperweight from Oban (1992)." [Quarry] (42:4) Mr 94, p. 95.
3181. KEENE, John R.
"Echoes That Come" (for Melvin Dixon). [JamesWR] (11:5) Fall 94, p. 10.
3182. KEENER, LuAnn (Lu Ann)
"The Blood-Tie." [LouisL] (11:2) Fall 94, p. 81.
"Feeding on High Branches." [Chelsea] (56) 94, p. 75.
"Giraffes." [Chelsea] (56) 94, p. 74-75.
3183. KEES, Weldon
"The Beach." [NoDaQ] (62:3) Sum 94-95, p. 198.
3184. KEFALA, Antigone
"Guided Tour." [MalR] (107) Sum 94, p. 188.
"Story." [MalR] (107) Sum 94, p. 189.
3185. KEITH, Bill
"ABCDEFG." [RagMag] (12:1) Sum 94, p. 19.
"Blues." [RagMag] (12:1) Sum 94, p. 20.
3186. KEITH, W. J.
"The Darwin Poems" (7 poems). [AntigR] (97) Spr 94, p. 78-84.
3187. KEITHLEY, George
"Dusk" (for Carol. Corrected reprint from issue #20). [Colum] (21) Fall 93, p. 158-159.
3188. KELLER, David
"About Rabbits." [Iowa] (24:3) Fall 94, p. 183-184.
"At the Stone Age Tombs" (for Ann Zell). [Pivot] (42) 94, p. 48.
"Fortune-Telling" (for Rachel Bellow). [Pivot] (42) 94, p. 47.
3189. KELLEY, Caffyn
"Magic." [SinW] (54) Wint 94-95, p. 91-93.
3190. KELLEY, Janine Soucie
"Paradise." [ChamLR] (14/15) Spr-Fall 94, p. 153.
"Requiem." [ChamLR] (14/15) Spr-Fall 94, p. 152.
3191. KELLEY, Karen
"Minus." [Talisman] (12) Spr 94, p. 244-245.
3192. KELLEY, Kathleen
"A Virtuous Woman Speaks." [EvergreenC] (9:2) Sum-Fall 94, p. 84.

3193. KELLEY, Paul
"All the unmoving moon-light anyone could bear" (in memory, Rob Dunham). [Quarry] (43:2) S 94, p. 42.
"Benear you, average" (for Annette Hurtig). [Quarry] (43:2) S 94, p. 41.
"Forty lines fast to the hour." [Quarry] (43:2) S 94, p. 40.
3194. KELLEY, Tina
"The Dark Side of Selene, the Moon." [CreamCR] (18:2) Fall 94, p. 174-175.
3195. KELLY, Anne M.
"Domestic." [MalR] (109) Wint 94, p. 98.
"Educating Planaria." [MalR] (109) Wint 94, p. 99.
"Picnic." [MalR] (109) Wint 94, p. 100.
3196. KELLY, Brigit Pegeen
"Cry of the Jay." [AntR] (52:1) Wint 94, p. 78.
"Divining the Field." [AntR] (52:1) Wint 94, p. 71.
"Field Song." [AntR] (52:1) Wint 94, p. 76-77.
"Of Royal Issue." [AntR] (52:1) Wint 94, p. 72.
"Past the Stations." [NoAmR] (279:2) Mr-Ap 94, p. 9.
"The Pear Tree." [AntR] (52:1) Wint 94, p. 73-75.
3197. KELLY, Erren Geraud
"Gospel Music." [Obs] (9:1) Spr-Sum 94, p. 91.
"To My Father." [Obs] (9:1) Spr-Sum 94, p. 92.
3198. KELLY, J. Patrick
"Smashing the Cathedrals." [BellArk] (10:6) N-D 94, p. 30.
3199. KELLY, Richard
"A Rising Sun." [AntigR] (97) Spr 94, p. 146.
"The Soul's Expanse." [AntigR] (97) Spr 94, p. 146.
3200. KELLY, Robert
"Doors." [GrandS] (13:2, #50) Fall 94, p. 16-22.
3201. KELLY, Robert A.
"From Purgatory Mary Flannery Speaks About Sgt. Rodney Maxwell Davis." [AntigR] (98) Sum 94, p. 74.
"Mary Flannery Speaks About Her Father." [AntigR] (98) Sum 94, p. 75.
"Mary Flannery Speaks About Madame Chiang Kai-Shek." [AntigR] (98) Sum 94, p. 76.
3202. KELLY, William
"Water Tiger." [Vis] (46) 94, p. 33.
3203. KELLY-DeWITT, Susan
"Odalisque." [Poetry] (164:2) My 94, p. 88.
3204. KEMALA
"Ainal Adnin: A Love Song" (tr. by Hafiz Arif). [InterQ] (1:3) 94, p. 180-184.
3205. KEMP, Penn
"Evolution #9." [Arc] (33) Fall 94, p. 27.
"Portrait of an Unfinished Marriage: Or, Let Byron Be Bygone." [PoetryC] (14:2) Mr 94, p. 24-25.
3206. KEMPHER, Ruth Moon
"Hedges." [SmPd] (31:2, #91) Spr 94, p. 21.
"Ms. Notes: Apricots and Their Odor." [DogRR] (26) Wint 94-95, p. 57-58.
"Revisions: The Alphabet Picture with a Red M at the Core." [HiramPoR] (55/56) Fall 93-Sum 94, p. 56-58.
"The Rivers That Feed the Sea." [LitR] (37:4) Sum 94, p. 571.
"Unofficial Log: S.S. Orizaba, April 26, 1932." [JlNJPo] (16:1) Spr 94, p. 9.
3207. KEMPTON, Karl
"Om Suite" (Selections). [Zyzzyva] (10:3) Fall 94, p. 75-78.
3208. KENDALL, Robert
"Adventures in Clean Living." [Pivot] (42) 94, p. 19.
"Eleven Clues" (Selections: 3-4). [Pivot] (41) 93, p. 30-31.
"The Grass Is Always Greener Where There's Grass." [Pivot] (42) 94, p. 19.
3209. KENDIG, Diane
"The Susan B. Anthony Coin Campaign." [SingHM] (21) 94, p. 16.
"Teaching in Prison." [MinnR] (41/42) Fall 93-Spr 94 (published Mr 95), p. 38.
3210. KENDRICK, Dolores
"Anne's Hideaway." [PlumR] (7) [94?], p. 20-22.
"The Cows Lie Down in Fog." [AmerPoR] (23:6) N-D 94, p. 37.
"Rya's Rainbow." [PlumR] (7) [94?], p. 18-19.
3211. KENDRICK, Jack
"My Father's Ghost Hangs on My Bones." [Confr] (52/53) Wint-Spr 94, p. 303-304.

3212. KENDRICK, Leatha
"What Binds Us." [Wind] (73) 94, p. 13-14.
3213. KENISTON, Ann
"Burial." [SouthernPR] (34:2) Wint 94, p. 65.
"Immunity." [BelPoJ] (45:1) Fall 94, p. 42.
"The Suitcases." [PoetL] (89:2) Sum 94, p. 51-52.
3214. KENNE, Mel
"The Messenger." [Border] (4) Spr-Sum 94, p. 49.
3215. KENNEDY, Anne
"Hy Brasil: Summer 1980." [FreeL] (13) Spr 94, p. 17.
"Rendezvous: Los Angeles, 1944." [FreeL] (13) Spr 94, p. 16-17.
3216. KENNEDY, B. L.
"Poet Arrested for Abduction of an Angel." [ContextS] (4:1) 94, p. 22.
3217. KENNEDY, David
"In Greenwich Foot Tunnel." [Stand] (35:2) Spr 94, p. 68.
3218. KENNEDY, John
"Starlings." [SouthernHR] (28:1) Wint 94, p. 63.
3219. KENNEDY, Mick
"Rhondala." [WindO] (58) Sum 94, p. 43.
3220. KENNEDY, X. J.
"Abou Ben Adman" (with apologies to Leigh Hunt). [Light] (12) Wint 94-95, p. 16.
"Aftermath." [Elf] (4:2) Sum 94, p. 26.
"Classical Dilemma." [Light] (10) Sum 94, p. 24.
"Composition Theory." [Light] (9) Spr 94, p. 16.
"A Death's-head in the Park." [Elf] (4:2) Sum 94, p. 27.
"Social Distinction." [Light] (9) Spr 94, p. 14.
"Taking Aspirin." [CarolQ] (47:1) Fall 94, p. 17.
3221. KENNY, Maurice
"Bear." [Callaloo] (17:1) Wint 94, p. 132.
"He Stands There." [Callaloo] (17:1) Wint 94, p. 133-134.
"Molly" (from *Tekonwatonki / Molly Brant*, 1992). [Kaleid] (29) Sum-Fall 94, p. 38.
"Molly: Report Back to the Village" (from *Tekonwatonki / Molly Brant*, 1992). [Kaleid] (29) Sum-Fall 94, p. 39.
3222. KENYON, Jane
"Man Eating." [Atlantic] (273:4) Ap 94, p. 90.
"Prognosis." [NewYorker] (70:37) 14 N 94, p. 96.
"Sleepers in Jaipur." [PartR] (61:1) Wint 94, p. 153.
3223. KEPLER, Tom
"My Son Sleeping." [HiramPoR] (55/56) Fall 93-Sum 94, p. 59.
"Winter Solstice." [HiramPoR] (55/56) Fall 93-Sum 94, p. 60.
3224. KEPLINGER, David
"Mercy." [BlackWR] (21:1) Fall-Wint 94, p. 108.
3225. KERANS, J. C.
"Colleen Elizabeth." [SingHM] (21) 94, p. 35.
3226. KERCHEVAL, Jesse Lee
"The Kindness of Strangers." [NewEngR] (16:2) Spr 94, p. 141-143.
"My Father Receives the First Visitation." [Agni] (39) 94, p. 83-84.
"Your Wife, a Widow, Waits for You." [DenQ] (29:2) Fall 94, p. 12.
3227. KERLEY, Gary
"The World's Business, 3 A.M." [SouthernPR] (34:2) Wint 94, p. 42.
3228. KERMAN, Judith
"The Butcher's Work." [HiramPoR] (55/56) Fall 93-Sum 94, p. 61.
3229. KERN, Carl
"Get a Dog" (Lines Composed for a Lady Who Lives Alone and Gardens). [FourQ] (8:1) Spr 94, p. 9.
3230. KERR, Don
"Breathless." [Descant] (25:1, #84) Spr 94, p. 41-42.
"Jules et Jim." [Descant] (25:1, #84) Spr 94, p. 43-44.
3231. KERR, Kathryn
"The Goddess." [IllinoisR] (1:2) Spr 94, p. 33.
3232. KERR, Lisa Drnec
"The Call" (First Sue Saniel Elkind National Poetry Award, Finalist). [Kalliope] (16:2) 94, p. 30.
3233. KERR, Meg
"Imagining You Whole." [Paint] (21) Aut 94, p. 125.

3234. KERR, Milton
"Cosmopolitan Ritual." [CoalC] (8) Ap 94, p. 32.
3235. KERR, Walter H.
"Shake 'N Bake." [Light] (10) Sum 94, p. 29.
"The Silence of the Iambs." [Light] (9) Spr 94, p. 20.
3236. KERSHNER, Ivan
"Upon Seeing a Dog Drown" (Saturday, Nov. 6, 1971. From "Airports Full of People a Long Time Dead"). [AmerPoR] (23:4) Jl-Ag 94, p. 28.
3237. KESLER, Russell (Russ)
"July." [SouthernHR] (28:3) Sum 94, p. 280.
"On the Bus." [WillowS] (34) Sum 94, p. 62.
"Skinning Squirrels." [NegC] (14:1/2) 94, p. 146.
"Waking at Night." [QW] (38) Winter-Spr 93-94, p. 127.
3238. KESSLER, Jascha
"This Breathing, Devouring Swamp" (tr. of Ottó Orbán, w. Mária Körösy). [GrahamHR] (18) Wint 94-95, p. 100.
3239. KESSLER, Ruth
"Deception." [NegC] (14:1/2) 94, p. 72.
3240. KESSLER, Sydney
"Just as the Birds Stopped Singing." [CarolQ] (46:2) Wint 94, p. 79.
"Sgt. Krieger" (from the poems of a winter soldier). [Parting] (7:1) Sum 94, p. 15.
3241. KESTLER, Erik
"Ars Scarlotica (of a Green Sailboat)." [PoetL] (89:4) Wint 94-95, p. 36.
3242. KETCHEK, Michael
"Doughnut Shop." [SlipS] (14) 94, p. 85.
KETHLEY, Fiona Pitt
See PITT-KETHLEY, Fiona
3243. KEYES, Claire
"Nauset Beach, October: A Memory." [SpoonR] (19:1) Wint-Spr 94, p. 102.
3244. KEYWORTH, Suzanne
"Landscape." [MidwQ] (35:2) Wint 94, p. 171.
"Watercolor." [PoetryE] (37/38) Spr 94, p. 16.
3245. KHAIYAT, Mahdy Y.
"Crystal." [SantaBR] (2:1) Spr-Sum 94, p. 79.
"Evening." [SantaBR] (2:1) Spr-Sum 94, p. 79.
"The Jogger on Los Carneros Road." [SantaBR] (2:1) Spr-Sum 94, p. 79.
3246. KHALVATI, Mimi
"Vine Leaves." [Pivot] (42) 94, p. 10.
3247. KHAN, Sharon
"Strategy" (tr. of Jorge Etcheverry, w. the author). [CanLit] (142/143) Fall-Wint 94, p. 62.
3248. KHARMS, Daniil
"Morning (Awakening of the Elements)" (tr. by Dean Furbish). [ChironR] (13:2) Sum 94, p. 7.
"Untitled: Everyone in the end advances" (tr. by Dean Furbish). [ChironR] (13:2) Sum 94, p. 7.
"Untitled: Spring arrived" (tr. by Dean Furbish). [ChironR] (13:2) Sum 94, p. 7.
"Wicked Gathering of the Faithless" (tr. by Dean Furbish). [ChironR] (13:2) Sum 94, p. 7.
KHIEM, Truong
See TRUONG, Khiem
3249. KHODZHER, Anna
"Duchenku" (tr. by Galina De Roeck). [Manoa] (6:2) Wint 94, p. 176-177.
"Kumbiak Kayuka" (tr. by Galina De Roeck). [Manoa] (6:2) Wint 94, p. 177-178.
"Patterns Sing" (tr. by Galina De Roeck). [Manoa] (6:2) Wint 94, p. 176.
3250. KHOSLA, Maya
"Pem-Pem's Story." [NewOR] (20:3/4) Fall-Wint 94, p. 140-141.
3251. KIDDER, Helga Karin
"The Poplar" (tr. of Michael Donhauser). [SpoonR] (19:1) Wint-Spr 94, p. 113.
"San Giustina. Night" (tr. of Michael Donhauser). [SpoonR] (19:1) Wint-Spr 94, p. 114.
"Your Back" (tr. of Michael Donhauser). [SpoonR] (19:1) Wint-Spr 94, p. 115.
3252. KIETLINSKA, Katarzyna
"Mother and Daughter" (tr. of Anna Czekanowicz, w. David Malcolm). [InterQ] (1:1) [93?], p. 106.

"A Poet's Worth" (tr. of Wladyslaw Zawistowski, w. David Malcolm). [InterQ] (1:1) [93?], p. 104.
"Report from a Distant City" (tr. of Anna Czekanowicz, w. David Malcolm). [InterQ] (1:1) [93?], p. 107.
"To Get Through the Night" (tr. of Anna Czekanowicz, w. David Malcolm). [InterQ] (1:1) [93?], p. 108-109.

3253. KIJIMA, Hajime
"After the Funeral" (tr. by the author and Larry Levis). [InterQ] (1:2) 93, p. 69.

3254. KIKAKU (1661-1707)
Haiku [AmerPoR] (23:4) Jl-Ag 94, p. 17.

3255. KIM, Ann
"The Upsidedown Waterfall." [Agni] (39) 94, p. 190.

3256. KIM, Jacqueline
"One Version of Cheese and Fruit." [BambooR] (60) Wint 94, p. 99-100.

3257. KIM, Myung Mi
"Cosmography" (Excerpt). [Avec] (7:1) 94, p. 89-93.

3258. KIM, Seung-Hee
"The Female Buddha" (at The Delivery Room in Severance General Hospital, tr. by Dr. Chang Young-hee). [BambooR] (63/64) Sum-Fall 94, p. 21-22.
"Life in the Egg 1." [BambooR] (63/64) Sum-Fall 94, p. 23-24.

3259. KIM, Sue Kwock
"Hwajon." [Nat] (258:23) Je 13 94, p. 838.
"Occupation." [Poetry] (164:4) Jl 94, p. 193.

3260. KIM, Yong
"Childhood." [Boulevard] (9:1/2, #25/26) Spr 94, p. 186.

3261. KIM, Yong U.
"Early Snow." [Jacaranda] (4:2) Spr 90, p. 54.

3262. KIMBALL, Michael
"In Emily Dickinson." [Amelia] (7:3, #22) 94, p. 101.
"Like Bread." [Amelia] (7:4, #23) 94, p. 112.
"New Can of Paint." [Amelia] (7:3, #22) 94, p. 113.
"Other Men." [Amelia] (7:3, #22) 94, p. 113.

3263. KIMBRELL, James
"Variation on a Theme by Chagall." [MidAR] (14:2) 94, p. 63-64.

3264. KIMM, Robert
"Chelan Fire." [CoalC] (8) Ap 94, p. 17-18.

3265. KINCAID, Joan Payne
"All Week She'd Worn the Garnet Ring Given for Luck." [Parting] (7:2) Wint 94-95, p. 21.
"Exhibition." [Parting] (7:1) Sum 94, p. 14.
"Sink Sonnet." [Parting] (7:1) Sum 94, p. 14.
"Sounds Like." [Parting] (7:2) Wint 94-95, p. 21.

3266. KINDEL, Marian
"Transition." [Kaleid] (Special Issue) 94, p. 24.

3267. KINER, Stacie M.
"For the Dead Come Back." [ApalQ] (40/41) 94, p. 113-114.

3268. KING, Ben
"If I Should Die." [Light] (11) Aut 94, p. 24.

3269. KING, David
"Night Trains." [SouthernPR] (34:1) Sum 94, p. 51.

3270. KING, Jane
"Domesticity." [MassR] (35:3/4) Aut-Wint 94, p. 410.
"Jealousy." [MassR] (35:3/4) Aut-Wint 94, p. 411-412.

3271. KING, Janna
"Boy, Thirteen." [NewEngR] (16:2) Spr 94, p. 56.
"Kissing Jace Goodbye." [SpoonR] (19:1) Wint-Spr 94, p. 38-39.
"Lilacs." [CapeR] (29:1) Spr 94, p. 7.
"Now Comes Regret." [SpoonR] (19:1) Wint-Spr 94, p. 40.

3272. KING, Julie
"Moon Song." [CimR] (109) O 94, p. 75.

3273. KING, Larry
"My Two Cents" (culled entirely from Larry King's column in *USA Today* by Sam Johnson and Chris Marcil). [NewRep] (211:1) 4 Jl 94, p. 9.

3274. KING, Lyn
"Travelogue." [Descant] (24:4, #83) Wint 93-94, p. 18-20.

3275. KING, Nancy
"From the Amazon." [Border] (3) Fall 93, p. 34-35.
3276. KING, Robert
"At Yellow Clay Village." [Plain] (14:3) Spr 94, p. 25.
"Field Research." [BellArk] (10:5) S-O 94, p. 3-10.
"Living Along the River." [Ascent] (18:2) Wint 94, p. 35.
"The Train." [Ascent] (18:2) Wint 94, p. 34.
3277. KING, Robert S.
"Condensation." [BlackBR] (19) Fall-Wint 94, p. 18.
"Earthen Well." [SpoonR] (19:1) Wint-Spr 94, p. 53.
"Epitaph for a Blind Man Murdered." [Hellas] (5:2) Fall-Wint 94, p. 42.
"For Art's Sake." [BlackBR] (19) Fall-Wint 94, p. 19.
"The Gentleman Who Woke Up As a Goat." [BlackBR] (18) Wint-Spr 94, p. 4-5.
"The Light Sedative of Dark." [SpoonR] (19:1) Wint-Spr 94, p. 52.
"Street Opera." [BlackBR] (19) Fall-Wint 94, p. 18.
"Traveller's Tale." [HolCrit] (31:2) Ap 94, p. 16-17.
"Treasure Hunt." [MidwQ] (35:4) Sum 94, p. 408.
"Under Gray Depot Skies." [BlackBR] (18) Wint-Spr 94, p. 37.
3278. KING, Rosamond S.
"Inauguration at the Dinner Table." [Obs] (9:2) Fall-Wint 94, p. 94.
"Stars." [Obs] (9:2) Fall-Wint 94, p. 95-96.
"Two Shes." [Obs] (9:2) Fall-Wint 94, p. 94-95.
3279. KING, Russell
"Family Farm" (recipient of the first annual Rosebud Award). [Rosebud] (1:2) Sum 94, p. 36-37.
3280. KING, Willie James
"A '93 Summer Song." [Obs] (9:1) Spr-Sum 94, p. 95.
"Angling on the Alabama." [Obs] (9:1) Spr-Sum 94, p. 93-94.
"The Hunter." [Obs] (9:1) Spr-Sum 94, p. 94.
"It Kept Me Warm." [Pembroke] (26) 94, p. 91.
3281. KINLOCH, David
"Dustie-Fute." [Jacaranda] (5:1) Wint-Spr 91, p. 88.
3282. KINNELL, Galway
"The Cellist." [Atlantic] (274:4) O 94, p. 100.
"The Deconstruction of Emily Dickinson." [AmerPoR] (23:6) N-D 94, p. 40.
"Flies." [NewYorker] (70:41) 12 D 94, p. 94-95.
"Lackawanna." [ParisR] (36:132) Fall 94, p. 16-18.
"The Music of Poetry." [Antaeus] (75/76) Aut 94, p. 290-291.
"Neverland." [Poetry] (165:1) O 94, p. 26-28.
"Parkinson's Disease." [NewYorker] (70:39) 28 N 94, p. 122-123.
"The Pen." [AmerPoR] (23:6) N-D 94, p. 41.
"Picnic." [NewYorker] (70:16) 6 Je 94, p. 72.
"Running on Silk." [Thrpny] (59) Fall 94, p. 23.
"The Striped Snake and the Goldfinch." [AmerPoR] (23:6) N-D 94, p. 39-40.
"Telephoning in Mexican Sunlight." [BostonR] (19:5) O-N 94, p. 34.
3283. KINSELLA, John
"To Mix in City Circles." [DogRR] (13:1, #25) Spr-Sum 94, p. 14.
3284. KINSOLVING, Susan
"In a Field of Black-Eyed Susans" (An Acrostic). [Light] (9) Spr 94, p. 20.
3285. KIPP, Karen
"Skunks" (for Linda). [AmerPoR] (23:3) My-Je 94, p. 23.
3286. KIRBY, Barney
"Possibility (Sampling with Rilke and Wright)." [Verse] (11:1) Spr 94, p. 49.
3287. KIRBY, David
"The Birth and Untimely Death of the Musical Legacy of the Outlaw Jesse James." [SlipS] (14) 94, p. 89-90.
"Broken Promises." [NegC] (14:1/2) 94, p. 147.
"Lurch, Whose Story Doesn't End." [Ploughs] (20:4) Wint 94-95, p. 117-122.
"The Possum Boyfriend." [Colum] ("The Lost Issues", [i.e. 18-19]) 93, p. 115-116.
"Something Wild." [ChiR] (40:2/3) 94, p. 39-43.
"Sub Rosa." [Writer] (107:3) Mr 94, p. 11.
"The Summer of the Cuban Missile Crisis." [KenR] (NS 16:4) Fall 94, p. 2-5.
"Your Momma Says Omnia Vincit Amor." [CoalC] (8) Ap 94, p. 3.
3288. KIRCHWEY, Karl
"Arcadia." [Antaeus] (73/74) Spr 94, p. 158-159.

"He Considers the Birds of the Air" (Matthew 8:20). [NewYorker] (70:3) 7 Mr 94, p. 78.
"Sonogram." [NewRep] (210:4) 24 Ja 94, p. 35.
"To Nature" (tr. of Friedrich Hölderlin). [Antaeus] (73/74) Spr 94, p. 160-162.
"The Wound" (Verrocchio's *Christ and Saint Thomas*). [Nat] (258:23) Je 13 94, p. 836.

3289. KIRKLAND, Leigh
"Field Guide to Identification." [Raritan] (13:4) Spr 94, p. 17-18.

3290. KIRKPATRICK, Robert
"Summer Triangles." [CarolQ] (46:2) Wint 94, p. 24-26.

3291. KIRSCHNER, Elizabeth
"Angel of My Poverty." [DenQ] (29:1) Sum 94, p. 18-19.

3292. KIRTS, Terry
"Attempting the J. Crew Photo spread." [ArtfulD] (26/27) 94, p. 58-59.
"Before You Called." [SycamoreR] (6:2) Sum 94, p. 23.
"Fertilizer Days." [Farm] (11:1) Spr-Sum 94, p. 151.
"First Frost." [SycamoreR] (6:2) Sum 94, p. 19-20.
"Remedial." [ArtfulD] (26/27) 94, p. 57.
"The Resiliency of Condiments." [ArtfulD] (26/27) 94, p. 56.
"Snowstorm '79: Terry." [SpoonR] (19:1) Wint-Spr 94, p. 50-51.
"Stream" (for John Howard, who fell down the sewer). [ArtfulD] (26/27) 94, p. 55.
"This Story." [SycamoreR] (6:2) Sum 94, p. 21-22.
"The Way It Was Told." [SycamoreR] (6:2) Sum 94, p. 24.

3293. KISHKAN, Theresa
"The Last Day of Summer." [PoetryC] (14:2) Mr 94, p. 23.
"La Rondine" (for F. & D.). [PoetryC] (14:2) Mr 94, p. 23.
"Small Lights for Cheyenne." [PoetryC] (14:2) Mr 94, p. 23.

3294. KITTELL, Linda
"Barracoon." [NewEngR] (16:1) Wint 94, p. 121.
"Braids." [NewEngR] (16:1) Wint 94, p. 119.
"On Her Knees." [NewEngR] (16:1) Wint 94, p. 118.
"Verso of #199: Dr. Syn." [NewEngR] (16:1) Wint 94, p. 117.
"Walking in Her Cape Coat." [NewEngR] (16:1) Wint 94, p. 120.

3295. KIZER, Carolyn
"Reunion." [Antaeus] (75/76) Aut 94, p. 292.

3296. KLAASSEN, Tonja Gunvaldsen
"Breath" (for Ethel Catherwood who set a world record at the 1928 Olympics). [Grain] (22:2) Fall 94, p. 82.
"Fall River." [PraF] (15:4, #69) Wint 94-95, p. 90.
"Mama." [Grain] (22:2) Fall 94, p. 81.
"My Sister's Moon Through My Window." [PraF] (15:4, #69) Wint 94-95, p. 91.

3297. KLARE, Judy
"Visiting Mayan Ruins During the Gulf War." [Plain] (14:3) Spr 94, p. 18.

3298. KLASS, Judy
"Turn Down the Leaves." [JlNJPo] (16:2) Aut 94, p. 21.

3299. KLASSEN, Sarah
"Crowned" (based on engravings by the Dutch artist Jan Luykin, 17th century, of martyrs executed in the 16th century: Two at Bamberg, 1550). [Event] (23:3) Wint 94-95, p. 62.
"A Proper Limit" (based on engravings by the Dutch artist Jan Luykin, 17th century, of martyrs executed in the 16th century: Asperen, 1569). [Event] (23:3) Wint 94-95, p. 63-64.
"Spoils" (based on engravings by the Dutch artist Jan Luykin, 17th century, of martyrs executed in the 16th century: Maeyken Wens, Antwerp, 1573). [Event] (23:3) Wint 94-95, p. 61.
"Stations" (Selections: 2, 4). [PraF] (15:4, #69) Wint 94-95, p. 93-94.

3300. KLEIN, Michael
"The Change." [GrahamHR] (18) Wint 94-95, p. 40.
"Churches." [KenR] (NS 16:2) Spr 94, p. 90.
"Dream: The House." [Colum] (22) Wint 94, p. 70.
"The Sorrow" (for Gregg Russo). [KenR] (NS 16:2) Spr 94, p. 89.
"What It Is Like for You." [KenR] (NS 16:2) Spr 94, p. 89-90.

3301. KLEINSCHMIDT, Edward
"Bee Loud." [Iowa] (24:3) Fall 94, p. 109.
"Chalktalk." [Manoa] (6:1) Sum 94, p. 22.
"Day Wait." [Boulevard] (9:3, #27) Fall 94, p. 146.

"The Death of the Field Mouse." [Iowa] (24:3) Fall 94, p. 108.
"Decalcomania." [TampaR] (8) Spr 94, p. 31.
"Last Actions of Autumn." [Manoa] (6:1) Sum 94, p. 21-22.
"Magnification." [Epoch] (43:3) 94, p. 300-301.
"My Eschatology." [TampaR] (8) Spr 94, p. 30.
"Subito." [IndR] (17:1) Spr 94, p. 117.
"What Gives" (for C. D. Wright). [BlackWR] (21:1) Fall-Wint 94, p. 20.

3302. KLEINZAHLER, August
"The Damselfly." [Poetry] (164:5) Ag 94, p. 263.
"Green River Cemetery: Springs." [NewYorker] (70:26) 22-29 Ag 94, p. 87.
"Hard-Boiled." [GrandS] (13:1, #49) Sum 94, p. 34-36.
"San Francisco / New York." [Thrpny] (56) Wint 94, p. 25.
"Watching Dogwood Blossoms Fall in the Parking Lot Off Route 46." [Poetry] (164:5) Ag 94, p. 262.

3303. KLIPSCHUTZ
"24 Lines Toward an Appreciation of Wallace Stevens." [PoetC] (26:1) Fall 94, p. 31.
"Delirium." [PoetC] (25:3) Spr 94, p. 4.
"Larkinesque." [PoetC] (25:3) Spr 94, p. 5.
"My Office My Self." [LaurelR] (28:2) Sum 94, p. 61.

3304. KLOEFKORN, William
"After the Divorce." [SoDakR] (32:3) Fall 94, p. 104-105.
"Granddaughter." [TarRP] (34:1) Fall 94, p. 23.
"Hardware." [SoDakR] (32:3) Fall 94, p. 102-103.
"Oceanside, Early August." [MidwQ] (35:2) Wint 94, p. 172-173.
"On the Oregon Trail in Western Nebraska, 14 July 1993." [MidwQ] (36:1) Aut 94, p. 62-63.
"Rope." [LaurelR] (28:1) Wint 94, p. 62.
"Saturday Night." [TarRP] (34:1) Fall 94, p. 22.
"Tattoos" (Camp Augustine, the first night). [SoDakR] (32:3) Fall 94, p. 101.
"Thinking More, Talking Less." [WillowS] (34) Sum 94, p. 50-51.

KLYZA, Sheila McGrory
See McGRORY-KLYZA, Sheila

3305. KNAPP, Trevor West
"Filling My Father's Pockets." [NoDaQ] (62:1) Wint 94-95, p. 38-39.
"Gabriella Does the Lippizan Ballet." [PoetL] (89:1) Spr 94, p. 13-14.

3306. KNAUTH, Stephen
"The Birch Field." [Pivot] (41) 93, p. 22-23.

3307. KNICK, Teri
"Avowal." [AnthNEW] (6) 94, p. 30.

3308. KNIGHT, Arthur Winfield
"Butch Cassidy: Bottled Water." [DogRR] (13:1, #25) Spr-Sum 94, p. 20-21.

3309. KNIGHT, John Cantey
"Chronos." [Poem] (72) N 94, p. 5.
"A Glimpse of Helen." [Poem] (72) N 94, p. 6.

3310. KNIGHT, Julie
"Good Enough." [ChironR] (13:4) Wint 94, p. 6.
"Thursday Afternoon at the Orange County Jail." [ChironR] (13:4) Wint 94, p. 6.

3311. KNIGHT, Kit
"Ellen Conkle, 1934: Gone in October." [SlipS] (14) 94, p. 101.
"Hot Chocolate Pudding." [SlipS] (14) 94, p. 102-103.

3312. KNIGHT, Lynne
"Appropriate Lover." [NoDaQ] (62:2) Spr 94-95, p. 53-54.
"Bedtime Story." [GettyR] (7:1) Wint 94, p. 128-129.
"Bloodstreams" (from *The Book of Common Betrayals*). [PoetryNW] (35:1) Spr 94, p. 9-10.
"The Cordoning." [NoDaQ] (62:2) Spr 94-95, p. 52.
"Dissolving Borders." [NewEngR] (16:4) Fall 94, p. 108.
"Eighteen." [PoetryE] (37/38) Spr 94, p. 17.
"The Grammar of Lost Gardens" (from *The Book of Common Betrayals*). [PoetryNW] (35:1) Spr 94, p. 10-11.
"Her Story." [Calyx] (15:3) Wint 94-95, p. 58-59.
"Her Story." [Poetry] (163:5) F 94, p. 263-264.

3313. KNOELLER, Christian
"Learning to Speak Again" (For Y. T.). [WestB] (34) 94, p. 70.

3314. KNOEPFLE, John
"Dark Space." [Farm] (11:1) Spr-Sum 94, p. 38.
"A Green Snake Interview: 'In the Picture'." [Farm] (11:2) Fall-Wint 94-95, p. 111-126.
"Rocks and Shoals: Translating the Psalms." [NewL] (60:4) 94, p. 197-199.
3315. KNOX, Ann B.
"Bereave." [Poetry] (165:1) O 94, p. 18.
3316. KNOX, Caroline
"Kilim." [ParisR] (36:131) Sum 94, p. 146.
3317. KNUTSON, Nancy Roxbury
"I Have Been Meaning to Tell You." [Elf] (4:1) Spr 94, p. 35.
"Thinning the Radishes." [Calyx] (15:2) Sum 94, p. 12-13.
"Tyranny in Spring." [Elf] (4:1) Spr 94, p. 35.
"Your Only Song." [Elf] (4:1) Spr 94, p. 34.
3318. KO, Chang-soo (Chang Soo)
"Fruit" (tr. of Cho Jung-kwon). [Vis] (45) 94, p. 17.
"On Translating Korean Poetry." [InterQ] (1:2) 93, p. 73.
3319. KOBYLARZ, P. (Philip)
"The Cold." [DenQ] (29:1) Sum 94, p. 20.
"Dead Men's Shoes." [PraF] (15:4, #69) Wint 94-95, p. 92-93.
"The Insubstantial Pageant." [ParisR] (36:133) Wint 94, p. 181-182.
"Like" (tr. of Jude Stéfan, w. M. Manopoulos). [PoetryE] (37/38) Spr 94, p. 225.
"To Cavafy" (tr. of Jude Stéfan, w. M. Manopoulos). [PoetryE] (37/38) Spr 94, p. 224.
3320. KOCH, Claude
"The Poem." [FourQ] (8:2) Fall 94, p. 38.
3321. KOCH, Kenneth
"A Heroine of the Greek Resistance." [AmerPoR] (23:5) S-O 94, p. 5-7.
"A New Guide." [AmerPoR] (23:5) S-O 94, p. 3-5.
3322. KOCHANOWSKI, Jan
"Lament 19 or: A Dream" (From *Laments*, tr. by Stanislaw Baranczak and Seamus Heaney). [HarvardR] (7) Fall 94, p. 7-10.
3323. KOCHER, Ruth Ellen
"At Home the People Sing." [GettyR] (7:2) Spr 94, p. 333-335.
"Drowning." [MissouriR] (17:3) 94, p. 77.
"February Leaving." [MissouriR] (17:3) 94, p. 78.
"The First Monsoon" (for A.K.). [MissouriR] (17:3) 94, p. 74-75.
"Gustav's Arc." [MissouriR] (17:3) 94, p. 76.
"Last Night in the Garden." [AfAmRev] (28:4) Wint 94, p. 599.
"The Long Arm Forward." [MissouriR] (17:3) 94, p. 79.
"Principle." [MissouriR] (17:3) 94, p. 73.
"Sestina Mouths the Object, the Word." [WillowS] (34) Sum 94, p. 52-53.
"Susan's Hair." [GettyR] (7:2) Spr 94, p. 336-337.
"Variable." [MissouriR] (17:3) 94, p. 80-81.
3324. KOCOT, Noelle
"The Last Time I Saw Him." [AlabamaLR] (8:1) 94, p. 49-50.
"The Number 4 Comforts a Sad Child." [ChatR] (14:3) Spr 94, p. 43.
"Words and Things" (for Michel Foucault). [CapeR] (29:2) Fall 94, p. 6.
3325. KOEHN, David
"Frogbeaters." [ApalQ] (40/41) 94, p. 98-99.
KOEHN, Lala Heine
See HEINE-KOEHN, Lala
3326. KOENIG, Brenda
"Drop Line Fishing, Gulf of St. Lawrence." [PoetL] (89:2) Sum 94, p. 40.
3327. KOENINGER, Kainoa
"Sojourner Truth Sings to the Woman Spirit." [CapeR] (29:1) Spr 94, p. 8.
"Sojourner Truth Sings to the Woman Spirit." [ChangingM] (27) Wint 94, p. 48.
3328. KOERTGE, Ron
"On the Tip of My Tongue." [ApalQ] (40/41) 94, p. 81.
3329. KOESTENBAUM, Phyllis
"Ars Poetica." [AmerLC] (6) 94, p. 124.
3330. KOESTENBAUM, Wayne
"1970." [NewYorker] (70:7) 4 Ap 94, p. 80.
"1975." [Boulevard] (9:1/2, #25/26) Spr 94, p. 109-110.
"The Garbo Index." [NewYorker] (70:5) 21 Mr 94, p. 146.
"Haunting Tune That Ends Too Soon." [AmerPoR] (23:2) Mr-Ap 94, p. 34.

"Rita, Time, and Space." [YaleR] (82:1) Ja 94, p. 55-56.

3331. KOETHE, John
"Falling Water." [WestHR] (48:4) Wint 94, p. 348-357.

3332. KOGAWA, Joy
"For A.D." [CanLit] (140) Spr 94, p. 12.

3333. KOH, Denise
"Whispers Between Weeds." [CanLit] (140) Spr 94, p. 59.

3334. KOHN, Deborah
"The Angel in the Closet." [Interim] (13:2) Fall-Wint 94-95, p. 33-34.

3335. KOLLAR, Mary
"Voyeur." [CrabCR] (8:2/3/9:1/2/3) 94, p. 42-43.

3336. KOLODJI, Deborah P.
"Wedding Veils." [Pearl] (20) Spr 94, p. 81.

3337. KOLODNY, Susan
"Patient." [GreenMR] (NS 17:2) Fall-Wint 94-95, p. 113.

3338. KOLT, Val
"Like the Wolf." [RagMag] (12:1) Sum 94, p. 86.

3339. KOLUMBAN, Nicholas
"Felix Dzerzhinsky." [ArtfulD] (26/27) 94, p. 10.
"People, Branches" (tr. of Sándor Csoóri). [InterQ] (1:1) [93?], p. 92.
"Remember the Time When I Flew." [ArtfulD] (26/27) 94, p. 11.
"Sarcophagus" (tr. of Elemér Horváth). [ArtfulD] (26/27) 94, p. 12.

3340. KOMPPA, Juha
"Sentimental Journey Through Indochina." [JamesWR] (11:5) Fall 94, p. 9.

3341. KOMUNYAKAA, Yusef
"Acalophiles." [IllinoisR] (2:1) Fall 94, p. 27.
"At the Red Sea." [Callaloo] (17:4) Fall 94, p. 957-958.
"Breasts." [Callaloo] (17:4) Fall 94, p. 956.
"Castrato." [Epoch] (43:2) 94, p. 179.
"Chiaroscuro." [SouthernR] (30:4) Aut 94, p. 777-778.
"Complicity." [NewEngR] (16:1) Wint 94, p. 152.
"The Deck." [Callaloo] (17:4) Fall 94, p. 955.
"Dia de los Muertos." [NewEngR] (16:1) Wint 94, p. 151.
"Doppelgangers." [HayF] (14) Spr-Sum 94, p. 37.
"Five Points." [Colum] (22) Wint 94, p. 25-27.
"Frontispiece." [SenR] (24:1) Spr 94, p. 7-8.
"The Hanoi Market." [Agni] (39) 94, p. 58.
"Homo Erectus." [NewEngR] (16:1) Wint 94, p. 150.
"Homunculus." [NewEngR] (16:1) Wint 94, p. 149.
"In Line at the Bank." [SenR] (24:1) Spr 94, p. 5-6.
"King of the Hill." [Epoch] (43:2) 94, p. 178.
"King of the Octaves." [Epoch] (43:2) 94, p. 180-182.
"Lingo." [SouthernR] (30:4) Aut 94, p. 775-777.
"Mud." [Thrpny] (58) Sum 94, p. 20.
"Never Land." [ChiR] (40:2/3) 94, p. 25-26.
"The Price of Blood" (after T.S. Noble's painting). [Colum] (22) Wint 94, p. 28-29.
"Queensland, Inc." [NewEngR] (16:1) Wint 94, p. 153.
"Russian Phantasia." [NewEngR] (16:1) Wint 94, p. 149-150.
"Semantics." [NewEngR] (16:1) Wint 94, p. 148.
"Significance." [HayF] (14) Spr-Sum 94, p. 36.
"Speed Ball." [NewEngR] (16:1) Wint 94, p. 151-152.
"Trueblood's Blues." [Agni] (39) 94, p. 56-57.
"Vigilante." [SenR] (24:1) Spr 94, p. 9-10.
"Watson & the Shark." [SouthernR] (30:4) Aut 94, p. 779-780.
"We Never Know." [OhioR] (52) 94, p. 136-137.

3342. KONCEL, Mary A.
"The Big Deep Voice of God." [ProseP] (3) 94, p. 59.
"Emanuel on the Tightrope." [ProseP] (3) 94, p. 60.

3343. KONO, Juliet
"A Scolding from My Father" (To R.H., D.K., M.M.). [BambooR] (63/64) Sum-Fall 94, p. 25-26.

3344. KONUK, Mutlu
"The Birth" (tr. of Nazim Hikmet, w. Randy Blasing). [AmerPoR] (23:2) Mr-Ap 94, p. 37.
"Last Letter to My Son" (tr. of Nazim Hikmet, w. Randy Blasing). [AmerPoR] (23:2) Mr-Ap 94, p. 38-39.

"The Mailman" (from Hungarian travel notes, tr. of Nazim Hikmet, w. Randy Blasing). [AmerPoR] (23:2) Mr-Ap 94, p. 38.
"One A.M." (tr. of Nazim Hikmet, w. Randy Blasing). [AmerPoR] (23:2) Mr-Ap 94, p. 37.
"Some Memories" (tr. of Nazim Hikmet, w. Randy Blasing). [AmerPoR] (23:2) Mr-Ap 94, p. 40-41.
"Thirty Years Ago" (tr. of Nazim Hikmet, w. Randy Blasing). [AmerPoR] (23:2) Mr-Ap 94, p. 41.
"To Samet Vurgun" (tr. of Nazim Hikmet, w. Randy Blasing). [AmerPoR] (23:2) Mr-Ap 94, p. 39.
"Windows" (tr. of Nazim Hikmet, w. Randy Blasing). [AmerPoR] (23:2) Mr-Ap 94, p. 39-40.

3345. KOONS, Cedar
"Hermit." [Sun] (222) Je 94, p. 12.
"High Priestess." [Sun] (222) Je 94, p. p. 12.

3346. KOONTZ, Haven
"Echo or Loss." [HopewellR] (6) 94, p. 106.
"It." [HopewellR] (6) 94, p. 107.

3347. KOOSER, Ted
"Assessment." [EngJ] (83:7) N 94, p. 43.
"At the End of a Branch." [EngJ] (83:7) N 94, p. 43.
"A Hatch of Flies." [Border] (3) Fall 93, p. 36.
"Interchange." [Border] (3) Fall 93, p. 37.
"Old Cobweb." [EngJ] (83:7) N 94, p. 43.
"The Simple-Minded." [EngJ] (83:7) N 94, p. 43.

3348. KOPEC, Karen
"Daily Behavior." [AnthNEW] (6) 94, p. 18.

3349. KOPELKE, Kendra
"Scream." [PoetL] (89:1) Spr 94, p. 42.

3350. KOPPLE, K. A.
"Cancer Gnaws from My Shoulderblades" (tr. of Mercedes Roffé). [SenR] (24:2) Fall 94, p. 64-68.

3351. KÖRÖSY, Mária
"Accident on a Stretch of Interstate 94 Between Chicago and Milwaukee" (tr. of Ottó Orbán, w. Bruce Berlind). [Boulevard] (9:1/2, #25/26) Spr 94, p. 226.
"American Station" (In the Grand Canyon, tr. of Agnes Nemes Nagy, w. Bruce Berlind). [AnotherCM] (27) 94, p. 147.
"Daydream" (tr. of György Petri, w. Bruce Berlind). [AmerPoR] (23:1) Ja-F 94, p. 34.
"The Drawbacks of Redemption" (tr. of György Petri, w. Bruce Berlind). [SenR] (24:2) Fall 94, p. 57.
"Elegy" (tr. of György Petri, w. Bruce Berlind). [AmerPoR] (23:1) Ja-F 94, p. 32.
"Execrable Cold" (tr. of Gyula Illyés, w. Bruce Berlind)." [WebR] (18) Fall 94, p. 6.
"From the Insomnia Songs" (In memory of Arnold Schönberg, tr. of György Petri, w. Bruce Berlind). [AmerPoR] (23:1) Ja-F 94, p. 33.
"Horace Has a Bad Day" (tr. of György Petri, w. Bruce Berland). [Poetry] (164:2) My 94, p. 85.
"I Like" (tr. of György Petri, w. Bruce Berlind). [Chelsea] (56) 94, p. 113.
"A Miscarried Meeting with János Pilinszky" (tr. of Sándor Kányádi, w. Bruce Berlind). [SenR] (24:2) Fall 94, p. 59.
"Night Song of the Personal Spook" (tr. of György Petri, w. Bruce Berlind). [AmerPoR] (23:1) Ja-F 94, p. 33.
"The Onion Speaks" (tr. of György Petri, w. Bruce Berlind). [Chelsea] (56) 94, p. 111.
"Our Relationship begins to be Intimate" (tr. of György Petri, w. Bruce Berlind). [AmerPoR] (23:1) Ja-F 94, p. 32.
"Remembering My First Master" (tr. of Szabolcs Várady, w. Bruce Berlind). [SenR] (24:2) Fall 94, p. 60-61.
"Self-Portrait 1990" (tr. of György Petri, w. Bruce Berlind). [Chelsea] (56) 94, p. 112.
"Snow" (tr. of Agnes Nemes Nagy, w. Bruce Berlind). [AnotherCM] (27) 94, p. 148.
"The Sun's Gone Down" (tr. of Agnes Nemes Nagy, w. Bruce Berlind). [AnotherCM] (27) 94, p. 149.
"There Will Be No War" (tr. of Gyula Illyes, w. Bruce Berlind). [ConnPR] (13:1) 94, p. 23.

"This Breathing, Devouring Swamp" (tr. of Ottó Orbán, w. Jascha Kessler). [GrahamHR] (18) Wint 94-95, p. 100.
"To A." (tr. of György Petri, w. Bruce Berlind). [AmerPoR] (23:1) Ja-F 94, p. 33.
"White" (tr. of Gyula Illyés, w. Bruce Berlind). [WebR] (18) Fall 94, p. 5-6.
"With a Consignment of Poems" (tr. of György Petri, w. Bruce Berlind). [Chelsea] (56) 94, p. 112.
"Woodcut" (tr. of Sándor Kányádi, w. Bruce Berlind). [SenR] (24:2) Fall 94, p. 58.

3352. KORT, S. (Susanne)
"Barrows." [PaintedB] (53/54) 94, p. 32.
"Blessed Quotidian." [CaribbeanW] (8) 94, p. 61.
"Champ." [PaintedB] (53/54) 94, p. 33.
"The Classics Club." [Nimrod] (38:1) Fall-Wint 94, p. 120.
"Grandson." [CaribbeanW] (8) 94, p. 60.
"Granny Smith." [Nimrod] (38:1) Fall-Wint 94, p. 119.
"Migraine." [GrahamHR] (18) Wint 94-95, p. 98-99.
"La Moda." [Plain] (14:3) Spr 94, p. 34.
"Recovery." [NowestR] (32:2) 94, p. 12.
"Rite of Passage." [Sonora] (27) Spr 94, p. 73.
"Vacation Snapshots." [ApalQ] (40/41) 94, p. 92.

3353. KOSSMAN, Nina
"At the curl of the eyelashes" (tr. of Marina Tsvetaeva). [PoetL] (89:3) Fall 94, p. 47.
"The Eyes" (tr. of Marina Tsvetaeva). [PoetL] (89:3) Fall 94, p. 45.
"In Memory of Berangé" (tr. of Marina Tsvetaeva). [PoetL] (89:3) Fall 94, p. 44.
"My Veins Slashed Open" (From "In the Inmost Hour of the Soul," tr. of Marina Tsvetayeva). [AmerPoR] (23:6) N-D 94, p. 38.
"Slowly" (tr. of Marina Tsvetaeva). [AntigR] (99) Aut 94, p. 51.
"Someone left, with a head" (tr. of Marina Tsvetaeva). [PoetL] (89:3) Fall 94, p. 43.
"To Genius" (tr. of Marina Tsvetaeva). [AntigR] (99) Aut 94, p. 49.
"The Valley of the Roses" (tr. of Marina Tsvetaeva). [PoetL] (89:3) Fall 94, p. 46.

3354. KOSTELANETZ, Richard
"Circular Poem" (Design by Beth Lin and Atif Toor). [FreeL] (13) Spr 94, p. 34.
"He folded his body into a ball that could roll fluently in every direction." [HeavenB] (11) 94, p. 41.
"Hysterical Pregnancy" (Typography by Keith Newton). [NoAmR] (279:5) S-O 94, p. 35.
"Minimal Audio Plays." [WestHR] (48:3) Fall 94, p. 268-269.
"On the verge of death" (from *1001 Stories*). [HeavenB] (11) 94, p. 43.
"A Poetry-Film Storyboard: Transformations" (from *Transformations: A Poetry Film Story Board*). [Talisman] (12) Spr 94, p. 219.
"Poetry I Shall Not Make." [NewYorkQ] (53) 94, p. 59.
"Spanglish Reparations" (Layout by Erik J. Ringerud). [Caliban] (14) 94, p. 118-119.
Two Circular Poems. [ChamLR] (14/15) Spr-Fall 94, p. 201-202.

3355. KOSTENKO, Lina
"The Clock" (tr. by Marta Sawczuk). [Vis] (44) 94, p. 39.

3356. KOSTKOWSKA, Justyna
"My Name Is Jocasta" (tr. of Katarzyna Borun-Jagodzinska, w. Kathleen Snodgrass). [ArtfulD] (26/27) 94, p. 22.
"A Patriotic Song" (tr. of Katarzyna Borun-Jagodzinska, w. Kathleen Snodgrass). [ArtfulD] (26/27) 94, p. 21.

3357. KOSTOS, Dean
"Elegy for a Living Man" (For Theodore, with Parkinson's disease). [Boulevard] (9:1/2, #25/26) Spr 94, p. 94-96.
"In a Desert, the Memory of an Ocean" (for my brother, Steve). [JamesWR] (11:5) Fall 94, p. 15.

3358. KOTT, Stefanie
"The Rose, the Thorn, and the Wind." [Confr] (52/53) Wint-Spr 94, p. 324.

3359. KOTZIN, Miriam N.
"Challenge." [Boulevard] (9:3, #27) Fall 94, p. 180-181.

3360. KOUMJIAN, Vaughn
"Arriviste." [Light] (9) Spr 94, p. 16.

3361. KOUROUS, Sharon
"Leaving." [HiramPoR] (55/56) Fall 93-Sum 94, p. 62.

3362. KOVAC, Deirdre
"A Field." [GlobalCR] (4) Fall 94, p. 18-19.

3363. KOVACS, Edna
"August." [BellArk] (10:6) N-D 94, p. 26.
"Mermaid Madness." [BellArk] (10:3) My-Je 94, p. 13.
"Morning Star Reflections." [BellArk] (10:2) Mr-Ap 94, p. 31.
"Morning Walk in Maui." [BellArk] (10:3) My-Je 94, p. 12.
"Mt. Jefferson." [BellArk] (10:5) S-O 94, p. 23.
"Newport." [BellArk] (10:5) S-O 94, p. 25.
"October." [BellArk] (10:2) Mr-Ap 94, p. 14.
"Sea Interlude." [BellArk] (10:6) N-D 94, p. 6.
"Slow Dancing with the Moon" (— Dolly Parton). [BellArk] (10:3 [i.e. 10:4]) Jl-Ag 94, p. 10.
3364. KOVACS, George
"Man" (from "From, to . . ."). [AmerPoR] (23:1) Ja-F 94, p. 30.
3365. KOVEN, Stephanie
"Compiègne." [Epoch] (43:3) 94, p. 299.
3366. KOZAK, Roberta
"Indiana Beach" (Associated Writing Programs Intro Award poem). [IndR] (17:2) Fall 94, p. 151-152.
"Prismatic" (for Debie). [GettyR] (7:3) Sum 94, p. 516.
"Recovery" (Associated Writing Programs Intro Award poem). [IndR] (17:2) Fall 94, p. 153-154.
3367. KOZER, José
"Lunch" (tr. by David Frye). [MichQR] (33:3) Sum 94, p. 577.
3368. KRABBENHOFT, Ken
"Ode to the Table" (tr. of Pablo Neruda). [Field] (51) Fall 94, p. 13-14.
3369. KRAMER, Aaron
"Bridge." [CumbPR] (13:2) Spr 94, p. 68.
"I and Moishe-Leib" (tr. of Moishe Nadir). [Vis] (46) 94, p. 6.
3370. KRAMER, Karen
"Untitled: in the dream I was wearing a robe and I didn't recognize it was a red terry cloth." [HangL] (65) 94, p. 95.
3371. KRAPF, Norbert
"Alfred's Double" (Greenwich Village, 1948). [Confr] (54/55) Fall 94-Wint 95, p. 329.
"Alfred's Wave." [Confr] (54/55) Fall 94-Wint 95, p. 328.
"Closest to Home." [AmerS] (63:4) Aut 94, p. 601.
"Meditation in the Israelite Cemetery, Würzburg." [AmerS] (63:1) Wint 94, p. 60-62.
3372. KRASZEWSKI, Charles
"Shame" (tr. of Zbigniew Herbert). [NewYorker] (69:48) 31 Ja 94, p. 52.
3373. KRATT, Mary
"Late Snow." [NoCarLR] (2:1) Spr 94, p. 60.
3374. KRAUS, Jim
"Islands." [ChamLR] (14/15) Spr-Fall 94, p. 4-5.
3375. KRAUS, Sharon
"The Gesture." [Agni] (40) 94, p. 147-148.
3376. KRAUSHAAR, Mark
"Life Is What It's All About" (— American Red Cross Slogan. For the woman in the blue Ford). [PoetL] (89:3) Fall 94, p. 25-26.
"The Neighbors." [PoetL] (89:3) Fall 94, p. 29.
"Someone's Number." [PoetL] (89:3) Fall 94, p. 27-28.
3377. KREBS, Michael
"Birdfeed." [ClockR] (9:1/2) 94-95, p. 19.
"Late News and Poultry." [SlipS] (14) 94, p. 94.
"Stick Figures & m Birds." [HolCrit] (31:2) Ap 94, p. 18.
3378. KRECHEL, Ursula
"Early November" (tr. by Reinhold Grimm). [Pembroke] (26) 94, p. 134.
3379. KRESH, David
"Every Place Is the Same." [Epoch] (43:1) 94, p. 82.
3380. KRESS, Leonard
"Coach." [MassR] (35:1) Spr 94, p. 128-130.
"Sappho's Apples." [QW] (39) Sum-Fall 94, p. 173-175.
"Shotputters and Discus Throwers." [Comm] (121:15) 9 S 94, p. 11.
"Veronica." [ArtfulD] (26/27) 94, p. 109-111.
3381. KRETZ, Thomas
"My Favorite Poem." [SmPd] (31:1, #90) Wint 94, p. 14.

"Orchard of Deterioration." [ChrC] (111:29) 19 O 94, p. 952.
"Striped Things and Food." [CapeR] (29:2) Fall 94, p. 23.

3382. KRMPOTIC, Vesna
"Where You Came From" (tr. by Dasha Culic Nisula). [InterQ] (1:1) [93?], p. 118.

3383. KROEKER, G. W.
"Econ I." [SmPd] (31:2, #91) Spr 94, p. 25.

3384. KROLL, Ernest
"Casino" (Atlantic City). [Light] (10) Sum 94, p. 17.
"Concert Tour." [Light] (9) Spr 94, p. 8.
"Endurance." [Light] (10) Sum 94, p. 8.
"Florida." [Light] (11) Aut 94, p. 12.

3385. KROLL, Judith
"Borrowed Gods." [KenR] (NS 16:3) Sum 94, p. 96-97.
"Our Breast" (for Alicia Ostriker). [KenR] (NS 16:3) Sum 94, p. 97-99.

3386. KRONEN, Steve
"Autobiography: The Early Yers." [ParisR] (36:133) Wint 94, p. 174-175.
"In the Hangar of Brisbee, Oklahoma, 1933." [VirQR] (70:3) Sum 94, p. 453-454.
"Marianne Moore Late at Night." [QW] (38) Winter-Spr 93-94, p. 129-130.
"The World Before Them." [ParisR] (36:133) Wint 94, p. 175.

3387. KRONENFELD, Judy
"Marital Discord." [CharR] (20:1) Spr 94, p. 64.
"Soft." [PassN] (15:2) Wint 94, p. 4.

3388. KRUGER, Michael
"Footnote" (tr. by Richard Dove). [NewYorker] (69:48) 31 Ja 94, p. 44.

3389. KRUGOVOY, Anya
"Vienna 1901." [Iowa] (24:3) Fall 94, p. 176.

3390. KRUKOWSKI, Damon
"The Antediluvian World." [GrandS] (13:1, #49) Sum 94, p. 208.

3391. KRUSE, Kristina
"Remaining a Soldier." [NewEngR] (16:2) Spr 94, p. 120-121.

3392. KRYSL, Marilyn
"Hymn to Hard Work." [SpoonR] (19:1) Wint-Spr 94, p. 12.
"Poem for Extraordinary Day." [SpoonR] (19:1) Wint-Spr 94, p. 10-11.
"Profit Motive." [SpoonR] (19:1) Wint-Spr 94, p. 13.
"Sestina: Eden of Water." [Vis] (45) 94, p. 24-25.
"Soulskin." [AnotherCM] (28) 94, p. 82-84.

3393. KUBICEK, J. L.
"One by One." [WritersF] (20) 94, p. 85.

3394. KUDERKO, Lynne (Lynne M.)
"3600 Lakeview, Chicago" (to Barrett. Associated Writing Programs Intro Award poem). [IndR] (17:2) Fall 94, p. 147-148.
"Assignation." [PraS] (68:2) Sum 94, p. 24.
"Charles A. Snyder & Company." [PassN] (15:2) Wint 94, p. 29.
"History Lesson: The Horse Latitudes." [PassN] (15:2) Wint 94, p. 30-31.
"The Man Who Came Home." [PraS] (68:2) Sum 94, p. 25.
"Moving from the Family Home after Divorce" (Associated Writing Programs Intro Award poem). [IndR] (17:2) Fall 94, p. 149-150.
"Seeds." [PraS] (68:2) Sum 94, p. 23.
"Shadows Joining Other Shadows." [PraS] (68:2) Sum 94, p. 26.

3395. KULAK, Lorne
"A.M. Walk in the Plant." [Grain] (22:1) Sum 94, p. 71.
"Bird's Eye View." [Grain] (22:1) Sum 94, p. 71.
"The Curling Rink." [Grain] (22:1) Sum 94, p. 72.

3396. KULIK, William
"1889-1916" (tr. of Max Jacob). [AmerPoR] (23:2) Mr-Ap 94, p. 3.
"1914" (tr. of Max Jacob). [AmerPoR] (23:2) Mr-Ap 94, p. 3.
"Achilles' Wheel" (tr. of Max Jacob). [AmerPoR] (23:2) Mr-Ap 94, p. 4.
"Ballad of the Night Visitor" (tr. of Max Jacob). [AmerPoR] (23:2) Mr-Ap 94, p. 4.
"A Bit of Art Criticism" (tr. of Max Jacob). [AmerPoR] (23:2) Mr-Ap 94, p. 3.
"Burial in Quimper" (tr. of Max Jacob). [AmerPoR] (23:2) Mr-Ap 94, p. 5.
"Christian Families" (tr. of Max Jacob). [AmerPoR] (23:2) Mr-Ap 94, p. 5.
"The Dice Cup" (4 selections, tr. of Max Jacob). [DenQ] (29:1) Sum 94, p. 81-82.
"Fear" (tr. of Max Jacob). [AmerPoR] (23:2) Mr-Ap 94, p. 3.
"The Feminist Question" (tr. of Max Jacob). [AmerPoR] (23:2) Mr-Ap 94, p. 3.
"Hell Has Gradations" (tr. of Max Jacob). [AmerPoR] (23:2) Mr-Ap 94, p. 4.

"If Guillaume's Death Had Been Christian" (tr. of Max Jacob). [AmerPoR] (23:2) Mr-Ap 94, p. 5.
"Infernal Visions" (tr. of Max Jacob). [AmerPoR] (23:2) Mr-Ap 94, p. 5.
"Jean Jacques" (tr. of Max Jacob). [AmerPoR] (23:2) Mr-Ap 94, p. 4.
"The Key" (tr. of Max Jacob). [AmerPoR] (23:2) Mr-Ap 94, p. 3.
"Poem: To erase the heads of the generals of the Empire!" (tr. of Max Jacob). [AmerPoR] (23:2) Mr-Ap 94, p. 3.
"Reconstruction" (tr. of Max Jacob). [AmerPoR] (23:2) Mr-Ap 94, p. 5.

3397. KUMAR, Mina
"After a Decade, and Pregnant, You Call Your Mother." [HangL] (65) 94, p. 26.
"Among the Gopis." [HangL] (65) 94, p. 27-28.
"Curried Rhythm." [HangL] (65) 94, p. 25.

3398. KUMBIER, William
"Three Nocturnes." [CentR] (38:1) Wint 94, p. 131-135.

3399. KUMIN, Maxine
"Cross-Country Skiing." [Poetry] (165:3) D 94, p. 131.
"In a Different Country" (Music Festival, Sewanee, Tennessee). [Poetry] (164:5) Ag 94, p. 249-250.
"In Praise of the New Transfer Station." [Hudson] (47:3) Aut 94, p. 423-424.
"The Word." [Atlantic] (273:3) Mr 94, p. 96.
"Youth Orchestra, with Dogs" (University of the South). [Poetry] (164:5) Ag 94, p. 250-251.

3400. KUNERT, Guenter (Günter)
"From My Life History" (tr. by Reinhold Grimm). [Pembroke] (26) 94, p. 139.
"Larmoyance" (tr. by Agnes Stein). [MidAR] (14:2) 94, p. 60.

3401. KUNITZ, Daniel
"Alternate Ends" (To Paul Galison). [Salm] (103) Sum 94, p. 107-108.

3402. KUNTZ, Laurie
"Benign." [NewDeltaR] (11:2) Spr-Sum 94, p. 58-59.

KUO-PIN, Huang
See WONG, Lawrence

3403. KUPPNER, Frank
"The Bridge: A Node." [Jacaranda] (5:1) Wint-Spr 91, p. 89.

3404. KURTZAHN, Leslie J.
"Moving." [DenQ] (28:4) Spr 94, p. 30-31.

KUSATAO, Ozaki
See OZAKI, Kusatao

3405. KUSHNER, Bill
"December." [HangL] (65) 94, p. 30-31.

3406. KUSHNER, Dale
"Ravaged Sarajevo." [Poetry] (164:4) Jl 94, p. 192.

3407. KUSZ, Natalie
"Persistent Heat." [AmerV] (34) 94, p. 20.

3408. KUUSISTO, Stephen
"Post-Orphic." [IndR] (17:2) Fall 94, p. 76.
"Tenth Muse." [IndR] (17:2) Fall 94, p. 77.

3409. KUYPERS, Janet
"Addict." [CoalC] (8) Ap 94, p. 33.

3410. KUZMA, Greg
"All That I Love." [VirQR] (70:1) Wint 94, p. 103-105.
"The Arrangement." [TriQ] (91) Fall 94, p. 220-226.
"The Chairs." [PoetC] (26:1) Fall 94, p. 24-26.
"Driving Past the Cemetery." [MidwQ] (35:2) Wint 94, p. 174-178.
"The Loon" (for Jeff). [CharR] (20:2) Fall 94, p. 98-100.
"Money." [NewL] (60:2) 94, p. 124-138.
"The Precautions." [Crazy] (46) Spr 94, p. 91-100.
"Putting in the Seeds." [LitR] (37:4) Sum 94, p. 662-663.
"Warren." [PoetryE] (37/38) Spr 94, p. 188-194.

3411. KUZMIN, Mikhail
"The End of Volume Two" (tr. with Scholia by John Barnstead). [AntigR] (99) Aut 94, p. 58-61.

3412. KWA, Lydia
"Scooter." [WestCL] (28:1/2, #13/14) Spr-Fall 94, p. 16.

KWANG-CHUNG, Yu
See YU, Kwang-chung

3413. KWASNY, Melissa
"Grass." [PoetryNW] (35:4) Wint 94-95, p. 24.
"Learning to Speak to Them." [PoetryNW] (35:4) Wint 94-95, p. 25.
"An Urban Poem." [PoetryNW] (35:4) Wint 94-95, p. 26.
3414. KWIATEK, Joellen
"On the Way to Tell My Sister." [AmerPoR] (23:4) Jl-Ag 94, p. 29.
"Still Life of the Martyrdom of St. Serapion" (for Edward Ruchalski). [AmerPoR] (23:4) Jl-Ag 94, p. 29.
3415. KYLE, Christiane Jacox
"A Late Epithalamion." [Poetry] (164:3) Je 94, p. 135.
"Old Woman" (tr. of Gabriela Mistral). [SenR] (24:1) Spr 94, p. 56-57.
"The Sea" (tr. of Gabriela Mistral). [SenR] (24:1) Spr 94, p. 58-59.
3416. KYLE, Garland Richard
"San Francisco." [ModernW] (2) Wint 94, p. 129.
"Sometimes." [ModernW] (2) Wint 94, p. 128.
"Thanos Villas (Merovigli)" (for Melina Mercouri). [ModernW] (2) Wint 94, p. 127.
"Vietnam 1973." [ModernW] (2) Wint 94, p. 129.
3417. KYMYTVAL', Antonina
"Under the Wing of My Yaranga" (tr. by Galina De Roeck). [Manoa] (6:2) Wint 94, p. 181.
KYOJIN, Okura
See OKURA, Kyojin
KYOKO, Mori
See MORI, Kyoko

LA . . .
See also names beginning with "La" without the following space, filed below in their alphabetic positions, e.g., LaSALLE.
3418. La FONTAINE, Jean de
"Ulysses' Shipmates" (tr. by Craig Hill). [Raritan] (13:4) Spr 94, p. 19-21.
La HOUSSAYE, Harry de
See De la HOUSSAYE, Harry
La MARE, Walter de
See De la MARE, Walter
3419. LABRA, Carilda Oliver
"After Papa" (tr. by Ruth Behar). [MichQR] (33:3) Sum 94, p. 599-600.
"Soil" (tr. by Ruth Behar). [MichQR] (33:3) Sum 94, p. 598.
LABRUNO, Carmen Michael
See LaBRUNO, Michael (Carmen Michael)
3420. LaBRUNO, Michael (Carmen Michael)
"San Juan Seduces the Holy Ghost." [Chelsea] (56) 94, p. 79-80.
3421. LADER, Bruce
"Wait Till You're Twenty-One." [Poetry] (164:3) Je 94, p. 153.
3422. LADIK, Katalin
"It is painful to feel desire" (tr. by Emoke B'Racz). [Vis] (46) 94, p. 18.
3423. LADIN, Jay
"Three Cents." [HayF] (14) Spr-Sum 94, p. 17.
3424. LaFEMINA, Gerry
"American Ideograph." [PennR] (6:1) 94, p. 14-15.
"The Long Drive Home from Club Soda to Comstock." [AmerLC] (6) 94, p. 50-51.
"Spirituals." [SenR] (24:1) Spr 94, p. 66-68.
3425. LaFOND, Carolyn Street
"After the Final Heat of Summer." [BellArk] (10:6) N-D 94, p. 10.
"Bird Mobile." [BellArk] (10:6) N-D 94, p. 10.
"Courtship" (for David). [BellArk] (10:6) N-D 94, p. 10.
LaFONTAINE, Jean de
See La FONTAINE, Jean de
3426. LAGIER, Jennifer
"Archetype." [SantaBR] (2:1) Spr-Sum 94, p. 81.
"Quantification of the Romance That Poisons Our Minds." [SlipS] (14) 94, p. 105.
3427. LaGORY, Michael
"Post Meridiem Reentry." [Hellas] (5:2) Fall-Wint 94, p. 51.
"Traffic Court." [ChamLR] (14/15) Spr-Fall 94, p. 238-240.

3428. LAHIRI, Chitra
"Ravaged Blossom" (tr. by Arlene Zide and Paramita Banerjee). [InterQ] (1:2) 93, p. 189.
"Where There Is No Rest" (tr. by Arlene Zide and Paramita Banerjee). [InterQ] (1:2) 93, p. 188.
3429. LAINO, E. J. Miller
"Hard Words." [MassR] (35:1) Spr 94, p. 60-61.
"The Night Before Surgery: A Love Poem." [PoetryE] (37/38) Spr 94, p. 51.
"Poem for Mrs. Miller." [PoetryE] (37/38) Spr 94, p. 52-53.
"Skimming the Turtle." [MassR] (35:1) Spr 94, p. 61-62.
3430. LAKE, Kathleen
"Prayers for Your Wife." [Sun] (227) N 94, p. 33.
3431. LAKE, Paul
"Eternal Recurrence." [Chelsea] (56) 94, p. 37-38.
"Narcissus Reflects" (For Frederick Turner). [Poetry] (163:5) F 94, p. 265-266.
3432. LALLY, Margaret
"Ceremony at Saks." [Hudson] (47:1) Spr 94, p. 48.
"Song on the River Seine." [Hudson] (47:1) Spr 94, p. 46-47.
3433. LAMBERT-NEIDIGH, Paula J.
"I Told My Mother in a Postcard." [Parting] (7:1) Sum 94, p. 65.
3434. LaMERS, Joyce
"Command Performance." [Light] (9) Spr 94, p. 8.
"Down the Snake, that untamed river." [Light] (10) Sum 94, p. 24.
"Dry Run." [Light] (11) Aut 94, p. 24.
"Family Values." [Light] (10) Sum 94, p. 18.
"Hoover Depression." [Light] (10) Sum 94, p. 11.
"Pollsters." [Light] (12) Wint 94-95, p. 11.
"Predictions." [Light] (11) Aut 94, p. 15.
"Where River Alph meets sunless sea." [Light] (12) Wint 94-95, p. 24.
3435. LAMMON, Martin
"The Emperor's Dog Finds the Way Home." [GettyR] (7:4) Aut 94, p. 624.
"How I Learned to Count." [GettyR] (7:4) Aut 94, p. 622-623.
"Valley Falls." [MidwQ] (35:4) Sum 94, p. 409.
3436. LAMPORT, Felicia
"Academic Asset." [Light] (11) Aut 94, p. 4.
"Alice's Variorum Quorum." [Light] (11) Aut 94, p. 5.
"The Boston Lady." [Light] (11) Aut 94, p. 3.
"Bringing Home the Beacon." [Light] (11) Aut 94, p. 6.
"Clothes Question." [Light] (11) Aut 94, p. 5.
"Eggomania." [Light] (11) Aut 94, p. 5.
"Gregious Error." [Light] (11) Aut 94, p. 6.
"It Takes a Heap of Compost to Make a House a Mess." [Light] (11) Aut 94, p. 6.
"Means Test." [Light] (11) Aut 94, p. 4.
"Our Garden Plot Won't Thicken If You're Stingy with The Chicken Wire." [Light] (11) Aut 94, p. 6.
"Overdrivers." [Light] (11) Aut 94, p. 4.
3437. LANDALE, Zoë
"Garden of Revelation." [TickleAce] (28) Fall-Wint 94, p. 120-121.
"Home." [Arc] (33) Fall 94, p. 59.
"Mother of the Dance." [TickleAce] (28) Fall-Wint 94, p. 119.
"Yellow." [Event] (23:3) Wint 94-95, p. 65-66.
3438. LANDERS, Susan
"Polar Twins of the Scottish Muse." [Verse] (11:1) Spr 94, p. 32.
3439. LANDFIELD, Anne
"Carnivores." [SantaBR] (1:1) Spr-Sum 93, p. 57.
3440. LANDGRAF, Susan
"Aristotle Called Them The Intestines of the Earth" (from "Cuttings." The Nimrod / Hardman Wards: Honorable Mention). [Nimrod] (38:1) Fall-Wint 94, p. 35.
"Between Worlds." [Nimrod] (38:1) Fall-Wint 94, p. 38.
"Out of a Long Dream Coming Sounds." [Nimrod] (38:1) Fall-Wint 94, p. 36.
"We Never Know What Womb We'll Go Back to." [Nimrod] (38:1) Fall-Wint 94, p. 37.
3441. LANE, Belden C.
"Poverty of Words." [ChrC] (111:36) 14 D 94, p. 1189.
3442. LANE, M. Travis
"D'Or." [AntigR] (96) Wint 94, p. 44.

"In Some Moods." [AntigR] (96) Wint 94, p. 45-46.
"Magritte Door" (for Sabrina: "When is a door not a door?"). [AntigR] (96) Wint 94, p. 43.

3443. LANE, Patrick
"The Calf." [SouthernR] (30:2) Ap, Spr 94, p. 294-295.
"The Deer." [SouthernR] (30:2) Ap, Spr 94, p. 293.
"Held Water." [CanLit] (141) Sum 94, p. 37.
"Held Water." [SouthernR] (30:2) Ap, Spr 94, p. 292.
"Wysteria." [CanLit] (141) Sum 94, p. 36-37.

3444. LANE, Suzanne
"Listening for the Phone." [ApalQ] (40/41) 94, p. 100-101.

LANG, Meng
See MENG, Lang

3445. LANG, Susanna
"Equinox." [GreenMR] (NS 17:2) Fall-Wint 94-95, p. 116.

3446. LANGAN, Steve
"The Black Pants." [ChiR] (40:4) 94, p. 26.
"The Black Pants, Day 2." [ChiR] (40:4) 94, p. 27.
"The Black Pants, Day 4." [ChiR] (40:4) 94, p. 29.
"The Black Pants, Day 6." [ChiR] (40:4) 94, p. 31.
"The Black Pants, Day 7." [ChiR] (40:4) 94, p. 32.
"The Black Pants, Evening, Day 3." [ChiR] (40:4) 94, p. 28.
"The Black Pants, Evening, Day 5." [ChiR] (40:4) 94, p. 30.
"Freezing." [ColR] (21:1) Spr 94, p. 108-109.
"Omaha." [Witness] (8:2) 94, p. 142-144.
"Stealing from the Till." [ColR] (21:1) Spr 94, p. 110-113.

3447. LANGHINRICHS, Ruth
"Away at School." [WindO] (58) Sum 94, p. 9.
"The Button." [WindO] (58) Sum 94, p. 7.
"The Formative Years." [WindO] (58) Sum 94, p. 5-6.
"The Movies." [WindO] (58) Sum 94, p. 8.
"The Romantic." [WindO] (58) Sum 94, p. 4.
"The Subversive." [WindO] (58) Sum 94, p. 6.

3448. LANGILLE, Carole
"Travel." [Event] (23:1) Spr 94, p. 24.

3449. LANGLAS, James
"Another Birthday." [Poetry] (164:3) Je 94, p. 149.
"Crossing" (For my father). [Poetry] (164:3) Je 94, p. 148.

3450. LANGRALL, Liza
"When Momma Was." [SouthernPR] (34:1) Sum 94, p. 33.

3451. LANIGAN-SCHMIDT, Therese
"And I Miss You Joann." [Writer] (107:1) Ja 94, p. 25.

LANILAU, Carolyn Lei
See LEI-LANILAU, Carolyn

3452. LANSKY, Bruce
"Georgie Porgie, what a shame" (New Adventures of Mother Goose Version). [Harp] (288:1726) Mr 94, p. 30.
"Peter, Peter, sugar eater" (New Adventures of Mother Goose Version). [Harp] (288:1726) Mr 94, p. 30.

3453. LANTHIER, Kateri
"Lake Road Knowledge." [Descant] (25:1, #84) Spr 94, p. 107.
"The Near Suburbs." [AntigR] (98) Sum 94, p. 77-78.
"Oscar Wilde at the City Hall Auditorium" (Belleville, Ontario, 1882). [Descant] (25:1, #84) Spr 94, p. 106.

3454. LAPIERRE, René
"1. New England View" (tr. by Myrna Delson-Karan). [AntigR] (98) Sum 94, p. 67.
"1. Vue de la Nouvelle-Angleterre." [AntigR] (98) Sum 94, p. 66.
"2. Couronne." [AntigR] (98) Sum 94, p. 68.
"2. Wreath" (tr. by Myrna Delson-Karan). [AntigR] (98) Sum 94, p. 69.
"3. Night Tunnel" (tr. by Myrna Delson-Karan). [AntigR] (98) Sum 94, p. 71.
"3. Nuit." [AntigR] (98) Sum 94, p. 70.
"4. Salamander's Nest" (tr. by Myrna Delson-Karan). [AntigR] (98) Sum 94, p. 73.
"4. Salamandre." [AntigR] (98) Sum 94, p. 72.
"Grasses of Eternity" (tr. by Myrna Delson-Karan). [InterPR] (20:2) Fall 94, p. 57.
"Il y eut cette image encore, un coin bas de campagne." [InterPR] (20:2) Fall 94, p. 56.

"A la lisière du petit bois l'herbe était piquée." [InterPR] (20:2) Fall 94, p. 54.
"New York 1957" (tr. by Myrna Delson-Karan). [InterPR] (20:2) Fall 94, p. 53.
"Promise" (tr. by Myrna Delson-Karan). [InterPR] (20:2) Fall 94, p. 55.
"Soir de printemps 1957, dans Lexington Avenue." [InterPR] (20:2) Fall 94, p. 52.

3455. LARAQUE, Paul
"The Season of Reckonings" (In Memory of My Brother, the Writer Guy F. Laraque, Assassinated Under the Cedras Regime, tr. by Jack Hirschman). [CentralP] (23) Spr 94, p. 70-72.

3456. LARDNER, Ted
"The Swallows at Dee's." [Caliban] (14) 94, p. 92.

3457. LARIOS VENDRELL, Luis
"Crepúsculo." [Nuez] (5:13/14/15) 94, p. 19.

3458. LARKIN, Joan
"Waste Not." [AmerPoR] (23:4) Jl-Ag 94, p. 37.

3459. LARKIN, Maryrose
"Alphabarbie" (for GB). [Jacaranda] (10) 94, p. 75.

3460. LARRAHONA KASTEN, Alfonso
"Desenjaulado" (Para el poeta cubano Rafael Bordao). [Nuez] (5:13/14/15) 94, p. 29.
"Diseño un Ojo Ahora" (Para *La Nuez*). [Nuez] (5:13/14/15) 94, p. 29.
"En Esta Voz" (a David Valjalo). [Nuez] (5:13/14/15) 94, p. 29.

3461. LARS, Krystyna
"(I) Night Journey" (tr. by Georgia Scott and David Malcolm). [InterQ] (1:1) [93?], p. 102-103.
"(I) She Writes with Fire" (tr. by Georgia Scott and David Malcolm). [InterQ] (1:1) [93?], p. 101.

3462. LARSEN, Jeanne
"The Muse of Sex." [NewEngR] (16:4) Fall 94, p. 102-105.

3463. LARSON, Lance
"Rhetoric Summer: Preparing for Comps." [Salm] (101/102) Wint-Spr 94, p. 154-155.

3464. LARSON, Rustin
"Loving the Good Driver." [PassN] (15:2) Wint 94, p. 24-25.
"The Woman in the National Gallery." [WilliamMR] (32) 94, p. 104-105.

3465. LARSON, Steve
"Mother and Father." [RagMag] (12:1) Sum 94, p. 85.
"To Honor the Particular." [RagMag] (12:1) Sum 94, p. 84.

3466. LASALA, Laura
"A Poor Memory." [AnthNEW] (6) 94, p. 33.

3467. LaSALLE, Peter
"Coffin Window." [ConnPR] (13:1) 94, p. 5.
"In Other Cities." [Witness] (8:2) 94, p. 188.
"Subway Golf." [ApalQ] (40/41) 94, p. 88.
"El Sueño del Hombre de Los BoSox: Austin Texas." [ApalQ] (40/41) 94, p. 86-87.

3468. LASSELL, Michael
"Casa de Colombo." [Jacaranda] (4:2) Spr 90, p. 59.
"The Indian Hunter" (Bronze, 1860, by John Quincy Adams Ward, American, 1830-1910). [CrabCR] (8:2/3/9:1/2/3) 94, p. 21.

3469. LATHBURY, Roger
"Clerihews" (George Bernard Shaw, James A. Joyce). [Light] (10) Sum 94, p. 15.

3470. LATIF, Tariq
"On Losing His Soul." [Verse] (11:2) Sum 94, p. 86.

3471. LATTA, John
"Epilogue City." [NewAW] (12) Spr-Sum 94, p. 112-114.
"A Letter Beginning with *The Stories*." [Epoch] (43:1) 94, p. 80-81.

3472. LAU, Barbara
"The Distance a Voice Carries Over the Lake." [SouthernPR] (34:2) Wint 94, p. 25-26.
"Promises." [Border] (5) Fall-Wint 94, p. 29.

3473. LAU, Carolyn
"Ballet as a Means of Translating Words into Flesh on Glissade Épaulement." [YellowS] (12:2, #46) Sum-Fall 94, p. 10.
"Butterfly Physics." [YellowS] (12:2, #46) Sum-Fall 94, p. 10.
"The Nineteen Seventies Practicing English Poems" (illustrated by Tony Speirs). [YellowS] (12:2, #46) Sum-Fall 94, p. 11.
"Speaking for Fresh Matisse." [YellowS] (12:2, #46) Sum-Fall 94, p. 10.

3474. LAU, Evelyn
"The Pictures." [KenR] (NS 16:1) Wint 94, p. 134-135.
"Pressure." [MichQR] (33:1) Wint 94, p. 66-67.
"Solipsism." [SouthernR] (30:2) Ap, Spr 94, p. 296-297.
3475. LAU, Lucius
"Ai" (love in Chinese). [BambooR] (60) Wint 94, p. 101.
3476. LAUBER, Peg Carlson
"The Amusement Park." [Kalliope] (16:1) 94, p. 11-13.
3477. LAUE, John
"Civilization." [ContextS] (4:1) 94, p. 23.
"Oblivion" (From the Kona Coast). [SantaBR] (2:1) Spr-Sum 94, p. 85.
"Paranoia." [SantaBR] (2:1) Spr-Sum 94, p. 84.
3478. LAUGHLIN, James
"Along the Meadow Stream." [PartR] (61:4) Fall 94, p. 641.
"Apokatastasis." [Agni] (39) 94, p. 33.
"At a Certain Point." [Agni] (39) 94, p. 34.
"Bittersweet." [Interim] (13:1) Spr-Sum 94, p. 14.
"The Chips Are Flying." [NewYorkQ] (53) 94, p. 50.
"The Day I Was Dead." [Thrpny] (57) Spr 94, p. 10.
"The Desert in Bloom" (from *Byways*). [GrandS] (13:1, #49) Sum 94, p. 91-94.
"The Hypnerotomachia" (Version of Colonna). [HarvardR] (7) Fall 94, p. 38.
"In Old Age." [PartR] (61:4) Fall 94, p. 640.
"In the Nursery." [NewYorker] (70:15) 30 My 94, p. 78.
"Is Memory." [YaleR] (82:4) O 94, p. 78.
"It's Difficult." [Agni] (39) 94, p. 31-32.
"Melissa" (From *Byways*). [Agni] (39) 94, p. 35-41.
"Penelope Venit Abit Helene" (after Martial, Ep. 1.62). [ParisR] (36:130) Spr 94, p. 147.
"Remembering William Carlos Williams" (Selection: "9 Ridge Road"). [Agni] (40) 94, p. 1-11.
"Sweet Childhood." [Interim] (13:1) Spr-Sum 94, p. 14.
"La Vita Nuova." [HarvardR] (6) Spr 94, p. 148.
"The Wood Nymph." [ParisR] (36:130) Spr 94, p. 146.
3479. LAUINGER, Ann
"Prehistory." [GlobalCR] (4) Fall 94, p. 34.
"The Sighting." [GlobalCR] (4) Fall 94, p. 32-33.
3480. LAURENCE, Alexander
"Codex" (Excerpts, tr. of Maurice Roche). [Talisman] (13) Fall 94-Wint 95, p. 16-34.
LAURENTIS, Louise Budde de
See DeLAURENTIS, Louise Budde
3481. LAURO, Alberto
"Hora de Partir." [Nuez] (5:13/14/15) 94, p. 49.
3482. LAUTERBACH, Ann
"Ashes, Ashes (Robert Tyman, Susan Crile)." [Conjunc] (22) 94, p. 311-314.
"Constellation." [Chelsea] (57) 94, p. 21-24.
"Eclipse." [DenQ] (28:3) Wint 94, p. 23.
"In the Museum of the Word (Henri Matisse)" (for Thomas Neurath). [Conjunc] (22) 94, p. 314-319.
3483. LAUX, Dorianne
"Aphasia" (for Honeya). [AmerV] (35) 94, p. 77.
"Fast Gas" (for Richard). [YellowS] (11:4, #44) Wint 93-94, p. 22.
"For My Daughter Who Loves Animals." [YellowS] (12:2, #46) Sum-Fall 94, p. 28.
"Interior." [AmerV] (35) 94, p. 80.
"Late October." [AmerV] (35) 94, p. 78.
"To My Best Friend, Turning Forty" (for Kim). [AmerV] (35) 94, p. 79.
3484. LAVALLE, Tomás Guido
"La Caverna" (para Keely Marina Weiss). [LindLM] (13:1) Mr 94, p. 13.
"En el Aire de Su Llama." [LindLM] (13:1) Mr 94, p. 13.
"Punta d'en Pampá." [LindLM] (13:1) Mr 94, p. 13.
3485. LAVENDER, William
"Buster on Plato." [NewOR] (20:1/2) Spr-Sum 94, p. 73.
"Clocking In." [NewOR] (20:1/2) Spr-Sum 94, p. 72.
"The Kine." [NewOR] (20:1/2) Spr-Sum 94, p. 70-71.
"The Poetry of Work." [NewOR] (20:1/2) Spr-Sum 94, p. 78-79.
"Road Narrative." [NewOR] (20:1/2) Spr-Sum 94, p. 74-76.

"The Therapy." [NewOR] (20:1/2) Spr-Sum 94, p. 77.

3486. LAVERGNE, Alfredo

"América." [InterPR] (20:2) Fall 94, p. 106.

"America" (tr. by Hugh Hazelton). [InterPR] (20:2) Fall 94, p. 108.

"Amérique" (tr. by Sylvie Perron). [InterPR] (20:2) Fall 94, p. 107.

3487. LAVIN, S. R.

"The War Between the States." [Stand] (35:4) Aut 94, p. 75.

"What Happened in Waco." [Stand] (35:4) Aut 94, p. 75.

3488. LAWRENCE, Anthony

"At the Seminar on Teenage Suicide." [GettyR] (7:3) Sum 94, p. 496-497.

"Mark and Lars." [GettyR] (7:3) Sum 94, p. 498.

3489. LAWS, Kyle

"Running Down the Song of Wind on Barbed Wire." [BlackBR] (19) Fall-Wint 94, p. 36.

3490. LAWSON, David

"More Than a Mouthful" (from *The News in Brief*). [SlipS] (14) 94, p. 87.

"Phineas Taylor Barnum." [NewYorkQ] (53) 94, p. 73.

3491. LAYTON, Elizabeth

"On Sending a Granddaughter Off to College." [NewL] (60:3) 94, p. 12.

3492. LAYTON, Peter

"Habeas Corpus." [WindO] (58) Sum 94, p. 44.

LE . . .

See also names beginning with "Le" without the following space, filed below in their alphabetic positions, e.g., LeFEVRE.

3493. Le DRESSAY, Anne

"In My Next Life." [CanLit] (141) Sum 94, p. 14.

"Last Words." [TickleAce] (28) Fall-Wint 94, p. 68-69.

3494. Le GUIN, Ursula

"In That Desert" (written for the AIDS Wall in Portland, 1989). [AmerV] (33) 94, p. 18.

3495. LEA, Sydney

"Aubade." [SouthernR] (30:3) Sum 94, p. 542-544.

3496. LEADER, Mary

"Photographs (For Our Children)" (after a film by Edit Koszegi, Sandor Simo, & Andras Suranyi). [WestHR] (48:3) Fall 94, p. 298.

3497. LEAHY, Anna

"Morning Musing." [MinnR] (41/42) Fall 93-Spr 94 (published Mr 95), p. 29-30.

3498. LEAKE, Brent T.

"No Hitter: 6-29-90." [BlackBR] (18) Wint-Spr 94, p. 20-21.

LEAN, Christopher M. Mac

See Mac LEAN, Christopher M.

3499. LEASE, Joseph

"George Techner: Listen with Pain." [DenQ] (29:1) Sum 94, p. 21.

"New World." [ColR] (21:1) Spr 94, p. 119.

"Orient Point." [ColR] (21:1) Spr 94, p. 114-118.

"The Sun Threshes, Seed Rains, a Cord of Wet Wood." [ColR] (21:1) Spr 94, p. 120.

3500. LEAVITT, M. S.

"Stealing Apples at Cocheco Farms" (After the poems and letters of Carolyn Page). [NegC] (14:1/2) 94, p. 11.

"Wyndham Gaol in Wyndham Towne." [NegC] (14:1/2) 94, p. 12-15.

3501. LEAX, John

"Family Story." [Image] (3) Spr 93, p. 70-71.

3502. LeBLANC, Jean

"Pilgrim Heights, Provincetown, Massachusetts." [SmPd] (31:3, #92) Fall 94, p. 28.

3503. LeBOX, Annette

"The Kiss as Signifier." [PraF] (15:3, #68) Aut 94, p. 115.

"Litany." [HiramPoR] (57) Fall 94-Wint 95, p. 37.

3504. LECHAY, Dan

"Quarry." [Iowa] (24:3) Fall 94, p. 177-178.

"Quiet Evening, Cat, Then Rain." [Iowa] (24:3) Fall 94, p. 179-180.

3505. LECKER, Sophia

"We Are Both Nice Canadian Women." [Grain] (22:2) Fall 94, p. 52.

3506. LECKIE, Ross

"At the Funeral" (In memory of Harold Oldham). [AntigR] (96) Wint 94, p. 69.

"First Break of Spring." [AntigR] (96) Wint 94, p. 70.

"The Watermelon." [DenQ] (28:4) Spr 94, p. 32.
LECOMTE, Roger Gilbert
See GILBERT-LECOMTE, Roger
3507. LECUONA, Ernesto
"Siempre en Mi Corazon." [Areíto] (4:15) Marzo 94, p. 42.
3508. LEDERHENDLER, Lazer
"Fifth Invention: Love Song." [PoetryC] (14:4) S 94, p. 13.
"First Invention: Pavement." [PoetryC] (14:4) S 94, p. 12.
"Fourth Invention: Litany." [PoetryC] (14:4) S 94, p. 12.
"Second Invention: Sidewalk (Almost a Story)." [PoetryC] (14:4) S 94, p. 12.
"Sixth Invention: Jazz." [PoetryC] (14:4) S 94, p. 13.
"Third Invention: Symbol." [PoetryC] (14:4) S 94, p. 12.
LEDRESSAY, Anne
See Le DRESSAY, Anne
3509. LEE, David
"No Lazy S Ranch." [PoetryE] (37/38) Spr 94, p. 179-187.
3510. LEE, Gregory
"The Boy Who Catches Wasps" (tr. of Duo Duo). [Manoa] (6:1) Sum 94, p. 155.
"When I Knew the Bell Sound Was Green" (tr. of Duo Duo). [Manoa] (6:1) Sum 94, p. 156.
3511. LEE, John B.
"Animals Hearing Guns." [Arc] (33) Fall 94, p. 22-23.
"It Was a Fall of Skunks." [Arc] (33) Fall 94, p. 19-20.
"Jimi Hendrix in the Company of Cows." [Arc] (33) Fall 94, p. 24.
"Please Finish Reading This Poem." [PraF] (15:3, #68) Aut 94, p. 60-61.
"Watching Hummingbirds with Garth and the Boys." [Arc] (33) Fall 94, p. 21.
"When Doris Day Was in My Living Room." [PraF] (15:3, #68) Aut 94, p. 59.
3512. LEE, Kristin W.
"Mugging." [WestHR] (48:3) Fall 94, p. 252-253.
"Shells." [WestHR] (48:3) Fall 94, p. 254-255.
"Soil." [WestHR] (48:3) Fall 94, p. 253.
3513. LEE, L. L.
"Odes" (Selections: 4.7, 2.14, tr. of Horace). [CharR] (20:1) Spr 94, p. 77-78.
3514. LEE, Lance
"Sleepwalking at Dawn." [CapeR] (29:2) Fall 94, p. 29.
3515. LEE, Lanniko L.
"Ishi's Reply." [Paint] (21) Aut 94, p. 123-124.
3516. LEE, Li-Young
"For a New Citizen of These United States." [WillowR] (21) Spr 94, p. 59-60.
"Mnemonic." [EngJ] (83:2) F 94, p. 87.
3517. LEE, Linda Caldwell
"At the Sistine Chapel." [HopewellR] (6) 94, p. 109.
"Inventory." [HopewellR] (6) 94, p. 108.
3518. LEE, Mabel
"Where the Sea Stands Still" (tr. of Yang Lian). [Talisman] (12) Spr 94, p. 182-190.
3519. LEE, Maria
"Exorcise." [SouthernPR] (34:2) Wint 94, p. 40.
3520. LEE, Priscilla
"All My Life." [Zyzzyva] (10:3) Fall 94, p. 103-104.
3521. LEE, Richard E.
"David Ignatow." [Pearl] (20) Spr 94, p. 54.
3522. LEE, Sharon
"Attack." [Amelia] (7:3, #22) 94, p. 26.
3523. LEEDS, Stephen
"In the Round." [ParisR] (36:132) Fall 94, p. 234.
"Unsound." [ParisR] (36:132) Fall 94, p. 233.
3524. LEEFLANG, Ed
"In the Other" (tr. by Pleuke Boyce). [Quarry] (43:1) Je 94, p. 28.
"Letters to Leporello" (tr. by Pleuke Boyce). [Quarry] (43:1) Je 94, p. 29-30.
3525. LEEN, Mary
"From Maria's Notebook of Thieves" (for Leslie Silko). [AmerPoR] (23:2) Mr-Ap 94, p. 56.
3526. LEFCOWITZ, Barbara F.
"Sophocles' Sestina for Sigmund Freud." [PoetL] (89:3) Fall 94, p. 15-16.
3527. LEFEBURE, Stephen
"Bisti." [WeberS] (11:3) Fall 94, p. 107.

"Canyonlands." [WeberS] (11:3) Fall 94, p. 106.
"The Cave." [WeberS] (11:3) Fall 94, p. 106.
"The Clearing." [WeberS] (11:3) Fall 94, p. 107.
"The Hike." [WeberS] (11:3) Fall 94, p. 106.
"Monument Valley." [WeberS] (11:3) Fall 94, p. 108.
"The Sandias." [WeberS] (11:3) Fall 94, p. 107.

3528. LEFTWICH, Jim
"All the Harm I've Done to Silence #1." [SycamoreR] (6:1) Wint 94, p. 43.
"All the Harm I've Done to Silence #2." [SycamoreR] (6:1) Wint 94, p. 44.
"Religion Comes Easily." [ClockR] (9:1/2) 94-95, p. 71.

3529. LEGASPI, Joseph O.
"Visiting the *Manongs* in a Convalescent Home in Delano." [BambooR] (63/64) Sum-Fall 94, p. 27-28.

3530. LÉGER, Ronald
"One of these mornings" (tr. of Daniel Dargis, w. Paul G. Croteau). [InterPR] (20:2) Fall 94, p. 23.

3531. LEGLER, Philip
"Parade." [PassN] (15:2) Wint 94, p. 46.
"Winter Afternoon." [PassN] (15:2) Wint 94, p. 47.

LEGUIN, Ursula K.
See Le GUIN, Ursula K.

3532. LEHBERT, Margitt
"Description of the Quadrilateral Lover" (tr. of Katja Wessels). [Chelsea] (56) 94, p. 114.
"The Dying of Bicycles" (tr. of Katja Wessels). [Chelsea] (56) 94, p. 116.
"The Loch Ness Expedition" (tr. of Katja Wesels). [Verse] (11:1) Spr 94, p. 16-17.
"The Meeting of the Meteorologists" (tr. of Katja Wessels). [Chelsea] (56) 94, p. 115.

3533. LEHMAN, David
"The Book of Dreams." [HarvardR] (7) Fall 94, p. 39.
"The Secret Life." [Boulevard] (9:3, #27) Fall 94, p. 41-44.
"Sixth Sense." [NewYorker] (69:48) 31 Ja 94, p. 62.
"Young Death." [ColR] (21:1) Spr 94, p. 168-171.

3534. LEHTO, Leevi
"Quite Another Eternity" (Selections: 1-6, 68-70, tr. by C. B. Hall). [Talisman] (12) Spr 94, p. 198-199.

3535. LEI, Tyana
"Contrivances." [NowestR] (32:1) 94, p. 59.

3536. LEI-LANILAU, Carolyn
"Kolohe or Communication." [Manoa] (6:2) Wint 94, p. 142-145.
"Leilani's Mele" (for Lokelani). [Manoa] (6:2) Wint 94, p. 146-147.

3537. LEIBLEIN, Adelle
"Uncle Harry" (The Nimrod / Hardman Wards: Honorable Mention). [Nimrod] (38:1) Fall-Wint 94, p. 39-40.

3538. LEIGH, Simon
"Christiane." [AntigR] (96) Wint 94, p. 71-73.
"Life After Life." [AntigR] (96) Wint 94, p. 73.

3539. LEIPER, Esther M.
"Confessions of a Junkie." [Amelia] (7:3, #22) 94, p. 121.
"The Heirloom Coverlet." [Amelia] (7:3, #22) 94, p. 58-59.

3540. LELAND, Blake
"Gift." [Comm] (121:3) 11 F 94, p. 14.

3541. LELAND, Kurt
"At the Home for Retired Piano Teachers." [BelPoJ] (44:4) Sum 94, p. 30-31.

3542. LELOS, Cynthia
"Going." [Kalliope] (16:1) 94, p. 41.

3543. LEM, Carol
"Ars Poetica." [IllinoisR] (2:1) Fall 94, p. 28.
"History." [IllinoisR] (2:1) Fall 94, p. 29-31.

3544. LeMASTER, J. R.
"Modern Love." [XavierR] (14:2) Fall 94, p. 55.
"The Nightingales Are Dead." [XavierR] (14:2) Fall 94, p. 56.

3545. LeMAY, Gabrielle
"Lullaby." [Confr] (52/53) Wint-Spr 94, p. 316.
"Sister Clara." [Confr] (52/53) Wint-Spr 94, p. 314.
"Small and Ugly." [Confr] (52/53) Wint-Spr 94, p. 315.

3546. LEMMON, Amy
"Kindred" (ELF 1994 Poetry Competition: The Ruth Cable Memorial Prize). [Elf] (4:2) Sum 94, p. 21.
"Propitiation." [BellR] (17:1/2) Spr-Fall 94, p. 51.
3547. LENGEL, Gena
"His Hand." [Blueline] (15) 94, p. 9-10.
3548. LENIER, Sue
"Donkeys." [NewRep] (211:11) 12 S 94, p. 40.
3549. LENTINI, Rosa
"Ahora que la noche me susurra que ella y el agua son una misma ausencia." [Inti] (39) Primavera 94, p. 259.
"Durante toda la noche han goteado flores." [Inti] (39) Primavera 94, p. 259-260.
"Existe una vasta tierra de árboles cubierta por las aguas." [Inti] (39) Primavera 94, p. 260-261.
"Habla de la noche vigía, de la noche de ojos envolventes." [Inti] (39) Primavera 94, p. 261.
"La luna tiembla en un mar en calma." [Inti] (39) Primavera 94, p. 260.
3550. LEON, Juan
"Sea's Path" (tr. of Minerva Salado). [MichQR] (33:4) Fall 94, p. 804.
3551. LEON, Peter
"Songs for the Unmapped Highways: Junk Girl Sleeps in the Rapid Tunnels of the New York Subway System." [HiramPoR] (55/56) Fall 93-Sum 94, p. 63-64.
3552. LEONG, Liew Geok
"Hawker Centre: Dramatis Personae." [MalR] (107) Sum 94, p. 78-79.
3553. LEONHARDT, Kenneth
"Advances to Antses." [Light] (10) Sum 94, p. 21.
"Back to Basie's." [Light] (9) Spr 94, p. 16.
"Fair Warning." [Light] (11) Aut 94, p. 22.
"Heir Apparent." [Light] (12) Wint 94-95, p. 13.
"Just Wandering." [Light] (9) Spr 94, p. 17.
"Let No Man Wrong My Epitaph." [DogRR] (26) Wint 94-95, p. 23.
"Mu-Tin-Ear." [Light] (9) Spr 94, p. 10.
"Old Ed Young." [SmPd] (31:3, #92) Fall 94, p. 31.
"The Passing Passion of Samuel Pepys." [Light] (9) Spr 94, p. 11.
"The Perfect Poem" (with response from John J. Brugaletta). [SoCoast] (17) Je 94, p. 26-27.
"Russian Roulette & the Lost Soul." [Light] (10) Sum 94, p. 24.
"Since I Meticulous, I Feel Ridiculous." [Light] (11) Aut 94, p. 9.
3554. LEOPARDI, Giacomo
"The Infinite" (tr. by John Frederick Nims). [AmerS] (63:3) Sum 94, p. 448.
3555. LEOPOLD, Nikia
"Centerpiece." [PoetL] (89:2) Sum 94, p. 55.
"Snow into Evening." [Poetry] (165:3) D 94, p. 129.
3556. LERNER, Linda
"What's All This Jazz?" [Vis] (44) 94, p. 14.
3557. LesCARBEAU, Mitchell
"Coyote Howling" (Temecula, California). [GrahamHR] (18) Wint 94-95, p. 78.
"Dead Man's Float." [PoetL] (89:2) Sum 94, p. 37.
"The Persistence of Polytheism." [PoetL] (89:2) Sum 94, p. 38-39.
LESLIE, Molara Ogundipe
See OGUNDIPE-LESLIE, Molara
3558. LESLIE, Naton
"Drought at the Kinzua." [WestB] (34) 94, p. 64-65.
"A Myth of Hands." [CimR] (108) Jl 94, p. 86-89.
"A Question of the Morning." [WestB] (34) 94, p. 65-66.
3559. LESSEN, Laurie Suzanne
"Shoulders and Skin." [SouthernPR] (34:1) Sum 94, p. 11-12.
3560. LESSER, Rika
"Epilogue: *Dödsdansen*." [ParisR] (36:133) Wint 94, p. 281-283.
3561. LESTER, J. C.
"Requiem for a Word." [SingHM] (21) 94, p. 61-62.
3562. LESTER-MASSMAN, G. (Gordon)
"135. Afterward he wondered about the enormous and complex connectedness." [HarvardR] (6) Spr 94, p. 50-51.

3563. LETKEMANN, Susan Rempel
"I Don't Know How Much There Is Left of My Mother" (Grain Contest Winners, Prose Poem: Honourable Mention). [Grain] (21:4) Spr 94, p. 24.
3564. LEUNG, Man Chui
"Ive Heard This Song Before." [WestCL] (28:1/2, #13/14) Spr-Fall 94, p. 114-116.
3565. LEUNG, Ping-kwan
"Distinguished Leaves" (tr. by Gordon T. Osing). [Talisman] (12) Spr 94, p. 173.
"The Leaf on the Edge" (tr. by Gordon T. Osing). [Talisman] (12) Spr 94, p. 173.
"Morning in a Foreign Land" (tr. by Gordon T. Osing and the author). [PoetryC] (14:3) My 94, p. 22.
"Streetlamp and Tin Leaf" (tr. by Gordon T. Osing). [Talisman] (12) Spr 94, p. 174.
LEV, Dina Ben
See BEN-LEV, Dina
3566. LEVCHEV, Vladimir
"Four Seekers of the Great Metaphor" (tr. by Lisa Sapinkopf and Georgi Belev). [PartR] (61:2) Spr 94, p. 319-320.
3567. LEVERTOV, Denise
"Dom Helder Camara at the Nuclear Test Site." [Image] (4) Fall 93, p. 37.
"For Those Whom the Gods Love Less." [AmerPoR] (23:3) My-Je 94, p. 21.
"For Those Whom the Gods Love Less." [GettyR] (7:2) Spr 94, p. 280.
"The Glittering Noise." [AmerPoR] (23:3) My-Je 94, p. 22.
"The Great Black Heron." [AmerPoR] (23:3) My-Je 94, p. 21.
"The Hymn." [AmerPoR] (23:3) My-Je 94, p. 22.
"What goes Unsaid." [AmerPoR] (23:3) My-Je 94, p. 21.
"Wondering." [Image] (4) Fall 93, p. 38.
3568. LEVI, Steven C.
"Chinese Squares." [Amelia] (7:3, #22) 94, p. 59.
"Monica was a bastard." [Pearl] (20) Spr 94, p. 62.
3569. LEVI, Tikva
"The Extent of the Tragedy" (tr. by Ammiel Alcalay). [LitR] (37:2) Wint 94, p. 346.
"Poor Bertolt Brecht Came from the Black Forest" (tr. by Ammiel Alcalay). [LitR] (37:2) Wint 94, p. 346.
"Purim Sequence" (tr. by Ammiel Alcalay). [LitR] (37:2) Wint 94, p. 347-355.
"To the Life of Plants on the Road" (tr. by Ammiel Alcalay). [LitR] (37:2) Wint 94, p. 345.
3570. LEVI, Toni Mergentime
"Lovesong" (for Paul). [HiramPoR] (55/56) Fall 93-Sum 94, p. 66-67.
"Undertow." [CapeR] (29:1) Spr 94, p. 39.
"Where It Happens." [HiramPoR] (55/56) Fall 93-Sum 94, p. 65.
3571. LEVIN, Dana
"The Speakers Are the Souls of Babies." [Colum] ("The Lost Issues", [i.e. 18-19]) 93, p. 119.
3572. LEVIN, Harriet
"What Stopped Her." [WestB] (35) 94, p. 83.
3573. LEVIN, Lynn E.
"Crazy Quilt." [Northeast] (5:11) Wint 94-95, p. 19.
3574. LEVIN, Phillis
"The Landing." [DenQ] (29:1) Sum 94, p. 22-23.
"The Third Day." [Atlantic] (273:2) F 94, p. 81.
"The White Line." [Nat] (259:16) N 14 94, p. 592.
3575. LEVINE, David
"It Would Have Been Enough." [NewYorkQ] (53) 94, p. 71-72.
3576. LEVINE, Elise
"Mercy Weather." [AntigR] (97) Spr 94, p. 136-137.
LEVINE, Judy Katz
See KATZ-LEVINE, Judy
3577. LEVINE, Julia
"Abduction under the Hubble Telescope." [Nimrod] (38:1) Fall-Wint 94, p. 2.
"Angels." [Nimrod] (38:1) Fall-Wint 94, p. 7.
"Fontanelle." [Nimrod] (38:1) Fall-Wint 94, p. 3-4.
"Sabbath in the Night of the Meteor Showers." [Nimrod] (38:1) Fall-Wint 94, p. 5.
"Thanksgiving in the Capay Valley." [Nimrod] (38:1) Fall-Wint 94, p. 6.
"Touching Wild Animals" (from "Practicing for Heaven." The Pablo Neruda Prize for Poetry: First Prize). [Nimrod] (38:1) Fall-Wint 94, p. 1.
3578. LEVINE, Mark
"Being Late." [CutB] (41) Wint 94, p. 38-39.

"Faces." [CutB] (41) Wint 94, p. 40-41.
"The Fish." [IndR] (17:1) Spr 94, p. 180-181.
"No Introduction Needed." [IndR] (17:1) Spr 94, p. 184.
"Song." [IndR] (17:1) Spr 94, p. 182-183.
"Spring." [Ploughs] (20:1) Spr 94, p. 168-169.
"Tribe." [Ploughs] (20:1) Spr 94, p. 166-167.
"Trilogy." [Epoch] (43:3) 94, p. 302-303.

3579. LEVINE, Philip
"Alba." [WestHR] (48:1) Spr 94, p. 6.
"Ask for Nothing." [Boulevard] (9:1/2, #25/26) Spr 94, p. 41.
"Dust and Memory." [NewYorker] (70:33) 17 O 94, p. 82.
"Edward Leiberman, Entrepreneur, Four Years After the Burnings on Okinawa." [ParisR] (36:131) Sum 94, p. 86-87.
"Holy Son and Mother of the Projects." [IndR] (17:1) Spr 94, p. 54.
"In a Village Near Paris." [ParisR] (36:131) Sum 94, p. 87-88.
"The Letters." [Boulevard] (9:1/2, #25/26) Spr 94, p. 42-43.
"Magpiety." [Atlantic] (274:5) N 94, p. 110-111.
"My Family under Caesar." [IndR] (17:1) Spr 94, p. 55.
"My Given Name." [Field] (50) Spr 94, p. 44.
"Nothing Means Nothing." [ColR] (21:1) Spr 94, p. 78-80.
"One Day." [Poetry] (164:1) Ap 94, p. 17-19.
"Photography." [Poetry] (164:1) Ap 94, p. 15-16.
"The Poem of Chalk." [Thrpny] (58) Sum 94, p. 8.
"Tristan." [Poetry] (164:1) Ap 94, p. 20-21.
"Trust." [Field] (50) Spr 94, p. 42-43.

3580. LEVINE, Suzanne Jill
"The Hour of the Wolf." [LindLM] (13:1) Mr 94, p. 23.
"To Sin, Divine." [LindLM] (13:1) Mr 94, p. 23.
"Traveling South." [LindLM] (13:1) Mr 94, p. 23.

3581. LEVINSON, David
"The Fix." [JamesWR] (11:2) Wint 94, p. 7.
"He." [JamesWR] (11:2) Wint 94, p. 15.

3582. LEVINSON, James Heller
"Steps." [DogRR] (13:1, #25) Spr-Sum 94, p. 8.
"Stump." [SpoonR] (19:1) Wint-Spr 94, p. 66-67.
"You Dreamed You Asked Your Brother Not to Eat the Tacos in My Livingroom." [SpoonR] (19:1) Wint-Spr 94, p. 68-70.

3583. LEVINSON, Zev
"Shel Zahav." [InterQ] (1:3) 94, p. 163.

3584. LEVIS, Larry
"After the Funeral" (tr. of Hajime Kijima, w. the author). [InterQ] (1:2) 93, p. 69.
"Elegy with a Thimbleful of Water in the Cage." [SouthernR] (30:2) Ap, Spr 94, p. 298-305.
"Elegy with the Sprawl of a Wave Inside It." [Field] (50) Spr 94, p. 7-10.
"Ocean Park No. 17, 1968: Homage to Diebenkorn." [ColR] (21:1) Spr 94, p. 145-149.

3585. LEVITIN, Alexis
"17. I find my friends with ease" (From *Solar Matter*, 1955, tr. of Eugenio de Andrade). [NewRena] (9:1, #27) 94, p. 113.
"34. Here I listen to the work of autumn" (From *Solar Matter*, 1995, tr. of Eugenio de Andrade). [NewRena] (9:1, #27) 94, p. 115.
"35. It doesn't startle me if an arm of the river" (From *Solar Matter*, 1995, tr. of Eugenio de Andrade). [NewRena] (9:1, #27) 94, p. 117.
"#47" (from *White Space*, tr. of Fiama Hasse Pais Brandão). [MassR] (35:1) Spr 94, p. 105.
"#49" (from *White Space*, tr. of Fiama Hasse Pais Brandão). [MassR] (35:1) Spr 94, p. 106.
"Adagio" (tr. of Eugenio de Andrade). [Os] (39) Fall-Wint 94, p. 23.
"Adagio Quasi Andante" (tr. of Eugenio de Andrade). [JamesWR] (11:4) Sum 94, p. 4.
"Almost Nothing" (tr. of Eugenio de Andrade). [Os] (39) Fall-Wint 94, p. 19.
"Between March and April" (tr. of Eugenio de Andrade). [ApalQ] (40/41) 94, p. 76-77.
"By Chance" (tr. of Eugenio de Andrade). [Os] (38) Spr 94, p. 19.
"Dedikation" (Selections from the poem-cycle: #4, #8, tr. of Egito Goncalves). [ArtfulD] (26/27) 94, p. 50-51.

"Dedikation" (Selection: #9, tr. of Egito Goncalves). [ConnPR] (13:1) 94, p. 26.
"Dunes" (tr. of Eugenio de Andrade). [HarvardR] (6) Spr 94, p. 172.
"From Summer's Side" (tr. of Eugenio de Andrade). [CrabCR] (8:2/3/9:1/2/3) 94, p. 73.
"Graphic 2" (tr. of Fiama Hasse Pais Brandao). [Vis] (46) 94, p. 20.
"In Memoriam" (tr. of Eugenio de Andrade). [Os] (39) Fall-Wint 94, p. 21.
"In My Favor" (tr. of Alexandre O'Neill). [Os] (39) Fall-Wint 94, p. 5.
"Last Poem" (tr. of Eugenio de Andrade). [WebR] (18) Fall 94, p. 26.
"Lines of Winter" (tr. of Eugenio de Andrade). [WebR] (18) Fall 94, p. 25.
"Nocturne" (tr. of Eugenio de Andrade). [Os] (39) Fall-Wint 94, p. 23.
"On Ground Now Bright Dances Air" (From *Shadow's Weight*, tr. of Eugenio de Andrade). [NewRena] (9:1, #27) 94, p. 121.
"Passeio Allegre" (tr. of Eugenio de Andrade). [WebR] (18) Fall 94, p. 25.
"Passion" (tr. of Eugenio de Andrade). [Os] (38) Spr 94, p. 21.
"Provisional Title" (tr. of Eugenio de Andrade). [PoetL] (89:3) Fall 94, p. 17-18.
"Solar Matter 38" (tr. of Eugenio de Andrade). [MidAR] (14:2) 94, p. 65.
"Those Bodies" (tr. of Eugenio de Andrade). [Sun] (223) Jl 94, p. 27.
"The Visit" (tr. of Eugenio de Andrade). [Os] (38) Spr 94, p. 19.
"With the Rushes" (From *Another Name for Earth*, tr. of Eugenio de Andrade). [NewRena] (9:1, #27) 94, p. 119.

3586. LEVY, Howard
"The Kabbalist's Pencil." [AmerLC] (6) 94, p. 39-40.
"Matisse in the Rotogravure: The Cutouts." [ParisR] (36:130) Spr 94, p. 109.
"To Aleksander Wat." [ParisR] (36:130) Spr 94, p. 108.

3587. LEVY, Primo
"For Adolf Eichmann" (tr. by Ruth Feldman and Brian Swann). [NewEngR] (16:2) Spr 94, p. 149.

3588. LEVY, Robert J.
"Mount Fuji and Flowers" (After David Hockney). [PraS] (68:2) Sum 94, p. 66.

3589. LEWIS, Diane Quintrall
"Corner Boy." [Border] (5) Fall-Wint 94, p. 30.

3590. LEWIS, Graham
"Baby." [NewL] (60:3) 94, p. 44-45.
"The Barker's Eulogy for the Human Wart." [NewL] (60:3) 94, p. 43.
"Lester's Tales." [WilliamMR] (32) 94, p. 20-21.

3591. LEWIS, Gwyneth
"A Fanciful Marriage." [Verse] (11:1) Spr 94, p. 98-100.

3592. LEWIS, J. Patrick
"Among the literati of the Thames." [Light] (11) Aut 94, p. 24.
"And God Made the Animals." [Light] (12) Wint 94-95, p. 22.
"Bride & Groom." [Light] (11) Aut 94, p. 22.
"A Street Light in July." [Light] (9) Spr 94, p. 20.

3593. LEWIS, Joel
"End Time Bagels." [HangL] (64) 94, p. 49.
"In Paterson — 4." [NewAW] (12) Spr-Sum 94, p. 126.
"In Paterson." [NewAW] (12) Spr-Sum 94, p. 125.
"Wallington (North Jersey Elegy)." [HangL] (64) 94, p. 50.

3594. LEWIS, Katherine
"I Am Not Gaia, she Says." [BellArk] (10:2) Mr-Ap 94, p. 10.
"I Find a Melody Horse Roaming on a Modern Meadow." [BellArk] (10:2) Mr-Ap 94, p. 10.
"I Write on the Sky. I Write on the Sea." [BellArk] (10:2) Mr-Ap 94, p. 10.
"On the Old Plain, Men and Women." [BellArk] (10:2) Mr-Ap 94, p. 10.
"Water and Rock." [BellArk] (10:2) Mr-Ap 94, p. 10.
"We See." [BellArk] (10:2) Mr-Ap 94, p. 10.

3595. LEWIS, Lisa
"Bridget." [AmerPoR] (23:5) S-O 94, p. 17.
"February." [AmerPoR] (23:5) S-O 94, p. 16.
"Goodbye, Moon." [PassN] (15:1) Sum 94, p. 45-47.
"The Heartland." [AmerPoR] (23:5) S-O 94, p. 17.
"Responsibility." [AmerPoR] (23:5) S-O 94, p. 18.

3596. LEWIS, Mark
"Burning the New Suburb." [Border] (5) Fall-Wint 94, p. 31-32.
"Meeting the Scarecrows." [LaurelR] (28:2) Sum 94, p. 35.
"When Blackbirds Eye." [Border] (5) Fall-Wint 94, p. 33.

3597. LEWIS, Melvin E.
"Waves." [Obs] (9:1) Spr-Sum 94, p. 96.
3598. LEWIS, Peggy Hapke
"Dowager's Hump." [HolCrit] (31:1) F 94, p. 15.
3599. LEY, Donald
"The Courier." [Pivot] (41) 93, p. 2.
3600. LI, Ch'ing-Chao
"To the Tune 'The Washing Stream'" (tr. by Sam Hamill). [CrabCR] (8:2/3/9:1/2/3) 94, p. 50.
3601. LI, Guohua
"When the People Arose from Cheese" (tr. of Duo Duo, w. Donald Finkel). [AnotherCM] (27) 94, p. 216-217.
3602. LI, He
"The Joys of Youth" (tr. by Jodi Varon). [Colum] (21) Fall 93, p. 82.
"A Song from Memory" (tr. by Jodi Varon). [Colum] (21) Fall 93, p. 81.
"Written Under Mt. Hua" (To the Tune: Throwing Off My Sadness, tr. by Jodi Varon). [Colum] (21) Fall 93, p. 79-80.
3603. LI, Mingxia
"Confession" (tr. of Zhai Yongming, w. Leonard Schwartz). [Talisman] (12) Spr 94, p. 163.
"Premonition" (tr. of Zhai Yongming, w. Leonard Schwartz). [Talisman] (12) Spr 94, p. 162.
"River Tale" (tr. of Chin Sung, w. Leonard Schwartz). [Talisman] (12) Spr 94, p. 177-178.
3604. LI, Peter C. T.
"Tai Chi Masters of Dim Sum Checks." [BambooR] (63/64) Sum-Fall 94, p. 29.
3605. LI, Po
"I Make My Home in the Mountains" (tr. by Sam Hamill). [NewEngR] (16:3) Sum 94, p. 31.
3606. LI, Po (c. 699-762)
"Drinking Alone Beneath the Moon" (tr. by David Lunde). [ChamLR] (14/15) Spr-Fall 94, p. 205.
"The River Merchant's Wife: A Litter" (tr. by Ezra Pound). [NewYorkQ] (53) 94, p. 8.
"Seeing Meng Hau-ran Off from Yellow Crane Tower" (tr. by David Lunde). [SpoonR] (19:1) Wint-Spr 94, p. 58.
3607. LI, Yan
"The Song of AIDS" (tr. by Denis Mair). [Talisman] (12) Spr 94, p. 176.
LIAN, Yang
See YANG, Lian
3608. LIARDET, Tim
"Do Poor Tom Some Charity." [MalR] (107) Sum 94, p. 178-179.
"In the Natural History Museum." [ChatR] (14:3) Spr 94, p. 29-30.
3609. LIATSOS, Sandra
"That Old Sombrero." [CrabCR] (8:2/3/9:1/2/3) 94, p. 74.
3610. LIBBY, Anthony
"Shunga *Warriors*." [SouthernR] (30:3) Sum 94, p. 545.
3611. LIBERTHSON, Daniel
"Suicide." [SoCoast] (17) Je 94, p. 13.
3612. LIEBERMAN, Laurence
"By the Light of One Star." [SouthernR] (30:2) Ap, Spr 94, p. 306-311.
"Carib's Leap." [NewEngR] (16:3) Sum 94, p. 137-140.
"Compass of the Dying." [Boulevard] (9:3, #27) Fall 94, p. 120-123.
"Cudjoe's Head." [AmerPoR] (23:1) Ja-F 94, p. 40.
"The Factories of Bay Leaf and Lime." [CimR] (106) Ja 94, p. 71-81.
"In Fear of the Music Scholar." [DenQ] (28:4) Spr 94, p. 33-35.
"Limey." [Journal] (18:2) Fall-Wint 94, p. 58-60.
"The Morning Star, Extinguished" (Trinidad, Summer '90). [CharR] (20:1) Spr 94, p. 56-59.
3613. LIEBERMAN, Michael
"At Autopsy." [TexasR] (15:1/2) Spr-Sum 94, p. 91.
"Prediction." [MidwQ] (36:1) Aut 94, p. 64.
"Without Allusion." [Border] (3) Fall 93, p. 38.
3614. LIEPERT, Susan
"Sunk." [Grain] (22:1) Sum 94, p. 117.

3615. LIETZ, Robert
"Flag Day." [IllinoisR] (1:2) Spr 94, p. 13-14.
"Fog Delay" (The Atlantic Coast remembered in Ohio). [CapeR] (29:1) Spr 94, p. 48-49.
"Stopping Off." [Border] (3) Fall 93, p. 39-40.
"Synagogue." [IllinoisR] (1:2) Spr 94, p. 19-21.

LIFSHIN, Lin
See LIFSHIN, Lyn

3616. LIFSHIN, Lyn
"African Violet Madonna." [WormR] (34:3, #135) 94, p. 92.
"After Gliding Back." [Rosebud] (1:2) Sum 94, p. 66.
"Afterward." [CrabCR] (8:2/3/9:1/2/3) 94, p. 91.
"Afterward." [HolCrit] (31:1) F 94, p. 17.
"Afterward." [MinnR] (41/42) Fall 93-Spr 94 (published Mr 95), p. 39.
"Afterward." [ShadowP] (4) 94, p. 35-36.
"Afterward" (2 poems). [Plain] (15:1) Fall 94, p. 19.
"All Afternoon We." [DogRR] (13:1, #25) Spr-Sum 94, p. 40.
"Amid Rotting Corpses." [BlackBR] (19) Fall-Wint 94, p. 12-13.
"Armenia." [BlackBR] (19) Fall-Wint 94, p. 15.
"As Bread Is Being Distributed." [NewYorkQ] (53) 94, p. 47.
"The Band of Dark Stings Like a Birthmark." [Parting] (7:1) Sum 94, p. 12.
"Black Ice" (2 poems). [Plain] (14:2) Wint 94, p. 28.
"Blue Tattoo." [ChamLR] (14/15) Spr-Fall 94, p. 67.
"Canopy Plant Madonna." [WormR] (34:3, #135) 94, p. 92.
"The Child We Will Not Have." [FourQ] (8:2) Fall 94, p. 25.
"The Daughter I Don't Have." [Kalliope] (16:3) 94, p. 49.
"Dream of Ivy." [LitR] (37:4) Sum 94, p. 665.
"The Erotic Mirror." [Ledge] (17) Wint 94, p. 62-63.
"First Day Out, First Warm Day." [Confr] (52/53) Wint-Spr 94, p. 326-327.
"First Thanksgiving." [HiramPoR] (55/56) Fall 93-Sum 94, p. 71-72.
"Found at the Vietnam Wall" (2 poems). [BlackBR] (19) Fall-Wint 94, p. 13-14.
"Getting My Mother Ice." [Confr] (52/53) Wint-Spr 94, p. 328.
"Going Shopping with My Mother." [ShadowP] (4) 94, p. 34-35.
"Hair." [CreamCR] (18:1) Spr 94, p. 46-47.
"Heat Wave, Middlebury." [ColEng] (56:6) O 94, p. 680-681.
"Help Us Or We Will All Die." [Plain] (14:3) Spr 94, p. 23.
"Hybrid Iris Madonna." [WormR] (34:3, #135) 94, p. 92.
"Hysteria." [BlackBR] (18) Wint-Spr 94, p. 22.
"I Take My Mother on a Stroll in DC." [Wind] (74) 94, p. 23.
"If in These Last Months." [ShadowP] (4) 94, p. 38-40.
"In That City." [DogRR] (26) Wint 94-95, p. 34.
"Indian Summer." [MidwQ] (35:3) Spr 94, p. 311.
"Iris Madonna." [WormR] (34:3, #135) 94, p. 92.
"It Was Like." [BlackBR] (18) Wint-Spr 94, p. 22-23.
"Jesse's Boy" (with the blessing of Jesse and Ollie). [NewYorkQ] (53) 94, p. 48-49.
"Lake Champlain." [Blueline] (15) 94, p. 39-40.
"The Last Words of Commander James T. 'Kinky' Kirk's Madonna." [Amelia] (7:4, #23) 94, p. 82.
"Last Year, Raking Leaves to Exhaustion." [RagMag] (12:1) Sum 94, p. 93.
"Like an Amulet of Blood." [Parting] (7:1) Sum 94, p. 12.
"The Mad Girl Feels the Latest Onslaught of Violence." [BlackBR] (18) Wint-Spr 94, p. 15-16.
"The Mad Girl Wonders About Donating Her Organs." [CrabCR] (8:2/3/9:1/2/3) 94, p. 91.
"Man Travelling into Birds." [BlackBR] (18) Wint-Spr 94, p. 14-15.
"May 21, 1911" (2 poems). [Wind] (73) 94, p. 15-16.
"Mint Leaves at Yaddo." [FourQ] (8:2) Fall 94, p. 26.
"Mint Leaves at Yaddo." [ShadowP] (4) 94, p. 30-31.
"Mother and Daughter Photos." [WilliamMR] (32) 94, p. 87.
"My Father Leaves Vilnius." [HolCrit] (31:5) D 94, p. 18-19.
"My Mother and I Tangle." [ShadowP] (4) 94, p. 40.
"My Mother Dozes in the Room with TV on Too Long, All Windows Closed." [ShadowP] (4) 94, p. 33-34.
"My Mother Is Too Sick for Her Gifts." [SlipS] (14) 94, p. 109-110.
"My Sister Says But Doesn't *Everyone* Waste Their Life?" [Ledge] (17) Wint 94, p. 60-61.

"New Orleans Madonna." [NegC] (13:2/3) 93, p. 245.
"Now, Going into the Orange Room." [ShadowP] (4) 94, p. 36.
"On a Night So Cottonwood So Chino Valley." [Border] (5) Fall-Wint 94, p. 34.
"On the Night They Dance on the Berlin Wall, Swill Champagne." [DogRR] (13:1, #25) Spr-Sum 94, p. 10-11.
"On the Way to the Gas, One Woman." [Calyx] (15:3) Wint 94-95, p. 35.
"Panic." [ShadowP] (4) 94, p. 36-37.
"Panic's." [ShadowP] (4) 94, p. 37-38.
"Parade" (A Wormwood Chapbook). [WormR] (34:2, #134) 94, p. 50-88.
"The Pearls." [HiramPoR] (55/56) Fall 93-Sum 94, p. 73.
"Photographs of Mothers and Daughters." [PaintedB] (53/54) 94, p. 36.
"The President's Arms Are Like Oak Branches." [Sun] (220) Ap 94, p. 36.
"The President's Arms Are Like Oak Branches." [ChiR] (40:2/3) 94, p. 111-112.
"The President's Hair." [AnotherCM] (27) 94, p. 139.
"The President's Thighs." [AnotherCM] (27) 94, p. 137.
"The President's Thighs Hide Out in the Rose Garden." [AnotherCM] (27) 94, p. 138.
"Putting Mother to Bed." [ShadowP] (4) 94, p. 32-33.
"Sarajevo." [BlackBR] (18) Wint-Spr 94, p. 26.
"Sarajevo." [BlackBR] (19) Fall-Wint 94, p. 12.
"Sarajevo" (3 poems). [Plain] (14:3) Spr 94, p. 22-23.
"So Many Bodies All Over." [Calyx] (15:3) Wint 94-95, p. 36-37.
"Sometimes It Seems Like Before." [ShadowP] (4) 94, p. 28-30.
"Sperm Bank Madonna's Slogan." [Amelia] (7:4, #23) 94, p. 52.
"That January We Pretended Things Were Normal." [HiramPoR] (55/56) Fall 93-Sum 94, p. 68-70.
"Thaw." [MidwQ] (35:2) Wint 94, p. 179.
"Those Nights." [Farm] (11:2) Fall-Wint 94-95, p. 100.
"Vietnam in the History Text Books." [NewYorkQ] (53) 94, p. 46.
"We Drive Two Hours Up the Roller Coaster." [Amelia] (7:3, #22) 94, p. 104-105.
"When I Saw Effie's Mother." [PaintedB] (53/54) 94, p. 34-35.
"Who Held the Camera So Steadily and Why" (photographs at the Holocaust Museum). [SlipS] (14) 94, p. 109.
"Wild Horses Dying." [MidwQ] (35:4) Sum 94, p. 410.
"Wisteria Madonna." [WormR] (34:3, #135) 94, p. 92.
"You Take for Granted." [ChamLR] (14/15) Spr-Fall 94, p. 65-66.
"A Young Girl's Diary, Lodsz Ghetto." [ChamLR] (14/15) Spr-Fall 94, p. 62.
"Young Girl's Diary, Wednesday March 11, 1942, Lodsz." [ChamLR] (14/15) Spr-Fall 94, p. 63-64.
"Your Words." [CreamCR] (18:1) Spr 94, p. 45.

3617. LIGNELL, Kathleen
"The Art of Self Defense." [Border] (3) Fall 93, p. 41.
"Northern Lights." [Gaia] (4) Je 94, p. 17.
"Wooden Fish." [CimR] (109) O 94, p. 59-60.

3618. LIHN, Enrique
"Diario de Muerte" (Selections: 18, 33, 45, tr. by Alastair Reid). [AmerPoR] (23:4) Jl-Ag 94, p. 38.

3619. LILLY, Rebecca
"August thunderstorm." [Amelia] (7:3, #22) 94, p. 19.
"The Diary." [Iowa] (24:3) Fall 94, p. 74.
"The Fortuneteller's Parlor." [Iowa] (24:3) Fall 94, p. 74.
"Leaf." [Stand] (36:1) Wint 94-95, p. 19.
"My heartbeat." [Amelia] (7:3, #22) 94, p. 19.
"Stone and Ash." [NoDaQ] (62:3) Sum 94-95, p. 120.

3620. LIM-WILSON, Fatima
"Amok." [SantaBR] (2:2) Fall-Wint 94, p. 60.
"Broken English" (for Manuel Fragante, dismissed from his government post because of his "heavy Filipino accent"). [Field] (50) Spr 94, p. 90.
"Cape Hatteras." [Field] (50) Spr 94, p. 88.
"Crossing Dreams" (for Agnes). [SantaBR] (2:2) Fall-Wint 94, p. 63.
"Raising the Dead." [Poetry] (164:6) S 94, p. 327.
"Raising the Dead." [SantaBR] (2:2) Fall-Wint 94, p. 62.
"The Rotten Fruit Series" (for the glass flower makers, Leopold and Rudolf Blaschka). [SantaBR] (2:2) Fall-Wint 94, p. 61.
"Things to Do in the Dark." [SantaBR] (2:2) Fall-Wint 94, p. 64.
"The Wave." [Field] (50) Spr 94, p. 89.

3621. LIMA, Robert
"Cay Birth." [CaribbeanW] (8) 94, p. 54.
3622. LIMEHOUSE, Capers
"The Farm" (Summer, 1956). [Poem] (72) N 94, p. 14-15.
"The Field" (For Walter). [Poem] (72) N 94, p. 16.
"Rain." [Poem] (72) N 94, p. 13.
LIN, Song
See SONG, Lin
3623. LIN, Tan
"Spent Cartridge + Dying Flame + Hieroglyph (Conceptual Trap to Conceptual Trap)." [Talisman] (12) Spr 94, p. 248-249.
3624. LINCOLN, Rachel
"Small Sacrifices." [AmerV] (34) 94, p. 129-130.
3625. LINDBERG, Loretta
"It Could Happen." [CrabCR] (8:2/3/9:1/2/3) 94, p. 121-123.
"Not Enough." [CrabCR] (8:2/3/9:1/2/3) 94, p. 120-121.
3626. LINDBERG, Peggy
"Stonehenge and the Dance." [Plain] (14:3) Spr 94, p. 17.
3627. LINDEMAN, Jack
"As If." [BellArk] (10:1) Ja-F 94, p. 24.
"Ode to Joy." [BellArk] (10:1) Ja-F 94, p. 24.
3628. LINDGREN, Joan
"Somewhere Else" (tr. of Juan Gelman). [InterQ] (1:4) 94, p. 50-51.
3629. LINDHOLDT, Paul
"Another Wild." [ChiR] (40:1) 94, p. 26-27.
"Cotton Mather." [ChiR] (40:1) 94, p. 31.
"Here and Now." [ChiR] (40:1) 94, p. 30.
"Magistrate." [SouthernHR] (28:3) Sum 94, p. 278-279.
"Rebecca Glover." [ChiR] (40:1) 94, p. 28-29.
3630. LINDNER, April
"Peep Show." [GreensboroR] (56) Sum 94, p. 49-50.
3631. LINDNER, Carl
"Outside Activities." [Poetry] (163:4) Ja 94, p. 214.
"Snake." [CreamCR] (18:1) Spr 94, p. 69.
3632. LINDOW, Sandra
"Of Wood and Will." [Kaleid] (Special Issue) 94, p. 7.
3633. LINDSAY, David
"My Grandmother." [AntigR] (97) Spr 94, p. 138.
3634. LINDSAY, Sarah
"Superman in Sunglasses." [CreamCR] (18:2) Fall 94, p. 134.
3635. LINEBARGER, Jim
"Chorus Line, 1952." [WormR] (34:4, #136) 94, p. 152.
"Failure to Communicate." [WormR] (34:4, #136) 94, p. 153.
3636. LINEBERGER, James
"Flowers Light the Sun." [CoalC] (8) Ap 94, p. 34.
"Judgment Call." [CoalC] (8) Ap 94, p. 26-28.
"Lazarus." [CentR] (38:2) Spr 94, p. 331.
"A Night at the Opera." [CentR] (38:2) Spr 94, p. 330.
"What Is It with All These Poets." [CentR] (38:2) Spr 94, p. 329-330.
3637. LINEHAN, Susan
"When You Are Where You Are." [Vis] (46) 94, p. 39.
3638. LINET, Valerie
"Heat." [HangL] (65) 94, p. 96.
"Wanting a Chimpanzee." [HangL] (65) 94, p. 97.
LING, Bei
See BEI, Ling
3639. LING, Gregory
"Arrival, Key Biscayne, FL." [PaintedHR] (11) Spr-Sum 94, p. 48-49.
3640. LINH, Tran Ngoc
"Untitled: The weather is gothic today." [PoetryC] (14:3) My 94, p. 21.
3641. LINSTEAD, Alex
"The Arab Children, Brussels, St. Servai." [JamesWR] (11:4) Sum 94, p. 14.
3642. LIOTTA, P. H.
"After Cavafy" (Fiskardo, Kephalonia). [ProseP] (3) 94, p. 62.
"Colossus." [Pivot] (41) 93, p. 24.
"Corrida de Toros." [Pivot] (42) 94, p. 23.

"Emigrés." [AntR] (52:2) Spr 94, p. 313.
"Everyone Will Write Poetry" (tr. of Branko Miljkovic). [InterQ] (1:3) 94, p. 189.
"Falling Towards Belgrade." [AntR] (52:2) Spr 94, p. 316-317.
"Fruit Tree, After a Rain" (tr. of Dobrisa Cesaric). [InterQ] (1:3) 94, p. 187.
"How It Must End." [AntR] (52:2) Spr 94, p. 318-321.
"Leaving Dubrovnik." [AntR] (52:2) Spr 94, p. 314-315.
"Melville's Room." [Pivot] (41) 93, p. 23.
"Mythologies" (Pella, Makedonia). [ProseP] (3) 94, p. 61.
"A Nation of Poets." [InterQ] (1:3) 94, p. 185-186.
"The Politics of Blood." [Pivot] (42) 94, p. 22.
"Struga Wedding." [Pivot] (42) 94, p. 23.
"Sun" (tr. of Branko Miljkovic). [InterQ] (1:3) 94, p. 188.

3643. LIPMAN, Joel
"Don't Cut, Don't Cut." [WorldL] (5) 94, p. 43.
"Then they drew the trees." [WorldL] (5) 94, p. 42.

3644. LIPPMAN, Matthew
"Country Has No Lights (for Galeano)." [Colum] ("The Lost Issues", [i.e. 18-19]) 93, p. 151-162.
"Got Got." [BrooklynR] (11) 94, p. 70-71.
"Primavera." [SenR] (24:1) Spr 94, p. 64-65.
"Saints." [Colum] ("The Lost Issues", [i.e. 18-19]) 93, p. 150.

3645. LIPS, Tom
"Act of Contrition." [Descant] (24:4, #83) Wint 93-94, p. 40.
"Priests." [Descant] (24:4, #83) Wint 93-94, p. 38-39.

3646. LIPSITZ, Lou
"Betty Adcock Tells Me There Are 1,086 Meanings of the Word 'Romantic'." [Sun] (228) D 94, p. 29.
"Old Self." [SouthernR] (30:3) Sum 94, p. 547.
"Seeking the Hook." [SouthernR] (30:3) Sum 94, p. 546.
"To S. After Years Apart." [Sun] (228) D 94, p. 28.

3647. LIPTON, Robert
"Cease-Fire." [Jacaranda] (5:1) Wint-Spr 91, p. 112.

3648. LISCHER, Diane
"In Winter, I Burn Poems." [AnthNEW] (6) 94, p. 20.

3649. LISHAN, Stuart
"When Penance Comes: Monkey Boy Talks to the Near-Suicide." [ChiR] (40:2/3) 94, p. 65.
"Why, When Some See Beauty, Some Don't: Monkey Boy and the Fox." [ChiR] (40:2/3) 94, p. 63.
"Withdrawals: Monkey Boy, Wandering the Forest Waiting for the Angels, Tells of His Death Moment." [ChiR] (40:2/3) 94, p. 64.

3650. LISK, Thomas
"The Transcendental Revolt Against Plastic Worms." [Border] (3) Fall 93, p. 42.
"Uncle Tonto Moore." [ApalQ] (42) Fall 94, p. 51.

3651. LISOWSKI, Joseph
"Breaking the Minute." [LitR] (37:4) Sum 94, p. 683.
"Hi Tech in Steel Town." [Amelia] (7:4, #23) 94, p. 149.
"Peasant Homes at Wei River." [ChamLR] (14/15) Spr-Fall 94, p. 206.
"Return to Wang River." [ChamLR] (14/15) Spr-Fall 94, p. 207.
"Waking to Watch You Sleep." [CaribbeanW] (8) 94, p. 43.

3652. LISOWSKI, Krzysztof
"School of Survival" (tr. by Ewa Hryniewicz-Yarbrough). [QW] (39) Sum-Fall 94, p. 148.

3653. LITHERLAND, S. J.
"Your Language." [Stand] (35:2) Spr 94, p. 31.

3654. LITTLE, Geraldine C.
"Viewpoints on Nora: Later." [SenR] (24:2) Fall 94, p. 38-39.

3655. LITWACK, Susan
"Just Kisses." [LaurelR] (28:1) Wint 94, p. 54-55.

3656. LIU, Manliu
"Manfly's Journal" (tr. by David Shapiro and Wang Ping). [Talisman] (12) Spr 94, p. 164-166.

3657. LIU, Timothy
"Cycling." [YellowS] (11:4, #44) Wint 93-94, p. 24.
"Desire As the Gesture Between Us." [YellowS] (11:4, #44) Wint 93-94, p. 24.
"Elegy." [NewEngR] (16:3) Sum 94, p. 88.

"For Those Who Do Not Dream." [YellowS] (11:4, #44) Wint 93-94, p. 24.
"Invocation." [HarvardR] (7) Fall 94, p. 31.
"Men Without." [WestHR] (48:1) Spr 94, p. 7.
"Nothing but the Truth So Help Me God." [ParisR] (36:132) Fall 94, p. 228.
"Reading Whitman in a Toilet Stall." [ParisR] (36:132) Fall 94, p. 227-228.
"Rest Stop, Highway 91." [ParisR] (36:132) Fall 94, p. 229.
"The Size of It." [ParisR] (36:132) Fall 94, p. 226.
"Winter." [QW] (38) Winter-Spr 93-94, p. 133.

LLOSA, Ricardo Pau
See PAU-LLOSA, Ricardo

3658. LLOYD, Margaret
"The Argument." [NewEngR] (16:4) Fall 94, p. 111-112.
"Backwards to Heaven." [PoetryE] (37/38) Spr 94, p. 54.
"Beyond the Maples and Pines." [NewEngR] (16:4) Fall 94, p. 112.
"In the Late Evening." [NewEngR] (16:4) Fall 94, p. 110.
"The Letter." [PoetryE] (37/38) Spr 94, p. 55.
"Turned." [GreenMR] (NS 17:2) Fall-Wint 94-95, p. 86.

3659. LLOYD, Martha
"He Lives in the Swamp, This Braque Bird." [PoetC] (25:3) Spr 94, p. 12.
"Vanilla Bean for the Creme Brulee." [PoetC] (25:3) Spr 94, p. 11.

3660. LOBE, Robert Aaron
"Giselle." [HolCrit] (31:5) D 94, p. 19-20.

3661. LOBER, George
"Wish." [Elf] (4:1) Spr 94, p. 37.

3662. LOCHHEAD, Douglas
"Wood Point Poems." [AntigR] (96) Wint 94, p. 7-16.

3663. LOCKE, Duane
"An Aphid." [DarkMoon] (1) 94, p. 42.
"Interpreters." [DarkMoon] (1) 94, p. 46.
"The Japanese Junk Sculptress." [DarkMoon] (1) 94, p. 45.
"Marmot." [ContextS] (4:1) 94, p. 40-41.
"Moonlit Carp." [ContextS] (4:1) 94, p. 40.
"Moving to the City's Poor Neighborhood." [SantaBR] (2:2) Fall-Wint 94, p. 143.
"Predicated Snow." [DarkMoon] (1) 94, p. 44.
"The Return." [SantaBR] (2:2) Fall-Wint 94, p. 142.
"Snails in Switzerland." [DarkMoon] (1) 94, p. 47.
"Three." [DarkMoon] (1) 94, p. 41.
"The Tropics." [PoetL] (89:4) Wint 94-95, p. 35.
"Watermelons and Cats." [DarkMoon] (1) 94, p. 43.

3664. LOCKE, Edward
"After Our Dinner." [ApalQ] (40/41) 94, p. 91.
"Shades." [Sonora] (27) Spr 94, p. 110.

3665. LOCKE, Mona
"Of Our Need to See Trees Leaning into the Wind." [SoDakR] (32:2) Sum 94, p. 122.

3666. LOCKETT, Andrea
"At Edgemont Park." [Pivot] (42) 94, p. 33.
"Ritual" (for L.E.L.). [Pivot] (42) 94, p. 33.

3667. LOCKETT, C. J.
"Of the Dawn." [AntigR] (97) Spr 94, p. 48.

3668. LOCKLIN, Gerald
"Am I Missing Something?" [WormR] (34:4, #136) 94, p. 178.
"André Derain: *Les Voiles Rouges*." [Pearl] (20) Spr 94, p. 55.
"The Bard of Amphibia" (Special Section: 43 poems). [WormR] (34:3, #135) 94, p. 107-124.
"But It Didn't Stop Me or the Dog." [ChironR] (13:2) Sum 94, p. 2.
"Do Not Go Gentle into That Chlorine." [SlipS] (14) 94, p. 125-126.
"A Faulknerian Etiology." [Amelia] (7:4, #23) 94, p. 69.
"Franz Locklin's Masterpiece." [WormR] (34:1, #133) 94, p. 4.
"Henri Fantin-Latour: *Sill Life with Pansies,* 1974" (A reprise). [ChironR] (13:2) Sum 94, p. 2.
"How Very Interesting (1992)." [WormR] (34:1, #133) 94, p. 4-5.
"I Like Cats That Catch Things." [WormR] (34:1, #133) 94, p. 1.
"*Imperial Crown Tritillaria in a Copper Vase*, 1987." [Pearl] (20) Spr 94, p. 55.
"In Sane Mind." [SlipS] (14) 94, p. 124.
"The Largesse of the Gentleman Poet." [WormR] (34:1, #133) 94, p. 4.

"Like Son, Like Father." [WormR] (34:1, #133) 94, p. 2-3.
"Lucian Freud: *Naked Man, Backview,* 1991-92." [ChironR] (13:2) Sum 94, p. 2.
"Magritte: *Illustrated Youth*." [Pearl] (20) Spr 94, p. 55.
"Maybe If I'd Worn It on My Wrist?" [ChironR] (13:2) Sum 94, p. 3.
"Moot Point." [WormR] (34:4, #136) 94, p. 177.
"The New Male." [ChironR] (13:2) Sum 94, p. 3.
"Oedipus Is Never Around When We Need Him." [WormR] (34:4, #136) 94, p. 178.
"Oh Well, Humans Eat Tripe." [ChironR] (13:2) Sum 94, p. 3.
"Or Maybe Ambrose Bierce." [WormR] (34:1, #133) 94, p. 2.
"Picasso: *Seated Woman,* April 27, 1938." [ChironR] (13:2) Sum 94, p. 2.
"Picasso: *The Studio,* 1934." [ChironR] (13:2) Sum 94, p. 2.
"Picasso: *Woman Reclining on a Couch,* 1939." [ChironR] (13:2) Sum 94, p. 2.
"Poop." [ChironR] (13:2) Sum 94, p. 9.
"Psychopathology of the After-Dinner Nap." [ChironR] (13:2) Sum 94, p. 3.
"A Remarkable Case of Sibling Specialization." [WormR] (34:1, #133) 94, p. 4.
"They'll Never Understand." [WormR] (34:1, #133) 94, p. 2.
"Waiting for Anything." [WormR] (34:1, #133) 94, p. 3.
"Whatever Happened to the Simple Things, Like Steroids." [WormR] (34:4, #136) 94, p. 178.
"Why Abbot and Costello Are in Heaven." [WormR] (34:4, #136) 94, p. 177.
"Will My *Chirons* Come Home to Roost?" [ChironR] (13:2) Sum 94, p. 3.

3669. LOCKWARD, Diane
"Making the World Safe for Children." [JlNJPo] (16:2) Aut 94, p. 22.

3670. LODEN, Rachel
"The Age of Miracles." [Caliban] (14) 94, p. 132.
"April in Helsinki." [ColEng] (56:1) Ja 94, p. 68-69.
"A Catechism for Imaginary Virgins." [SenR] (24:2) Fall 94, p. 49.
"Five Minute Agoraphobic Holidays." [AmerLC] (6) 94, p. 62.
"General Dudayev Enters the New World." [NewAW] (12) Spr-Sum 94, p. 116.
"The Little Richard Story (II)." [NewAW] (12) Spr-Sum 94, p. 117.
"Notes on the Borderline." [GrahamHR] (18) Wint 94-95, p. 41.
"The Pork Latitudes." [PoetL] (89:4) Wint 94-95, p. 11-12.
"The Rowboat at Vladivostok." [Caliban] (14) 94, p. 133.
"Woman on the Road Near Ithaca." [PoetL] (89:4) Wint 94-95, p. 13.

3671. LOEHLE, Craig
"Bahá'í Riddles." [WorldO] (26:2) Wint 94-95, p. 43.

3672. LOEWEN, Ann
"Fresh Water Meets Salt." [TickleAce] (28) Fall-Wint 94, p. 99.
"Strawberry Summer." [TickleAce] (28) Fall-Wint 94, p. 98.

3673. LOGAN
"Zopilotes" (for Manual Zamora). [NewDeltaR] (11:1) Fall 93-Wint 94, p. 97-98.

3674. LOGAN, William
"The Embarrassment of Riches." [YaleR] (82:2) Ap 94, p. 70-71.
"The High Summer of Capital." [PartR] (61:2) Spr 94, p. 317-318.
"The Lost Birds of Venice." [NewRep] (210:8) 21 F 94, p. 38.
"Seductions of the Swimming Club." [Agni] (39) 94, p. 59.
"Sunday in the South." [ParisR] (36:130) Spr 94, p. 112-113.
"Vesuvius." [Nat] (258:25) Je 27 94, p. 919.

3675. LOGGINS, Vernon Porter
"Tables." [Poem] (71) My 94, p. 19.

3676. LOGSDON, Lucy
"The Elders." [PoetL] (89:4) Wint 94-95, p. 16.

3677. LOHMANN, Jeanne
"The Hawk." [BellArk] (10:3 [i.e. 10:4]) Jl-Ag 94, p. 10.
"Instructions for Moving." [BellArk] (10:5) S-O 94, p. 26.
"Setting Out the Pansies." [BellArk] (10:5) S-O 94, p. 27.
"Tulips." [BellArk] (10:3 [i.e. 10:4]) Jl-Ag 94, p. 12.

3678. LOIZOU, Doros
"Between a Good Morning and a Good Night" (tr. by Nicholas Samaras). [DenQ] (29:1) Sum 94, p. 83-85.

3679. LoLORDO, Ann
"Azrael's Sleep." [SoDakR] (32:2) Sum 94, p. 91.
"The Smell of Rain." [GreensboroR] (56) Sum 94, p. 34.

LOMAS, Estela Alicia Lopez
See LOPEZ LOMAS, Estela Alicia

3680. LOMBARDO, Gian
"The Crash and Its Sound." [Iowa] (24:3) Fall 94, p. 69.
"The Heart Grows an Inch Measured Against the Wall." [Iowa] (24:3) Fall 94, p. 69.
3681. LOMKE, Evander
"The Still Kingdom" (for F. S. L.). [Confr] (52/53) Wint-Spr 94, p. 320.
3682. LONE, D. M.
"8" (tr. by Arlene Zide and Tilottama Daswani). [InterQ] (1:2) 93, p. 161.
LONERGAN, Janet Gill
See GILL-LONERGAN, Janet
3683. LONG, Alison
"Silently Shouting." [ConnPR] (13:1) 94, p. 22.
3684. LONG, Barbara Meetze
"As If." [TarRP] (33:2) Spr 94, p. 17.
3685. LONG, Joel
"Waiting for the Best Things." [ChatR] (14:2) Wint 94, p. 45.
3686. LONG, Philomene
"4:31 A.M." [Jacaranda] (10) 94, p. 90-91.
3687. LONG, Richard
"The Attic Box." [NewDeltaR] (11:2) Spr-Sum 94, p. 61.
3688. LONG, Robert (Robert Hill)
"Betrayal of the Muse." [IllinoisR] (1:2) Spr 94, p. 65.
"Burn This." [Hudson] (47:1) Spr 94, p. 56.
"The Conspiracy." [Poetry] (163:4) Ja 94, p. 195-196.
"Dust on Dust." [Pivot] (41) 93, p. 57.
"The Horizon Pain Opens." [Hudson] (47:1) Spr 94, p. 54-55.
"The Muse and I Are Alone." [IllinoisR] (1:2) Spr 94, p. 68.
"The Muse Gets Back on the Bus." [SycamoreR] (6:1) Wint 94, p. 51.
"The Muse Is Gone." [IllinoisR] (1:2) Spr 94, p. 69.
"The Muse Lends a Hand." [SycamoreR] (6:1) Wint 94, p. 49.
"The Muse Off-Duty." [SycamoreR] (6:1) Wint 94, p. 50.
"The Muse Shivers." [IllinoisR] (1:2) Spr 94, p. 64.
"The Muse Smokes." [SycamoreR] (6:1) Wint 94, p. 48.
"The Muse Speaks." [IllinoisR] (1:2) Spr 94, p. 67.
"The Muse Squints." [IllinoisR] (1:2) Spr 94, p. 66.
"The Muse Stares." [SycamoreR] (6:1) Wint 94, p. 47.
"Refuge." [Manoa] (6:1) Sum 94, p. 41-42.
"The River Kept from Us." [Hudson] (47:1) Spr 94, p. 53-54.
"Where the Muse Lives." [SycamoreR] (6:1) Wint 94, p. 46.
3689. LONG, Toni
"EX Marks the Spot" (for anyone who has ever had a broken heart). [EvergreenC] (9:2) Sum-Fall 94, p. 64-66.
"A Poem about Nothing in Particular." [EvergreenC] (9:2) Sum-Fall 94, p. 60-63.
3690. LONGENBACH, James
"The Threshold of the Visible World." [WestHR] (48:4) Wint 94, p. 316-320.
"What You Find in the Woods." [YaleR] (82:4) O 94, p. 81.
3691. LONGLEY, Judy
"Jimson Weed." [SouthernPR] (34:2) Wint 94, p. 55-56.
"Matisse in Morocco" (Selections: I-III). [ParisR] (36:133) Wint 94, p. 219-220.
"Sleep" (for Bill). [LouisL] (11:1) Spr 94, p. 179-180.
"Uprooted." [LouisL] (11:1) Spr 94, p. 178.
3692. LONGLEY, Michael
"Behind a Cloud." [NewYorker] (70:10) 25 Ap 94, p. 69.
"Couplets." [YaleR] (82:3) Jl 94, p. 33.
"The Ghost Orchid." [Thrpny] (58) Sum 94, p. 34.
"Snow-Hole." [NewYorker] (69:47) 24 Ja 94, p. 40.
"Spiderwoman." [NewYorker] (70:39) 28 N 94, p. 108.
3693. LONGWELL, Jeff
"Verrazano-Narrows Bridge" (tr. of Jesús J. Barquet, w. the author). [MichQR] (33:3) Sum 94, p. 636-637.
3694. LOO, Jeffrey
"The Angel of Pain." [SlipS] (14) 94, p. 76.
3695. LOOMIS, Jon
"Bathers" (Philadelphia Museum of Art, 1993). [Field] (50) Spr 94, p. 31.
"Church Street." [IndR] (17:2) Fall 94, p. 28.
"The Day of the Comet." [Field] (51) Fall 94, p. 86.
"Easter." [Field] (51) Fall 94, p. 85.

"In the Year of the Great Flood." [IndR] (17:2) Fall 94, p. 29.
"On the 1st Tee with Charles Wright." [Field] (51) Fall 94, p. 83.
"The Patience of the Muse." [Field] (51) Fall 94, p. 84.
"Vanitas Motel." [Field] (50) Spr 94, p. 32.
"Watching *Wings of Desire* with a Bad Cold." [Field] (50) Spr 94, p. 33.

3696. LOONEY, George
"Morning Visitation." [Sonora] (28) Fall 94, p. 27-28.

3697. LOPEZ LOMAS, Estela Alicia
"Quincunce" (in Spanish and English, tr. by Angela McEwan). [Luz] (7) N 94, p. 22-26.

3698. LOPEZ PACHECO, Alexandra
"First Ecologue" (from *Ecologues and Urban Pieces*, work in progress, tr. of Jesús López-Pacheco). [CanLit] (142/143) Fall-Wint 94, p. 139-141.

3699. LOPEZ-PACHECO, Jesús
"Ecologia Primera" (de *Ecologas y Urbanas*, obra en preparacion). [CanLit] (142/143) Fall-Wint 94, p. 136-138.
"First Ecologue" (from *Ecologues and Urban Pieces*, work in progress, tr. by Alexandra López Pacheco). [CanLit] (142/143) Fall-Wint 94, p. 139-141.

3700. LORD, John Mason, Jr.
"Atlantic Parting." [DogRR] (26) Wint 94-95, p. 60-61.
"The Lesson." [DogRR] (26) Wint 94-95, p. 60.

3701. LORD, Ted
"Grafting." [CreamCR] (18:2) Fall 94, p. 123.
"Landscape." [Nimrod] (38:1) Fall-Wint 94, p. 121.
"Transit." [SycamoreR] (6:2) Sum 94, p. 53.

LORDO, Ann Lo
See LoLORDO, Ann

3702. LORENZO, Alejandro
"Aprende." [LindLM] (13:1) Mr 94, p. 15.
"Lo Que Pronto Desaparece." [LindLM] (13:1) Mr 94, p. 15.

3703. LORRAINE, J.
"Brother Percey." [Comm] (121:18) 21 O 94, p. 16.

LOS SANTOS, Marisa de
See SANTOS, Marisa de los

3704. LOTT, April
"Fire Safety." [AnthNEW] (6) 94, p. 15.

3705. LOTT, David G.
"Among the Hmung." [Light] (12) Wint 94-95, p. 21.

3706. LOUDIN, Robert
"In the Can." [CoalC] (8) Ap 94, p. 33.

3707. LOUDON, Stephen
"6.9.92." [BlackBR] (19) Fall-Wint 94, p. 17.
"Hey Man." [BlackBR] (19) Fall-Wint 94, p. 16-17.

3708. LOUGHLIN, John
"Heritage." [Ploughs] (20:4) Wint 94-95, p. 129-130.
"Laplacian Dream." [Sonora] (28) Fall 94, p. 1-2.

3709. LOUIS, Adrian C.
"The Boys Cruise Seattle." [TriQ] (90) Spr-Sum 94, p. 143.
"Fever Journal" (Dakotah Territory: September 22, 1992). [SouthernR] (30:3) Sum 94, p. 548-549.
"For My Lakota Woman." [TriQ] (90) Spr-Sum 94, p. 138-139.
"Graffiti Dialogue in a Nebraska Bordertown Laundromat." [TriQ] (90) Spr-Sum 94, p. 146.
"How Verdell and Doctor Zhivago Disassembled the Soviet Union." [TriQ] (90) Spr-Sum 94, p. 141-142.
"Human Brain Song." [ContextS] (4:1) 94, p. 9.
"Last Song of the Dove." [TriQ] (90) Spr-Sum 94, p. 145.
"A Rudimentary Lesson in American Indian Journalism." [TriQ] (90) Spr-Sum 94, p. 147-149.
"A Savage Blood Thirst." [TriQ] (90) Spr-Sum 94, p. 144.
"Sonnenkinder." [Chelsea] (56) 94, p. 34.
"Sonny's Purple Heart." [ChiR] (40:2/3) 94, p. 66-68.
"Spirit-Deer Deep in Pine Forests" (for Leslie Marmon Silko). [TriQ] (90) Spr-Sum 94, p. 140.
"Statue of Liberty." [ContextS] (4:1) 94, p. 28.
"That Great Wingless Bird" (for David Reeve). [Chelsea] (56) 94, p. 35-36.

3710. LOUIS-DREYFUS, William
"The Alley" (tr. of Jules Supervielle, w. Molly Peacock). [Agni] (39) 94, p. 25.
"God Thinks of Man" (tr. of Jules Supervielle, w. Molly Peacock). [Boulevard] (9:3, #27) Fall 94, p. 109-110.
"Prophecy" (tr. of Jules Supervielle, w. Molly Peacock). [Agni] (39) 94, p. 23.
"The Raindrop (God Speaking)" (tr. of Jules Supervielle, w. Molly Peacock). [Boulevard] (9:3, #27) Fall 94, p. 110.
"Whisper of Agony" (tr. of Jules Supervielle, w. Molly Peacock). [Agni] (39) 94, p. 24.
3711. LOVE, B. D.
"Preliminaries." [Poem] (71) My 94, p. 64-65.
"Salt" (for Mabel Young). [Poem] (71) My 94, p. 66.
"Speed." [Poem] (71) My 94, p. 62-63.
"Weight." [Poem] (71) My 94, p. 61.
3712. LOVE, Monifa A.
"Green Times Remembered" (for Romare Bearden). [InterQ] (1:2) 93, p. 147.
"Maximum Security." [InterQ] (1:2) 93, p. 150-151.
"Testimony" (found in Terry Tempest Williams' *Refuge: An Unnatural History of Family and Place*). [InterQ] (1:2) 93, p. 148-149.
3713. LOVE, Raymond D.
"My Thinking Cap." [Light] (12) Wint 94-95, p. 22.
3714. LOVE, Shirley
"Mulberry." [SpoonR] (19:1) Wint-Spr 94, p. 26.
"Who Can Say Why a Single Bird's Note." [SpoonR] (19:1) Wint-Spr 94, p. 25.
3715. LOVE, Tim
"Thames." [Stand] (36:1) Wint 94-95, p. 77.
3716. LOVELL, Shelly
"Perder de Vista." [Sonora] (27) Spr 94, p. 59-60.
3717. LOVELL,Thoreau
"Out of the Wilderness" (for John High, exiled in Russia). [ProseP] (3) 94, p. 64.
"Potential Birds." [ProseP] (3) 94, p. 63.
3718. LOVELOCK, Yann
"Pardon" (tr. of Louis Remacle). [Os] (39) Fall-Wint 94, p. 9.
"Snow" (tr. of Louis Remacle). [Os] (39) Fall-Wint 94, p. 7.
3719. LOVING, A. L.
"The Completion." [Kalliope] (16:3) 94, p. 31.
"For My Friend Who Dreams" (for T.C.J.). [NegC] (14:1/2) 94, p. 61.
"Glass." [Kalliope] (16:3) 94, p. 31.
LOW, Jackson Mac
See Mac LOW, Jackson
3720. LOWELL, James
"Immortal Turtle." [CaribbeanW] (8) 94, p. 69.
3721. LOWELL, Robert
"Epilogue" (from *Dolphin*). [NewEngR] (16:3) Sum 94, p. 58.
3722. LOWENSTEIN, Robert
"The Ferryman." [JINJPo] (16:1) Spr 94, p. 10.
3723. LOWENTHAL, Jessica
"Between These Two Eyes" (for Issa Clubb). [Talisman] (13) Fall 94-Wint 95, p. 7-8.
"Manifesto." [Talisman] (13) Fall 94-Wint 95, p. 7.
3724. LOWENTHAL, Michael F.
"The Carpenter." [EvergreenC] (9:2) Sum-Fall 94, p. 30.
"Family Resemblance." [EvergreenC] (9:2) Sum-Fall 94, p. 31-32.
3725. LOWERY, Joanne
"Backward Poem." [HangL] (65) 94, p. 32.
"Basso Profundo" (third prize in the 1994 *Chiron Review* Poetry Contest). [ChironR] (13:4) Wint 94, p. 14.
"Creve Coeur: The Display." [WebR] (18) Fall 94, p. 103-104.
"Dirty Trees." [NegC] (13:2/3) 93, p. 31-32.
"November Inventory." [HangL] (65) 94, p. 33.
"Poem to Plato." [Verse] (11:1) Spr 94, p. 86.
"Transylvania, 1992." [WebR] (18) Fall 94, p. 104.
"Van Eyck's View" (Second Runner-Up, Poetry Award). [NewL] (60:2) 94, p. 72.
"Van Eyck's Wings" (Second Runner-Up, Poetry Award). [NewL] (60:2) 94, p. 73.

3726. LOWITZ, Leza
"Ah, my pocketbook" (Tanka, tr. of Motoko Michiura, w. Miyuki Aoyama and Akemi Tomioka). [Zyzzyva] (10:2) Sum 94, p. 61.
"Haiku: Someone else's wife" (tr. of Nobuko Katsura, w. Miyuki Aoyama). [YellowS] (11:4, #44) Wint 93-94, p. 44.
"My nipples still erect" (Tanka, tr. of Motoko Michiura, w. Miyuki Aoyama and Akemi Tomioka). [Zyzzyva] (10:2) Sum 94, p. 61.
"The Second to Last Kiss (Tanka)" (tr. of Amari Hayashi, w. Miyuki Aoyama). [YellowS] (11:4, #44) Wint 93-94, p. 45.
"Someday I'll turn to water" (Tanka, tr. of Motoko Michiura, w. Miyuki Aoyama and Akemi Tomioka). [Zyzzyva] (10:2) Sum 94, p. 61.
"Tanka: Washing and combing" (tr. of Motoko Michiura, w. Akemi Tomioka). [YellowS] (11:4, #44) Wint 93-94, p. 44.
"Whenever I see poppies" (Tanka, tr. of Motoko Michiura, w. Miyuki Aoyama and Akemi Tomioka). [Zyzzyva] (10:2) Sum 94, p. 61.

3727. LOWMAN, Anthony W.
"When in Doubt, or Washington State." [ChironR] (13:2) Sum 94, p. 25.

3728. LOYDELL, Rupert M.
"No Joke." [ChironR] (13:2) Sum 94, p. 27.
"Separations." [ChironR] (13:2) Sum 94, p. 27.
"Zigzag." [ChironR] (13:2) Sum 94, p. 27.

3729. LOZANO, Vicente
"Digression on an Enameled Watchcase from the Chicago World's Fair." [Border] (3) Fall 93, p. 43-44.

3730. LU, Yimin
"Awakening at Dawn" (tr. by Cheng Baolin and Richard Terrill). [AnotherCM] (27) 94, p. 90.
"Sand Castle" (tr. by Cheng Baolin and Richard Terrill). [AnotherCM] (27) 94, p. 88.
"Wind and Rain Were Approaching" (tr. by Cheng Baolin and Richard Terrill). [AnotherCM] (27) 94, p. 89.

3731. LU, Yu
"Autumn Lift" (tr. by David Gordon). [WorldL] (5) 94, p. 17.
"In Twin Clear Hall, a Night Piece" (tr. by David Gordon). [WorldL] (5) 94, p. 19.
"Neighbor Without Food Being Taken to the Outskirts: Pitying Him I Wrote This" (tr. by David Gordon). [WorldL] (5) 94, p. 18.

3732. LUBESKI, Lori
"The Collaborator" (to Jennifer Hoff). [Chain] (1) Spr-Sum 94, p. 212-215.

LUBIN, Yves
See SAINT, Assotto

LUCCA, Rafael Arraiz
See ARRAIZ LUCCA, Rafael

3733. LUCERO, Anthony
"Dear X." [Pearl] (20) Spr 94, p. 54.
"Wet." [Amelia] (7:3, #22) 94, p. 47.

3734. LUCIA, Joseph P.
"Reclaiming the Id." [ColEng] (56:6) O 94, p. 682.

3735. LUCINA, Mary
"Footprints." [Poetry] (164:5) Ag 94, p. 272.

3736. LUCKMANN, W.
"Children Yearn for Rain." [BlackBR] (18) Wint-Spr 94, p. 6-7.
"Modern Bushman." [BlackBR] (18) Wint-Spr 94, p. 7-8.

3737. LUDVIGSON, Susan
"God Speaks to Emily Dickinson about Her Absent Father." [SouthernR] (30:4) Aut 94, p. 832.
"God Speaks to Emily Dickinson about Her Dreams." [SouthernR] (30:4) Aut 94, p. 831-832.
"Gratitude." [Poetry] (164:4) Jl 94, p. 222.
"Listening." [Poetry] (164:4) Jl 94, p. 220.
"So Many Ways to Tell Ourselves the Truths." [GeoR] (48:2) Sum 94, p. 239.
"This Move into the Abstract." [Poetry] (164:4) Jl 94, p. 221.

3738. LUDWIN, Deanna Kern
"More Doctor Stories." [AnotherCM] (28) 94, p. 93-94.
"Saving Geraniums." [CimR] (108) Jl 94, p. 82.

3739. LUDWIN, Peter
"Among the Hopi at Walpi, First Mesa." [ChamLR] (14/15) Spr-Fall 94, p. 154-156.

3740. LUFT, Daniel
"Signatures." [Ledge] (17) Wint 94, p. 68-69.

3741. LUFT, David A.
"A Love Poem." [AntigR] (96) Wint 94, p. 97.

3742. LUKILIUS (mid-1st c. A.D.)
"Epitaph of a Boxer" (tr. by John J. Brugaletta). [SoCoast] (16) Ja 94, p. 57.

3743. LUM, Wing Tek
"The Caretaker." [BambooR] (63/64) Sum-Fall 94, p. 31-32.
"Childhood Memories." [BambooR] (60) Wint 94, p. 106-107.
"The Last Oldtimers." [BambooR] (63/64) Sum-Fall 94, p. 30.
"This Secret Charge." [BambooR] (60) Wint 94, p. 102-103.
"The Youngest Child." [BambooR] (60) Wint 94, p. 104-105.

3744. LUMMIS, Suzanne
"To the Man in the Parking Lot of Sunset and Western." [ChironR] (13:2) Sum 94, p. 8.
"A Woman With a Chameleon on Her Hat." [SouthernPR] (34:1) Sum 94, p. 64-65.

3745. LUMSDEN, Tom, Jr.
"Encounter." [HiramPoR] (57) Fall 94-Wint 95, p. 38.
"On the Left Bank." [HiramPoR] (57) Fall 94-Wint 95, p. 39.

LUNA, Blas Manuel de
See DeLUNA, Blas Manuel

3746. LUNDAY, Robert
"The Deaf in the Subway." [SouthernPR] (34:1) Sum 94, p. 48-49.
"Enochville." [SouthernPR] (34:1) Sum 94, p. 49-50.

3747. LUNDBERG, Carol Wade
"Is This How It Is?" [CumbPR] (14:1) Fall 94, p. 69-70.
"To Long John Silver and Friends" (from "The Secret Life"). [AmerPoR] (23:3) My-Je 94, p. 24.

3748. LUNDE, David
"Drinking Alone Beneath the Moon" (tr. of Li Po, c. 699-762). [ChamLR] (14/15) Spr-Fall 94, p. 205.
"Poem Sent to Old Friends While Staying Overnight on the Tung-Lu River" (tr. of Meng Hau-ran). [SpoonR] (19:1) Wint-Spr 94, p. 59.
"Seeing Meng Hau-ran Off from Yellow Crane Tower" (tr. of Li Po). [SpoonR] (19:1) Wint-Spr 94, p. 58.
"To My Love" (from "Heart Transplants & Other Misappropriations"). [AmerPoR] (23:1) Ja-F 94, p. 30.

3749. LUNDIN, Deanne
"Changing Portrait of You in New Mexico." [Jacaranda] (10) 94, p. 31.
"Dinner at the Reel Inn" (for Katherine Swiggart). [Jacaranda] (10) 94, p. 30.
"Having Wonderful Time Wish You Were Here." [Jacaranda] (5:1) Wint-Spr 91, p. 118.

3750. LUOMA, Bill
"My Trip to New York City" (Excerts). [RiverC] (14:2) Spr 94, p. 77-80.

3751. LUPTON, Carmen
"St. Cecelia's Abbey." [WashR] (19:5) F-Mr 94, p. 9.
"Water Tells All." [WashR] (19:5) F-Mr 94, p. 9.
"Wind Due South Opens Hand." [WashR] (19:5) F-Mr 94, p. 9.

3752. LUQUE, María de la Peña
"Los Perfiles de la Luz." [Luz] (7) N 94, p. 34-38.
"The Profiles of Light" (tr. by Margaret Saine). [Luz] (7) N 94, p. 35-39.

3753. LURIE, Alison
"New Orleans: Some Impressions." [NegC] (13:2/3) 93, p. 246.

3754. LUSH, Laura
"Force." [Event] (23:1) Spr 94, p. 25.
"Hook." [Quarry] (43:3) n 94, p. 129.
"Lamb." [Quarry] (43:3) n 94, p. 128.
"The Last Morning." [Quarry] (42:4) Mr 94, p. 115.
"Sandbags." [Event] (23:1) Spr 94, p. 26-27.
"What You Are Made Of" (for Gabriele). [Dandel] (21:1) 94, p. 9.

3755. LUSK, Daniel
"Axe." [CumbPR] (14:1) Fall 94, p. 9.
"Dung Light." [LaurelR] (28:2) Sum 94, p. 51-52.
"A Foreign Country." [LaurelR] (28:2) Sum 94, p. 50.
"Taking a Bath" (Robert Penn Warren Poetry Prize Winner: Second Prize). [CumbPR] (14:1) Fall 94, p. 7-8.

"Telling." [NewL] (61:1) 94, p. 152.

3756. LUTERMAN, Alison
"Broken Water Glass" (for Dana Keefer). [Sun] (217) Ja 94, p. 18-19.
"Don't Stop." [Sun] (226) O 94, p. 37.
"Kitchen Sink Drama." [Sun] (227) N 94, p. 36.
"Ode to the Jacuzzi at the 23rd St. Y." [Sun] (225) S 94, p. 30.

3757. LUTZ, Jeanne
"Romantic Notions." [BellR] (17:1/2) Spr-Fall 94, p. 46.

3758. LUX, Thomas
"Gorgeous Surfaces." [Atlantic] (273:5) My 94, p. 117.
"Onomatopoeia." [Antaeus] (73/74) Spr 94, p. 81.

3759. LUXTON, Steve
"Yucatan." [CanLit] (142/143) Fall-Wint 94, p. 204.

3760. LUZZARO, Susan
"Begin with the Body." [Kalliope] (16:3) 94, p. 32-33.
"Utopia." [Iowa] (24:3) Fall 94, p. 72-73.

3761. LYLE, K. Curtis
"Electric Church" (excerpted from *Warrior Poet Voodoo Jimi Hendrix*). [Eyeball] (3) 93, p. 24.

3762. LYNCH, Doris
"Departures." [ArtfulD] (26/27) 94, p. 52.
"Rainy Twilight." [HopewellR] (6) 94, p. 110.

3763. LYNCH, Kathleen
"Motel Baby." [PoetryNW] (35:2) Sum 94, p. 16-17.
"Only Trees." [PoetryNW] (35:2) Sum 94, p. 15.
"You Go." [SycamoreR] (6:2) Sum 94, p. 37.

3764. LYNCH, Thomas
"Byzance." [Vis] (45) 94, p. 25.
"Maura." [Vis] (45) 94, p. 26.
"The Nines." [NewYorker] (70:34) 24 O 94, p. 73.
"Tongue and Groove." [SouthernR] (30:3) Sum 94, p. 550-551.
"Vigil." [SouthernR] (30:3) Sum 94, p. 550.

3765. LYNES, Jeanette
"My Mother and Roberta Bondar." [PraF] (15:2, #67) Sum 94, p. 64.
"Season of Lies." [AntigR] (97) Spr 94, p. 132.
"Sonnet on the Remarkably Tiny Waist of Lucy Maude Montgomery." [AntigR] (97) Spr 94, p. 131.

3766. LYNN, Catherine
"Better Than Nothing" (Boston, 1938). [SlipS] (14) 94, p. 104.

3767. LYNSKEY, Edward C.
"The Appalachian Snake Man." [Pembroke] (26) 94, p. 96.
"Circe Rode a Blue Mule." [HampSPR] Wint 94, p. 46.
"Cleburne's Rude Coming." [ChironR] (13:2) Sum 94, p. 30.
"Damselfly." [DogRR] (26) Wint 94-95, p. 13.
"Eight-Cylinder Shrine." [PoetryNW] (35:2) Sum 94, p. 44.
"The Fiddler Rests at Last." [ChironR] (13:4) Wint 94, p. 29.
"Giving the Tongue of Life to Wire." [CarolQ] (47:1) Fall 94, p. 63.
"Hanging the Horse Thief Whose Second Life Is a Spider." [ChironR] (13:2) Sum 94, p. 30.
"Harum-Scarums." [Pivot] (41) 93, p. 50.
"Ice Fishing on Lake Huron, Christmas Night." [ChironR] (13:4) Wint 94, p. 29.
"In Search of Our Father's Guitar and Gin." [ColEng] (56:2) F 94, p. 193.
"Mrs. Lincoln's Game of Bone Chess." [Plain] (14:2) Wint 94, p. 27.
"My Father's Native City." [Amelia] (7:4, #23) 94, p. 150.
"Night the Waxworks Came to Corinth." [Plain] (15:1) Fall 94, p. 31.
"Sad Romances of Winston Links." [HampSPR] Wint 94, p. 46-47.
"Skunk Pranks." [WindO] (58) Sum 94, p. 38.
"A Snake Prayer" (news item in the *Washington Post*). [Pivot] (42) 94, p. 35.
"Town Remembers Tyler's Suicide Fifty Years Late." [ChironR] (13:4) Wint 94, p. 29.

3768. LYON, George Ella
"Mother's Day." [Wind] (73) 94, p. 17.

3769. LYONS, Jim
"Skid." [MalR] (106) Spr 94, p. 76.

3770. LYONS, Richard
"The Black Venus: For Max Ernst." [ParisR] (36:133) Wint 94, p. 284-287.

"For Dianne Wherever She May Be." [PassN] (15:1) Sum 94, p. 12-14.
"Like Glass Pyramids at Midnight." [PassN] (15:1) Sum 94, p. 19.
"Some Weeks before an Autumn Wedding." [Crazy] (47) Wint 94, p. 29-42.

3771. LYONS, Robert
"A Letter to Glenda." [BellArk] (10:2) Mr-Ap 94, p. 11.
"The Visitors." [BellArk] (10:6) N-D 94, p. 16.

3772. LYSAGHT, Seán
"Phases of the Flap-Man." [Stand] (35:4) Aut 94, p. 76-77.

3773. LYSENKO, Gennadii
"Between This September and That One" (tr. by G. S. Smith). [Manoa] (6:2) Wint 94, p. 77.
"In the Middle of All This Idle Running Around" (tr. by G. S. Smith). [Manoa] (6:2) Wint 94, p. 79.
"It's Not Because the Music Is the Way It Is" (tr. by G. S. Smith). [Manoa] (6:2) Wint 94, p. 78.
"Once More, Everything Is Blindingly Dull" (tr. by G. S. Smith). [Manoa] (6:2) Wint 94, p. 78.
"That Which I Sowed" (tr. by G. S. Smith). [Manoa] (6:2) Wint 94, p. 79.

3774. LYTLE, Leslie
"My Grandfather's Journey to the New World." [GrahamHR] (18) Wint 94-95, p. 86-87.

3775. M., Paul
"Tiny hands." [Amelia] (7:4, #23) 94, p. 24.

MAC . . .
See also names beginning with Mc . . .

3776. Mac LEAN, Christopher M.
"All for a Night in June" (by Aris Aterian). [HawaiiR] (18:1, #40) Spr 94, p. 113-114.

3777. Mac LOW, Jackson
"Banal Axiom Follicle" (Forties 29). [Talisman] (12) Spr 94, p. 7-8.
"Underlingers Cope" (Forties 22). [Talisman] (12) Spr 94, p. 5-6.

MACATANGAY, Maria Silvagnia
See SILVAGNIA-MACATANGAY, Maria

3778. MacCASH, Doug
"Very Hot for a Penguin." [NewOR] (20:1/2) Spr-Sum 94, p. 118-121.

3779. MacDONALD, C. G.
"Cardiac Pantoum." [HampSPR] Wint 94, p. 15.
"Living Fossils" (for Charles Bukowski and Raymond Carver). [WestHR] (48:2) Sum 94, p. 169.
"Rejection Note." [WestHR] (48:2) Sum 94, p. 167.
"Tripod and Eunuch." [WestHR] (48:2) Sum 94, p. 168.

3780. MacDONALD, Calum
"The Genealogy of Goraidh." [Verse] (11:2) Sum 94, p. 43.
"The Highest Apple." [Verse] (11:2) Sum 94, p. 42.
"Siol Ghoraihd." [Verse] (11:2) Sum 94, p. 43.
"Sraidean No Rionn-Eorpa." [Verse] (11:2) Sum 94, p. 44.
"Streets of Europe." [Verse] (11:2) Sum 94, p. 45.
"An Ubhal As Airde." [Verse] (11:2) Sum 94, p. 41.

3781. MacDONALD, Cynthia
"Children Who Fall Off the Edge of the World Because of Secrets." [Antaeus] (75/76) Aut 94, p. 293-294.

3782. MacDONALD, Ranald
"The Fireworks Display." [Verse] (11:2) Sum 94, p. 28.

3783. MacDONALD, Tanis
"Angel." [Dandel] (21:2) 94, p. 6-7.
"Bread and Salt." [Grain] (22:2) Fall 94, p. 34-35.
"Holding Ground" (2nd Place, 1994 Poetry Contest). [Dandel] (21:1) 94, p. 6.

3784. MACE, Carroll E.
"Fatherland, I Do Not Forget You" (tr. of Marco Tulio del Arca Saravia). [XavierR] (14:2) Fall 94, p. 65.

3785. MACEIRA, Karen
"Days Off" (For Esther, Irene, and Margie). [NegC] (13:2/3) 93, p. 35-37.
"Sestina From the Other side of Town." [NegC] (13:2/3) 93, p. 33-34.

3786. MacFHIONNLAIGH, Fearghas
"Eagle, Robin, Pine (For Catherine Nugent)" (Selections: 1-8, 35). [Verse] (11:2) Sum 94, p. 48-49.
"Iolair, Brùdhearg, Giuthas (Airson Catherine Nugent)" (Selections: 1-8, 35). [Verse] (11:2) Sum 94, p. 46-47.
3787. MacGOWAN, Blanche
"Clerihew: Cantankerous Charles de Gaulle." [Light] (11) Aut 94, p. 22.
3788. MACH, Jean
"Scenes from the Freeway." [SingHM] (21) 94, p. 27-29.
3789. MACHAN, Katharyn Howd
"Grandmother." [Amelia] (7:3, #22) 94, p. 149.
"How to Eat in the House of Death." [SlipS] (14) 94, p. 26-27.
"Nettie Sturges, 1888." [SenR] (24:1) Spr 94, p. 71.
"Refrigerator." [SlipS] (14) 94, p. 27.
"Whale Watch." [AnthNEW] (6) 94, p. 9.
"When Radio Was a Young Kid Just Starting Out" (for Samuel Kashner). [BellR] (17:1/2) Spr-Fall 94, p. 91.
3790. MACIEL, Gerónimo
"Campanas del Desierto." [Luz] (7) N 94, p. 40-44.
"Desert's Bells" (tr. by Angela McEwan). [Luz] (7) N 94, p. 41-45.
3791. MACIGEWSKI, Margaret
"Soul Mating." [Vis] (46) 94, p. 18.
3792. MacINNES, Mairi
"At the Gericault Exhibition." [SewanR] (102:1) Wint 94, p. 18-21.
"Two Kinds of Bird." [NewRep] (210:19) 9 My 94, p. 38.
3793. MACIOCI, R. Nikolas
"The Intimacy of Sustained Silent Reading." [InterPR] (20:1) Spr 94, p. 93.
"Young Love in the 1950s." [ApalQ] (42) Fall 94, p. 52.
3794. MacKENNA, Karen
"Sisters." [AntigR] (96) Wint 94, p. 74.
3795. MacKENZIE, Robert
"Airs." [Verse] (11:1) Spr 94, p. 46.
"Like Pornography." [Verse] (11:1) Spr 94, p. 46.
"Streep." [Verse] (11:1) Spr 94, p. 46.
3796. MACKEY, Mary
"The Best Sex of the Century." [YellowS] (12:1, #45) Spr-Sum 94, p. 12.
3797. MACKEY, Nathaniel
"Song of the Andoumboulou: 16." [RiverC] (14:2) Spr 94, p. 90-95.
"Song of the Andoumboulou" (Selections: 23-25). [Sulfur] (34) Spr 94, p. 73-83.
3798. MACKIE, James
"The Abyss on Grace Street." [Poem] (72) N 94, p. 63.
"An Afternoon in the Rain" (for Jim Delaney). [Poem] (72) N 94, p. 66-67.
"Blue Letters." [Poem] (72) N 94, p. 64-65.
"Chasing a Savage God." [Poem] (72) N 94, p. 62.
"Heart of the Story." [Poem] (72) N 94, p. 68.
"Homeless." [Poem] (72) N 94, p. 61.
3799. MacKINNON, Alistair
"Wasp Byke." [Verse] (11:1) Spr 94, p. 68.
3800. MacKINNON, Bruce
"Astrodon Johnstoni." [Salm] (103) Sum 94, p. 94.
"Cruelties." [Salm] (103) Sum 94, p. 93-94.
"Stigmata." [Boulevard] (9:3, #27) Fall 94, p. 147.
3801. MACKLIN, Elizabeth
"A Chance Small Fruit." [SouthwR] (79:1) Wint 94, p. 84.
"The Homeland." [NewYorker] (70:27) 5 S 94, p. 85.
"Into the Change-Train Landscape." [SouthwR] (79:1) Wint 94, p. 84-85.
"One Thing Alone." [NewYorker] (70:6) 28 Mr 94, p. 96.
"Our Dear River." [Thrpny] (58) Sum 94, p. 34.
"What She Said Afterward." [NewYorker] (70:36) 7 N 94, p. 187.
MacLEAN, Christopher M.
See Mac LEAN, Christopher M.
3802. MACLEAR, Kyo
"Mapless Departures." [WestCL] (28:1/2, #13/14) Spr-Fall 94, p. 224-225.
"The Walls Between Us Are Paper Thin." [WestCL] (28:1/2, #13/14) Spr-Fall 94, p. 222-223.

3803. MacLEOD, Joseph Gordon
"Cancer, or, The Crab." [Sulfur] (34) Spr 94, p. 142-146.
3804. MacLEOD, Kathryn
"Blessings" (to Susan Clark). [Chain] (1) Spr-Sum 94, p. 273-274.
3805. MacLEOD, Sue
"My Own Creation Story" (in memory of Isabelle MacLeod Suffidy). [AntigR] (97) Spr 94, p. 7-8.
MACLOW, Jackson
See Mac LOW, Jackson
3806. MacMAHON, Bruce D.
"Twelve Madmen Visit." [SmPd] (31:2, #91) Spr 94, p. 23-24.
3807. MacNEACAIL, Aonghas
"Beside the River." [Verse] (11:2) Sum 94, p. 53.
"Hymn to a Young Demon." [Verse] (11:2) Sum 94, p. 51.
"In the Season When Crocuses." [Verse] (11:2) Sum 94, p. 52.
"Laoidh An Donius Oig." [Verse] (11:2) Sum 94, p. 50.
"Ri Linn Nan Crócus." [Verse] (11:2) Sum 94, p. 52.
"Taobh Na H-Aibhne." [Verse] (11:2) Sum 94, p. 53.
3808. MACRI, Angie
"Nights Like These." [WestB] (34) 94, p. 47.
"Texas Panhandle Roadsong." [CapeR] (29:1) Spr 94, p. 37.
3809. MADDAH, Marita
"The Breakfast." [Verse] (11:2) Sum 94, p. 15.
3810. MADDEN, Ed
"On the Road to Abilene." [Border] (5) Fall-Wint 94, p. 35.
"Wooden Bridge, Cache River, on Algoa Road" (for Scott). [Border] (5) Fall-Wint 94, p. 36-37.
3811. MADDOX, Everette
"Cleaning the Cruiser." [NewOR] (20:3/4) Fall-Wint 94, p. 34-35.
"Flowing on the Bench." [NewOR] (20:3/4) Fall-Wint 94, p. 60.
"Geographical Poem." [NewOR] (20:3/4) Fall-Wint 94, p. 58.
"The Great Man's Death: An Anecdote." [NewOR] (20:3/4) Fall-Wint 94, p. 55.
"Heaven" (For my Mother & Rupert Brooke). [NewOR] (20:3/4) Fall-Wint 94, p. 59-60.
"How I Got In" (For Wade). [NewOR] (20:3/4) Fall-Wint 94, p. 47.
"How I Start My Day." [NegC] (13:2/3) 93, p. 63.
"The Miracle." [NewOR] (20:3/4) Fall-Wint 94, p. 39.
"New Orleans" (for Ralph Adamo). [NewOR] (20:3/4) Fall-Wint 94, p. 55-56.
"No New Tabs" (Sign in the Chukker, October 25th, 1971). [NewOR] (20:3/4) Fall-Wint 94, p. 53-54.
"Of Fashion." [NewOR] (20:3/4) Fall-Wint 94, p. 56-57.
"The Old Man Croaks." [NegC] (13:2/3) 93, p. 64.
"The Outbound Dog." [NegC] (13:2/3) 93, p. 65.
"Suzy in Sunlight." [PoetL] (89:1) Spr 94, p. 56.
"Things I'd Like to Do Preferably Before I Die." [NegC] (13:2/3) 93, p. 66.
"Thirteen Ways of Being Looked at by a Possum." [NewOR] (20:3/4) Fall-Wint 94, p. 52-53.
"Tick Tock." [NewOR] (20:3/4) Fall-Wint 94, p. 54-55.
"Where I Had Been." [NewOR] (20:3/4) Fall-Wint 94, p. 58.
"Why He Did It." [NewOR] (20:3/4) Fall-Wint 94, p. 57.
3812. MADDOX, Marjorie
"Body and Soul." [PaintedB] (53/54) 94, p. 66.
"Cross." [PaintedB] (53/54) 94, p. 70.
"Crying Wolf." [LaurelR] (28:1) Wint 94, p. 36.
"Elocution Lessons." [ColEng] (56:8) D 94, p. 934.
"Father's Day." [Farm] (11:2) Fall-Wint 94-95, p. 14-15.
"God and the Tightrope." [PaintedB] (53/54) 94, p. 69.
"God Goes Fishing." [PaintedB] (53/54) 94, p. 68.
"God Trick-or-Treating." [PaintedB] (53/54) 94, p. 67.
"Golden Hair." [ContextS] (4:1) 94, p. 18-19.
"Hope." [Farm] (11:1) Spr-Sum 94, p. 39.
"How to Fit God into a Poem." [PaintedB] (53/54) 94, p. 64-65.
"Inside the Wolf." [LaurelR] (28:1) Wint 94, p. 37.
"Magnificat." [PaintedB] (53/54) 94, p. 71.
"The Truth of Lies, the Lies of Truth." [Image] (5) Spr 94, p. 37-38.

3813. MADDOX, William S.
"Do Not Shove This product Up Your Nose." [Outbr] (25) 94, p. 60.
3814. MADDUX, Carolyn
"Dewatto Dancer." [BellArk] (10:3) My-Je 94, p. 25.
"Pocatello Summer." [BellArk] (10:3 [i.e. 10:4]) Jl-Ag 94, p. 10.
"Star Dance." [BellArk] (10:3 [i.e. 10:4]) Jl-Ag 94, p. 10.
"Sunset at Bear River." [BellArk] (10:5) S-O 94, p. 23.
"Wild Strawberries." [BellArk] (10:3 [i.e. 10:4]) Jl-Ag 94, p. 10.
3815. MADERA, Osiris
"Anillos." [CuadP] (8:23) My-Ag 94, p. 71.
"Bajo la Lluvia." [CuadP] (8:23) My-Ag 94, p. 70.
"Dueña del Sueño." [CuadP] (8:23) My-Ag 94, p. 70.
"Ejecutivos." [CuadP] (8:23) My-Ag 94, p. 70.
"Fina Copa." [CuadP] (8:23) My-Ag 94, p. 71.
"Mejor Yo Invito." [CuadP] (8:23) My-Ag 94, p. 71.
"Mi Memoria." [CuadP] (8:23) My-Ag 94, p. 72.
"El Tanca." [CuadP] (8:23) My-Ag 94, p. 69.
"Tanca del Amor sin Recuerdos." [CuadP] (8:23) My-Ag 94, p. 72.
"Vanguardias." [CuadP] (8:23) My-Ag 94, p. 70-71.
3816. MADIGAN, Rich
"Lanternfishing." [SouthernPR] (34:1) Sum 94, p. 37-38.
3817. MADIGAN, Rick
"Odysseus in Florida." [Crazy] (47) Wint 94, p. 22.
"Shout!" [IndR] (17:2) Fall 94, p. 56-57.
"Wild Horses." [IndR] (17:2) Fall 94, p. 54-55.
3818. MADONICK, Michael David
"Abide" (for Rashied Robinson). [SycamoreR] (6:2) Sum 94, p. 10-11.
"Dance." [SycamoreR] (6:2) Sum 94, p. 12-13.
"The Fireman Takes His Bride to the Christian Cock-fights." [SycamoreR] (6:2) Sum 94, p. 14-15.
"Peas." [SycamoreR] (6:2) Sum 94, p. 16-17.
"Revelation in the Lobby of the Grand Hotel." [Boulevard] (9:3, #27) Fall 94, p. 186-187.
3819. MADRID, Anthony
"The Abominable Snowman." [PoetryNW] (35:3) Aut 94, p. 40-41.
3820. MADSON, Art
"Wars." [SoCaR] (27:1/2) Fall 94-Spr 95, p. 7.
3821. MADUEÑO, Amalio
"Garcia Dies." [PraS] (68:4) Wint 94, p. 170-171.
"Mexican Bob in Silver City" (for Bill Gersh). [PraS] (68:4) Wint 94, p. 172.
3822. MAERZ, Florence Szerlag
"Auto Heat" (3rd Prize, The Amelia Short Humor Awards). [Amelia] (7:4, #23) 94, p. 102.
"Progress?" (Honorable Mention, The Amelia Short Humor Awards). [Amelia] (7:4, #23) 94, p. 130.
"Stick with the label of the address." [Amelia] (7:3, #22) 94, p. 61.
3823. MAGARRELL, Elaine
"Time Zones" (tr. of Moshe Dor). [WebR] (18) Fall 94, p. 10.
3824. MAGAVERN, Sam
"Master, Man, and Woman." [Poetry] (164:2) My 94, p. 84.
3825. MAGED, Sergey
"Paradise County Seat" (tr. by J. Kates). [Writ] (26) 94, p. 20-27.
3826. MAGEE, Kevin
"Tedium Drum III" (Excerpt. With the texts published in *Sulfer* #32, this section completes the work). [Avec] (7:1) 94, p. 59-62.
3827. MAGEE, Michael
"In the Tide Pool." [FloridaR] (20:1) Fall 94, p. 40-41.
3828. MAGER, Don
"Antistrophes" (tr. of Rainer Maria Rilke). [RiverS] (40) 94, p. 27, 29.
"Mirror." [CapeR] (29:2) Fall 94, p. 43.
"Song" (tr. of Jaroslav Seifert). [NewRena] (9:1, #27) 94, p. 65.
"Sparrow." [BlackBR] (19) Fall-Wint 94, p. 26.
"Sun." [CoalC] (8) Ap 94, p. 36.
"Untitled Stanzas" (tr. of Rainer Maria Rilke). [RiverS] (40) 94, p. 31.
"Veering." [NewRena] (9:1, #27) 94, p. 145.
"Willow." [CapeR] (29:2) Fall 94, p. 42.

3829. MAGGI, Maria
"There Is Just the Breath." [PraS] (68:2) Sum 94, p. 123-124.
MAGHUT, Mohammad al-
See Al-MAGHUT, Mohammad
3830. MAGILL, Robert
"The Most Telling Death." [Kaleid] (29) Sum-Fall 94, p. 21.
3831. MAGINNES, Al
"The Angels of Our Daily Bread." [GeoR] (48:1) Spr 94, p. 23-24.
"Bread." [Pembroke] (26) 94, p. 109-110.
"Counting Toward Harmony." [TampaR] (8) Spr 94, p. 12-13.
"Moonvine." [Ledge] (17) Wint 94, p. 40-41.
"Perfume." [LouisL] (11:2) Fall 94, p. 66-67.
"The Riverman Writes His Love." [Pembroke] (26) 94, p. 110.
"Sharks in Kansas." [MidAR] (14:2) 94, p. 45-47.
"The Sound of One Voice." [GreenMR] (NS 17:2) Fall-Wint 94-95, p. 117-118.
"Terminal Street." [Ledge] (17) Wint 94, p. 42-44.
"Trails." [LouisL] (11:2) Fall 94, p. 68-69.
"Want." [SouthernPR] (34:1) Sum 94, p. 27-28.
3832. MAGORIAN, James
"Book of the Dead." [SlipS] (14) 94, p. 96-99.
"Kamikaze Pilots in Retirement." [SewanR] (102:3) Sum 94, p. 335-337.
3833. MAGOWAN, Robin
"Spoke Song." [NewRep] (210:24) 13 Je 94, p. 50.
3834. MAGRELLI, Valerio
"Other Still Lives" (Excerpts, tr. by Marco Fazzini and Douglas Reid Skinner). [Verse] (11:1) Spr 94, p. 44-45.
3835. MAGUINESS, Nancy
"Canticle of a Twig." [JINJPo] (16:1) Spr 94, p. 11.
"Elan Vital." [JINJPo] (16:1) Spr 94, p. 12.
3836. MAHAPATRA, Anuradha
"Crow" (tr. by Paramita Banerjee and Carolyne Wright). [PartR] (61:1) Wint 94, p. 155.
"Tambura" (tr. by Carolyne Wright, w. Paramita Banerjee). [Calyx] (15:2) Sum 94, p. 61.
3837. MAHAPATRA, Jayanta
"The Absence of Knowledge." [SewanR] (102:1) Wint 94, p. 22-23.
"Japan" (Two Poems). [InterQ] (1:2) 93, p. 162-163.
"Landscape." [InterQ] (1:2) 93, p. 165.
"Late." [InterQ] (1:2) 93, p. 164.
"Octave." [InterQ] (1:2) 93, p. 166.
"Someone in My room." [MalR] (107) Sum 94, p. 47-49.
"Waiting for the Summer of 1994 (after the rioting in India)." [InterQ] (1:2) 93, p. 167.
3838. MAHARAJ, Robyn
"Candle Maker." [Dandel] (21:2) 94, p. 69.
"The Prisoner." [Dandel] (21:2) 94, p. 70.
3839. MAHDI, Sami
"The Ants" (tr. by Mohammed Darweesh). [Vis] (45) 94, p. 37.
3840. MAHONEY, Dorothy
"A Thinly Painted Line." [AntigR] (97) Spr 94, p. 147.
3841. MAHONEY, Gene
"Arthur Rimbaud (1854-1891)." [WormR] (34:4, #136) 94, p. 139-140.
"Jack of Lanterns." [WormR] (34:4, #136) 94, p. 140.
3842. MAHONEY, Lisa
"Metamorphosis." [Amelia] (7:3, #22) 94, p. 107-108.
3843. MAHONEY, MaryJo
"Aesthetic Transport." [NoCarLR] (2:1) Spr 94, p. 128.
3844. MAHOOD, Shirley
"Squamish." [CanLit] (142/143) Fall-Wint 94, p. 37.
3845. MAIA
"Stars on the Water*" (*an ancient star-group in Egyptian lore). [Gaia] (4) Je 94, p. 5.
"Talking in Our Sleep" (for Will Inman). [Gaia] (4) Je 94, p. 5-6.
3846. MAIER, Jennifer
"Cockroach." [NegC] (13:2/3) 93, p. 38-39.
"Vegitable Man" [sic]." [NegC] (13:2/3) 93, p. 40-41.

3847. MAILLARD, Keith
"The Author Recalls His Adolescence." [AntigR] (96) Wint 94, p. 99-100.
"The Author Recalls His Childhood." [AntigR] (96) Wint 94, p. 98.
"Gloss on a Text of John Ashbery's." [MalR] (106) Spr 94, p. 27-28.
"Solving an Old Thriller." [PoetryC] (14:3) My 94, p. 24.
3848. MAIR, Denis
"The Song of AIDS" (tr. of Yan Li). [Talisman] (12) Spr 94, p. 176.
3849. MAJAJ, Lisa Suhair
"Tata Bahiyeh" (for that generation). [InterQ] (1:3) 94, p. 176-178.
3850. MAJOR, Alice
"A Creation Myth: How Men and Women Came to Be." [PoetryC] (15:1) N 94, p. 25.
3851. MAJOR, Clarence
"Descendant of Solomon and the Queen of Sheba." [NewL] (60:4) 94, p. 91-93.
"I Was Looking for the University." [AfAmRev] (28:1) Spr 94, p. 28.
"On Trying to Imagine the Kiwi Pregnant." [AfAmRev] (28:1) Spr 94, p. 25-26.
"On Watching a Caterpillar Become a Butterfly." [AfAmRev] (28:1) Spr 94, p. 23-24.
"The Slave Trade: View from the Middle Passage." [AfAmRev] (28:1) Spr 94, p. 11-22.
"View from a Rock at Dusk" (New Mexico). [AfAmRev] (28:1) Spr 94, p. 27.
3852. MAK, Lev
"Eden After" (tr. by Dan Jaffe). [DenQ] (29:1) Sum 94, p. 86.
3853. MAKIKO
"Sidewinder." [Amelia] (7:4, #23) 94, p. 8.
3854. MAKOFSKE, Mary
"Bare-Hearted Frog." [Blueline] (15) 94, p. 55.
"Dragonfly Fossil." [Blueline] (15) 94, p. 56.
"The Iceman." [CumbPR] (13:2) Spr 94, p. 31-32.
"A Personal History of the Early Fifties." [CreamCR] (18:1) Spr 94, p. 26-27.
"Shy with Each Other As a Boy and Girl." [Kalliope] (16:3) 94, p. 38.
"A Woman in the Cloister of Her Mind" (for May Sarton). [CumbPR] (13:2) Spr 94, p. 33.
3855. MAKUCK, Peter
"Against Distance." [SewanR] (102:1) Wint 94, p. 24-28.
"Bloodstone." [PoetryNW] (35:4) Wint 94-95, p. 14-16.
"The Fluteman." [SouthernPR] (34:2) Wint 94, p. 46-48.
"Flying Fish." [PoetryNW] (35:4) Wint 94-95, p. 16-17.
"Woodsmoke." [Poetry] (165:1) O 94, p. 5-6.
3856. MALANCIOIU, Ileana
"Another Hour" (tr. by Eveline L. Kanes and Mihai Zaharia). [InterPR] (20:1) Spr 94, p. 37.
"Bufonul." [InterPR] (20:1) Spr 94, p. 42.
"Ca un Iepure." [InterPR] (20:1) Spr 94, p. 38.
"Inca un Ceas." [InterPR] (20:1) Spr 94, p. 36.
"The Jester" (tr. by Eveline L. Kanes and Mihai Zaharia). [InterPR] (20:1) Spr 94, p. 43.
"The Last Memory" (tr. by Eveline L. Kanes and Mihai Zaharia). [InterPR] (20:1) Spr 94, p. 45.
"Like a Rabbit" (tr. by Eveline L. Kanes and Mihai Zaharia). [InterPR] (20:1) Spr 94, p. 39.
"Pe Cind Calatoream." [InterPR] (20:1) Spr 94, p. 46.
"Prada Visului Meu." [InterPR] (20:1) Spr 94, p. 40.
"Ultima Amintire." [InterPR] (20:1) Spr 94, p. 44.
"Victim of My Dream" (tr. by Eveline L. Kanes and Mihai Zaharia). [InterPR] (20:1) Spr 94, p. 41.
"When I Sailed" (tr. by Eveline L. Kanes and Mihai Zaharia). [InterPR] (20:1) Spr 94, p. 47.
3857. MALANGA, Gerard
"L'Amour Fou." [Arshile] (3) 94, p. 22-23.
"Calvinized" (for Josie Borain). [Arshile] (3) 94, p. 20-21.
"Scent" (for Sally Mann, photographer). [Arshile] (3) 94, p. 18-19.
3858. MALCOLM, Bruce
"Actual Size." [BrooklynR] (11) 94, p. 46-47.
"Found a Peanut." [BrooklynR] (11) 94, p. 48-49.
"Messenger." [BrooklynR] (11) 94, p. 50-52.

3859. MALCOLM, David
"(I) Night Journey" (tr. of Krystyna Lars, w. Georgia Scott). [InterQ] (1:1) [93?], p. 102-103.
"(I) She Writes with Fire" (tr. of Krystyna Lars, w. Georgia Scott). [InterQ] (1:1) [93?], p. 101.
"In Fourteen Red Tramcars" (tr. of Wladyslaw Zawistowski, w. Georgia Scott). [InterQ] (1:1) [93?], p. 105.
"Mother and Daughter" (tr. of Anna Czekanowicz, w. Katarzyna Kietlinska). [InterQ] (1:1) [93?], p. 106.
"A Poet's Worth" (tr. of Wladyslaw Zawistowski, w. Katarzyna Kietlinska). [InterQ] (1:1) [93?], p. 104.
"Report from a Distant City" (tr. of Anna Czekanowicz, w. Katarzyna Kietlinska). [InterQ] (1:1) [93?], p. 107.
"To Get Through the Night" (tr. of Anna Czekanowicz, w. Katarzyna Kietlinska). [InterQ] (1:1) [93?], p. 108-109.
3860. MALCOLM, River
"Looking for My First Kitten." [SoCoast] (17) Je 94, p. 28.
3861. MALDEN, Ann-Britt
"Coffee." [Sonora] (27) Spr 94, p. 95-101.
3862. MALEY, Sandra
"The Suicide" (tr. of Jorge Luis Borges). [PlumR] (7) [94?], p. 67.
"The Unending Rose" (to Susana Bombal, tr. of Jorge Luis Borges). [PlumR] (7) [94?], p. 66.
3863. MALI, Taylor
"I Could Be a Poet" (A poem for people who know how poems are supposed to be read). [BelPoJ] (45:2) Wint 94-95, p. 20-21.
3864. MALIK, Irfan
"Her Hands Clasp One Another" (tr. by Lisa Sapinkopf and the author). [InterQ] (1:3) 94, p. 179.
3865. MALINOVSKI, Nina
"Civilization's Children" (tr. by Per Brask and Patrick Friesen). [PoetryC] (14:2) Mr 94, p. 22.
"Untitled: In dreams" (tr. by Per Brask and Patrick Friesen). [PoetryC] (14:2) Mr 94, p. 22.
3866. MALLARMÉ, Stéphane
"Sonnets" (Selections: II-III, tr. by Henry Weinfield). [DenQ] (29:1) Sum 94, p. 87-88.
"Windows" (tr. by Rachel Hadas). [HarvardR] (6) Spr 94, p. 158-159.
3867. MALLEY, Ern
"Culture as Exhibit" (by James McAuley and Harold Stewart, under the pseudonym of Ern Malley). [InterQ] (1:2) 93, p. 117-118.
3868. MALLOY, Dorothy D.
"Timepiece." [Amelia] (7:3, #22) 94, p. 143.
3869. MALONE, Carol
"Persephone to Demeter." [Boulevard] (9:3, #27) Fall 94, p. 188.
3870. MALONE, Jaquelyn
"For Julie." [SycamoreR] (6:2) Sum 94, p. 51.
3871. MALONE, Pamela
"It Sits There." [BellArk] (10:1) Ja-F 94, p. 24.
3872. MALONEY, Dana Holley
"Imagining the Man in the Station." [JINJPo] (16:2) Aut 94, p. 23-24.
"Maintenance." [EngJ] (83:2) F 94, p. 91.
"When the Dinner Guest Comes." [JINJPo] (16:2) Aut 94, p. 25.
3873. MALROUX, Claire
"Exploded Landscape" (tr. by Marilyn Hacker). [ColR] (21:2) Fall 94, p. 108.
"The Lamp Set Down" (tr. by Marilyn Hacker). [ColR] (21:2) Fall 94, p. 109-111.
"Precepts" (tr. by Marilyn Hacker). [Agni] (39) 94, p. 210.
"The rain shakes a disheveled head" (tr. by Marilyn Hacker). [PraS] (68:1) Spr 94, p. 29.
"She speaks to us of a country not our own" (tr. by Marilyn Hacker). [PraS] (68:1) Spr 94, p. 30.
"Time Has Doors Has Windows" (tr. by Marilyn Hacker). [ColR] (21:2) Fall 94, p. 107.
3874. MALTMAN, Kim
"One Hundred Views of Edo." [Nimrod] (37:2) Spr-Sum 94, p. 60-61.

3875. MALYON, Carol
"Blurred Buffalo" (from a painting by Milt Jewell). [Arc] (33) Fall 94, p. 38-39.
"You Wake Up Beside a Stranger." [Grain] (22:2) Fall 94, p. 59-61.
MAN, Chui Leung
See LEUNG, Man Chui
3876. MANDELL, Charlotte
"Xenias" (tr. of Jean-Paul Auxemery). [Sulfur] (35) Fall 94, p. 131-138.
3877. MANDELSTAM, Osip
"The Stalin Epigram" (tr. by Clarence Brown and W. S. Merwin). [Agni] (39) 94, p. 94-95.
3878. MANESIOTIS, Joy
"Anesthesia." [Journal] (18:2) Fall-Wint 94, p. 56.
"Crossing Over." [Journal] (18:2) Fall-Wint 94, p. 57.
"Fugue." [DenQ] (28:4) Spr 94, p. 36-37.
"Howard Johnson's." [SycamoreR] (6:1) Wint 94, p. 17-18.
"Night Watchman at the Aquarium." [SycamoreR] (6:1) Wint 94, p. 16.
"The Pianist." [SycamoreR] (6:1) Wint 94, p. 15.
3879. MANGAN, Kathy
"The Fallen." [CimR] (107) Ap 94, p. 82.
"Headwaters." [SenR] (24:2) Fall 94, p. 33.
"Island Cemetery." [CimR] (107) Ap 94, p. 81-82.
"Leavings." [SenR] (24:2) Fall 94, p. 31-32.
"St. Paul Street Seasonal." [GettyR] (7:2) Spr 94, p. 278.
"Thatch." [GettyR] (7:2) Spr 94, p. 279.
3880. MANGAN, Pat
"Acid." [TriQ] (90) Spr-Sum 94, p. 181-182.
"Boil." [TriQ] (90) Spr-Sum 94, p. 185.
"Calf's Head in the Mountains Above Mexico City." [TriQ] (91) Fall 94, p. 188.
"F Train." [TriQ] (91) Fall 94, p. 187.
"Roots." [TriQ] (90) Spr-Sum 94, p. 184.
"Thompson." [TriQ] (90) Spr-Sum 94, p. 183.
3881. MANKIEWICZ, Angela Consolo
"Freak." [SlipS] (14) 94, p. 69-70.
"Radiation Order: 5 Days a Week — 6 Weeks." [ChironR] (13:3) Aut 94, p. 32.
MANLIU, Liu
See LIU, Manliu
3882. MANN, Charles Edward
"Answering Machine." [HolCrit] (31:5) D 94, p. 17-18.
"At the Museum of Natural History." [FourQ] (8:2) Fall 94, p. 39.
"Losing Count." [Border] (4) Spr-Sum 94, p. 50.
"Such Freedom." [CapeR] (29:2) Fall 94, p. 32.
"Walking to Heaven." [CreamCR] (18:2) Fall 94, p. 135.
3883. MANN, Emily
"To Know a Monster: The Story of the Greensboro Massacre" (Selection: Prologue — The Present "W. A. R."). [OntR] (41) Fall-Wint 94, p. 48-53.
3884. MANN, John
"July 16, 1942." [IllinoisR] (1:2) Spr 94, p. 7-8.
"Mercy." [IllinoisR] (1:2) Spr 94, p. 17.
"Why Should There Not Be Nothing?" (— George Steiner). [NoDaQ] (62:1) Wint 94-95, p. 111-112.
3885. MANN, Jules
"Left for Summer." [ModernW] (1) Summer 94, p. 71.
"Ode to J." [EvergreenC] (9:1) Wint-Spr 94, p. 21.
"Ten Years." [ModernW] (1) Summer 94, p. 72.
"Untitled: It finally started raining." [ModernW] (1) Summer 94, p. 73.
3886. MANN, Randall
"The Robe of Lady Philosophy." [CumbPR] (14:1) Fall 94, p. 54.
3887. MANNING, Jennifer
"Nitrogen." [GreensboroR] (56) Sum 94, p. 97-98.
3888. MANNING, Sylvia
"Lantana Dreams Zapata in the Room." [Border] (5) Fall-Wint 94, p. 38-41.
3889. MANOO-RAHMING, Lelawattee
"Love Up De Culture." [CaribbeanW] (8) 94, p. 8-9.
3890. MANOPOULOS, Monique
"Like" (tr. of Jude Stéfan, w. P. Kobylarz). [PoetryE] (37/38) Spr 94, p. 225.
"To Cavafy" (tr. of Jude Stéfan, w. P. Kobylarz). [PoetryE] (37/38) Spr 94, p. 224.

3891. MANSOUR, Joyce
"All the Nights" (tr. by Molly Bendall). [DenQ] (29:1) Sum 94, p. 89.
"The Amazon" (tr. by Carol Poster). [PoetryE] (37/38) Spr 94, p. 230.
"Going and Coming of Sequins" (tr. by Molly Bendall). [AmerPoR] (23:4) Jl-Ag 94, p. 16.
"In the Gloom on the Left" (tr. by Molly Bendall). [AmerPoR] (23:4) Jl-Ag 94, p. 15.
"Mirror" (tr. by Molly Bendall). [DenQ] (29:1) Sum 94, p. 90.
"Modesty" (tr. by Molly Bendall). [AmerPoR] (23:4) Jl-Ag 94, p. 15.
"The Sun in Capricorn" (tr. by Molly Bendall). [AmerPoR] (23:4) Jl-Ag 94, p. 15.
3892. MANYARROWS, Victoria
"Today." [Callaloo] (17:1) Wint 94, p. 353.
3893. MANYÉ i MARTI, Lourdes
"Desert of the Days" (tr. of Miquel Martí i Pol, w. Wayne Cox). [SouthernHR] (28:2) Spr 94, p. 157.
"The Other Struggle" (tr. of Miquel Martí i Pol, w. Wayne Cox). [SouthernHR] (28:2) Spr 94, p. 159.
3894. MANZOR, Yanai
"My Key" (tr. by David Frye). [MichQR] (33:4) Fall 94, p. 731.
3895. MARBAUGH, Wade
"Riverside Birth." [InterQ] (1:4) 94, p. 104.
3896. MARCELLO, Leo (Leo Luke)
"The Loop, Chincoteague, Virginia." [LouisL] (11:2) Fall 94, p. 71-72.
"Names and Numbers." [XavierR] (14:1) Spr 94, p. 30-32.
"Red Cloud's Confession." [XavierR] (14:1) Spr 94, p. 28-29.
"A Sister Writes from the Missions, 1888." [XavierR] (14:1) Spr 94, p. 26-27.
3897. MARCH, Joseph Moncure
"The Wild Party" (Drawings by Art Spiegelman). [NewYorker] (70:19) 27 Je-4 Jl 94, p. 155-163.
3898. MARCHAMPS, Guy
"A Love Poem to Humanity" (Excerpt, to Kypris, tr. by Judith Cowan). [InterPR] (20:2) Fall 94, p. 87-91.
"Poème d'Amour à l'Humanité" (Excerpt, à Kypris). [InterPR] (20:2) Fall 94, p. 86-90.
3899. MARCHAND, Blaine
"Discovering Buoyancy." [Arc] (32) Spr 94, p. 14-15.
"Travelling Alone." [Arc] (32) Spr 94, p. 16-17.
3900. MARCHAND, Clément
"Snow Solo" (tr. by Judith Cowan). [InterPR] (20:2) Fall 94, p. 63, 65.
"Solo de Neige." [InterPR] (20:2) Fall 94, p. 62, 64.
3901. MARCHANT, Fred
"The Afterlife on Squaw Peak." [HarvardR] (6) Spr 94, p. 42-43.
"Boraxo." [Agni] (39) 94, p. 89.
"Butterfly Chair." [BostonR] (19:1) Fe-Mr 94, p. 27.
"Song of the Stomach." [HarvardR] (2) Fall 92, p. 102-103.
"Tipping Point." [HarvardR] (6) Spr 94, p. 41-42.
3902. MARCIL, Chris
"My Two Cents" (culled entirely from Larry King's column in *USA Today* by Sam Johnson and Chris Maril). [NewRep] (211:1) 4 Jl 94, p. 9.
3903. MARCUS, Jacqueline
"Sycamore Bay" (corrected reprint from 5:2). [SycamoreR] (6:1) Wint 94, p. 39-40.
3904. MARCUS, Mordecai
"Blood Wedding." [Plain] (15:1) Fall 94, p. 18.
"Edward Hopper's 'Excursion into Philosophy'." [Gaia] (4) Je 94, p. 6.
3905. MARCUS, Morton
"Every Morning." [ProseP] (3) 94, p. 67.
"My Triangle." [ProseP] (3) 94, p. 68.
"Odysseus." [BellR] (17:1/2) Spr-Fall 94, p. 36-37.
"Penelope." [BellR] (17:1/2) Spr-Fall 94, p. 35.
"Who Can Tell the Dreamer from the Dream?" [ProseP] (3) 94, p. 65-66.
3906. MARCUS, Peter
"Help." [Ploughs] (20:1) Spr 94, p. 170.
"The Teaching." [TarRP] (33:2) Spr 94, p. 24.
"Whitefish." [PlumR] (7) [94?], p. 68-69.

3907. MARCUS, Sharon
"Non-Existent Poems" (1, 3-4, 31, 50, 55, 61). [Descant] (25:1, #84) Spr 94, p. 114-120.
3908. MARCUS, Stanley
"The Short Guy." [Confr] (52/53) Wint-Spr 94, p. 333-334.
3909. MARDER, Daniel
"Having Kanchenjunga." [Nimrod] (38:1) Fall-Wint 94, p. 122.
MARE, Walter de la
See De la MARE, Walter
3910. MARES, E. A.
"Chisme entre los Viejos (Gossip among the Old Ones)." [PraS] (68:4) Wint 94, p. 151-152.
"I-40/Route 66 Alburquerque to Amarillo: Petty Gossip." [PraS] (68:4) Wint 94, p. 153-154.
"Time Traveller Dance." [PraS] (68:4) Wint 94, p. 155.
3911. MARGOLIS, Gary
"The Flare." [GreenMR] (NS 17:2) Fall-Wint 94-95, p. 112.
"For a Stable of Horses." [PoetryNW] (35:1) Spr 94, p. 12-13.
"A Shadow of a Nest." [PoetryNW] (35:1) Spr 94, p. 14.
3912. MARGOSHES, Dave
"Eat Their Own." [Grain] (22:1) Sum 94, p. 27.
"The Sound of My Voice." [Grain] (22:1) Sum 94, p. 28.
3913. MARIANI, Paul
"Ghost." [Image] (4) Fall 93, p. 12-13.
"The Great Wheel." [Image] (4) Fall 93, p. 11-12.
3914. MARINO, Gigi
"The Elevator." [Pivot] (41) 93, p. 54-55.
3915. MARINOVICH, Matt
"How to Look Suspicious in the Public Library." [QW] (38) Winter-Spr 93-94, p. 116-117.
"Mr. Moro Successfully Frozen in a Block of Ice." [PoetryE] (37/38) Spr 94, p. 120-121.
"Night School." [PoetryE] (37/38) Spr 94, p. 118-119.
"Yardwork." [QW] (38) Winter-Spr 93-94, p. 118-119.
3916. MARIO, Luis
"Primera Vez." [Nuez] (5:13/14/15) 94, p. 67.
3917. MARION, Jeff Daniel
"For My Friends Who Missed Me in the Public Places Where They Thought I Would Be." [Wind] (74) 94, p. 24-25.
"Letting Go: A Letter to Libba." [Wind] (74) 94, p. 24.
"The Man Who Made Color" (for the memory of my father J. D. Marion 1915-1990). [SouthernPR] (34:2) Wint 94, p. 8-9.
3918. MARKHAM, E. A.
"A Family Gift." [Jacaranda] (5:1) Wint-Spr 91, p. 74-77.
"This Might Have Been a Lucky House for Us." [Pivot] (42) 94, p. 25.
3919. MARKOS, Don
"Splitting Wood." [Northeast] (5:11) Wint 94-95, p. 40.
3920. MARKOTIC, Nicole
"Portage." [CapilR] (2:12) Wint 94, p. 59-66.
"Talk-Talking." [CapilR] (2:12) Wint 94, p. 56-58.
3921. MARLATT, Daphne
"Small Print" (for Bet). [WestCL] (28:3, #15) Wint 94-95, p. 26-28.
3922. MARLIS, Stefanie
"Dog." [AmerPoR] (23:5) S-O 94, p. 47.
"Riots." [PoetryE] (37/38) Spr 94, p. 18.
"Saturn." [Poetry] (164:2) My 94, p. 68.
MARLIS, Stephanie
See MARLIS, Stefanie
3923. MARMOL, Jose
"Atina el Deseo." [CuadP] (8:23) My-Ag 94, p. 66.
"Costa del Este." [CuadP] (8:23) My-Ag 94, p. 64.
"Destallar el Horizonte." [CuadP] (8:23) My-Ag 94, p. 65.
"Idioma de los Dioses." [CuadP] (8:23) My-Ag 94, p. 63-64.
"Retrato de Muher." [CuadP] (8:23) My-Ag 94, p. 65-66.
"Seduccion." [CuadP] (8:23) My-Ag 94, p. 66-67.

3924. MARPLE, Vivian
"Clothes Line — a Rope or Wire to Hang Clothes on in Order to Air or Dry Them." [PraF] (15:3, #68) Aut 94, p. 36.
"Sitting on the furnace grate." [Grain] (22:1) Sum 94, p. 134.
"This is the night you judge other pain by." [PraF] (15:3, #68) Aut 94, p. 37.
"When I was little, I wanted a horse named Flicka." [Grain] (22:1) Sum 94, p. 135.
3925. MARQUART, Debra
"I Am Upstairs, Trying to Be Quiet." [CumbPR] (14:1) Fall 94, p. 81.
"Missing Wife." [CumbPR] (14:1) Fall 94, p. 82-83.
"Sweet Light Crude." [CumbPR] (14:1) Fall 94, p. 79-80.
3926. MARRON, Thomas
"Songs for the Angels. Five: Michael after the Fall." [Conscience] (15:1) Spr 94, p. 24.
"Songs for the Angels. Four: Lucifer Bedazzled." [Conscience] (15:1) Spr 94, p. 22.
"Songs for the Angels. One: First Visitation." [Conscience] (15:1) Spr 94, p. 16.
"Songs for the Angels. Six: Lucifer Surprised by Age." [Conscience] (15:1) Spr 94, p. 26.
"Songs for the Angels. Three: Gabriel Considers His Horn." [Conscience] (15:1) Spr 94, p. 20.
"Songs for the Angels. Two: Rebellion of the Angels." [Conscience] (15:1) Spr 94, p. 18.
MARRUZ, Fina Garcia
See GARCIA MARRUZ, Fina
3927. MARSH, Irene Eberling
"If You Were Here." [Parting] (7:1) Sum 94, p. 59.
3928. MARSHALL, Jack
"Wing and Prayer." [Pequod] (37) 94, p. 9-11.
3929. MARSHALL, John
"Mackey MacLaren." [AntigR] (97) Spr 94, p. 148.
"Postcard." [MalR] (108) Fall 94, p. 57.
3930. MARSHALL, Tod
"Academic, Waiting for Spring Break." [BellArk] (10:3) My-Je 94, p. 9.
"The American Side of the Falls." [SouthernR] (30:3) Sum 94, p. 552-554.
"Instant Historical." [DenQ] (28:3) Wint 94, p. 24-25.
"Mother Tells the Girl of Fish." [Boulevard] (9:1/2, #25/26) Spr 94, p. 78.
"A New Martyrdom." [ColR] (21:2) Fall 94, p. 129.
"Psalm 62: Spring." [BellArk] (10:3) My-Je 94, p. 9.
3931. MARSHBURN, Sandra
"Northbound." [Parting] (7:1) Sum 94, p. 64.
"November Funeral." [TarRP] (33:2) Spr 94, p. 37.
3932. MARTEAU, Robert
"Août sur les Chaumes Abandonnés" (tr. by Andrea Moorhead). [PoetryE] (37/38) Spr 94, p. 228.
"Etude pour une Muse" (extraits). [Os] (39) Fall-Wint 94, p. 28-31.
"Le Lavis Mouvant" (tr. by Andrea Moorhead). [PoetryE] (37/38) Spr 94, p. 227.
"Peignez l'ombre en couleur et vous avez un autre." [Os] (38) Spr 94, p. 2.
MARTHA ELIZABETH
See ELIZABETH, Martha
MARTI, Lourdes Manyé i
See MANYÉ i MARTI, Lourdes
3933. MARTI i POL, Miquel
"L'Altre Combat." [SouthernHR] (28:2) Spr 94, p. 158.
"Desert Dels Dies." [SouthernHR] (28:2) Spr 94, p. 156.
"Desert of the Days" (tr. by Wayne Cox and Lourdes Manyé i Martí). [SouthernHR] (28:2) Spr 94, p. 157.
"The Other Struggle" (tr. by Wayne Cox and Lourdes Manyé i Martí). [SouthernHR] (28:2) Spr 94, p. 159.
3934. MARTIAL
"Martial Translation" (12 selection, tr. by William Matthews). [Light] (10) Sum 94, p. 4-5.
"Martial's Epigrams" (Selection: X, xlvii, tr. by William Matthews). [Poetry] (165:3) D 94, p. 157.
"Three Poems: IV.41, VI.93, XII.12" (tr. by Joseph S. Salemi). [CrabCR] (8:2/3/9:1/2/3) 94, p. 101-102.
"Translations from Martial" (X.lix, IX.xiv, IX.x, X.lxxiv, X.lxi, tr. by William Matthews). [ColR] (21:2) Fall 94, p. 90-91.

3935. MARTIN, Camille
"The Screen, the Beach" (Selections: XII-XIII, tr. of Lionel Ray). [LitR] (37:4) Sum 94, p. 658-659.
3936. MARTIN, Charles
"Victoria's Secret." [Hellas] (5:2) Fall-Wint 94, p. 43.
3937. MARTIN, D. S.
"Tribal Burial Customs." [AntigR] (99) Aut 94, p. 77-78.
3938. MARTIN, Herbert Woodward
"Black Jazz." [Obs] (9:2) Fall-Wint 94, p. 98.
"The Broken Vessel." [Obs] (9:2) Fall-Wint 94, p. 98.
"The Garden of Earthly Delight" (for: Robert Hayden). [WritersF] (20) 94, p. 41.
"Letter to Freedom" (a found poem). [AfAmRev] (28:4) Wint 94, p. 598.
"Wilderness." [Obs] (9:2) Fall-Wint 94, p. 97.
3939. MARTIN, Kathi
"How to Be Fat — How to Be Thin." [Sonora] (28) Fall 94, p. 25.
3940. MARTIN, Lynn
"By the River." [PoetryNW] (35:1) Spr 94, p. 19-20.
"Carolina Handler." [PoetryNW] (35:1) Spr 94, p. 18-19.
"Seeds." [PoetryNW] (35:1) Spr 94, p. 18.
3941. MARTIN, Paul
"The Blue Silk Sportcoat." [ChironR] (13:4) Wint 94, p. 11.
"Living in the Combat Zone." [ChironR] (13:2) Sum 94, p. 30.
3942. MARTIN, Richard
"The Bartender Remembers Raising His Son." [BellR] (17:1/2) Spr-Fall 94, p. 56-57.
"Projection." [AnotherCM] (27) 94, p. 140-142.
3943. MARTIN, Stephen-Paul
"The center is the ghost of an absent king." [HeavenB] (11) 94, p. 17.
3944. MARTIN, Terry
"Mother's Day, 1991." [EngJ] (83:3) Mr 94, p. 103.
3945. MARTIN, W.
"Beautiful Moments." [Iowa] (24:3) Fall 94, p. 38.
"Marzipan." [Iowa] (24:3) Fall 94, p. 34-38.
"Spain" (tr. of Nico Graf). [ArtfulD] (26/27) 94, p. 16-20.
3946. MARTINAITIS, Marcelijus
"A Worldwide Pain in Kukutis' Detached Leg" (tr. by Laima Sruoginis). [Vis] (45) 94, p. 38-39.
3947. MARTINEZ, Dionisio (Dionisio D.)
"An Absolute Certainty." [InterQ] (1:4) 94, p. 155-156.
"The Architect." [Chelsea] (56) 94, p. 99.
"Better Days" (for Ricardo Pau-Llosa). [PraS] (68:4) Wint 94, p. 111.
"Erik Satie: Préludes." [Caliban] (14) 94, p. 44-45.
"Frank Lloyd Wright: The Land." [Caliban] (14) 94, p. 43.
"Gustav Klimt: The Kiss." [PraS] (68:4) Wint 94, p. 114-115.
"Gymnopédis." [MidAR] (14:2) 94, p. 8-9.
"History, Vacationing in Cuba Circa 1993, Refuses to Absolve Rip Van Winkle's Children." [PraS] (68:4) Wint 94, p. 114.
"Interpretaciones del realismo." [InterQ] (1:4) 94, p. 159.
"Interpretations of Realism" (tr. by Sandra Teichmann). [InterQ] (1:4) 94, p. 158.
"Laura Hereda un Charlatán." [InterQ] (1:4) 94, p. 157.
"Laura Inherits a Charlatan" (tr. by Sandra Teichmann). [InterQ] (1:4) 94, p. 157.
"Lost in the Streets" (for Eddie Steele). [KenR] (NS 16:2) Spr 94, p. 129.
"Marcel Duchamp Descending a Staircase" (Associated Writing Programs Intro Award poem). [IndR] (17:2) Fall 94, p. 142-144.
"Matisse: Blue Nude, 1952" (Associated Writing Programs Intro Award poem). [IndR] (17:2) Fall 94, p. 141.
"The Perfect Circle" (for Stephen Dunn). [KenR] (NS 16:2) Spr 94, p. 128.
"Sarabande." [MidAR] (14:2) 94, p. 10-11.
"The Scream That Peaks Past Fear" (after Christopher Fulkerson). [Chelsea] (56) 94, p. 97-98.
"The Search Party." [PraS] (68:4) Wint 94, p. 112.
"Simplicity." [GeoR] (48:1) Spr 94, p. 135-138.
"A Single Voice." [PraS] (68:4) Wint 94, p. 113.
"Tableau." [Confr] (52/53) Wint-Spr 94, p. 297-298.
"Treason." [Confr] (52/53) Wint-Spr 94, p. 299.
"Valse-Ballet." [InterQ] (1:4) 94, p. 160.

"What the Men Talk About When the Women Leave the Room." [Chelsea] (56) 94, p. 96-97.

MARTINEZ, Enrique González
See GONZALEZ MARTINEZ, Enrique

3948. MARTINEZ, Marcos L.
"Coming Out: A Sensual Sestina." [JamesWR] (11:5) Fall 94, p. 9.

3949. MARTINEZ, Ruben Gerard
"Toasting a Side Show of Lives." [IndR] (17:1) Spr 94, p. 25.
"Under Lights" (L. A. Riots '92). [IndR] (17:1) Spr 94, p. 24.

MARTINEZ ALLEN, Valerie
See ALLEN, Valerie Martínez

3950. MARTLAND, Robert
"Eagle." [CoalC] (8) Ap 94, p. 6.

3951. MARTONE, John
"Alone in our house." [Northeast] (5:10) Sum 94, p. 25.

3952. MARVEL, Catherine
"Crazy Quilt." [ColR] (21:1) Spr 94, p. 164-165.
"Shadow of an Idea." [ColR] (21:1) Spr 94, p. 166-167.

3953. MARVIN, Jay
"The First Time." [ChironR] (13:2) Sum 94, p. 31.

3954. MARX, Anne
"A Token to Be Taken on Faith." [Amelia] (7:3, #22) 94, p. 90.

3955. MARX, Doug
"In a Large Family" (a response to Galway Kinnell's "When One Has Lived a Long Time Alone"). [Harp] (288:1725) F 94, p. 34.

3956. MARZAHL, Kevin
"From Liverpool." [SouthernPR] (34:2) Wint 94, p. 36-37.

3957. MARZAN, Julio
"Call Out My Number" (tr. of Julia de Burgos). [Callaloo] (17:3) Sum 94, p. 671.
"Pentachromatic" (tr. of Julia de Burgos). [Callaloo] (17:3) Sum 94, p. 705-706.
"Poem of the Intimate Agony" (tr. of Julia de Burgos). [Callaloo] (17:3) Sum 94, p. 670.
"Poem with the Final Tune" (tr. of Julia de Burgos). [Callaloo] (17:3) Sum 94, p. 669.

3958. MASAHIDE (1657-1723)
Haiku [AmerPoR] (23:4) Jl-Ag 94, p. 18.

3959. MASON, Clif
"In the Animal Park" (Parc National de l'Akagera, Rwanda). [Amelia] (7:4, #23) 94, p. 116-117.
"Lakota Hoop Dancer" (for Kevin Locke). [WorldO] (25:3) Spr 94, p. 48-49.
"Night Song." [Plain] (14:3) Spr 94, p. 37.

3960. MASON, David
"The Escape." [Hudson] (47:2) Sum 94, p. 249-252.
"No One Had Told Us." [Hudson] (47:2) Sum 94, p. 254.
"On Being Dismissed As a Pastoral Poet." [SouthernR] (30:3) Sum 94, p. 555.
"September 1971" (to D.K. who wrote, tr. of Yiorgos Chouliaras, w. the author). [Pequod] (37) 94, p. 119.
"The Summer of Love." [Hudson] (47:2) Sum 94, p. 252-253.

3961. MASON, Herbert
"Nothing." [AmerPoR] (23:3) My-Je 94, p. 55.

3962. MASON, Janet
"Gloria in Excelsis Deo." [EvergreenC] (9:2) Sum-Fall 94, p. 44.
"My Father's Two Eyes." [Pearl] (20) Spr 94, p. 76-77.
"No Complaints." [EvergreenC] (9:2) Sum-Fall 94, p. 41-43.
"A Week Before Spring." [Blueline] (15) 94, p. 37.

3963. MASON, Jerry
"When One Leaves." [HampSPR] Wint 94, p. 36.

3964. MASON, Lucinda
"Soldiers of their childhood." [ChangingM] (27) Wint 94, p. 46.

3965. MASSMAN, Gordon
See also LESTER-MASSMAN, G. (Gordon)

MASTER, J. R. le
See LeMASTER, J. R.

3966. MASUDA, Barry
"Auto-Sonnet Machine." [HawaiiR] (18:1, #40) Spr 94, p. 78.
"Detonating Sentences." [HawaiiR] (18:1, #40) Spr 94, p. 79.

"A Louse's Parousia." [HawaiiR] (18:1, #40) Spr 94, p. 80.

3967. MATAMOROS, Miguel
"Lagrimas Negras." [Areíto] (4:15) Marzo 94, p. 44.
"Olvido." [Areíto] (4:15) Marzo 94, p. 44.

3968. MATEO, Noel
"Noble Cabbage." [BambooR] (63/64) Sum-Fall 94, p. 33.

3969. MATHENEY, Barbara K.
"Mr. Raymond in the Lobby of the Palomar Hotel." [Jacaranda] (5:1) Wint-Spr 91, p. 20-21.

3970. MATHERN, Eric
"Servants' Day Off." [NewRep] (211:25) 19 D 94, p. 36.

3971. MATHERNE, Beverly
"Fabrique de Tabac (Tobacco Harvest)." [Verse] (11:2) Sum 94, p. 79-80.

3972. MATHEWS, Harry
"Miss Unity's Book of Reminders." [NewAW] (12) Spr-Sum 94, p. 17-20.

3973. MATHIS, Cleopatra
"Little Lie." [Pivot] (41) 93, p. 44.
"A Text in Forgiveness." [Pivot] (41) 93, p. 43-44.

MATHISEN, Aina Gerner
See GERNER-MATHISEN, Aina

3974. MATHUR, Shakunt
"Chilka Lake" (tr. by Arlene Zide and Aruna Sitesh). [InterQ] (1:2) 93, p. 180-181.

3975. MATSIKIDZE, Isabella Pupurai
"Memorials of Our Redemption: A Woman-Epic of Zimbabwe" (Excerpt). [InterQ] (1:3) 94, p. 41-42.

3976. MATSON, Clive
"Shadow Traffic." [Vis] (46) 94, p. 36-37.

3977. MATTAWA, Khaled
"Atta" (Benghazi, 1968). [Callaloo] (17:2) Sum 94, p. 600-601.
"Bright Yellow, Ketchup Red." [NewEngR] (16:4) Fall 94, p. 159-160.
"Celebrating Her" (tr. of Adonis). [InterQ] (1:3) 94, p. 126-127.
"Days of 1933." [Callaloo] (17:2) Sum 94, p. 599.
"Hunger" (in memory of Joe Bolton). [InterQ] (1:3) 94, p. 124-125.
"The Mail from Tunis, 1992." [InterQ] (1:3) 94, p. 121-123.
"The Mouse" (tr. of Sa'adi Yusuf). [InterQ] (1:3) 94, p. 133.
"Night in Hamdan" (tr. of Sa'adi Yusuf). [InterQ] (1:3) 94, p. 134.
"Perfume" (tr. of Hashim Shafiq). [InterQ] (1:3) 94, p. 132.
"Questions and Their Retinue" (tr. of Hatif Janabi). [InterQ] (1:3) 94, p. 128-130.
"The River" (tr. of Hashim Shafiq). [InterQ] (1:3) 94, p. 131.
"What She Said on a Lewd Lute Night." [HayF] (14) Spr-Sum 94, p. 72-73.
"White Nile Elegy." [Callaloo] (17:2) Sum 94, p. 598.

3978. MATTERN, Evelyn
"Applause." [ChrC] (111:19) 15-22 Je 94, p. 598.

3979. MATTHAIS, John
"Mozart Variations #15" (tr. of Goran Sonnevi, w. G. Printz-Pahlson).). [Vis] (46) 94, p. 11.
"Mozart Variations #9" (tr. of Goran Sonnevi, w. G. Printz-Pahlson). [Vis] (45) 94, p. 13.

3980. MATTHEW, Antonia
"Hard to Move." [SingHM] (21) 94, p. 32-33.

3981. MATTHEWS, Mary
"Ten Shots." [WillowR] (21) Spr 94, p. 19.

3982. MATTHEWS, Sebastian
"And What It Mustn't." [Jacaranda] (4:2) Spr 90, p. 33.

3983. MATTHEWS, William
"After the Storm" (tr. of Moshe Dor, w. the author). [TarRP] (34:1) Fall 94, p. 29.
"Angels and Cave" (tr. of Moshe Dor, w. the author). [TarRP] (34:1) Fall 94, p. 28.
"Blind Tasting." [Light] (10) Sum 94, p. 6.
"Cancer Talk." [Antaeus] (75/76) Aut 94, p. 295.
"Cheap Seats, the Cincinnati Gardens, Professional Basketball, 1959." [Atlantic] (274:6) D 94, p. 119.
"Dead Languages." [GeoR] (48:4) Wint 94, p. 709-710.
"Forms." [ColR] (21:2) Fall 94, p. 89.
"Grandmother Talking." [PassN] (15:1) Sum 94, p. 30.
"House Sitting." [AmerV] (35) 94, p. 56.
"Lust Acts." [Light] (10) Sum 94, p. 26.

"Martial Translations" (12 selections). [Light] (10) Sum 94, p. 4-5.
"Martial's Epigrams" (Selection: X, xlvii, tr. of Martial). [Poetry] (165:3) D 94, p. 157.
"Negligence." [PassN] (15:1) Sum 94, p. 31-32.
"A Night at the Opera." [AmerV] (35) 94, p. 54.
"Open City" (tr. of Moshe Dor, w. the author). [TarRP] (34:1) Fall 94, p. 29.
"Pavarotti in Transport, 1990" (Un Ballo in Maschera). [Pivot] (42) 94, p. 45.
"Pledge of Allegiance." [AmerV] (35) 94, p. 55.
"Premature Ejaculation." [Light] (10) Sum 94, p. 26.
"The Reason." [ColR] (21:2) Fall 94, p. 88.
"Refuge" (tr. of Moshe Dor, w. the author). [TarRP] (34:1) Fall 94, p. 28.
"The Sale of the Good Life." [Light] (10) Sum 94, p. 5.
"Stubbornness" (tr. of Moshe Dor, w. the author). [TarRP] (34:1) Fall 94, p. 29.
"Sweatballs." [ColR] (21:2) Fall 94, p. 86-87.
"Tomorrow." [AmerV] (35) 94, p. 51-52.
"Translations from Martial" (X.lix, IX.xiv, IX.x, X.lxxiv, X.lxi). [ColR] (21:2) Fall 94, p. 90-91.
"Va, Pensiero." [NewYorker] (70:42) 19 D 94, p. 81.
"Wasps." [AmerV] (35) 94, p. 53.
"Why Superboy Left." [Light] (10) Sum 94, p. 3.

3984. MATTHIAS, John
"After Years Away." [Stand] (35:3) Sum 94, p. 36-37.
"Dedication." [Image] ([2]) Sum 92, p. 61-62.
"The Silence of Stones." [Image] ([2]) Sum 92, p. 58-59.
"The Singer of Tales" (for Charles Simic). [Image] ([2]) Sum 92, p. 59-61.

MATTHIAS JOHANNESSEN
See JOHANNESSEN, Matthias

3985. MATTINGLY, Tracy
"Ouija." [PoetL] (89:2) Sum 94, p. 21-22.

3986. MATTOX, Gretchen
"The Hanging Gardens." [Pequod] (37) 94, p. 12.

3987. MAULDIN, Chelsea
"Adultery." [PaintedB] (53/54) 94, p. 7.
"Story of the Beggars." [PaintedB] (53/54) 94, p. 6.

3988. MAULSBY, Vernon
"Movements." [EvergreenC] (9:1) Wint-Spr 94, p. 81.

3989. MAURER-ALVAREZ, Pansy
"Dahlias." [Kalliope] (16:1) 94, p. 23.

3990. MAURICE, Carlotta
"Rampage." [Chelsea] (56) 94, p. 102.

3991. MAX, Lin
"When the Tules Are Peppered with Red-Winged Blackbirds." [Calyx] (15:2) Sum 94, p. 50-51.

3992. MAXWELL, Glyn
"As You Walk Out One Morning." [Verse] (11:2) Sum 94, p. 13-14.
"Car Game." [Verse] (11:2) Sum 94, p. 11.
"Conquest." [Verse] (11:2) Sum 94, p. 12.
"The Devil at War." [Verse] (11:2) Sum 94, p. 10.
"Just Like Us II, or, The Plot Thins." [Verse] (11:2) Sum 94, p. 12.

3993. MAXWELL, Mary
"Beckett in Roussillon." [ParisR] (36:133) Wint 94, p. 176.
"The Oxbow" (after the painting, *View from Mount Holyoke*, by Tomas Cole). [Salm] (104/105) Fall 94-Wint 95, p. 158-162.

MAY, Gabrielle le
See LeMAY, Gabrielle

3994. MAYER, Bernadette
"Instead of Always Doing Old Things." [Talisman] (13) Fall 94-Wint 95, p. 117.
"Introduction" (to Helen Decker). [Chelsea] (57) 94, p. 39.
"'W' Sonnet" (for Fanny Howe). [Chelsea] (57) 94, p. 40.

3995. MAYER, Rachael
"A Crumb Dance." [HiramPoR] (55/56) Fall 93-Sum 94, p. 74-75.
"Letters to the Baby." [KenR] (NS 16:2) Spr 94, p. 68-70.
"The Lights on the Harbor." [KenR] (NS 16:2) Spr 94, p. 66-68.
"The Small Earth." [ChatR] (14:3) Spr 94, p. 44.
"Waiting." [HiramPoR] (55/56) Fall 93-Sum 94, p. 76-77.

MAYER, Rachel
See MAYER, Rachael
3996. MAYES, Frances
"Ancient Air: A Stony Sestina, Doubled in Time." [SouthernR] (30:1) Ja, Wint 94, p. 91-94.
"Devotion." [Manoa] (6:2) Wint 94, p. 214.
"Malaria / *Palimpsest*." [ColR] (21:2) Fall 94, p. 146-147.
"Midsummer." [SouthernR] (30:4) Aut 94, p. 704.
"Rubric." [Manoa] (6:2) Wint 94, p. 213.
"Shaving My Legs with Ockham's Razor." [SouthernR] (30:4) Aut 94, p. 702-703.
"This Morning They Read 'Loveliest of Trees ...'." [Manoa] (6:2) Wint 94, p. 211-212.
3997. MAYNARD, L.
"At the Finest." [Vis] (45) 94, p. 40.
3998. MAYNARD, Theodore
"The World's Miser." [CimR] (107) Ap 94, p. 118-119.
3999. MAYRÖCKER, Friederike
"With Each Cloudy Peak / Je Ein Umwölkter Gipfel" (Selections: 4 poems, tr. by Rosmarie Waldrop). [Avec] (8:1) 94, p. 110-115.
4000. MAYS, J. L.
"I Was One with You This Morning." [ModernW] (2) Wint 94, p. 49.
"The Matador." [ModernW] (2) Wint 94, p. 50-51.
4001. MAZUR, Gail
"The Acorn." [HarvardR] (Premier Issue) Spr 92, p. 113.
"Fracture Santa Monica." [ColR] (21:2) Fall 94, p. 143-144.
"On the River: *Tableau Vivant*." [HarvardR] (7) Fall 94, p. 47.
"Revenant." [BostonR] (19:6) D-Ja 94-95, p. 17.
"Right Now." [ColR] (21:2) Fall 94, p. 145.
4002. MAZZOCCO, Robert
"Elegy for Three." [Antaeus] (75/76) Aut 94, p. 296.
4003. MAZZOTTI, Jose A. (José Antonio)
"Codo Empinado." [Inti] (39) Primavera 94, p. 266.
" *Mare* Is the Female of the Horse" (after an essay by Roman Jakobson, tr. by G. J. Racz). [PoetL] (89:1) Spr 94, p. 18.
"Nymph and Navigator" (tr. by G. J. Racz). [PoetL] (89:1) Spr 94, p. 19-20.
"Por la Orilla del Rio." [Inti] (39) Primavera 94, p. 263.
"Saqsaywaman." [Inti] (39) Primavera 94, p. 264.
"Sonqoruru." [Inti] (39) Primavera 94, p. 264-265.
4004. MBERI, Antar S. K.
"Nothing Went Untouched This morning" (Excerpt. From "A Song Out of Harlem"). [AmerPoR] (23:6) N-D 94, p. 38.
Mc . . .
See also names beginning with Mac . . .
4005. McADAMS, Janet
"The Children's Corner." [NoAmR] (279:3) My-Je 94, p. 27.
4006. McALEAVEY, David
"Hunting Season." [Amelia] (7:3, #22) 94, p. 13.
4007. McALLASTER, Elva
"Pedagese: Convention Level." [ChrC] (111:4) 2-9 F 94, p. 103.
4008. McALLISTER, Michael
"Stories Swallowed." [JamesWR] (11:4) Sum 94, p. 12.
4009. McALPINE, Cam
"(Canada Day, Moose Jaw, Saskatchewan)." [WestCL] (28:3, #15) Wint 94-95, p. 91.
"(Flin Flon, Manitoba)." [WestCL] (28:3, #15) Wint 94-95, p. 92.
"Near Brandon, Manitoba." [CanLit] (141) Sum 94, p. 70.
"(North Battleford, Saskatchewan)." [WestCL] (28:3, #15) Wint 94-95, p. 89.
"(Saskatoon, Saskatchewan)." [WestCL] (28:3, #15) Wint 94-95, p. 90.
"(Slave Lake, Alberta)." [WestCL] (28:3, #15) Wint 94-95, p. 88.
"Winnipeg, Manitoba." [CanLit] (141) Sum 94, p. 71.
4010. McALPINE, Katherine
"Idyll Tears." [Light] (9) Spr 94, p. 15.
"My Own Two Cents Worth" (for Gail White & Tom Riley). [Light] (11) Aut 94, p. 31.
"A New Age Iliad." [CumbPR] (14:1) Fall 94, p. 46.

"Of Thee I Sing" (variations on a theme by W.W., with several G.G. titles hiding within). [Light] (11) Aut 94, p. 19.
"The Ungay Cavalier." [Light] (9) Spr 94, p. 10.

4011. McANDREW, Donald A.
"Fountain Pen." [EngJ] (83:1) Ja 94, p. 90.

4012. McARTHUR, Catherine
"Clouds." [BellArk] (10:6) N-D 94, p. 9.
"Our Wedding." [BellArk] (10:6) N-D 94, p. 9.

4013. McARTHUR, Mac
"A Trick of Light." [JamesWR] (11:2) Wint 94, p. 3.

4014. McAULEY, James
"Culture as Exhibit" (w. Harold Stewart, under the pseudonym of Ern Malley). [InterQ] (1:2) 93, p. 117-118.

4015. McBRIDE, Mekeel
"The Transparent Rose" (for Ruth). [SenR] (24:2) Fall 94, p. 37.

4016. McBRIDE, Regina
"The Blood Doll." [Pequod] (37) 94, p. 13-15.
"The Doll Maker." [Pequod] (37) 94, p. 16-18.

4017. McBRIDE-AHEBEE, Octavia
"The Iron Market." [InterQ] (1:4) 94, p. 96.

4018. McCABE, Victoria
"Gathering in the Old Orbits of Our Dead." [PraS] (68:1) Spr 94, p. 104.
"Grief Moves In." [LitR] (37:4) Sum 94, p. 666.
"Letter to Celine: Why Live?" [NewYorkQ] (53) 94, p. 98-99.

4019. McCANLESS, Katherine
"Circus." [Poem] (71) My 94, p. 48.
"Genealogy of a Southern Girl." [Poem] (71) My 94, p. 49.
"Soul Food." [Poem] (71) My 94, p. 46-47.

4020. McCANN, Janet
"Answering Machine." [Pivot] (42) 94, p. 35.
"Instructions for the Young." [CentR] (38:1) Wint 94, p. 120.
"The Neighbor." [CentR] (38:1) Wint 94, p. 121.
"Sunday Supplement." [SycamoreR] (6:1) Wint 94, p. 20.
"What Is Wrong." [Border] (3) Fall 93, p. 45.

4021. McCANN, Kathleen (Kathleen M.)
"Cather's Cottage, Grand Manan Island, N.B., Canada." [Blueline] (15) 94, p. 20.
"Pitch." [Interim] (13:2) Fall-Wint 94-95, p. 26.
"Things Women Say to Feel Safe." [Interim] (13:2) Fall-Wint 94-95, p. 25.
"Up the Ante" (for Marny Muir). [Interim] (13:2) Fall-Wint 94-95, p. 27.

4022. McCARTHY, Eugene J.
"James Dickey." [SoCaR] (26:2) Spr 94, p. 6-7.

4023. McCARTHY, Maureen
"Drag the Body." [Quarry] (43:1) Je 94, p. 54.
"Fredericton." [Quarry] (43:1) Je 94, p. 53.
"A Nasty Wind." [Quarry] (43:1) Je 94, p. 56.
"Secret." [Quarry] (43:1) Je 94, p. 55.
"Thoughts." [Quarry] (43:1) Je 94, p. 52.

4024. McCARTNEY, Sharon
"Bathing with Martin." [Event] (23:2) Sum 94, p. 29-30.

4025. McCARTY, Neil
"R&R on the Interstate." [RagMag] (12:1) Sum 94, p. 46.
"Selene." [RagMag] (12:1) Sum 94, p. 47.

4026. McCASKILL, Kerry
"The Essential Lurid Details: Death of a Wood-Be Poet." [SlipS] (14) 94, p. 19.

4027. McCASLIN, Susan
"Songs of the Beloved" (16 poems). [BellArk] (10:1) Ja-F 94, p. 12-13.

4028. McCLANAHAN, Rebecca
"Demons." [QW] (39) Sum-Fall 94, p. 170-172.
"First Husband." [QW] (39) Sum-Fall 94, p. 169.
"Open Swim at the Y." [GettyR] (7:3) Sum 94, p. 435-436.

4029. McCLATCHY, J. D.
"My Mammogram." [Poetry] (164:4) Jl 94, p. 210-212.

McCLELLAN, Jan
See McCLELLAN, Jane

4030. McCLELLAN, Jane
"No Empty Stare." [CentR] (38:3) Fall 94, p. 506-507.

"Raven Rock." [Blueline] (15) 94, p. 17-18.
"Transience." [Parting] (7:1) Sum 94, p. 60.
"An Unseasonal Freeze on Jekyll Island." [FourQ] (8:2) Fall 94, p. 12.
"When Bifocals Are Not a Pair." [SouthernPR] (34:1) Sum 94, p. 12-13.

McCLEOD, Maria L.
See McLEOD, Maria L.

4031. McCLURE, Michael
"American Dream." [HeavenB] (11) 94, p. 90.
"Through the Bars." [HeavenB] (11) 94, p. 91.

4032. McCLURE, Michael Jay
"Break." [VirQR] (70:4) Aut 94, p. 672.
"Haunted." [VirQR] (70:4) Aut 94, p. 670-672.
"The Poem Emerges." [VirQR] (70:4) Aut 94, p. 668-669.
"Song." [VirQR] (70:4) Aut 94, p. 669-670.

4033. McCOLLOUGH, Joel (Joel A.)
"Apple Festival Time." [CimR] (109) O 94, p. 65.
"Matutinal" (a romance). [Poem] (71) My 94, p. 70.
"Night-Driving Solo." [Poem] (71) My 94, p. 67.
"Stumphouse Mountain Tunnel." [Poem] (71) My 94, p. 68.
"Weaver's Hitch." [Poem] (71) My 94, p. 69.

4034. McCOMBS, Judith
"Love Poem, Later." [Calyx] (15:2) Sum 94, p. 33.

4035. McCONNEL, Frances Ruhlen
"Something Like Faith." [MassR] (35:1) Spr 94, p. 132-134.
"Villanelle." [MassR] (35:1) Spr 94, p. 131.

4036. McCORD, Andrew
"Five Beirut Poems" (tr. of Faiz Ahmed Faiz). [Conjunc] (23) 94, p. 84-88.

4037. McCORKLE, James
"The Cloak." [PlumR] (7) [94?], p. 72-73.
"Driving Westward from Connecticut." [GreenMR] (NS 17:2) Fall-Wint 94-95, p. 54.

4038. McCORKLE, Kate
"Second World." [ColR] (21:2) Fall 94, p. 169-170.

4039. McCORMICK, James
"I Know That Summer." [NegC] (13:2/3) 93, p. 42.

4040. McCORMICK, James Scannell
"Huntington Beach." [PassN] (15:2) Wint 94, p. 18-19.

4041. McCORMICK, Jeri
"At Effigy Mounds." [CumbPR] (14:1) Fall 94, p. 13.
"Miners' Morning." [CumbPR] (14:1) Fall 94, p. 14.
"Your Mother's Grandma" (for Celia Mary Whitaker. Robert Penn Warren Poetry Prize Winner: Honorable Mention). [CumbPR] (14:1) Fall 94, p. 12.

4042. McCORMICK, Jim
"The Hammer." [NewOR] (20:1/2) Spr-Sum 94, p. 114.
"The King and I." [NewOR] (20:1/2) Spr-Sum 94, p. 117.
"The Roach Sonnet." [NewOR] (20:1/2) Spr-Sum 94, p. 116.
"Sparrows for Cathedrals." [NewOR] (20:1/2) Spr-Sum 94, p. 115.

4043. McCRORIE, Edward
"Christmas Introductions." [SpiritSH] (59) 94, p. 23.

4044. McCULLOUGH, Ken
"Autocriticism Meeting (1987)" (tr. of U Sam Oeur, w. the author). [Manoa] (6:2) Wint 94, p. 129-130.
"Dream After Composing the Appeal of the Cambodian League for Freedom and Democracy" (for Rose Rutherford, tr. of U Sam Oeur). [ArtfulD] (26/27) 94, p. 38.
"Exodus" (tr. of U Sam Oeur, w. the author). [Manoa] (6:2) Wint 94, p. 125.
"I Try to Survive Only for the Nation" (tr. of U Sam Oeur, w. the author). [Manoa] (6:2) Wint 94, p. 130-131.
"Instructions" (for Shivani Arjuna). [CrabCR] (8:2/3/9:1/2/3) 94, p. 5.
"My Invisible Sisters and Death by Execution" (tr. of U Sam Oeur, w. the author). [Manoa] (6:2) Wint 94, p. 126-129.
"Sacred Vows" (for Michael Dennis Browne, tr. of U Sam Oeur). [ArtfulD] (26/27) 94, p. 35-37.
"Searching for Dad" (March 1979, for Lorraine Ciancio, tr. of U Sam Oeur). [ArtfulD] (26/27) 94, p. 39-40.

4045. McDADE, Thomas Michael
"I Saw Williams Play." [Spitball] (47) Sum 94, p. 27.
4046. McDANIEL, Douglas
"Flame Delhi." [Spitball] (47) Sum 94, p. 89.
4047. McDANIEL, Wilma Elizabeth
"Academic Career of Orville Kincaid." [Amelia] (7:3, #22) 94, p. 167-168.
"Beauty Contest of 1934." [ChironR] (13:4) Wint 94, p. 2.
"Black Roses." [ChironR] (13:4) Wint 94, p. 3.
"Death in a Sacred Porsche." [WormR] (34:1, #133) 94, p. 11-12.
"Doubting John Mayfis." [WormR] (34:4, #136) 94, p. 138-139.
"Evaluation of Cabo San Lucas." [WormR] (34:1, #133) 94, p. 10-11.
"Family Traditions." [WormR] (34:4, #136) 94, p. 138.
"Family Transportation, 1936." [ChironR] (13:4) Wint 94, p. 4.
"Flawed Existence." [WormR] (34:1, #133) 94, p. 11.
"Holiday Disclosure." [WormR] (34:4, #136) 94, p. 137-138.
"Lament of a Tidy Housekeeper." [ChironR] (13:4) Wint 94, p. 4.
"The Little Mean Gene." [ChironR] (13:4) Wint 94, p. 3.
"Merle Aint No Stranger to Me." [Amelia] (7:4, #23) 94, p. 150.
"Poor Timing." [ChironR] (13:4) Wint 94, p. 4.
"Power." [ChironR] (13:4) Wint 94, p. 3.
"Sleeping Arrangements." [ChironR] (13:4) Wint 94, p. 2.
"Sleepwalker." [ChironR] (13:4) Wint 94, p. 2.
"Substitutes." [ChironR] (13:4) Wint 94, p. 3.
"Today and Yesterday." [ChironR] (13:4) Wint 94, p. 4.
4048. McDERMOTT, George
"Woodward Hill Cemetery" (Lancaster, Pa.). [Pivot] (41) 93, p. 39.
4049. McDERMOTT, Sharon Fagan
"At the Station." [JINJPo] (16:2) Aut 94, p. 26.
"Before the Rains." [JINJPo] (16:2) Aut 94, p. 27.
McDONALD, Hazel Simmons
See SIMMONS-McDONALD, Hazel
4050. McDONALD, Ian
"Any Poem." [Pivot] (41) 93, p. 18.
"Fragments." [CaribbeanW] (8) 94, p. 13-14.
"On the Headland." [CaribbeanW] (8) 94, p. 11-12.
4051. McDONALD, Paul
"Hats in the Air." [CoalC] (8) Ap 94, p. 46.
4052. McDONALD, Peter
"Endtime." [Pivot] (41) 93, p. 22.
4053. McDONALD, Walter
"After Fifty." [MissouriR] (17:1) 94, p. 72.
"After the Random Tornado." [MissouriR] (17:1) 94, p. 67.
"August on Padre Island." [Outbr] (25) 94, p. 61.
"Baptizing the Dog at Nine." [SenR] (24:1) Spr 94, p. 28.
"Burning in Dry July." [CharR] (20:2) Fall 94, p. 101.
"But It Was Water." [MissouriR] (17:1) 94, p. 70.
"Chimes on the Patio." [EngJ] (83:6) O 94, p. 32.
"Coyotes and Dogs." [PoetC] (25:3) Spr 94, p. 13.
"Dogs and the Laws of Duty." [EngJ] (83:6) O 94, p. 50.
"Dreams and the Laws of Mercy." [SoCoast] (16) Ja 94, p. 18.
"Fame at Eleven." [ColEng] (56:2) F 94, p. 192.
"Farms at Auction." [MissouriR] (17:1) 94, p. 68.
"For Friends Missing in Action." [IllinoisR] (1:2) Spr 94, p. 12.
"For God in My Sorrows." [NoDaQ] (62:4) Fall 94-95, p. 95-96.
"Frogs in a Dry Zone." [HiramPoR] (57) Fall 94-Wint 95, p. 40.
"Graves of Unknown Soldiers." [TexasR] (15:1/2) Spr-Sum 94, p. 92.
"The Invention of Courage." [MissouriR] (17:1) 94, p. 73.
"Kindling for a Thousand Fires." [Border] (5) Fall-Wint 94, p. 42.
"Letting Go." [PraS] (68:2) Sum 94, p. 67.
"Old Men Fishing at Brownwood." [Border] (5) Fall-Wint 94, p. 43.
"The Ranch in Escondido." [Outbr] (25) 94, p. 63.
"Rembrandt and the Art of Mercy." [NewEngR] (16:3) Sum 94, p. 68.
"Scanning the Range for Strays." [MissouriR] (17:1) 94, p. 69.
"The Songs of Country Girls." [MissouriR] (17:1) 94, p. 74.
"Stalls and the Laws of Order." [Descant] (25:1, #84) Spr 94, p. 9.
"The Summer Before Saigon." [PoetL] (89:3) Fall 94, p. 13.

"This Night and Others Like It." [CharR] (20:2) Fall 94, p. 102.
"Uncle Carl and the Art of Taxidermy." [MissouriR] (17:1) 94, p. 71.
"Uncle Oscar and the Art of Carving." [PraS] (68:2) Sum 94, p. 68.
"Under Hardscrabble Skies." [SoDakR] (32:1) Spr 94, p. 103.
"When the Children Have Gone." [ConnPR] (13:1) 94, p. 16.
"The Winter of Desert Storm." [Outbr] (25) 94, p. 62.

4054. McDOUGALL, Jo
"Circus." [LouisL] (11:2) Fall 94, p. 70.
"What Happens When We Leave?" [Journal] (18:2) Fall-Wint 94, p. 52.

4055. McDOWELL, John
"Held for Viewing" (sculpture and poetry: 4 poems with illustrations of sculpture). [Dandel] (20:2) 93, p. 57-65.

4056. McDOWELL, Robert
"Already a Good Day." [ClockR] (9:1/2) 94-95, p. 63.
"Nothing for It." [Pequod] (37) 94, p. 19.
"Some Things They Should Learn to Live Without." [Pequod] (37) 94, p. 20.

4057. McELROY, Delmore
"Order Police." [SmPd] (31:1, #90) Wint 94, p. 17.

4058. McELROY, Gil
"Hurricane Sky." [Nimrod] (37:2) Spr-Sum 94, p. 63.
"The Legitimate Use of Population." [Nimrod] (37:2) Spr-Sum 94, p. 64.
"Unfathomed Folk." [Nimrod] (37:2) Spr-Sum 94, p. 62.

4059. McEWAN, Angela
"Desert's Bells" (tr. of Gerónimo Maciel). [Luz] (7) N 94, p. 41-45.
"The One Who Never Was" (tr. of Ester de Izaguirre). [Luz] (6) My 94, p. 11.
"Quincunce" (English tr. of Estela Alicia López Lomas). [Luz] (7) N 94, p. 22-26.
"Theatre" (tr. of Ester de Izaguirre). [Luz] (6) My 94, p. 13.
"To a Young Couple Embracing in the Street" (tr. of Ester de Izaguirre). [Luz] (6) My 94, p. 15.

4060. McEWEN, R. F.
"Old Rags and Iron." [PraS] (68:1) Spr 94, p. 109-112.

4061. McFADDEN, David W.
"Elizabeth." [PoetryC] (15:1) N 94, p. 14.
"Problem Child X's and O's Paradox." [PoetryC] (15:1) N 94, p. 15.
"Sunflower." [PoetryC] (15:1) N 94, p. 15.

4062. McFADDEN, Joyce
"Will Work for Food — California 1993." [Pearl] (20) Spr 94, p. 20.

4063. McFADDEN, Mary Ann
"Disco Saturday Night." [SouthernPR] (34:1) Sum 94, p. 67-69.
"Marriage." [AmerV] (33) 94, p. 32-39.

4064. McFALL, Gardner
"Begin." [DarkMoon] (1) 94, p. 67.
"Day Lily." [DarkMoon] (1) 94, p. 70.
"The Encounter." [ParisR] (36:133) Wint 94, p. 116.
"Epithalamium" (for Dodge and Mimi). [DarkMoon] (1) 94, p. 68.
"May." [DarkMoon] (1) 94, p. 69.
"Mission in Hong Kong." [Pequod] (37) 94, p. 21-22.
"Mother Love." [ParisR] (36:133) Wint 94, p. 117.

4065. McFARLAND, Ron
"Doing What I Can for the Trade Deficit." [BlackBR] (18) Wint-Spr 94, p. 24-25.
"Faire l'Amour." [HampSPR] Wint 94, p. 41.
"A Random Encounter with Wallace Stevens." [HiramPoR] (57) Fall 94-Wint 95, p. 41.

4066. McFEE, Michael
"Barnum's Animal Crackers." [VirQR] (70:3) Sum 94, p. 452-453.
"Colander." [TarRP] (34:1) Fall 94, p. 7.
"Colander." [VirQR] (70:3) Sum 94, p. 453.
"Nap." [TarRP] (34:1) Fall 94, p. 6.
"Pearly Gates." [CarolQ] (46:3) Sum 94, p. 30.
"Pencil." [Shen] (44:1) Spr 94, p. 50-51.
"Spirit Paper." [ApalQ] (40/41) 94, p. 65.
"Thirteen Ways of Looking at a Blackboard." [TarRP] (34:1) Fall 94, p. 4-6.
"To a Muse." [Hudson] (46:4) Wint 94, p. 681-682.
"The Tunnel." [ApalQ] (40/41) 94, p. 64.

4067. McGEE, Karen
"The Kiss." [EvergreenC] (9:2) Sum-Fall 94, p. 10.

"Sleeping Beauty with Baby." [EvergreenC] (9:2) Sum-Fall 94, p. 11.

4068. McGEE, Lynn
"Air Show." [OntR] (40) Spr-Sum 94, p. 36-37.
"How to Cook." [OntR] (40) Spr-Sum 94, p. 38-39.
"Incognito, And Not." [OntR] (40) Spr-Sum 94, p. 45.
"Seattle in July." [OntR] (40) Spr-Sum 94, p. 42-44.
"Three Views of the Human Body." [OntR] (40) Spr-Sum 94, p. 40-41.

4069. McGINN, Florence
"At The Wall." [BlackBR] (19) Fall-Wint 94, p. 42.
"Holding the Words." [Elf] (4:4) Wint 94, p. 36.
"Perched on Thistle Stalks." [BlackBR] (19) Fall-Wint 94, p. 42.
"Swollen shadows." [BlackBR] (19) Fall-Wint 94, p. 42.

4070. McGLINN, Sen
"Ascending Poem." [WorldO] (25:3) Spr 94, p. 57.

4071. McGOLDRICK, James A.
"Lace." [Vis] (45) 94, p. 8.

4072. McGOVERN, Robert
"The Magi." [ChrC] (111:36) 14 D 94, p. 1189.

4073. McGOWIN, Kevin
"Elephant Love." [Rosebud] (1:3) Aut-Wint 94, p. 59.
"Equinox." [Rosebud] (1:3) Aut-Wint 94, p. 54-55.
"Lines Spoken by the World's Oldest Witch, on Halloween." [Rosebud] (1:3) Aut-Wint 94, p. 52-53.
"More Than a Life of Edmund Kean" (An opera, or play, in one act). [Rosebud] (1:3) Aut-Wint 94, p. 56-58.

4074. McGRATH, Campbell
"The First Trimester." [Antaeus] (75/76) Aut 94, p. 297-299.
"Sunset, Route 90, Brewster County, Texas." [Bomb] (46) Wint 94, p. 56.
"Untitled: Box cars and electric guitars." [Bomb] (46) Wint 94, p. 56.

4075. McGRATH, Carmelita
"Adam and Eve on a Winter Afternoon." [TickleAce] (28) Fall-Wint 94, p. 32-33.
"Solar Eclipse, St. John's, Newfoundland." [TickleAce] (28) Fall-Wint 94, p. 34.
"The Way You Walk into the Water." [TickleAce] (28) Fall-Wint 94, p. 35.

4076. McGRATH, Lynette
"Tarragona" (tr. of Vicent Andrés Estellés, w. Nathaniel Smith). [SenR] (24:2) Fall 94, p. 63.

4077. McGRATH, Wendy
"Brown Boots." [Dandel] (21:2) 94, p. 9.

4078. McGRAW, Marcus
"Praha 9." [ArtfulD] (26/27) 94, p. 46.

4079. McGRORY-KLYZA, Sheila
"Heirs Apparent." [WestB] (35) 94, p. 36.
"Wallpapering the Kitchen with My Mother." [Kalliope] (16:1) 94, p. 24.

4080. McGUCKIAN, Medbh
"The Albert Chain." [AmerV] (35) 94, p. 34-35.
"The Nearness of the Grape Arbour to the Fruit Cellar." [AmerV] (35) 94, p. 37-38.
"Skull-Light." [AmerV] (35) 94, p. 33.
"Waxwing Winter." [AmerV] (35) 94, p. 36.

4081. McHADDAD, Kris
"She Asks for Conversation." [ChironR] (13:2) Sum 94, p. 26.
"This Day." [ChironR] (13:2) Sum 94, p. 26.
"Weather." [ChironR] (13:2) Sum 94, p. 26.

4082. McHUGH, Heather
"A Boomerang on Breath" (tr. of Paul Celan, w. Niko McHugh). [SenR] (24:1) Spr 94, p. 48.
"Chance Having Been Rigged" (tr. of Paul Celan, w. Niko McHugh). [SenR] (24:1) Spr 94, p. 46.
"Close to Yclept." [Colum] (21) Fall 93, p. 30-31.
"Curve." [BelPoJ] (45:1) Fall 94, p. 46.
"Dry Time." [Jacaranda] (10) 94, p. 28.
"The Island of the Visible" (tr. of Paul Celan, w. Niko McHugh). [SenR] (24:1) Spr 94, p. 47.
"Out of Angel Substance" (tr. of Paul Celan, w. Niko McHugh). [SenR] (24:1) Spr 94, p. 52.
"Pain, the Syllable" (tr. of Paul Celan, w. Niko McHugh). [SenR] (24:1) Spr 94, p. 50-51.

"Some Kind of Pine." [Jacaranda] (10) 94, p. 26-27.
"Two St. Petersburgs." [Jacaranda] (10) 94, p. 25.
"Unbroken Water." [Colum] (21) Fall 93, p. 29.
"You with the Dark Slingshot" (tr. of Paul Celan, w. Niko McHugh). [SenR] (24:1) Spr 94, p. 49.

4083. McHUGH, Niko
"A Boomerang on Breath" (tr. of Paul Celan, w. Heather McHugh). [SenR] (24:1) Spr 94, p. 48.
"Chance Having Been Rigged" (tr. of Paul Celan, w. Heather McHugh). [SenR] (24:1) Spr 94, p. 46.
"The Island of the Visible" (tr. of Paul Celan, w. Heather McHugh). [SenR] (24:1) Spr 94, p. 47.
"Out of Angel Substance" (tr. of Paul Celan, w. Heather McHugh). [SenR] (24:1) Spr 94, p. 52.
"Pain, the Syllable" (tr. of Paul Celan, w. Heather McHugh). [SenR] (24:1) Spr 94, p. 50-51.
"You with the Dark Slingshot" (tr. of Paul Celan, w. Heather McHugh). [SenR] (24:1) Spr 94, p. 49.

4084. McILVOY, Kevin
"Baker's Apprentice." [HayF] (15) Fall-Wint 94, p. 78.
"Census." [Witness] (8:1) 94, p. 178.

4085. McINTOSH, Joan
"The Missing Woman." [CumbPR] (13:2) Spr 94, p. 38.
"One Time." [CumbPR] (13:2) Spr 94, p. 37.

4086. McKAY, Don
"Big Alberta Clouds." [PoetryC] (14:3) My 94, p. 4.
"Black Box." [PoetryC] (14:3) My 94, p. 4.
"Camouflage." [PoetryC] (14:3) My 94, p. 4.
"Old Growth Hemlock." [PoetryC] (14:3) My 94, p. 4.

4087. McKAY, Linda Back
"High." [Parting] (7:1) Sum 94, p. 53.
"Reaching Adulthood." [Farm] (11:1) Spr-Sum 94, p. 98-99.
"Suicides." [Farm] (11:2) Fall-Wint 94-95, p. 80.

4088. McKEAN, James
"Rowboat." [Journal] (18:2) Fall-Wint 94, p. 19.
"This Way Please" (— Restaurante El Coral). [Journal] (18:2) Fall-Wint 94, p. 20-21.
"Whale Rock." [HighP] (9:2) Ag 94, p. 73.

4089. McKEE, Katherine E.
"Amela." [Dandel] (21:1) 94, p. 42-43.

4090. McKEE, Lucie
"Seamstress." [SouthernR] (30:1) Ja, Wint 94, p. 95.

4091. McKELVIE, Scott
"Accepting Losses by Associative Reasoning." [WebR] (18) Fall 94, p. 63.

4092. McKENTY, Bob
"High-Tech Low." [Light] (9) Spr 94, p. 10.
"In-Irons Mike." [Light] (9) Spr 94, p. 11.
"The Nauga." [Light] (10) Sum 94, p. 10.
"The Oddest Animal." [Light] (11) Aut 94, p. 9.
"La-Z-Boy." [Light] (10) Sum 94, p. 15.

4093. McKENZIE, Carter
"The Wedding" (to Jennifer Arin). [Chain] (1) Spr-Sum 94, p. 255.

4094. McKENZIE, Jeffrey
"Diaspora." [PoetryNW] (35:2) Sum 94, p. 43.

4095. McKENZIE, Lee
"Independence Day at the Mall." [Calyx] (15:2) Sum 94, p. 6-7.
"Late Spring Snow." [CimR] (108) Jl 94, p. 90.

4096. McKERNAN, John
"The Papers and Speeches." [Parting] (7:2) Wint 94-95, p. 66.
"Sunflower." [WindO] (58) Sum 94, p. 46-47.
"Your Fingers." [Parting] (7:2) Wint 94-95, p. 64.

4097. McKINNEY, Joshua
"The Abolitionist." [DenQ] (29:2) Fall 94, p. 13-14.
"Casting." [ChatR] (14:3) Spr 94, p. 45-47.
"Dump." [LaurelR] (28:1) Wint 94, p. 61.
"In Other Words." [InterQ] (1:4) 94, p. 152.

"Quick." [Boulevard] (9:3, #27) Fall 94, p. 185.
"Remainder." [InterQ] (1:4) 94, p. 151.

4098. McKINSEY, Martin
"Evacuation" (tr. of Yannis Ritsos). [Field] (50) Spr 94, p. 37.
"Illicit Spring" (tr. of Yannis Ritsos). [HarvardR] (7) Fall 94, p. 30.
"In the Garden" (tr. of Yannis Ritsos). [HarvardR] (7) Fall 94, p. 29.
"On Silence" (tr. of Yannis Ritsos). [TriQ] (92) Wint 94-95, p. 257.
"The Original Position" (tr. of Yannis Ritsos). [Field] (50) Spr 94, p. 40.
"The Other Fear" (tr. of Yannis Ritsos). [TriQ] (92) Wint 94-95, p. 256.
"Stages of Weariness" (tr. of Yannis Ritsos). [Field] (50) Spr 94, p. 41.
"The Trail" (tr. of Yannis Ritsos). [Field] (50) Spr 94, p. 38.
"Until One Night" (tr. of Yannis Ritsos). [Field] (50) Spr 94, p. 39.

4099. McLACHLAN, Ian
"Five Vietnamese Words." [Witness] (8:1) 94, p. 156-157.
"Remembering Té." [Witness] (8:1) 94, p. 158-160.

4100. McLAUGHLIN, Catherine
"Identity." [Border] (3) Fall 93, p. 46.
"Instinct." [Comm] (121:9) 6 My 94, p. 16.

4101. McLAUGHLIN, Walt
"That Vague Odor." [SlipS] (14) 94, p. 58.

4102. McLAURIN, Ken
"The Bee Constellation." [PoetC] (25:2) Wint 94, p. 13.

4103. McLEAN, Dirk
"Cricket Loses." [PraF] (15:4, #69) Wint 94-95, p. 101.

4104. McLEAN, Julia
"Biochemical Disorder." [CoalC] (8) Ap 94, p. 45.

4105. McLENNAN, Rob
"Playing Scrabble w/ Michael Dennis." [AntigR] (97) Spr 94, p. 135.

4106. McLEOD, Maria L.
"Cursing Sheep." [CentralP] (23) Spr 94, p. 108-109.

4107. McLURE, Pam
"Glass Wall." [BrooklynR] (11) 94, p. 116.

4108. McMAHON, Brendan
"Captain Cook." [ChamLR] (14/15) Spr-Fall 94, p. 79-80.

4109. McMAHON, Lynne
"All Lycra and Spandex." [Poetry] (164:2) My 94, p. 65.
"Peter Pan." [ChiR] (40:2/3) 94, p. 27.
"Post Natal." [Atlantic] (273:5) My 94, p. 104.
"Zachary at Three." [Poetry] (164:2) My 94, p. 66.

4110. McMAHON, M. (Michael)
"The Apple Peeler." [Blueline] (15) 94, p. 73-74.
"Clear Dreams." [Blueline] (15) 94, p. 3-5.
"The Dog in Her First Heat." [Farm] (11:2) Fall-Wint 94-95, p. 70.
"Naming the Beasts." [Farm] (11:2) Fall-Wint 94-95, p. 69.
"Pulling the Beets." [Farm] (11:2) Fall-Wint 94-95, p. 71.
"Randy Goes to the Bank." [Pearl] (20) Spr 94, p. 60.

4111. McMAHON, Michael B.
"Quiet Time." [SoCoast] (16) Ja 94, p. 54-55.

4112. McMASTER, Susan
"Young Crows." [Arc] (33) Fall 94, p. 56-57.

4113. McMICHAEL, James
"Before." [AmerPoR] (23:1) Ja-F 94, p. 17.

4114. McMILLAN, Ian
"Essential Engineering Works." [Jacaranda] (5:1) Wint-Spr 91, p. 42.

4115. McMILLAN, Peter
"Ostrich." [Light] (12) Wint 94-95, p. 10.

4116. McMORRIS, Mark
"Apple Colloquies." [KenR] (NS 16:2) Spr 94, p. 122-124.

4117. McMULLEN, Richard E.
"The Door." [ColEng] (56:7) N 94, p. 827.
"He Noticed." [Comm] (121:9) 6 My 94, p. 13.
"The Next Question." [HangL] (65) 94, p. 39.

4118. McMURRAY, Earl
"Snow." [SouthernPR] (34:1) Sum 94, p. 59.

4119. McNAIR, Wesley
"Love Handles." [NewEngR] (16:3) Sum 94, p. 128-129.

"The Lover." [PoetryNW] (35:1) Spr 94, p. 11.
"Poem for My Feet." [NewEngR] (16:3) Sum 94, p. 129-130.

4120. McNALL, Sally Allen
"Hinge" (for Jane Bradley). [PraS] (68:2) Sum 94, p. 70.
"Old Story" (Clark Art Institute, July, 1991). [PraS] (68:2) Sum 94, p. 71.
"Wolfsong." [PraS] (68:2) Sum 94, p. 69.

4121. McNALLY, Richard
"Some Years Ago at the Lumber Yard." [WindO] (58) Sum 94, p. 21.

4122. McNAMARA, Robert
"In the Cage." [CreamCR] (18:2) Fall 94, p. 168.

4123. McNAUGHTON, Duncan
"White Rain Like in Ticino." [Zyzzyva] (10:4) Wint 94, p. 28-31.

4124. McNEIL, Jean
"The Anthropologist." [AntigR] (98) Sum 94, p. 83-85.
"Feeding Love on England." [PoetryC] (14:4) S 94, p. 16.
"Unpoetic Drunk." [PoetryC] (14:4) S 94, p. 16.

4125. McNEILL, Christine
"Conveyance." [Verse] (11:2) Sum 94, p. 82-83.

4126. McNEILLEY, Michael
"How Erasers Are Made." [NewDeltaR] (10:2) Spr-Sum 93, p. 67.
"Like Trains into Tunnels." [SlipS] (14) 94, p. 30-31.
"Replication and Rejoinder." [WritersF] (20) 94, p. 204.

4127. McNEW, Christopher
"Eye Bank" (For Nathan Leopold). [ChiR] (40:2/3) 94, p. 8.

4128. McNULTY, Ted
"Labor Day." [Ploughs] (20:1) Spr 94, p. 171.

4129. McNULTY, Tim
"As a Heron Unsettles a Shallow Pool" (for Mary). [CrabCR] (8:2/3/9:1/2/3) 94, p. 12-13.

4130. McORMOND, Steve
"From the Top of the Web." [AntigR] (97) Spr 94, p. 45.

4131. McPHERSON, Carolyn Flanders
"Somebody Stole George Washington's False Teeth." [EngJ] (83:4) Ap 94, p. 103.

4132. McPHERSON, Michael
"Fruit of the Poison Tree" (for N.H.). [BambooR] (63/64) Sum-Fall 94, p. 34-35.
"Hakalau Bridge." [ChamLR] (14/15) Spr-Fall 94, p. 12.
"Hilina Pali." [BambooR] (63/64) Sum-Fall 94, p. 36.
"Kaimuki." [BambooR] (60) Wint 94, p. 110-111.
"The Point Roberts Ferry." [ChamLR] (14/15) Spr-Fall 94, p. 15-16.
"Pololu." [ChamLR] (14/15) Spr-Fall 94, p. 13.
"Studio." [ChamLR] (14/15) Spr-Fall 94, p. 14.
"Testimony." [BambooR] (60) Wint 94, p. 108-109.
"Up Mauka." [BambooR] (63/64) Sum-Fall 94, p. 37-38.
"The Walking Stone." [BambooR] (63/64) Sum-Fall 94, p. 39.
"The Walking Stone." [ChamLR] (14/15) Spr-Fall 94, p. 17.

4133. McPHERSON, Sandra
"Beach Journal, May: Concepts and Measurements." [Shen] (44:2) Sum 94, p. 28-29.
"Geode." [Shen] (44:2) Sum 94, p. 31.
"I could not be scary when I screamed." [AmerV] (34) 94, p. 96.
"Outsider: Juanita Rogers." [KenR] (NS 16:1) Wint 94, p. 152-153.
"Outsider: Minnie Evans." [KenR] (NS 16:1) Wint 94, p. 153-154.
"Paths Rounding Timberline, Mt. Hood, Last Week of Summer." [YaleR] (82:3) Jl 94, p. 25-30.
"Phlox Diffusa: A Poem for My Fiftieth Birthday." [YaleR] (82:3) Jl 94, p. 24.
"Preliminary Designs." [SouthernR] (30:3) Sum 94, p. 556-558.
"*Reposoir:* Four Legends for Mose Tolliver's 'Flowering Tree'." [AmerPoR] (23:3) My-Je 94, p. 6.
"Sonnet: Purple Ochre Sea Star" (Pisaster ochraceus). [Shen] (44:2) Sum 94, p. 30.
"The Study of Genius" (Laurel and Hardy Convention, Las Vegas, 1992). [Poetry] (164:2) My 94, p. 63-64.

4134. McRAY, Paul
"Bedell Bridge Poem" (Haverhill, New Hampshire, 1990). [IllinoisR] (1:2) Spr 94, p. 52.
"Is This the Way It Happens." [IllinoisR] (1:2) Spr 94, p. 15.

4135. McROBBIE, Kenneth
"The French Revolution's Bicentenary." [AntigR] (96) Wint 94, p. 121.
"The Politics of Censorship" (For M.L.). [AntigR] (96) Wint 94, p. 119.
"Why You Can Now Get a Bolshoi Mac in Moscow." [AntigR] (96) Wint 94, p. 120.
4136. McROBERTS, Robert
"Famous People." [Northeast] (5:10) Sum 94, p. 8.
4137. McSEVENEY, Angela
"Cataloguing Manuscripts." [Jacaranda] (5:1) Wint-Spr 91, p. 84-85.
4138. McSWEEN, Harold B.
"Darkest Houston." [PoetC] (25:3) Spr 94, p. 36.
4139. McWHIRTER, George
"Ali Baba & the Forty Thousand Bees." [PoetryC] (14:2) Mr 94, p. 5.
"Last Firs." [PoetryC] (14:2) Mr 94, p. 5.
4140. MEAD, Jane
"Delphi, Coming Around the Corner." [AmerPoR] (23:5) S-O 94, p. 20.
"Passing a Truck Full of Chickens at Night on Highway Eighty." [AmerPoR] (23:5) S-O 94, p. 20.
4141. MEADE, Mary Ann
"Ward for Anorexic Women." [CrabCR] (8:2/3/9:1/2/3) 94, p. 90.
4142. MEALER, Bryan
"Lost Dog." [HangL] (64) 94, p. 78.
4143. MEAS, M. Minford
"Ground Cover." [Light] (10) Sum 94, p. 14.
4144. MEDENICA, Susan
"Aster Day." [SmPd] (31:2, #91) Spr 94, p. 32.
"Bear Camp." [Poem] (72) N 94, p. 30.
"Plowing Under." [SmPd] (31:2, #91) Spr 94, p. 32.
"Taxidermy." [Poem] (72) N 94, p. 31.
"Ursa." [Poem] (72) N 94, p. 29.
4145. MEDINA, Pablo
"The New Circus." [Pivot] (41) 93, p. 56.
"Nocturno de Towanda" (for Joseph and Deborah Szabo). [SenR] (24:1) Spr 94, p. 60-62.
"Operation." [SenR] (24:1) Spr 94, p. 63.
4146. MEDINA, Tony
"Traneing In." [Eyeball] (3) 93, p. 42-43.
4147. MEDNICK, Lisa
"Columbus Day." [NewOR] (20:1/2) Spr-Sum 94, p. 124.
"Homelands." [NewOR] (20:1/2) Spr-Sum 94, p. 123.
4148. MEEHAN, Charlotte
"Photograph." [BrooklynR] (11) 94, p. 114.
4149. MEEHAN, Maude
"Imperfect Silence" (First Sue Saniel Elkind National Poetry Award, Finalist). [Kalliope] (16:2) 94, p. 31.
4150. MEEHAN, Paula
"Her Dream." [QW] (38) Winter-Spr 93-94, p. 198-199.
4151. MEEK, Ed
"Chekhov Gives Directions After the Wedding." [Amelia] (7:3, #22) 94, p. 127-128.
"Drought." [Poem] (71) My 94, p. 35.
"The Monkey's Dream." [Amelia] (7:3, #22) 94, p. 127.
"Nothing Means Anything." [Amelia] (7:3, #22) 94, p. 128-129.
4152. MEEK-HENSON, Sandra
"Chameleon." [GeoR] (48:4) Wint 94, p. 665.
4153. MEGAW, Neill
"Adversity." [Light] (11) Aut 94, p. 13.
"At the Wet Edges." [Nimrod] (38:1) Fall-Wint 94, p. 123.
"The Aubade Gambit." [Hellas] (5:2) Fall-Wint 94, p. 33.
"Down-home Dialectics." [Hellas] (5:1) Spr-Sum 94, p. 55.
"First Notes for a Major Motion Picture, Found Crumpled in a Kansas Motel Room." [HampSPR] Wint 94, p. 25.
"Fooled Again." [SoCoast] (17) Je 94, p. 56.
"French Country-House Interior" (Jacques Petit). [SoCoast] (16) Ja 94, p. 9.
"Genius." [Light] (11) Aut 94, p. 19.
"Limits." [Light] (10) Sum 94, p. 20.
"London: Waterloo Bridge." [CapeR] (29:2) Fall 94, p. 40.

"Morning in the Suburbs, Late 20th Century." [Nimrod] (38:1) Fall-Wint 94, p. 124.
"Morning Mist, Waquoit Bay." [CapeR] (29:2) Fall 94, p. 39.
"Ode to a Lost Nightingale." [Hellas] (5:2) Fall-Wint 94, p. 49.
"Pointed Finger." [Light] (11) Aut 94, p. 15.
"Shelley in South Dakota." [Nimrod] (38:1) Fall-Wint 94, p. 125.
"Sundown." [Elf] (4:1) Spr 94, p. 29.
"The Tears of Odysseus." [SoCoast] (16) Ja 94, p. 8.
"Top of the World." [SoCoast] (17) Je 94, p. 18.
"Very Brief Encounter." [SoCoast] (16) Ja 94, p. 6-7.
"Visitation." [Hellas] (5:1) Spr-Sum 94, p. 54.

4154. MEHIGAN, Joshua
"Casually, Another One." [Pequod] (37) 94, p. 26.

4155. MEHMEDINOVIC, Semezdin
"Curfew" (prose poem, tr. by Ammiel Alcalay). [Conjunc] (23) 94, p. 269-270.
"Glass" (prose poem, tr. by Ammiel Alcalay). [Conjunc] (23) 94, p. 268.
"Lion's" (prose poem, tr. by Ammiel Alcalay). [Conjunc] (23) 94, p. 270.
"A Martyr's Resting Place" (prose poem, tr. by Ammiel Alcalay). [Conjunc] (23) 94, p. 269.
"White Death" (prose poem, tr. by Ammiel Alcalay). [Conjunc] (23) 94, p. 268-269.

4156. MEHRHOFF, Charlie
"Done w/ Mirrors" (for Phyllis Walsh). [DogRR] (26) Wint 94-95, p. 35-38.
"Just Hollow Enough." [Elf] (4:1) Spr 94, p. 36.

4157. MEHROTRA, Arvind Krishna
"Locking Up" (for I. Allan Sealy). [GettyR] (7:3) Sum 94, p. 395.
"Nautical." [GettyR] (7:3) Sum 94, p. 396.

4158. MEHTA, Diane S.
"Elegy." [Journal] (18:1) Spr-Sum 94, p. 113.

4159. MEIDAV, Edie
"Zeno's Paradox." [NewL] (60:3) 94, p. 96-99.

4160. MEIKSIN, Judy
"Sex First, Date Later." [SlipS] (14) 94, p. 111-112.

4161. MEINHARD, Hermine
"Flying" (First Sue Saniel Elkind National Poetry Award, Grand Award Winner). [Kalliope] (16:2) 94, p. 11.
"The Mother." [Kalliope] (16:3) 94, p. 26.
"Yellow Sun." [Kalliope] (16:3) 94, p. 25-26.

4162. MEINHOFF, Michael
"Permanent Resident." [ChamLR] (14/15) Spr-Fall 94, p. 111.
"Waterlogue." [ChamLR] (14/15) Spr-Fall 94, p. 110.

4163. MEINKE, Peter
"Acorns." [InterQ] (1:4) 94, p. 108-109.
"The Bartok Choir in Castelnuovo." [BlackWR] (21:1) Fall-Wint 94, p. 109.
"Constellation" (for V.M.). [TampaR] (9) Fall 94, p. 59.
"Fortunato Pietro." [CarolQ] (47:1) Fall 94, p. 64.
"Rondini." [TampaR] (9) Fall 94, p. 60.
"Tolstoy at Yasnaya Polyana." [SouthernHR] (28:4) Fall 94, p. 332.

4164. MELICK, Linda
"Auschwitz, 1943" (First Sue Saniel Elkind National Poetry Award, Finalist). [Kalliope] (16:2) 94, p. 32-33.

4165. MELLARD, Joan
"Super-Suds" (for Dad). [Border] (3) Fall 93, p. 47-48.

MELLENGER, Maria
See MELLINGER, Maria

4166. MELLIN, Lilace A.
"Rearview Mirror / Crystal Ball." [Parting] (7:1) Sum 94, p. 2.

4167. MELLINGER, Maria
"10/22/91 Yesterday." [BellArk] (10:3 [i.e. 10:4]) Jl-Ag 94, p. 8.
"And While I've Got My Dictionary Out, Did You Know 'Love Apple' Means Tomato?" [BellArk] (10:3 [i.e. 10:4]) Jl-Ag 94, p. 8.
"Baltimore." [BellArk] (10:1) Ja-F 94, p. 24.
"Bzz." [BellArk] (10:6) N-D 94, p. 27.
"Do Saints Read Personal Ads?" [BellArk] (10:5) S-O 94, p. 11.
"Gardening with Kim." [BellArk] (10:1) Ja-F 94, p. 24.
"Memories of East Texas." [BellArk] (10:6) N-D 94, p. 8.
"Shanti in a Sari." [BellArk] (10:6) N-D 94, p. 6.
"Untitled: I opened a letter from Jerry and found." [BellArk] (10:6) N-D 94, p. 26.

4168. MELNYCZUK, Askold
"There." [GreensboroR] (56) Sum 94, p. 64.
4169. MELTZER, C. Rips
"Nocturnal Hunter." [Jacaranda] (4:2) Spr 90, p. 84.
4170. MEMMER, Philip
"Letter to a Friend." [Poetry] (163:5) F 94, p. 256.
4171. MEMMOLO, Dan
"Floating Air Biscuits." [NewYorkQ] (53) 94, p. 74-75.
"Venezuela." [ApalQ] (42) Fall 94, p. 33.
4172. MENASHE, Samuel
"High Fever." [Boulevard] (9:3, #27) Fall 94, p. 124.
"Self-Portrait." [Pivot] (42) 94, p. 49.
4173. MENDEL, Stephanie
"They Killed the Silence of the Drive by Pretending" (for Claire). [CreamCR] (18:1) Spr 94, p. 90.
4174. MÉNDEZ, José Antonio
"Novia Mia." [Areíto] (4:15) Marzo 94, p. 41.
4175. MENEBROKER, Ann
"Poem from the Alley" (for Kell). [Pearl] (20) Spr 94, p. 20.
4176. MENG, Hau-ran (ca. 730 A.D.)
"Poem Sent to Old Friends While Staying Overnight on the Tung-Lu River" (tr. by David Lunde). [SpoonR] (19:1) Wint-Spr 94, p. 59.
4177. MENG, Lang
"The Cemetery of Language" (tr. by Yanbing Chen). [AnotherCM] (27) 94, p. 65.
"Not Letting Grief Go" (tr. by Yanbing Chen). [AnotherCM] (27) 94, p. 67.
"The Prop Gun" (tr. by Yanbing Chen). [AnotherCM] (27) 94, p. 66.
"Winter" (tr. by Yanbing Chen). [AnotherCM] (27) 94, p. 68.
MENOZZI, Wallis Wilde
See WILDE-MENOZZI, Wallis
4178. MERCURIO, Katherine M.
"For Poe and Plath." [Ledge] (17) Wint 94, p. 84-85.
"Remembering Thoreau." [CapeR] (29:2) Fall 94, p. 3.
"Returning to School." [CapeR] (29:2) Fall 94, p. 4-5.
4179. MEREDITH, Connie
"Fidelity." [Wind] (74) 94, p. 25.
4180. MEREDITH, Cynthia
"Wedding Night Disturbance on the Loop." [Border] (5) Fall-Wint 94, p. 44-45.
4181. MERGEN, Barney
"Extinction, or, How Many Hypotheses Does It Take to Kill a Dinosaur?" [Light] (11) Aut 94, p. 14.
4182. MERRILL, Christopher
"A Face in the Delta" (New Orleans, December 1988, tr. of Ales Debeljak, w. the author). [NegC] (13:2/3) 93, p. 12.
"Woman and Bird" (tr. of André Breton, w. Jeanie Puleston Fleming). [NewRena] (9:1, #27) 94, p. 77.
4183. MERRILL, James
"After Cavafy." [NewYRB] (41:13) 14 Jl 94, p. 34.
"Cosmo." [YaleR] (82:2) Ap 94, p. 43-45.
"Scrapping the Computer." [Antaeus] (75/76) Aut 94, p. 300-301.
"Tony: Ending the Life." [ParisR] (36:131) Sum 94, p. 81-85.
4184. MERRIN, Jeredith
"Blue Skies." [Agni] (40) 94, p. 156.
"Dream-View of Delft" (in memory of Elizabeth Bishop). [ParisR] (36:132) Fall 94, p. 225.
"The Shadow Plant." [ParisR] (36:132) Fall 94, p. 224.
"Sublunar." [Agni] (40) 94, p. 154-155.
4185. MERRITT, Catherine
"Visiting Uncle Albert in Four Sonnet Variations." [Hellas] (5:2) Fall-Wint 94, p. 101-104.
4186. MERRITT, Constance
"The Mute Swan." [Callaloo] (17:4) Fall 94, p. 1051.
4187. MERRITT, Henry
"Questioning Wittgenstein (A Largely True Story)." [Stand] (35:4) Aut 94, p. 48-53.
MERS, Joyce la
See LaMERS, Joyce

4188. MERSMANN, James
"Lighting the Lamp." [BelPoJ] (45:1) Fall 94, p. 38-39.
"Watching My Mother's Breath" (for Regina Mersmann, born Oct. 15, 1899, died Aug. 28, 1990). [BelPoJ] (45:1) Fall 94, p. 40-41.
4189. MERTON, Andrew
"Blessing" (Peru, 1964). [Conscience] (15:3) Aut 94, p. 25.
"Christians." [Conscience] (15:4) Wint 94-95, p. 31.
"Rachel at Eighteen Months." [Conscience] (15:3) Aut 94, p. 29.
"Time Travel in the Grand Canyon." [Conscience] (15:3) Aut 94, p. 20.
4190. MERTON, Thomas
"Chant to Be Used in Processions Around a Site with Furnaces." [AntigR] (97) Spr 94, p. 110-113.
"Figures for an Apocalypse: VII. Landscape: Beast." [AntigR] (97) Spr 94, p. 106-107.
"The Guns of Fort Knox." [AntigR] (97) Spr 94, p. 105.
"Landscape." [AntigR] (97) Spr 94, p. 108-109.
"The Legacy of Herakleitos: XI. All Things Are Fire." [AntigR] (97) Spr 94, p. 114.
4191. MERWIN, W. S.
"3 French Poems." [Atlantic] (274:3) S 94, p. 56-57.
"Ancestral Voices." [NewYRB] (41:16) 6 O 94, p. 23.
"Battues." [Nat] (259:1) Jl 4 94, p. 30.
"The Bird." [Poetry] (164:1) Ap 94, p. 2.
"The Blind Seer of Ambon." [Nat] (259:20) D 12 94, p. 734.
"The Blind Seer of Ambon." [TampaR] (9) Fall 94, p. 29-30.
"December Night." [GettyR] (7:1) Wint 94, p. 150.
"Emergence." [NewYorker] (70:9) 18 Ap 94, p. 75.
"The Furrow." [NewYorker] (70:20) 11 Jl 94, p. 74.
"Left Open" (from *Travels*). [AntR] (52:1) Wint 94, p. 26.
"Old Walls." [NewYorker] (70:32) 10 O 94, p. 76.
"On the Old Way." [Nat] (259:20) D 12 94, p. 734.
"One Story." [Nat] (259:20) D 12 94, p. 734.
"Passing." [Poetry] (164:6) S 94, p. 314.
"Possessions." [Antaeus] (75/76) Aut 94, p. 302-303.
"Purgatory I." [ColR] (21:1) Spr 94, p. 64-69.
"Returning Season." [Poetry] (164:1) Ap 94, p. 3.
"The Stalin Epigram" (tr. of Osip Mandelstam, w. Clarence Brown). [Agni] (39) 94, p. 94-95.
"Traces." [Poetry] (164:1) Ap 94, p. 1.
"Untouched." [Poetry] (164:6) S 94, p. 315.
"The View." [Poetry] (164:6) S 94, p. 313.
"Vixen." [NewYorker] (70:43) 26 D 94-2 Ja 95, p. 97.
"Walking Around" (tr. of Pablo Neruda). [Field] (51) Fall 94, p. 22-23.
4192. MERZLAK, Regina
"The Wind" (from "Earth Tones"). [AmerPoR] (23:3) My-Je 94, p. 24.
4193. MESLER, Corey
"The Man with the Perfect Jump Shot." [Vis] (46) 94, p. 11-12.
4194. MESSER, Sarah
"1898, Chittenden Hotel Suicide." [ParisR] (36:132) Fall 94, p. 28-29.
"After Wildflower." [CreamCR] (18:2) Fall 94, p. 160-161.
"Banished, 1665." [CreamCR] (18:2) Fall 94, p. 162-163.
"Rendered Dog." [ParisR] (36:132) Fall 94, p. 27-28.
4195. MESSERLI, Douglas
"Closure." [Zyzzyva] (10:1) Spr 94, p. 60.
"Despair" (after Baudelaire). [Arshile] (3) 94, p. 11.
"Scrooge" (after Laforgue). [Arshile] (3) 94, p. 12.
"Shame" (after Rimbaud). [Arshile] (3) 94, p. 9.
"Snow White" (after Guillaume Apollinaire). [Zyzzyva] (10:1) Spr 94, p. 61.
"Spleen" (after Baudelaire). [Arshile] (3) 94, p. 10.
4196. MESSO, George
"After the Flood" (tr. of Arhtur Rimbaud). [Pearl] (20) Spr 94, p. 84.
4197. METHVIN, Susan Herport
"Christ Dancing." [ChrC] (111:2) 19 Ja 94, p. 46.
"Looking at a Photograph of a Man Heading for Market in Senegal." [SouthernPR] (34:1) Sum 94, p. 32.

4198. METRES, Philip
"Untitled: It's time to change the record" (tr. of Sergey Gandlevsky, w. Dmitry Psurtsev). [ArtfulD] (26/27) 94, p. 15.
"Untitled: Oh, how the lilacs are this May!" (tr. of Sergey Gandlevsky, w. Dmitry Psurtsev). [ArtfulD] (26/27) 94, p. 14.
"Untitled: To land a job at the garage" (tr. of Sergey Gandlevsky, w. Dmitry Psurtsev). [ArtfulD] (26/27) 94, p. 13.
4199. MEYER, David C.
"Daddy's Little Girl." [CapeR] (29:2) Fall 94, p. 48.
"Hawk." [Elf] (4:4) Wint 94, p. 39.
"Kin." [Elf] (4:4) Wint 94, p. 38-39.
4200. MEYER, Thomas
"The Artifact." [JamesWR] (11:2) Wint 94, p. 12.
"September." [JamesWR] (11:2) Wint 94, p. 12.
"The Waiter Replaces the Fork I Dropped." [JamesWR] (11:2) Wint 94, p. 12.
4201. MEYER-ZEUNER, Gwen
"Main Channel, Night: The Mississippi." [Northeast] (5:10) Sum 94, p. 27.
4202. MEYERS, Brad
"Before the Storm" (interlude). [BellArk] (10:5) S-O 94, p. 23.
"Before the Storm" (interlude). [BellArk] (10:6) N-D 94, p. 26.
4203. MEYERS, Richard
"The Threshold of Awakening." [InterPR] (20:1) Spr 94, p. 91-92.
4204. MEZEY, Robert
"1972" (tr. of Jorge Luis Borges). [AmerPoR] (23:1) Ja-F 94, p. 26.
"Adrogué" (tr. of Jorge Luis Borges, w. Richard Barnes). [Descant] (25:1, #84) Spr 94, p. 65-66.
"Alexander Selkirk" (tr. of Jorge Luis Borges). [Descant] (25:1, #84) Spr 94, p. 61.
"Alexander Selkirk" (tr. of Jorge Luis Borges). [WestHR] (48:3) Fall 94, p. 234.
"Blake" (tr. of Jorge Luis Borges). [AmerPoR] (23:1) Ja-F 94, p. 25.
"Einar Tambarskelver (Heimskringla, I, 117)" (tr. of Jorge Luis Borges). [AmerPoR] (23:1) Ja-F 94, p. 29.
"Elegy for a Park" (tr. of Jorge Luis Borges). [NewYRB] (41:21) 22 D 94, p. 22.
"Elvira de Alvear" (tr. of Jorge Luis Borges). [AmerPoR] (23:1) Ja-F 94, p. 25.
"Endymion on Latmos" (tr. of Jorge Luis Borges, w. Richard Barnes). [Descant] (25:1, #84) Spr 94, p. 67-68.
"The Engraving" (tr. of Jorge Luis Borges). [PartR] (61:4) Fall 94, p. 631.
"The Enigmas" (tr. of Jorge Luis Borges, w. Richard Barnes). [Agni] (40) 94, p. 119.
"Flowing or Being" (tr. of Jorge Luis Borges, w. Richard Barnes). [Agni] (40) 94, p. 121.
"Fragments of an Apocryphal Evangelist" (12 selections, tr. of Jorge Luis Borges). [Poetry] (164:2) My 94, p. 72.
"G. A. Bürger" (tr. of Jorge Luis Borges). [SoCoast] (17) Je 94, p. 25.
"Hengist Wants Men (449 A.D.)" (tr. of Jorge Luis Borges). [AmerPoR] (23:1) Ja-F 94, p. 29.
"*Inferno*, V, 129" (tr. of Jorge Luis Borges, w. Richard Barnes). [AmerPoR] (23:1) Ja-F 94, p. 27.
"Luke XXIII" (tr. of Jorge Luis Borges, w. Richard Barnes). [Agni] (40) 94, p. 120.
"Matthew XXV, 30" (tr. of Jorge Luis Borges, w. Richard Barnes). [AmerPoR] (23:1) Ja-F 94, p. 27.
"Matthew XXV, 30" (tr. of Jorge Luis Borges, w. Richard Barnes). [Descant] (25:1, #84) Spr 94, p. 74.
"Metaphors of the Thousand and One Nights" (tr. of Jorge Luis Borges). [Descant] (25:1, #84) Spr 94, p. 72-73.
"Metaphors of the Thousand and One Nights" (tr. of Jorge Luis Borges). [WestHR] (48:3) Fall 94, p. 236-237.
"Mexico" (tr. of Jorge Luis Borges). [Thrpny] (56) Wint 94, p. 30.
"The Mirror" (tr. of Jorge Luis Borges). [AmerPoR] (23:1) Ja-F 94, p. 25.
"Museum" (tr. of Jorge Luis Borges). [PartR] (61:4) Fall 94, p. 631-632.
"Nineteen Twenty-something" (tr. of Jorge Luis Borges). [AmerPoR] (23:1) Ja-F 94, p. 25.
"The Odyssey, Book XXIII" (tr. of Jorge Luis Borges, w. Richard Barnes). [AmerPoR] (23:1) Ja-F 94, p. 27.
"On His Blindness" (tr. of Jorge Luis Borges). [Poetry] (164:2) My 94, p. 71.
"One-Rime Dream" (in memory of Henri Coulette). [YaleR] (82:1) Ja 94, p. 84.
"The Other" (tr. of Jorge Luis Borges). [WestHR] (48:3) Fall 94, p. 233.

"La Recoleta" (tr. of Jorge Luis Borges, w. Richard Barnes). [AmerPoR] (23:1) Ja-F 94, p. 28.
"Ricardo Güiraldes" (tr. of Jorge Luis Borges). [Descant] (25:1, #84) Spr 94, p. 64.
"Saturdays" (To C.G., tr. of Jorge Luis Borges). [AmerPoR] (23:1) Ja-F 94, p. 26.
"Swords" (tr. of Jorge Luis Borges, w. Richard Barnes). [Descant] (25:1, #84) Spr 94, p. 69.
"Tamerlane (1336-1405)" (tr. of Jorge Luis Borges). [Descant] (25:1, #84) Spr 94, p. 62-63.
"Tea Dance at the Nautilus Hotel (1925)" (on a painting by Donald Justice). [NewRep] (210:5) 31 Ja 94, p. 39.
"To France" (tr. of Jorge Luis Borges). [SoCoast] (17) Je 94, p. 23.
"To Francisco López Merino" (tr. of Jorge Luis Borges). [AmerPoR] (23:1) Ja-F 94, p. 26.
"To Manuel Mujica Lainez" (tr. of Jorge Luis Borges, w. Richard Barnes). [AmerPoR] (23:1) Ja-F 94, p. 26.
"To the One Reading Me" (tr. of Jorge Luis Borges). [Descant] (25:1, #84) Spr 94, p. 60.

4205. MICCICHE, Laura
"Poem of Definitions." [Sonora] (27) Spr 94, p. 61.

4206. MICHAEL, Brien
"Walk on the Pavement." [SmPd] (31:1, #90) Wint 94, p. 16.

4207. MICHAUD, Michael Gregg
"Genesis 1992." [Amelia] (7:3, #22) 94, p. 11.
"Juan Carlo." [JamesWR] (11:4) Sum 94, p. 7.
"June 28, 1993." [Amelia] (7:4, #23) 94, p. 179-180.
"My Book of Dreams." [Amelia] (7:4, #23) 94, p. 179.

4208. MICHAUX, Henri
"Poteaux d'Angle (Angle Markers)" (tr. by Lynn Hoggard). [GrahamHR] (18) Wint 94-95, p. 81-82.

4209. MICHEL, Jean-Claude
"Bitter Strata" (tr. of Maurice Cadet). [InterPR] (20:2) Fall 94, p. 25.

4210. MICHELSON, Peter
"Enduring Witness, the Mosques of Kattankudi." [SpoonR] (19:1) Wint-Spr 94, p. 48-49.

4211. MICHELSON, Richard
"The Scream." [NewL] (60:2) 94, p. 87-88.

4212. MICHIURA, Motoko
"Ah, my pocketbook" (Tanka, tr. by Miyuki Aoyama, Akemi Tomioka, and Leza Lowitz). [Zyzzyva] (10:2) Sum 94, p. 61.
"My nipples still erect" (Tanka, tr. by Miyuki Aoyama, Akemi Tomioka, and Leza Lowitz). [Zyzzyva] (10:2) Sum 94, p. 61.
"Someday I'll turn to water" (Tanka, tr. by Miyuki Aoyama, Akemi Tomioka, and Leza Lowitz). [Zyzzyva] (10:2) Sum 94, p. 61.
"Tanka: Washing and combing" (tr. by Akemi Tomioka and Leza Lowitz). [YellowS] (11:4, #44) Wint 93-94, p. 44.
"Whenever I see poppies" (Tanka, tr. by Miyuki Aoyama, Akemi Tomioka, and Leza Lowitz). [Zyzzyva] (10:2) Sum 94, p. 61.

4213. MICHOD, Alec
"Because the TV Exploded." [AnotherCM] (28) 94, p. 95.

4214. MICUS, Edward
"Canopy." [LaurelR] (28:1) Wint 94, p. 52.
"Minnesota: March." [LaurelR] (28:1) Wint 94, p. 53.

4215. MIDDELPLAATS, Marina
"My Cousin in Messines." [Vis] (46) 94, p. 6.

4216. MIDDLETON, Christopher
"A Breeze in Derveni." [GrandS] (13:2, #50) Fall 94, p. 63-64.
"Fishing Boats at Assos." [Thrpny] (58) Sum 94, p. 17.
"A Landscape by Delacroix." [NewYorker] (70:18) 20 Je 94, p. 72.

4217. MIDDLETON, David
"Ex Nihilo." [Image] ([2]) Sum 92, p. 41-44.
"The Sunday School Lesson." [SewanR] (102:1) Wint 94, p. 29-31.

4218. MIECZKOWSKI, Rondo
"Paperwhite Narcissus." [ModernW] (1) Summer 94, p. 25-26.

4219. MIHAILOVA, Zhana
"The Time of the Blue Haze" (tr. of Damian Damianov, w. Karl Elder). [AnotherCM] (28) 94, p. 34.

4220. MIHAIU, Virgil
"Every Hope" (tr. by Brenda Walker). [PoetryC] (14:4) S 94, p. 21.
"I Know Him" (tr. by Brenda Walker). [PoetryC] (14:4) S 94, p. 21.
4221. MIKOFSKY, Bernard S.
"Silentium" (tr. of Fyodor Ivanovich Tyutchev). [Talisman] (12) Spr 94, p. 197.
"To My Sister Florence." [WorldL] (5) 94, p. 40.
"We Are Two" (tr. of Karel Capek). [WorldL] (5) 94, p. 40.
4222. MIKOLEY, Jim
"The 9th Day." [Pearl] (20) Spr 94, p. 74.
"California Handjob." [SlipS] (14) 94, p. 14.
"The Cuban Sandwich." [SlipS] (14) 94, p. 13.
"Officer Fenton's Last Words." [ContextS] (4:1) 94, p. 31.
"Universal Sign for Dead." [SlipS] (14) 94, p. 15.
4223. MIKULEC, Patrick B.
"Barbed Wire." [HiramPoR] (55/56) Fall 93-Sum 94, p. 78.
4224. MILANES, Cecilia R.
"Your Tongue." [Vis] (44) 94, p. 27.
4225. MILANÉS, Pablo
"El Breve Espacio en Que No Estas." [Areíto] (4:15) Marzo 94, p. 44.
4226. MILBURN, Michael
"In the Frame." [NewEngR] (16:1) Wint 94, p. 68.
"Loose Ends." [HarvardR] (2) Fall 92, p. 39.
"Poem in Place of Goodbye." [NewEngR] (16:1) Wint 94, p. 70.
"Words for a Child." [NewEngR] (16:1) Wint 94, p. 69.
4227. MILES, Jeff
"Before the First Snow." [Pembroke] (26) 94, p. 93.
"Jezebel in the Garden." [Pembroke] (26) 94, p. 94.
"Late February." [Pembroke] (26) 94, p. 92.
4228. MILES, Kirk R.
"First Aid for the Choking Victim." [PraF] (15:1, #66) Spr 94, p. 112.
4229. MILES, S. Phillip
"Kyrie Eleison." [Pembroke] (26) 94, p. 95.
4230. MILES, Steve
"Come Morning." [Poem] (71) My 94, p. 44-45.
"Easter." [Poem] (71) My 94, p. 42-43.
"Owl." [Poem] (71) My 94, p. 40-41.
4231. MILJKOVIC, Branko
"Everyone Will Write Poetry" (tr. by P. H. Liotta). [InterQ] (1:3) 94, p. 189.
"Sun" (tr. by P. H. Liotta). [InterQ] (1:3) 94, p. 188.
4232. MILLER, Bernice Ybarra
"A New Love." [SinW] (53) Sum-Fall 94, p. 91.
4233. MILLER, Carol E.
"No Lady of the House." [SoCoast] (17) Je 94, p. 48-49.
4234. MILLER, Carolyn
"A Dream of Flying: The Amelia Earhart Story." [QW] (38) Winter-Spr 93-94, p. 125-126.
"In the Arboretum." [Zyzzyva] (10:2) Sum 94, p. 88-89.
4235. MILLER, D. C.
"Driven by Obscurity." [SouthernPR] (34:1) Sum 94, p. 53-54.
"I Saw that Softness." [SouthernPR] (34:1) Sum 94, p. 54.
4236. MILLER, Derek
"Cashing in with The Night." [HangL] (65) 94, p. 36-37.
"Etiquette on Dealing with Other Relatives." [HangL] (65) 94, p. 35.
"How the Outfield Is Positioned." [HangL] (65) 94, p. 34-35.
"Things Bothered with Knowing Dreamlessness." [HangL] (65) 94, p. 38-39.
4237. MILLER, E. Ethelbert
"And Then Mr. Dorsey Wrote Precious Lord." [Callaloo] (17:4) Fall 94, p. 1102.
4238. MILLER, Elizabeth Gamble
"Guaro Even 100 Proof Fails" (tr. of Carlos Ernesto García). [InterQ] (1:4) 94, p. 32.
4239. MILLER, Eric
"An Incident from the War of 1912." [MalR] (109) Wint 94, p. 49-50.
4240. MILLER, Errol
"Beloved Infidel." [CentR] (38:3) Fall 94, p. 512-514.
"Blues-Men of the Delta." [ChatR] (14:2) Wint 94, p. 35-36.
"The End of the String." [GrahamHR] (18) Wint 94-95, p. 22.
"Even with Answers." [Plain] (15:1) Fall 94, p. 24-25.

"In the Innermost Parts of the Continent." [HampSPR] Wint 94, p. 12-13.
"Jake Comes Home." [Parting] (7:2) Wint 94-95, p. 65.
"Leachville." [LaurelR] (28:1) Wint 94, p. 101-102.
"The Long Hours Settling In" (A Plainsongs Award Poem). [Plain] (14:2) Wint 94, p. 39.
"Love Poem." [SlipS] (14) 94, p. 25.
"The More I Could Not Do." [GrahamHR] (18) Wint 94-95, p. 21.
"Not Far to the South." [Elf] (4:2) Sum 94, p. 42-43.
"On the Lower East Side of the South." [BlackBR] (19) Fall-Wint 94, p. 6-7.
"Outwrite Fiction." [SantaBR] (2:2) Fall-Wint 94, p. 146-147.
"Papa, Your Personality Is Showing." [CumbPR] (13:2) Spr 94, p. 27.
"Pavilion of Ruin." [CentR] (38:3) Fall 94, p. 514-516.
"Striving for Reality." [Plain] (14:3) Spr 94, p. 24.
"This Year, in Autumn." [MidwQ] (35:4) Sum 94, p. 411.
"A Treasury of Modern Thought." [FourQ] (8:1) Spr 94, p. 48-49.
"Wilsonville Story." [Border] (3) Fall 93, p. 49.

4241. MILLER, Heather Ross
"Even Swap." [SouthernR] (30:4) Aut 94, p. 772-773.
"Keeping Peace." [SouthernR] (30:4) Aut 94, p. 773-774.
"Thoreau at Night." [TarRP] (33:2) Spr 94, p. 49.

4242. MILLER, Jane
"Fooling Around by the Light of the Moon." [ChiR] (40:4) 94, p. 1-2.

4243. MILLER, Jennifer
"Blues Song for a Showgirl" (for José, 1948-1990). [ParisR] (36:132) Fall 94, p. 129-130.
"Bronco Busting." [ParisR] (36:132) Fall 94, p. 131.

4244. MILLER, John N.
"Hailing to Byzantium." [CapeR] (29:1) Spr 94, p. 44.
"Moving Upstream, South." [CapeR] (29:1) Spr 94, p. 43.

4245. MILLER, Kevin
"The Light Left." [CrabCR] (8:2/3/9:1/2/3) 94, p. 89.

4246. MILLER, Leslie Adrienne
"Mermaid in the U-Bahn Station." [NoDaQ] (62:1) Wint 94-95, p. 7-8.

4247. MILLER, Lisa C.
"Promises." [Conscience] (15:4) Wint 94-95, p. 35.

4248. MILLER, Marlene
"How to Get More Life Out of an Eggroll." [CapeR] (29:1) Spr 94, p. 23.

4249. MILLER, Matthew
"Factory Work." [Amelia] (7:4, #23) 94, p. 138-139.

4250. MILLER, Michael
"The Concept of the Poet with Three Heads" (Associated Writing Programs Intro Award poem). [IndR] (17:2) Fall 94, p. 136-138.
"Procession." [NewRep] (210:25) 20 Je 94, p. 30.

4251. MILLER, Patricia Cleary
"Mother Won't Wear Walking Shoes." [NewL] (61:1) 94, p. 153.

4252. MILLER, Philip
"Abandonment Anxiety." [ColEng] (56:5) S 94, p. 575-576.
"Darkening." [Plain] (14:2) Wint 94, p. 36.
"Deeply." [Poem] (72) N 94, p. 60.
"Eternity." [Pivot] (41) 93, p. 40-41.
"Fingers." [SmPd] (31:3, #92) Fall 94, p. 32-33.
"Fried Fish." [Poem] (72) N 94, p. 58-59.
"In the Presence of Others." [ColEng] (56:5) S 94, p. 574-575.
"Others." [PoetC] (26:1) Fall 94, p. 9-10.
"The Song the Bird Sings." [Pivot] (41) 93, p. 41.
"Through Strange Eyes" (for Zada Vogel). [Pivot] (42) 94, p. 27.
"Vick's Salve." [AmerS] (63:3) Sum 94, p. 440.
"We Can't Get Off." [CoalC] (8) Ap 94, p. 37-38.

4253. MILLER, Ray
"Bar Story." [Parting] (7:1) Sum 94, p. 74.

4254. MILLER, Robert
"My Wife." [PaintedB] (53/54) 94, p. 10.
"Outline for a Romantic Narrative." [PaintedB] (53/54) 94, p. 8-9.

4255. MILLER, Sean
"The Guitar Player." [Confr] (54/55) Fall 94-Wint 95, p. 317.

4256. MILLER, Stephen Paul
"Squash Omelette." [Talisman] (13) Fall 94-Wint 95, p. 271.
4257. MILLER, William R.
"Amish Barns." [CumbPR] (14:1) Fall 94, p. 50.
"Hair Day." [CumbPR] (14:1) Fall 94, p. 51.
4258. MILLER-DUGGAN, Devon
"Busy in a Cold, Cold Gloom." [Plain] (14:3) Spr 94, p. 16.
"Nativity." [SmPd] (31:3, #92) Fall 94, p. 33-34.
MILLER LAINO, E. J.
See LAINO, E. J. Miller
4259. MILLETT, John
"The Fruit Ripens." [Vis] (45) 94, p. 22.
"Ore." [Vis] (46) 94, p. 20.
"O'Reilly." [Vis] (45) 94, p. 22.
4260. MILLIGAN, Paula
"The Gaia Hypothesis." [BellArk] (10:3) My-Je 94, p. 27.
"The Man Underground." [BellArk] (10:3) My-Je 94, p. 27.
"Reflections." [BellArk] (10:3) My-Je 94, p. 27.
"Truing." [Gaia] (4) Je 94, p. 43.
4261. MILLIS, Christopher
"Visual Field Exam." [HarvardR] (6) Spr 94, p. 83.
4262. MILLMAN, Lawrence
"Beothucks." [TickleAce] (28) Fall-Wint 94, p. 100.
"Glacial Erratic" (for Elliott Merrick). [TickleAce] (28) Fall-Wint 94, p. 102.
"Snail." [TickleAce] (28) Fall-Wint 94, p. 101.
4263. MILLS, Jess
"My Mother, Going Blind." [TarRP] (33:2) Spr 94, p. 36.
4264. MILLS, Ralph J., Jr.
"The Dwarf / Moon's." [IllinoisR] (2:1) Fall 94, p. 33.
"In Late May." [IllinoisR] (2:1) Fall 94, p. 32.
"Maybe." [IllinoisR] (2:1) Fall 94, p. 34.
"Trees" (after Jaccottet). [TarRP] (34:1) Fall 94, p. 21.
"A Wind / Laps." [IllinoisR] (2:1) Fall 94, p. 32.
4265. MILLS, Todd E.
"The Fruit Mask." [YellowS] (11:4, #44) Wint 93-94, p. 25.
"A Party at a Rented House." [YellowS] (11:4, #44) Wint 93-94, p. 25.
4266. MILLS, Wilmer Hastings
"Morning Song." [PoetC] (26:1) Fall 94, p. 15.
4267. MILNER, Joseph O.
"Convention Going." [EngJ] (83:7) N 94, p. 19.
4268. MILOSZ, Czeslaw
"At a Certain Age" (tr. by the author and Robert Hass). [NewYorker] (69:46) 17 Ja 94, p. 68.
"The Bridge" (tr. of Oscar V. de L. Milosz, w. Robert Hass). [Thrpny] (58) Sum 94, p. 11.
"I Would Like to Describe" (tr. of Zbigniew Herbert, w. Peter Dale Scott). [NewEngR] (16:1) Wint 94, p. 105-106.
"Incantation" (tr. by the author and Robert Pinsky). [GrahamHR] (18) Wint 94-95, p. 106.
"Incantation" (tr. by the author and Robert Pinsky). [TriQ] (92) Wint 94-95, p. 21-22.
"A Polka Dot Dress." [HarvardR] (Premier Issue) Spr 92, p. 34.
"Realism" (tr. by the author and Robert Hass). [NewYorker] (70:8) 11 Ap 94, p. 70.
"This World" (tr. by the author and Robert Hass). [Antaeus] (75/76) Aut 94, p. 304.
"Window" (tr. by the author and Lillian Vallée). [NewEngR] (16:3) Sum 94, p. 23.
4269. MILOSZ, Oscar V. de L.
"The Bridge" (tr. by Czeslaw Milosz and Robert Hass). [Thrpny] (58) Sum 94, p. 11.
"Le Pont." [Thrpny] (58) Sum 94, p. 11.
4270. MILTNER, Robert
"Past the Starting Line." [ContextS] (4:1) 94, p. 44.
4271. MIMS, Kevin
"Argument in Favor of the Letter-Box Format." [Pearl] (20) Spr 94, p. 19.
"Confessions to My Sister." [SoCoast] (17) Je 94, p. 54-55.
"Storeless." [Pearl] (20) Spr 94, p. 19.
"Traveling Apart." [FloridaR] (19:2) 94, p. 66.

4272. MINARD, Nancy
"This View." [AntigR] (98) Sum 94, p. 103.
"What the White Bird Speaks." [AntigR] (98) Sum 94, p. 104.
"Wind." [AntigR] (98) Sum 94, p. 102.
4273. MINCZESKI, John
"Starting to Hate." [AnotherCM] (27) 94, p. 143-144.
4274. MINETT, Amy J.
"Family Matters." [Jacaranda] (5:1) Wint-Spr 91, p. 5.
MING, Hsiang
See HSIANG, Ming
MINGXIA, Li
See LI, Mingxia
4275. MINOR, Marisa
"I Did Not Know You." [SpiritSH] (59) 94, p. 16.
MINORU, Yoshioka
See YOSHIOKA, Minoru
4276. MIRABAI
"His Hair" (version by Robert Bly). [HarvardR] (6) Spr 94, p. 113.
4277. MIRABAI, Princess (1489-1550)
"For Love of the Dark One: Mirabai Translations" (tr. by Andrew Schelling). [YellowS] (11:4, #44) Wint 93-94, p. 8-9.
4278. MIRANDA, Veronica
"Asleep, Dead or Bewitched" (tr. of Alejandro Schmidt). [Luz] (7) N 94, p. 29-33.
"Notion of Reality" (Selections, tr. of Carlos Vitale). [Luz] (7) N 94, p. 17-20.
"Renuevo tras la Lluvia Equilibrio del Ansia" (Premio Agustín Acosta de Poesía 1992. Selections: 3 poems, English tr. of Arminda Valdés-Ginebra). [Luz] (6) My 94, p. 20-26.
4279. MIRCEA, Ion
"Forma Mentis" (tr. by Adam J. Sorkin and Liliana Ursu). [NewEngR] (16:1) Wint 94, p. 116.
"Kind of Bright" (tr. by Adam J. Sorkin and Liviu Cotrau). [HayF] (14) Spr-Sum 94, p. 15.
"The Mold" (tr. by Adam J. Sorkin and Liliana Ursu). [NewEngR] (16:1) Wint 94, p. 115.
"River in the Dark" (tr. by Adam J. Sorkin and Liviu Cotrau). [HayF] (14) Spr-Sum 94, p. 16.
"S.F." (tr. by Adam J. Sorkin and Liliana Ursu). [NewEngR] (16:1) Wint 94, p. 115-116.
4280. MIROLLO, Gabriella
"The Poet at Two Rejects the Beach." [Poetry] (164:5) Ag 94, p. 270.
4281. MIROSEVICH, Toni
"Gandhi Joins the Work Force." [KenR] (NS 16:2) Spr 94, p. 119-120.
"Virginia Woolf Joins the Work Force." [KenR] (NS 16:2) Spr 94, p. 120-121.
4282. MISTRAL, Gabriela
"Old Woman" (tr. by Christiane Jacox Kyle). [SenR] (24:1) Spr 94, p. 56-57.
"The Sea" (tr. by Christiane Jacox Kyle). [SenR] (24:1) Spr 94, p. 58-59.
4283. MISTRY, Manek
"Spoon." [Parting] (7:1) Sum 94, p. 72.
4284. MITCHAM, Judson
"Deadpan." [NewEngR] (16:3) Sum 94, p. 91-92.
"The Foolishness of God Is Wiser Than Men" (1 Corinthians 1:25). [Poetry] (164:2) My 94, p. 73.
"A Postcard to My Father." [NewEngR] (16:3) Sum 94, p. 91.
"Preface to an Omnibus Review." [GeoR] (48:2) Sum 94, p. 359-360.
"Preface to an Omnibus Review" (From the Summer issue of *The Georgia Review*). [Harp] (289:1734) N 94, p. 32.
"The Secret of Humility Is Excellence." [NewEngR] (16:3) Sum 94, p. 90.
"Surrender." [GeoR] (48:1) Spr 94, p. 106.
4285. MITCHELL, Elaine
"Clerihew: Gerard Manley Hopkins." [Light] (10) Sum 94, p. 12.
"Clerihew: Karl Marx." [Light] (9) Spr 94, p. 13.
"Form." [Light] (9) Spr 94, p. 16.
4286. MITCHELL, Hayley R.
"Bitter." [SlipS] (14) 94, p. 92.
"I Never Knew You Loved White Tulips." [Pearl] (20) Spr 94, p. 7.
"You Wait a Year or Two or Four." [SlipS] (14) 94, p. 91.

4287. MITCHELL, Mark
"Past Ten Sleep." [SpoonR] (19:1) Wint-Spr 94, p. 107.
"Two Poverties" (From the portrait, "Agua," by Flor Garduno). [SpoonR] (19:1) Wint-Spr 94, p. 108-109.
4288. MITCHELL, Rick
"Giving Back." [CimR] (108) Jl 94, p. 81.
4289. MITCHELL, Roger
"Cardamom." [NewEngR] (16:3) Sum 94, p. 87.
"Looking Back at the Sky." [Pequod] (37) 94, p. 27.
"Taxi Dancer, Montana, 1936" (from a photo by Margaret Bourke-White). [HopewellR] (6) 94, p. 111.
"Whole Way Down." [Pequod] (37) 94, p. 28.
4290. MITCHELL, Susan
"Music." [Antaeus] (75/76) Aut 94, p. 305-309.
4291. MITCHELL-FOUST, Michelle
"Abacus of Birds for Eurydice." [DenQ] (28:4) Spr 94, p. 38-40.
4292. MITCHNER, Gary
"On the Western Edge." [ParisR] (36:131) Sum 94, p. 106-107.
4293. MITCHNER, Stuart
"At Stephen Crane's Funeral." [Poetry] (163:4) Ja 94, p. 215.
"Coleridge." [Poetry] (163:4) Ja 94, p. 216.
"Verisimilitude." [Poetry] (163:4) Ja 94, p. 215.
4294. MITRA, Debarati
"He Gets Well" (tr. by Carolyne Wright and Paramita Banerjee). [InterQ] (1:2) 93, p. 156.
"In White Moonlight" (tr. by Carolyne Wright and Paramita Banerjee). [InterQ] (1:2) 93, p. 155.
MITSUHARU, Kaneko
See KANEKO, Mitsuharu
4295. MITTENTHAL, Robert
"Social Sculpture" (Selections: 1-12). [Avec] (8:1) 94, p. 5-11.
"Sunburn." [Avec] (8:1) 94, p. 1-4.
4296. MIXON, Victoria
"The Diseased." [CreamCR] (18:2) Fall 94, p. 114.
MIYUKI, Aoyama
See AOYAMA, Miyuki
4297. MIZER, Ray
"Apple Festival Numero Uno." [Elf] (4:2) Sum 94, p. 35.
"Elemental Artistry." [BellArk] (10:3 [i.e. 10:4]) Jl-Ag 94, p. 25.
"Gallery Twist." [BellArk] (10:3) My-Je 94, p. 7.
"No Fire, No Ice." [SmPd] (31:1, #90) Wint 94, p. 24.
"Not Euclid Alone." [BellArk] (10:3 [i.e. 10:4]) Jl-Ag 94, p. 9.
"Sonnet for a Stricken Lady." [BellArk] (10:1) Ja-F 94, p. 23.
"Waterworld Blues." [Elf] (4:2) Sum 94, p. 36.
"Way-up-North Camp." [BellArk] (10:1) Ja-F 94, p. 23.
4298. MIZUNO, Ruriko
"Dora's Island" (tr. by Edwin A. Cranston). [TriQ] (91) Fall 94, p. 58-59.
"Hänsel and Gretel's Island" (tr. by Edwin A. Cranston). [TriQ] (91) Fall 94, p. 56-57.
"On the Island of Elephant Trees" (tr. by Edwin A. Cranston). [TriQ] (91) Fall 94, p. 62-63.
"The Sky Where the Moas Were" (tr. by Edwin A. Cranston). [TriQ] (91) Fall 94, p. 60-61.
"The Tree House" (tr. by Edwin A. Cranston). [TriQ] (91) Fall 94, p. 64-65.
4299. MLADINIC, Peter
"Houses." [PoetryE] (37/38) Spr 94, p. 19.
4300. MLINKO, Ange
"The beautiful catherine Deneuve." [Talisman] (12) Spr 94, p. 17.
"Hologram arctic — rabbit." [Talisman] (12) Spr 94, p. 16.
"On L." [Talisman] (13) Fall 94-Wint 95, p. 221.
MO, Chang
See CHANG, Mo
4301. MOBBY, William
"Larch Tree." [ConnPR] (13:1) 94, p. 25.
4302. MOBILIO, Albert
"A Dust Having Filled My Eyes (ii)." [Talisman] (13) Fall 94-Wint 95, p. 9-10.

"I Woke in a Room So Dark (i)." [Talisman] (13) Fall 94-Wint 95, p. 9.
"To Get Rid of This Blinded Face (iii)." [Talisman] (13) Fall 94-Wint 95, p. 10.
"What I Could Throw Off I Threw (iv)." [Talisman] (13) Fall 94-Wint 95, p. 11.

4303. MOCK, Jeff
"Although You Can't Step into the Same River Twice." [LaurelR] (28:2) Sum 94, p. 58.
"Cartography: Here There Be Dragons." [WebR] (18) Fall 94, p. 90.
"Jeff Mock, 1960-1991." [PassN] (15:2) Wint 94, p. 22-23.
"Joan's Birthday" (14 February). [DenQ] (29:1) Sum 94, p. 24-25.
"Lazarus About to Drink a Glass of Water." [Farm] (11:1) Spr-Sum 94, p. 115-116.
"The One Nice Street in Town." [IndR] (17:2) Fall 94, p. 53.
"When She Wakes to the Strange Early Light." [PoetryNW] (35:1) Spr 94, p. 3-8.

4304. MODRCIN, Ines
"Surrendering (No. 4)" (tr. of Goran Tomcic, w. the author). [SenR] (24:2) Fall 94, p. 55.

4305. MOE, Frederick (Fredrick)
"Conversations with My Grandfather." [BellArk] (10:3 [i.e. 10:4]) Jl-Ag 94, p. 15.
"The Passing of Shakers at Canterbury." [Elf] (4:3) Fall 94, p. 31.
"Three Scenes from Pitcher Mountain." [BellArk] (10:3) My-Je 94, p. 11.

4306. MOFFET, Penelope
"Ching / The Well." [PaintedHR] (11) Spr-Sum 94, p. 53.
"Fuel." [PaintedHR] (11) Spr-Sum 94, p. 51.
"Solstice." [PaintedHR] (11) Spr-Sum 94, p. 52.

4307. MOHRING, Ron
"Written." [ArtfulD] (26/27) 94, p. 82.

4308. MOHYLNY, Attila
"Archipenko's Plasticity" (tr. by Michael M. Naydan). [DenQ] (29:1) Sum 94, p. 91.

4309. MOLDAW, Carol
"Bosque del Apache." [NewRep] (211:21) 21 N 94, p. 36.

MOLEN, Robert vander
See VanderMOLEN, Robert

4310. MOMADAY, Scott
"Believe This." [Ploughs] (20:1) Spr 94, p. 37.

4311. MONACO, Cory
"The '80s." [WormR] (34:3, #135) 94, p. 93.
"Apt. Filling Up." [WormR] (34:3, #135) 94, p. 93.
"The Cannibal." [WormR] (34:3, #135) 94, p. 92.
"Christmas Eve '92." [WormR] (34:1, #133) 94, p. 20.
"The Cold-Medication Commercial." [WormR] (34:3, #135) 94, p. 94.
"Competition." [WormR] (34:3, #135) 94, p. 95.
"Couldn't Really Tell You." [WormR] (34:3, #135) 94, p. 95.
"The Dog Mirage." [WormR] (34:1, #133) 94, p. 22.
"Eavesdropping." [WormR] (34:1, #133) 94, p. 21.
"Elmer to Daffy." [WormR] (34:1, #133) 94, p. 22.
"The Flying Saucer." [WormR] (34:1, #133) 94, p. 22.
"It Takes One to Know One." [WormR] (34:1, #133) 94, p. 22.
"Jerking Con Edison Around." [WormR] (34:1, #133) 94, p. 24.
"The Lazy Worm." [WormR] (34:1, #133) 94, p. 21.
"Like." [WormR] (34:3, #135) 94, p. 92.
"My Moth." [WormR] (34:3, #135) 94, p. 93.
"New Jersey." [WormR] (34:1, #133) 94, p. 23.
"Orange." [WormR] (34:3, #135) 94, p. 95.
"P.F.C. Morgan." [WormR] (34:3, #135) 94, p. 95.
"Results." [WormR] (34:3, #135) 94, p. 96.
"Robin Jaynes." [WormR] (34:3, #135) 94, p. 95.
"Sarcasm." [WormR] (34:3, #135) 94, p. 92.
"The Traitor." [WormR] (34:3, #135) 94, p. 94.
"Ugly Woman." [WormR] (34:1, #133) 94, p. 23.
"Vodka." [WormR] (34:3, #135) 94, p. 94.
"What Ashbery et Al. Said at the Big Poetry Meeting." [WormR] (34:3, #135) 94, p. 95.

4312. MONAGAN, George C.
"Uncle Jack." [Blueline] (15) 94, p. 63.

4313. MONAGHAN, Timothy
"Getting Up." [Elf] (4:3) Fall 94, p. 35.
"The Kicker." [NegC] (14:1/2) 94, p. 154-155.

4314. MONAHAN, Jean
"Animal Fair" (for Karen Silverstein. 1993 John Williams Andrews Narrative Poetry Contest Prize Winner). [PoetL] (89:1) Spr 94, p. 7-12.
"Medusa Cuts Her Hair." [SenR] (24:2) Fall 94, p. 50-51.
4315. MONETTE, Paul
"The Bee-Eater" (For Carol Muske). [Thrpny] (59) Fall 94, p. 6.
4316. MONEY, Peter
"Six-Forty-Nine." [Talisman] (12) Spr 94, p. 83-84.
4317. MONNIER, Pascalle
"Locations" (tr. by John Ashbery). [Conjunc] (23) 94, p. 274-278.
"Para Siempre Teresita? Para Siempre Rodrigo" (tr. by John Ashbery). [Conjunc] (23) 94, p. 272-274.
4318. MONROE, Melissa
"Inside the Chinese Room" (suggested by John Searle's thought experiment). [Ploughs] (20:4) Wint 94-95, p. 131-133.
MONT, Steve de
See DeMONT, Steve
4319. MONTAGUE, John
"The Horse" (tr. of Francis Ponge). [AmerPoR] (23:4) Jl-Ag 94, p. 32-33.
"The Nuptial Habits of Dogs" (tr. of Francis Ponge). [AmerPoR] (23:4) Jl-Ag 94, p. 32.
4320. MONTALE, Eugenio
"Giorno e Notte" (tr. by Jane Stuart). [TampaR] (8) Spr 94, p. 49.
"Serenata Indiana" (tr. by Jane Stuart). [TampaR] (8) Spr 94, p. 48.
4321. MONTANHAGOL, Guilhem de
"No Sap Per Que Va Son Joy Pus Tarzan" (in Provençal and English, tr. by Joseph S. Salemi). [CumbPR] (13:2) Spr 94, p. 40-45.
4322. MONTEJO, Eugenio
"At the End of Things" (tr. by Alastair Reid). [Trans] (29) Spr 94, p. 38.
"Certain Words" (tr. by Alastair Reid). [Trans] (29) Spr 94, p. 36.
"In This City" (tr. by Alastair Reid). [Trans] (29) Spr 94, p. 40.
"Life" (tr. by Alastair Reid). [Trans] (29) Spr 94, p. 37.
"The Orinoco" (tr. by Alastair Reid). [Trans] (29) Spr 94, p. 39.
"Two Bodies" (tr. by Alastair Reid). [Trans] (29) Spr 94, p. 35.
4323. MONTEZ, Susan
"Buckingham Alba." [MinnR] (41/42) Fall 93-Spr 94 (published Mr 95), p. 19.
"Eking Out a Living in the Third Poorest County in Virginia." [MinnR] (41/42) Fall 93-Spr 94 (published Mr 95), p. 19.
"Faculty Meeting." [PoetryE] (37/38) Spr 94, p. 98.
"Meditations on the Day Abbey Hoffman Died." [PoetryE] (37/38) Spr 94, p. 94.
"South Bronx I.S. 193 Social Studies Class Takes a Field Trip to Bronx Criminal Court." [PoetryE] (37/38) Spr 94, p. 95-97.
4324. MONTGOMERY, Missy Marie
"The Fish Beneath the Words." [SouthernPR] (34:2) Wint 94, p. 39.
4325. MONTGOMERY-FATE, Tom
"Manila Squatter." [ChrC] (111:13) 20 Ap 94, p. 416.
4326. MOODY, Rodger
"Simple Love" (for Julian). [Zyzzyva] (10:1) Spr 94, p. 45.
4327. MOODY, Shirley
"Arcimboldo's 'Water'" (Giuseppe Arcimboldo, Italian Painter, 1527-1593). [SouthernPR] (34:1) Sum 94, p. 36-37.
4328. MOOLTEN, David
"Blue Moon." [PoetryE] (37/38) Spr 94, p. 40-41.
"Camille Claudel and Auguste Rodin." [SewanR] (102:4) Fall 94, p. 547-548.
"Decisions." [PraS] (68:2) Sum 94, p. 126-127.
"Gypsy." [Poetry] (163:4) Ja 94, p. 193-194.
"Last Words." [NowestR] (32:1) 94, p. 117-118.
"Magnavox." [PraS] (68:2) Sum 94, p. 125-126.
"Midwest" (for Robyn Young). [QW] (38) Winter-Spr 93-94, p. 107-108.
"Moths." [PoetryE] (37/38) Spr 94, p. 42-43.
"Phase." [QW] (38) Winter-Spr 93-94, p. 109-110.
"Salem, Massachusetts." [SewanR] (102:4) Fall 94, p. 548-549.
4329. MOON, Janell
"Equal Rights Amendment." [SingHM] (21) 94, p. 2.
"I Rent." [SingHM] (21) 94, p. 47-48.

4330. MOONEY, Martin
"Cleaning the Statues." [Verse] (11:1) Spr 94, p. 96.
4331. MOORE, Barbara
"The Big School." [NewEngR] (16:2) Spr 94, p. 102-103.
"The Flame Tree." [NewEngR] (16:2) Spr 94, p. 101.
"The Room, the Crows." [NewEngR] (16:2) Spr 94, p. 103.
4332. MOORE, Berwyn J.
"The Decisive Moment" (After the photograph, "Suicide," by Russell Sorgi, 1942). [CimR] (107) Ap 94, p. 90-91.
MOORE, Cynthia Gerard
See GERARD-MOORE, Cynthia
4333. MOORE, Edward
"The Democrat." [ChironR] (13:2) Sum 94, p. 31.
4334. MOORE, George B.
"Sewing the Whale's Mouth Shut." [HiramPoR] (57) Fall 94-Wint 95, p. 42.
4335. MOORE, Honor
"Aubade" (For R.). [YellowS] (12:2, #46) Sum-Fall 94, p. 20.
"Citizenship." [AmerPoR] (23:1) Ja-F 94, p. 18.
"Double Curse." [YellowS] (12:2, #46) Sum-Fall 94, p. 20.
"Equinox." [YellowS] (12:2, #46) Sum-Fall 94, p. 20.
"Roses and Orchids." [YellowS] (12:2, #46) Sum-Fall 94, p. 20.
"Undertow." [AmerPoR] (23:1) Ja-F 94, p. 18.
4336. MOORE, Jim
"Freshman Papers." [ParisR] (36:133) Wint 94, p. 289-290.
"The Young Men." [ParisR] (36:133) Wint 94, p. 288.
4337. MOORE, Lenard D.
"Black women shaking." [XavierR] (14:2) Fall 94, p. 29.
"Blues artist leafing." [XavierR] (14:2) Fall 94, p. 29.
"Jazz shadows." [XavierR] (14:2) Fall 94, p. 29.
"Late evening birdsong." [XavierR] (14:2) Fall 94, p. 29.
"Near Spring" (Tennessee, 1993 — for Christopher Buckley). [MidwQ] (35:4) Sum 94, p. 412.
"Old black men standing." [XavierR] (14:2) Fall 94, p. 29.
4338. MOORE, Mary
"Doors." [Poetry] (164:2) My 94, p. 91.
4339. MOORE, Michele Spring
"Adolescent Rag: Greece, New York, 1981" (for Patrick, Shari, and TJ). [HangL] (64) 94, p. 51.
"Ghost Stories." [HangL] (64) 94, p. 52.
"Mom's Working Class" (to all my friends with "poverty mentality"). [HangL] (64) 94, p. 54.
"The Night Before You Left the State." [HangL] (64) 94, p. 53.
4340. MOORE, Miles David
"The Bears of Paris." [Pivot] (41) 93, p. 42.
"Cave Canem." [Pivot] (42) 94, p. 5.
"Trappers." [Light] (12) Wint 94-95, p. 10.
4341. MOORE, Richard
"At Her Party." [Light] (11) Aut 94, p. 15.
"Brit Abroad." [Light] (10) Sum 94, p. 19.
"Children." [PoetC] (25:2) Wint 94, p. 33.
"Daydeath." [Salm] (103) Sum 94, p. 101.
"The Incorruptibility of the Heavens." [Light] (12) Wint 94-95, p. 7.
"Malcolm." [Light] (9) Spr 94, p. 12.
"Nighthood." [CumbPR] (13:2) Spr 94, p. 67.
"Old Fools" (Selections: Part I, Numbers 3-4). [Hellas] (5:2) Fall-Wint 94, p. 40-41.
"Poem Inspired by a Dictionary Entry" (Wavell, Archibald Percival, 1st Earl Wavell, 1883-1950, British Field Marshal). [Light] (10) Sum 94, p. 16.
"Sunset Watching" (in memory of a marriage). [PoetC] (25:2) Wint 94, p. 31-32.
"Tough Beef." [Light] (12) Wint 94-95, p. 8.
4342. MOORE, Richard O.
"Holding On." [Talisman] (12) Spr 94, p. 98-102.
4343. MOORE, Todd
"I Was Trying." [CoalC] (8) Ap 94, p. 43.
"When I Saw" (Sept 13, 1988). [CoalC] (8) Ap 94, p. 44.

4344. MOORHEAD, Andrea
"Août sur les Chaumes Abandonnés" (tr. of Robert Marteau). [PoetryE] (37/38) Spr 94, p. 228.
"Le Lavis Mouvant" (tr. of Robert Marteau). [PoetryE] (37/38) Spr 94, p. 227.
"Outside My Window, Niagara." [Os] (39) Fall-Wint 94, p. 32-35.
"Shadows on the Heart." [Os] (38) Spr 94, p. 28-32.
4345. MOR, Barbara
"Linguistic Duplex." [Sulfur] (35) Fall 94, p. 26-49.
4346. MORA, Pat
"Coatlicue's Rules: Advice from an Aztec Goddess." [PraS] (68:4) Wint 94, p. 76-78.
"Mangos y Limones." [PraS] (68:4) Wint 94, p. 80.
"The Shadow." [PraS] (68:4) Wint 94, p. 81.
"Spring Shining." [PraS] (68:4) Wint 94, p. 79.
4347. MORAN, Ronald
"Honeymooning at the Bizarre Coffee House." [WebR] (18) Fall 94, p. 91-92.
"The Rent-a-Hand Registry." [Northeast] (5:10) Sum 94, p. 24-25.
"Shirley and the Lost Muse Society." [WebR] (18) Fall 94, p. 93.
"Waiting in Memphis." [WebR] (18) Fall 94, p. 94.
4348. MORÉ, Benny
"Amor Fugaz." [Areíto] (4:15) Marzo 94, p. 42.
4349. MOREJON, Nancy
"Ana Mendieta" (tr. by David Frye). [MichQR] (33:3) Sum 94, p. 618-620.
"Before a Mirror" (To Sonia Rivera Valdés, tr. by David Frye). [MichQR] (33:3) Sum 94, p. 621-622.
"A Chronicle That Swoons Before the Immigrant Tree" (tr. by Ruth Behar). [MichQR] (33:3) Sum 94, p. 623.
4350. MORELAND, Jane
"Freedom Oak." [Border] (4) Spr-Sum 94, p. 51.
4351. MORENCY, Pierre
"I Know" (tr. by Brenda Casey and Elizabeth Hahn). [InterPR] (20:2) Fall 94, p. 75.
"I Must Say" (tr. by Brenda Casey and Elizabeth Hahn). [InterPR] (20:2) Fall 94, p. 73.
"Je Dois Dire." [InterPR] (20:2) Fall 94, p. 72.
"Je Le Sais." [InterPR] (20:2) Fall 94, p. 74.
4352. MORENO JIMENEZ, Domingo
"¡Extraviado!" [CuadP] (8:22) Enero-Abril 94, p. 69.
"Oracion." [CuadP] (8:22) Enero-Abril 94, p. 70.
"Postumismo." [CuadP] (8:22) Enero-Abril 94, p. 80.
"¡Viejas Heridas!" [CuadP] (8:22) Enero-Abril 94, p. 68.
4353. MORGAN, Edwin
"Virtual and Other Realities" (4, 6). [Verse] (11:1) Spr 94, p. 15-16.
"Virtual and Other Realities" (7-8, 12, 21). [Verse] (11:2) Sum 94, p. 23-25.
4354. MORGAN, Elizabeth Seydel
"Atlanta." [SouthernR] (30:4) Aut 94, p. 785-786.
"Perseid Night." [EngJ] (83:8) D 94, p. 40.
"Sensing Winter." [SouthernR] (30:4) Aut 94, p. 786-787.
"Ways to Go." [EngJ] (83:8) D 94, p. 40.
"Willem DeKooning Declared Incompetent" (News item, August 1989). [Poetry] (164:2) My 94, p. 95.
4355. MORGAN, Frederick
"At Large." [AmerS] (63:4) Aut 94, p. 590.
"I Call It Back." [AmerS] (63:2) Spr 94, p. 286.
4356. MORGAN, James
"Digging a Hole in the Earth." [HiramPoR] (55/56) Fall 93-Sum 94, p. 79-80.
4357. MORGAN, John
"Whistler's Mother." [Jacaranda] (4:2) Spr 90, p. 106.
4358. MORGAN, Peadar
"After an Accident." [Verse] (11:2) Sum 94, p. 58.
"Aig Ceann An Tunail." [Verse] (11:2) Sum 94, p. 56.
"At the Tunnel's End." [Verse] (11:2) Sum 94, p. 56-57.
"An Dèidh Tubaist." [Verse] (11:2) Sum 94, p. 57.
"Gun Fhios." [Verse] (11:2) Sum 94, p. 54.
"Unknowingly." [Verse] (11:2) Sum 94, p. 55.
4359. MORGAN, Robert
"Attraction." [CarolQ] (46:2) Wint 94, p. 36.

"Fulgurite." [CarolQ] (46:2) Wint 94, p. 35.
"Heat Lightning." [AmerS] (63:1) Wint 94, p. 76.
"The Light of Motion." [CarolQ] (46:2) Wint 94, p. 37.
"Long Fast." [CarolQ] (46:2) Wint 94, p. 34.
"Mountain Sickness." [VirQR] (70:3) Sum 94, p. 451.
"Offering." [WilliamMR] (32) 94, p. 31.
"Sanghoe." [VirQR] (70:3) Sum 94, p. 451-452.
"Thaw Fires." [VirQR] (70:3) Sum 94, p. 450.
"Translumination." [CarolQ] (46:2) Wint 94, p. 33.

4360. MORGENSTERN, Christian
"The Fence" (tr. by Simon Darragh). [Light] (11) Aut 94, p. 9.

4361. MORI, Kyoko
"In an American Landscape." [WillowR] (21) Spr 94, p. 61-62.

4362. MORIARTY, Laura
"Forever" (Selections: 11 poems). [Avec] (7:1) 94, p. 131-139.
"Symmetry" (Selections: 10 items). [Avec] (8:1) 94, p. 141-147.
"Triumph" (to Abigail Child). [Chain] (1) Spr-Sum 94, p. 179-182.

4363. MORIARTY, Michael
"A Memory of London." [NewYorkQ] (53) 94, p. 44-45.

4364. MORIARTY, Susan Repetto
"Under Wraps." [GreensboroR] (56) Sum 94, p. 17.

4365. MORITZ, A. F.
"The Door." [SpoonR] (19:1) Wint-Spr 94, p. 55.
"Given." [Nimrod] (37:2) Spr-Sum 94, p. 65-66.
"Sculptures." [Pequod] (37) 94, p. 29-32.
"The Woman." [SpoonR] (19:1) Wint-Spr 94, p. 56-57.

4366. MORLEY, David
"What You Do and What You Say." [Quarry] (43:2) S 94, p. 130-132.
"A Whispering Child." [Quarry] (43:2) S 94, p. 133-134.

4367. MORLEY, Hilda
"Untitled: To know the fullness of the weight of time." [GrandS] (13:1, #49) Sum 94, p. 109-110.
"Visit to Stefan's Grave, August 25, 1992." [IllinoisR] (2:1) Fall 94, p. 35.
"With Cavafy." [IllinoisR] (2:1) Fall 94, p. 36.

4368. MORLEY, Marjorie
"Afternoon at Hurricane Ridge." [BellArk] (10:3) My-Je 94, p. 12.
"Answers for a Girl with a Notebook." [BellArk] (10:2) Mr-Ap 94, p. 31.

4369. MORLEY, Pamela
"Dearest Lisa." [PaintedB] (53/54) 94, p. 84-85.

4370. MORPHEW, Melissa
"The Missionary Writes to Her Fiancé Concerning a Small Death." [PoetL] (89:3) Fall 94, p. 36.
"The Missionary Writes to Her Fiancé Concerning the Nature of God." [PoetL] (89:3) Fall 94, p. 37.

4371. MORRIEN, Adriaan
"Angels" (tr. by Pleuke Boyce). [Quarry] (43:1) Je 94, p. 24-25.
"Longing to Fly" (tr. by Pleuke Boyce). [Quarry] (43:1) Je 94, p. 23.
"Love and Friendship" (tr. by Pleuke Boyce). [Quarry] (43:1) Je 94, p. 27.
"Old Age" (tr. by Pleuke Boyce). [Quarry] (43:1) Je 94, p. 26.
"Ten Lines" (tr. by Pleuke Boyce). [Quarry] (43:1) Je 94, p. 22.

4372. MORRILL, Donald
"Elegy" (for M.D., 1949-1991). [MidwQ] (36:1) Aut 94, p. 65-66.

4373. MORRIS, Bernard E.
"Be Perfect, True." [DogRR] (26) Wint 94-95, p. 12.
"New Orleans Might Be Nice." [Poem] (72) N 94, p. 46.
"To Hold Together." [SmPd] (31:2, #91) Spr 94, p. 33.
"You'll Drive Me Wild." [Poem] (72) N 94, p. 47.

4374. MORRIS, Cecil
"At School." [HiramPoR] (55/56) Fall 93-Sum 94, p. 82-83.
"Crossings." [HiramPoR] (55/56) Fall 93-Sum 94, p. 81.
"The Dance Instructor Talks." [EngJ] (83:1) Ja 94, p. 91.

4375. MORRIS, Daniel
"Psalm" (Irwin Walter Morris, 1929-1972). [SycamoreR] (6:2) Sum 94, p. 27-28.
"Self Portrait." [DenQ] (28:4) Spr 94, p. 41.

4376. MORRIS, Herbert
"Boy and Father" (Ernest Hemingway and his son Gregory, Sun Valley, Idaho, October, 1941 — a photograph by Robert Capa). [Crazy] (46) Spr 94, p. 71-76.
"Duesenberg, 1929." [Poetry] (165:2) N 94, p. 74-75.
"The Dusk Which Falls Each Evening in Look Park." [Crazy] (46) Spr 94, p. 65-70.
"How It May Have Happened, Had It Happened." [DenQ] (29:2) Fall 94, p. 15-24.
"On the Plight of Us in the Caravaggio" (A detail from *The Sacrifice of Isaac* painted by Michelangelo Amerighi da Caravaggio). [KenR] (NS 16:3) Sum 94, p. 22-27.
"Soir Bleu" (Edward Hopper, oil on canvas, 1914, for Steven Millhauser). [Crazy] (46) Spr 94, p. 38-64.
"Sometimes, Late" (for Donald Revell). [AntR] (52:1) Wint 94, p. 110-124.
4377. MORRIS, John
"View from the Spanish Steps." [NegC] (14:1/2) 94, p. 86.
4378. MORRIS, Miriam W.
"Nothing But a Crow?" [NegC] (14:1/2) 94, p. 64.
4379. MORRIS, Paul
"The Geography of Weather." [CumbPR] (13:2) Spr 94, p. 28-29.
4380. MORRIS, Peter
"Capricornucopia." [WormR] (34:4, #136) 94, p. 146.
"Gaining on Me." [WormR] (34:4, #136) 94, p. 146-147.
"One of the Worst Things." [WormR] (34:4, #136) 94, p. 145.
"The Scrutinies." [WormR] (34:4, #136) 94, p. 146.
4381. MORRISON, Rusane
"The Way Back." [SlipS] (14) 94, p. 67.
4382. MORRO, Henry J.
"The Burning Voice." [Pearl] (20) Spr 94, p. 78.
"Gilbert Roland / El Macho." [Pearl] (20) Spr 94, p. 78.
4383. MORT, Graham
"Cowrie Shells." [Nimrod] (38:1) Fall-Wint 94, p. 126-127.
"Sperm." [Nimrod] (38:1) Fall-Wint 94, p. 128-129.
"Waking Somewhere Else." [Nimrod] (38:1) Fall-Wint 94, p. 130.
4384. MORTAL, Anna
"Mother's Refrigerator." [Kalliope] (16:3) 94, p. 13.
4385. MORTENSEN, Arthur
"Life at the Ballpark." [Hellas] (5:2) Fall-Wint 94, p. 63.
4386. MORTENSON, Chris
"O Men, O Mighty Men." [ChironR] (13:4) Wint 94, p. 25.
4387. MORTON, Colin
"All Those Years." [Descant] (25:1, #84) Spr 94, p. 40.
"The Coastlines of the Archipelago." [Descant] (25:1, #84) Spr 94, p. 38.
"The Good Place." [PoetryC] (14:4) S 94, p. 5.
"Neighbours." [PoetryC] (14:4) S 94, p. 5.
"Night Bus." [PoetryC] (14:4) S 94, p. 5.
"Signs of Change." [Descant] (25:1, #84) Spr 94, p. 39.
4388. MORTON, Colleen
"Amanthophobia: Fear of Dust." [SpoonR] (19:1) Wint-Spr 94, p. 112.
"Chromophobia: Fear of Colors." [SpoonR] (19:1) Wint-Spr 94, p. 110-111.
"Trail Horses in a Field." [SycamoreR] (6:1) Wint 94, p. 32.
4389. MORTON, Leith
"At the Bathhouse" (tr. of Ishigaki Rin). [Stand] (35:3) Sum 94, p. 17.
"Cliff" (tr. of Ishigaki Rin). [Stand] (35:3) Sum 94, p. 16.
"Deer" (tr. of Shiro Murano). [Stand] (35:3) Sum 94, p. 15.
"Living" (tr. of Ishigaki Rin). [Stand] (35:3) Sum 94, p. 16.
4390. MOSER, Cheryl
"The Way You Are." [Kalliope] (16:1) 94, p. 58.
4391. MOSES, Daniel David
"Bus Lines." [Arc] (32) Spr 94, p. 33.
"A Resurrection Song." [Nimrod] (37:2) Spr-Sum 94, p. 67.
"Shorts Lines." [Arc] (32) Spr 94, p. 32.
4392. MOSKOP, Susan
"The Ladies in Challis." [NegC] (13:2/3) 93, p. 43.
4393. MOSKUS, Charles D.
"Los Angeles, 1965, 1992." [HiramPoR] (57) Fall 94-Wint 95, p. 43.
"Blythe, California." [Border] (5) Fall-Wint 94, p. 46.

"Doppelganger." [HiramPoR] (57) Fall 94-Wint 95, p. 44.
"Fast Eddie Explains." [BellArk] (10:2) Mr-Ap 94, p. 31.
"Lonely Is a Place." [BellArk] (10:1) Ja-F 94, p. 25.
"Prayer." [BellArk] (10:1) Ja-F 94, p. 16.
"Stop." [HiramPoR] (57) Fall 94-Wint 95, p. 45.

4394. MOSS, Jennifer
"A Man Had a Bird." [HayF] (15) Fall-Wint 94, p. 80-81.

4395. MOSS, Stanley
"Near Machpelah/Heron." [PartR] (61:4) Fall 94, p. 641.

4396. MOSS, Thylias
"Mornings." [Ploughs] (20:1) Spr 94, p. 72-74.

4397. MOSSIN, Andrew
"Lines for a Continuing Narrative." [Talisman] (12) Spr 94, p. 246-247.
"Lyric." [RiverC] (14:2) Spr 94, p. 59-68.

MOTHER GOOSE
See ANONYMOUS (Mother Goose)

MOTOKIYU, Tosa
See TOSA, Motokiyu

MOTOKO, Michiura
See MICHIURA, Motoko

4398. MOTT, Michael
"Add to Old Battles" (from "Pyder Hundred"). [Vis] (45) 94, p. 11.
"Birthplace." [VirQR] (70:3) Sum 94, p. 448.
"Hightide of Evening" (from "Pyder Hundred"). [Vis] (45) 94, p. 12.
"Homage to Pontormo." [Vis] (45) 94, p. 13.
"In Memory of William Stafford 1914-1993." [SewanR] (102:3) Sum 94, p. 387.
"Pyder Hundred" (Excerpt). [Verse] (11:1) Spr 94, p. 50.
"Red Leaves." [Vis] (45) 94, p. 10.
"Tree Struck by Lightning." [VirQR] (70:3) Sum 94, p. 447-448.

MOTT, Robert de
See DeMOTT, Robert

4399. MOUL, James
"Waves." [AnthNEW] (6) 94, p. 36.

4400. MOULDS, Julie
"Plucked Eyes." [PassN] (15:1) Sum 94, p. 44.

4401. MOUNTAIN, Judevine
"No Zen Master Me!" [Sun] (226) O 94, p. 7.
"Quoting T'ao Ch'ien." [Sun] (226) O 94, p. 7.

4402. MOURÉ, Erin
"4 Translations from Rilke" (for my friends — a sequence). [MalR] (108) Fall 94, p. 58-61.
"The Life of St. Teresa" (a sequence). [MalR] (108) Fall 94, p. 62-68.
"The Voice." [Arc] (32) Spr 94, p. 8-9.

4403. MOVIUS, Geoffrey
"Dream." [HarvardR] (7) Fall 94, p. 25.
"Morning Walk." [HarvardR] (2) Fall 92, p. 113.

4404. MOWREY, Vincent
"Losing the Muse." [Sun] (221) My 94, p. 33.

4405. MOXLEY, Jennifer
"What are these winged words" (to Kate Rushin). [Chain] (1) Spr-Sum 94, p. 207-208.

4406. MOYANO, José Repiso
"Desde Cualquier Eternidad Es Posible." [Nuez] (5:13/14/15) 94, p. 14.
"Poema: Instalado ya en un día." [Nuez] (5:13/14/15) 94, p. 14.

4407. MOZGA, Anna
"Leon'todon." [CanLit] (141) Sum 94, p. 13.

4408. MUDHAFFAR, May
"A Calm Moment" (tr. by Pauline Kaldas). [InterQ] (1:3) 94, p. 156.
"A Man and a Woman" (tr. by Pauline Kaldas). [InterQ] (1:3) 94, p. 157.

4409. MUELLER, Lisel
"Curriculum Vitae." [SenR] (24:2) Fall 94, p. 28-29.
"Night Voyage: a Dream." [SenR] (24:2) Fall 94, p. 30.
"Silence and Dancing" (Elektra's imperative at the end of the opera by Richard Strauss). [TriQ] (91) Fall 94, p. 186.

4410. MUENCH, Simone
"Cleaning" (for B.R.). [Calyx] (15:3) Wint 94-95, p. 54.

"Insomnia" (2nd runner-up, 8th annual *Louisiana Literature* Prize for Poetry). [LouisL] (11:1) Spr 94, p. 6-7.
"Walking." [LouisL] (11:2) Fall 94, p. 75-76.

4411. MUKHERJEE, Mithi
"Household Shrine" (tr. of Rajlakshimi Devi, w. Carolyne Wright). [InterQ] (1:2) 93, p. 158.

4412. MUKHOPADHYAY, Vijaya
"Blue Pills" (tr. by Sunil B. Ray and Carolyne Wright). [KenR] (NS 16:4) Fall 94, p. 92.
"Film" (tr. by Sunil B. Ray and Carolyne Wright). [KenR] (NS 16:4) Fall 94, p. 91-92.
"That's Not for Puti" (tr. by Paramita Banerjee and Carolyne Wright). [KenR] (NS 16:4) Fall 94, p. 93.
"Woman" (tr. by Carolyne Wright and Sunil B. Ray, w. the author). [InterQ] (1:2) 93, p. 159.

4413. MULCAHY, Barbara
"Like My Father." [Dandel] (21:1) 94, p. 10-11.
"The Straw Stack in January." [Dandel] (21:1) 94, p. 11.

4414. MULDOON, Paul
"The Frog." [Poetry] (165:2) N 94, p. 104.
"Incantata" (In memory of Mary Farl Powers). [AmerPoR] (23:5) S-O 94, p. 48-51.
"The Train." [NewYorker] (70:40) 5 D 94, p. 93.

4415. MULHERN, Maureen
"The Earthly World above." [Crazy] (47) Wint 94, p. 16-17.

4416. MULLAN, Zarina
"For Women Who Have Run Over Liquid Cement." [ClockR] (9:1/2) 94-95, p. 35.

4417. MULLEN, Harryette
"Jesus Is My Airplane." [Callaloo] (17:2) Sum 94, p. 493.
"Just As I Am I Come." [Callaloo] (17:2) Sum 94, p. 492.
"*Muse* & Drudge." [AntR] (52:1) Wint 94, p. 104-107.
"That Her Body Bleeds." [Callaloo] (17:2) Sum 94, p. 494.

4418. MULLEN, Laura
"Another Version." [SycamoreR] (6:2) Sum 94, p. 40-41.
"The Audience." [DenQ] (28:4) Spr 94, p. 42-43.
"Autumn." [Bomb] (50) Wint 94-95, p. 85.
"Banyans." [VirQR] (70:2) Spr 94, p. 309-314.
"The Book When It's Shut." [Jacaranda] (4:2) Spr 90, p. 53.
"The Catch" (Monday, December 7, 1987. Nice. for C.S.). [DenQ] (28:4) Spr 94, p. 44.
"Drive." [Antaeus] (73/74) Spr 94, p. 80.
"Heirloom." [ColR] (21:1) Spr 94, p. 160-161.
"House." [VirQR] (70:2) Spr 94, p. 309.
"Immigrations." [Bomb] (50) Wint 94-95, p. 84.
"Keys." [ColR] (21:1) Spr 94, p. 158-159.
"Tours of the Architecture." [SycamoreR] (6:2) Sum 94, p. 42-43.
"Traffic Jam." [VirQR] (70:2) Spr 94, p. 308.

4419. MULLIGAN, Mary-Margaret
"A Swan Song." [CapeR] (29:1) Spr 94, p. 38.

4420. MULLINS, Cecil J.
"Claire." [Hellas] (5:2) Fall-Wint 94, p. 50.

4421. MULLOY, Marcia
"Evensong." [Elf] (4:2) Sum 94, p. 40-41.
"The Name of a Thing." [EvergreenC] (9:2) Sum-Fall 94, p. 59.

4422. MULRANE, Scott (Scott H.)
"Across the Straits." [DogRR] (26) Wint 94-95, p. 31.
"One May Have Too Many Friends to Lose." [Poem] (71) My 94, p. 54.
"Strangers." [Poem] (71) My 94, p. 55.
"Taking the Waters." [Poem] (71) My 94, p. 56.

4423. MULROONEY,C.
"Jerusalem." [Jacaranda] (5:1) Wint-Spr 91, p. 26.

4424. MUNN, Carol
"View of the Dead." [Poetry] (164:3) Je 94, p. 144.

4425. MUÑOZ, Charles
"Cain, in the Desert, Sings the End of Warfare." [WritersF] (20) 94, p. 203.
"Lockerbie." [BelPoJ] (45:2) Wint 94-95, p. 9-11.
"My Great-Grandparents' Daguerreotype." [Pivot] (42) 94, p. 29.

"Osiris in Arizona." [BelPoJ] (45:2) Wint 94-95, p. 12-13.

4426. MUNRO, David
"Oscar (Man Overboard)." [PaintedB] (53/54) 94, p. 87-89.

4427. MUNRO, Peter
"Tea." [SantaBR] (2:2) Fall-Wint 94, p. 33.

4428. MUNROE, Peter
"Exodus." [BelPoJ] (44:4) Sum 94, p. 36-38.

MUNTANER, Frances Negrón
See NEGRON-MUNTANER, Frances

4429. MURANAKA, D. N.
"Yukimi" (snow viewing). [BambooR] (60) Wint 94, p. 112.

4430. MURANO, Shiro
"Deer" (tr. by Leith Morton). [Stand] (35:3) Sum 94, p. 15.

4431. MURATORI, Fred
"Breathing Spell." [Vis] (44) 94, p. 24.
"Nobody Out There." [Jacaranda] (5:1) Wint-Spr 91, p. 115.

4432. MURAWSKI, Elisabeth
"Promise, Breaking." [CumbPR] (14:1) Fall 94, p. 67-68.
"To All Climbers." [Journal] (18:2) Fall-Wint 94, p. 25.
"Towards Five." [Journal] (18:2) Fall-Wint 94, p. 26-27.

4433. MURGUIA, Alejandro
"The Girl Can't Help It." [NewL] (60:3) 94, p. 45.

MURONG, Xi
See XI, Murong

4434. MURPHY, Barbara
"Bedtime Story." [NewEngR] (16:1) Wint 94, p. 17.
"Clarity." [NewEngR] (16:1) Wint 94, p. 16.
"In Chekhov's *Three Sisters*." [NewEngR] (16:1) Wint 94, p. 18.
"PHIL 255: Logic." [NewEngR] (16:1) Wint 94, p. 18-19.

4435. MURPHY, Carol
"Remembered in the Bone." [Confr] (52/53) Wint-Spr 94, p. 312.

4436. MURPHY, Christine
"Fest Notes." [NegC] (13:2/3) 93, p. 260.

4437. MURPHY, Jean
"Car Hop." [Light] (11) Aut 94, p. 21.

4438. MURPHY, Kay
"The Man Who Heard Vincent." [NewOR] (20:1/2) Spr-Sum 94, p. 97-99.
"Oh, Everette, There Is Not Reason Why" (for Everette Maddox). [NegC] (13:2/3) 93, p. 74-75.
"Those Art Deco Days." [NewOR] (20:1/2) Spr-Sum 94, p. 100.

4439. MURPHY, Michelle
"Lattitudes." [Zyzzyva] (10:1) Spr 94, p. 43.

4440. MURPHY, Patricia
"Drives" (Associated Writing Programs Intro Award poem). [IndR] (17:2) Fall 94, p. 123-124.

4441. MURPHY, Reen
"Easter Sunday" (First Sue Saniel Elkind National Poetry Award, Finalist). [Kalliope] (16:2) 94, p. 34.

4442. MURPHY, Sheila E.
"Fluency." [Talisman] (12) Spr 94, p. 228-231.
"Squaw Peak — June Morning, 6:00." [Parting] (7:2) Wint 94-95, p. 68.

4443. MURPHY, Timothy
"Harvest of Sorrows." [Hellas] (5:2) Fall-Wint 94, p. 68.
"Jasper Lake." [Hellas] (5:2) Fall-Wint 94, p. 70.
"Paul Among the Corinthians." [Hellas] (5:2) Fall-Wint 94, p. 34.
"Razing the Woodlot." [Hellas] (5:2) Fall-Wint 94, p. 95.
"Return to the Beartooth." [Hellas] (5:2) Fall-Wint 94, p. 69.

4444. MURPHY, Y. C.
"After Hours." [PassN] (15:2) Wint 94, p. 13.
"Mona Lisa I." [PassN] (15:2) Wint 94, p. 11.
"Mona Rides." [Epoch] (43:1) 94, p. 84.
"Mona Thinks of Crying." [Epoch] (43:1) 94, p. 85.
"Sad Mona." [Epoch] (43:1) 94, p. 83.
"Scat, Mona, Scat!" [PassN] (15:2) Wint 94, p. 12.
"Skunk Lady." [BlackWR] (20:2) Spr-Sum 94, p. 21-22.

4445. MURRAY, Eugene
"God Knows." [Northeast] (5:11) Wint 94-95, p. 18.
4446. MURRAY, G. E.
"Clearances." [GrahamHR] (18) Wint 94-95, p. 30-32.
"Le Corps Bleu." [IllinoisR] (2:1) Fall 94, p. 37.
"Selling Quietly in a Time of Madness Turned Sad." [InterQ] (1:2) 93, p. 80.
4447. MURRAY, Jesse
"At Dusk It Is Etc." [GlobalCR] (4) Fall 94, p. 59-60.
"Stance." [GlobalCR] (4) Fall 94, p. 58.
4448. MURRAY, Les (Les A.)
"Corniche." [Image] (7) Fall 94, p. 16-17.
"Crankshaft." [Colum] (21) Fall 93, p. 120-125.
"Each Morning Once More Seamless." [Image] (7) Fall 94, p. 14-15.
"The Goose Feet." [Verse] (11:2) Sum 94, p. 3.
"It Allows a Portrait in Line-Scan at Fifteen." [Image] (7) Fall 94, p. 13-14.
"Like Wheeling Stacked Water." [ColR] (21:2) Fall 94, p. 98-99.
"The Middle Sea" (Book 1 of a Verse Novel in Progress). [Pequod] (38) 94, p. 111-166.
"Suspended Vessels" (for Joanna Gooding and Simon Curtis). [ColR] (21:2) Fall 94, p. 96-97.
4449. MURRAY, Simone G.
"Émilie Printemps." [InterPR] (20:2) Fall 94, p. 84.
"Springtime Emily" (tr. by the author). [InterPR] (20:2) Fall 94, p. 85.
4450. MURRAY, Stephanie
"The Warrior." [Callaloo] (17:1) Wint 94, p. 188.
4451. MURREY, Matthew
"Crow." [MidwQ] (35:2) Wint 94, p. 181.
"For the Joy, for Nothing." [PoetC] (25:2) Wint 94, p. 26.
"Swallow." [MidwQ] (35:2) Wint 94, p. 180.
"Water on My Back, Chicago." [PaintedB] (53/54) 94, p. 94.
4452. MUSGRAVE, Susan
"Depression in Debrecen" (Budapest Spring Festival, Hungary, 1993). [MalR] (106) Spr 94, p. 8-11.
"Effort of Love." [MalR] (106) Spr 94, p. 6-7.
"Effort of Love." [SouthernR] (30:2) Ap, Spr 94, p. 313-314.
"Exchange of Fire" (from "Hair Dreams, a sequence"). [Nimrod] (37:2) Spr-Sum 94, p. 69-70.
"If You Dream of Finding Hairpins of a Rival Woman" (from "Hair Dreams, a sequence"). [Nimrod] (37:2) Spr-Sum 94, p. 68.
"Imagine." [MalR] (106) Spr 94, p. 5.
"The Spiritualization of Cruelty." [SouthernR] (30:2) Ap, Spr 94, p. 312-313.
4453. MUSIAL, Grzegorz
"On Campus" (tr. by Lia Purpura and the author). [LitR] (37:4) Sum 94, p. 573.
4454. MUSKE, Carol
"Theories of Education." [Jacaranda] (10) 94, p. 128.
4455. MUSSER, Geoffrey
"Comes a Young Man with Thunder in His Voice." [Amelia] (7:3, #22) 94, p. 23.
4456. MUTIS, Alvaro
"City" (tr. by Anthony Edkins). [WebR] (18) Fall 94, p. 22.
"The Death of Captain Cook" (tr. by Anthony Edkins). [WebR] (18) Fall 94, p. 24.
"Sonata" (tr. by Anthony Edkins). [WebR] (18) Fall 94, p. 23.
4457. MYATT, Treva
"Mother?" [Hellas] (5:1) Spr-Sum 94, p. 48.
4458. MYCUE, Edward
"Darkness." [HeavenB] (11) 94, p. 36.
"Fence for a Glass House." [HeavenB] (11) 94, p. 35.
"Political Speech." [Caliban] (14) 94, p. 136.
"To the Foot That Dangles: Hymn to San Francisco." [RagMag] (12:1) Sum 94, p. 10.
4459. MYERS, Douglas
"Under the Garden Wall." [CrabCR] (8:2/3/9:1/2/3) 94, p. 145.
4460. MYERS, Jack
"Look." [AmerPoR] (23:4) Jl-Ag 94, p. 33.
"Mr. Muscle Beach and the Aerobics Instructor." [ChiR] (40:2/3) 94, p. 75.
"Taking the Children Away." [AmerPoR] (23:4) Jl-Ag 94, p. 33.
"Training Horses." [SouthernR] (30:3) Sum 94, p. 559-560.

4461. MYERS, Neil
"Patching." [HopewellR] (6) 94, p. 112.
4462. MYLES, Eileen
"Twilight Train." [Chelsea] (57) 94, p. 50-52.
4463. MYSKO, Madeleine
"Note to My Mother in Summer." [Pivot] (42) 94, p. 43.
"Out of the Blue" (For Elizabeth Spires). [Hudson] (47:1) Spr 94, p. 80.
"Silver Maple." [SouthernHR] (28:3) Sum 94, p. 260.
"Teeth" (for Joyce Brown). [Pivot] (42) 94, p. 43.
MYUNG, Mi Kim
See KIM, Myung Mi
4464. MYVETTE, Sharmane
"Casting Down Arms." [CaribbeanW] (8) 94, p. 40.

4465. NACCA, Judy M.
"Tracking You Down." [RagMag] (12:1) Sum 94, p. 23.
"What You Ask of Night." [RagMag] (12:1) Sum 94, p. 22.
4466. NADEAU, Marcel
"Les Mariés du Niagara" (à l'épousée). [InterPR] (20:2) Fall 94, p. 34.
"Newly Married at Niagara" (to the bride, tr. by Judith Cowan). [InterPR] (20:2) Fall 94, p. 35.
"Les Recluses." [InterPR] (20:2) Fall 94, p. 32.
"The Recluses" (tr. by Judith Cowan). [InterPR] (20:2) Fall 94, p. 33.
4467. NADELMAN, Cynthia
"All That Fall (In Memory of Samuel Beckett)." [DenQ] (28:4) Spr 94, p. 45-46.
4468. NADIR, Moishe
"I and Moishe-Leib" (tr. by Aaron Kramer). [Vis] (46) 94, p. 6.
NAGAMURA, Kit Pancoast
See PANCOAST-NAGAMURA, Kit
4469. NAGEL, Gwen L.
"Mount Auburn Cemetery." [AlabamaLR] (8:1) 94, p. 10-11.
4470. NAGLER, Robert
"Ball." [CoalC] (8) Ap 94, p. 40.
"Dulces y Juguetes" (The Indian District, Calle 7 de Mayo, Guanajuato). [ChamLR] (14/15) Spr-Fall 94, p. 159-160.
"He Thinks His Self-Effacing Talk Forwards the Seduction." [AnotherCM] (27) 94, p. 145-146.
"Mme. Hellu Is 94." [ChamLR] (14/15) Spr-Fall 94, p. 236-237.
"On a Painting by Gericault, 'A Madman Afflicted with Kleptomania'." [CentR] (38:1) Wint 94, p. 129.
"On an Etching, 'Antiope', by Dunoyer de Segozac." [CentR] (38:1) Wint 94, p. 128.
"On 'The Limekiln' by Gericault, 1823/1824." [CentR] (38:1) Wint 94, p. 130.
4471. NAGY, Agnes Nemes
"American Station" (In the Grand Canyon, tr. by Bruce Berlind and Mária Körösy). [AnotherCM] (27) 94, p. 147.
"In the Garden" (to Lajos Aprily and Zoltán Jékely, tr. by Bruce Berlind). [AmerPoR] (23:1) Ja-F 94, p. 34.
"Snow" (tr. by Bruce Berlind and Mária Körösy). [AnotherCM] (27) 94, p. 148.
"The Sun's Gone Down" (tr. by Bruce Berlind and Mária Körösy). [AnotherCM] (27) 94, p. 149.
4472. NAKADA, Mark
"Deformed." [WestCL] (28:1/2, #13/14) Spr-Fall 94, p. 30.
"E Face." [WestCL] (28:1/2, #13/14) Spr-Fall 94, p. 31-32.
"Marginalia." [WestCL] (28:1/2, #13/14) Spr-Fall 94, p. 29.
4473. NANCE, Thomas
"Dionysius N." [SmPd] (31:2, #91) Spr 94, p. 9.
"Dionysius N. Remembers the Christmas Fire." [SmPd] (31:2, #91) Spr 94, p. 11-12.
"Dionysius N. Wants Shy Girl." [SmPd] (31:2, #91) Spr 94, p. 10-11.
4474. NAPARSTECK, Martin
"The Importance of Names." [HiramPoR] (55/56) Fall 93-Sum 94, p. 84.
4475. NAPIER, Alan
"Errors." [ApalQ] (40/41) 94, p. 80.
4476. NASH, Roger
"A Desperate Woman." [PoetryC] (14:4) S 94, p. 25.

"Marriage of Opposites." [PoetryC] (14:4) S 94, p. 25.
"My Lady of Journeys." [PoetryC] (14:4) S 94, p. 25.
"Where Our Voices Go" (for Aida). [PoetryC] (14:4) S 94, p. 25.
4477. NASH, Susan Smith
"At the Mall" (to Lisa Houston). [Chain] (1) Spr-Sum 94, p. 153.
"A Half-Dozen Eclairs" (Selections: 5 works). [Avec] (8:1) 94, p. 84-92.
"Venice in Furs" (to Lisa Houston). [Chain] (1) Spr-Sum 94, p. 154.
4478. NASON, Jim
"The Poetess." [AntigR] (96) Wint 94, p. 137-138.
"Ubiquitous Tiff." [AntigR] (96) Wint 94, p. 135-136.
4479. NASR, Najwa
"Address Unknown" (tr. of Fuad Rifqa). [LitR] (37:3) Spr 94, p. 517.
"Another Picking Season" (tr. of Fuad Rifqa). [LitR] (37:3) Spr 94, p. 517.
"The Beirut Sea" (tr. of May Rihani). [LitR] (37:3) Spr 94, p. 521-522.
"I Was Born Under the sign of Leo" (tr. of Ounsi al-Haj). [LitR] (37:3) Spr 94, p. 488.
"In Tübingen" (tr. of Fuad Rifqa). [LitR] (37:3) Spr 94, p. 518.
"Note from a Soldier" (tr. of Fuad Rifqa). [LitR] (37:3) Spr 94, p. 515-516.
"Olives Are My Hymns" (tr. of Henri Zoghaib). [LitR] (37:3) Spr 94, p. 531-532.
"A Scattered Hymn" (tr. of Ounsi al-Haj). [LitR] (37:3) Spr 94, p. 486.
"The Silence Which Passes by Like Scandal" (Excerpt, tr. of Ounsi al-Haj). [LitR] (37:3) Spr 94, p. 487-488.
"A Song for the Evening" (tr. of Fuad Rifqa). [LitR] (37:3) Spr 94, p. 516.
"Under Logs of Anger" (tr. of Ounsi al-Haj). [LitR] (37:3) Spr 94, p. 489-490.
4480. NASREEN, Taslima
"Character" (tr. by Carolyne Wright and Farida Sarkar). [NewYorker] (70:26) 22-29 Ag 94, p. 77.
"The Game in Reverse" (tr. by Mohammed Nurul Huda and Carolyne Wright, w. the author). [IndR] (17:1) Spr 94, p. 97.
"Happy Marriage" (tr. by Carolyne Wright and Mohammad Nurul Huda, w. the author). [NewYorker] (70:28) 12 S 94, p. 55.
NASRIN, Taslima
See NASREEN, Taslima
NATALE, Nanci Roth
See ROTH-NATALE, Nanci
4481. NATHAN, Leonard
"Departures." [PoetL] (89:3) Fall 94, p. 38.
"Faith." [NewEngR] (16:4) Fall 94, p. 139-140.
"Minna." [NewEngR] (16:4) Fall 94, p. 138.
"Museum Piece." [Salm] (101/102) Wint-Spr 94, p. 156.
"Silhouette." [Salm] (101/102) Wint-Spr 94, p. 157.
"We Took Her Death." [NewEngR] (16:4) Fall 94, p. 137.
"Winter Ode." [NewEngR] (16:4) Fall 94, p. 139.
4482. NATHAN, Norman
"Back to Basics." [SpiritSH] (59) 94, p. 36.
"Gems." [NewRena] (9:1, #27) 94, p. 61.
"Kuan Yin" (who listens to the prayers of the world). [ChamLR] (14/15) Spr-Fall 94, p. 203.
"The World of Us Curators." [NewRena] (9:1, #27) 94, p. 60.
4483. NATHANIEL, Isabel
"Cartography." [Journal] (18:1) Spr-Sum 94, p. 32-34.
"The Dominion of Lights." [Journal] (18:1) Spr-Sum 94, p. 25-26.
"The Grackles." [Journal] (18:1) Spr-Sum 94, p. 31.
"The Lake." [Journal] (18:1) Spr-Sum 94, p. 27-28.
"The Lake Revisited." [Journal] (18:1) Spr-Sum 94, p. 29-30.
"The Lie." [PraS] (68:2) Sum 94, p. 86.
"Sunrise from the Seventh Floor." [PraS] (68:2) Sum 94, p. 87-88.
4484. NAUGHTON, John
"Wind and Smoke" (tr. of Yves Bonnefoy). [GrahamHR] (18) Wint 94-95, p. 7-11.
4485. NAVARRO, Ophelia
"When Mexicans Die They Build Houses to God" (for Norma). [Ploughs] (20:1) Spr 94, p. 147.
4486. NAWROCKI, James J.
"Abscence: Three Elegies." [JamesWR] (11:2) Wint 94, p. 10.
"In Dante." [JamesWR] (11:2) Wint 94, p. 5.

4487. NAYDAN, Michael M.
"100 Years of Youth" (tr. of Natalka Bilotserkivets). [Agni] (39) 94, p. 42.
"Archipenko's Plasticity" (tr. of Attila Mohylny). [DenQ] (29:1) Sum 94, p. 91.
4488. NAYLOR, Paul
"Los Cabos." [Talisman] (12) Spr 94, p. 19.
"Intersecting Socket" (for Lindsay Hill). [NewAW] (12) Spr-Sum 94, p. 136-137.
"Material Implication" (for Michael Davidson). [Talisman] (12) Spr 94, p. 19.
"Theses on the Philosophy of History" (Selections: V, VII, A). [Caliban] (14) 94, p. 125-127.
4489. NAZARIE, Mia
"Cheshire Cat" (tr. of Daniela Crasnaru, w. Adam J. Sorkin). [PraS] (68:1) Spr 94, p. 67-68.
4490. NEAL, Iris
"A Death in Tonasket." [Plain] (14:2) Wint 94, p. 22.
4491. NEALON, Chris
"Ideal Genealogy." [JamesWR] (11:4) Sum 94, p. 9.
"Red Pepper at Dusk." [QW] (38) Winter-Spr 93-94, p. 124.
4492. NECHVATAL, Joseph
"viral attaque: moRal twiliGht" (from "Computer Virus Project," 1993). [Bomb] (46) Wint 94, p. 44-45.
4493. NEELY, Letta Simone-Nefertari
"Gawd and Alluh Huh Sistahs." [SinW] (54) Wint 94-95, p. 13-14.
"I Don't Kneel." [SinW] (54) Wint 94-95, p. 122.
4494. NEGRON-MUNTANER, Frances
"Bodypolitics." [EvergreenC] (9:1) Wint-Spr 94, p. 22.
"Cicatrices." [EvergreenC] (9:1) Wint-Spr 94, p. 25.
"Scars." [EvergreenC] (9:1) Wint-Spr 94, p. 24.
4495. NEGRONI, María
"Islandia" (Selections: I-VI, tr. by Anne Twitty). [ParisR] (36:130) Spr 94, p. 152-155.
4496. NEHRING, Tina
"Blanks." [Jacaranda] (10) 94, p. 80-81.
NEIDIGH, Paula J. Lambert
See LAMBERT-NEIDIGH, Paula J.
4497. NEILL, Sidney
"Sound." [SmPd] (31:3, #92) Fall 94, p. 10-11.
4498. NEILL, Uilleam
"Arann Na N-Oigheadh N-Iomdha." [Verse] (11:2) Sum 94, p. 60.
"Arran of the Many Stags." [Verse] (11:2) Sum 94, p. 61.
"Ciod Am Bealach Am Buail Sinn?" [Verse] (11:2) Sum 94, p. 59.
"What Pass Shall We Take?" [Verse] (11:2) Sum 94, p. 59-60.
4499. NEILSON, Melanie
"Blue of the Sky Black to the Eye." [Conjunc] (22) 94, p. 226.
"Childhood Insert." [Conjunc] (22) 94, p. 221-223.
"Flat Serialized Space Was Why I Turned." [Conjunc] (22) 94, p. 226.
"Prefers to Look at Birds She Says Chapter." [Conjunc] (22) 94, p. 224.
"River." [Conjunc] (22) 94, p. 216-219.
"Romance of Cherries." [Conjunc] (22) 94, p. 215.
4500. NELMS, Sheryl L.
"Abuse." [SingHM] (21) 94, p. 66.
"Empathy." [SingHM] (21) 94, p. 68.
"Eva Mae Eitner." [Kaleid] (29) Sum-Fall 94, p. 33.
"Exwife." [SingHM] (21) 94, p. 67.
"Kansas Cold." [Kaleid] (28) Wint-Spr 94, p. 43.
"Kansas Homestead." [Kaleid] (29) Sum-Fall 94, p. 19.
"Sliding Toward a Texas Winter." [Kaleid] (29) Sum-Fall 94, p. 45.
4501. NELSON, Chris
"Adultery" (1st runner-up, 8th annual *Louisiana Literature* Prize for Poetry). [LouisL] (11:1) Spr 94, p. 4-5.
4502. NELSON, Crawdad
"Sexual Expression / Repression in the Workplace." [ContextS] (4:1) 94, p. 34.
4503. NELSON, George
"Precept Shuddered." [NewAW] (12) Spr-Sum 94, p. 140.
4504. NELSON, Howard
"Rain in the Mountains." [TarRP] (33:2) Spr 94, p. 25.

4505. NELSON, James E.
"Daybreak." [Plain] (15:1) Fall 94, p. 15.
4506. NELSON, Jo
"Another Trail of Tears." [Plain] (14:3) Spr 94, p. 15.
4507. NELSON, Paul
"Night Crawlers." [LaurelR] (28:1) Wint 94, p. 26.
"Springfall." [LaurelR] (28:1) Wint 94, p. 27.
4508. NELSON, Sandra
"The Alchemist's Alphabet." [PoetryE] (37/38) Spr 94, p. 10.
"When a Woman Holds a Letter." [RagMag] (12:1) Sum 94, p. 5.
"Written While Waiting for J. M. Coetzee's Magistrate." [RiverS] (40) 94, p. 48.
4509. NELSON-DEIGHAN, Shannon
"For the Imagists at the British Museum." [Poetry] (164:6) S 94, p. 319.
"Victorian Hummingbird Case." [Poetry] (164:5) Ag 94, p. 281.
4510. NENLYUMKINA, Zoya
"Old Tale" (tr. by Galina De Roeck). [Manoa] (6:2) Wint 94, p. 179-180.
4511. NERUDA, Pablo
"Bird" (tr. by William O'Daly). [Field] (51) Fall 94, p. 33.
"Melancholy inside Families" (tr. by Robert Bly and James Wright). [Field] (51) Fall 94, p. 8-9.
"Ode to the Table" (tr. by Ken Krabbenhoft). [Field] (51) Fall 94, p. 13-14.
"Walking Around" (tr. by W. S. Merwin). [Field] (51) Fall 94, p. 22-23.
4512. NESANOVICH, Stella
"The Threat of Bremen." [XavierR] (14:1) Spr 94, p. 65-66.
4513. NEVILL, Sue
"Bulls." [Grain] (22:1) Sum 94, p. 86.
"Divided Highway." [AntigR] (99) Aut 94, p. 12.
"Lady Dahlia." [Event] (23:2) Sum 94, p. 31.
"Respect for Blackberries." [AntigR] (96) Wint 94, p. 109.
4514. NEVILLE, Tam Lin
"First Child, Narcissa Whitman 1808-1847." [SingHM] (21) 94, p. 3-4.
4515. NEW, Joan Cockrell
"311 Mataro Court, North Port, Florida." [SouthernR] (30:4) Aut 94, p. 855-856.
4516. NEWBERN, Laura
"The Walking Stick." [TriQ] (92) Wint 94-95, p. 93-95.
4517. NEWCOMB, P. F.
"White Dreams." [Elf] (4:1) Spr 94, p. 42.
4518. NEWELL, Michael L.
"At the Ashland Oregon Old-Time Fiddlers' Concert" (Lithia Park, 1981). [BellArk] (10:3) My-Je 94, p. 12.
"The Character of Hats." [BellArk] (10:5) S-O 94, p. 23.
"Dividing Line." [BellArk] (10:6) N-D 94, p. 7.
"Duncan Quincannon." [BellArk] (10:5) S-O 94, p. 12.
"A Memory of Water." [BellArk] (10:6) N-D 94, p. 6.
"My Parents Phone Me Overseas." [BellArk] (10:6) N-D 94, p. 7.
"Recidivist." [BellArk] (10:5) S-O 94, p. 25.
4519. NEWLAND, Emily
"Dust." [Light] (11) Aut 94, p. 13.
"Things We Don't Want to Know" (To a Prospective Suitor). [Light] (11) Aut 94, p. 21.
4520. NEWLING, Bruce E.
"Up the Orinoco." [Light] (10) Sum 94, p. 17.
4521. NEWMAN, Amy
"Curving the Past Tense" (Chapbook: 10 poems). [OhioR] (52) 94, p. 41-56.
"Design." [Kalliope] (16:1) 94, p. 60.
4522. NEWMAN, Christopher (Chris)
"A Polonaise of Oginski" (tr. of Eugene Dubnov, w. the author). [Grain] (21:4) Spr 94, p. 98.
"White Night" (tr. of Eugene Dubnov, w. Carol Rumens). [SouthernPR] (34:2) Wint 94, p. 42-43.
4523. NEWMAN, David
"Bad Cop." [WormR] (34:3, #135) 94, p. 96-97.
"Counter Guy." [WormR] (34:3, #135) 94, p. 98.
"Missing the Whole Point." [Pearl] (20) Spr 94, p. 59.
"Things I've Been When drunk." [WormR] (34:3, #135) 94, p. 98-99.
"The Value of Literature." [WormR] (34:3, #135) 94, p. 97-98.

4524. NEWMAN, Harry
"The Last Days of Oskar." [SlipS] (14) 94, p. 49-51.
4525. NEWMAN, Lesléa
"Lunch on Sixth Ave." [Art&Und] (3:4) O-N 94, p. 14-15.
4526. NEWMAN, P. B.
"Actress." [ApalQ] (40/41) 94, p. 60-61.
"Doll Collector." [ApalQ] (40/41) 94, p. 58-59.
"Ex-Missionary." [ApalQ] (40/41) 94, p. 62-63.
4527. NEWTON, Keith
"Hysterical Pregnancy" (w. Richard Kostelanetz). [NoAmR] (279:5) S-O 94, p. 35.
4528. NEWTON RIOS, Alexandra (*See also* RIOS, Alexandra)
"Intimacy." [Americas] (22:1/2) Spr-Sum 94, p. 104-105.
4529. NGAI, Sianne
"Eighth Century Suite" (Selections: 2-7). [Avec] (8:1) 94, p. 127-140.
"Renga" (February 9, 1994, Chinese New Year's Eve, w. Judith Goldman, Lee Ann Brown, and Lisa Jarnot). [Chain] (1) Spr-Sum 94, p. 197-199.
"Some Brief Histories of Time" (Selection: #2). [Talisman] (12) Spr 94, p. 234-237.
4530. NICHOL, B. P.
"The Natural Thing." [CapilR] (2:13) Spr 94, p. 9.
4531. NICHOLS, Grace
"Blackout." [MassR] (35:3/4) Aut-Wint 94, p. 381-382.
"Configurations." [Jacaranda] (5:1) Wint-Spr 91, p. 43.
4532. NICHOLS, Judith
"Mother, Muse." [HayF] (15) Fall-Wint 94, p. 76-77.
4533. NICHOLSON, Catherine
"The View After 70 Is Breathtaking." [SinW] (53) Sum-Fall 94, p. 84-85.
4534. NICK, Dagmar
"Late Fall" (tr. by Jim Barnes). [DenQ] (29:1) Sum 94, p. 92.
4535. NICKERSON, Sheila
"Flying Over Montana." [DogRR] (13:1, #25) Spr-Sum 94, p. 28.
"Traveling East, from the Oregon Coast." [DogRR] (13:1, #25) Spr-Sum 94, p. 26.
"Visit to My Daughter, Living on the Wallkill: Spring Flood." [DogRR] (13:1, #25) Spr-Sum 94, p. 27.
"When the House Pipes Speak." [DogRR] (13:1, #25) Spr-Sum 94, p. 27.
4536. NICKSON, Richard
"Lineage." [Light] (9) Spr 94, p. 12.
4537. NIDITCH, B. Z.
"History Was Made In Our Time." [DogRR] (26) Wint 94-95, p. 27.
"Kazimir Malevich." [DenQ] (29:2) Fall 94, p. 25.
"My Century." [ChamLR] (14/15) Spr-Fall 94, p. 68.
"Outdoors: Prague, 1988." [SpiritSH] (59) 94, p. 18.
"The Road to Serfdom." [SpiritSH] (59) 94, p. 17.
"Rome" (to Ungaretti, in memoriam). [ApalQ] (42) Fall 94, p. 41-42.
4538. NIED, Susanna
"Untitled: To lose everything and carry it with you" (tr. of Søren Ulrik Thomsen). [GrandS] (12:4, #48) Wint 94, p. 28-29.
4539. NIELSEN, Aldon
"A Good Place to Raise a Boy." [Talisman] (12) Spr 94, p. 94-95.
4540. NIELSEN, Dan
"An American Family." [Pearl] (20) Spr 94, p. 71.
"Bone Cancer." [ChironR] (13:3) Aut 94, p. 15.
"Breaking Up." [Pearl] (20) Spr 94, p. 60.
"A Career in the Arts." [ChironR] (13:3) Aut 94, p. 15.
"The Present." [ChironR] (13:3) Aut 94, p. 15.
4541. NIELSEN, Kristy
"The Hummingbird Between My Legs" (The Amelia Prose Poem Award). [Amelia] (7:4, #23) 94, p. 146.
4542. NIGRO, Nic
"Joe B." [BellArk] (10:6) N-D 94, p. 7.
"Omega." [BellArk] (10:3 [i.e. 10:4]) Jl-Ag 94, p. 26.
"A Riddle." [BellArk] (10:6) N-D 94, p. 6.
"Romney's Last Fall Term to Emeritus." [BellArk] (10:3 [i.e. 10:4]) Jl-Ag 94, p. 25.
4543. NIMMO, Kurt
"1-800-Death." [SlipS] (14) 94, p. 40-42.
"Drive Home." [WormR] (34:4, #136) 94, p. 158-159.
"Maria Vasquez." [SlipS] (14) 94, p. 38-40.

"Sheila's Friends." [WormR] (34:4, #136) 94, p. 157-158.
"Three Rooms." [WormR] (34:4, #136) 94, p. 155-157.

4544. NIMNICHT, Nona
"Digression on a Shirt: Ravenna." [QW] (38) Winter-Spr 93-94, p. 112.

4545. NIMS, John Frederick
"Blasphemer." [Light] (9) Spr 94, p. 4.
"Cajolery." [Light] (9) Spr 94, p. 4.
"Celebrating a Birthday." [HarvardR] (6) Spr 94, p. 39.
"Cosmology." [Light] (9) Spr 94, p. 5.
"Darwin in the Zoo." [Light] (9) Spr 94, p. 5.
"Etymology." [Light] (9) Spr 94, p. 4.
"Experimental." [Light] (9) Spr 94, p. 5.
"Further Reflections on 'Trees'." [Light] (9) Spr 94, p. 3.
"Good Night!" [Light] (9) Spr 94, p. 6.
"How Noble in Reason! How Infinite in Faculty!" [Light] (9) Spr 94, p. 3.
"The Infinite" (tr. of Giacomo Loepardi). [AmerS] (63:3) Sum 94, p. 448.
"'Light' Verse." [Light] (9) Spr 94, p. 3.
"Limerick." [Light] (9) Spr 94, p. 5.
"Love's Progress." [Hudson] (47:3) Aut 94, p. 425-426.
"Loving One's Neighbor." [Light] (9) Spr 94, p. 4.
"Naif." [Light] (9) Spr 94, p. 3.
"Old Silver Tongue's Habeas Corpus." [Light] (9) Spr 94, p. 6.
"Parting." [Light] (9) Spr 94, p. 5.
"Pascal on Ultrasound." [KenR] (NS 16:1) Wint 94, p. 55-56.
"Philosopher." [Light] (9) Spr 94, p. 5.
"Po'-Biz Verse." [Light] (9) Spr 94, p. 5.
"Prayer." [Light] (9) Spr 94, p. 3.
"The Seizure" (Bernini in Winter). [KenR] (NS 16:1) Wint 94, p. 55.
"She Objects." [Light] (9) Spr 94, p. 6.
"Skin and Skull." [Light] (9) Spr 94, p. 4.
"Strange!" [Hudson] (47:3) Aut 94, p. 426.
"Trivia." [Light] (9) Spr 94, p. 4.
"You Pious People." [Light] (9) Spr 94, p. 4.

4546. NIÑO, Raúl
"My Work." [SantaBR] (2:1) Spr-Sum 94, p. 96.

NIORD, Chard de
See DeNIORD, Chard

NIRO, Alan de
See DeNIRO, Alan

4547. NISETICH, Frank
"Eight Goodbyes to a Brief Affair." [NegC] (14:1/2) 94, p. 101-108.

4548. NISHIOKA, L.
"In His Absence" (for S.N.). [BambooR] (60) Wint 94, p. 113-114.
"Kilani Bakery *Obaasan*." [BambooR] (60) Wint 94, p. 115-116.
"On Walking by the Widelia Patch a Year Later." [BambooR] (63/64) Sum-Fall 94, p. 40-41.

4549. NISONSON, Evan J.
"On Broadway." [SantaBR] (2:1) Spr-Sum 94, p. 92.

4550. NISULA, Dasha Culic
"Famous Surrealist's Slippers" (tr. of Bozica Jelusic, w. the author). [InterQ] (1:1) [93?], p. 124-125.
"The Ground in Labrador (After Lawrence)" (tr. of Bozica Jelusic, w. the author). [InterQ] (1:1) [93?], p. 122-123.
"Key of the Vanishing Kingdom" (Homage to Sylvia Plath, tr. of Bozica Jelusic). [PennR] (6:1) 94, p. 21.
"Metaphor — Simulation" (tr. of Neda Miranda Blazevic). [InterQ] (1:1) [93?], p. 120-121.
"A Quote from Russian Literature" (tr. of Irena Vrkljan). [InterQ] (1:1) [93?], p. 126-127.
"Solution" (tr. of Jagoda Zamoda). [InterQ] (1:1) [93?], p. 119.
"Where You Came From" (tr. of Vesna Krmpotic). [InterQ] (1:1) [93?], p. 118.
"Women" (tr. of Sasa Vegri). [InterQ] (1:1) [93?], p. 100.

4551. NITCHIE, George W.
"Reflection on a Pretentious Commencement Speaker." [Light] (11) Aut 94, p. 15.

4552. NIVEN, Julie
"Hunting Crawdads." [Elf] (4:3) Fall 94, p. 39.

4553. NIXON, John, Jr.
"Blessed Were the Poor." [Comm] (121:12) 17 Je 94, p. 17.
"Four Feet around the Square." [Comm] (121:4) 25 F 94, p. 16.
"Franco-American." [ChamLR] (14/15) Spr-Fall 94, p. 95.
"Writing about Writing about Writing." [CarolQ] (47:1) Fall 94, p. 39.

4554. NIXON, Sallie
"Zion" (Naitonal Park, Utah). [Pembroke] (26) 94, p. 112.

4555. NOBILE, A. M.
"Winter Afternoon." [AntigR] (96) Wint 94, p. 110.

4556. NOBLES, Edward
"After So Many Years, a First Love (On First Looking into Robert Hughes' *The Shock of the New)*." [DenQ] (28:4) Spr 94, p. 47-48.
"The Current Cinema." [DenQ] (29:1) Sum 94, p. 26-27.
"Hearing Them." [DenQ] (29:1) Sum 94, p. 28.
"History." [Boulevard] (9:3, #27) Fall 94, p. 145.
"Into Light." [PoetL] (89:4) Wint 94-95, p. 8.
"Stone-Bird-Hunter." [PoetL] (89:4) Wint 94-95, p. 7.
"The Unwanted." [PoetL] (89:4) Wint 94-95, p. 9-10.
"Visitation 1994." [TarRP] (34:1) Fall 94, p. 7.

NOBUKO, Katsura
See KATSURA, Nobuko

4557. NOEL, Roger
"Autumn" (tr. of Paule Doyon). [InterPR] (20:2) Fall 94, p. 61.
"Spring" (tr. of Paule Doyon). [InterPR] (20:2) Fall 94, p. 59.

4558. NOGUCHI, Rick
"When for Weeks the Sea Is Flat." [BambooR] (63/64) Sum-Fall 94, p. 42-43.

4559. NOGUERE, Suzanne
"The Music Box." [Pivot] (41) 93, p. 3.

4560. NOLAN, James
"Over the Oysters" (For Lee Meitzen Grue). [NegC] (13:2/3) 93, p. 44-45.

4561. NOLDE, Carol
"Comfort in Stone." [Hellas] (5:1) Spr-Sum 94, p. 82-83.
"Promise of Flowers" (a sestina for Frank). [Hellas] (5:1) Spr-Sum 94, p. 84-85.

4562. NOLL, Bruce A.
"Old Missionary's 1950 Furlough." [ChrC] (111:9) 16 Mr 94, p. 280.

4563. NOLLA, Olga
"Abrahan Lincoln Sin Cabeza." [CuadP] (8:22) Enero-Abril 94, p. 16-17.
"Cosas Que Ahora Prefiero." [CuadP] (8:22) Enero-Abril 94, p. 16.
"Sacerdotisa." [CuadP] (8:22) Enero-Abril 94, p. 15.

4564. NOMEZ, Naín
"When a Man and a Woman Separate" (To Enrique Molina with paraphrase, tr. by Lake Sagaris). [CanLit] (142/143) Fall-Wint 94, p. 118-119.

NOORD, Barbara van
See Van NOORD, Barbara

4565. NORBURY, Christopher
"Emma Noreen." [Amelia] (7:4, #23) 94, p. 166-167.

4566. NORDBRANDT, Henrik
"Kastelorizon" (tr. by Alex Taylor). [Vis] (44) 94, p. 15.
"Our Love Is Like Byzantium" (tr. by Alex Taylor). [Vis] (46) 94, p. 17.
"A Recollection from 1967" (tr. by Anne Born). [ProseP] (3) 94, p. 70.
"The Rose from Lesbos" (tr. by Alex Taylor). [Vis] (45) 94, p. 10.
"The Train" (tr. by Anne Born). [ProseP] (3) 94, p. 69.

4567. NORDFORS, Douglas
"Home." [SycamoreR] (6:2) Sum 94, p. 49.

4568. NORDHAUS, Jean
"Escalator." [WestB] (35) 94, p. 8-9.
"The Natural Sonneteer." [Poetry] (164:2) My 94, p. 69.
"Night Return from Nepal." [PoetL] (89:3) Fall 94, p. 30.
"The Physical." [WestB] (34) 94, p. 84.
"The Pool" (for KEZ). [PlumR] (7) [94?], p. 50-51.

4569. NORDSTROM, Tracy
"Sidewalk Sale." [RagMag] (12:1) Sum 94, p. 6.
"St. Valentine." [RagMag] (12:1) Sum 94, p. 7.

NORINAGA, Ojiu
See OJIU, Norinaga

4570. NORMAN, Chad
"Mosquito Nursing." [Arc] (33) Fall 94, p. 12.
4571. NORMAN, Leslie
"Sometimes the Girls Played Funeral." [SlipS] (14) 94, p. 72.
4572. NORMINGTON, Jim
"Here They Are" (tr. of Efraín Huerta). [Talisman] (12) Spr 94, p. 202-203.
4573. NORRIS, Lisa
"We Walked the Road from Missoula." [SouthernPR] (34:2) Wint 94, p. 50-51.
4574. NORTHROP, Kate
"The Fifth English Letter to Jana Kavkova from Her Smaller Sister in Prague." [PoetL] (89:1) Spr 94, p. 29-30.
4575. NORTHSUN, Nila
"Peeping Toms." [Callaloo] (17:1) Wint 94, p. 301-302.
4576. NORTHUP, Harry E.
"Absolute." [Pearl] (20) Spr 94, p. 15.
4577. NOSTRAND, Jennifer
"Behind the statues." [HiramPoR] (55/56) Fall 93-Sum 94, p. 87.
"Children run through pools of color." [HiramPoR] (55/56) Fall 93-Sum 94, p. 86.
"We had lunch in a Utrillo painting." [HiramPoR] (55/56) Fall 93-Sum 94, p. 85.
4578. NOTO, John
"Jardin des Tuileries: A Split-Screen Offers April Rain As Hands." [Talisman] (12) Spr 94, p. 148-149.
"The Mating Drill of Psycho-Motor Shadows: [City-Quake]." [Talisman] (13) Fall 94-Wint 95, p. 266-267.
"Rain Paintings Breathed Through Sudden Lips Distress the Grain of Leaves in the Dream-Book of a City." [Caliban] (14) 94, p. 114-116.
4579. NOVAK, Victoria B.
"Spiritwalker." [Kaleid] (29) Sum-Fall 94, p. 59.
4580. NOVAKOVICH, Josip
"Cobbles." [PoetL] (89:4) Wint 94-95, p. 5-6.
"Missouri in Nebraska." [SoDakR] (32:4) Wint 94, p. 61-62.
4581. NOWAK, Mark
"Looking to the Four Rivers." [WritersF] (20) 94, p. 158.
"Ranek." [MidwQ] (35:4) Sum 94, p. 413.
4582. NOWAK, Michael
"On the Persistence of Bathos." [AnthNEW] (6) 94, p. 27.
4583. NOWLAN, Alden
"In Our Time" (from *Bread, Wine & Salt*, 1967). [Kaleid] (29) Sum-Fall 94, p. 51.
"The War Lost" (from *Bread, Wine & Salt*, 1967). [Kaleid] (29) Sum-Fall 94, p. 58.
4584. NOYES, H. F.
"Moonless tor." [Amelia] (7:3, #22) 94, p. 85.
"Wind lifting swings." [Amelia] (7:3, #22) 94, p. 32.
4585. NOYES, Steve
"Gold Seal, Raw silk." [MalR] (109) Wint 94, p. 52.
"The Infolded Question." [MalR] (109) Wint 94, p. 53.
"Woman of the Island" (for Sue Donaldson). [MalR] (109) Wint 94, p. 51.
4586. NUÑEZ, N.
"Veinte Años" (de María Teresa Vera). [Areíto] (4:15) Marzo 94, p. 41.
4587. NURKSE, D.
"The Background Chords Return in Minor." [AntR] (52:2) Spr 94, p. 302.
"Black River." [HarvardR] (7) Fall 94, p. 41.
"The Interior." [WestB] (35) 94, p. 14.
"Interior Highway." [PoetryNW] (35:4) Wint 94-95, p. 46-47.
"The Last Husband." [PoetryNW] (35:4) Wint 94-95, p. 45-46.
"The Master Surgeon." [MassR] (35:1) Spr 94, p. 45-46.
"Night Walk in Binney's Wood." [NoDaQ] (62:3) Sum 94-95, p. 150.
"Rosewood Handles." [HangL] (64) 94, p. 57.
"Things I Forgot to Tell My Doctor." [HangL] (64) 94, p. 55.
"Transience." [HangL] (64) 94, p. 56.
"The Twenty-Four-Hour War." [HangL] (64) 94, p. 58.
4588. NUTTER, Geoffrey
"Tea, Chairs, and Cormorants." [ColR] (21:1) Spr 94, p. 105-107.
"Tea, Chairs, and Cormorants." [HayF] (14) Spr-Sum 94, p. 60-61.
"Turning the Pegs." [ColR] (21:1) Spr 94, p. 103-104.

4589. NUTTER, Jude
"Aunt Alice's Ashes" (Empied on a slough on Sergief Island, Stikine River Flats, Alaska). [Stand] (36:1) Wint 94-95, p. 58.
"A True Story: Mourning Cloaks." [WeberS] (11:3) Fall 94, p. 119.
"A True Story: The Beech Trees." [Stand] (36:1) Wint 94-95, p. 59.
4590. NWABUEZE, Chim
"Flowers for the Inferno" (Excerpt). [Caliban] (14) 94, p. 36-37.
"Flowers for the Inferno" (Excerpt). [Callaloo] (17:4) Fall 94, p. 1119-1122.
4591. NYE, Naomi Shihab
"Boy and Egg." [HawaiiR] (18:1, #40) Spr 94, p. 91.
"La Feria." [ProseP] (3) 94, p. 72.
"Hammer and Nail." [ProseP] (3) 94, p. 71.
"Inside the Riddle." [Vis] (45) 94, p. 19.
"Linked." [EngJ] (83:4) Ap 94, p. 109.
4592. NYHART, Al
"Admin Man." [ChironR] (13:4) Wint 94, p. 24.
"In Between." [FreeL] (13) Spr 94, p. 14.
4593. NYHART, Nina
"Coming to Terms with the Feminine." [ProseP] (3) 94, p. 73.
"Dream Letter." [Field] (51) Fall 94, p. 60.
"Winternet." [Field] (51) Fall 94, p. 58-59.
4594. NYONG'O, Tav
"Drag." [ModernW] (2) Wint 94, p. 79.
"This World." [ModernW] (2) Wint 94, p. 78.
"Words." [ModernW] (2) Wint 94, p. 77.
4595. NYSTROM, Debra
"Fly-fishing on Tommy's Lake" (to Dan). [Shen] (44:2) Sum 94, p. 54-55.
"Night Before the Fertility Clinic" (to Jane Ellen Harrison). [Shen] (44:2) Sum 94, p. 53.
4596. NYSTROM, Karen
"In Itself." [DenQ] (28:4) Spr 94, p. 49-50.
"Movements Shown to Her." [DenQ] (28:4) Spr 94, p. 51.
4597. NYTE, Gregory
"Resonance." [AntigR] (98) Sum 94, p. 7.
"To the Farmer in the Dell." [AntigR] (98) Sum 94, p. 8.
4598. NZUJI, Clémentine
"Kasala" (tr. by Julia Older). [InterQ] (1:3) 94, p. 39-40.

4599. OAKES, J. Cailin
"Icarus, Tired of Falling, Hails a Cab." [QW] (39) Sum-Fall 94, p. 207-208.
4600. OAKLEY, Wayne
"Hunting the Sun." [PoetryC] (14:3) My 94, p. 13.
"Just Like Him." [PoetryC] (14:3) My 94, p. 13.
"The Neophyte." [PoetryC] (14:3) My 94, p. 13.
"Untitled: If the sky is clear." [PoetryC] (14:3) My 94, p. 13.
"Where Does She Keep Him." [PoetryC] (14:3) My 94, p. 13.
4601. OAKS, Jeff
"Raccoons." [Nimrod] (38:1) Fall-Wint 94, p. 131.
"The Sandpit." [Nimrod] (38:1) Fall-Wint 94, p. 132.
4602. OATES, Joyce Carol
"Like Walking to the Drug Store, When I Get Out." [ParisR] (36:133) Wint 94, p. 229-230.
"The Lord Is My Shepherd I Shall Not Want." [NewRep] (211:22) 28 N 94, p. 72.
"On This Morning of Grief." [NewRep] (210:2/3) 10-17 Ja 94, p. 44.
4603. OBADIAH, Silas
"The Caller" (for a haunting ghost). [Obs] (9:1) Spr-Sum 94, p. 97.
"A Root in the Dark." [Obs] (9:1) Spr-Sum 94, p. 98.
4604. OBEJAS, Achy
"Sunday." [MichQR] (33:4) Fall 94, p. 774-775.
4605. OBERG, Robert J.
"Rooster." [Comm] (121:5) 11 Mr 94, p. 8.
4606. OBINO, Maria
"Lampi e Acqua" (Excerpt, tr. by Kathleen Fraser). [Avec] (7:1) 94, p. 83-88.

4607. O'BRIAN, Catherine
"Salvation, White Lies and Millyard Light." [GreenMR] (NS 17:2) Fall-Wint 94-95, p. 81.
"Undone." [GreenMR] (NS 17:2) Fall-Wint 94-95, p. 80.
4608. O'BRIEN, Gregory
"Sat Up and Watched Go By." [Verse] (11:1) Spr 94, p. 26-30.
"There Is Only One." [MalR] (107) Sum 94, p. 198.
"There Is Only One." [Verse] (11:1) Spr 94, p. 31.
"Variations on a Theme by Saint John of the Cross." [MalR] (107) Sum 94, p. 199-200.
4609. O'BRIEN, Laurie
"Ave Verum Corpus." [NegC] (14:1/2) 94, p. 157.
"Schema." [PoetL] (89:3) Fall 94, p. 19.
"Sixth Century." [ApalQ] (42) Fall 94, p. 30-32.
4610. O'BRIEN, Sean
"Before." [Jacaranda] (5:1) Wint-Spr 91, p. 58-59.
4611. OCHESTER, Ed
"Bad Muffler / Bare Feet." [PraS] (68:3) Fall 94, p. 24.
"Unreconstructed." [PraS] (68:3) Fall 94, p. 23.
4612. O'CONNELL, Richard
"Lopez Vaz" (From his History, 1586 — Valdivia's Feast, circa 1540-41). [ApalQ] (42) Fall 94, p. 39-40.
4613. O'CONNOR, Flannery
"The First Book." [AntigR] (99) Aut 94, p. 141.
4614. O'CONNOR, Mary
"Het Lezende Vrouwtje: A Woman in Blue Reading a Letter, Vermeer, 1664." [Jacaranda] (4:2) Spr 90, p. 55.
4615. O'DALY, William
"Bird" (tr. of Pablo Neruda). [Field] (51) Fall 94, p. 33.
4616. ODAM, Joyce
"Clear Nights." [Parting] (7:2) Wint 94-95, p. 60.
"Sometimes the Train Comes Through." [Parting] (7:2) Wint 94-95, p. 58.
"Toward Their Happiness." [Parting] (7:1) Sum 94, p. 62.
"Withdrawn." [NegC] (14:1/2) 94, p. 156.
4617. O'DAY, Jeanne
"The 5th Grade Atlas." [CaribbeanW] (8) 94, p. 41-42.
4618. ODOI, Nori
"In China, They Breed Roses from Tigers." [AnthNEW] (6) 94, p. 28.
4619. O'DONNELL, Mark
"Evening" (AIDS Zen). [Poz] (1:3) Ag-S 94, p. 35.
"Morning" (AIDS Zen). [Poz] (1:2) Je-Jl 94, p. 37.
"A Night on the Town" (AIDS Zen). [Poz] (1:1) Ap-My 94, p. 41.
"Party" (AIDS Zen). [Poz] (1:4) O-N 94, p. 29.
"A Walk on the Street" (AIDS Zen). [Poz] (1:1) Ap-My 94, p. 41.
4620. O'DONNELL, Mary
"At the Zoological Gardens." [CharR] (20:2) Fall 94, p. 84-85.
4621. O'DRISCOLL, Dennis
"Water." [SouthernR] (30:2) Ap, Spr 94, p. 315.
4622. O'DWYER, Tess
"Empire of Dreams" (tr. of Giannina Braschi, w. José Vazquez-Amaral). [ApalQ] (40/41) 94, p. 49-53.
"Exercise (Reflection Poem)" (to José Balza, tr. of Alfredo Silva Estrada). [Trans] (29) Spr 94, p. 66-67.
"From two slow roads, two fast stops, I take the wind" (tr. of Giannina Braschi). [ProseP] (3) 94, p. 20.
"I always knew that a bit farther or closer but never in the exact spot" (tr. of Giannina Braschi). [ProseP] (3) 94, p. 19.
"I Don't Have It, and I Wanted It" (from *Empire of Dreams*, tr. of Giannina Braschi). [Callaloo] (17:3) Sum 94, p. 938.
"I Want to Talk to You, Word" (tr. of Alfredo Chacón). [Trans] (29) Spr 94, p. 146.
"It's Not Fair" (tr. of María Auxiliadora Alvarez). [Trans] (29) Spr 94, p. 90-91.
"Once the Voice Is Herself" (tr. of Alfredo Chacón). [Trans] (29) Spr 94, p. 145.
"The Red Bird of My Air" (tr. of María Auxiliadora Alvarez). [Trans] (29) Spr 94, p. 92.
"The Scream of Images" (tr. of Alfredo Silva Estrada). [Trans] (29) Spr 94, p. 68-69.
"Sure, it's true" (tr. of Giannina Braschi). [ProseP] (3) 94, p. 18.

"Utter" (tr. of Alfredo Chacón). [Trans] (29) Spr 94, p. 144.
4623. OERKE, Andrew
"A Certain Wednesday Night" (tr. of May Rihani). [LitR] (37:3) Spr 94, p. 520-521.
4624. OESTREICHER, Deb
"Instructions for Egyptian Foreplay." [PoetryNW] (35:2) Sum 94, p. 39-40.
"Lecture on Glass." [PoetryNW] (35:2) Sum 94, p. 40-41.
"The Mother Is on the Table." [PoetryNW] (35:2) Sum 94, p. 41-42.
"What the Maiden Said When Approached." [PoetryNW] (35:2) Sum 94, p. 42-43.
OEUR, U Sam
See U, Sam Oeur
4625. OFFEN, Ron
"Gift of Tongues." [Pearl] (20) Spr 94, p. 45.
"Holmes Poem: The Poetry Stalker" (for Kate Fericano). [Zyzzyva] (10:1) Spr 94, p. 62-63.
"Visions." [SoCoast] (16) Ja 94, p. 19.
4626. OFNER, Terry
"Not Quite Afternoon." [WorldO] (26:2) Wint 94-95, p. 37.
4627. OGDEN, Hugh
"The Androscoggin, September." [TarRP] (34:1) Fall 94, p. 9.
"The Lesson." [NoDaQ] (62:3) Sum 94-95, p. 94-95.
"Oblations" (for Annette). [CapeR] (29:2) Fall 94, p. 46.
4628. O'GRADY, Jennifer
"Buster's Last Hand." [Colum] (21) Fall 93, p. 98.
"The Miraculous Draft of Fishes." [Colum] (21) Fall 93, p. 96-97.
4629. OGUNDIPE-LESLIE, Molara
"For Audre Lorde." [MalR] (107) Sum 94, p. 216-224.
4630. O'HAY, Charles
"Passions of a Man" (for Charles Mingus, 1922-1979). [NewYorkQ] (53) 94, p. 76.
4631. O'HEERON, G. Antoinette
"Song of the Cicada." [CapeR] (29:2) Fall 94, p. 50.
4632. O'HEHIR, Diana
"Child." [PoetryNW] (35:3) Aut 94, p. 43.
"Climbing." [PoetryNW] (35:3) Aut 94, p. 44.
"Dialogue Between Body and Soul." [PoetryNW] (35:3) Aut 94, p. 46-47.
"Empty God." [PoetryNW] (35:3) Aut 94, p. 44.
"Map." [PoetryNW] (35:3) Aut 94, p. 42.
"Recovery Spells: The Ordinary Run of Things." [PoetryNW] (35:3) Aut 94, p. 45-46.
4633. OHNESORGE-FICK, Marlon
"The Flood." [NewEngR] (16:4) Fall 94, p. 93-94.
4634. OJAIDE, Tanure
"The Life Belt." [SouthernPR] (34:1) Sum 94, p. 21-22.
"New Rivers" (for Gail Peck, author of *New River*). [SouthernPR] (34:1) Sum 94, p. 62.
4635. OJIU, Norinaga
"Autumn Grasses Renga" (tr. of Araki Yasusada, Ozaki Kusatao and Akutagawa Fusei, w. Tosa Motokiyu and Okura Kyojin). [Conjunc] (23) 94, p. 72-73.
"Dream and Charcoal" (tr. of Araki Yasusada, w. Tosa Motokiyu and Okura Kyojin). [Conjunc] (23) 94, p. 69-70.
"Geisha and Iris" (tr. of Araki Yasusada, w. Tosa Motokiyu and Okura Kyojin). [Conjunc] (23) 94, p. 70-71.
"Horsehide and Sunspot" (July 17, 1962, Hiroshima Municipal Stadium, tr. of Araki Yasusada, w. Tosa Motokiyu and Okura Kyojin). [Conjunc] (23) 94, p. 72.
"Sentences for Jack Spicer Renga" (tr. of Araki Yasusada and Akutagawa Fusei, w. Tosa Motokiyu and Okura Kyojin). [Conjunc] (23) 94, p. 75-76.
"Suitor Renga" (tr. of Araki Yasusada, Ozaki Kusatao and Akutagawa Fusei, w. Tosa Motokiyu and Okura Kyojin). [Conjunc] (23) 94, p. 74.
"Telescope with Urn" (tr. of Araki Yasusada, w. Tosa Motokiyu and Okura Kyojin). [Conjunc] (23) 94, p. 69.
"Untitled Haiku" (tr. of Araki Yasusada, w. Tosa Motokiyu and Okura Kyojin). [Conjunc] (23) 94, p. 71.
"Utterances and Hepatica" (tr. of Araki Yasusada, w. Tosa Motokiyu and Okura Kyojin). [Conjunc] (23) 94, p. 76-77.
4636. OKITA, Dwight
"Notes for a Poem on Being Asian American." [WillowR] (21) Spr 94, p. 63-64.

4637. OKTENBERG, Adrian
"Woman, Embracing Tree." [AmerV] (33) 94, p. 26.
4638. OKUN, Mikhail
"Poete Maudit" (tr. by J. Kates). [PlumR] (7) [94?], p. 8.
4639. OKURA, Kyojin
"Autumn Grasses Renga" (tr. of Araki Yasusada, Ozaki Kusatao and Akutagawa Fusei, w. Tosa Motokiyu and Ojiu Norinaga). [Conjunc] (23) 94, p. 72-73.
"Dream and Charcoal" (tr. of Araki Yasusada, w. Tosa Motokiyu and Ojiu Norinaga). [Conjunc] (23) 94, p. 69-70.
"Geisha and Iris" (tr. of Araki Yasusada, w. Tosa Motokiyu and Ojiu Norinaga). [Conjunc] (23) 94, p. 70-71.
"Horsehide and Sunspot" (July 17, 1962, Hiroshima Municipal Stadium, tr. of Araki Yasusada, w. Tosa Motokiyu and Ojiu Norinaga). [Conjunc] (23) 94, p. 72.
"Sentences for Jack Spicer Renga" (tr. of Araki Yasusada and Akutagawa Fusei, w. Tosa Motokiyu and Ojiu Norinaga). [Conjunc] (23) 94, p. 75-76.
"Suitor Renga" (tr. of Araki Yasusada, Ozaki Kusatao and Akutagawa Fusei, w. Tosa Motokiyu and Ojiu Norinaga). [Conjunc] (23) 94, p. 74.
"Telescope with Urn" (tr. of Araki Yasusada, w. Tosa Motokiyu and Ojiu Norinaga). [Conjunc] (23) 94, p. 69.
"Untitled Haiku" (tr. of Araki Yasusada, w. Tosa Motokiyu and Ojiu Norinaga). [Conjunc] (23) 94, p. 71.
"Utterances and Hepatica" (tr. of Araki Yasusada, w. Tosa Motokiyu and Ojiu Norinaga). [Conjunc] (23) 94, p. 76-77.
4640. OLDEN, Megan
"The Beautiful Child." [SantaBR] (2:2) Fall-Wint 94, p. 96-97.
"Snow White and Rose-Red: the Untold Story." [SantaBR] (2:2) Fall-Wint 94, p. 96.
4641. OLDER, Julia
"Chante-moi" (tr. of Véronique Tadjo). [InterQ] (1:3) 94, p. 73-74.
"Kasala" (tr. of Clémentine Nzuji). [InterQ] (1:3) 94, p. 39-40.
4642. OLDS, Sharon
"Sunday Night." [Antaeus] (75/76) Aut 94, p. 310-311.
4643. OLDS-ELLINGSON, Alice (*See also* ELLINGSON, Alice)
"Ashok Prahbu." [SlipS] (14) 94, p. 24-25.
"My Daddy." [SlipS] (14) 94, p. 23.
4644. OLESCHINSKI, Brigitte
"Ebb and Flow, Along" (tr. by Gary Sea). [GrahamHR] (18) Wint 94-95, p. 71.
"Heiress to Her Own Express Train" (For E.O., tr. by Gary Sea). [WebR] (18) Fall 94, p. 31.
"Mental Heat Control" (tr. by Gary Sea). [GrahamHR] (18) Wint 94-95, p. 72.
"Something Empty, Something Silent Stays Behind" (tr. by Gary Sea). [GrahamHR] (18) Wint 94-95, p. 73.
4645. OLIENSIS, Jenny
"Greek Homework, April's Tomb, or The Raft Refused." [Salm] (103) Sum 94, p. 103-104.
"High School." [Salm] (103) Sum 94, p. 102.
4646. OLINKA, Sharon
"Bird of Death" (For Everette Maddox). [NegC] (13:2/3) 93, p. 76-77.
4647. OLIVE, Harry
"In All the Worlds of If." [Elf] (4:2) Sum 94, p. 39.
"Inside the Limits of the Day." [Plain] (15:1) Fall 94, p. 13.
"Instructions." [Elf] (4:2) Sum 94, p. 39.
"On Days Far From Extraordinary Visions." [Elf] (4:2) Sum 94, p. 38.
"Yes Bird." [Elf] (4:4) Wint 94, p. 35.
4648. OLIVEIRA, David
"Reporter" (from Storytelling). [EvergreenC] (9:2) Sum-Fall 94, p. 91-92.
4649. OLIVER, Douglas
"The Borrowed Bow." [NewRep] (210:20) 16 My 94, p. 48.
4650. OLIVER, Mary
"Fall." [Poetry] (165:1) O 94, p. 1.
"Grass." [OhioR] (52) 94, p. 38.
"Herons in Winter in the Frozen Marsh." [NewEngR] (16:3) Sum 94, p. 27-28.
"Mockingbirds." [Atlantic] (273:2) F 94, p. 80.
"Morning Glories." [Poetry] (165:1) O 94, p. 2.
"Mushrooms." [SantaBR] (2:2) Fall-Wint 94, p. 6.
"October." [OhioR] (52) 94, p. 39.
"Roses." [OhioR] (52) 94, p. 37.

"September." [OhioR] (52) 94, p. 40.
"Spring." [SantaBR] (2:2) Fall-Wint 94, p. 9.
"A Summer Afternoon." [Witness] (8:2) 94, p. 107.
"The Sun." [SantaBR] (2:2) Fall-Wint 94, p. 14-15.
"Wild Geese." [SantaBR] (2:2) Fall-Wint 94, p. 11.

4651. OLLIVIER, L. L.
"The Calling." [ChamLR] (14/15) Spr-Fall 94, p. 193.

4652. OLSCAMP, Marcel
"Credo" (in French). [InterPR] (20:2) Fall 94, p. 48, 50.
"Credo" (tr. by Michael Gilson). [InterPR] (20:2) Fall 94, p. 49, 51.

4653. OLSEN, Lance
"Stories." [WillowS] (34) Sum 94, p. 63.

4654. OLSEN, William
"Heraclitus, Fragment 16." [SouthernR] (30:3) Sum 94, p. 561-562.
"In the Time of Blithe Astonishments." [TriQ] (91) Fall 94, p. 216-217.
"The Mist Nets." [TriQ] (91) Fall 94, p. 218-219.
"The Storm Chasers." [GettyR] (7:2) Spr 94, p. 230-232.

4655. OLSON, David
"Continental Divide." [CrabCR] (8:2/3/9:1/2/3) 94, p. 56.

4656. OLSON, John
"Arctic Parlor." [NewAW] (12) Spr-Sum 94, p. 118-119.
"Henry IV Part Three." [AnotherCM] (27) 94, p. 167-168.
"Iridescent Caulk." [Sulfur] (34) Spr 94, p. 30-31.
"Nose and Throat." [Sulfur] (34) Spr 94, p. 31-32.
"Restrictions Unbound." [Caliban] (14) 94, p. 140-141.
"Weights and Measures." [NewAW] (12) Spr-Sum 94, p. 120-121.

4657. OLSON, Sandra
"Tradition." [Parting] (7:2) Wint 94-95, p. 41-42.

4658. OLSSON, Kurt S.
"The Unblessed" (Ham to his father). [CarolQ] (47:1) Fall 94, p. 79.

4659. O'MALLEY, Nancy
"And the Clapper Filled Her Belly." [SmPd] (31:2, #91) Spr 94, p. 19.

4660. O'MEARA, David
"The Death of Fellini." [TickleAce] (28) Fall-Wint 94, p. 66.
"Debut." [AntigR] (98) Sum 94, p. 12-13.
"Spain" (for Jeff Hardill and Amy Allan). [AntigR] (98) Sum 94, p. 9-10.
"St. Patrick's Day." [TickleAce] (28) Fall-Wint 94, p. 64-65.
"Ways to Be Gored." [AntigR] (98) Sum 94, p. 11.

4661. ONCINA, Lori
"A Friend." [BellArk] (10:1) Ja-F 94, p. 15.
"Waiting." [BellArk] (10:3) My-Je 94, p. 25.

4662. ONDAATJE, Michael
"Night Fever." [Antaeus] (75/76) Aut 94, p. 312.

4663. O'NEILL, Alexandre
"A Meu Favor." [Os] (39) Fall-Wint 94, p. 4.
"In My Favor" (tr. by Alexis Levitin). [Os] (39) Fall-Wint 94, p. 5.

4664. O'NEILL, Brian
"After Reading Roethke's 'Rose' the Ladies Are Happy and Still" (for Jerry Thaden). [HopewellR] (6) 94, p. 113-114.

4665. O'NEILL, John
"Antler." [Descant] (24:4, #83) Wint 93-94, p. 14.
"Light." [PraF] (15:1, #66) Spr 94, p. 115.
"The Loon." [Descant] (24:4, #83) Wint 93-94, p. 15.
"Midnight Sun." [Descant] (24:4, #83) Wint 93-94, p. 17.
"The Photographer of Wolves" (Second Prize, Long Poem Category). [PraF] (15:4, #69) Wint 94-95, p. 30-42.
"Whales." [PraF] (15:1, #66) Spr 94, p. 114.
"Wilderness Directive." [Descant] (24:4, #83) Wint 93-94, p. 16.

4666. O'NEILL, Jordan
"Do Not Imagine Me." [Kalliope] (16:1) 94, p. 25.

4667. ONESS, Chad
"Easter Burrito" (for Ern Merritt). [SantaBR] (2:1) Spr-Sum 94, p. 71.
"Talking to Hinkmet." [NegC] (14:1/2) 94, p. 165-168.

4668. ONESS, Elizabeth
"What I Know." [SantaBR] (2:2) Fall-Wint 94, p. 29-30.
"Woman Holding a Balance." [SantaBR] (2:2) Fall-Wint 94, p. 28.

4669. ONITSURA
Haiku [AmerPoR] (23:4) Jl-Ag 94, p. 18.
4670. ONOPA, Paul
"A Tool Box Full of Your Tools." [PoetL] (89:3) Fall 94, p. 5-6.
4671. OPENGART, Bea
"Nude" (after Duane Michals). [ApalQ] (40/41) 94, p. 84-85.
"Walls." [InterQ] (1:3) 94, p. 164.
4672. OPPENHEIMER, Priscilla
"Clerihew: Stephen Spender." [Light] (9) Spr 94, p. 20.
"Musical Clerihew." [Light] (9) Spr 94, p. 11.
"Thinker." [Light] (10) Sum 94, p. 15.
4673. OPSTEDAL, Kevin
"Big Sur." [DarkMoon] (1) 94, p. 72.
"Ground Zero." [DarkMoon] (1) 94, p. 74.
"Night Sounds." [DarkMoon] (1) 94, p. 73.
"Out the window are lands to be discovered." [DarkMoon] (1) 94, p. 71.
"Radio Twinkling in Venusian Ionophere." [DarkMoon] (1) 94, p. 75.
4674. OPYR, Linda E.
"Vantage Point." [EngJ] (83:6) O 94, p. 61.
4675. ORAVECZ, Imre
"According to My Friend H." (tr. by Bruce Berlind). [DenQ] (29:1) Sum 94, p. 93.
"And Afterwards You Came" (tr. by Bruce Berlind). [DenQ] (29:1) Sum 94, p. 94.
"I Came Again" (tr. by Bruce Berlind). [Nimrod] (38:1) Fall-Wint 94, p. 133.
"Today I Had to Wait Outside a Door" (tr. by Bruce Berlind). [DenQ] (29:1) Sum 94, p. 95.
4676. ORBAN, Judith
"The Blue Notebook" (tr. of Zafer Senocak). [Descant] (24:4, #83) Wint 93-94, p. 122.
"Recognitions" (tr. of Zafer Senocak). [Descant] (24:4, #83) Wint 93-94, p. 120-121.
4677. ORBAN, Ottó
"Accident on a Stretch of Interstate 94 Between Chicago and Milwaukee" (tr. by Bruce Berlind, w. Mária Körösy). [Boulevard] (9:1/2, #25/26) Spr 94, p. 226.
"This Breathing, Devouring Swamp" (tr. by Jascha Kessler, w. Mária Körösy). [GrahamHR] (18) Wint 94-95, p. 100.
4678. ORLEN, Steve
"Shyness." [NewEngR] (16:4) Fall 94, p. 95-96.
4679. ORLOWSKY, Dzvinia
"Dogs Days." [Journal] (18:2) Fall-Wint 94, p. 22-23.
"First Communion." [TarRP] (34:1) Fall 94, p. 48.
"A Handful of Bees." [Agni] (39) 94, p. 88.
"A Handful of Bees." [TarRP] (34:1) Fall 94, p. 47.
"Nests." [Journal] (18:2) Fall-Wint 94, p. 24.
"The Slaughter." [Jacaranda] (10) 94, p. 116.
4680. ORMSBY, Eric
"Baudelaire to Mme. Aupick, at Honfleur (1867)." [Descant] (25:3/4, #86/87) Fall-Wint 94, p. 202-203.
"Fragrances." [Descant] (25:3/4, #86/87) Fall-Wint 94, p. 201.
"Grasses in November" (Reprinted with corrections from Bluelines 1993). [Blueline] (15) 94, p. 83.
"Hate." [Descant] (25:3/4, #86/87) Fall-Wint 94, p. 204.
"Of Paradise as a Garden." [Descant] (25:3/4, #86/87) Fall-Wint 94, p. 205.
"Rain." [Blueline] (15) 94, p. 8.
"Rain in Childhood." [NewYorker] (70:17) 13 Je 94, p. 62.
"Spider Silk." [Blueline] (15) 94, p. 7.
"Starlings." [Blueline] (15) 94, p. 8.
4681. O'ROURKE, Meghan
"Acceleration." [HangL] (64) 94, p. 79-81.
"The Fire I Refuse" (for Timothy Doherty, 1954-1977). [HangL] (64) 94, p. 85-86.
"Mary's Breast." [HangL] (64) 94, p. 84.
"The Physicist's Wife." [HangL] (64) 94, p. 82-83.
4682. ORR, Ed
"Gide: African Dry Spell." [YellowS] (11:4, #44) Wint 93-94, p. 22.
"Watching the Sky Break Blue Again." [AnotherCM] (28) 94, p. 96.
4683. ORR, Gregory
"The City of Salt." [AmerPoR] (23:2) Mr-Ap 94, p. 16.

"Dark Prayer." [AmerPoR] (23:2) Mr-Ap 94, p. 17.
"Elegy for a Child." [AmerPoR] (23:2) Mr-Ap 94, p. 16.
"Everything" (for my mother). [OntR] (40) Spr-Sum 94, p. 105.
"The Gray Fox." [AmerPoR] (23:2) Mr-Ap 94, p. 17.
"House of Childhood." [OntR] (40) Spr-Sum 94, p. 103.
"A Litany." [AmerPoR] (23:2) Mr-Ap 94, p. 16.
"A Moment." [OntR] (40) Spr-Sum 94, p. 104.
"The Motorcycle." [SouthernR] (30:1) Ja, Wint 94, p. 96.
"My Father's Voice." [AmerPoR] (23:2) Mr-Ap 94, p. 17.
"A Photo of My Mother in Haiti." [SouthernR] (30:1) Ja, Wint 94, p. 97-98.
"The Vase." [AmerPoR] (23:2) Mr-Ap 94, p. 17.
"A Visitor." [AmerPoR] (23:2) Mr-Ap 94, p. 17.
"Who'd Want to Be a Man?" [AmerPoR] (23:2) Mr-Ap 94, p. 16.

4684. ORR, Stephen K.
"Haiku" (2 poems). [Amelia] (7:3, #22) 94, p. 66.

4685. ORR, Thomas Alan
"Gnat Dancing." [HopewellR] (6) 94, p. 115.

4686. ORR, Verlena
"Alone with the Cat." [PoetC] (25:2) Wint 94, p. 30.

4687. ORTH, Ghita
"Breaking the Silence." [NewEngR] (16:1) Wint 94, p. 71.
"Healing." [NewEngR] (16:1) Wint 94, p. 74-75.
"Knowing." [NewEngR] (16:1) Wint 94, p. 73-74.
"Speaking as Mother." [NewEngR] (16:1) Wint 94, p. 72.
"Understanding Bonsai." [NewEngR] (16:1) Wint 94, p. 76-77.

4688. ORTIZ, Chris
"Findings in a Wrinkled Piece of Paper." [WindO] (58) Sum 94, p. 48-49.
"Living Under the Mango Shade." [BilingR] (19:2) My-Ag 94, p. 164.

4689. ORTIZ, Simon
"Seed." [Ploughs] (20:1) Spr 94, p. 34-36.

ORTIZ COFER, Judith
See COFER, Judith Ortiz

4690. OSBEY, Brenda Marie
"Mother Catherine." [SouthernR] (30:4) Aut 94, p. 833-836.

4691. OSBORN, Andrew
"Continuous Correspondence from *EIDOS*." [ColR] (21:1) Spr 94, p. 125.
"Hermes Has His Way." [ColR] (21:1) Spr 94, p. 126-127.

4692. OSBORN, Bud
"Drapetomania." [Grain] (21:4) Spr 94, p. 84.
"Mullin's Brother." [Grain] (21:4) Spr 94, p. 86.
"Outside This Hotel a Man Is Freezing to Death" (for preston blount). [Grain] (21:4) Spr 94, p. 85.

4693. O'SHEA-NOONAN, Mary-Beth
"After the Funeral." [Ledge] (17) Wint 94, p. 37.
"On Wyndam Road." [Ledge] (17) Wint 94, p. 38-39.

4694. OSHEROW, Jacqueline
"Conversations with Survivors." [SenR] (24:1) Spr 94, p. 29-38.
"Late Night Tête-à-Tête with a Moon in Transit." [WestHR] (48:4) Wint 94, p. 328-337.
"A Poem for Ptolemy." [NewRep] (210:6) 7 F 94, p. 40.

4695. OSING, Gordon T.
"Distinguished Leaves" (tr. of Leung Ping-kwan). [Talisman] (12) Spr 94, p. 173.
"The Leaf on the Edge" (tr. of Leung Ping-kwan). [Talisman] (12) Spr 94, p. 173.
"Morning in a Foreign Land" (tr. of Ping-kwan Leung, w. the author). [PoetryC] (14:3) My 94, p. 22.
"Streetlamp and Tin Leaf" (tr. of Leung Ping-kwan). [Talisman] (12) Spr 94, p. 174.

4696. OSMAN, Jena
"The Agrarian." [Avec] (8:1) 94, p. 13-17.
"Character Derive." [Avec] (8:1) 94, p. 18-20.
"Hydra Village." [Avec] (8:1) 94, p. 21-22.
"Lecture Notes." [Avec] (8:1) 94, p. 23-24.
"The Parrot: Distincition of Awkward Shape, Allure of Deep Color." [Avec] (8:1) 94, p. 12.

4697. OSSIP, Kathleen
"A Change in the Weather." [Elf] (4:2) Sum 94, p. 29.

4698. OSSMANN, April
"Bikini." [SenR] (24:2) Fall 94, p. 47-48.
"Something About Desire." [AntR] (52:2) Spr 94, p. 312.
4699. OSSOTT, Hanni
"Ignorance" (tr. by Pamela Carmell). [Trans] (29) Spr 94, p. 89.
"The Illness" (tr. by Pamela Carmell). [Trans] (29) Spr 94, p. 86-88.
"Ownership" (tr. by Pamela Carmell). [Trans] (29) Spr 94, p. 89.
4700. OSTERHAUS, Joe
"The Summer Storms." [Journal] (18:1) Spr-Sum 94, p. 79.
"To an Aborted Child." [Journal] (18:1) Spr-Sum 94, p. 73-74.
"Two on Film" (part 2 for Gerald Mast). [Journal] (18:1) Spr-Sum 94, p. 75-78.
4701. OSTRIKER, Alicia
"After the Reunion." [Antaeus] (73/74) Spr 94, p. 69-70.
"The Book for Life" (for Sheila Solomon. The Nimrod / Hardman Wards: Honorable Mention). [Nimrod] (38:1) Fall-Wint 94, p. 43-49.
"The Boys, the Broomhandle, the Retarded Girl." [ParisR] (36:133) Wint 94, p. 177.
"Extended Sonnet." [AmerS] (63:3) Sum 94, p. 420.
"The Glassblower's Breath." [PraS] (68:1) Spr 94, p. 57-58.
"The Mastectomy Poems" (Selections: 2-3, 6, 8-12). [KenR] (NS 16:1) Wint 94, p. 3-8.
"Neoplatonic Riff." [PraS] (68:1) Spr 94, p. 59.
"Taylor Lake." [ColR] (21:2) Fall 94, p. 113-116.
"Translation" (for Judith Hemschemeyer). [ColR] (21:2) Fall 94, p. 112.
"A Walker in the City." [Witness] (8:2) 94, p. 67-69.
4702. O'SULLIVAN, Maggie
"Narrow Bandages Even Tombs" (to Denise Riley. In memoriam Ellen O'Donovan 1880-1945). [Chain] (1) Spr-Sum 94, p. 220-222.
4703. O'SULLIVAN, Sibbie
"Killing the Wasp." [ApalQ] (40/41) 94, p. 96-97.
4704. OTERO, Blas de
"Surge" (tr. by James Brasfield). [Talisman] (12) Spr 94, p. 200-201.
4705. O'TOOLE, John M.
"Corsage." [Ascent] (18:2) Wint 94, p. 50.
"Menu." [Ascent] (18:2) Wint 94, p. 51.
"Northern Pacific." [Ascent] (19:1) Fall 94, p. 27.
4706. OTT, Kelly Elizabeth
"West Texas." [Border] (5) Fall-Wint 94, p. 47-48.
4707. OTT, Martin
"To Burn." [BlackBR] (18) Wint-Spr 94, p. 34.
4708. OTT, Rita
"Silence." [BellArk] (10:5) S-O 94, p. 24.
"Thanksgiving in May." [BellArk] (10:5) S-O 94, p. 24.
"To Build a Rock Wall." [BellArk] (10:5) S-O 94, p. 24.
4709. OTTEN, Charlotte F.
"Piers." [SoCoast] (16) Ja 94, p. 43.
4710. OTTEN, Elizabeth
"3.36 Young Maiden" (from the 16th c. Sanskrit treatise *Blazing Sapphire*, tr. of Rupa Gosvamin, w. Neal Delmonico). [WebR] (18) Fall 94, p. 37.
"4.35 Bashful Radha" (from the 16th c. Sanskrit treatise *Blazing Sapphire*, tr. of Rupa Gosvamin, w. Neal Delmonico). [WebR] (18) Fall 94, p. 37.
4711. OUTLAW, Keddy Ann
"Men Don't Carry Mirrors." [Border] (5) Fall-Wint 94, p. 49.
"Moon Monk." [Border] (5) Fall-Wint 94, p. 51.
4712. OVERSTREET, Roy
"Ode to the Sea." [Border] (3) Fall 93, p. 50-51.
4713. OVID
"Ceyx and Alcyone" (From Book XI of *Metamorphoses*, tr. by David R. Slavitt). [NewEngR] (16:1) Wint 94, p. 26-33.
"Tristia III.3" (tr. by Peter Green). [SouthernHR] (28:1) Wint 94, p. 42-44.
4714. OWEN, Maureen
"A History of the English-Speaking Peoples or Tea in the Shape of a Kite." [Chelsea] (57) 94, p. 26-27.
"Now Even the Jungle Wanted Him Dead or She Closed the Door Behind Her." [Chelsea] (57) 94, p. 25-26.
4715. OWEN, Sue
"Curiosity Kills the Cat." [NewDeltaR] (10:1) Fall 92-Wint 93, p. 64-65.

"The Devil's Cookbook." [NewDeltaR] (10:1) Fall 92-Wint 93, p. 62-63.
"Hen's Teeth." [NewDeltaR] (10:1) Fall 92-Wint 93, p. 66-67.

4716. OWENS, Collie
"Three Poems about Childhood." [LaurelR] (28:1) Wint 94, p. 40-41.
"Wilderness Experience." [NegC] (14:1/2) 94, p. 62-63.

4717. OWENS, John
"There once was a feeling named Hate" (3rd Prize, The A & C Limericks Awards). [Amelia] (7:4, #23) 94, p. 15.

4718. OWENS, June
"Chagall's Angel" (third prize in the 1994 *Chiron Review* Poetry Contest). [ChironR] (13:4) Wint 94, p. 15.
"Old Bones and Baubles." [Amelia] (7:3, #22) 94, p. 137.

4719. OWENS, Rochelle
"Luca: Discourse on Life and Death" (Excerpts). [Talisman] (12) Spr 94, p. 125-128.

4720. OWENS, Scott
"The Ashes and the Poplars Bent Down Toward Her Corolla" (after Robert Desnos). [GeoR] (48:1) Spr 94, p. 78-79.
"Returning to the Father, the Son." [LaurelR] (28:1) Wint 94, p. 81-82.

4721. OWENS, Suzanne
"Flying Back to Chalk River." [Nimrod] (37:2) Spr-Sum 94, p. 71.
"I Stare at Your Skull." [Nimrod] (37:2) Spr-Sum 94, p. 72.
"St. Peter's Chapel of the Pieta." [CumbPR] (14:1) Fall 94, p. 36-37.

4722. OWNBEY, Brian
"Despite Ourselves a Window in a Field." [TarRP] (33:2) Spr 94, p. 34.

4723. OZAKI, Kusatao
"Autumn Grasses Renga" (w. Araki Yasusada and Akutagawa Fusei, tr. by Tosa Motokiyu, Ojiu Norinaga and Okura Kyojin). [Conjunc] (23) 94, p. 72-73.
"Suitor Renga" (w. Araki Yasusada and Akutagawa Fusei, tr. by Tosa Motokiyu, Ojiu Norinaga and Okura Kyojin). [Conjunc] (23) 94, p. 74.

4724. PACE, Barbara G.
"Talking with Edna." [EngJ] (83:4) Ap 94, p. 108.

4725. PACERNICK, Gary
"Beach Scene." [Confr] (54/55) Fall 94-Wint 95, p. 299.
"Proverbs." [Confr] (54/55) Fall 94-Wint 95, p. 300.

PACHECO, Alexandra López
See LOPEZ PACHECO, Alexandra

PACHECO, Jesús López
See LOPEZ-PACHECO, Jesús

4726. PACK, Robert
"Reversing." [ColR] (21:2) Fall 94, p. 81-83.
"The Snowy Owl." [ColR] (21:2) Fall 94, p. 79-80.
"South Bronx 1939." [PraS] (68:1) Spr 94, p. 126-127.
"Stellar Thanksgiving." [PraS] (68:1) Spr 94, p. 124-125.
"The Trees Will Die." [GeoR] (48:2) Sum 94, p. 311-313.

4727. PACKARD, William
"Deplorable creative writing workshops." [NewYorkQ] (53) 94, p. 109.
"He was key student in my playwriting class." [WorldL] (5) 94, p. 26.
"The Poet." [WorldL] (5) 94, p. 27.
"When you were young there were none of these fancy creative writing programs." [WorldL] (5) 94, p. 26.

4728. PADDOCK, Harold
"It Was Summer." [TickleAce] (28) Fall-Wint 94, p. 108.
"It Was Winter." [TickleAce] (28) Fall-Wint 94, p. 107.

4729. PADEL, Ruth
"Bad Dream." [Verse] (11:1) Spr 94, p. 5.
"Birdlime" (from William Turner's *Herbal*, 1551). [KenR] (NS 16:3) Sum 94, p. 121.
"Britain's First Banana." [KenR] (NS 16:3) Sum 94, p. 121-122.
"Gecko." [HarvardR] (7) Fall 94, p. 24.
"Intercity." [Verse] (11:1) Spr 94, p. 7.
"Movement in Copper." [KenR] (NS 16:3) Sum 94, p. 122-123.
"Skin." [Verse] (11:1) Spr 94, p. 6.
"Vodka." [Verse] (11:1) Spr 94, p. 6.

4730. PADGETT, Ron
"Fish" (tr. of Yu Jian, w. Wang Ping). [Talisman] (12) Spr 94, p. 160-161.
4731. PADGETT, Tom
"Dirty Books." [HampSPR] Wint 94, p. 29-30.
"Post-Partum Sonogram." [HampSPR] Wint 94, p. 29.
4732. PADUNOV, Vladimir
"15 Wise Exhortations" (tr. of Dmitrii Aleksandrovich Prigov, w. Nancy Condee). [MinnR] (41/42) Fall 93-Spr 94 (published Mr 95), p. 11-12.
"Telegrams" (tr. of Dmitrii Aleksandrovich Prigov, w. Nancy Condee). [MinnR] (41/42) Fall 93-Spr 94 (published Mr 95), p. 12-14.
"The Weather on the Planet" (tr. of Dmitrii Aleksandrovich Prigov, w. Nancy Condee). [MinnR] (41/42) Fall 93-Spr 94 (published Mr 95), p. 14-15.
4733. PAGE, Carolyn
"Barn Flight." [NegC] (14:1/2) 94, p. 178.
"J. J. Newberry's." [NegC] (14:1/2) 94, p. 180.
"Neighbor." [NegC] (14:1/2) 94, p. 179.
"Newberry's Lunch Counter Clerk." [NegC] (14:1/2) 94, p. 181.
4734. PAGE, Dorothy
"Endings." [AnthNEW] (6) 94, p. 21.
4735. PAGE, Geoff
"Southwest." [InterQ] (1:2) 93, p. 110.
4736. PAGE, P. K.
"Could I Write a Poem Now?" [CanLit] (142/143) Fall-Wint 94, p. 112.
4737. PAGE, Ra
"The Silk Division." [SoCoast] (17) Je 94, p. 50.
4738. PAGE, William
"The Artist of Dust." [WritersF] (20) 94, p. 139.
"For Autumn." [WritersF] (20) 94, p. 142.
"Sand." [WritersF] (20) 94, p. 140-141.
"Standing on Edge." [NoAmR] (279:5) S-O 94, p. 22.
"Truth." [WritersF] (20) 94, p. 138.
PAHLSON, Goran Printz
See PRINTZ-PAHLSON, Goran
4739. PAINO, Frankie
"Alchemy" (John William Polidori, M.D., 1795-1821). [KenR] (NS 16:4) Fall 94, p. 123-124.
"Desire." [KenR] (NS 16:4) Fall 94, p. 125-126.
"Each Bone of the Body." [GettyR] (7:3) Sum 94, p. 425-429.
"The Martyrdom of St. Sebastian." [Iowa] (24:3) Fall 94, p. 31-32.
"Necromancy." [Iowa] (24:3) Fall 94, p. 29-30.
"The Old Religion." [KenR] (NS 16:4) Fall 94, p. 126-128.
"Ophelia." [Journal] (18:2) Fall-Wint 94, p. 53.
4740. PAINO, Gerrie
"In the Chapel of the Virgin, Zaragoza, Spain." [CreamCR] (18:1) Spr 94, p. 16-17.
"Part of the Story." [ChatR] (14:2) Wint 94, p. 40-41.
"With the Woman in the Cancer Ward." [CreamCR] (18:1) Spr 94, p. 14-15.
4741. PAIR, Grant
"Papermaking" (for Catherine Roemer). [Jacaranda] (4:2) Spr 90, p. 75.
4742. PAKER, Saliha
"Caka Bey" (tr. of Özdemir Ince, for Anthony Bryer). [Talisman] (13) Fall 94-Wint 95, p. 250.
4743. PAKRAVAN, Saideh
"Balloons." [PoetL] (89:4) Wint 94-95, p. 15.
4744. PALENCIA, Elaine Fowler
"Taking the Train." [WillowR] (21) Spr 94, p. 4-5.
"Tracks." [WillowR] (21) Spr 94, p. 6-7.
4745. PALEOLOGO, M. P.
"Caparina." [JlNJPo] (16:1) Spr 94, p. 13.
4746. PALING, Stephen
"The Gnostic Serpent." [Hellas] (5:1) Spr-Sum 94, p. 73.
4747. PALMA, Michael
"Burlesque." [Pivot] (42) 94, p. 51.
"Ray Charles at the Copa." [Pivot] (41) 93, p. 1.
"Song." [Pivot] (42) 94, p. 51.

4748. PALMA, Michel
"Testament" (tr. of Roger Gilbert-Lecomte, w. Lee Whittier). [PoetryE] (37/38) Spr 94, p. 236.
"The Wind After, The Wind Before" (tr. of Roger Gilbert-Lecomte, w. Lee Whittier). [PoetryE] (37/38) Spr 94, p. 234-235.

PALMA, Ray di
See DiPALMA, Ray

4749. PALMER, Joanne
"On Sunday, Other Couples Clean the House and Go to Brunch." [BellArk] (10:1) Ja-F 94, p. 11.

4750. PALMER, John
"Houses by Cezanne." [IndR] (17:1) Spr 94, p. 37.

4751. PALMER, Lesley E.
"Birthday." [Sun] (217) Ja 94, p. 15.
"Purge." [HiramPoR] (55/56) Fall 93-Sum 94, p. 88.

4752. PALMER, Leslie
"To the Post, Athlon Flaubert." [CapeR] (29:2) Fall 94, p. 28.

4753. PANCOAST-NAGAMURA, Kit
"Haiku on the Lijiang River." [CreamCR] (18:1) Spr 94, p. 20.

4754. PANDE, Mrinal
"Her Home" (tr. by Arlene Zide and the author). [InterQ] (1:2) 93, p. 185.

4755. PANKEY, Eric
"The Crow's Complaint." [Image] (8) Wint 94-95, p. 17-18.
"Evening with Swallows." [Image] (8) Wint 94-95, p. 18.
"June Vagaries." [Poetry] (164:3) Je 94, p. 125.
"The Kingdom Likened to a Field of Weeds." [Image] (8) Wint 94-95, p. 17.
"The Language of Flowers." [Poetry] (164:3) Je 94, p. 126.
"Nocturne and Refrain." [ColR] (21:1) Spr 94, p. 187.
"The Phrase of Thine Actions." [NewL] (60:4) 94, p. 89.
"The Relic." [WebR] (18) Fall 94, p. 46.
"Tulip." [ColR] (21:1) Spr 94, p. 186.
"Two-Part Invention." [SenR] (24:1) Spr 94, p. 70.

4756. PANNU, Raj
"For Those Who Have Come Before Me." [WestCL] (28:1/2, #13/14) Spr-Fall 94, p. 191-192.
"Lotus Land." [WestCL] (28:1/2, #13/14) Spr-Fall 94, p. 190.

4757. PANTIN, Yolanda
"I Didn't Want to Speak with Anyone" (tr. by Steven F. White). [Trans] (29) Spr 94, p. 109-110.
"There Are Three Vultures" (tr. by Steven F. White). [Trans] (29) Spr 94, p. 111.
"Who Are They Eating?" (tr. by Steven F. White). [Trans] (29) Spr 94, p. 111.

4758. PAOLA, Suzanne
"Genesis." [Thrpny] (58) Sum 94, p. 20.
"New Year's Eve." [PartR] (61:4) Fall 94, p. 636-637.

4759. PAPAGEORGIOU, Mary Ann
"Brutal Delicacy." [PoetL] (89:4) Wint 94-95, p. 37.

4760. PAPE, Greg
"Evening News." [BlackWR] (20:2) Spr-Sum 94, p. 26-27.
"Likeness." [Sonora] (28) Fall 94, p. 48.
"Whatever Happened to J.C.?" [BlackWR] (20:2) Spr-Sum 94, p. 24-25.

PAPPAS, Rita Signorelli
See SIGNORELLI-PAPPAS, Rita

4761. PARHAM, Robert
"The Kid." [SoCoast] (17) Je 94, p. 32.
"Old Stumps." [CapeR] (29:1) Spr 94, p. 34.
"Self Portrait." [SouthernPR] (34:1) Sum 94, p. 56.

4762. PARINI, Jay
"Near Pitlochry." [WilliamMR] (32) 94, p. 106.

4763. PARIS, Philip
"The Mourner." [WestHR] (48:1) Spr 94, p. 109.

4764. PARK, Joon
"The Practice of Ethics." [AntR] (52:1) Wint 94, p. 94-95.

4765. PARKER, Alan Michael
"Days Like Prose." [ParisR] (36:130) Spr 94, p. 160.
"The Geese." [Raritan] (14:2) Fall 94, p. 17-18.
"Hopscotch." [NewRep] (211:6) 8 Ag 94, p. 40.

"Hush." [ParisR] (36:130) Spr 94, p. 158.
"The Margin." [WestHR] (48:3) Fall 94, p. 231.
"Recessional." [ParisR] (36:130) Spr 94, p. 157.
"The Sears Catalogue." [ParisR] (36:130) Spr 94, p. 156.
"Strawberry Jam." [WestHR] (48:3) Fall 94, p. 230.
"The Ticket." [ParisR] (36:130) Spr 94, p. 159.
"Winter Motet." [Raritan] (14:2) Fall 94, p. 15-16.

4766. PARKER, Pam A.
"Another Sweaty Dream." [AmerV] (33) 94, p. 87.
"Stone." [KenR] (NS 16:1) Wint 94, p. 136.

4767. PARKES, Ian
"Overnight." [Jacaranda] (5:1) Wint-Spr 91, p. 81.

4768. PARKHURST, Carolyn K.
"Made Of." [MinnR] (41/42) Fall 93-Spr 94 (published Mr 95), p. 41-47.

4769. PARKIN, Andrew
"Discourse from an Immortal" (tr. of Lawrence Wong, w. Evangeline Almberg). [PoetryC] (14:3) My 94, p. 22.
"The Shattered Cliff" (tr. of Lawrence Wong, w. Evangeline Almberg). [PoetryC] (14:3) My 94, p. 22.

4770. PARMAN, Sue
"Morning Becomes Perseids" (August 11, 1993: falling stars from the constellation Perseus). [HiramPoR] (55/56) Fall 93-Sum 94, p. 89-90.
"Noel." [HiramPoR] (55/56) Fall 93-Sum 94, p. 91-92.

4771. PARNES, Uzi
"Carnaval" (drama — a work in progress, w. Carmelita Tropicana). [MichQR] (33:4) Fall 94, p. 733-747.

4772. PARRIS, Ed
"Our Islands." [Blueline] (15) 94, p. 19.

4773. PARRISH, Karen
"Glass." [ApalQ] (40/41) 94, p. 109-110.
"Harbinger." [ApalQ] (40/41) 94, p. 107-108.

4774. PARRY, Hugh J.
"Double Dactyl." [Light] (12) Wint 94-95, p. 17.

4775. PARSLEY, Jamie
"For the Winter Angels" (from "The Loneliness of Blizzards"). [AmerPoR] (23:4) Jl-Ag 94, p. 28.

4776. PARSONS, Kenneth A.
"Nightmusic" (for Travelin' Dave). [Wind] (73) 94, p. 18.

4777. PARSONS, Linda
"Keeping House." [Wind] (73) 94, p. 19-20.
"The Life You Save" (for Rachel). [Wind] (73) 94, p. 19.

4778. PARTINGTON, Stephen Derwent
"Biochemistry Lab by Night." [Verse] (11:2) Sum 94, p. 85.

4779. PARTRIDGE, Dixie
"After Looking Up Lapwing in the Encyclopedia" (for my mother). [Kaleid] (Special Issue) 94, p. 29.
"Earthly Effects." [Comm] (121:1) 14 Ja 94, p. 22.
"House of My Serial Dreams." [HiramPoR] (57) Fall 94-Wint 95, p. 46-47.
"Loss." [HiramPoR] (57) Fall 94-Wint 95, p. 49.
"November Turning" (for my mother at 70). [Comm] (121:20) 18 N 94, p. 28.
"Out of the Dark." [Comm] (121:17) 7 O 94, p. 18.
"That Day at the County Fair." [HiramPoR] (57) Fall 94-Wint 95, p. 48.

4780. PARULSKIS, Sigitas
"Border Village" (from *Journey Along the Edge of the Sand*, tr. by Laima Sruoginis). [ArtfulD] (26/27) 94, p. 8-9.
"Landscape" (from *Journey Along the Edge of the Sand*, tr. by Laima Sruoginis). [ArtfulD] (26/27) 94, p. 7.

4781. PASCHEN, Elise
"Graffiti." [WestHR] (48:3) Fall 94, p. 292.
"The Other Mother." [NewRep] (211:24) 12 D 94, p. 40.
"Woman Dreaming of Escape" (Saturday at the Miró Retrospective, MOMA). [WestHR] (48:3) Fall 94, p. 293.

4782. PASQUALI, Thelma V.
"Ash Form." [CapeR] (29:1) Spr 94, p. 47.

4783. PASSALACQUA, Rose
"The House of the Soul" (tr. of Miguel-Angel Zapata). [NewL] (60:4) 94, p. 87.

"In the Beginning the Moon Did Not Inspire Song" (tr. of Miguel Angel Zapata). [WritersF] (20) 94, p. 178.
"Paul Celan" (tr. of Miguel Angel Zapata). [WritersF] (20) 94, p. 179.
"Variations for My Brother Alfonso" (tr. of Carlos Germán Belli). [Conjunc] (23) 94, p. 111-114.

4784. PASSARELLA, Lee
"The Leap" (Hickory Nut Falls, August 1991). [Gaia] (4) Je 94, p. 38.
"Off Broadway" (for Philip Levine). [Elf] (4:1) Spr 94, p. 39.
"Winter as Sibyl." [Gaia] (4) Je 94, p. 38.

PASSEK, Valeri Brainin
See BRAININ-PASSEK, Valeri

4785. PASSER, Jay
"Free Enterprise Messiah." [Caliban] (14) 94, p. 104.

4786. PASSIKOFF, Ben
"And Nowhere Was to Go." [SmPd] (31:3, #92) Fall 94, p. 10.

4787. PAST, Ambar
"Family Portrait" (in memory of Old Emeterio, my father. Tr. of Joaquín Vásquez Aguilar, w. Reginald Gibbons). [TriQ] (91) Fall 94, p. 154-155.
"Found in the Armory of a Cyclone" (tr. of Raúl Garduño, w. Reginald Gibbons). [TriQ] (91) Fall 94, p. 146-147.
"Landscape with Dead Anthems" (tr. by Reginald Gibbons). [TriQ] (91) Fall 94, p. 115-116.

4788. PASTAN, Linda
"The Bronx, 1942." [TriQ] (91) Fall 94, p. 229.
"City of Ambition" (Alfred Steiglitz, photogravure, 1910). [Witness] (8:2) 94, p. 9.
"Courbet's 'Still Life with Apples and Pomegranate'." [GettyR] (7:1) Wint 94, p. 26.
"Daylight Savings." [GettyR] (7:1) Wint 94, p. 27.
"The Law of Primogeniture." [GettyR] (7:4) Aut 94, p. 596.
"The Lumberjacks." [Poetry] (165:2) N 94, p. 82.
"MD 67." [NewRep] (211:2) 11 Jl 94, p. 39.
"Mercy." [Pivot] (42) 94, p. 3.
"Migraine." [Poetry] (165:1) O 94, p. 11.
"Poetry Reading." [Poetry] (163:4) Ja 94, p. 221.
"Requiem." [Poetry] (165:2) N 94, p. 81.
"The Silent Treatment." [GettyR] (7:4) Aut 94, p. 595.
"Smoke Screen." [GettyR] (7:1) Wint 94, p. 28.
"Stationary Bicycle." [GettyR] (7:4) Aut 94, p. 594.
"Vermilion." [Thrpny] (59) Fall 94, p. 37.
"With the Passing of the Leaves." [Vis] (45) 94, p. 9.

4789. PASTOR, Ned
"Discombobulated." [Light] (12) Wint 94-95, p. 18.
"Distinguished But Indistinguishable." [Amelia] (7:3, #22) 94, p. 119.

4790. PATERSON, Don
"19:00: Auchterhouse." [Verse] (11:2) Sum 94, p. 3.

4791. PATERSON, Stuart A.
"Enlisting." [Verse] (11:2) Sum 94, p. 90-91.

4792. PATERSON, Veronica
"Barring Unforeseen Circumstances." [NegC] (14:1/2) 94, p. 46.

4793. PATRICK, Kathleen
"Sitting Bull's Bones" (honorable mention, Social Concern Poetry Competition, 1993). [BlackBR] (18) Wint-Spr 94, p. 45-46.

4794. PATRICK, William B.
"Turner's *The Slave Ship*." [SouthernR] (30:3) Sum 94, p. 563-576.

4795. PATTEN, Karl
"Mid-July." [MidwQ] (36:1) Aut 94, p. 67.
"Open Eyes." [PoetL] (89:3) Fall 94, p. 14.

4796. PATTERSON, Tori
"Kiss Old Ship." [DenQ] (29:1) Sum 94, p. 29.

4797. PATTON, Christopher
"My Father Strokes the Saw." [PraF] (15:4, #69) Wint 94-95, p. 43.
"River Parts." [CanLit] (141) Sum 94, p. 55-56.

4798. PATTON, Kelli Rae
"Notes on a Phoenix" (for Nettie). [HarvardA] (129:1) Sum 94, p. 23.
"Sunday Drive." [HarvardA] (128:2) Wint 94, p. 17.

4799. PAU-LLOSA, Ricardo
"Contemplating the Distinct Possibilities of Failure." [Caliban] (14) 94, p. 56-57.

"Fidelio Ponce de Leon." [Colum] ("The Lost Issues", [i.e. 18-19]) 93, p. 143-144.
"Grave." [PraS] (68:4) Wint 94, p. 116.
"The Raft of the Medusa." [PraS] (68:4) Wint 94, p. 120.

4800. PAUL, Martin
"Marea del Silencio — 41" (tr. of Gabriel Celaya, w. José A. Elgorriaga). [GrandS] (13:1, #49) Sum 94, p. 222-223.

PAUL M.
See M., Paul

4801. PAULIN, Tom
"Linda Nicklin." [GrandS] (13:1, #49) Sum 94, p. 186-187.

4802. PAVESE, Cesare
"San Martino Summer (Indian Summer)" (tr. by Scott Davison). [PraS] (68:1) Spr 94, p. 114.
"Two Poems of 1946" (tr. by Scott Davison). [PraS] (68:1) Spr 94, p. 113.

4803. PAVLICH, Walter
"Bad Nerves." [Poetry] (165:1) O 94, p. 12.
"Big Noise Mornings." [PoetL] (89:4) Wint 94-95, p. 39.
"Black Grapes." [CharR] (20:1) Spr 94, p. 61.
"Casting Off on a Meteor." [Pivot] (41) 93, p. 50.
"Faintness." [GreensboroR] (56) Sum 94, p. 51-52.
"My Glasses Make Her Sad." [AmerPoR] (23:4) Jl-Ag 94, p. 22.
"October Blue." [Shen] (44:2) Sum 94, p. 87.
"Of the Wind." [CharR] (20:1) Spr 94, p. 62.
"Past the Last Exit." [CharR] (20:1) Spr 94, p. 62.
"Seaside Church." [PoetL] (89:2) Sum 94, p. 41-43.
"Somebody Has to Be the Coroner." [LaurelR] (28:2) Sum 94, p. 92-93.

4804. PAVLOV, Konstantin
"Poem about the Poet's Stockyard" (tr. by Ludmilla Popova-Wightman). [Vis] (46) 94, p. 34-35.
"The Satirist" (tr. by Ludmilla Popova-Wightman). [Vis] (46) 94, p. 35.
"Why Adam Fell" (tr. by Ludmilla Popova-Wightman). [Vis] (45) 94, p. 43.

4805. PAYNE, Gerrye
"Le Jardin des Plantes." [HiramPoR] (57) Fall 94-Wint 95, p. 50.
"The Marriage." [WillowR] (21) Spr 94, p. 15-16.

4806. PAZ, Octavio
"Breathing" (tr. by Eliot Weinberger). [NewYorker] (70:13) 16 My 94, p. 74.
"Soliloquio." [ParisR] (36:130) Spr 94, p. 14-18.
"Soliloquy" (tr. by Eliot Weinberger). [ParisR] (36:130) Spr 94, p. 15-19.

4807. PEACHER, Georgiana
"Elizabeth of Mariana." [Amelia] (7:4, #23) 94, p. 159-160.

4808. PEACOCK, Molly
"The Alley" (tr. of Jules Supervielle, w. William Louis-Dreyfus). [Agni] (39) 94, p. 25.
"God Thinks of Man" (tr. of Jules Supervielle, w. William Louis-Dreyfus). [Boulevard] (9:3, #27) Fall 94, p. 109-110.
"The Gown." [AmerLC] (6) 94, p. 71-72.
"Have You Ever Faked an Orgasm?" [ParisR] (36:130) Spr 94, p. 256.
"I Consider the Possibility." [ParisR] (36:130) Spr 94, p. 257.
"My College Sex Group." [ParisR] (36:130) Spr 94, p. 254.
"Prophecy" (tr. of Jules Supervielle, w. William Louis-Dreyfus). [Agni] (39) 94, p. 23.
"The Raindrop (God Speaking)" (tr. of Jules Supervielle, w. William Louis-Dreyfus). [Boulevard] (9:3, #27) Fall 94, p. 110.
"The Return." [ParisR] (36:130) Spr 94, p. 255.
"The Rule." [ParisR] (36:130) Spr 94, p. 255.
"Whisper of Agony" (tr. of Jules Supervielle, w. William Louis-Dreyfus). [Agni] (39) 94, p. 24.

4809. PEARLBERG, Gerry Gomez
"First Date with the D.J." [ModernW] (2) Wint 94, p. 38.
"Happy Birthday, Baby." [ModernW] (2) Wint 94, p. 39.
"The National Council of Jewish Women's Thrift Shop." [ModernW] (2) Wint 94, p. 35-37.
"Shave." [ModernW] (1) Summer 94, p. 97-98.

4810. PEARN, Victor
"Colorado University" (for Spirit and Dede). [NegC] (14:1/2) 94, p. 65.
"Hard Corn." [Parting] (7:1) Sum 94, p. 57.

4811. PEARSALL, Amy Lee
"Memory Jars." [Border] (4) Spr-Sum 94, p. 53-54.
4812. PEARSON, Miranda
"Father's Day." [Grain] (22:1) Sum 94, p. 116.
4813. PEARSON, Ted
"Seven Acoustic Masks." [Epoch] (43:3) 94, p. 292-298.
4814. PEASE, Deborah
"Even Though." [GettyR] (7:1) Wint 94, p. 100.
"Flutter." [Chelsea] (56) 94, p. 76-77.
"Such a Hug." [Chelsea] (56) 94, p. 77-78.
4815. PECK, John
"For Radovan Lorkovic." [Salm] (104/105) Fall 94-Wint 95, p. 165-167.
4816. PECK, Steven
"Carpenter's Song." [SantaBR] (2:1) Spr-Sum 94, p. 87.
"Début." [SantaBR] (2:1) Spr-Sum 94, p. 87.
"Young girls in bright spring dresses." [SantaBR] (2:1) Spr-Sum 94, p. 86.
4817. PECKHAM, Ellen
"Fragments of Letters — 1965." [LitR] (37:4) Sum 94, p. 579.
4818. PEDDLE, Marcus
"A Curious Subtraction." [TickleAce] (28) Fall-Wint 94, p. 67.
4819. PEDEN, Margaret Sayers
"Amante" (poem excerpts: I, III, tr. of Rafael Cadenas). [Trans] (29) Spr 94, p. 48-49.
"The Great Forgotten" (tr. of Rafael Cadenas). [Trans] (29) Spr 94, p. 46.
"In the Midst of Uncertainty" (tr. of Rafael Cadenas). [Trans] (29) Spr 94, p. 50-51.
"Late, I Take Up the Thread" (tr. of Rafael Cadenas). [Trans] (29) Spr 94, p. 45.
"You Tear Me" (tr. of Rafael Cadenas). [Trans] (29) Spr 94, p. 47.
4820. PEELER, Tim
"So I've Got the Class." [Spitball] (46) Spr 94, p. 70.
"My Ten Year Old Said He Didn't Want to Play This Year." [Spitball] (47) Sum 94, p. 30-31.
PEENEN, H. J. van
See Van PEENEN, H. J.
4821. PEIRCE, Kathleen
"Figure with Trees." [ParisR] (36:133) Wint 94, p. 183.
"Height." [ParisR] (36:133) Wint 94, p. 183-184.
"Mother and Son." [ParisR] (36:133) Wint 94, p. 184.
4822. PELIZZON, V. Penelope
"Keeping." [Zyzzyva] (10:2) Sum 94, p. 131.
4823. PELLERIN, Suzanne
"La Cité des Interdits." [InterPR] (20:2) Fall 94, p. 44, 46.
"The City of the Forbidden" (tr. by the author and Peter Couto). [InterPR] (20:2) Fall 94, p. 45, 47.
4824. PELLETIER, Jean-Pierre
"Gloria" (in French, tr. of Jody Freeman). [InterPR] (20:2) Fall 94, p. 101, 103.
4825. PELLETIERE, Marcia
"Draw." [SouthernPR] (34:2) Wint 94, p. 18.
4826. PENCE, Amy
"Eclipse, or Small River Stones." [NewAW] (12) Spr-Sum 94, p. 128.
"Spectators in Eden." [Sonora] (27) Spr 94, p. 22-25.
"A Trinity." [Sonora] (27) Spr 94, p. 20-21.
4827. PENFOLD, Maia
"Sturm and Drang." [Nimrod] (37:2) Spr-Sum 94, p. 73.
"Time to Kill." [Nimrod] (37:2) Spr-Sum 94, p. 74-75.
4828. PENN, Peggy
"Dancing in the Dark" (for Nancy Goldberger). [ParisR] (36:131) Sum 94, p. 158-159.
"The Soup." [ParisR] (36:131) Sum 94, p. 160.
4829. PENNANT, Edmund
"The Art of Dowsing." [Pivot] (41) 93, p. 47-48.
"Cronus." [NewYorkQ] (53) 94, p. 58.
"Incident on Times Square" (third prize in the 1994 *Chiron Review* Poetry Contest). [ChironR] (13:4) Wint 94, p. 14.
"Nonage." [Pivot] (41) 93, p. 47.
"The Spring." [Gaia] (4) Je 94, p. 14.
"Tahara." [Callaloo] (17:4) Fall 94, p. 1052.

"Tisha B'Av." [Jacaranda] (4:2) Spr 90, p. 34.
4830. PENNER, Cheryl
"Someone, Somewhere." [Sonora] (27) Spr 94, p. 74.
4831. PENNY, Michael
"The Best Laid Plans." [AntigR] (96) Wint 94, p. 80.
"I Make a Mistake." [AntigR] (96) Wint 94, p. 79.
"Injured." [AntigR] (96) Wint 94, p. 76.
"Like Music." [AntigR] (96) Wint 94, p. 77.
"Lizard." [TickleAce] (28) Fall-Wint 94, p. 114.
"Turbulence." [AntigR] (96) Wint 94, p. 81.
"Turning Over Rocks." [AntigR] (96) Wint 94, p. 78.
4832. PERCHAN, Robert
"Truth." [ProseP] (3) 94, p. 74.
4833. PERCHIK, Simon
"46. Luke warm, I monitor." [Parting] (7:1) Sum 94, p. 46.
"80. Like those old men on the ward." [Nimrod] (38:1) Fall-Wint 94, p. 134.
"89. These shadows I grow in my good arm." [Nimrod] (38:1) Fall-Wint 94, p. 135.
"243. Again you set the clock :this stove." [Parting] (7:1) Sum 94, p. 47.
"383. To erase their tracks my eyes." [ChamLR] (14/15) Spr-Fall 94, p. 107.
"386. Not the kind ponds pull up, the ice." [ChamLR] (14/15) Spr-Fall 94, p. 108.
"400. You close your eyes as if the sun too." [SmPd] (31:2, #91) Spr 94, p. 8.
"407. These rusting wires whose hooks." [ChamLR] (14/15) Spr-Fall 94, p. 109.
"421. Step by step my heart goes on." [Parting] (7:1) Sum 94, p. 48.
"602. For your birth date a raft." [CentR] (38:2) Spr 94, p. 332.
"608. You limp the way a caterpillar." [CentR] (38:2) Spr 94, p. 333.
"Again you set the clock :this stove." [DogRR] (13:1, #25) Spr-Sum 94, p. 12.
"All that rain is behind them now." [WilliamMR] (32) 94, p. 49.
"And this scar still hungry." [CharR] (20:2) Fall 94, p. 110.
"And Under the Warning Lights." [Pequod] (37) 94, p. 33.
"And your upper jaw." [NowestR] (32:3) 94, p. 34.
"As if once and head down." [NowestR] (32:1) 94, p. 63.
"Bedtime Story." [FreeL] (13) Spr 94, p. 22.
"Before you even saw a lake." [Pembroke] (26) 94, p. 80.
"Even this envelope carries in its breath." [Os] (39) Fall-Wint 94, p. 27.
"Even without their feathers, kisses." [Os] (38) Spr 94, p. 23.
"I bring you a cake and your birthday." [CharR] (20:2) Fall 94, p. 111.
"In this dark room two walls." [Farm] (11:2) Fall-Wint 94-95, p. 44.
"Instead these leaves." [AmerLC] (6) 94, p. 75-76.
"There Will Be Hearings." [CrabCR] (8:2/3/9:1/2/3) 94, p. 88.
"They Must Learn It from the Sun." [Epoch] (43:2) 94, p. 192-193.
"This handle slopes the way each fountain." [Os] (38) Spr 94, p. 24.
"This Scar." [SoDakR] (32:1) Spr 94, p. 104.
"This twig needs leaves, its bark." [Os] (39) Fall-Wint 94, p. 26.
"With each step and practice." [Farm] (11:2) Fall-Wint 94-95, p. 45.
"You are dead for hours, years." [NowestR] (32:3) 94, p. 35.
"You try to make sense, the radiator." [Os] (38) Spr 94, p. 25.
"You wet one hand with the other." [DenQ] (28:4) Spr 94, p. 52.
"You wet one hand with the other." [Northeast] (5:11) Wint 94-95, p. 34.
4834. PERDUE, James
"Surprising Hunters." [WestB] (34) 94, p. 80-81.
4835. PEREIRA, Peter
"Angel of death." [SlipS] (14) 94, p. 9.
"The Climbing Rose." [BellArk] (10:1) Ja-F 94, p. 25.
"Fetus Papyraceous." [SlipS] (14) 94, p. 10.
"In August, My Sister." [SlipS] (14) 94, p. 10-11.
"The Wages of Mercy." [SlipS] (14) 94, p. 8.
"The Wine Press." [BellArk] (10:1) Ja-F 94, p. 25.
4836. PERELMAN, Bob
"Chaim Soutine." [ColR] (21:1) Spr 94, p. 128-134.
"Have You Heard the One." [NewAW] (12) Spr-Sum 94, p. 37-38.
"The Ideal Poem." [NewAW] (12) Spr-Sum 94, p. 35-36.
"News Is News, Poetry Poetry." [RiverC] (14:2) Spr 94, p. 23-27.
"Two Poems." [IndR] (17:1) Spr 94, p. 21-22.
4837. PERETZ, Maya
"Overheard" (tr. of Halina Poswiatowska). [WebR] (18) Fall 94, p. 13.

4838. PÉREZ, Anthony
"Doña Rosa: the Rest of the Story." [Border] (4) Spr-Sum 94, p. 55.
4839. PEREZ, Moira
"My Profound Vocation" (tr. of Angel Gonzalez, w. Steven Ford Brown). [InterQ] (1:1) [93?], p. 153.
4840. PÉREZ GUTIÉRREZ, Amparo
"Fragmento" (I, II). [Nuez] (5:13/14/15) 94, p. 17.
4841. PERI ROSSI, Cristina
"Evohé" (tr. by Diana Decker). [AmerV] (33) 94, p. 19-25.
4842. PERILLO, Lucia Maria
"Annunciation at a Foreign Film." [AmerV] (35) 94, p. 9-10.
"At Saint Placid's." [AmerV] (35) 94, p. 4.
"Cairn for Future Travel." [AmerV] (35) 94, p. 3.
"Kilned." [AmerV] (35) 94, p. 6.
"Lazy Jesus." [AmerV] (35) 94, p. 5.
"On Belay." [AmerV] (35) 94, p. 7.
"Tripe." [AmerV] (35) 94, p. 8.
4843. PERKINS, James Ashbrook
"Birds of a Feather." [CapeR] (29:1) Spr 94, p. 9.
"This, Whitebread, Is Something You Will Never Know" (for Worthia Thomas). [CapeR] (29:1) Spr 94, p. 10.
4844. PERKINS, Leialoha Apo
"In Honour of the Grandmothers of the Plaza of May, Argentina" (for Mary Claire Smith, Berkeley). [ChamLR] (14/15) Spr-Fall 94, p. 42-45.
"Makaha Coast." [ChamLR] (14/15) Spr-Fall 94, p. 18-20.
4845. PERKINS, Leslie D.
"The Ocelot." [Light] (10) Sum 94, p. 10.
"Romance Writer's Lament." [Light] (10) Sum 94, p. 15.
4846. PERLBERG, Mark
"Cartography." [IllinoisR] (2:1) Fall 94, p. 38.
"The Last Meeting." [PraS] (68:1) Spr 94, p. 117-118.
"Return to the Island" (after Wang Wei). [WillowR] (21) Spr 94, p. 67.
"Up in Maine." [PraS] (68:1) Spr 94, p. 117.
4847. PERLMAN, John
"After 'Easement'" (for SS). [Talisman] (12) Spr 94, p. 88.
"Easement." [Talisman] (12) Spr 94, p. 87.
"The High Peaks at Lake Lila." [Talisman] (12) Spr 94, p. 86.
"The High Peaks from Blue Mt." [Talisman] (12) Spr 94, p. 86.
"However the nexus." [Talisman] (12) Spr 94, p. 90-91.
"Regalia of the world & person." [Talisman] (12) Spr 94, p. 85.
"We keep carrying inscriptions." [Talisman] (12) Spr 94, p. 89.
4848. PERLONGO, Bob
"One Early Woman." [Boulevard] (9:3, #27) Fall 94, p. 125.
4849. PERRINE, Laurence
"The Amazing Antics of Two Tranquil Tourists, or A Grim Tale Made Gay" (With apologies to Guy Wetmore Carryl). [Light] (12) Wint 94-95, p. 3.
"Class Exercise." [Light] (12) Wint 94-95, p. 4.
"Cow Poem." [Light] (12) Wint 94-95, p. 5.
"Daybreak." [Light] (12) Wint 94-95, p. 4.
"Epitaph on Parnassus' Side." [Light] (12) Wint 94-95, p. 4.
"The Final Solution." [Light] (12) Wint 94-95, p. 6.
"For a Friend, Turned 50 This January" (With a bottle of Scotch). [Light] (12) Wint 94-95, p. 6.
"Fourteen Lines But Not a Sonnet." [Light] (9) Spr 94, p. 17.
"Limerick." [Light] (12) Wint 94-95, p. 6.
"On Joining the Race to Conquer Space, Yet Sweetly Chime in 2/4 Time." [Light] (12) Wint 94-95, p. 4.
4850. PERRON, Sylvie
"Amérique" (tr. of Alfredo Lavergne). [InterPR] (20:2) Fall 94, p. 107.
4851. PERRONE, Charles A.
"The Book of Fracta" (Selections, tr. of Horacio Costa). [Sulfur] (34) Spr 94, p. 150-157.
4852. PERRY, Candace
"Long Term Therapy." [Sun] (217) Ja 94, p. 23.
4853. PERRY, Stephen
"Adam and Eve." [CimR] (109) O 94, p. 76-77.

"Descartes' Baby's Asshole." [Jacaranda] (10) 94, p. 12-13.
"Giraffes and Wells." [Jacaranda] (5:1) Wint-Spr 91, p. 22-23.
"Homecoming." [CimR] (109) O 94, p. 77-78.

PERSHIK, Simon
See PERCHIK, Simon

4854. PERSINGER, Allan
"Apricot Preserves." [ChironR] (13:3) Aut 94, p. 30.

4855. PERSUN, Terry (Terry L.)
"Flickering." [ChironR] (13:4) Wint 94, p. 30.
"In the Midwest." [Parting] (7:1) Sum 94, p. 69.
"Learning to Drink." [HiramPoR] (55/56) Fall 93-Sum 94, p. 93.
"Prayer." [Parting] (7:2) Wint 94-95, p. 19.
"The Quiet." [ContextS] (4:1) 94, p. 37.

4856. PESEROFF, Joyce
"To Miss the Mark" (Literal translation of "sin" from the Hebrew). [Agni] (40) 94, p. 166-170.

4857. PESTANA, Emily
"The Bible Coloring Book." [HawaiiR] (18:1, #40) Spr 94, p. 95.

4858. PETERNEL, Joan
"The Birthday." [Luz] (6) My 94, p. 34.
"El Cumpleaños" (tr. by Joyce Mc. Gregor del Castillo). [Luz] (6) My 94, p. 35.
"La Familia" (tr. by Joyce Mc. Gregor del Castillo). [Luz] (6) My 94, p. 37.
"The Family." [Luz] (6) My 94, p. 36.
"¿Propulsion o Traccion?" (tr. by Joyce Mc. Gregor del Castillo). [Luz] (6) My 94, p. 39.
"Propulsion or Traction?" [Luz] (6) My 94, p. 38.
"Us and Our Shadows." [Amelia] (7:4, #23) 94, p. 160.

4859. PETERS, Erskine
"Blues Cycle." [Obs] (9:1) Spr-Sum 94, p. 99-102.

4860. PETERS, Robert
"Blemish." [Pearl] (20) Spr 94, p. 72.

4861. PETERSEN, Inez
"What Grandmother Said." [KenR] (NS 16:2) Spr 94, p. 23-26.

4862. PETERSEN, Paulann
"Admission." [WeberS] (11:3) Fall 94, p. 47.
"Lullaby." [Poetry] (164:5) Ag 94, p. 273.
"This Owl Is a Song for the Hunter." [WeberS] (11:3) Fall 94, p. 48.
"When I Walk." [Poetry] (164:5) Ag 94, p. 274-275.
"Yes, Walt Whitman." [WeberS] (11:3) Fall 94, p. 46-47.

4863. PETERSON, Allan
"At Four." [Ascent] (19:1) Fall 94, p. 76.
"Civil War." [SouthernHR] (28:1) Wint 94, p. 14.
"Famous Canaries." [AnotherCM] (27) 94, p. 169-170.
"Jittery Leaves." [Ascent] (18:2) Wint 94, p. 9.
"Lost." [Ascent] (18:2) Wint 94, p. 9.
"Making Things Worse." [Agni] (40) 94, p. 137.
"Odd Moment at Grand Tower." [Ascent] (19:1) Fall 94, p. 77.
"Patience." [MidwQ] (36:1) Aut 94, p. 68.
"Poemissimo." [Agni] (40) 94, p. 135-136.
"Rapture." [AnotherCM] (27) 94, p. 171.
"A Short Bio." [IndR] (17:2) Fall 94, p. 49.
"Talk Talk Talk." [AmerLC] (6) 94, p. 54.
"Those Tattooed." [NewDeltaR] (11:2) Spr-Sum 94, p. 40.
"White Man's Lies." [PennR] (6:1) 94, p. 38.

4864. PETERSON, Eugene H.
"The Psalms: A New Translation" (14, 51, 58, 88, 90, 131, 139). [Image] (5) Spr 94, p. 21-28.

4865. PETERSON, Jim
"The Men." [LaurelR] (28:2) Sum 94, p. 27-30.
"Remission." [LaurelR] (28:2) Sum 94, p. 24-26.

4866. PETERSON, Lorinda
"How to See in the Dark." [Quarry] (43:2) S 94, p. 91-92.

4867. PETIC, Zorika
"Horses in a Summer Pasture." [TarRP] (34:1) Fall 94, p. 30.

4868. PETOSKEY, Barbara J.
"Birth of the Blues." [Confr] (54/55) Fall 94-Wint 95, p. 320.

4869. PETREMAN, David A.
"Bernabé." [AntigR] (99) Aut 94, p. 79.
"The Evening Toast." [TampaR] (8) Spr 94, p. 41.
"Trauco." [TampaR] (8) Spr 94, p. 42-43.
4870. PETRI, György
"Daydream" (tr. by Bruce Berlind, w. Mária Körösy). [AmerPoR] (23:1) Ja-F 94, p. 34.
"The Drawbacks of Redemption" (tr. by Bruce Berlind and Mária Körösy). [SenR] (24:2) Fall 94, p. 57.
"Elegy" (tr. by Bruce Berlind, w. Mária Körösy). [AmerPoR] (23:1) Ja-F 94, p. 32.
"From the Insomnia Songs" (In memory of Arnold Schönberg, tr. by Bruce Berlind, w. Mária Körösy). [AmerPoR] (23:1) Ja-F 94, p. 33.
"Horace Has a Bad Day" (tr. by Bruce Berland and Mária Körösy). [Poetry] (164:2) My 94, p. 85.
"I Like" (tr. by Bruce Berlind, w. Mária Körösy). [Chelsea] (56) 94, p. 113.
"Night Song of the Personal Spook" (tr. by Bruce Berlind, w. Mária Körösy). [AmerPoR] (23:1) Ja-F 94, p. 33.
"The Onion Speaks" (tr. by Bruce Berlind, w. Mária Körösy). [Chelsea] (56) 94, p. 111.
"Our Relationship begins to be Intimate" (tr. by Bruce Berlind, w. Mária Körösy). [AmerPoR] (23:1) Ja-F 94, p. 32.
"Self-Portrait 1990" (tr. by Bruce Berlind, w. Mária Körösy). [Chelsea] (56) 94, p. 112.
"To A." (tr. by Bruce Berlind, w. Mária Körösy). [AmerPoR] (23:1) Ja-F 94, p. 33.
"With a Consignment of Poems" (tr. by Bruce Berlind, w. Mária Körösy). [Chelsea] (56) 94, p. 112.
4871. PETRIE, Mark
"Summer Salsa." [Pearl] (20) Spr 94, p. 56.
4872. PETROSKY, Anthony
"The Unpredictability of Comfort and Tradition." [ColEng] (56:1) Ja 94, p. 67-68.
PETROV, David Shrayer
See SHRAYER-PETROV, David
4873. PFAU, Thomas
"A Certain Uncertainty." [DenQ] (28:4) Spr 94, p. 53.
"The End of the Private Self." [ParisR] (36:133) Wint 94, p. 291.
"Rest Area." [ParisR] (36:133) Wint 94, p. 293.
"Suburban Exquisites." [ParisR] (36:133) Wint 94, p. 292.
4874. PFEIFER, Michael
"Among the Stars." [WebR] (18) Fall 94, p. 89.
"The Argument." [LaurelR] (28:1) Wint 94, p. 78.
4875. PFEIFER, Teresa M.
"And She Does." [FreeL] (13) Spr 94, p. 15.
4876. PFINGSTON, Roger
"Housing in the Okefenokee." [ArtfulD] (26/27) 94, p. 89.
4877. PHILIP, Marlene Nourbese
"Crossed Stitch." [RiverC] (14:2) Spr 94, p. 72-73.
"A Good Neighbour." [RiverC] (14:2) Spr 94, p. 69-71.
4878. PHILIPS, Elizabeth
"Leaving the Air." [Arc] (32) Spr 94, p. 34.
"On the Road to Redberry Lake." [Arc] (32) Spr 94, p. 35-36.
4879. PHILLIPS, Adam
"The Given." [Raritan] (13:4) Spr 94, p. 15.
"Looser." [Raritan] (13:4) Spr 94, p. 16.
"Quid Pro Quo." [Raritan] (13:4) Spr 94, p. 16.
"Rites of Spring." [Raritan] (13:4) Spr 94, p. 15.
4880. PHILLIPS, Carl
"Aubade for Eve Under the Arbor." [Witness] (8:1) 94, p. 87.
"The Captain, Back by Popular Demand, Decides Against a World Tour." [WebR] (18) Fall 94, p. 100.
"Cortège." [Agni] (40) 94, p. 179-184.
"Cotillion." [KenR] (NS 16:3) Sum 94, p. 73-74.
"Dream for Pilate." [KenR] (NS 16:3) Sum 94, p. 72-73.
"Glads." [KenR] (NS 16:3) Sum 94, p. 71-72.
"Hermaphrodite." [Chelsea] (56) 94, p. 50-51.
"I See a Man." [Witness] (8:1) 94, p. 86.
"Kit." [WebR] (18) Fall 94, p. 101.

"One Sees Pictures of Dante." [WebR] (18) Fall 94, p. 97.
"Our Lady." [KenR] (NS 16:3) Sum 94, p. 74-75.
"Pygmalion." [WebR] (18) Fall 94, p. 96-97.
"Seminar: Problems in Renaissance Painting." [Chelsea] (56) 94, p. 49.
"Teaching Ovid to Sixth-Graders." [Chelsea] (56) 94, p. 51-52.
"Two Versions of the Very Same Story" (After Borges). [HarvardR] (7) Fall 94, p. 50.
"Your Dream" (a reinterpretation for Doug). [WebR] (18) Fall 94, p. 98-99.

4881. PHILLIPS, Louis
"Avernus Shoe Co." [SouthernPR] (34:1) Sum 94, p. 55.
"Baron Von Hügel." [Light] (9) Spr 94, p. 11.
"John Keats Returns to Earth & Looks at Television." [EngJ] (83:8) D 94, p. 22.
"The Krazy Kat Rag" (Selection: 22). [Light] (9) Spr 94, p. 21.
"The Krazy Kat Rag" (Selection: 23). [Light] (10) Sum 94, p. 23.
"The Krazy Kat Rag" (Selection: 24). [Light] (11) Aut 94, p. 23.
"The Krazy Kat Rag" (3 selections: 25-26, 26 — two selections numbered 26). [Light] (12) Wint 94-95, p. 23.
"Music Brings on This Feeling More Than Once." [Confr] (54/55) Fall 94-Wint 95, p. 321.

4882. PHILLIPS, Robert
"Breakdown Lane." [OntR] (40) Spr-Sum 94, p. 106-107.
"Drive Friendly" (Texas Interstate Road Sign). [Border] (4) Spr-Sum 94, p. 56-57.
"Easy Street" (For Billy Collins). [IllinoisR] (1:2) Spr 94, p. 54-55.
"Elegy for an Art Critic" (John I. H. Baur, 1909-1987). [Border] (3) Fall 93, p. 55-57.
"Flower Fires" (To the memory of Muriel Rukeyser, 1913-1980). [Border] (3) Fall 93, p. 52-53.
"Recovery." [TriQ] (91) Fall 94, p. 227-228.

4883. PHILLIPS, Walt
"Cyrus the Movie Man." [Amelia] (7:4, #23) 94, p. 180.
"Glory." [Amelia] (7:4, #23) 94, p. 180.
"Long Ago." [Amelia] (7:4, #23) 94, p. 180.
"Notation." [BlackBR] (18) Wint-Spr 94, p. 28.
"Status." [BlackBR] (18) Wint-Spr 94, p. 28.

4884. PHILLIS, Randy
"Sleeping on My Side." [HiramPoR] (55/56) Fall 93-Sum 94, p. 94-95.

4885. PHILP, Geoffrey
"Una Carta para Andrew." [InterQ] (1:4) 94, p. 95.
"The Garden." [CaribbeanW] (8) 94, p. 39.

4886. PHILPOT, Tracy
"A Bad Marriage." [IndR] (17:1) Spr 94, p. 155-156.
"Illegitimacy." [IndR] (17:1) Spr 94, p. 157-159.
"(Language Apes) in a Forest without Narrative." [DenQ] (28:4) Spr 94, p. 54-55.

4887. PHIPPS, Marilene
"Auxilia." [InterQ] (1:4) 94, p. 76.
"Dieudonne." [InterQ] (1:4) 94, p. 77.
"Gaetan." [InterQ] (1:4) 94, p. 78.
"Haitian Masks." [InterQ] (1:4) 94, p. 74-75.

4888. PHIPPS, Wanda
"Rose Window (or Prosettes)" (2 excerpts). [Agni] (39) 94, p. 170-171.

4889. PICARD, Jane Whittington
"Bull" (First Sue Saniel Elkind National Poetry Award, Finalist). [Kalliope] (16:2) 94, p. 35-36.

4890. PICARD, Meredith
"Morning Coffee." [HampSPR] Wint 94, p. 10.

4891. PICHÉ, Alphonse
"Brumes." [InterPR] (20:2) Fall 94, p. 70.
"Chant Marin." [InterPR] (20:2) Fall 94, p. 68.
"Childhood" (tr. by Judith Cowan). [InterPR] (20:2) Fall 94, p. 67.
"Enfances." [InterPR] (20:2) Fall 94, p. 66.
"Fog" (tr. by Gary Wilson). [InterPR] (20:2) Fall 94, p. 71.
"Remous." [InterPR] (20:2) Fall 94, p. 70.
"Sailor Song" (tr. by Judith Cowan). [InterPR] (20:2) Fall 94, p. 69.
"Whirlpool" (tr. by Gary Wilson). [InterPR] (20:2) Fall 94, p. 71.

4892. PICKARD, Deanna
"Another Self." [NewEngR] (16:4) Fall 94, p. 113.

"Ke Ke's Brother in Pegged Jeans." [AntR] (52:4) Fall 94, p. 603.
"Lilacs with One Poppy." [NewEngR] (16:4) Fall 94, p. 114.

4893. PICKRELL, Lee Ann
"On Nights When I Can't Sleep." [SantaBR] (1:2) Fall-Wint 93, p. 11.
"The T.G.&Y." [SantaBR] (2:1) Spr-Sum 94, p. 97.

4894. PIEDRA, Ramblazo
"Conversación con Mi Alter Ego." [Nuez] (5:13/14/15) 94, p. 71.

4895. PIEPMEIER, Alison
"After Her Brother Died." [Rosebud] (1:3) Aut-Wint 94, p. 110.

4896. PIERCE, Edith Lovejoy
"Fifty Years Later." [ChrC] (111:26) 21-28 S 94, p. 846.
"The Fruit." [ChrC] (111:8) 9 Mr 94, p. 256.

4897. PIERCY, Marge
"The Altneushul in the Old Prague Ghetto." [Vis] (44) 94, p. 34.
"Death of a Doe on Chequesset Neck." [HeavenB] (11) 94, p. 86.
"I Am Not a House." [NegC] (14:1/2) 94, p. 7.
"The Music Wars." [Vis] (45) 94, p. 14.
"October Sizzles." [HeavenB] (11) 94, p. 4.
"The Retreat." [HeavenB] (11) 94, p. 3.
"The White Stasis." [NegC] (14:1/2) 94, p. 6.

4898. PIERMAN, Carol J.
"The Apparition." [ChiR] (40:2/3) 94, p. 121-122.
"Museum of Human Response." [BlackWR] (21:1) Fall-Wint 94, p. 88-89.

PIERO, W. S. di
See Di PIERO, W. S.

4899. PIERPOINT, Katherine
"Sleeper." [NewYorker] (70:27) 5 S 94, p. 96.

4900. PIGGFORD, George
"Good Friday 1988" (To John). [EvergreenC] (9:2) Sum-Fall 94, p. 57-58.

4901. PIHEL, Eric
"Chase." [HampSPR] Wint 94, p. 17.
"Letter to Mario Cuomo on Why I Spray-Painted Some of My Poems on a NY Thruway Bridge." [HampSPR] Wint 94, p. 18.

4902. PIKE, Lawrence
"On Healing." [Light] (11) Aut 94, p. 18.

4903. PILIBOSIAN, Helene
"Sharp Edges Curved." [HampSPR] Wint 94, p. 14.
"The Triangular Era." [HawaiiR] (18:1, #40) Spr 94, p. 98-99.
"Weaning the Moon." [CapeR] (29:1) Spr 94, p. 36.

4904. PILINSZKY, János
"Ravensbrück Passion" (from "Metropolitan Icons," tr. by Emery George). [AmerPoR] (23:6) N-D 94, p. 22.
"Under a Winter Sky" (For Tamás Cholnoky, tr. by Emery George). [DenQ] (29:1) Sum 94, p. 96.

4905. PILKINTON, Mary Lou
"Mr. Small Isn't Here." [Border] (4) Spr-Sum 94, p. 58.
"Ride 'em Cowboy." [Border] (4) Spr-Sum 94, p. 59.

4906. PILZER, Fred K.
"A certain young Pilgrim named Fox" (Honorable Mention, The A & C Limericks Awards). [Amelia] (7:4, #23) 94, p. 21.

4907. PINCKNEY, Diana
"Falling for Fantasy." [Light] (11) Aut 94, p. 20.
"Strangers Who Sit." [Pembroke] (26) 94, p. 125.

4908. PINES, Paul
"The Cry of Merlin" (Selections: 3 poems). [GlobalCR] (4) Fall 94, p. 3-5.

4909. PING, Wang
"Born in the Year of Chicken." [Talisman] (12) Spr 94, p. 170-172.
"Fish" (tr. of Yu Jian, w. Ron Padgett). [Talisman] (12) Spr 94, p. 160-161.
"A Flash of Thought from the River." [ChiR] (40:1) 94, p. 120.
"The Gleaner" (Van Gogh, *Peasant Woman Stooping*, 1885, tr. of Xue Di, w. Keith Waldrop). [Manoa] (6:1) Sum 94, p. 84-85.
"Interplay" (tr. of Xue Di, w. Keith Waldrop). [Manoa] (6:1) Sum 94, p. 84.
"Manfly's Journal" (tr. of Liu Manliu, w. David Shapiro). [Talisman] (12) Spr 94, p. 164-166.

PING-KWAN, Leung
See LEUNG, Ping-kwan

4910. PINK, David
"Deer Stand." [SoDakR] (32:3) Fall 94, p. 49.
"Window Box Garden." [SoDakR] (32:3) Fall 94, p. 50.
PIÑON, Evangelina Vigil
See VIGIL-PIÑON, Evangelina
4911. PINSKER, Sanford
"Fair Youth Beneath the Spanish Steps." [CentR] (38:2) Spr 94, p. 322.
"People Much Married." [CentR] (38:3) Fall 94, p. 510.
"Surprised by Summer, I Weep." [CentR] (38:3) Fall 94, p. 511.
4912. PINSKY, Robert
"Body" (tr. of Boris Christov). [PartR] (61:1) Wint 94, p. 159.
"Canto XXI — The Inferno of Dante Algierhi" (tr. of Dante Algierhi). [Colum] (21) Fall 93, p. 7-13.
"Creation According to Ovid." [NewRep] (210:11) 14 Mr 94, p. 44.
"Dante, Inferno XXVI: Ulysses" (tr. of Dante). [HarvardR] (6) Spr 94, p. 137-140.
"Dante's *Inferno*, Canto XVIII: Among the Pimps and Seducers" (tr. of Dante). [Verse] (11:1) Spr 94, p. 59-62.
"Dante's *Inferno*, Canto XXV: Among the Thieves" (tr. of Dante). [Raritan] (14:1) Sum 94, p. 18-25.
"Dante's *Inferno*, Canto XXXI: The Giants" (tr. of Dante). [QW] (39) Sum-Fall 94, p. 150-157.
"Dante's *Inferno*, Canto XXXIV (The Final Canto)." [Agni] (39) 94, p. 242-246.
"The Day Dreamers." [NewYorker] (70:18) 20 Je 94, p. 58.
"If You Could Write One Great Poem, What Would You Want It to Be About?" (Asked of 4 student poets at the Illinois Schools for the Deaf and Visually Impaired). [NewRep] (210:16) 18 Ap 94, p. 47.
"Incantation" (tr. of Czeslaw Milosz, w. the author). [GrahamHR] (18) Wint 94-95, p. 106.
"Incantation" (tr. of Czeslaw Milosz, w. the author). [TriQ] (92) Wint 94-95, p. 21-22.
"Inferno, Canto II: The Beginning of the Journey" (tr. of Dante). [AmerPoR] (23:4) Jl-Ag 94, p. 36-37.
"Newcomer." [Salm] (104/105) Fall 94-Wint 95, p. 157.
"Poem with Refrains." [Antaeus] (75/76) Aut 94, p. 313-315.
"Spirit" (tr. of Boris Christov). [PartR] (61:1) Wint 94, p. 158.
4913. PINSON, Douglas
"The Iconoclast Begs the Question." [Pembroke] (26) 94, p. 140-141.
4914. PINSON, Jean-Claude
"Eel Season" (tr. by Robert Hackett). [ConnPR] (13:1) 94, p. 18-19.
4915. PIOMBINO, Nick
"The Disappearance." [Avec] (8:1) 94, p. 126.
"Fantasy." [Avec] (8:1) 94, p. 121-122.
"Indeterminate Rhapsody." [Avec] (8:1) 94, p. 123-125.
"A Poet's Apology" (for Cydney). [Avec] (8:1) 94, p. 116-117.
"Seven Plus Four." [Avec] (8:1) 94, p. 119-120.
"Variations on a Theme of Stevens." [Avec] (8:1) 94, p. 118.
4916. PISCAL, Michael D.
"In My Word, a Constellation." [ChironR] (13:3) Aut 94, p. 16.
4917. PITA, Juana Rosa
"Sips of Light" (11 selections, tr. by Mario Salvatierra, w. the author). [Luz] (7) N 94, p. 11-15.
"Sorbos de Luz" (11 selections). [Luz] (7) N 94, p. 10-14.
4918. PITKIN, Joe
"Prelude to a Shout That Wakes the Apartment Building." [WritersF] (20) 94, p. 190.
4919. PITT-KETHLEY, Fiona
"Lying." [Jacaranda] (5:1) Wint-Spr 91, p. 44-45.
4920. PITTMAN-SCHULZ, Kimberly
"Gourd." [PaintedHR] (11) Spr-Sum 94, p. 54.
4921. PIXLEY, Jennifer Craig
"Love Song." [BelPoJ] (45:1) Fall 94, p. 15.
"Site Specific." [BelPoJ] (45:1) Fall 94, p. 14.
"A Tendency Toward Order." [BelPoJ] (45:1) Fall 94, p. 12-13.
4922. PIZARRO, Michele
"Saturn Sequence" (Selection: 1 — "Her Worries"). [Jacaranda] (5:1) Wint-Spr 91, p. 4.

4923. PLANTOS, Ted
"Iguana Soup" (Ruinas El Rey — Cancun, Mexico, 1990). [CanLit] (142/143) Fall-Wint 94, p. 49.
4924. PLASTIRA, Alexándra
"Ascent" (tr. by Yannis Goumas). [Os] (38) Spr 94, p. 12.
"Endowment" (tr. by Yannis Goumas). [Os] (38) Spr 94, p. 13.
"The Lord's Day" (tr. by Yannis Goumas). [Os] (38) Spr 94, p. 11.
4925. PLATH, James
"Courbet, on the Rocks." [ApalQ] (40/41) 94, p. 95.
4926. PLATH, Sylvia
"Balloons." [AmerPoR] (23:2) Mr-Ap 94, p. 30.
4927. PLATT, Donald
"Keys to No Doors." [NewEngR] (16:4) Fall 94, p. 88-90.
4928. PLEASANT, Sina-Aurelia
"My Things." [SantaBR] (1:2) Fall-Wint 93, p. 97.
PLESSIS, Rachel Blau du
See DuPLESSIS, Rachel Blau
4929. PLEVIN-FOUST, Mimi
"Good-bye, Raul." [Poz] (1:4) O-N 94, p. 25.
PLUMB, Andy
See SHELPHARD, Selena Anna / Andy Plumb
4930. PLUMLY, Stanley
"Panegyric for Gee." [Antaeus] (75/76) Aut 94, p. 316-317.
"A Passage for the Poet, Citizen, Inventor, William Drummond, 1585-1649 ..." [PlumR] (7) [94?], p. 12.
4931. PLUMMER, Pamela
"Lush Life" (listening to the World Saxophone Quartet). [Eyeball] (3) 93, p. 46.
4932. PLUMPP, Sterling D.
"Ordinariness Birthed" (for Shirley Turner). [Epoch] (43:3) 94, p. 304-307.
PO, Li
See LI, Po
4933. POBO, Kenneth
"Bad Hair Day." [Poem] (71) My 94, p. 22-23.
"Closet Boy." [Outbr] (25) 94, p. 65.
"Dream of Hands." [AntigR] (97) Spr 94, p. 9-10.
"Fork, Spoon and Knife." [AntigR] (97) Spr 94, p. 11.
"Jennifer Bakes a Potato." [WestB] (35) 94, p. 7.
"Jennifer's Dream Garden." [Poem] (71) My 94, p. 24.
"Leather Sky." [OgalalaR] (5:1) Wint 94, p. 45.
"Mary Alice Visits Jennifer." [Poem] (71) My 94, p. 20-21.
"Young Redon at Peyrelebade." [Outbr] (25) 94, p. 64.
4934. POCH, John E.
"America." [NewDeltaR] (10:1) Fall 92-Wint 93, p. 44-45.
POL, Miquel Marti i
See MARTI i POL, Miquel
4935. POLINER, Elizabeth
"October." [SmPd] (31:2, #91) Spr 94, p. 31.
"Penelope's Choice." [Poem] (71) My 94, p. 51.
"Phobia." [Poem] (71) My 94, p. 50.
4936. POLIZZI, Allessandria
"American Dreaming." [ContextS] (4:1) 94, p. 27.
4937. POLLACK, Carrie
"Ode to a Balding Medieval Saint." [HiramPoR] (55/56) Fall 93-Sum 94, p. 96-97.
4938. POLLENTIER, Nicole
"Origami Rabbits and Secret Suns." [HangL] (64) 94, p. 87.
4939. POLLOCK, Philip James
"The Christmas Flood." [WestHR] (48:3) Fall 94, p. 300-302.
4940. POMALES, Luis
"Babel." [Americas] (22:1/2) Spr-Sum 94, p. 89.
"Grandma's Notions about Life." [Americas] (22:1/2) Spr-Sum 94, p. 87-88.
"New-Port." [Americas] (22:1/2) Spr-Sum 94, p. 90.
4941. POND, Judith
"In Paradisum" (Die Unerträgliche Leictigkeit des Seins). [MalR] (106) Spr 94, p. 35.
4942. PONGE, Francis
"The Cycle of Seasons" (tr. by C. K. Williams). [AmerPoR] (23:4) Jl-Ag 94, p. 30.

"The Horse" (tr. by John Montague). [AmerPoR] (23:4) Jl-Ag 94, p. 32-33.
"Notes Towards a Shellfish" (tr. by C. K. Williams). [AmerPoR] (23:1) Ja-F 94, p. 48.
"The Nuptial Habits of Dogs" (tr. by John Montague). [AmerPoR] (23:4) Jl-Ag 94, p. 32.
"The Shrimp" (tr. by C. K. Williams). [AmerPoR] (23:4) Jl-Ag 94, p. 31-32.
"Snails" (tr. by C. K. Williams). [AmerPoR] (23:4) Jl-Ag 94, p. 30-31.

4943. PONSOT, Marie
"Evening the Ark." [ParisR] (36:133) Wint 94, p. 168.
"For My Old Self, at Notre-Dame de Paris: *fluctuat nec mergitur*." [ParisR] (36:133) Wint 94, p. 167-168.
"Old Mama Saturday." [WestHR] (48:1) Spr 94, p. 93.

4944. POOL, Michael
"The Lonesome Portable Detail." [TampaR] (9) Fall 94, p. 53.

4945. POOLE, Francis
"Cantaloupes." [PoetryE] (37/38) Spr 94, p. 77.
"A Spring Morning in Santa Ana." [PoetryE] (37/38) Spr 94, p. 76.

4946. POOLE, Joan Lauri
"Sister." [LitR] (37:4) Sum 94, p. 685.

4947. POORTSTRA, Margryt
"As a Rule" (tr. by Fridsma Bernard Sr.). [Vis] (46) 94, p. 10.

4948. POPA, Vasko
"Big city Poem" (tr. by Charles Simic). [HarvardR] (Premier Issue) Spr 92, p. 47.

4949. POPE, Deborah
"As the Children's Carpool Departs." [TarRP] (34:1) Fall 94, p. 25.
"Biopsy." [GeoR] (48:1) Spr 94, p. 105.
"Boy Blowing Bubbles." [Shen] (44:3) Fall 94, p. 91.
"Circle of Night." [SouthernR] (30:1) Ja, Wint 94, p. 100-101.
"In the Night of the Heart." [LaurelR] (28:2) Sum 94, p. 46-47.
"In the Parking Lot of the County Regional Hospital." [Thrpny] (57) Spr 94, p. 20.
"In the Poetry Workshop." [PoetryNW] (35:2) Sum 94, p. 27-28.
"Mammogram." [SouthernPR] (34:2) Wint 94, p. 22-23.
"Once in Your Rooms." [TarRP] (34:1) Fall 94, p. 26-27.
"Sunrise, Interchange, Ithaca." [Shen] (44:3) Fall 94, p. 92.
"Turning Point." [SouthernR] (30:1) Ja, Wint 94, p. 99-100.
"The Woman Question" (after Friesecke's "The Garden Parasol," 1907). [PoetryNW] (35:2) Sum 94, p. 26-27.

4950. POPE, Deidre
"Temporary Separation." [NowestR] (32:1) 94, p. 113-114.
"What the Garden Grows" (First Sue Saniel Elkind National Poetry Award, Finalist). [Kalliope] (16:2) 94, p. 37-38.

4951. POPOVA, Olga
"Among Black Trees" (tr. by J. Kates). [CrabCR] (8:2/3/9:1/2/3) 94, p. 46.

4952. POPOVA-WIGHTMAN, Ludmilla
"Poem about the Poet's Stockyard" (tr. of Konstantin Pavlov). [Vis] (46) 94, p. 34-35.
"The Satirist" (tr. of Konstantin Pavlov). [Vis] (46) 94, p. 35.
"Why Adam Fell" (tr. of Konstantin Pavlov). [Vis] (45) 94, p. 43.

4953. PORTER, Anne
"A Carol." [Comm] (121:22) 16 D 94, p. 13.
"A Fragment." [Comm] (121:19) 4 N 94, p. 15.
"The Icon." [Comm] (121:22) 16 D 94, p. 13.
"In Another World." [Comm] (121:20) 18 N 94, p. 14.
"A Morning Dream." [Comm] (121:19) 4 N 94, p. 15.
"Old in the City." [Comm] (121:19) 4 N 94, p. 15.

4954. PORTER, Pamela Rice
"Emaline." [Vis] (44) 94, p. 25-27.
"Perpetuity." [Border] (3) Fall 93, p. 58-59.

4955. PORTER, William
"A Sort of Diary From the Black River." [SycamoreR] (6:2) Sum 94, p. 35-36.

4956. PORTERFIELD, Susan
"Metaphysics." [IllinoisR] (1:2) Spr 94, p. 28.

4957. PORTUGAL, Anne
"The Exhibition" (tr. by Norma Cole). [Chelsea] (57) 94, p. 62-64.

4958. POST, Robert
"Don't Ask." [WindO] (58) Sum 94, p. 31.

"Waiting for D-Day." [WindO] (58) Sum 94, p. 30.
4959. POSTER, Carol
"The Amazon" (tr. of Joyce Mansour). [PoetryE] (37/38) Spr 94, p. 230.
"Falling on Earth" (tr. of Andre-ferdinand Herold). [PoetryE] (37/38) Spr 94, p. 233.
"I Dream" (tr. of Albert Samain). [PoetryE] (37/38) Spr 94, p. 226.
4960. POSWIATOWSKA, Halina
"Overheard" (tr. by Maya Peretz). [WebR] (18) Fall 94, p. 13.
4961. POTOK, Rena
"Absalom" (tr. of Anton Shammas). [InterQ] (1:3) 94, p. 159.
"You Sit" (tr. of Anton Shammas). [InterQ] (1:3) 94, p. 160.
4962. POTOS, Andrea
"Depending on the Flight." [Calyx] (15:3) Wint 94-95, p. 55.
"A Faint Breath of Peach." [Kalliope] (16:1) 94, p. 15.
"The One Red-Haired Summer." [Calyx] (15:2) Sum 94, p. 5.
4963. POTTER, Carol
"Block Island Ferry." [Journal] (18:2) Fall-Wint 94, p. 17-18.
"Pumpkin Pie." [Journal] (18:2) Fall-Wint 94, p. 15-16.
"Salt-wind Off Truro." [Journal] (18:2) Fall-Wint 94, p. 14.
4964. POULAKOS, James
"What Birds Dream." [WeberS] (11:1) Wint 94, p. 68.
4965. POULIN, A., Jr.
"Day Has No Equal But Night" (tr. of Anne Hébert). [AmerPoR] (23:4) Jl-Ag 94, p. 10.
"The Executed" (tr. of Anne Hébert). [AmerPoR] (23:4) Jl-Ag 94, p. 10.
"The Old" (tr. of Anne Hébert). [AmerPoR] (23:4) Jl-Ag 94, p. 10.
"The Piano" (tr. of Anne Hébert). [AmerPoR] (23:4) Jl-Ag 94, p. 10.
4966. POUND, Ezra
"Fan Piece, for Her Imperial Lord." [AmerPoR] (23:2) Mr-Ap 94, p. 45.
"The River Merchant's Wife: A Letter" (tr. of Li Po). [NewYorkQ] (53) 94, p. 8.
4967. POUND, Omar
"Industry Needs You." [WorldL] (5) 94, p. 37.
"Vitriol and the Prison Visitor." [WorldL] (5) 94, p. 36.
4968. POUNDS, Wayne
"In Asia, in Blindness." [CharR] (20:1) Spr 94, p. 60.
4969. POVERNY, Rick
"Prospecting Topanga." [JlNJPo] (16:1) Spr 94, p. 14.
"Showing the Opals." [JlNJPo] (16:1) Spr 94, p. 15.
4970. POWELL, Dannye Romine
"Fairest of Them All." [CreamCR] (18:1) Spr 94, p. 12.
"My Father and Johnny" (Miami, February, 1950). [SouthernR] (30:1) Ja, Wint 94, p. 102-104.
4971. POWELL, Gregory
"Harlem." [Obs] (9:1) Spr-Sum 94, p. 104-105.
"Solo." [Obs] (9:1) Spr-Sum 94, p. 103-104.
4972. POWELL, Jonathan
"Excavation." [NegC] (13:2/3) 93, p. 46-47.
4973. POWELL, Joseph
"Pioneer Square: Spare Change." [Poetry] (165:2) N 94, p. 66.
4974. POWELL, Susan
"What Was Given." [NegC] (14:1/2) 94, p. 66-67.
4975. POWER, Marjorie
"The Chess Game." [ChrC] (111:1) 5-12 Ja 94, p. 14.
"The Night I Gave His Laugh Enough Room." [SouthernPR] (34:1) Sum 94, p. 17-18.
"Tishku Recognizes Me." [Jacaranda] (4:2) Spr 90, p. 111.
4976. POWER, S. Stanford
"Strength." [Parting] (7:2) Wint 94-95, p. 15.
4977. POWERS, Dan W.
"Lilith." [ApalQ] (40/41) 94, p. 78-79.
4978. POWERS, Richard L.
"Country Ham." [Pembroke] (26) 94, p. 149.
"Diagnostic Center." [LouisL] (11:1) Spr 94, p. 183.
"Flora Macdonald College, 12/7/41." [Pembroke] (26) 94, p. 148.
4979. POZIER, Bernard
"Career's Sunset" (tr. by Roch Smith). [InterPR] (20:2) Fall 94, p. 79.
"Fin de Carrière." [InterPR] (20:2) Fall 94, p. 78.

4980. PRAHLAD, Sw. Anand
"Hold-Up on Lime Cay." [CharR] (20:2) Fall 94, p. 107.
"Tuning, for Elsie." [CharR] (20:2) Fall 94, p. 108-109.
4981. PRAISNER, Wanda S.
"Quo Fata Ferunt" (island motto: "Whither the fates carry us"). [JlNJPo] (16:1) Spr 94, p. 16.
4982. PRATT, Charles W.
"Baudelaire" (from the French of Baudelaire). [Light] (11) Aut 94, p. 20.
"Firstborn." [Comm] (121:22) 16 D 94, p. 9.
"Homesteader in the Orchard." [PennR] (6:1) 94, p. 25.
"Stone Child in the Herb Garden." [LitR] (37:4) Sum 94, p. 602.
"Summer Music." [Light] (10) Sum 94, p. 7.
"A Taste of Country." [HiramPoR] (55/56) Fall 93-Sum 94, p. 98.
"Watching the Eclipse from the Bedroom Window." [Light] (10) Sum 94, p. 16.
"When in Dublin." [Light] (11) Aut 94, p. 24.
"Wolsey's Hole." [BelPoJ] (45:2) Wint 94-95, p. 34.
4983. PRATT, Priscilla E.
"Letter to the Editor." [Light] (11) Aut 94, p. 30.
"Storm in August." [Light] (10) Sum 94, p. 7.
4984. PRAXILLA of Sicyon (mid-5th c. B.C.)
"First among the lovely things I leave" (tr. by John J. Brugaletta). [SoCoast] (16) Ja 94, p. 57.
4985. PREFONTAINE, Jay R.
"After Death." [BellR] (17:1/2) Spr-Fall 94, p. 26.
"The Bird Man." [WritersF] (20) 94, p. 121.
"Crazy Without Her." [BellR] (17:1/2) Spr-Fall 94, p. 27.
"Keeper of the Flightless Birds." [BellR] (17:1/2) Spr-Fall 94, p. 28-29.
4986. PRESNELL, Barbara
"His Pearl." [Kalliope] (16:1) 94, p. 26-27.
"June Bride." [NewDeltaR] (10:2) Spr-Sum 93, p. 65-66.
4987. PRESTI, Michael
"Everette Maddox in Heaven." [NewOR] (20:1/2) Spr-Sum 94, p. 141-144.
"Seven Accidents" (3 selections). [NewOR] (20:1/2) Spr-Sum 94, p. 138-140.
4988. PREVALLET, Kristin
"Electric, ignite the surface" (to Elizabeth Willis). [Chain] (1) Spr-Sum 94, p. 226-228.
4989. PRÉVERT, Jacques
"Right to Watch" (tr. by Connie Sanderson). [PoetryE] (37/38) Spr 94, p. 229.
PREZ, Eleanor des
See DesPREZ, Eleanor
4990. PRICE, Caroline
"Double Act." [Stand] (35:2) Spr 94, p. 28-29.
4991. PRICE, Katie
"Gaze (Otherwise the Curved Breast Could Not Dazzle You So)." [CreamCR] (18:1) Spr 94, p. 34.
4992. PRICE, Lynette
"Music in Me" (In honor of the Caribana). [Eyeball] (3) 93, p. 17.
4993. PRICE, Matthew
"Doubt." [Verse] (11:2) Sum 94, p. 87-88.
4994. PRICE, Ron
"Persimmon." [Pivot] (42) 94, p. 50.
"The Sea-Cave" (after Seferis). [Pivot] (42) 94, p. 49-50.
4995. PRIGOV, Dmitrii Aleksandrovich
"15 Wise Exhortations" (tr. by Nancy Condee and Vladimir Padunov). [MinnR] (41/42) Fall 93-Spr 94 (published Mr 95), p. 11-12.
"Telegrams" (tr. by Nancy Condee and Vladimir Padunov). [MinnR] (41/42) Fall 93-Spr 94 (published Mr 95), p. 12-14.
"The Weather on the Planet" (tr. by Nancy Condee and Vladimir Padunov). [MinnR] (41/42) Fall 93-Spr 94 (published Mr 95), p. 14-15.
PRIMA, Diane di
See Di PRIMA, Diane
4996. PRINTZ-PAHLSON, G. (Goran)
"Mozart Variations #9" (tr. of Goran Sonnevi, w. John Matthais). [Vis] (45) 94, p. 13.
"Mozart Variations #15" (tr. of Goran Sonnevi, w. John Matthais).). [Vis] (46) 94, p. 11.

PRISCO, Joseph di
See Di PRISCO, Joseph
4997. PRISK, David
"Ars Poetica." [HayF] (15) Fall-Wint 94, p. 60.
4998. PRITCHARD, Selwyn
"Dear Kate, Kind Daughter." [Descant] (25:1, #84) Spr 94, p. 46.
"Dear Kate, Kind Daughter." [PartR] (61:2) Spr 94, p. 324.
"Ganeesh at Night." [Descant] (25:1, #84) Spr 94, p. 45.
"How Sweetly Birds Sing on Sunday." [Descant] (25:1, #84) Spr 94, p. 47.
"In Aubrey's Place." [KenR] (NS 16:4) Fall 94, p. 63-65.
"Last Word." [KenR] (NS 16:4) Fall 94, p. 63.
"Video" (For Stan Smith). [Descant] (25:1, #84) Spr 94, p. 48-50.
4999. PRITIKIN, Renny
"For a Kid." [Zyzzyva] (10:1) Spr 94, p. 59.
5000. PROPER, Stan
"Bella." [Amelia] (7:3, #22) 94, p. 138.
5001. PROULX, Suzanne
"Underwater." [Wind] (74) 94, p. 26-27.
5002. PRUITT, William
"Laughter." [Blueline] (15) 94, p. 62.
5003. PRYOR, Josh
"Fishing in L.A." [ChironR] (13:2) Sum 94, p. 19.
5004. PRYPUTNIEWICZ, Tania
"The Chanter's Daughter" (First Sue Saniel Elkind National Poetry Award, Finalist). [Kalliope] (16:2) 94, p. 39-40.
5005. PSURTSEV, Dmitry
"Untitled: It's time to change the record" (tr. of Sergey Gandlevsky, w. Philip Metres). [ArtfulD] (26/27) 94, p. 15.
"Untitled: Oh, how the lilacs are this May!" (tr. of Sergey Gandlevsky, w. Philip Metres). [ArtfulD] (26/27) 94, p. 14.
"Untitled: To land a job at the garage" (tr. of Sergey Gandlevsky, w. Philip Metres). [ArtfulD] (26/27) 94, p. 13.
5006. PULLEY, Nancy
"Dove Song." [SycamoreR] (6:2) Sum 94, p. 47-48.
5007. PULTZ, Constance
"The Biggest Mall in the World." [ContextS] (4:1) 94, p. 12.
"Cross-Dressing." [ContextS] (4:1) 94, p. 26.
"The Real Thing." [ContextS] (4:1) 94, p. 42-43.
5008. PURCELL, J. Q.
"The Village Alchemist (1620)." [CarolQ] (46:3) Sum 94, p. 44-45.
5009. PURDY, Al
"Earle Birney in Hospital." [Quarry] (43:2) S 94, p. 18-19.
"Pound." [Quarry] (43:2) S 94, p. 20-21.
"A Sorrow for Tom." [Quarry] (43:2) S 94, p. 26-28.
"To —." [Quarry] (43:3) n 94, p. 34.
"Wandering Through Troy." [Quarry] (43:2) S 94, p. 24-25.
"Yeats." [Quarry] (43:2) S 94, p. 22-23.
5010. PURDY, Carol
"On the Beach." [NewYorkQ] (53) 94, p. 77.
5011. PURKINGE
"Ectomorph." [Talisman] (13) Fall 94-Wint 95, p. 297-300.
5012. PURPURA, Lia
"Cardinal." [PlumR] (7) [94?], p. 7.
"Construction." [NegC] (14:1/2) 94, p. 84.
"Museum Horse." [AntR] (52:2) Spr 94, p. 326.
"On Campus" (tr. of Grzegorz Musial, w. the author). [LitR] (37:4) Sum 94, p. 573.
5013. PUST, Sara
"Cross-Country." [RagMag] (12:1) Sum 94, p. 61-62.
"A Derivation." [RagMag] (12:1) Sum 94, p. 58-59.
"On Hearing Adrienne Rich." [RagMag] (12:1) Sum 94, p. 60.
"Poem for the Woman I Am Missing." [RagMag] (12:1) Sum 94, p. 63.

QI, Qiu
See QIU, Qi
5014. QIU, Qi
"Monument" (tr. of Qiu Zhenzhong, w. Jeff Twitchell). [Talisman] (12) Spr 94, p. 180.
"Scene" (tr. of Qiu Zhenzhong, w. Jeff Twitchell). [Talisman] (12) Spr 94, p. 179.
"Sound of the Universe" (tr. of Qiu Zhenzhong, w. Jeff Twitchell). [Talisman] (12) Spr 94, p. 179.
5015. QIU, Xiaolong
"In Exile." [WebR] (18) Fall 94, p. 39.
5016. QIU, Zhenzhong
"Monument" (tr. by Qiu Qi and Jeff Twitchell). [Talisman] (12) Spr 94, p. 180.
"Scene" (tr. by Qiu Qi and Jeff Twitchell). [Talisman] (12) Spr 94, p. 179.
"Sound of the Universe" (tr. by Qiu Qi and Jeff Twitchell). [Talisman] (12) Spr 94, p. 179.
5017. QUADE, Mary R.
"Widowed." [ChiR] (40:4) 94, p. 57-58.
5018. QUAGLIANO, Tony
"A Jazz Note." [NegC] (13:2/3) 93, p. 263.
"An Occasional Poem to Czeslaw Milosz." [HarvardR] (6) Spr 94, p. 104.
"The Whacko and Shrink on the Freeway." [NewYorkQ] (53) 94, p. 102.
"Wolfsbane for Cantwell." [ChamLR] (14/15) Spr-Fall 94, p. 69-71.
5019. QUALLS, Suzanne
"Focusing." [Agni] (40) 94, p. 142-146.
5020. QUAN, Andy
"Family." [TickleAce] (28) Fall-Wint 94, p. 89-90.
"Inheritance." [TickleAce] (28) Fall-Wint 94, p. 93-94.
"My Past Sheds Down Around Me." [TickleAce] (28) Fall-Wint 94, p. 91-92.
"Suite for Two Lovers" (Selections: 2 poems). [Arc] (32) Spr 94, p. 52-53.
5021. QUANT, Brenda Dyer
"Under the Weather." [NegC] (13:2/3) 93, p. 264-266.
5022. QUATTLEBAUM, Mary
"Addressing Thalia, Muse of Comedy." [Light] (12) Wint 94-95, p. 17.
"A Celebration, with Gravity." [GettyR] (7:4) Aut 94, p. 651-652.
5023. QUAY, Sara
"Midnight Bar." [SingHM] (21) 94, p. 53.
5024. QUENNEVILLE, Freda
"The Movements of Stars." [SoCoast] (16) Ja 94, p. 40.
5025. QUINLAN, Linda
"Family" (for Sean). [NewOR] (20:1/2) Spr-Sum 94, p. 128.
"If Wishes Were Horses" (for Dad). [NewOR] (20:1/2) Spr-Sum 94, p. 127.
"Twelve." [NewOR] (20:1/2) Spr-Sum 94, p. 125-126.
5026. QUINN, Harold
"Swinging." [NegC] (14:1/2) 94, p. 182.
5027. QUINN, James P.
"Mother's Hands." [Rosebud] (1:2) Sum 94, p. 68.
5028. QUINN, John
"Which Ones to Kill, Which Not, & How & Why" (for Turley & Foley). [Interim] (13:1) Spr-Sum 94, p. 29-31.
5029. QUIÑONES, Magaly
"Travelling Baggage" (tr. by Elizabeth Hernández). [Callaloo] (17:3) Sum 94, p. 808.
5030. QUINTANA, Leroy V.
"Filemon can say a lot of foolish things sometimes." [PraS] (68:4) Wint 94, p. 131.
"Filemon has a theory about Mexican music." [PraS] (68:4) Wint 94, p. 131.
"Grandmother, how quickly the days pass, how quickly." [PraS] (68:4) Wint 94, p. 129-130.
"Grandmother's father was killed by some Tejanos." [PraS] (68:4) Wint 94, p. 133-134.
"Granizo." [PraS] (68:4) Wint 94, p. 132.
"He was a tailor and came to be known as Juan Agujas." [PraS] (68:4) Wint 94, p. 130.
"Landmarks in the History of a Northern New Mexico Village." [PraS] (68:4) Wint 94, p. 135.
"Long before Styrofoam." [PraS] (68:4) Wint 94, p. 134.
"My mother says my grandmother told her." [PraS] (68:4) Wint 94, p. 132.

"Vecino." [PraS] (68:4) Wint 94, p. 133.

5031. QUINTANALES, Mirtha N.
"Moving" (November 1983, tr. by David Frye). [MichQR] (33:3) Sum 94, p. 590-591.

5032. QUINTILIUS
"The Key" (tr. by Peter Russell, from *Quintilii Apocalypsos Fragmenta*). [BellArk] (10:3 [i.e. 10:4]) Jl-Ag 94, p. 16.

5033. RAAB, Lawrence
"All Day." [Antaeus] (73/74) Spr 94, p. 67-68.
"Daily Life." [VirQR] (70:1) Wint 94, p. 95-96.
"My Soul Is a Light Housekeeper." [NewYorker] (70:29) 19 S 94, p. 58.
"The Uses of Nostalgia." [VirQR] (70:1) Wint 94, p. 96-98.

5034. RABBITT, Thomas
"Road Kills" (Chapbook: 13 poems). [BlackWR] (20:2) Spr-Sum 94, p. 49-71.
"The Secret Life of Agnes Quinn." [GettyR] (7:3) Sum 94, p. 532.

5035. RABÉARIVELO, Jean-Joseph
"Cactus." [InterQ] (1:3) 94, p. 19.

5036. RABESS, Gregory
"Carib Lament." [CaribbeanW] (8) 94, p. 79-80.
"Eruption Karifuna." [CaribbeanW] (8) 94, p. 77-78.
"Pegoua Rock." [CaribbeanW] (8) 94, p. 81-82.

5037. RABINOWITZ, Anna
"Of Two Minds." [NewAW] (12) Spr-Sum 94, p. 130-132.

5038. RABY, Elizabeth
"6 PM, Hotel Colón, Cathedral Square, Barcelona, Spain." [JlNJPo] (16:2) Aut 94, p. 28.
"To Maudie from Your Anders, 1903" (from the courtship letters of Andrew F. Nuquist to Maud Edgerton). [JlNJPo] (16:2) Aut 94, p. 29.

5039. RACHLIN, Ellen
"Sedation." [AmerPoR] (23:2) Mr-Ap 94, p. 55.

RACZ, Emoke B'
See B'RACZ, Emoke

5040. RACZ, G. J.
"*Mare* Is the Female of the Horse" (after an essay by Roman Jakobson, tr. of José Antonio Mazzotti). [PoetL] (89:1) Spr 94, p. 18.
"Nymph and Navigator" (tr. of José Antonio Mazzotti). [PoetL] (89:1) Spr 94, p. 19-20.

5041. RADAVICH, David
"Grass Springing." [Light] (9) Spr 94, p. 7.
"Man with the Snow-Blower." [PoetC] (25:3) Spr 94, p. 10.

5042. RADOEV, Ivan
"Ballad for the Future" (tr. by Lisa Sapinkopf and Georgi Belev). [InterQ] (1:1) [93?], p. 77.

5043. RADULESCU, Stella Vinitchi
"Now When Wè Are Seeds Again" (from "Blood and White Applies"). [AmerPoR] (23:5) S-O 94, p. 32.

5044. RAE, Simon
"Vision 2020." [Jacaranda] (5:1) Wint-Spr 91, p. 46-47.

5045. RAFFEL, Burton
"Generation after Generation." [ParisR] (36:130) Spr 94, p. 111.
"Inventing Space and Time." [ParisR] (36:130) Spr 94, p. 110.
"Sonnet (Half-Italian) to Poisonous Tongues." [DenQ] (29:1) Sum 94, p. 30.

5046. RAFFERTY, Charles
"Another Night in Fayetteville." [WestB] (34) 94, p. 18.
"The Arsonist Tells His Story to the Attorney." [OgalalaR] (5:1) Wint 94, p. 78-79.
"Behind the Vineland Gun Club." [WestB] (34) 94, p. 18-19.
"The Man Who Invented Urinal Mints Attends His Class Reunion." [CapeR] (29:1) Spr 94, p. 40-41.
"New Year's Eve." [OgalalaR] (5:1) Wint 94, p. 70-71.
"Night Fishing." [OgalalaR] (5:1) Wint 94, p. 74-75.
"Nostalgia." [OgalalaR] (5:1) Wint 94, p. 76-77.
"Poem for a Patient Neighbor." [LouisL] (11:1) Spr 94, p. 181.
"Saving for a Bike." [LouisL] (11:1) Spr 94, p. 182.
"Stealing the Corn." [OgalalaR] (5:1) Wint 94, p. 73.

"Testimony." [Hellas] (5:2) Fall-Wint 94, p. 39.
"Understanding the Pond." [OgalalaR] (5:1) Wint 94, p. 72.
"The Voices Below." [OgalalaR] (5:1) Wint 94, p. 80-81.

5047. RAGAN, Jacie
"Marking Time." [NegC] (14:1/2) 94, p. 191.

5048. RAGAN, James
"The Mortar and the Pestle." [NewL] (61:1) 94, p. 155.
"The Old Prague Jewish Cemetery." [NewL] (60:4) 94, p. 33.

5049. RAGAN, Sam
"The Patriot." [NoCarLR] (2:1) Spr 94, p. 236.
"Poetry Reading." [NoCarLR] (2:1) Spr 94, p. 236.

5050. RAGLAND, Scott
"Wondering." [Parting] (7:1) Sum 94, p. 76.

5051. RAHBANI, Mansour
"Don't Let Them Take Me Away" (tr. by Mansour Ajami). [LitR] (37:3) Spr 94, p. 512-513.
"Neither One Is Staying With the Other" (tr. by Mansour Ajami). [LitR] (37:3) Spr 94, p. 513-514.

5052. RAHIM, Jennifer
"The Felling of a Tree." [CaribbeanW] (8) 94, p. 45.
"This May Be a Train." [MalR] (107) Sum 94, p. 36-37.
"Walk Like Trees." [CaribbeanW] (8) 94, p. 46-47.

RAHMING, Lelawattee Manoo
See MANOO-RAHMING, Lelawattee

RAI, Harivansh
See BACCHAN

5053. RAINE, Craig
"History: The Home Movie" (1924). [NewYorker] (70:20) 11 Jl 94, p. 62-64.
"History: The Home Movie" (1931). [NewYorker] (70:21) 18 Jl 94, p. 42-43.
"History: The Home Movie" (1934). [NewYorker] (70:22) 25 Jl 94, p. 52-53.
"History: The Home Movie" (1937, 1941, 1946). [NewYorker] (70:23) 1 Ag 94, p. 66-67.

5054. RAKOSI, Carl
"Jazz" (a compote of titles). [Arshile] (3) 94, p. 29.

5055. RALPH, Brett
"The Ladies Room." [ChironR] (13:3) Aut 94, p. 32.

5056. RAMAIYA, Nita
"I Am" (tr. by the author and edited by Arlene Zide). [InterQ] (1:2) 93, p. 182-183.

5057. RAMANUJAN, A. K.
"Foundlings in the Yukon." [Poetry] (164:5) Ag 94, p. 283-284.
"How Can One Write About Bosnia." [Poetry] (164:4) Jl 94, p. 207.
"In March." [Poetry] (164:4) Jl 94, p. 206.
"Pain." [Poetry] (164:4) Jl 94, p. 208.
"Sonnet: Time moves in and out of me." [Poetry] (164:4) Jl 94, p. 205.

5058. RAMBO, Jody
"On Returning to the Beachhouse." [CreamCR] (18:2) Fall 94, p. 131.

RAMDWAR, Camille Hernandez
See HERNANDEZ-RAMDWAR, Camille

5059. RAMKE, Bin
"Art. Love. Geology." [ParisR] (36:131) Sum 94, p. 97-99.
"As If the Past." [ParisR] (36:133) Wint 94, p. 221-225.
"How Light Is Spent." [Pequod] (37) 94, p. 34-35.
"My Older Brother's Hobby." [WestHR] (48:1) Spr 94, p. 67.
"Never To Heaven Go." [DenQ] (29:1) Sum 94, p. 142-143.
"On Reading D.H. Lawrence's 'Lightning'." [WestHR] (48:1) Spr 94, p. 66.
"When Culture Was Popular." [OhioR] (52) 94, p. 30-34.

5060. RAMKISSOON-CHEN, Rajandaye
"The Old Lieutenant's Charm." [MalR] (107) Sum 94, p. 38.
"With Cancer and with Child." [MalR] (107) Sum 94, p. 39.

5061. RAMSDELL, Heather
"Bridge Segments" (Selections: 1-9A). [Sulfur] (35) Fall 94, p. 13-25.

5062. RAMSDEN, Margery
"Joe." [Verse] (11:2) Sum 94, p. 90.

5063. RAMSEY, Paul
"Pythagoras." [BellArk] (10:3 [i.e. 10:4]) Jl-Ag 94, p. 25.

5064. RAMSEY, William M.
"A Strange Telepathy." [SoCaR] (27:1/2) Fall 94-Spr 95, p. 11.
5065. RANAIVO, Flavien
"An Ordinary Love Song." [InterQ] (1:3) 94, p. 20.
5066. RANCOURT, Suzanne
"Soft." [Callaloo] (17:1) Wint 94, p. 131.
"Whose Mouth Do I Speak With." [Callaloo] (17:1) Wint 94, p. 130.
5067. RANDALL, Julia
"Battle Day" (Bennington, August 16, 1777, August 16, 1992). [SouthernR] (30:4) Aut 94, p. 783-784.
5068. RANDALL, Julie Malvase
"Where Orion Hunts" (A Plainsongs Award Poem). [Plain] (14:3) Spr 94, p. 4-5.
RANDOLPH, Meg Hill Fitz
See FITZ-RANDOLPH, Meg Hill
5069. RANDOLPH, Sarah
"Work." [PlumR] (7) [94?], p. 11.
5070. RANKIN, Paula
"Blue Moon." [TarRP] (34:1) Fall 94, p. 31.
"Country Song: July" (to my husband). [TarRP] (34:1) Fall 94, p. 32.
"Glamour." [SenR] (24:1) Spr 94, p. 73.
"Strange Winter." [SenR] (24:1) Spr 94, p. 74-75.
5071. RANKINE, Claudia
"Birthright." [KenR] (NS 16:2) Spr 94, p. 17-18.
"Him." [Pequod] (38) 94, p. 13.
"New Windows." [KenR] (NS 16:2) Spr 94, p. 19-20.
"Out of Many, One." [Pequod] (38) 94, p. 7-12.
"She." [Pequod] (38) 94, p. 14.
5072. RANNEY, Michael
"Prediction." [Wind] (73) 94, p. 21.
"Trench Master." [SmPd] (31:2, #91) Spr 94, p. 22.
5073. RAPHAEL, Dan
"The Light Goes North to Gain Wings." [HeavenB] (11) 94, p. 46.
"Untitled: a threat, a molecule-wide thread, cold, so cold light cant move here." [CentralP] (23) Spr 94, p. 119-120.
5074. RAPOPORT, Janis
"After Paradise" (for Bill and Vina Percy). [Nimrod] (37:2) Spr-Sum 94, p. 81-82.
"A Ceremony of Oysters." [Nimrod] (37:2) Spr-Sum 94, p. 76-78.
"Clam Harbour." [Nimrod] (37:2) Spr-Sum 94, p. 80.
"Parrsboro: Looking for Fossils." [Nimrod] (37:2) Spr-Sum 94, p. 79.
5075. RAPTOSH, Diane
"The Idea of North." [PoetryC] (15:1) N 94, p. 22.
"Lullaby for the Unborn." [MichQR] (33:2) Spr 94, p. 372-373.
"The Quickening." [PoetryC] (15:1) N 94, p. 22.
5076. RAS, Barbara
"The Correct Analysis." [Zyzzyva] (10:1) Spr 94, p. 86-87.
5077. RASH, Ron
"1934." [SoCaR] (27:1/2) Fall 94-Spr 95, p. 4.
"Flying Squadron." [SoCaR] (27:1/2) Fall 94-Spr 95, p. 5.
"Grabbling." [SoCaR] (26:2) Spr 94, p. 40.
"Local Color." [Hellas] (5:1) Spr-Sum 94, p. 45-46.
"The Old Men at Hamrick's Carp Pond." [SoCaR] (27:1/2) Fall 94-Spr 95, p. 6.
5078. RASHID, Ian Iqbal
"Knowing Your Place." [WestCL] (28:1/2, #13/14) Spr-Fall 94, p. 243-245.
"You Are What You Were." [Arc] (32) Spr 94, p. 11.
5079. RATCLIFFE, Stephen
"Act." [SantaBR] (1:1) Spr-Sum 93, p. 94.
"Context = One Less Person." [CentralP] (23) Spr 94, p. 40.
"Fiction." [SantaBR] (1:1) Spr-Sum 93, p. 92.
"M." [Talisman] (12) Spr 94, p. 226.
"N." [SantaBR] (1:1) Spr-Sum 93, p. 93.
"Paradise." [SantaBR] (1:1) Spr-Sum 93, p. 93.
"Part II." [CentralP] (23) Spr 94, p. 41.
"Pause." [SantaBR] (1:1) Spr-Sum 93, p. 94.
"Present Tense" (Excerpts). [Conjunc] (22) 94, p. 209-213.
"Q." [Talisman] (12) Spr 94, p. 227.
"Story." [SantaBR] (1:1) Spr-Sum 93, p. 92.

5080. RATNER, Rochelle
"Thankstaking." [IllinoisR] (2:1) Fall 94, p. 39-40.
5081. RATTAN, Cleatus
"Childish" (to Martin). [WormR] (34:4, #136) 94, p. 147.
"Good Days." [WormR] (34:4, #136) 94, p. 147.
5082. RATTAN, Walter
"The Protector." [SmPd] (31:2, #91) Spr 94, p. 29.
5083. RATTEE, Michael
"Making It Right." [Pivot] (41) 93, p. 4-5.
5084. RATZLAFF, Keith
"Composition with the Yellow Half Moon." [Journal] (18:1) Spr-Sum 94, p. 54-55.
"Leonardo Sketches an Old Man from Memory." [NewEngR] (16:3) Sum 94, p. 69-70.
"Medicinal Fora" (After Paul Klee's Officinale Flora). [ArtfulD] (26/27) 94, p. 48.
"Roof Flower" (After Paul Klee's Dächerblume). [ArtfulD] (26/27) 94, p. 49.
"Torrential Angel." [Journal] (18:1) Spr-Sum 94, p. 56.
5085. RAU, Aurel
"Around the Fire" (tr. by Adam J. Sorkin and Liviu Bleoca). [HiramPoR] (55/56) Fall 93-Sum 94, p. 100.
"The Gift" (tr. by Adam J. Sorkin and Liviu Bleoca). [HiramPoR] (55/56) Fall 93-Sum 94, p. 99.
"Writing with a Ballpoint" (tr. by Adam J. Sorkin and Liviu Bleoca). [HiramPoR] (55/56) Fall 93-Sum 94, p. 101.
5086. RAWLINS, C. L.
"Paths, Crossing" (for Gary Holthaus, near Longmont, Colorado). [Ploughs] (20:4) Wint 94-95, p. 134-135.
5087. RAWLS, Alex
"4% Pantomime." [NewOR] (20:1/2) Spr-Sum 94, p. 96.
"American Caesar." [NewOR] (20:1/2) Spr-Sum 94, p. 95.
"Elvis Called Me at 4:30 One Morning Last year." [NewOR] (20:1/2) Spr-Sum 94, p. 92-93.
"A Few Comments About My Head." [NewOR] (20:1/2) Spr-Sum 94, p. 94.
5088. RAWSON, Eric
"Seclusion at Nine O'Clock." [SycamoreR] (6:1) Wint 94, p. 33.
5089. RAY, David
"Alzheimer's." [Agni] (39) 94, p. 90-91.
"American Gothic." [PoetL] (89:1) Spr 94, p. 37-38.
"At the Blue Mist." [Amelia] (7:3, #22) 94, p. 41-42.
"The Convention for Twins." [Confr] (52/53) Wint-Spr 94, p. 308.
"A Few Words About Prayer." [NewL] (60:4) 94, p. 192-193.
"For the Biographer." [Nat] (259:2) Jl 11 94, p. 67.
"Fremantle." [DarkMoon] (1) 94, p. 11.
"Hearsay." [WillowR] (21) Spr 94, p. 9-10.
"In Shadow's Beside the Sea." [PoetL] (89:1) Spr 94, p. 39-41.
"Inland Ode." [DarkMoon] (1) 94, p. 10.
"Intertextuality" (for A.D. Hope). [PoetC] (25:2) Wint 94, p. 9.
"The Monologue." [PoetC] (25:2) Wint 94, p. 6-8.
"The Orphan Train." [PoetC] (25:2) Wint 94, p. 10-11.
"Orphanage." [WillowR] (21) Spr 94, p. 8.
"A Pair of Shoes." [DarkMoon] (1) 94, p. 12-13.
"The Roadster." [DarkMoon] (1) 94, p. 7-10.
"Spain, As I Was Growing Up." [Confr] (54/55) Fall 94-Wint 95, p. 50.
"Twins." [Confr] (52/53) Wint-Spr 94, p. 306-307.
"Vigil." [DarkMoon] (1) 94, p. 5-6.
"A Wall of Heartwood." [MidwQ] (36:1) Aut 94, p. 69.
5090. RAY, Elle
"Now the Darkness." [CrabCR] (8:2/3/9:1/2/3) 94, p. 7-8.
5091. RAY, Judy
"Memories of Silence." [DarkMoon] (1) 94, p. 14.
"More Than a Generation Gap." [DarkMoon] (1) 94, p. 15.
"The Steps" (A site-specific sculpture at the Djerassi Foundation). [DarkMoon] (1) 94, p. 16.
5092. RAY, Lionel
"The Screen, the Beach" (Selections: XII-XIII, tr. by Camille Martin). [LitR] (37:4) Sum 94, p. 658-659.

5093. RAY, Sunil B.
"Blue Pills" (tr. of Vijaya Mukhopadhyay, w. Carolyne Wright). [KenR] (NS 16:4) Fall 94, p. 92.
"Film" (tr. of Vijaya Mukhopadhyay, w. Carolyne Wright). [KenR] (NS 16:4) Fall 94, p. 91-92.
"Woman" (tr. of Vijaya Mukhopadhyay, w. Carolyne Wright and the author). [InterQ] (1:2) 93, p. 159.
5094. RAYMOND, Clarinda Harriss
"Mason Jars." [SoCoast] (17) Je 94, p. 12.
5095. RAYMOND, Monica
"3. Two sopranos, a mezzo" (to Catherine Draycott). [Chain] (1) Spr-Sum 94, p. 234.
"Farewell to Felicia" (On Her Departing from the Harvard Expository Writing Program). [Light] (11) Aut 94, p. 7.
5096. RAZ, Hilda
"Cobb's Hill Pond." [ColR] (21:2) Fall 94, p. 174-175.
"I Hear the Name of the Moon and Am Afraid." [ColR] (21:2) Fall 94, p. 178.
"Sarah Among Animals" (— Priam's Green Bird Wing). [ColR] (21:2) Fall 94, p. 179.
"Sarah's Response." [ColR] (21:2) Fall 94, p. 176-177.
5097. RAZAVI, Rebecca Hopkins
"Hunting the Lamb." [PoetL] (89:2) Sum 94, p. 24.
"World Under" (for Suzanne). [SouthernPR] (34:2) Wint 94, p. 66.
5098. RE, Lucia
"Four Poems" (tr. of Amelia Rosselli, w. Paul Vangelisti). [Chelsea] (57) 94, p. 79-81.
5099. REA, Susan
"Firebird Suite." [LouisL] (11:1) Spr 94, p. 177.
"The Painting" (for Gail). [LouisL] (11:1) Spr 94, p. 175-176.
"Train Suite." [ColR] (21:2) Fall 94, p. 92-95.
5100. REAGLER, Robin
"From This Garden I Chose." [DenQ] (28:4) Spr 94, p. 56.
"Self-Portrait, Still a Little Wet." [ColR] (21:1) Spr 94, p. 121-124.
5101. REARDON, Alissa
"The Hysterial Woman Reorders Her World." [HawaiiR] (18:1, #40) Spr 94, p. 100.
"Letter Across Fort Collins" (To Laura). [CreamCR] (18:2) Fall 94, p. 118-119.
"Sister" (Associated Writing Programs Intro Award poem). [IndR] (17:2) Fall 94, p. 114.
5102. REBAZA-SORALUZ, Luis
"Epilogue" (In memoriam Nelson Arrunátegui, tr. by Elizabeth Doonan). [PlumR] (7) [94?], p. 2-3.
"The Lake" (for Stephanie — 2 March 1983, tr. by Elizabeth Doonan). [PlumR] (7) [94?], p. 1.
"Of the Sonorous Labyrinth" (for Pilar and José Luis Malpartida, tr. by Elizabeth Doonan Kauffman). [Boulevard] (9:1/2, #25/26) Spr 94, p. 257-258.
5103. RECHNER, Mary
"Dreams of Sisters and Brothers." [Parting] (7:2) Wint 94-95, p. 35.
"What I Did for the Opera" (for Jessica). [Parting] (7:2) Wint 94-95, p. 24.
5104. RECIPUTI, Natalie
"Silk Dreams." [BellArk] (10:3) My-Je 94, p. 12.
5105. RECTOR, Liam
"Elizabeth Bishop." [Boulevard] (9:1/2, #25/26) Spr 94, p. 240-241.
"Our Own Ones." [Ploughs] (20:4) Wint 94-95, p. 136-139.
"Uncle Snort." [Ploughs] (20:4) Wint 94-95, p. 141.
"We Should Not Let Munich Slip Away." [Ploughs] (20:4) Wint 94-95, p. 140.
RED, Rockin'
See ROCKIN' RED
5106. REDDY, Chicu
"1,000 Cuts." [HarvardA] (129:2) Fall 94, p. 17.
5107. REDEL, Victoria
"Press." [PassN] (15:2) Wint 94, p. 3.
"Talk the Big Hand Down." [Field] (50) Spr 94, p. 91-93.
5108. REDEN, Lisa
"One Year Later" (A love poem). [Blueline] (15) 94, p. 14.
5109. REDHILL, Michael
"In darkness, barefoot." [Descant] (25:1, #84) Spr 94, p. 24.

"A Murder" (For Andrea Atkinson). [Descant] (25:1, #84) Spr 94, p. 21.
"Outside Quebec City." [Descant] (25:1, #84) Spr 94, p. 18.
"Pioneer Graves" (For Jeanne). [Descant] (25:1, #84) Spr 94, p. 17.
"Sur le Pont." [Descant] (25:1, #84) Spr 94, p. 23.
"Tattoo." [Descant] (25:1, #84) Spr 94, p. 16.
"Trial-End at the Municipal Buildings." [Descant] (25:1, #84) Spr 94, p. 22.
"Viewing Detroit." [Descant] (25:1, #84) Spr 94, p. 19-20.

5110. REDLIN, Josephine
"Grandfather." [NoDaQ] (62:1) Wint 94-95, p. 35-36.
"The Passing" (for Louie L. Costa). [NewEngR] (16:2) Spr 94, p. 122-123.
"A Rosary for Rain Before Mass, 1953." [Journal] (18:2) Fall-Wint 94, p. 28-29.
"Salt Block." [AntR] (52:2) Spr 94, p. 304.

5111. REDMAN, Randall
"Cafe (Where Love Has Ended)." [NegC] (14:1/2) 94, p. 174.

REECE, Erik Anderson
See ANDERSON-REECE, Erik

5112. REECE, Spencer
"For a Modern Bestiary." [Boulevard] (9:1/2, #25/26) Spr 94, p. 44-45.
"What Anne Frank Never Wrote in Her Diary." [ChamLR] (14/15) Spr-Fall 94, p. 61.

5113. REED, Helen
"The Poison Bottle and the Dangerous Man." [WillowR] (21) Spr 94, p. 13.

5114. REED, John R.
"Magdalene." [RiverS] (40) 94, p. 46-47.

5115. REED, John Richard
"Leaves from a Partbook" (Fantasia for Viol Consort). [Poetry] (163:5) F 94, p. 270.
"Second Coming" (For Duane Michals). [Poetry] (164:2) My 94, p. 74.
"Two for Roethke." [Poetry] (163:5) F 94, p. 269.

5116. REED, Kjersti A.
"Hands." [MinnR] (41/42) Fall 93-Spr 94 (published Mr 95), p. 36.

5117. REED, Lori
"Gangster Crap." [Eyeball] (3) 93, p. 34.

5118. REED, Marthe
"Axiology of image, or images piled one on top of another." [Writ] (26) 94, p. 10.
"Blue tull, a wash of blue tulle (falls)." [Writ] (26) 94, p. 9.
"A fox clutches her shoulder (bare shoulders)." [Writ] (26) 94, p. 5.
"In habitual kitchen, dark cupboards, linoleum floor." [Writ] (26) 94, p. 6.
"Memory abandons him, and he. Has none." [Writ] (26) 94, p. 11.
"Spring, maybe February: snow clusters, clusters of red-stamened blossoms." [Writ] (26) 94, p. 8.
"Venus rises out of mist-draped night." [Writ] (26) 94, p. 7.

5119. REEDY, Penelope
"Houseguests." [ContextS] (4:1) 94, p. 36.

5120. REES-JONES, Deryn
"Blue" (for Ian). [Verse] (11:1) Spr 94, p. 38.
"Connections." [MalR] (107) Sum 94, p. 164-165.
"Interim." [MalR] (107) Sum 94, p. 163.
"Metamorphoses." [Jacaranda] (10) 94, p. 136.

5121. REESE, Steven
"Broadway Limited for Johnstown." [PoetC] (25:3) Spr 94, p. 37.
"Christian in the Den of Produce." [CreamCR] (18:1) Spr 94, p. 73-74.
"With My Sons at the Milky Way Show." [WestB] (34) 94, p. 43.
"Woodshed." [SouthernHR] (28:2) Spr 94, p. 165." [SouthernHR] (28:2) Spr 94, p. 165.

5122. REEVE, Davd
"Certainly." [ChironR] (13:2) Sum 94, p. 23.
"Staying Alive." [ChironR] (13:4) Wint 94, p. 15.

5123. REEVE, F. D.
"On Appledore." [Poetry] (164:1) Ap 94, p. 7.
"A Sonnet for Christmas." [Poetry] (165:3) D 94, p. 132.

5124. REGIER, G. Travis (Gail)
"Aubade." [HayF] (14) Spr-Sum 94, p. 58.
"A Childhood in Springfield, Missouri." [HayF] (14) Spr-Sum 94, p. 57.
"Means of Production." [QW] (38) Winter-Spr 93-94, p. 96.
"Sleeping in Public." [Poetry] (165:2) N 94, p. 67.

5125. REHM, Pam
"1. It is often said that underlying diversity" (to Barbara Jordan). [Chain] (1) Spr-Sum 94, p. 232.
5126. REIBETANZ, John
"A Chain for Stephanie." [MalR] (108) Fall 94, p. 92-95.
"Rembrandt." [MalR] (108) Fall 94, p. 89-91.
"Wyeth." [CanLit] (141) Sum 94, p. 73-74.
5127. REICHARD, William
"Bonsai." [Vis] (44) 94, p. 21.
"Rodeo Beach, CA" (Creation). [Vis] (44) 94, p. 20.
5128. REICHMAN, Sebastian
"Sweeper Before His Door" (Selections: 4 poems, tr. by Nina Zivancevic). [Talisman] (13) Fall 94-Wint 95, p. 35-36.
5129. REICHOW, Victoria
"Swallowing the Moon." [PassN] (15:2) Wint 94, p. 15.
5130. REID, Alastair
"At the End of Things" (tr. of Eugenio Montejo). [Trans] (29) Spr 94, p. 38.
"Certain Words" (tr. of Eugenio Montejo). [Trans] (29) Spr 94, p. 36.
"Diario de Muerte" (Selections: 18, 33, 45, tr. of Enrique Lihn). [AmerPoR] (23:4) Jl-Ag 94, p. 38.
"In This City" (tr. of Eugenio Montejo). [Trans] (29) Spr 94, p. 40.
"Life" (tr. of Eugenio Montejo). [Trans] (29) Spr 94, p. 37.
"The Orinoco" (tr. of Eugenio Montejo). [Trans] (29) Spr 94, p. 39.
"Two Bodies" (tr. of Eugenio Montejo). [Trans] (29) Spr 94, p. 35.
5131. REID, Bethany
"My Mother Hanging Clothes to Dry." [Calyx] (15:3) Wint 94-95, p. 48-49.
5132. REID, Monty
"Flat Side." [WestCL] (28:3, #15) Wint 94-95, p. 56-60.
"Near the Beisecker Bio-Medical Waste Incinerator." [Dandel] (21:2) 94, p. 26-33.
5133. REIDEL, James
"Beelzebub" (for Richard Howard). [PoetL] (89:2) Sum 94, p. 33.
"An Evening" (tr. of Thomas Bernhard). [ArtfulD] (26/27) 94, p. 61.
"Living and Dead" (tr. of Thomas Bernhard). [ArtfulD] (26/27) 94, p. 62.
"My Parents' House" (tr. of Thomas Bernhard). [ArtfulD] (26/27) 94, p. 60.
5134. REIFF, Sandra
"Cousteau Goes to Antarctica to Film the Great White Shark." [Border] (3) Fall 93, p. 60.
5135. REISS, James
"Eclipse the Dark, My Fiftieth Birthday: July 11, 1991" (for my mother). [AntR] (52:3) Sum 94, p. 482-485.
5136. REITER, David P.
"Mutton Birds" (Lord Howe Island). [Descant] (25:3/4, #86/87) Fall-Wint 94, p. 185.
"Nude in a Forest" (after *nu, paysage ensoleillé* by Matisse). [Descant] (25:3/4, #86/87) Fall-Wint 94, p. 188.
"Le Poéte" (an analytical cubist painting by Picasso). [Descant] (25:3/4, #86/87) Fall-Wint 94, p. 186-187.
"Rules for Prisoners, Port Arthur, 1843." [Amelia] (7:4, #23) 94, p. 119.
"Tame Cattle, 1805." [Amelia] (7:4, #23) 94, p. 118.
5137. REITER, Thomas
"Amichon and the Gods" (1875, the Windward Islands). [CaribbeanW] (8) 94, p. 66-68.
"The Claim." [PoetC] (26:1) Fall 94, p. 21.
"Roots and Powers." [Ascent] (19:1) Fall 94, p. 75.
"Spiderwort." [IllinoisR] (2:1) Fall 94, p. 41.
5138. REMACLE, Louis
"Iviêr." [Os] (39) Fall-Wint 94, p. 6.
"Pardon" (in Walloon). [Os] (39) Fall-Wint 94, p. 8.
"Pardon" (tr. by Yann Lovelock). [Os] (39) Fall-Wint 94, p. 9.
"Snow" (tr. by Yann Lovelock). [Os] (39) Fall-Wint 94, p. 7.
5139. REMINGTON, Rebekah
"My Wall." [SycamoreR] (6:1) Wint 94, p. 30-31.
"Variations on a Theme after Flaubert." [SycamoreR] (6:1) Wint 94, p. 27-29.
5140. REMPLE, Margaret
"Looking into Firs outside My Window." [PraS] (68:2) Sum 94, p. 90-93.
"My Country." [PraS] (68:2) Sum 94, p. 88-90.

5141. REMUND, Marcella
"Old Family Photo." [SoDakR] (32:2) Sum 94, p. 133.
5142. RENKL, Margaret
"At the Tennessee State Fair I Think of You." [SouthernR] (30:1) Ja, Wint 94, p. 105-106.
"The Mantis." [PaintedB] (53/54) 94, p. 82-83.
"Secret Anniversaries." [SouthernR] (30:1) Ja, Wint 94, p. 106-107.
5143. RENNING, Charles H.
"Homo Ludens." [Light] (10) Sum 94, p. 23.
"The Meter Maid." [Light] (12) Wint 94-95, p. 11.
5144. RENZONI, Scott
"The Leaves." [ConnPR] (13:1) 94, p. 20.
5145. REPOSA, Carol Coffee
"Apache Family Portrait." [Border] (5) Fall-Wint 94, p. 52.
5146. REPP, John
"Cooking." [Iowa] (24:3) Fall 94, p. 181-182.
"Day Off." [BellArk] (10:5) S-O 94, p. 13.
"Mosaic." [Journal] (18:2) Fall-Wint 94, p. 50-51.
"Mr. Ernie Interrupts a Dividing Creek Daydream." [Journal] (18:2) Fall-Wint 94, p. 46-49.
5147. RESS, Lisa
"Can a Girl from a Small Mining Town in the West Find Happiness as the Wife of a Wealthy and Titled Englishman?" (Radio announcer's query, *Our Gal Sunday*, 1945). [IllinoisR] (2:1) Fall 94, p. 42.
"River and Sea" (For Theodore Roethke). [IllinoisR] (2:1) Fall 94, p. 43.
5148. RETALLACK, Joan
"9/26/93." [Chain] (1) Spr-Sum 94, p. 196.
"Steinzas In Mediation" (to Tina Darragh). [Chain] (1) Spr-Sum 94, p. 238-241.
5149. RETSOV, Samuel
"Carless Love." [Talisman] (13) Fall 94-Wint 95, p. 254.
"Comfort." [Talisman] (13) Fall 94-Wint 95, p. 254.
5150. REVARD, Carter
"When We Get Manhattan Back." [Callaloo] (17:1) Wint 94, p. 351-352.
5151. REVELL, Donald
"After the News." [Agni] (39) 94, p. 120.
"Annie" (tr. of Guillaume Apollinaire). [AmerPoR] (23:6) N-D 94, p. 5.
"Arranged to Meet in Aix." [AmerLC] (6) 94, p. 37-38.
"Autumn" (tr. of Guillaume Apollinaire). [AmerPoR] (23:6) N-D 94, p. 5.
"The Brazier" (tr. of Guillaume Apollinaire). [Colum] (22) Wint 94, p. 112-114.
"The Door" (tr. of Guillaume Apollinaire). [AmerPoR] (23:6) N-D 94, p. 5.
"An Evening" (tr. of Guillaume Apollinaire). [PartR] (61:4) Fall 94, p. 629-630.
"The Farewell" (tr. of Guillaume Apollinaire). [Pequod] (38) 94, p. 100.
"Fewer Than Music." [NewAW] (12) Spr-Sum 94, p. 12.
"The Harvest Month" (tr. of Guillaume Apollinaire). [Pequod] (38) 94, p. 90-95.
"Hunting Horns" (tr. of Guillaume Apollinaire). [AmerPoR] (23:6) N-D 94, p. 5.
"Inquire." [SouthwR] (79:1) Wint 94, p. 112.
"Marie" (tr. of Guillaume Appollinaire). [WillowS] (34) Sum 94, p. 67.
"Mephisto." [NewAW] (12) Spr-Sum 94, p. 14.
"Once Divided." [Antaeus] (73/74) Spr 94, p. 153.
"Orison." [Conjunc] (22) 94, p. 320-321.
"Palace" (to Max Jacob, tr. of Guillaume Apollinaire). [Pequod] (38) 94, p. 98-99.
"Parts." [SouthwR] (79:1) Wint 94, p. 112-113.
"Poem Read at the Marriage of André Salmon" (July 13, 1909, tr. of Guillaume Apollinaire). [SenR] (24:1) Spr 94, p. 53-54.
"Rosemonde" (to André Derain, tr. of Guillaume Apollinaire). [SenR] (24:1) Spr 94, p. 55.
"Sail." [Boulevard] (9:3, #27) Fall 94, p. 129.
"Saltimbanques" (tr. of Guillaume Apollinaire). [AmerPoR] (23:6) N-D 94, p. 5.
"Sickly Autumn" (tr. of Guillaume Apollinaire). [PartR] (61:4) Fall 94, p. 630.
"Singer" (tr. of Guillaume Apollinaire). [AmerPoR] (23:6) N-D 94, p. 5.
"There Are Three." [NewAW] (12) Spr-Sum 94, p. 13.
"The Traveller" (to Fernand Fleuret, tr. of Guillaume Apollinaire). [Pequod] (38) 94, p. 96-97.
"The Wind by Night" (tr. of Guillaume Appollinaire). [WillowS] (34) Sum 94, p. 66.
"Zone" (tr. of Guillaume Apollinaire). [AmerPoR] (23:6) N-D 94, p. 3-5.

5152. REVERDY, Pierre
"Clandestine Passage" (tr. by Tom Hibbard). [WillowS] (34) Sum 94, p. 65.
5153. REWAK, William J.
"Ebony Grace." [NegC] (14:1/2) 94, p. 175.
"It's Been So Long." [NegC] (14:1/2) 94, p. 177.
"Poppies." [NegC] (14:1/2) 94, p. 176.
5154. REYNOLDS, Diane
"Foraminifera: Her Architecture." [Border] (5) Fall-Wint 94, p. 53-54.
5155. REYNOLDS, Mark
"Left." [NewYorkQ] (53) 94, p. 104.
5156. RHENISCH, Harold
"Absolute Zero." [MalR] (109) Wint 94, p. 38-40.
"Barbarossa." [Event] (23:2) Sum 94, p. 34-36.
"Birdsong." [MalR] (106) Spr 94, p. 48-49.
"Grasshoppers." [PoetryC] (14:3) My 94, p. 6.
"The Kingfisher." [Event] (23:2) Sum 94, p. 32-33.
"Moon on the Olympic Peninsula." [PoetryC] (14:3) My 94, p. 6.
"The Poor Shall Inherit the Earth." [PoetryC] (14:3) My 94, p. 7.
"Shaman." [PoetryC] (14:3) My 94, p. 7.
"Zazen." [PoetryC] (14:3) My 94, p. 7.
5157. RHOADES, Lisa
"Lift." [Kalliope] (16:1) 94, p. 43.
5158. RHODENBAUGH, Suzanne
"The Darning Egg." [SoDakR] (32:2) Sum 94, p. 92-93.
"Polly Wadleigh Hay Smith Calling." [CimR] (107) Ap 94, p. 87-88.
5159. RHODES, Martha
"Neither of Us." [GlobalCR] (3) Spr 94, p. 68-69.
"The Robe." [Jacaranda] (5:1) Wint-Spr 91, p. 30.
"This Cottage, This Dream." [HarvardR] (7) Fall 94, p. 49.
5160. RIBOVICH, John
"Envy." [Poem] (71) My 94, p. 14.
"Gluttony." [Poem] (71) My 94, p. 13.
"Lust." [Poem] (71) My 94, p. 12.
5161. RICE, Dorothy Marie
"3 Views on Elvis." [Obs] (9:1) Spr-Sum 94, p. 110.
"BayBra." [Obs] (9:1) Spr-Sum 94, p. 108.
"The Children of Clay." [Obs] (9:1) Spr-Sum 94, p. 109-110.
"Jah Dance." [Obs] (9:1) Spr-Sum 94, p. 109.
"Sweetgrass." [Obs] (9:1) Spr-Sum 94, p. 106-107.
"A Taste for Blood (or Thoughts after a Punk Breaks into My Car)." [Obs] (9:1) Spr-Sum 94, p. 107.
"Two Boys." [Obs] (9:1) Spr-Sum 94, p. 108.
"Why R You Still Dancing 2 This Beat?" [Obs] (9:1) Spr-Sum 94, p. 108-109.
5162. RICE, Oliver
"Annus Mirabilis." [GeoR] (48:4) Wint 94, p. 693-694.
"A Birdlog, A Lottery Ticket." [Ascent] (18:3) Spr 94, p. 55.
"The One Light Town." [CarolQ] (46:3) Sum 94, p. 29.
5163. RICH, Adrienne
"Final Notations." [VirQR] (70:4) Aut 94, p. 682.
5164. RICH, Martin
"Bloomsday, 1983." [MinnR] (41/42) Fall 93-Spr 94 (published Mr 95), p. 32-33.
5165. RICH, Susan
"Nomadic Life" (Republic of Niger). [SouthernPR] (34:1) Sum 94, p. 61.
"The One" (for Giovani Soto, 1972-1990). [PassN] (15:2) Wint 94, p. 37.
"Welcome to the Mapparium." [SouthernPR] (34:1) Sum 94, p. 60.
5166. RICHARD, Brad
"Order of Effects." [Border] (4) Spr-Sum 94, p. 60.
"Wallace Stevens Fishing: August 3, 1955." [AmerLC] (6) 94, p. 33-36.
5167. RICHARDS, Marilee
"How an Older Man Makes Love." [PoetL] (89:4) Wint 94-95, p. 38.
"Old Cows." [PoetryNW] (35:1) Spr 94, p. 26.
5168. RICHARDS, Peter
"Because There Is No Soft." [DenQ] (29:1) Sum 94, p. 31-32.
"Such Adjustments." [YaleR] (82:3) Jl 94, p. 34-35.
5169. RICHARDSON, Kelley Logan
"Abel Was I." [Paint] (21) Aut 94, p. 121.

5170. RICHARDSON, Peter
"Addendum." [Poetry] (164:3) Je 94, p. 156.
"Daydreams." [Poetry] (163:6) Mr 94, p. 330.
RICHARDSON, S. Banks
See BANKS-RICHARDSON, S. (Stan)
5171. RICHARDSON, Steve
"The Portuguese Man-o'-War." [Light] (10) Sum 94, p. 8.
"Schooling." [YellowS] (12:3, #47) Fall-Wint 94-95, p. 20.
"Weathering." [YellowS] (12:3, #47) Fall-Wint 94-95, p. 21.
5172. RICHARDSON, Timothy
"In the Tracks of a Stag." [PartR] (61:4) Fall 94, p. 638-639.
5173. RICHEY, Aubrey
"The Snow Queen's Kiss Was." [NowestR] (32:1) 94, p. 61-62.
5174. RICHMAN, Jan
"Rockabye." [Zyzzyva] (10:3) Fall 94, p. 52.
5175. RICHMAN, Norma Hope
"A Daughter's House" (in memory of my mother). [EngJ] (83:4) Ap 94, p. 104.
5176. RICHMAN, Robert
"The Countryside You Knew." [NewRep] (211:17) 24 O 94, p. 41.
"First Light." [PartR] (61:2) Spr 94, p. 318.
5177. RICHMAN, Steven
"First Strike." [LitR] (37:4) Sum 94, p. 667.
5178. RICHSTONE, May
"Going Going." [Light] (10) Sum 94, p. 19.
"Heavenly Days." [Light] (9) Spr 94, p. 8.
"Pall." [Light] (12) Wint 94-95, p. 12.
"Plan Ahead." [Light] (12) Wint 94-95, p. 10.
"The Real Reason." [Light] (12) Wint 94-95, p. 18.
"Thankless." [Light] (11) Aut 94, p. 12.
"ZZZ." [Light] (10) Sum 94, p. 11.
5179. RICHTER, Karl
"All Things Pointy." [NewDeltaR] (10:1) Fall 92-Wint 93, p. 28-29.
5180. RICKEY, R.
"Language (Skin) Scrapes" (w. Jacqueline Turner). [WestCL] (28:1/2, #13/14) Spr-Fall 94, p. 258-261.
5181. RICKS, David
"The Character of the Country." [Poem] (71) My 94, p. 8.
"The Disappearing Languages." [Pivot] (42) 94, p. 17.
"The Discovery of the Mind." [Poetry] (165:2) N 94, p. 63-64.
"Klokkestenen" (Lyø, Denmark). [Poem] (71) My 94, p. 7.
"New Year." [Poem] (71) My 94, p. 6.
"Revoked." [Poetry] (165:2) N 94, p. 64.
"Shreds and Patches." [Poetry] (165:2) N 94, p. 65.
"Vacuum." [Pivot] (42) 94, p. 18.
5182. RIDGEWELL, Peter
"You Who Are High and Dry" (tr. of Arni Ibsen, w. the author). [Vis] (45) 94, p. 18-19.
5183. RIDL, Jack (Jack R.)
"A Month in the Summer: a Suite for My Daughter." [PoetryE] (37/38) Spr 94, p. 164-174.
"Morning: Mid July." [DenQ] (29:1) Sum 94, p. 33.
"Worn Morning." [PassN] (15:2) Wint 94, p. 26-27.
5184. RIFENBURGH, Daniel
"Major Molineux Recalls." [WestHR] (48:2) Sum 94, p. 191.
"To My Opposite Number in Samarkand." [WestHR] (48:2) Sum 94, p. 188-189.
"Uncle Kenny." [WestHR] (48:2) Sum 94, p. 190.
5185. RIFQA, Fuad
"Address Unknown" (tr. by Najwa Nasr). [LitR] (37:3) Spr 94, p. 517.
"Another Picking Season" (tr. by Najwa Nasr). [LitR] (37:3) Spr 94, p. 517.
"In Tübingen" (tr. by Najwa Nasr). [LitR] (37:3) Spr 94, p. 518.
"Note from a Soldier" (tr. by Najwa Nasr). [LitR] (37:3) Spr 94, p. 515-516.
"A Song for the Evening" (tr. by Najwa Nasr). [LitR] (37:3) Spr 94, p. 516.
5186. RIGSBEE, David
"Sketches of Spain." [SouthernPR] (34:2) Wint 94, p. 48-50.
"Suite for Susan Rankaitis." [CarolQ] (47:1) Fall 94, p. 20-29.

5187. RIHANI, May
"The Beirut Sea" (tr. by Najwa Nasr). [LitR] (37:3) Spr 94, p. 521-522.
"A Certain Wednesday Night" (tr. by Andrew Oerke). [LitR] (37:3) Spr 94, p. 520-521.
"Ghurba — In an Alien Land" (tr. by Zuheir al-Faqih). [LitR] (37:3) Spr 94, p. 519-520.
"Voyage 2" (tr. by Zuheir al-Faqih). [LitR] (37:3) Spr 94, p. 520.
5188. RIKER, William H.
"So Said Mistress Coke*" (*per John Aubrey). [Light] (9) Spr 94, p. 15.
5189. RILEY, Denise
"December." [Chain] (1) Spr-Sum 94, p. 223-224.
5190. RILEY, Joanne M. (Joanne Mokosh)
"Braiding at Nightfall." [Poem] (71) My 94, p. 58-59.
"Chimera." [Poem] (71) My 94, p. 60.
"Crossing without Daughters." [CimR] (107) Ap 94, p. 99-100.
"March in Alder Country." [Poem] (71) My 94, p. 57.
"The Salt Marsh." [Parting] (7:2) Wint 94-95, p. 57-58.
5191. RILEY, Michael D.
"EKG." [CumbPR] (14:1) Fall 94, p. 28.
"November." [LaurelR] (28:2) Sum 94, p. 84.
"Poetry at Hayfield House." [CumbPR] (14:1) Fall 94, p. 30.
"The Reader." [CumbPR] (14:1) Fall 94, p. 29.
"The Visit." [CumbPR] (14:1) Fall 94, p. 31-32.
5192. RILEY, Patricia
"The Patriarchs." [Callaloo] (17:1) Wint 94, p. 76.
"Tryin to Get Back Home." [Callaloo] (17:1) Wint 94, p. 74-75.
5193. RILEY, Tom
"Advice to the Lion" (for Gail White). [Light] (11) Aut 94, p. 31.
5194. RILKE, Rainer Maria
"4 Translations from Rilke" (tr. by Erin Mouré, for my friends — a sequence). [MalR] (108) Fall 94, p. 58-61.
"Antistrophes" (tr. by Don Mager). [RiverS] (40) 94, p. 27, 29.
"Blue Hydrangeas" (tr. by David Young). [Field] (50) Spr 94, p. 23.
"The Bowl of Roses" (tr. by David Young). [Field] (50) Spr 94, p. 24-26.
"Buddha" (tr. by Bernhard Frank). [HeavenB] (11) 94, p. 38.
"Death-Experience" (tr. by David Young). [Field] (50) Spr 94, p. 21.
"Eros" (tr. by Jane Hirshfield, w. Samuel Michael Halevi). [DenQ] (29:1) Sum 94, p. 97.
"Gegen-Strophen." [RiverS] (40) 94, p. 26, 28.
"The Glory of Buddha" (tr. by Bernhard Frank). [HeavenB] (11) 94, p. 38.
"Happens a Man" (tr. by Steven Heighton). [Quarry] (43:3) n 94, p. 42.
"Untitled: From almost all things, It flashes toward feeling" (tr. by Jane Hirshfield, w. Samuel Michael Halevi). [DenQ] (29:1) Sum 94, p. 98.
"Untitled Stanzas" (in German and English, tr. by Don Mager). [RiverS] (40) 94, p. 30-31.
"Venice in Late Autumn" (tr. by David Young). [Field] (50) Spr 94, p. 22.
5195. RIMBAUD, Arthur
"After the Flood" (tr. by George Messo). [Pearl] (20) Spr 94, p. 84.
"Ophelia" (tr. by Rachel Hadas). [HarvardR] (Premier Issue) Spr 92, p. 21-22.
5196. RIMBEY, Anne Giles
"Silk." [Rosebud] (1:3) Aut-Wint 94, p. 125.
"What We Learn First." [Rosebud] (1:3) Aut-Wint 94, p. 124.
RIN, Ishigaki
See ISHIGAKI, Rin
5197. RIND, Sherry
"Breakfast Music." [PoetryNW] (35:2) Sum 94, p. 35-36.
"Plotting a Novel." [PoetryNW] (35:2) Sum 94, p. 32.
"The Silliness of the Ostrich." [PoetryNW] (35:2) Sum 94, p. 33.
"We Are Fun" (Monkey Mia Beach, Australia). [PoetryNW] (35:2) Sum 94, p. 34-35.
RING, Wendy White
See WHITE-RING, Wendy
5198. RINGEL, Marcia
"Our guests, displaying faultless breeding." [Light] (11) Aut 94, p. 30.
5199. RINGMA, Nick
"For You." [PraF] (15:1, #66) Spr 94, p. 113.

5200. RINKA, Stephanie
"Knowing What I've Got" (third prize in the 1994 *Chiron Review* Poetry Contest). [ChironR] (13:4) Wint 94, p. 14.
RIO, Zaida del
See Del RIO, Zaida
5201. RIORDAN, Maurice
"Apples." [Pivot] (42) 94, p. 1.
5202. RIOS, Alberto (Alberto Alvaro)
"Chinese Food in the Fifties." [Pequod] (38) 94, p. 85-87.
"Common Crows in the Winter Tree" (Pratt House, Vassar College). [PraS] (68:4) Wint 94, p. 17-19.
"Domingo Limón." [PraS] (68:4) Wint 94, p. 12-15.
"If I Leave You" (For Joaquín). [Pequod] (38) 94, p. 79-84.
"In My Hurry." [PraS] (68:4) Wint 94, p. 16-17.
"A Simple Thing to Know." [CreamCR] (18:2) Fall 94, p. 139.
"A Small Motor." [WilliamMR] (32) 94, p. 7.
5203. RIOS, Alexandra (*See also* NEWTON-RIOS, Alexandra)
"Languages of Leaving." [Jacaranda] (4:2) Spr 90, p. 78-79.
5204. RISTAU, Harland
"Enigma." [Northeast] (5:10) Sum 94, p. 18.
5205. RISTOVIC, Aleksandar (Aleksander)
"About Hope and Dissipation" (tr. by Charles Simic). [Agni] (40) 94, p. 176-177.
"Comparison" (tr. by Charles Simic). [Field] (51) Fall 94, p. 75.
"Mythology" (tr. by Charles Simic). [Field] (51) Fall 94, p. 76.
"Simple Desire" (tr. by Charles Simic). [Agni] (40) 94, p. 178.
"Wine of Collusion" (tr. by Charles Simic). [Agni] (40) 94, p. 175.
5206. RITCHESON, Brendan
"Ghazals." [AntR] (52:1) Wint 94, p. 100-102.
"Medication Song: Pierced by Her Look I Succumb." [AntR] (52:1) Wint 94, p. 103.
"A Night Alone in the Haunted Motel." [AntR] (52:1) Wint 94, p. 96-97.
"Running into Bierce Just North of Chihuahua City, Easter, 1985." [AntR] (52:1) Wint 94, p. 98-99.
5207. RITCHIE, Elisavietta
"Instructions for Collected Works." [NewYorkQ] (53) 94, p. 70.
"One Wedding Night." [Kalliope] (16:3) 94, p. 37.
5208. RITCHINGS, Joan Drew
"Ant." [Light] (10) Sum 94, p. 9.
"Dilemma." [Light] (10) Sum 94, p. 14.
"Wild Party." [Light] (10) Sum 94, p. 10.
5209. RITSOS, Yannis
"3 x 111 Tristychs" (Selections, tr. by José García and Adamantia García-Baltatzi). [PaintedHR] (11) Spr-Sum 94, p. 28.
"Evacuation" (tr. by Martin McKinsey). [Field] (50) Spr 94, p. 37.
"Illicit Spring" (tr. by Martin McKinsey). [HarvardR] (7) Fall 94, p. 30.
"In the Garden" (tr. by Martin McKinsey). [HarvardR] (7) Fall 94, p. 29.
"On Silence" (tr. by Martin McKinsey). [TriQ] (92) Wint 94-95, p. 257.
"The Original Position" (tr. by Martin McKinsey). [Field] (50) Spr 94, p. 40.
"The Other Fear" (tr. by Martin McKinsey). [TriQ] (92) Wint 94-95, p. 256.
"Stages of Weariness" (tr. by Martin McKinsey). [Field] (50) Spr 94, p. 41.
"The Trail" (tr. by Martin McKinsey). [Field] (50) Spr 94, p. 38.
"Until One Night" (tr. by Martin McKinsey). [Field] (50) Spr 94, p. 39.
5210. RITTER, Kelly
"Given." [GreensboroR] (56) Sum 94, p. 62.
5211. RIVARD, David
"Big Mood Swing." [HarvardR] (6) Spr 94, p. 82-83.
"Curious Forces." [TriQ] (92) Wint 94-95, p. 79-80.
"God the Broken Lock." [HayF] (14) Spr-Sum 94, p. 69-70.
"It Could Be." [HayF] (14) Spr-Sum 94, p. 67-68.
"Jihad." [TriQ] (92) Wint 94-95, p. 77-78.
"Self Portrait." [HarvardR] (Premier Issue) Spr 92, p. 15-16.
"The Shy." [Ploughs] (20:4) Wint 94-95, p. 161-162.
"Welcome, Fear." [Ploughs] (20:4) Wint 94-95, p. 159-160.
5212. RIVERO, Mario
"Ballad of Things Lost" (For Giovanni Quessep, tr. by Elizabeth B. Clark). [ApalQ] (42) Fall 94, p. 44-48.

"Suddenly Someone Is Knocking" (tr. by Elizabeth B. Clark). [ApalQ] (42) Fall 94, p. 43.

ROBB, Maria Elena Caballero
See CABALLERO-ROBB, Maria Elena

5213. ROBBINS, Anthony
"Quince, Too, in the Gloom More Radiant: Vide Cor Tuum." [YellowS] (12:1, #45) Spr-Sum 94, p. 13.

5214. ROBBINS, Michael
"1380 19th St. #2" (for Deirdre). [Plain] (14:2) Wint 94, p. 13.
"For Deirdre." [Plain] (14:3) Spr 94, p. 31.
"Memories of the Island." [PoetL] (89:3) Fall 94, p. 34.
"Rumors of the Hellhound." [PoetL] (89:3) Fall 94, p. 35.

5215. ROBBINS, Richard
"First Grade." [GreensboroR] (56) Sum 94, p. 63.
"Pioneer Reburied Near Casper" (Quintinna Snodderly, Oregon Trail, 1852). [CumbPR] (14:1) Fall 94, p. 52-53.
"Reversals." [LaurelR] (28:1) Wint 94, p. 65-66.

5216. ROBBINS, Sheryl
"Ahab." [DenQ] (29:2) Fall 94, p. 26-27.

5217. ROBBINS, Tim
"Eskimo Tale." [HangL] (64) 94, p. 60.
"Mayberry" (for Marc). [JamesWR] (11:4) Sum 94, p. 14.
"Takahashi Mutsuo." [HangL] (64) 94, p. 61.
"Tannenbaum." [JamesWR] (11:2) Wint 94, p. 8.
"Upanishads." [JamesWR] (11:2) Wint 94, p. 9.

5218. ROBERTI, Rem
"A Twelve Step Lament." [Amelia] (7:4, #23) 94, p. 128.

5219. ROBERTS, Andy
"Chestnuts and Hazels." [BellArk] (10:2) Mr-Ap 94, p. 31.
"Discus, Laps, Javelin." [BellArk] (10:5) S-O 94, p. 27.
"Girl Gangs." [BlackBR] (18) Wint-Spr 94, p. 27.
"A Point in Time." [HiramPoR] (55/56) Fall 93-Sum 94, p. 102-103.

5220. ROBERTS, David Thomas
"Inanimate Intimacy." [HeavenB] (11) 94, p. 47.
"The Jack of Diamonds Goes to Silo-Land." [HeavenB] (11) 94, p. 48-49.

5221. ROBERTS, Gildas
"Home-thoughts, from Abroad" (or Sod You, Robert Browning). [TickleAce] (28) Fall-Wint 94, p. 59-60.
"The Long Weekend of Mister Kilby." [TickleAce] (28) Fall-Wint 94, p. 61-63.

5222. ROBERTS, Ginger
"Watching a Sleeping Pig." [PoetL] (89:2) Sum 94, p. 20.

5223. ROBERTS, Katrina
"Vendange." [SouthernPR] (34:2) Wint 94, p. 37-38.

5224. ROBERTS, Kevin
"Interns." [Descant] (24:4, #83) Wint 93-94, p. 9-10.
"Narrows." [MalR] (108) Fall 94, p. 48.
"Phone Calls." [Descant] (24:4, #83) Wint 93-94, p. 7-8.

5225. ROBERTS, Kim
"The Double-Breasted Pepper Project." [RiverS] (40) 94, p. 25.
"Truro Dunes, Cape Cod." [Confr] (54/55) Fall 94-Wint 95, p. 314.

5226. ROBERTS, Len
"After the Fight." [PraS] (68:3) Fall 94, p. 103-104.
"After the Second Operation." [PraS] (68:3) Fall 94, p. 104-105.
"Climbing the Three Hills in Search of the Best Christmas Tree." [GreenMR] (NS 17:2) Fall-Wint 94-95, p. 12-13.
"The Day after Easter" (tr. of Sandor Csoori). [SouthernR] (30:2) Ap, Spr 94, p. 282-283.
"Diary, Early Fall of 1982" (tr. of Sándor Csoóri). [NowestR] (32:2) 94, p. 24.
"Ecclesiastes Ch. 1, V. 9" (tr. of Sandor Knayadi, w. Eva Bordisne). [Boulevard] (9:3, #27) Fall 94, p. 138-139.
"First the Girdle and Brown." [PoetL] (89:4) Wint 94-95, p. 29-30.
"Fleeing Soldier, 1944" (tr. of Sándor Csoóri). [NowestR] (32:2) 94, p. 25.
"He's Alone." [AmerPoR] (23:3) My-Je 94, p. 48.
"Holy and Wicked Time" (tr. of Sándor Csoóri, w. Miklos Horvath). [NowestR] (32:2) 94, p. 26.

"I Look Back and Don't See Myself" (tr. of Sandor Csoori). [AnotherCM] (28) 94, p. 30-31.
"I Shall Go, I'm Going" (tr. of Sándor Csoóri). [NowestR] (32:2) 94, p. 29.
"I Surrender Myself" (tr. of Sándor Csoóri, w. László Vertes). [NowestR] (32:2) 94, p. 28.
"If Forgetting What You Know." [BlackWR] (20:2) Spr-Sum 94, p. 118-119.
"If I Had Believed" (tr. of Sandor Csoori, w. Laszlo Vertes). [AnotherCM] (28) 94, p. 32.
"Injured Poem" (For Ferenc Kiss, who's learning to speak after his stroke. Tr. of Sándor Csoóri). [DenQ] (29:1) Sum 94, p. 55.
"My Mother's Trailer." [WestB] (34) 94, p. 45-46.
"My Son Reminds Me." [PoetryE] (37/38) Spr 94, p. 91.
"My Wife Wants Me to Cut." [GrahamHR] (18) Wint 94-95, p. 46-47.
"The Orange Tiger Lilies Opened." [Journal] (18:1) Spr-Sum 94, p. 116-117.
"Parting the Sheets." [Journal] (18:1) Spr-Sum 94, p. 114-115.
"Reconsidering the Commandments." [SouthernPR] (34:1) Sum 94, p. 24-25.
"Refusal." [GreenMR] (NS 17:2) Fall-Wint 94-95, p. 14-15.
"Rich." [PoetryE] (37/38) Spr 94, p. 92-93.
"Ripping Slate Off the Barn Roof." [PoetL] (89:4) Wint 94-95, p. 27-28.
"Sister Ann Zita Shows Us the Foolishness of the Forbidden Books." [WestB] (34) 94, p. 44-45.
"The Smile of My Exile" (tr. of Sándor Csoóri, w. Miklos Horvath). [NowestR] (32:2) 94, p. 23.
"There Are No Angels on These Walls." [Journal] (18:1) Spr-Sum 94, p. 118-120.
"There Are Only Days" (tr. of Sándor Csoóri). [NowestR] (32:2) 94, p. 27.
"The Way of the Cross." [AmerPoR] (23:3) My-Je 94, p. 48.
"Well." [GrahamHR] (18) Wint 94-95, p. 44-45.

5227. ROBERTS, Michael Symmons
"A Free Lunch." [Verse] (11:1) Spr 94, p. 63.
"A Near Collision of Free Agents." [Verse] (11:1) Spr 94, p. 63.

5228. ROBERTS, Michèle
"Lacrimae Rerum." [Jacaranda] (5:1) Wint-Spr 91, p. 82-83.

5229. ROBERTS, Nora Ruth
"One Day While I Was Walking Home." [ContextS] (4:1) 94, p. 8.

5230. ROBERTS, Stephen R.
"Brainstorming or Why the Birds Are Not Singing." [SoCoast] (17) Je 94, p. 39.
"Chinese Restaurant Dream." [Plain] (14:2) Wint 94, p. 16.

5231. ROBERTS, Teresa Noelle
"At Judy's Loft Diner, Candor, NY." [BellArk] (10:2) Mr-Ap 94, p. 28.
"College Dining Hall" (for Lauren). [BellArk] (10:2) Mr-Ap 94, p. 28.
"Lost on a Back Road Near Seneca Lake While Contemplating Moving to Boston." [BellArk] (10:6) N-D 94, p. 10.
"The Place in Wood Where the Fire Hides." [BellArk] (10:3) My-Je 94, p. 9.
"She Praises Her Lover's Bones." [BellArk] (10:2) Mr-Ap 94, p. 28.
"Spring Tonic." [BellArk] (10:6) N-D 94, p. 10.
"Stillroom." [BellArk] (10:5) S-O 94, p. 26.
"Tenacity." [BellArk] (10:2) Mr-Ap 94, p. 28.
"Tortoiseshell Logic." [BellArk] (10:2) Mr-Ap 94, p. 28.
"Vernal." [BellArk] (10:3) My-Je 94, p. 9.
"When Wildlife and Agriculture Become Incompatible, I Know Which to Choose." [BellArk] (10:5) S-O 94, p. 26.
"Your Business Trip Was Badly Timed, Beloved: A Pagan Lust-Song." [BellArk] (10:5) S-O 94, p. 26.

5232. ROBERTS, Tony
"J i.m." [SouthernR] (30:2) Ap, Spr 94, p. 316.

5233. ROBERTSON, Hugh
"Horror Vacui." [Sonora] (27) Spr 94, p. 108-109.

5234. ROBERTSON, Lisa
"I want someone to say what you say" (w. Susan Clark and Catriona Strang). [Chain] (1) Spr-Sum 94, p. 29.

5235. ROBERTSON, Robin
"Artichoke." [NewYorker] (70:41) 12 D 94, p. 120.

5236. ROBERTSON, Trevor
"Into Another Man's House." [PraF] (15:3, #68) Aut 94, p. 72.
"Woman Is, Comma." [PraF] (15:3, #68) Aut 94, p. 73.

5237. ROBERTSON, William
"Bird Dog." [Grain] (21:4) Spr 94, p. 119.
"Boys to Men." [Event] (23:2) Sum 94, p. 37-39.
"Signals." [Grain] (21:4) Spr 94, p. 118.
5238. ROBERTUS, Polly M.
"The Lion Tamer's Wife." [CapeR] (29:1) Spr 94, p. 26.
5239. ROBINER, Linda Goodman
"As You Lay Dying." [ChironR] (13:2) Sum 94, p. 31.
"Poet." [HiramPoR] (55/56) Fall 93-Sum 94, p. 104.
5240. ROBINS, Corinne
"Review." [AnotherCM] (27) 94, p. 176.
5241. ROBINSON, Blake
"Some Distichs." [Border] (3) Fall 93, p. 61.
5242. ROBINSON, Elizabeth
"i. Let's begin again." [Chain] (1) Spr-Sum 94, p. 263-265.
"Creases." [Avec] (7:1) 94, p. 79-82.
5243. ROBINSON, James Miller
"Heading Back to Tuscaloosa." [ChatR] (14:2) Wint 94, p. 44.
5244. ROBINSON, John
"Mongoose." [AnthNEW] (6) 94, p. 24.
5245. ROBISON, Margaret
"The Bridge of Flowers." [NegC] (14:1/2) 94, p. 95.
"Counting." [NegC] (14:1/2) 94, p. 96.
"My Father." [Parting] (7:2) Wint 94-95, p. 50.
"Red." [Parting] (7:2) Wint 94-95, p. 50.
5246. ROBY, Gayle
"Still-fishing." [Iowa] (24:1) Wint 94, p. 77.
ROCA, Daniel Jacome
See JACOME-ROCA, Daniel
ROCCA, L. (Lenny) della
See DellaROCCA, L. (Lenny)
5247. ROCHE, Dale
"Vienna." [SouthernPR] (34:1) Sum 94, p. 10-11.
5248. ROCHE, Maurice
"Codex" (Excerpts, tr. by Alexander Laurence). [Talisman] (13) Fall 94-Wint 95, p. 16-34.
5249. ROCHE, Paul
"The Dinner Candle (Positano, July 1984)." [Confr] (52/53) Wint-Spr 94, p. 332.
5250. ROCHELEAU, Linda
"After the Hurricane." [ChironR] (13:3) Aut 94, p. 17.
"The Bitch." [ChironR] (13:3) Aut 94, p. 17.
"Standing Ovation." [ChironR] (13:3) Aut 94, p. 17.
5251. ROCHESTER, John Wilmot, Earl of
"The Latter End of the Chorus of the Second Act of Seneca's *Troades*" (tr. of Seneca). [SoCoast] (16) Ja 94, p. 59.
5252. ROCK, David
"En la Finca de Mi Abuelo." [LindLM] (13:1) Mr 94, p. 30.
"Making to Westward the Caravel." [HiramPoR] (57) Fall 94-Wint 95, p. 51.
5253. ROCKEL, Nicholas
"Alkaios 347." [Descant] (25:1, #84) Spr 94, p. 26.
"Alkaios Fr. 130." [Descant] (25:1, #84) Spr 94, p. 35.
"Alkaios Fr. 332." [Descant] (25:1, #84) Spr 94, p. 25.
"Alkman Fr. 58." [Descant] (25:1, #84) Spr 94, p. 33.
"Archilochos Fr. 71." [Descant] (25:1, #84) Spr 94, p. 28.
"Catullus 2." [Descant] (25:1, #84) Spr 94, p. 27.
"Catullus 8." [Descant] (25:1, #84) Spr 94, p. 32.
"Catullus 43." [Descant] (25:1, #84) Spr 94, p. 34.
"Catullus 73." [Descant] (25:1, #84) Spr 94, p. 30.
"Catullus 75." [Descant] (25:1, #84) Spr 94, p. 31.
"Ibykos Fr. 286." [Descant] (25:1, #84) Spr 94, p. 29.
5254. ROCKIN' RED
"On the Euphemisms of Entombment." [Light] (12) Wint 94-95, p. 20.
5255. ROCKWELL, Tom
"Sexual Politics." [NewYorkQ] (53) 94, p. 113.
5256. RODE, Curt
"The Poet at Five." [SycamoreR] (6:2) Sum 94, p. 52.

5257. RODEMAN, Juliet
"In the House of God." [AnthNEW] (6) 94, p. 12.
5258. RODENBECK, John
"1914-1915" (Excerpt, tr. of Giuseppe Ungaretti). [Iowa] (24:1) Wint 94, p. 164.
"First Love" (tr. of Giuseppe Ungaretti). [Iowa] (24:1) Wint 94, p. 163-164.
"Intervention of the Gods" (tr. of C. P. Cavafy). [Iowa] (24:1) Wint 94, p. 162.
"On the Actual Site" (tr. of C. P. Cavafy). [Iowa] (24:1) Wint 94, p. 162.
"Phase" (Mariano, 25 June 1916, tr. of Giuseppe Ungaretti). [Iowa] (24:1) Wint 94, p. 163.
5259. RODGERS, Mary Columbro
"I Looked for Loveliness" (from "Catholic Marriage Poems 1962-1979"). [AmerPoR] (23:4) Jl-Ag 94, p. 28.
5260. RODIA, Becky
"Embrace." [LaurelR] (28:2) Sum 94, p. 53.
5261. RODIN, Renee
"For Florence." [CapilR] (2:12) Wint 94, p. 23-24.
"For Luck." [CapilR] (2:12) Wint 94, p. 17-19.
"Readers and Company." [CapilR] (2:12) Wint 94, p. 20-22.
5262. RODNING, Charles Bernard
"Haiku / Senryu Sequence." [NegC] (14:1/2) 94, p. 8.
5263. RODRIGUEZ, Aleida
"History." [KenR] (NS 16:1) Wint 94, p. 98-99.
"Landscape." [KenR] (NS 16:1) Wint 94, p. 99-100.
"My Mother in Two Photographs, Among Other things." [PraS] (68:4) Wint 94, p. 19-21.
5264. RODRIGUEZ, Andrés
"Papa Cayo." [BilingR] (19:1) Ja-Ap 94, p. 58-59.
"Summer." [BilingR] (19:1) Ja-Ap 94, p. 59-60.
5265. RODRIGUEZ, Carmen
"Destiny." [WestCL] (28:1/2, #13/14) Spr-Fall 94, p. 19.
"Lights." [WestCL] (28:1/2, #13/14) Spr-Fall 94, p. 19.
"Naked Out There." [WestCL] (28:1/2, #13/14) Spr-Fall 94, p. 20.
"What Does Not Exist." [WestCL] (28:1/2, #13/14) Spr-Fall 94, p. 19.
5266. RODRIGUEZ, Lola
"ManhattAntilles." [CaribbeanW] (8) 94, p. 15-16.
5267. RODRIGUEZ, Michael
"Archeologist." [FreeL] (13) Spr 94, p. 20-21.
"The Thresholds of Pain." [FreeL] (13) Spr 94, p. 18-20.
5268. RODRIGUEZ, Osvaldo
"El Amor Se Acaba." [Areíto] (4:15) Marzo 94, p. 43.
5269. RODRIGUEZ, Rebecca (age 11)
"Just a Gust of Wind." [AnthNEW] (6) 94, p. 38.
5270. RODRIGUEZ, Reina María
"The Islands" (tr. by Ruth Behar). [MichQR] (33:4) Fall 94, p. 783-784.
"Letter to a Woman Friend" (tr. by Ruth Behar). [MichQR] (33:4) Fall 94, p. 784.
5271. RODRIGUEZ-RODRIGUEZ, Jorge
"Niño watching mounted police." [Amelia] (7:3, #22) 94, p. 8.
5272. ROE, Margie McCreless
"Holy Saturday." [ChrC] (111:10) 23-30 Mr 94, p. 304.
"Talking in the Dark." [Border] (3) Fall 93, p. 63-64.
"Whitman." [Border] (3) Fall 93, p. 62.
ROECK, Galina de
See De ROECK, Galina
5273. ROESKE, Paulette
"The Absence of Edges" (to Lisel Mueller). [PoetryNW] (35:2) Sum 94, p. 30-31.
"Accordion." [PoetryE] (37/38) Spr 94, p. 155-163.
"High Image Therapy." [PoetryNW] (35:2) Sum 94, p. 29-30.
5274. ROFFÉ, Mercedes
"Cancer Gnaws from My Shoulderblades" (tr. by K. A. Kopple). [SenR] (24:2) Fall 94, p. 64-68.
5275. ROGERS, Bertha
"Japanese Beetle Trap." [Pivot] (42) 94, p. 14.
"Night Song." [Pivot] (42) 94, p. 13.
"Turkey Buzzard." [Pivot] (41) 93, p. 24.
5276. ROGERS, Daryl
"I Finally Gave In and Called Her Tonight." [WormR] (34:1, #133) 94, p. 19-20.

"James Joyce Goes to a Biker Bar." [WormR] (34:1, #133) 94, p. 19.
"June 10, Malibu Drive." [SlipS] (14) 94, p. 7.
"Rattletrap." [WormR] (34:1, #133) 94, p. 20.
"Sacrifice." [SlipS] (14) 94, p. 6.

5277. ROGERS, Del Marie
"High-flying Man" (after James Surls' sculpture). [Border] (3) Fall 93, p. 66.

5278. ROGERS, Denise
"Sleeping with God." [Border] (5) Fall-Wint 94, p. 55-56.

5279. ROGERS, K. S.
"Just This Side of Ripe." [Blueline] (15) 94, p. 75.

5280. ROGERS, Linda
"Mother Board." [MalR] (109) Wint 94, p. 73-74.
"Someone Who Rode Horses." [MalR] (109) Wint 94, p. 72.
"Surprised by the Flood." [MalR] (109) Wint 94, p. 70-71.

5281. ROGERS, Pattiann
"Egg." [GeoR] (48:4) Wint 94, p. 640-641.
"The Fallacy of Thinking Flesh Is Flesh." [ParisR] (36:133) Wint 94, p. 278-279.
"Idée Fixe." [WeberS] (11:3) Fall 94, p. 30-31.
"Rapture of the Deep: The Pattern of Poseidon's Love Song." [Poetry] (164:5) Ag 94, p. 268-269.
"Sensual Deprivation." [WeberS] (11:3) Fall 94, p. 31-32.
"The Singing Place." [ParisR] (36:133) Wint 94, p. 279-280.

5282. ROGERS-GREEN, Carmen
"Election Time — Again." [CaribbeanW] (8) 94, p. 48-49.
"Tonight." [CaribbeanW] (8) 94, p. 50-51.

5283. ROGET, Gwendoline Lewis
"Farewell to Summer" (from "Elans under a Wynnewood Sky"). [AmerPoR] (23:5) S-O 94, p. 32.

5284. ROGOFF, Jay
"Laughter." [KenR] (NS 16:3) Sum 94, p. 18-21.
"Welcome to the Family." [PraS] (68:3) Fall 94, p. 21-22.

5285. ROHRER, Matthew
"Hotel de l'Etoile." [DenQ] (29:1) Sum 94, p. 34.

5286. ROJAS, Gonzalo
"Carta a Huidobro." [Inti] (39) Primavera 94, p. 243-244.
"Flores para Humberto" (A.H. Días-Casanueva). [Inti] (39) Primavera 94, p. 244-245.
"Four Epigrams" (tr. by Ben Belitt). [Colum] (22) Wint 94, p. 154.
"Numen" (tr. by Ben Belitt). [Colum] (22) Wint 94, p. 152-153.
"La Sedentaria" (A Mercedes come era, gorda y protentosa). [Inti] (39) Primavera 94, p. 245.

5287. ROLLINGS, Alane
"To Be a Different Person." [GettyR] (7:1) Wint 94, p. 176-177.
"The Uncontrollability of Things." [GettyR] (7:1) Wint 94, p. 174-175.

5288. ROLLINSON, Neil
"Interference." [Pivot] (41) 93, p. 31.

5289. ROMAN, Aurelia
"Ballade" (tr. of Eugene Ionescu, w. Bradley R. Strahan). [Vis] (46) 94, p. 5.
"Croquis Humoristique" (tr. of Eugene Ionescu, w. Bradley R. Strahan). [Vis] (46) 94, p. 4.
"The Exhausted One" (tr. of Eugene Ionescu, w. Bradley R. Strahan). [Vis] (46) 94, p. 5.

5290. ROMANENKO, Alexander Petrovich
"The Third Degree of Freedom" (2 selections, tr. by Galina De Roeck). [Manoa] (6:2) Wint 94, p. 80-81.

5291. ROMANO, Rose
"Breaking Legs." [SlipS] (14) 94, p. 79.

5292. ROMOND, Edwin
"Classroom Fight on Monday." [Sun] (228) D 94, p. 23.
"Dravecky Dreams." [Spitball] (46) Spr 94, p. 41.

5293. ROMOSAN, Petru
"A Ride at Daybreak" (for Nichita Stanescu as a young poet, tr. by Adam J. Sorkin). [Vis] (44) 94, p. 39.
"Winter Tale" (tr. by Adam J. Sorkin and Radu Surdulescu). [Vis] (46) 94, p. 29.

5294. ROMTVEDT, David
"Having a Rest." [Border] (3) Fall 93, p. 67.

"Ho Chi Minh City." [Pivot] (42) 94, p. 12.
"Who Owes Us." [Ploughs] (20:4) Wint 94-95, p. 163.

5295. RONAN, John
"Rite of Spring." [CrabCR] (8:2/3/9:1/2/3) 94, p. 72-73.

5296. RONCI, Ray
"My Skull." [Agni] (40) 94, p. 150-151.

5297. RONK, Martha
"The mind of another wants nothing you can see." [Talisman] (12) Spr 94, p. 232.
"Not Just a Pronoun." [DenQ] (29:2) Fall 94, p. 28-38.
"The question of why another lifts your spirits so." [Talisman] (12) Spr 94, p. 232.
"A State of Mind." [Chelsea] (57) 94, p. 57-58.

5298. ROOT, William Pitt
"Crossing the Rez." [HighP] (9:2) Ag 94, p. 42-43.

5299. ROPPEL, Katherine
"Metamorphoses." [Amelia] (7:3, #22) 94, p. 156.

5300. ROQUEPLAN, Fernand
"King of Wounds." [IndR] (17:1) Spr 94, p. 161.
"What Vishnu Dreamed." [Vis] (46) 94, p. 32.

5301. RORIPAUGH, Lee Ann
"Pearls." [NewEngR] (16:2) Spr 94, p. 124-125.

5302. ROSBERG, Rose
"Double Vision." [NewRena] (9:1, #27) 94, p. 59.
"Reopened Accounts." [NewRena] (9:1, #27) 94, p. 57-58.

5303. ROSE, Carol
"Election Day — Israel — 1992." [Quarry] (42:4) Mr 94, p. 33.
"Fleshing Out the Rib: Revisioning Women in Biblical Myth" (Honourable Mention, Long Poem Category). [PraF] (15:4, #69) Wint 94-95, p. 50-61.
"Jerusalem: Another Version of the Story" (for Di Brandt). [Quarry] (42:4) Mr 94, p. 35.
"Lamentations." [Quarry] (42:4) Mr 94, p. 31.
"Married, Forever." [Quarry] (42:4) Mr 94, p. 37.
"Occupied Territories: An Argument in Poetry" (w. Di Brandt). [Quarry] (42:4) Mr 94, p. 29-37.

5304. ROSE, Dorothy L.
"Wish Book." [Rosebud] (1:2) Sum 94, p. 30-31.

5305. ROSE, Judith
"Gift." [PraS] (68:2) Sum 94, p. 128-129.
"Off Range Road, La Porte County." [PraS] (68:2) Sum 94, p. 130-131.
"What She Ate Last Night, Dreaming." [PraS] (68:2) Sum 94, p. 129.

5306. ROSE, Rachel
"Opening the Storm Eye." [PraF] (15:3, #68) Aut 94, p. 77.

5307. ROSEN, Kenneth
"Equinox." [BelPoJ] (45:1) Fall 94, p. 26-27.
"Prospectors." [WestHR] (48:1) Spr 94, p. 27-29.

5308. ROSEN, Michael J.
"Green Thumb, Blue Tail, White Lie" (for M. V.). [Thrpny] (58) Sum 94, p. 29.
"The Night Before His Parents' First Trip to Europe His Mother Writes a Letter 'To Our Children'." [Salm] (103) Sum 94, p. 97-98.
"Penn's Rescue." [PraS] (68:1) Spr 94, p. 118-124.

5309. ROSEN, Rachael
"Subjected." [SinW] (54) Wint 94-95, p. 80.
"Words." [SinW] (52) Spr-Sum 94, p. 7.

5310. ROSEN, Sally
"The Artist of My Own Sitting Down." [PoetryNW] (35:2) Sum 94, p. 13-14.
"Letter Home: Hydrangeas." [PoetryNW] (35:2) Sum 94, p. 14-15.
"To Eve." [PoetryNW] (35:2) Sum 94, p. 12.

5311. ROSENBERG, Victoria H.
"Thoughts on Leaving a Board Meeting." [AntigR] (98) Sum 94, p. 14.

5312. ROSENFELD, Natania
"The End of Summer." [AntR] (52:4) Fall 94, p. 606-607.

5313. ROSENFIELD, Kim
"Hot Place" (to Joan Retallack). [Chain] (1) Spr-Sum 94, p. 195.

5314. ROSENSTOCK, S. X.
"Doyenne du Comice." [WestHR] (48:3) Fall 94, p. 229.
"Pretext." [WestHR] (48:4) Wint 94, p. 321-323.

"Le Réalisme Fantastique de Berthe Bovary Lipshitz en Anglais Americain" (for my Alison Blythe). [ParisR] (36:130) Spr 94, p. 141-145.
"The Women of Jekyll & Hyde." [WestHR] (48:3) Fall 94, p. 228-229.

5315. ROSENTHAL, M. L.
"The Beautiful Angels." [Nat] (258:17) My 2 94, p. 608.

5316. ROSENWALD, John
"The Cat at a Friend's House" (tr. of Zhang Zhen, w. Yanbing Chen). [AnotherCM] (27) 94, p. 76-77.
"The City" (4 selections, tr. of Gu Cheng, w. Chen Yanbing and the Beloit/Fudan Translation Workshop). [Manoa] (6:1) Sum 94, p. 118-120.
"Garden" (tr. of Chen Dongdong, w. Yanbing Chen). [AnotherCM] (27) 94, p. 75.
"In Sickness" (tr. of Chen Dongdong, w. Yanbing Chen). [AnotherCM] (27) 94, p. 74.
"The North" (tr. of Chen Dongdong, w. Yanbing Chen). [AnotherCM] (27) 94, p. 72.
"Poetry" (tr. of Chen Dongdong, w. Yanbing Chen). [AnotherCM] (27) 94, p. 73.
"When the People Rise from Cheese" (Statement #1, tr. of Duo Duo). [AnotherCM] (27) 94, p. 216.

5317. ROSENWASSER, Rena
"The Right Plate over the Panic Grasses." [Chelsea] (57) 94, p. 74.
"Triptych." [Zyzzyva] (10:1) Spr 94, p. 104-108.
"Undoing Herself." [Chelsea] (57) 94, p. 73.

5318. ROSENZWEIG, Geri
"The Flaxen God." [AntigR] (96) Wint 94, p. 139-140.

5319. ROSENZWEIG, Phyllis
"Wet" (to Diane Ward). [Chain] (1) Spr-Sum 94, p. 245-246.

5320. ROSNAY, Jean-Pierre
"France" (tr. by J. Kates). [PoetryE] (37/38) Spr 94, p. 210.
"I Write Books" (tr. by J. Kates). [PoetryE] (37/38) Spr 94, p. 208.
"There Is No Heaven" (tr. by J. Kates). [PoetryE] (37/38) Spr 94, p. 209.

5321. ROSS, David
"Afternoon." [BellArk] (10:6) N-D 94, p. 27.
"Earthed." [BellArk] (10:6) N-D 94, p. 27.
"Turn." [BellArk] (10:3 [i.e. 10:4]) Jl-Ag 94, p. 26.
"A View from the Hill." [BellArk] (10:3 [i.e. 10:4]) Jl-Ag 94, p. 25.
"Wild Parrots." [TampaR] (8) Spr 94, p. 40.

5322. ROSS, Emily
"At the Horse Show." [Amelia] (7:4, #23) 94, p. 91.

5323. ROSS, Linwood M.
"For Fire Escape Women." [Wind] (74) 94, p. 27-28.
"The Murphy Gang." [ChironR] (13:2) Sum 94, p. 24.
"My Black Mama Poem." [PaintedB] (53/54) 94, p. 103-104.

5324. ROSSELLI, Amelia
"Four Poems" (tr. by Lucia Re and Paul Vangelisti). [Chelsea] (57) 94, p. 79-81.

5325. ROSSER, J. Allyn
"Coming Your Way." [Poetry] (163:5) F 94, p. 253-254.
"Delayed Response." [MichQR] (33:2) Spr 94, p. 346-347.
"Late Elvis." [MichQR] (33:2) Spr 94, p. 345.
"Late Letter." [Poetry] (165:3) D 94, p. 152.
"Square Dance, Fourth Grade." [GeoR] (48:4) Wint 94, p. 741-742.

ROSSI, Cristina Peri
See PERI ROSSI, Cristina

5326. ROSSI, J.
"Blackout." [BambooR] (63/64) Sum-Fall 94, p. 44-45.

5327. ROSSI, Lee
"Patrimony." [Jacaranda] (4:2) Spr 90, p. 104-105.

5328. ROSSI, Mark Antony
"The Fix." [ContextS] (4:1) 94, p. 33.

5329. ROSSI, Michele
"The Horned Moon Ditty." [Amelia] (7:3, #22) 94, p. 53.
"Winter." [Amelia] (7:3, #22) 94, p. 65.

5330. ROSSINI, Clare
"Nightmare." [NewEngR] (16:2) Spr 94, p. 57.

5331. ROTELLA, Alexis
"Deep inside the Blizzard." [Amelia] (7:4, #23) 94, p. 160.

5332. ROTH, Paul
"Holding the Moon." [DarkMoon] (1) 94, p. 21.
"Husk of a Secret." [DarkMoon] (1) 94, p. 19.
"Old Heart." [DarkMoon] (1) 94, p. 18.
"Onondaga." [DarkMoon] (1) 94, p. 20.
"Quicksand Sky." [DarkMoon] (1) 94, p. 22.
"Staying Outside." [DarkMoon] (1) 94, p. 17.
5333. ROTH, Ron
"No One Told Him It's a Gift." [SoDakR] (32:3) Fall 94, p. 47-48.
5334. ROTH-NATALE, Nanci
"Boris at Play." [BellArk] (10:2) Mr-Ap 94, p. 27.
5335. ROTHMAN, David J.
"Apollo to the Athletes." [Agni] (39) 94, p. 26-27.
"Bird, Beast, and Flower." [GettyR] (7:2) Spr 94, p. 349.
"The Death of the Unicorn." [Hellas] (5:2) Fall-Wint 94, p. 64-65.
"One of the Lords of Life." [Poetry] (163:6) Mr 94, p. 320-321.
"The Year of Wind." [GettyR] (7:2) Spr 94, p. 348.
5336. ROTHMAN, Susan Noe
"Pencil Test." [SlipS] (14) 94, p. 19.
5337. ROTTNER, Brendelle
"Thin gnarled finger." [Amelia] (7:3, #22) 94, p. 7.
5338. ROUBAUD, Jacques
"I Dream" (tr. by Harriet Zinnes). [DenQ] (29:1) Sum 94, p. 99.
"Under the Colors of" (from *La pluralité des mondes de Lewis*, tr. by Rosmarie Waldrop). [CentralP] (23) Spr 94, p. 33-37.
"You Are Safe" (tr. by Harriet Zinnes). [DenQ] (29:1) Sum 94, p. 100.
5339. ROUSE, Michael
"Wood Finishes." [Dandel] (21:1) 94, p. 13.
5340. ROUZIER, Agnès
"Non, Rien" (Excerpt, tr. by Chet Wiener). [Avec] (8:1) 94, p. 77-83.
5341. ROWE, Candice
"Promise." [Border] (3) Fall 93, p. 68.
5342. ROXMAN, Susanna
"Interior with a Kitchen Maid." [Vis] (45) 94, p. 28.
"Interior with a Kitchen Maid." [WebR] (18) Fall 94, p. 87.
"Old Executioners." [WebR] (18) Fall 94, p. 88.
"The Salt Lick." [WebR] (18) Fall 94, p. 86.
5343. ROY, Lucinda
"Genesis." [AmerPoR] (23:2) Mr-Ap 94, p. 8.
5344. ROYNESDAL, John A.
"The Watchers." [ChamLR] (14/15) Spr-Fall 94, p. 112-114.
5345. RRESHPJA, Frederik
"The Forest at Night" (tr. by Uk Bucpapa and Henry Israeli). [DenQ] (29:1) Sum 94, p. 101.
"The Sea" (tr. by Uk Bucpapa and Henry Israeli). [DenQ] (29:1) Sum 94, p. 102.
5346. RUBIN, Larry
"The Bachelor, Reconsidering." [NewEngR] (16:4) Fall 94, p. 87.
5347. RUBIN, Mark
"God and Country." [SycamoreR] (6:2) Sum 94, p. 34.
"Reconciliation." [GettyR] (7:3) Sum 94, p. 469.
"Springtime in Tompkins Square." [GettyR] (7:3) Sum 94, p. 470.
"Third Wing." [Sonora] (27) Spr 94, p. 130-131.
5348. RUBINO, Diane
"Who She Was." [AmerV] (34) 94, p. 92.
5349. RUBINSTEIN, Raphael
"Sparks from a Hammer." [Talisman] (13) Fall 94-Wint 95, p. 246-249.
5350. RUCKER, James D.
"Said the Albatross to Macbeth." [Writer] (107:1) Ja 94, p. 26.
5351. RUCKER, Trish
"Elegy." [ApalQ] (42) Fall 94, p. 50.
"Nursery Rhyme." [NewOR] (20:3/4) Fall-Wint 94, p. 142.
5352. RUDEN, Sarah
"Chartres Cathedral." [Northeast] (5:10) Sum 94, p. 11.
"Johnna's Rape." [Northeast] (5:10) Sum 94, p. 10.
5353. RUDMAN, Mark
"The Couple (I)." [YellowS] (12:1, #45) Spr-Sum 94, p. 28-29.

"The Daughters of Troy" (Excerpts, tr. of Euripides, w. Katharine Washburn). [DenQ] (29:1) Sum 94, p. 57-78.
"Gratuitous Act." [Boulevard] (9:3, #27) Fall 94, p. 148-151.
"Holderlin in Tubingen" (tr. of Johannes Bobrowski). [Pequod] (37) 94, p. 128.
"In the Torrent" (tr. of Johannes Bobrowski). [Pequod] (37) 94, p. 129.
"Kenwood Elementary." [PoetryE] (37/38) Spr 94, p. 175-178.
"Postscript: An Elegy" (to the memory of James Schuyler). [PartR] (61:2) Spr 94, p. 322.
"Rider" (Excerpts). [AmerPoR] (23:2) Mr-Ap 94, p. 42-44.

5354. RUDOLF, Anthony
"The Idols of Terah" (tr. of Claude Vigée). [Stand] (35:4) Aut 94, p. 38-40.

5355. RUEFLE, Mary
"The Death of Shelley." [Ploughs] (20:4) Wint 94-95, p. 166-167.
"Evangelical." [BlackWR] (21:1) Fall-Wint 94, p. 110.
"Glory." [Ploughs] (20:4) Wint 94-95, p. 164-165.
"The March." [BlackWR] (21:1) Fall-Wint 94, p. 111.
"Perpetually Attempting to Soar." [ChiR] (40:1) 94, p. 60.
"Rising Bodies." [Ploughs] (20:4) Wint 94-95, p. 168.
"Trust Me." [DenQ] (28:4) Spr 94, p. 57.

5356. RUESCHER, Scott
"Grampa." [Gaia] (4) Je 94, p. 56.
"Waiting for the Light to Change." [Gaia] (4) Je 94, p. 54-56.

5357. RUFFO, Armand Garnet
"Night Vision." [Callaloo] (17:1) Wint 94, p. 263.
"On Lake Titicaca." [Callaloo] (17:1) Wint 94, p. 264.
"The Season" (for Linda). [Callaloo] (17:1) Wint 94, p. 265.
"A Tangled Perfection" (for Judith). [Callaloo] (17:1) Wint 94, p. 266.

5358. RUGEBREGT, Carol
"Oma Bep (Grandmother in Holland)." [Amelia] (7:3, #22) 94, p. 154-155.

5359. RUGO, Mariève
"Cancer." [KenR] (NS 16:3) Sum 94, p. 93-94.
"Entropy." [KenR] (NS 16:3) Sum 94, p. 94-95.
"Limitations of Dusk." [GrahamHR] (18) Wint 94-95, p. 17.
"Making Love." [Chelsea] (56) 94, p. 53.
"The Messengers." [SouthernHR] (28:4) Fall 94, p. 378.
"Survivor." [SenR] (24:2) Fall 94, p. 44.

RUISSEAUX, Pierre des
See DesRUISSEAUX, Pierre

5360. RUIZ, Jean Marie
"Thirty-Three." [Jacaranda] (5:1) Wint-Spr 91, p. 9.

5361. RUMENS, Carol
"White Night" (tr. of Eugene Dubnov, w. Christopher Newman). [SouthernPR] (34:2) Wint 94, p. 42-43.

5362. RUMMEL, Mary Kay
"A Story She Wraps Around Herself." [SingHM] (21) 94, p. 12-14.
"Without Her, Nothing." [Northeast] (5:10) Sum 94, p. 26-27.

5363. RUNGE, Doris
"Angerichtet." [SouthernHR] (28:3) Sum 94, p. 257.
"Brotherhood" (tr. by Edda Hodnett). [SouthernHR] (28:3) Sum 94, p. 256.
"Bruderschaft." [SouthernHR] (28:3) Sum 94, p. 256.
"Dressed Up" (tr. by Edda Hodnett). [SouthernHR] (28:3) Sum 94, p. 257.
"Fliegen." [SouthernHR] (28:3) Sum 94, p. 251.
"Flying" (tr. by Edda Hodnett). [SouthernHR] (28:3) Sum 94, p. 251.
"Hunting Song" (tr. by Edda Hodnett). [SouthernHR] (28:3) Sum 94, p. 259.
"Jagdlied." [SouthernHR] (28:3) Sum 94, p. 258.
"The Last Line" (tr. by Edda Hodnett). [SouthernHR] (28:3) Sum 94, p. 254.
"Die Letzte Zeile." [SouthernHR] (28:3) Sum 94, p. 254.
"Market Woman in Siena" (tr. by Edda Hodnett). [SouthernHR] (28:3) Sum 94, p. 253.
"Marktfrau in Siena." [SouthernHR] (28:3) Sum 94, p. 253.
"Nachtasyl." [SouthernHR] (28:3) Sum 94, p. 255.
"Night Asylum" (tr. by Edda Hodnett). [SouthernHR] (28:3) Sum 94, p. 255.
"Ophelias Blumen." [SouthernHR] (28:3) Sum 94, p. 252.
"Ophelia's Flowers" (tr. by Edda Hodnett). [SouthernHR] (28:3) Sum 94, p. 252.

5364. RUPCHEV, Georgi
"Attraction" (tr. by Lisa Sapinkopf, w. Georgi Belev). [CrabCR] (8:2/3/9:1/2/3) 94, p. 111.
RURIKO, Mizuno
See MIZUNO, Ruriko
5365. RUSHIN, Kate
"This Is Not a Dangerous Poem." [Chain] (1) Spr-Sum 94, p. 209-210.
5366. RUSHING, W. Jackson
"Crossing the Blanco River." [Border] (5) Fall-Wint 94, p. 57.
"Mexican Road." [Border] (5) Fall-Wint 94, p. 58.
5367. RUSS, Don
"At the End of the Woods." [PoetryNW] (35:1) Spr 94, p. 25.
5368. RUSS-SPAAR, Lisa
"A Doubt." [Poetry] (164:4) Jl 94, p. 217.
"February 29, 1992." [VirQR] (70:1) Wint 94, p. 106-107.
"String Quartet, Festung Concert, Salzburg" (for Pete). [VirQR] (70:1) Wint 94, p. 108-109.
5369. RUSSELL, C. C.
"Katie." [HiramPoR] (55/56) Fall 93-Sum 94, p. 105.
5370. RUSSELL, Peter
"Four Snowmen and a Fifth." [BellArk] (10:5) S-O 94, p. 14-15.
"From the Elegies of Quintilius." [BellArk] (10:3) My-Je 94, p. 3.
"Girl Painting." [BellArk] (10:6) N-D 94, p. 3.
"The Key" (tr. from *Quintilii Apocalypsos Fragmenta*). [BellArk] (10:3 [i.e. 10:4]) Jl-Ag 94, p. 16.
"Last Judgments" (from Quintilii Apocalypseos Fragmenta). [NoDaQ] (62:1) Wint 94-95, p. 61-63.
"Missing a Bus." [BellArk] (10:2) Mr-Ap 94, p. 16.
"Monday Morning." [BellArk] (10:6) N-D 94, p. 3.
"Ode." [BellArk] (10:6) N-D 94, p. 3.
"Three Sonnets." [BellArk] (10:3) My-Je 94, p. 3.
"The Wild Cats in November." [BellArk] (10:6) N-D 94, p. 3.
5371. RUSSELL, Thomas
"An Elegy for Liberace." [NowestR] (32:2) 94, p. 18-21.
5372. RUSSELL, Timothy
"Jade Plant." [Poetry] (163:5) F 94, p. 257.
5373. RUSSO, Albert
"Cablegram from Greta Garbo Suitor." [Amelia] (7:3, #22) 94, p. 38-39.
"The Prisons of Love" (Honorable Mention, The Amelia Awards). [Amelia] (7:4, #23) 94, p. 47.
"The Unforgiven Star." [Amelia] (7:3, #22) 94, p. 38.
5374. RUSSO, Gianna
"Migrants." [Sun] (219) Mr 94, p. 19.
"Penitenti (The Repentant Ones)." [SlipS] (14) 94, p. 29.
"The Revenge of the Poetess." [Sun] (219) Mr 94, p. 19.
5375. RUSSO, Linda
"Accident & Phenomenon (2 dreams about you)." [HarvardR] (7) Fall 94, p. 53.
5376. RUSTED, Brian
"Rain Lies." [WestCL] (28:1/2, #13/14) Spr-Fall 94, p. 255-257.
5377. RUTH, Barbara
"If Kathy Power Surrenders, Can the Millennium Be Far Behind?" [SinW] (54) Wint 94-95, p. 30-36.
5378. RUTHERFORD, Bonnie
"Desert Rain." [BellArk] (10:2) Mr-Ap 94, p. 9.
5379. RUTSALA, Vern
"Listening to a Russian Choir." [Poetry] (164:2) My 94, p. 79-81.
5380. RUTSKY, Randy
"Note on Letter and Photograph." [Jacaranda] (5:1) Wint-Spr 91, p. 114.
5381. RUYBALID, Mariana
"Remembering Manchuria." [Kaleid] (28) Wint-Spr 94, p. 57.
5382. RUZESKY, Jay
"Crocuses." [PoetryC] (14:2) Mr 94, p. 4.
"Ink Lake." [PoetryC] (14:2) Mr 94, p. 4.
"Night of the Skagit County Parade." [Quarry] (43:1) Je 94, p. 102-103.
"Something About the Rain Falling on the Ocean That Sounds Like a Chorus of Missing Children." [PoetryC] (14:2) Mr 94, p. 4.

5383. RYALS, Mary Jane
"In the Motel Room." [NewDeltaR] (10:2) Spr-Sum 93, p. 50-51.
"Mary Elks." [TampaR] (8) Spr 94, p. 21.
5384. RYAN, Gregory A.
"Chocolate Santa Claus." [JINJPo] (16:2) Aut 94, p. 30.
"Sidereal." [LitR] (37:4) Sum 94, p. 679.
5385. RYAN, John Allen
"Child-Beater." [HangL] (65) 94, p. 46-47.
"The Last Time I Saw Kerouac" (Greenwich Village). [HangL] (65) 94, p. 48.
5386. RYAN, Kay
"Connections." [GeoR] (48:4) Wint 94, p. 773.
"Losses." [GeoR] (48:3) Fall 94, p. 583.
"Matrigupta" (of Ujjain, India). [ParisR] (36:131) Sum 94, p. 295.
"Outsider Art." [PartR] (61:2) Spr 94, p. 323-324.
5387. RYAN, Margaret
"Against Romance." [BelPoJ] (44:4) Sum 94, p. 20.
"Daylily." [Pivot] (41) 93, p. 8.
"Fuchsia." [BelPoJ] (44:4) Sum 94, p. 21.
"A Happy Childhood." [Pivot] (41) 93, p. 7.
"Prometheus at Rockefeller Center." [BelPoJ] (44:4) Sum 94, p. 23.
"Spring: Snapshots." [Pivot] (42) 94, p. 12-13.
5388. RYAN, Nigel
"Eleven Stars Over Andalusia" (tr. of Mahmoud Darwish, w. Mona Anis, Aga Shahid Ali and Ahmad Dallal). [GrandS] (12:4, #48) Wint 94, p. 100-111.
5389. RYAN, R. M.
"Absent Minded." [Light] (10) Sum 94, p. 16.
"Taking Turns" (Prague). [AnotherCM] (28) 94, p. 97-98.
5390. RYBERG, Maureen
"He Looked Like Nijinsky, Except." [PoetL] (89:3) Fall 94, p. 21-22.
5391. RYBICKI, John
"Bass." [ProseP] (3) 94, p. 75.
"First Storm, Day Off Work." [PoetryE] (37/38) Spr 94, p. 113.
"Ringing In." [PoetryE] (37/38) Spr 94, p. 112.
RYDBERG, Amy Shea
See SHEA-RYDBERG, Amy
5392. RYERSON, Alice
"My Childhood Is My Firstborn Child." [SpoonR] (19:1) Wint-Spr 94, p. 54.
"Preparation for Winter" (for Susan Moon). [PraS] (68:2) Sum 94, p. 148.

5393. SABINES, Jaime
"All the Buried Voices" (tr. by Reginald Gibbons). [TriQ] (91) Fall 94, p. 147.
"Like the Night" (tr. by Reginald Gibbons). [TriQ] (91) Fall 94, p. 107.
5394. SABINI, Meredith
"It Doesn't Compute." [Pearl] (20) Spr 94, p. 21.
5395. SACKS, Peter
"Three Mourning Songs." [Pequod] (37) 94, p. 36-37.
5396. SADOFF, Ira
"In the Heat." [DenQ] (28:4) Spr 94, p. 58.
"One We Knew." [TriQ] (92) Wint 94-95, p. 74-75.
"Poem: I like waking up by the lake." [TriQ] (92) Wint 94-95, p. 76.
"When I Come Home" (after the Xenia tornado of 1974). [Boulevard] (9:1/2, #25/26) Spr 94, p. 134-135.
5397. SADOW, Stephen
"Diptych: I. Cycle, II. Transmission" (tr. of Ricardo Feierstein, w. J. Kates). [PlumR] (7) [94?], p. 55-57.
SADOWSKI, Jennifer Young
See YOUNG-SADOWSKI, Jennifer
5398. SAFRANSKY, Sy
"Those Men." [Sun] (223) Jl 94, p. 39.
"Who Forgets My Name." [Sun] (218) F 94, p. 35.
5399. SAGAN, Miriam
"Baby Baby" (30 poems). [Noctiluca] (3) 94, p. 45-84.
"Renga" (2 poems, w. Judy Katz-Levine). [Noctiluca] (3) 94, p. 39-44.
5400. SAGARIS, Lake
"Awakening." [CanLit] (142/143) Fall-Wint 94, p. 101.

"When a Man and a Woman Separate" (To Enrique Molina with paraphrase, tr. of Naín Nómez). [CanLit] (142/143) Fall-Wint 94, p. 118-119.

5401. SAGEL, Jim
"Entrada." [PraS] (68:4) Wint 94, p. 189.

5402. SAGSTETTER, Karen
"Leaving." [PoetL] (89:4) Wint 94-95, p. 24.

5403. SAHAFI, Janet E.
"Child's Play." [BellR] (17:1/2) Spr-Fall 94, p. 90.

SA'ID, 'Ali Ahmad
See ADONIS

5404. SAIJO, Albert
"Earth Slanguage with English on It." [BambooR] (60) Wint 94, p. 117-118.

5405. SAINE, Margaret
"The Profiles of Light" (tr. of María de la Peña Luque). [Luz] (7) N 94, p. 35-39.

5406. SAINT, Assotto
"Devils in America." [JamesWR] (11:5) Fall 94, p. 13.
"Going Home Celebration" (for donald woods, from *Wishing for Wings*). [JamesWR] (11:5) Fall 94, p. 13.
"Heart & Soul" (To Essex Hemphill" (from *The Road Before Us: 100 Gay Black Poets*). [JamesWR] (11:5) Fall 94, p. 13.
"Heaven in Hell" (for counsel wright, from *Stations*). [JamesWR] (11:5) Fall 94, p. 13.
"In the Fast Lane" (from *Stations*). [JamesWR] (11:5) Fall 94, p. 13.
"Nuclear Lovers" (from *Stations*). [JamesWR] (11:5) Fall 94, p. 12.
"The Queen's Etiquette." [Art&Und] (3:3) Ag 94, p. 12.
"Shuffle Along." [Art&Und] (3:3) Ag 94, p. 12.
"Souvenir" (from *Stations*). [JamesWR] (11:5) Fall 94, p. 13.
"Vital Signs" (for David Frechette). [Art&Und] (3:3) Ag 94, p. 12.

5407. SAINT-DENIS, Janou
"The Measure of Time" (tr. by Katherine Beeman). [InterPR] (20:2) Fall 94, p. 77.
"Mesure du Temps." [InterPR] (20:2) Fall 94, p. 76.

5408. SAISER, Marjorie
"As If Wind Wants In." [WestB] (34) 94, p. 82-83.
"Cold Morning, High Country." [MidwQ] (35:2) Wint 94, p. 182.
"If Sky Were a Sea to Float Face Down In." [WestB] (34) 94, p. 83.
"In the Dream the Horse." [Crazy] (46) Spr 94, p. 87-90.
"Kathy in the Swing." [GeoR] (48:1) Spr 94, p. 118-120.
"On Hearing of the Suicide of a Young Farmer." [MidwQ] (35:2) Wint 94, p. 183-184.

5409. SAITO, Etsuko
"Frosted Glass" (in Japanese and English, tr. by Matthew Forrest and Henry Hughes). [SycamoreR] (6:2) Sum 94, p. 94-95.
"I Learned on the Right Side of the Sea" (in Japanese and English, tr. by Matthew Forrest and Henry Hughes). [SycamoreR] (6:2) Sum 94, p. 96-98.

5410. SAJE, Natasha
"Agoraphobia." [VirQR] (70:4) Aut 94, p. 673-674.
"Appetites." [Salm] (101/102) Wint-Spr 94, p. 165-166.
"Edith Wharton After the Death of Henry James." [GettyR] (7:2) Spr 94, p. 324.
"Red Under the Skin." [Ploughs] (20:1) Spr 94, p. 135-142.
"Salsify." [Salm] (101/102) Wint-Spr 94, p. 167.
"What I Want to Make for You." [AmerV] (33) 94, p. 118-119.

5411. SAKNUSSEMM, Kristopher
"The Shoveler." [CrabCR] (8:2/3/9:1/2/3) 94, p. 68-69.

5412. SALA, Jerome
"Meditation #3." [Talisman] (13) Fall 94-Wint 95, p. 289.
"Meditation #8." [Talisman] (13) Fall 94-Wint 95, p. 289-290.

5413. SALADO, Minerva
"Sea's Path" (tr. by Juan Leon). [MichQR] (33:4) Fall 94, p. 804.

5414. SALAMONE, Karen
"Tea and Oranges." [BellArk] (10:6) N-D 94, p. 13.
"Walking in February." [BellArk] (10:6) N-D 94, p. 13.
"Winter Strategies." [BellArk] (10:6) N-D 94, p. 13.

5415. SALASIN, Sal
"But keep listening." [AnotherCM] (28) 94, p. 112.
"In my dreams I can't remember how to." [AnotherCM] (28) 94, p. 110-111.

5416. SALAZAR, Dixie
"The Chameleon" (In Memory of Sylvia). [BlackWR] (20:2) Spr-Sum 94, p. 19-20.
"The Human Body Library." [SantaBR] (2:1) Spr-Sum 94, p. 82.
"If I Should Die Before I Wake." [SantaBR] (2:1) Spr-Sum 94, p. 83.
"Lullabies of the Spider." [InterQ] (1:4) 94, p. 112-113.
"White Night." [InterQ] (1:4) 94, p. 114.
"Why I'm Not Someone Else." [InterQ] (1:4) 94, p. 110-111.
5417. SALDAÑA, Excilia
"My Name (A Family Anti-Elegy)" (Excerpts, tr. by Ruth Behar and David Frye). [MichQR] (33:3) Sum 94, p. 543-547.
5418. SALEH, Dennis
"Dec. 29." [SantaBR] (2:2) Fall-Wint 94, p. 98.
"The Negative Confession of the Scribe." [HangL] (65) 94, p. 49-50.
5419. SALEMI, Joseph S.
"Anti-Smoking Fanatic." [Hellas] (5:1) Spr-Sum 94, p. 43.
"Corrective Maxims for Miseducated Young Poets." [Hellas] (5:2) Fall-Wint 94, p. 21-25.
"Health Food Freak." [Hellas] (5:1) Spr-Sum 94, p. 43.
"No Sap Per Que Va Son Joy Pus Tarzan" (tr. of Guilhem de Montanhagol). [CumbPR] (13:2) Spr 94, p. 40-45.
"Three Poems: IV.41, VI.93, XII.12" (tr. of Martial). [CrabCR] (8:2/3/9:1/2/3) 94, p. 101-102.
"A welcome spring breeze dulls the whetted edge of the winter" (I.4, tr. of Horace). [CarolQ] (46:3) Sum 94, p. 51.
5420. SALERNO, Joe
"Shadows." [CrabCR] (8:2/3/9:1/2/3) 94, p. 140-141.
5421. SALERNO, Mark
"Gone to Reno" (for R. Stephen Posey). [Zyzzyva] (10:1) Spr 94, p. 103.
"Romania or Someplace." [Arshile] (3) 94, p. 41.
"To Paul Zollo." [Arshile] (3) 94, p. 40.
"Too Late." [Arshile] (3) 94, p. 39.
5422. SALIM, Leyzman
"The Land Is Screaming" (tr. of Feliciano Acosta, w. Lauren Schick). [InterQ] (1:4) 94, p. 22.
"Pomberi" (tr. of Feliciano Acosta, w. Lauren Schick). [InterQ] (1:4) 94, p. 23.
5423. SALINAS, Pedro
"The Dispersed Woman" (tr. by Robert Bly). [HarvardR] (6) Spr 94, p. 165.
SALLE, Peter la
See LaSALLE, Peter
5424. SALLIS, James
"Elements of Style." [PoetryE] (37/38) Spr 94, p. 20.
"Hunter." [XavierR] (14:1) Spr 94, p. 45.
"Memory at 3 A.M." [SoDakR] (32:3) Fall 94, p. 128.
"Poems." [SoDakR] (32:3) Fall 94, p. 129.
5425. SALOM, Philip
"Catacomb di St Callisto." [NewL] (60:4) 94, p. 190-191.
"A Roman Journal" (Selections: 5 poems). [MalR] (107) Sum 94, p. 50-56.
5426. SALOY, Mona Lisa
"On My Block." [SouthernR] (30:4) Aut 94, p. 789-790.
"Song for Elder Sisters." [SouthernR] (30:4) Aut 94, p. 788-789.
5427. SALTER, Jennifer
"Words You Didn't Send." [Dandel] (21:2) 94, p. 10-11.
5428. SALTER, Mary Jo
"The Age of Reason." [Thrpny] (57) Spr 94, p. 13.
5429. SALTMAN, Benjamin
"Carpet City." [PoetL] (89:1) Spr 94, p. 43-44.
5430. SALTMAN, Bethany
"Dream" ([I]-V). [PaintedB] (53/54) 94, p. 73-77.
"The Lake." [BrooklynR] (11) 94, p. 20.
"Sarah." [NewYorkQ] (53) 94, p. 87.
"Small Boats." [Nimrod] (38:1) Fall-Wint 94, p. 136.
5431. SALVATIERRA, Mario
"Sips of Light" (11 selections, tr. of Juana Rosa Pita, w. the author). [Luz] (7) N 94, p. 11-15.
5432. SALZMAN, Eva
"Grief." [NewYorker] (70:7) 4 Ap 94, p. 74.

5433. SAMAIN, Albert
"I Dream" (tr. by Carol Poster). [PoetryE] (37/38) Spr 94, p. 226.
5434. SAMARAS, Nicholas
"Between a Good Morning and a Good Night" (tr. of Doros Loizou). [DenQ] (29:1) Sum 94, p. 83-85.
"Easter in the Cancer Ward" (from *Hands of the Saddlemaker*, Yale UP, 1992). [Hellas] (5:1) Spr-Sum 94, p. 57-63.
"Eve Naming Other Animals." [NewEngR] (16:3) Sum 94, p. 115-116.
"Injury." [MichQR] (33:1) Wint 94, p. 111-113.
"Movable Feasts." [HarvardR] (Premier Issue) Spr 92, p. 31.
5435. SAMPERI, Frank
"Late turning of leaves." [WorldL] (5) 94, p. 39.
"'Tis love." [WorldL] (5) 94, p. 39.
5436. SAMPSON, Dennis
"The Anaconda." [AmerV] (35) 94, p. 85-86.
"The Leopard." [AmerV] (35) 94, p. 87-88.
"The Tight-Rope Walker." [AmerV] (35) 94, p. 83-84.
5437. SAMS, Jeffrey
"The Finding." [DarkMoon] (1) 94, p. 56.
"In Need of a Spider." [DarkMoon] (1) 94, p. 53.
"Mistress and Ceremony." [DarkMoon] (1) 94, p. 54-55.
"Physical Illusion." [DarkMoon] (1) 94, p. 58.
"Sunny Morning." [DarkMoon] (1) 94, p. 57.
5438. SAMYN, Mary Ann
"Driving." [HiramPoR] (57) Fall 94-Wint 95, p. 54.
"Duet." [RagMag] (12:1) Sum 94, p. 98-99.
"Gulls." [HiramPoR] (57) Fall 94-Wint 95, p. 53.
"Heat." [LaurelR] (28:1) Wint 94, p. 86.
"My Mother Who Grows Needy." [RagMag] (12:1) Sum 94, p. 101.
"Storm Warnings." [HiramPoR] (57) Fall 94-Wint 95, p. 52.
5439. SANAZARO, Leonard
"Hillside." [CentR] (38:1) Wint 94, p. 126-127.
"The Romanov Bones." [CentR] (38:1) Wint 94, p. 124-125.
5440. SANCHEZ, Carol Lee
"Journey's End, Santa Barbara." [Callaloo] (17:1) Wint 94, p. 68-71.
"Unpacking the Years" (for mother). [Callaloo] (17:1) Wint 94, p. 72-73.
5441. SANDERS, Kristine
"Fire Truck." [ChironR] (13:3) Aut 94, p. 12.
"Hit While Running" (for K.J.P.). [ChironR] (13:3) Aut 94, p. 12.
"Tiling." [Pearl] (20) Spr 94, p. 46.
5442. SANDERS, Mark
"Children on the Clouds." [MidwQ] (35:3) Spr 94, p. 314.
"For My Sister, 1961." [MidwQ] (35:3) Spr 94, p. 312.
"The Old Man and the Sea." [MidwQ] (35:3) Spr 94, p. 313.
"The Poem" (for Dana Gioia). [AntigR] (97) Spr 94, p. 12.
5443. SANDERS, Tony
"After Berenice Abbott." [ParisR] (36:130) Spr 94, p. 241-245.
"Equally Incapable of Seeing the Nothingness From Which He Emerges and the Infinity In Which He Is Engulfed." [Confr] (54/55) Fall 94-Wint 95, p. 293-294.
"Expatriate Hours Return to Their Homeland." [Confr] (54/55) Fall 94-Wint 95, p. 295.
"Token Symmetry." [GettyR] (7:4) Aut 94, p. 575.
"Transit Authority." [YaleR] (82:4) O 94, p. 79-80.
"West Street" (after Berenice Abbott). [GettyR] (7:4) Aut 94, p. 576.
5444. SANDERSON, Connie
"Right to Watch" (tr. of Jacques Prévert). [PoetryE] (37/38) Spr 94, p. 229.
5445. SANDOVAL, José-Luis
"Ti Jean." [MoodySI] (28, also labeled 29) Fall 94, p. 33.
5446. SANDY, Stephen
"A Common." [NewYorker] (70:17) 13 Je 94, p. 76.
"Denny." [ParisR] (36:130) Spr 94, p. 98.
"For Charlie, Reading." [WestHR] (48:1) Spr 94, p. 12.
"Force of Nature." [ParisR] (36:130) Spr 94, p. 99.
"Hard By." [ParisR] (36:130) Spr 94, p. 98.

"Not Visiting the Dalai Lama in Vermont." [Salm] (104/105) Fall 94-Wint 95, p. 168-169.
"Photo of Melville, Back Room, Old Bookstore." [ParisR] (36:130) Spr 94, p. 97.
"A Standing Egg." [HarvardR] (6) Spr 94, p. 91.
"Threads." [ParisR] (36:130) Spr 94, p. 95-97.

5447. SANELLI, Mary Lou
"Where the Love Went." [Calyx] (15:2) Sum 94, p. 58.

5448. SANER, Reg
"Forest Mornings I Can't Ask to Happen." [Poetry] (163:6) Mr 94, p. 318.
"North of Wupatki." [Poetry] (163:6) Mr 94, p. 319.

5449. SANFORD, Alice
"Transparent Eyeball" (for Ralph Waldo Emerson). [SantaBR] (2:2) Fall-Wint 94, p. 91.
"Words are strokes." [SantaBR] (2:2) Fall-Wint 94, p. 90.

5450. SANFORD, John
"Okie Madonna" (from "Scenes of the National Life," 9). [SantaBR] (2:1) Spr-Sum 94, p. 9-10.
"Two Hundred Girls in a Caramel Facotry" (from "Scenes of the National Life," 7). [SantaBR] (2:1) Spr-Sum 94, p. 8-9.

5451. SANGE, Gary
"Personal Belonging." [BellR] (17:1/2) Spr-Fall 94, p. 94-95.
"Soapbox Derby." [LitR] (37:4) Sum 94, p. 687.

5452. SANGER, Richard
"Magical Flurries" (for Ricardo Lobo Da Silveira O'Reilly Sternberg). [CanLit] (142/143) Fall-Wint 94, p. 21.

5453. SANSOM, Peter
"Translating Hans Carossa." [Stand] (35:3) Sum 94, p. 76.

5454. SANTANA, Ernesto
"Knots in the Handkerchief" (tr. by Ruth Behar). [MichQR] (33:4) Fall 94, p. 677.

5455. SANTEK, Jerod
"HIV Research Project." [JamesWR] (11:3) Spr 94, p. 11.
"Outside Radiology." [JamesWR] (11:3) Spr 94, p. 10.
"Sestina for Beth in Her Third Month." [JamesWR] (11:3) Spr 94, p. 11.
"Unexpected Frosts." [JamesWR] (11:3) Spr 94, p. 11.

5456. SANTELLO, Rob
"To Know It's Not the End." [RagMag] (12:1) Sum 94, p. 24.

SANTIAGO BACA, Jimmy
See BACA, Jimmy Santiago

5457. SANTOS, Marisa de los
"For Susan." [WestHR] (48:3) Fall 94, p. 299.

5458. SANTOS, Sherod
"The Asylum Sonnets" (for Sarah Santos Knoeppel). [SouthernHR] (28:3) Sum 94, p. 230-231.
"The Tyrant." [Jacaranda] (4:2) Spr 90, p. 32.

5459. SANZ CALLIS, Amparo
"La Bruja." [Nuez] (5:13/14/15) 94, p. 49.

5460. SAPINKOPF, Lisa
"And When the Winter Wind Rushed Straight into My Heart" (tr. of Georgi Borisov, w. Georgi Belev). [InterQ] (1:1) [93?], p. 86.
"Arrival" (tr. of Fedya Filkova, w. Georgi Belev). [InterQ] (1:1) [93?], p. 85.
"Attraction" (tr. of Georgi Rupchev, w. Georgi Belev). [CrabCR] (8:2/3/9:1/2/3) 94, p. 111.
"Ballad for the Future" (tr. of Ivan Radoev, w. Georgi Belev). [InterQ] (1:1) [93?], p. 77.
"De Natura Rerum" (tr. of Yves Bonnefoy). [HarvardR] (2) Fall 92, p. 155.
"Four Seekers of the Great Metaphor" (tr. of Vladimir Levchev, w. Georgi Belev). [PartR] (61:2) Spr 94, p. 319-320.
"Grass" (tr. of Blaga Dimitrova, w. Georgi Belev). [InterQ] (1:1) [93?], p. 79.
"Her Hands Clasp One Another" (tr. of Irfan Malik, w. the author). [InterQ] (1:3) 94, p. 179.
"Hotel Room (Vienna, 1966)" (tr. of Blaga Dimitrova, w. Georgi Belev). [InterQ] (1:1) [93?], p. 78-79.
"Morning" (tr. of Miriana Basheva, w. Georgi Belev). [CrabCR] (8:2/3/9:1/2/3) 94, p. 109.
"Ortamezar — The Jewish Quarter" (tr. of Ivan Teofilov, w. Georgi Belev). [InterQ] (1:1) [93?], p. 82-83.

"Psyché and the Palace of Love" (tr. of Yves Bonnefoy). [BostonR] (19:1) Fe-Mr 94, p. 17.
"Repentance" (tr. of Blaga Dimitrova, w. Georgi Belev). [InterQ] (1:1) [93?], p. 80.
"Silence" (tr. of Marin Georgiev, w. Georgi Belev). [InterQ] (1:1) [93?], p. 81.
"Song" (tr. of Georgi Belev, w. the author). [InterQ] (1:1) [93?], p. 87.
"A Tale That's Not a Tale" (tr. of Binyo Ivanov, w. Georgi Belev). [CrabCR] (8:2/3/9:1/2/3) 94, p. 109-110.
"Teenagers" (tr. of Ivan Teofilov, w. Georgi Belev). [InterQ] (1:1) [93?], p. 84.
"Vulnerability" (tr. of Fedya Filkova, w. Georgi Belev). [InterQ] (1:1) [93?], p. 85.
"The Wind Is Coming and I Love You" (tr. of Binyo Ivanov, w. Georgi Belev). [PartR] (61:2) Spr 94, p. 320-321.

5461. SAPPHIRE
"1965 / Gorilla in the Midst" (#2-#3). [CentralP] (23) Spr 94, p. 28-32.

5462. SAPPHO (Fl. 600 B.C.)
"Behind the laurel bush you stood" (tr. by Robin Skelton). [Arc] (32) Spr 94, p. 38.
"Fragments" (105(a), 105(c), tr. by Anita George)." [Poetry] (164:3) Je 94, p. 140.
"Three Fragments" (tr. by Anita George). [AntigR] (97) Spr 94, p. 66.
"Two Fragments" (tr. by Jack Flavin). [ApalQ] (40/41) 94, p. 69-70.

5463. SARAH, Robyn
"Astronomy." [PoetryC] (14:3) My 94, p. 25.

5464. SARAI, Sarah
"First Appearance of the Angel Evelyn." [Zyzzyva] (10:1) Spr 94, p. 67.

SARAVIA, Marco Tulio del Arca
See ARCA SARAVIA, Marco Tulio del

5465. SARGENT, Robert
"Faulkner." [NegC] (14:1/2) 94, p. 70-71.
"Mr. Mencken." [PoetryE] (37/38) Spr 94, p. 31.
"Oh Play That Thing!" [Pembroke] (26) 94, p. 78-79.
"Passing a Flowerbed." [PoetryE] (37/38) Spr 94, p. 30.
"Young Man Away from Home." [HolCrit] (31:2) Ap 94, p. 17.

5466. SARKAR, Farida
"Character" (tr. of Taslima Nasrin, w. Carolyne Wright). [NewYorker] (70:26) 22-29 Ag 94, p. 77.

5467. SARRIS, Nikos
"The Elegies of Jutting Rock" (Selections: 6 poems, tr. of Odysseus Elytis, w. Jeffrey Carson). [AmerPoR] (23:6) N-D 94, p. 27-30.
"Elegy of Grüningen" (In memory of Friedrich von Hardenberg. Tr. of Odysseus Elytis, w. Jeffrey Carson).). [NoDaQ] (62:4) Fall 94-95, p. 9-10.
"The Garden Was Entering the Sea" (tr. of Odysseus Elytis, w. Jeffrey Carson). [NoDaQ] (62:4) Fall 94-95, p. 7-8.
"The Icon" (tr. of Odysseus Elytis, w. Jeffrey Carson). [AmerPoR] (23:4) Jl-Ag 94, p. 48.

5468. SARTARELLI, Stephen
"In These Skies." [Talisman] (12) Spr 94, p. 145.
"Reading the Numbers." [Talisman] (12) Spr 94, p. 145-146.
"Winter Garden." [Talisman] (12) Spr 94, p. 146.

5469. SARTEL, Moshe
"Lamenting of the Birds" (tr. by Ammiel Alcalay). [LitR] (37:2) Wint 94, p. 291-303.
"A Stone I Lay from Marble of Marmara" (tr. by Ammiel Alcalay). [LitR] (37:2) Wint 94, p. 288-290.

5470. SARTORIUS, Joachim
"Alexandrie, Boulevard de Ramleh, 1903" (tr. by Rosmarie Waldrop). [Conjunc] (23) 94, p. 137-138.
"A Fig for the Way Home" (tr. by Sibylle Schlesier). [Conjunc] (23) 94, p. 139.
"Hoarfrostwatch" (tr. by Rosmarie Waldrop). [Conjunc] (23) 94, p. 138.
"In This Black Stillness" (tr. by Sibylle Schlesier and Nathaniel Tarn). [Conjunc] (23) 94, p. 140-143.
"(Love)" (tr. by Sibylle Schlesier). [Conjunc] (23) 94, p. 139.
"To a Dolphin in Batumi" (tr. by Rosmarie Waldrop). [Conjunc] (23) 94, p. 140.

5471. SASSMANN, Steven
"America's Golden Age." [ChironR] (13:3) Aut 94, p. 20.
"He'll Remember." [ChironR] (13:3) Aut 94, p. 20.
"Me and Robert and God." [ChironR] (13:3) Aut 94, p. 20.
"Tonya." [ChironR] (13:3) Aut 94, p. 20.

5472. SATER, Steven
"Canyon of Enough." [Confr] (52/53) Wint-Spr 94, p. 322.
"Midnight Omnipotence." [Confr] (52/53) Wint-Spr 94, p. 323.
"Out on the Island." [Confr] (52/53) Wint-Spr 94, p. 321.
5473. SATO, Hiroaki
"Figure" (tr. of Ishihara Yoshiro). [Conjunc] (23) 94, p. 220.
"Horse and Riot" (tr. of Ishihara Yoshiro). [Conjunc] (23) 94, p. 215-216.
"Mist & Town" (tr. of Ishihara Yoshiro). [Conjunc] (23) 94, p. 219-220.
"Myth" (tr. of Ishihara Yoshiro). [Conjunc] (23) 94, p. 217.
"Night Robbers" (tr. of Ishihara Yoshiro). [Conjunc] (23) 94, p. 216-217.
"Song of the Ringing in the Ear" (tr. of Ishihara Yoshiro). [Conjunc] (23) 94, p. 218.
"Structure" (tr. of Ishihara Yoshiro). [Conjunc] (23) 94, p. 215.
5474. SATTELEE, Thom
"Loop Trails." [Blueline] (15) 94, p. 61.
5475. SAVAGE, Tom
"Fireflies in Tompkins Square." [HangL] (65) 94, p. 51-54.
"On Approval." [Talisman] (12) Spr 94, p. 216-217.
"You'd Be Amazed to Find Yourself Here." [Talisman] (13) Fall 94-Wint 95, p. 149-150.
5476. SAVOIE, Paul
"Maëlstrom." [Descant] (24:4, #83) Wint 93-94, p. 143.
"Painter's Reach." [Descant] (24:4, #83) Wint 93-94, p. 144.
"Serpentine." [Descant] (24:4, #83) Wint 93-94, p. 142.
5477. SAVORY, Elaine
"Cutting the Vine." [CaribbeanW] (8) 94, p. 59.
5478. SAWCZUK, Marta
"The Clock" (tr. of Lina Kostenko). [Vis] (44) 94, p. 39.
5479. SAWYER, Virginia
"Isabel Archer." [SouthernHR] (28:1) Wint 94, p. 64-65.
5480. SAYA, Tom
"House of Horrors." [PoetryE] (37/38) Spr 94, p. 9.
"A Thin Arc." [SoCaR] (27:1/2) Fall 94-Spr 95, p. 9.
SAYED, Mahmud al-
See Al-SAYED, Mahmud
5481. SCAFIDI, Steve
"Lies." [AmerPoR] (23:2) Mr-Ap 94, p. 55.
"Love Story River." [CreamCR] (18:1) Spr 94, p. 70.
"Of Trees, Iced." [SouthernPR] (34:2) Wint 94, p. 51.
"The Swing." [CreamCR] (18:1) Spr 94, p. 71.
5482. SCALAPINO, Leslie
"The Front Matter, Dead Souls" (Excerpt, for Jerry Estrin). [Avec] (7:1) 94, p. 39.
"The Front Matter, Dead Souls" (Selection). [Sonora] (28) Fall 94, p. 38-44.
"The Front Matter, Dead Souls, a Serial Novel for Publication in the Newspaper" (Exceprts). [RiverC] (14:2) Spr 94, p. 81-85.
"New Time" (Excerpts). [Chelsea] (57) 94, p. 32-38.
5483. SCALF, Sue
"First Reader, Political Incorrect." [Poem] (72) N 94, p. 34.
"The Lost Children." [NegC] (14:1/2) 94, p. 110-111.
"Solitude's Small Voice." [Poem] (72) N 94, p. 32-33.
5484. SCAMMELL, William
"Bleeding Heart Yard." [Jacaranda] (5:1) Wint-Spr 91, p. 48-49.
5485. SCANNELL, Vernon
"A Cemetery Revisited." [Stand] (35:2) Spr 94, p. 65.
"Climacterics." [Stand] (36:1) Wint 94-95, p. 56.
5486. SCARBROUGH, George
"Dead Weight." [SpiritSH] (59) 94, p. 3.
"Mule." [SpiritSH] (59) 94, p. 4.
"The Question." [SpiritSH] (59) 94, p. 5-7.
5487. SCATES, Maxine
"Leaping" (for D.). [SycamoreR] (6:2) Sum 94, p. 57-59.
"Strings" (After hearing a recording of Shostakovich's Quartet No. 8 as played by the Kronos Quartet). [SycamoreR] (6:2) Sum 94, p. 62-65.
"Two Fridas." [SycamoreR] (6:2) Sum 94, p. 60-61.
5488. SCATTERGOOD, Amy
"Eleanor Roosevelt Looking Through the Window of a Cross-Country Train." [DenQ] (29:2) Fall 94, p. 39-40.

"Magellan's Straits." [Border] (5) Fall-Wint 94, p. 59-60.
"The Patriarch Fields." [IndR] (17:2) Fall 94, p. 73.

5489. SCHAAF, Richard
"In Oaxaca" (tr. of Marjorie Agosin). [HarvardR] (6) Spr 94, p. 168.

5490. SCHAAFSMA, David
"Easter Tribute, Leningrad." [EngJ] (83:3) Mr 94, p. 102.

5491. SCHACHTER, Esty
"Bernarda." [SingHM] (21) 94, p. 10-11.

5492. SCHAEDLER, Brad
"Birds That Flew." [ChironR] (13:4) Wint 94, p. 24.
"Jacob's Funeral." [Plain] (15:1) Fall 94, p. 17.
"We Are" (from "Angle of the Sun"). [AmerPoR] (23:5) S-O 94, p. 32.

5493. SCHAEFFER, Susan
"Monday." [BrooklynR] (11) 94, p. 107.

5494. SCHAFFER, Amanda
"The People v. Horatio M. Loomis, 1850" (First Prize). [HarvardA] (128:3) Spr 94, p. 15.
"Postcard, 1912." [HarvardA] (129:2) Fall 94, p. 14.

5495. SCHAFFNER, M. A. (Michael)
"Logan Circle." [CapeR] (29:2) Fall 94, p. 13.
"The March Rains." [Vis] (46) 94, p. 24.
"Tom's Cove." [Pivot] (41) 93, p. 16.
"View of the Potomac from Memorial Bridge." [SmPd] (31:1, #90) Wint 94, p. 25.
"Western Dreams." [HampSPR] Wint 94, p. 16.

5496. SCHEELE, Roy
"Apology." [Poetry] (165:2) N 94, p. 83.
"Eohippus." [Poetry] (165:2) N 94, p. 83.

5497. SCHEETZ, Nancy B.
"A Single Thread." [SouthernHR] (28:2) Spr 94, p. 180.

5498. SCHEFFLER, Laura
"Cemetery at Lambert International Airport, St. Louis." [ArtfulD] (26/27) 94, p. 54.
"The Souvenir." [ArtfulD] (26/27) 94, p. 53.

5499. SCHEIBLI, Silvia
"Caffeine Kisses." [DarkMoon] (1) 94, p. 38.
"Frijole Beach." [DarkMoon] (1) 94, p. 39.
"Poems." [DarkMoon] (1) 94, p. 40.
"Review." [DarkMoon] (1) 94, p. 35.
"There Is Time." [DarkMoon] (1) 94, p. 37.
"Walking." [DarkMoon] (1) 94, p. 36.

5500. SCHEIN, Lorraine
"Ephemera." [BrooklynR] (11) 94, p. 13.

5501. SCHELLING, Andrew
"For a Tribal Girl in Bangkok." [Sulfur] (34) Spr 94, p. 148.
"For Love of the Dark One: Mirabai Translations" (tr. of Princess Mirabai, 1489-1550). [YellowS] (11:4, #44) Wint 93-94, p. 8-9.
"Landrover" (for Anne Waldman, 2 April 1994). [Talisman] (13) Fall 94-Wint 95, p. 104-115.
"On the Wall." [Sulfur] (34) Spr 94, p. 147-148.
"Run My Hand Under." [Sulfur] (34) Spr 94, p. 149.

5502. SCHEMM, Ripley
"Building Fence." [Ploughs] (20:1) Spr 94, p. 115-116.
"Melissa's Abstract." [Ploughs] (20:1) Spr 94, p. 117.

5503. SCHERER, Catherine
"Latch On." [Kalliope] (16:1) 94, p. 51.

5504. SCHEXNAYDER, Kenneth
"The Gray Heron." [SouthernPR] (34:1) Sum 94, p. 57.

5505. SCHICK, Lauren
"The Land Is Screaming" (tr. of Feliciano Acosta, w. Leyzman Salim). [InterQ] (1:4) 94, p. 22.
"Pomberi" (tr. of Feliciano Acosta, w. Leyzman Salim). [InterQ] (1:4) 94, p. 23.

5506. SCHIELE, Evelyn
"Sunday Afternoon in Winter." [WillowR] (21) Spr 94, p. 14.

5507. SCHILLER, Laura
"The Marine." [SpoonR] (19:1) Wint-Spr 94, p. 91-92.

5508. SCHILPP, Margot
"Non Sequitur." [GettyR] (7:1) Wint 94, p. 127.

5509. SCHIMMEL, Harold
"Island to Island" (Excerpt, tr. by Peter Cole). [Conjunc] (23) 94, p. 105-110.
5510. SCHLAGEL, Anthony
"The Secret Music." [Talisman] (13) Fall 94-Wint 95, p. 231-232.
5511. SCHLANGER, Eugene
"Cavafy." [AmerS] (63:3) Sum 94, p. 402.
5512. SCHLECHT, Andrea
"Icarus of Another World" (An Early Chapter of Our History: The First Aviator). [PraF] (15:2, #67) Sum 94, p. 51-55.
5513. SCHLEGEL, Victoria
"Like Unnatural Words." [ParisR] (36:132) Fall 94, p. 252.
5514. SCHLESIER, Sibylle
"A Fig for the Way Home" (tr. of Joachim Sartorius). [Conjunc] (23) 94, p. 139.
"In This Black Stillness" (tr. of Joachim Sartorius, w. Nathaniel Tarn). [Conjunc] (23) 94, p. 140-143.
"(Love)" (tr. of Joachim Sartorius). [Conjunc] (23) 94, p. 139.
5515. SCHLOESSINGK, Sebastian
"The Complaint." [Verse] (11:1) Spr 94, p. 97.
"Dents." [Verse] (11:1) Spr 94, p. 97.
5516. SCHLOSS, Henry
"Cave Hill" (Louisville). [WestHR] (48:2) Sum 94, p. 142.
"Olive Culture." [WestHR] (48:2) Sum 94, p. 137-141.
5517. SCHLUN, Betsy van
"Dorothea." [SantaBR] (2:2) Fall-Wint 94, p. 152-154.
5518. SCHMIDT, Alejandro
"Asleep, Dead or Bewitched" (tr. by Veronica Miranda). [Luz] (7) N 94, p. 29-33.
"Dormida, Muerta o Hechizada." [Luz] (7) N 94, p. 28-32.
5519. SCHMIDT, Jan Zlotnik
"Parable" (from "We Speak in Tongues"). [AmerPoR] (23:1) Ja-F 94, p. 30.
5520. SCHMIDT, Paul
"Austin City Limits." [WestHR] (48:4) Wint 94, p. 377-385.
5521. SCHMIDT, Paulette
"The Evening Holds Out Its Arms" (tr. of Philippe Soupault). [Vis] (44) 94, p. 24.
SCHMIDT, Therese Lanigan
See LANIGAN-SCHMIDT, Therese
5522. SCHMIT, David
"Crackle." [BlackBR] (19) Fall-Wint 94, p. 32.
"Native village." [BlackBR] (19) Fall-Wint 94, p. 32.
"Postcard world." [BlackBR] (19) Fall-Wint 94, p. 32.
5523. SCHMITZ, Barbara
"The Mother of the Schizophrenic." [SlipS] (14) 94, p. 120-121.
5524. SCHMITZ, Dennis
"Klauer's Dog." [Field] (51) Fall 94, p. 66-68.
5525. SCHNEBERG, Willa
"Harem" (for Hudda Shaarawi, 1879-1947, first to remove the veil in Egypt). [SingHM] (21) 94, p. 15.
5526. SCHNEEMAN, Elio
"Curved Reality." [Talisman] (13) Fall 94-Wint 95, p. 153.
"For the New Year." [Talisman] (13) Fall 94-Wint 95, p. 153.
5527. SCHNEIDER, Aaron
"Breakfast of Bears." [Nimrod] (37:2) Spr-Sum 94, p. 83.
"Need." [Nimrod] (37:2) Spr-Sum 94, p. 84.
5528. SCHNEIDER, Annerose D.
"Good Luck." [Pearl] (20) Spr 94, p. 43.
"He Is Afraid." [Pearl] (20) Spr 94, p. 43.
"I Think of You." [Pearl] (20) Spr 94, p. 43.
"Shadow." [Pearl] (20) Spr 94, p. 43.
5529. SCHNEIDER, J. L.
"Christmas Dinner." [Amelia] (7:3, #22) 94, p. 109.
5530. SCHNEIDER, Martin
"(For Cove)." [Talisman] (12) Spr 94, p. 253.
"Nightmare." [Talisman] (12) Spr 94, p. 253.
5531. SCHNEIDER, Pat
"The Aunts." [NegC] (14:1/2) 94, p. 189-190.
"Don't Look at the Moon." [NegC] (14:1/2) 94, p. 186.
"Shape and Line. Tomorrow." [NegC] (14:1/2) 94, p. 187-188.

5532. SCHNEIDERS, Jay
"Bay of Pigs." [WillowS] (34) Sum 94, p. 60-61.
"A brief Nosology of Misunderstandings in the Nineties." [AntigR] (99) Aut 94, p. 108-109.
"That It Will Not Happen This Time." [GeoR] (48:1) Spr 94, p. 66.
5533. SCHOEBERLEIN, Marion
"Winter's Way." [Amelia] (7:3, #22) 94, p. 159.
5534. SCHOENBERGER, Nancy
"The Blue Hour." [Verse] (11:1) Spr 94, p. 118.
"Burning the Child." [IllinoisR] (1:2) Spr 94, p. 51.
"Complacency of a Room." [Verse] (11:1) Spr 94, p. 119.
"Dear Boy." [IllinoisR] (1:2) Spr 94, p. 53.
"Recipe." [WilliamMR] (32) 94, p. 89-91.
5535. SCHOFIELD, Don
"Comp I." [Gaia] (4) Je 94, p. 42.
"Dead Shepherd's Hut." [Gaia] (4) Je 94, p. 41.
"Drystone Wall." [SouthernPR] (34:2) Wint 94, p. 27-28.
"Volcano." [Gaia] (4) Je 94, p. 42-43.
5536. SCHOONOVER, Amy Jo
"Rock, Paper, Scissors." [HiramPoR] (55/56) Fall 93-Sum 94, p. 106.
5537. SCHORB, E. M.
"Copperheads: The New York Draft Riots." [AmerS] (63:1) Wint 94, p. 86-88.
"Sharp" (Poet of Parris Island). [BelPoJ] (45:1) Fall 94, p. 30-33.
"Wallace Stevens Contemplates Sunday Service in Haddam." [PoetryNW] (35:2) Sum 94, p. 25.
5538. SCHOTT, Penelope Scambly
"Hedgerow in Spring Thaw." [PlumR] (7) [94?], p. 70-71.
5539. SCHRAF, Mark
"Maybe." [Spitball] (47) Sum 94, p. 33-34.
"Question and Answer." [Spitball] (46) Spr 94, p. 52-53.
5540. SCHRAMM, Darrell G. H.
"At the Border." [Border] (5) Fall-Wint 94, p. 61.
"A Confession." [SlipS] (14) 94, p. 103.
"Grillwork." [Border] (5) Fall-Wint 94, p. 62.
5541. SCHRECK, Dean A.
"Man in the Wood." [Amelia] (7:4, #23) 94, p. 123.
5542. SCHREINER, Steven
"Chuck-a-Burger Drive-in." [PoetC] (25:3) Spr 94, p. 22-23.
"The Weather." [PoetC] (25:3) Spr 94, p. 24.
5543. SCHROCK, Michael
"Adam & Eve." [PoetryE] (37/38) Spr 94, p. 29.
5544. SCHULMAN, Grace
"After the Storm." [NewRep] (211:12/13) 19-26 S 94, p. 50.
"Bestiaries." [ParisR] (36:131) Sum 94, p. 205-207.
"Crossing the Square." [CreamCR] (18:2) Fall 94, p. 132.
"Expulsion." [Antaeus] (75/76) Aut 94, p. 319-321.
"God's Letters." [Nat] (259:7) S 5-12 94, p. 250.
"Home Movie." [Boulevard] (9:1/2, #25/26) Spr 94, p. 136.
"New Netherland, 1654." [KenR] (NS 16:4) Fall 94, p. 25-26.
"Notes from Underground: W.H. Auden on the Lexington Avenue I.R.T." [NewYorker] (70:27) 5 S 94, p. 78.
"The Present Perfect." [Boulevard] (9:1/2, #25/26) Spr 94, p. 137-138.
"Río Grande de Loíza" (tr. of Julia de Burgos). [Callaloo] (17:3) Sum 94, p. 667.
"Site." [Pequod] (37) 94, p. 38.
"Somewhere in Brittany." [Pivot] (42) 94, p. 52-53.
"Street Scene." [CreamCR] (18:2) Fall 94, p. 133.
5545. SCHULTZ, Susan (Susan M.)
"Body Surfer." [BambooR] (60) Wint 94, p. 121-122.
"Declensions of Is." [NewAW] (12) Spr-Sum 94, p. 133-135.
"Drive ME" (for John and Rebecca Ernest). [DenQ] (28:4) Spr 94, p. 59-60.
"Final Destinations" (In Memoriam F.W.S., 1913-1992). [PoetryE] (37/38) Spr 94, p. 195-200.
"Sinister Wisdom" (to R.M. Ernest). [Chain] (1) Spr-Sum 94, p. 252-253.
"The Sky's the Limit." [BambooR] (60) Wint 94, p. 119-120.
SCHULZ, Kimberly Pittman
See PITTMAN-SCHULZ, Kimberly

5546. SCHWARTZ, Dan
"Letter from a Younger Brother." [MoodySI] (28, also labeled 29) Fall 94, p. 35.
5547. SCHWARTZ, Hillel
"Mount St. Peter, Maastricht." [BelPoJ] (45:1) Fall 94, p. 22-23.
"Rancho Coastal Humane Society Thrift Shop Sutra." [BelPoJ] (45:1) Fall 94, p. 24-25.
"Twenty Days Into the Wind." [ChamLR] (14/15) Spr-Fall 94, p. 91-92.
5548. SCHWARTZ, Leonard
"Chinese Honey" (tr. of Zhang Er, w. the author). [Talisman] (12) Spr 94, p. 167.
"Confession" (tr. of Zhai Yongming, w. Mingxia Li). [Talisman] (12) Spr 94, p. 163.
"Fake Abdication." [DenQ] (28:3) Wint 94, p. 26-27.
"Premonition" (tr. of Zhai Yongming, w. Mingxia Li). [Talisman] (12) Spr 94, p. 162.
"River Tale" (tr. of Chin Sung, w. Mingxia Li). [Talisman] (12) Spr 94, p. 177-178.
"Story" (tr. of Zhang Er, w. the author). [Talisman] (12) Spr 94, p. 168-169.
5549. SCHWARTZ, Lloyd
"Friendly Song" (printed on the Brazilian 50 Cruzeiros note, tr. of Carlos Drummond de Andrade). [HarvardR] (Premier Issue) Spr 92, p. 109.
5550. SCHWARTZ, Magi
"Skinscape." [SlipS] (14) 94, p. 51.
5551. SCHWARTZ, Ruth L.
"The City at Sunset." [Chelsea] (56) 94, p. 54-57.
5552. SCHWARTZMAN, Adam
"The Sanctuary" (For Alice). [Verse] (11:1) Spr 94, p. 84.
"The Unmoored Boat." [Verse] (11:1) Spr 94, p. 85.
"Westpark" (For PRS and GF). [Verse] (11:1) Spr 94, p. 84.
5553. SCHWARZ, Ghita
"English as a Second Language: Advanced." [Caliban] (14) 94, p. 111.
"English as a Second Language: Beginner." [Caliban] (14) 94, p. 110.
5554. SCHWINDT, Vila
"Carbon Steel." [SantaBR] (2:2) Fall-Wint 94, p. 35.
"Dollface." [SantaBR] (2:2) Fall-Wint 94, p. 34.
"Enigma" (one of Four Proverb Poems). [SantaBR] (2:2) Fall-Wint 94, p. 36.
"Tenor" (one of Four Proverb Poems). [SantaBR] (2:2) Fall-Wint 94, p. 36.
"Tinder in the Night" (one of Four Proverb Poems). [SantaBR] (2:2) Fall-Wint 94, p. 36.
"Widow" (one of Four Proverb Poems). [SantaBR] (2:2) Fall-Wint 94, p. 36.
"Wishbone." [SantaBR] (2:2) Fall-Wint 94, p. 34.
5555. SCOBIE, Stephen
"Driving from Helsinki to Turku." [PoetryC] (15:1) N 94, p. 13.
"Rostock Craving." [PoetryC] (15:1) N 94, p. 13.
5556. SCOFIELD, James
"Also on Thursday." [Outbr] (25) 94, p. 66.
"The Children's Corner." [Elf] (4:3) Fall 94, p. 38-39.
"Elegy." [SmPd] (31:3, #92) Fall 94, p. 12-13.
"The Last Spring." [MidwQ] (36:1) Aut 94, p. 70.
"Requietory for Relativism." [Iowa] (24:1) Wint 94, p. 106.
"Spring Sparkle and the Cock-Bird Shriek." [Iowa] (24:1) Wint 94, p. 107.
"Young Love." [YellowS] (12:1, #45) Spr-Sum 94, p. 39.
5557. SCOFIELD, Michael
"Curmudgeon." [Amelia] (7:3, #22) 94, p. 135.
"Heading Down Hill." [BellArk] (10:6) N-D 94, p. 6.
"Prayer on My 57th Birthday." [BellArk] (10:6) N-D 94, p. 6.
"Strawberry Pie." [BellArk] (10:6) N-D 94, p. 6.
"Tom Dusts Himself Off Rather Quickly." [Amelia] (7:4, #23) 94, p. 73.
5558. SCOON, Karen
"Fish Derby." [AntigR] (96) Wint 94, p. 108.
"The Fishcleaner." [AntigR] (96) Wint 94, p. 107.
"Midnight Shift at the Respite Center." [AntigR] (96) Wint 94, p. 106.
5559. SCOTT, Georgia
"(I) Night Journey" (tr. of Krystyna Lars, w. David Malcolm). [InterQ] (1:1) [93?], p. 102-103.
"(I) She Writes with Fire" (tr. of Krystyna Lars, w. David Malcolm). [InterQ] (1:1) [93?], p. 101.

"In Fourteen Red Tramcars" (tr. of Wladyslaw Zawistowski, w. David Malcolm). [InterQ] (1:1) [93?], p. 105.

5560. SCOTT, Giles
"Second Anniversary." [FreeL] (13) Spr 94, p. 11.
"The Strangest Thing." [SlipS] (14) 94, p. 20.

5561. SCOTT, James
"Howard" (Lament for a pickle player who strangled on his instrument in Carnegie Hall). [SoCoast] (16) Ja 94, p. 48.

5562. SCOTT, Mark
"Stinson Lake, New Hampshire." [NegC] (14:1/2) 94, p. 132-133.

5563. SCOTT, Peter Dale
"I Would Like to Describe" (tr. of Zbigniew Herbert, w. Czeslaw Milosz). [NewEngR] (16:1) Wint 94, p. 105-106.

5564. SCRIMGEOUR, J. D.
"Pick-Up." [HiramPoR] (55/56) Fall 93-Sum 94, p. 107.
"Under the Ghost" (for Harriet Jacobs). [MidAR] (14:2) 94, p. 12-13.

5565. SCRIMGEOUR, James R.
"Coastal Flood Warnings." [SmPd] (31:1, #90) Wint 94, p. 27.
"Monomoy National Wildlife Sanctuary." [NegC] (14:1/2) 94, p. 121-122.
"On the Breaker." [SmPd] (31:1, #90) Wint 94, p. 26.
"Pulling in the Rebound." [SmPd] (31:1, #90) Wint 94, p. 27.
"Sitting on the Orange Granite Rock." [SmPd] (31:1, #90) Wint 94, p. 26.

5566. SCROGGINS, Mark
"The Encroachment of History in October 1993." [Talisman] (13) Fall 94-Wint 95, p. 258.

5567. SCRUTON, James
"Bats." [Farm] (11:2) Fall-Wint 94-95, p. 99.
"Charon." [Poetry] (165:1) O 94, p. 4.
"The Gravedigger's Soliloquy." [NegC] (14:1/2) 94, p. 135.
"The Man with the Metal Detector." [NegC] (14:1/2) 94, p. 134.
"On the Feast of Saint Blaise." [CumbPR] (13:2) Spr 94, p. 64.
"Through Kudzu." [CumbPR] (13:2) Spr 94, p. 65.
"Tire Swing." [CarolQ] (47:1) Fall 94, p. 30.
"View Through a Fence." [Farm] (11:2) Fall-Wint 94-95, p. 97.
"What Gathers." [Farm] (11:2) Fall-Wint 94-95, p. 98.

5568. SCULLY, Maurice
"In Praise of Painting Doors" (for Louis' recovery). [WorldL] (5) 94, p. 28-29.

5569. SEA, Gary
"Ebb and Flow, Along" (tr. of Brigitte Oleschinski). [GrahamHR] (18) Wint 94-95, p. 71.
"Heiress to Her Own Express Train" (For E.O., tr. of Brigitte Oleschinski). [WebR] (18) Fall 94, p. 31.
"Mental Heat Control" (tr. of Brigitte Oleschinski). [GrahamHR] (18) Wint 94-95, p. 72.
"Something Empty, Something Silent Stays Behind" (tr. of Brigitte Oleschinski). [GrahamHR] (18) Wint 94-95, p. 73.
"Tuesday" (tr. of Iren Baumann). [Vis] (45) 94, p. 23.

5570. SEALE, Jan Epton
"Begging at St. Mark's." [CapeR] (29:2) Fall 94, p. 10-11.
"Dealing in Futures." [CapeR] (29:2) Fall 94, p. 9.

5571. SEAMAN, Barbara
"Hospital Gown." [Kaleid] (29) Sum-Fall 94, p. 15.
"Overalls." [Farm] (11:1) Spr-Sum 94, p. 149-150.
"Red Cross Orthopedic Hospital, Kabul." [Kaleid] (29) Sum-Fall 94, p. 57.
"Willow with Two Hearts." [WestB] (35) 94, p. 80-81.

5572. SEARCY, Darlene
"I Interview the Artists." [AntigR] (99) Aut 94, p. 76.

5573. SEARS, Donald A.
"Winter's Solstice" (Excerpt, in memoriam, Donald A. Sears, 1923-1994). [SoCoast] (17) Je 94, p. 66.

5574. SEARSMITH, Kelly
"Father." [MinnR] (41/42) Fall 93-Spr 94 (published Mr 95), p. 17.

5575. SEATON, Maureen
"After Sinead O'Connor Appears on 'Saturday Night Life,' The Pope" (for Janet Bloch. Editors' Prize Winner). [MissouriR] (17:1) 94, p. 118-119.
"The Age of Reason." [PoetryE] (37/38) Spr 94, p. 131.

"Blame It on the Weather in Each of Us." [PoetryE] (37/38) Spr 94, p. 129.
"Clarinets." [KenR] (NS 16:1) Wint 94, p. 157-158.
"During the Eclipse I Remember You Sent Me *Playboy*." [IndR] (17:2) Fall 94, p. 25.
"Eggshell Seas" (Editors' Prize Winner). [MissouriR] (17:1) 94, p. 120.
"The Exquisite Corpse." [IndR] (17:2) Fall 94, p. 22.
"Far Rockaway" (After "The Pyramids to the Projects," Charles Burchette). [KenR] (NS 16:1) Wint 94, p. 155-156.
"Furious Cooking" (for Vanessa and Susan). [NewEngR] (16:3) Sum 94, p. 132-133.
"L.A. Dream #1." [HarvardR] (7) Fall 94, p. 44-45.
"The Mall." [PoetryE] (37/38) Spr 94, p. 127.
"The Queen of Jersey." [IndR] (17:2) Fall 94, p. 26-27.
"Sisters." [PoetryE] (37/38) Spr 94, p. 128.
"Tasha and the Pope." [PoetryE] (37/38) Spr 94, p. 130.
"Theories of Illusion" (after Stephen Jay Gould's *The Panda's Thumb*. Editors' Prize Winner). [MissouriR] (17:1) 94, p. 116-117.
"An Unofficial Interpretation of Pieter Aertsen's 'A Butcher Stall with the Holy Family Giving Alms on the Flight to Egypt,' c. 1550" (for Jennie). [Colum] (22) Wint 94, p. 126-127.
"The West Room." [IndR] (17:2) Fall 94, p. 23-24.
"White Dancing." [KenR] (NS 16:1) Wint 94, p. 158-159.

5576. SEAWARD, Alexander
"Cri de Corps." [Light] (11) Aut 94, p. 18.

5577. SEAY, James
"Tidal Rivers" (for Tim McLaurin, during transplant, 1990). [SouthernR] (30:4) Aut 94, p. 857-858.

5578. SEBASTIAN, Robert M.
"For a Garrulous Prestidigitator." [Light] (12) Wint 94-95, p. 12.
"Some Ept Observations." [Light] (9) Spr 94, p. 17.

5579. SEDAKOVA, Olga
"Chinese Travelogue" (tr. by Andrew Wachtel). [Conjunc] (23) 94, p. 9-20.

5580. SEDEORA, Irene
"Cocoon." [Parting] (7:1) Sum 94, p. 56.

5581. SEFERIS, George
"The Cats of St. Nicholas" (tr. by George Economou). [HarvardR] (2) Fall 92, p. 123-124.

5582. SEIBLES, Tim
"The Stupid." [HangL] (64) 94, p. 62-63.

5583. SEID, Christopher
"Wards Island." [FreeL] (13) Spr 94, p. 4-5.

5584. SEIDEN, Henry M.
"Tinnitus" (For my father). [Poetry] (164:3) Je 94, p. 147.

5585. SEIDMAN, Hugh
"Alms." [HangL] (65) 94, p. 55.
"Aluminum Bowl." [HangL] (65) 94, p. 56.
"Napalm." [HangL] (65) 94, p. 55.

5586. SEIFERLE, Rebecca
"The Ripped-Out Seam." [Jacaranda] (10) 94, p. 124-125.

5587. SEIFERT, Jaroslav
"Písen." [NewRena] (9:1, #27) 94, p. 64.
"The Skeleton of A Whale" (tr. by Vera Bokovec). [Vis] (45) 94, p. 32-33.
"Song" (tr. by Don Mager). [NewRena] (9:1, #27) 94, p. 65.

5588. SEILER, Barry
"The Presley Scarf." [LitR] (37:4) Sum 94, p. 606-607.

5589. SEKOU, Lasana M.
"Liberation Theology." [MassR] (35:3/4) Aut-Wint 94, p. 540-543.

5590. SELAWSKY, John (John T.)
"Echo." [Blueline] (15) 94, p. 36.
"Homage." [WestB] (35) 94, p. 32.
"Spring Rain." [Blueline] (15) 94, p. 35.

5591. SELBY, Spencer
"Close." [DenQ] (29:2) Fall 94, p. 41-42.

5592. SELLAND, Eric
"Kusudama" (Selection: "A Spring Ode," tr. of Yoshioka Minoru). [ChiR] (40:1) 94, p. 118-119.

5593. SELLERS, Heather (Heather Laurie)
"Amateur Naturalism." [Ascent] (18:3) Spr 94, p. 27.
"Apartment Complex Calendula Bed." [HawaiiR] (18:1, #40) Spr 94, p. 101-102.

5594. SELLEY, April
"Cleaning the Refrigerators of the Dead." [SlipS] (14) 94, p. 95.
"Still Dancing." [Parting] (7:1) Sum 94, p. 29-30.

5595. SELMAN, Robyn
"Amazing Feats of Strength." [BostonR] (19:5) O-N 94, p. 39.
"Avec Amour." [AmerV] (33) 94, p. 73-79.
"Bullet Train to Mecca." [BostonR] (19:5) O-N 94, p. 39.
"Directions to My House." [BostonR] (19:5) O-N 94, p. 39.
"For the Field." [KenR] (NS 16:4) Fall 94, p. 1.
"Hagiographies." [WestHR] (48:4) Wint 94, p. 324-327.
"New Language This Meaning." [BostonR] (19:5) O-N 94, p. 39.

5596. SELVING, Jan
"Spy." [DenQ] (28:4) Spr 94, p. 61-63.

5597. SEMANSKY, Chris
"Dear John." [NewDeltaR] (10:2) Spr-Sum 93, p. 25-26.
"The Guest." [SlipS] (14) 94, p. 43.

5598. SEMONES, Charles
"All Saints' Day." [Wind] (74) 94, p. 28.
"Bad Blood." [Wind] (73) 94, p. 22.
"Burning Bush, Kentucky." [CapeR] (29:1) Spr 94, p. 2.
"Geography Lesson" (for J.K.). [CapeR] (29:1) Spr 94, p. 1.
"Hard Love." [Wind] (73) 94, p. 23.
"In the Upper Cumberland." [Wind] (74) 94, p. 29.

5599. SEN, Sudeep
"April's Air." [MalR] (107) Sum 94, p. 71.
"Govind Dev Temple, Vrindavan." [MalR] (107) Sum 94, p. 70.
"Scattered Pieces of a Quarrel." [Pembroke] (26) 94, p. 142.

5600. SENARATNE, Shamina
"Catching Falling Fruit" (Selections). [WestCL] (28:1/2, #13/14) Spr-Fall 94, p. 214-217.

5601. SENECA
"Hercules Conquers the Underworld" (Choral Ode from the tragedy *Hercules Furens*, tr. by Dana Gioia). [CarolQ] (46:2) Wint 94, p. 76-77.
"Hercules Furens" (Excerpt from Act III, tr. by Dana Gioia). [Image] (3) Spr 93, p. 13-15.
"The Latter End of the Chorus of the Second Act of Seneca's *Troades*" (in Latin and English, tr. by John Wilmot, Earl of Rochester). [SoCoast] (16) Ja 94, p. 58-59.

5602. SENG, Goh Poh
"Hornby Island" (for Billy Little, who shared loved spots and fond friends). [CanLit] (140) Spr 94, p. 60-61.

5603. SENGUPTA, Mallika
"The Earth Chooses Her Own Husband" (tr. by Carolyne Wright. w. Paramita Banerjee). [Calyx] (15:2) Sum 94, p. 59.

5604. SENOCAK, Zafer
"The Blue Notebook" (tr. by Judith Orban). [Descant] (24:4, #83) Wint 93-94, p. 122.
"Recognitions" (tr. by Judith Orban). [Descant] (24:4, #83) Wint 93-94, p. 120-121.

5605. SENS, Jean-Marc
"Bread Making." [CimR] (106) Ja 94, p. 86.
"Debriefed." [CimR] (108) Jl 94, p. 85.
"Detour." [XavierR] (14:1) Spr 94, p. 77.
"In de Sica's *Bicycle Thief*." [CimR] (106) Ja 94, p. 85.

5606. SERAFINO, Alan
"The Last Bear in the Bosnia Zoo." [Arc] (33) Fall 94, p. 40-41.

5607. SERRI, Bracha
"Aliza Says" (tr. by Yonina Borvick). [LitR] (37:2) Wint 94, p. 337-338.
"And to Return, Who Is a Jew?" (tr. by Yonina Borvick). [LitR] (37:2) Wint 94, p. 338-339.
"I Am the Daughter of Lot" (tr. by Yonina Borvick). [LitR] (37:2) Wint 94, p. 335.
"Wife of Lot" (tr. by Yonina Borvick). [LitR] (37:2) Wint 94, p. 336-337.

5608. SERVISS, Shirley
"The Power of the Printed Word." [Dandel] (21:1) 94, p. 74.

"Sowing Words." [Dandel] (21:1) 94, p. 73.
5609. SESAR, Carl
"Poems to Eat" (12 poems tr. of Takuboku Ishikawa). [InterQ] (1:2) 93, p. 60-61.
5610. SETH, Rajee
"Bungalow on the Mountain" (tr. by Arlene Zide and Aruna Sitesh). [InterQ] (1:2) 93, p. 178-179.
5611. SETTLES, Phyllis
"Voices" (third prize in the 1994 *Chiron Review* Poetry Contest). [ChironR] (13:4) Wint 94, p. 15.
SEUNG-HEE, Kim
See KIM, Seung-Hee
5612. SEUSS-BRAKEMAN, Diane
"Lost." [CumbPR] (14:1) Fall 94, p. 63-65.
5613. SEWELL, Brad
"Bluegill (after Caravaggio's *The Conversion of Saint Paul,* c. 1601)." [DenQ] (28:4) Spr 94, p. 64-65.
5614. SEXTON, Megan
"Kosode." [Poem] (72) N 94, p. 40.
"Ramps." [Poem] (72) N 94, p. 37.
"Untitled: I'm trying hard to remember." [Poem] (72) N 94, p. 38-39.
5615. SEXTON, Tom
"Beluga." [WeberS] (11:3) Fall 94, p. 94.
"Caribou." [WeberS] (11:3) Fall 94, p. 94.
"Epitaph." [WeberS] (11:3) Fall 94, p. 93.
"Naming." [WeberS] (11:3) Fall 94, p. 93.
5616. SHABAZZ, Phillip
"Dance Blues." [AmerV] (35) 94, p. 25-26.
"Orange Light." [AmerV] (35) 94, p. 27.
"Recent Memories." [AmerV] (35) 94, p. 28.
"Sister Telling." [AmerV] (35) 94, p. 29-30.
5617. SHADDEN, William
"Turpentine." [Pearl] (20) Spr 94, p. 6.
5618. SHADOIAN, Jack
"Murder in Massachusetts." [NewYorkQ] (53) 94, p. 83.
5619. SHAFER, Audrey
"Holocaust Museum, October, 1993." [HiramPoR] (55/56) Fall 93-Sum 94, p. 110-111.
"Loss." [HiramPoR] (55/56) Fall 93-Sum 94, p. 108-109.
5620. SHAFFER, Ann
"Disturbing the Season." [Poetry] (164:3) Je 94, p. 142-143.
5621. SHAFIQ, Hashim
"Perfume" (tr. by Khaled Mattawa). [InterQ] (1:3) 94, p. 132.
"The River" (tr. by Khaled Mattawa). [InterQ] (1:3) 94, p. 131.
SHAGHAGHI, María Luisa Arroyo
See ARROYO SHAGHAGHI, María Luisa
5622. SHAMLU, Ahmad
"In the Moment" (tr. by Ali Zarrin). [Vis] (46) 94, p. 20.
5623. SHAMMAS, Anton
"Absalom" (tr. by Rena Potok). [InterQ] (1:3) 94, p. 159.
"You Sit" (tr. by Rena Potok). [InterQ] (1:3) 94, p. 160.
SHAN, Han
See HAN, Shan
5624. SHANG, Zhongmin
"Homeland" (tr. by Cheng Baolin and Richard Terrill). [TampaR] (9) Fall 94, p. 9.
"Mother" (tr. by Cheng Baolin and Richard Terrill). [TampaR] (9) Fall 94, p. 8.
5625. SHANLEY, Helen
"Fog." [Amelia] (7:4, #23) 94, p. 70-71.
5626. SHANNON, L. A.
"The Wait." [QW] (39) Sum-Fall 94, p. 205-206.
5627. SHAPCOTT, Jo
"Love Song with a Flock of Sheep." [Jacaranda] (5:1) Wint-Spr 91, p. 50-51.
5628. SHAPCOTT, Thomas
"Mouth Feathers." [Pivot] (41) 93, p. 17.
5629. SHAPIRO, Alan
"The Basement." [TriQ] (92) Wint 94-95, p. 38-40.
"Ex-Wife: Infatuation." [Thrpny] (59) Fall 94, p. 30.

"In the Land of the Inheritance." [BostonR] (19:6) D-Ja 94-95, p. 24.
"Lethe." [TriQ] (90) Spr-Sum 94, p. 71.
"Manufacturing." [TriQ] (90) Spr-Sum 94, p. 72-74.
"Mother: Sunbathing." [TriQ] (92) Wint 94-95, p. 42-43.
"Single Mother." [TriQ] (92) Wint 94-95, p. 44-48.
"Woman Friend." [TriQ] (92) Wint 94-95, p. 41.

5630. SHAPIRO, David
"Christ in Prague." [NewAW] (12) Spr-Sum 94, p. 29.
"For Seifert's Mozart in Prague." [NewAW] (12) Spr-Sum 94, p. 30-31.
"Manfly's Journal" (tr. of Liu Manliu, w. Wang Ping). [Talisman] (12) Spr 94, p. 164-166.
"Mary with Sleeping Child" (For Michal). [Boulevard] (9:3, #27) Fall 94, p. 193-194.
"A Scientific American." [NewAW] (12) Spr-Sum 94, p. 28.

5631. SHAPIRO, Gregg
"Technicolor Chalk." [ChamLR] (14/15) Spr-Fall 94, p. 190.

5632. SHAPIRO, Harvey
"Mercy." [HangL] (64) 94, p. 64.
"Traveling Through Ireland." [HangL] (64) 94, p. 65-66.

5633. SHAPIRO, Karl
"The Bourgeois Poet" (Selections: 1-7, 64, 69-78, 85-89, 95-96). [AmerPoR] (23:3) My-Je 94, p. 25-34.
"The Day That Painting Died" (for Joseph Niepce, 1826). [NewYorkQ] (53) 94, p. 36.

5634. SHAPIRO, Myra
"A Brother." [HarvardR] (7) Fall 94, p. 52.

5635. SHAQRA, Shawqi Abi
"The Box" (tr. by Mansour Ajami). [LitR] (37:3) Spr 94, p. 449.
"The Neighbors Think I Am a Star" (tr. by Mansour Ajami). [LitR] (37:3) Spr 94, p. 447-448.
"The Road" (tr. by Mansour Ajami). [LitR] (37:3) Spr 94, p. 450.

SHARAT CHANDRA, G. S.
See CHANDRA, G. S. Sharat

5636. SHARE, Don
"Dialogue" (tr. of Valeri Brainin-Passek, w. Deborah Cohen). [PartR] (61:2) Spr 94, p. 315-316.
"For Laura." [Poetry] (164:5) Ag 94, p. 258.
"The World Is As It Appears" (tr. of Miguel Hernandez). [HarvardR] (2) Fall 92, p. 140.

5637. SHARKEY, Lee
"Between Worlds" (at the Writing Workshop). [Kaleid] (28) Wint-Spr 94, p. 51.
"Ruth Revised" (for Ruth Cohen). [Kaleid] (28) Wint-Spr 94, p. 58.
"Slicing Bread in Air" (Syktyvkar, Komi Republic, Russia, 1992). [CreamCR] (18:2) Fall 94, p. 143-159.
"Warsaw, 1937." [MinnR] (41/42) Fall 93-Spr 94 (published Mr 95), p. 37.

5638. SHATTUCK, M. Lisa
"Emergence." [CapeR] (29:2) Fall 94, p. 18.

5639. SHAVIT, Dean
"Four Rabbis." [ChiR] (40:4) 94, p. 68-70.

5640. SHAW, Angela
"October Snowfall." [ChatR] (14:3) Spr 94, p. 48.

5641. SHAW, Catherine
"Resolution." [AmerV] (33) 94, p. 149-150.

5642. SHAW, Catherine Harnett
"Magnets" (tr. of Moshe Dor). [WebR] (18) Fall 94, p. 11.

5643. SHAW, Janet
"Kinderlieder." [SouthernPR] (34:2) Wint 94, p. 34-36.

5644. SHAW, Luci
"Eucalyptus." [Image] (6) Sum 94, p. 61-62.
"Making a Path: Tuolumne Meadows." [Image] (6) Sum 94, p. 60.
"Shore, Aberystwyth, Wales." [Image] (6) Sum 94, p. 58-59.

5645. SHAW, Robert B.
"12:00 M." [PartR] (61:2) Spr 94, p. 321-322.
"Back Yard Archaeology." [Boulevard] (9:1/2, #25/26) Spr 94, p. 220-221.
"First Bird." [Poetry] (164:5) Ag 94, p. 280.
"Man with Metal Detector." [Poetry] (164:5) Ag 94, p. 276-277.

"On Their Anniversary It Rained." [YaleR] (82:1) Ja 94, p. 85.
"The Porch Swing." [Poetry] (164:5) Ag 94, p. 279-280.
"Proscenium Masks." [Poetry] (164:5) Ag 94, p. 278-279.

5646. SHEA, Amy
"Thoughts during a Sermon on Women and Hunger." [CharR] (20:2) Fall 94, p. 112.

SHEA, Rachel Davis
See DAVIS-SHEA, Rachel

5647. SHEA-RYDBERG, Amy
"June Thirteenth." [NegC] (14:1/2) 94, p. 123.

5648. SHEARER, Laura
"The Incantation." [HampSPR] Wint 94, p. 42.

5649. SHEBELSKI, R. C.
"The Great Indoors." [Light] (10) Sum 94, p. 11.

5650. SHECK, Laurie
"The Book of Persephone." [SouthernHR] (28:1) Wint 94, p. 28.

5651. SHEEHAN, Aurelie
"Irish Like Us." [Kalliope] (16:3) 94, p. 28-29.

5652. SHEEHAN, Kathleen
"Harbor." [SantaBR] (2:2) Fall-Wint 94, p. 149.
"Poetry Reading." [SantaBR] (2:2) Fall-Wint 94, p. 149.

5653. SHEEHAN, Marc J.
"The Empty Present." [Parting] (7:1) Sum 94, p. 55.
"The New World Order." [Parting] (7:1) Sum 94, p. 20.
"Shame." [Parting] (7:1) Sum 94, p. 19.

5654. SHEFFER, Roger
"Breaking Camp, Raquette Lake, 1960." [Blueline] (15) 94, p. 1-2.
"Family Photo, Full of Elbows." [SoDakR] (32:2) Sum 94, p. 132.
"The Guy Who Got Lost at West Canada." [Blueline] (15) 94, p. 2.

5655. SHEFFER, Susannah
"Lower East Side." [PoetL] (89:3) Fall 94, p. 41.
"Mistakes." [PoetL] (89:3) Fall 94, p. 42.
"Strangers." [CreamCR] (18:2) Fall 94, p. 102.

5656. SHEIKH, Mansour Y. (Mansoor Y.)
"Poem: There is a silence that delves for pain" (tr. by Daud Kamal). [Vis] (45) 94, p. 21.
"Still Life" (tr. by Daud Kamal). [Vis] (46) 94, p. 10.

5657. SHELDON, Glenn
"Home: 12 Sylvan Street." [Wind] (74) 94, p. 30.
"Image Indigo." [ApalQ] (42) Fall 94, p. 56-58.
"Image Indigo." [Border] (3) Fall 93, p. 69-71.

5658. SHELDON, Kathleen
"A Different Life." [FloridaR] (20:1) Fall 94, p. 103.
"One Thing." [FloridaR] (20:1) Fall 94, p. 104-105.

5659. SHELLER, Gayle Hunter
"Crux of It All." [BellArk] (10:1) Ja-F 94, p. 16.
"Fire and Smoke." [BellArk] (10:3) My-Je 94, p. 13.
"Grandpa's Hymn" (for Leonard). [BellArk] (10:2) Mr-Ap 94, p. 29.
"Her Place." [BellArk] (10:2) Mr-Ap 94, p. 29.
"Kitchen Crones" (Selections: 3 poems). [BellArk] (10:5) S-O 94, p. 10.
"Laundry Day." [BellArk] (10:2) Mr-Ap 94, p. 29.
"Making the Crooked Straight" (for Wilbur). [BellArk] (10:2) Mr-Ap 94, p. 29.
"Poet Lavender" (for L.L.). [BellArk] (10:1) Ja-F 94, p. 16.

5660. SHELLY, Elaine
"A Question of Audre." [EvergreenC] (9:1) Wint-Spr 94, p. 88-89.
"Tituba" (A slave and one of the first women accused of witchcraft in colonial Salem). [EvergreenC] (9:1) Wint-Spr 94, p. 87.

5661. SHELTON, Richard
"The Little Town of West Texas." [GeoR] (48:1) Spr 94, p. 94-95.

5662. SHEPARD, J. Michael
"Out of Florida." [ChironR] (13:2) Sum 94, p. 10.

5663. SHEPARD, Neil
"Ghost Talk." [CharR] (20:1) Spr 94, p. 75-76.

5664. SHEPHARD, Selena Anna / Andy Plumb
"Pretty Persuasion." [ModernW] (2) Wint 94, p. 121-124.

5665. SHEPHERD, Gail
"Love Letters." [YaleR] (82:1) Ja 94, p. 57-58.

5666. SHEPHERD, J. Barrie
"Christmas Mail." [ChrC] (111:36) 14 D 94, p. 1189.
"Cosmicology." [ChrC] (111:21) 13-20 Jl 94, p. 671.
"Going to Bethlehem." [ChrC] (111:37) 21-28 D 94, p. 1220.
"Nunc Dimittis." [ChrC] (111:16) 11 My 94, p. 498.
"Rwanda." [ChrC] (111:27) 7 O 94, p. 886.
"Seasonal Exit." [ChrC] (111:7) 2 Mr 94, p. 226.
5667. SHEPHERD, Melissa
"Acoustics." [Border] (3) Fall 93, p. 72.
"The Need of Hands" (to Jeannine Keenan). [PraS] (68:3) Fall 94, p. 51-52.
5668. SHEPHERD, Reginald
"Amaranth." [PassN] (15:1) Sum 94, p. 43.
"Apparently." [LitR] (37:4) Sum 94, p. 688.
"Bacchus." [WestHR] (48:1) Spr 94, p. 65.
"Black Is the Color of My True Love's Hair." [ParisR] (36:131) Sum 94, p. 104-105.
"Black Money." [KenR] (NS 16:4) Fall 94, p. 129.
"Blindsided." [BrooklynR] (11) 94, p. 31.
"A Brief Manual for Swimmers." [Poetry] (164:5) Ag 94, p. 266.
"Brotherhood." [ColR] (21:1) Spr 94, p. 137-138.
"Clair De Lune." [PraS] (68:2) Sum 94, p. 96.
"Crush." [ChiR] (40:2/3) 94, p. 30-32.
"Daylight for a Stranger." [HighP] (9:2) Ag 94, p. 104-105.
"Desire and the Slave Trade." [Callaloo] (17:2) Sum 94, p. 495-496.
"Hero." [AnotherCM] (28) 94, p. 128.
"Hygiene." [ChiR] (40:2/3) 94, p. 33-34.
"Later That Same Day." [RiverS] (40) 94, p. 57-58.
"A Man Named Troy." [Callaloo] (17:2) Sum 94, p. 497-498.
"Miscegenation." [Callaloo] (17:2) Sum 94, p. 499.
"A Muse." [ParisR] (36:131) Sum 94, p. 103.
"My Foolish Friend." [KenR] (NS 16:4) Fall 94, p. 130.
"My Mother Dated Otis Redding." [Confr] (52/53) Wint-Spr 94, p. 311.
"Narcissus and the Namesake River." [LaurelR] (28:1) Wint 94, p. 122.
"The New World." [ColR] (21:1) Spr 94, p. 139-140.
"North Pearl." [WestHR] (48:1) Spr 94, p. 64.
"Notes From Ariadne at Sea." [ApalQ] (42) Fall 94, p. 34.
"Phenomenology." [Poetry] (164:5) Ag 94, p. 267.
"Pindaric Ode to Yet Another White Man as Apollo." [RiverS] (40) 94, p. 59.
"Provisional." [Iowa] (24:3) Fall 94, p. 110.
"Sebastian's Summer Poem." [PraS] (68:2) Sum 94, p. 95-96.
"Self-Portrait As Shards of Mirror." [Callaloo] (17:2) Sum 94, p. 500.
"Self-Portrait Surviving Spring." [PassN] (15:1) Sum 94, p. 42.
"Shipbuilding." [DenQ] (29:2) Fall 94, p. 43-44.
"Song to the Siren." [ParisR] (36:131) Sum 94, p. 104.
"Soul Music." [ChiR] (40:2/3) 94, p. 35-36.
"Stop on By." [AnotherCM] (28) 94, p. 129-130.
"Three A.M. Eternal." [QW] (38) Winter-Spr 93-94, p. 97.
"Two or Three Things I Know About Him." [ColR] (21:1) Spr 94, p. 135-136.
"Two Versions of Midsummer." [BlackWR] (21:1) Fall-Wint 94, p. 112-113.
5669. SHEPPARD, Simon
"For the Thrift Store." [Art&Und] (3:1) Ap 94, p. 6.
"The Map of a New Country." [Art&Und] (3:1) Ap 94, p. 6.
"One Perfect Day." [JamesWR] (11:4) Sum 94, p. 1.
5670. SHERIDAN, Virginia G.
"Origami." [CapeR] (29:1) Spr 94, p. 45.
5671. SHERMAN, Kenneth
"Jumbo." [Arc] (33) Fall 94, p. 37.
5672. SHERRILL, Steven
"Hymn for Granite." [GeoR] (48:2) Sum 94, p. 274.
"Lament of the Sheet Metal Worker." [PlumR] (7) [94?], p. 9.
5673. SHERRY, Pearl Andelson
"Fermi Lab: Sisyphus of Quarks." [Poetry] (165:3) D 94, p. 143.
5674. SHEVIN, David
"The Music of Asian Carolina" (for Christina). [XavierR] (14:1) Spr 94, p. 63-64.

5675. SHIEL, Leslie
"Andre." [SantaBR] (2:2) Fall-Wint 94, p. 94-95.
5676. SHIKATANI, Gerry
"Follow the River." [WestCL] (28:1/2, #13/14) Spr-Fall 94, p. 134-139.
5677. SHIKI (1867-1902)
Haiku [AmerPoR] (23:4) Jl-Ag 94, p. 18.
5678. SHINDER, Jason
"Once Before the Ocean." [Colum] ("The Lost Issues", [i.e. 18-19]) 93, p. 141.
"The Storm, After" (Provincetown, Mass.). [Colum] ("The Lost Issues", [i.e. 18-19]) 93, p. 142.
5679. SHINING BEAR
"Ursu Monarch." [Pearl] (20) Spr 94, p. 85.
SHINKICKI, Takahashi (1901-1987)
See TAKAHASHI, Shinkicki (1901-1987)
5680. SHIPLEY, Vivian
"Black Mussel, Leo." [NegC] (14:1/2) 94, p. 223.
"Fungus-Yum." [HampSPR] Wint 94, p. 32.
"Here's Looking at You." [NegC] (14:1/2) 94, p. 222.
"Hitchhiking Mass Pike." [NegC] (14:1/2) 94, p. 224.
"Moonshine." [HampSPR] Wint 94, p. 31.
"Night Fishing at Morgan Point." [Nimrod] (38:1) Fall-Wint 94, p. 78.
"No Six Pounders" (The Nimrod / Hardman Wards: Finalist). [Nimrod] (38:1) Fall-Wint 94, p. 77.
"Stony Creek Granite." [NegC] (14:1/2) 94, p. 115-116.
"Why I Fish." [HampSPR] Wint 94, p. 33.
5681. SHIPPY, Peter Jay
"Creepy About Being." [Ploughs] (20:4) Wint 94-95, p. 171.
"Where Everything Is When." [Ploughs] (20:4) Wint 94-95, p. 169-170.
5682. SHIRAZI, Reza
"Chor Bazaar" (*Chor Bazaar:* Hindi for Thieves Market). [CoalC] (8) Ap 94, p. 30.
5683. SHIRLEY, Aleda
"The Day of the Dead Bride and Groom." [AmerV] (34) 94, p. 53-54.
SHIRO, Murano
See MURANO, Shiro
5684. SHOAF, Diann Blakely
"Bad Blood." [AntR] (52:1) Wint 94, p. 90-91.
"Delta Funeral." [SouthernR] (30:4) Aut 94, p. 716-718.
"Foucault in Vermont." [Ploughs] (20:1) Spr 94, p. 175.
"Her Accusers — Topsfield, Massachusetts, 1692." [Jacaranda] (4:2) Spr 90, p. 110.
"High Tide." [HarvardR] (6) Spr 94, p. 56.
"Lee at Arlington, 1866." [NegC] (14:1/2) 94, p. 136.
"Multiple Exposure." [ColR] (21:1) Spr 94, p. 162-163.
"Polyphemus." [Shen] (44:2) Sum 94, p. 52.
"Solo, New Orleans." [AntR] (52:1) Wint 94, p. 88-89.
"Summer Closing." [TarRP] (34:1) Fall 94, p. 24.
"The Triumph of Style." [AntR] (52:1) Wint 94, p. 92-93.
"Trompe l'Oeil." [DenQ] (28:4) Spr 94, p. 66-67.
"Vertigo." [HarvardR] (2) Fall 92, p. 163.
5685. SHOLL, Betsy
"Behind the Saint-Lazare Station" (After the photo by Henri Cartier-Bresson). [Field] (50) Spr 94, p. 66-67.
"Valentines." [Field] (50) Spr 94, p. 68-69.
5686. SHOMER, Enid
"At Freud's House." [OntR] (41) Fall-Wint 94, p. 108-109.
"A Floridian Swimming in Brooklyn." [Kalliope] (16:1) 94, p. 61.
"In Greensboro" (Woolworth's lunch counter. For Jibreel A-A. K-A. Khazan (Ezell Blair, Jr.), Franklin McCain, Joseph McNeil, and David Richmond).). [OgalalaR] (5:1) Wint 94, p. 26-27.
"The Lonely Ones" (Color woodcut by Edvard Munch, 1899). [OgalalaR] (5:1) Wint 94, p. 24-25.
"The Mystery of My Father's Cleanliness." [MassR] (35:1) Spr 94, p. 102.
"Notes from the Sketchbook of Gustav Klimt." [SouthernPR] (34:1) Sum 94, p. 5-9.
"Snoop." [MassR] (35:1) Spr 94, p. 101-102.
5687. SHORB, Michael
"Antonin Artaud on Madison Avenue." [HeavenB] (11) 94, p. 12.
"Something Good On." [HeavenB] (11) 94, p. 10-11.

5688. SHORE, Jane
"Peak Season." [Salm] (104/105) Fall 94-Wint 95, p. 174-176.
5689. SHORR, Kathy
"At the Arboretum." [QW] (39) Sum-Fall 94, p. 164-165.
"Wolf Den." [QW] (39) Sum-Fall 94, p. 161-163.
5690. SHORT, Gary
"Church." [LaurelR] (28:2) Sum 94, p. 43-44.
"Given Back." [LaurelR] (28:2) Sum 94, p. 45.
"Little Makeweights of Guilt." [WritersF] (20) 94, p. 71.
"One Summer." [QW] (38) Winter-Spr 93-94, p. 134-135.
"Rain." [HayF] (15) Fall-Wint 94, p. 24.
"The Stars That Fell." [WritersF] (20) 94, p. 70.
"When I Look Outside." [HayF] (15) Fall-Wint 94, p. 25.
5691. SHOWS, Hal Steven
"Waterlude." [CarolQ] (47:1) Fall 94, p. 19.
5692. SHRAYER, Maxim
"Villa Borghese" (tr. of David Shrayer-Petrov, w. Dolores Stewart). [Salm] (101/102) Wint-Spr 94, p. 151-153.
5693. SHRAYER-PETROV, David
"Villa Borghese" (tr. by Dolores Stewart and Maxim Shrayer). [Salm] (101/102) Wint-Spr 94, p. 151-153.
5694. SHRESTHA, Bandana
"Ghazal." [InterQ] (1:2) 93, p. 152-154.
5695. SHRIVER, Peggy L.
"Lines on History." [ChrC] (111:23) 10-17 Ag 94, p. 754.
5696. SHUCARD, Alan
"Training" (from "We Will Raise a Family"). [AmerPoR] (23:4) Jl-Ag 94, p. 28.
5697. SHUFORD, Kelly
"Dusk in Tuscumbia." [Pivot] (42) 94, p. 23.
"To My Zoologist Husband." [SoCoast] (17) Je 94, p. 33.
5698. SHULKLAPPER, Lucille Gang
"On the Death of Mining Towns." [Parting] (7:1) Sum 94, p. 41.
5699. SHULTZ, George E.
"Silent Noise." [Pearl] (20) Spr 94, p. 21.
5700. SHUMATE, Kathleen
"E. J. Bellocq, Storyville Photographer." [NegC] (13:2/3) 93, p. 52-56.
5701. SHURIN, Aaron
"Subliminal Sweat." [Zyzzyva] (10:3) Fall 94, p. 79-81.
5702. SHUTTLE, Penelope
"From the Window." [Stand] (36:1) Wint 94-95, p. 73.
"Long Walks." [Verse] (11:2) Sum 94, p. 26.
"Tigers." [Verse] (11:2) Sum 94, p. 27.
5703. SHUTTLEWORTH, Red
"Ghazal for Gaelic Translation." [WestB] (35) 94, p. 11.
"Gonna Drink My Chocolate Rodeo." [BellR] (17:1/2) Spr-Fall 94, p. 30.
5704. SICOLI, Dan
"House of Satan." [Pearl] (20) Spr 94, p. 64.
5705. SIDJAK, Dave
"Mexican Bus." [Event] (23:3) Wint 94-95, p. 68-69.
"Speed." [Event] (23:3) Wint 94-95, p. 70.
"Will." [Event] (23:3) Wint 94-95, p. 67.
5706. SIEGEL, Joan I.
"Arctic Tern." [Comm] (121:21) 2 D 94, p. 11.
"I Am Angry at You." [CumbPR] (13:2) Spr 94, p. 75.
"Photograph: In the Old Neighborhood." [CumbPR] (13:2) Spr 94, p. 76.
"Shadow Life." [PoetC] (25:3) Spr 94, p. 32.
"Spring Poem." [CumbPR] (13:2) Spr 94, p. 77.
5707. SIEGEL, Robert
"Digging Out the Cellar Under the Front Porch." [Image] (7) Fall 94, p. 30.
"Opening Day." [Image] (7) Fall 94, p. 29.
"Seer" (Winner of the 1994 Milton Center Poetry Contest). [Image] (7) Fall 94, p. 27-28.
5708. SIEVERS, Tere
"Freeze Frame." [Pearl] (20) Spr 94, p. 82.
"To New York with Gram When I Am Twelve." [Pearl] (20) Spr 94, p. 82.

5709. SIGNORELLI-PAPPAS, Rita
"Dante Writes the *Rime Petrose*." [HolCrit] (31:1) F 94, p. 18.
"Face in the Glass." [CumbPR] (13:2) Spr 94, p. 78-79.
"Metaphors." [SoCoast] (17) Je 94, p. 3.
"Polly Put the Kettle On" (After Paula Rego). [InterPR] (20:1) Spr 94, p. 98-99.
"Themes of Initiation." [MidwQ] (35:3) Spr 94, p. 316-317.
"Wind." [MidwQ] (35:3) Spr 94, p. 315.
5710. SIKÉLIANOS, Eléni
"At Night, Two" (for t.). [Zyzzyva] (10:4) Wint 94, p. 116-117.
"Home-Fries." [Talisman] (13) Fall 94-Wint 95, p. 199.
5711. SIKELIANOS, Eleni
"Little Pasha." [Caliban] (14) 94, p. 91.
5712. SILANO, Martha
"For a Friend Who'd Prefer a Sestina." [PoetryNW] (35:1) Spr 94, p. 39.
"For a Friend Who'd Prefer a Sestina." [PoetryNW] (35:3) Aut 94, p. 39.
5713. SILBERG, Richard
"So to Speak." [Zyzzyva] (10:1) Spr 94, p. 95.
5714. SILÉN, Iván
"El Cielo de Oriente." [Nuez] (5:13/14/15) 94, p. 71.
5715. SILENT THUNDER
"The Story of Er Mao and Me" (Selections: 2 poems, tr. by Zhang Ziqing). [Talisman] (13) Fall 94-Wint 95, p. 157-158.
5716. SILESKY, Barry
"The Political Unconscious." [IllinoisR] (2:1) Fall 94, p. 46.
"What Happened." [IllinoisR] (2:1) Fall 94, p. 44-46.
5717. SILEX, Edgar
"The Beautiful Thread" (Some things my grandfather said my grandfathers said to tell me). [Americas] (22:3/4) Fall-Wint 94, p. 80-81.
"For Beauty." [Americas] (22:3/4) Fall-Wint 94, p. 82.
"Leaving Cibola." [Americas] (22:3/4) Fall-Wint 94, p. 78-79.
"Short-Lived Journal." [Callaloo] (17:1) Wint 94, p. 128-129.
"The Truth." [Americas] (22:3/4) Fall-Wint 94, p. 83.
"Washington D.C." [Americas] (22:3/4) Fall-Wint 94, p. 76-77.
5718. SILK, Dennis
"Figment of Crabb Robinson's *Reminiscences*." [Stand] (36:1) Wint 94-95, p. 55.
5719. SILKIN, Jon
"Fuji" (tr. of Mitsuharu Kaneko, w. Tomoyuki Iino). [Stand] (35:3) Sum 94, p. 18.
"A Noiseless Place." [Quarry] (42:4) Mr 94, p. 55.
"The Two Are Dead." [Quarry] (42:4) Mr 94, p. 56-57.
5720. SILLIMAN, Deborah
"Mother." [CaribbeanW] (8) 94, p. 58.
5721. SILLIMAN, Ron
"Non" (Excerpt. For Jackson Mac Low). [NewAW] (12) Spr-Sum 94, p. 66-72.
5722. SILLINGS, Elizabeth
"Correction Facility." [Kalliope] (16:3) 94, p. 73.
5723. SILNA, Amy
"This Strange Hour." [WestHR] (48:3) Fall 94, p. 257.
5724. SILVA, Lynda S.
"Chocolate Craving." [Dandel] (20:2) 93, p. 47-48.
"Doin' the Streets in Dark Glasses." [CoalC] (8) Ap 94, p. 11.
"If I Were Water." [Nimrod] (38:1) Fall-Wint 94, p. 137.
"Leaves of an Autumn Past." [CoalC] (8) Ap 94, p. 8.
"Leaves of Autumn Past." [Nimrod] (38:1) Fall-Wint 94, p. 138.
5725. SILVA, Sam
"In the Nature of All Eternal Hypocrisy." [DogRR] (26) Wint 94-95, p. 10.
"Keeping the Unfaith." [DogRR] (26) Wint 94-95, p. 10.
"The Mother of the Sweet Several." [DogRR] (26) Wint 94-95, p. 11.
"Rhetorical Deaths on the Altar." [DogRR] (26) Wint 94-95, p. 11.
5726. SILVA ESTRADA, Alfredo
"Exercise (Reflection Poem)" (to José Balza, tr. by Tess O'Dwyer). [Trans] (29) Spr 94, p. 66-67.
"The Scream of Images" (tr. by Tess O'Dwyer). [Trans] (29) Spr 94, p. 68-69.
5727. SILVAGNIA-MACATANGAY, Maria
"A Long, Hard Look." [CoalC] (8) Ap 94, p. 38.
5728. SILVERMAN, Herschel
"Cittee Cittee Cittee II." [Talisman] (13) Fall 94-Wint 95, p. 144-148.

"A Niftee Chickee Cittee Serenade" (Celebrating John Zorn solo at the Kniting Factory 1/28/94 [sic]). [Talisman] (13) Fall 94-Wint 95, p. 143-144.
"On the Road Again" (information highway, for Jack Kerouac). [MoodySI] (28, also labeled 29) Fall 94, p. 13.

5729. SILVERTHORNE, Marty
"Conversation on the Leavings." [Pembroke] (26) 94, p. 70-71.

5730. SIMIC, Amela
"The Apprentice" (tr. of Goran Simic). [AntR] (52:2) Spr 94, p. 214.
"The Arrival of the Wolf" (tr. of Goran Simic). [AntR] (52:2) Spr 94, p. 218.
"Beauty and the Beast" (tr. of Ferida Durakovic). [AntR] (52:2) Spr 94, p. 213.
"The Bridge" (tr. of Goran Simic). [ParisR] (36:133) Wint 94, p. 120.
"Imagination Lost" (tr. of Goran Simic). [AntR] (52:2) Spr 94, p. 216.
"Lament for Vijecnica" (tr. of Goran Simic). [ParisR] (36:133) Wint 94, p. 119.
"November, Raging Through the Rooms" (tr. of Ferida Durakovic). [AntR] (52:2) Spr 94, p. 215.
"The Town and the Dogs" (tr. of Goran Simic). [ParisR] (36:133) Wint 94, p. 118.

5731. SIMIC, Charles
"About Hope and Dissipation" (tr. of Aleksander Ristovic). [Agni] (40) 94, p. 176-177.
"Big city Poem" (tr. of Vasko Popa). [HarvardR] (Premier Issue) Spr 92, p. 47.
"Childhood at the Movies." [ColR] (21:1) Spr 94, p. 93.
"The Church of Insomnia." [ProseP] (3) 94, p. 77.
"Comparison" (tr. of Aleksandar Ristovic). [Field] (51) Fall 94, p. 75.
"Elegy." [GettyR] (7:3) Sum 94, p. 513.
"Euphemia Gray's Pubis" (For John Yau). [ProseP] (3) 94, p. 76.
"The Gambler." [HarvardR] (7) Fall 94, p. 15.
"Grim Contingencies." [GeoR] (48:3) Fall 94, p. 497.
"If I Knew I'd Bear Myself Proudly" (tr. of Matija Bickovic). [HarvardR] (Premier Issue) Spr 92, p. 75.
"In Ecstasy of Surrender." [Field] (51) Fall 94, p. 56.
"In Strange Cities." [GettyR] (7:3) Sum 94, p. 514.
"Jones Very." [HarvardR] (7) Fall 94, p. 15.
"My Insomnia and I." [Field] (50) Spr 94, p. 53-54.
"Mystery Writer." [Field] (51) Fall 94, p. 57.
"Mythology" (tr. of Aleksandar Ristovic). [Field] (51) Fall 94, p. 76.
"October Light." [NewYorker] (70:34) 24 O 94, p. 66.
"On Dreams." [HarvardR] (7) Fall 94, p. 13-14.
"The Philosopher." [HarvardR] (7) Fall 94, p. 15.
"Pocket Theater." [ColR] (21:1) Spr 94, p. 94.
"Raskolnikov." [GeoR] (48:3) Fall 94, p. 498.
"Relaxing in a Madhouse." [Antaeus] (75/76) Aut 94, p. 322.
"The Secret." [GettyR] (7:3) Sum 94, p. 515.
"Shaving." [HarvardR] (2) Fall 92, p. 22.
"Simple Desire" (tr. of Aleksander Ristovic). [Agni] (40) 94, p. 178.
"The Story of Crucifixion." [Agni] (39) 94, p. 22.
"Two Dreams and a Memoir about Chess." [HarvardR] (7) Fall 94, p. 14.
"Wanted Poster." [NewYorker] (70:2) 28 F 94, p. 74.
"Wine of Collusion" (tr. of Aleksander Ristovic). [Agni] (40) 94, p. 175.
"Winter Poem." [HarvardR] (7) Fall 94, p. 15.

5732. SIMIC, Goran
"The Apprentice" (tr. by Amela Simic). [AntR] (52:2) Spr 94, p. 214.
"The Arrival of the Wolf" (tr. by Amela Simic). [AntR] (52:2) Spr 94, p. 218.
"The Bridge" (tr. by Amelia Simic). [ParisR] (36:133) Wint 94, p. 120.
"Imagination Lost" (tr. by Amela Simic). [AntR] (52:2) Spr 94, p. 216.
"Lament for Vijecnica" (tr. by Amelia Simic). [ParisR] (36:133) Wint 94, p. 119.
"The Town and the Dogs" (tr. by Amelia Simic). [ParisR] (36:133) Wint 94, p. 118.

5733. SIMMERMAN, Jim
"Maddy's Woods." [CharR] (20:2) Fall 94, p. 103-104.

5734. SIMMONS, Shan
"Her Hands." [BlackBR] (19) Fall-Wint 94, p. 43-44.
"Last Lines for Little Brother." [WestB] (34) 94, p. 48.
"Little River Canyon." [Poem] (72) N 94, p. 28.
"Observation and Prayer." [Poem] (72) N 94, p. 26.
"Ways." [Poem] (72) N 94, p. 27.

5735. SIMMONS-MCDONALD, Hazel
"School Play" (for Pat-Allan). [MalR] (107) Sum 94, p. 80-81.

5736. SIMMS, Kristina
"Downstream." [ChatR] (14:2) Wint 94, p. 29.
5737. SIMON, Beth
"Audit." [Northeast] (5:10) Sum 94, p. 3-4.
"Before and After the Lake Birds." [Northeast] (5:10) Sum 94, p. 5-6.
"Before and After the Lake Birds." [SouthernPR] (34:1) Sum 94, p. 28-29.
"Giving Over." [MidwQ] (35:4) Sum 94, p. 414.
"Spirits." [Arc] (33) Fall 94, p. 44.
5738. SIMON, Maurya
"Bark with Authority." [SpoonR] (19:1) Wint-Spr 94, p. 118.
"Crèche." [Ploughs] (20:4) Wint 94-95, p. 172-173.
"Keeping Track." [SpoonR] (19:1) Wint-Spr 94, p. 116.
"Maya." [Poetry] (164:4) Jl 94, p. 202.
"Merry-Go-Round." [PraS] (68:1) Spr 94, p. 152.
"Russell Market." [Poetry] (164:4) Jl 94, p. 204.
"San Gabriels" (For Bob Chapman). [SpoonR] (19:1) Wint-Spr 94, p. 117.
"Taj Mahal." [Poetry] (164:4) Jl 94, p. 203.
"The Yogi Speaking." [PraS] (68:1) Spr 94, p. 151.
5739. SIMONIDES of Ceos (556-468 B.C.)
"Tourist, take this message to your hawkish nation" (tr. by John J. Brugaletta). [SoCoast] (16) Ja 94, p. 57.
5740. SIMPKINS, Kate
"The Last Time I Saw Joy" (This is about Posession). [BlackBR] (19) Fall-Wint 94, p. 21.
"What the Flowers Do" (Associated Writing Programs Intro Award poem). [IndR] (17:2) Fall 94, p. 139-140.
5741. SIMPSON, Anne
"Tomatoes, Apples." [Event] (23:2) Sum 94, p. 40-41.
5742. SIMPSON, Jamie
"The Bee Charmer." [CapeR] (29:1) Spr 94, p. 14.
5743. SIMPSON, Louis
"Al and Beth." [SouthernR] (30:2) Ap, Spr 94, p. 321-322.
"The Clearing." [SouthernR] (30:2) Ap, Spr 94, p. 317-320.
"Fame." [NewEngR] (16:1) Wint 94, p. 162.
"The Iverson Boy." [Hudson] (47:1) Spr 94, p. 27-28.
"Returning to Paris." [HarvardR] (7) Fall 94, p. 22-23.
"Two Friends." [HarvardR] (6) Spr 94, p. 16-19.
"The Walker on Main Street." [Vis] (45) 94, p. 30.
"The Yardman's Story." [Vis] (45) 94, p. 31-32.
5744. SIMPSON, Matt
"Illicit in Grasmere." [Stand] (35:2) Spr 94, p. 71.
5745. SIMPSON, Nancy
"Now in Another Land." [PraS] (68:2) Sum 94, p. 97.
"Pangloss Speaks to the Freshman Class." [PraS] (68:2) Sum 94, p. 98.
"The Skin Diver's Memory." [PraS] (68:2) Sum 94, p. 98-99.
"Studying Winter." [PraS] (68:2) Sum 94, p. 100.
5746. SIMS, Ann
"Details." [Kalliope] (16:3) 94, p. 17.
5747. SIMS, Roberta
"Drought." [PaintedHR] (11) Spr-Sum 94, p. 55.
SIN, Aseret
See WASHINGTON, Teresa (Aseret Sin)
5748. SINAGUB, Jonathan
"City of Peace, Nature, Science — City of Oneness" (w. Katherine Keane). [Caliban] (14) 94, p. 74-88.
5749. SINDALL, Susan
"Fantasy." [Pivot] (41) 93, p. 36.
5750. SINDT, Christopher
"My Name Is Micah Jellison And." [HayF] (14) Spr-Sum 94, p. 30.
5751. SINGER, Darren A.
"Alchemy and Art." [NegC] (14:1/2) 94, p. 137.
5752. SINGER, Katie
"Road Side Stand." [SoDakR] (32:2) Sum 94, p. 77.
5753. SIRIUS, Nicolae
"Concealment in Self" (tr. by Walter Tonetto). [CentR] (38:2) Spr 94, p. 337.
"The White Century" (tr. by Walter Tonetto). [CentR] (38:2) Spr 94, p. 338.

5754. SIROWITZ, Hal
"At My Grave." [SlipS] (14) 94, p. 63.
"Crumbs." [SlipS] (14) 94, p. 62.
"Let Me Die First." [SlipS] (14) 94, p. 61.
"My Thoughtful Son." [SlipS] (14) 94, p. 63.
"News of My Death." [SlipS] (14) 94, p. 62.
"No More Birthdays." [SlipS] (14) 94, p. 61.
"Two Burials for the Same Person." [HangL] (65) 94, p. 71.
5755. SISSON, C. H.
"Credence." [Image] (5) Spr 94, p. 19.
"Now." [Image] (5) Spr 94, p. 20.
5756. SITESH, Aruna
"Bungalow on the Mountain" (tr. of Rajee Seth, w. Arlene Zide). [InterQ] (1:2) 93, p. 178-179.
"Chilka Lake" (tr. of Shakunt Mathur, w. Arlene Zide). [InterQ] (1:2) 93, p. 180-181.
"Song of Separation" (tr. of Teji Grover, w. Arlene Zide and the author). [InterQ] (1:2) 93, p. 190-191.
5757. SKALSKY, Askold
"Losing Face." [Poem] (72) N 94, p. 23.
"Millville." [JINJPo] (16:1) Spr 94, p. 17.
"Moon Poem." [Blueline] (15) 94, p. 53-54.
"The Ponies of Chuang Tzu." [Wind] (74) 94, p. 32-33.
"Summer of '62." [JINJPo] (16:1) Spr 94, p. 18-19.
"Summers in Miletus." [Poem] (72) N 94, p. 20-21.
"Sweetbriers in Yakutia*" (*Republic in Eastern Siberia and once a site of Stalin's labor camps). [Wind] (74) 94, p. 31-32.
"Wish List." [Poem] (72) N 94, p. 22.
5758. SKEEN, Anita
"In the Rare Book Room: Three Versions." [Nimrod] (38:1) Fall-Wint 94, p. 139-140.
5759. SKELLEY, Jack
"City Hall." [IllinoisR] (2:1) Fall 94, p. 47-48.
5760. SKELTON, Robin
"Behind the laurel bush you stood" (tr. of Sappho, fl. 600 B.C.). [Arc] (32) Spr 94, p. 38.
"Happy the man that has at last found out" (tr. of Theognis, born 544 B.C.). [Arc] (32) Spr 94, p. 39.
"Julian, who's begun to grow" (tr. of Statyllius Flaccus, 1st Century B.C./A.D.). [Arc] (32) Spr 94, p. 39.
"Perugia: A Hallowe'en Triptych." [Nimrod] (37:2) Spr-Sum 94, p. 85-87.
"You, boy, with the girlish eyes" (tr. of Anakreon, 563-478 B.C.). [Arc] (32) Spr 94, p. 38.
5761. SKENE, K. V.
"Lunch at the Trout." [Grain] (22:2) Fall 94, p. 15.
5762. SKILLMAN, Judith
"The Fingerboard." [SouthernHR] (28:2) Spr 94, p. 155.
"Notes for Another Alice" (First Sue Saniel Elkind National Poetry Award, Finalist). [Kalliope] (16:2) 94, p. 41-42.
"Oodles of Tiny Fiddles." [NowestR] (32:3) 94, p. 30-31.
"Oral History." [NowestR] (32:1) 94, p. 111-112.
5763. SKINNER, Douglas Reid
"Other Still Lives" (Excerpts, tr. of Valerio Magrelli, w. Marco Fazzini). [Verse] (11:1) Spr 94, p. 44-45.
5764. SKINNER, Jeffrey
"Bill Evans and the Birds of Appetite." [AmerV] (35) 94, p. 119.
"Had students, once — Lennox in the Berkshires." [AmerV] (35) 94, p. 123.
"I played the time like shadow letters." [AmerV] (35) 94, p. 124.
"Prayer to Owl Hiding in Daylight." [Writer] (107:2) F 94, p. 16-17.
"The trend of each age is its thumbprint virus." [AmerV] (35) 94, p. 121.
"When Lees bashed knee to cannon in the Chateau." [AmerV] (35) 94, p. 122.
"You have to work hard in order to relax." [AmerV] (35) 94, p. 120.
5765. SKINNER, Knute
"At Ease." [HolCrit] (31:1) F 94, p. 19.
"One Good Turn Deserves Another." [HolCrit] (31:2) Ap 94, p. 15.
"Sundays." [Amelia] (7:3, #22) 94, p. 56.

"Thematic Variations: Three Songs." [SewanR] (102:3) Sum 94, p. 388-391.
"The Young Man." [Amelia] (7:3, #22) 94, p. 56-57.

5766. SKLAR, David
"Manifesto." [WormR] (34:4, #136) 94, p. 155.
"A Sestina to Piss Off the Scholars." [WormR] (34:4, #136) 94, p. 153-154.
"Walking in Town on a Snowy Evening." [WormR] (34:4, #136) 94, p. 154-155.

5767. SKLAREW, Myra
"April 1943: Borszczow." [Vis] (45) 94, p. 16.
"In Unfamiliar Air." [Vis] (45) 94, p. 15-16.
"Song of the Lost Days." [Confr] (54/55) Fall 94-Wint 95, p. 301.

5768. SKLOOT, Floyd
"The Ambassador Apartments." [PoetC] (26:1) Fall 94, p. 20.
"Coffee." [Crazy] (47) Wint 94, p. 77-78.
"Dancing in the Cosmos." [GettyR] (7:1) Wint 94, p. 78-79.
"Day of the Rainbow." [PoetryNW] (35:2) Sum 94, p. 9-10.
"Delius in Florida." [PraS] (68:1) Spr 94, p. 61-62.
"Dizzy." [PraS] (68:1) Spr 94, p. 62.
"Home Remedies." [Crazy] (46) Spr 94, p. 101-105.
"Indian Summer." [Crazy] (47) Wint 94, p. 79.
"Poppies." [GettyR] (7:1) Wint 94, p. 80.
"River Walk." [PraS] (68:1) Spr 94, p. 63.
"Smoke." [PoetC] (25:2) Wint 94, p. 12.
"Touches." [PraS] (68:1) Spr 94, p. 60-61.
"The Winter Branch." [Crazy] (47) Wint 94, p. 80-81.

5769. SKOBLOW, Jeffrey
"Mingus in the Flesh." [Eyeball] (3) 93, p. 28.

5770. SKRUPSKELIS, Viktoria
"Jasmine Bush" (tr. of Judita Vaiciunaite, w. Stuart Friebert). [Field] (51) Fall 94, p. 64.
"Still Life with Window Frosted Over" (tr. of Judita Vaiciunaite, w. Stuart Friebert). [Field] (51) Fall 94, p. 65.

5771. SKVARLA, Jeanne
"Instructions for the Anxious." [PoetryE] (37/38) Spr 94, p. 70.
"Meditation in the Grove of the Thinking Trees." [PoetryE] (37/38) Spr 94, p. 71.
"Moroccan Hash." [PoetryE] (37/38) Spr 94, p. 73.
"Once I Was Chased Out of Galveston Bay." [PoetryE] (37/38) Spr 94, p. 74.
"The Patient." [PoetryE] (37/38) Spr 94, p. 72.
"Poem: I needed to become more lifelike." [PoetryE] (37/38) Spr 94, p. 75.

5772. SLADE, Giles
"Two Borsalinos." [AntigR] (99) Aut 94, p. 123-126.

5773. SLAPIKAS, Carolyn
"2 Things You Must Know." [NewYorkQ] (53) 94, p. 115.

5774. SLATTERY, Dennis Patrick
"Dropping Out" (for Matt). [Border] (4) Spr-Sum 94, p. 61.

5775. SLAUGHTER, Adèle
"The Book of Denial." [VirQR] (70:4) Aut 94, p. 666-667.
"Piano Lesson." [VirQR] (70:4) Aut 94, p. 665-666.
"Sleeping with My Sisters." [VirQR] (70:4) Aut 94, p. 663-665.
"Wrestling with My Brother." [VirQR] (70:4) Aut 94, p. 667-668.

5776. SLAUGHTER, William
"The Face, Also, Has Bruised Dignity" (tr. of Bei Ling, w. Jin Zhong). [Manoa] (6:1) Sum 94, p. 82-83.

5777. SLAVITT, David (David R.)
"Ceyx and Alcyone" (From Book XI of Ovid's *Metamorphoses*). [NewEngR] (16:1) Wint 94, p. 26-33.
"Domitian at Ostia." [Light] (9) Spr 94, p. 9.
"The Gravid Mares" (from *Georgics*, tr. of Virgil). [NewEngR] (16:3) Sum 94, p. 28.
"Niagara Falls." [Light] (12) Wint 94-95, p. 10.

5778. SLEBODA, Steve
"The Call of Genius." [DarkMoon] (1) 94, p. 50-51.
"Each Adjective." [DarkMoon] (1) 94, p. 49.
"Hate." [DarkMoon] (1) 94, p. 52.
"Tiny Brush." [DarkMoon] (1) 94, p. 48.

5779. SLEIGH, Tom (Thomas)
"Child's Drawing: 'Boy Holding a Ball at a Funeral'" (Jewish Museum in Prague). [TriQ] (92) Wint 94-95, p. 49-50.
"The Explanation" (for Jared Baker, 1960-1992). [ParisR] (36:133) Wint 94, p. 294.
"Some Larger Motion." [ParisR] (36:133) Wint 94, p. 295-296.
"The Souls." [Ploughs] (20:4) Wint 94-95, p. 178.
"The Tank." [TriQ] (92) Wint 94-95, p. 53-55.
"The Word." [TriQ] (92) Wint 94-95, p. 51-52.
"The Work" (for my father). [Ploughs] (20:4) Wint 94-95, p. 174-177.
5780. SLEIN, Tracy
"I Guess He's Dead Now." [CoalC] (8) Ap 94, p. 12.
5781. SLETTEDAHL, Heidi
"Absence." [RagMag] (12:1) Sum 94, p. 50.
"Housebound." [RagMag] (12:1) Sum 94, p. 51.
5782. SLIVA, Gayle
"Disappearing Acts." [Interim] (13:2) Fall-Wint 94-95, p. 4.
"The Husband." [Interim] (13:2) Fall-Wint 94-95, p. 5.
5783. SLOAN, Kay
"Breakfast in Keseberg's Diner" (Sacramento, 1848). [ParisR] (36:131) Sum 94, p. 100-101.
5784. SLOAN, Margy
"Abduction's Query." [Avec] (7:1) 94, p. 14-21.
5785. SLOSS, Henry
"Between Lives." [ParisR] (36:133) Wint 94, p. 169-173.
"Fairy Tales." [ParisR] (36:130) Spr 94, p. 149.
"Irregular Exercise." [ParisR] (36:130) Spr 94, p. 150-151.
"New Year's Eve." [WestHR] (48:2) Sum 94, p. 143.
"An Old World Setting." [WestHR] (48:4) Wint 94, p. 358-376.
"Slice of Art." [ParisR] (36:130) Spr 94, p. 148.
5786. SLYMAN, Ernest
"Goldfish." [Light] (11) Aut 94, p. 8.
5787. SMAILS, William
"Aphrodite." [BellArk] (10:3 [i.e. 10:4]) Jl-Ag 94, p. 14-15.
"Sand." [BellArk] (10:1) Ja-F 94, p. 28.
5788. SMALL, Abbott
"Spain by Summer Light." [Wind] (74) 94, p. 33-34.
5789. SMALL, Michael
"Camille Claudel." [HarvardR] (2) Fall 92, p. 52.
5790. SMALL, Virginia
"Loose Ends." [Kalliope] (16:3) 94, p. 50-51.
5791. SMALLFIELD, Edward
"Epithalamion" (for Lina and Neil, October 2, 1993). [PaintedHR] (11) Spr-Sum 94, p. 6-7.
"Football." [Caliban] (14) 94, p. 137.
5792. SMART, Harry
"Am Einunddreissigsten Mai, 1992." [Stand] (36:1) Wint 94-95, p. 33.
5793. SMELCER, John (John E.)
"Crow Pass." [DogRR] (13:1, #25) Spr-Sum 94, p. 6.
"Kesugi Ridge" (for Tom Sexton). [Zyzzyva] (10:1) Spr 94, p. 125.
"Ritual." [BelPoJ] (44:4) Sum 94, p. 35.
"Tazlina." [DogRR] (13:1, #25) Spr-Sum 94, p. 7.
"Weir Fisher." [BelPoJ] (44:4) Sum 94, p. 34.
5794. SMITH, Arthur
"Kudzu in Winter." [KenR] (NS 16:4) Fall 94, p. 122.
"Labor Day." [KenR] (NS 16:4) Fall 94, p. 120-121.
"Once in Ohio." [KenR] (NS 16:4) Fall 94, p. 121-122.
"One Life." [SouthernR] (30:3) Sum 94, p. 577-578.
5795. SMITH, Bruce
"After the *Evening News*." [TriQ] (90) Spr-Sum 94, p. 173-174.
"Blue Cornflowers Framing the Resurrection." [IllinoisR] (1:2) Spr 94, p. 32.
"Catullan." [HarvardR] (6) Spr 94, p. 27.
"Delinquent." [TriQ] (90) Spr-Sum 94, p. 175.
"Like This." [Ploughs] (20:1) Spr 94, p. 146.
"Stroke." [Pequod] (37) 94, p. 67-70.
"Students." [BostonR] (19:3/4) Je-S 94, p. 31.
"To the Executive Director of the Fallen World." [HarvardR] (6) Spr 94, p. 26-27.

"War Baby, Breast-Bone." [HarvardR] (6) Spr 94, p. 25.

5796. SMITH, Charlie
"Appetite." [Thrpny] (57) Spr 94, p. 29.
"Conceit." [Poetry] (163:4) Ja 94, p. 209.
"The Essential Story." [Poetry] (163:4) Ja 94, p. 210.
"February 2." [Pivot] (41) 93, p. 21.
"The Gesture." [SouthernR] (30:4) Aut 94, p. 782.
"I don't Want a Son." [Agni] (39) 94, p. 87.
"Invention of the Land." [GeoR] (48:2) Sum 94, p. 298.
"The Miniature City." [Poetry] (163:4) Ja 94, p. 208.
"Ransom." [SouthernR] (30:4) Aut 94, p. 781-782.
"Ruffians." [Poetry] (163:4) Ja 94, p. 211.
"The Small Sound the Night Makes." [Pivot] (41) 93, p. 21.

5797. SMITH, Cheryl D.
"Slam Funk." [Eyeball] (3) 93, p. 18.

5798. SMITH, D. J.
"And You Will Wake." [PoetryC] (15:1) N 94, p. 21.
"Everywhere the Light." [SouthernPR] (34:1) Sum 94, p. 40-41.
"In the Brief Light of Summer." [GreenMR] (NS 17:2) Fall-Wint 94-95, p. 52.
"Jimmy Finds-a-Feather Speaks for Me" (for Johnny). [PassN] (15:2) Wint 94, p. 5-6.
"Maggie's Legacy." [PoetryC] (15:1) N 94, p. 21.
"Of Fathers and Sons." [PoetryC] (15:1) N 94, p. 21.
"Pilgrim." [PassN] (15:2) Wint 94, p. 7.
"Prayers for the Dead Ventriloquist." [Stand] (36:1) Wint 94-95, p. 34.
"A Thread." [GreenMR] (NS 17:2) Fall-Wint 94-95, p. 51.

5799. SMITH, D. M.
"Mantra for Spring Time." [Amelia] (7:4, #23) 94, p. 22.

5800. SMITH, Dave
"A Boy with Ringworm." [Poetry] (164:1) Ap 94, p. 13-14.
"Brittany." [PraS] (68:3) Fall 94, p. 31.
"Can of Beans." [NoAmR] (279:4) Jl-Ag 94, p. 20-21.
"The Carmelite Nun" (tr. of Franco Buffoni, w. the author). [SouthernR] (30:2) Ap, Spr 94, p. 272-274.
"The Crystal Set." [PraS] (68:3) Fall 94, p. 33-34.
"Dog Walk." [NoAmR] (279:3) My-Je 94, p. 36.
"Edwin Muir's Palm Tree" (St. Andrews, Scotland). [PraS] (68:3) Fall 94, p. 28-29.
"In the Library." [VirQR] (70:3) Sum 94, p. 444-445.
"Little Ode to the Wheelchair Boys." [NoAmR] (279:2) Mr-Ap 94, p. 48.
"Littoral Memory." [ColR] (21:2) Fall 94, p. 165-166.
"Mighty Joe Turner's Blues." [Poetry] (164:1) Ap 94, p. 11-12.
"One Hundred Twenty-nine Dollars." [PraS] (68:3) Fall 94, p. 31.
"Palm Trees at 1430 Knollwood Dr." [PraS] (68:3) Fall 94, p. 30.
"Power Lunch." [PraS] (68:3) Fall 94, p. 32.
"Taking the Field." [Shen] (44:3) Fall 94, p. 111-113.
"To the Dutch Poet's Shoes" (for Maria Van Daalen). [ColR] (21:2) Fall 94, p. 167-168.
"Unknown Daughter." [VirQR] (70:3) Sum 94, p. 446-447.
"Velvet Running." [PraS] (68:3) Fall 94, p. 30.
"Wolves." [PraS] (68:3) Fall 94, p. 32.

5801. SMITH, David-Glen
"Canticle." [ChangingM] (27) Wint 94, p. 18.
"The Myth of Fear" (for Mary Lou Brockett). [AnotherCM] (27) 94, p. 177-178.

5802. SMITH, David James
"Beauty." [AlabamaLR] (8:1) 94, p. 8-9.
"Pigeons." [WilliamMR] (32) 94, p. 72.
"Sparrow." [FloridaR] (20:1) Fall 94, p. 106-107.
"Winter Memory." [HiramPoR] (57) Fall 94-Wint 95, p. 55.

5803. SMITH, Dean
"After Two Years." [PoetryE] (37/38) Spr 94, p. 56.
"Diver." [PoetryE] (37/38) Spr 94, p. 57.

5804. SMITH, Donald
"Where She'd Like to Settle Down." [CoalC] (8) Ap 94, p. 7.

5805. SMITH, Douglas Burnet
"Fiesole Lament." [Event] (23:2) Sum 94, p. 42.

5806. SMITH, E. W.
"Evelina Weaving." [CreamCR] (18:1) Spr 94, p. 13.
5807. SMITH, Ellen McGrath
"Embers in the Shape of the Map of America, 1975." [SouthernPR] (34:1) Sum 94, p. 18-19.
"Off Friendship Avenue." [SouthernPR] (34:1) Sum 94, p. 18.
5808. SMITH, Francis J.
"Charter Flight." [Light] (9) Spr 94, p. 9.
"Spring Is a Two-Faced Metaphor." [Light] (9) Spr 94, p. 7.
5809. SMITH, G. S.
"Between This September and That One" (tr. of Gennadii Lysenko). [Manoa] (6:2) Wint 94, p. 77.
"In the Middle of All This Idle Running Around" (tr. of Gennadii Lysenko). [Manoa] (6:2) Wint 94, p. 79.
"It's Not Because the Music Is the Way It Is" (tr. of Gennadii Lysenko). [Manoa] (6:2) Wint 94, p. 78.
"Once More, Everything Is Blindingly Dull" (tr. of Gennadii Lysenko). [Manoa] (6:2) Wint 94, p. 78.
"That Which I Sowed" (tr. of Gennadii Lysenko). [Manoa] (6:2) Wint 94, p. 79.
5810. SMITH, Greg
"The Man Who Couldn't Go." [AntigR] (96) Wint 94, p. 125.
"Never Far From Camp." [AntigR] (98) Sum 94, p. 106.
"Never Far From the Camp." [AntigR] (96) Wint 94, p. 124.
5811. SMITH, Iain Crichton
"Day after Day." [MalR] (107) Sum 94, p. 125-126.
"In Israel." [Stand] (35:3) Sum 94, p. 19.
5812. SMITH, J. D.
"Komboloi." [NewDeltaR] (10:2) Spr-Sum 93, p. 1-2.
5813. SMITH, J. Mark
"Mummery." [Dandel] (20:2) 93, p. 13-14.
5814. SMITH, Jack
"A Platform Before the Castle." [HiramPoR] (57) Fall 94-Wint 95, p. 56-57.
5815. SMITH, Jared
"Erie." [IllinoisR] (2:1) Fall 94, p. 49.
5816. SMITH, Joan Jobe
"More Secrets About Beans" (Special Section: 22 poems). [WormR] (34:1, #133) 94, p. 25-40.
"On the Way to Heaven." [SlipS] (14) 94, p. 113.
5817. SMITH, Jonathan
"Conquistadoras." [RiverS] (40) 94, p. 4.
"Two Tone Town." [RiverS] (40) 94, p. 5-6.
5818. SMITH, Jordan
"After *Die Walküre*." [ParisR] (36:133) Wint 94, p. 226.
"The Dream of Horses." [ParisR] (36:131) Sum 94, p. 217-218.
"Matthew 5:22." [Salm] (104/105) Fall 94-Wint 95, p. 163-164.
"Tristan." [Poetry] (164:1) Ap 94, p. 22.
SMITH, Jordan Fisher
See FISHER-SMITH, Jordan
5819. SMITH, Katherine
"First Snow." [Vis] (44) 94, p. 17.
"Nude." [Vis] (45) 94, p. 37.
5820. SMITH, Kirsten
"Doctor's Visit." [Witness] (8:1) 94, p. 122.
"First Words." [Witness] (8:1) 94, p. 124.
"Foliage." [BellR] (17:1/2) Spr-Fall 94, p. 31.
"Getaway." [NoDaQ] (62:1) Wint 94-95, p. 129-130.
"The Girl Next Door." [GettyR] (7:1) Wint 94, p. 163-164.
"Marlene." [Witness] (8:1) 94, p. 123.
"Tattoo Parlor." [QW] (38) Winter-Spr 93-94, p. 120.
"This Dangerous Music." [FloridaR] (20:1) Fall 94, p. 82-83.
"Typical Bobby." [Witness] (8:1) 94, p. 125.
5821. SMITH, Linda Fuller
"Stuck Outside." [SoCoast] (16) Ja 94, p. 11.
5822. SMITH, Linda Wasmer
"Why I Am Propped Up in Bed, Reading the *Selected Poems of William Carlos Williams*, at 10:00 on a Monday Morning." [CoalC] (8) Ap 94, p. 51.

5823. SMITH, Malachi D.
"Time Keeper." [CaribbeanW] (8) 94, p. 36.
5824. SMITH, Michael C.
"The Infants at the Shoreline." [NowestR] (32:1) 94, p. 115.
"This Is the Way." [Jacaranda] (10) 94, p. 14.
5825. SMITH, Michael P.
"Making Shit Happen." [ChangingM] (27) Wint 94, p. 45.
5826. SMITH, Michael S.
"Father's Cufflinks." [Plain] (14:2) Wint 94, p. 24.
"Indian Summer." [WindO] (58) Sum 94, p. 39-40.
"Managers' Meeting." [Ledge] (17) Wint 94, p. 66-67.
"Mother Works the Nursing Home Crowd." [WindO] (58) Sum 94, p. 41-42.
"Wood Works." [Ledge] (17) Wint 94, p. 64-65.
5827. SMITH, Nathaniel
"I Can't Say Your Name" (tr. of Vicent Andrés Estellés). [SenR] (24:2) Fall 94, p. 62.
"Tarragona" (tr. of Vicent Andrés Estellés, w. Lynette McGrath). [SenR] (24:2) Fall 94, p. 63.
5828. SMITH, Noel
"October in the White Mountains." [Blueline] (15) 94, p. 44.
5829. SMITH, Norman H. C.
"The Ruined Prince." [DogRR] (26) Wint 94-95, p. 28.
5830. SMITH, R. T.
"Before the Breakup." [SouthernR] (30:4) Aut 94, p. 838-840.
"Chore." [Gaia] (4) Je 94, p. 35.
"Cryptic." [Elf] (4:1) Spr 94, p. 21.
"End of Summer, the City of The Tribes." [Stand] (35:2) Spr 94, p. 60-61.
"A Holy Well in Clare" (for Brendan Galvin). [Poem] (71) My 94, p. 2-3.
"Jumble Sale." [Stand] (35:2) Spr 94, p. 62.
"The Magdalene." [Poetry] (164:6) S 94, p. 328-330.
"Mushrooms" (In Sneem, County Kerry). [GeoR] (48:2) Sum 94, p. 324-325.
"Old Nuns." [Poem] (71) My 94, p. 4-5.
"Passage to Kilronin." [Poem] (71) My 94, p. 1.
"Red Dog." [Elf] (4:1) Spr 94, p. 24.
"Renaissance." [Gaia] (4) Je 94, p. 34.
"Sabbath in Donegal." [PoetC] (25:2) Wint 94, p. 22.
"Shells." [Gaia] (4) Je 94, p. 34-35.
"Teresa." [PoetC] (25:2) Wint 94, p. 23.
"Tinder." [AlabamaLR] (8:1) 94, p. 36-37.
"To Write The New Yorker Poem." [SouthernPR] (34:1) Sum 94, p. 63.
"Tooth Fairy." [Elf] (4:1) Spr 94, p. 22-23.
"Walter Anderson's J." [SouthernPR] (34:2) Wint 94, p. 56-57.
"Waterford" (County Cavan). [SouthernR] (30:4) Aut 94, p. 837-838.
5831. SMITH, Robert L.
"At Least Once." [ContextS] (4:1) 94, p. 39.
"Bones, Dry Bones." [SoCaR] (26:2) Spr 94, p. 154.
5832. SMITH, Roch
"Career's Sunset" (tr. of Bernard Pozier). [InterPR] (20:2) Fall 94, p. 79.
"Hermine and Her Mother" (tr. of Jean Ethier-Blais). [InterPR] (20:2) Fall 94, p. 83.
5833. SMITH, Rod
"For Loss" (Selections: 3 poems). [WashR] (20:4) D 94-Ja 95, p. 29.
5834. SMITH, Ron
"The Light That Dwells in Names." [Nimrod] (37:2) Spr-Sum 94, p. 90.
"The Radiant Gift." [Nimrod] (37:2) Spr-Sum 94, p. 89.
"Things As They Are." [Nimrod] (37:2) Spr-Sum 94, p. 88.
5835. SMITH, Shannon Mark
"Another Country." [NewOR] (20:3/4) Fall-Wint 94, p. 143.
"I Was Born in Keokuk." [NewOR] (20:3/4) Fall-Wint 94, p. 144.
SMITH, Shelli Jankowski
See JANKOWSKI-SMITH, Shelli
5836. SMITH, Stephen E.
"Bomb Dream." [SouthernPR] (34:1) Sum 94, p. 26-27.
5837. SMITH, Steven M.
"The Visit." [ChironR] (13:2) Sum 94, p. 19.
5838. SMITH, Steven Ross
"Cracks." [PraF] (15:2, #67) Sum 94, p. 82.

5839. SMITH, Thomas R.
"The Road from Genghis Khan." [ProseP] (3) 94, p. 78.
5840. SMITH, Todd
"Macy's Annual Thanksgiving Day Parade." [SycamoreR] (6:2) Sum 94, p. 46.
5841. SMITH, Tracy K.
"The Anxious" (Second Prize). [HarvardA] (128:3) Spr 94, p. 9.
"Voice of the Master." [Eyeball] (3) 93, p. 11.
5842. SMITHER, Elizabeth
"Karate Class." [MalR] (107) Sum 94, p. 116.
"A Whole Day's Rain." [MalR] (107) Sum 94, p. 117.
5843. SMITS, Ronald F.
"The Rose Petunia." [TarRP] (34:1) Fall 94, p. 18.
"Still Life." [TarRP] (34:1) Fall 94, p. 18.
5844. SMOCK, Frederick
"Ballad of Externals." [InterQ] (1:4) 94, p. 125-127.
"Quaestio." [Wind] (73) 94, p. 24.
5845. SMOKEWOOD, Elaine
"It's Not the Heat." [CapeR] (29:2) Fall 94, p. 2.
5846. SMUKLER, Linda
"I Know You." [KenR] (NS 16:1) Wint 94, p. 137.
"Married." [AmerV] (33) 94, p. 40.
"Prayer." [ProseP] (3) 94, p. 79.
"Sign." [KenR] (NS 16:1) Wint 94, p. 137-138.
"Suits and Ties." [KenR] (NS 16:1) Wint 94, p. 138-139.
5847. SMYTH, Richard
"The Day of Rain." [ApalQ] (42) Fall 94, p. 55.
"The Holding." [ApalQ] (42) Fall 94, p. 54.
"The Method of Weedflowers." [FloridaR] (19:2) 94, p. 83.
5848. SNEEDEN, Ralph
"Coltrane and My Father." [NewEngR] (16:1) Wint 94, p. 156.
5849. SNEFF, Priscilla
"Chance Becomes My Science." [Ploughs] (20:4) Wint 94-95, p. 179.
5850. SNIDER, Clifton
"Branding Iron" (for River Phoenix). [Pearl] (20) Spr 94, p. 13.
5851. SNIDER, Michael
"Pantoum." [Colum] ("The Lost Issues", [i.e. 18-19]) 93, p. 153-154.
5852. SNODGRASS, Ann
"American Suite" (tr. of Luciano Erba). [QW] (39) Sum-Fall 94, p. 149.
5853. SNODGRASS, Kathleen
"My Name Is Jocasta" (tr. of Katarzyna Borun-Jagodzinska, w. Justyna Kostkowska). [ArtfulD] (26/27) 94, p. 22.
"A Patriotic Song" (tr. of Katarzyna Borun-Jagodzinska, w. Justyna Kostkowska). [ArtfulD] (26/27) 94, p. 21.
5854. SNODGRASS, W. D.
"A Presence." [NewRep] (211:18) 31 O 94, p. 47.
5855. SNOOK, Joann
"Merlin." [EngJ] (83:3) Mr 94, p. 103.
5856. SNOW, Carol
"Dear." [Pequod] (37) 94, p. 71-73.
"For." [DenQ] (29:1) Sum 94, p. 35-38.
"Recollection." [DenQ] (29:1) Sum 94, p. 39.
5857. SNYDER, Bob
"Grandma." [Epoch] (43:2) 94, p. 183.
5858. SNYDER, Gary
"Covers the Ground." [Thrpny] (58) Sum 94, p. 28.
"Daconstruction." [Antaeus] (75/76) Aut 94, p. 323.
"Reeds." [Sulfur] (35) Fall 94, p. 9-12.
"Surrounded by Wild Turkeys." [AntR] (52:1) Wint 94, p. 20.
5859. SNYDER, Jennifer
"1983." [AmerPoR] (23:6) N-D 94, p. 6.
"Fathers." [IndR] (17:2) Fall 94, p. 79-80.
"Funeral." [IndR] (17:2) Fall 94, p. 78.
"Kiss." [AmerPoR] (23:6) N-D 94, p. 6-7.
"Kiss Me Until I'm Filled with People" (Selections: 7-10). [MidAR] (14:2) 94, p. 154-158.
"Minnesota." [MidAR] (14:2) 94, p. 152-153.

"Sonnet: Who can remember their childhood?" [PassN] (15:2) Wint 94, p. 41.
SNYDER, Kaye Bache
See BACHE-SNYDER, Kaye
5860. SNYDER, L. A.
"The Connection." [WestB] (35) 94, p. 33.
"Touch and Time." [WestB] (35) 94, p. 34-35.
5861. SNYDER, Molly B.
"The Ten-Minute Mile." [CreamCR] (18:2) Fall 94, p. 138.
5862. SNYDER, William, Jr.
"Anastasia." [Amelia] (7:4, #23) 94, p. 38.
"If This Doesn't Change Your Mind, Read It Again While Sitting in Your Truck: a Pantoum." [Border] (5) Fall-Wint 94, p. 63-64.
"Parentheses" (To Andrew Ramsay, killed in France, December 21, 1915). [ChamLR] (14/15) Spr-Fall 94, p. 40-41.
5863. SOBIN, Anthony
"The Appointment." [SoCoast] (17) Je 94, p. 15.
5864. SOBIN, Gustaf
"Seventh Ode: The Relics." [Sulfur] (35) Fall 94, p. 127-130.
"Sixth Ode: The Grottoes." [Sulfur] (35) Fall 94, p. 124-126.
5865. SOBRINO, Gabriella
"Spaces" (tr. by Donald Gecewicz). [Vis] (46) 94, p. 37.
5866. SOBSEY, Cynthia
"Alzheimer" (for Fran). [Kalliope] (16:1) 94, p. 22.
5867. SODERLING, Janice
"Another White Cloud of Moths." [BelPoJ] (45:1) Fall 94, p. 36.
"Cutting." [Interim] (13:1) Spr-Sum 94, p. 12.
"It's a Sorry Sight." [Interim] (13:1) Spr-Sum 94, p. 13.
"Silence Leans Askew." [Interim] (13:1) Spr-Sum 94, p. 13.
5868. SOFIELD, David
"Think-Piece." [NewRep] (211:23) 5 D 94, p. 44.
5869. SOIFER, Mark
"Barry Schuler's Spectacular Model Train Display." [Pembroke] (26) 94, p. 88.
5870. SOKOL, John
"Aubade." [NegC] (14:1/2) 94, p. 138.
"Ganymede" (A Plainsongs Award Poem). [Plain] (14:3) Spr 94, p. 21.
"Inflatable 'Scream'." [NewYorkQ] (53) 94, p. 80.
"Picasso's Last Self-Portrait" (June 30, 1972). [Plain] (15:1) Fall 94, p. 12.
5871. SOLDOFSKY, Alan
"First Day." [Manoa] (6:1) Sum 94, p. 16-17.
"Poplar Catkins." [Manoa] (6:1) Sum 94, p. 15-16.
"Starry Night." [Manoa] (6:1) Sum 94, p. 16.
"Thirteen." [MichQR] (33:1) Wint 94, p. 117-118.
5872. SOLEDAD, Starfire
"Old Crows." [NegC] (14:1/2) 94, p. 60.
5873. SOLHEIM, James
"Garbage(I)." [AnotherCM] (28) 94, p. 138-142.
5874. SOLOMON, Mark
"Box Turtle." [Bomb] (47) Spr 94, p. 77.
"Falling Asleep, Book in My Lap" (for Larry Levis). [CumbPR] (14:1) Fall 94, p. 66.
"These Are the Streets." [TriQ] (91) Fall 94, p. 185.
5875. SOLOMON, Marvin
"Four Stone Lions." [NegC] (14:1/2) 94, p. 10.
"Mourning Doves." [Light] (10) Sum 94, p. 8.
"Traveling Through Louisiana on One Shirt." [SouthernPR] (34:1) Sum 94, p. 52-53.
5876. SOLOMON, Suzanne A.
"Chikatilo's Confession." [NewYorkQ] (53) 94, p. 81.
5877. SOLONCHE, J. R.
"Because That Was the Only Vision." [PoetryNW] (35:3) Aut 94, p. 38-39.
"I Read a Poem Today About a Spider, Who." [PoetC] (25:3) Spr 94, p. 34.
"I Read in the Newspaper That Andrew Wiles." [PoetryNW] (35:3) Aut 94, p. 38.
"Questionnaire." [PoetryNW] (35:3) Aut 94, p. 37.
"Slug." [PoetC] (25:3) Spr 94, p. 33.
5878. SOLWAY, Arthur
"Elegy." [PraS] (68:2) Sum 94, p. 133.

"Like Air." [PraS] (68:2) Sum 94, p. 134.
"Wild Sage." [PraS] (68:2) Sum 94, p. 135.

5879. SOLWAY, David
"East Peninsula." [Nimrod] (37:2) Spr-Sum 94, p. 94-95.
"Off Telendos." [Nimrod] (37:2) Spr-Sum 94, p. 92-93.
"West Peninsula." [Nimrod] (37:2) Spr-Sum 94, p. 91.

5880. SOMECK, Ronny
"7 Lines on the Miraculous Yarkon" (tr. by Ammiel Alcalay). [LitR] (37:2) Wint 94, p. 341.
"Dimona Blues" (tr. by Ammiel Alcalay). [LitR] (37:2) Wint 94, p. 342.
"Embroidered Rag. Poem on Umm Kulthum" (tr. by Ammiel Alcalay). [LitR] (37:2) Wint 94, p. 343.
"The First Law of the Jungle: A Poem Missing-in-Action" (to my uncle, m.i.a., palestine, 1947). [QW] (38) Winter-Spr 93-94, p. 123.
"The Girl and the Butcher's Window" (tr. by Ammiel Alcalay). [LitR] (37:2) Wint 94, p. 341-342.
"HaMasger Street. Wedding Singer" (tr. by Ammiel Alcalay). [LitR] (37:2) Wint 94, p. 343.
"Handcuffs. Street Poem" (tr. by Ammiel Alcalay). [LitR] (37:2) Wint 94, p. 342.
"Jasmine. Poem on Sandpaper" (tr. by Ammiel Alcalay). [LitR] (37:2) Wint 94, p. 344.
"Nelson. Trafalgar Square" (tr. by Ammiel Alcalay). [LitR] (37:2) Wint 94, p. 344.
"Niva" (tr. by Ammiel Alcalay). [LitR] (37:2) Wint 94, p. 341.
"Poverty Line" (tr. by Ammiel Alcalay). [LitR] (37:2) Wint 94, p. 340.
"Sunscape" (tr. by Ammiel Alcalay). [LitR] (37:2) Wint 94, p. 342.

5881. SOMMER, Jason
"Adam Naming Himself." [TriQ] (92) Wint 94-95, p. 73.
"The Wound." [TriQ] (92) Wint 94-95, p. 71-72.

5882. SOMMER, Piotr
"The January Star" (tr. by the author and Michael Kasper). [Thrpny] (56) Wint 94, p. 30.

5883. SONDE, Susan
"Persimmon." [NowestR] (32:1) 94, p. 60.

5884. SONG, Lin
"Blank" (tr. by Yanbing Chen). [AnotherCM] (27) 94, p. 70-71.
"Sickroom" (tr. by Yanbing Chen). [AnotherCM] (27) 94, p. 69.

5885. SONIAT, Katherine
"Along the Way." [PoetL] (89:2) Sum 94, p. 49-50.
"Approaching New Orleans: A Summer Scene." [NegC] (13:2/3) 93, p. 57-58.
"The Celebrants." [NewOR] (20:3/4) Fall-Wint 94, p. 136-137.
"Child Care." [Shen] (44:4) Wint 94, p. 113-114.
"The Eel Hour." [NoAmR] (279:5) S-O 94, p. 17.
"Hot Air." [Witness] (8:1) 94, p. 170.
"Love and Transfiguration." [PoetC] (25:3) Spr 94, p. 18-19.
"Scrim." [Shen] (44:4) Wint 94, p. 115.
"Selecting Thoughts for Rouen." [NegC] (13:2/3) 93, p. 59-60.
"Storyville, November 12, 1917: Midnight." [Witness] (8:2) 94, p. 156-157.
"Street Kisses." [YellowS] (12:1, #45) Spr-Sum 94, p. 21.
"Triolette." [Witness] (8:1) 94, p. 168-169.
"Veils" (for Christine). [LaurelR] (28:2) Sum 94, p. 85.
"Wild Apples." [ColR] (21:2) Fall 94, p. 126-128.

5886. SONNENFELD, Mark
"Grids of Life." [BlackBR] (19) Fall-Wint 94, p. 27.
"Oxen-Women Snap Finger-Tentacle." [BlackBR] (19) Fall-Wint 94, p. 27.
"Tonite." [BlackBR] (19) Fall-Wint 94, p. 30.
"Wiretapper." [BlackBR] (19) Fall-Wint 94, p. 30-31.

5887. SONNENSCHEIN, Dana
"Hat Six Road." [WritersF] (20) 94, p. 192.

5888. SONNEVI, Goran
"Mozart Variations #9" (tr. by John Matthais and G. Printz-Pahlson). [Vis] (45) 94, p. 13.
"Mozart Variations #15" (tr. by John Matthais and G. Printz-Pahlson).). [Vis] (46) 94, p. 11.

5889. SONNIER, Keith
"I believe in architecture." [Bomb] (46) Wint 94, p. 23.

5890. SOOPKIAN, Touba
"The Loveliest." [Pearl] (20) Spr 94, p. 42.
"My Persian Carpet Hanging Over My American Wall." [Pearl] (20) Spr 94, p. 42.

5891. SOPER, Constance L.
"Gustavo Swimming" (for Doug). [Calyx] (15:2) Sum 94, p. 52-53.

SORALUZ, Luis Rebaza
See REBAZA-SORALUZ, Luis

5892. SORBY, Angela
"Glossolalia." [AnotherCM] (27) 94, p. 179.
"Gold Rush." [BrooklynR] (11) 94, p. 18-19.
"Museum Piece." [Nat] (258:19) My 16 94, p. 674.
"Timber Queen" (Olympia Peninsula, Washington State). [BrooklynR] (11) 94, p. 16-17.

5893. SORCIC, Jim
"The Blossom." [YellowS] (12:3, #47) Fall-Wint 94-95, p. 28-29.

5894. SORENSEN, Sally Jo
"A Woman From a Fundamentalist Sect in Which Females Do Not Speak Opens St. Mark." [WestB] (34) 94, p. 88-89.

5895. SORESTAD, Glen
"The Man Who Couldn't Go." [AntigR] (98) Sum 94, p. 88.
"Old Fisherman." [Dandel] (20:2) 93, p. 19-20.

5896. SORKIN, Adam (Adam J.)
"Around the Fire" (tr. of Aurel Rau, w. Liviu Bleoca). [HiramPoR] (55/56) Fall 93-Sum 94, p. 100.
"Ars Exilum Mundi" (tr. of Magda Carneci, w. the author). [Vis] (46) 94, p. 29.
"At the Bus Stop, in Winter" (tr. of Ioana Ieronim). [ChatR] (14:3) Spr 94, p. 41.
"Bison Hunting" (tr. of Liliana Ursu, w. the author). [Vis] (46) 94, p. 38.
"Cheshire Cat" (tr. of Daniela Crasnaru, w. Mia Nazarie). [PraS] (68:1) Spr 94, p. 67-68.
"Couple" (tr. of Liliana Ursu, w. the author). [Vis] (44) 94, p. 11.
"Curtsy" (tr. of Daniela Crasnaru, w. Maria-Ana Tupan). [PraS] (68:1) Spr 94, p. 68.
"Double Portrait" (tr. of Liliana Ursu, w. the author). [Vis] (46) 94, p. 38.
"Forma Mentis" (tr. of Ion Mircea, w. Liliana Ursu). [NewEngR] (16:1) Wint 94, p. 116.
"The Gift" (tr. of Aurel Rau, w. Liviu Bleoca). [HiramPoR] (55/56) Fall 93-Sum 94, p. 99.
"The Herald's Ballad" (Excerpt, tr. of Dan Verona, w. Mihaela A. Irimia). [Vis] (46) 94, p. 30.
"Kind of Bright" (tr. of Ion Mircea, w. Liviu Cotrau). [HayF] (14) Spr-Sum 94, p. 15.
"Memory of an October Evening in 1984" (tr. of Mircea Cartarescu, w. Ileana Ciocarlie). [AnotherCM] (27) 94, p. 13-14.
"The Mold" (tr. of Ion Mircea, w. Liliana Ursu). [NewEngR] (16:1) Wint 94, p. 115.
"Not a Thing About Survival Technique" (tr. of Mircea Cartarescu, w. Ileana Ciocârlie). [NewDeltaR] (10:2) Spr-Sum 93, p. 68.
"Our Love Has Gone" (tr. of Mircea Cartarescu, w. Ileana Ciocarlie). [AnotherCM] (27) 94, p. 15-16.
"Partisans" (tr. of Ioana Ieronim, w. the author). [Vis] (46) 94, p. 28.
"A Ride at Daybreak" (for Nichita Stanescu as a young poet, tr. of Petru Romosan). [Vis] (44) 94, p. 39.
"River in the Dark" (tr. of Ion Mircea, w. Liviu Cotrau). [HayF] (14) Spr-Sum 94, p. 16.
"S.F." (tr. of Ion Mircea, w. Liliana Ursu). [NewEngR] (16:1) Wint 94, p. 115-116.
"Scripta" (tr. of Daniela Crasnaru, w. Ioana Ieronim). [Vis] (46) 94, p. 39.
"Silent Voices" (For Cella Delavrancea and Gabriela Melinescu, tr. of Liliana Ursu, w. the poet). [Kalliope] (16:2) 94, p. 66-67.
"Slope" (tr. of Daniela Crasnaru). [Vis] (44) 94, p. 16.
"Winter Tale" (tr. of Petru Romosan, w. Radu Surdulescu). [Vis] (46) 94, p. 29.
"With One Eye We Cry, with the Other We Laugh" (tr. of Liliana Ursu). [Vis] (45) 94, p. 36.
"Writing with a Ballpoint" (tr. of Aurel Rau, w. Liviu Bleoca). [HiramPoR] (55/56) Fall 93-Sum 94, p. 101.

5897. SORNBERGER, Judith
"She Considers Christmas Past." [WestB] (35) 94, p. 79-80.

5898. SOSEKI (b. 1867)
Haiku [AmerPoR] (23:4) Jl-Ag 94, p. 20.

5899. SOSSEN, Rhea
"An Enigma Inside a Paradox." [Light] (12) Wint 94-95, p. 11.
5900. SOTO, Francisco
"As If in a Game" (tr. of Roberto Valero). [MichQR] (33:4) Fall 94, p. 655.
5901. SOTO, Gary
"Afternoon Memory." [Thrpny] (57) Spr 94, p. 28.
"Bench Life on the Day of the Dead." [IllinoisR] (2:1) Fall 94, p. 50.
"The Charity of La Señora Lara." [PraS] (68:4) Wint 94, p. 41-42.
" *Chisme* at Rivera's Studio." [PraS] (68:4) Wint 94, p. 45-46.
"Everything Twice." [BostonR] (19:2) Ap-My 94, p. 30.
"Evolved People." [OntR] (41) Fall-Wint 94, p. 122-124.
"Fair Trade." [PraS] (68:4) Wint 94, p. 42-43.
"Guilt and the Iron Lung." [GreenMR] (NS 17:2) Fall-Wint 94-95, p. 5-6.
"Listening to Jets." [TriQ] (91) Fall 94, p. 173.
"The Old House in My 40th Year." [Poetry] (163:4) Ja 94, p. 198.
"Phone Calls." [OntR] (41) Fall-Wint 94, p. 121.
"Small Talk and Checkers." [PraS] (68:4) Wint 94, p. 44.
"The Tuba Player." [TriQ] (91) Fall 94, p. 174-175.
"Water Wheel." [Poetry] (163:4) Ja 94, p. 197.
"What Are You Speaking?" [GreenMR] (NS 17:2) Fall-Wint 94-95, p. 7-8.
5902. SOULAR, James
"The Longing of Bones." [MidwQ] (36:1) Aut 94, p. 71.
5903. SOUPAULT, Philippe
"The Evening Holds Out Its Arms" (tr. by Paulette Schmidt). [Vis] (44) 94, p. 24.
5904. SOVIERO, Marcelle M.
"When He Is Here." [SlipS] (14) 94, p. 44.
"The Wrong of It." [SlipS] (14) 94, p. 45.
5905. SOWDER, Michael
"Drawing Down Words" (for Melanie Gordon McManus). [NegC] (14:1/2) 94, p. 26.
SPAAR, Lisa Russ
See RUSS-SPAAR, Lisa
5906. SPACKS, Barry
"Blizzards of Metaphor." [PraS] (68:2) Sum 94, p. 94.
"New Year's Monkey." [Light] (12) Wint 94-95, p. 7.
"Progress of Orpheus." [PraS] (68:2) Sum 94, p. 94-95.
"Shell." [PraS] (68:2) Sum 94, p. 93.
5907. SPAGNOLI, Laura
"Corn." [SpiritSH] (59) 94, p. 13.
"Marigold." [SpiritSH] (59) 94, p. 15.
"Mathematics Review." [SpiritSH] (59) 94, p. 14.
5908. SPAHIU, Xhevahir
"Debts" (tr. by Uk Bucpapa and Henry Israeli). [DenQ] (29:1) Sum 94, p. 103.
5909. SPALDING, Esta
"After the Drought." [PraF] (15:3, #68) Aut 94, p. 35.
"Fall." [MalR] (108) Fall 94, p. 78-79.
"Love's Back." [MalR] (108) Fall 94, p. 76.
"Shipbuilding." [MalR] (108) Fall 94, p. 77.
5910. SPANN, Jeri
"Nose." [Light] (10) Sum 94, p. 21.
5911. SPARENBERG, David
"Beggar of Sorrow" (tr. of Tadeusz Gajcy, w. Aleksandra Szostalo). [WebR] (18) Fall 94, p. 14.
"Request of Thyme" (tr. of Malgorzata Hillar, w. Aleksandra Szostalo). [WebR] (18) Fall 94, p. 15.
5912. SPARK, Muriel
"The Dark Music of the Rue du Cherche-Midi." [NewYorker] (70:1) 21 F 94, p. 104.
5913. SPARLING, George
"The Dark Entity Beneath the Glint of Sun." [Elf] (4:4) Wint 94, p. 29.
5914. SPARROW
"A Bus." [Border] (3) Fall 93, p. 73.
"On the F Train." [Sun] (218) F 94, p. 23.
5915. SPEAKES, Richard
"Red Lilies" (For Joan Didion). [Poetry] (165:3) D 94, p. 144.
"A Rose That Remembers Itself." [Poetry] (165:3) D 94, p. 145.

5916. SPEAR, Roberta
"Eating Blackberries in the Dark." [CreamCR] (18:1) Spr 94, p. 29.
"Good Men." [Crazy] (47) Wint 94, p. 8-9.
"Paleta." [Crazy] (47) Wint 94, p. 10-11.
"Star Gazers." [Crazy] (47) Wint 94, p. 14-15.
"The Window." [Crazy] (47) Wint 94, p. 12-13.
5917. SPEARS, Jeremy
"Dream of the Voyeur." [JamesWR] (11:5) Fall 94, p. 15.
"Mud Dancing" (after Richard Ronan). [JamesWR] (11:5) Fall 94, p. 6.
"Second Sight." [JamesWR] (11:2) Wint 94, p. 10.
"Young." [JamesWR] (11:2) Wint 94, p. 17.
5918. SPEARS, Monroe K.
"Lines Spoken to James Dickey on His Sixtieth Birthday" (Columbia, South Carolina, February 1983). [SoCaR] (26:2) Spr 94, p. 7.
5919. SPECTOR, Donna
"Going Down into the Dark." [Gaia] (4) Je 94, p. 44-45.
"In Grandmother's House." [Gaia] (4) Je 94, p. 44.
"My Son Calls Me from Los Angeles." [Gaia] (4) Je 94, p. 45.
5920. SPEER, Laurel
"Alexis & Nick." [BellR] (17:1/2) Spr-Fall 94, p. 38.
"Come Back John Hay and Give Us Wisdom." [CoalC] (8) Ap 94, p. 13.
"Drifting in the Sea of My Dreaming Sheets." [SlipS] (14) 94, p. 95.
"Having a Conversation That Has Killed Me." [SantaBR] (2:2) Fall-Wint 94, p. 148.
"A Movie Script of Paradise Lost." [CrabCR] (8:2/3/9:1/2/3) 94, p. 4-5.
"My Pit Pony." [NegC] (14:1/2) 94, p. 58.
"A Sorry Story about a Dog & Love." [Pearl] (20) Spr 94, p. 47.
5921. SPEES, Benjamin
"The Long Way to Carver's Grave." [BellArk] (10:2) Mr-Ap 94, p. 13.
"One William James Missed." [BellArk] (10:2) Mr-Ap 94, p. 13.
5922. SPENCE, Michael
"Mother Dreaming." [SewanR] (102:2) Spr 94, p. 211-212.
5923. SPENCER, Beth
"Fishwife." [RagMag] (12:1) Sum 94, p. 27.
"The Get-Away." [RagMag] (12:1) Sum 94, p. 26.
"We Are Sunflowers Too Late Planted" (Notes on an Untimely Flirtation). [RagMag] (12:1) Sum 94, p. 25.
5924. SPENCER, Patricia
"As You Read This Acrostic." [SouthernPR] (34:2) Wint 94, p. 43.
"For Rachel and Reuben Sanders." [Poem] (71) My 94, p. 33.
"On Writing." [HampSPR] Wint 94, p. 8.
"Storm: Young Boy Struck by Lightning." [Poem] (71) My 94, p. 34.
5925. SPERANZA, Anthony
"The Sailor." [Plain] (14:3) Spr 94, p. 16.
5926. SPERBER, Anna Victoria
"Skinny Dip." [HangL] (65) 94, p. 98.
5927. SPHERES, Duane R.
"Our Cornucopia Again." [BellArk] (10:3 [i.e. 10:4]) Jl-Ag 94, p. 25.
5928. SPIDEL, Lianne
"Lab Partners." [HiramPoR] (55/56) Fall 93-Sum 94, p. 112-113.
5929. SPIGLE, Naomi
"Allergies." [WindO] (58) Sum 94, p. 36.
"Houdini." [WindO] (58) Sum 94, p. 37.
"Mirror of the Moon." [WindO] (58) Sum 94, p. 35.
5930. SPIRENG, Matthew J.
"Ashokan Reservoir." [Outbr] (25) 94, p. 67.
"Beatrice Houdini Announces Before Her Death That Despite Their Vow, Her Husband Never Communicated with Her Once During the Sixteen Years After His Death." [PoetC] (25:3) Spr 94, p. 20.
"Beyond Mountains." [BellArk] (10:3 [i.e. 10:4]) Jl-Ag 94, p. 15.
"Cloud Nine." [HolCrit] (31:3) Je 94, p. 18.
"Emptiness." [Plain] (14:3) Spr 94, p. 14.
"Hiking the Northeast Trail." [MidwQ] (35:4) Sum 94, p. 415.
"In This World of Infinite." [Poem] (72) N 94, p. 17.
"Lost Lives." [CumbPR] (13:2) Spr 94, p. 9.
"Mathematics." [ColEng] (56:6) O 94, p. 679.
"Mother's Singing." [Outbr] (25) 94, p. 68.

"Moving the Woodpile." [CumbPR] (13:2) Spr 94, p. 10.
"October Night after Rain." [BellArk] (10:2) Mr-Ap 94, p. 11.
"Perrine's Bridge." [CapeR] (29:1) Spr 94, p. 24.
"The Radish." [SmPd] (31:3, #92) Fall 94, p. 20.
"Slap Shot" (In memory of John Currier). [AmerS] (63:4) Aut 94, p. 544.
"The Stone." [Poem] (72) N 94, p. 18.
"Sun Dog." [Poem] (72) N 94, p. 19.
"Thinking of Things That Come From Above." [SouthernHR] (28:1) Wint 94, p. 65.
"While the Women Waited." [BellArk] (10:2) Mr-Ap 94, p. 11.

5931. SPIRES, Elizabeth
"The First Day." [PartR] (61:4) Fall 94, p. 632-633.

5932. SPIRES, Lisa M.
"In Defense of Free-Spirited Verse" (Honorable Mention, The Amelia Awards). [Amelia] (7:4, #23) 94, p. 43-44.

5933. SPIRO, Barry
"Monologue to a Mummy (with Receptionist Rising)." [JlNJPo] (16:1) Spr 94, p. 20-22.

5934. SPIRO, Peter
"Foreign Bars with Familiar Names." [GreenMR] (NS 17:2) Fall-Wint 94-95, p. 121-122.
"Pigs." [SlipS] (14) 94, p. 66-67.

5935. SPISAK, Dagmar Jill
"Whispers Call My Childhood Name." [ChatR] (14:2) Wint 94, p. 47.

5936. SPITZER, Mark
"Beneath 3M." [Elf] (4:1) Spr 94, p. 40-41.
"She Slit Her Wrists But Lived by Accident." [SlipS] (14) 94, p. 122.

5937. SPIVACK, Susan Fantl
"Any Old Music." [Kalliope] (16:3) 94, p. 19-20.
"Mother-in-Law Tongue's." [Kalliope] (16:3) 94, p. 20.

5938. SPROLES, Sara
"A Satori." [MidwQ] (35:3) Spr 94, p. 318.

5939. SPYDELL, Cat
"Star Songs." [Pearl] (20) Spr 94, p. 83.

5940. SRUOGINIS, Laima
"Border Village" (from *Journey Along the Edge of the Sand*, tr. of Sigitas Parulskis). [ArtfulD] (26/27) 94, p. 8-9.
"Landscape" (from *Journey Along the Edge of the Sand*, tr. of Sigitas Parulskis). [ArtfulD] (26/27) 94, p. 7.
"Three Letters to Vilnius." [ArtfulD] (26/27) 94, p. 4-6.
"A Worldwide Pain in Kukutis' Detached Leg" (tr. of Marcelijus Martinaitis). [Vis] (45) 94, p. 38-39.

5941. SRYGLEY, Carolyn
"The Procreative Passing." [PennR] (6:1) 94, p. 36-37.

ST. . . .
See also Saint . . .

5942. ST. ANDREWS, B. A.
"Aztecs." [ChamLR] (14/15) Spr-Fall 94, p. 157-158.
"Making Soup." [HighP] (9:2) Ag 94, p. 46.
"Unless Soul Clap Its Hands and Sing." [ChamLR] (14/15) Spr-Fall 94, p. 191-192.

5943. ST. CLAIR, Philip
"Absent Fathers." [ArtfulD] (26/27) 94, p. 84.
"Cancer Families." [GettyR] (7:3) Sum 94, p. 430.
"Cancer Families" (From the Summer issue of *The Gettysburg Review*). [Harp] (289:1735) D 94, p. 28.
"Society." [IllinoisR] (1:2) Spr 94, p. 49.
"Sparks." [ArtfulD] (26/27) 94, p. 85.

5944. ST. GERMAIN, Sheryl
"At Paisano Ranch, Thinking About Making God." [NewL] (60:4) 94, p. 196.
"Getting Rid of the Accent." [NegC] (13:2/3) 93, p. 50-51.
"Hurricane Season" (For Eddie). [NegC] (13:2/3) 93, p. 48-49.
"Jesus Gets Drunk in the Andes." [NewL] (60:4) 94, p. 194-195.

5945. ST. JACQUES, Elizabeth
"Haiku" (2 poems). [Amelia] (7:3, #22) 94, p. 99.

5946. ST. JOHN, David
"The Figure *You*." [Antaeus] (75/76) Aut 94, p. 318.
"Fleurs Mystiques." [ColR] (21:1) Spr 94, p. 154-157.

"Lost Magic." [Field] (50) Spr 94, p. 11-12.
"Study for the World's Body: The Body of Desire — Of Time & The Body" (To HM, 1922-1987). [AmerPoR] (23:5) S-O 94, p. 21-26.

5947. ST. LOUIS, Ralph
"Great Grandmother." [Poem] (71) My 94, p. 31.
"Valley Springs." [Poem] (71) My 94, p. 32.

5948. ST. MARTIN, Hardie
"The Days That Fill Time" (tr. of Guillermo Sucre). [Trans] (29) Spr 94, p. 63.
"The House We're Born and Die in" (tr. of Guillermo Sucre). [Trans] (29) Spr 94, p. 62-63.
"In the Open Air" (tr. of Guillermo Sucre). [Trans] (29) Spr 94, p. 65.
"Like His Likeness" (homage to J. L. L., tr. of Guillermo Sucre). [Trans] (29) Spr 94, p. 64.
"There's the Head Born in the Mirror" (tr. of Guillermo Sucre). [Trans] (29) Spr 94, p. 65.

5949. STAFFORD, William
"Humanities 101." [Light] (11) Aut 94, p. 14.
"Listening at Little Lake Elkhart." [CrabCR] (8:2/3/9:1/2/3) 94, p. 3.
"Little Rooms" (*An Oregon Message*, 1988). [Border] (4) Spr-Sum 94, p. 86.
"A Memorial: Son Bret." [PlumR] (7) [94?], p. 83.
"Sometimes, Reading." [OhioR] (51) 94, p. 120.
"The Tulip Tree." [Border] (4) Spr-Sum 94, p. 87-88.
"The Way It Is." [SoCoast] (16) Ja 94, p. 3.
"The World." [WeberS] (11:3) Fall 94, p. 65.

5950. STAHL, Dick
"Meeting the Tin Man." [Farm] (11:2) Fall-Wint 94-95, p. 110.

5951. STAHL, Jayne Lyn
"USA Donuts." [Jacaranda] (4:2) Spr 90, p. 62-63.

5952. STAHLECKER, Beth
"Halfway House." [Jacaranda] (10) 94, p. 94.
"Paul." [Jacaranda] (10) 94, p. 95.
"Stray." [Pequod] (37) 94, p. 74.

5953. STAHLKUPPE, Jackson
"Tommy T. Awaits Visits from His Late Wife." [CreamCR] (18:1) Spr 94, p. 28.

5954. STAINSBY, Martha
"After the Abortion." [HampSPR] Wint 94, p. 23.

5955. STAKER, Brian
"Mediatations." [WestHR] (48:3) Fall 94, p. 270.

5956. STALLINGS, A. E.
"Another Winter in England." [Light] (12) Wint 94-95, p. 11.

5957. STALLINGS, Alicia
"In Wonderland." [NegC] (14:1/2) 94, p. 141.

5958. STALLONE, Barbara
"Female in the Pavilion." [BellR] (17:1/2) Spr-Fall 94, p. 52-53.

5959. STAMBLER, Peter
"After Dinner, I Close My Door" (tr. of Han Shan). [SouthernHR] (28:4) Fall 94, p. 347.
"Carelessly, I Drop My Inkstone in the Pool" (tr. of Han Shan). [GrahamHR] (18) Wint 94-95, p. 74.
"Every Morning, He Takes Breakfast with Me" (tr. of Han Shan). [GrahamHR] (18) Wint 94-95, p. 75.
"Leaping Upwards, I Clap My Heels and Bruise Them" (tr. of Han Shan). [SouthernHR] (28:4) Fall 94, p. 347.
"Useless, These Absent Thoughts" (tr. of Han Shan). [Stand] (35:3) Sum 94, p. 54.
"The Uses of Poetry" (tr. of Han Shan). [GrahamHR] (18) Wint 94-95, p. 77.
"We Come Ashore Far from Home" (tr. of Han Shan). [GrahamHR] (18) Wint 94-95, p. 76.

5960. STANDER, Anne C.
"Story at Eye Level." [HayF] (15) Fall-Wint 94, p. 102-103.

5961. STANDING, Sue
"Alba." [Iowa] (24:1) Wint 94, p. 2.
"Lamu." [HarvardR] (7) Fall 94, p. 40-41.
"Montpeyroux." [BostonR] (19:2) Ap-My 94, p. 36.
"St. Francis in Ecstasy (Bellini)." [Iowa] (24:1) Wint 94, p. 2.
"Translations from Colonial Swahili." [Iowa] (24:1) Wint 94, p. 1.

5962. STANDLEY, Gerald
"Le Chambon." [ChatR] (14:2) Wint 94, p. 48.
5963. STANESCU, Nichita
"Ars Poetica" (in Romanian). [InterPR] (20:1) Spr 94, p. 60, 62.
"The Art of Poetry" (tr. by Eveline L. Kanes and Mihai Zaharia). [InterPR] (20:1) Spr 94, p. 61, 63.
"Cain and Abel" (tr. by Eveline L. Kanes and Mihai Zaharia). [InterPR] (20:1) Spr 94, p. 51.
"Cain si Abel." [InterPR] (20:1) Spr 94, p. 50.
"A Confession" (tr. by Richard Collins). [Vis] (46) 94, p. 8.
"On the Field of Stone" (tr. by Eveline L. Kanes and Mihai Zaharia). [InterPR] (20:1) Spr 94, p. 53.
"Pe Cimpul de Piatra." [InterPR] (20:1) Spr 94, p. 52.
"Poem: Tu plutesti ca un vis de noapte." [InterPR] (20:1) Spr 94, p. 48.
"Poem: You float like a nocturnal dream" (tr. by Eveline L. Kanes and Mihai Zaharia). [InterPR] (20:1) Spr 94, p. 49.
"Testament" (in Romanian). [InterPR] (20:1) Spr 94, p. 54, 56.
"Testament" (tr. by Eveline L. Kanes and Mihai Zaharia). [InterPR] (20:1) Spr 94, p. 55, 57.
"Veghe Linga Metale." [InterPR] (20:1) Spr 94, p. 58.
"Vigil Near Metals" (tr. by Eveline L. Kanes and Mihai Zaharia). [InterPR] (20:1) Spr 94, p. 59.
5964. STANKO, Mary Rudbeck
"Almsgiver." [Plain] (14:2) Wint 94, p. 11.
"Walls." [InterPR] (20:1) Spr 94, p. 90.
5965. STANLEY, George
"Another Monastery" (for Jay & Pete). [Arc] (32) Spr 94, p. 37.
5966. STANLEY, Jean W.
"Blue Birds." [SoDakR] (32:2) Sum 94, p. 123.
"Galls." [SoDakR] (32:2) Sum 94, p. 124.
"What Day." [SoDakR] (32:2) Sum 94, p. 125.
5967. STANLEY, Thomas
"Music for My Mother (December 1992)." [Eyeball] (3) 93, p. 26.
"Voodoo in the Hour of Conscience (April 1993)." [Eyeball] (3) 93, p. 26.
5968. STANNISH, Dianne
"Married Men." [HayF] (15) Fall-Wint 94, p. 101.
5969. STANTON, Joseph
"Daumier's *The Third Class Carriage*." [ChamLR] (14/15) Spr-Fall 94, p. 226-227.
"The Incredible Shrinking Man." [SouthernPR] (34:1) Sum 94, p. 56-57.
"Ironwoods." [HarvardR] (2) Fall 92, p. 80.
"Izutsu." [ChamLR] (14/15) Spr-Fall 94, p. 228.
"Magritte Variations." [ChamLR] (14/15) Spr-Fall 94, p. 224-225.
5970. STANTON, Kay
"Mother's Recipe." [SoCoast] (16) Ja 94, p. 22.
"Under Snow" (Honorable Mention, 8th Annual Contest). [SoCoast] (16) Ja 94, p. 23.
5971. STANTON, Maura
"Computer Map of the Early Universe." [HopewellR] (6) 94, p. 116.
"Freshman English Poetry Anthology" (University of Minnesota, 1964. Winner, Lynda Hull Memorial Poetry Award). [Crazy] (46) Spr 94, p. 22-25.
"A History of Criticism." [Crazy] (46) Spr 94, p. 26-30.
5972. STAP, Don
"Fish Crows." [TriQ] (91) Fall 94, p. 183-184.
5973. STAPLES, Catherine
"Mr. Elliot Fitch Shepard Returns Sargent's Portrait of His Wife." [WestB] (35) 94, p. 58.
"The Poet's Wife." [NewDeltaR] (11:2) Spr-Sum 94, p. 60.
5974. STARKE, Anthony
"Rooms." [Chelsea] (56) 94, p. 100-101.
5975. STARKEY, David
"Afternoon Tea." [ApalQ] (40/41) 94, p. 89.
"Aspects of Dale." [ChatR] (14:2) Wint 94, p. 37-38.
"Codicil" (For my son Stephen, at three weeks). [Pivot] (41) 93, p. 35-36.
"I Recognized Myself in a Biography of Dylan Thomas." [CapeR] (29:2) Fall 94, p. 7.
"Portland." [PoetL] (89:3) Fall 94, p. 11-12.

"Pottawatomie Creek." [BelPoJ] (45:2) Wint 94-95, p. 32-33.
"Pyrolatry." [CapeR] (29:2) Fall 94, p. 8.
"The Shopping Channel." [Jacaranda] (4:2) Spr 90, p. 30-31.
"Trotz Alledem." [Jacaranda] (4:2) Spr 90, p. 29.

5976. STARKEY, John
"Yaw." [CutB] (41) Wint 94, p. 30-31.

5977. STARNINO, Carmine
"After Caravaggio's Doubting Thomas." [Quarry] (43:2) S 94, p. 111.
"Birthday Morning." [AntigR] (97) Spr 94, p. 33.
"From the Childhood of Jesus." [Quarry] (43:2) S 94, p. 109-110.
"Ghost." [PoetryC] (14:3) My 94, p. 16.
"Lullaby." [AntigR] (97) Spr 94, p. 35-36.
"Pepino's Anniversary." [PoetryC] (14:3) My 94, p. 16.
"Photograph Taken During My Cousin's 1959 Prom." [AntigR] (97) Spr 94, p. 34.
"Picking the Last Tomatoes with My Uncle." [PoetryC] (14:3) My 94, p. 16.
"Shopping for Turtles" (for Anthony, at six). [PoetryC] (14:3) My 94, p. 16.

5978. STARR, Jean
"Flight." [Callaloo] (17:1) Wint 94, p. 303-304.
"Sac and Fox Pow-Wow, Stroud, Oklahoma" (Intertribal). [Callaloo] (17:1) Wint 94, p. 305.

5979. STARR, Teresa
"Beauty" (for Mark Strand). [Poem] (72) N 94, p. 24.
"Storm." [Poem] (72) N 94, p. 25.

5980. STARRETT, Virginia
"Dante" (tr. of Anna Akhmatova). [SoCoast] (17) Je 94, p. 62.

5981. STASIOWSKI, Carole A.
"Approaching the Temple." [SpoonR] (19:1) Wint-Spr 94, p. 32-33.
"Slit." [SpoonR] (19:1) Wint-Spr 94, p. 34-35.

5982. STATYLLIUS FLACCUS (1st Century B.C./A.D.)
"Julian, who's begun to grow" (tr. by Robin Skelton). [Arc] (32) Spr 94, p. 39.

5983. STAUDACHER, Carol
"Calling Forth the Tenderness in Men." [CumbPR] (13:2) Spr 94, p. 46-48.

5984. STAUDT, David
"Dream of Pines." [SouthernHR] (28:2) Spr 94, p. 179.
"A Reading." [ChatR] (14:2) Wint 94, p. 39.
"Red Sumac." [CarolQ] (46:3) Sum 94, p. 12.

5985. STAYNER, M. L.
"Consider the Woman Who." [ModernW] (1) Summer 94, p. 101-103.

5986. STAYTON, Corey
"St. Louis Black." [XavierR] (14:2) Fall 94, p. 70.

5987. STEELE, Lani
"God Has No Balls." [ContextS] (4:1) 94, p. 13-14.

5988. STÉFAN, Jude
"Like" (tr. by M. Manopoulos and P. Kobylarz). [PoetryE] (37/38) Spr 94, p. 225.
"To Cavafy" (tr. by M. Manopoulos and P. Kobylarz). [PoetryE] (37/38) Spr 94, p. 224.

5989. STEFENHAGENS, Lyn
"Love Me in Tall Woods." [DogRR] (26) Wint 94-95, p. 5.
"Plinko." [Parting] (7:2) Wint 94-95, p. 24.

5990. STEHNO, F. Patrick
"Sierra November." [Amelia] (7:3, #22) 94, p. 70.

5991. STEIDLMAYER, Heidy
"Cutlery." [TriQ] (91) Fall 94, p. 171.
"Lamp." [TriQ] (91) Fall 94, p. 170.
"Turnstile." [TriQ] (91) Fall 94, p. 172.

5992. STEIN, Agnes
"Larmoyance" (tr. of Gunter Kunert). [MidAR] (14:2) 94, p. 60.

5993. STEIN, Donna Baier
"Troilus on Horseback." [AnthNEW] (6) 94, p. 14.

5994. STEIN, Hannah
"Hand-Me-Downs." [CreamCR] (18:1) Spr 94, p. 32-33.
"Lighthouse at Point Reyes." [PraS] (68:2) Sum 94, p. 136-137.
"A View of the Lagoon." [PraS] (68:2) Sum 94, p. 138-139.
"Woman and Horse on the Beach." [PraS] (68:2) Sum 94, p. 137-138.

5995. STEIN, Jessica
"The Last Supper." [SinW] (54) Wint 94-95, p. 105.

5996. STEIN, Jill
"Dangers on the Rooftop in Ninth Grade." [NegC] (14:1/2) 94, p. 112-113.
5997. STEIN, Kevin
"Body and Soul." [PoetC] (25:3) Spr 94, p. 16.
"His Blue Period." [Shen] (44:1) Spr 94, p. 102-103.
"Past Midnight, My Daughter Awakened by Miles Davis' *Kind of Blue*." [Shen] (44:2) Sum 94, p. 64-65.
"What Passes for Paradise." [Shen] (44:1) Spr 94, p. 104-105.
5998. STEIN, Michael
"Bonsai." [SouthwR] (79:4) Aut 94, p. 716.
"Diving." [TarRP] (34:1) Fall 94, p. 14.
"Expatriate." [DenQ] (29:2) Fall 94, p. 45.
5999. STEINBERG, Hugh
"Musical." [IndR] (17:1) Spr 94, p. 56-57.
6000. STEINBERG, Martin
"A One Winged Bee." [JINJPo] (16:1) Spr 94, p. 23-24.
6001. STEINBERG, Paul Charles
"Untitled: If you are sitting in a square, opposite." [Amelia] (7:3, #22) 94, p. 126.
6002. STEINGASS, David
"Porkbomb." [ApalQ] (40/41) 94, p. 105-106.
6003. STEINGESSER, Martin
"Call Into Evening." [Border] (4) Spr-Sum 94, p. 62-63.
6004. STEINMAN, Louise
"The Flag of Yoshio Shimizu" (for my father). [Zyzzyva] (10:2) Sum 94, p. 114-128.
6005. STEINWACHS, Mark
"One Art." [AntigR] (96) Wint 94, p. 122-123.
6006. STELIGA, Heather S. J.
"Game of Lies" (tr. of Yang Lian, w. Chen Shi-Zheng). [Manoa] (6:1) Sum 94, p. 157-158.
"Winter Garden" (tr. of Yang Lian, w. Chen Shi-Zheng). [Manoa] (6:1) Sum 94, p. 158-159.
6007. STELMACH, Marjorie
"Draft of an Answer." [CumbPR] (14:1) Fall 94, p. 58.
"How to Walk on Water." [Ascent] (18:2) Wint 94, p. 39.
"The Middle Spaces." [TampaR] (9) Fall 94, p. 18-19.
"Preservation." [CapeR] (29:2) Fall 94, p. 20.
"Why She Stays." [CumbPR] (14:1) Fall 94, p. 57.
"Yesterday's Story." [CumbPR] (14:1) Fall 94, p. 55-56.
6008. STEPANCHEV, Stephen
"Born in December." [Poetry] (165:3) D 94, p. 125.
"Darkness Snowing." [Poetry] (165:3) D 94, p. 127.
"A Wound That Never Heals." [Poetry] (165:3) D 94, p. 126.
6009. STEPHENS, Christine
"Dreaming Our Life." [Nimrod] (38:1) Fall-Wint 94, p. 141.
"Spring Day in February." [Nimrod] (38:1) Fall-Wint 94, p. 141.
6010. STEPHENSON, Melissa
"The Hitchhiker." [HangL] (64) 94, p. 88-89.
6011. STEPTOE, Lamont (Lamont B.)
"Baldwin: A Black Cat." [NegC] (14:1/2) 94, p. 118.
"Crap Shoot." [NegC] (14:1/2) 94, p. 117.
"Disappearance." [NegC] (14:1/2) 94, p. 119-120.
"Jam/dancin'." [Eyeball] (3) 93, p. 43.
6012. STERLE, Francine
"Deciphering the Alphabet." [NoAmR] (279:1) Ja-F 94, p. 30-31.
6013. STERLING, Phillip
"Heartsick." [GeoR] (48:3) Fall 94, p. 459-460.
"Marriage." [CapeR] (29:1) Spr 94, p. 32-33.
6014. STERN, Gerald
"Blacker Than Ever." [TriQ] (91) Fall 94, p. 238-242.
"Did I Say." [Poetry] (164:3) Je 94, p. 133.
"Knowledge." [SycamoreR] (6:2) Sum 94, p. 87-88.
"Light." [Poetry] (164:3) Je 94, p. 131-132.
"Mimi." [Poetry] (164:3) Je 94, p. 127-131.
"Only Elegy." [Field] (51) Fall 94, p. 97.
"Progress and Poverty." [Field] (51) Fall 94, p. 98-99.

6015. STERN, Peter
"Siroh." [Amelia] (7:3, #22) 94, p. 57.
6016. STERN, Robert
"To the Memory of My Mother." [AntigR] (97) Spr 94, p. 128-129.
6017. STERNLIEB, Barry
"Standing Her Ground" (for Sister Durette). [Farm] (11:1) Spr-Sum 94, p. 133.
6018. STEVENS, A. Wilber
"Letter to Greece" (for Kenneth O. Hanson). [BellArk] (10:3) My-Je 94, p. 10.
"My Dry Cleaner Bronko Reads of the Shelling of Dubrovnik in the New York Times." [WebR] (18) Fall 94, p. 95.
6019. STEVENS, Beth
"Ancient Garden." [CapeR] (29:1) Spr 94, p. 19.
"Come to Me." [CapeR] (29:1) Spr 94, p. 18.
6020. STEVENS, Elizabeth
"Homage." [AntigR] (99) Aut 94, p. 112.
6021. STEVENS, Geoff
"The Farnes." [CoalC] (8) Ap 94, p. 10.
6022. STEVENS, Jim
"Douce France." [Descant] (25:1, #84) Spr 94, p. 36-37.
"The Thoughts of Agammemnon." [NegC] (14:1/2) 94, p. 143-144.
6023. STEVENS, Wallace
"The Emperor of Ice-Cream" (the original in English, 2 Polish translations, and 2 English retranslations of the Polish versions). [HarvardR] (6) Spr 94, p. 99-102.
"Theory." [WestHR] (48:2) Sum 94, p. 147.
6024. STEVENSON, David
"Afternoon with Birds." [WritersF] (20) 94, p. 235.
6025. STEWARD, D. E.
"Agosto." [NoDaQ] (62:2) Spr 94-95, p. 41-46.
6026. STEWART, Deborah
"Shadow Box South." [PoetL] (89:3) Fall 94, p. 39-40.
6027. STEWART, Dolores
"Villa Borghese" (tr. of David Shrayer-Petrov, w. Maxim Shrayer). [Salm] (101/102) Wint-Spr 94, p. 151-153.
6028. STEWART, Harold
"Culture as Exhibit" (w. James McAuley, under the pseudonym of Ern Malley). [InterQ] (1:2) 93, p. 117-118.
6029. STEWART, Jack
"At Home with Angels." [Poetry] (164:2) My 94, p. 75.
6030. STEWART, Pamela
"1960." [Journal] (18:1) Spr-Sum 94, p. 48.
"Living on the Hill." [Journal] (18:1) Spr-Sum 94, p. 47.
"The Oblivious Earth." [HighP] (9:2) Ag 94, p. 51.
"On Innocence." [PassN] (15:1) Sum 94, p. 11.
6031. STEWART, Shannon
"Archaeology." [MalR] (106) Spr 94, p. 81.
"Architecture." [MalR] (106) Spr 94, p. 80.
"Barnacles." [Arc] (33) Fall 94, p. 29.
"Geneaology" [sic]. [MalR] (106) Spr 94, p. 82.
6032. STEWART, Sheila
"Stepped Out." [AntigR] (99) Aut 94, p. 81-82.
"Ulster." [AntigR] (99) Aut 94, p. 80.
6033. STEWART, Shirley
"Modestly Epicurean." [Light] (12) Wint 94-95, p. 8.
"Two Nits for Miss Muffet." [Light] (12) Wint 94-95, p. 21.
6034. STEWART, Susan
"The Book of Lamentations" (Selections: 1-5, tr. from the Hebrew). [DenQ] (29:1) Sum 94, p. 47-52.
"The Desert (1990-1993)." [AmerPoR] (23:1) Ja-F 94, p. 13-15.
"Slaughter: On the Properties Generally Required of the Syntax of a Formal System." [AmerPoR] (23:1) Ja-F 94, p. 12-13.
6035. STEWART, W. Gregory
"Gatling found the way to cast." [Amelia] (7:3, #22) 94, p. 21.
"What Is This in the Wind." [Amelia] (7:4, #23) 94, p. 148-149.
6036. STIEBER, Chris
"The Giraffe in the World Book Encyclopedia." [WindO] (58) Sum 94, p. 26.

6037. STILLWELL, Marie
"A Place Called Enigma." [WebR] (18) Fall 94, p. 54.
"The Prize Lambs." [WebR] (18) Fall 94, p. 52-53.
"Reflections in the Slow Lane" (On following a truckload of telephone poles). [WebR] (18) Fall 94, p. 53.
6038. STIX, Judith Saul
"Vines." [WebR] (18) Fall 94, p. 66.
6039. STIX, Nicholas
"Making Pancakes Is an Exact Art." [NegC] (14:1/2) 94, p. 85.
6040. STOCK, Norman
"The Poem Eaten As Written." [NewYorkQ] (53) 94, p. 68.
6041. STOCKTON, Chris
"Shadows in the Okavango Delta." [SantaBR] (1:1) Spr-Sum 93, p. 67-73.
6042. STOCKWELL, Elsie Wear
"Brighton" (from "For a Stranger Here"). [AmerPoR] (23:5) S-O 94, p. 32.
"Prehistory" (from "The Light Between the Leaves"). [AmerPoR] (23:2) Mr-Ap 94, p. 33.
"Where's the Moon?" [Plain] (14:3) Spr 94, p. 13.
6043. STOCKWELL, Samn
"Prologue." [NewYorker] (70:12) 9 My 94, p. 74.
6044. STOICA, Ion
"The Only Shelter" (tr. by Brenda Walker). [PoetryC] (14:4) S 94, p. 21.
"You Can Never Leave" (tr. by Brenda Walker). [PoetryC] (14:4) S 94, p. 21.
6045. STOKES, Ann
"Chalice of Green." [SinW] (53) Sum-Fall 94, p. 76-77.
6046. STOLOFF, Carolyn
"Clean It Up, Shut It Down." [AnotherCM] (27) 94, p. 180-181.
"Full Moon" (Vence, France). [PoetL] (89:2) Sum 94, p. 25-26.
"Honored Guest." [AnotherCM] (27) 94, p. 182.
"Tasting the Stuff of Clouds." [Talisman] (12) Spr 94, p. 141.
"Thresholds." [NegC] (14:1/2) 94, p. 87-88.
"What I Miss, What I Want." [HangL] (64) 94, p. 67.
6047. STONE, Alison
"After the Accident." [IllinoisR] (2:1) Fall 94, p. 51-52.
"I'll Take Her Heart." [NewYorkQ] (53) 94, p. 93-94.
"Nicked on Old Compton Street." [IllinoisR] (2:1) Fall 94, p. 53.
"Persephone Returning." [Poetry] (164:3) Je 94, p. 134.
6048. STONE, Ira F.
"Atoning for the Abusive Parent" (From "A Yizkor Prayer for Victims of Abuse," in the second issue of *Kerem: A journal of creative explorations of Judaism*, Jewish Study Center, Washington, DC). [Harp] (288:1727) Ap 94, p. 30.
STONE, Robin Cooper
See COOPER-STONE, Robin
6049. STONE, Ruth
"Coffee and Sweet Rolls." [Boulevard] (9:1/2, #25/26) Spr 94, p. 15-16.
"Columbus, Ohio." [AmerPoR] (23:5) S-O 94, p. 34.
"Look to the Future." [AmerPoR] (23:5) S-O 94, p. 34.
"Medium for Stasis." [Boulevard] (9:3, #27) Fall 94, p. 69-74.
"Music." [Boulevard] (9:1/2, #25/26) Spr 94, p. 17.
"The Usual." [AmerPoR] (23:5) S-O 94, p. 34.
6050. STONE, Sophia
"From an Expressionist Painting." [NewOR] (20:1/2) Spr-Sum 94, p. 132-133.
"Leaving a Freshman at College." [SouthernR] (30:3) Sum 94, p. 579-580.
"Shortly After His Death in 1344, the Painter Simone Martini Visits His Brother-in-Law in Siena." [NewOR] (20:1/2) Spr-Sum 94, p. 134-135.
6051. STONEHOUSE, Cathy
"Illuminations." [CapilR] (2:13) Spr 94, p. 41-45.
"Magic Lantern." [CapilR] (2:13) Spr 94, p. 46-47.
"Phantom Pain." [CapilR] (2:13) Spr 94, p. 48.
6052. STORER, Norman W.
"Double Dactyl." [Light] (9) Spr 94, p. 13.
"Limerick." [Light] (12) Wint 94-95, p. 20.
6053. STOTT, Libby
"After the Heart Attack." [Poetry] (164:4) Jl 94, p. 218.
6054. STOUT, Barbara F.
"Frostline." [Hellas] (5:1) Spr-Sum 94, p. 81.

"Orphan." [Hellas] (5:1) Spr-Sum 94, p. 79-80.

6055. STOUT, Robert Joe
"Careers." [Pivot] (42) 94, p. 24.
"Che." [DogRR] (13:1, #25) Spr-Sum 94, p. 21.

6056. STOWELL, Phyllis
"#100 and 7." [Kalliope] (16:1) 94, p. 74.
"#100 and 11." [Kalliope] (16:1) 94, p. 40.
"Alchemical Green." [InterQ] (1:4) 94, p. 133.
"Ce Chemin, a Dialogue." [InterQ] (1:4) 94, p. 130-132.
"A Possible Life." [NewRena] (9:1, #27) 94, p. 126-127.

6057. STRAHAN, Bradley R.
"After the Deluge." [NegC] (14:1/2) 94, p. 142.
"Ballade" (tr. of Eugene Ionescu, w. Aurelia Roman). [Vis] (46) 94, p. 5.
"Croquis Humoristique" (tr. of Eugene Ionescu, w. Aurelia Roman). [Vis] (46) 94, p. 4.
"The Exhausted One" (tr. of Eugene Ionescu, w. Aurelia Roman). [Vis] (46) 94, p. 5.

6058. STRANEY, Susan
"November." [Amelia] (7:3, #22) 94, p. 136.

6059. STRANG, Catriona
"I want someone to say what you say" (w. Susan Clark and Lisa Robertson). [Chain] (1) Spr-Sum 94, p. 29.

6060. STRATTON, Dirk
"Fragment." [WebR] (18) Fall 94, p. 106.
"Let the Facts Speak for Themselves." [WebR] (18) Fall 94, p. 105-106.

6061. STRAUS, Marc (Marc J.)
"A Big Black Crow." [TriQ] (90) Spr-Sum 94, p. 91.
"The Bogeymen." [TriQ] (90) Spr-Sum 94, p. 90.
"Dr. Gold and Dr. Green." [TriQ] (90) Spr-Sum 94, p. 92.
"Dr. Gold and Dr. Green, II." [TriQ] (90) Spr-Sum 94, p. 93.
"The List." [BlackWR] (20:2) Spr-Sum 94, p. 78.
"Luck." [BlackWR] (20:2) Spr-Sum 94, p. 80.
"My Seventh Brithday." [PassN] (15:2) Wint 94, p. 39.
"Neuroanatomy Summer." [BlackWR] (20:2) Spr-Sum 94, p. 79.
"Red Polka Dot Dress." [PassN] (15:2) Wint 94, p. 38.

6062. STRAUSS, Gwen
"The Cyclops." [Conscience] (15:2) Sum 94, p. 13.

6063. STRAUSS, Lawrence
"The Flood." [Confr] (54/55) Fall 94-Wint 95, p. 327.

6064. STRICKLAND, Stephanie
"Heaven and Earth, 1666." [PraS] (68:3) Fall 94, p. 8.
"A History of Bearing Greek Gifts" (For Briseis). [ParisR] (36:132) Fall 94, p. 128.
"Iris an Illusion." [ParisR] (36:132) Fall 94, p. 127.
"Real Toads." [PraS] (68:3) Fall 94, p. 9-11.
"The Romans Captured Archimedes." [PraS] (68:3) Fall 94, p. 7.

6065. STROBOS, Semon
"Family Album." [NegC] (14:1/2) 94, p. 145.

6066. STROFFOLINO, Chris
"After Long Conversation." [Avec] (8:1) 94, p. 95-96.
"Debris." [Avec] (8:1) 94, p. 99-100.
"In the Lap." [Avec] (8:1) 94, p. 97-98.
"Now That Its April and January Is Back in America." [Avec] (8:1) 94, p. 94.
"Vive La différence." [AmerPoR] (23:3) My-Je 94, p. 54.
"Written in White." [Avec] (8:1) 94, p. 93.

6067. STRONG, Christina
"I Liken Myself to Terry Anderson." [AnthNEW] (6) 94, p. 29.

6068. STRONGIN, Lynn
"Evening Reading." [SouthernHR] (28:1) Wint 94, p. 16.
"Shipped Off to the Prairies." [Confr] (52/53) Wint-Spr 94, p. 335.

6069. STROUD, Diane
"First Boy." [EngJ] (83:1) Ja 94, p. 91.

6070. STRUTHERS, Ann
"Catherine Holtzman (1954-1990)." [PoetC] (26:1) Fall 94, p. 23.
"Ice Bison." [PoetC] (26:1) Fall 94, p. 22.

6071. STRUTHERS, Betsy
"Country Matters." [MalR] (108) Fall 94, p. 75.

6072. STRYK, Dan
"Lizard." [HolCrit] (31:2) Ap 94, p. 18-19.
"Solace of the Aging Mare." [HampSPR] Wint 94, p. 24.
"Toadfish." [HampSPR] Wint 94, p. 24.
6073. STRYK, Lucien
"Shrine of the Crane" (Yamaguchi, Japan). [PartR] (61:2) Spr 94, p. 313-314.
"Shrine of the Crane" (Yamaguchi, Japan). [WillowR] (21) Spr 94, p. 58.
"Student." [IllinoisR] (1:2) Spr 94, p. 34.
6074. STUART, Dabney
"Appalachian Spring." [SouthernR] (30:4) Aut 94, p. 841.
"Bedtime Story." [PoetC] (25:2) Wint 94, p. 20.
"Commencement." [SouthernR] (30:1) Ja, Wint 94, p. 108.
"Fence." [SouthernR] (30:1) Ja, Wint 94, p. 109.
"Lines for a Guestbook." [Light] (11) Aut 94, p. 15.
"Making Honey." [PoetC] (25:2) Wint 94, p. 16-19.
"Palm Reader." [QW] (38) Winter-Spr 93-94, p. 121-122.
"Plates" (South Island, New Zealand). [SouthernR] (30:4) Aut 94, p. 842-843.
"Presence." [TarRP] (33:2) Spr 94, p. 27.
"The Tapawera Raspberry Festival." [SouthernR] (30:4) Aut 94, p. 843-845.
"Tending." [TarRP] (33:2) Spr 94, p. 26.
6075. STUART, Jane
"Abracadabra." [BellArk] (10:6) N-D 94, p. 26.
"Giorno e Notte" (tr. of Eugenio Montale). [TampaR] (8) Spr 94, p. 49.
"Gypsy Poems." [Pembroke] (26) 94, p. 69.
"Orange." [BellArk] (10:6) N-D 94, p. 26.
"The Red Fox." [BellArk] (10:1) Ja-F 94, p. 24.
"Ribbons." [BellArk] (10:1) Ja-F 94, p. 24.
"Roses." [BellArk] (10:6) N-D 94, p. 9.
"Serenata Indiana" (tr. of Eugenio Montale). [TampaR] (8) Spr 94, p. 48.
"Wind Walker." [HiramPoR] (55/56) Fall 93-Sum 94, p. 114.
STUBBS, John Heath
See HEATH-STUBBS, John
6076. STUCK, Anne F.
"Perrault (Again)." [Hellas] (5:2) Fall-Wint 94, p. 100.
6077. STULL, Charlene
"Down This Hill." [Poetry] (164:2) My 94, p. 89-90.
6078. STURGEON, Shawn
"Christ Our Lord." [ParisR] (36:132) Fall 94, p. 125-126.
"Either Ur." [ParisR] (36:132) Fall 94, p. 124.
"Happy as Walt Whitman." [ParisR] (36:132) Fall 94, p. 125.
"The Roman Way." [ParisR] (36:132) Fall 94, p. 126.
6079. STYMEIST, David Sanders
"Mitla, Oaxaca." [PraF] (15:4, #69) Wint 94-95, p. 96-97.
6080. SU, Adrienne
"Francine, 1949." [GreensboroR] (56) Sum 94, p. 114-115.
6081. SUAREZ, María del Carmen
"Eterno Retorno." [Luz] (6) My 94, p. 44.
"Tiempo Primordial." [Luz] (6) My 94, p. 45.
6082. SUAREZ, Virgil
"Monks of Mood" (for the Beats). [NewDeltaR] (10:2) Spr-Sum 93, p. 21-24.
"Ode to a Torch Song Girl" (for V.B.). [ApalQ] (42) Fall 94, p. 26-29.
6083. SUBRAMAN, Belinda
"Bird/Brain Chatter." [Border] (3) Fall 93, p. 74.
"Clutching the Known." [HeavenB] (11) 94, p. 37.
"Explaining the Trinity, Or Three Losses." [CoalC] (8) Ap 94, p. 32.
"Walking Poem." [HeavenB] (11) 94, p. 37.
6084. SUCRE, Guillermo
"The Days That Fill Time" (tr. by Hardie St. Martin). [Trans] (29) Spr 94, p. 63.
"The House We're Born and Die in" (tr. by Hardie St. Martin). [Trans] (29) Spr 94, p. 62-63.
"In the Open Air" (tr. by Hardie St. Martin). [Trans] (29) Spr 94, p. 65.
"Like His Likeness" (homage to J. L. L., tr. by Hardie St. Martin). [Trans] (29) Spr 94, p. 64.
"There's the Head Born in the Mirror" (tr. by Hardie St. Martin). [Trans] (29) Spr 94, p. 65.

6085. SUERMONDT, Tim
"Briefly Eavesdropping on Walt Whitman, Virginia, 1863." [Poetry] (164:4) Jl 94, p. 195.
6086. SULLIVAN, Anne McCrary
"The Assignment." [EngJ] (83:4) Ap 94, p. 108.
"Notes from a Marine Biologist's Daughter." [GettyR] (7:4) Aut 94, p. 703.
6087. SULLIVAN, C. (Chris)
"Pruning." [Border] (4) Spr-Sum 94, p. 64-65.
"Redeye." [Farm] (11:2) Fall-Wint 94-95, p. 67-68.
6088. SULLIVAN, Gary
"Among the Living" (for Marta). [CentralP] (23) Spr 94, p. 24-27.
"Oscillating Wildly." [Talisman] (13) Fall 94-Wint 95, p. 264.
"Phoenix." [Talisman] (13) Fall 94-Wint 95, p. 265.
6089. SULLIVAN, James
"Arthritic Rain" (for emma's stillborn child). [SpiritSH] (59) 94, p. 21.
"The Mississippi Fugue." [SpiritSH] (59) 94, p. 22.
6090. SULLIVAN, John
"Texas Highway Love Poem." [BlackBR] (19) Fall-Wint 94, p. 8-9.
6091. SULTANA, Nasima
"I'll Go Away and I Won't Say a Thing" (tr. by Carolyne Wright and Mohammad Nurul Huda). [InterQ] (1:2) 93, p. 160.
"Let There Be Some Rage" (tr. by Mohammed Nurul Huda and Carolyne Wright, w. the author). [IndR] (17:1) Spr 94, p. 98.
6092. SULU, Nolon
"The Deer." [Callaloo] (17:1) Wint 94, p. 189.
6093. SUMMERHAYES, Don
"Family Reunion." [Descant] (25:3/4, #86/87) Fall-Wint 94, p. 233-235.
"North Dakota, December 1954." [Descant] (25:3/4, #86/87) Fall-Wint 94, p. 232.
6094. SUMMERS, Merna
"Chinese Paintings" (Selections: 4 poems). [Arc] (33) Fall 94, p. 46-47.
6095. SUNDAHL, Daniel James
"Easter Morning, Luna Pier, Two Men Fishing in a Boat." [SmPd] (31:3, #92) Fall 94, p. 23-24.
"Good Friday, April, 1963, Seining for Minnows, Death and Transfiguration." [SmPd] (31:3, #92) Fall 94, p. 22-23.
SUNG, Chin
See CHIN, Sung
6096. SUPERVIELLE, Jules
"The Alley" (tr. by William Louis-Dreyfus and Molly Peacock). [Agni] (39) 94, p. 25.
"Behind This Faded Sky" (tr. by Geoffrey Gardner). [CrabCR] (8:2/3/9:1/2/3) 94, p. 136.
"God Thinks of Man" (tr. by William Louis-Dreyfus and Molly Peacock). [Boulevard] (9:3, #27) Fall 94, p. 109-110.
"Prophecy" (tr. by William Louis-Dreyfus and Molly Peacock). [Agni] (39) 94, p. 23.
"The Raindrop (God Speaking)" (tr. by William Louis-Dreyfus and Molly Peacock). [Boulevard] (9:3, #27) Fall 94, p. 110.
"This Innocent Child" (tr. by Geoffrey Gardner). [CrabCR] (8:2/3/9:1/2/3) 94, p. 137.
"Whisper of Agony" (tr. by William Louis-Dreyfus and Molly Peacock). [Agni] (39) 94, p. 24.
6097. SUPOWIT, Sandy
"Ode to Chocolate." [CapeR] (29:1) Spr 94, p. 6.
6098. SUPRANER, Robyn
"Abstract Expressionists in Connecticut." [Gaia] (4) Je 94, p. 20.
"Uneasy in Taos." [Gaia] (4) Je 94, p. 20.
6099. SURDULESCU, Radu
"Winter Tale" (tr. of Petru Romosan, w. Adam J. Sorkin). [Vis] (46) 94, p. 29.
6100. SURINSKY, Wendy
"After Talking About the Photographs of Robert Mapplethorpe." [YellowS] (11:4, #44) Wint 93-94, p. 37.
6101. SURVANT, Joe
"Anniversary." [AmerV] (34) 94, p. 107.
6102. SUSKO, Mario
"Paper Tea" (tr. of Ferida Durakovic). [AntR] (52:2) Spr 94, p. 217.

6103. SUTE-JO, Lady (1633—1698)
Haiku [AmerPoR] (23:4) Jl-Ag 94, p. 18.
6104. SUTPHEN, Joyce
"Death Becomes Me." [Poetry] (164:4) Jl 94, p. 209.
"A Kind of Deliverance." [Vis] (45) 94, p. 4.
6105. SUTTON, Dorothy
"Legacy" (for John Preston Moseley, 1897-1976). [Wind] (73) 94, p. 25-26.
"This Is Just to Say" (after a poem by William Carlos Williams). [Wind] (73) 94, p. 25.
6106. SUTTON, Pamela
"Archaeopteryx Lithographica." [DenQ] (29:1) Sum 94, p. 40-41.
6107. SVENVOLD, Mark
"Vesper Music" (Four Poems. First Place, Poetry Award). [NewL] (60:2) 94, p. 9-19.
6108. SVOBODA, Terese
"A Cure for Hiccups." [ParisR] (36:133) Wint 94, p. 122.
"Death for Franchise." [Pequod] (37) 94, p. 123.
"Donkey." [Pequod] (37) 94, p. 124.
"Epithalmion For K.S. and S.H." [HawaiiR] (18:1, #40) Spr 94, p. 94.
"Horse's Hooves." [Verse] (11:2) Sum 94, p. 127-128.
"A Moo from a Can with a Cow on It." [GeoR] (48:1) Spr 94, p. 80.
"Mother's Minotaur." [HawaiiR] (18:1, #40) Spr 94, p. 93.
"The Septic Conversation." [KenR] (NS 16:4) Fall 94, p. 69-70.
"The Smell of Burning Pennies." [KenR] (NS 16:4) Fall 94, p. 69.
"Stations." [HawaiiR] (18:1, #40) Spr 94, p. 92.
"Sudanese Ghost House." [Boulevard] (9:3, #27) Fall 94, p. 127-128.
"Unicorn." [Salm] (103) Sum 94, p. 99-100.
"Wait." [Verse] (11:2) Sum 94, p. 128.
6109. SWAN, Marc
"Always Moving." [WormR] (34:4, #136) 94, p. 145.
"Clip Job." [WormR] (34:4, #136) 94, p. 145.
"Good Hands." [SlipS] (14) 94, p. 114.
"In Her Sunday Dress." [OgalalaR] (5:1) Wint 94, p. 82.
"Rubber Skull." [BlackBR] (19) Fall-Wint 94, p. 24.
"The Vortex." [WormR] (34:4, #136) 94, p. 144-145.
6110. SWANDER, Mary
"Take Two." [TarRP] (33:2) Spr 94, p. 1-3.
6111. SWANEY, George
"The Shortest Note I Ever Wrote to Myself: Yesterday, 12/11/93." [PoetryE] (37/38) Spr 94, p. 137.
6112. SWANGER, David
"Something About Love." [CharR] (20:1) Spr 94, p. 73-74.
"This Waking Unafraid." [CharR] (20:1) Spr 94, p. 72.
6113. SWANN, Brian
"Adam and Eve Name the Animals" (Excerpt). [Light] (10) Sum 94, p. 8.
"Crow." [InterQ] (1:4) 94, p. 97.
"For Adolf Eichmann" (tr. of Primo Levy, w. Ruth Feldman). [NewEngR] (16:2) Spr 94, p. 149.
"Once in Prague." [HarvardR] (6) Spr 94, p. 165.
"Proserpina." [Boulevard] (9:3, #27) Fall 94, p. 189.
"This House." [Shen] (44:1) Spr 94, p. 66-67.
"Whiteness." [YaleR] (82:1) Ja 94, p. 86-87.
6114. SWANNELL, Anne
"Sitting on Her Lawn's So Difficult." [Dandel] (21:1) 94, p. 70-71.
6115. SWANSON, Eleanor
"Field." [SingHM] (21) 94, p. 1.
6116. SWANSON, Suzanne M.
"The Crow Reaches the Middle of Her Life." [Gaia] (4) Je 94, p. 40.
6117. SWARTS, Helene
"Moving to the Island." [AnthNEW] (6) 94, p. 23.
6118. SWARTWOUT, Susan
"Freak Love: a Sequence." [ClockR] (9:1/2) 94-95, p. 65-70.
6119. SWARTZ, David
"Maybe in the Army." [SlipS] (14) 94, p. 35.
6120. SWEENEY, Bill
"The Everly Brothers (Tet, 1968)." [CapeR] (29:2) Fall 94, p. 44-45.

6121. SWEENEY, Matthew
"The House." [SouthernR] (30:2) Ap, Spr 94, p. 323-324.
"Keep Him In." [SouthernR] (30:2) Ap, Spr 94, p. 324-325.
"The Shadow Home." [Jacaranda] (5:1) Wint-Spr 91, p. 52.
"Sleep with a Suitcase." [Pivot] (42) 94, p. 8.
"Try Biting." [Pivot] (42) 94, p. 7.
6122. SWEET, Denise
"The Origin of Envy." [AnotherCM] (28) 94, p. 153-154.
"Song for Discharming." [AnotherCM] (28) 94, p. 151-152.
6123. SWEET, Victoria
"To Those in Future Evenings" (tr. of Renée Vivien). [PoetryE] (37/38) Spr 94, p. 222.
"You for Whom I've Written" (tr. of Renée Vivien). [PoetryE] (37/38) Spr 94, p. 223.
6124. SWEETING, Lynn
"Going Home" (for my grandmother Winnifred Sweeting). [CaribbeanW] (8) 94, p. 22-24.
"Living on the Lee." [CaribbeanW] (8) 94, p. 19-21.
6125. SWENSEN, Cole
"Cathedral." [Avec] (8:1) 94, p. 61.
"Crowd" (to Elizabeth Robinson). [Chain] (1) Spr-Sum 94, p. 260-262.
"Fulcrum." [Avec] (8:1) 94, p. 67.
"Harvest." [Avec] (8:1) 94, p. 63.
"The Inviolable Sanctity of Animals" (after Max Ernst). [Avec] (8:1) 94, p. 62.
"A Love of Daily Living." [Avec] (8:1) 94, p. 63.
"The Ones That Are the Same." [Avec] (8:1) 94, p. 65.
"To Ant." [Avec] (8:1) 94, p. 61.
"To In and Done." [Avec] (8:1) 94, p. 66.
"To One." [Avec] (8:1) 94, p. 64.
"Watching." [Avec] (8:1) 94, p. 64.
6126. SWENSON, Karen
"Bayon, Angkor Thom." [PraS] (68:1) Spr 94, p. 77-78.
"The Cham Towers at Danang." [NewL] (60:2) 94, p. 92.
"Cultural Exchange" (for Madonna). [NewL] (60:2) 94, p. 89-90.
"Getting a Purchase." [PraS] (68:1) Spr 94, p. 78-79.
"Market Women: Lake Toba." [PraS] (68:1) Spr 94, p. 77.
"Share Taxi to Singapore." [NewL] (60:2) 94, p. 91.
"Sulawesi: Balconies of the Dead." [NewL] (60:2) 94, p. 93.
"Time and the Perfume River." [Pivot] (41) 93, p. 27.
"Uncoupling in Bali." [Confr] (52/53) Wint-Spr 94, p. 300.
"Wedding Bed in Mangkutana." [DenQ] (28:3) Wint 94, p. 28.
6127. SWENSON, May
"Assuming the Lotus." [AmerPoR] (23:5) S-O 94, p. 8.
"Dear Elizabeth" (A reply to Elizabeth Bishop in Brazil). [ParisR] (36:131) Sum 94, p. 172-173.
"Death, Great Smoothener." [AmerPoR] (23:5) S-O 94, p. 13.
"The Kiss." [AmerPoR] (23:5) S-O 94, p. 8.
"The Lightning." [AmerPoR] (23:5) S-O 94, p. 11-12.
"Something Goes By." [AmerPoR] (23:5) S-O 94, p. 52.
"Standing Torso." [KenR] (NS 16:3) Sum 94, p. 140-141.
6128. SWENSON, Paul
"The Meeting." [WeberS] (11:2) Spr-Sum 94, p. 108.
"The Plunge." [WeberS] (11:2) Spr-Sum 94, p. 106-107.
6129. SWERDLOW, David
"Beautiful." [CreamCR] (18:1) Spr 94, p. 42-43.
"Self and Duende." [AmerLC] (6) 94, p. 4.
6130. SWIFT, Doug
"Jewelweed." [Pivot] (42) 94, p. 39.
"My Old, Sweet Song." [ArtfulD] (26/27) 94, p. 147.
6131. SWIFT, Joan
"At the Whitehorse Rearing Ponds: Letting the Fry Go." [PoetryNW] (35:4) Wint 94-95, p. 44.
"Looking at African-American Quilts in Eli's Basement." [Calyx] (15:3) Wint 94-95, p. 33.
6132. SWISS, Thomas
"Flood." [Outbr] (25) 94, p. 71.

"Poem Ending with a Stanza by Rilke." [Iowa] (24:3) Fall 94, p. 111-113.
"Shy Boy." [Outbr] (25) 94, p. 72.
"Sun Going Down." [Outbr] (25) 94, p. 69-70.

6133. SWIST, Wally
"August." [Os] (39) Fall-Wint 94, p. 12.
"Helping Hands." [Outbr] (25) 94, p. 73.
"Winter Nap" (for Bob Arnold). [ShadowP] (4) 94, p. 27.

6134. SYLVAIN, Patrick
"Army of Draculas." [CaribbeanW] (8) 94, p. 10.

6135. SYLVESTER, Everton
"Way to Wendell Wedding." [MassR] (35:3/4) Aut-Wint 94, p. 574-575.

6136. SYLVESTER, Janet
"The Compact." [Shen] (44:3) Fall 94, p. 114-115.
"Neap and High." [Shen] (44:3) Fall 94, p. 116.

6137. SZCZEPANSKI, Marian
"Castle in the Air (1922)" (From a sequence of poems "Paul Klee in the Kunstmuseam, Bern" [sic]). [Vis] (44) 94, p. 22.
"Fete des Vendanges." [Vis] (46) 94, p. 22-23.

6138. SZIRTES, George
"Chinese White." [Jacaranda] (5:1) Wint-Spr 91, p. 53.

6139. SZOSTALO, Aleksandra
"Beggar of Sorrow" (tr. of Tadeusz Gajcy, w. David Sparenberg). [WebR] (18) Fall 94, p. 14.
"Request of Thyme" (tr. of Malgorzata Hillar, w. David Sparenberg). [WebR] (18) Fall 94, p. 15.

6140. SZPORLUK, Larissa
"Prowler's Universe." [NowestR] (32:3) 94, p. 32-33.

6141. SZUMIGALSKI, Anne
"Untitled: The woman who lived alone on the edge of the moor." [Arc] (33) Fall 94, p. 65-67.

6142. SZUMOWSKI, Margaret C.
"The Dent." [PoetryE] (37/38) Spr 94, p. 106.
"Tenderness in the Midst of War." [PoetryE] (37/38) Spr 94, p. 104-105.

6143. SZYMASZEK, Stacy
"Lombardy, Italy." [SinW] (54) Wint 94-95, p. 113-114.

6144. SZYMBORSKA, Wislawa
"Allegro Ma Non Troppo" (tr. by Stanislaw Baranczak and Clare Cavanagh). [Salm] (103) Sum 94, p. 266-267.
"A Byzantine Mosaic" (tr. by Stanislaw Baranczak and Clare Cavanagh). [HarvardR] (2) Fall 92, p. 150-151.
"Coloratura" (tr. by Stanislaw Baranczak and Clare Cavanagh). [Salm] (103) Sum 94, p. 268-269.
"Epitaph" (tr. by Stanislaw Baranczak and Clare Cavanagh). [PartR] (61:4) Fall 94, p. 633.
"May 16, 1973" (tr. by Stanislaw Baranczak and Clare Cavanagh). [HarvardR] (7) Fall 94, p. 36-37.
"On the Banks of the Styx" (tr. by Stanislaw Baranczak and Clare Cavanagh). [Salm] (103) Sum 94, p. 269-270.
"Poetry Reading" (tr. by Stanislaw Baranczak and Clare Cavanagh). [PartR] (61:4) Fall 94, p. 634.
"Sky" (tr. by Stanislaw Baranczak and Clare Cavanagh). [Agni] (39) 94, p. 20-21.
"We're Extremely Fortunate" (tr. by Stanislaw Baranczak and Clare Cavanagh). [Salm] (103) Sum 94, p. 270-271.
"Writing a Curriculum Vitae" (tr. by Grazyna Drabik and Austin Flint). [Crazy] (47) Wint 94, p. 100-101.

T., H.
See H. T.

6145. TADJO, Véronique
"Chante-moi" (tr. by Julia Older). [InterQ] (1:3) 94, p. 73-74.

TAEKO, Tomioka (b. 1935)
See TOMIOKA, Taeko (b. 1935)

6146. TAFDRUP, Pia
"A" (tr. by Roger Greenwald). [Pequod] (38) 94, p. 50.
"De Profundis" (tr. by Roger Greenwald). [Pequod] (38) 94, p. 54.

"Destination" (tr. by Roger Greenwald). [Pequod] (38) 94, p. 57.
"Frost Chord" (tr. by Roger Greenwald). [Pequod] (38) 94, p. 51.
"Leaf-fall among Red Oaks in Maine" (tr. by Roger Greenwald). [Pequod] (38) 94, p. 55.
"Lumière Cendrée" (tr. by Roger Greenwald). [Pequod] (38) 94, p. 56.
"Shadow-figure" (tr. by Roger Greenwald). [Pequod] (38) 94, p. 52.
"Tabernacles" (tr. by Roger Greenwald). [Pequod] (38) 94, p. 53.

6147. TAGGART, John
"How Sweet It Is." [Talisman] (12) Spr 94, p. 22-23.
"A Queen Not the Queen." [Talisman] (12) Spr 94, p. 21.
"Right Tool" (for Ted Enslin). [Talisman] (12) Spr 94, p. 24.

6148. TAGLIABUE, John
"Like 14 Tiny Disciples of St. Valentine." [Elf] (4:2) Sum 94, p. 30.
"The Lunatic, the Lover, and the Poet, and the Common Reader." [Elf] (4:2) Sum 94, p. 31.

6149. TAKAHASHI, Shinkicki (1901-1987)
Haiku [AmerPoR] (23:4) Jl-Ag 94, p. 20.

6150. TAKARA, Kathryn Waddell
"Bittersweet." [ChamLR] (14/15) Spr-Fall 94, p. 104-106.
"Tra-lang-a-lang, Cha-lang-a-land Blues." [ChamLR] (14/15) Spr-Fall 94, p. 102-103.

6151. TAKATA, Ellen
"The Miracle of the Parasitic Twin." [HangL] (65) 94, p. 100.
"Siblings (from a Photograph of Franz and Ottla Kafka)." [HangL] (65) 94, p. 99.

6152. TAKSA, Mark
"Opera, Peppers and the Old Ocean." [PaintedHR] (11) Spr-Sum 94, p. 29.
"The Rainbow and the Stronger." [SouthernPR] (34:2) Wint 94, p. 10.
"The Rebellion." [LaurelR] (28:1) Wint 94, p. 28.

TAKUBOKU, Ishikawa
See ISHIKAWA, Takuboku

6153. TALAMANTES, Rosina R.
"Impalpable Web." [SoDakR] (32:4) Wint 94, p. 81.
"The Rage of Sausages." [SoDakR] (32:4) Wint 94, p. 80.
"Tequia y Piñata." [SoDakR] (32:4) Wint 94, p. 82.

6154. TALENTINO, Arnold
"Descartes Watching His Cat." [NoDaQ] (62:3) Sum 94-95, p. 160.

6155. TALLIE, Mariahadessa
"Baby Got More Than Back." [Eyeball] (3) 93, p. 16.

6156. TAMMARO, Thom
"Go Figure." [Sun] (220) Ap 94, p. 32-33.
"'mericn fst fd." [ChiR] (40:2/3) 94, p. 29.

TAMS FUQUEN, Ruth V.
See FUQUEN, Ruth V. Tams

6157. TAN, Janet
"Faces" (tr. of Xue Di, w. Keith Waldrop). [Manoa] (6:1) Sum 94, p. 85-86.

TAN, Lin
See LIN, Tan

6158. TANEMURA, Kenneth
"Haiku" (5 poems). [Northeast] (5:10) Sum 94, p. 9.

6159. TANGORRA, Joanne
"In the Country." [LaurelR] (28:1) Wint 94, p. 83-85.

6160. TANNY, Marlaina B.
"Dance of the Unheralded." [WorldO] (26:2) Wint 94-95, p. 13.
"From the Proper Angle." [WorldO] (26:1) Fall 94, p. 15.

6161. TANYOL, Tugrul
"Fathers Far Off" (tr. by Ruth Christie). [Stand] (35:2) Spr 94, p. 69.

6162. TAPIA, Michael J.
"Part II. Abraham's Secret." [Poem] (72) N 94, p. 44-45.

6163. TARN, Natasha
"T(w)alks: Seven." [Talisman] (12) Spr 94, p. 207.
"T(w)alks: Six." [Talisman] (12) Spr 94, p. 206.

6164. TARN, Nathaniel
"ARC67.94." [RiverC] (14:2) Spr 94, p. 6.
"In This Black Stillness" (tr. of Joachim Sartorius, w. Sibylle Schlesier). [Conjunc] (23) 94, p. 140-143.
"Meditation: First and Last Trek, Zangskar." [Conjunc] (22) 94, p. 184-189.

6165. TARNOWSKI, Alice
"Mary, Mary." [ChrC] (111:35) 7 D 94, p. 1162.
6166. TARNOWSKI, Alice Marie
"High Tea." [Light] (10) Sum 94, p. 18.
6167. TARTARILLA, Susan
"After Ironweed." [EngJ] (83:2) F 94, p. 90.
6168. TARTT, Peggy Ann
"Taking Her In." [HolCrit] (31:3) Je 94, p. 19.
6169. TATE, James
"Abandoned Conceptions." [ColR] (21:1) Spr 94, p. 172.
"Becoming a Scout." [GettyR] (7:2) Spr 94, p. 304-305.
"Desire." [Iowa] (24:3) Fall 94, p. 142.
"The Documentary We Were Making." [CutB] (41) Wint 94, p. 71-72.
"The Great Root System." [ColR] (21:1) Spr 94, p. 173-174.
"Happy As the Day Is Long." [HarvardR] (Premier Issue) Spr 92, p. 11.
"How the Pope Is Chosen." [HarvardR] (7) Fall 94, p. 19-20.
"Loyalty." [GettyR] (7:2) Spr 94, p. 308.
"A Manual of Enlargement." [HarvardR] (7) Fall 94, p. 20-21.
"A Missed Opportunity." [Antaeus] (75/76) Aut 94, p. 324.
"A New Beginning." [GettyR] (7:2) Spr 94, p. 306-307.
"The Nitrogen Cycle." [CutB] (41) Wint 94, p. 69-70.
"The Parade and After the Parade." [Iowa] (24:3) Fall 94, p. 143.
"We Go to a Fire." [Iowa] (24:3) Fall 94, p. 141.
6170. TATE, Joan
"Route Tournante" (tr. of Kjell Espmark). [ParisR] (36:130) Spr 94, p. 100-101.
6171. TAUB, Yermiyahu Ahron
"By the Grave: Historian and Craft." [JamesWR] (11:4) Sum 94, p. 16.
"The Night I Returned to Pornography" (with love and thanks to Melanie Search). [EvergreenC] (9:1) Wint-Spr 94, p. 28-30.
"Preparing to Dance." [JamesWR] (11:4) Sum 94, p. 16.
"The Question of Moishe Oysher." [JamesWR] (11:4) Sum 94, p. 5.
6172. TAWFALL, Mary
"Tambourine." [HangL] (64) 94, p. 90.
6173. TAWFIQ, Badr
"The Dream Tree" (tr. by Abdelwahab Elmessiri). [Vis] (45) 94, p. 20-21.
6174. TAYLOR, Alex
"Kastelorizon" (tr. of Henrik Nordbrandt). [Vis] (44) 94, p. 15.
"Our Love Is Like Byzantium" (tr. of Henrik Nordbrandt). [Vis] (46) 94, p. 17.
"The Rose from Lesbos" (tr. of Henrik Nordbrandt). [Vis] (45) 94, p. 10.
6175. TAYLOR, Bruce
"Arabesque." [Poetry] (165:1) O 94, p. 23.
"Calling It the Given." [Poetry] (165:1) O 94, p. 21.
"Gray Drapes." [Poetry] (165:1) O 94, p. 24.
"Like." [Poetry] (165:1) O 94, p. 22.
"Poetry Beauty Truth Love Respect & Wonder: A Child's First Sestina." [Northeast] (5:10) Sum 94, p. 28-29.
"Rising out of Love." [ChiR] (40:2/3) 94, p. 11.
"The World's Best Bad Example" (for Harry Newman, 1921-1992). [Light] (12) Wint 94-95, p. 19.
6176. TAYLOR, Eleanor Ross
"The Diary." [SouthernR] (30:4) Aut 94, p. 690-692.
"Homecoming." [SouthernR] (30:4) Aut 94, p. 692.
"Katydids Sewanee." [SouthernR] (30:4) Aut 94, p. 689-690.
6177. TAYLOR, Henry
"Afternoons with a Boomerang." [NewRep] (211:26) 26 D 94, p. 38.
"Circe" (tr. of Moshe Dor). [WebR] (18) Fall 94, p. 9.
"In Another's Hands." [EngJ] (83:5) S 94, p. 60.
6178. TAYLOR, Judith
"Brief Affair." [TarRP] (34:1) Fall 94, p. 3.
"Natural History of Los Angeles." [PoetL] (89:2) Sum 94, p. 29-30.
"Prayer in the British Museum" (Woodcuts of the floating world, Ukiyo-E). [SouthernPR] (34:2) Wint 94, p. 32.
6179. TAYLOR, Keith
"An Afternoon at Lake Michigan." [Parting] (7:1) Sum 94, p. 39.
"Hitchhiking." [Parting] (7:1) Sum 94, p. 35-37.
"Livy, Abridged." [Pivot] (41) 93, p. 32.

"They're Out There, Waiting." [Pivot] (41) 93, p. 32-33.
"White Fire" (an extract from a renga). [Parting] (7:1) Sum 94, p. 38.

6180. TAYLOR, Koko
"63 Year Old Mama." [ClockR] (9:1/2) 94-95, p. 132.

6181. TAYLOR, Linda
"Eyes." [PoetryNW] (35:4) Wint 94-95, p. 20-21.
"Night Walking, Dream Pillow." [PoetryNW] (35:4) Wint 94-95, p. 21-23.
"Prodigal." [IndR] (17:1) Spr 94, p. 126.
"Returning to the Cuyahoga." [PoetryNW] (35:4) Wint 94-95, p. 18-20.
"Saul on the Road to Damascus." [IndR] (17:1) Spr 94, p. 127.
"Way Down to the End of the Road" (for Mike, Wayne, and Davy). [IndR] (17:2) Fall 94, p. 95-96.

6182. TAYLOR, Mervyn
"Homefire." [Bomb] (46) Wint 94, p. 64.
"Next" (for Suchitha). [Bomb] (46) Wint 94, p. 64.
"R.S.V.P." (for Fatisha). [Bomb] (46) Wint 94, p. 64.

6183. TAYLOR, Thomas Lowe
"Storm." [WashR] (19:6) Ap-My 94, p. 5.

6184. TAYSON, Richard
"Blood Test." [KenR] (NS 16:3) Sum 94, p. 42-43.
"Fever." [KenR] (NS 16:3) Sum 94, p. 43-44.
"The Gift." [JamesWR] (11:3) Spr 94, p. 12.
"Love as an Argument in Time and Loss" (Patroclus and Achilles). [JamesWR] (11:3) Spr 94, p. 13.
"My Mother Asks If Men Make Love Face to Face." [HangL] (65) 94, p. 68-69.
"Nightsweats." [HangL] (65) 94, p. 70-71.
"Remembering the Man Who Molested Me." [JamesWR] (11:3) Spr 94, p. 13.
"Sacraments." [Crazy] (46) Spr 94, p. 82-86.
"Sacred Anus." [JamesWR] (11:3) Spr 94, p. 13.

6185. TEARAWAY, Tom
"Angry Moon-Cloud." [Writer] (107:5) My 94, p. 19-20.

6186. TEDESCO, Cynthia
"Study of Absence." [CapeR] (29:1) Spr 94, p. 16.

6187. TEICHMANN, Sandra (Sandra Gail)
"Bird on a Fence Post, 1992." [Border] (4) Spr-Sum 94, p. 66.
"For All That the Ground Still Yields to Our Steps." [Border] (4) Spr-Sum 94, p. 67.
"Interpretations of Realism" (tr. of Dionisio D. Martinez). [InterQ] (1:4) 94, p. 158.
"Laura Inherits a Charlatan" (tr. of Dionisio D. Martinez). [InterQ] (1:4) 94, p. 157.

6188. TEILLIER, Jorge
"In the Sun of the Hazelnut Trees" (tr. by Carolyne Wright). [InterQ] (1:1) [93?], p. 63.
"So Long." [HarvardR] (2) Fall 92, p. 144-145.
"Week in Valdivia" (For my old friends in the Trilce Group, and those from Indice, and for Jorge Torres Ulloa. Tr. by Carolyne Wright). [Agni] (39) 94, p. 119.

6189. TEITELBOIM, Dora
"What good?" [Vis] (46) 94, p. 10.

6190. TEMESVARI, Agnes
"Purple Lantern." [Os] (38) Spr 94, p. 5.
"Sybil." [Os] (38) Spr 94, p. 4.

6191. TEMPLE, Frédéric Jacques
"Sur L'Ile de Groix" (à Gérard Le Gouic). [Os] (39) Fall-Wint 94, p. 11.

6192. TEMPLETON, Fiona
"Fa me s' Mutual Cha in" (to Kathryn MacLeod). [Chain] (1) Spr-Sum 94, p. 268-272.

6193. TENENBAUM, Molly
"Apple Ladder." [PoetryNW] (35:1) Spr 94, p. 21-22.
"The Aptitutde Test." [BelPoJ] (45:2) Wint 94-95, p. 22-23.
"As I Set Out." [BelPoJ] (45:2) Wint 94-95, p. 24-25.
"Cooking Song." [PoetryNW] (35:1) Spr 94, p. 22-23.
"The Spiders in the Fruit of their Year." [PoetryNW] (35:1) Spr 94, p. 20-21.
"Spring Vase." [BelPoJ] (45:2) Wint 94-95, p. 26-27.

6194. TEOFILOV, Ivan
"Ortamezar — The Jewish Quarter" (tr. by Lisa Sapinkopf and Georgi Belev). [InterQ] (1:1) [93?], p. 82-83.
"Teenagers" (tr. by Lisa Sapinkopf and Georgi Belev). [InterQ] (1:1) [93?], p. 84.

6195. TERAN, Ana Enriqueta
"Her Head Bowed in Acceptance" (tr. by Steven F. White). [Trans] (29) Spr 94, p. 41.
"Remnants" (tr. by Steven F. White). [Trans] (29) Spr 94, p. 41.
"Short Stretches" (tr. by Steven F. White). [Trans] (29) Spr 94, p. 42.
"Sole Sign" (tr. by Steven F. White). [Trans] (29) Spr 94, p. 42.
6196. TERENZI, John
"Dinner by Candle." [Northeast] (5:11) Wint 94-95, p. 37.
6197. TERPSTRA, John
"Our Loves Quit the Places We Bury Them, and Ascend." [Image] (7) Fall 94, p. 64-65.
6198. TERRANOVA, Elaine
"Blind Man." [Boulevard] (9:1/2, #25/26) Spr 94, p. 260-261.
"Merry-Go-Round." [Boulevard] (9:1/2, #25/26) Spr 94, p. 259.
6199. TERRILL, Mark
"Metaphors, Money, and Madness." [ContextS] (4:1) 94, p. 38.
6200. TERRILL, Richard
"Aiming" (tr. of Jing Bute, w. Cheng Baolin). [AnotherCM] (27) 94, p. 87.
"An Anonymous Woman Visited My Home" (tr. of Cheng Baolin, w. the author). [AnotherCM] (27) 94, p. 97.
"Awakening at Dawn" (tr. of Lu Yimin, w. Cheng Baolin). [AnotherCM] (27) 94, p. 90.
"Blowing Wind" (tr. of Xi Chuan, w. Cheng Baolin). [AnotherCM] (27) 94, p. 85.
"Correspondent" (tr. of Yu Jian, w. Cheng Baolin). [NoDaQ] (62:1) Wint 94-95, p. 93-94.
"Experience" (tr. of Xi Chuan, w. Cheng Baolin). [AnotherCM] (27) 94, p. 86.
"Fish" (tr. of Cheng Baolin, w. the author). [AnotherCM] (27) 94, p. 93.
"Glass" (tr. of Cheng Baolin, w. the author). [AnotherCM] (27) 94, p. 91.
"Growing Grapes" (tr. of Cheng Baolin, w. the author). [AnotherCM] (27) 94, p. 95.
"Homeland" (tr. of Shang Zhongmin, w. Cheng Baolin). [TampaR] (9) Fall 94, p. 9.
"Mother" (tr. of Shang Zhongmin, w. Cheng Baolin). [TampaR] (9) Fall 94, p. 8.
"Occurrence" (tr. of Cheng Baolin, w. the author). [AnotherCM] (27) 94, p. 98.
"Running Across My Wife at a Subway Station" (tr. of Cheng Baolin, w. the author). [AnotherCM] (27) 94, p. 92.
"Sand Castle" (tr. of Lu Yimin, w. Cheng Baolin). [AnotherCM] (27) 94, p. 88.
"Spring" (tr. of Cheng Baolin, w. the author). [AnotherCM] (27) 94, p. 94.
"The Sunset Above the Square" (tr. of Xi Chuan, w. Cheng Baolin). [AnotherCM] (27) 94, p. 84.
"Tympanist" (tr. of Cheng Baolin, w. the author). [AnotherCM] (27) 94, p. 96.
"Walt Whitman" (tr. of Wang Yin, w. Cheng Baolin). [NowestR] (32:1) 94, p. 110.
"Wind and Rain Were Approaching" (tr. of Lu Yimin, w. Cheng Baolin). [AnotherCM] (27) 94, p. 89.
6201. TERRIS, Susan
"Flesh." [PoetC] (25:3) Spr 94, p. 25.
"Gumbo." [CapeR] (29:2) Fall 94, p. 24-25.
"In Loco Parentis." [SpoonR] (19:1) Wint-Spr 94, p. 45.
"Kali Ma." [Kalliope] (16:3) 94, p. 35-36.
"Moon Calling." [SpoonR] (19:1) Wint-Spr 94, p. 46.
"Post Mortem." [Kalliope] (16:3) 94, p. 34.
6202. TERRIS, Viginia (Virginia R.)
"Black River Dam." [JINJPo] (16:1) Spr 94, p. 25.
"The Jolly Hour." [ProseP] (3) 94, p. 80.
6203. TESCHKE, Holger
"Manhattan Transfer" (tr. by Reinhold Grimm). [Pembroke] (26) 94, p. 135.
6204. TESSIER, Vanna
"Frostbitten." [Dandel] (21:1) 94, p. 14-15.
6205. TESSITORE
"Sister." [FloridaR] (20:1) Fall 94, p. 36-39.
6206. TETTE, Sharan Flynn
"Cana." [ChrC] (111:21) 13-20 Jl 94, p. 688.
6207. TETZLOFF, David
"The Neighborhood." [SmPd] (31:3, #92) Fall 94, p. 24.
6208. THACKREY, Susan
"Or." [Avec] (7:1) 94, p. 69-72.
6209. THALMAN, Mark
"Monsieur Perdreau's Garden." [Pearl] (20) Spr 94, p. 79.

6210. THAM, Hilary
"The First Apple Farmer" (Runner Up, 1993 John Williams Andrews Narrative Poetry Contest). [PoetL] (89:2) Sum 94, p. 5-11.
6211. THANIEL, George
"Poems for Gwendolyn MacEwen" (8 poems, tr. of Nikolas Tsingos). [Descant] (24:4, #83) Wint 93-94, p. 41-52.
6212. THATCHER, Timothy E.
"Wet Stones" (Winner, The Mary Elinore Smith Poetry Prize). [AmerS] (63:3) Sum 94, p. 349-350.
6213. THEIS, Dick
"The Constellations, Northern Wisconsin." [TampaR] (8) Spr 94, p. 11.
6214. THEOGNIS (born 544 B.C.)
"Happy the man that has at last found out" (tr. by Robin Skelton). [Arc] (32) Spr 94, p. 39.
6215. THEOGNIS of Mègara (late-6th - early-5th c. B.C.)
"The Exile" (tr. by John J. Brugaletta). [SoCoast] (16) Ja 94, p. 57.
6216. THINNES, Christopher Dylan
"Divorce." [Jacaranda] (4:2) Spr 90, p. 107.
6217. THOMAS, Amy
"Father's Insomnia." [GrahamHR] (18) Wint 94-95, p. 27.
"Quahog." [GrahamHR] (18) Wint 94-95, p. 25.
"Ripe Tonight." [GrahamHR] (18) Wint 94-95, p. 23-24.
"Visiting a Coma." [GrahamHR] (18) Wint 94-95, p. 27-29.
6218. THOMAS, Denise
"How West Becomes the West." [HighP] (9:2) Ag 94, p. 44-45.
"In the Hallway of Love." [Manoa] (6:1) Sum 94, p. 92-93.
"What You Heard Calling You." [Manoa] (6:1) Sum 94, p. 91.
6219. THOMAS, Elizabeth
"Atlantic City." [NewOR] (20:1/2) Spr-Sum 94, p. 84.
"Incident." [NewOR] (20:1/2) Spr-Sum 94, p. 85-87.
"Sex." [NewOR] (20:1/2) Spr-Sum 94, p. 80-81.
"Tina Modotti Visits Guanajuato." [NewOR] (20:1/2) Spr-Sum 94, p. 82-83.
6220. THOMAS, F. Richard
"Butter." [EngJ] (83:7) N 94, p. 79.
6221. THOMAS, G. Murray
"Cows on the Freeway." [Pearl] (20) Spr 94, p. 11.
6222. THOMAS, George T.
"7. She was skinny my stepmother." [ChironR] (13:3) Aut 94, p. 24.
6223. THOMAS, Jim
"Bog Thing." [Wind] (73) 94, p. 28.
"Driving into Early Fall." [Wind] (73) 94, p. 29.
"Off-White Collar." [Wind] (73) 94, p. 27.
6224. THOMAS, Joan E.
"Billie's Blues." [Eyeball] (3) 93, p. 42.
6225. THOMAS, Lamar
"And the Sun Dreams of Night's Bride — Slowly" (The Nimrod / Hardman Wards: Finalist). [Nimrod] (38:1) Fall-Wint 94, p. 41-42.
6226. THOMAS, Larry D.
"Of His Presence." [WebR] (18) Fall 94, p. 46.
6227. THOMAS, P. L.
"3 1/2's (Three Halves)." [Outbr] (25) 94, p. 74.
6228. THOMAS, Randolph
"Distant Music." [TarRP] (34:1) Fall 94, p. 20.
"First Days." [PoetryNW] (35:1) Spr 94, p. 24.
"She Believes in Magic." [LaurelR] (28:1) Wint 94, p. 121.
6229. THOMAS, Scott E.
"The Outside World." [WebR] (18) Fall 94, p. 70.
"Red Umbrella in a Snow Squall." [WebR] (18) Fall 94, p. 70.
6230. THOMAS, Terry
"Facing the Snake." [Plain] (14:3) Spr 94, p. 8.
"The Forgotten Citizen" (This Cheap Stone Is Neglected by the State). [Plain] (14:3) Spr 94, p. 10.
"The Hump Backed Beast." [Plain] (15:1) Fall 94, p. 37.
"My Last Roomie." [Plain] (14:3) Spr 94, p. 11.
"Roll My Number." [Plain] (14:2) Wint 94, p. 23.
"Romeo and the Abby." [HampSPR] Wint 94, p. 48.

"Summer of the Hired Hand." [Plain] (14:3) Spr 94, p. 9.

6231. THOMIM, Jeannnette Barnes

"For Jakie." [AnthNEW] (6) 94, p. 10.

6232. THOMPSON, Gary

"Birthday Psalm." [SoCoast] (16) Ja 94, p. 16.
"Dancing Mad." [HayF] (15) Fall-Wint 94, p. 82.
"The Lesson of Birds." [WritersF] (20) 94, p. 58-60.
"Noyo: Edge of the World." [ColR] (21:2) Fall 94, p. 137-138.
"Of California" (for Emily Malaga). [ColR] (21:2) Fall 94, p. 139.
"Water." [HayF] (15) Fall-Wint 94, p. 83.

6233. THOMPSON, Jeanie

"Just Sex." [Poem] (72) N 94, p. 41.
"Self-Portraits as Mother and Child." [Poem] (72) N 94, p. 42-43.

6234. THOMPSON, Jerry

"Work." [Zyzzyva] (10:4) Wint 94, p. 115.

6235. THOMPSON, Jim

"Bee's Head." [PoetryNW] (35:4) Wint 94-95, p. 39-40.

6236. THOMPSON, Karen

"Q & A: So you want to know what it means to be a dyke." [SinW] (52) Spr-Sum 94, p. 96-97.

6237. THOMPSON, Kate

"Land Rover." [TriQ] (91) Fall 94, p. 211.
"Teaboy." [TriQ] (91) Fall 94, p. 212.

6238. THOMPSON, Michael

"To Shit-Disturber Lövberg at the Dantobom Death-House, Written at Graveside" (Dedicated to Doctor Blad, tr. of Carl Michael Bellman). [Quarry] (43:1) Je 94, p. 44-45.
"On an Unexpected Farewell, Announced at Ulla Winblad's Breakfast One Summer Morning in the Country" (Pastoral Dedicated to Ryl. Secretary Leopold, tr. of Carl Michael Bellman). [Quarry] (43:1) Je 94, p. 46-48.
"To Ulla in the Window at Fiskartorp, about Noon, One Summer's Day" (Pastoral Dedic. to Herr Assessor Lunström, tr. of Carl Michael Bellman). [Quarry] (43:1) Je 94, p. 42-43.

6239. THOMPSON, Ricki

"Still Life: Turtle Sex." [Thrpny] (58) Sum 94, p. 14.

6240. THOMPSON, W. B.

"Nemerov." [WestHR] (48:1) Spr 94, p. 108.

6241. THOMPSON, William

"Bus." [Callaloo] (17:1) Wint 94, p. 190.

6242. THOMSEN, Søren Ulrik

"Untitled: To lose everything and carry it with you" (tr. by Susanna Nied). [GrandS] (12:4, #48) Wint 94, p. 28-29.

6243. THOMSON, Christopher

"Witching Hour." [SoCoast] (16) Ja 94, p. 20-21.

6244. THOMSON, David

"Misterioso" (after Monk). [NewEngR] (16:4) Fall 94, p. 162-163.
"Smoke Signs." [BellArk] (10:3 [i.e. 10:4]) Jl-Ag 94, p. 13.
"Variation on Mingus's *Sweet Sucker Dance*." [NewEngR] (16:4) Fall 94, p. 161-162.

6245. THORBURN, Russell

"Dubin, the Murderer." [Parting] (7:1) Sum 94, p. 71.
"The Ravine." [Parting] (7:1) Sum 94, p. 70.
"The Swiss Club." [Parting] (7:1) Sum 94, p. 70.

6246. THORNBURGH, Tim

"Sayonara Saipan" (Winner Marguerette Cummins Broadside Award. Composed in commemoration of the 50th anniversary of the battle for Saipan). [Amelia] (7:3, #22) 94, Supplement.

6247. THORNTON, Russell

"The Prophetess." [Event] (23:3) Wint 94-95, p. 71-72.

6248. THORPE, Allison

"Charity." [Poem] (72) N 94, p. 55-57.

6249. THRASHER, T.

"10-27-93" (for Renae). [Pearl] (20) Spr 94, p. 10.
"I see you've found it easy to leave." [Pearl] (20) Spr 94, p. 10.
"A love song means nothing to me." [Pearl] (20) Spr 94, p. 10.

THRETHEWEY, Eric
See TRETHEWEY, Eric
6250. THUMBOO, Edwin
"Father — 4." [MalR] (107) Sum 94, p. 201.
"The Visitor." [MalR] (107) Sum 94, p. 202-203.
6251. TIBBETTS, Frederick
"Before the Revolution." [Antaeus] (73/74) Spr 94, p. 156-157.
"Descending Ode." [OhioR] (52) 94, p. 78.
"Dissonant Interval." [ParisR] (36:133) Wint 94, p. 130.
"Etrurian Gates." [DenQ] (29:1) Sum 94, p. 42.
"First Persons." [AntR] (52:4) Fall 94, p. 604-605.
"The Great Gate of Kiev." [NewRep] (210:9) 28 F 94, p. 44.
"The Logic of Hegel" (For Peter Middleton). [SenR] (24:1) Spr 94, p. 21-22.
"Pyotr and the Wolf." [SenR] (24:1) Spr 94, p. 17-18.
"Venetian Ode." [Salm] (104/105) Fall 94-Wint 95, p. 170-171.
"War Sonata." [SenR] (24:1) Spr 94, p. 19-20.
6252. TIERNEY, Karl
"Jinx." [Colum] (22) Wint 94, p. 141.
"Mission Dolores." [Colum] (21) Fall 93, p. 113-114.
6253. TIFFANY, Monica
"For Teachers' Throats." [EngJ] (83:8) D 94, p. 46.
6254. TILLETT, Robert James
"At the Paradise Inn" (Effingham, Illinois). [PoetryNW] (35:2) Sum 94, p. 37-38.
"Gold in the Black Hills." [Border] (5) Fall-Wint 94, p. 65.
"Protected Land." [PoetryNW] (35:2) Sum 94, p. 37.
"Stone Fish." [Border] (5) Fall-Wint 94, p. 66.
"Stone Fish." [PoetryNW] (35:2) Sum 94, p. 36.
6255. TILLINGHAST, Richard
"The Adirondack." [Boulevard] (9:3, #27) Fall 94, p. 190.
"Afternoon at Griffin's." [Nat] (259:18) N 28 94, p. 660.
"An Elegist's Tour of Dublin." [SewanR] (102:2) Spr 94, p. 255-256.
"Hooded Crow and Speedwell." [NewRep] (210:23) 6 Je 94, p. 40.
"The Ornament." [SouthernR] (30:4) Aut 94, p. 714-715.
"Osman's Dream." [GettyR] (7:4) Aut 94, p. 668-669.
"Sighted in Belgrade." [GettyR] (7:4) Aut 94, p. 670.
6256. TIMAR, Josef
"As Caravaggio." [CanLit] (141) Sum 94, p. 35-36.
6257. TIMM, Steve
"After 39 Years." [RagMag] (12:1) Sum 94, p. 52-53.
"Do-It-Yourself." [SmPd] (31:3, #92) Fall 94, p. 13.
"From a Beach." [RagMag] (12:1) Sum 94, p. 55.
"Want, Part Fifteen." [RagMag] (12:1) Sum 94, p. 54.
6258. TIMS, Jane Spavold
"Appetites." [AntigR] (99) Aut 94, p. 97.
6259. TIUS, Mary M.
"Fools." [Light] (9) Spr 94, p. 13.
"The McTavity Test." [Light] (11) Aut 94, p. 22.
"Two Riddles." [Light] (12) Wint 94-95, p. 18.
6260. TOBE, Dorothy
"Crayola Jesus." [SouthernHR] (28:4) Fall 94, p. 333.
6261. TOBIN, Anne M.
"Midnight Train from Moscow" (First Sue Saniel Elkind National Poetry Award, Finalist). [Kalliope] (16:2) 94, p. 43.
6262. TOBIN, Daniel
"The Barber." [CumbPR] (13:2) Spr 94, p. 54-55.
"Five Exegetical Poems: A Palimpsest" (after Martin Buber). [CumbPR] (13:2) Spr 94, p. 56-59.
"Homage to Bosch." [Image] (8) Wint 94-95, p. 57-62.
"A Life Not Lived" (Summer 1980, for M. H.). [SouthernHR] (28:1) Wint 94, p. 45.
"Lycanthropy." [Confr] (54/55) Fall 94-Wint 95, p. 306-307.
"The Withness of the Body." [TampaR] (9) Fall 94, p. 10.
6263. TOBIN, Philip
"All This Time." [MidwQ] (35:4) Sum 94, p. 416-417.
6264. TOCA, Kay
"Mental Notes on No. 1463." [NewOR] (20:1/2) Spr-Sum 94, p. 90.
"Night Season." [NewOR] (20:1/2) Spr-Sum 94, p. 88.

"To Love and Listen." [NewOR] (20:1/2) Spr-Sum 94, p. 89.
"What Heaven Is." [NewOR] (20:1/2) Spr-Sum 94, p. 91.

6265. TODD, Harris
"A Tattered Flannel Shirt." [Wind] (73) 94, p. 30-31.

6266. TODD, J. C.
"Men Kissing." [ParisR] (36:132) Fall 94, p. 235-236.

6267. TOFER, Merle
"Jesus." [ChironR] (13:3) Aut 94, p. 31.

6268. TOHE, Laura
"Joe-Babes." [Callaloo] (17:1) Wint 94, p. 320-321.
"Snake Lover." [Callaloo] (17:1) Wint 94, p. 322-324.

6269. TOKUNO, Ken
"Incense." [BellArk] (10:3 [i.e. 10:4]) Jl-Ag 94, p. 7.

6270. TOLEK
"Say Cheese." [SlipS] (14) 94, p. 115.
"Young Winter." [Pearl] (20) Spr 94, p. 47.

6271. TOMCIC, Goran
"Benediction de Dieu Dans la Solitude." [Confr] (54/55) Fall 94-Wint 95, p. 287.
"By Nightfall." [Confr] (54/55) Fall 94-Wint 95, p. 288.
"The Fear." [Confr] (54/55) Fall 94-Wint 95, p. 286.
"Look! I'm Writing in English." [SenR] (24:2) Fall 94, p. 53.
"Suddenly." [SenR] (24:2) Fall 94, p. 54.
"Surrendering (No. 4)" (tr. by the author and Inex Modrcin). [SenR] (24:2) Fall 94, p. 55.
"To Be Alone." [SenR] (24:2) Fall 94, p. 56.

6272. TOMES, Marta
"Goshen Lane, Spring 1992." [Wind] (74) 94, p. 35.

6273. TOMIOKA, Akemi
"Ah, my pocketbook" (Tanka, tr. of Motoko Michiura, w. Miyuki Aoyama and Leza Lowitz). [Zyzzyva] (10:2) Sum 94, p. 61.
"My nipples still erect" (Tanka, tr. of Motoko Michiura, w. Miyuki Aoyama and Leza Lowitz). [Zyzzyva] (10:2) Sum 94, p. 61.
"Someday I'll turn to water" (Tanka, tr. of Motoko Michiura, w. Miyuki Aoyama and Leza Lowitz). [Zyzzyva] (10:2) Sum 94, p. 61.
"Tanka: Washing and combing" (tr. of Motoko Michiura, w. Leza Lowitz). [YellowS] (11:4, #44) Wint 93-94, p. 44.
"Whenever I see poppies" (Tanka, tr. of Motoko Michiura, w. Miyuki Aoyama and Leza Lowitz). [Zyzzyva] (10:2) Sum 94, p. 61.

6274. TOMIOKA, Taeko (b. 1935)
"Girl Friend" (tr. by Graeme Wilson). [Jacaranda] (5:1) Wint-Spr 91, p. 117.

6275. TOMLINSON, Charles
"Above the Rio Grande." [Hudson] (46:4) Wint 94, p. 734-735.
"Autumn." [Hudson] (47:2) Sum 94, p. 218.
"For a Granddaughter." [Hudson] (47:2) Sum 94, p. 213-216.
"Melville on the Acropolis" (for Vincent Scully). [ParisR] (36:132) Fall 94, p. 31.
"On the Late Plane." [Hudson] (47:2) Sum 94, p. 219.
"Roman Fugue." [PartR] (61:1) Wint 94, p. 152.
"The Shadow." [ParisR] (36:132) Fall 94, p. 30.
"To My Daughter." [Hudson] (47:2) Sum 94, p. 217.
"Transaction at Mallards Pike." [Hudson] (47:2) Sum 94, p. 217-218.
"Varenna." [PartR] (61:1) Wint 94, p. 151-152.

6276. TOMLINSON, Rawdon
"The Cabin at Elk Falls." [Quarry] (42:4) Mr 94, p. 86.
"Coyote Nights." [PoetC] (26:1) Fall 94, p. 29.
"Dance" (Geronimo). [WritersF] (20) 94, p. 218.
"Lightning Struck Pine." [Quarry] (42:4) Mr 94, p. 87.
"Repetition and Variation." [PoetC] (26:1) Fall 94, p. 30.
"Run-Off." [HolCrit] (31:1) F 94, p. 16-17.
"Sister's Drawings after Little Brother's Death, III." [LaurelR] (28:2) Sum 94, p. 48.
"Waiting at San Antonio, 1886" (Geronimo). [WritersF] (20) 94, p. 219.
"War Story Told in the Backyard on a Sunday Afternoon." [HiramPoR] (55/56) Fall 93-Sum 94, p. 115.

TOMOYUKI, Iino
See IINO, Tomoyuki

6277. TONETTO, Walter
"The Angler's Vacant Hook." [CentR] (38:2) Spr 94, p. 336.

"Concealment in Self" (tr. of Nicolae Sirius). [CentR] (38:2) Spr 94, p. 337.
"The White Century" (tr. of Nicolae Sirius). [CentR] (38:2) Spr 94, p. 338.

6278. TONG, Frank
"Elephants." [Quarry] (43:2) S 94, p. 45-46.
"Paper Bodies." [Quarry] (43:2) S 94, p. 43-44.

6279. TORRES, Eddie
"American Dream." [Callaloo] (17:1) Wint 94, p. 191-192.

6280. TORRES-GUZMAN, Esteban
"The River's Mouth." [Vis] (45) 94, p. 34.

6281. TORRESON, Rodney
"Jim Bouton: Unwriting." [NewYorkQ] (53) 94, p. 84-86.
"Trapped Muskrat." [Parting] (7:1) Sum 94, p. 63.

6282. TOSA, Motokiyu
"Autumn Grasses Renga" (tr. of Araki Yasusada, Ozaki Kusatao and Akutagawa Fusei, w. Ojiu Norinaga and Okura Kyojin). [Conjunc] (23) 94, p. 72-73.
"Dream and Charcoal" (tr. of Araki Yasusada, w. Ojiu Norinaga and Okura Kyojin). [Conjunc] (23) 94, p. 69-70.
"Geisha and Iris" (tr. of Araki Yasusada, w. Ojiu Norinaga and Okura Kyojin). [Conjunc] (23) 94, p. 70-71.
"Horsehide and Sunspot" (July 17, 1962, Hiroshima Municipal Stadium, tr. of Araki Yasusada, w. Ojiu Norinaga and Okura Kyojin). [Conjunc] (23) 94, p. 72.
"Sentences for Jack Spicer Renga" (tr. of Araki Yasusada and Akutagawa Fusei, w. Ojiu Norinaga and Okura Kyojin). [Conjunc] (23) 94, p. 75-76.
"Suitor Renga" (tr. of Araki Yasusada, Ozaki Kusatao and Akutagawa Fusei, w. Ojiu Norinaga and Okura Kyojin). [Conjunc] (23) 94, p. 74.
"Telescope with Urn" (tr. of Araki Yasusada, w. Ojiu Norinaga and Okura Kyojin). [Conjunc] (23) 94, p. 69.
"Untitled Haiku" (tr. of Araki Yasusada, w. Ojiu Norinaga and Okura Kyojin). [Conjunc] (23) 94, p. 71.
"Utterances and Hepatica" (tr. of Araki Yasusada, w. Ojiu Norinaga and Okura Kyojin). [Conjunc] (23) 94, p. 76-77.

6283. TOSTESON, Heather
"Epiphany." [SouthernPR] (34:1) Sum 94, p. 39.
"Reification" (for V). [Pequod] (37) 94, p. 75-82.

6284. TOSTEVIN, Lola Lemire
"Flesh, Song(e) et Promenade" (tr. of Nicole Brossard). [WestCL] (28:3, #15) Wint 94-95, p. 6-25.

6285. TOTA, Frank
"Celestina and the Vollard Suite" (After the engravings of Pablo Picasso). [CarolQ] (46:3) Sum 94, p. 71-72.
"The Last White Ship." [CarolQ] (46:3) Sum 94, p. 70.

TOV, S. Ben
See BEN-TOV, S.

6286. TOWLE, Tony
"Downtown Song." [HangL] (65) 94, p. 73-75.
"Storytelling." [Arshile] (3) 94, p. 30-38.

6287. TOWNER, Daniel
"At Serpent Mound." [DenQ] (28:4) Spr 94, p. 68.

6288. TOWNSEND, Ann
"At the Depot." [Crazy] (47) Wint 94, p. 55.
"The Baby Finds Her Hand." [Crazy] (47) Wint 94, p. 59.
"Cameo." [Crazy] (47) Wint 94, p. 56-57.
"Eighteenth-Century Medical Illustration: The Infant in Its Little Room." [NoAmR] (279:1) Ja-F 94, p. 19.
"From a Window." [Crazy] (47) Wint 94, p. 58.
"How It Hurts." [Nat] (259:11) O 10 94, p. 394.
"Trimmings." [Nat] (258:19) My 16 94, p. 674.

6289. TOWNSEND, Cheryl A.
"She Opened Her Blouse." [SlipS] (14) 94, p. 7.

6290. TOZEUR, Djanet
"Lessons on Foreign Languages in a Reeperbahn Cafe" (for Cordula). [SlipS] (14) 94, p. 115-117.

6291. TRABER, Mike
"The Ancestors." [Kaleid] (29) Sum-Fall 94, p. 37.
"Cruising." [Kaleid] (29) Sum-Fall 94, p. 37.

TRAC, Vu
See VU, Trac
6292. TRAD, Michel
"A Kiss" (tr. by Mansour Ajami). [LitR] (37:3) Spr 94, p. 526.
"Souvenir" (tr. by Mansour Ajami). [LitR] (37:3) Spr 94, p. 526.
"We Have a Cottage" (tr. by Mansour Ajami). [LitR] (37:3) Spr 94, p. 525.
6293. TRALE, Marianne McGinn
"Photograph of My Child." [GreenMR] (NS 17:2) Fall-Wint 94-95, p. 125.
6294. TRAN, Barbara
"Departure's Museum." [Pequod] (37) 94, p. 83.
TRAN, Ngoc Linh
See LINH, Tran Ngoc
6295. TRAN, Truong (Truong D.)
"1. Fork is used." [Zyzzyva] (10:2) Sum 94, p. 96.
"2. Bottle of beer." [Zyzzyva] (10:2) Sum 94, p. 96.
"3. Since California adopted the Lottery." [Zyzzyva] (10:2) Sum 94, p. 97.
"4. Eat an artichoke." [Zyzzyva] (10:2) Sum 94, p. 97.
"No Pictures No Sins." [Crazy] (47) Wint 94, p. 26-27.
"The Washing." [Crazy] (47) Wint 94, p. 28.
6296. TRANSTRÖMER, Tomas
"The Cuckoo" (tr. by Robert Bly). [Field] (50) Spr 94, p. 101.
"The Kingdom of Uncertainty" (tr. by Robert Bly). [Field] (50) Spr 94, p. 100.
"La Lugubre Gondola No. 2" (tr. by Joanna Bankier). [ParisR] (36:130) Spr 94, p. 236-238.
6297. TRANTER, John
"Decalcomania." [NewAW] (12) Spr-Sum 94, p. 44-46.
"The Duck Abandons Hollywood." [GrandS] (13:1, #49) Sum 94, p. 82.
"Pantoum: Amulet." [KenR] (NS 16:4) Fall 94, p. 61-62.
"Pantoum: The Morning After." [KenR] (NS 16:4) Fall 94, p. 62.
"Rimbaud in Sydney." [Verse] (11:1) Spr 94, p. 14.
"The Un-American Women." [GrandS] (13:1, #49) Sum 94, p. 81.
6298. TRASK, Haunani-Kay
"Chant of Lamentation." [Calyx] (15:2) Sum 94, p. 10-11.
"Ko'olau." [Callaloo] (17:1) Wint 94, p. 63.
"Refusal" (For K. W. class of '67, Kamehameha Schools). [Callaloo] (17:1) Wint 94, p. 65-67.
"Waikiki." [Calyx] (15:2) Sum 94, p. 8-9.
"You Will Be Undarkened." [Callaloo] (17:1) Wint 94, p. 64.
6299. TRAUNSTEIN, Russ
"Buck Starr Writes Agin'" (eina vestern phantasie-buchrevoo). [SoCoast] (16) Ja 94, p. 44-45.
"That's Amazing, Grace!" (for Peri Murdock). [Light] (9) Spr 94, p. 12.
"To a Chicken." [Light] (10) Sum 94, p. 9.
6300. TRAXLER, Patricia
"Confession." [KenR] (NS 16:1) Wint 94, p. 57-60.
"The Visit." [KenR] (NS 16:1) Wint 94, p. 60-61.
6301. TREDE, Meredith
"On Seeing an Ex-Husband on the Cheese Line of the Gourmet Grocery Store." [ParisR] (36:132) Fall 94, p. 132.
6302. TREFETHEN, Tracy
"An Anonymous Belgian Trio, 1920." [PaintedB] (53/54) 94, p. 46.
"Ars Poetica." [Quarry] (42:4) Mr 94, p. 15.
"Carnival." [Quarry] (42:4) Mr 94, p. 14.
"Elegy." [PaintedB] (53/54) 94, p. 47.
"Grounding." [Quarry] (42:4) Mr 94, p. 13.
"Still Life with the Tidal River Ouse" (for Virginia Woolf). [PaintedB] (53/54) 94, p. 48.
6303. TREGEBOV, Rhea
"The Big Picture." [Event] (23:2) Sum 94, p. 46.
"Confessional Poetry." [Event] (23:2) Sum 94, p. 44-45.
"Coquelicots." [PoetryC] (15:1) N 94, p. 25.
"Very Pretty." [Event] (23:2) Sum 94, p. 43.
"Whoever I Think I Am." [MalR] (108) Fall 94, p. 26-34.
6304. TREITEL, Renata
"Eclipse." [SoCoast] (17) Je 94, p. 36.
"Like the Bosom of an Artichoke." [CreamCR] (18:1) Spr 94, p. 51.

6305. TREMBLAY, Clarisse
"Behind the little woolly clouds the sky is writing its anguish" (tr. by Geoffrey Edwards). [InterPR] (20:2) Fall 94, p. 39.
"Derrière les petits nuages laineux le ciel écrit l'angoisse." [InterPR] (20:2) Fall 94, p. 38.
"I am a bloodthought pierced with rebellious dawns" (tr. by Geoffrey Edwards). [InterPR] (20:2) Fall 94, p. 39.
"Je suis une pensée de sang transpercée d'aubes." [InterPR] (20:2) Fall 94, p. 38.
6306. TREMMEL, Robert
"Fatherhood." [SouthernPR] (34:2) Wint 94, p. 11-12.
"Sunday Afternoon." [Border] (4) Spr-Sum 94, p. 68.
"Who Built My Neighbor's Shed, Then?" [NewDeltaR] (11:1) Fall 93-Wint 94, p. 59-60.
6307. TRENT, Luke
"Selecting a Statue in Your Father's Likeness." [HayF] (14) Spr-Sum 94, p. 71.
6308. TRESSLER, Clyde
"Maxine Recalls Singing for the Troops." [NewEngR] (16:4) Fall 94, p. 164-165.
6309. TRETHEWEY, Eric
"Blueberry." [PoetC] (25:3) Spr 94, p. 14-15.
"The Cellar." [NewRep] (210:17) 25 Ap 94, p. 40.
6310. TRIGGS, Jeffery Alan
"For Charlotte Elena, Age 10, January 2, 1993." [LitR] (37:4) Sum 94, p. 682.
6311. TRILLIN, Calvin
"Adieu, Justice Blackmun." [Nat] (258:17) My 2 94, p. 582.
"Adieu, Speaker Foley." [Nat] (259:19) D 5 94, p. 678.
"Airwave Pols." [Nat] (258:18) My 9 94, p. 618.
"An Attempt to Summarize the Latest 400,000 Words Written About Bill and Hillary Clinton." [Nat] (259:1) Jl 4 94, p. 6.
"A Cheer for an Exile's Return to Mother Russia." [Nat] (258:24) Je 20 94, p. 859.
"Christmas in Qatar" (A New Holiday Classic for Those Tiring of "White Christmas" and "Jingle Bells"). [NewYorker] (70:42) 19 D 94, p. 88.
"Cyberlament." [Nat] (259:9) S 26 94, p. 298.
"Dole, Cheney, Baker, Bennett, Kemp and Quayle." [Nat] (259:6) Ag 22-29 94, p. 186.
"Don't Whine Bill" (A Sing-along to the tune of that old standard "Don't Blame Me for Falling in Love with You"). [Nat] (259:3) Jl 18 94, p. 78.
"Empty Suit." [Nat] (259:15) N 7 94, p. 518.
"Extol Dole?" [Nat] (259:21) D 19 94, p. 750.
"Heat Wave, 1994." [Nat] (259:7) S 5-12 94, p. 222.
"Just How Do You Suppose That Alice Knows?" [NewYorker] (70:36) 7 N 94, p. 224.
"Knowing Nothing." [Nat] (259:16) N 14 94, p. 566.
"More Awful News." [Nat] (258:19) My 16 94, p. 654.
"A Note to Michael and Lisa Marie." [Nat] (259:22) D 26 94, p. 786.
"On Bruce E. Babbitt's Not Being Nominated to the Supreme Court." [Nat] (258:22) Je 6 94, p. 774.
"On Satanic Jews, As Seen in the Haldeman Diaries." [Nat] (258:23) Je 13 94, p. 822.
"On the Court's Latest 7-2 Reversal of a Death Penalty." [Nat] (259:2) Jl 11 94, p. 42.
"Pataki." [Nat] (259:17) N 21 94, p. 602.
"Peace Mission." [Nat] (259:14) O 31 94, p. 482.
"Reflections on the Congressional Testimony of Tobacco Company Executives." [Nat] (258:21) My 30 94, p. 738.
"A Short Conversation Encompassing All the News of the Day." [Nat] (259:4) Jl 25-Ag 1 94, p. 114.
"A Small Point Re the Nixon Homages." [Nat] (258:20) My 23 94, p. 690.
"Status Report on the President." [Nat] (259:10) O 3 94, p. 334.
"There's Always Paula Jones" (A She Shanty). [Nat] (259:5) Ag 8-15 94, p. 149.
"Thinking Back." [Nat] (259:8) S 19 94, p. 262.
"Third-Down-Long-Yardage Football." [Nat] (259:11) O 10 94, p. 370.
"Two Old Warriers." [Nat] (259:18) N 28 94, p. 638.
"Unless You're Newt." [Nat] (259:20) D 12 94, p. 715.
"A Virginia Republican Cheer For Oliver North." [Nat] (258:25) Je 27 94, p. 893.
6312. TRINIDAD, David
"It." [Colum] ("The Lost Issues", [i.e. 18-19]) 93, p. 127.

6313. TRIPATHY, Sunanda
"Poem in Motion" (tr. by Arlene Zide and J. P. Das). [InterQ] (1:2) 93, p. 186.
6314. TRIPLETT, Pimone
"On Giving Up the Child, a Dream." [NegC] (14:1/2) 94, p. 78-79.
"On Pattern." [CreamCR] (18:2) Fall 94, p. 170-171.
6315. TRITICA, John
"Improvisations with Lines by Charles Alexander." [Talisman] (12) Spr 94, p. 117-119.
"Residence in the High Desert" (Selection: 3). [Talisman] (13) Fall 94-Wint 95, p. 222-223.
"The Tune of Chance." [CentralP] (23) Spr 94, p. 130-131.
6316. TRIVELPIECE, Laurel
"Calling." [Amelia] (7:3, #22) 94, p. 138.
"The Nursery." [Witness] (8:1) 94, p. 84-85.
"White-Crowned Sparrows." [Witness] (8:1) 94, p. 85.
6317. TROPICANA, Carmelita
"Carnaval" (drama — a work in progress, w. Uzi Parnes). [MichQR] (33:4) Fall 94, p. 733-747.
6318. TROUPE, Quincy
"&, or And" (For Roberta Hill Whiteman & Miles Dewey Davis). [Eyeball] (3) 93, p. 46.
"The Architecture of Speech" (For Oliver Jackson, Allan Kornblum, Carolyn Holbrook-Montgomery & Lois Vosson). [Eyeball] (3) 93, p. 45.
6319. TROWBRIDGE, William
"The Band Director's Farewell." [Pivot] (42) 94, p. 24-25.
"Break." [SpoonR] (19:1) Wint-Spr 94, p. 20.
"Cinema des Beaux Arts." [TarRP] (34:1) Fall 94, p. 1.
"Dump Rats." [TarRP] (34:1) Fall 94, p. 2.
"Foxfire." [GettyR] (7:2) Spr 94, p. 262-264.
"Phantom Sleep." [ColR] (21:2) Fall 94, p. 154.
"Prayer." [NewL] (60:3) 94, p. 100.
"Rosebud." [NewL] (60:3) 94, p. 101.
"Scot-free." [Shen] (44:2) Sum 94, p. 110.
"Visit" (Georgetown Medical Center, 1991). [SpoonR] (19:1) Wint-Spr 94, p. 21-22.
"Why Astaire." [ColR] (21:2) Fall 94, p. 155.
6320. TRUDELL, Dennis
"Dushay's Friend." [ContextS] (4:1) 94, p. 29.
6321. TRUMBULL, Richard
"How to Bow." [Parting] (7:1) Sum 94, p. 72.
6322. TRUONG, Khiem
"Meditation." [HayF] (15) Fall-Wint 94, p. 106-107.
"Weather Vane." [HayF] (15) Fall-Wint 94, p. 104-105.
TRUONG, Tran
See TRAN, Truong
6323. TSINGOS, Nikolas
"Poems for Gwendolyn MacEwen" (8 poems, tr. by George Thaniel). [Descant] (24:4, #83) Wint 93-94, p. 41-52.
6324. TSIRIOTAKIS, Helen
"As Voices Stretch." [Quarry] (42:4) Mr 94, p. 108-109.
6325. TSVETAEVA, Marina
"At the curl of the eyelashes" (tr. by Nina Kossman). [PoetL] (89:3) Fall 94, p. 47.
"The Eyes" (tr. by Nina Kossman). [PoetL] (89:3) Fall 94, p. 45.
"In Memory of Berangé" (tr. by Nina Kossman). [PoetL] (89:3) Fall 94, p. 44.
"Slowly" (in Russian and English, tr. by Nina Kossman). [AntigR] (99) Aut 94, p. 50-51.
"Someone left, with a head" (tr. by Nina Kossman). [PoetL] (89:3) Fall 94, p. 43.
"To Genius" (in Russian and English, tr. by Nina Kossman). [AntigR] (99) Aut 94, p. 48-49.
"The Valley of the Roses" (tr. by Nina Kossman). [PoetL] (89:3) Fall 94, p. 46.
6326. TSVETAYEVA, Marina
"My Veins Slashed Open" (From "In the Inmost Hour of the Soul," tr. by Nina Kossman). [AmerPoR] (23:6) N-D 94, p. 38.
TU, Fu
See DU, Fu

6327. TUCKER, Jean
"Oil" (in the cafeteria of the night ferry Ariadne). [CumbPR] (13:2) Spr 94, p. 50-51.
"Other Places in Our Lives" (for Hans-Peter). [CumbPR] (13:2) Spr 94, p. 49.
6328. TUCKER, Leonore
"Yearning." [Obs] (9:1) Spr-Sum 94, p. 111.
6329. TUCKER, Martin
"Alfred Whole." [Confr] (54/55) Fall 94-Wint 95, p. 331.
6330. TUCKER, Memye Curtis
"The Mentalist." [ColR] (21:2) Fall 94, p. 156-157.
6331. TUÉNI, Nadia
"Balamand" (tr. by Samuel Hazo). [LitR] (37:3) Spr 94, p. 529.
"Beirut" (tr. by Samuel Hazo). [LitR] (37:3) Spr 94, p. 527-528.
"A Beirut Summer Day" (tr. by the author). [LitR] (37:3) Spr 94, p. 530.
"Beit-Eddine" (tr. by Samuel Hazo). [LitR] (37:3) Spr 94, p. 528-529.
"In the Lebanese Mountains" (tr. by Samuel Hazo). [LitR] (37:3) Spr 94, p. 528.
"It's Man's Fate" (tr. by friends). [LitR] (37:3) Spr 94, p. 529-530.
6332. TUFTS, Carol
"Hades and Persephone." [Poetry] (165:1) O 94, p. 3.
"Thinking About American Communists, 1992" (for Eugene and Peggy Dennis). [MinnR] (41/42) Fall 93-Spr 94 (published Mr 95), p. 18.
6333. TULLY, John
"House Is a Language." [ChrC] (111:5) 16 F 94, p. 168.
6334. TUPAN, Maria-Ana
"Curtsy" (tr. of Daniela Crasnaru, w. Adam J. Sorkin). [PraS] (68:1) Spr 94, p. 68.
6335. TURCO, Lewis (Lewis Putnam)
"Deja-Vu" (On four lines by Vern Rutsala). [NewYorkQ] (53) 94, p. 61.
"Jason Pullen, 1920-1943." [HampSPR] Wint 94, p. 45.
"Jeremy Carr, 1840-1861." [HampSPR] Wint 94, p. 44.
" *Parturiphobia*: The Fear of Childbirth." [CreamCR] (18:2) Fall 94, p. 126.
6336. TURNBULL, Gael
"Dry Leaves." [Stand] (36:1) Wint 94-95, p. 45.
"Estuaries" (9 selections). [Sulfur] (34) Spr 94, p. 59-62.
"An Oran (The Song)." [Stand] (36:1) Wint 94-95, p. 46.
"Wedding Anniversary Thought in Terms of a Raku Firing." [Stand] (36:1) Wint 94-95, p. 46.
"Whin." [Stand] (36:1) Wint 94-95, p. 46.
6337. TURNER, Barbara Murray
"Lone Mountain Haiku." [WorldO] (25:4) Sum 94, p. 62.
6338. TURNER, Daniel Drew
"Where I Live / Stream." [SantaBR] (2:2) Fall-Wint 94, p. 140.
"Wind, Sun, Moon." [SantaBR] (2:2) Fall-Wint 94, p. 141.
6339. TURNER, Gordon
"Rough Edges." [Event] (23:1) Spr 94, p. 36-37.
6340. TURNER, Jacqueline
"Language (Skin) Scrapes" (w. R. Rickey). [WestCL] (28:1/2, #13/14) Spr-Fall 94, p. 258-261.
6341. TURPIN, Mark
"Aubade." [Agni] (40) 94, p. 133.
"The Box." [BostonR] (19:3/4) Je-S 94, p. 22.
"In Winter." [BostonR] (19:3/4) Je-S 94, p. 22.
"Last Hired." [Agni] (40) 94, p. 131-132.
"Photograph from Antietam" (— "Dead Confederate Soldier," Gardner, Catalog #554). [BostonR] (19:3/4) Je-S 94, p. 22.
"Pickwork." [BostonR] (19:3/4) Je-S 94, p. 22.
"Shithouse." [Agni] (40) 94, p. 134.
"Shithouse." [BostonR] (19:3/4) Je-S 94, p. 22.
"Will Turpin b. 1987." [BostonR] (19:3/4) Je-S 94, p. 22.
6342. TUTOR, Bobby
"I will have entered and you will have seen." [GrahamHR] (18) Wint 94-95, p. 79.
6343. TUZMAN, Ani
"Thumbnail Sketch." [Calyx] (15:3) Wint 94-95, p. 34.
6344. TWAIN, Mark
"Those Annual Bills" (A parody on "those Evening Bells" by Thomas Moore). [Light] (9) Spr 94, p. 22.

6345. TWICHELL, Chase
"The City in the Lilac." [YaleR] (82:4) O 94, p. 75-77.
"Corporate Geese." [BlackWR] (20:2) Spr-Sum 94, p. 75-77.
"The Ghost of Eden" (Selections: 3 poems). [OntR] (41) Fall-Wint 94, p. 19-29.
"Recorded Birds." [Antaeus] (75/76) Aut 94, p. 325-326.
6346. TWITCHELL, Jeff
"Monument" (tr. of Qiu Zhenzhong, w. Qiu Qi). [Talisman] (12) Spr 94, p. 180.
"Scene" (tr. of Qiu Zhenzhong, w. Qiu Qi). [Talisman] (12) Spr 94, p. 179.
"Sound of the Universe" (tr. of Qiu Zhenzhong, w. Qiu Qi). [Talisman] (12) Spr 94, p. 179.
6347. TWITTY, Anne
"Islandia" (Selections: I-VI, tr. of María Negroni). [ParisR] (36:130) Spr 94, p. 152-155.
6348. TYUTCHEV, Fyodor Ivanovich
"Silentium" (tr. by Bernard S. Mikofsky). [Talisman] (12) Spr 94, p. 197.

6349. U, Sam Oeur
"Autocriticism Meeting (1987)" (tr. by the author and Ken McCullough). [Manoa] (6:2) Wint 94, p. 129-130.
"Dream After Composing the Appeal of the Cambodian League for Freedom and Democracy" (for Rose Rutherford, tr. by Ken McCullough). [ArtfulD] (26/27) 94, p. 38.
"Exodus" (tr. by the author and Ken McCullough). [Manoa] (6:2) Wint 94, p. 125.
"I Try to Survive Only for the Nation" (tr. by the author and Ken McCullough). [Manoa] (6:2) Wint 94, p. 130-131.
"My Invisible Sisters and Death by Execution" (tr. by the author and Ken McCullough). [Manoa] (6:2) Wint 94, p. 126-129.
"Sacred Vows" (for Michael Dennis Browne, tr. by Ken McCullough). [ArtfulD] (26/27) 94, p. 35-37.
"Searching for Dad" (March 1979, for Lorraine Ciancio, tr. by Ken McCullough). [ArtfulD] (26/27) 94, p. 39-40.
6350. UBA, Umaru
"The Crude Farmer." [Paint] (21) Aut 94, p. 120.
6351. UDALL, Jay
"Accidents of Survival." [BellArk] (10:6) N-D 94, p. 25.
"Baptism." [BellArk] (10:1) Ja-F 94, p. 22.
"Beautiful Confusion." [BellArk] (10:5) S-O 94, p. 23.
"The Gift Given." [BellArk] (10:6) N-D 94, p. 25.
"Going." [BellArk] (10:5) S-O 94, p. 25.
"He Contemplates Having Children." [BellArk] (10:6) N-D 94, p. 25.
"Heading Out." [BellArk] (10:5) S-O 94, p. 23.
"Homecoming." [BellArk] (10:6) N-D 94, p. 25.
"In Winter." [BellArk] (10:3) My-Je 94, p. 9.
"Listen" (in memory of Wallace Stevens). [BellArk] (10:1) Ja-F 94, p. 22.
"Messages." [BellArk] (10:3) My-Je 94, p. 8.
"My Mother-in-Law at the Grand Canyon." [BellArk] (10:1) Ja-F 94, p. 22.
"Parting Words." [BellArk] (10:5) S-O 94, p. 23.
"People Are Not Ideas." [BellArk] (10:1) Ja-F 94, p. 22.
"Pilgrimage." [BellArk] (10:1) Ja-F 94, p. 22.
"Preparation." [BellArk] (10:1) Ja-F 94, p. 22.
"Song to Emptiness." [BellArk] (10:1) Ja-F 94, p. 22.
"To an Egg Roll Disappeared." [BellArk] (10:3 [i.e. 10:4]) Jl-Ag 94, p. 26.
"Trails" (A Short History). [BellArk] (10:6) N-D 94, p. 25.
6352. UKRAINETZ, Elizabeth
"Bygones." [Quarry] (43:2) S 94, p. 80.
6353. ULLMAN, Leslie
"Black Onyx." [Pequod] (37) 94, p. 84-85.
"Night Trade." [Pequod] (37) 94, p. 90.
"Visitations." [Pequod] (37) 94, p. 86-89.
6354. ULLRICH, David
"Old Moons, Artifacts, and Dreams." [NegC] (14:1/2) 94, p. 98.
"Phases of the Moon" (Father and Daughter). [NegC] (14:1/2) 94, p. 97.
6355. ULMER, James
"Crossing." [Border] (4) Spr-Sum 94, p. 69-70.
"On the Estuary." [Crazy] (47) Wint 94, p. 20-21.

"White Connecticut Fences." [Border] (4) Spr-Sum 94, p. 71-72.

6356. ULMER, Spring

"Touch girl and your cheeks." [Chain] (1) Spr-Sum 94, p. 160-161.

6357. UNGAR, Barbara Louise

"Magic Carpet Edition" (from *The Book of Knowledge*). [GlobalCR] (4) Fall 94, p. 29.

6358. UNGARETTI, Giuseppe

"1914-1915" (Excerpt, tr. by John Rodenbeck). [Iowa] (24:1) Wint 94, p. 164.
"First Love" (tr. by John Rodenbeck). [Iowa] (24:1) Wint 94, p. 163-164.
"Phase" (Mariano, 25 June 1916, tr. by John Rodenbeck). [Iowa] (24:1) Wint 94, p. 163.

6359. UNGER, Barbara

"Hatsuko Unpacks the Dolls." [NewDeltaR] (11:2) Spr-Sum 94, p. 20-21.

6360. UNGER, David

"This Is My City" (tr. of Sonia Chocrón). [Trans] (29) Spr 94, p. 179.
"Through the Streets" (tr. of Sonia Chocrón). [Trans] (29) Spr 94, p. 179.

6361. UNRAU, John

"Bereavement." [NewRena] (9:1, #27) 94, p. 123.
"Brother Dryhthelm of Melrose" (Ecclesiastical History of England, Book 5, Chapter 12). [NewRena] (9:1, #27) 94, p. 124-125.

6362. UPDIKE, John

"61 and 2/3." [Poetry] (164:5) Ag 94, p. 261.
"Compliment." [Poetry] (164:5) Ag 94, p. 260.
"Down Time." [Poetry] (164:5) Ag 94, p. 259.
"In the Cemetery High Above Shillington." [OntR] (40) Spr-Sum 94, p. 24-29.
"New York City." [NewRep] (211:8/9) 22-29 Ag 94, p. 44.
"Not Cancelled Yet." [Poetry] (164:5) Ag 94, p. 261.

6363. UPTON, Lee

"The Arrest of Christ in the Book of Kells." [Field] (50) Spr 94, p. 87.
"Beatrix Potter." [Field] (50) Spr 94, p. 85.
"Dorothy in Exile." [Field] (50) Spr 94, p. 86.
"A Familiar Woman." [CreamCR] (18:2) Fall 94, p. 164-165.
"Herb Gatherers Off I-80." [BlackWR] (20:2) Spr-Sum 94, p. 28.
"The Hysteric's Divan." [Journal] (18:1) Spr-Sum 94, p. 39.
"The Rip in the Tapestry." [HayF] (15) Fall-Wint 94, p. 53.
"The Scarlet Letter." [Field] (50) Spr 94, p. 84.
"Tattoo of the New World." [Journal] (18:1) Spr-Sum 94, p. 38.
"Translation into a New Tongue." [Journal] (18:1) Spr-Sum 94, p. 40.
"The Wanderers." [Field] (50) Spr 94, p. 83.

6364. URBANUS, Andrew

"Slice of the American Pie." [ChironR] (13:4) Wint 94, p. 24.

6365. URSU, Liliana

"About Sacrifice" (tr. by Bruce Weigl). [AmerPoR] (23:2) Mr-Ap 94, p. 15.
"Bison Hunting" (tr. by Adam J. Sorkin and the author). [Vis] (46) 94, p. 38.
"Couple" (tr. by Adam J. Sorkin, w. the author). [Vis] (44) 94, p. 11.
"Depression Before the Equinox (or: Words for the Portraits of Poets Dreamed by Jan Cordua)" (tr. by Bruce Weigl). [AmerPoR] (23:2) Mr-Ap 94, p. 14.
"Double Portrait" (tr. by Adam J. Sorkin and the author). [Vis] (46) 94, p. 38.
"Eating Blackberries in a February Night" (tr. by the author and Bruce Weigl). [PoetL] (89:1) Spr 94, p. 33.
"Forma Mentis" (tr. of Ion Mircea, w. Adam J. Sorkin). [NewEngR] (16:1) Wint 94, p. 116.
"Heart Washed Like a Brain, Europe for Sale" (tr. by the author and Bruce Weigl). [WilliamMR] (32) 94, p. 74-75.
"Memories from the Arc in the Mountains" (tr. by the author and Bruce Weigl). [PoetL] (89:1) Spr 94, p. 34.
"The Mistaken Road" (tr. by Bruce Weigl). [AmerPoR] (23:2) Mr-Ap 94, p. 13.
"The Mold" (tr. of Ion Mircea, w. Adam J. Sorkin). [NewEngR] (16:1) Wint 94, p. 115.
"Moment with Thunder" (for Tess, tr. by Tess Gallagher, w. the poet). [Kalliope] (16:2) 94, p. 68.
"The Music Room" (tr. by Brenda Walker). [PoetryC] (14:4) S 94, p. 20.
"My Body" (tr. by Bruce Weigl). [QW] (38) Winter-Spr 93-94, p. 114.
"Poets' Corner" (tr. by Brenda Walker). [PoetryC] (14:4) S 94, p. 20.
"Prayer for Brother Alexander" (tr. by Bruce Weigl). [AmerPoR] (23:2) Mr-Ap 94, p. 15.

"Prelude" (for Sylvia Plath, tr. by the author and Bruce Weigl). [PoetL] (89:1) Spr 94, p. 35.
"Ruins of the Monastery at Cirtisoara" (tr. by Bruce Weigl). [AmerPoR] (23:2) Mr-Ap 94, p. 14.
"S.F." (tr. of Ion Mircea, w. Adam J. Sorkin). [NewEngR] (16:1) Wint 94, p. 115-116.
"Silent Voices" (For Cella Delavrancea and Gabriela Melinescu, tr. by Adam J. Sorkin. w. the poet). [Kalliope] (16:2) 94, p. 66-67.
"Society of Consumers" (tr. by Bruce Weigl). [AmerPoR] (23:2) Mr-Ap 94, p. 14.
"Window Cut into White Pine" (in memory of Ezra Pound, tr. by Bruce Weigl). [QW] (38) Winter-Spr 93-94, p. 115.
"With One Eye We Cry, with the Other We Laugh" (tr. by Adam Sorkin). [Vis] (45) 94, p. 36.

6366. USCHUK, Pamela
"Finding Peaches in the Desert." [AmerV] (33) 94, p. 125-126.

6367. UTLEY, Constance
"Rook's Creek." [AnthNEW] (6) 94, p. 25.

6368. UYEMATSU, Amy
"Mother's Day Poem to Myself." [BambooR] (63/64) Sum-Fall 94, p. 46.
"Prospect Avenue." [Pivot] (42) 94, p. 11.

6369. VAICIUNAITE, Judita
"Jasmine Bush" (tr. by Viktoria Skrupskelis and Stuart Friebert). [Field] (51) Fall 94, p. 64.
"Still Life with Window Frosted Over" (tr. by Viktoria Skrupskelis and Stuart Friebert). [Field] (51) Fall 94, p. 65.

6370. VALDÉS, Grisel
"Isla Negra." [LindLM] (13:1) Mr 94, p. 10.

6371. VALDÉS-GINEBRA, Arminda
"Renuevo tras la Lluvia Equilibrio del Ansia" (Premio Agustín Acosta de Poesía 1992. Selections: 3 poems, in Spanish and English, tr. by Veronica Miranda). [Luz] (6) My 94, p. 20-26.

6372. VALENTE, Lynn Manning
"Ozone." [AnthNEW] (6) 94, p. 16.

6373. VALENTE, Peter
"After Spicer." [Talisman] (13) Fall 94-Wint 95, p. 219.

6374. VALENTINE, Jean
"The Angel." [AmerPoR] (23:3) My-Je 94, p. 47.
"Bees." [AmerPoR] (23:3) My-Je 94, p. 47.
"Green for the Land." [NewYorker] (70:3) 7 Mr 94, p. 71.
"Home." [NewYorker] (70:16) 6 Je 94, p. 66.
"Red for Blood." [Field] (50) Spr 94, p. 20.
"We Don't Even Know We're Born." [AmerPoR] (23:3) My-Je 94, p. 47.

6375. VALERIO, R. D.
"Assemble These Bones." [WormR] (34:3, #135) 94, p. 101-102.
"Conspiracy Theory Number 27." [WormR] (34:3, #135) 94, p. 102.
"Horizon." [CapeR] (29:2) Fall 94, p. 38.
"Old Habits." [WormR] (34:3, #135) 94, p. 101.
"To Be Broken Is the Destiny of Glass." [WormR] (34:3, #135) 94, p. 102-103.

6376. VALERO, Roberto
"As If in a Game" (tr. by Francisco Soto). [MichQR] (33:4) Fall 94, p. 655.
"Heyoehkah." [Nuez] (5:13/14/15) 94, p. 36.
"Recordando a San Francisco de Asís" (Umbría 1182-1226). [Nuez] (5:13/14/15) 94, p. 36.
"Tu Imagen y Semejanza." [Nuez] (5:13/14/15) 94, p. 36.

6377. VALÉRY, Paul
"Helen" (tr. by Rachel Hadas). [HarvardR] (6) Spr 94, p. 143.

6378. VALLÉE, Lillian
"Window" (tr. of Czeslaw Milosz, w. the author). [NewEngR] (16:3) Sum 94, p. 23.

6379. VALLEJO, Cesar
"Circa 1926" (tr. by Clayton Eshleman, w. Jorge Guzmán). [PartR] (61:4) Fall 94, p. 635-636.

6380. VALLONE, Antonio
"Still Life." [Border] (3) Fall 93, p. 75-76.

6381. Van ARKEL, Jo
"The Art of Giving." [ContextS] (4:1) 94, p. 17.
6382. Van BEEK, Edith
"Desecrations (Lamentations)." [Event] (23:1) Spr 94, p. 43.
6383. Van BRUNT, Lloyd
"Baby Doll." [DarkMoon] (1) 94, p. 62-63.
"Bobcat." [DarkMoon] (1) 94, p. 61.
"China Blue" (for Laura). [DarkMoon] (1) 94, p. 66.
"Untitled: I want the stillness of snow in woods." [DarkMoon] (1) 94, p. 59-60.
"Weighing the Balance." [DarkMoon] (1) 94, p. 64-65.
Van DAALEN, Maria
See DAALEN, Maria van
Van den BEUKEL, Karlien
See BEUKEL, Karlien van den
6384. Van GERVEN, Claudia
"Beauty Considers Her Homelife." [PraS] (68:1) Spr 94, p. 105-106.
"Dear Anger." [PraS] (68:1) Spr 94, p. 108.
"Faith Sings." [PraS] (68:1) Spr 94, p. 106-107.
6385. Van NOORD, Barbara
"A Day in April." [AmerS] (63:3) Sum 94, p. 400-401.
"In Memoriam: Remind Me of Mercy." [SpoonR] (19:1) Wint-Spr 94, p. 47.
6386. Van PEENEN, H. J.
"Candelilla." [BellArk] (10:5) S-O 94, p. 29.
"Doing Post-Mortems" (San Francisco General Hospital, 1957). [BellArk] (10:6) N-D 94, p. 23.
"Prehistory on a Cliff." [BellArk] (10:5) S-O 94, p. 29.
"Salsipuedes Canyon" (Salsipuedes means "get out if you can"). [BellArk] (10:5) S-O 94, p. 29.
Van SCHLUN, Betsy
See SCHLUN, Betsy van
6387. Van WALLEGHEN, Michael
"Beauty." [CimR] (108) Jl 94, p. 78-80.
"Garage." [CimR] (108) Jl 94, p. 77-78.
"Tools and Provisions." [CimR] (108) Jl 94, p. 75-76.
6388. Van WINCKEL, Nance
"Aubade on Pacifico Bluffs." [QW] (38) Winter-Spr 93-94, p. 98.
"Coincidentally." [PoetryNW] (35:3) Aut 94, p. 28-29.
"Help, Help!" [NewEngR] (16:1) Wint 94, p. 21.
"Here's Hoping for One More Snow." [HighP] (9:2) Ag 94, p. 106-107.
"His Hands Were Empty, Mine Were Full." [BlackWR] (21:1) Fall-Wint 94, p. 19.
"I Forget Myself." [QW] (38) Winter-Spr 93-94, p. 99-100.
"Injunction." [SouthernR] (30:2) Ap, Spr 94, p. 328-329.
"Last Trip to Balfour." [DenQ] (29:1) Sum 94, p. 43.
"Nothing in the World." [NewEngR] (16:1) Wint 94, p. 20.
"What Are You Looking At?" [NowestR] (32:3) 94, p. 26-27.
6389. Van ZANT, Frank
"To the Man in Isolation Slapping Baloney on His Head, Nassau County Correctional Facility, East Meadow, NY 5/18/94." [ProseP] (3) 94, p. 81-82.
VANBRUNT, Lloyd
See Van BRUNT, Lloyd
6390. VANCE, Bob
"Dozens of Green Frogs Flip Away from My Feet." [HiramPoR] (57) Fall 94-Wint 95, p. 58.
VanDAALEN, Maria
See DAALEN, Maria van
6391. Vande ZANDE, Jeff
"Sometimes, When I See." [Wind] (74) 94, p. 38.
VANDER . . .
See also names beginning with "Vander" without the following space, filed below in their alphabetic positions, e.g. VanderMOLEN.
6392. Vander WAL, Jane Aaron
"After He Left We Bought His Chair from the Restaurant." [PoetryC] (15:1) N 94, p. 17.
"Bill Eaves." [AntigR] (99) Aut 94, p. 9-10.
"Leak." [AntigR] (99) Aut 94, p. 7-8.
"Neighbors — a True Story." [PoetryC] (15:1) N 94, p. 17.

"A Portrait." [PoetryC] (15:1) N 94, p. 17.
"Wild Animals' Teeth Dissolve Like That." [AntigR] (99) Aut 94, p. 11.
6393. VANDERLIP, Brian
"Modern Religion." [PraF] (15:1, #66) Spr 94, p. 117.
"Sunday School." [PraF] (15:1, #66) Spr 94, p. 116.
6394. VanderMOLEN, Robert
"Dune." [Epoch] (43:2) 94, p. 186-189.
VANDERWAL, Jane Aaron
See Vander WAL, Jane Aaron
6395. VANDO, Gloria
"Swallows of Salangan." [WestHR] (48:1) Spr 94, p. 106-107.
6396. VANEK, Mary
"Good Taste in a Crisis of Civility, Potlatch Creek." [IllinoisR] (2:1) Fall 94, p. 54.
6397. VANGELISTI, Paul
"Four Poems" (tr. of Amelia Rosselli, w. Lucia Re). [Chelsea] (57) 94, p. 79-81.
VANGERVEN, Claudia
See Van GERVEN, Claudia
VANNOORD, Barbara
See Van NOORD, Barbara
VANPEENEN, H. J.
See Van PEENEN, H. J.
VanSCHLUN, Betsy
See SCHLUN, Betsy van
VANWALLEGHEN, Michael
See Van WALLEGHEN, Michael
VANWINCKEL, Nance
See Van WINCKEL, Nance
VanZANT, Frank
See Van ZANT, Frank
6398. VARADY, Szabolcs
"Remembering My First Master" (tr. by Bruce Berlind and Mária Körösy). [SenR] (24:2) Fall 94, p. 60-61.
VARELA, Maria Elena Cruz
See CRUZ VARELA, Maria Elena
6399. VARGAS, Juan Carlos
"Topiary" (Zarcero, Costa Rica). [CaribbeanW] (8) 94, p. 25-26.
6400. VARNER, William
"The Inner Life." [GreenMR] (NS 17:2) Fall-Wint 94-95, p. 57.
"A Palmful of Evening." [GreenMR] (NS 17:2) Fall-Wint 94-95, p. 56.
6401. VARON, Jodi
"The Joys of Youth" (tr. of Li He). [Colum] (21) Fall 93, p. 82.
"A Song from Memory" (tr. of Li He). [Colum] (21) Fall 93, p. 81.
"Written Under Mt. Hua" (To the Tune: Throwing Off My Sadness, tr. of Li He). [Colum] (21) Fall 93, p. 79-80.
6402. VARON, Susan
"The House Was Quiet As an Alien Planet." [SoCoast] (17) Je 94, p. 19.
"Roxbury Flurry" (After a mobile by Alexander Calder). [SoCoast] (17) Je 94, p. 42-43.
6403. VASCONCELLOS, Cherry Jean
"End in Sight." [Pearl] (20) Spr 94, p. 8.
6404. VASQUEZ AGUILAR, Joaquín
"Family Portrait" (in memory of Old Emeterio, my father. Tr. by Reginald Gibbons and Ambar Past). [TriQ] (91) Fall 94, p. 154-155.
6405. VAUGHAN, Rachael
"Trade Wind." [Vis] (45) 94, p. 27.
6406. VAUGHN, Michael J.
"Henry Miller's Marshmallow Stick." [Elf] (4:4) Wint 94, p. 30.
6407. VAUSE, Mikel
"I've Always Feared Rattlesnakes." [WeberS] (11:1) Wint 94, p. 98.
6408. VAZIRANI, Reetika
"Housekeeping in the New World" (Maryland, 1969). [KenR] (NS 16:4) Fall 94, p. 86.
"In the War, 1966-67." [KenR] (NS 16:4) Fall 94, p. 85-86.
"The King's Doctor Attending to the Queen." [AmerV] (34) 94, p. 8.
"Mrs. Biswas Breaks Her Connection with Another Relative." [Agni] (39) 94, p. 121.

"Mrs. Biswas Remembers Mookherjee." [Nat] (258:19) My 16 94, p. 674.
"Postcards & Telegrams." [Nat] (259:1) Jl 4 94, p. 30.
"Rupa, at 14, upon Hearing the Poet from Bilaspur." [MalR] (108) Fall 94, p. 96.
"Underground" (Patiala, Punjab, 1966-67). [KenR] (NS 16:4) Fall 94, p. 84-85.

6409. VAZQUEZ-AMARAL, José
"Empire of Dreams" (tr. of Giannina Braschi, w. Tess O'Dwyer). [ApalQ] (40/41) 94, p. 49-53.

6410. VAZQUEZ DIAZ, René
"La Borrasca." [LindLM] (13:1) Mr 94, p. 3.
"Donde Se Pudre la Belleza." [LindLM] (13:1) Mr 94, p. 3.
"Homenaje." [LindLM] (13:1) Mr 94, p. 3.

6411. VEAZEY, Mary
"Crooked Man Blues: Two Conundrums." [Light] (12) Wint 94-95, p. 18.

6412. VECCHIONE, Glen
"Big Bands." [Jacaranda] (5:1) Wint-Spr 91, p. 28-29.

6413. VECERA, Grant
"Trout Creek, Utah (circa 1939)." [InterQ] (1:4) 94, p. 134.

6414. VEGA, Eduardo
"And He Became / Their Natural." [PlumR] (7) [94?], p. 6.

6415. VEGA, Janine Pommy
"Doorway." [HeavenB] (11) 94, p. 94.
"Island of the Sun." [HeavenB] (11) 94, p. 94.

6416. VEGRI, Sasa
"Women" (tr. by Dasha Culic Nisula). [InterQ] (1:1) [93?], p. 100.

6417. VEINBERG, Jon
"The Moth-Burning." [BlackWR] (20:2) Spr-Sum 94, p. 29-30.

6418. VENART, Sarah
"Rib." [AntigR] (97) Spr 94, p. 37.

VENDRELL, Luis Larios
See LARIOS VENDRELL, Luis

6419. VENIT, J. S.
"A Form of Telegram Cut from the Trees." [PartR] (61:4) Fall 94, p. 637-638.

6420. VERA, María Teresa
"Veinte Años" (Versos de N. Nuñez). [Areíto] (4:15) Marzo 94, p. 41.

6421. VERDECCHIA, Guillermo
"Building a House" (Grain Contest Winners, Prose Poem: Third). [Grain] (21:4) Spr 94, p. 18-19.

6422. VERMILYA, Miriam
"Heartwood." [NewEngR] (16:4) Fall 94, p. 91-92.

6423. VERONA, Dan
"The Herald's Ballad" (Excerpt, tr. by Adam J. Sorkin and Mihaela A. Irimia). [Vis] (46) 94, p. 30.

6424. VERTES, László
"I Surrender Myself" (tr. of Sándor Csoóri, w. Len Roberts). [NowestR] (32:2) 94, p. 28.
"If I Had Believed" (tr. of Sandor Csoori, w. Len Roberts). [AnotherCM] (28) 94, p. 32.

6425. VERTREACE, Martha M.
"At Le Bistro." [Kalliope] (16:3) 94, p. 58-59.
"Cyclogenesis." [Kalliope] (16:3) 94, p. 59-60.

6426. VESAAS, Tarjei
"Farther and Farther Away" (to a Writer, tr. by Roger Greenwald). [Pequod] (37) 94, p. 118.

6427. VIANT, William
"No Evil." [WillowS] (34) Sum 94, p. 37.

6428. VIENNA, Cris
"The Bad Life." [HangL] (65) 94, p. 101.
"Generals." [HangL] (65) 94, p. 101.

6429. VIERECK, Peter
"Pluto Incognito." [Boulevard] (9:1/2, #25/26) Spr 94, p. 175-185.

6430. VIGÉE, Claude
"The Idols of Terah" (tr. by Anthony Rudolf). [Stand] (35:4) Aut 94, p. 38-40.

6431. VIGIL, Mary Black
"The Tokens (Mittitur)" (tr. of anonymous poem from *Bodleian Latin Miscellany*, ca. 1500, w. John J. Brugaletta). [SoCoast] (16) Ja 94, p. 61.

6432. VIGIL-PIÑON, Evangelina
"Altamirano, Chiapas, México" (1 enero 1994). [Americas] (22:1/2) Spr-Sum 94, p. 101-103.
"India María." [Americas] (22:1/2) Spr-Sum 94, p. 100.
"Susto." [Americas] (22:1/2) Spr-Sum 94, p. 99.
"Tiempos Abandonados Cobbled and Dusty." [Americas] (22:1/2) Spr-Sum 94, p. 91-98.
6433. VILLAIRE, Louis A.
"La Esperanza." [ChangingM] (27) Wint 94, p. 72.
"Hope." [ChangingM] (27) Wint 94, p. 72.
"Tree of Heaven." [ChangingM] (27) Wint 94, p. 72.
6434. VILLANUEVA, Alma Luz
"Crazy Courage" (To Michael B.). [PraS] (68:4) Wint 94, p. 127-128.
6435. VILLANUEVA, Tino
"Jugábamos / We Played." [PraS] (68:4) Wint 94, p. 106-108.
6436. VILLEMAIRE, Yolande
"A Prayer to India" (tr. by Judith Cowan). [InterPR] (20:2) Fall 94, p. 93, 95.
"Prière Indienne." [InterPR] (20:2) Fall 94, p. 92, 94.
6437. VINCENT, Eleanor
"Maya's Bones." [SantaBR] (1:1) Spr-Sum 93, p. 59.
6438. VINCENTI, David F.
"I'm What Goes Bump in the Night (Again)" (for Lynda, rather than waking her up a third time). [Outbr] (25) 94, p. 75.
"Legacies" (in memory of Joseph Schneider — whose stories are still told — for Jim and the rest of the legacy). [Outbr] (25) 94, p. 76.
6439. VINOGRAD, Julia
"For a Young Man." [Art&Und] (3:1) Ap 94, p. 10.
"Listening to the Radio." [ChironR] (13:2) Sum 94, p. 6.
"Not Exactly the Way It Happened, But Close Enough." [ChironR] (13:2) Sum 94, p. 6.
"Praise." [Art&Und] (3:1) Ap 94, p. 10.
6440. VINZ, Mark
"Getting Used to the Water." [HighP] (9:1) Spr 94, p. 69-70.
"Learning to Read the X-Rays." [SoDakR] (32:4) Wint 94, p. 16.
"Return." [SoDakR] (32:4) Wint 94, p. 14-15.
"Tax Time." [HighP] (9:1) Spr 94, p. 68.
"Working Man." [HighP] (9:1) Spr 94, p. 71.
6441. VIRGIL
"The Gravid Mares" (from *Georgics*, tr. by David Slavitt). [NewEngR] (16:3) Sum 94, p. 28.
6442. VIRGILIO, Peter
"Dreamobile Francis Bacon I." [Ploughs] (20:4) Wint 94-95, p. 181.
"Dreamobile Joseph Cornell." [Ploughs] (20:4) Wint 94-95, p. 180.
6443. VITACCHIO, Alberto
"Alberto Vitacchio da Carabane West." [RagMag] (12:1) Sum 94, p. 34.
"The Counterpane." [RagMag] (12:1) Sum 94, p. 35.
"The Spouter-Inn." [RagMag] (12:1) Sum 94, p. 36.
6444. VITALE, Carlos
"Noción de Realidad" (Selections). [Luz] (7) N 94, p. 16-20.
"Notion of Reality" (Selections, tr. by Veronica Miranda). [Luz] (7) N 94, p. 17-20.
"Sombras Dibujadas" (tr. of Pietro Civitareale). [Luz] (7) N 94, p. 47-48.
VITO, E. B. de
See De VITO, E. B.
6445. VIVIEN, Renée
"To Those in Future Evenings" (tr. by Victoria Sweet). [PoetryE] (37/38) Spr 94, p. 222.
"You for Whom I've Written" (tr. by Victoria Sweet). [PoetryE] (37/38) Spr 94, p. 223.
6446. VLASOPOLOS, Anca
"Middle-Aged Crisis." [SpoonR] (19:1) Wint-Spr 94, p. 63.
6447. VOEGTLEN, Anne Reynolds
"Kit." [TriQ] (90) Spr-Sum 94, p. 169.
"Moonsnail and Cockle." [TriQ] (90) Spr-Sum 94, p. 168.
"Night Dive." [TriQ] (90) Spr-Sum 94, p. 167.
"Red Dahlias." [TriQ] (90) Spr-Sum 94, p. 166.

6448. VOGEL, Angela
"Southside Jersey." [CreamCR] (18:1) Spr 94, p. 58.
6449. VOGEL, Constance
"Elbow." [EngJ] (83:1) Ja 94, p. 90.
"Lines." [EngJ] (83:5) S 94, p. 64.
6450. VOGEL, Frank
"Why I'm Late." [Light] (11) Aut 94, p. 13.
6451. VOGELSANG, Arthur
"Arizona." [Zyzzyva] (10:1) Spr 94, p. 135.
"Days of '68, Dogs of Yore." [Jacaranda] (10) 94, p. 77.
"Empire." [AntR] (52:1) Wint 94, p. 79.
"Epic." [AntR] (52:1) Wint 94, p. 80.
"Forked." [AntR] (52:1) Wint 94, p. 81.
"Is It Him or Us?" [Jacaranda] (10) 94, p. 76.
"The Nose, the Grand Canyon, and the Sixties." [AntR] (52:1) Wint 94, p. 82.
6452. VOISINE, Connie
"Glass" (for R. Voisine). [Ploughs] (20:4) Wint 94-95, p. 183.
"Gretel and the Oven." [CreamCR] (18:1) Spr 94, p. 67.
"Hearing the Snow." [CreamCR] (18:1) Spr 94, p. 66.
"Hot." [Ploughs] (20:4) Wint 94-95, p. 182.
"Hungry." [Thrpny] (57) Spr 94, p. 29.
"The Miracle." [CreamCR] (18:1) Spr 94, p. 64-65.
"True Stories." [Ploughs] (20:4) Wint 94-95, p. 184.
6453. VOLBORTH, Judith Mtn. Leaf
"Rainmaker's Visit." [Callaloo] (17:1) Wint 94, p. 219.
6454. VOLDSETH, Beverly
"A Story." [RagMag] (12:1) Sum 94, p. 31.
6455. VOLKMAN, Karen
"From Shore." [Poetry] (164:5) Ag 94, p. 271.
"The Gold Book." [AmerPoR] (23:5) S-O 94, p. 47.
"Reflections." [WestHR] (48:2) Sum 94, p. 173.
6456. VOLLMER, Judith
"My Sublimation." [Witness] (8:2) 94, p. 58-59.
6457. VOLO, Alfonso
"Untitled: I am gazing at Edward Hicks'." [MoodySI] (28, also labeled 29) Fall 94, p. 16.
6458. Von HENDY, Gerry
"A Modern Crane." [WindO] (58) Sum 94, p. 24.
"The Prop." [WindO] (58) Sum 94, p. 22-23.
"Put Up Your Arms." [WindO] (58) Sum 94, p. 15.
"Say Nothing." [WindO] (58) Sum 94, p. 14.
"A Scrum by the Lincoln Memorial." [WindO] (58) Sum 94, p. 22.
"Tomatoes Remain in the Rain." [WindO] (58) Sum 94, p. 23.
"When the Winds Blow Wild." [WindO] (58) Sum 94, p. 16.
6459. VOSS, Fred
"The Front." [Pearl] (20) Spr 94, p. 53.
"Good Customer." [SlipS] (14) 94, p. 21.
"One of the Joys of the Job" (Secial Sections: 32 poems). [WormR] (34:4, #136) 94, p. 161-176.
"Silent Pictures." [Pearl] (20) Spr 94, p. 53.
6460. VRKLJAN, Irena
"A Quote from Russian Literature" (tr. by Dasha Culic Nisula). [InterQ] (1:1) [93?], p. 126-127.
6461. VU, Trac
"1975." [ModernW] (1) Summer 94, p. 43-44.
"Among Others." [ModernW] (1) Summer 94, p. 45.
"Honesty." [ModernW] (1) Summer 94, p. 46.

6462. W. T. K.
"Of Little Swallow" (for Siu Yin). [HiramPoR] (57) Fall 94-Wint 95, p. 36.
"Voice of the River." [HiramPoR] (57) Fall 94-Wint 95, p. 35.
6463. WACHMAN, Gay
"As Full of Sorrows As the Sea of Sands." [EvergreenC] (9:2) Sum-Fall 94, p. 82.
"Father." [FourQ] (8:2) Fall 94, p. 51.
"Guy Fawkes' Day." [EvergreenC] (9:2) Sum-Fall 94, p. 83.

6464. WACHTEL, Andrew
"Chinese Travelogue" (tr. of Olga Sedakova). [Conjunc] (23) 94, p. 9-20.
6465. WACHTEL, Chuck
"Again." [HangL] (64) 94, p. 73-74.
"The Chinchintora" (tr. of Manlio Argueta, from his collection *La Guerra Florida*). [HangL] (64) 94, p. 12-14.
"The Chronicler of the Indies, 1548" (tr. of Manlio Argueta, from his collection *La Guerra Florida*). [HangL] (64) 94, p. 8-9.
"Gentle Homeland" (tr. of Manlio Argueta, from his collection *La Guerra Florida*). [HangL] (64) 94, p. 10.
"Head-Hunters" (tr. of Manlio Argueta, from his collection *La Guerra Florida*). [HangL] (64) 94, p. 11.
"Her Husband, Standing Beside Her on the Platform of 125th Street Station, Holding Their Newborn Child ..., Points to the Conductor, Leaning Out the Window of an Incoming Train" (for Robin T.). [HangL] (65) 94, p. 76-78.
"A Horizon of Dogs" (tr. of Manlio Argueta). [Pequod] (37) 94, p. 125-126.
"My Country" (tr. of Manlio Argueta). [Pequod] (37) 94, p. 127.
"Our Love" (for Eileen). [HangL] (65) 94, p. 81.
"Sin Embargo." [HangL] (64) 94, p. 68-72.
"Supply Side." [HangL] (65) 94, p. 80.
"When the Dust Settled the Dow, Which Tracks Thirty of the Nation's Leading Companies, Was Down Nearly 4 Percent" (— New York Times, 11/16/91). [HangL] (65) 94, p. 79.
6466. WADE, Cheryl Marie
"She Says / He Says: Another Midnight Conversation." [Kaleid] (28) Wint-Spr 94, p. 34.
6467. WADE, Evelyn Amuedo
"From Bed to Worse." [Light] (12) Wint 94-95, p. 18.
6468. WADE, James
"Empty" (from the author's journal). [TickleAce] (28) Fall-Wint 94, p. 74.
"In darkness far away" (from the author's journal). [TickleAce] (28) Fall-Wint 94, p. 75.
6469. WADE, Seth
"Zen Goat." [DogRR] (26) Wint 94-95, p. 58-59.
6470. WADE, Sidney
"Catalogue Raisonné" (First Sue Saniel Elkind National Poetry Award, Finalist). [Kalliope] (16:2) 94, p. 44-45.
6471. WAGNER, Anneliese
"Black Soap." [WestB] (35) 94, p. 12.
"It Never Stops." [WestB] (35) 94, p. 13.
6472. WAGNER, Lynn
"White Blues." [PaintedB] (53/54) 94, p. 102.
6473. WAGNER, Maryfrances
"Saying Goodbye to the Children." [SingHM] (21) 94, p. 30.
6474. WAGNER, Shari
"His Silence." [HopewellR] (6) 94, p. 117.
6475. WAGONER, David
"Blindman." [Nat] (258:18) My 9 94, p. 638.
"Clancy the Burro's First Day in Heaven." [Poetry] (163:6) Mr 94, p. 326-327.
"For a Woman Who Phoned *Poetry Northwest*, Thinking It Was *Poultry Northwest*." [Poetry] (163:4) Ja 94, p. 213.
"Homecoming." [Poetry] (163:4) Ja 94, p. 212-213.
"Let Us Put You in Your Dream Car." [Poetry] (165:2) N 94, p. 72.
"Love Still Has Something of the Sea." [ParisR] (36:133) Wint 94, p. 113.
"My Mother and Father." [NewRep] (210:14) 4 Ap 94, p. 40.
"Taming a Bear." [Poetry] (163:6) Mr 94, p. 323-324.
"Vital Signs." [NewRep] (211:16) 17 O 94, p. 44.
"Walt Whitman Bathing." [YaleR] (82:4) O 94, p. 82-83.
"A Woman Photographing Holsteins." [Poetry] (163:6) Mr 94, p. 325.
6476. WAH, Fred
"Seasons Greetings from the Diamond Grill" (Excerpts). [CanLit] (140) Spr 94, p. 8-11.
WAI-LIM, Yip
See YIP, Wai-lim
6477. WAIDTLOW, Donna J.
"This Stone Holds a Dance." [ChamLR] (14/15) Spr-Fall 94, p. 6-7.

6478. WAINWRIGHT, J. A.
"Her Story." [AntigR] (99) Aut 94, p. 62-63.
"Solo at Perry Creek Falls." [AntigR] (99) Aut 94, p. 64.
"Young Charon" (for Christopher). [AntigR] (99) Aut 94, p. 65.
6479. WAKEFIELD, Kathleen
"On a Line by Rumi." [SouthernPR] (34:2) Wint 94, p. 43-44.
6480. WAKIDA, Patty
"Kenji's Pantoum." [SantaBR] (2:1) Spr-Sum 94, p. 94-95.
6481. WAKOSKI, Diane
"Emerald City." [Caliban] (14) 94, p. 32.
"Seeing the World Through Hopper's Glasses." [Caliban] (14) 94, p. 30-31.
WAL, Jane Aaron Vander
See Vander WAL, Jane Aaron
6482. WALDEN, Gale
"The Falling of Objects." [HarvardR] (2) Fall 92, p. 47-48.
6483. WALDEN, Gale R.
"The Archaeologist of Frank." [LaurelR] (28:2) Sum 94, p. 104.
6484. WALDEN, William
"Given Taken." [Light] (11) Aut 94, p. 12.
"In the Groove." [Light] (11) Aut 94, p. 10.
6485. WALDMAN, Anne
"Belated Transmission Request" (for Chogyam Trungpa, Rinpoche). [NewL] (60:4) 94, p. 128-131.
"IOVIS 2" (2 selections). [Talisman] (13) Fall 94-Wint 95, p. 79-103.
"So Help Me Sappho." [Chelsea] (57) 94, p. 71-72.
6486. WALDMAN, Ken
"40th Birthday" (for Kate Brown). [Border] (5) Fall-Wint 94, p. 67.
"Equinox Shopping." [PaintedHR] (11) Spr-Sum 94, p. 31.
"Fairbanks Cabin." [HighP] (9:2) Ag 94, p. 99.
"Frigidity." [Pearl] (20) Spr 94, p. 59.
"The Galax Sound" (for Bev, June, Rose, and Tara). [CapeR] (29:1) Spr 94, p. 42.
"The Genius." [DogRR] (26) Wint 94-95, p. 4.
"Hot Springs Road Trip." [PaintedHR] (11) Spr-Sum 94, p. 30.
"January Flight: Nome to Kotzebue." [SoDakR] (32:3) Fall 94, p. 45.
"Nome Magistrate" (for B. G.). [HighP] (9:2) Ag 94, p. 98.
"Red Lantern." [SoDakR] (32:4) Wint 94, p. 27-28.
"Swimmers." [Hellas] (5:1) Spr-Sum 94, p. 47.
"Tennis Without a Net." [TarRP] (33:2) Spr 94, p. 5.
"The Visitation." [SoDakR] (32:3) Fall 94, p. 46.
"Writing Class: the Correctional Center." [NewDeltaR] (11:1) Fall 93-Wint 94, p. 92.
6487. WALDNER, Liz
"Creation Story." [Iowa] (24:1) Wint 94, p. 188-189.
"The Gaiety That Is Being." [WashR] (20:3) O-N 94, p. 6.
"My Hand." [Iowa] (24:1) Wint 94, p. 189-190.
"The Night Your Father Is (H./er(r)e)." [WashR] (20:3) O-N 94, p. 7.
"Truth, Beauty, Tree." [DenQ] (29:2) Fall 94, p. 46.
"The Uses of Things." [DenQ] (29:2) Fall 94, p. 47.
6488. WALDROP, Jason
"Neglect." [Ploughs] (20:4) Wint 94-95, p. 185.
6489. WALDROP, Keith
"Faces" (tr. of Xue Di, w. Janet Tan). [Manoa] (6:1) Sum 94, p. 85-86.
"The Gleaner" (Van Gogh, *Peasant Woman Stooping*, 1885, tr. of Xue Di, w. Wang Ping). [Manoa] (6:1) Sum 94, p. 84-85.
"The House Seen From Nowhere" (Selections: 3 texts). [Avec] (8:1) 94, p. 58-60.
"Interplay" (tr. of Xue Di, w. Wang Ping). [Manoa] (6:1) Sum 94, p. 84.
"Memory Stand-Ins." [Avec] (8:1) 94, p. 55-57.
6490. WALDROP, Rosmarie
"Alexandrie, Boulevard de Ramleh, 1903" (tr. of Joachim Sartorius). [Conjunc] (23) 94, p. 137-138.
"Dante's Hell" (tr. of Edmond Jabès). [Avec] (7:1) 94, p. 141-147.
"Hoarfrostwatch" (tr. of Joachim Sartorius). [Conjunc] (23) 94, p. 138.
"It Is a Question." [Chelsea] (57) 94, p. 29.
"A Key into the Language of America" (Selections: Chapters XXII, XXVII-XXIX). [CentralP] (23) Spr 94, p. 148-151.
"The Kitchen" (tr. of Elke Erb). [WorldL] (5) 94, p. 11.

"Ruppiner Street" (tr. of Elke Erb). [WorldL] (5) 94, p. 11.
"'Shi,' or: The Invention of Writing" (for Per Aage Brandt). [Caliban] (14) 94, p. 14.
"To a Dolphin in Batumi" (tr. of Joachim Sartorius). [Conjunc] (23) 94, p. 140.
"Touch." [Chelsea] (57) 94, p. 28.
"Under the Colors of" (from *La pluralité des mondes de Lewis*, tr. of Jacques Roubaud). [CentralP] (23) Spr 94, p. 33-37.
"Visit" (tr. of Elke Erb). [WorldL] (5) 94, p. 10.
"Vivat, Crescat, Floreat!" (tr. of Elke Erb). [WorldL] (5) 94, p. 10.
"Voluntary Control." [Caliban] (14) 94, p. 15.
"With Each Cloudy Peak / Je Ein Umwölkter Gipfel" (Selections: 4 poems, tr. of Friederike Mayröcker). [Avec] (8:1) 94, p. 110-115.

6491. WALDSTEIN, Gail
"Gravity Slack Belly." [HighP] (9:1) Spr 94, p. 72-73.
"Visceral Pleasures" (for Margaret). [NegC] (14:1/2) 94, p. 163-164.

6492. WALEY, Arthur
"Alas and alas" (tr. of Cho Wen-chün). [NewYorkQ] (53) 94, p. 7.

6493. WALKER, Anne F.
"Dencity." [SantaBR] (1:1) Spr-Sum 93, p. 51.
"Fantastics." [SantaBR] (1:1) Spr-Sum 93, p. 51.

6494. WALKER, Brenda
"After the Fall" (tr. of Daniela Crasnaru). [PoetryC] (14:4) S 94, p. 22.
"The Arena" (tr. of Maria Banus). [PoetryC] (14:4) S 94, p. 24.
"At the Table" (To Sorin, tr. of Maria Banus). [PoetryC] (14:4) S 94, p. 24.
"Every Hope" (tr. of Virgil Mihaiu). [PoetryC] (14:4) S 94, p. 21.
"The Face of Smoke" (tr. of Carmen Firan). [PoetryC] (14:4) S 94, p. 23.
"The Family's Wednesday" (tr. of Danisa Comanescu). [PoetryC] (14:4) S 94, p. 23.
"I Know Him" (tr. of Virgil Mihaiu). [PoetryC] (14:4) S 94, p. 21.
"In Praise of the Month of April" (tr. of Daniela Crasnaru). [PoetryC] (14:4) S 94, p. 22.
"The Music Room" (tr. of Liliana Ursu). [PoetryC] (14:4) S 94, p. 20.
"The Only Shelter" (tr. of Ion Stoica). [PoetryC] (14:4) S 94, p. 21.
"Poets' Corner" (tr. of Liliana Ursu). [PoetryC] (14:4) S 94, p. 20.
"Separation" (tr. of Carmen Firan). [PoetryC] (14:4) S 94, p. 23.
"You Can Never Leave" (tr. of Ion Stoica). [PoetryC] (14:4) S 94, p. 21.

6495. WALKER, Dale
"The Sentencing." [WebR] (18) Fall 94, p. 64.

6496. WALKER, Del Casey
"The Eve of St. Agnes." [Amelia] (7:3, #22) 94, p. 93.

6497. WALKER, Jeanne Murray
"Cousin." [Image] (3) Spr 93, p. 39.
"Cutting." [WestB] (34) 94, p. 15-16.
"Expiation." [Pivot] (42) 94, p. 44.
"Looking for Ruby Earrings on Portobello Road." [Image] (3) Spr 93, p. 38.
"The Money Poem." [WestB] (34) 94, p. 14.
"Planetarium" (for Jack). [Image] (3) Spr 93, p. 37.
"Saving the Past." [Shen] (44:3) Fall 94, p. 56-59.
"The Taproom Bar." [Pivot] (41) 93, p. 6.
"Turnabout." [Pivot] (41) 93, p. 6-7.
"Why the Fiddler's Wife Is Thinking of Leaving Town." [Shen] (44:3) Fall 94, p. 54-55.
"Write About Something You Know." [WestB] (34) 94, p. 14-15.

6498. WALKER, Sue
"Foo-ra-de-ack-a-sa-ki — Have Some Seafood, Mama, in La Capitale Mondale de l'Ecrevisse." [ApalQ] (40/41) 94, p. 93.
"Speaking of Alexander" (Recounting Gossip & History). [SoCoast] (16) Ja 94, p. 53.

6499. WALKER, Victoria
"White Skin." [WestCL] (28:1/2, #13/14) Spr-Fall 94, p. 153.

6500. WALLACE, Anthony
"Poi Dog." [ChamLR] (14/15) Spr-Fall 94, p. 183.

6501. WALLACE, George
"I'll Take My Winters Cold." [Confr] (52/53) Wint-Spr 94, p. 336.

6502. WALLACE, Janet
"Autumnal" (from "Plenty." The Nimrod / Hardman Wards: Finalist). [Nimrod] (38:1) Fall-Wint 94, p. 79-80.

6503. WALLACE, Mark
"The Displaced Blizzard." [Talisman] (13) Fall 94-Wint 95, p. 224-228.
6504. WALLACE, Patricia
"Home from the Hospital." [NoDaQ] (62:4) Fall 94-95, p. 187-188.
6505. WALLACE, Rob
"Addition." [LouisL] (11:1) Spr 94, p. 185.
"The Peregrine Falcon" (at Overton Park Zoo, Memphis). [LouisL] (11:1) Spr 94, p. 184.
6506. WALLACE, Robert
"Creek." [PoetryNW] (35:1) Spr 94, p. 16-17.
"The Typewriter." [OhioR] (52) 94, p. 79.
6507. WALLACE, Ronald
"Career Day." [BlackWR] (21:1) Fall-Wint 94, p. 29.
"The Cup." [TampaR] (9) Fall 94, p. 37.
"Days Like This." [Hellas] (5:1) Spr-Sum 94, p. 91.
"The Drink." [IllinoisR] (1:2) Spr 94, p. 48.
"Hardware." [Poetry] (164:3) Je 94, p. 154.
"Hunger." [BlackWR] (21:1) Fall-Wint 94, p. 30.
"In Miniature." [TampaR] (9) Fall 94, p. 38.
"In the Cave." [Hellas] (5:1) Spr-Sum 94, p. 92.
"Man and Machine." [LaurelR] (28:1) Wint 94, p. 74-75.
"Masculine Endings." [PoetryNW] (35:4) Wint 94-95, p. 27.
"The McPoem." [PoetryNW] (35:4) Wint 94-95, p. 27.
"Saints." [LaurelR] (28:1) Wint 94, p. 75-76.
"The Story of New Zealand." [BlackWR] (21:1) Fall-Wint 94, p. 28.
6508. WALLACE-CRABBE, Chris
"Delivering Tact." [InterQ] (1:2) 93, p. 109.
"Glorying." [Verse] (11:2) Sum 94, p. 88.
WALLEGHEN, Michael van
See Van WALLEGHEN, Michael
6509. WALLER, Margaret
"Bay Mare." [TickleAce] (28) Fall-Wint 94, p. 115-116.
6510. WALN, Vi
"Tsoai-Talee" (for N. Scott Momaday). [Paint] (21) Aut 94, p. 122.
6511. WALSH, Agnes
"Tea Ceremony." [TickleAce] (28) Fall-Wint 94, p. 8.
"The Time That Passes." [TickleAce] (28) Fall-Wint 94, p. 7.
6512. WALSH, Marty
"Furniture Out In the Woods." [Plain] (14:3) Spr 94, p. 35.
"I Saw the Carcass of a Deer." [Plain] (14:2) Wint 94, p. 17.
6513. WALSH, Sean Patrick
"Water Crossing." [Border] (3) Fall 93, p. 78.
6514. WALSH-BOYD, Liz
"Drowning the Heart." [BellArk] (10:6) N-D 94, p. 8.
"Telling a Dream." [BellArk] (10:6) N-D 94, p. 8.
6515. WALTER, Eugene
"Lizard Fever." [NegC] (14:1/2) 94, p. 192-194.
6516. WALTERS, Pia
"Visit." [ColEng] (56:7) N 94, p. 826.
6517. WALTERS, Stella
"Sylvia." [CoalC] (8) Ap 94, p. 14.
6518. WALTON, Gary
"Love Song." [SlipS] (14) 94, p. 33-34.
6519. WALZER, Kevin
"Prodigal" (Christ the King Newman Center, Athens, Ohio). [WestB] (34) 94, p. 31.
"To Be Human." [Elf] (4:3) Fall 94, p. 34-35.
6520. WAMSLEY, Lisa A.
"Freight." [Border] (4) Spr-Sum 94, p. 73.
6521. WANDOR, Michelene
"After the Renaissance." [Jacaranda] (5:1) Wint-Spr 91, p. 54-55.
6522. WANG, Hui-Ming
"A Sixteen Character Lyric" (tr. of Chou Ching Chuan). [PaintedB] (53/54) 94, p. 92-93.
6523. WANG, Jiaxin
"Diary" (tr. by Michelle Yeh). [Manoa] (6:1) Sum 94, p. 112.
"A Visit" (tr. by Michelle Yeh). [Manoa] (6:1) Sum 94, p. 112-113.

WANG, Ping
See PING, Wang
6524. WANG, Wei
"Bird-Singing Stream" (variation by Wai-lim Yip). [Talisman] (12) Spr 94, p. 157-158.
"You Asked About My Life. I Send You, Pei Di, These Lines" (tr. by Tony Barnstone, Willis Barnstone and Xu Haixin). [NewEngR] (16:3) Sum 94, p. 31.
6525. WANG, Weiqing
"Words of Autumn" (tr. of Bei Ling, w. Jin Zhong). [Manoa] (6:1) Sum 94, p. 81.
6526. WANG, Yin
"Walt Whitman" (tr. by Richard Terrill and Cheng Baolin). [NowestR] (32:1) 94, p. 110.
6527. WANG, Yun
"Elegy for the Piano." [InterQ] (1:2) 93, p. 14-16.
"Loss in Spring." [WebR] (18) Fall 94, p. 38.
6528. WANIEK, Marilyn (Marilyn Nelson)
"Blessing the Boats." [AmerPoR] (23:4) Jl-Ag 94, p. 11.
"Don't Throw Out Wine Bottles." [GettyR] (7:3) Sum 94, p. 416-417.
"Fish and Floor-Dust Bouquet." [GettyR] (7:3) Sum 94, p. 415.
"Is She Okay?" [GettyR] (7:4) Aut 94, p. 573.
"Memento." [GettyR] (7:3) Sum 94, p. 418.
"Minor Miracle." [Obs] (9:1) Spr-Sum 94, p. 113-114.
"Paul Kamphaus, 1958." [Obs] (9:1) Spr-Sum 94, p. 112-113.
"La Peste." [GettyR] (7:4) Aut 94, p. 574.
6529. WANNBERG, Scott
"Make It Up (As You Go)." [Arshile] (3) 94, p. 27-28.
"Muse River." [Arshile] (3) 94, p. 24.
"Unease." [Arshile] (3) 94, p. 25-26.
"When the Colleagues Run Out of Ammunition." [Zyzzyva] (10:1) Spr 94, p. 143.
6530. WARA, Manden
"Le Chant de Nedjma" (Pour Kateb). [Callaloo] (17:2) Sum 94, p. 602-604.
"The Song of Nedjma" (For Kateb, tr. by Carrol F. Coates). [Callaloo] (17:2) Sum 94, p. 605-607.
6531. WARD, Adam
"Days." [BrooklynR] (11) 94, p. 54-59.
6532. WARD, Diane
"Between — two legs erase." [Chain] (1) Spr-Sum 94, p. 248-249.
"Mediate." [Chain] (1) Spr-Sum 94, p. 244.
6533. WARD, Jerry W., Jr.
"Serious." [GeoR] (48:3) Fall 94, p. 486-487.
6534. WARD, Scott
"Penelope in the Garden." [HiramPoR] (57) Fall 94-Wint 95, p. 59-60.
6535. WARD, Thom
"Cleaning Grandma's Gutters." [Confr] (54/55) Fall 94-Wint 95, p. 303-304.
"Cycling Through Adam's Basin." [PoetL] (89:3) Fall 94, p. 20.
"The End Won't Be So Bad." [TarRP] (33:2) Spr 94, p. 16.
6536. WARDEN, Marine Robert
"Twenty-Five Circuits of the Sun." [Pearl] (20) Spr 94, p. 75.
6537. WARING, Belle
"It Was My First Nursing Job." [AmerV] (35) 94, p. 143-145.
"October Crows." [AmerV] (35) 94, p. 149-152.
"People Think All Wrong About Manhood." [AmerV] (35) 94, p. 146-148.
6538. WARN, Emily
"Tower of Babel." [SouthernPR] (34:1) Sum 94, p. 47-48.
6539. WARNER, Alan
"Biography of the Poet." [Verse] (11:1) Spr 94, p. 69.
6540. WARNER, James
"The Blue Heights." [PoetryC] (14:2) Mr 94, p. 17.
"Jump." [PoetryC] (14:2) Mr 94, p. 17.
"Messengers." [PoetryC] (14:2) Mr 94, p. 17.
"Via Negativa." [PoetryC] (14:2) Mr 94, p. 17.
6541. WARNER, Marilyn
"I'd Argue That." [BellArk] (10:3) My-Je 94, p. 28.
"Lifequake." [BellArk] (10:2) Mr-Ap 94, p. 9.

6542. WARNER, Rebecca
"Inheritance." [GrahamHR] (18) Wint 94-95, p. 80.
6543. WARREN, Louise
"Confronting the sea, the shift of skies, beauty" (tr. by D. G. Jones). [PoetryC] (14:4) S 94, p. 28.
"In my house there are no mirrors" (tr. by D. G. Jones). [PoetryC] (14:4) S 94, p. 28.
"Stream of lightning, I love sweat" (tr. by D. G. Jones). [PoetryC] (14:4) S 94, p. 28.
"Your belly betrays light tremors" (tr. by D. G. Jones). [PoetryC] (14:4) S 94, p. 28.
6544. WARREN, Shirley
"For My Jenny." [JINJPo] (16:2) Aut 94, p. 31.
"Graveside, Mother, I Become You." [CrabCR] (8:2/3/9:1/2/3) 94, p. 57-58.
6545. WARSAW, Irene
"Gone with the Windy Speeches." [Light] (10) Sum 94, p. 15.
6546. WARSH, Lewis
"Montgomery Clift." [Journal] (18:1) Spr-Sum 94, p. 49.
6547. WARSHAWSKI, Morrie
"Floating By." [IndR] (17:1) Spr 94, p. 151.
6548. WARWICK, Ioanna-Veronika (I. V., Joanna-Veronika)
"Factories in Lodz." [Poetry] (163:4) Ja 94, p. 191.
"From the Lost Letters of Felice Bauer to Kafka." [PraS] (68:2) Sum 94, p. 140-141.
"Garden View (Grudziadz, Pomerania)." [Pembroke] (26) 94, p. 72.
"Holding the Python." [Poetry] (163:6) Mr 94, p. 322.
"A Hopeless Case." [Pembroke] (26) 94, p. 73-74.
"The Lost Name." [PraS] (68:2) Sum 94, p. 141-142.
"Lot's Wife." [NewDeltaR] (10:1) Fall 92-Wint 93, p. 14-15.
"My Father-in-Law From the Country of the Dead." [Plain] (14:3) Spr 94, p. 7.
"My Grandmother's Laughing" (Selection. The Nimrod / Hardman Wards: Honorable Mention). [Nimrod] (38:1) Fall-Wint 94, p. 50-55.
"Wheatchild." [Plain] (14:2) Wint 94, p. 7.
6549. WASHBURN, Katharine
"The Daughters of Troy" (Excerpts, tr. of Euripides, w. Mark Rudman). [DenQ] (29:1) Sum 94, p. 57-78.
6550. WASHINGTON, Teresa (Aseret Sin)
"Sister." [Obs] (9:2) Fall-Wint 94, p. 100-101.
"Things Unseen." [Obs] (9:2) Fall-Wint 94, p. 99-100.
6551. WASHINGTON, Willie D.
"Mixed Nuts." [Outbr] (25) 94, p. 85.
6552. WATERHOUSE, Philip A.
"Fools Paradise." [Parting] (7:2) Wint 94-95, p. 56.
"Mt. Red." [Parting] (7:2) Wint 94-95, p. 4.
6553. WATERS, Chocolate
"Junkfood Man." [FreeL] (13) Spr 94, p. 30.
6554. WATERS, Chris
"Chumming." [CimR] (109) O 94, p. 72.
"When the Pheasant Dies." [FloridaR] (19:2) 94, p. 82.
6555. WATERS, Michael
"Airing the Mattress." [IllinoisR] (2:1) Fall 94, p. 55.
"Assateague" (in memoriam John Logan). [AmerV] (35) 94, p. 138-139.
"The Floating Wreaths." [IllinoisR] (2:1) Fall 94, p. 56.
"Herbs." [AmerV] (35) 94, p. 136.
"Homeless Elvis." [AmerV] (35) 94, p. 137.
"Last Joke." [AmerV] (35) 94, p. 135.
"Renaissance." [DarkMoon] (1) 94, p. 34.
"Simple Happiness." [Crazy] (47) Wint 94, p. 82.
"Ssss." [Crazy] (47) Wint 94, p. 83.
6556. WATERSON, Michael
"Terrible Twos." [SantaBR] (1:2) Fall-Wint 93, p. 62-63.
6557. WATKINS, Clive
"Hedger." [MalR] (107) Sum 94, p. 152.
"Jigsaw." [MalR] (107) Sum 94, p. 150-151.
6558. WATKINS, Klyd
"Radnor Lake: April 18, 1992." [Poem] (71) My 94, p. 36-37.
6559. WATKINS, Nancy R.
"As If Eating Breakfast Alone Were Not Enough." [NewOR] (20:1/2) Spr-Sum 94, p. 129-131.

6560. WATKINS, William John
"All Things Have End." [Elf] (4:4) Wint 94, p. 32.
"Central Park West." [Elf] (4:4) Wint 94, p. 33.
"Color Commentator." [Elf] (4:4) Wint 94, p. 32.
"Day Late and a Sonnet Short." [Hellas] (5:1) Spr-Sum 94, p. 52.
"Done with Mirrors." [Hellas] (5:1) Spr-Sum 94, p. 53.
"Love's Bankrupt." [WindO] (58) Sum 94, p. 52.
"Philosophy." [HiramPoR] (55/56) Fall 93-Sum 94, p. 116.
"The Power of Cold." [MidwQ] (35:3) Spr 94, p. 319.
"Wife of My Youth, Look Back, Look Back." [Hellas] (5:2) Fall-Wint 94, p. 37.
6561. WATNIK, Harry
"St. Works." [HampSPR] Wint 94, p. 34-35.
"Stardust Physics." [HampSPR] Wint 94, p. 34.
6562. WATSKY, Paul
"Four Stories of My Body." [CreamCR] (18:2) Fall 94, p. 97.
6563. WATSON, Craig
"E^2" (Excerpts). [Talisman] (13) Fall 94-Wint 95, p. 294-296.
6564. WATSON, Ellen
"Anything But Empty." [PoetryNW] (35:4) Wint 94-95, p. 12-13.
"Gone Fishin'." [PoetryNW] (35:4) Wint 94-95, p. 13-14.
6565. WATSON, M. C.
"Because Cheap Is How I Feel." [NewYorkQ] (53) 94, p. 91-92.
6566. WATSON, R. H.
"The Lover." [Shen] (44:2) Sum 94, p. 108-109.
6567. WATSON, Ron
"Duet" (for Ellen). [Wind] (73) 94, p. 31-32.
6568. WATTISON, Meredith
"Edvard Munch's Feet." [Vis] (45) 94, p. 39.
"Grape." [Vis] (45) 94, p. 39.
"Husband Bread." [NewEngR] (16:3) Sum 94, p. 89.
6569. WATTS, David
"Let Me Blow Out the Light, She Said." [YellowS] (12:3, #47) Fall-Wint 94-95, p. 20.
6570. WAYBRANT, Linda
"Father Poems" (First Prize, Long Poem Category). [PraF] (15:4, #69) Wint 94-95, p. 11-23.
"Marilyn." [PraF] (15:1, #66) Spr 94, p. 133-134.
6571. WAYMAN, Tom
"The Astonishing Weight of the Dead" (Selections: 2 poems). [OntR] (41) Fall-Wint 94, p. 88-91.
"The Bald Man." [Caliban] (14) 94, p. 112-113.
"Billy and Women." [PassN] (15:2) Wint 94, p. 43.
"Billy on the Valley." [PassN] (15:2) Wint 94, p. 43.
"Casualties." [PassN] (15:2) Wint 94, p. 44-45.
"Eye Mountains." [CanLit] (141) Sum 94, p. 72.
"In the Birth Canal." [Event] (23:2) Sum 94, p. 47-49.
"Poetry Overdose." [TriQ] (90) Spr-Sum 94, p. 179-180.
"War on a Round Planet." [MalR] (106) Spr 94, p. 42-44.
6572. WAYNE, Jane O.
"In a Mood." [Poetry] (165:1) O 94, p. 10.
"In the Runaway's House." [Poetry] (165:1) O 94, p. 9-10.
6573. WEARNE, Alan
"Making the World Revolve" (Excerpt). [MalR] (107) Sum 94, p. 168-169.
6574. WEATHERFORD, Carole Boston
"The Gospel According to Minnie" (commissioned by the James Diggs Gallery, Winston Salem State University, for an exhibit of works by the late Minnie Evans). [Obs] (9:2) Fall-Wint 94, p. 103.
"Guarding the Gates" (commissioned by the James Diggs Gallery, Winston Salem State University, for an exhibit of works by the late Minnie Evans). [Obs] (9:2) Fall-Wint 94, p. 103-104.
"Home in Glory" (commissioned by the James Diggs Gallery, Winston Salem State University, for an exhibit of works by the late Minnie Evans). [Obs] (9:2) Fall-Wint 94, p. 102-103.

"In the Garden" (commissioned by the James Diggs Gallery, Winston Salem State University, for an exhibit of works by the late Minnie Evans). [Obs] (9:2) Fall-Wint 94, p. 104.
"No Cutting" (commissioned by the James Diggs Gallery, Winston Salem State University, for an exhibit of works by the late Minnie Evans). [Obs] (9:2) Fall-Wint 94, p. 102.
"The Secret Life of Plants" (commissioned by the James Diggs Gallery, Winston Salem State University, for an exhibit of works by the late Minnie Evans). [Obs] (9:2) Fall-Wint 94, p. 104.
"The Tan Chanteuse." [Callaloo] (17:4) Fall 94, p. 966.

6575. WEATHERS, Winston
"The Shopper's Prayer." [Light] (10) Sum 94, p. 18.

6576. WEAVER, Katie McAllaster
"Black Without Blue Horses." [WritersF] (20) 94, p. 84.

6577. WEAVER, Roger
"Horizontal, Vertical." [DogRR] (26) Wint 94-95, p. 18.
"A Poet." [DogRR] (26) Wint 94-95, p. 18.

6578. WEBB, Charles (Charles H., Charles Harper)
"Advice for New Singles." [Amelia] (7:4, #23) 94, p. 88.
"Behaviorists." [Agni] (40) 94, p. 164-165.
"Blind." [WestB] (35) 94, p. 35.
"Cops Always Treat You Like You've Got Something to Hide." [Amelia] (7:4, #23) 94, p. 86-87.
"Dinosaurs." [Jacaranda] (5:1) Wint-Spr 91, p. 24-25.
"Ex-Jocks." [CrabCR] (8:2/3/9:1/2/3) 94, p. 98.
"Holiday Inn." [WestHR] (48:3) Fall 94, p. 291.
"In the War Zone." [Agni] (40) 94, p. 162-163.
"Mastery." [WestHR] (48:3) Fall 94, p. 291.
"My Muse." [Iowa] (24:1) Wint 94, p. 78.
"My Umbrella Doesn't Care If I Kick It." [Amelia] (7:4, #23) 94, p. 87-88.
"Patients in Therapy." [CimR] (109) O 94, p. 61.
"Poets at the Sock Hop." [ApalQ] (40/41) 94, p. 94.
"Pomades." [ProseP] (3) 94, p. 83.
"The Shape of History." [MichQR] (33:2) Spr 94, p. 374.
"Spiders." [PoetryE] (37/38) Spr 94, p. 58-59.
"Thumping the Fat." [ChironR] (13:4) Wint 94, p. 11.
"True Prophets." [Ploughs] (20:1) Spr 94, p. 103-104.
"Waking to Rain." [PoetL] (89:4) Wint 94-95, p. 48.
"The Weight of Knowledge." [SouthernPR] (34:2) Wint 94, p. 58-59.
"Werewolf of L.A." [Pearl] (20) Spr 94, p. 14.
"Without Being a Wimp." [Amelia] (7:4, #23) 94, p. 89-90.

6579. WEBB, Margaret
"Arrival Time." [Descant] (25:1, #84) Spr 94, p. 58.
"The Dream Is Woman." [Descant] (25:1, #84) Spr 94, p. 51-52.
"Haying." [Dandel] (20:2) 93, p. 17-18.
"Over Easy." [Descant] (25:1, #84) Spr 94, p. 56.
"Seven A.M." [Descant] (25:1, #84) Spr 94, p. 59.
"Spring Summer Fall." [Descant] (25:1, #84) Spr 94, p. 54-55.
"The Visit." [Descant] (25:1, #84) Spr 94, p. 53.
"Walking with My Husband One Night." [Descant] (25:1, #84) Spr 94, p. 57.

6580. WEBB, Martha
"The Door on Its Hinges" (Volcano, Hawai'i). [ChamLR] (14/15) Spr-Fall 94, p. 1.
"The garden of hands." [ChamLR] (14/15) Spr-Fall 94, p. 2.
"Two Dragons Dancing in August." [ChamLR] (14/15) Spr-Fall 94, p. 3.

6581. WEBB, Robert (Robert T.)
"Applying an Old Photograph of My Mother to Her Recent Mid-Life Shenanigans." [Confr] (54/55) Fall 94-Wint 95, p. 318.
"Beach Scene, Tybee Island." [Amelia] (7:3, #22) 94, p. 103.
"Democracy of Nature" (for Maxine Kumin). [Amelia] (7:4, #23) 94, p. 83.
"The Gift of Magi" (Overheard at Wanda Rae's Beauty Emporium). [NegC] (14:1/2) 94, p. 76-77.
"The Last Photograph of Truman Capote." [Amelia] (7:4, #23) 94, p. 161.
"On an Occasional Poet." [Light] (10) Sum 94, p. 14.

6582. WEBB, Sean
"Big Bang." [Amelia] (7:4, #23) 94, p. 125.
"Hemisphere Dance." [PoetL] (89:4) Wint 94-95, p. 40.

"Table." [CumbPR] (13:2) Spr 94, p. 66.
6583. WEBER, Mark
"Politics." [Pearl] (20) Spr 94, p. 52.
6584. WEBSTER, Ed
"San Joaquin Valley Poems: 1969." [WestHR] (48:4) Wint 94, p. 338-340.
6585. WEBSTER, Kerri
"Landlocked, Idaho." [MidAR] (14:2) 94, p. 40-41.
6586. WEE, Rebecca (Rebecca Liv)
"Crossings." [Iowa] (24:1) Wint 94, p. 80-81.
"A Few Words on Penis Envy." [MinnR] (41/42) Fall 93-Spr 94 (published Mr 95), p. 16.
6587. WEEKS, Robert Lewis
"Crisis." [PoetC] (25:3) Spr 94, p. 3.
6588. WEES, Coreen Dwyer
"Collecting Sleep and Flight." [MidwQ] (35:2) Wint 94, p. 185.
WEI, Wang
See WANG, Wei
6589. WEIERLINGER, Jesse
"And Marvelous Conviction." [Amelia] (7:3, #22) 94, p. 155.
6590. WEIGEL, John A.
"An Alternative." [Light] (12) Wint 94-95, p. 7.
6591. WEIGL, Bruce
"About Sacrifice" (tr. of Liliana Ursu). [AmerPoR] (23:2) Mr-Ap 94, p. 15.
"Depression Before the Equinox (or: Words for the Portraits of Poets Dreamed by Jan Cordua)" (tr. of Liliana Ursu). [AmerPoR] (23:2) Mr-Ap 94, p. 14.
"Eating Blackberries in a February Night" (tr. of Liliana Ursu, w. the author). [PoetL] (89:1) Spr 94, p. 33.
"Fever Dream in Hanoi." [TriQ] (90) Spr-Sum 94, p. 83-85.
"From the House on Nguyen Du." [Antaeus] (75/76) Aut 94, p. 327-328.
"Heart Washed Like a Brina, Europe for Sale" (tr. of Liliana Ursu, w. the author). [WilliamMR] (32) 94, p. 74-75.
"Memories from the Arc in the Mountains" (tr. of Liliana Ursu, w. the author). [PoetL] (89:1) Spr 94, p. 34.
"The Mistaken Road" (tr. of Liliana Ursu). [AmerPoR] (23:2) Mr-Ap 94, p. 13.
"My Body" (tr. of Liliana Ursu). [QW] (38) Winter-Spr 93-94, p. 114.
"Prayer for Brother Alexander" (tr. of Liliana Ursu). [AmerPoR] (23:2) Mr-Ap 94, p. 15.
"Prelude" (for Sylvia Plath, tr. of Liliana Ursu, w. the author). [PoetL] (89:1) Spr 94, p. 35.
"Ruins of the Monastery at Cirtisoara" (tr. of Liliana Ursu). [AmerPoR] (23:2) Mr-Ap 94, p. 14.
"Society of Consumers" (tr. of Liliana Ursu). [AmerPoR] (23:2) Mr-Ap 94, p. 14.
"That Finished Feeling." [SouthernR] (30:3) Sum 94, p. 581.
"Three Meditations at Nguyen Du." [TriQ] (90) Spr-Sum 94, p. 86-87.
"What I Saw, What I Did, in the Alley." [TriQ] (90) Spr-Sum 94, p. 88.
"Window Cut into White Pine" (in memory of Ezra Pound, tr. of Liliana Ursu). [QW] (38) Winter-Spr 93-94, p. 115.
"Words for the Husky Girl." [TriQ] (90) Spr-Sum 94, p. 89.
6592. WEIL, James L.
"Arts of the Book." [Confr] (54/55) Fall 94-Wint 95, p. 325.
"The Gift." [Confr] (54/55) Fall 94-Wint 95, p. 326.
6593. WEIL, Joe
"Father and Son." [JlNJPo] (16:1) Spr 94, p. 27-28.
"Hopper's Shoes." [JlNJPo] (16:1) Spr 94, p. 26.
6594. WEINBERGER, Eliot
"Breathing" (tr. of Octavio Paz). [NewYorker] (70:13) 16 My 94, p. 74.
"Soliloquy" (tr. of Octavio Paz). [ParisR] (36:130) Spr 94, p. 15-19.
6595. WEINBLATT, Jennifer
"Passover." [PoetL] (89:2) Sum 94, p. 23.
6596. WEINER, Joshua
"The Not-Yet Child." [BostonR] (19:3/4) Je-S 94, p. 25.
6597. WEINFIELD, Henry
"Sonnets" (Selections: II-III, tr. of Stéphane Mallarmé). [DenQ] (29:1) Sum 94, p. 87-88.
6598. WEINGARTEN, Robert
"Against Friendship." [PoetryE] (37/38) Spr 94, p. 88-90.

"The New Confessions." [PoetryE] (37/38) Spr 94, p. 85-87.
6599. WEINMAN, Paul
"Night Hooves." [BlackBR] (18) Wint-Spr 94, p. 17.
"Oyster Talk." [SlipS] (14) 94, p. 54.
6600. WEINRAUB, Richard Marx
"Hector in Synagogue." [EvergreenC] (9:1) Wint-Spr 94, p. 49-50.
6601. WEINSTEIN, Debra
"The Dead." [GlobalCR] (3) Spr 94, p. 86-87.
"Last Night." [AmerV] (33) 94, p. 86.
6602. WEINSTEIN, Marsha
"Then Slake Him From" (tr. of Amira Hess). [LitR] (37:2) Wint 94, p. 307.
6603. WEINSTEIN, Muriel Harris
"Leah Julia." [Outbr] (25) 94, p. 86-87.
"Momma's Tongue." [CapeR] (29:1) Spr 94, p. 5.
6604. WEINTRAGER, Richard
"The Living Room" (Grain Contest Winners, Prose Poem: Second). [Grain] (21:4) Spr 94, p. 16-17.
WEIQING, Wang
See WANG, Weiqing
6605. WEISBERG, Barbara
"Diary Entries." [NewYorkQ] (53) 94, p. 89-90.
"Naming Grief." [SlipS] (14) 94, p. 34.
6606. WEISERT, Hilde
"Poems of Domestic Life, 2: The Mouse Upstairs." [CumbPR] (13:2) Spr 94, p. 11-12.
6607. WEISS, David
"The City of the Dead." [Salm] (103) Sum 94, p. 95-96.
6608. WEISS, Jan
"Sweeping" (First Runner-Up, Poetry Award). [NewL] (60:2) 94, p. 75.
"Traveling" (First Runner-Up, Poetry Award). [NewL] (60:2) 94, p. 74-75.
6609. WEISS, Jason
"The Mechanical Rose." [LindLM] (13:1) Mr 94, p. 8.
"Out." [LindLM] (13:1) Mr 94, p. 8.
"The Whispers." [LindLM] (13:1) Mr 94, p. 8.
6610. WEISSBORT, Daniel
"Transplanted" (for Michael Hamburger). [Pivot] (41) 93, p. 49.
6611. WELBURN, Ron
"Peopling Winter." [Callaloo] (17:1) Wint 94, p. 117.
"Yellow Wolf Spirit." [Callaloo] (17:1) Wint 94, p. 115-116.
6612. WELCH, Don
"At the Road's Edge." [TarRP] (34:1) Fall 94, p. 10.
"The Dream of the Sloth." [MidwQ] (35:3) Spr 94, p. 320.
"L'Envoi." [LaurelR] (28:2) Sum 94, p. 95.
"Good Mondays." [LaurelR] (28:2) Sum 94, p. 94.
"Ruth." [TarRP] (34:1) Fall 94, p. 10.
"They Came Over Fields." [MidwQ] (35:3) Spr 94, p. 321.
6613. WELCH, Enid Santiago
"In My Mind." [BilingR] (19:2) My-Ag 94, p. 162.
"Papi." [BilingR] (19:2) My-Ag 94, p. 163.
"Project Women." [NegC] (14:1/2) 94, p. 19.
6614. WELCH, John
"After the Blast." [BellArk] (10:3 [i.e. 10:4]) Jl-Ag 94, p. 9.
"Bolero." [BellArk] (10:1) Ja-F 94, p. 16.
"Full Circle." [ChatR] (14:2) Wint 94, p. 49-50.
"Market Street." [BellArk] (10:1) Ja-F 94, p. 25.
"Roadhouse, Dakotas." [BellArk] (10:3 [i.e. 10:4]) Jl-Ag 94, p. 9.
"These leaves." [BellArk] (10:1) Ja-F 94, p. 16.
"What in the World Are They Doing?" [BellArk] (10:3 [i.e. 10:4]) Jl-Ag 94, p. 9.
6615. WELCH, Liliane
"Nursing Home." [CanLit] (141) Sum 94, p. 33.
6616. WELCH, Michael Dylan
"Between tricks." [Amelia] (7:4, #23) 94, p. 146.
6617. WELFORD, Gabrielle
"A Day(m) in Brooklyn." [SoCoast] (16) Ja 94, p. 46.
"Seawalk and Speech of the Stubbornhearted." [SoCoast] (16) Ja 94, p. 31.

6618. WELIN, Richard
"The Abbey and Cathedral of St. Gallen." [Ascent] (18:3) Spr 94, p. 37.
"Dream of the Next Thing." [Ascent] (18:3) Spr 94, p. 37.
6619. WELISH, Marjorie
"Equinoxes of Glass." [ColR] (21:1) Spr 94, p. 141-142.
"Of or On Dominoes." [ColR] (21:1) Spr 94, p. 143-144.
6620. WELLS, Dorothy
"Night Funeral in New Orleans." [NegC] (13:2/3) 93, p. 61-62.
"Waterlogged." [NegC] (14:1/2) 94, p. 18.
6621. WELLS, Shanna
"On a Soldier's Funeral." [Amelia] (7:3, #22) 94, p. 153.
6622. WELLS, Will
"Hard Water." [SouthernPR] (34:1) Sum 94, p. 34.
"Upon Hearing a Recording of the Big Bang." [DenQ] (28:4) Spr 94, p. 69.
6623. WELSH, Lawrence
"Mass Transit Rebirth." [Pearl] (20) Spr 94, p. 15.
"Obituary." [WormR] (34:1, #133) 94, p. 43-44.
WEN-CHÜN, Cho
See CHO, Wen-chün
6624. WENDELL, Julia
"Shade of Wings." [PraS] (68:3) Fall 94, p. 140.
6625. WENDEROTH, Joe
"Alone Throwing Stones." [BlackWR] (21:1) Fall-Wint 94, p. 21.
6626. WENDT, Albert
"A Sequence." [MalR] (107) Sum 94, p. 9-18.
6627. WENDT, Ingrid
"10:30 Sunday Morning." [CharR] (20:1) Spr 94, p. 65-66.
"First Morning in the Santa Caterina: Villa Serbelloni, Bellagio." [CharR] (20:1) Spr 94, p. 68-69.
"Italy: Singing the Map." [AntR] (52:2) Spr 94, p. 311.
"Scaffolding." [CharR] (20:1) Spr 94, p. 66-67.
"St. Martin's Day, 1992." [CharR] (20:1) Spr 94, p. 69-71.
6628. WENGER, Gigi
"Of All the Men I Have Known." [Dandel] (21:2) 94, p. 71.
6629. WENTHE, William
"For the Dwarf on the Altar." [PoetryE] (37/38) Spr 94, p. 122-123.
"Fountains Abbey." [PoetryE] (37/38) Spr 94, p. 124-125.
"In Early Spring." [PoetryE] (37/38) Spr 94, p. 126.
6630. WENTZ, Stephen W.
"River Muskie." [BellArk] (10:2) Mr-Ap 94, p. 31.
6631. WERNER, Judith
"Stillborn." [ChrC] (111:9) 16 Mr 94, p. 268.
6632. WESELS, Katja
"The Loch Ness Expedition" (tr. by Margitt Lehbert). [Verse] (11:1) Spr 94, p. 16-17.
6633. WESLEY, Marilyn
"The Poppet" (for Graham Duncan). [Pivot] (42) 94, p. 46-47.
6634. WESLOWSKI, Dieter
"Let Us Swim Out." [Sonora] (27) Spr 94, p. 19.
"Munich." [ChamLR] (14/15) Spr-Fall 94, p. 60.
"To Your Fiction." [LitR] (37:4) Sum 94, p. 664.
6635. WESSELS, Katja
"Description of the Quadrilateral Lover" (tr. by Margitt Lehbert). [Chelsea] (56) 94, p. 114.
"The Dying of Bicycles" (tr. by Margitt Lehbert). [Chelsea] (56) 94, p. 116.
"The Meeting of the Meteorologists" (tr. by Margitt Lehbert). [Chelsea] (56) 94, p. 115.
6636. WEST, Jean
"Jazz." [Kalliope] (16:1) 94, p. 52-53.
6637. WEST, Kathleene
"Capitalism As We Know It." [KenR] (NS 16:2) Spr 94, p. 125-126.
"Cravings." [KenR] (NS 16:2) Spr 94, p. 126-127.
6638. WEST, Richard M.
"The Shimmering Wall." [WormR] (34:1, #133) 94, p. 44-45.
"Something Was Lost in the Translation." [Pearl] (20) Spr 94, p. 61.

6639. WEST, Satori
"I walk the dirt road." [Amelia] (7:4, #23) 94, p. 7.
6640. WESTERFIELD, Nancy G.
"Bathtubs I Have Known." [Plain] (14:3) Spr 94, p. 29.
"Beneath the Cloverleaf." [Plain] (15:1) Fall 94, p. 36.
"His First Death." [Nimrod] (38:1) Fall-Wint 94, p. 143.
"The Husband Who Turned Into a Houseplant." [Nimrod] (38:1) Fall-Wint 94, p. 142.
"The Indifference of a Winter's Day." [NegC] (14:1/2) 94, p. 73.
"The Moon As Onion." [Light] (10) Sum 94, p. 22.
"The view at the End of Nebraska" (A Plainsongs Award Poem). [Plain] (14:2) Wint 94, p. 5.
6641. WESTLER, Max
"Cave Painting." [HayF] (15) Fall-Wint 94, p. 49.
"Civil Defense Exercise, 1955." [PoetryE] (37/38) Spr 94, p. 60-61.
"Complete Simplicity." [PoetryE] (37/38) Spr 94, p. 62.
6642. WETZSTEON, Rachel
"Clubfoot." [Thrpny] (57) Spr 94, p. 30.
"Coming Back to the Cave." [Salm] (101/102) Wint-Spr 94, p. 172.
"Poem for a New Year." [NewRep] (211:20) 14 N 94, p. 36.
"Stage Directions for a Short Play." [KenR] (NS 16:1) Wint 94, p. 68.
"Three Poems after Montale." [Raritan] (14:2) Fall 94, p. 13-14.
"The Triumph of Marsyas." [SouthwR] (79:4) Aut 94, p. 660-661.
6643. WEUVE, Denise R.
"Dancing in the Laundromat" (Honorable Mention, 8th Annual Contest). [SoCoast] (17) Je 94, p. 44-45.
6644. WEVILL, Sharon
"Of the Same/Other." [Border] (4) Spr-Sum 94, p. 74.
6645. WEXELBLATT, Robert
"Shiksas." [CumbPR] (14:1) Fall 94, p. 40.
6646. WEXLER, Evelyn
"All in Season." [CapeR] (29:2) Fall 94, p. 1.
6647. WEXLER, Philip
"Dear Minister of Justice." [Jacaranda] (5:1) Wint-Spr 91, p. 27.
"Grandmother Going Downhill." [NewDeltaR] (11:1) Fall 93-Wint 94, p. 61-63.
"The Last Hopes of Greco Pirelli." [Parting] (7:1) Sum 94, p. 13.
6648. WHALEN, John James
"Black Velvet." [VirQR] (70:3) Sum 94, p. 455.
"Chlorophyll Angels." [VirQR] (70:3) Sum 94, p. 454-455.
6649. WHALEN, Maryann
"Sad Southern Girls." [AntigR] (98) Sum 94, p. 31-32.
6650. WHALEN, Tom
"Traveller." [GreenMR] (NS 17:2) Fall-Wint 94-95, p. 53.
6651. WHALLEY, Karen
"Some Thoughts on the Afterlife." [CrabCR] (8:2/3/9:1/2/3) 94, p. 58.
6652. WHEAT, Maxwell Corydon, Jr.
"The Bear." [ChrC] (111:2) 19 Ja 94, p. 39.
6653. WHEATCROFT, John
"The Relique." [FourQ] (8:1) Spr 94, p. 10.
"Waking in an Inn on a Tidal Stream." [LitR] (37:4) Sum 94, p. 608.
6654. WHEATLEY, David
"These Are the Wars." [Stand] (36:1) Wint 94-95, p. 75.
6655. WHEELER, Charles B.
"D. H. Lawrence Does the Dishes." [PoetC] (25:3) Spr 94, p. 6-7.
"Doctor Will See You Now." [CentR] (38:2) Spr 94, p. 334-335.
"The Idea-Balloon." [LaurelR] (28:1) Wint 94, p. 56-58.
"Supermarket." [CumbPR] (14:1) Fall 94, p. 73.
"Visiting the Sick." [CumbPR] (14:1) Fall 94, p. 71-72.
6656. WHEELER, Sue
"13th Anniversary." [CreamCR] (18:2) Fall 94, p. 98.
"Child of the Times." [MalR] (109) Wint 94, p. 96.
"A Conversation of Blackbirds" (for Lynn and Karen). [MalR] (109) Wint 94, p. 97.
"Deep and Crisp and Even." [Grain] (22:1) Sum 94, p. 14.
"Hey Diddle Diddle." [Arc] (33) Fall 94, p. 25.
"Personal Effects." [MalR] (108) Fall 94, p. 40-47.
"Sari Shop, Bangalore." [MalR] (106) Spr 94, p. 63-64.

"Solstice on the Anacortes Ferry" (for Peter). [Grain] (22:1) Sum 94, p. 13.
"We Two Kings." [CreamCR] (18:2) Fall 94, p. 99.
"What'll You Have?" [Event] (23:1) Spr 94, p. 32-33.
"Winging It." [Event] (23:1) Spr 94, p. 30-31.
"Yes Sir, Yes Sir." [Event] (23:2) Sum 94, p. 50.

6657. WHEELER, Susan
"The Arbiter of Desire & the Wreath." [NewAW] (12) Spr-Sum 94, p. 15.
"Independence Day, Chicago" (for the late mayor of Chicago, Harold Washington). [Pequod] (37) 94, p. 91-92.
"O.K." [NewAW] (12) Spr-Sum 94, p. 16.

6658. WHITE, Beverley
"Captain Vic's Lobster Pound." [AnthNEW] (6) 94, p. 26.

6659. WHITE, Calvin
"Crow Cries." [TickleAce] (28) Fall-Wint 94, p. 110-111.
"Snapping." [TickleAce] (28) Fall-Wint 94, p. 109.

6660. WHITE, Claire Nicolas
"The Orchard." [Confr] (54/55) Fall 94-Wint 95, p. 302.

6661. WHITE, Danny
"When Farmers Pray for Rain." [SoCaR] (27:1/2) Fall 94-Spr 95, p. 8.

6662. WHITE, E. B.
"An Earthbound Boy" (After Seeing the Movie "Test Pilot"). [NewYorker] (70:5) 21 Mr 94, p. 164.

6663. WHITE, Gail
"Advice to the Lioness." [Light] (11) Aut 94, p. 31.
"Ballade of a Latter-Day Faust." [Light] (12) Wint 94-95, p. 12.
"Boating on the Mississippi" (Second Prize, Second Annual River Rhyme Competition). [Light] (9) Spr 94, p. 22.
"The Escape." [Calyx] (15:3) Wint 94-95, p. 11.
"Garnered Wisdom." [Grain] (21:4) Spr 94, p. 62.
"My Secret Faith." [Calyx] (15:3) Wint 94-95, p. 11.
"Sitting in a French Cafe Without Knowing French." [DogRR] (26) Wint 94-95, p. 49.
"Song for the N.E.A." [DogRR] (26) Wint 94-95, p. 12.
"Summing Up." [Poem] (72) N 94, p. 35.
"Teacher and Students." [Poem] (72) N 94, p. 36.

6664. WHITE, J. P.
"121 Waverly Place." [OntR] (41) Fall-Wint 94, p. 106-107.
"The Beautician." [Crazy] (47) Wint 94, p. 63-65.
"The Birth of Violence." [HighP] (9:2) Ag 94, p. 71-72.
"The Cats." [CumbPR] (13:2) Spr 94, p. 14-15.
"Colette's Last Cat." [OntR] (41) Fall-Wint 94, p. 105.
"The Contortionist." [HighP] (9:2) Ag 94, p. 68-70.
"Elephant Land." [CreamCR] (18:1) Spr 94, p. 68.
"Essay on the Snake." [GreenMR] (NS 17:2) Fall-Wint 94-95, p. 87-88.
"Woman with Turtles." [TarRP] (33:2) Spr 94, p. 38-39.

6665. WHITE, John
"II. Coda." [Eyeball] (3) 93, p. 32.
"For Miles." [Eyeball] (3) 93, p. 32.

6666. WHITE, Kevin E.
"Eating a Piece of Cold BBQ Chicken at 1 AM." [SlipS] (14) 94, p. 124.

6667. WHITE, Laura
"Warm." [Parting] (7:2) Wint 94-95, p. 48.

6668. WHITE, Marvin K.
"Last Rites" (Meant to be read out loud and proud). [Poz] (1:2) Je-Jl 94, p. 23.

6669. WHITE, Michael
"The Woman on the Steps of the *Bella Vista Apts.*" [ParisR] (36:133) Wint 94, p. 231-232.

6670. WHITE, Mimi
"Zaydee's Short Career in the Russian Army." [Poetry] (163:4) Ja 94, p. 192.

6671. WHITE, Patti
"Our Lady of Perpetual Help Business School" (Award of Excellence: Poetry). [HopewellR] (6) 94, p. 82-84.

6672. WHITE, Philip
"Wings" (for LeeAnn). [NewEngR] (16:3) Sum 94, p. 136.

6673. WHITE, Sarah
"Sonnet Lesson" (for S.J. Marks). [NegC] (14:1/2) 94, p. 80.

6674. WHITE, Steven F.
"Her Head Bowed in Acceptance" (tr. of Ana Enriqueta Terán). [Trans] (29) Spr 94, p. 41.
"I Didn't Want to Speak with Anyone" (tr. of Yolanda Pantin). [Trans] (29) Spr 94, p. 109-110.
"Remnants" (tr. of Ana Enriqueta Terán). [Trans] (29) Spr 94, p. 41.
"Short Stretches" (tr. of Ana Enriqueta Terán). [Trans] (29) Spr 94, p. 42.
"Sole Sign" (tr. of Ana Enriqueta Terán). [Trans] (29) Spr 94, p. 42.
"There Are Three Vultures" (tr. of Yolanda Pantin). [Trans] (29) Spr 94, p. 111.
"Who Are They Eating?" (tr. of Yolanda Pantin). [Trans] (29) Spr 94, p. 111.

6675. WHITE-RING, Wendy
"States of Emergency." [Parting] (7:1) Sum 94, p. 17.

6676. WHITEHEAD, Gary J.
"My Grandfather Dying." [Parting] (7:1) Sum 94, p. 62.

6677. WHITEHEAD, Jett W.
"After the Ice" (Higgins Lake, April 29). [AntigR] (96) Wint 94, p. 31.
"Early Morning Walk." [AntigR] (96) Wint 94, p. 32.

6678. WHITEHOUSE, Lisa
"At Great Grandma's House." [BellArk] (10:6) N-D 94, p. 8.
"On Christmas Eve Awake." [BellArk] (10:6) N-D 94, p. 26.
"Thoughts on a Snow Storm." [BellArk] (10:6) N-D 94, p. 8.

6679. WHITENECK, Margaret
"Perennial Crossing." [XavierR] (14:2) Fall 94, p. 66.

6680. WHITLOW, Carolyn Beard
"The Hour of Blue." [KenR] (NS 16:3) Sum 94, p. 80-81.

6681. WHITMAN, Ruth
"The Accident, 1901." [NewRep] (211:1) 4 Jl 94, p. 40.

6682. WHITNEY, Ross R.
"Dr. Barth." [CumbPR] (14:1) Fall 94, p. 49.

6683. WHITT, Harold
"Son of American Lit" (Selections: 4 poems). [BellArk] (10:5) S-O 94, p. 15.

6684. WHITTEMORE, Christine
"Lily of the Valley." [AmerS] (63:4) Aut 94, p. 556.

6685. WHITTEMORE, Reed
"Boathouse." [VirQR] (70:3) Sum 94, p. 458-459.
"I'm Inside" (tr. of Yisrael Eliraz, w. Moshe Dor). [HarvardR] (7) Fall 94, p. 32-34.
"Soaps." [Light] (9) Spr 94, p. 14.
"The Stories." [VirQR] (70:3) Sum 94, p. 459-460.

6686. WHITTEN, Kathleen
"Vietnam Reliquary." [GrahamHR] (18) Wint 94-95, p. 70.

6687. WHITTEN, Leslie H.
"The Cat" (tr. of Charles Baudelaire). [Outbr] (25) 94, p. 88-89.

6688. WHITTIER, Lee
"Testament" (tr. of Roger Gilbert-Lecomte, w. Michel Palma). [PoetryE] (37/38) Spr 94, p. 236.
"The Wind After, The Wind Before" (tr. of Roger Gilbert-Lecomte, w. Michel Palma). [PoetryE] (37/38) Spr 94, p. 234-235.

6689. WHITTINGHAM, Brian
"Assembly Line Hysteria." [Verse] (11:1) Spr 94, p. 71.

6690. WHITTINGTON, Donald R.
"Meditations of Thanksgiving" (Presented in Three Parts). [Amelia] (7:4, #23) 94, p. 156-158.
"Upon Reading in the Paper That Joe Garagiola and Abraham Lincoln Share a Birthday." [Amelia] (7:3, #22) 94, p. 105.

6691. WHITTINGTON, Jancie
"Bloodlines." [BelPoJ] (44:4) Sum 94, p. 6-7.

6692. WHYTE, Christopher
"The Garden." [Verse] (11:2) Sum 94, p. 67.
"An Garradh." [Verse] (11:2) Sum 94, p. 66.
"Monsieur Franck's Quintet." [Verse] (11:2) Sum 94, p. 68.
"An Quintette le Monsieur Franck." [Verse] (11:2) Sum 94, p. 68.

6693. WICKS, Susan
"Caves." [BelPoJ] (45:2) Wint 94-95, p. 36.
"Holiday Season." [Verse] (11:2) Sum 94, p. 17.
"On Re-Recording Mozart." [Stand] (35:3) Sum 94, p. 55.

"On Re-Recording Mozart" (reprinted to correct errors in 35:3). [Stand] (35:4) Aut 94, p. 32.
"Stuffing Hearts." [SouthernR] (30:2) Ap, Spr 94, p. 330-331.
"Understairs." [SouthernR] (30:2) Ap, Spr 94, p. 330.
"Voice." [NewYorker] (70:11) 2 My 94, p. 72.
"Wake." [BelPoJ] (45:2) Wint 94-95, p. 35.

6694. WIDERKEHR, Richard
"The Alligators in My Computer." [CrabCR] (8:2/3/9:1/2/3) 94, p. 130-134.
"Night Watchman's Afternoon." [CrabCR] (8:2/3/9:1/2/3) 94, p. 134-135.

6695. WIEDER, Laurance
"Dumb." [Pequod] (37) 94, p. 93.

6696. WIEGEL, Nancy J.
"The Psalm of the Pallbearers." [TampaR] (8) Spr 94, p. 57.

6697. WIENER, Chet
"Non, Rien" (Excerpt, tr. of Agnès Rouzier). [Avec] (8:1) 94, p. 77-83.

6698. WIER, Dara
"Enough Said." [CutB] (41) Wint 94, p. 35-37.
"I Remember Rilke." [CutB] (41) Wint 94, p. 33-34.

6699. WIERSMA, G.
"Morning, Looking into the Distance" (tr. of Bei Ling). [Manoa] (6:1) Sum 94, p. 82.

6700. WIESE, Brooke
"Glory on Great Jones Street." [LaurelR] (28:2) Sum 94, p. 62-63.

6701. WIGGS, Terry
"The Beauteous Castrato Harmonies of Academe." [ChironR] (13:2) Sum 94, p. 17.

WIGHTMAN, Ludmilla Popova
See POPOVA-WIGHTMAN, Ludmilla

6702. WILBORN, William
"In February." [CumbPR] (13:2) Spr 94, p. 61.
"On the Virgin and Child of Botticelli in the Petit Palais, Avignon." [CumbPR] (13:2) Spr 94, p. 60.

6703. WILBUR, Frederick
"Skirmish." [HampSPR] Wint 94, p. 27.
"A Whittler's Tale." [HampSPR] Wint 94, p. 28.

6704. WILCOX, Patricia
"Three-Part Invention for Celan." [DenQ] (28:4) Spr 94, p. 70-72.

6705. WILD, Peter
"The Bear." [ArtfulD] (26/27) 94, p. 106.
"Choir." [PoetL] (89:3) Fall 94, p. 33.
"Engineer's Wife." [LaurelR] (28:1) Wint 94, p. 127.
"The Failed Eclipse." [ApalQ] (40/41) 94, p. 71.
"Great Trombonists." [ArtfulD] (26/27) 94, p. 107.
"The Green River Ordinance." [ApalQ] (40/41) 94, p. 72.
"On the Court." [Outbr] (25) 94, p. 90.
"Orphans." [ArtfulD] (26/27) 94, p. 108.

6706. WILDE-MENOZZI, Wallis
"Bees." [MalR] (109) Wint 94, p. 83-84.
"Black." [ProseP] (3) 94, p. 85.
"Fire." [ProseP] (3) 94, p. 86.
"Forest." [ProseP] (3) 94, p. 84.
"Oranges." [MalR] (109) Wint 94, p. 85-87.
"Rare." [Verse] (11:2) Sum 94, p. 83-84.

6707. WILDER, Rex
"On the Eve of the millennium." [BelPoJ] (45:2) Wint 94-95, p. 6-8.
"Still Life." [Poetry] (163:5) F 94, p. 275.

6708. WILDING, Margo
"Red Shift." [PraS] (68:2) Sum 94, p. 143-144.

6709. WILENSKY, Ben
"Coffee on the Morning Watch" (from "The Psalms of a Sailor Jew"). [AmerPoR] (23:6) N-D 94, p. 22.

6710. WILES, Clifton A.
"An Ed Buffaloe Photograph." [Border] (4) Spr-Sum 94, p. 75.

6711. WILEY, Catherine
"Lake Steam Baths" (for Gertie. First Sue Saniel Elkind National Poetry Award, Finalist). [Kalliope] (16:2) 94, p. 46-47.

6712. WILKES, Kennette
"What You Can See in March." [SouthernHR] (28:1) Wint 94, p. 46.
6713. WILLARD, Nancy
"Gabriel Returns from the Annunciation." [Confr] (54/55) Fall 94-Wint 95, p. 277.
"An Inconvenience of Wings." [PassN] (15:1) Sum 94, p. 29.
"The Lesson on Guardian Angels at Star of the Sea Elementary." [NewL] (60:4) 94, p. 85.
"The Mission of the Puffball." [Field] (50) Spr 94, p. 99.
"Tobias and the Fish." [Confr] (54/55) Fall 94-Wint 95, p. 278.
"Visitation in a Pewter Dish." [Caliban] (14) 94, p. 35.
"What Wings Give Away." [NewL] (60:4) 94, p. 83.
"The Winged Ones." [NewYorker] (70:35) 31 O 94, p. 78.
6714. WILLERTON, Chris
"Plains Battleground." [Border] (3) Fall 93, p. 79.
6715. WILLEY, Rosemary
"The House We Pass Through." [Ploughs] (20:4) Wint 94-95, p. 205.
"Wishing the Neighbors Goodnight." [GreenMR] (NS 17:2) Fall-Wint 94-95, p. 55.
6716. WILLIAMS, Barbara
"Artist's Concept, 1838" (from "Portrait of a Gentlewoman Artist"). [Nimrod] (37:2) Spr-Sum 94, p. 120.
"Burning Bush" (from "Portrait of a Gentlewoman Artist"). [Nimrod] (37:2) Spr-Sum 94, p. 122.
"There Is a Season, 1846" (from "Portrait of a Gentlewoman Artist"). [Nimrod] (37:2) Spr-Sum 94, p. 121.
6717. WILLIAMS, C. K.
"The Cycle of Seasons" (tr. of Francis Ponge). [AmerPoR] (23:4) Jl-Ag 94, p. 30.
"Notes Towards a Shellfish" (tr. of Francis Ponge). [AmerPoR] (23:1) Ja-F 94, p. 48.
"Secrets." [Antaeus] (75/76) Aut 94, p. 329-331.
"The Shrimp" (tr. of Francis Ponge). [AmerPoR] (23:4) Jl-Ag 94, p. 31-32.
"Snails" (tr. of Francis Ponge). [AmerPoR] (23:4) Jl-Ag 94, p. 30-31.
"Thirst." [NewYorker] (70:37) 14 N 94, p. 103.
6718. WILLIAMS, Donna Glee
"The Rescue." [NewOR] (20:1/2) Spr-Sum 94, p. 122.
6719. WILLIAMS, Gerald
"Gaps, Guns, Targets." [AmerPoR] (23:4) Jl-Ag 94, p. 47.
"New Suit, Just Like Mayakovsky." [SycamoreR] (6:1) Wint 94, p. 21-22.
6720. WILLIAMS, Godffrey
"You Ask Me What Hip Hop Is." [Eyeball] (3) 93, p. 11-12.
6721. WILLIAMS, Hugo
"Waiting to Go On." [NewYorker] (70:9) 18 Ap 94, p. 72.
6722. WILLIAMS, James
"Stillborn." [CreamCR] (18:1) Spr 94, p. 19.
6723. WILLIAMS, Jay G.
"Saturday Night Vigil." [ChrC] (111:10) 23-30 Mr 94, p. 300.
6724. WILLIAMS, Lisa
"After the Wedding." [ClockR] (9:1/2) 94-95, p. 134-135.
"Cemetery." [CreamCR] (18:1) Spr 94, p. 48-49.
"Iowa." [ChatR] (14:2) Wint 94, p. 51-52.
"Let Us Banish God." [SinW] (54) Wint 94-95, p. 67-68.
"Reading." [LouisL] (11:1) Spr 94, p. 172-174.
6725. WILLIAMS, Mary
"Hiali Give Us Strength." [CaribbeanW] (8) 94, p. 83.
6726. WILLIAMS, Melissa
"How My Mother Loved Me." [QW] (39) Sum-Fall 94, p. 247.
"Wheels." [QW] (39) Sum-Fall 94, p. 248-249.
6727. WILLIAMS, Miller
"Beside an Open Grave the Mind of the Young Preacher Comes Almost to Terms." [Image] (6) Sum 94, p. 20.
"God." [Image] (6) Sum 94, p. 21-22.
"Jonah on His Deathbed." [NewL] (60:4) 94, p. 143-147.
"Muse of the Evening." [NewEngR] (16:4) Fall 94, p. 99.
"The Sense of Loneliness in Spite of Everything." [Image] (6) Sum 94, p. 22.
"Six Lines Probably in F-Minor." [NewL] (60:4) 94, p. 143.
"Sleeping with Friends." [NewEngR] (16:4) Fall 94, p. 99.
"A Visitor's Guide to the Blue Planet." [SouthernR] (30:4) Aut 94, p. 824-825.

6728. WILLIAMS, Norman
"Games in the Darkening Air." [Hudson] (47:3) Aut 94, p. 422.
6729. WILLIAMS, Peter
"Thirties Eclogue." [Spitball] (47) Sum 94, p. 32.
6730. WILLIAMS, Philip Lee
"Camping with My Brother." [Confr] (54/55) Fall 94-Wint 95, p. 271.
"Rosie, a Plastic Dog." [Confr] (54/55) Fall 94-Wint 95, p. 272.
6731. WILLIAMS, Ralph T.
"Esteban" (with apologies to Gabriel Garcia Marquez). [ChamLR] (14/15) Spr-Fall 94, p. 93-94.
6732. WILLIAMS, Robert
"And Are We No Turned at Hard Angles?" [GettyR] (7:3) Sum 94, p. 446.
"The First Sunday of Advent Nineteen Fifty-Seven." [GettyR] (7:3) Sum 94, p. 447.
"The Old School." [GettyR] (7:3) Sum 94, p. 448.
6733. WILLIAMS, Roger
"Buffalo Creek." [BelPoJ] (45:2) Wint 94-95, p. 28.
"Delirium." [BelPoJ] (45:2) Wint 94-95, p. 28.
6734. WILLIAMS, Rynn
"The Dance." [Manoa] (6:1) Sum 94, p. 39-40.
"Hunger." [WillowR] (21) Spr 94, p. 11-12.
"Longing" (After Edward Hopper). [Nat] 774.(259:21) D 19 94, p. 776.
"Women by a Road as the Sun Sets." [Manoa] (6:1) Sum 94, p. 38-39.
6735. WILLIAMS, Theresa A.
"The Darkness You Came From." [Vis] (46) 94, p. 9.
6736. WILLIAMS, Tyrone
"A Wager on Transcendence." [DenQ] (28:3) Wint 94, p. 29.
6737. WILLIAMS, Zarle K.
"Juárez." [Pivot] (41) 93, p. 26.
6738. WILLIAMSON, Alan
"Deb's Dream About Pavese." [AmerPoR] (23:2) Mr-Ap 94, p. 12.
"The Etruscan Couple in the Villa Giulia." [Jacaranda] (4:2) Spr 90, p. 51.
"The Harvest Moon." [YaleR] (82:2) Ap 94, p. 84-88.
"Rilke's Argument with Don Giovanni." [BostonR] (19:5) O-N 94, p. 27.
"Toward the New Year" (Lower Manhattan). [AmerPoR] (23:2) Mr-Ap 94, p. 12.
6739. WILLIAMSON, Greg
"Ballade for Dead Poets." [Pequod] (37) 94, p. 94.
"Taxidermy." [Poetry] (164:5) Ag 94, p. 282.
6740. WILLIAMSON, Tharin
"Who Call for the Sun." [HolCrit] (31:1) F 94, p. 15-16.
6741. WILLINGHAM, Sara
"Still Grieving." [PoetryE] (37/38) Spr 94, p. 32.
6742. WILLIS, David James
"Night Log." [JamesWR] (11:2) Wint 94, p. 5.
"Stood Up for Lunch at the Chic Cafe Downtown." [JamesWR] (11:2) Wint 94, p. 10.
6743. WILLIS, Dawn Diez
"The Verses in Ash" (for William Tyndale, first translator of the New Testament into English ..., burned as a heretic in Oct. 1536). [DogRR] (26) Wint 94-95, p. 3.
6744. WILLIS, Elizabeth
"The Human Abstract" (Excerpt). [Avec] (8:1) 94, p. 44-45.
"It's sweetness makes her lean with watered longing." [Chain] (1) Spr-Sum 94, p. 229.
"My soul herself, myself" (to Julie Kalendek). [Chain] (1) Spr-Sum 94, p. 280-281.
"Songs for A." [Avec] (8:1) 94, p. 46-54.
6745. WILLIS, Irene
"Acme." [LaurelR] (28:2) Sum 94, p. 102-103.
"The Butcher's Wife." [FloridaR] (20:1) Fall 94, p. 100-101.
"Fire." [HiramPoR] (55/56) Fall 93-Sum 94, p. 117-118.
"Two Apples." [FloridaR] (20:1) Fall 94, p. 102.
6746. WILLIS, Paul
"Convoy." [SantaBR] (2:1) Spr-Sum 94, p. 89.
"How We Go On." [SantaBR] (2:1) Spr-Sum 94, p. 88.
"Late and Soon." [WeberS] (11:3) Fall 94, p. 64.
"Meeting Like This." [WeberS] (11:3) Fall 94, p. 62.
"Mission Pine Spring" (San Rafael Wilderness). [WeberS] (11:3) Fall 94, p. 63.

"Penn Valley." [SantaBR] (2:1) Spr-Sum 94, p. 90.
"Piedra Blanca" (Sespe Wilderness). [WeberS] (11:3) Fall 94, p. 62-63.
"Roma Potrero" (San Rafael Wilderness). [SantaBR] (2:1) Spr-Sum 94, p. 91.
"Surfers on the Earth." [SantaBR] (2:1) Spr-Sum 94, p. 90.

6747. WILLITTS, Martin, Jr.
"Coyote and Bear." [InterQ] (1:4) 94, p. 103.
"Raven Was Traveling." [InterQ] (1:4) 94, p. 102.

6748. WILLMOTT, Glenn
"Seventh Day in Durham, North Carolina." [AntigR] (96) Wint 94, p. 126-128.

6749. WILLOUGHBY, N. C. Dylan
"Another on the Same." [DenQ] (29:2) Fall 94, p. 48-49.
"Unwound." [Pembroke] (26) 94, p. 89.

WILMOT, John, Earl of Rochester
See ROCHESTER, John Wilmot, Earl of

6750. WILNER, Eleanor
"The Bird in the Laurel's Song." [ChamLR] (14/15) Spr-Fall 94, p. 197-198.
"Job's Wife, a 20th Century Casting Script." [SycamoreR] (6:2) Sum 94, p. 66-67.
"The Love of What Is Not." [Calyx] (15:3) Wint 94-95, p. 38-41.
"When Asked to Lie Down on the Altar" (for Marie Howe, and her "Isaac"). [ChamLR] (14/15) Spr-Fall 94, p. 194-196.

6751. WILOCH, Thomas
"My Television and I." [WormR] (34:3, #135) 94, p. 89-90.
"Period Piece." [WormR] (34:3, #135) 94, p. 90.
"Something About Sidewalks." [WormR] (34:3, #135) 94, p. 89.

6752. WILSON, Alan R.
"Canis Minor the Little Dog" (from "The Sonneteer's Sky Atlas"). [Nimrod] (37:2) Spr-Sum 94, p. 124.
"Circinus the Compasses." [MalR] (109) Wint 94, p. 102.
"Columba the Dove." [MalR] (109) Wint 94, p. 101.
"Five Winter Cinquains." [AntigR] (98) Sum 94, p. 86-87.
"Horologium the Clock." [MalR] (109) Wint 94, p. 103.
"Reticulum the Net" (from "The Sonneteer's Sky Atlas"). [Nimrod] (37:2) Spr-Sum 94, p. 123.

6753. WILSON, Audrey
"Opera Afternoons." [ApalQ] (40/41) 94, p. 75.

6754. WILSON, Dede
"English Garden, American Style." [Light] (10) Sum 94, p. 19.
"One Nightstand." [Light] (10) Sum 94, p. 16.
"To the Girl in the Tower." [SouthernPR] (34:1) Sum 94, p. 19-20.
"Whirligigs." [CreamCR] (18:1) Spr 94, p. 50.

6755. WILSON, E. Milton
"The Rainbow Series" (Selections: "1. Light Physics"). [ChamLR] (14/15) Spr-Fall 94, p. 139.

WILSON, Fatima Lim
See LIM-WILSON, Fatima

6756. WILSON, Gary
"Fog" (tr. of Alphonse Piché). [InterPR] (20:2) Fall 94, p. 71.
"Whirlpool" (tr. of Alphonse Piché). [InterPR] (20:2) Fall 94, p. 71.

6757. WILSON, Graeme
"Civil War" (tr. of Emperor Hanazono, 1297-1348). [Jacaranda] (5:1) Wint-Spr 91, p. 116.
"Conscript" (tr. of Imamatsuribe no Yosafu, written in 755). [Jacaranda] (5:1) Wint-Spr 91, p. 116.
"Girl Friend" (tr. of Tomioka Taeko, b. 1935). [Jacaranda] (5:1) Wint-Spr 91, p. 117.
"Stairway" (tr. of Yosano Akiko, 1878-1942). [Jacaranda] (5:1) Wint-Spr 91, p. 116.

6758. WILSON, Ian Randall
"How Much of It Is True?" [PoetryE] (37/38) Spr 94, p. 12-13.

6759. WILSON, James Webb
"After the Game." [SmPd] (31:1, #90) Wint 94, p. 21.

6760. WILSON, Joyce
"Norwegian Spruce." [Agni] (39) 94, p. 62-63.
"Spruce Down, Fifty Dollars." [HarvardR] (Premier Issue) Spr 92, p. 80.

6761. WILSON, Ken G.
"90 West." [Border] (4) Spr-Sum 94, p. 78-79.
"Expectations of Angels" (Guanajuato, Mexico). [Border] (4) Spr-Sum 94, p. 76-77.

6762. WILSON, Leonore
"Amado." [YellowS] (12:2, #46) Sum-Fall 94, p. 37.
"Black Dawn." [YellowS] (12:2, #46) Sum-Fall 94, p. 38.
"Blind Flowers." [YellowS] (12:2, #46) Sum-Fall 94, p. 37.
"Good Dawn." [YellowS] (12:2, #46) Sum-Fall 94, p. 37.
"Late August Sunflowers." [YellowS] (12:2, #46) Sum-Fall 94, p. 36.
"Nightclub in Moonlight." [PoetC] (25:3) Spr 94, p. 17.
"Vetch." [YellowS] (12:2, #46) Sum-Fall 94, p. 36.
"White Grass." [YellowS] (12:2, #46) Sum-Fall 94, p. 38.
"White Water." [YellowS] (12:2, #46) Sum-Fall 94, p. 36.
6763. WILSON, Ralph
"Following the Wrong Star." [SoDakR] (32:4) Wint 94, p. 19-20.
"Fragments." [MidwQ] (35:4) Sum 94, p. 418.
"Inventing Blue River." [SoDakR] (32:4) Wint 94, p. 17-18.
6764. WILSON, Rob
"Local Motions." [BambooR] (60) Wint 94, p. 123.
"National Geographic." [ChamLR] (14/15) Spr-Fall 94, p. 39.
6765. WILSON, Steve
"Baby #2 Leaps From the Womb." [NegC] (14:1/2) 94, p. 158.
"The Grand Hotel." [NewAW] (12) Spr-Sum 94, p. 138.
"A Parcel of Bones." [MidwQ] (35:4) Sum 94, p. 419.
"Sleeping on the Singapore Express" (2:00 A.M., Malaysia). [NewAW] (12) Spr-Sum 94, p. 139.
6766. WIMAN, Christian
"Anteater." [ColEng] (56:4) Ap 94, p. 453.
"Fisherman." [PoetC] (25:3) Spr 94, p. 29.
"Hearing Loss." [PoetC] (25:3) Spr 94, p. 30-31.
"The Long Home" (Excerpt). [PlumR] (7) [94?], p. 13-17.
"Mesquites." [SouthernPR] (34:2) Wint 94, p. 52-53.
6767. WIMAN, Richard
"Mujer Cubana." [WeberS] (11:2) Spr-Sum 94, p. 96.
6768. WINANS, Allan
"For All Those Kids Who Keep Writing Poems for Bukowski." [DogRR] (26) Wint 94-95, p. 14-15.
"The System." [BlackBR] (19) Fall-Wint 94, p. 28-29.
6769. WINCH, Terence
"Blank Expressions." [NewAW] (12) Spr-Sum 94, p. 40.
"The Green Room." [NewAW] (12) Spr-Sum 94, p. 42.
"Isolated Territory." [NewAW] (12) Spr-Sum 94, p. 39.
"Jumper on the Line." [NewAW] (12) Spr-Sum 94, p. 41.
"Taste Wars." [NewAW] (12) Spr-Sum 94, p. 43.
WINCKEL, Nance van
See Van WINCKEL, Nance
6770. WINDERS, R. Lightbulb
"The Honey-Hall" (Selections: 3, 6, 21, 99, 119, 128, tr. of Bacchan). [GrahamHR] (18) Wint 94-95, p. 60-61.
6771. WINE, Wayne
"Small Reality." [Plain] (14:3) Spr 94, p. 12.
WING, Tek Lum
See LUM, Wing Tek
6772. WINKLER, M.
"A Year Later" (tr. by Bernhard Frank). [WebR] (18) Fall 94, p. 12.
6773. WINNER, Robert
"Recovery Room." [NewYorker] (70:12) 9 My 94, p. 63.
6774. WINOGRAD, Kathryn Burt
"It Is Spring, Yes." [Farm] (11:2) Fall-Wint 94-95, p. 11.
"Living Will." [Farm] (11:2) Fall-Wint 94-95, p. 12-13.
WINTER, Corrine de
See DeWINTER, Corrine
6775. WINTER, Jonah
"Art." [Talisman] (13) Fall 94-Wint 95, p. 270.
"Doc Severinsen's Diary." [ChiR] (40:2/3) 94, p. 4.
"Duet for Channel Three and Channel Seven." [ChiR] (40:2/3) 94, p. 3.
"Lines Composed a Few Miles Below the World Trade Center." [Thrpny] (56) Wint 94, p. 28.
"Love." [Ploughs] (20:4) Wint 94-95, p. 206-207.

"Ode on Complexity." [ChiR] (40:2/3) 94, p. 5-7.
"The 'Unexpected Mariachi Band' Factor, or Logic 101 ..." [HawaiiR] (18:1, #40) Spr 94, p. 115-116.

6776. WINTERER, Heather
"The Long Illness." [DenQ] (29:1) Sum 94, p. 44-45.

6777. WINTERS, Anne
"The Mill-Race." [TriQ] (90) Spr-Sum 94, p. 53-55.
"Sonnet: Three Images." [TriQ] (90) Spr-Sum 94, p. 56.

6778. WINTERS, Mary
"Barber Shop." [ColEng] (56:2) F 94, p. 191.
"Dreams of a Spoon." [WestB] (35) 94, p. 10-11.
"Golden." [SmPd] (31:3, #92) Fall 94, p. 26-27.
"Her Mother Pretended Not to Notice." [Parting] (7:2) Wint 94-95, p. 44.
"High-Flown Design." [Interim] (13:1) Spr-Sum 94, p. 34.
"Lawyer's Office." [FourQ] (8:2) Fall 94, p. 11.
"Mentors." [Interim] (13:1) Spr-Sum 94, p. 32.
"Near the Stream." [ChatR] (14:3) Spr 94, p. 49.
"Tests." [OgalalaR] (5:1) Wint 94, p. 83.
"Time Bomb." [Border] (4) Spr-Sum 94, p. 81.
"To Be Hollow." [Interim] (13:1) Spr-Sum 94, p. 33.

6779. WINTERS, Nancy
"Ars Poetica." [Light] (10) Sum 94, p. 15.

6780. WINTHROP, Jeanette
"Saturday Morning at the Supermarket." [Sun] (220) Ap 94, p. 22.

6781. WINTZ, Anita
"Spaghettini Fini." [Light] (11) Aut 94, p. 11.

6782. WINWOOD, David
"Frog." [WritersF] (20) 94, p. 24-26.
"Lovers and Friends." [WritersF] (20) 94, p. 27.

6783. WISE, Jessie L., Jr.
"No Brownstones, Just Alleyways & Corner Pockets Full." [Obs] (9:2) Fall-Wint 94, p. 105-107.

6784. WISEMAN, Christopher
"Belated Thanks." [Dandel] (20:2) 93, p. 28.
"Out of Season." [Dandel] (20:2) 93, p. 29-30.
"Suddenly (Last Summer)" (for D.). [Dandel] (20:2) 93, p. 31-32.

6785. WISHNER, Nan
"Silver Bracelets." [CreamCR] (18:2) Fall 94, p. 127.

6786. WISNIEWSKI, Terry
"Making Tea at Two A.M." [SycamoreR] (6:2) Sum 94, p. 18.

6787. WITEK, Terri
"The Balanced Aquarium." [NewEngR] (16:3) Sum 94, p. 64-67.
"Blackboard." [Shen] (44:4) Wint 94, p. 32.
"The Robbers." [Shen] (44:4) Wint 94, p. 33.

6788. WITHEROW, Judith K.
"Are You a Gypsy." [SinW] (52) Spr-Sum 94, p. 57.

6789. WITT, Harold
"American Lit: Fiction." [NewYorkQ] (53) 94, p. 62.
"The Art of Poetry." [Wind] (74) 94, p. 95.
"Betatakin." [BellArk] (10:2) Mr-Ap 94, p. 14.
"California Roller Baby." [Wind] (74) 94, p. 37.
"The Call of the Wild." [Light] (10) Sum 94, p. 10.
"Christmas Eve at Grandpa's." [WritersF] (20) 94, p. 38-39.
"Fame." [Wind] (74) 94, p. 36.
"The Lady or the Tiger." [Wind] (74) 94, p. 94.
"Painting Over the 60's." [PoetC] (25:2) Wint 94, p. 34.
"Son of American Lit" (for David Alpaugh). [Wind] (74) 94, p. 36.
"Who I Really Wanted to Be." [Light] (11) Aut 94, p. 17.
"Writing America." [Wind] (74) 94, p. 93-94.

6790. WITT, Samuel Brown
"Elegy of a Living Man" (winner, 8th annual *Louisiana Literature* Prize for Poetry). [LouisL] (11:1) Spr 94, p. 1-3.
"Pastoral." [LouisL] (11:2) Fall 94, p. 73-74.

WITT, Susan Kelly de
See KELLY-DeWITT, Susan

6791. WITTE, Francine
"Perception." [GreenMR] (NS 17:2) Fall-Wint 94-95, p. 85.
6792. WITTE, George
"The Apparitioners." [GettyR] (7:1) Wint 94, p. 69-70.
"Clipping an Obituary." [Confr] (52/53) Wint-Spr 94, p. 329.
"Holiday Cake." [GettyR] (7:1) Wint 94, p. 66-67.
"My Mother in Her Garden, Turning a Kaleidoscope." [KenR] (NS 16:1) Wint 94, p. 62-67.
"Star Rhyme." [GettyR] (7:1) Wint 94, p. 68.
6793. WITTE, Phyllis
"To Grow Up in the Borough of Queens." [BrooklynR] (11) 94, p. 75.
6794. WITTWER, Rodney
"Sunglasses & Hats." [Ploughs] (20:4) Wint 94-95, p. 209.
"We Are Not Like Other People & Do Not Need Them." [Ploughs] (20:4) Wint 94-95, p. 208.
6795. WOHL, Jane Elkington
"Orion Wanders into Wyoming." [CumbPR] (14:1) Fall 94, p. 39.
6796. WOHLFELD, Valerie
"Ashes and Cinders of Burnt Things." [DenQ] (28:4) Spr 94, p. 73.
"Notes of Dictation for a Formal Lecture Concerning a Concise History of the Sea." [NoAmR] (279:2) Mr-Ap 94, p. 28-29.
6797. WOJAHN, David
"Among the Joshua Trees" (G.P., 1947-74 — for Rick Madigan). [MissouriR] (17:1) 94, p. 34-35.
"Burned Tract" (BWR Chapbook: 4 poems). [BlackWR] (21:1) Fall-Wint 94, p. 43-72.
"Cienfuegos Road" (August, 1992). [ChiR] (40:2/3) 94, p. 44-45.
"Elegy and Periphere." [MissouriR] (17:1) 94, p. 27-31.
"Emanations." [ChiR] (40:2/3) 94, p. 46-48.
"Homage to Ryszard Kapuscinski." [Poetry] (164:4) Jl 94, p. 187-190.
"In Memory of Primo Levi." [MissouriR] (17:1) 94, p. 32-33.
"It's Only Rock and Roll But I Like It: The Fall of Saigon, 1975." [Crazy] (47) Wint 94, p. 103.
"A Print of the Expulsion." [Crazy] (46) Spr 94, p. 77-81.
"Tribute and Ash." [Poetry] (163:5) F 94, p. 280-282.
"Truth-Taking Stare." [PassN] (15:1) Sum 94, p. 20-22.
"Westchester Tours, Day Eight: 'A Morning Visit to Some Great War Battlefields'." [PassN] (15:1) Sum 94, p. 23-24.
6798. WOLBACH, Sarah
"Boot Fence." [Border] (5) Fall-Wint 94, p. 68-69.
6799. WOLF, David
"Be Sure to Shake the Orange Juice." [NewYorkQ] (53) 94, p. 95.
"The Exchange." [HiramPoR] (55/56) Fall 93-Sum 94, p. 120.
"Glory Road." [RiverS] (40) 94, p. 54-55.
"Mid August." [HiramPoR] (55/56) Fall 93-Sum 94, p. 119.
6800. WOLF, Manfred
"Message About the Times" (tr. of Remco Campert). [GrahamHR] (18) Wint 94-95, p. 18.
"Poetry" (tr. of Remco Campert). [GrahamHR] (18) Wint 94-95, p. 19.
"Sunday" (tr. of Remco Campert). [GrahamHR] (18) Wint 94-95, p. 20.
6801. WOLF, Michele
"Lucky Smile." [Pequod] (37) 94, p. 95.
6802. WOLF, William A., Jr.
"But Joy Came to Us Naturally, Then." [Outbr] (25) 94, p. 91-92.
6803. WOLFE, Digby
"Taking the Rap: From Columbus to Clinton in Twenty Minutes." [SantaBR] (1:2) Fall-Wint 93, p. 110-125.
6804. WOLFF, Daniel
"How to Hop a Freight." [Thrpny] (59) Fall 94, p. 35.
6805. WOLFF, Rebecca
"Press Play." [AnotherCM] (28) 94, p. 165.
6806. WOLLOCH, Yona
"Outside the Body" (tr. by Linda Zisquit). [HarvardR] (7) Fall 94, p. 34.
6807. WOLOCH, Cecilia
"My Mother's Dreams." [AntR] (52:4) Fall 94, p. 615.
"Your Back." [AntR] (52:4) Fall 94, p. 614.

6808. WONG, Lawrence
"Discourse from an Immortal" (tr. by Evangeline Almberg and Andrew Parkin). [PoetryC] (14:3) My 94, p. 22.
"The Shattered Cliff" (tr. by Evangeline Almberg and Andrew Parkin). [PoetryC] (14:3) My 94, p. 22.
6809. WONG, Rita
"Rat Traps." [WestCL] (28:1/2, #13/14) Spr-Fall 94, p. 279-280.
6810. WONG-CHU, Jim
"Recipe for Tea." [CanLit] (140) Spr 94, p. 31-33.
"Sensitivity Test." [WestCL] (28:1/2, #13/14) Spr-Fall 94, p. 133.
6811. WOOD, Eve
"Arranged Marriage, China, 1921." [Poetry] (164:3) Je 94, p. 138.
"To My Wife." [PoetC] (26:1) Fall 94, p. 11.
6812. WOOD, Renate
"The Patience of Ice." [SenR] (24:1) Spr 94, p. 24-26.
6813. WOODCOCK, George
"The Cherry Tree on Cherry Street." [CanLit] (141) Sum 94, p. 84-85.
"The Diamond Bowler of the Khmer Kings, Pnom Penh, 1964." [CanLit] (140) Spr 94, p. 69-70.
"Dream of the Afternoon." [Descant] (24:4, #83) Wint 93-94, p. 90.
"Kampong Chhnang." [CanLit] (140) Spr 94, p. 64-65.
"Obsidian." [Descant] (24:4, #83) Wint 93-94, p. 91.
"Of Birdies in Byzantium." [Descant] (24:4, #83) Wint 93-94, p. 89.
"Ta Promh." [CanLit] (140) Spr 94, p. 68-69.
6814. WOODING, Robert
"My Love Is a Many-Splintered Thing." [Light] (9) Spr 94, p. 15.
6815. WOODLEY, Ken
"Excavation." [HampSPR] Wint 94, p. 49.
"The Serpent." [HampSPR] Wint 94, p. 50.
6816. WOODMAN, Christopher
"Like Every Angel Born." [CharR] (20:2) Fall 94, p. 82-83.
"The Whitetailed Deer." [CharR] (20:2) Fall 94, p. 81-82.
6817. WOODRUFF, William
"Coyotes howling." [WormR] (34:1, #133) 94, p. 10.
"Flashing in my cornering headlight beams." [WormR] (34:1, #133) 94, p. 10.
"Needed to vacuum." [WormR] (34:1, #133) 94, p. 10.
"On the frayed carpet." [WormR] (34:1, #133) 94, p. 10.
"Reeling, blood-splotched, two boxers." [WormR] (34:1, #133) 94, p. 10.
6818. WOODS, Christopher
"The Fire That Night." [XavierR] (14:1) Spr 94, p. 81.
6819. WOODSUM, Douglas
"Calm after a Little Madness." [NewEngR] (16:3) Sum 94, p. 134.
"Lines for Juliet." [ColR] (21:2) Fall 94, p. 142.
"No Scion of Daedalus." [NewEngR] (16:3) Sum 94, p. 134-135.
"Pear." [ColR] (21:2) Fall 94, p. 140-141.
"Two Planes." [DenQ] (29:2) Fall 94, p. 50.
6820. WOODWARD, Gerard
"The Wonders of the World." [Verse] (11:1) Spr 94, p. 8-13.
6821. WOODWORTH, Marc
"Adrian Leverkühn's Song for the Clearwings." [ParisR] (36:133) Wint 94, p. 128-129.
"Letter from Ryder." [WestHR] (48:3) Fall 94, p. 294-297.
6822. WOODY, Elizabeth
"The Girlfriends." [Ploughs] (20:1) Spr 94, p. 8.
"Perfidy." [Ploughs] (20:1) Spr 94, p. 9-10.
"Straight and Clear." [Ploughs] (20:1) Spr 94, p. 11-14.
6823. WOOLLEY, David
"Driving." [CoalC] (8) Ap 94, p. 23.
6824. WORFOLK, Dorothy
"Comparisons." [BellArk] (10:6) N-D 94, p. 22.
6825. WORLEY, James
"He Clears the Lichens from Her Graveyard Name." [ChrC] (111:22) 27 Jl-3 Ag 94, p. 724.
"A Peak in Darien" (Of the Hubble Telescope). [ChrC] (111:13) 20 Ap 94, p. 418.
"What I Do for a Living." [ChrC] (111:24) 24-31 Ag 94, p. 786.
"You Go First!" [ChrC] (111:36) 14 D 94, p. 1189.

6826. WORLEY, Jeff
"Happy Hour at the Two Keys Tavern." [NewEngR] (16:4) Fall 94, p. 60-61.
"March." [MidwQ] (35:3) Spr 94, p. 322-323.
"Raison d'être" (For my friend Logan). [CreamCR] (18:2) Fall 94, p. 120-121.
"Reckless." [PoetryNW] (35:3) Aut 94, p. 32-33.
"Traffic." [PoetryNW] (35:3) Aut 94, p. 31.
6827. WORMSER, Baron
"At the Lincoln Memorial." [TampaR] (8) Spr 94, p. 56.
"Colonial" (After Conrad). [IllinoisR] (2:1) Fall 94, p. 59.
"Death of a Woodcutter (1954)." [IllinoisR] (2:1) Fall 94, p. 58.
"Dramatis Personae (1957)" (for Sandy Phippen)." [NewEngR] (16:3) Sum 94, p. 10.
"Dreams." [IllinoisR] (2:1) Fall 94, p. 57.
"Dying in the Hospital." [Crazy] (47) Wint 94, p. 54.
"If Vietnam Is Only a Memory, Then I'm a Ghost" (1980). [IllinoisR] (1:2) Spr 94, p. 9-10.
"It's a Party (1959)." [NewEngR] (16:3) Sum 94, p. 8-9.
"Kissing." [Crazy] (47) Wint 94, p. 53.
"My Father Fought in World War Two." [Crazy] (47) Wint 94, p. 49-50.
"Pico." [Crazy] (47) Wint 94, p. 51-52.
"Pikesville." [GrahamHR] (18) Wint 94-95, p. 83-84.
"Sister Angela (1947)" (for Christopher Corkery). [NowestR] (32:2) 94, p. 13-14.
"Squares." [NewEngR] (16:3) Sum 94, p. 7-8.
"Weather." [NewEngR] (16:3) Sum 94, p. 5-6.
6828. WOROZBYT, Theodore, Jr.
"Blue Note." [TarRP] (34:1) Fall 94, p. 11-12.
"The Guitar." [Poetry] (164:5) Ag 94, p. 255.
"Knitting." [PoetC] (26:1) Fall 94, p. 12.
"Leaving Bucharest." [PoetL] (89:2) Sum 94, p. 27-28.
"Scheduled Return." [NegC] (14:1/2) 94, p. 25.
6829. WORTH, Jan
"Master Plan." [PassN] (15:2) Wint 94, p. 20-21.
6830. WORTSMAN, Peter
"Gertrude and Alice Pose." [ProseP] (3) 94, p. 87.
6831. WOUND, Lily
"Film" (Third Prize). [HarvardA] (128:3) Spr 94, p. 18.
6832. WRAY, Bettye K.
"Staten Island Memorabilia." [NegC] (14:1/2) 94, p. 149-150.
6833. WRIGHT, Bobbie Wallace
"Unclassified Ad." [Obs] (9:2) Fall-Wint 94, p. 108.
6834. WRIGHT, C. D.
"Flame." [Field] (50) Spr 94, p. 81.
"Floating Trees." [Chelsea] (57) 94, p. 44-45.
"Girl Friend Poem #5." [SouthernR] (30:4) Aut 94, p. 859.
"Girl Friend Poem #7." [SouthernR] (30:4) Aut 94, p. 860.
"Lake Echo, Dear." [Field] (50) Spr 94, p. 80.
"Oneness." [Field] (50) Spr 94, p. 82.
6835. WRIGHT, Carolyne
"Another Look at 'Albion on the Rock': Plate 38 of Blake's *Milton*." [HarvardR] (2) Fall 92, p. 70-71.
"Blue Pills" (tr. of Vijaya Mukhopadhyay, w. Sunil B. Ray). [KenR] (NS 16:4) Fall 94, p. 92.
"Character" (tr. of Taslima Nasrin, w. Farida Sarkar). [NewYorker] (70:26) 22-29 Ag 94, p. 77.
"Crow" (tr. of Anuradha Mahapatra, w. Paramita Banerjee). [PartR] (61:1) Wint 94, p. 155.
"The Earth Chooses Her Own Husband" (tr. of Mallika Sengupta, w. Paramita Banerjee). [Calyx] (15:2) Sum 94, p. 59.
"Film" (tr. of Vijaya Mukhopadhyay, w. Sunil B. Ray). [KenR] (NS 16:4) Fall 94, p. 91-92.
"The Game in Reverse" (tr. of Taslima Nasreen, w. Mohammed Nurul Huda and the author). [IndR] (17:1) Spr 94, p. 97.
"Happy Marriage" (tr. of Taslima Nasrin, w. Mohammad Nurul Huda and the author). [NewYorker] (70:28) 12 S 94, p. 55.
"He Gets Well" (tr. of Debarati Mitra, w. Paramita Banerjee). [InterQ] (1:2) 93, p. 156.

"Household Shrine" (tr. of Rajlakshimi Devi, w. Mithi Mukherjee). [InterQ] (1:2) 93, p. 158.
"I Go" (tr. of Rama Ghosh, w. Paramita Banerjee). [BostonR] (19:2) Ap-My 94, p. 9.
"I'll Go Away and I Won't Say a Thing" (tr. of Nasima Sultana, w. Mohammad Nurul Huda). [InterQ] (1:2) 93, p. 160.
"In the Sun of the Hazelnut Trees" (tr. of Jorge Teillier). [InterQ] (1:1) [93?], p. 63.
"In White Moonlight" (tr. of Debarati Mitra, w. Paramita Banerjee). [InterQ] (1:2) 93, p. 155.
"Let There Be Some Rage" (tr. of Nasima Sultana, w. Mohammed Nurul Huda and the author). [IndR] (17:1) Spr 94, p. 98.
"Tambura" (tr. of Anuradha Mahapatra, w. Paramita Banerjee). [Calyx] (15:2) Sum 94, p. 61.
"That's Not for Puti" (tr. of Vijaya Mukhopadhyay, w. Paramita Banerjee). [KenR] (NS 16:4) Fall 94, p. 93.
"Thirty-Five Parganas" (tr. of Gita Chattopadhyay, w. Paramita Banerjee). [Calyx] (15:2) Sum 94, p. 60.
"Thou Art Durga" (tr. of Gita Chattopadhyay, w. Paramita Banerjee). [InterQ] (1:2) 93, p. 157.
"Week in Valdivia" (For my old friends in the Trilce Group, and those from Indice, and for Jorge Torres Ulloa. Tr. of Jorge Teillier). [Agni] (39) 94, p. 119.
"Woman" (tr. of Vijaya Mukhopadhyay, w. Sunil B. Ray and the author). [InterQ] (1:2) 93, p. 159.

6836. WRIGHT, Charles
"Looking Across Laguna Canyon at Dusk, West-by-Northwest." [NewYorker] (70:18) 20 Je 94, p. 67.
"Meditation on Form and Measure." [Field] (51) Fall 94, p. 81-82.
"Omaggio a Montale." [Antaeus] (75/76) Aut 94, p. 332.
"Poem Half in the Manner of Li Ho." [Field] (50) Spr 94, p. 64-65.
"Sky Valley Rider." [NoCarLR] (2:1) Spr 94, p. 177.
"Still-Life with Stick and Word." [ColR] (21:1) Spr 94, p. 60-61.
"Yard Work." [PartR] (61:2) Spr 94, p. 309.

6837. WRIGHT, Charles S.
"Of Wine and Water." [NegC] (14:1/2) 94, p. 131.

6838. WRIGHT, Dorothy Winslow
"In Search of Harmony." [Outbr] (25) 94, p. 93.

6839. WRIGHT, Franz
"The Comedian." [NewYorker] (69:47) 24 Ja 94, p. 58.
"Ending." [Field] (51) Fall 94, p. 63.
"The Family's Windy Summer Night." [Field] (51) Fall 94, p. 62.
"The Mailman." [Field] (51) Fall 94, p. 61.
"This was the first time I knelt." [PartR] (61:4) Fall 94, p. 705.

6840. WRIGHT, Howard
"Interior." [AntigR] (99) Aut 94, p. 111.
"Rathlin." [Verse] (11:1) Spr 94, p. 72.
"A Return." [AntigR] (99) Aut 94, p. 110.

6841. WRIGHT, James
"Complaint." [Pequod] (37) 94, p. 111-112.
"Melancholy inside Families" (tr. of Pablo Neruda, w. Robert Bly). [Field] (51) Fall 94, p. 8-9.

6842. WRIGHT, Jay
"The Cradle Logic of Autumn." [Callaloo] (17:2) Sum 94, p. 458-459.
"The Economy of Power." [Callaloo] (17:2) Sum 94, p. 456-457.
"Leaving the Buenos Aires Cemetery." [Callaloo] (17:2) Sum 94, p. 450.
"Naming the Asturian Bird." [Callaloo] (17:2) Sum 94, p. 452-453.
"Popper's Dlimma." [Callaloo] (17:2) Sum 94, p. 454-455.
"Seguidilla with a Double Heart." [Callaloo] (17:2) Sum 94, p. 451.

6843. WRIGHT, Kirby
"Community Garden." [Plain] (14:2) Wint 94, p. 18.
"Poem for Ironwood." [Plain] (14:3) Spr 94, p. 32.

6844. WRIGHT, Leilani
"Autopsy." [SlipS] (14) 94, p. 11.
"The Photo Critic's Last Request." [ChironR] (13:2) Sum 94, p. 31.

6845. WRIGHT, Nancy Means
"The Freshening" (for Tom Buttolph, Shoreham, Vermont). [ClockR] (9:1/2) 94-95, p. 108-109.

6846. WRIGLEY, Robert
"Angels." [GeoR] (48:3) Fall 94, p. 569-570.
"Aubade." [PoetryNW] (35:3) Aut 94, p. 27-28.
"Fires." [EngJ] (83:8) D 94, p. 71.
"Gold" (for Dennis and Claire). [Shen] (44:2) Sum 94, p. 25.
"Habitat." [Manoa] (6:2) Wint 94, p. 207-208.
"Killing the Snakes" (for Kim). [SouthernR] (30:1) Ja, Wint 94, p. 110-111.
"The Longing of Eagles." [PoetryNW] (35:3) Aut 94, p. 26-27.
"Lucky." [Manoa] (6:2) Wint 94, p. 209.
"Meadowlark." [Manoa] (6:2) Wint 94, p. 210.
"Seeing the Lynx Again." [GettyR] (7:1) Wint 94, p. 77.
"Spider Light." [IllinoisR] (2:1) Fall 94, p. 60-61.
"Spontaneous." [Manoa] (6:2) Wint 94, p. 206.
"Two Horses, Two Men" (for Bob & Ashley Jackson). [Shen] (44:2) Sum 94, p. 26-27.
6847. WYATT, Charles
"Beggar Couple with Children and a Dog" (Rembrandt, c. 1648). [HangL] (64) 94, p. 75.
"Camera Obscura." [Journal] (18:1) Spr-Sum 94, p. 108-110.
"The Cows." [Jacaranda] (4:2) Spr 90, p. 82.
"Dismantling a Child's Playhouse." [AnotherCM] (28) 94, p. 181.
"Doors." [Journal] (18:1) Spr-Sum 94, p. 111-112.
"A Fish's Head." [Jacaranda] (4:2) Spr 90, p. 83.
"A Fragile Thing." [DarkMoon] (1) 94, p. 32-33.
"From *Rembrandt Drawings:* A Coach, c1655." [CumbPR] (13:2) Spr 94, p. 62.
"From *Rembrandt Drawings:* Christ as a Gardner Appears to Mary Magdalen c. 1638 (studies for a painting)." [CumbPR] (13:2) Spr 94, p. 63.
"I Am Growing Tired." [Jacaranda] (5:1) Wint-Spr 91, p. 113.
"It Was, Uncertainly." [NewDeltaR] (11:2) Spr-Sum 94, p. 18-19.
"Motif." [DarkMoon] (1) 94, p. 29.
"Spirits for S.M. Jones, 1836-1899." [Interim] (13:1) Spr-Sum 94, p. 24-29.
"Stars." [DarkMoon] (1) 94, p. 28.
"(Study for a) Portrait of Maria Trip, C.1693" (drawing, Rembrandt van Rijn. ELF 1994 Poetry Competition: Honorable Mention). [Elf] (4:2) Sum 94, p. 24.
"Tree Turtles." [DarkMoon] (1) 94, p. 30-31.
"Whale in Philadelphia." [CarolQ] (46:3) Sum 94, p. 69.
"Winter Honeysuckle." [Farm] (11:1) Spr-Sum 94, p. 100.
"Woman in North Holland Costume" (c. 1638-40). [HangL] (64) 94, p. 76.
6848. WYATT, Thomas, Sir, the Elder (1526)
"Whoso List to Hunt." [SoCoast] (17) Je 94, p. 61.
6849. WYCKOFF, Derek
"Modern Diplomacy." [HiramPoR] (57) Fall 94-Wint 95, p. 61.
6850. WYLAM, John
"House Without Curtains." [Northeast] (5:11) Wint 94-95, p. 38.
"One Winter or Another." [Northeast] (5:11) Wint 94-95, p. 39.
6851. WYNAND, Derk
"Free Speech." [Quarry] (43:2) S 94, p. 83-84.
"French Poets, We Love." [Grain] (22:2) Fall 94, p. 42.
"Head." [Quarry] (43:2) S 94, p. 81.
"Parade." [Quarry] (43:2) S 94, p. 82.
6852. WYREBEK, M.
"Near Death." [PraS] (68:1) Spr 94, p. 116.
"Trendelenburg Position." [PraS] (68:1) Spr 94, p. 115.
6853. WYTTENBERG, Victoria
"Circlet." [PoetryC] (15:1) N 94, p. 20.
"Flowers Have Beauty and Roots Have Worth." [PoetryC] (15:1) N 94, p. 20.

6854. XI, Chuan
"Blowing Wind" (tr. by Cheng Baolin and Richard Terrill). [AnotherCM] (27) 94, p. 85.
"Experience" (tr. by Cheng Baolin and Richard Terrill). [AnotherCM] (27) 94, p. 86.
"Memory" (tr. of Bei Ling, w. Tony Barnstone). [Talisman] (12) Spr 94, p. 175.
"The Sunset Above the Square" (tr. by Cheng Baolin and Richard Terrill). [AnotherCM] (27) 94, p. 84.
"Void" (tr. of Bei Ling, w. Tony Barnstone). [Talisman] (12) Spr 94, p. 175.

6855. XI, Murong
"Burning" (tr. by Zheng Jianqing and Angela Ball). [LitR] (37:4) Sum 94, p. 684.
XIAOLONG, Qiu
See QIU, Xiaolong
6856. XIRINACS, Olga
"Eau Folle (1)" (tr. by Hillary J. Gardner). [DenQ] (29:1) Sum 94, p. 113.
6857. XU, Haixin
"You Asked About My Life. I Send You, Pei Di, These Lines" (tr. of Wang Wei, w. Tony Barnstone and Willis Barnstone). [NewEngR] (16:3) Sum 94, p. 31.
6858. XUE, Di
"Faces" (tr. by Janet Tan and Keith Waldrop). [Manoa] (6:1) Sum 94, p. 85-86.
"The Gleaner" (Van Gogh, *Peasant Woman Stooping*, 1885, tr. by Wang Ping and Keith Waldrop). [Manoa] (6:1) Sum 94, p. 84-85.
"Interplay" (tr. by Wang Ping and Keith Waldrop). [Manoa] (6:1) Sum 94, p. 84.
XUELIANG, Chen
See CHEN, Xueliang

6859. YAACOBI, Gad
"Calm Reconciliation or Latest Impressions" (tr. by Keren Alklai-Gut). [AmerLC] (6) 94, p. 125-126.
6860. YAKE, William (Bill)
"Into the Desert." [BellArk] (10:2) Mr-Ap 94, p. 11.
"Myth, Wind, Stone, Seed" (A poem for fractals, myth, chaos). [BellArk] (10:3) My-Je 94, p. 14.
6861. YAKIN, Heather D.
"Sangsara (Pastoral)." [HeavenB] (11) 94, p. 85.
6862. YAMAMOTO, Judith
"If Earth Is One of Seven." [Ploughs] (20:1) Spr 94, p. 118.
6863. YAMANAKA, Lois-Ann
"Dead Dogs RIP." [Bomb] (46) Wint 94, p. 62.
"My Eyes Adore You." [Bomb] (46) Wint 94, p. 60-61.
YAN, Li
See LI, Yan
YANBING, Chang
See CHEN, Yanbing
YANBING, Chen
See CHEN, Yanbing
6864. YANG, Lian
"Altitude of a Dream" (tr. by Michelle Yeh). [Manoa] (6:1) Sum 94, p. 160.
"Before Daybreak" (tr. by Brian Holton). [Conjunc] (23) 94, p. 43.
"A City of Dead Poets" (tr. by Michelle Yeh). [Manoa] (6:1) Sum 94, p. 159-160.
"The Foundations of Terror" (tr. by Brian Holton). [Conjunc] (23) 94, p. 46.
"Game of Lies" (tr. by Heather S. J. Steliga and Chen Shi-Zheng). [Manoa] (6:1) Sum 94, p. 157-158.
"The Garden on a Winter's Day, 1" (tr. by Brian Holton). [Conjunc] (23) 94, p. 44.
"The Garden on a Winter's Day, 3" (tr. by Brian Holton). [Conjunc] (23) 94, p. 45.
"Mountain Valley" (tr. by Brian Holton). [Conjunc] (23) 94, p. 43-44.
"Where the Sea Stands Still" (tr. by Mabel Lee). [Talisman] (12) Spr 94, p. 182-190.
"Winter Garden" (tr. by Heather S. J. Steliga and Chen Shi-Zheng). [Manoa] (6:1) Sum 94, p. 158-159.
6865. YANOVER, Lisa
"First Hebrew Lesson" (3 selections). [PraS] (68:3) Fall 94, p. 48-50.
YARBROUGH, Ewa Hryniewicz
See HRYNIEWICZ-YARBROUGH, Ewa
6866. YARKER, Patrick
"Actual Size." [Verse] (11:1) Spr 94, p. 65.
YASUSADA, Araki
See ARAKI, Yasusada
6867. YATES, Katie
"Amana Girl in Black Winter Coat" (to Spring Ulmer). [Chain] (1) Spr-Sum 94, p. 159.
"A Psalm As Essay About Anne Waldman's Work." [Talisman] (13) Fall 94-Wint 95, p. 118-119.
6868. YATES, Steve
"Honing." [TampaR] (8) Spr 94, p. 66-67.

"Sawhorse with a Wife Sitting Against It." [Border] (4) Spr-Sum 94, p. 82-83.

6869. YAU, Emily
"Spring Birdsong." [ConnPR] (13:1) 94, p. 8.

6870. YAU, John
"Bare Sheets" (I-III). [PlumR] (7) [94?], p. 77-78.
"Hospital Parking Lot Rendezvous." [PlumR] (7) [94?], p. 4-5.

6871. YEH, Michelle
"Altitude of a Dream" (tr. of Yang Lian). [Manoa] (6:1) Sum 94, p. 160.
"A City of Dead Poets" (tr. of Yang Lian). [Manoa] (6:1) Sum 94, p. 159-160.
"Diary" (tr. of Wang Jiaxin). [Manoa] (6:1) Sum 94, p. 112.
"A Visit" (tr. of Wang Jiaxin). [Manoa] (6:1) Sum 94, p. 112-113.

6872. YELLE, Gerald
"Prayer for Standing on Hind Legs." [Sonora] (28) Fall 94, p. 64.
"Vote with Your Aeroflot, I'll Shoot with My Dame's Rocket." [Sonora] (28) Fall 94, p. 65-66.

6873. YENSER, Stephen
"Lo-Cal Elegy." [AntR] (52:1) Wint 94, p. 108.
"Pentimento." [Jacaranda] (10) 94, p. 129.
"Salle Archaique ("Archaischer Torso Apollos")." [AntR] (52:1) Wint 94, p. 109.
"Valentine." [Poetry] (163:5) F 94, p. 249-250.

YIMIN, Lu
See LU, Yimin

YIN, Wang
See WANG, Yin

6874. YIP, Wai-lim
"Quest." [Talisman] (12) Spr 94, p. 156.
"Temple of Thirty-Three Rooms" (tr. of Chang Mo). [Talisman] (12) Spr 94, p. 154-155.
"Travelling in Spring." [InterQ] (1:2) 93, p. 58-59.
"Variation of a Poem by Wang Wei: Bird-Singing Stream." [Talisman] (12) Spr 94, p. 157-158.
"Walking Toward Wang Wei (1989)" (tr. of Fu Lo). [InterQ] (1:2) 93, p. 56-57.

6875. YODER, Jonathan
"Big Dan de Lion" (in memory of Sterling Allen Brown, also for other bluesmen). [Callaloo] (17:4) Fall 94, p. 969-972.
"Coltrane." [Callaloo] (17:4) Fall 94, p. 973.

YONG, Kim
See KIM, Yong

YONG, U. Kim
See KIM, Yong U.

YONGMING, Zhai
See ZHAI, Yongming

6876. YORK, Maggie
"The Bachelor." [Stand] (35:4) Aut 94, p. 4.

YOSAFU, Imamatsuribe no
See IMAMATSURIBE no Yosafu

6877. YOSANO, Akiko (1878-1942)
"Stairway" (tr. by Graeme Wilson). [Jacaranda] (5:1) Wint-Spr 91, p. 116.

6878. YOSHIOKA, Minoru
"Kusudama" (Selection: "A Spring Ode," tr. by Eric Selland). [ChiR] (40:1) 94, p. 118-119.

6879. YOUMANS, Marly
"Testament for the Paisley Loom-Workers." [SoCaR] (27:1/2) Fall 94-Spr 95, p. 12.

6880. YOUMANS, Rich
"Alignments." [Northeast] (5:11) Wint 94-95, p. 15.

6881. YOUNG, Annette
"The Oracle" (for Sheryl Stover). [BellArk] (10:6) N-D 94, p. 4.

6882. YOUNG, Bard
"Fast Food and Metaphysics." [NegC] (14:1/2) 94, p. 59.

6883. YOUNG, Brian
"Deadline." [AnotherCM] (27) 94, p. 204-205.
"Into the Previously Dying Wind." [ColR] (21:1) Spr 94, p. 87-90.
"An Old Song in the Middle of the Night." [QW] (38) Winter-Spr 93-94, p. 136-137.
"Summer Tanager." [ChiR] (40:2/3) 94, p. 106-108.
"Test Section." [Arshile] (3) 94, p. 17.

"Wellness Center." [ColR] (21:1) Spr 94, p. 81-86.
6884. YOUNG, C. Dale
"Sunday Afternoon." [PartR] (61:2) Spr 94, p. 323.
6885. YOUNG, David
"Blue Hydrangeas" (tr. of Rainer Maria Rilke). [Field] (50) Spr 94, p. 23.
"The Bowl of Roses" (tr. of Rainer Maria Rilke). [Field] (50) Spr 94, p. 24-26.
"Death-Experience" (tr. of Rainer Maria Rilke). [Field] (50) Spr 94, p. 21.
"The Good Kings Wenceslases" (tr. of Miroslav Holub, w. Dana Hábová). [HarvardR] (Premier Issue) Spr 92, p. 52.
"Intensive Care Unit" (tr. of Miroslav Holub, w. Dana Hábová). [InterQ] (1:1) [93?], p. 93.
"Pompeii" (tr. of Miroslav Holub, w. Dana Hábová). [HarvardR] (Premier Issue) Spr 92, p. 117.
"Pompeii" (tr. of Miroslav Holub, w. Dana Hábová). [InterQ] (1:1) [93?], p. 94-95.
"Venice in Late Autumn" (tr. of Rainer Maria Rilke). [Field] (50) Spr 94, p. 22.
6886. YOUNG, Dean
"All Told." [IndR] (17:2) Fall 94, p. 5.
"Charm School." [PoetryE] (37/38) Spr 94, p. 64-65.
"The Last I Heard from My Father." [PoetryE] (37/38) Spr 94, p. 63.
"Lives of Composers." [Thrpny] (57) Spr 94, p. 34.
"Love Poem with Hole in the Wall." [PoetryE] (37/38) Spr 94, p. 68-69.
"Poem of Eternals for the New Year." [PoetryE] (37/38) Spr 94, p. 66-67.
"Post-Ovidian." [IndR] (17:2) Fall 94, p. 1-2.
"While Tony Hoagland Reads at the Poetry Society of America." [IndR] (17:2) Fall 94, p. 3-4.
6887. YOUNG, Gary
"Brave Deeds" (a work in progress). [SantaBR] (2:2) Fall-Wint 94, p. 32.
"Four Poems." [SantaBR] (1:2) Fall-Wint 93, p. 99.
"I discovered a journal in the children's ward." [ProseP] (3) 94, p. 88.
"My son is learning about death, about the possibilities." [ProseP] (3) 94, p. 89.
6888. YOUNG, George
"The Anguish of Bears." [LitR] (37:4) Sum 94, p. 574.
"Calligraphy." [ChamLR] (14/15) Spr-Fall 94, p. 138.
"Drinking Confusion to Newton's Rainbow." [NegC] (14:1/2) 94, p. 56-57.
"Oh Savage Spirit." [PoetC] (25:3) Spr 94, p. 35.
"A Postcard from the Prairie." [LitR] (37:4) Sum 94, p. 575.
6889. YOUNG, Jim
"Sidewalk Sale." [Light] (11) Aut 94, p. 10.
6890. YOUNG, John Allen
"I Remember My Father Weeping." [Amelia] (7:4, #23) 94, p. 170.
"Walking the Bike Path." [Amelia] (7:4, #23) 94, p. 171-172.
6891. YOUNG, Karl
"Milestones. Set Two" (2 excerpts). [RiverS] (40) 94, p. 63.
6892. YOUNG, Linda
"Along Every Street, All Night Diners." [NewYorkQ] (53) 94, p. 96-97.
"A Progression." [Plain] (14:2) Wint 94, p. 10-11.
6893. YOUNG, Mary Macrina
"Lamaze." [AmerV] (35) 94, p. 60.
"Lifecry" (age 5). [AmerV] (35) 94, p. 63.
"Maggie in Spring." [AmerV] (35) 94, p. 64.
"Poem for My Father." [AmerV] (35) 94, p. 59.
"A Praise with Eyes." [AmerV] (35) 94, p. 63.
"Whitley County." [AmerV] (35) 94, p. 61.
"Woman at Our Lady of Peace Asking." [AmerV] (35) 94, p. 62.
6894. YOUNG, Patricia
"Crow's Apology." [Arc] (33) Fall 94, p. 28.
6895. YOUNG BEAR, Ray (Ray A.)
"Our Bird Aegis." [Callaloo] (17:1) Wint 94, p. 213.
6896. YOUNG-ESQUIBEL, David
"Oil of Royal Pine, August 22, 1993." [BilingR] (19:1) Ja-Ap 94, p. 57.
YOUNG-HEE, Chang
See CHANG, Young-hee
6897. YOUNG-SADOWSKI, Jennifer
"Accepting the Inexplicable Gift." [BellArk] (10:2) Mr-Ap 94, p. 12.
"Andy Hits the Big Time." [BellArk] (10:2) Mr-Ap 94, p. 12.
"Mrs. Clancy's Grand Piano." [BellArk] (10:2) Mr-Ap 94, p. 12.

"Mucking Out." [SycamoreR] (6:1) Wint 94, p. 23.
"The Questions of Vocation." [BellArk] (10:2) Mr-Ap 94, p. 12.
6898. YOUNGBLOM, Tracy
"Hard Work." [Shen] (44:1) Spr 94, p. 101.
6899. YOUNGS, Anne Ohman
"Anniversary." [Elf] (4:4) Wint 94, p. 34-35.
"Hot August Light." [CreamCR] (18:1) Spr 94, p. 62-63.
"Recognizing Ever-Changing Landscapes." [ProseP] (3) 94, p. 90-91.
6900. YOURCENAR, Marguerite
"The Thirty-Three Names of God: Essay from a Journal with No Dates or Personal Pronouns" (tr. by Brooke Bergan). [PoetryE] (37/38) Spr 94, p. 203-207.
6901. YOVU, Peter
"Weasel." [CrabCR] (8:2/3/9:1/2/3) 94, p. 17.
6902. YSKAMP, Amanda
"Demolition Derby." [GeoR] (48:4) Wint 94, p. 758-760.
6903. YU, Jian
"Correspondent" (tr. by Cheng Baolin and Richard Terrill). [NoDaQ] (62:1) Wint 94-95, p. 93-94.
"Fish" (tr. by Wang Ping and Ron Padgett). [Talisman] (12) Spr 94, p. 160-161.
6904. YU, Kwang-chung
"The Mirror." [PoetryC] (14:3) My 94, p. 20.
YU, Lu
See LU, Yu
6905. YU, Timothy
"Fragrant Harbor." [HarvardA] (129:2) Fall 94, p. 26.
YUE, Ming Chen
See CHEN, Yue Ming
6906. YUEN, Che-hung
"Grandma Is Dead." [PoetryC] (14:3) My 94, p. 21.
YUN, Wang
See WANG, Yun
6907. YURANA, Matt
"Houdini's Boyhood." [PoetryNW] (35:2) Sum 94, p. 3-4.
"Ontogeny." [PoetryNW] (35:2) Sum 94, p. 7-9.
"The Wheelchair Repairman Watches a Storm, Agnews State Mental Hospital." [PoetryNW] (35:2) Sum 94, p. 5-7.
6908. YURDANA, Matt
"Killing Birds." [Plain] (14:2) Wint 94, p. 6-7.
"Last Day in Portugal." [Plain] (15:1) Fall 94, p. 34-35.
"Leaving the Yolo County Raptor Center." [Plain] (14:3) Spr 94, p. 19.
6909. YURMAN, R.
"Anatomy." [ChironR] (13:2) Sum 94, p. 15.
"Green Vegetables." [SlipS] (14) 94, p. 106-107.
6910. YUSUF, Sa'adi
"The Mouse" (tr. by Khaled Mattawa). [InterQ] (1:3) 94, p. 133.
"Night in Hamdan" (tr. by Khaled Mattawa). [InterQ] (1:3) 94, p. 134.
6911. YUZNA, Susan
"The Great Divide." [AntR] (52:3) Sum 94, p. 476-477.
"Lake Winnibigoshish." [Ploughs] (20:1) Spr 94, p. 119-120.
"North Avenue East" (for my son). [AntR] (52:3) Sum 94, p. 475.
"The Radio." [LaurelR] (28:2) Sum 94, p. 90-91.

6912. ZAGAJEWSKI, Adam
"Late Feast" (English translation). [PartR] (61:4) Fall 94, p. 708.
6913. ZAGER, Sophie
"Her Daughter at the Exhibition of Helga's Pictures by Andrew Wyeth." [PoetL] (89:2) Sum 94, p. 35-36.
6914. ZAHARIA, Mihai
"Another Hour" (tr. of Ileana Malancioiu, w. Eveline L. Kanes). [InterPR] (20:1) Spr 94, p. 37.
"The Art of Poetry" (tr. of Nichita Stanescu, w. Eveline L. Kanes). [InterPR] (20:1) Spr 94, p. 61, 63.
"Autumn Exhibition" (tr. of Mircea Dinescu, w. Eveline L. Kanes). [InterPR] (20:1) Spr 94, p. 19.

"Cain and Abel" (tr. of Nichita Stanescu, w. Eveline L. Kanes). [InterPR] (20:1) Spr 94, p. 51.
"Caudine Forks" (tr. of Horia Badescu, w. Eveline L. Kanes). [InterPR] (20:1) Spr 94, p. 77.
"The Churches Have No Roofs" (tr. of Ana Blandiana, w. Eveline L. Kanes). [InterPR] (20:1) Spr 94, p. 25.
"Death has climbed on our house" (tr. of Mircea Dinescu, w. Eveline L. Kanes). [InterPR] (20:1) Spr 94, p. 13.
"The Father" (tr. of Ana Blandiana, w. Eveline L. Kanes). [InterPR] (20:1) Spr 94, p. 33.
"Guilty Star" (tr. of Stefan A. Doinas, w. Eveline L. Kanes). [InterPR] (20:1) Spr 94, p. 69.
"Hell" (tr. of Ana Blandiana, w. Eveline L. Kanes). [InterPR] (20:1) Spr 94, p. 31.
"The Hypocritical Corpse" (tr. of Mircea Dinescu, w. Eveline L. Kanes). [InterPR] (20:1) Spr 94, p. 23.
"Jericho Waltz" (tr. of Mircea Dinescu, w. Eveline L. Kanes). [InterPR] (20:1) Spr 94, p. 15.
"The Jester" (tr. of Ileana Malancioiu, w. Eveline L. Kanes). [InterPR] (20:1) Spr 94, p. 43.
"Journey into the Light" (tr. of Stefan A. Doinas, w. Eveline L. Kanes). [InterPR] (20:1) Spr 94, p. 67.
"The Lamentations of Solomon" (X, XXVI, tr. of Horia Badescu, w. Eveline L. Kanes). [InterPR] (20:1) Spr 94, p. 83, 85.
"The Last Memory" (tr. of Ileana Malancioiu, w. Eveline L. Kanes). [InterPR] (20:1) Spr 94, p. 45.
"Like a Rabbit" (tr. of Ileana Malancioiu, w. Eveline L. Kanes). [InterPR] (20:1) Spr 94, p. 39.
"Lorenzo's Decree" (tr. of Stefan A. Doinas, w. Eveline L. Kanes). [InterPR] (20:1) Spr 94, p. 65.
"Maieutics" (tr. of Horia Badescu, w. Eveline L. Kanes). [InterPR] (20:1) Spr 94, p. 87.
"Medical Advice" (tr. of Mircea Dinescu, w. Eveline L. Kanes). [InterPR] (20:1) Spr 94, p. 21.
"Molecules of Calcium" (tr. of Ana Blandiana, w. Eveline L. Kanes). [InterPR] (20:1) Spr 94, p. 27.
"On the Field of Stone" (tr. of Nichita Stanescu, w. Eveline L. Kanes). [InterPR] (20:1) Spr 94, p. 53.
"Poem: Who can still dream, and of what" (tr. of Ana Blandiana, w. Eveline L. Kanes). [InterPR] (20:1) Spr 94, p. 35.
"Poem: You float like a nocturnal dream" (tr. of Nichita Stanescu, w. Eveline L. Kanes). [InterPR] (20:1) Spr 94, p. 49.
"Psalm: You who have taught bears" (tr. of Ana Blandiana, w. Eveline L. Kanes). [InterPR] (20:1) Spr 94, p. 29.
"Song" (1-2, tr. of Horia Badescu, w. Eveline L. Kanes). [InterPR] (20:1) Spr 94, p. 79, 81.
"The Story of the Rats" (tr. of Stefan A. Doinas, w. Eveline L. Kanes). [InterPR] (20:1) Spr 94, p. 71.
"Testament" (tr. of Nichita Stanescu, w. Eveline L. Kanes). [InterPR] (20:1) Spr 94, p. 55, 57.
"Trace of a Voyage" (tr. of Mircea Dinescu, w. Eveline L. Kanes). [InterPR] (20:1) Spr 94, p. 17.
"Ulysses" (tr. of Stefan A. Doinas, w. Eveline L. Kanes). [InterPR] (20:1) Spr 94, p. 75.
"Victim of My Dream" (tr. of Ileana Malancioiu, w. Eveline L. Kanes). [InterPR] (20:1) Spr 94, p. 41.
"Vigil Near Metals" (tr. of Nichita Stanescu, w. Eveline L. Kanes). [InterPR] (20:1) Spr 94, p. 59.
"When I Sailed" (tr. of Ileana Malancioiu, w. Eveline L. Kanes). [InterPR] (20:1) Spr 94, p. 47.
"The Wounded Veteran" (tr. of Stefan A. Doinas, w. Eveline L. Kanes). [InterPR] (20:1) Spr 94, p. 73.

6915. ZAMODA, Jagoda
"Solution" (tr. by Dasha Culic Nisula). [InterQ] (1:1) [93?], p. 119.

6916. ZAMORA, Juan Carlos
"Infancia Oblicua." [LindLM] (13:1) Mr 94, p. 9.

ZANDE, Jeff Vande
See Vande ZANDE, Jeff
ZANT, Frank Van
See Van ZANT, Frank
6917. ZAPATA, Miguel-Angel
"The House of the Soul" (tr. by Rose Passalacqua). [NewL] (60:4) 94, p. 87.
"In the Beginning the Moon Did Not Inspire Song" (tr. by Rose Passalacqua). [WritersF] (20) 94, p. 178.
"Paul Celan" (tr. by Rose Passalacqua). [WritersF] (20) 94, p. 179.
6918. ZARIN, Cynthia
"The Astronomical Hen." [NewYorker] (70:29) 19 S 94, p. 86.
"Primrose." [NewYorker] (70:8) 11 Ap 94, p. 60.
6919. ZARRIN, Ali
"In the Moment" (tr. of Ahmad Shamlu). [Vis] (46) 94, p. 20.
6920. ZAWINSKI, Andrena
"Chiaroscuro for Reflected Light." [Plain] (14:3) Spr 94, p. 36.
"Sacrilege of Dream." [PaintedB] (53/54) 94, p. 78-80.
6921. ZAWISTOWSKI, Wladyslaw
"In Fourteen Red Tramcars" (tr. by Georgia Scott and David Malcolm). [InterQ] (1:1) [93?], p. 105.
"A Poet's Worth" (tr. by Katarzyna Kietlinska and David Malcolm). [InterQ] (1:1) [93?], p. 104.
6922. ZEALAND, Karen
"A Field Guide." [Ascent] (19:1) Fall 94, p. 16.
"With Winter Coming." [Ascent] (19:1) Fall 94, p. 17.
6923. ZECCHINO, Mike
"Reconciled in Nome." [NegC] (14:1/2) 94, p. 23.
6924. ZEGERS, Kip
"8th Grade." [Northeast] (5:11) Wint 94-95, p. 13.
"The Facts" (From "The Promise Is"). [AmerPoR] (23:6) N-D 94, p. 38.
"In Place." [Northeast] (5:11) Wint 94-95, p. 12.
"The One Kid." [Northeast] (5:11) Wint 94-95, p. 14.
6925. ZEIGER, Gene
"At Metacomet." [PraS] (68:2) Sum 94, p. 145.
"Best Intentions." [NegC] (14:1/2) 94, p. 74.
"Cheek to Cheek." [PraS] (68:2) Sum 94, p. 147.
"The Old Days." [PraS] (68:2) Sum 94, p. 146.
6926. ZELCER, Brook
"At a Kissing Booth." [WormR] (34:3, #135) 94, p. 106.
"Ducks Land." [WormR] (34:3, #135) 94, p. 106.
"Embarrassed." [WormR] (34:3, #135) 94, p. 105.
"Just One." [WormR] (34:3, #135) 94, p. 106.
"Tiny Anchors." [WormR] (34:3, #135) 94, p. 106.
6927. ZENITH, Richard
"The Art of Poetry" (tr. of Mario Benedetti). [AmerPoR] (23:3) My-Je 94, p. 49.
"Everything Is Distant" (tr. of Mario Benedetti). [AmerPoR] (23:3) My-Je 94, p. 50.
"I Am My Guest" (tr. of Mario Benedetti). [AmerPoR] (23:3) My-Je 94, p. 49.
"Life This Parenthesis" (tr. of Mario Benedetti). [AmerPoR] (23:3) My-Je 94, p. 49.
"Transgressions" (tr. of Mario Benedetti). [AmerPoR] (23:3) My-Je 94, p. 49.
"Traveling" (tr. of Mario Benedetti). [AmerPoR] (23:3) My-Je 94, p. 49.
6928. ZEPPA, Mary
"A Rose Tattoo." [Vis] (44) 94, p. 9.
6929. ZERDEN, D. L.
"Spring Market on Canal Street." [Poetry] (164:1) Ap 94, p. 9-10.
ZEUNER, Gwen Meyer
See MEYER-ZEUNER, Gwen
6930. ZHAI, Yongming
"Confession" (tr. by Leonard Schwartz and Mingxia Li). [Talisman] (12) Spr 94, p. 163.
"Premonition" (tr. by Leonard Schwartz and Mingxia Li). [Talisman] (12) Spr 94, p. 162.
6931. ZHANG, Er
"Chinese Honey" (tr. by the author and Leonard Schwartz). [Talisman] (12) Spr 94, p. 167.
"Story" (tr. by the author and Leonard Schwartz). [Talisman] (12) Spr 94, p. 168-169.

6932. ZHANG, Zhen
"Beijing Two" (tr. by the author). [Manoa] (6:1) Sum 94, p. 115-116.
"The Cat at a Friend's House" (tr. by Yanbing Chen and John Rosenwald). [AnotherCM] (27) 94, p. 76-77.
"A New Emperor's Almanac Begins" (January 1989, the first year of the Heisei reign in Japan, tr. by the author). [Manoa] (6:1) Sum 94, p. 116-117.
6933. ZHANG, Ziqing
"The Story of Er Mao and Me" (Selections: 2 poems, tr. of Silent Thunder). [Talisman] (13) Fall 94-Wint 95, p. 157-158.
ZHAO, Zhenkai
See BEI DAO
ZHEN, Zhang
See ZHANG, Zhen
6934. ZHENG, Jianqing
"Burning" (tr. of Xi Murong, w. Angela Ball). [LitR] (37:4) Sum 94, p. 684.
ZHENKAI, Zhao
See BEI DAO
ZHENZHONG, Qiu
See QIU, Zhenzhong
ZHONG, Jin
See JIN, Zhong
ZHONGMIN, Shang
See SHANG, Zhongmin
6935. ZIDE, Arlene
"8" (tr. of D. M. Lone, w. Tilottama Daswani). [InterQ] (1:2) 93, p. 161.
"Bungalow on the Mountain" (tr. of Rajee Seth, w. Aruna Sitesh). [InterQ] (1:2) 93, p. 178-179.
"Chilka Lake" (tr. of Shakunt Mathur, w. Aruna Sitesh). [InterQ] (1:2) 93, p. 180-181.
"The Fish — 2" (tr. of Gagan Gill, w. J. P. Das and Madhu Joshi). [InterQ] (1:2) 93, p. 184.
"Her Home" (tr. of Mrinal Pande, w. the author). [InterQ] (1:2) 93, p. 185.
"I Am" (tr. of Nita Ramaiya, w. the author). [InterQ] (1:2) 93, p. 182-183.
"My Whole Life for Him" (tr. of Manorama Mahapatra Biswal, w. J. P. Das). [InterQ] (1:2) 93, p. 177.
"Poem in Motion" (tr. of Sunanda Tripathy, w. J. P. Das). [InterQ] (1:2) 93, p. 186.
"Ravaged Blossom" (tr. of Chitra Lahiri, w. Paramita Banerjee). [InterQ] (1:2) 93, p. 189.
"Song of Separation" (tr. of Teji Grover, w. Aruna Sitesh and the author). [InterQ] (1:2) 93, p. 190-191.
"Street Drama" (tr. of Chaitali Chattopadhyay, w. Paramita Banerjee). [InterQ] (1:2) 93, p. 187.
"Where There Is No Rest" (tr. of Chitra Lahiri, w. Paramita Banerjee). [InterQ] (1:2) 93, p. 188.
6936. ZIEROTH, David
"Endhome." [SouthernR] (30:2) Ap, Spr 94, p. 332-333.
"The Father of the Workaholic." [MalR] (109) Wint 94, p. 36-37.
"Thinking My Neighbour's Thoughts." [PoetryC] (15:1) N 94, p. 24.
"The Way Past Words." [PoetryC] (15:1) N 94, p. 24.
"Workaholic Addresses His Wife." [MalR] (109) Wint 94, p. 32-33.
"Workaholic Says Goodbye to Daughter." [MalR] (109) Wint 94, p. 34-35.
6937. ZILLES, Luke
"Chapel." [Pivot] (42) 94, p. 37-38.
6938. ZIMAN, Larry
"1+1=3." [ContextS] (4:1) 94, p. 24.
"1945." [ContextS] (4:1) 94, p. 24.
"Astronauts." [ContextS] (4:1) 94, p. 24.
"Buddha." [ContextS] (4:1) 94, p. 25.
"Bureaucracy." [ContextS] (4:1) 94, p. 25.
"Curiosity." [ContextS] (4:1) 94, p. 25.
"Despair." [ContextS] (4:1) 94, p. 24.
"Divorce." [ContextS] (4:1) 94, p. 24.
"Earth." [ContextS] (4:1) 94, p. 24.
"Ideology." [ContextS] (4:1) 94, p. 24.
"Love." [ContextS] (4:1) 94, p. 24.
"Militarism." [ContextS] (4:1) 94, p. 25.

"Mystic." [ContextS] (4:1) 94, p. 25.
"Nostalgia." [ContextS] (4:1) 94, p. 24.
"Philosophy." [ContextS] (4:1) 94, p. 24.
"Poetry." [ContextS] (4:1) 94, p. 25.
"Sci-Fi Flick." [ContextS] (4:1) 94, p. 15-16.
"Sundown." [ContextS] (4:1) 94, p. 25.
"Television." [ContextS] (4:1) 94, p. 25.

6939. ZIMMER, Paul
"And Then I Drove On." [PlumR] (7) [94?], p. 54.
"Aurora Borealis." [SouthernR] (30:1) Ja, Wint 94, p. 113-114.
"The Books." [GeoR] (48:2) Sum 94, p. 296-297.
"Diz's Face" (January 6, 1993). [SouthernR] (30:1) Ja, Wint 94, p. 114-115.
"Romance." [SouthernR] (30:1) Ja, Wint 94, p. 112.

6940. ZIMMERMAN, Daniel
"Scarecrow." [NewYorkQ] (53) 94, p. 69.

6941. ZIMMERMAN, Irene
"Backyard Performance." [ChrC] (111:11) 6 Ap 94, p. 340.
"The Un-Bent Woman" (Luke 13:10-17). [ChrC] (111:8) 9 Mr 94, p. 245.

6942. ZIMMERMAN, Laurie
"Circling Ellis" (for Edward Cassells, one of the "names" inscribed on the American Immigrant Wall of Honor). [BellArk] (10:5) S-O 94, p. 16.
"Cygnus Rising." [BellArk] (10:6) N-D 94, p. 22.

6943. ZINNES, Harriet
"I Dream" (tr. of Jacques Roubaud). [DenQ] (29:1) Sum 94, p. 99.
"You Are Safe" (tr. of Jacques Roubaud). [DenQ] (29:1) Sum 94, p. 100.

6944. ZIPTER, Yvonne
"Climbers." [WillowR] (21) Spr 94, p. 17-18.
"Guarding Our Grief." [EvergreenC] (9:1) Wint-Spr 94, p. 40.

ZIQING, Zhang
See ZHANG, Ziqing

6945. ZISQUIT, Linda
"Outside the Body" (tr. of Yona Wolloch). [HarvardR] (7) Fall 94, p. 34.

6946. ZIVANCEVIC, Nina
"Sweeper Before His Door" (Selections: 4 poems, tr. of Sebastian Reichman). [Talisman] (13) Fall 94-Wint 95, p. 35-36.

6947. ZOGHAIB, Henri
"Digoenes / Pillar of Salt" (tr. by Adnan Haydar and Michael Beard). [LitR] (37:3) Spr 94, p. 533-535.
"I Long for a Moment" (tr. by Adnan Haydar and Michael Beard). [LitR] (37:3) Spr 94, p. 532.
"Olives Are My Hymns" (tr. by Najwa Nasr). [LitR] (37:3) Spr 94, p. 531-532.

6948. ZOLLER, James A.
"The Sky Upon Us" (for Stefan, 8). [ProseP] (3) 94, p. 92.
"Sunday Morning" (for Stefan, four). [ChrC] (111:29) 19 O 94, p. 956.

6949. ZOLO, Amerigo
"1492 Christopher Columbus 1992." [ChamLR] (14/15) Spr-Fall 94, p. 81-90.

6950. ZUBER, Isabel
"Bane and Simples." [Poetry] (165:1) O 94, p. 14.
"Missing the Milky Way." [Poetry] (165:1) O 94, p. 15.

6951. ZUBICK, Kelleen
"Loro at the Onsen." [AntR] (52:4) Fall 94, p. 616.

6952. ZUCKERMAN, Ryki
"Carol Ann." [MoodySI] (28, also labeled 29) Fall 94, p. 16.

6953. ZUKOWSKI, Jenn
"Father." [Elf] (4:1) Spr 94, p. 38.

6954. ZWEIG, Martha
"Cosmos." [NowestR] (32:1) 94, p. 65.
"Envoy." [Manoa] (6:2) Wint 94, p. 27.
"North." [Manoa] (6:2) Wint 94, p. 28.
"Spooked." [NowestR] (32:1) 94, p. 66.
"Spring Sentiment." [NowestR] (32:1) 94, p. 67.
"Unison." [NowestR] (32:1) 94, p. 64.
"Ward's Field." [GettyR] (7:3) Sum 94, p. 533.
"What Becomes of Them." [Manoa] (6:2) Wint 94, p. 27-28.

6955. ZWICKY, Ian
"Goalie." [Nimrod] (37:2) Spr-Sum 94, p. 125.

"Rain Shadow." [Nimrod] (37:2) Spr-Sum 94, p. 127.
"Recovery." [Nimrod] (37:2) Spr-Sum 94, p. 126.
"Small Song for the Wind Among the Eaves." [Nimrod] (37:2) Spr-Sum 94, p. 125.

6956. ZWICKY, Jan
"Kant and Bruckner: Twelve Variations." [Descant] (25:1, #84) Spr 94, p. 75-89.

6957. ZYDEK, Fredrick
"Doing Kaddish" (for Darrell Cole). [HolCrit] (31:3) Je 94, p. 19.
"Letter to Light: New Year's Eve 1988." [CharR] (20:2) Fall 94, p. 114.
"Letter to Wallis in L.A." [CharR] (20:2) Fall 94, p. 113.
"Three Small Bare-Skinned Swallows" (for S.J. Holmes). [NewEngR] (16:4) Fall 94, p. 44.
"Visiting the Relic Museum." [Conscience] (15:4) Wint 94-95, p. 38.

6958. ZYMBOLY, Melissa
"Folding Clothes After the Stroke" (for S. Z.). [SingHM] (21) 94, p. 17.

Title Index

Titles are arranged alphanumerically, with numerals filed in numerical order before letters. Each title is followed by one or more author entry numbers, which refer to the numbered entries in the first part of the volume. Entry numbers are preceded by a space colon space (:). Any numeral which preceeds the space colon space (:) is part of the title, not an entry number. Poems with "Untitled" in the title position are entered under "Untitled" followed by the first line of the poem and also directly under the first line. Numbered titles are entered under the number and also under the part following the number.

About the Authors

RAFAEL CATALA (B.A., M.A., Ph.D., New York University) is president of The Ometeca Institute and editor-in-chief of *The Ometeca Journal*, both dedicated to the study and encouragement of relations between the sciences and the humanities. He was born in Las Tunas, Cuba in 1942 and came to the United States in 1961. His books of poetry and literary criticism, as well as many essays and poems, have been published in the United States, Canada, Latin America, and Europe. He has taught Latin American Literature at NYU, Lafayette College, and Seton Hall University. In 1993-94 he was visiting professor at the University of Costa Rica. In 1995 and 1996 he held the Gates-Ferry Distinguished Lecturer Chair at Centenary College, where he led seminars on the creative process. Catalá is a major proponent and practitioner of *cienciapoesía* (sciencepoetry), an embodiment of the integration of aesthetics, ethics, and the sciences. A new book of critical essays about Catalá's poetry and literary work was published in 1994: *Rafael Catalá: del Círculo cuadrado a la cienciapoesía — Hacia una nueva poética latinoamericana* (Ed. by Luis A. Jiménez. Kent, WA: Ventura One).

JAMES D. ANDERSON (B.A., Harvard College, M.S.L.S., D.L.S., Columbia University) is associate dean and professor of the School of Communication, Information, and Library Studies, at Rutgers the State University of New Jersey. His library career has included service at Sheldon Jackson College, Sitka, Alaska, and the Portland (Oregon) Public Library. He taught at Columbia, St. John's, and the City University of New York before coming to Rutgers in 1977, where he specializes in the design of textual databases for information retrieval. Major projects have included the international bibliography and database of the Modern Language Association of America and the bilingual (French & English) *Bibliography of the History of Art*, sponsored by the J. Paul Getty Trust and the French Centre National de la Recherche Scientifique in Paris. At Rutgers he also chairs the President's Select Committee for Lesbian and Gay Concerns, and for the Presbyterian Church (U.S.A.), he edits and publishes the monthly journal *More Light Update*, on lesbian and gay issues within that denomination.